The
TOP TWENTY
Book

Fifth Edition

The Official British Record
Charts 1955 – 1990

Compiled by
Tony Jasper

BLANDFORD

A BLANDFORD BOOK

This edition first published in the UK 1991
by Blandford
(a Cassell imprint)
Villiers House
41/47 Strand
LONDON
WC2N 5JE

First edition 1983
Second edition 1984
Third edition 1986
Fourth edition 1987

Copyright © 1991 (Top Twenty) Music
Week/BRMB/Gallup/CNI.
Supporting text, additional material and layout
copyright © 1976, 1978, 1979, 1983, 1984, 1986, 1988 and
1991 Tony Jasper

Distributed in the United States by
Sterling Publishing Co., Inc., 387 Park Avenue South,
New York, NY 10016-8810

Distributed in Australia by
Capricorn Link (Pty) Ltd., PO Box 665,
Lane Cove, NSW 2066

ISBN 0–7137–2207–X Hbk
        0–7137–2208–8 Pbk

Typeset by Litho Link Ltd., Welshpool
Printed in Great Britain by HarperCollins Manufacturing, Glasgow

INTRODUCTION

This new and fully updated volume brings the Top Twenty charts up to the last week of 1990 and supersedes any of the previous versions and editions. There are also best selling and album listings for most years. There is an index of titles so that a record's location in the appropriate chart can be found easily.

Various music chart information has appeared over the years. However, this volume (as opposed to, say, the *Guinness Book of Hit Singles*) has a consistent 'take' from a common copyright source – the *Record Mirror*. This musical paper has printed the accepted major chart, that of the music industry and the one utilised by the BBC for Radio One and Top Of The Pops since 1968, with the publishing rights resting with *Music Week*, and radio rights with the BBC. Thus there are some differences in data here and in the Guinness Book as it affects some of the very early years. Guinness for a period uses chart material from the *New Musical Express*. Due to length and subsequent cost of purchasing it was decided in 1975 to print the Top Twenty and not the complete 50 and later 75. In any case major record sales only apply to records making the 20 and for many years the BBC – as Radio Luxembourg – featured the Top Twenty. This decision has again been confirmed, though the compiler would enjoy seeing a complete chart run-down printed.

To Use The Book

The system employed provides easy access to anyone compiling a 20 from weeks other than the first of a month. Dates of week-endings are printed across the page for each month. Beneath the first week is listed the Top Twenty. If you trace along the line you can see where a particular record is the next week – and so forth. A glance *down* the column gives you the performance of the other records; thus a 20 can be easily assembled.

Record titles which appear below the first week's 20 are those which have entered in the other weeks of the month. If a record has entered the top 20 the second week of a month, then its entry should occur in the second column below the second week-ending of the month. Preceding

3

Top Twenty positions are also given and records which drop out of a 20 during a month have their fall down the chart plotted! For example:

```
7                                                      14  21  28
5 Running Up That Hill Kate Bush (EMI(12)KB1)           8  15  23
```

This tells how Kate's record was at Number 5 on September 7 and in subsequent weeks it moved to 8, 15 and 23. Another example:

```
— If I Was Midge Ure (Chrysalis URE(X)1)               29   8   4
```

This shows how *If I Was* was not chart listed until September 14 and subsequently moved into position 8 and 4 on the last two weeks of the month.

Provided a record has a Top 20 listing during a month its positions outside of that area are listed, and confined to the Top 75 as printed in the official industry chart.

In addition there is a list of Number Ones (please note that in the early years differences between this book and other similar listings elsewhere arise because of a different source being utilised), of the best artists and records each year and a generalised summary continues before each year.

In a book of this nature and containing thousands and thousands of figures it would be surprising, even after all the careful checking, if there is not the occasional incorrect figure. We will be pleased to hear of any inaccuracies for later correction – but we hope the miracle has happened and there are none! However, since the 1987 (fourth) edition, a few inaccuracies, or misprints, have been noticed; these have now received attention.

Dedicated to Alan and Theresa Wall, and Claire; Peter and Suzi Thornton, and Daniel.

Thanks to Andrew Brain (Music Week), Adrian Wistreich (CIN), Peter Scaping (BPI). John Jude Owens, Lance Daniels, A. Davies, Ken Jones, Darren Spencer, Robert Clement, Derek Whitcombe, Peter Barnes, R. B. Stott, C. G. Bradley.

Tony Jasper, January 1991   4

1955

Ballads were the order of the day in 1955, with a host of hits from singers such as Johnny Ray, Frankie Laine, Guy Mitchell, Tony Bennett, Rosemary Clooney and Doris Day.

Ray was in the charts by April 1955 singing 'If You Believe', and ended the year with 'Song Of The Dreamer'. This pencil-slim half-Red Indian wept real tears as he emotionally sang songs such as 'Cry' and 'Little White Cloud That Cried'. A childhood accident had left him 52 per cent deaf, so he wore a hearing aid. Unkind critics said that he switched it off when he was performing so that he couldn't hear himself sing.

However, the hysteria which Ray created was phenomenal. George Cooper, an ex-stage doorman at the London Palladium, lived through all the crazes in music and he has said that nobody, not even The Beatles, created the fan furore that Ray did at that particular theatre. One night after a show Ray serenaded a vast crowd in Argyll Street from the Palladium roof, for his fans had made it clear that they were not going to leave the theatre until he had provided an unaccompanied encore.

Rosemary Clooney sang more jovial, fun songs, such as 'Mambo Italiano', and 'Where Will The Dimple Be'. Doris Day entered the Top Twenty in April 1955 with 'Ready, Willing And Able', and Tony Bennett found a Number One with 'Stranger In Paradise' and engaged in a chart battle with both The Four Aces and Tony Martin who also entered the Top Ten with the same song.

Frankie Laine had already achieved an 18-week Number One hit in 1951 (the *New Musical Express* had begun the first pop chart ever that year) with 'I Believe', and he went on to record a string of classic hit discs. His first record of 1955 was 'Rain Rain Rain', and he followed this with five other hits. Frankie Laine made a visit to Britain during the same year and was highly insulted for being criticised by the show business critic of one mass circulation newspaper, not for his voice but for the cut of his suit! Laine stood on the stage of the London Palladium and retorted 'Knock my talent if you must, but not my tailor'. He was sporting the new line in Italian-cut suits, with a square-shouldered short jacket, known as a 'bum freezer', and shoes with pointed toes.

Laine invited the audience on his second night at the Palladium to approve his suit, which they did in the same way as they approved his voice which had bellowed its way through hits such as 'Shine', 'Mule Train' and 'Cry Of The Wild Goose'. Suitably mollified, Laine finished his act, but he had learned something that was to become more and more marked as pop music developed — that music and clothes were already linked. Clothes maketh the man, but they also help to make the music.

Apart from these American balladeers, Britain had her own hit makers, one of whom was Ruby Murray, a totally unsophisticated Irish girl who achieved five singles in the Top Twenty in one week. Ballads also came from singers such as Jimmy Young, Dickie Valentine, David Whitfield and Malcolm Vaughan. Many of these balladeers came from the most unlikely backgrounds — for example, Vaughan's high tenor voice had previously been one half of a knockabout comedy act. David Whitfield had been mixing cement on building sites in Hull until he entered the charts, and Dave King had been a mime artist in vaudeville until he learned how to sing suspiciously like Perry Como and Dean Martin.

Jimmy Young, who is now a successful Radio 2 disc-jockey, had two hits in 1955 — 'Unchained Melody' and the Number One 'Man From Laramie'. Al Hibbler also achieved a Number One with 'Unchained Melody'.

1955 was a memorable year for Pat Boone, not in terms of a huge number of hits, but for his first British chart entry, 'Ain't That A Shame'. He reached Number Seven with this hit, which is perhaps more associated with Fats Domino in most people's minds.

Pop music was on the way in 1955, but generally speaking it was in the form of predictable songs from predictable artists. A new trend was needed and it came with the emergence of Bill Haley and The Comets who arrived in the Top Twenty with 'Shake, Rattle and Roll', a song which had been recorded on 12 April 1954 in the same session as 'Rock Around The Clock', which was to become their next hit. 'Rock Around The Clock' made little chart impression when it was first released in January 1955, but on its re-release and chart entry in October the record was in the charts for four months.

The new craze brought its own Teddy Boy fashion following. Drainpipe trousers, bootlace ties, patches of velvet on lapels and pockets of drape jackets, 'brothel creeper' shoes, and the liberal application of Brylcreem to plastered-back quiffs of hair all added up to the Teddy Boy's uniform. However, the 'Teds' and their music certainly injected some much-needed excitement into the music scene of 1955.

	22	29
1 Mambo Italiano *Rosemary Clooney* (Philips)		1
2 Finger of Suspicion *Dickie Valentine* (Decca)		2
3 Mr Sandman *The Chordettes* (Columbia)		–
4 Shake Rattle And Roll *Bill Haley* (Brunswick)		6
5 Naughty Lady Of Shady Lane *Dean Martin* (Capitol)		3
6 Happy Days And Lonely Nights *Suzi Miller* (Decca)		–
7 No One But You *Billy Eckstine* (MGM)		
8 Softly Softly *Ruby Murray* (Columbia)		5
9 Don't Go To Strangers *Ronnie Harris* (Columbia)		8
10 Let Me Go *Teresa Brewer* (Vogue/Coral)		10
– Mr Sandman *The Four Aces* (Brunswick)		4
– Give Me Your Word *Tennessee Ernie Ford* (Capitol)		7
– Mobile *Ray Burns* (Columbia)		9

22 January 1955 saw the first published chart, which consisted of a Top Ten only until 8 October 1955.

	5	12	19	26
1 Mambo Italiano *Rosemary Clooney* (Philips)		2	4	3
2 Finger Of Suspicion *Dickie Valentine* (Decca)		6	8	7
3 Softly Softly *Ruby Murray* (Columbia)		3	2	2
4 Shake Rattle And Roll *Bill Haley* (Brunswick)		5	6	5
5 Naughty Lady Of Shady Lane *Dean Martin* (Capitol)		1	3	4
6 Give Me Your Word *Tennessee Ernie Ford* (Capitol)		4	1	1
7 Let Me Go *Teresa Brewer* (Vogue/Coral)		7	7	6
8 Mobile *Ray Burns* (Columbia)		8	–	10
9 A Blossom Fell *Various Artists* (Decca)		10	–	–
10 Mr Sandman *The Chordettes* (Columbia)		–	–	–
– Beyond The Stars *David Whitfield* (Decca)		9	5	8
– Serenade/Drinking Song *Mario Lanza* (HMV)		–	10	–
– Heartbeat *Ruby Murray* (Columbia)		–	–	9

In the Record Mirror *issue of 19 February Dickie Valentine was credited with A Blossom Fell at the Number Nine position. The record was not listed for 26 February 1955.*

	5	12	19	26
1 Give Me Your Word *Tennessee Ernie Ford* (Capitol)		2	1	1
2 Softly Softly *Ruby Murray* (Columbia)		1	2	2
3 Let Me Go *Teresa Brewer* (Vogue/Coral)		3	3	6
4 Naughty Lady Of Shady Lane *Dean Martin* (Capitol)		8	6	7
5 Shake Rattle And Roll *Bill Haley* (Brunswick)		9	10	–
6 Mambo Italiano *Rosemary Clooney* (Philips)		6	–	–
7 Mobile *Ray Burns* (Columbia)		5	4	4
8 Heartbeat *Ruby Murray* (Columbia)		–	–	–
9 Finger Of Suspicion *Dickie Valentine* (Decca)		–	–	–
10 A Blossom Fell *Nat 'King' Cole* (Capitol)		4	5	5
– Tomorrow *Johnny Brandon* (Polygon)		7	7	–
– Cherry Pink Apple Blossom *Perez Prado* (HMV)		–	8	3
– If You Believe *Johnny Ray* (Philips)		10	–	–
– Let Me Go *Ruby Murray* (Columbia)		–	9	9
– If Anyone Finds This I Love You *Ruby Murray* (Columbia)		–	–	8
– A Blossom Fell *Dickie Valentine* (Decca)		–	–	10

APRIL 1955

2	16–23	30
1 Give Me Your Word *Tennessee Ernie Ford* (Capitol)	1	1
2 Softly Softly *Ruby Murray* (Columbia)	5	8
3 Cherry Pink Apple Blossom *Perez Prado* (HMV)	2	2
4 A Blossom Fell *Nat 'King' Cole* (Capitol)	–	–
5 Prize Of Old Gold *Joan Regan* (Decca)	6	–
6 Mobile *Ray Burns* (Columbia)	–	–
7 If Anyone Finds This I Love You *Ruby Murray* (Columbia)	10	9
8 Tomorrow *Johnny Brandon* (Polygon)	–	–
9 Mambo Rock *Bill Haley* (Brunswick)	–	–
10 Let Me Go *Teresa Brewer* (Vogue/Coral)	–	–
– Stranger In Paradise *Tony Bennett* (Philips)	3	3
– Wedding Bells *Eddie Fisher* (HMV)	4	7
– Cherry Pink Apple Blossom *Eddie Calvert* (Columbia)	7	4
– Earth Angel *The Crew Cuts* (Mercury)	8	5
– Under The Bridges Of Paris *Eartha Kitt* (HMV)	9	–
– Stranger In Paradise *Tony Martin* (HMV)	–	6
– Ready Willing And Able *Doris Day* (Philips)	–	10

The chart for 2 April was an official listing owing to a small number of shop returns caused by the Easter holidays. The 2 April chart was described by Record Mirror as for 'laughs'. There was no chart for 9 April and that of the 16 April was printed both to cover that week and the previous one.

MAY 1955

7	14	21	28
1 Stranger In Paradise *Tony Bennett* (Philips)	1	1	1
2 Cherry Pink Apple Blossom *Perez Prado* (HMV)	2	2	3
3 Earth Angel *The Crew Cuts* (Mercury)	5	3	5
4 Cherry Pink Apple Blossom *Eddie Calvert* (Columbia)	3	4	4
5 Give Me Your Word *Tennessee Ernie Ford* (Capitol)	4	6	7
6 Stranger In Paradise *Tony Martin* (HMV)	7	9	10
7 Ready Willing And Able *Doris Day* (Philips)	10	–	–
8 Wedding Bells *Eddie Fisher* (HMV)	9	–	–
9 If You Believe *Johnny Ray* (Philips)	6	7	6
10 You, My Love *Frank Sinatra* (Capitol)	–	–	–
– Unchained Melody *Al Hibbler* (Brunswick)	8	5	2
– Stranger In Paradise *The Four Aces* (Brunswick)	–	8	9
– Unchained Melody *Les Baxter* (Capitol)	–	10	–
– Unchained Melody *Jimmy Young* (Decca)	–	–	8

JUNE 1955

4	11	18	25
1 Stranger In Paradise *Tony Bennett* (Philips)	6	7	8
2 Unchained Melody *Al Hibbler* (Brunswick)	1	1	1
3 Cherry Pink *Perez Prado* (HMV)	4	6	6
4 Cherry Pink *Eddie Calvert* (Columbia)	2	2	5
5 Earth Angel *The Crew Cuts* (Mercury)	3	3	2
6 If You Believe *Johnny Ray* (Philips)	5	–	9
7 Give Me Your Word *Tennessee Ernie Ford* (Capitol)	–	10	–
8 Unchained Melody *Jimmy Young* (Decca)	7	4	4
9 Stranger In Paradise *The Four Aces* (Brunswick)	10	9	–
10 Stranger In Paradise *Tony Martin* (HMV)	8	8	7
– Dreamboat *Alma Cogan* (HMV)	9	5	3
– Cool Water *Frankie Laine* (Philips)	–	–	10

The chart for 4 June was a repeat of that for 28 May.

9

JULY 1955

2	9	16	23	30
1 Unchained Melody *Al Hibbler* (Brunswick)	2	3	4	6
2 Dreamboat *Alma Cogan* (HMV)	1	1	2	3
3 Unchained Melody *Jimmy Young* (Decca)	3	2	5	5
4 Earth Angel *The Crew Cuts* (Mercury)	5	7	9	10
5 Cherry Pink *Eddie Calvert* (Columbia)	6	9	8	–
6 Stranger In Paradise *Tony Bennett* (Philips)	–	–	–	–
7 I Wonder *Dickie Valentine* (Decca)	4	5	7	7
8 Cool Water *Frankie Laine* (Philips)	7	6	3	2
9 Cherry Pink *Perez Prado* (HMV)	10	–	–	–
10 Where Will The Dimple Be *Rosemary Clooney* (Philips)	9	9	–	–
– Evermore *Ruby Murray* (Columbia)	8	8	6	4
– Rose Marie *Slim Whitman* (London)	–	4	1	1
– Mama *David Whitfield* (Decca)	–	–	10	–
– Strange Lady In Town *Frankie Laine* (Philips)	–	–	–	8
– Ev'ry Day Of My Life *Malcolm Vaughan* (HMV)	–	–	–	9

AUGUST 1955

13	20	27
1 Rose Marie *Slim Whitman* (London)	1	1
2 Cool Water *Frankie Laine* (Philips)	2	3
3 Unchained Melody *Jimmy Young* (Decca)	9	–
4 Strange Lady In Town *Frankie Laine* (Philips)	6	5
5 Ev'ry Day Of My Life *Malcolm Vaughan* (HMV)	7	9
6 Evermore *Ruby Murray* (Columbia)	5	7
7 Ev'rywhere *David Whitfield* (Decca)	4	4
8 Dreamboat *Alma Cogan* (HMV)	–	–
9 Learnin' The Blues *Frank Sinatra* (Capitol)	3	2
10 I Wonder *Dickie Valentine* (Decca)	–	–
– Indian Love Call *Slim Whitman* (London)	8	8
– Unchained Melody *Al Hibbler* (Brunswick)	10	10
– The Breeze And I *Caterina Valente* (Polydor)	–	6

The chart for 6 August was the same as that for 30 July, due to the August Bank Holiday.

SEPTEMBER 1955

3	10	17	24
1 Rose Marie *Slim Whitman* (London)	1	1	1
2 Cool Water *Frankie Laine* (Philips)	2	2	2
3 Learnin' The Blues *Frank Sinatra* (Capitol)	3	3	3
4 Ev'rywhere *David Whitfield* (Decca)	4	4	4
5 The Breeze And I *Caterina Valente* (Polydor)	5	6	7
6 Indian Love Call *Slim Whitman* (London)	7	5	6
7 Strange Lady In Town *Frankie Laine* (Philips)	6	7	10
8 Ev'ry Day Of My Life *Malcolm Vaughan* (HMV)	8	–	–
9 Evermore *Ruby Murray* (Columbia)	9	8	9
10 John And Julie *Eddie Calvert* (Columbia)	–	10	–
– Love Me Or Leave Me *Sammy Davis Jnr.* (Brunswick)	–	9	8
– The Man From Laramie *Jimmy Young* (Decca)	10	–	5

OCTOBER 1955

	1	8	15	22	29
1 Cool Water *Frankie Laine* (Philips)		2	2	6	9
2 Rose Marie *Slim Whitman* (London)		3	3	3	6
3 The Man From Laramie *Jimmy Young* (Decca)		1	1	1	1
4 Learnin' The Blues *Frank Sinatra* (Capitol)		5	8	15	14
5 Ev'rywhere *David Whitfield* (Decca)		4	6	10	10
6 Indian Love Call *Slim Whitman* (London)		7	13	13	15
7 The Breeze And I *Caterina Valente* (Polydor)		9	9	11	12
8 Blue Star *Cyril Stapleton* (Decca)		6	5	4	4
9 Strange Lady In Town *Frankie Laine* (Philips)		17	–	–	–
10 Ev'ry Day Of My Life *Malcolm Vaughan* (HMV)		10	15	–	–
– Yellow Rose Of Texas *Mitch Miller* (Philips)		8	4	2	2
– Close The Door *The Stargazers* (Decca)		11	18	19	–
– Hey, There *Rosemary Clooney* (Philips)		12	7	8	8
– Humming Bird *Frankie Laine* (Philips)		13	16	16	18
– Hernando's Hideaway *The Johnston Brothers* (Decca)		14	10	7	5
– Love Me Or Leave Me *Sammy Davis Jnr.* (Brunswick)		15	17	19	–
– Hernando's Hideaway *Johnny Ray* (Philips)		16	10	9	11
– Hey, There *Johnny Ray* (Philips)		18	14	12	7
– John And Julie *Eddie Calvert* (Columbia)		19	–	–	–
– The Dam Busters March *R.A.F. Band* (HMV)		20	–	–	–
– Rock Around The Clock *Bill Haley* (Brunswick)		–	12	5	3
– Hey, There *Sammy Davis Jnr.* (Brunswick)		–	19	17	20
– Love Me Or Leave Me *Doris Day* (Philips)		–	20	–	–
– Yellow Rose Of Texas *Ronnie Hilton* (HMV)		–	20	–	–
– I'll Come When You Call *Ruby Murray* (Columbia)		–	–	14	13
– Hey, There *The Johnston Brothers* (Decca)		–	–	18	16
– Bring Your Smile Along *Frankie Laine* (Philips)		–	–	–	17
– That Old Black Magic *Sammy Davis Jnr.* (Brunswick)		–	–	–	18

It was for the first time that Record Mirror *published a Top Twenty on 8 October 1955.*

NOVEMBER 1955

	5	12	19	26
1 The Man From Laramie *Jimmy Young* (Decca)		2	4	6
2 Yellow Rose Of Texas *Mitch Miller* (Philips)		3	2	3
3 Blue Star *Cyril Stapleton* (Decca)		5	8	10
4 Rock Around The Clock *Bill Haley* (Brunswick)		1	1	1
5 Hernando's Hideaway *The Johnston Brothers* (Decca)		4	3	4
6 Hey, There *Rosemary Clooney* (Philips)		6	7	7
7 Rose Marie *Slim Whitman* (London)		9	13	17
8 Cool Water *Frankie Laine* (Philips)		–	–	–
9 Hey, There *Johnny Ray* (Philips)		8	9	12
10 The Breeze And I *Caterina Valente* (Polydor)		15	–	–
11 Hey, There *The Johnston Brothers* (Decca)		–	–	14
12 I'll Come When You Call *Ruby Murray* (Columbia)		11	11	–
13 Hernando's Hideaway *Johnny Ray* (Philips)		12	14	–
14 Everywhere *David Whitfield* (Decca)		17	–	15
15 Indian Love Call *Slim Whitman* (London)		–	–	–
16 Love Is A Many Splendored Thing *The Four Aces* (Brunswick)		13	6	2
17 Yellow Rose Of Texas *Gary Miller* (Nixa)		–	–	–
18 Let's Have A Ding-Dong *Winifred Atwell* (Decca)		7	5	9
19 Love Is A Many Splendored Thing *Nat 'King' Cole* (Capitol)		–	15	–
20 Dam Busters March *Billy Cotton* (Decca)		–	–	–
– Bring Your Smile Along *Frankie Laine* (Philips)		10	–	–
– Ain't That A Shame *Pat Boone* (London)		14	10	5
– Meet Me On The Corner *Max Bygraves* (HMV)		16	12	13

5

	12	19	26
– Singing Dogs *The Singing Dogs* (Nixa)	–	15	–
– Join In And Sing Again *The Johnston Brothers* (Decca)	–	17	–
– Seventeen *The Fontaine Sisters* (London)	–	18	–
– Twenty Tiny Fingers *The Stargazers* (Decca)	–	19	8
– Blue Star *Eve Boswell* (Parlophone)	–	20	20
– When You Lose The One You Love *David Whitfield* (Decca)	–	–	11
– Christmas Alphabet *Dickie Valentine* (Decca)	–	–	18
– Hawk Eye *Frankie Laine* (Philips)	–	–	16
– Suddenly There's A Valley *Lee Lawrence* (Columbia)	–	–	19

Only 17 records were listed in the chart published for the 12 November 1955 issue of Record Mirror.

DECEMBER 1955

3

	10	17	24
1 Rock Around The Clock *Bill Haley* (Brunswick)	1	1	1
2 Love Is A Many Splendored Thing *The Four Aces* (Brunswick)	2	2	3
3 Let's Have A Ding-Dong *Winifred Atwell* (Decca)	5	4	4
4 Twenty Tiny Fingers *The Stargazers* (Decca)	4	5	6
5 Ain't That A Shame *Pat Boone* (London)	6	6	7
6 Christmas Alphabet *Dickie Valentine* (Decca)	3	3	2
7 Yellow Rose Of Texas *Mitch Miller* (Philips)	7	8	10
8 Hernando's Hideaway *The Johnston Brothers* (Decca)	15	–	–
9 Hey, There *Rosemary Clooney* (Philips)	11	–	–
10 The Man From Laramie *Jimmy Young* (Decca)	19	–	–
11 Blue Star *Cyril Stapleton* (Decca)	16	17	–
12 Meet Me On The Corner *Max Bygraves* (HMV)	8	7	5
13 Hawk Eye *Frankie Laine* (Philips)	9	9	11
14 Hey, There *The Johnston Brothers* (Decca)	13	19	–
15 Cloudburst *Don Lang* (HMV)	10	13	14
16 Hey, There *Johnny Ray* (Philips)	–	–	–
17 I'll Come When You Call *Ruby Murray* (Columbia)	–	–	–
18 Caribbean *Mitchell Torok* (London)	–	–	–
19 Suddenly There's A Valley *Petula Clark* (Nixa)	14	10	8
20 I'll Never Stop Loving You *Doris Day* (Philips)	–	–	–
– When You Lose The One You Love *David Whitfield* (Decca)	12	14	15
– Singing Dogs *The Singing Dogs* (Nixa)	17	20	–
– The Very First Christmas Of All *Ruby Murray* (Columbia)	17	11	9
– Seventeen *The Fontaine Sisters* (London)	20	–	–
– Suddenly There's A Valley *Lee Lawrence* (Columbia)	20	–	19
– The Shifting Whispering Sands *Billy Vaughan* (London)	–	12	13
– Suddenly There's A Valley *Julius La Rosa* (London)	–	14	16
– Join In And Sing Again *The Johnston Frothers* (Decca)	–	16	12
– Bluebell Polka *Jimmy Shand* (Parlophone)	–	18	20
– Tina Marie *Perry Como* (HMV)	–	–	17
– Pickin' A Chicken *Eve Boswell* (Parlophone)	–	–	18

1956

1956 saw the emergence of Elvis Presley, was an event which dwarfed even the debut of Bill Haley during the previous year. The first year for Elvis meant no less than six hits in the Top Twenty, the first being the memorable 'Heartbreak Hotel', which was followed by 'Blue Suede Shoes'. Such was his popularity, particularly in his home country, that by the summer of that year Elvis was making a film, *Love Me Tender*. According to Derek Johnson in his book *Beat Music* (Wilhelm Hansen, 1969), Presley had sold ten million records by the end of 1956.

1956 began with Rock 'n' Roll and beat music, for the year opened with Bill Haley at Number One with 'Rock Around The Clock'. Haley achieved other hits during the year, including 'See You Later Alligator', 'Rockin' Through The Rye' and 'Saints Rock And Roll'. 'Rock Around The Clock' made a re-entry in October 1956, which was its third appearance in the charts.

The new Rock sounds resulted in some ballad singers having a thin time. Ruby Murray only managed one hit in 1956 in contrast to her seven hits of 1955, but Nat 'King' Cole continued some successful forays on the Top Twenty with three entries.

Another American singer, Perry Como, appeared on the British scene and was fairly successful with 'Hot Diggity', 'More' and 'Glendora' but, in comparison to Como's many chart appearances which were to occur in 1958, these three Top Twenty entries were just the beginning. Alma Cogan retained her popularity, while Pat Boone's first quiet one-hit quest for fame in 1955 blossomed into four hits in 1956, including the Forces' favourite, 'I'll Be Home'.

The arrival of Presley might possibly overshadow one other major event of 1956 – the arrival of Lonnie Donegan and skiffle music. Even if most of his records were derived from American music, Donegan was British and with his arrival, skiffle became the newest trend across the country. This one-time traditional jazzman had a staggering eight-year run of hits, beginning with 'Rock Island Line' and, even though Ken Colyer had more claim to fame as the

13

gentleman responsible for bringing skiffle to the British public, it was Donegan who received media coverage.

Even though the sartorial style of skiffle was undistinguished, it did set off a trend for 'do-it-yourself' music, and thousands of skiffle groups throughout the British Isles made their own instruments such as tea-chest basses and home-made drum kits. One such skiffle group included a certain Richard Starkey, who was later to become the percussionist with a group called The Beatles. His first gig earned him 15 shillings (75p), but the club secretary concerned was allegedly drunk and forgot to pay him!

Britain looked for her own rival to Presley and adopted American Gene Vincent, who became famous for 'Be Bop A Lula', but apart from this hit, Vincent was not a success in terms of the charts. 'Be Bop A Lula' stayed only two weeks in the Top Twenty and his follow-up hit, 'Bluejean Bop', had a one-week residence only.

Another British answer to Presley was an ex-Merchant Navy sailor known as Tommy Steele, whose image was carefully moulded by John Kennedy, a smart-talking publicist and ex-Fleet Street photographer. Kennedy stated 'Tommy is a natural to be the British Presley. But . . . Presley's sullen approach, and all that hip-swivelling which gets him criticised so much isn't right. Nor is the fact that most people think Rock is a lower-class form of music, appealing only to the poor-paid yobboes. We must make Tommy into an upper-class hero'. So Steele was launched at a debutante party and for three weeks his 'Rock With The Caveman' remained in the Top Twenty.

Steele, in the same way as many other British singers of this era, then cast an eye to the American charts. Steele covered two successive American hits of Guy Mitchell, reaching Number One with 'Singing The Blues' and Number Fifteen with 'Knee Deep In The Blues'. In February Guy Mitchell also reached Number One with 'Singing The Blues', and he won easily with his version of the latter song and reached Number Three.

After Steele came umpteen other British rockers blessed with surnames such as Goode, Power, Eager, Wilde and Fury, and by that time it was acceptable for rockers on stage to wear Italian-cut suits without being criticised as Frankie Laine had been.

Oddly enough, 1956 produced few one-hit wonders, but the ones who do belong in this category include Mitchell

Torok with 'When Mexico Gave Up The Rhumba', Don Cherry and 'Band Of Gold' and Joe 'Fingers' Carr with his 'Portuguese Washer Woman'. There were also several good instrumentals from one-hit orchestras such as those of Frank Chacksfield with 'In Old Lisbon' and the splendid 'Autumn Concerto' by The Melachrino Orchestra. But despite every ballad, orchestral piece or comedy record, 1956 was really concerned with solo singer Rock 'n' Roll, with Presley as the undisputed King.

JANUARY 1956

7		14	21	28
1 Rock Around The Clock *Bill Haley* (Brunswick)		2	4	8
2 Love Is A Many Splendored Thing *The Four Aces* (Brunswick)		4	3	6
3 Rock-A-Beatin' Boogie *Bill Haley* (Brunswick)		5	6	7
4 Christmas Alphabet *Dickie Valentine* (Decca)		–	–	–
5 Meet Me On The Corner *Max Bygraves* (HMV)		8	13	16
6 Let's Have A Ding-Dong *Winifred Atwell* (Decca)		–	–	–
7 Ain't That A Shame *Pat Boone* (London)		12	17	–
8 Rock Island Line *Lonnie Donegan* (Decca)		9	8	9
9 The Ballad Of Davy Crockett *Bill Hayes* (London)		3	2	2
10 Twenty Tiny Fingers *The Stargazers* (Decca)		17	–	–
11 Sixteen Tons *Tennessee Ernie Ford* (Capitol)		1	1	1
12 Pickin' A Chicken *Eve Boswell* (Parlophone)		10	12	13
13 Tina Marie *Perry Como* (HMV)		–	–	–
14 When You Lose The One You Love *David Whitfield* (Decca)		13	10	10
15 Yellow Rose Of Texas *Mitch Miller* (Philips)		–	–	–
16 The Shifting Whispering Sands *Billy Vaughan* (London)		14	9	13
17 Suddenly There's A Valley *Petula Clark* (Nixa)		16	15	–
18 Cloudburst *Don Lang* (HMV)		11	–	–
19 Arrivederci, Darling *Edna Savage* (Parlophone)		–	20	–
20 Never Do A Tango With An Eskimo *Alma Cogan* (HMV)		20	16	–
20 Sixteen Tons *Frankie Laine* (Philips)		15	–	18
– Ballad Of Davy Crockett *Tennessee Ernie Ford* (Capitol)		6	7	4
– Love And Marriage *Frank Sinatra* (Capitol)		7	5	3
– Groce Di Oro *Joan Regan* (Decca)		18	–	–
– Robin Hood *Gary Miller* (Nixa)		19	13	12
– Love Is A Tender Trap *Frank Sinatra* (Capitol)		–	11	5
– Ballad Of Davy Crocket *Gary Miller* (Nixa)		–	18	–
– Robin Hood *Dick James* (Parlophone)		–	18	–
– Only You *The Hilltoppers* (London)		–	–	11
– Yellow Rose Of Texas *Stan Freburg* (Capitol)		–	–	15
– Zambesi *Lou Busch* (Capitol)		–	–	17
– Dreams Can Tell A Lie *Nat 'King' Cole* (Capitol)		–	–	18
– The Shifting Whispering Sands *Eamonn Andrews* (Parlophone)		–	–	20

FEBRUARY 1956

4		11	18	25
1 Sixteen Tons *Tennessee Ernie Ford* (Capitol)		1	3	5
2 Ballad Of Davy Crockett *Bill Hayes* (London)		4	8	10
3 Love Is A Tender Trap *Frank Sinatra* (Capitol)		2	5	4
4 Love And Marriage *Frank Sinatra* (Capitol)		10	11	17
5 Ballad Of Davy Crockett *Tennessee Ernie Ford* (Capitol)		6	7	13
6 Rock-A-Beatin' Boogie *Bill Haley* (Brunswick)		9	19	15
7 Rock Island Line *Lonnie Donegan* (Decca)		6	12	11
8 When You Lose The One You Love *David Whitfield* (Decca)		15	–	–
9 Love Is A Many Splendored Thing *The Four Aces* (Brunswick)		14	–	–
10 Rock Around The Clock *Bill Haley* (Brunswick)		–	18	19
11 Robin Hood *Gary Miller* (Nixa)		13	15	–
12 Dreams Can Tell A Lie *Nat 'King' Cole* (Capitol)		20	16	16
13 Zambesi *Lou Busch* (Capitol)		5	1	1
14 Pickin' A Chicken *Eve Boswell* (Parlophone)		16	20	–
15 Only You *The Hilltoppers* (London)		8	6	6
16 It's Almost Tomorrow *The Dream Weavers* (Brunswick)		11	4	3
17 The Shifting Whispering Sands *Eamonn Andrews* (Parlophone)		–	–	–
18 Ain't That A Shame *Fats Domino* (London)		–	–	–
19 Sixteen Tons *Frankie Laine* (Philips)		18	–	–

4	11	18	25
20 With Your Love *Malcolm Vaughan* (HMV)	17	–	–
– Memories Are Made Of This *Dean Martin* (Capitol)	3	2	2
– Young And Foolish *Ronnie Hilton* (HMV)	12	–	–
– Young And Foolish *Edmund Hockeridge* (Nixa)	19	14	12
– Rock And Roll Waltz *Kay Starr* (HMV)	–	9	8
– Band Of Gold *Don Cherry* (Philips)	–	10	7
– Memories Are Made Of This *Dave King* (Decca)	–	13	9
– Who's Sorry Now *Johnny Ray* (Philips)	–	17	–
– With Your Love *Robert Earl* (Philips)	–	–	13
– Ballad Of Davy Crockett *Gary Miller* (Nixa)	–	–	18
– Young And Foolish *Dean Martin* (Capitol)	–	–	20

MARCH 1956

3	10	17	24	31
1 Memories Are Made Of This *Dean Martin* (Capitol)	1	3	4	5
2 Zambesi *Lou Busch* (Capitol)	2	2	3	4
3 It's Almost Tomorrow *The Dream Weavers* (Brunswick)	3	1	1	1
4 Only You *The Hilltoppers* (London)	4	6	7	6
5 Rock And Roll Waltz *Kay Starr* (HMV)	6	4	2	2
6 Band Of Gold *Don Cherry* (Philips)	7	9	9	10
7 Love Is A Tender Trap *Frank Sinatra* (Capitol)	9	12	–	–
8 Memories Are Made Of This *Dave King* (Decca)	5	5	6	7
9 Sixteen Tons *Tennessee Ernie Ford* (Capitol)	12	–	–	–
10 Rock Island Line *Lonnie Donegan* (Decca)	10	10	10	–
11 Young And Foolish *Edmund Hockeridge* (Nixa)	11	15	17	–
12 Ballad Of Davy Crockett *Bill Hayes* (London)	12	19	–	–
13 Jimmy Unknown *Lita Rosa* (Decca)	13	20	13	17
14 Rock-A-Beatin' Boogie *Bill Haley* (Brunswick)	–	–	–	–
14 Ballad Of Davy Crockett *Tennessee Ernie Ford* (Capitol)	–	–	–	–
16 Dreams Can Tell A Lie *Nat 'King' Cole* (Capitol)	14	–	–	–
16 Love And Marriage *Frank Sinatra* (Capitol)	–	–	–	–
18 With Your Love *Robert Earl* (Philips)	–	–	–	–
19 Rock Around The Clock *Bill Haley* (Brunswick)	–	–	–	–
20 Tumbling Tumbleweeds *Slim Whitman* (London)	16	15	20	–
– Chain Gang *Jimmy Young* (Decca)	17	11	11	9
– Poor People Of Paris *Winifred Atwell* (Decca)	17	7	5	3
– My September Love *David Whitfield* (Decca)	20	–	18	19
– Rudder And Rock *David Whitfield* (Decca)	–	19	–	–
– See You Later Alligator *Bill Haley* (Brunswick)	8	8	8	8
– Great Pretender *Jimmy Parkinson* (Columbia)	15	13	11	11
– My September Love *Robert Earl* (Philips)	–	14	19	–
– I Hear You Knocking *Gale Storm* (London)	–	17	–	–
– Theme From The Threepenny Opera *Dick Hyman* (MGM)	–	–	16	12
– Seven Days *Anne Shelton* (Philips)	–	–	14	16
– Zambesi *Eddie Calvert* (Columbia)	–	–	15	13
– Theme From The Threepenny Opera *Billy Vaughan* (London)	–	–	20	15
– I'm A Fool *Slim Whitman* (London)	–	–	–	14
– A Tear Fell *Teresa Brewer* (Vogue/Coral)	–	–	–	20
– Willie Can *Alma Cogan* (HMV)	–	–	–	17

	14	21	28
7			
1 Poor People Of Paris *Winifred Atwell* (Decca)	1	1	1
2 It's Almost Tomorrow *The Dream Weavers* (Brunswick)	2	2	2
3 Rock And Roll Waltz *Kay Starr* (HMV)	3	3	5
4 Zambesi *Lou Busch* (Capitol)	4	5	10
5 Memories Are Made Of This *Dave King* (Decca)	5	7	7
6 Only You *The Hilltoppers* (London)	6	4	5
7 Memories Are Made Of This *Dean Martin* (Capitol)	7	7	9
8 See You Later Alligator *Bill Haley* (Brunswick)	7	4	5
9 Chain Gang *Jimmy Young* (Decca)	16	–	–
10 Great Pretender *Jimmy Parkinson* (Columbia)	11	–	–
11 I'm A Fool *Slim Whitman* (London)	17	16	18
12 Band Of Gold *Don Cherry* (Philips)	18	–	–
12 Theme From The Threepenny Opera *Dick Hyman* (HMV)	9	11	11
14 Zambesi *Eddie Calvert* (Columbia)	–	–	–
15 Willie Can *Alma Cogan* (HMV)	14	14	15
16 Theme From The Threepenny Opera *Billy Vaughan* (London)	–	–	–
17 My September Love *David Whitfield* (Decca)	12	9	8
17 A Tear Fell *Teresa Brewer* (Vogue/Coral)	10	13	6
19 Rock Island Line *Lonnie Donegan* (Decca)	15	20	–
20 Seven Days *Anne Shelton* (Philips)	19	18	–
– You Can't Be True To Two *Dave King* (Decca)	12	10	13
– In A Little Spanish Town *Bing Crosby* (Brunswick)	20	–	–
– Nothin' To Do *Michael Holliday* (Columbia)	20	16	–
– No Other Love *Ronnie Hilton* (HMV)	–	12	4
– Theme From The Threepenny Opera *Louis Armstrong* (Philips)	–	15	16
– I'll Be Home *Pat Boone* (London)	–	19	14
– Lost John *Lonnie Donegan* (Nixa)	–	–	17
– Ain't Misbehavin' *Johnny Ray* (Philips)	–	–	18
– Main Title *Billy May* (Capitol)	–	–	20

	12	19	26
5			
1 Poor People Of Paris *Winifred Atwell* (Decca)	2	2	5
2 No Other Love *Ronnie Hilton* (HMV)	1	1	1
3 It's Almost Tomorrow *The Dream Weavers* (Brunswick)	5	10	12
4 A Tear Fell *Teresa Brewer* (Vogue/Coral)	3	3	2
5 Rock And Roll Waltz *Kay Starr* (HMV)	6	6	7
6 Only You *The Hilltoppers* (London)	8	8	10
7 My September Love *David Whitfield* (Decca)	4	5	4
8 Main Title *Billy May* (Capitol)	9	7	9
9 Theme From The Threepenny Opera *Dick Hyman* (HMV)	19	14	–
10 I'll Be Home *Pat Boone* (London)	7	4	3
11 Lost John *Lonnie Donegan* (Nixa)	10	9	6
12 Memories Are Made Of This *Dave King* (Decca)	12	–	–
13 Theme From The Threepenny Opera *Louis Armstrong* (Philips)	11	11	13
14 Memories Are Made Of This *Dean Martin* (Capitol)	19	–	18
15 See You Later Alligator *Bill Haley* (Brunswick)	16	18	19
16 Zambesi *Lou Busch* (Capitol)	–	–	–
17 You Can't Be True To Two *Dave King* (Decca)	14	13	14
18 Willie Can *Alma Cogan* (HMV)	17	19	–
19 Ain't Misbehavin' *Johnny Ray* (Philips)	–	–	–
20 Rock Island Line *Lonnie Donegan* (Decca)	13	–	16
– Mountain Greenery *Mel Torme* (Victor/Coral)	15	–	–
– No Other Love *Edmund Hockeridge* (Nixa)	18	16	–
– Port Au Prince *Winifred Atwell* (Decca)	–	20	–

5	12	19	26
– Heartbreak Hotel *Elvis Presley* (HMV)	–	17	11
– Too Young To Go Steady *Nat 'King' Cole* (Capitol)	–	15	17
– The Happy Whistler *Don Robertson* (Capitol)	–	12	8
– Blue Suede Shoes *Carl Perkins* (London)	–	–	15
– Hot Diggity *Perry Como* (HMV)	–	–	19

JUNE 1956

2	9	16	23	30
1 No Other Love *Ronnie Hilton* (HMV)	3	3	5	6
2 A Tear Fell *Teresa Brewer* (Vogue/Coral)	4	4	7	7
3 I'll Be Home *Pat Boone* (London)	1	1	1	1
4 Lost John *Lonnie Donegan* (Nixa)	2	2	2	2
5 My September Love *David Whitfield* (Decca)	7	8	8	9
5 Heartbreak Hotel *Elvis Presley* (HMV)	5	6	4	3
7 Poor People Of Paris *Winifred Atwell* (Decca)	9	14	–	–
8 The Happy Whistler *Don Robertson* (Capitol)	8	9	13	–
9 Main Title *Billy May* (Capitol)	10	11	16	–
10 Rock And Roll Waltz *Kay Starr* (HMV)	11	15	–	–
11 Saints Rock And Roll *Bill Haley* (Brunswick)	6	5	3	5
12 Only You *The Hilltoppers* (London)	20	–	–	–
13 Too Young To Go Steady *Nat 'King' Cole* (Capitol)	12	18	12	13
14 Theme From The Threepenny Opera *Louis Armstrong* (Philips)	20	–	–	–
15 Hot Diggity *Perry Como* (HMV)	13	7	6	4
16 You Can't Be True To Two *Dave King* (Decca)	–	–	–	–
17 Blue Suede Shoes *Carl Perkins* (London)	15	13	15	19
18 Blue Suede Shoes *Elvis Presley* (HMV)	14	9	10	12
19 Rock Island Line *Lonnie Donegan* (Decca)	–	–	–	–
19 It's Almost Tomorrow *The Dream Weavers* (Brunswick)	–	–	–	–
– Take It Satch (E.P.) *Louis Armstrong* (Philips)	20	–	–	–
– Out Of Town *Max Bygraves* (HMV)	18	–	–	–
– Hot Diggity *The Stargazers* (Decca)	17	–	–	–
– Moonglow And Theme From The Picnic *Morris Stoloff* (Brunswick)	16	12	9	11
– Hot Diggity *Michael Holliday* (Columbia)	–	16	11	15
– Gal In The Yaller Shoes *Michael Holliday* (Columbia)	–	20	17	10
– Mountain Greenery *Mel Torme* (Vogue)	19	18	19	–
– Carousel (L.P.) *Soundtrack* (Capitol)	–	–	19	–
– Experiments In Mice *Johnny Dankworth* (Parlophone)	–	–	17	–
– Songs For Swingin' Lovers (L.P.) *Frank Sinatra* (Capitol)	–	–	13	13
– Why Do Fools Fall In Love *Frankie Lymon and The Teenagers* (Columbia)	–	–	–	15
– All Star Hit Parade *Various Artists* (Decca)	–	–	–	8
– Wayward Wind *Gogi Grant* (London)	–	–	–	17
– Portuguese Washer Woman *Joe 'Fingers' Carr* (Capitol)	–	–	–	19
– Wayward Wind *Tex Ritter* (Capitol)	–	–	–	18

No Number Seventeen was listed for 16 June 1956.

JULY 1956

7	14	21	28
1 I'll Be Home *Pat Boone* (London)	1	3	3
2 Lost John *Lonnie Donegan* (Nixa)	7	7	14
3 All Star Hit Parade *Various Artists* (Decca)	2	2	2
4 Heartbreak Hotel *Elvis Presley* (HMV)	6	6	5
5 Hot Diggity *Perry Como* (HMV)	9	9	12
6 Saints Rock And Roll *Bill Haley* (Brunswick)	8	11	9

7	**14**	**21**	**28**
7 Bluebottle Blues *The Goons* (Decca)	3	4	4
8 Experiments In Mice *Johnny Dankworth* (Parlophone)	5	5	8
9 Wayward Wind *Gogi Grant* (London)	10	8	10
10 No Other Love *Ronnie Hilton* (HMV)	16	–	–
11 My September Love *David Whitfield* (Decca)	15	–	–
12 Wayward Wind *Tex Ritter* (Capitol)	13	9	11
13 Why Do Fools Fall In Love *Frankie Lymon and The Teenagers* (Columbia)	4	1	1
14 Blue Suede Shoes *Elvis Presley* (HMV)	14	–	–
15 A Tear Fell *Teresa Brewer* (Vogue/Coral)	–	18	20
16 Songs For Swingin' Lovers (L.P.) *Frank Sinatra* (Capitol)	11	13	–
17 Moonglow And Theme From The Picnic *Morris Stoloff* (Brunswick)	12	16	18
18 I'm Walking Backwards *The Goons* (Decca)	–	–	–
20 Carousel (L.P.) *Various Artists* (Capitol)	–	–	–
20 Skiffle Session (E.P.) *Lonnie Donegan* (Nixa)	–	–	–
– Who Are We *Ronnie Hilton* (HMV)	17	15	13
– Whatever Will Be Will Be *Doris Day* (Philips)	18	14	9
– Badpenny Blues *Humphrey Lyttleton* (Parlophone)	19	17	18
– Portuguese Washer Woman *Joe 'Fingers' Carr* (Capitol)	20	–	–
– Walk Hand In Hand *Tony Martin* (HMV)	–	12	6
– A Sweet Old Fashioned Girl *Teresa Brewer* (Vogue/Coral)	–	19	15
– Hot Diggity *Michael Holliday* (Columbia)	–	20	–
– Mountain Greenery *Mel Tormel* (Vogue Coral)	–	–	16
– Be Bop A Lula *Gene Vincent* (Capitol)	–	–	17
– Serenade *Slim Whitman* (London)	–	–	20

AUGUST 1956

4	**11**	**18**	**25**
1 Why Do Fools Fall In Love *Frankie Lymon and The Teenagers* (Columbia)	2	2	2
2 Whatever Will Be Will Be *Doris Day* (Philips)	1	1	1
3 A Sweet Old Fashioned Girl *Teresa Brewer* (Vogue/Coral)	3	3	3
4 I'll Be Home *Pat Boone* (London)	6	6	8
5 Walk Hand In Hand *Tony Martin* (HMV)	4	5	4
6 Bluebottle Blues *The Goons* (Decca)	16	–	17
7 Mountain Greenery *Mel Torme* (Vogue Coral)	5	4	5
8 All Star Hit Parade *Various Artists* (Decca)	7	9	12
9 Wayward Wind *Tex Ritter* (Capitol)	8	8	9
10 Wayward Wind *Gogi Grant* (Capitol)	11	11	16
11 Saints Rock And Roll *Bill Haley* (Brunswick)	10	9	13
12 Heartbreak Hotel *Elvis Presley* (HMV)	9	13	7
13 Who Are We *Ronnie Hilton* (HMV)	12	16	–
14 Experiments In Mice *Johnny Dankworth* (Columbia)	20	15	–
15 Serenade *Slim Whitman* (London)	14	14	11
16 Lost John *Lonnie Donegan* (Nixa)	17	–	–
17 The Faithful Hussar *Ted Heath* (Decca)	15	–	–
18 Walk Hand In Hand *Ronnie Carroll* (Philips)	13	12	10
19 Walk Hand In Hand *Jimmy Parkinson* (Columbia)	–	18	–
20 Hot Diggity *Perry Como* (HMV)	17	–	–
– Blue Suede Shoes *Elvis Presley* (HMV)	19	–	–
– Why Do Fools Fall In Love *Alma Cogan* (HMV)	20	19	–
– I Want You, I Need You, I Love You *Elvis Presley* (HMV)	–	20	15
– Rockin' Through The Rye *Bill Haley* (Brunswick)	–	7	6
– Be Bop A Lula *Gene Vincent* (Capitol)	–	17	20
– My Son John *David Whitfield* (Decca)	–	–	18
– You Are My First Love *Ruby Murray* (Columbia)	–	–	19
– I Almost Lost My Mind *Pat Boone* (London)	–	–	13
– Long Tall Sally *Little Richard* (London)	–	–	20

SEPTEMBER 1956

1	8	15	22	29
1 Whatever Will Be Will Be *Doris Day* (Philips)	1	1	2	2
2 Why Do Fools Fall In Love *Frankie Lymon and The Teenagers* (Columbia)	2	3	5	17
3 A Sweet Old Fashioned Girl *Teresa Brewer* (Vogue/Coral)	5	5	8	11
4 Rockin' Through The Rye *Bill Haley* (Brunswick)	4	4	3	3
5 Walk Hand In Hand *Tony Martin* (HMV)	6	6	7	14
6 Mountain Greenery *Mel Torme* (Vogue Coral)	7	7	13	15
7 I Almost Lost My Mind *Pat Boone* (London)	8	18	18	–
8 Wayward Wind *Tex Ritter* (Capitol)	15	19	–	–
9 Heartbreak Hotel *Elvis Presley* (HMV)	10	19	–	–
9 Serenade *Slim Whitman* (London)	13	12	17	20
11 I'll Be Home *Pat Boone* (London)	11	–	19	–
12 Born To Be With You *The Chordettes* (London)	13	14	15	16
13 My Son John *David Whitfield* (Decca)	–	–	–	–
14 I'm In Love Again *Fats Domino* (London)	9	17	–	19
15 Lay Down Your Arms *Anne Shelton* (Philips)	3	2	1	1
16 Saints Rock And Roll *Bill Haley* (Brunswick)	12	10	12	12
17 Walk Hand In Hand *Ronnie Carroll* (Philips)	16	–	–	–
18 Who Are We *Ronnie Hilton* (HMV)	–	–	–	–
19 Long Tall Sally *Little Richard* (London)	–	–	–	–
20 I Want You, I Need You, I Love You *Elvis Presley* (HMV)	19	19	–	–
– The Great Pretender *The Platters* (Mercury)	16	9	6	6
– Only You *The Platters* (Mercury)	18	11	11	10
– A Woman In Love *Frankie Laine* (Philips)	–	15	10	7
– Bring A Little Water Sylvia *Lonnie Donegan* (Nixa)	–	16	9	8
– Dead Or Alive *Lonnie Donegan* (Nixa)	–	13	14	9
– Ying Tong Song *The Goons* (Decca)	–	8	4	4
– Rock Around The Clock *Bill Haley* (Brunswick)	–	–	19	13
– Hound Dog *Elvis Presley* (HMV)	–	–	16	5
– When Mexico Gave Up The Rhumba *Mitchell Torok* (Brunswick)	–	–	–	18
– Moonglow And Theme From The Picnic *Morris Stoloff* (Brunswick)	19	–	–	–

OCTOBER 1956

6	13	20	27
1 Lay Down Your Arms *Anne Shelton* (Philips)	1	2	3
2 Woman In Love *Frankie Laine* (Philips)	2	1	1
3 Whatever Will Be Will Be *Doris Day* (Philips)	3	5	8
4 Hound Dog *Elvis Presley* (HMV)	5	3	2
5 Giddy Up A Ding Dong *Freddy Bell and The Bell Boys* (Mercury)	4	4	4
6 Rockin' Through The Rye *Bill Haley* (Brunswick)	6	6	6
7 Ying Tong Song *The Goons* (Decca)	8	7	10
8 The Great Pretender *The Platters* (Mercury)	11	12	–
9 Only You *The Platters* (Mercury)	7	8	15
10 Rock Around The Clock *Bill Haley* (Brunswick)	10	9	7
11 Bring A Little Water Sylvia *Lonnie Donegan* (Nixa)	9	10	11
12 Saints Rock And Roll *Bill Haley* (Brunswick)	15	19	19
13 Dead Or Alive *Lonnie Donegan* (Nixa)	13	15	17
14 See You Later Alligator *Bill Haley* (Brunswick)	17	13	16
15 When Mexico Gave Up The Rhumba *Mitchell Torok* (Brunswick)	14	11	9
16 Born To Be With You *The Chordettes* (London)	12	18	–
17 Walk Hand In Hand *Tony Martin* (HMV)	–	–	–
18 Razzle Dazzle *Bill Haley* (Brunswick)	16	16	20

6

	13	20	27
19 Why Do Fools Fall In Love *Frankie Lymon and The Teenagers* (Columbia)	20	–	–
20 Woman In Love *Ronnie Hilton* (HMV)	–	–	–
– More *Perry Como* (HMV)	18	17	12
– Guys And Dolls (E.P.) *Marlon Brando and Jean Simmons* (Brunswick)	19	–	–
– Just Walking In The Rain *Johnny Ray* (Philips)	–	14	5
– Woman In Love *The Four Aces* (Brunswick)	–	20	–
– More *Jimmy Young* (Decca)	–	–	13
– Bluejean Bop *Gene Vincent* (Capitol)	–	–	14
– Rock With The Caveman *Tommy Steele* (Decca)	–	–	17

NOVEMBER 1956

3

	10	17	24
1 Woman In Love *Frankie Laine* (Philips)	2	2	2
2 Hound Dog *Elvis Presley* (HMV)	3	3	4
3 Just Walking In The Rain *Johnny Ray* (Philips)	1	1	1
4 Lay Down Your Arms *Anne Shelton* (Philips)	7	11	18
5 Rockin' Through The Rye *Bill Haley* (Brunswick)	5	9	11
6 My Prayer *The Platters* (Mercury)	6	4	3
7 Giddy Up A Ding Dong *Freddie Bell and The Bell Boys* (Mercury)	8	13	–
8 More *Jimmy Young* (Decca)	4	5	6
9 When Mexico Gave Up The Rhumba *Mitchell Torok* (Brunswick)	10	7	8
10 Rock Around The Clock *Bill Haley* (Brunswick)	9	18	15
11 Rock With The Caveman *Tommy Steele* (Decca)	13	20	–
12 More *Perry Como* (HMV)	11	17	–
13 Whatever Will Be Will Be *Doris Day* (Philips)	20	–	–
14 Bluejean Bop *Gene Vincent* (Capitol)	12	–	–
15 Ying Tong Song *The Goons* (Decca)	–	–	–
16 Love Me As Though There Were No Tomorrow *Nat 'King' Cole* (Capitol)	–	16	20
17 See You Later Alligator *Bill Haley* (Brunswick)	–	–	–
18 Only You *The Platters* (Mercury)	17	18	17
18 Bring A Little Water Sylvia *Lonnie Donegan* (Nixa)	–	–	–
18 Make It A Party *Winifred Atwell* (Decca)	18	15	12
18 Autumn Concerto *George Melachrino* (HMV)	–	–	–
– Don't Be Cruel *Elvis Presley* (HMV)	19	–	–
– Green Door *Jim Lowe* (London)	13	10	12
– Green Door *Frankie Vaughan* (Philips)	15	6	5
– Rip It Up *Bill Haley* (Brunswick)	16	8	7
– Blue Moon (E.P.) *Elvis Presley* (HMV)	–	12	10
– St Theresa Of The Roses *Malcolm Vaughan* (HMV)	–	14	9
– True Love *Bing Crosby and Grace Kelly* (Capitol)	–	–	16
– Rudy's Rock *Bill Haley* (Brunswick)	–	–	18
– Cindy, Oh Cindy *Eddie Fisher* (HMV)	–	–	14

DECEMBER 1956

1

	8	15	22
1 Just Walking In The Rain *Johnny Ray* (Philips)	1	1	1
2 Woman In Love *Frankie Laine* (Philips)	6	9	10
3 Green Door *Frankie Vaughan* (Philips)	3	2	3
4 My Prayer *The Platters* (Mercury)	4	6	7
5 Rip It Up *Bill Haley* (Brunswick)	2	4	5
6 St Theresa Of The Roses *Malcolm Vaughan* (HMV)	5	3	4
7 More *Perry Como* (HMV)	10	12	13

1

	8	15	22
8 Hound Dog *Elvis Presley* (HMV)	7	8	8
9 Blue Moon (E.P.) *Elvis Presley* (HMV)	8	11	14
10 When Mexico Gave Up The Rhumba *Mitchell Torok* (Brunswick)	11	16	19
11 True Love *Bing Crosby and Grace Kelly* (Capitol)	12	10	9
12 Cindy, Oh Cindy *Eddie Fisher* (HMV)	9	7	6
13 Make It A Party *Winifred Atwell* (Decca)	15	13	11
14 Green Door *Jim Lowe* (London)	16	14	15
15 Rockin' Through The Rye *Bill Haley* (Brunswick)	14	16	18
16 Only You *The Platters* (Mercury)	17	20	–
17 Two Different Worlds *Ronnie Hilton* (HMV)	–	19	–
18 Giddy Up A Ding Dong *Freddie Bell and The Bell Boys* (Mercury)	–	–	–
19 Sing With Shand *Jimmy Shand* (Parlophone)	–	–	–
20 Don't Be Cruel *Elvis Presley* (HMV)	17	–	–
– Singing The Blues *Guy Mitchell* (Philips)	13	5	2
– Love Me Tender *Elvis Presley* (HMV)	20	15	12
– Singing The Blues *Tommy Steele* (Decca)	–	18	17
– Christmas Island *Dickie Valentine* (Decca)	–	–	20
– Rock Around The Clock *Bill Haley* (Brunswick)	19	–	16

No chart was published in Record Mirror *for 29 December 1956.*

1956–BEST-SELLING SINGLES

1 I'll Be Home *Pat Boone* (London)
2 It's Almost Tomorrow *The Dream Weavers* (Brunswick)
3 Whatever Will Be Will Be *Doris Day* (Philips)
4 Poor People Of Paris *Winifred Atwell* (Decca)
5 Why Do Fools Fall In Love *Frankie Lymon and The Teenagers* (Columbia)
6 Rock And Roll Waltz *Kay Starr* (HMV)
7 Zambesi *Lou Busch* (Capitol)
8 A Woman In Love *Frankie Laine* (Philips)
9 Just Walking In The Rain *Johnny Ray* (Philips)
10 Hound Dog *Elvis Presley* (HMV)
11 Memories Are Made Of This *Dean Martin* (Capitol)
12 No Other Love *Ronnie Hilton* (HMV)
13 Only You *The Hilltoppers* (London)
14 Lost John *Lonnie Donegan* (Nixa)
15 A Tear Fell *Teresa Brewer* (Vogue/Coral)
16 Lay Down Your Arms *Anne Shelton* (Philips)
17 Rockin' Through The Rye *Bill Haley* (Brunswick)
18 Sixteen Tons *Tennessee Ernie Ford* (Capitol)
19 A Sweet Old Fashioned Girl *Teresa Brewer* (Vogue/Coral)
20 Heartbreak Hotel *Elvis Presley* (HMV)

1957

Bill Haley had arrived in the charts in January 1955 and, with 14 hits to his credit, he all but disappeared from the charts in 1957. Indeed, he was to return with 'Rock Around The Clock' in 1968 and 1974, but to all intents and purposes his chart impetus was never as strong once 'Rock The Joint' had left the Top Twenty.

However, there were several good newcomers on the music scene, including The Everly Brothers, Jerry Lee Lewis, Tab Hunter and Sonny James. Hunter and James both had a hit with 'Young Love', after which James did not appear in the charts again, and Hunter did not do much better, for he could only manage one more Top Ten hit, 'Ninety-Nine Ways' before he, too, faded into obscurity.

The Everley Brothers began their 19-hit trail in July 1957 with 'Bye Bye Love', and with their third record, 'All I Have To Do Is Dream' during the following year, they achieved their first Number One. Jerry Lee Lewis began with 'Whole Lotta Shakin' Goin' On', and in December 1957 he produced 'Great Balls Of Fire', a deserved Number One and one of pop's many classics.

For several newcomers of 1956, 1957 saw their fortunes continue to improve. Lonnie Donegan achieved five hits, of which two, 'Cumberland Gap' and 'Puttin' On The Style', reached the Number One position. The latter disc's B-side was the equally popular 'Gambling Man'.

Tommy Steele had four hits in 1957, as did Johnny Ray, but whereas Steele had a rosy future stretching ahead of him, Ray's chart career was drawing to an end, despite the fact that he achieved a Number One in 1957 with 'Yes Tonight Josephine'. However, his follow-up record, 'Build Your Love', only reached Number Seventeen and spent under a month in the Top Twenty.

Ray's recording company, Philips, had continued to have some measure of success with Frankie Laine, another of their artists, for he managed to achieve one hit with 'Love Is A Golden Ring', and the third of the famous Philips trio, Guy Mitchell, entered the Top Twenty three times throughout the year. One of his hits, 'Rock-A-Billy', reached the Number One position and he beat Tommy Steele in the chart listings with 'Knee Deep In The Blues'.

1957 also saw the first Number One record for the British singer, Frankie Vaughan, who covered 'Garden Of Eden', which had been an American hit. He was chased up the charts by Gary Miller but Miller's challenge proved weak, for he only reached the Number Fourteen position. Vaughan had three more hits including 'Gotta Have Something In The Bank Frank', for which he was joined by The Kaye Sisters.

Apart from the Top Twenty, 1957 also saw the birth of *6.5 Special*, the first British television pop series, which also tended to affect the charts themselves. Programme regulars such as Jim Dale, Terry Dene and Marty Wilde saw chart success following their television appearances. Dene promised much, but following two hits in 1957 and one in 1958, he disappeared from the charts.

Another major event was the advent of The Crickets and their lead singer, Buddy Holly in September 1957. Buddy Holly and The Crickets were living proof that for every trend in pop, there was a reaction countering it. For every menacing Gene Vincent, there was a melodic, clean-cut Buddy Holly. If the elder statesmen of pop became rather too old, there were always child stars of 13 or 14 years of age such as Laurie London, Jackie Dennis or Frankie Lymon ready to fill the gaps.

JANUARY 1957

5	12	19	26
1 Singing The Blues *Guy Mitchell* (Philips)	1	2	1
2 Just Walking In The Rain *Johnny Ray* (Philips)	3	8	12
3 Green Door *Frankie Vaughan* (Philips)	4	5	7
4 Singing The Blues *Tommy Steele* (Decca)	2	1	2
5 St Theresa Of The Roses *Malcolm Vaughan* (HMV)	5	7	6
6 Rip It Up *Little Richard* (London)	10	14	20
7 True Love *Bing Crosby and Grace Kelly* (Capitol)	6	4	4
7 Cindy, Oh Cindy *Eddie Fisher* (HMV)	7	9	11
9 Hound Dog *Elvis Presley* (HMV)	9	10	13
10 My Prayer *The Platters* (Mercury)	–	–	–
11 A Woman In Love *Frankie Laine* (Philips)	20	–	–
12 Love Me Tender *Elvis Presley* (HMV)	15	15	14
13 Blue Moon *Elvis Presley* (HMV)	19	17	–
14 Rock Around The Clock *Bill Haley* (Brunswick)	16	–	–
14 Rockin' Through The Rye *Bill Haley* (Brunswick)	–	–	–
16 Sing With Shand *Jimmy Shand* (Parlophone)	–	–	–
17 Make It A Party *Winifred Atwell* (Decca)	–	–	–
18 Blueberry Hill *Fats Domino* (London)	11	11	10
19 Friendly Persuasion *Pat Boone* (London)	8	6	5
20 A House With Love In It *Vera Lynn* (Decca)	–	–	–
– Moonlight Gambler *Frankie Laine* (Philips)	12	13	9
– Garden Of Eden *Gary Miller* (Nixa)	12	16	17
– Garden Of Eden *Frankie Vaughan* (Philips)	14	3	3
– More *Jimmy Young* (Decca)	16	–	–
– When Mexico Gave Up The Rhumba *Mitchell Torok* (Brunswick)	16	–	–
– Don't Be Cruel *Elvis Presley* (HMV)	20	–	–
– Don't You Rock Me Daddy-O *Lonnie Donegan* (Nixa)	–	12	8
– Garden Of Eden *Dick James* (Parlophone)	–	18	–
– Garden Of Eden *Joe Valino* (HMV)	–	19	17
– Two Different Worlds *Ronnie Hilton* (HMV)	–	20	–
– You Don't Owe Me A Thing *Johnny Ray* (Philips)	–	–	19
– Don't You Rock Me Daddy-O *The Vipers* (Parlophone)	–	–	15
– Adoration Waltz *David Whitfield* (Decca)	–	–	16

FEBRUARY 1957

2	9	16	23
1 Garden of Eden *Frankie Vaughan* (Philips)	1	1	2
2 Singing The Blues *Guy Mitchell* (Philips)	2	3	3
3 Singing The Blues *Tommy Steele* (Decca)	6	12	13
4 Friendly Persuasion *Pat Boone* (London)	3	6	8
5 True Love *Bing Crosby and Grace Kelly* (Capitol)	4	5	7
6 St Theresa Of The Roses *Malcolm Vaughan* (HMV)	9	9	12
7 Blueberry Hill *Fats Domino* (London)	7	7	11
8 Don't You Rock Me Daddy-O *Lonnie Donegan* (Nixa)	5	4	5
9 Moonlight Gambler *Frankie Laine* (Philips)	13	–	–
10 Hound Dog *Elvis Presley* (HMV)	12	20	–
11 Cindy, Oh Cindy *Eddie Fisher* (HMV)	16	17	–
12 Green Door *Frankie Vaughan* (Philips)	–	–	–
13 Don't You Rock Me Daddy-O *The Vipers* (Parlophone)	8	13	15
14 Garden Of Eden *Gary Miller* (Nixa)	–	19	–
15 You Don't Owe Me A Thing *Johnny Ray* (Philips)	19	15	14
15 Adoration Waltz *David Whitfield* (Decca)	16	20	17
17 Just Walking In The Rain *Johnny Ray* (Philips)	18	–	–
18 Love Me Tender *Elvis Presley* (HMV)	–	–	–
19 Rock The Joint *Bill Haley* (Brunswick)	15	18	20

	9	16	23
20 Ain't That A Shame *Fats Domino* (London)	–	–	–
– Don't Forbid Me *Pat Boone* (London)	14	8	4
– Young Love *Tab Hunter* (London)	10	2	1
– Don't Knock The Rock *Bill Haley* (Brunswick)	11	10	10
– Rip It Up *Little Richard* (London)	20	–	–
– Young Love *Sonny James* (Capitol)	–	11	9
– Long Tall Sally *Little Richard* (London)	–	15	19
– Rock A Bye Your Baby *Jerry Lewis* (Brunswick)	–	14	16
– Knee Deep In The Blues *Tommy Steele* (Decca)	–	–	18
– Knee Deep In The Blues *Guy Mitchell* (Philips)	–	–	6
– You, Me And Us *Alma Cogan* (HMV)	–	–	20

MARCH 1957

2	9	16	23	30
1 Young Love *Tab Hunter* (London)	1	1	1	1
2 Don't Forbid Me *Pat Boone* (London)	2	2	2	2
3 Knee Deep In The Blues *Guy Mitchell* (Philips)	3	3	3	4
4 Garden Of Eden *Frankie Vaughan* (Philips)	5	9	10	–
5 Singing The Blues *Guy Mitchell* (Philips)	6	7	8	11
6 Don't You Rock Me Daddy-O *Lonnie Donegan* (Nixa)	4	4	5	6
7 True Love *Bing Crosby and Grace Kelly* (Capitol)	8	8	9	7
8 Long Tall Sally *Little Richard* (London)	7	5	4	3
9 Friendly Persuasion *Pat Boone* (London)	10	10	12	20
10 Young Love *Sonny James* (Capitol)	11	13	17	–
11 Adoration Waltz *David Whitfield* (Decca)	12	14	16	–
12 Blueberry Hill *Fats Domino* (London)	16	–	–	–
13 Banana Boat Song *Harry Belafonte* (HMV)	9	6	6	5
14 You Don't Owe Me A Thing *Johnny Ray* (Philips)	19	15	13	16
15 Don't Knock The Rock *Bill Haley* (Brunswick)	13	16	–	–
16 Knee Deep In The Blues *Tommy Steele* (Decca)	17	–	–	–
16 Banana Boat Song *The Tarriers* (Columbia)	14	12	11	15
18 Rip It Up *Little Richard* (London)	18	19	–	–
18 St Theresa Of The Roses *Malcolm Vaughan* (HMV)	–	–	–	–
20 Rock A Bye Your Baby *Jerry Lewis* (Capitol)	19	18	–	19
– Banana Boat Song *Shirley Bassey* (Philips)	15	11	7	8
– Wisdom Of A Fool *Norman Wisdom* (Columbia)	–	20	20	–
– Look Homeward Angel *Johnny Ray* (Philips)	–	17	18	12
– She's Got It *Little Richard* (London)	–	–	14	13
– Only You *The Platters* (Mercury)	–	–	14	10
– The Girl Can't Help It *Little Richard* (London)	–	–	18	14
– The Great Pretender *The Platters* (Mercury)	–	–	20	17
– Cumberland Gap *The Vipers* (Parlophone)	–	–	–	9
– Freight Train *Chas McDevitt and Nancy Whiskey* (Oriole)	–	–	–	18

APRIL 1957

6	13	20	27
1 Young Love *Tab Hunter* (London)	2	2	2
2 Don't Forbid Me *Pat Boone* (London)	3	5	6
3 Long Tall Sally *Little Richard* (London)	4	4	4
4 Knee Deep In The Blues *Guy Mitchell* (Philips)	6	8	20
5 Banana Boat Song *Harry Belafonte* (HMV)	5	3	3
6 Cumberland Gap *Lonnie Donegan* (Nixa)	1	1	1
7 Don't You Rock Me Daddy-O *Lonnie Donegan* (Nixa)	9	15	–
8 Look Homeward Angel *Johnny Ray* (Philips)	7	10	8
9 Cumberland Gap *The Vipers* (Parlophone)	12	–	–
10 Only You *The Platters* (Mercury)	17	–	–
11 The Girl Can't Help It *Little Richard* (London)	10	12	11

	13	**20**	**27**
12 Banana Boat Song *Shirley Bassey* (Philips)	18	–	–
13 She's Got It *Little Richard* (London)	8	13	17
14 True Love *Bing Crosby and Grace Kelly* (Capitol)	14	20	20
15 Singing The Blues *Guy Mitchell* (Philips)	–	–	–
16 Friendly Persuasion *Pat Boone* (London)	–	–	–
17 The Great Pretender *The Platters* (Mercury)	–	–	–
18 Tutti Frutti *Little Richard* (London)	–	–	–
18 Heart *Max Bygraves* (Decca)	19	17	14
20 Banana Boat Song *The Tarriers* (Columbia)	–	–	–
– Freight Train *Chas McDevitt and Nancy Whiskey* (Oriole)	11	8	9
– I'm Not A Juvenile Delinquent *Frankie Lymon and The Teenagers* (Columbia)	13	7	12
– Ninety-Nine Ways *Tab Hunter* (London)	15	11	13
– Singing The Blues *Tommy Steele* (Decca)	19	19	–
– Baby Baby *Frankie Lymon and The Teenagers* (Columbia)	16	6	5
– I'll Take You Home Again Kathleen *Slim Whitman* (London)	–	13	7
– Love Is A Golden Ring *Frankie Laine* (Philips)	–	16	–
– Butterfly *Andy Williams* (London)	–	18	16
– I'm Walkin' *Fats Domino* (London)	–	20	15
– Maggie May *The Vipers* (Parlophone)	–	20	–
– When I Fall In Love *Nat 'King' Cole* (Capitol)	–	–	10
– Butterfly *Charlie Gracie* (Parlophone)	–	–	17
– Butterfingers *Tommy Steele* (Decca)	–	–	19

MAY 1957

	11	**18**	**25**
1 Cumberland Gap *Lonnie Donegan* (Nixa)	2	5	8
2 Baby Baby *Frankie Lymon and The Teenagers* (Columbia)	4	6	6
3 Banana Boat Song *Harry Belafonte* (HMV)	6	11	13
4 Long Tall Sally *Little Richard* (London)	10	13	16
5 Rock-A-Billy *Guy Mitchell* (Philips)	3	2	2
6 Young Love *Tab Hunter* (London)	11	15	–
7 When I Fall In Love *Nat 'King' Cole* (Capitol)	7	3	4
8 Butterfly *Andy Williams* (London)	1	1	1
9 Look Homeward Angel *Johnny Ray* (Philips)	13	12	18
10 Ninety-Nine Ways *Tab Hunter* (London)	5	8	10
11 I'll Take You Home Again Kathleen *Slim Whitman* (London)	9	9	5
12 Don't Forbid Me *Pat Boone* (London)	17	–	–
13 The Girl Can't Help It *Little Richard* (London)	4	14	20
14 Freight Train *Chas McDevitt and Nancy Whiskey* (Oriole)	8	10	9
15 I'm Not A Juvenile Delinquent *Frankie Lymon and The Teenagers* (Columbia)	19	18	–
16 I'm Walkin' *Fats Domino* (London)	16	20	15
17 Love Is A Golden Ring *Frankie Laine* (Philips)	–	–	–
18 Butterfingers *Tommy Steele* (Decca)	–	–	11
19 Butterfly *Charlie Gracie* (Parlophone)	–	19	14
20 She's Got It *Little Richard* (London)	20	–	–
– Yes Tonight Josephine *Johnny Ray* (Philips)	12	4	3
– Too Much *Elvis Presley* (HMV)	15	7	7
– Chapel Of The Roses *Malcolm Vaughan* (HMV)	18	16	19
– Why Baby Why *Pat Boone* (London)	–	17	–
– Party Doll *Buddy Knox* (Columbia)	–	–	17
– Mr Wonderful *Peggy Lee* (Brunswick)	–	–	12

JUNE 1957

	8	15	22	29
1 Butterfly *Andy Williams* (London)	2	3	5	9
2 Yes Tonight Josephine *Johnny Ray* (Philips)	1	1	1	1
3 Rock-A-Billy *Guy Mitchell* (Philips)	4	4	7	12
4 When I Fall In Love *Nat 'King' Cole* (Capitol)	3	2	3	3
5 I'll Take You Home Again Kathleen *Slim Whitman* (London)	6	14	17	–
6 Freight Train *Chas McDevitt and Nancy Whiskey* (Oriole)	5	11	12	18
7 Baby Baby *Frankie Lymon and The Teenagers* (Columbia)	14	19	18	–
8 Cumberland Gap *The Vipers* (Columbia)	11	13	15	19
9 Cumberland Gap *Lonnie Donegan* (Nixa)	–	–	–	–
10 Mr Wonderful *Peggy Lee* (Brunswick)	9	9	8	11
11 Ninety-Nine Ways *Tab Hunter* (London)	17	20	–	–
12 Around The World *Bing Crosby* (Brunswick)	8	7	4	7
13 Butterfingers *Tommy Steele* (Decca)	12	16	14	16
14 Around The World *Gracie Fields* (Columbia)	10	10	10	13
15 Around The World *Ronnie Hilton* (HMV)	7	6	6	5
16 Long Tall Sally *Little Richard* (London)	–	–	–	–
17 Look Homeward Angel *Johnny Ray* (Philips)	–	–	–	–
18 I'm Sorry *The Platters* (Mercury)	–	–	20	–
19 Chapel Of The Roses *Malcolm Vaughan* (HMV)	18	18	–	–
20 The Girl Can't Help It *Little Richard* (London)	–	–	–	–
– A White Sports Coat *Terry Dene* (Decca)	19	–	16	17
– Puttin' On The Style *Lonnie Donegan* (Nixa)	–	15	–	–
– A White Sports Coat *The King Brothers* (Parlophone)	19	17	11	10
– We Will Make Love *Russ Hamilton* (Oriole)	16	12	13	8
– Gambling Man *Lonnie Donegan* (Nixa)	15	8	2	2
– Little Darlin' *The Diamonds* (Mercury)	13	5	9	4
– Island In The Sun *Harry Belafonte* (RCA)	–	–	19	15
– All Shook Up *Elvis Presley* (HMV)	–	–	–	6
– Another School Day *Chuck Berry* (London)	–	–	–	20
– Fabulous *Charlie Gracie* (Parlophone)	–	–	–	14

JULY 1957

	13	20	27
1 Gambling Man *Lonnie Donegan* (Nixa)	2	2	2
2 All Shook Up *Elvis Presley* (RCA)	1	1	1
3 Yes Tonight Josephine *Johnny Ray* (Philips)	4	7	7
4 Little Darlin' *The Diamonds* (Mercury)	6	5	5
5 Around The World *Ronnie Hilton* (HMV)	5	6	8
6 We Will Make Love *Russ Hamilton* (Oriole)	3	3	4
7 When I Fall In Love *Nat 'King' Cole* (Capitol)	7	13	11
8 Around The World *Bing Crosby* (Brunswick)	9	10	13
9 A White Sports Coat *The King Brothers* (Parlophone)	8	11	12
10 Mr Wonderful *Peggy Lee* (Capitol)	13	17	18
11 Butterfingers *Tommy Steele* (Decca)	10	9	9
12 Butterfly *Andy Williams* (London)	–	–	–
13 Fabulous *Charlie Gracie* (Parlophone)	16	15	20
14 Freight Train *Chas McDevitt and Nancy Whiskey* (Oriole)	17	19	–
15 Around The World *Gracie Fields* (Columbia)	19	–	–
16 Rock-A-Billy *Guy Mitchell* (Philips)	–	–	–
17 Island In The Sun *Harry Belafonte* (RCA)	12	16	15
18 Lucille *Little Richard* (London)	15	12	10
19 I'm Sorry *The Platters* (Mercury)	–	–	–
20 I Like Your Kind Of Love *Andy Williams* (London)	18	18	19
– Last Train To San Fernando *Johnny Duncan* (Columbia)	–	–	17
– Teddy Bear *Elvis Presley* (RCA)	14	4	3

6	13	20	27
– Love Letters In The Sand *Pat Boone* (London)	11	8	6
– A White Sports Coat *Terry Dene* (Decca)	20	–	–
– Start Movin' *Sal Mineo* (Philips)	–	20	–
– Bye Bye Love *The Everly Brothers* (London)	–	14	14
– All Star Hit Parade Vol. 2 *Various Artists* (Decca)	–	–	16

AUGUST 1957

3	10	17	24	31
1 All Shook Up *Elvis Presley* (HMV)	1	1	1	3
2 Teddy Bear *Elvis Presley* (RCA)	3	2	4	5
3 Gambling Man/Puttin' On The Style *Lonnie Donegan* (Nixa)	2	5	8	12
4 We Will Make Love *Russ Hamilton* (Oriole)	4	6	10	10
5 Little Darlin' *The Diamonds* (Mercury)	6	9	9	16
6 Love Letters In The Sand *Pat Boone* (London)	5	3	3	2
7 Lucille *Little Richard* (London)	9	16	–	–
8 Around The World *Ronnie Hilton* (HMV)	12	18	18	–
9 Island In The Sun *Harry Belafonte* (RCA)	7	4	2	4
10 Yes Tonight Josephine *Johnny Ray* (Philips)	14	20	19	–
11 Butterfingers *Tommy Steele* (Decca)	11	15	15	17
12 Bye Bye Love *The Everly Brothers* (London)	8	7	6	7
13 Around The World *Bing Crosby* (Brunswick)	19	19	–	–
14 Start Movin' *Terry Dene* (Decca)	16	14	17	20
15 When I Fall In Love *Nat 'King' Cole* (Capitol)	15	17	–	–
16 Last Train To San Fernando *Johnny Duncan* (Columbia)	10	8	7	6
17 All Star Hit Parade Vol. 2 *Various Artists* (Decca)	13	10	11	19
18 A White Sports Coat *The King Brothers* (Parlophone)	–	–	–	–
19 Start Movin' *Sal Mineo* (Philips)	18	11	13	15
20 With All My Heart *Petula Clark* (Nixa)	17	12	14	9
– Fabulous *Charlie Gracie* (Parlophone)	20	–	16	13
– Diana *Paul Anka* (Columbia)	–	13	5	1
– Water Water/Handful Of Songs *Tommy Steele* (Decca)	–	–	12	8
– I'm Gonna Sit Right Down And Write Myself A Letter *Billy Williams* (Vogue Coral)	–	–	20	–
– Wanderin' Eyes *Charlie Gracie* (London)	–	–	–	11
– Shiralee *Tommy Steele* (Decca)	–	–	–	14
– Paralysed *Elvis Presley* (HMV)	–	–	–	18

SEPTEMBER 1957

7	14	21	28
1 Diana *Paul Anka* (Columbia)	1	1	1
2 Love Letters In The Sand *Pat Boone* (London)	2	2	2
3 Last Train To San Fernando *Johnny Duncan* (Columbia)	3	3	3
4 All Shook Up *Elvis Presley* (HMV)	5	7	7
5 Island In The Sun *Harry Belafonte* (RCA)	4	4	4
6 Water Water/Handful Of Songs *Tommy Steele* (Decca)	6	5	5
7 Teddy Bear *Elvis Presley* (RCA)	10	12	14
8 Bye Bye Love *The Everly Brothers* (London)	11	11	13
9 With All My Heart *Petula Clark* (Nixa)	7	8	6
10 Paralysed *Elvis Presley* (HMV)	9	9	10
11 Wanderin' Eyes *Charlie Gracie* (London)	8	6	8
12 Fabulous *Charlie Gracie* (Parlophone)	13	16	–
13 We Will Make Love *Russ Hamilton* (Oriole)	17	–	16
14 Little Darlin' *The Diamonds* (Mercury)	18	19	–
15 Gambling Man/Puttin' On The Style *Lonnie Donegan* (Nixa)	14	14	–
16 Shiralee *Tommy Steele* (Decca)	16	15	17
17 Tammy *Debbie Reynolds* (Vogue/Coral)	12	10	9

7		14	21	28
18 Butterfingers *Tommy Steele* (Decca)		–	–	–
19 All Star Hit Parade Vol. 2 *Various Artists* (Decca)		–	–	–
20 Start Movin' *Sal Mineo* (Philips)		–	–	–
– Jenny Jenny *Little Richard* (London)		15	13	11
– Build Your Love *Johnny Ray* (Philips)		19	17	18
– Man On Fire *Frankie Vaughan* (Philips)		20	–	–
– Stardust *Billy Ward* (London)		–	20	20
– Whole Lotta Shakin' Goin' On *Jerry Lee Lewis* (London)		–	–	19
– That'll Be The Day *The Crickets* (Vogue/Coral)		–	–	12
– Short Fat Fannie *Larry Williams* (London)		–	18	15

OCTOBER 1957

5	12	19	26
1 Diana *Paul Anka* (Columbia)	1	1	2
2 Love Letters In The Sand *Pat Boone* (London)	2	5	6
3 Last Train To San Fernando *Johnny Duncan* (Columbia)	4	6	15
4 Wanderin' Eyes *Charlie Gracie* (London)	6	7	7
5 Island In The Sun *Harry Belafonte* (RCA)	9	8	12
6 Tammy *Debbie Reynolds* (Vogue/Coral)	3	3	4
7 Water Water/Handful Of Songs *Tommy Steele* (Decca)	8	9	9
8 With All My Heart *Petula Clark* (Nixa)	11	12	10
9 All Shook Up *Elvis Presley* (HMV)	10	13	16
10 That'll Be The Day *The Crickets*(Vogue Coral)	5	2	1
11 Paralysed *Elvis Presley* (HMV)	13	17	18
12 Jenny Jenny *Little Richard* (London)	20	–	–
13 Teddy Bear *Elvis Presley* (RCA)	14	15	8
14 Remember You're Mine *Pat Boone* (London)	16	10	5
15 Whole Lotta Shakin' Goin' On *Jerry Lee Lewis* (London)	12	14	11
16 Bye Bye Love *The Everly Brothers* (London)	17	–	–
17 Stardust *Billy Ward* (London)	–	–	–
18 Let's Have A Party *Elvis Presley* (RCA)	7	4	3
19 Short Fat Fannie *Larry Williams* (London)	–	–	–
20 In The Middle Of An Island *The King Brothers* (Parlophone)	–	–	–
– My Dixie Darlin' *Lonnie Donegan* (Nixa)	15	11	14
– Wedding Ring *Russ Hamilton* (Oriole)	18	19	20
– Man On Fire/Wanderin' Eyes *Frankie Vaughan* (Philips)*	19	16	13
– Call Rosie On The Phone *Guy Mitchell* (Philips)	–	18	17
– Be My Girl *Jim Dale* (Parlophone)	–	20	19

* Record Mirror *first listed this record as a one-selling side, namely 'Man On Fire', as seen in the September listings.*

NOVEMBER 1957

2	9	16	23	30
1 That'll Be The Day *The Crickets* (Vogue/Coral)	1	1	3	6
2 Let's Have A Party *Elvis Presley* (RCA)	2	2	2	3
3 Tammy *Debbie Reynolds* (Vogue/Coral)	3	3	9	12
4 Diana *Paul Anka* (Columbia)	4	9	11	16
5 Remember You're Mine *Pat Boone* (London)	5	8	8	7
6 Man On Fire/Wanderin' Eyes *Frankie Vaughan* (Philips)	7	10	12	15
7 Be My Girl *Jim Dale* (Parlophone)	6	6	5	2
8 Whole Lotta Shakin' Goin' On *Jerry Lee Lewis* (London)	9	14	20	–
9 Love Letters In The Sand *Pat Boone* (London)	13	17	–	–
10 Wanderin' Eyes *Charlie Gracie* (London)	16	–	–	–
11 Teddy Bear *Elvis Presley* (RCA)	14	19	–	–
12 Water Water/Handful Of Songs *Tommy Steele* (Decca)	15	–	–	–

2	9	16	23	30
13 Island In The Sun *Harry Belafonte* (RCA)	18	–	–	–
14 With All My Heart *Petula Clark* (Nixa)	17	15	–	–
15 My Dixie Darlin' *Lonnie Donegan* (Nixa)	10	13	16	19
16 Last Train To San Fernando *Johnny Duncan* (Columbia)	20	–	–	–
17 Gotta Have Something In The Bank Frank *Frankie Vaughan and The Kaye Sisters* (Philips)	8	7	7	8
18 Lawdy Miss Clawdy/Tryin' To Get You *Elvis Presley* (HMV)	11	12	13	20
19 He's Got The Whole Wide World In His Hands *Laurie London* (Parlophone)	–	20	–	13
20 Honeycombe *Jimmy Rodgers* (Columbia)	–	–	–	–
– I Love You Baby *Paul Anka* (Columbia)	12	5	4	4
– Santa Bring Back My Baby to Me *Elvis Presley* (RCA)	–	16	10	9
– Mary's Boy Child *Harry Belafonte* (RCA)	–	4	1	1
– Wake Up Little Susie *The Everly Brothers* (London)	19	11	6	5
– Reet Petite *Jackie Wilson* (Coral)	–	18	17	18
– Alone *Petula Clark* (Pye/Nixa)	–	–	14	10
– Alone *The Shepherd Sisters* (HMV)	–	–	15	14
– Ma He's Making Eyes At Me *Johnny Otis Show* (Capitol)	–	–	18	11
– Alone *The Southlanders* (Decca)	–	–	19	17
– Keep A Knocking *Little Richard* (London)	–	–	–	20

DECEMBER 1957

7	14	21
1 Mary's Boy Child *Harry Belafonte* (RCA)	1	1
2 Wake Up Little Susie *The Everly Brothers* (London)	2	3
3 I Love You Baby *Paul Anka* (Columbia)	3	3
4 Be My Girl *Jim Dale* (Parlophone)	4	6
5 Let's Have A Party *Elvis Presley* (RCA)	9	8
6 Ma He's Making Eyes At Me *Johnny Otis Show* (Capitol)	6	2
7 Remember You're Mine *Pat Boone* (London)	11	8
8 Santa Bring Back My Baby To Me *Elvis Presley* (RCA)	7	11
9 Alone *Petula Clark* (Pye/Nixa)	8	13
10 That'll Be The Day *The Crickets* (Vogue/Coral)	17	15
11 My Special Angel *Malcolm Vaughan* (HMV)	5	5
12 He's Got The Whole Wide World In His Hands *Laurie London* (Parlophone)	13	12
13 Gotta Have Something In The Bank Frank *Frankie Vaughan and The Kaye Sisters* (Philips)	–	–
14 Diana *Paul Anka* (Columbia)	15	17
15 Keep A Knocking *Little Richard* (London)	–	–
16 My Special Angel *Bobby Helms* (Brunswick)	18	20
17 Reet Petite *Jackie Wilson* (Coral)	12	14
17 Alone *The Southlanders* (Decca)	–	–
19 Tammy *Debbie Reynolds* (Vogue/Coral)	–	–
20 Alone *The Shepherd Sisters* (HMV)	–	–
– Wake Up Little Susie *The King Brothers* (Parlophone)	–	19
– Great Balls Of Fire *Jerry Lee Lewis* (London)	–	16
– Let's Have A Ball *Winifred Atwell* (Decca)	10	7
– All The Way *Frank Sinatra* (Capitol)	14	8
– April Love *Pat Boone* (London)	16	18

No chart was published for 28 December 1957.
We have found no record of the paper being published on 14 December and the listings for this date has been derived from the 'last week' figures of 21 December. However, such figures do not indicate the complete Top Twenty owing to records dropping out and being replaced in the charts.

1   Love Letters In The Sand *Pat Boone* (London)
2   Diana *Paul Anka* (Columbia)
3   All Shook Up *Elvis Presley* (RCA)
4   Young Love *Tab Hunter* (London)
5   Island In The Sun *Harry Belafonte* (RCA)
6   Teddy Bear *Elvis Presley* (RCA)
7   Yes Tonight Josephine *Johnny Ray* (Philips)
8   Don't Forbid Me *Pat Boone* (London)
9   When I Fall In Love *Nat 'King' Cole* (Capitol)
10 Long Tall Sally *Little Richard* (London)
11 Let's Have A Party *Elvis Presley* (RCA)
12 Gambling Man/Puttin' On The Style *Lonnie Donegan* (Nixa)
13 Mary's Boy Child *Harry Belafonte* (RCA)
14 That'll Be The Day *The Crickets* (Vogue/Coral)
15 All The Way *Frank Sinatra* (Capitol)
16 Wake Up Little Susie *The Everly Brothers* (London)
17 Tammy *Debbie Reynolds* (Vogue/Coral)
18 I Love You Baby *Paul Anka* (Columbia)
19 Remember You're Mine *Pat Boone* (London)
20 April Love *Pat Boone* (London)

1958

1957 saw the arrival of Cliff Richard who, once he had been persuaded not to act like a direct copy of Elvis Presley, began a long and successful chart career. His first chart entry was in October 1958 with the classic song 'Move It', a number which was re-recorded in a different style in 1975 by Alvin Stardust.

1958 was also the year of Duane Eddy's first twanging guitar hit, and the emergence of Johnny Mathis, a singer who was still to be found enjoying increasing success as late as 17 years hence in 1975.

There was also the start of a somewhat brief but amazingly successful career in the charts for Connie Francis. She began with a Number One, 'Who's Sorry Now', and by the end of 1958 she had achieved another four hits.

The chart regulars managed fairly well, for Pat Boone had four hit records, Elvis achieved six and Lonnie Donegan mustered three. 'Tom Dooley', one of Donegan's hits, gave 1958 chart followers an exciting time as it battled in the charts with the original version by the American group, The Kingston Trio, a slightly folky group.

Even Ruby Murray reappeared after remaining dormant in the 1957 charts, and the year also saw seven hits from Perry Como. Como had indeed made chart impressions in 1956 with 'Hot Diggity', 'More' and 'Glendora', but had disappeared from the charts in 1957. However, few could have expected his startling comeback of 1958. though his television show of the time obviously brought him back into the public eye and aided his success a great deal.

The year also produced some pop classics including 'Twilight Time' from The Platters, 'Purple People Eater' from Sheb Wooley, Vic Damone's 'On The Street Where You Live', and 'Oh! Boy', 'Maybe Baby' and 'Think It Over' from The Crickets with Buddy Holly. Buddy Holly began his solo hit run with the mighty 'Peggy Sue', a record which was followed up by 'Listen To Me', 'Rave On' and 'Early In The Morning'.

As always, big stars of the past failed to make the charts and therefore disappeared from the public eye. Winifred

Atwell's piano records failed to sell, although her Christmas hit of 1957 did mean that her name appeared in the 1958 listings. Eddie Calvert ended his trumpet successes with 'Mandy', and The Chordettes faded with the sickly strains of 'Lollipop'. The same song was also the swan-song of The Mudlarks.

However, another pianist appeared in the charts to fill the gaps left by both Joe Henderson and Winifred Atwell. This was Russ Conway, whose first hit was 'More Party Pops'.

Terry Dene appeared in the charts for the last time with 'Stairway Of Love', and Jackie Dennis had but a brief chart innings with 'La Dee Dah', not one of pop's most celebrated lyrics. The Four Preps came and went with the bouncy 'Big Man', a song best remembered for its piano chords. There was also a new but short-lived sound from Elias and his Zig Zag Jive Flutes with 'Tom Hark'.

Charlie Gracie was unsuccessful in 1958 despite four hits in 1957, including 'Fabulous' which had sounded very much like an early Presley record. Tab Hunter never found his way back into the charts, and the most important demise from the charts was that of Slim Whitman, who had achieved seven hits since 1955.

JANUARY 1958

4	11	18	25
1 Ma He's Making Eyes At Me *Johnny Otis Show* (Capitol)	1	2	3
2 Mary's Boy Child *Harry Belafonte* (RCA)	11	–	–
3 Wake Up Little Susie *The Everly Brothers* (London)	4	7	12
4 I Love You Baby *Paul Anka* (Columbia)	5	10	15
5 Great Balls Of Fire *Jerry Lee Lewis* (London)	2	1	2
6 My Special Angel *Malcolm Vaughan* (HMV)	3	5	7
7 Reet Petite *Jackie Wilson* (Coral)	7	3	9
8 All The Way *Frank Sinatra* (Capitol)	8	8	5
9 Kisses Sweeter Than Wine *Jimmy Rodgers* (Columbia)	6	9	8
10 Diana *Paul Anka* (Columbia)	14	–	–
11 Alone *Petula Clark* (Pye)	15	–	–
12 Party *Elvis Presley* (HMV)	16	13	–
13 Peggy Sue *Buddy Holly* (Coral)	10	4	6
14 Let's Have A Ball *Winifred Atwell* (Decca)	19	–	–
15 April Love *Pat Boone* (London)	12	12	16
16 Alone *The Southlanders* (Decca)	18	14	20
17 Oh! Boy *The Crickets* (Coral)	9	5	4
18 Jack O'Diamonds *Lonnie Donegan* (Pye)	17	16	–
19 Be My Girl *Jim Dale* (Parlophone)	–	–	–
20 Remember You're Mine *Pat Boone* (London)	–	20	–
– Kisses Sweeter Than Wine *Frankie Vaughan* (Philips)	13	11	14
– He's Got The Whole Wide World *Laurie London* (Parlophone)	20	17	–
– Story Of My Life *Michael Holliday* (Columbia)	–	15	10
– Wake Up Little Susie *The King Brothers* (Parlophone)	–	19	–
– I'm Left, You're Right, She's Gone *Elvis Presley* (RCA)	–	18	17
– The Story Of My Life *Gary Miller* (Nixa)	–	–	11
– Bony Maronie *Larry Williams* (London)	–	–	13
– Bye Bye Baby *Johnny Otis Show* (Capitol)	–	–	18
– At The Hop *Danny and The Juniors* (HMV)	–	–	19
– Jailhouse Rock *Elvis Presley* (RCA)	–	–	1

FEBRUARY 1958

1	8	15	22
1 Jailhouse Rock *Elvis Presley* (RCA)	1	2	3
2 The Story Of My Life *Michael Holliday* (Columbia)	2	1	1
3 Great Balls Of Fire *Jerry Lee Lewis* (London)	5	7	11
4 Oh! Boy *The Crickets* (Coral)	3	3	5
5 All The Way *Frank Sinatra* (Capitol)	6	6	7
6 Ma He's Making Eyes At Me *Johnny Otis Show* (Capitol)	11	14	17
7 Peggy Sue *Buddy Holly* (Coral)	8	11	10
8 Kisses Sweeter Than Wine *Jimmy Rodgers* (Columbia)	11	17	–
9 My Special Angel *Malcolm Vaughan* (HMV)	15	19	–
10 The Story Of My Life *Gary Miller* (Nixa)	10	13	14
11 April Love *Pat Boone* (London)	9	8	9
12 At The Hop *Danny and The Juniors* (HMV)	4	4	4
13 Bony Moronie *Larry Williams* (London)	14	12	12
14 Kisses Sweeter Than Wine *Frankie Vaughan* (Philips)	16	15	16
15 Reet Petite *Jackie Wilson* (Coral)	19	–	–
16 Love Me Forever *Marion Ryan* (Pye)	7	9	8
17 Bye Bye Baby *Johnny Otis Show* (Capitol)	18	18	–
18 Wake Up Little Susie *The Everly Brothers* (London)	–	–	–
19 I Love You Baby *Paul Anka* (Columbia)	–	–	–
20 I'm Left, You're Right, She's Gone *Elvis Presley* (RCA)	–	–	–
– You Are My Destiny *Paul Anka* (Columbia)	13	10	6
– Jailhouse Rock (E.P.) *Elvis Presley* (RCA)	16	16	15
– Love Me Forever *Edyie Gormie* (CBS)	20	–	–

1	**8**	**15**	**22**
– Magic Moments *Perry Como* (RCA)	–	5	2
– Put A Light In The Window *The Southlanders* (Decca)	–	20	–
– Mandy *Eddie Calvert* (Columbia)	–	–	13
– Stood Up *Ricky Nelson* (London)	–	–	18
– At The Hop *Nick Todd* (London)	–	–	19
– Raunchy *Bill Justis* (London)	–	–	20

MARCH 1958

1	**8**	**15**	**22**	**29**
1 Magic Moments/Catch A Falling Star *Perry Como* (RCA)	1	1	1	1
2 The Story Of My Life *Michael Holliday* (Columbia)	2	2	3	4
3 Jailhouse Rock *Elvis Presley* (RCA)	3	4	5	6
4 At The Hop *Danny and The Juniors* (HMV)	4	5	6	9
5 Oh! Boy *The Crickets* (Coral)	7	7	11	13
6 You Are My Destiny *Paul Anka* (Columbia)	6	8	10	11
7 Love Me Forever *Marion Ryan* (Nixa)	8	12	13	–
8 All The Way/Chicago *Frank Sinatra* (Capitol)	10	13	15	12
9 April Love *Pat Boone* (London)	9	11	12	14
10 Peggy Sue *Buddy Holly* (Coral)	11	15	19	–
11 Don't/I Beg Of You *Elvis Presley* (RCA)	5	3	2	2
12 Great Balls Of Fire *Jerry Lee Lewis* (London)	–	–	–	–
13 Bony Moronie *Larry Williams* (London)	17	–	–	–
14 At The Hop *Nick Todd* (London)	–	–	–	–
15 Whole Lotta Woman *Marvin Rainwater* (MGM)	16	16	8	5
16 Mandy *Eddie Calvert* (Columbia)	19	18	18	15
17 Witchcraft *Frank Sinatra* (Capitol)	–	20	–	–
18 Raunchy *Bill Justis* (London)	–	–	–	–
19 Kisses Sweeter Than Wine *Frankie Vaughan* (Philips)	–	–	–	–
20 Sugartime *The McGuire Sisters* (Coral)	–	–	–	–
– Nairobi *Tommy Steele* (Decca)	12	6	4	3
– We Are Not Alone/Can't Get Along Without You *Frankie Vaughan* (Philips)	13	10	14	17
– Good Golly Miss Molly *Little Richard* (London)	14	9	7	8
– Baby Lover *Petula Clark* (Pye)	15	17	17	18
– Sugar Time/Don't Let Go *Jim Dale* (Parlophone)	17	–	–	–
– Jailhouse Rock (E.P.) *Elvis Presley* (RCA)	20	–	–	–
– Maybe Baby *The Crickets* (Coral)	–	14	9	7
– To Be Loved *Jackie Wilson* (Coral)	–	19	–	19
– Why Don't They Understand *George Hamilton IV* (HMV)	–	20	16	20
– Swingin' Shepherd Blues *Mo Kauffman* (London)	–	–	20	–
– La Dee Dah *Jackie Dennis* (Decca)	–	–	–	10
– Big Beat *Fats Domino* (London)	–	–	–	16

APRIL 1958

5	**12**	**19**	**26**
1 Magic Moments/Catch A Falling Star *Perry Como* (RCA)	1	2	3
2 Don't/I Beg Of You *Elvis Presley* (RCA)	3	6	10
3 Whole Lotta Woman *Marvin Rainwater* (MGM)	2	1	1
4 Nairobi *Tommy Steele* (Decca)	5	5	9
5 Maybe Baby *The Crickets* (Coral)	4	4	5
6 La Dee Dah *Jackie Dennis* (Decca)	6	9	11
7 The Story Of My Life *Michael Holliday* (Columbia)	11	–	–
8 Good Golly Miss Molly *Little Richard* (London)	10	13	–
9 Swingin' Shepherd Blues *Ted Heath* (Decca)	7	8	4
10 Jailhouse Rock *Elvis Presley* (RCA)	12	–	–
11 At The Hop *Danny and The Juniors* (HMV)	–	–	–

5

	12	19	26
12 Too Soon To Know/A Wonderful Time Up There *Pat Boone* (London)	8	3	2
13 Tequila *The Champs* (London)	9	7	7
14 April Love *Pat Boone* (London)	15	14	15
15 Big Beat *Fats Domino* (London)	16	–	–
16 Mandy *Eddie Calvert* (Columbia)	14	19	–
17 Baby Lover *Petula Clark* (Pye)	18	–	–
18 Oh I I'm Falling In Love Again *Jimmy Rodgers* (Columbia)	–	15	–
19 To Be Loved *Jackie Wilson* (Coral)	17	17	17
20 You Are My Destiny *Paul Anka* (Columbia)	–	–	–
– Who's Sorry Now *Connie Francis* (MGM)	13	10	6
– To Be Loved *Malcolm Vaughan* (HMV)	17	20	16
– Breathless *Jerry Lee Lewis* (London)	20	11	8
– Happy Guitar/Princess *Tommy Steele* (Decca)	–	16	14
– Grand Coolie Dam/Nobody Loves Like An Irishman *Lonnie Donegan* (Pye)	–	12	12
– Sweet Little Sixteen *Chuck Berry* (London)	–	17	19
– Lollipop *The Chordettes* (London)	–	–	13
– Tom Hark *Elias and his Zig Zag Jive Flutes* (Columbia)	–	–	18
– The Clouds Will Soon Roll By *Tony Brent* (Columbia)	–	–	20

Record Mirror *in its issue of 12 April published a chart with two discs at Number Seventeen and then printed Number Eighteen and not a Nineteen and continued in numerical order.*

MAY 1958

3

	10	17	24	31
1 Whole Lotta Woman *Marvin Rainwater* (MGM)	1	4	7	7
2 It's Too Soon To Know/Wonderful Time Up There *Pat Boone* (London)	2	3	3	2
3 Who's Sorry Now *Connie Francis* (MGM)	3	1	1	1
4 Swingin' Shepherd Blues *Ted Heath* (Decca)	5	9	10	19
5 Magic Moments/Catch A Falling Star *Perry Como* (RCA)	10	10	–	–
6 Tequila *The Champs* (London)	11	13	20	–
6 Nobody Loves Like An Irishman/Grand Coolie Dam *Lonnie Donegan* (Nixa)	6	7	6	6
8 Lollipop *The Chordettes* (London)	7	8	8	20
9 Breathless *Jerry Lee Lewis* (London)	13	14	19	–
10 Maybe Baby *The Crickets* (Coral)	12	20	–	–
11 Don't/I Beg Of You *Elvis Presley* (RCA)	17	–	–	–
12 Tom Hark *Elias and his Zig Zag Jive Flutes* (Columbia)	8	6	4	4
13 Sweet Little Sixteen *Chuck Berry* (London)	19	11	15	–
14 To Be Loved *Malcolm Vaughan* (HMV)	14	15	–	–
15 Lollipop *The Mudlarks* (Columbia)	9	5	5	5
16 Wear My Ring Around Your Neck *Elvis Presley* (RCA)	4	2	2	3
17 Princess/Happy Guitar *Tommy Steele* (Decca)	15	–	–	–
18 Nairobi *Tommy Steele* (Decca)	–	–	–	–
19 The Clouds Will Soon Roll By *Tony Brent* (Columbia)	16	–	–	–
20 April Love *Pat Boone* (London)	–	–	–	–
– La Dee Dah *Jackie Dennis* (Decca)	18	–	–	–
– I May Never Pass This Way Again *Robert Earl* (Philips)	20	–	–	–
– Stairway Of Love *Terry Dene* (Decca)	–	12	12	16
– Tulips From Amsterdam/Hands *Max Bygraves* (Decca)	–	16	13	13
– Kewpie Doll *Perry Como* (RCA)	–	17	11	11
– Stairway Of Love *Michael Holliday* (Columbia)	–	18	16	9
– On The Street Where You Live *David Whitfield* (Decca)	–	19	18	–
– Kewpie Doll *Frankie Vaughan* (Philips)	–	–	9	8
– Swingin' Shepherd Blues *Ella Fitzgerald* (HMV)	–	–	17	18
– Witch Doctor *Don Lang* (HMV)	–	–	–	10

3	10	17	24	31
– Witch Doctor *David Seville* (London)	–	–	–	15
– All I Have To Do Is Dream/Claudette *The Everly Brothers* (London)	–	–	–	12
– Twilight Time *The Platters* (Mercury)	–	–	–	17
– On The Street Where You Live *Vic Damone* (Philips)	–	–	14	14

JUNE 1958

7	14	21	28
1 Who's Sorry Now *Connie Francis* (MGM)	1	1	3
2 It's Too Soon To Know/Wonderful Time Up There *Pat Boone* (London)	3	5	11
3 Tom Hark *Elias and his Zig Zag Jive Flutes* (Columbia)	2	3	7
4 Wear My Ring Around Your Neck *Elvis Presley* (RCA)	8	12	15
5 Grand Coolie Dam/Nobody Loves Like An Irishman *Lonnie Donegan* (Nixa)	7	11	17
6 Lollipop *The Mudlarks* (Columbia)	11	18	–
7 Stairway Of Love *Michael Holliday* (Columbia)	6	8	6
8 Witch Doctor *Don Lang* (HMV)	4	6	8
9 All I Have To Do Is Dream/Claudette *The Everly Brothers* (London)	5	2	1
10 Tulips From Amsterdam/Hands *Max Bygraves* (Decca)	10	7	4
11 On The Street Where You Live *Vic Damone* (Philips)	9	4	2
12 Kewpie Doll *Frankie Vaughan* (Philips)	13	14	16
13 Whole Lotta Woman *Marvin Rainwater* (MGM)	19	–	–
14 Twilight Time *The Platters* (Mercury)	14	10	13
15 Witch Doctor *David Seville* (London)	17	16	19
16 Kewpie Doll *Perry Como* (RCA)	15	–	–
17 Johnny B Goode *Chuck Berry* (London)	–	–	–
18 Stairway Of Love *Terry Dene* (Decca)	–	–	–
19 The Army Game *TV Cast* (HMV)	12	9	5
20 Swingin' Shepherd Blues *Ella Fitzgerald* (HMV)	–	–	–
– Book Of Love *The Mudlarks* (Columbia)	16	13	10
– I Dig You Baby *Marvin Rainwater* (MGM)	18	20	14
– I May Never Pass This Way Again *Perry Como* (RCA)	20	–	20
– Big Man *The Four Preps* (Capitol)	–	15	9
– Purple People Eater *Sheb Wooley* (MGM)	–	17	12
– On The Street Where You Live *David Whitfield* (Decca)	–	18	–
– Rave On *Buddy Holly* (Coral)	–	–	18

JULY 1958

5	12	19	26
1 All I Have To Do Is Dream/Claudette *The Everly Brothers* (London)	1	1	1
2 On The Street Where You Live *Vic Damone* (Philips)	2	4	5
3 Tulips From Amsterdam/Hands *Max Bygraves* (Decca)	3	3	3
4 Big Man *The Four Preps* (Capitol)	4	2	2
5 Who's Sorry Now *Connie Francis* (MGM)	5	9	10
6 Book Of Love *The Mudlarks* (Columbia)	9	10	16
7 The Army Game *TV Cast* (HMV)	11	17	–
8 Witch Doctor *Don Lang* (HMV)	12	12	20
9 Stairway Of Love *Michael Holliday* (Columbia)	15	15	–
10 Tom Hark *Elias and his Zig Zag Jive Flutes* (Columbia)	14	16	–
11 Purple People Eater *Sheb Wooley* (MGM)	13	13	14
12 Twilight Time *The Platters* (Mercury)	6	8	8
13 Sugar Moon *Pat Boone* (London)	7	5	11
14 Rave On *Buddy Holly* (Coral)	8	6	4

	5		12	19	26
15 Wonderful Time Up There/It's Too Soon To Know *Pat Boone* (London)			20	–	–
16 Grand Coolie Dam/Nobody Loves Like An Irishman *Lonnie Donegan* (Nixa)			17	–	–
17 Kewpie Doll *Frankie Vaughan* (Philips)			–	–	–
18 On The Street Where You Live *David Whitfield* (Decca)			19	19	19
19 Lady Is A Tramp (E.P.) *Frank Sinatra* (Capitol)			–	–	–
20 Sally Don't You Grieve/Betty, Betty, Betty *Lonnie Donegan* (Pye)			10	7	7
– I'm Sorry I Made You Cry *Connie Francis* (MGM)			16	14	12
– I May Never Pass This Way Again *Perry Como* (RCA)			18	–	–
– The Only Man On The Island *Tommy Steele* (Decca)			20	18	15
– Endless Sleep *Marty Wilde* (Philips)			20	11	9
– A Very Precious Love *Doris Day* (Philips)			–	20	–
– Hard Headed Woman *Elvis Presley* (RCA)			–	–	6
– When *The Kalin Twins* (Brunswick)			–	–	13
– Return To Me *Dean Martin* (Capitol)			–	–	17
– Patricia *Perez Prado* (RCA)			–	–	18

AUGUST 1958

2	9	16	23	30
1 All I Have To Do Is Dream/Claudette *The Everly Brothers* (London)	1	1	1	2
2 Hard Headed Woman *Elvis Presley* (RCA)	2	2	3	5
3 Big Man *The Four Preps* (Capitol)	3	4	6	7
4 Rave On *Buddy Holly* (Coral)	4	6	8	8
5 When *The Kalin Twins* (Brunswick)	5	3	2	1
6 Tulips From Amsterdam/Hands *Max Bygraves* (Decca)	6	7	7	6
7 Endless Sleep *Marty Wilde* (Philips)	7	5	4	4
8 Twilight Time *The Platters* (Mercury)	8	9	9	14
9 On The Street Where You Live *Vic Damone* (Philips)	9	10	13	18
10 Return To Me *Dean Martin* (Capitol)	10	8	5	3
11 Sally Don't You Grieve/Betty, Betty, Betty *Lonnie Donegan* (Pye)	11	14	18	–
12 Sugar Moon *Pat Boone* (London)	12	12	10	13
13 I'm Sorry I Made You Cry *Connie Francis* (MGM)	13	15	19	20
14 Who's Sorry Now *Connie Francis* (MGM)	14	17	–	–
15 The Only Man On The Island *Tommy Steele* (Decca)	15	16	17	–
16 Think It Over *The Crickets* (Coral)	16	13	14	15
17 Patricia *Perez Prado* (RCA)	17	11	11	11
18 Yakety Yak *The Coasters* (London)	18	18	16	10
19 Stairway Of Love *Michael Holliday* (Columbia)	19	–	–	–
20 Purple People Eater *Sheb Wooley* (MGM)	20	20	–	–
– Splish Splash *Bobby Darin* (London)	–	19	15	16
– Splish Splash/Hello My Darlings *Charlie Drake* (Parlophone)	–	–	12	9
– Poor Little Fool *Ricky Nelson* (London)	–	–	20	12
– Fever *Peggy Lee* (Capitol)	–	–	–	17
– Early In The Morning *Buddy Holly* (Coral)	–	–	–	19

The 9 August chart was a repeat of that for 2 August.

SEPTEMBER 1958

6		13	20	27
1	When *The Kalin Twins* (Brunswick)	1	1	1
2	All I Have To Do Is Dream *The Everly Brothers* (London)	4	5	6
3	Return To Me *Dean Martin* (Capitol)	2	4	4
4	Endless Sleep *Marty Wilde* (Philips)	5	9	11
5	Hard Headed Woman *Elvis Presley* (RCA)	13	11	–
6	Carolina Moon/Stupid Cupid *Connie Francis* (MGM)	3	2	2
7	Tulips From Amsterdam/Hands *Max Bygraves* (Decca)	12	10	16
8	Rave On *Buddy Holly* (Coral)	14	17	–
9	Patricia *Perez Prado* (RCA)	10	16	12
10	Yakety Yak *The Coasters* (London)	11	12	14
11	Poor Little Fool *Ricky Nelson* (London)	8	7	5
12	Fever *Peggy Lee* (Capitol)	6	8	9
13	Splish Splash/Hello My Darlings *Charlie Drake* (Parlophone)	9	6	7
14	Big Man *The Four Preps* (Capitol)	17	–	–
15	Splish Splash *Bobby Darin* (London)	18	20	–
16	Volare *Dean Martin* (Capitol)	7	3	3
17	Early In The Morning *Buddy Holly* (Coral)	15	–	–
18	Little Bernadette *Harry Belafonte* (RCA)	19	–	–
19	Sugar Moon *Pat Boone* (London)	–	–	–
20	Think It Over *The Crickets* (Coral)	20	–	–
–	Volare *Domenico Modugno* (Oriole)	16	15	13
–	Mad Passionate Love *Bernard Bresslaw* (HMV)	–	13	8
–	Bird Dog *The Everly Brothers* (London)	–	14	10
–	If Dreams Came True *Pat Boone* (London)	–	18	18
–	Rebel Rouser *Duane Eddy* (London)	–	19	17
–	Girl Of My Dreams *Tony Brent* (Columbia)	–	≥	15
–	Moon Talk *Perry Como* (RCA)	–	–	19
–	Born Too Late *The Poni-Tails* (HMV)	–	–	20

OCTOBER 1958

4		11	18	25
1	Stupid Cupid/Carolina Moon *Connie Francis* (MGM)	1	1	1
2	When *The Kalin Twins* (Brunswick)	3	3	7
3	Volare *Dean Martin* (Capitol)	2	2	3
4	Bird Dog *The Everly Brothers* (London)	4	6	5
5	Return To Me *Dean Martin* (Capitol)	8	12	20
6	Mad Passionate Love *Bernard Bresslaw* (HMV)	5	9	10
7	Poor Little Fool *Ricky Nelson* (London)	6	8	9
8	Splish Splash/Hello My Darlings *Charlie Drake* (Parlophone)	11	18	–
9	Endless Sleep *Marty Wilde* (Philips)	12	–	–
10	Fever *Peggy Lee* (Capitol)	13	15	–
11	All I Have To Do Is Dream/Claudette *The Everly Brothers* (London)	18	–	–
12	Born Too Late *The Poni-Tails* (HMV)	9	7	6
13	Rebel Rouser *Duane Eddy* (London)	–	17	19
14	If Dreams Came True *Pat Boone* (London)	16	–	18
15	Patricia *Perez Prado* (RCA)	19	20	16
16	Volare *Domenico Modugno* (Oriole)	17	14	14
17	Yakety Yak *The Coasters* (London)	–	–	–
18	Girl Of My Dreams *Tony Brent* (Columbia)	14	–	–
19	Move It *Cliff Richard* (Columbia)	10	5	4
20	Tulips From Amsterdam/Hands *Max Bygraves* (Decca)	–	–	–
–	King Creole *Elvis Presley* (RCA)	7	4	2
–	A Certain Smile *Johnny Mathis* (Fontana)	15	10	8
–	Little Star *The Elegants* (HMV)	20	–	–
–	Volare *Marino Marini* (Durium)	–	11	11

	11	18	25
– It's All In The Game *Tommy Edwards* (MGM)	–	13	12
– Western Movies *The Olympics* (HMV)	–	16	13
– Someday *Jodi Sands* (HMV)	–	17	17
– More Than Ever *Malcolm Vaughan* (HMV)	–	· –	14

NOVEMBER 1958

1

	8	15	22	29
1 Stupid Cupid/Carolina Moon *Connie Francis* (MGM)	2	3	6	9
2 King Creole *Elvis Presley* (RCA)	5	8	9	12
3 Move It *Cliff Richard* (Columbia)	3	4	7	7
4 Bird Dog *The Everly Brothers* (London)	1	1	1	3
5 A Certain Smile *Johnny Mathis* (Fontana)	7	7	4	5
6 Come Prima *Marino Marini* (Durium)	4	5	5	8
7 Born Too Late *The Poni-Tails* (HMV)	8	9	12	–
8 Volare *Dean Martin* (Capitol)	11	15	–	–
9 It's All In The Game *Tommy Edwards* (MGM)	6	2	2	2
10 More Than Ever *Malcolm Vaughan* (HMV)	10	10	8	6
11 Mad Passionate Love *Bernard Bresslaw* (HMV)	17	20	–	–
12 When *The Kalin Twins* (Brunswick)	16	17	–	–
13 Western Movies *The Olympics* (HMV)	12	13	18	20
14 Poor Little Fool *Ricky Nelson* (London)	14	14	20	–
15 Hoots Mon *Lord Rockingham's XI* (Decca)	9	6	3	1
16 Volare *Domenico Modugno* (Oriole)	–	–	–	–
17 Someday *Jodi Sands* (HMV)	18	16	17	18
18 Tea For Two Cha-Cha *Tommy Dorsey Orchestra* (Brunswick)	15	12	14	16
19 Patricia *Perez Prado* (RCA)	–	–	–	–
20 Rebel Rouser *Duane Eddy* (London)	19	–	–	–
– My True Love *Jack Scott* (London)	13	11	10	10
– Moon Talk *Perry Como* (RCA)	20	19	–	–
– Love Makes The World Go Round *Perry Como* (RCA)	–	18	13	11
– It's Only Make Believe *Conway Twitty* (MGM)	–	–	11	4
– Come On Let's Go *Tommy Steele* (Decca)	–	–	15	14
– Someday *Ricky Nelson* (London)	–	–	16	13
– It's So Easy *The Crickets* (Coral)	–	–	19	–
– Tom Dooley *Lonnie Donegan* (Nixa)	–	–	–	15
– High Class Baby *Cliff Richard* (Columbia)	–	–	–	17
– I'll Get By/Fallin' *Connie Francis* (MGM)	–	–	–	19

DECEMBER 1958

5

	12	19	26
1 Hoots Mon *Lord Rockingham's XI* (Decca)	1	1	2
2 It's Only Make Believe *Conway Twitty* (MGM)	2	2	1
3 It's All In The Game *Tommy Edwards* (MGM)	4	5	8
4 Tom Dooley *Lonnie Donegan* (Nixa)	3	3	3
5 Bird Dog *The Everly Brothers* (London)	11	14	20
6 A Certain Smile *Johnny Mathis* (Fontana)	10	9	15
7 More Than Ever *Malcolm Vaughan* (HMV)	6	11	14
8 Come Prima/Volare *Marino Marini* (Durium)	9	12	12
9 Come On Let's Go *Tommy Steele* (Decca)	12	10	11
10 High Class Baby *Cliff Richard* (Columbia)	7	6	5
11 Love Makes The World Go Round *Perry Como* (RCA)	13	8	9
12 Someday/I Got A Feeling *Ricky Nelson* (London)	14	13	13
13 Stupid Cupid/Carolina Moon *Connie Francis* (MGM)	15	20	–
14 Tea For Two Cha-Cha *Tommy Dorsey Orchestra* (Brunswick)	8	7	6
15 Move It *Cliff Richard* (Columbia)	16	16	17
16 My True Love *Jack Scott* (London)	–	–	–

	12	19	26
17 Tom Dooley *Kingston Trio* (Capitol)	5	4	4
18 Someday *Jodi Sands* (HMV)	19	17	19
19 King Creole *Elvis Presley* (RCA)	17	18	–
20 I'll Get by/Fallin' *Connie Francis* (MGM)	–	–	–
– The Day The Rains Came *Jane Morgan* (London)	18	15	7
– It's So Easy *The Crickets* (Coral)	20	–	–
– Mr Success *Frank Sinatra* (Capitol)	–	19	18
– Mary's Boy Child *Harry Belafonte* (RCA)	–	–	10
– More Party Pops *Russ Conway* (Columbia)	–	–	16

1958–BEST-SELLING SINGLES

1 All I Have To Do Is Dream/Claudette *The Everly Brothers* (London)
2 Who's Sorry Now *Connie Francis* (MGM)
3 Magic Moments/Catch A Falling Star *Perry Como* (RCA)
4 Stupid Cupid/Carolina Moon *Connie Francis* (MGM)
5 Hoots Mon *Lord Rockingham's XI* (Decca)
6 Tulips From Amsterdam/Hands *Max Bygraves* (HMV)
7 When *The Kalin Twins* (Brunswick)
8 It's Too Soon To Know/Wonderful Time Up There *Pat Boone* (London)
9 It's Only Make Believe *Conway Twitty* (MGM)
10 Whole Lotta Woman *Marvin Rainwater* (MGM)
11 Bird Dog *The Everly Brothers* (London)
12 Jailhouse Rock *Elvis Presley* (RCA)
13 The Story Of My Life *Michael Holliday* (Columbia)
14 Oh! Boy *The Crickets* (Coral)
15 On The Street Where You Live *Vic Damone* (Philips)
16 Return To Me *Dean Martin* (Capitol)
17 Tea For Two Cha-Cha *Tommy Dorsey Orchestra* (Brunswick)
18 It's All In The Game *Tommy Edwards* (MGM)
19 A Certain Smile *Johnny Mathis* (Fontana)
20 Tom Dooley *Lonnie Donegan* (Nixa)

1959

Most American Rock 'n' Roll heroes had hits during 1959 but Britain brought out some new pop heroes of her own for chart display. The American contingent included Pat Boone, Paul Anka, The Platters, Connie Francis, Buddy Holly, Ricky Nelson, Eddie Cochran and Fats Domino. On the British side, Tommy Steele continued in his flourishing career, and Billy Fury with 'Maybe To-morrow' and Adam Faith with 'What Do You Want' both entered the charts for the first time. One of Britain's home-grown black singers made the charts with the catchy 'What Do You Want To Make Those Eyes At Me For?'. His name was Emile Ford, and his chart life was short when compared to other singers of the time, although he did have four hits in 1960.

Frankie Vaughan, Russ Conway and Shirley Bassey all had hits in 1958. Bassey, after an absence from the charts in 1958, leapt to the fore with 'Kiss Me Honey Honey Kiss Me' and 'As I Love You'. Her success owed much to the Philips record company who took months in breaking the songs, such was their perseverance and faith in them, despite sceptical views from other record companies.

Chart fanatics observed some interesting battles in the record charts, for in the 1950s, unlike the 1970s, artists frequently competed for the top position with the same songs. Three versions of 'Come Softly To Me' made the Top Twenty. One of these was the original American version by The Fleetwoods, and the other two versions were by Craig Douglas and Frankie Vaughan, the latter being assisted by The Kaye Sisters, his high-stepping act and his Victor Mature type of beefcake appeal. The American version was the most popular, for it reached Number Six, while Frankie Vaughan and The Kaye Sisters lagged behind at Number Nine. However, both versions enjoyed two months in the charts. Craig Douglas' version only entered *Record Mirror*'s Top Ten British listing on several occasions, but with speed and alacrity he entered the charts for the first time with the disc's B-side, 'Teenager In Love'.

Douglas was a newcomer in 1959 and although 'Teenager In Love' was his first Top Twenty entry, he still lost to the more experienced opposition provided by Philips' recording artist, Marty Wilde, who took his version of the same song to the Number Two position.

Less exciting were the chart battles over the songs 'Only Sixteen' and 'Battle Of New Orleans'. Douglas featured again in the fight to take his version of the former song up the charts. This time he won and grabbed the Number One position. The classic version by the American singer, Sam Cooke, only reached Number Thirteen, and remained in the Top Twenty for only three weeks.

Lonnie Donegan spent 14 weeks in the Top Twenty, reaching Number Two with 'Battle Of New Orleans'. This was a case of a British artist, well-known in the popularity stakes, grabbing a song from an unknown American artist who had first made it a hit across the Atlantic. The 'unknown American' in this case was Johnny Horton, whose version of 'Battle Of New Orleans' stayed one solitary week in the British charts.

1959 saw a brief return of three heroes of the early 1950s, and at one time the charts almost contained all three at once. Frankie Laine galloped back with 'Rawhide', Guy Mitchell sang 'Heartaches By The Number', and Johnny Ray almost entered the Top Twenty with one of his best-ever, but unrecognised, discs called 'I'll Never Fall In Love Again'.

The early 1960s Trad Jazz boom in the charts was given its first breath of life in 1959 with 'Petite Fleur' by Chris Barber. The year's classics included 'To Know Him Is To Love Him' from The Teddy Bears, 'Dream Lover' by Bobby Darin, 'Here Comes Summer' from Jerry Keller, and Johnny and The Hurricanes' 'Red River Rock'. The most unexpected hit was 'A Pub With No Beer' from the Australian singer, Slim Dusty.

JANUARY 1959

3		10	17	24	31
1	It's Only Make Believe *Conway Twitty* (MGM)	1	1	3	7
2	Hoots Mon *Lord Rockingham's XI* (Decca)	2	2	8	14
3	Tom Dooley *Lonnie Donegan* (Nixa)	3	3	11	12
4	Tom Dooley *The Kingston Trio* (Capitol)	4	8	6	9
5	Love Makes The World Go Round *Perry Como* (RCA)	6	7	12	15
6	Tea For Two Cha-Cha *Tommy Dorsey Orchestra* (Brunswick)	5	9	9	11
7	It's All In The Game *Tommy Edwards* (MGM)	13	17	–	–
8	High Class Baby *Cliff Richard* (Columbia)	7	10	16	–
9	The Day The Rains Came *Jane Morgan* (London)	8	5	5	4
10	More Party Pops *Russ Conway* (Columbia)	15	–	–	–
11	Come On Let's Go *Tommy Steele* (Decca)	9	13	15	18
12	More Than Ever *Malcolm Vaughan* (HMV)	17	–	–	–
13	Someday *Ricky Nelson* (London)	16	19	–	–
14	Mary's Boy Child *Harry Belafonte* (RCA)	–	–	–	–
15	A Certain Smile *Johnny Mathis* (Fontana)	–	–	–	–
16	Come Prima *Marino Marini* (Durium)	–	–	–	–
17	Cannon Ball *Duane Eddy* (London)	14	14	20	–
18	Skiffle Party *Lonnie Donegan* (Nixa)	–	–	–	–
19	Son Of Mary *Harry Belafonte* (RCA)	–	–	–	–
20	Kiss Me Honey *Shirley Bassey* (Philips)	12	11	7	5
–	Baby Face *Little Richard* (London)	10	6	4	2
–	To Know Him Is To Love Him *The Teddy Bears* (London)	11	4	2	3
–	You Always Hurt The One You Love *Connie Francis* (MGM)	18	12	18	17
–	My Ukelele *Max Bygraves* (Decca)	19	16	–	–
–	King Creole *Elvis Presley* (RCA)	20	–	–	–
–	Smoke Gets In Your Eyes *The Platters* (Mercury)	–	15	10	8
–	Chantilly Lace *Big Bopper* (Mercury)	–	18	14	16
–	As I Love You *Shirley Bassey* (Philips)	–	20	13	10
–	High School Confidential *Jerry Lee Lewis* (London)	–	–	17	13
–	Problems *The Everly Brothers* (London)	–	–	19	6
–	All Of A Sudden My Heart Sings *Paul Anka* (Columbia)	–	–	–	19
–	I'll Remember Tonight *Pat Boone* (London)	–	–	–	20
–	I Got Stung/One Night *Elvis Presley* (RCA)	–	–	1	1

FEBRUARY 1959

7		14	21	28
1	I Got Stung/One Night *Elvis Presley* (RCA)	1	1	3
2	Baby Face *Little Richard* (London)	3	7	13
3	To Know Him Is To Love Him *The Teddy Bears* (London)	2	4	5
4	Kiss Me Honey *Shirley Bassey* (Philips)	4	6	8
5	Problems *The Everly Brothers* (London)	7	8	10
6	As I Love You *Shirley Bassey* (Philips)	6	2	2
7	Smoke Gets In Your Eyes *The Platters* (Mercury)	8	5	1
8	The Day The Rains Came *Jane Morgan* (London)	9	15	–
9	It's Only Make Believe *Conway Twitty* (MGM)	15	–	–
10	High School Confidential *Jerry Lee Lewis* (London)	13	13	–
11	Tea For Two Cha-Cha *Tommy Dorsey Orchestra* (Brunswick)	–	–	–
12	Does Your Chewing Gum Lose Its Flavour *Lonnie Donegan* (Nixa)	5	3	4
13	All Of A Sudden My Heart Sings *Paul Anka* (Columbia)	14	10	12
14	Tom Dooley *The Kingston Trio* (Capitol)	–	–	–
15	Hoots Mon *Lord Rockingham's XI* (Decca)	–	–	–
16	Wee Tom *Lord Rockingham's XI* (Decca)	11	12	16
17	I'll Be With You In Apple Blossom Time *Rosemary June* (Pye)	12	16	20

	14	21	28
18 Chantilly Lace *Big Bopper* (Mercury)	20	20	–
19 Tom Dooley *Lonnie Donegan* (Nixa)	–	–	–
20 You Always Hurt The One You Love *Connie Francis* (MGM)	–	–	–
– Pub With No Beer *Slim Dusty* (Columbia)	10	9	6
– Petite Fleur *Chris Barber* (Nixa)	15	16	7
– I'll Remember Tonight *Pat Boone* (London)	17	–	–
– Stagger Lee *Lloyd Price* (HMV)	18	18	14
– Little Drummer Boy *The Beverley Sisters* (Decca)	19	14	9
– My Happiness *Connie Francis* (MGM)	–	11	11
– Gigi *Billy Eckstine* (Mercury)	–	19	17
– Side Saddle *Russ Conway* (Columbia)	–	–	15
– Tomboy *Perry Como* (RCA)	–	–	18
– Wait For Me *Malcolm Vaughan* (HMV)	–	–	19

MARCH 1959

7	14	21	28
1 Smoke Gets In Your Eyes *The Platters* (Mercury)	1	1	1
2 As I Love You *Shirley Bassey* (Philips)	2	2	4
3 Does Your Chewing Gum Lose Its Flavour *Lonnie Donegan* (Nixa)	5	8	10
4 I Got Stung/One Night *Elvis Presley* (RCA)	8	12	17
5 Pub With No Beer *Slim Dusty* (Columbia)	3	5	7
6 Side Saddle *Russ Conway* (Columbia)	4	3	2
7 My Happiness *Connie Francis* (MGM)	7	4	3
8 Petite Fleur *Chris Barber* (Nixa)	6	6	5
9 Little Drummer Boy *The Beverley Sisters* (Decca)	9	9	9
10 To Know Him Is To Love Him *The Teddy Bears* (London)	15	–	–
11 Kiss Me Honey *Shirley Bassey* (Philips)	12	14	18
12 Stagger Lee *Lloyd Price* (HMV)	10	7	6
13 Problems *The Everly Brothers* (London)	17	–	–
14 It Doesn't Matter Any More *Buddy Holly* (Coral)	11	10	8
15 All Of A Sudden My Heart Sings *Paul Anka* (Columbia)	13	16	14
16 Baby Face *Little Richard* (London)	16	19	–
17 Tomboy *Perry Como* (RCA)	14	15	12
18 Gigi *Billy Eckstine* (Mercury)	20	11	11
19 Manhattan Spiritual *Reg Owen* (Pye)	17	18	–
20 C'mon Everybody *Eddie Cochran* (London)	–	13	15
– I'll Remember Tonight *Pat Boone* (London)	19	–	–
– Sing Little Birdie *Pearl Carr and Teddy Johnson* (Columbia)	–	17	19
– Donna *Marty Wilde* (Philips)	–	20	16
– Charlie Brown *The Coasters* (London)	–	–	13
– Donna *Ritchie Valens* (London)	–	–	20

APRIL 1959

4	11	18	25
1 Side Saddle *Russ Conway* (Columbia)	1	2	2
2 Smoke Gets In Your Eyes *The Platters* (Mercury)	3	3	7
3 It Doesn't Matter Any More *Buddy Holly* (Coral)	2	1	1
4 My Happiness *Connie Francis* (MGM)	4	7	10
5 As I Love You *Shirley Bassey* (Philips)	5	9	13
6 Petite Fleur *Chris Barber* (Nixa)	5	6	4
7 Stagger Lee *Lloyd Price* (HMV)	7	10	11
8 Pub With No Beer *Slim Dusty* (Columbia)	10	13	14
9 Little Drummer Boy *The Beverley Sisters* (Decca)	13	14	19
10 Gigi *Billy Eckstine* (Mercury)	11	11	16
11 Donna *Marty Wilde* (Philips)	8	4	6
12 Tomboy *Perry Como* (RCA)	14	15	15

	11	18	25
4			
13 Charlie Brown *The Coasters* (London)	9	5	5
14 C'mon Everybody *Eddie Cochran* (London)	12	8	8
15 Wait For Me *Malcolm Vaughan* (HMV)	16	19	–
16 Does Your Chewing Gum Lose Its Flavour *Lonnie Donegan* (Nixa)	19	–	–
17 By The Light Of The Silvery Moon *Little Richard* (London)	15	18	–
18 I Got Stung/One Night *Elvis Presley* (RCA)	–	19	–
19 Sing Little Birdie *Pearl Carr and Teddy Johnson* (Columbia)	17	12	–
20 Lonely One *Duane Eddy* (London)	–	–	–
– Maybe Tomorrow *Billy Fury* (Decca)	18	17	18
– Donna *Ritchie Valens* (London)	20	–	–
– It's Late/There'll Never Be Anyone But You *Ricky Nelson* (London)	–	16	9
– A Fool Such As I/I Need Your Love Tonight *Elvis Presley* (RCA)	–	–	3
– Come Softly To Me *The Fleetwoods* (London)	–	–	12
– Never Mind/Mean Streak *Cliff Richard* (Columbia)	–	–	17
– Come Softly To Me *Frankie Vaughan* (Philips)	–	–	20

MAY 1959

	9	16	23	30
2				
1 A Fool Such As I/I Need Your Love Tonight *Elvis Presley* (RCA)	1	1	1	1
2 It Doesn't Matter Any More *Buddy Holly* (Coral)	2	2	2	2
3 Side Saddle *Russ Conway* (Columbia)	5	4	5	9
4 Donna *Marty Wilde* (Philips)	4	7	7	6
5 Petite Fleur *Chris Barber* (Pye)	7	8	8	14
6 It's Late/There'll Never Be Anyone Else But You *Ricky Nelson* (London)	3	3	3	3
7 Charlie Brown *The Coasters* (London)	9	11	14	20
8 C'mon Everybody *Eddie Cochran* (London)	11	18	17	–
9 Smoke Gets In Your Eyes *The Platters* (Mercury)	15	16	18	–
10 Come Softly To Me *The Fleetwoods* (London)	6	6	6	10
11 Come Softly To Me *Frankie Vaughan and The Kaye Sisters* (Philips)	10	10	9	12
12 I Go Ape *Neil Sedaka* (RCA)	12	9	13	11
13 Idle On Parade (E.P.) *Anthony Newley* (Decca)	14	–	–	–
14 I've Waited So Long *Anthony Newley* (Decca)	8	5	4	4
15 My Happiness *Connie Francis* (MGM)	–	–	–	–
16 Mean Streak/Never Mind *Cliff Richard* (Columbia)	13	13	11	8
17 Stagger Lee *Lloyd Price* (HMV)	18	–	–	–
18 Tomboy *Perry Como* (RCA)	–	–	–	–
19 Wait For Me *Malcolm Vaughan* (HMV)	–	17	–	–
20 Lovin' Up A Storm *Jerry Lee Lewis* (London)	–	–	–	–
– Fort Worth Jail *Lonnie Donegan* (Nixa)	16	12	12	17
– Where Were You On Our Wedding Day *Lloyd Price* (HMV)	17	15	16	15
– Guitar Boogie Shuffle *Bert Weedon* (Top Rank)	19	14	10	7
– Maybe Tomorrow *Billy Fury* (Decca)	20	–	–	–
– Guitar Boogie Shuffle *The Virtues* (HMV)	–	19	19	19
– Hey Little Lucy *Conway Twitty* (MGM)	–	20	–	–
– Roulette *Russ Conway* (Columbia)	–	–	15	5
– Three Stars *Ruby Wright* (Parlophone)	–	–	20	18
– Poor Jenny/Take A Message To Mary *The Everly Brothers* (London)	–	–	–	13
– Margie *Fats Domino* (London)	–	–	–	16

JUNE 1959

6		13	20	27
1	A Fool Such As I/I Need Your Love Tonight *Elvis Presley* (RCA)	1	2	–
2	It Doesn't Matter Any More *Buddy Holly* (Coral)	4	7	–
3	Roulette *Russ Conway* (Columbia)	2	1	–
4	It's Late/There'll Never Be Anyone Else But You *Ricky Nelson* (London)	3	6	–
5	I've Waited So Long *Anthony Newley* (Decca)	6	5	–
6	Guitar Boogie Shuffle *Bert Weedon* (Top Rank)	7	8	–
7	Donna *Marty Wilde* (Philips)	15	20	–
8	Side Saddle *Russ Conway* (Columbia)	12	12	–
9	Mean Streak/Never Mind *Cliff Richard* (Columbia)	14	15	–
10	I Go Ape *Neil Sedaka* (RCA)	10	17	–
11	Take A Message To Mary/Poor Jenny *The Everly Brothers* (London)	11	13	–
12	Come Softly To Me *Frankie Vaughan and The Kaye Sisters* (Philips)	13	–	–
13	Dream Lover *Bobby Darin* (London)	5	3	–
14	Three Stars *Ruby Wright* (Parlophone)	8	9	–
15	Where Were You *Lloyd Price* (HMV)	–	–	–
16	May You Always *Joan Regan* (HMV)	20	16	–
17	Come Softly To Me *The Fleetwoods* (London)	18	–	–
18	Petite Fleur *Chris Barber* (Pye)	19	–	–
19	Margie *Fats Domino* (London)	–	–	–
20	A Teenager In Love *Marty Wilde* (Philips)	9	4	–
–	A Teenager In Love *Craig Douglas* (Top Rank)	16	14	–
–	Personality *Lloyd Price* (HMV)	17	11	–
–	Peter Gunn/Yep! *Duane Eddy* (London)	–	10	–
–	Personality *Anthony Newley* (Decca)	–	18	–
–	Goodbye Jimmy Goodbye *Ruby Murray* (Columbia)ʻ	–	19	–

There were no Top Twenty charts from 27 June until 8 August owing to a newspaper strike. During this time Record Mirror was not published.

AUGUST 1959

8	15		22	29
1	1	Livin' Doll *Cliff Richard* (Columbia)	1	2
2	2	Dream Lover *Bobby Darin* (London)	5	6
3	3	Battle Of New Orleans *Lonnie Donegan* (Pye)	4	5
6	4	Lipstick On Your Collar *Connie Francis* (MGM)	6	4
4	5	Big Hunk Of Love *Elvis Presley* (RCA)	7	9
5	6	A Teenager In Love *Marty Wilde* (Philips)	8	11
18	7	Lonely Boy *Paul Anka* (Columbia)	3	3
7	8	Roulette *Russ Conway* (Columbia)	10	14
9	9	Heart Of A Man *Frankie Vaughan* (Philips)	9	7
–	10	Only Sixteen *Craig Douglas* (Top Rank)	2	1
8	11	Peter Gunn *Duane Eddy* (London)	–	–
12	12	It's Late/There'll Never Be Anyone Else But You *Ricky Nelson* (London)	–	–
10	13	Personality *Anthony Newley* (Decca)	16	19
11	14	Ragtime Cowboy Joe *The Chipmunks* (London)	13	–
13	15	Someone *Johnny Mathis* (Fontana)	12	10
14	16	I Know *Perry Como* (RCA)	11	–
–	17	Give, Give, Give *Tommy Steele* (Decca)	20	20
16	18	Twixt, Twelve And Twenty *Pat Boone* (London)	–	18
19	19	Personality *Lloyd Price* (HMV)	–	–
–	20	Mona Lisa *Conway Twitty* (MGM)	19	16

	8	15		22	29
–	–	Only Sixteen *Sam Cooke* (HMV)		14	13
–	–	China Tea *Russ Conway* (Columbia)		15	8
–	–	Goodbye Jimmy Goodbye *Ruby Murray* (Columbia)		17	–
–	–	Tallahassie Lassie *Freddie Cannon* (Top Rank)		18	15
–	–	Here Comes Summer *Jerry Keller* (London)		–	12
–	–	Only Sixteen *Al Saxon* (Fontana)		–	17

Owing to the newspaper strike, no chart was published in Record Mirror for 8 August 1959, so those figures which appear under 8 August column were published as the 'last week' figures for 15 August 1959.

SEPTEMBER 1959

5		12	19	26
1	Only Sixteen *Craig Douglas* (Top Rank)	1	1	1
2	Livin' Doll *Cliff Richard* (Columbia)	2	2	2
3	Lonely Boy *Paul Anka* (Columbia)	3	4	4
4	Lipstick On Your Collar *Connie Francis* (MGM)	9	10	13
5	China Tea *Russ Conway* (Columbia)	4	5	5
6	Heart Of A Man *Frankie Vaughan* (Philips)	7	9	10
7	Battle Of New Orleans *Lonnie Donegan* (Pye)	6	11	15
8	Someone *Johnny Mathis* (Fontana)	11	12	12
9	Here Comes Summer *Jerry Keller* (London)	5	3	3
10	Dream Lover *Bobby Darin* (London)	13	19	–
11	Mona Lisa *Conway Twitty* (MGM)	10	6	6
12	Forty Miles Of Bad Road *Duane Eddy* (London)	8	7	7
13	Big Hunk Of Love *Elvis Presley* (RCA)	20	–	–
14	Just A Little Too Much *Ricky Nelson* (London)	12	8	9
15	Roulette *Russ Conway* (Columbia)	16	–	–
16	I Know *Perry Como* (RCA)	–	–	–
17	A Teenager In Love *Marty Wilde* (Philips)	–	–	–
18	Ragtime Cowboy Joe *The Chipmunks* (London)	–	–	–
19	Plenty Of Good Lovin' *Connie Francis* (MGM)	14	15	–
20	Only Sixteen *Sam Cooke* (HMV)	–	–	–
–	'Til I Kissed You *The Everly Brothers* (London)	15	13	8
–	Three Bells *The Browns* (RCA)	17	18	11
–	Peggy Sue Got Married *Buddy Holly* (Coral)	18	14	17
–	Just Keep It Up *Dee Clarke* (London)	19	–	–
–	Sal's Got A Sugar Lip *Lonnie Donegan* (Nixa)	–	16	18
–	High Hopes *Frank Sinatra* (Capitol)	–	17	16
–	I'm Gonna Get Married *Lloyd Price* (HMV)	–	20	20
–	Sea Of Love *Marty Wilde* (Philips)	–	–	14
–	Broken Hearted Melody *Sarah Vaughan* (Mercury)	–	–	19

OCTOBER 1959

3		10	17	24	31
1	Only Sixteen *Craig Douglas* (Top Rank)	1	6	7	8
2	Here Comes Summer *Jerry Keller* (London)	2	4	6	7
3	Livin' Doll *Cliff Richard* (Columbia)	4	8	10	15
4	'Til I Kissed You *The Everly Brothers* (London)	3	2	3	3
5	China Tea *Russ Conway* (Columbia)	11	17	19	–
6	Forty Miles Of Bad Road *Duane Eddy* (London)	12	16	16	–
7	Mona Lisa *Conway Twitty* (MGM)	8	10	12	18
8	Lonely Boy *Paul Anka* (Columbia)	10	12	18	–
9	Just A Little Too Much *Ricky Nelson* (London)	13	13	14	–
10	Three Bells *The Browns* (RCA)	6	7	5	6
11	Mack The Knife *Bobby Darin* (London)	5	3	2	2
12	Someone *Johnny Mathis* (Fontana)	14	15	17	–

	10	17	24	31
13 Sea Of Love *Marty Wilde* (Philips)	9	5	4	4
14 Peggy Sue Got Married *Buddy Holly* (Coral)	16	18	15	16
15 Heart Of A Man *Frankie Vaughan* (Philips)	20	–	–	–
16 Broken Hearted Melody *Sarah Vaughan* (Mercury)	15	9	11	11
17 Lipstick On Your Collar *Connie Francis* (MGM)	–	–	–	–
18 High Hopes *Frank Sinatra* (Capitol)	18	20	13	10
19 Sal's Got A Sugar Lip *Lonnie Donegan* (Nixa)	–	–	–	–
20 Hold Back Tomorrow *Miki and Griff* (Pye)	–	–	–	–
– Travellin' Light *Cliff Richard* (Columbia)	7	1	1	1
– Red River Rock *Johnny and The Hurricanes* (London)	17	11	9	5
– Sleep Walk *Santo and Johnny* (Pye)	19	14	–	–
– Makin' Love *Floyd Robinson* (RCA)	–	19	8	9
– Mr Blue *Mike Preston* (Decca)	–	–	20	13
– What Do You Want To Make Those Eyes At Me For? *Emile Ford* (Pye)	–	–	–	12
– Put Your Head On My Shoulder *Paul Anka* (Columbia)	–	–	–	14
– Teen Beat *Sandy Nelson* (Top Rank)	–	–	–	17
– Mr Blue *David Macbeth* (Pye)	–	–	–	19
– One More Sunrise *Dickie Valentine* (Pye)	–	–	–	20

NOVEMBER 1959

7	14	21	28
1 Travellin' Light *Cliff Richard* (Columbia)	1	1	1
2 Mack The Knife *Bobby Darin* (London)	2	4	5
3 Sea Of Love *Marty Wilde* (Philips)	4	5	9
4 Red River Rock *Johnny and The Hurricanes* (London)	3	2	3
5 'Til I Kissed You *The Everly Brothers* (London)	6	6	8
6 Three Bells *The Browns* (RCA)	11	12	–
7 Makin' Love *Floyd Robinson* (RCA)	8	14	17
8 Put Your Head On My Shoulder *Paul Anka* (Columbia)	7	7	7
9 What Do You Want To Make Those Eyes At Me For? *Emile Ford* (Pye)	5	3	2
10 Broken Hearted Melody *Sarah Vaughan* (Mercury)	10	12	14
11 Here Comes Summer *Jerry Keller* (London)	15	–	–
12 High Hopes *Frank Sinatra* (Capitol)	9	15	–
13 Mr Blue *Mike Preston* (Decca)	12	9	11
14 Mr Blue *David Macbeth* (Pye)	–	–	–
14 Teen Beat *Sandy Nelson* (Top Rank)	13	11	–
16 Only Sixteen *Craig Douglas* (Top Rank)	–	–	–
17 Mona Lisa *Conway Twitty* (MGM)	–	–	–
18 Livin' Doll *Cliff Richard* (Columbia)	–	–	–
19 I Want To Walk You Home *Fats Domino* (London)	19	–	–
20 One More Sunrise *Dickie Valentine* (Pye)	14	17	–
– Snow Coach *Russ Conway* (Columbia)	16	10	12
– Oh! Carol *Neil Sedaka* (RCA)	17	8	6
– Rawhide *Frankie Laine* (Philips)	18	19	–
– Always *Sammy Turner* (London)	20	–	–
– Seven Little Girls Sitting In The Back Seat *The Avons* (Columbia)	–	16	10
– What Do You Want *Adam Faith* (Parlophone)	–	18	4
– Poison Ivy *The Coasters* (London)	–	20	15
– More And More Party Pops *Russ Conway* (Columbia)	–	–	13
– Little White Bull *Tommy Steele* (Decca)	–	–	16
– The Best Of Everything *Johnny Mathis* (Fontana)	–	–	18
– Seven Little Girls Sitting In The Back Seat *P. Evans* (London)	–	–	18
– Heartaches By The Number *Guy Mitchell* (Philips)	–	–	20
– Little Donkey *The Beverley Sisters* (Decca)	–	–	20

5		12	19	26
1	What Do You Want *Adam Faith* (Parlophone)	1	1	1
2	What Do You Want To Make Those Eyes At Me For? *Emile Ford* (Pye)	2	2	2
3	Travellin' Light *Cliff Richard* (Columbia)	4	4	5
4	Oh! Carol *Neil Sedaka* (RCA)	3	3	3
5	Red River Rock *Johnny and The Hurricanes* (London)	6	6	12
6	Mack The Knife *Bobby Darin* (London)	8	16	–
7	Seven Little Girls Sitting In The Back Seat *The Avons* (Columbia)	5	5	4
8	Teen Beat *Sandy Nelson* (Top Rank)	7	8	14
8	Put Your Head On My Shoulder *Paul Anka* (Columbia)	9	18	–
10	'Til I Kissed You *The Everly Brothers* (London)	17	–	–
11	Snow Coach *Russ Conway* (Columbia)	10	9	6
12	Little White Bull *Tommy Steele* (Decca)	13	11	20
13	Sea Of Love *Marty Wilde* (Philips)	16	–	–
14	Rawhide *Frankie Laine* (Philips)	11	14	13
15	More And More Party Pops *Russ Conway* (Columbia)	15	11	9
16	Bad Boy *Marty Wilde* (Philips)	19	20	20
17	Heartaches By The Number *Guy Mitchell* (Philips)	–	–	–
18	Ivy Will Cling *Arnold Stang* (Fontana)	–	–	–
19	Piano Party *Winifred Atwell* (Decca)	20	15	18
20	Mr Blue *Mike Preston* (Decca)	–	–	–
–	Among My Souvenirs *Connie Francis* (MGM)	12	10	8
–	Some Kind-A-Earthquake *Duane Eddy* (London)	14	7	7
–	Seven Little Girls In The Back Seat *Paul Evans* (London)	18	–	16
–	Johnny Staccato Theme *Elmer Bernstein* (Capitol)	–	13	10
–	Be My Guest *Fats Domino* (London)	–	17	19
–	Deck Of Cards *Wink Martindale* (London)	–	19	–
–	Jingle Bell Rock *Max Bygraves* (Decca)	–	–	11
–	Reveille Rock *Johnny and The Hurricanes* (London)	–	–	15
–	Little Donkey *The Beverley Sisters* (Decca)	–	–	16

1959–BEST-SELLING SINGLES

1. Livin' Doll *Cliff Richard* (Columbia)
2. What Do You Want To Make Those Eyes At Me For? *Emile Ford* (Pye)
3. It Doesn't Matter Any More *Buddy Holly* (Coral)
4. Travellin' Light *Cliff Richard* (Columbia)
5. Smoke Gets In Your Eyes *The Platters* (Mercury)
6. Side Saddle *Russ Conway* (Columbia)
7. Dream Lover *Bobby Darin* (London)
8. A Fool Such As I/I Need Your Love Tonight *Elvis Presley* (RCA)
9. Battle Of New Orleans *Lonnie Donegan* (Pye)
10. Only Sixteen *Craig Douglas* (Top Rank)
11. Roulette *Russ Conway* (Columbia)
12. As I Love You *Shirley Bassey* (Philips)
13. Petite Fleur *Chris Barber* (Nixa)
14. It's Late/There'll Never Be Anyone Else But You *Ricky Nelson* (London)
15. I've Waited So Long *Anthony Newley* (Decca)
16. Oh! Carol *Neil Sedaka* (RCA)
17. What Do You Want *Adam Faith* (Parlophone)
18. 'Til I Kissed You *The Everly Brothers* (London)
19. Mack The Knife *Bobby Darin* (London)
20. Lipstick On Your Collar *Connie Francis* (MGM)

1960

1960 was the year of the 'Itsy Bitsy Teeny Weeny Yellow Polka Dot Bikini', 'Beatnik Fly', 'Tie Me Kangaroo Down Sport', 'Even More Party Pops' and 'Ooh! La La'. Such a list is hardly likely to excite any pop connoisseur.

However, the year was a good one for such artists as The King Brothers, who finally made the charts once more with their cover version of The Four Lads' American hit 'Standing On The Corner'. The Kaye Sisters, noble assistants to several Frankie Vaughan hits, had their only Top Twenty hit in their own right with 'Paper Roses'. Johnny Kidd stirred females with his swashbuckling image and his first-ever Hit Parade successes with 'Shakin' All Over' and 'Restless'. The wait for further triumph for Kidd was long.

Gary Mills enjoyed brief fame with two hits, 'Look For A Star' and 'Top Teen Baby'. Johnny Mathis had his fifth and sixth hits, but then had to wait until 1975 for his next one. Ricky Valance had his one and only taste of fame in 1960 with 'Tell Laura I Love Her', and this record sparked off some predictions that there would be a spate of 'death' discs. However, four years were to pass until Twinkle's 'Terry' and 'Leader Of The Pack' from The Shangri-Las.

Freddie Cannon must have wondered what had happened to his chart career after his 1958 smash hit 'Tallahassie Lassie', particularly as he had ousted Tommy Steele's version of the same song from the top listings. However, 1960 saw a short but happy comeback for Cannon, as no less than three of his records made the Top Twenty throughout the year, starting with 'Way Down Yonder In New Orleans'.

Max Bygraves saw a nine-hit run end with 'Fings Ain't What They Used To Be', while Gene Vincent's chart career also came to an end with 'Pistol Packing Mama'. But if some stars disappeared, as always, newcomers saw a career of sorts begin. There was Mark Wynter embarking on his six-hit disc career with 'Image Of A Girl', and The Shadows began their careers in their own right without Cliff Richard. 'Apache' and 'Man Of Mystery' began their hit trail, and a year later they achieved four more hits. They had begun as The Drifters, and had to change this name to

53

avoid confusion with the American band of the same name. They then changed it to The Shadows and learned that they now had the same name as Bobby Vee's American band, but they ignored *that* problem!

For some chart-established artists, life was good. Cliff Richard had no less than six hits; The Everly Brothers had four; and four hits were achieved by Duane Eddy. Adam Faith, with five hit records, almost equalled the amazing success of Cliff Richard, but Billy Fury remained comparatively quiet with only two hits.

Pat Boone did not appear in the 1960 charts, following his hit trail which had begun in 1955. However, he did have hits to come in 1961 and 1962.

For Frankie Laine it was goodbye with 'Rawhide', the fast-moving cowboy song of 1959, for after 1960 Laine did not appear in the charts again, in spite of continuing popularity into the 1970s.

In terms of success, then, 1960 belonged to Cliff Richard – with or without his Shadows.

	9	16	23	30
1 What Do You Want To Make Those Eyes At Me For? *Emile Ford* (Pye)		1	3	5
2 What Do You Want *Adam Faith* (Parlophone)		2	4	7
3 Oh! Carol *Neil Sedaka* (RCA)		3	5	8
4 Seven Little Girls Sitting In The Back Seat *The Avons* (Columbia)		7	11	—
5 Johnny Staccato Theme *Elmer Bernstein* (Capitol)		5	6	12
6 Little White Bull *Tommy Steele* (Decca)		6	8	9
7 Bad Boy *Marty Wilde* (Philips)		8	14	19
8 Reveille Rock *Johnny and The Hurricanes* (London)		10	14	—
9 Travellin' Light *Cliff Richard* (Columbia)		14	.—	—
10 Some Kind-A-Earthquake *Duane Eddy* (London)		13	17	—
11 Rawhide *Frankie Laine* (Philips)		15	12	17
12 Red River Rock *Johnny and The Hurricanes* (London)		20	—	—
13 Snow Coach *Russ Conway* (Columbia)		—	—	—
14 Starry-Eyed *Michael Holliday* (Columbia)		4	2	2
15 Teen Beat *Sandy Nelson* (Top Rank)		16	—	—
16 Be My Guest *Fats Domino* (London)		12	—	15
17 Among My Souvenirs *Connie Francis* (MGM)		17	—	—
18 More And More Party Pops *Russ Conway* (Columbia)		—	—	—
19 Too Good *Little Tony* (Decca)		19	13	13
20 Way Down Yonder *Freddie Cannon* (Top Rank)		9	7	4
– Why? *Anthony Newley* (Decca)		10	1	1
– In The Mood *Ernie Fields* (London)		18	—	—
– Heartaches By The Number *Guy Mitchell* (Philips)		—	9	6
– A Voice In The Wilderness *Cliff Richard* (Columbia)		—	10	3
– Expresso Bongo (E.P.) *Cliff Richard* (Columbia)		—	16	10
– Summer Set *Acker Bilk* (Columbia)		—	18	11
– Dance With Me *The Drifters* (London)		—	19	18
– Why? *Frankie Avalon* (HMV)		—	20	15
– Pretty Blue Eyes *Craig Douglas* (Top Rank)		—	—	14
– El Paso *Marty Robbins* (Fontana)		—	—	20

The chart for 2 January was a repeat of that for the last week in 1959.

	6	13	20	27
1 Why? *Anthony Newley* (Decca)		1	1	1
2 A Voice In The Wilderness *Cliff Richard* (Columbia)		2	2	3
3 Starry-Eyed *Michael Holliday* (Columbia)		3	7	11
4 Way Down Yonder *Freddie Cannon* (Top Rank)		4	4	4
5 Heartaches By The Number *Guy Mitchell* (Philips)		6	10	20
6 Poor Me *Adam Faith* (Parlophone)		5	3	2
7 What Do You Want To Make Those Eyes At Me For? *Emile Ford* (Pye)		9	11	18
8 Expresso Bongo (E.P.) *Cliff Richard* (Columbia)		16	—	—
9 Pretty Blue Eyes *Craig Douglas* (Top Rank)		7	5	6
10 Summer Set *Acker Bilk* (Columbia)		13	13	14
11 What Do You Want *Adam Faith* (Parlophone)		11	19	—
12 Oh! Carol *Neil Sedaka* (RCA)		19	—	—
13 Little White Bull *Tommy Steele* (Decca)		—	—	—
14 Beyond The Sea *Bobby Darin* (London)		10	9	8
15 Johnny Staccato Theme *Elmer Bernstein* (Columbia)		20	—	—
16 Misty *Johnny Mathis* (Fontana)		14	17	13
17 El Paso *Marty Robbins* (Fontana)		—	—	—

6	13	20	27
18 Why? *Frankie Avalon* (HMV)	–	–	–
19 Be My Guest *Fats Domino* (London)	17	18	–
20 Harbour Lights *The Platters* (Mercury)	14	12	16
20 Slow Boat To China *Emile Ford* (Pye)	8	6	7
– Running Bear *Johnny Preston* (Mercury)	12	8	5
– You Got What It Takes *Marv Johnson* (London)	18	15	12
– Rawhide *Frankie Laine* (Philips)	20	–	–
– Be Mine *Lance Fortune* (Columbia)	–	14	10
– Bonnie Came Back *Duane Eddy* (London)	–	16	9
– Happy Anniversary *Joan Regan* (HMV)	–	20	–
– Royal Event *Russ Conway* (Columbia)	–	–	14
– Who Could Be Bluer *Jerry Lordan* (Parlophone)	–	–	17
– Delaware *Perry Como* (RCA)	–	–	19

MARCH 1960

5	12	19	26
1 Poor Me *Adam Faith* (Parlophone)	2	2	4
2 Running Bear *Johnny Preston* (Mercury)	1	1	2
3 Why? *Anthony Newley* (Decca)	6	7	8
4 A Voice In The Wilderness *Cliff Richard* (Columbia)	5	11	13
5 Slow Boat To China *Emile Ford* (Pye)	4	8	10
6 Way Down Yonder *Freddie Cannon* (Top Rank)	10	–	–
7 Delaware *Perry Como* (RCA),	3	3	3
8 Pretty Blue Eyes *Craig Douglas* (Top Rank)	8	9	18
9 Be Mine *Lance Fortune* (Pye)	7	5	11
10 Beyond The Sea *Bobby Darin* (London)	15	–	–
11 Summer Set *Acker Bilk* (Columbia)	11	13	–
12 Bonnie Came Back *Duane Eddy* (London)	19	–	–
13 Theme From A Summer Place *Percy Faith* (Philips)	12	5	5
14 You Got What It Takes *Marv Johnson* (London)	9	4	6
15 Royal Event *Russ Conway* (Columbia)	16	19	–
16 Who Could Be Bluer *Jerry Lordan* (Parlophone)	14	16	15
17 Harbour Lights *The Platters* (Mercury)	–	–	–
18 Starry-Eyed *Michael Holliday* (Columbia)	–	–	–
19 California Here I Come *Freddie Cannon* (Top Rank)	20	–	–
20 Hit And Miss *The John Barry Seven* (Columbia)	16	12	19
20 What In The World's Come Over You *Jack Scott* (Top Rank)	13	10	7
– Colette *Billy Fury* (London)	18	18	–
– Beatnik Fly *Johnny and The Hurricanes* (London)	–	14	12
– Fings Ain't What They Used To Be *Max Bygraves* (Decca)	–	15	14
– Handyman *Jimmy Jones* (MGM)	–	17	17
– Wild One *Bobby Rydell* (Columbia)	–	20	20
– My Old Man's A Dustman *Lonnie Donegan* (Pye)	–	–	1
– Fall In Love With You *Cliff Richard* (Columbia)	–	–	9
– Do You Mind? *Anthony Newley* (Decca)	–	–	16

APRIL 1960

2	9	16	23	30
1 My Old Man's A Dustman *Lonnie Donegan* (Pye)	1	1	1	7
2 Running Bear *Johnny Preston* (Mercury)	4	8	16	–
3 Fall In Love With You *Cliff Richard* (Columbia)	2	3	3	4
4 Theme From A Summer Place *Percy Faith* (Philips)	6	7	11	13
5 Delaware *Perry Como* (RCA)	10	11	–	–
6 What In The World's Come Over You *Jack Scott* (Top Rank)	11	18	–	18
7 Fings Ain't What They Used To Be *Max Bygraves* (Decca)	8	6	9	12
8 Poor Me *Adam Faith* (Parlophone)	15	–	–	–

56

	9	16	23	30
9 Handy man *Jimmy Jones* (MGM)	3	4	5	5
10 Do You Mind? *Anthony Newley* (Decca)	7	5	4	2
11 You Got What It Takes *Marv Johnson* (London)	14	15	–	–
12 Beatnik Fly *Johnny and The Hurricanes* (London)	9	9	12	14
13 Wild One *Bobby Rydell* (Columbia)	12	13	18	19
14 Hit And Miss *The John Barry Seven* (Columbia)	16	20	19	–
15 Who Could Be Bluer *Jerry Lordan* (Parlophone)	–	–	–	–
16 Slow Boat To China *Emile Ford* (Pye)	20	–	–	–
16 Why? *Anthony Newley* (Decca)	–	–	–	–
18 Willie And The Hand Jive *Cliff Richard* (Columbia)	–	–	–	–
19 Clementine *Bobby Darin* (London)	13	14	13	19
20 Summer Set *Acker Bilk* (Columbia)	19	–	–	–
– Stuck On You *Elvis Presley* (RCA)	5	2	2	6
– Looking High, High, High *Bryan Johnson* (Decca)	17	–	–	–
– Country Boy *Fats Domino* (London)	18	–	–	–
– Sweet Nuthin's *Brenda Lee* (Brunswick)	20	10	8	8
– Someone Else's Baby *Adam Faith* (Parlophone)	–	12	7	3
– Cathy's Clown *The Everly Brothers* (Warner Bros.)	–	16	6	1
– Footsteps *Steve Lawrence* (HMV)	–	17	10	11
– He'll Have To Go *Jim Reeves* (RCA)	–	19	15	16
– Standing On The Corner *The King Brothers* (Parlophone)	–	–	14	9
– Ooh! La La *Keith Kelly* (Parlophone)	–	–	17	17
– Heart Of A Teenage Girl *Craig Douglas* (Top Rank)	–	–	20	15
– Shazam *Duane Eddy* (London)	–	–	–	10

MAY 1960

7	14	21	28
1 Cathy's Clown *The Everly Brothers* (Warner Bros.)	1	1	1
2 Do You Mind? *Anthony Newley* (Decca)	3	3	8
3 Someone Else's Baby *Adam Faith* (Parlophone)	2	2	3
4 Fall In Love With You *Cliff Richard* (Columbia)	6	7	11
5 Handyman *Jimmy Jones* (MGM)	5	6	7
6 Shazam *Duane Eddy* (London)	4	4	4
7 Sweet Nuthin's *Brenda Lee* (Brunswick)	7	8	5
8 Stuck On You *Elvis Presley* (RCA)	8	14	16
9 My Old Man's A Dustman *Lonnie Donegan* (Pye)	14	19	–
10 Standing On The Corner *The King Brothers* (Parlophone)	12	11	–
11 Footsteps *Steve Lawrence* (HMV)	13	10	9
12 Heart Of A Teenage Girl *Craig Douglas* (Top Rank)	10	12	14
13 Cradle Of Love *Johnny Preston* (Mercury)	9	5	2
14 Tease Me/Ooh! La La *Keith Kelly* (Parlophone)	17	13	17
15 Beatnik Fly *Johnny and The Hurricanes* (London)	15	16	–
16 Theme From A Summer Place *Percy Faith* (Philips)	16	18	–
17 He'll Have To Go *Jim Reeves* (RCA)	19	17	12
18 Fings Ain't What They Used To Be *Max Bygraves* (Decca)	–	–	–
19 Greenfields *The Brothers Four* (Philips)	–	–	–
20 Kookie-Kookie *Ed Byrnes* (Warner Bros.)	–	–	–
20 Mack The Knife *Ella Fitzgerald* (HMV)	–	–	–
– Three Steps To Heaven *Eddie Cochran* (London)	11	9	6
– Let The Little Girl Dance *Billy Bland* (London)	18	–	–
– Stairway To Heaven *Neil Sedaka* (RCA)	20	–	13
– Mama/Robot Man *Connie Francis* (MGM)	–	15	10
– Sixteen Reasons *Connie Stevens* (Warner Bros.)	–	20	–
– I Wanna Go Home *Lonnie Donegan* (Pye)	–	–	15
– The Urge *Freddie Cannon* (Top Rank)	–	–	18
– Lucky Five *Russ Conway* (Columbia)	–	–	19
– That's You *Nat 'King' Cole* (Capitol)	–	–	20

	4	11	18	25
1 Cathy's Clown *The Everly Brothers* (Warner Bros.)	1	1	1	
2 Cradle Of Love *Johnny Preston* (Mercury)	2	4	6	
3 Shazam *Duane Eddy* (London)	7	7	13	
4 Handyman *Jimmy Jones* (MGM)	5	6	7	
5 Sweet Nuthin's *Brenda Lee* (Brunswick)	6	8	14	
6 Three Steps To Heaven *Eddie Cochran* (London)	3	3	3	
7 Mama/Robot Man *Connie Francis* (MGM)	3	2	2	
8 Someone Else's Baby *Adam Faith* (Parlophone)	11	–	–	
9 I Wanna Go Home *Lonnie Donegan* (Pye)	8	5	8	
10 Footsteps *Steve Lawrence* (HMV)	10	–	–	
11 Lucky Five *Russ Conway* (Columbia)	9	12	–	
12 Heart Of A Teenage Girl *Craig Douglas* (Top Rank)	15	–	–	
13 Stairway To Heaven *Neil Sedaka* (RCA)	16	14	17	
14 Do You Mind? *Anthony Newley* (Decca)	–	–	–	
15 He'll Have To Go *Jim Reeves* (RCA)	14	11	11	
16 Fall In Love With You *Cliff Richard* (Columbia)	–	–	–	
17 That's You *Nat 'King' Cole* (Capitol)	19	19	19	
18 The Urge *Freddie Cannon* (Top Rank)	–	–	–	
19 Sixteen Reasons *Connie Stevens* (Warner Bros.)	17	12	12	
20 Let The Little Girl Dance *Billy Bland* (London)	–	–	–	
– Ain't Misbehavin' *Tommy Bruce* (Columbia)	12	9	4	
– Down Yonder *Johnny and The Hurricanes* (London)	12	10	9	
– You'll Never Know What You're Missing Till You Try *Emile Ford* (Pye)	18	18	–	
– That's Love *Billy Fury* (Decca)	20	–	–	
– Good Timin' *Jimmy Jones* (MGM)	–	15	5	
– River Stay Away From My Door *Frank Sinatra* (Capitol)	–	16	16	
– Angela Jones *Michael Cox* (Triumph)	–	17	10	
– Pistol Packing Mama *Gene Vincent* (Capitol)	–	20	15	
– Made You/When Johnny Comes Marching Home *Adam Faith* (Parlophone)	–	–	18	
– Talkin' Army Blues *Josh McCrae* (Top Rank)	–	–	20	

	2	9	16	23	30
1 Good Timin' *Jimmy Jones* (MGM)	1	1	1	2	
2 Mama/Robot Man *Connie Francis* (MGM)	6	6	8	9	
3 Three Steps To Heaven *Eddie Cochran* (London)	8	9	15	19	
4 Ain't Misbehavin' *Tommy Bruce* (Columbia)	4	5	6	8	
5 Cathy's Clown *The Everly Brothers* (Warner Bros.)	10	12	20	–	
6 What A Mouth *Tommy Steele* (Decca)	5	7	9	13	
7 Please Don't Tease *Cliff Richard* (Columbia)	2	2	2	1	
8 Made You/When Johnny Comes Marching Home *Adam Faith* (Parlophone)	3	4	4	7	
9 Angela Jones *Michael Cox* (Triumph)	9	8	10	18	
10 Shakin' All Over *Johnny Kidd* (HMV)	6	3	3	3	
11 Handyman *Jimmy Jones* (MGM)	13	–	–	–	
12 Cradle Of Love *Johnny Preston* (Mercury)	–	–	–	–	
13 I Wanna Go Home *Lonnie Donegan* (Pye)	16	15	17	–	
13 Down Yonder *Johnny and The Hurricanes* (London)	12	16	–	–	
15 He'll Have To Go *Jim Reeves* (RCA)	15	17	–	17	
16 Sixteen Reason *Connie Stevens* (Warner Bros.)	18	–	–	–	
17 Pistol Packing Mama *Gene Vincent* (Capitol)	11	19	–	–	
18 Shazam *Duane Eddy* (London)	–	–	–	–	
19 Talkin' Army Blues *Josh McCrae* (Top Rank)	14	18	16	15	
20 Sweet Nuthin's *Brenda Lee* (Brunswick)	20	–	–	–	

	9	16	23	30
– Look For A Star *Gary Mills* (Top Rank)	17	10	5	6
– I'm Sorry *Brenda Lee* (Brunswick)	19	11	14	15
– Yellow Polka Dot Bikini *Brian Hyland* (London)	–	13	12	14
– When Will I Be Loved *The Everly Brothers* (Warner Bros.)	–	14	7	5
– Elvis Is Back (L.P.) *Elvis Presley* (RCA)	–	20	–	–
– If She Should Come To You *Anthony Newley* (Decca)	–	–	11	12
– Because They're Young *Duane Eddy* (London)	–	–	13	11
– Love Is Like A Violin *Ken Dodd* (Decca)	–	–	18	–
– Apache *The Shadows* (Columbia)	–	–	19	10
– The Girl Of My Best Friend *Elvis Presley* (RCA)	–	–	–	4
– Tie Me Kangaroo Down Sport *Rolf Harris* (Columbia)	–	–	–	20

AUGUST 1960

	6	13	20	27
1 Please Don't Tease *Cliff Richard* (Columbia)		1	2	2
2 The Girl Of My Best Friend *Elvis Presley* (RCA)		3	3	3
3 Shakin' All Over *Johnny Kidd* (HMV)		4	6	6
4 Good Timin' *Jimmy Jones* (MGM)		7	11	–
5 Apache *The Shadows* (Columbia)		2	1	1
6 When Will I Be Loved *The Everly Brothers* (Warner Bros.)		5	4	5
7 Because They're Young *Duane Eddy* (London)		6	5	4
8 If She Should Come To You *Anthony Newley* (Decca)		9	7	8
9 Look For A Star *Gary Mills* (Top Rank)		11	17	20
10 Yellow Polka Dot Bikini *Brian Hyland* (London)		10	9	11
11 Made You/Johnny Comes Marching Home *Adam Faith* (Parlophone)		13	–	–
12 Tie Me Kangaroo Down Sport *Rolf Harris* (Columbia)		8	8	7
13 Talkin' Army Blues *Josh McCrae* (Top Rank)		12	14	13
14 I'm Sorry *Brenda Lee* (Brunswick)		18	10	10
15 Mama/Robot Man *Connie Francis* (MGM)		19	–	–
16 What A Mouth *Tommy Steele* (Decca)		14	–	–
17 Ain't Misbehavin' *Tommy Bruce* (Columbia)		15	–	–
18 Listen Little Girl *Keith Kelly* (Parlophone)		16	15	19
19 Love Is Like A Violin *Ken Dodd* (Decca)		20	19	15
20 Paper Roses *The Kaye Sisters* (Philips)		16	13	18
20 As Long As He Needs Me *Shirley Bassey* (Columbia)		–	20	–
– Everybody's Somebody's Fool *Connie Francis* (MGM)		–	12	9
– Please Help Me, I'm Falling *The Brook Brothers* (Top Rank)		–	16	–
– Only The Lonely *Roy Orbison* (London)		–	17	14
– Lorelei *Lonnie Donegan* (Pye)		–	–	12
– Tell Laura I Love Her *Ricky Valance* (Columbia)		–	–	15
– Image Of A Girl *Mark Wynter* (Decca)		–	–	17

SEPTEMBER 1960

	3	10	17	24
1 Apache *The Shadows* (Columbia)		1	1	1
2 Because They're Young *Duane Eddy* (London)		3	3	5
3 The Girl Of My Best Friend *Elvis Presley* (RCA)		2	2	2
4 Please Don't Tease *Cliff Richard* (Columbia)		4	5	9
5 When Will I Be Loved *The Everly Brothers* (Warner Bros.)		6	7	14
6 Everybody's Somebody's Fool *Connie Francis* (MGM)		7	9	8
7 Shakin' All Over *Johnny Kidd* (HMV)		10	16	–
8 If She Should Come To You *Anthony Newley* (Decca)		11	19	–
9 Tie Me Kangaroo Down Sport *Rolf Harris* (Columbia)		14	20	–
10 Tell Laura I Love Her *Ricky Valance* (Columbia)		5	4	3
11 Lorelei *Lonnie Donegan* (Pye)		–	–	–

3

	10	17	24
12 Only The Lonely *Roy Orbison* (London)	8	6	4
13 Love Is Like A Violin *Ken Dodd* (Decca)	12	15	–
14 I'm Sorry *Brenda Lee* (Brunswick)	–	–	–
15 Yellow Polka Dot Bikini *Brian Hyland* (London)	–	–	–
16 Talkin' Army Blues *Josh McCrae* (Top Rank)	–	17	–
17 As Long As He Needs Me *Shirley Bassey* (Columbia)	9	8	12
18 Caribbean Honeymoon *Frank Weir* (Oriole)	20	18	20
19 Paper Roses *The Kaye Sisters* (Philips)	15	10	15
20 Image Of A Girl *Mark Wynter* (Decca)	19	11	19
– How About That *Adam Faith* (Parlophone)	–	12	6
– Walk, Don't Run *The Ventures* (Top Rank)	–	14	10
– Nice 'n' Easy *Frank Sinatra* (Capitol)	–	20	–
– Nine Times Out Of Ten *Cliff Richard* (Columbia)	–	–	7
– So Sad/Lucille *The Everly Brothers* (Warner Bros.)	–	–	10
– Fish Man *Ian Menzies* (Pye)	–	–	16
– Walk, Don't Run *The John Barry Seven* (Columbia)	–	–	17
– I'll Be Your Hero/Jet Black Machine *Vince Taylor* (Palette)	–	–	18
– Please Help Me I'm Falling *Hank Locklin* (RCA)	13	13	13

For an unknown reason a chart was not published for 10 September 1960 in Record Mirror, so those figures which appear under 10 September column were published as the 'last week' figures for 17 September 1960.

OCTOBER 1960

1

	8	15	22	29
1 Tell Laura I Love Her *Ricky Valance* (Columbia)	1	2	3	5
2 Nine Times Out Of Ten *Cliff Richard* (Columbia)	3	4	6	7
3 Only The Lonely *Roy Orbison* (London)	2	1	1	1
4 How About That *Adam Faith* (Parlophone)	4	3	2	3
5 Apache *The Shadows* (Columbia)	7	10	13	16
6 The Girl Of My Best Friend/A Mess Of Blues *Elvis Presley* (RCA)	6	7	10	12
7 So Sad/Lucille *The Everly Brothers* (Warner Bros.)	5	5	5	4
8 Because They're Young *Duane Eddy* (London)	11	14	–	–
9 Walk, Don't Run *The Ventures* (Top Rank)	8	9	11	15
10 Please Help Me I'm Falling *Hank Locklin* (RCA)	10	12	14	17
11 Walk, Don't Run *The John Barry Seven* (Columbia)	9	8	7	10
12 Everybody's Somebody's Fool *Connie Francis* (MGM)	14	15	17	–
13 Image Of A Girl *Mark Wynter* (Decca)	18	–	–	–
14 As Long As He Needs Me *Shirley Bassey* (Columbia)	12	6	4	2
15 Fish Man *Ian Menzies* (Philips)	15	–	–	–
16 I'll Be Your Hero/Jet Black Machine *Vince Taylor* (Palette)	17	15	–	–
17 Please Don't Tease *Cliff Richard* (Columbia)	–	–	–	–
18 Let's Think About Living *Bob Luman* (Warner Bros.)	13	13	8	8
19 Chain Gang *Sam Cooke* (RCA)	16	11	9	11
20 When Will I Be Loved *The Everly Brothers* (Warner Bros.)	–	–	–	–
– Lonely/Sweetie Pie *Eddie Cochran* (London)	19	–	–	–
– Along Came Caroline *Michael Cox* (HMV)	20	20	–	–
– My Love For You *Johnny Mathis* (Fontana)	20	–	–	–
– McDonald's Cave *The Piltdown Men* (Capitol)	–	17	15	14
– Restless *Johnny Kidd* (HMV)	–	18	–	18
– Dreaming *Johnny Burnette* (London)	–	19	12	9
– Shortnin' Bread *The Viscounts* (Pye)	–	–	16	13
– Rocking Goose *Johnny and The Hurricanes* (London)	–	–	18	6
– Never On Sunday *Lyn Cornell* (Decca)	–	–	18	20
– Them There Eyes *Emile Ford* (Pye)	–	–	20	–
– Save The Last Dance For Me *The Drifters* (London)	–	–	–	18
– Top Teen Baby *Gary Mills* (Top Rank)	–	–	–	20

NOVEMBER 1960

5		12	19	26
1 It's Now Or Never *Elvis Presley* (RCA)		1	1	1
2 Only The Lonely *Roy Orbison* (London)		2	4	9
3 As Long As He Needs Me *Shirley Bassey* (Columbia)		3	5	6
4 Rocking Goose *Johnny and The Hurricanes* (London)		4	3	3
5 Nine Times Out Of Ten *Cliff Richard* (Columbia)		8	15	–
6 So Sad/Lucille *The Everly Brothers* (Warner Bros.)		11	–	–
7 Let's Think About Living *Bob Luman* (Warner Bros.)		9	11	16
8 Dreaming *Johnny Burnette* (London)		6	8	8
9 How About That *Adam Faith* (Parlophone)		15	20	–
10 Walk, Don't Run *The John Barry Seven* (Columbia)		17	18	–
11 Tell Laura I Love Her *Ricky Valance* (Columbia)		–	–	–
12 Chain Gang *Sam Cooke* (RCA)		14	–	–
13 My Heart Has A Mind Of Its Own *Connie Francis* (HMV)		5	2	5
14 My Love For You *Johnny Mathis* (Fontana)		–	16	–
15 McDonald's Cave *The Piltdown Men* (Capitol)		13	12	–
16 Please Help Me I'm Falling *Hank Locklin* (RCA)		18	–	–
16 Save The Last Dance For Me *The Drifters* (London)		7	6	4
18 Blue Angel/Today's Tear-Drops *Roy Orbison* (London)		16	13	15
19 Shortnin' Bread *The Viscounts* (Pye)		19	–	–
20 Mr Custer *Charlie Drake* (Parlophone)		20	14	17
20 The Girl Of My Best Friend/A Mess of Blues *Elvis Presley* (RCA)		–	–	–
– Man Of Mystery *The Shadows* (Columbia)		10	7	2
– Kommotion *Duane Eddy* (London)		12	10	12
– Goodness Gracious Me *Peter Sellers and Sophia Loren* (Parlophone)		–	9	7
– Milord *Edith Piaf* (Columbia)		–	17	19
– Sorry Robbie *Bert Weedon* (Top Rank)		–	18	–
– Lively *Lonnie Donegan* (Pye)		–	–	10
– Strawberry Fair *Anthony Newley* (Decca)		–	–	11
– Little Donkey *Nina and Frederik* (Columbia)		–	–	13
– Ole McDonald *Frank Sinatra* (Capitol)		–	–	14
– Wild Side Of Life *Josh McCrae* (Pye)		–	–	18
– Poetry In Motion *Johnny Tilliston* (London)		–	–	20

DECEMBER 1960

3		10	17–24	31
1 It's Now Or Never *Elvis Presley* (RCA)		1	1	1
2 Save The Last Dance For Me *The Drifters* (London)		2	2	3
3 Man Of Mystery/The Stranger *The Shadows* (Columbia)		5	11	12
4 Strawberry Fair *Anthony Newley* (Decca)		3	4	5
5 Goodness Gracious Me *Peter Sellers and Sophia Loren* (Parlophone)		7	7	8
6 Rocking Goose *Johnny and The Hurricanes* (London)		8	8	11
7 My Heart Has A Mind Of Its Own *Connie Francis* (MGM)		11	13	–
8 I Love You *Cliff Richard* (Columbia)		4	3	2
9 As Long As He Needs Me *Shirley Bassey* (Columbia)		12	–	–
10 Little Donkey *Nina and Frederik* (Columbia)		6	5	6
11 Dreaming *Johnny Burnette* (London)		14	14	–
12 Poetry In Motion *Johnny Tilliston* (London)		9	6	4
13 Gurney Slade *Max Harris* (Fontana)		10	10	10
14 Ole McDonald *Frank Sinatra* (Capitol)		17	15	–
15 Lively *Lonnie Donegan* (Pye)		–	18	18
16 My Love For You *Johnny Mathis* (Fontana)		18	20	20
17 Wild Side Of Life *Josh McCrae* (Pye)		15	16	16
18 Blue Angel/Today's Tear-Drops *Roy Orbison* (London)		18	–	–

3

	10	17–24	31
19 Kicking Up The Leaves *Mark Wynter* (Decca)	–	–	–
20 Only The Lonely *Roy Orbison* (London)	–	–	–
– Lonely Pup *Adam Faith* (Parlophone)	13	9	7
– Perfidia *The Ventures* (London)	16	12	9
– Time Will Tell *Ian Gregory* (Pye)	20	17	19
– You Talk Too Much *Johnny Carson* (Fontana)	–	18	–
– Strawberry Blonde *Frank D'Rone* (Mercury)	–	–	13
– Ten Swinging Bottles *Pete Chester and The Chesternuts* (Pye)	–	–	14
– Pepe *Russ Conway* (Columbia)	–	–	15
– Portrait Of My Love *Matt Monro* (Parlophone)	–	–	17
– It's·You That I Love *Marion Ryan* (Pye)	–	–	20

There was no Record Mirror for 24 December 1960.

1960–BEST-SELLING SINGLES

1 Cathy's Clown *The Everly Brothers* (Warner Bros.)
2 Please Don't Tease *Cliff Richard* (Columbia)
3 The Girl Of My Best Friend/A Mess Of Blues *Elvis Presley* (RCA)
4 Handyman *Jimmy Jones* (MGM)
5 Apache *The Shadows* (Columbia)
6 It's Now Or Never *Elvis Presley* (RCA)
7 Why? *Anthony Newley* (Decca)
8 Save The Last Dance For Me *The Drifters* (London)
9 Because They're Young *Duane Eddy* (London)
10 Shakin' All Over *Johnny Kidd* (HMV)
11 Poetry In Motion *Johnny Tillotson* (London)
12 Tell Laura I Love Her *Ricky Valance* (Columbia)
13 Running Bear *Johnny Preston* (Mercury)
14 Mama/Robot Man *Connie Francis* (MGM)
15 As Long As He Needs Me *Shirley Bassey* (Columbia)
16 Fall In Love With You *Cliff Richard* (Columbia)
{17 Poor Me *Adam Faith* (Parlophone)
{17 Good Timin' *Jimmy Jones* (MGM)
{18 Do You Mind? *Anthony Newley* (Decca)
{18 Three Steps To Heaven *Eddie Cochran* (London)
19 I Love You *Cliff Richard* (Columbia)
20 A Voice In The Wilderness *Cliff Richard* (Columbia)

In its listing of top songs for 1960 Record Mirror printed two Number Seventeens and two Number Eighteens.

1961

1961 chart statistics provided very little evidence for those people who suggested that the British Top Twenty merely reflected the hits which had been in the American Hit Parade some weeks previously. During the year, of some 42 records which had made the American Top Three, only seven reached the same positions in the British Top Twenty. Six of these were Number One hits on both sides of the Atlantic and a further 17 made the British Top Twenty, but 24 hits which had been in the American Top Three failed to enter the British charts at all.

The six chart toppers on both sides of the Atlantic were 'Are You Lonesome Tonight' and 'Surrender' by Elvis Presley; 'Blue Moon' from The Marcels; 'Runaway' by Del Shannon; The Highwaymen's version of 'Michael Row The Boat'; and 'Take Good Care Of My Baby' from Bobby Vee.

Among the American discs failing to enter the British Top Twenty were 'Goodbye, Cruel World' by James Darren; 'A Hundred Pounds Of Clay' by Gene McDaniels; 'Let's Twist Again' from Chubby Checker; 'Dedicated To The One I Love' from The Shirelles; 'Stand By Me' from Ben E. King; and 'Please Mr Postman' from The Marvelettes.

One American artist, however, was busily chalking up hits on both sides of the Atlantic. This was Elvis Presley, who had five chart hits, all of which reached the Number One position except for 'Wild In The Country/Feel So Fine'.

A newcomer to the British charts from America was Del Shannon. Shannon's hit 'Runaway' started his hit trail which ended in a total of eight hits by 1965. Neil Sedaka, another American, had his most successful year with three Top Twenty hits, though only 'Happy Birthday Sweet Sixteen' reached the Top Five.

Anyway, there were plenty of British hit-makers. Cliff Richard had 'Theme For A Dream' in the February listings, and ended the year with 'When The Girl In Your Arms Is The Girl In Your Heart', his fourth hit of 1961. His backing group, The Shadows, had one hit less than he, but they achieved something which Cliff failed to do in 1961 – they reached the Number One position with 'Kon-Tiki'.

The popularity of Trad Jazz continued, and Acker Bilk's run of hits continued after his 1960 success. He had three hits in 1961, one of which, 'Stranger On The Shore', was both a Number One and a record which sold a phenomenal number of copies. Kenny Ball entered the charts in February 1961 with 'Samantha' which he followed up with two more hits that year. 1962 was to yield a further three hits for Ball. Dave Brubeck, with a different Jazz sound, also made the charts with 'Take Five' a catchy, off-beat tune.

Adam Faith and Marty Wilde were also in the Hit Parade of 1961, but the latter was gradually running out of steam; he managed only one hit while Faith achieved four. The Allisons became one-hit wonders with the very successful Eurovision song 'Are You Sure?', but they then faded quickly from the scene. Tongue-in-cheek nostalgia came from The Temperance Seven, who had no less than four hits, though their popularity was waning by the time 'Pasadena', their second hit, reached its chart zenith of Number Four.

It was almost the last 1960s triumph for the twanging guitar of Duane Eddy, who achieved five hits in 1961. Three more lay in store for him in 1962, and then he disappeared into obscurity until he made a comeback in 1975 with 'Play Me Like You Play Your Guitar'.

Pop had began to see the wane of the rockers, with the leather clothes, the motorbikes and conversations filled with ton-up chat and argumentative clashes with authority. Certainly the onset of the Twist, spearheaded by Chubby Checker, changed dancehall tactics. Jiving turned to twisting, and the casualty wards of hospitals were full of ageing twisters whose enthusiasm got the better of their discretion. The Twist was only acceptable to the young until the old, too, cashed in on its popularity, by which time youth had dismissed such a dance and continued with its search for something or someone new.

JANUARY 1961

7	14	21	28
1 Poetry In Motion *Johnny Tilliston* (London)	1	1	2
2 Save The Last Dance For Me *The Drifters* (London)	3	5	12
3 I Love You *Cliff Richard* (Columbia)	2	3	4
4 It's Now Or Never *Elvis Presley* (RCA)	4	9	14
5 Lonely Pup *Adam Faith* (Parlophone)	10	–	–
6 Perifidia *The Ventures* (London)	5	8	15
7 Strawberry Fair *Anthony Newley* (Decca)	–	–	–
8 Man Of Mystery/The Stranger *The Shadows* (Columbia)	18	–	–
9 Counting Teardrops *Emile Ford* (Pye)	6	7	8
9 Goodness Gracious Me *Peter Sellers and Sophia Loren* (Parlophone)	11	16	–
11 Little Donkey *Nina and Frederik* (Columbia)	–	–	–
12 Portrait Of My Love *Matt Monro* (Parlophone)	7	6	5
13 Wild Side Of Life *Josh McCrae* (Pye)	–	–	–
14 Rocking Goose *Johnny and The Hurricanes* (London)	19	–	–
15 Strawberry Blonde *Frank D'Rone* (Mercury)	–	–	–
16 Ten Swinging Bottles *Pete Chester* (Pye)	–	–	–
17 Little Girl *Marty Wilde* (Philips)	20	20	20
18 Blue Angel *Roy Orbison* (London)	17	–	–
19 Stay *Maurice Williams* (Top Rank)	13	12	11
20 Buona Sera *Acker Bilk* (Columbia)	9	10	13
20 Like Strangers *The Everly Brothers* (London)	12	17	–
– Pepe *Duane Eddy* (London)	8	4	3
– Sway *Bobby Rydell* (Columbia)	14	18	–
– Black Stockings *The John Barry Seven* (Columbia)	15	–	–
– Piltdown Rides Again *The Piltdown Men* (Capitol)	15	13	18
– Are You Lonesome Tonight *Elvis Presley* (RCA)	–	2	1
– You're Sixteen *Johnny Burnette* (London)	–	11	9
– Pepe *Russ Conway* (Columbia)	–	14	–
– North To Alaska *Johnny Horton* (Philips)	–	15	16
– Chariot *Rhet Stoller* (Decca)	–	19	–
– Rubber Ball *Bobby Vee* (London)	–	20	7
– Sailor *Petula Clark* (Pye)	–	–	6
– Rubber Ball *Marty Wilde* (Philips)	–	–	10
– Many Years Ago *Connie Francis* (MGM)	–	–	17
– Sailor *Anne Shelton* (Philips)	–	–	19
– First Taste Of Love *Ben E. King* (London)	–	–	20

FEBRUARY 1961

4	11	18	25
1 Are You Lonesome Tonight *Elvis Presley* (RCA)	1	1	2
2 Sailor *Petula Clark* (Pye)	2	2	3
3 Pepe *Duane Eddy* (London)	4	9	12
4 Rubber Ball *Bobby Vee* (London)	3	5	7
5 Poetry In Motion *Johnny Tilliston* (London)	6	11	–
6 You're Sixteen *Johnny Burnette* (London)	5	6	11
7 Portrait Of My Love *Matt Monro* (Parlophone)	9	14	–
8 Sailor *Anne Shelton* (Philips)	7	10	15
9 Counting Teardrops *Emile Ford* (Pye)	13	–	–
10 Rubber Ball *Marty Wilde* (Philips)	10	–	16
11 I Love You *Cliff Richard* (Columbia)	17	18	–
12 Stay *Maurice Williams* (Top Rank)	–	–	–
13 Many Tears Ago *Connie Francis* (MGM)	–	–	–
14 Pepe *Russ Conway* (Columbia)	18	–	–
15 North To Alaska *Johnny Horton* (Philips)	19	–	–
16 Messing About On The River *Josh McCrae* (Pye)	16	15	–

65

	11	18	25
4			
17 First Taste Of Love *Ben E. King* (London)	–	16	–
18 Buona Sera *Acker Bilk* (Columbia)	11	12	14
19 It's Now Or Never *Elvis Presley* (RCA)	–	–	–
20 Calendar Girl *Neil Sedaka* (RCA)	20	13	10
– F.B.I. *The Shadows* (Columbia)	8	4	4
– Walk Right Back *The Everly Brothers* (Warner Bros.)	12	3	1
– Will You Love Me Tomorrow *The Shirelles* (Top Rank)	14	8	5
– Who Am I? /This Is It *Adam Faith* (Parlophone)	15	7	6
– Riders In The Sky *The Ramrods* (London)	–	17	8
– Pepy's Diary/Gather In The Mushrooms *Benny Hill* (Pye)	–	19	13
– Calcutta *Lawrence Welk* (London)	–	19	–
– Are You Sure? *The Allisons* (Fontana)	–	–	9
– Let's Jump The Broomstick *Brenda Lee* (Brunswick)	–	–	17
– Ja-Da *Johnny and The Hurricanes* (London)	–	–	17
– Wheels *The String-A-Longs* (London)	–	–	19
– New Orleans *The U.S. Bonds* (Top Rank)	–	–	20

MARCH 1961

	11	18	25
4			
1 Walk Right Back/Ebony Eyes *The Everly Brothers* (Warner Bros.)	1	1	2
2 Are You Sure? *The Allisons* (Fontana)	2	3	3
3 Sailor *Petula Clark* (Pye)	6	10	13
4 Will You Love Me Tomorrow *The Shirelles* (Top Rank)	3	5	5
5 Are You Lonesome Tonight *Elvis Presley* (RCA)	11	–	–
6 F.B.I. *The Shadows* (Columbia)	7	6	10
7 Theme For A Dream *Cliff Richard* (Columbia)	4	4	4
8 Riders In The Sky *The Ramrods* (London)	8	7	8
9 Who Am I?/This Is It *Adam Faith* (Parlophone)	9	11	20
10 Rubber Ball *Bobby Vee* (London)	–	–	–
11 Calendar Girl *Neil Sedaka* (RCA)	10	13	15
12 Wheels *The String-A-Longs* (London)	16	12	12
13 Samantha *Kenny Ball* (Pye)	12	14	13
14 Ja-Da *Johnny and The Hurricanes* (London)	18	–	–
15 Let's Jump The Broomstick *Brenda Lee* (Brunswick)	15	–	–
16 Baby Sittin' Boogie *Buzz Clifford* (Philips)	19	19	17
17 Pepe *Duane Eddy* (London)	–	–	–
18 Pepy's Diary/Gather In The Mushrooms *Benny Hill* (Pye)	20	–	–
18 Dream Girl *Mark Wynter* (Decca)	14	15	–
20 You're Sixteen *Johnny Burnette* (London)	–	–	–
– And The Heavens Cried *Anthony Newley* (Decca)	–	16	11
– Lazy River *Bobby Darin* (London)	–	17	9
– Goodnight Mrs Flintstone *The Piltdown Men* (Capitol)	–	18	19
– Warpaint *The Brook Brothers* (Pye)	–	20	17
– Wooden Heart *Elvis Presley* (RCA)	5	2	1
– My Kind Of Girl *Matt Monro* (Parlophone)	13	9	7
– Exodus *Ferrante and Teicher* (London)	17	8	6
– Marry Me *Mike Preston* (Decca)	–	–	16

APRIL 1961

	8	15	22	29
1				
1 Wooden Heart *Elvis Presley* (RCA)	1	2	2	1
2 Walk Right Back/Ebony Eyes *The Everly Brothers* (Warner Bros.)	3	3	5	13
3 Are You Sure? *The Allisons* (Fontana)	2	1	1	4
4 Theme For A Dream *Cliff Richard* (Columbia)	4	6	6	17

66

1	8	15	22	29
5 My Kind Of Girl *Matt Monro* (Parlophone)	6	12	16	18
6 Lazy River *Bobby Darin* (London)	5	4	7	5
7 Exodus *Ferranti and Teicher* (London)	9	10	14	14
8 And The Heavens Cried *Anthony Newley* (Decca)	8	8	9	19
8 Will You Love Me Tomorrow *The Shirelles* (Top Rank)	12	16	15	–
10 Riders In The Sky *The Ramrods* (London)	16	20	–	–
11 F.B.I. *The Shadows* (Columbia)	10	5	8	–
12 Warpaint *The Brook Brothers* (Pye)	13	11	11	7
13 Where The Boys Are *Connie Francis* (MGM)	7	9	10	16
13 Marry Me *Mike Preston* (Decca)	15	–	–	–
15 African Waltz *Johnny Dankworth* (Columbia)	–	13	17	12
16 Baby Sittin' Boogie *Buzz Clifford* (Fontana)	17	18	19	20
17 Calendar Girl *Neil Sedaka* (RCA)	–	–	–	–
17 Samantha *Kenny Ball* (Pye)	13	18	18	–
19 Goodnight Mrs Flintstone *The Piltdown Men* (Capitol)	–	–	–	–
20 Gee Whiz It's You *Cliff Richard* (Columbia)	–	15	12	8
– You're Driving Me Crazy *The Temperance Seven* (Parlophone)	11	7	4	1
– Blue Moon *The Marcels* (Pye)	18	14	3	3
– Pony Time *Chubby Checker* (Columbia)	19	–	–	–
– Exodus *Mantovani* (Decca)	20	–	–	–
– A Hundred Pounds Of Clay *Craig Douglas* (Top Rank)	–	17	13	11
– Theme From Dixie *Duane Eddy* (London)	–	–	20	6
– Little Boy Sad *Johnny Burnette* (London)	–	–	20	15
– Don't Treat Me Like A Child *Helen Shapiro* (Columbia)	–	–	–	9
– On The Rebound *Floyd Cramer* (RCA)	–	–	–	10

MAY 1961

6	13	20	27
1 You're Driving Me Crazy *The Temperance Seven* (Parlophone)	2	2	8
2 Blue Moon *The Marcels* (Pye)	1	1	3
3 Wooden Heart *Elvis Presley* (RCA)	3	7	12
4 Don't Treat Me Like A Child *Helen Shapiro* (Columbia)	4	8	7
5 On The Rebound *Floyd Cramer* (RCA)	5	5	5
6 Warpaint *The Brook Brothers* (Pye)	11	18	–
7 Theme From Dixie *Duane Eddy* (London)	8	16	15
8 A Hundred Pounds of Clay *Craig Douglas* (Top Rank)	10	13	16
9 Gee Whiz It's You *Cliff Richard* (Columbia)	17	11	–
10 Lazy River *Bobby Darin* (London)	19	20	–
11 African Waltz *Johnny Dankworth* (Columbia)	12	15	20
12 Are You Sure *The Allisons* (Fontana)	15	–	–
13 Little Boy Sad *Johnny Burnette* (London)	16	19	17
14 Runaway *Del Shannon* (London)	7	3	1
15 More Than I Can Say *Bobby Vee* (London)	6	6	6
16 Easy Going Me *Adam Faith* (Parlophone)	14	9	18
17 Exodus *Ferranti and Teicher* (London)	20	–	–
18 Walk Right Back/Ebony Eyes *The Everly Brothers* (Warner Bros.)	–	–	–
19 Where The Boys Are *Connie Francis* (MGM)	–	–	–
20 Baby Sittin' Boogie *Buzz Clifford* (Fontana)	–	–	–
– The Frightened City *The Shadows* (Columbia)	9	4	4
– What'd I Say? *Jerry Lee Lewis* (London)	13	10	11
– Have A Drink On Me *Lonnie Donegan* (Pye)	18	17	14
– But I Do *Clarence Frogman Henry* (Pye)	–	12	10
– You'll Never Know *Shirley Bassey* (Columbia)	–	14	9
– Little Devil *Neil Sedaka* (RCA)	–	–	13
– Surrender *Elvis Presley* (RCA)	–	–	1
– Travellin' Man *Ricky Nelson* (London)	–	–	19

3		10	17	24
1 Surrender *Elvis Presley* (RCA)		1	1	1
2 Runaway *Del Shannon* (London)		2	2	2
3 More Than I Can Say *Bobby Vee* (London)		5	6	14
4 The Frightened City *The Shadows* (Columbia)		4	3	5
5 Blue Moon *The Marcels* (Pye)		9	–	–
6 On The Rebound *Floyd Cramer* (RCA)		13	18	–
7 You'll Never Know *Shirley Bassey* (Columbia)		3	8	7
8 What'd I Say? *Jerry Lee Lewis* (London)		10	13	17
9 But I Do *Clarence Frogman Henry* (Pye)		6	5	8
10 Don't Treat Me Like A Child *Helen Shapiro* (Columbia)		11	17	–
11 Have A Drink On Me *Lonnie Donegan* (Pye)		7	12	15
12 Little Devil *Neil Sedaka* (RCA)		14	19	18
13 You're Driving Me Crazy *The Temperance Seven* (Parlophone)		17	–	–
14 Hello Mary Lou/Travellin' Man *Ricky Nelson* (London)		12	4	6
15 Wooden Heart *Elvis Presley* (RCA)		15	20	–
16 Easy Going Me *Adam Faith* (Parlophone)		–	–	–
17 African Waltz *Johnny Dankworth* (Columbia)		–	–	–
18 I Still Love You All *Kenny Ball* (Pye)		19	–	–
19 Runnin' Scared *Roy Orbison* (London)		16	16	13
20 Halfway To Paradise *Billy Fury* (Decca)		8	10	10
– Well I Ask You *Eden Kane* (Decca)		20	14	16
– I Told Every Little Star *Linda Scott* (Columbia)		18	9	11
– Pop Goes The Weasel/Bee-Bom *Anthony Newley* (Decca)		–	15	9
– Temptation *The Everly Brothers* (Warner Bros.)		–	11	3
– Pasadena *The Temperance Seven* (Parlophone)		–	7	4
– A Girl Like You *Cliff Richard* (Columbia)		–	–	12
– Weekend *Eddie Cochran* (London)		–	–	19
– Ring Of Fire *Duane Eddy* (London)		–	–	20

1		8	15	22	29
1 Runaway *Del Shannon* (London)		2	2	4	4
2 Surrender *Elvis Presley* (RCA)		6	8	9	14
3 Temptation *The Everly Brothers* (Warner Bros.)		1	1	1	1
4 Pasadena *The Temperance Seven* (Parlophone)		4	7	7	8
5 A Girl Like You *Cliff Richard* (Columbia)		5	3	3	6
6 Hello MaryLou/Travellin' Man *Ricky Nelson* (London)		3	4	5	3
7 Halfway To Paradise *Billy Fury* (Decca)		7	6	6	5
8 But I Do *Clarence Frogman Henry* (Pye)		8	13	19	16
9 The Frightened City *The Shadows* (Columbia)		12	19	–	–
10 You'll Never Know *Shirley Bassey* (Columbia)		19	–	–	–
11 Pop Goes The Weasel *Anthony Newley* (Decca)		10	11	15	–
12 Runnin' Scared *Roy Orbison* (London)		11	9	12	17
13 Well I Ask You *Eden Kane* (Decca)		9	5	2	2
14 I Told Every Little Star *Linda Scott* (Columbia)		17	–	–	–
15 Little Devil *Neil Sedaka* (RCA)		–	–	–	–
16 Have A Drink On Me *Lonnie Donegan* (Pye)		18	–	–	–
17 More Than I Can Say *Bobby Vee* (London)		–	–	–	20
18 Marcheta *Karl Denver* (Decca)		20	–	–	–
19 Ring Of Fire *Duane Eddy* (London)		13	15	20	–
20 Weekend *Eddie Cochran* (London)		15	18	18	15
– Breakin' In A Brand New Heart *Connie Francis* (MGM)		14	–	–	–
– Time *Craig Douglas* (Top Rank)		16	20	11	11
– You Don't Know *Helen Shapiro* (Columbia)		–	10	8	7
– Old Smokie/High Voltage *Johnny and The Hurricanes* (London)		–	12	14	19

1

	8	15	22	29
– Romeo *Petula Clark* (Pye)	8	15	22	29
– Baby I Don't Care/Valley Of Tears *Buddy Holly* (Coral)	–	14	13	10
– Moody River *Pat Boone* (London)	–	16	16	13
– You Always Hurt The One You Love *Clarence Frogman Henry* (Pye)	–	17	16	–
– Don't You Know It *Adam Faith* (Parlophone)	–	–	10	9
– Quarter To Three *The U.S. Bonds* (Top Rank)	–	–	–	12
– That's My Home *Acker Bilk* (Columbia)	–	–	–	18
	–	–	–	20

AUGUST 1961

5

	·12	19	26
1 Well I Ask You *Eden Kane* (Decca)	2	2	3
2 You Don't Know *Helen Shapiro* (Columbia)	1	1	2
3 Temptation *The Everly Brothers* (Warner Bros.)	5	12	11
4 Halfway To Paradise *Billy Fury* (Decca)	4	4	5
5 Pasadena *The Temperance Seven* (Parlophone)	12	9	15
6 A Girl Like You *Cliff Richard* (Columbia)	10	7	7
7 Runaway *Del Shannon* (London)	7	14	17
8 Hello Mary Lou/Travellin' Man *Ricky Nelson* (London)	8	10	9
9 Romeo *Petula Clark* (Pye)	6	5	6
10 Don't You Know It *Adam Faith* (Parlophone)	14	15	12
11 You Always Hurt The One You Love *Clarence Frogman Henry* (Pye)	12	11	10
12 Time *Craig Douglas* (Top Rank)	9	8	8
13 Johnny Remember Me *John Leyton* (Top Rank)	3	3	1
14 Baby I Don't Care/Valley Of Tears *Buddy Holly* (Coral)	13	–	14
15 Weekend *Eddie Cochran* (London)	–	–	19
16 Quarter To Three *The U.S. Bonds* (Top Rank)	15	13	13
17 Marcheta *Karl Denver* (Decca)	16	–	16
18 Reach For The Stars/Climb Every Mountain *Shirley Bassey* (Columbia)	–	6	4
19 Surrender *Elvis Presley* (RCA)	–	–	–
20 Runnin' Scared *Roy Orbison* (London)	–	–	–
– Cupid *Sam Cooke* (RCA)	17	17	18
– Moody River *Pat Boone* (London)	18	–	–
– But I Do *Clarence Frogman Henry* (Pye)	19	–	–
– Quite A Party *The Fireballs* (Pye)	20	–	–
– The Frightened City *The Shadows* (Columbia)	–	16	–
– The Writing On The Wall *Tommy Steele* (Decca)	–	18	–
– That's My Home *Acker Bilk* (Columbia)	–	19	–
– How Many Tears *Bobby Vee* (London)	–	20	–
– Ain't Gonna Wash For A Week *The Brook Brothers* (Pye)	–	–	20
– Too Many Beautiful Girls *Clinton Ford* (Oriole)	–	–	20

SEPTEMBER 1961

2

	9	16	23	30
1 Johnny Remember Me *John Leyton* (Top Rank)	1	1	1	2
2 You Don't Know *Helen Shapiro* (Columbia)	2	3	4	5
3 Reach For The Stars/Climb Every Mountain *Shirley Bassey* (Columbia)	4	5	5	8
4 Romeo *Petula Clark* (Pye)	8	7	17	–
5 Well I Ask You *Eden Kane* (Decca)	5	8	14	–
6 Halfway To Paradise *Billy Fury* (Decca)	6	13	19	17
7 A Girl Like You *Cliff Richard* (Columbia)	–	–	–	–
8 Ain't Gonna Wash For A Week *The Brook Brothers* (Pye)	10	12	11	18
9 Cupid *Sam Cooke* (RCA)	12	9	9	14
10 Time *Craig Douglas* (Top Rank)	15	–	–	–

69

	9	16	23	30
11 Quarter To Three *The U.S. Bonds* (Top Rank)	13	20	–	–
12 That's My Home *Acker Bilk* (Columbia)	11	16	12	19
13 How Many Tears *Bobby Vee* (London)	17	17	18	–
14 Hello Mary Lou/Travellin' Man *Ricky Nelson* (London)	–	–	–	–
15 You Always Hurt The One You Love *Clarence Frogman Henry* (Pye)	20	–	–	–
16 Baby I Don't Care/Valley Of Tears *Buddy Holly* (Coral)	–	–	–	–
17 Marcheta *Karl Denver* (Decca)	–	–	–	–
18 Pasadena *The Temperance Seven* (Parlophone)	–	–	–	–
19 Pepito *Los Machucambos* (Decca)	19	–	–	–
20 Temptation *The Everly Brothers* (Warner Bros.)	–	–	–	–
– Kon-Tiki *The Shadows* (Columbia)	7	4	2	1
– Wild In The Country/I Feel So Bad *Elvis Presley* (RCA)	3	2	3	3
– Michael Row The Boat/Lumbered *Lonnie Donegan* (Pye)	9	6	7	12
– Sea Of Heartbreak *Don Gibson* (RCA)	14	18	20	15
– Hats Off To Larry *Del Shannon* (London)	16	14	15	9
– Drivin' Home *Duane Eddy* (London)	18	19	–	–
– Michael Row The Boat *The Highwaymen* (HMV)	–	10	6	4
– Together *Connie Francis* (MGM)	–	11	13	10
– Jealousy *Billy Fury* (Decca)	–	15	8	6
– Get Lost *Eden Kane* (Decca)	–	–	10	7
– You'll Answer To Me *Cleo Laine* (Fontana)	–	–	16	11
– Walkin' Back To Happiness *Helen Shapiro* (Columbia)	–	–	–	13
– Granada *Frank Sinatra* (Reprise)	–	–	–	16
– I'm Gonna Knock On Your Door *Eddie Hodges* (London)	–	–	–	20

OCTOBER 1961

	14	21	28
1 Michael Row The Boat *The Highwaymen* (HMV)	3	3	4
2 Wild In The Country/I Feel So Bad *Elvis Presley* (RCA)	6	10	14
3 Walkin' Back To Happiness *Helen Shapiro* (Columbia)	1	1	1
4 Kon-Tiki *The Shadows* (Columbia)	7	8	15
5 Johnny Remember Me *John Leyton* (Top Rank)	9	15	–
6 Jealousy *Billy Fury* (Decca)	4	7	10
7 You'll Answer To Me *Cleo Laine* (Fontana)	5	4	6
8 Wild Wind *John Leyton* (Top Rank)	2	2	3
9 Sucu Sucu *Laurie Johnson* (Pye)	8	5	5
10 You Don't Know *Helen Shapiro* (Columbia)	12	–	–
11 Together *Connie Francis* (MGM)	10	12	–
12 Get Lost *Eden Kane* (Decca)	11	14	–
13 Hats Off To Larry *Del Shannon* (London)	14	9	11
14 Reach For The Stars/Climb Every Mountain *Shirley Bassey* (Columbia)	–	–	–
15 Granada *Frank Sinatra* (Reprise)	13	–	–
16 Muskrat *The Everly Brothers* (Warner Bros.)	–	–	–
17 Michael Row The Boat/Lumbered *Lonnie Donegan* (Pye)	16	17	–
18 Bless You *Tony Orlando* (Fontana)	19	11	7
19 Hard Hearted Hannah/Chilli Bom-Bom *The Temperance Seven* (Parlophone)	20	–	–
20 Sea Of Heartbreak *Don Gibson* (RCA)	–	20	20
– Who Put The Bomp *The Viscounts* (Nixa)	15	–	–
– Sucu Sucu *Nina and Frederik* (Columbia)	17	–	–
– My Boomerang Won't Come Back *Charlie Drake* (Parlophone)	18	16	13
– When The Girl In Your Arms Is The Girl In Your Heart *Cliff Richard* (Columbia)	–	6	2
– Mexicali Rose *Karl Denver* (Decca)	–	13	9
– You Must Have Been A Beautiful Baby *Bobby Darin* (London)	–	18	18
– Let's Get Together *Hayley Mills* (Decca)	–	19	12
– Hit The Road Jack *Ray Charles* (HMV)	–	–	8

7

	14	21	28
– Big Bad John *Jimmy Dean* (Philips)	–	–	16
– Take Five *Dave Brubeck* (Fontana)	–	–	17
– The Time Has Come *Adam Faith* (Parlophone)	–	–	19

NOVEMBER 1961

4

	11	18	25
1 Walkin' Back To Happiness *Helen Shapiro* (Columbia)	2	2	7
2 His Latest Flame *Elvis Presley* (RCA)	1	1	1
3 When The Girl In Your Arms Is The Girl In Your Heart			
Cliff Richard (Columbia)	3	5	11
4 Big Bad John *Jimmy Dean* (Philips)	5	4	2
5 Hit The Road Jack *Ray Charles* (HMV)	7	8	13
6 Wild Wind *John Leyton* (Top Rank)	9	13	–
7 Mexicali Rose *Karl Denver* (Decca)	11	16	14
8 Sucu Sucu *Laurie Johnson* (Pye)	12	18	16
9 Take Five *Dave Brubeck* (Fontana)	6	7	8
10 Michael Row The Boat *The Highwaymen* (HMV)	16	–	–
11 You'll Answer To Me *Cleo Laine* (Fontana)	14	17	–
12 Let's Get Together *Hayley Mills* (Decca)	13	11	–
13 Bless You *Tony Orlando* (Fontana)	10	15	19
14 Take Good Care Of My Baby *Bobby Vee* (London)	4	3	3
15 The Time Has Come *Adam Faith* (Parlophone)	8	6	5
16 You Don't Know What You've Got *Ral Donner* (Parlophone)	18	–	–
17 Sucu Sucu *Nina and Frederik* (Columbia)	–	–	–
18 Tribute To Buddy Holly *Mike Berry* (HMV)	–	–	–
19 Kon-Tiki *The Shadows* (Columbia)	–	–	–
20 My Boomerang Won't Come Back *Charlie Drake*			
(Parlophone)	15	–	–
– Creole Jazz *Acker Bilk* (Columbia)	17	–	–
– Moon River *Danny Williams* (HMV)	19	9	6
– Runaround Sue *Dion* (Top Rank)	20	20	12
– Tower Of Strength *Frankie Vaughan* (Philips)	–	10	4
– The Savage *The Shadows* (Columbia)	–	12	9
– Midnight In Moscow *Kenny Ball* (Pye)	–	14	10
– Married *The Brook Brothers* (Pye)	–	19	17
– I'll Get By *Shirley Bassey* (Columbia)	–	–	15
– Fool No. 1 *Brenda Lee* (Brunswick)	–	–	18
– My Friend The Sea *Petula Clark* (Pye)	–	–	20

DECEMBER 1961

2

	9	16	23	30
1 Take Good Care Of My Baby *Bobby Vee* (London)	2	3	5	20
2 His Latest Flame/Little Sister *Elvis Presley* (RCA)	3	4	15	–
3 Big Bad John *Jimmy Dean* (Philips)	6	8	14	–
4 Tower Of Strength *Frankie Vaughan* (Philips)	1	1	1	1
5 Moon River *Danny Williams* (HMV)	4	2	3	3
6 The Time Has Come *Adam Faith* (Parlophone)	5	16	16	–
7 Walkin' Back To Happiness *Helen Shapiro* (Columbia)	8	6	9	14
8 Take Five *Dave Brubeck* (Fontana)	7	15	12	8
9 The Savage *The Shadows* (Columbia)	11	9	–	–
10 I'll Get By *Shirley Bassey* (Columbia)	9	12	10	–
11 When The Girl In Your Arms Is The Girl In Your Heart				
Cliff Richard (Columbia)	16	–	13	–
12 Midnight In Moscow *Kenny Ball* (Pye)	10	5	4	7
13 Runaround Sue *Dion* (Top Rank)	–	–	–	–
14 This Time *Troy Shondell* (London)	–	–	–	–
15 Hit The Road Jack *Ray Charles* (HMV)	18	–	–	–

2

	9	**16**	**23**	**30**
16 Mexicali Rose *Karl Denver* (Decca)	–	–	–	–
17 September In The Rain *Dinah Washington* (Mercury)	–	–	–	–
18 Stranger On The Shore *Acker Bilk* (Columbia)	13	7	2	–
19 Married *The Brook Brothers* (Pye)	–	–	–	–
20 Fool No. 1 *Brenda Lee* (Brunswick)	–	–	–	–
– You're The Only Good Thing That's Happened To Me *Jim Reeves* (RCA)	12	–	–	–
– The Charleston *The Temperance Seven* (Parlophone)	14	20	–	–
– Johnny Will *Pat Boone* (London)	15	14	6	4
– Toy Balloons *Russ Conway* (Columbia)	17	20	7	9
– Let True Love Begin *Nat 'King' Cole* (Capitol)	19	–	–	–
– Ever Lovin' *Ricky Nelson* (London)	20	–	–	–
– So Long Baby *Del Shannon* (London)	–	10	19	11
– Let There Be Drums *Sandy Nelson* (London)	–	11	8	5
– My Friend The Sea *Petula Clark* (Pye)	–	13	11	12
– Baby's First Christmas *Connie Francis* (MGM)	–	17	–	–
– I'd Never Find Another You *Billy Fury* (Decca)	–	18	–	10
– Son, This Is She *John Leyton* (HMV)	–	19	–	–
– I Love How You Love Me *Jimmy Crawford* (Columbia)	–	–	17	–
– Happy Birthday Sweet Sixteen *Neil Sedaka* (RCA)	–	–	18	18
– I Understand *The G-Clefs* (London)	–	–	20	–
– Multiplication *Bobby Darin* (London)	–	–	–	13
– Don't Bring Lulu *Dorothy Provine* (Warner Bros)	–	–	–	15

A chart described as a 'skeleton' compilation was published in Record Mirror on 30 December 1961, and in the issue of 6 January 1962, a complete 'last week' column was published. We have not published the 30 December 'skeleton' chart as it was said at the time to be incorrect, and does not agree with the 'last week' placings of 6 January. However, the paper never a complete rundown of the 30 December listing; there is no real idea of chart positions of titles which dropped out of the Top 20.

1961–BEST-SELLING SINGLES

1 Runaway *Del Shannon* (London)
2 Wooden Heart *Elvis Presley* (RCA)
3 You Don't Know *Helen Shapiro* (Columbia)
4 Halfway To Paradise *Billy Fury* (Decca)
5 Well I Ask You *Eden Kane* (Decca)
6 Are You Sure? *The Allisons* (Fontana)
7 Walkin' Back To Happiness *Helen Shapiro* (Columbia)
8 Walk Right Back/Ebony Eyes *The Everly Brothers* (Warner Bros.)
9 Johnny Remember Me *John Leyton* (Top Rank)
10 His Latest Flame *Elvis Presley* (RCA)
11 Hello Mary Lou/Travellin' Man *Ricky Nelson* (London)
12 Surrender *Elvis Presley* (RCA)
13 A Girl Like You *Cliff Richard* (Columbia)
14 Temptation *The Everly Brothers* (Warner Bros.)
15 F.B.I. *The Shadows* (Columbia)
16 Blue Moon *The Marcels* (Pye)
17 Sailor *Petula Clark* (Pye)
18 Are You Lonesome Tonight *Elvis Presley* (RCA)
19 Theme For A Dream *Cliff Richard* (Columbia)
20 The Frightened City *The Shadows* (Columbia)
20 Reach For The Stars/Climb Every Mountain *Shirley Bassey* (Columbia)

1962

The early 1960s heroes continued their successes, with three hits each for Adam Faith and The Everly Brothers, Billy Fury achieved four hits, as did Elvis Presley, but 1962 also saw the end of Lonnie Donegan's 26-hit chart career which had included three Number One records, and six others in the Top Five. The end of Donegan's career was slightly unexpected, even though his last Top Five disc had been in 1960.

Very similar to Donegan was the case of Pat Boone. His famous song 'Speedy Gonzales' reached the Number Two position in July, and 'The Main Attraction' took the Number Twelve position in December, after which Boone also departed from the charts. Apart from 'Speedy Gonzales' and 'Johnny Will', Pat Boone had made a series of discs beginning with 'If Dreams Came True' in 1958, and he had continued with six discs which reached no higher position in the charts than Number Sixteen.

Connie Francis had but one Top Twenty song, 'Vacation', in 1962. She lacked good material, as did Pat Boone.

It was also the end for Craig Douglas, whose 'Oh Lonesome Me' was as good a title as any with which to say goodbye! Douglas had scored a total of nine hits, including 'A Hundred Pounds Of Clay', a cover version which effectively prevented the American version from repeating its Stateside chart positioning.

Marty Wilde achieved his eighth hit during 1962 with 'Jezebel', but this version of the Frankie Laine song remained in the charts for only two weeks. But if the demise of Wilde was drawing near, the pace was beginning to quicken for American 'Little Miss Dynamite', Brenda Lee, for she achieved four hits records in 1962, as opposed to her two-hit track performance of the previous year.

Other new names appeared, though few of these made very much chart impression. The Four Seasons entered the Top Ten with 'Sherry', a song which made a comeback in 1975, sung by Adrian Baker. It was The Four Seasons' only 1962 hit. The Tornados promised much with their arrival on the scene, and their 'Telstar' stayed almost five months in the Top Twenty.

However, 1962 also marked the demise of the memorable Nat 'King' Cole and the pianist Russ Conway. Cole had achieved 10 hits since 1955, and there had been 12 hits for Russ Conway.

1962 was a historic year for a Liverpool foursome called The Beatles – the most significant new group of the year. The date of their first chart entry with 'Love Me Do' was 15 December 1962, the highest position they reached in the charts was Number Seventeen, and they remained in the Top Twenty for just two weeks. John, George, Paul and Ringo created a whole new trend of haircuts, neat suits and an explosion of music from the Merseyside areas.

Apart from the birth of the Mersey Sound in the charts, 1962 was also a year for television themes finding their way into the Top Twenty, including two versions of the 'Theme From Z Cars', two versions of the 'Dr Kildare Theme', and two instrumentals – the 'Theme From The Man With The Golden Arm' and 'Cutty Sark'.

Possibly the most surprising hit of the year was 'September In The Rain' from Dinah Washington and, according to some, the funniest discs of the year were 'Hole In The Ground' and 'Right, Said Fred' from Bernard Cribbins.

JANUARY 1962

6

	13	20	27
1 Stranger On The Shore *Acker Bilk* (Columbia)	1	3	2
2 Moon River *Danny Williams* (HMV)	6	7	11
3 Let There Be Drums *Sandy Nelson* (London)	2	2	6
4 Johnny Will *Pat Boone* (London)	5	8	8
5 Tower Of Strength *Frankie Vaughan* (Philips)	9	17	–
6 Midnight In Moscow *Kenny Ball* (Pye)	4	9	15
7 So Long Baby *Del Shannon* (London)	11	11	19
8 Toy Balloons *Russ Conway* (Columbia)	13	20	–
9 I'd Never Find Another You *Billy Fury* (Decca)	8	4	4
10 My Friend The Sea *Petula Clark* (Pye)	–	–	–
11 Multiplication *Bobby Darin* (London)	10	5	3
12 Take Five *Dave Brubeck* (Fontana)	–	–	–
13 Happy Birthday Sweet Sixteen *Neil Sedaka* (RCA)	7	6	5
14 Don't Bring Lulu *Dorothy Provine* (Warner Bros.)	19	–	–
15 Banbino *The Springfields* (Philips)	–	–	–
16 September In The Rain *Dinah Washington* (Mercury)	–	–	–
17 Goodbye Cruel World *James Darren* (Pye)	15	15	–
18 Walkin' Back To Happiness *Helen Shapiro* (Columbia)	–	–	–
19 Run To Him *Bobby Vee* (London)	20	10	10
20 Take Good Care Of My Baby *Bobby Vee* (London)	–	–	–
– The Young Ones *Cliff Richard* (Columbia)	3	1	1
– Son, This Is She *John Leyton* (HMV)	12	–	20
– The Twist *Chubby Checker* (Columbia)	14	12	12
– Walk On By *Leroy Vandyke* (Mercury)	16	14	9
– The Lion Sleeps Tonight *The Tokens* (London)	18	19	18
– Peppermint Twist *Joey Dee and The Starlights* (Columbia)	17	16	13
– Let's Twist Again *Chubby Checker* (Columbia)	–	18	7
– The Language Of Love *John D. Loudermilk* (RCA)	–	13	14
– Forget Me Not *Eden Kane* (Decca)	–	–	16
– Crying In The Rain *The Everly Brothers* (Warner Bros.)	–	–	17
– The Comancheros *Lonnie Donegan* (Pye)	–	–	20

FEBRUARY 1962

3

	10	17	24
1 The Young Ones *Cliff Richard* (Columbia)	1	1	2
2 Rock-A-Hula Baby/Can't Help Falling In Love *Elvis Presley* (RCA)	2	2	1
3 Multiplication *Bobby Darin* (London)	8	11	20
4 Happy Birthday Sweet Sixteen *Neil Sedaka* (RCA)	7	6	11
5 Stranger On The Shore *Acker Bilk* (Columbia)	5	9	9
6 Let's Twist Again *Chubby Checker* (Columbia)	3	3	3
7 Forget Me Not *Eden Kane* (Decca)	4	4	4
8 I'd Never Find Another You *Billy Fury* (Decca)	9	7	10
9 Walk On By *Leroy Vandyke* (Mercury)	6	5	5
10 Let There Be Drums *Sandy Nelson* (London)	16	17	–
11 Crying In The Rain *The Everly Brothers* (Warner Bros.)	10	8	8
12 The Twist *Chubby Checker* (Columbia)	–	18	–
13 Run To Him *Bobby Vee* (London)	11	10	15
14 Lonesome *Adam Faith* (Parlophone)	12	16	–
15 Peppermint Twist *Joey Dee and The Starlights* (Columbia)	17	19	–
16 The Lion Sleeps Tonight *The Tokens* (RCA)	–	–	–
17 The Comancheros *Lonnie Donegan* (Pye)	–	20	–
18 Wimoweh *Karl Denver* (Decca)	–	12	6
19 Midnight In Moscow *Kenny Ball* (Pye)	15	–	–
20 The Language of Love *John D. Loudermilk* (RCA)	–	–	–
– Little Bitty Tear *Burl Ives* (Brunswick)	13	13	12

75

	10	**17**	**24**
– Jeannie *Danny Williams* (HMV)	14	15	18
– Moon River *Danny Williams* (HMV)	18	–	–
– Johnny Will *Pat Boone* (London)	19	–	–
– Don't Stop, Twist *Frankie Vaughan* (Philips)	20	14	19
– March Of The Siamese Children *Kenny Ball* (Pye)	–	–	7
– Hole In The Ground *Bernard Cribbins* (Parlophone)	–	–	13
– Lesson No. 1 *Russ Conway* (Columbia)	–	–	14
– Tell Me What He Said *Helen Shapiro* (Columbia)	–	–	16
– The Wanderer *Dion* (HMV)	–	–	17

MARCH 1962

3

	10	**17**	**24**	**31**
1 Rock-A-Hula Baby/Can't Help Falling In Love *Elvis Presley* (RCA)	1	1	3	3
2 Let's Twist Again *Chubby Checker* (Columbia)	4	6	5	5
3 March Of The Siamese Children *Kenny Ball* (Pye)	5	4	4	8
4 The Young Ones *Cliff Richard* (Columbia)	3	7	7	11
5 Tell Me What He Said *Helen Shapiro* (Columbia)	6	3	2	2
6 Walk On By *Leroy Vandyke* (Mercury)	12	11	15	17
7 Forget Me Not *Eden Kane* (Decca)	8	13	14	20
8 Wimoweh *Karl Denver* (Decca)	7	5	6	6
9 Wonderful Land *The Shadows* (Columbia)	2	2	1	1
10 Crying In The Rain *The Everly Brothers* (Warner Bros.)	9	8	13	16
11 Hole In The Ground *Bernard Cribbins* (Parlophone)	15	10	12	9
12 Little Bitty Tear *Burl Ives* (Brunswick)	14	18	16	–
13 The Wanderer *Dion* (HMV)	10	14	10	13
14 Softly As I Leave You *Matt Monro* (Parlophone)	13	12	11	10
15 Run To Him *Bobby Vee* (London)	–	–	–	–
16 Stranger On The Shore *Acker Bilk* (Columbia)	11	9	8	7
17 Happy Birthday Sweet Sixteen *Neil Sedaka* (RCA)	–	–	–	–
18 Don't Stop, Twist *Frankie Vaughan* (Philips)	17	–	–	–
19 I'd Never Find Another You *Billy Fury* (Decca)	–	–	–	–
20 Lesson No. 1 *Russ Conway* (Columbia)	16	–	–	–
– Theme From Z Cars *Johnny Keating* (Piccadilly)	18	15	17	14
– I'll See You In My Dreams *Pat Boone* (London)	19	19	–	–
– Frankie And Johnny *Acker Bilk* (Columbia)	20	–	–	–
– Dream Baby *Roy Orbison* (London)	–	16	9	4
– Twistin' The Night Away *Sam Cooke* (RCA)	–	17	18	15
– Letter Full Of Tears *Billy Fury* (Decca)	–	20	–	–
– Little Bitty Tear *Miki and Griff* (Pye)	–	–	19	–
– Jeannie *Danny Williams* (HMV)	–	–	20	–
– Hey! Baby *Bruce Channel* (Mercury)	–	–	25	12
– Hey Little Girl *Del Shannon* (London)	–	–	24	18
– Dr Kildare Theme *Johnny Spence* (Parlophone)	–	–	23	19

On 24 March 1962 Record Mirror *began to list a Top Fifty. Its 'last week' figures at this date were those of its new chart source and did not correspond with its own former chart listing.*

APRIL 1962

7

	14	**21**	**28**
1 Wonderful Land *The Shadows* (Columbia)	1	1	1
2 Tell Me What He Said *Helen Shapiro* (Columbia)	3	5	5
3 Dream Baby *Roy Orbison* (London)	2	2	3
4 Can't Help Falling In Love/Rock-A-Hula Baby *Elvis Presley* (RCA)	4	6	6
5 Wimoweh *Karl Denver* (Decca)	8	11	20

	14	21	28
7			
6 Stranger On The Shore *Acker Bilk* (Columbia)	7	13	12
7 Twistin' The Night Away *Sam Cooke* (RCA)	6	7	7
8 Hey Little Girl *Del Shannon* (London)	9	3	4
9 Hole In The Ground *Bernard Cribbins* (Parlophone)	3	4	15
10 Softly As I Leave You *Matt Monro* (Parlophone)	14	16	–
11 Theme From Z Cars *Johnny Keating* (Piccadilly)	11	8	11
12 Hey! Baby *Bruce Channel* (Mercury)	5	4	2
13 Let's Twist Again *Chubby Checker* (Columbia)	13	15	19
14 March Of The Siamese Children *Kenny Ball* (Pye)	20	–	–
15 The Wanderer *Dion* (HMV)	18	–	–
16 The Young Ones *Cliff Richard* (Columbia)	17	19	–
17 Dr Kildare Theme *Johnny Spence* (Parlophone)	15	18	18
18 Never Goodbye *Karl Denver* (Decca)	12	9	10
19 Love Me Warm And Tender *Paul Anka* (RCA)	19	–	–
20 When My Little Girl Is Smiling *Craig Douglas* (Top Rank)	16	10	9
24 When My Little Girl Is Smiling *Jimmy Justice* (Pye)	22	12	13
47 Speak To Me Pretty *Brenda Lee* (Brunswick)	29	17	8
21 The Maigret Theme *Joe Loss* (HMV)	21	20	–
– Nut Rocker *B. Bumble* (Top Rank)	–	31	14
– Wonderful World Of The Young *Danny Williams* (HMV)	37	22	16
46 The Party's Over *Lonnie Donegan* (Pye)	25	21	17

MAY 1962

	12	19	26
5			
1 Wonderful Land *The Shadows* (Columbia)	1	3	6
2 Hey Little Girl *Del Shannon* (London)	5	8	8
3 Hey! Baby *Bruce Channel* (Mercury)	4	10	14
4 Nut Rocker *B. Bumble* (Top Rank)	2	1	2
5 Dream Baby *Roy Orbison* (London)	7	14	–
6 Tell Me What He Said *Helen Shapiro* (Columbia)	17	–	–
7 Speak To Me Pretty *Brenda Lee* (Brunswick)	3	5	7
8 Can't Help Falling In Love/Rock-A-Hula Baby *Elvis Presley* (RCA)	14	16	16
9 Never Goodbye *Karl Denver* (Decca)	10	11	15
10 Stranger On The Shore *Acker Bilk* (Columbia)	15	13	12
11 Wonderful World Of The Young *Danny Williams* (HMV)	8	12	13
12 Twistin' The Night Away *Sam Cooke* (RCA)	11	18	–
13 Theme From Z Cars *Johnny Keating* (Piccadilly)	18	–	–
14 When My Little Girl Is Smiling *Craig Douglas* (Top Rank)	13	20	–
15 When My Little Girl Is Smiling *Jimmy Justice* (Pye)	12	9	9
16 The Party's Over *Lonnie Donegan* (Pye)	9	17	19
17 Love Letters *Ketty Lester* (London)	6	6	4
18 Let's Twist Again *Chubby Checker* (Columbia)	–	–	–
19 Young World *Ricky Nelson* (London)	19	–	–
20 Dr Kildare Theme *Johnny Spence* (Parlophone)	–	–	–
– Good Luck Charm *Elvis Presley* (RCA)	16	2	1
– Do You Want To Dance *Cliff Richard* (Columbia)	20	4	3
42 As You Like It *Adam Faith* (Parlophone)	23	7	5
36 Last Night Was Made For Love *Billy Fury* (Decca)	26	15	11
– Ginny Come Lately *Brian Hyland* (HMV)	36	19	10
– Come Outside *Mike Sarne* (Parlophone)	46	29	17
– I Don't Know Why *Eden Kane* (Decca)	50	28	18
48 Lonely City *John Leyton* (HMV)	35	25	20

77

	9	16	23	30
1 Good Luck Charm *Elvis Presley* (RCA)	1	1	1	3
2 I'm Looking Out The Window/Do You Want To Dance *Cliff Richard* (Columbia)	2	2	3	4
3 Nut Rocker *B. Bumble* (Top Rank)	3	5	9	10
4 Last Night Was Made For Love *Billy Fury* (Decca)	6	8	6	6
5 As You Like It *Adam Faith* (Parlophone)	5	6	8	14
6 Come Outside *Mike Sarne* (Parlophone)	4	3	2	1
7 Love Letters *Ketty Lester* (London)	11	13	–	–
8 I Don't Know Why *Eden Kane* (Decca)	9	7	7	11
9 Wonderful Land *The Shadows* (Columbia)	8	15	–	–
10 Ginny Come Lately *Brian Hyland* (HMV)	7	9	5	5
11 Stranger On The Shore *Acker Bilk* (Columbia)	12	11	11	9
12 When My Little Girl Is Smiling *Jimmy Justice* (Pye)	–	–	–	–
13 Wonderful World Of The Young *Danny Williams* (HMV)	19	–	–	–
14 Speak To Me Pretty *Brenda Lee* (Brunswick)	15	–	–	–
15 Hey Little Girl *Del Shannon* (London)	17	–	–	–
16 The Party's Over *Lonnie Donegan* (Pye)	20	–	–	–
17 Green Leaves Of Summer *Kenny Ball and his Jazzmen* (Pye)	13	10	10	12
18 A Picture Of You *Joe Brown* (Piccadilly)	10	4	4	2
19 How Can I Meet Her *The Everly Brothers* (Warner Bros.)	14	12	13	16
20 Lonely City *John Leyton* (HMV)	16	14	15	–
24 Unsquare Dance *Dave Brubeck* (CBS)	18	17	14	18
22 Lover Please *Maureen and The Vernon Girls* (Decca)	21	16	17	–
– Sharing You *Bobby Vee* (Liberty)	41	18	–	17
30 Jezebel *Marty Wilde* (Philips)	23	19	20	–
– A Little Love A Little Kiss *Karl Denver* (Decca)	32	20	–	19
– Ain't That Funny *Jimmy Justice* (Pye)	–	30	18	15
– I Can't Stop Loving You *Ray Charles* (HMV)	–	43	16	8
29 Deep In The Heart Of Texas *Duane Eddy* (RCA)	29	24	19	–
– English Country Garden *Jimmy Rodgers* (Columbia)	–	34	21	7
– Theme From Dr Kildare *Richard Chamberlain* (MGM)	40	23	12	13
– Yes My Darling Daughter *Eydie Gorme* (CBS)	–	–	34	20

	14	21	28
1 Come Outside *Mike Sarne* (Parlophone)	2	4	7
2 A Picture Of You *Joe Brown* (Piccadilly)	3	3	3
3 Good Luck Charm *Elvis Presley* (RCA)	4	6	6
4 I Can't Stop Loving You *Ray Charles* (HMV)	1	1	2
5 Ginny Come Lately *Brian Hyland* (HMV)	5	8	11
6 I'm Looking Out The Window/Do You Want To Dance *Cliff Richard* (Columbia)	6	10	19
7 Green Leaves Of Summer *Kenny Ball and his Jazzmen* (Pye)	15	18	–
8 Ain't That Funny *Jimmy Justice* (Pye)	9	15	12
9 Stranger On The Shore *Acker Bilk* (Columbia)	17	19	18
10 Sharing You *Bobby Vee* (Liberty)	13	16	16
11 Last Night Was Made For Love *Billy Fury* (Decca)	12	14	20
12 English Country Garden *Jimmy Rodgers* (Columbia)	8	5	9
13 As You Like It *Adam Faith* (Parlophone)	19	–	–
14 Here Comes That Feeling *Brenda Lee* (Brunswick)	7	7	5
15 I Don't Know Why *Eden Kane* (Decca)	18	–	–
16 Yes My Darling Daughter *Eydie Gorme* (CBS)	10	11	17
17 Theme From Dr Kildare *Richard Chamberlain* (MGM)	–	–	–
18 Don't Ever Change *The Crickets* (Liberty)	14	12	8
19 Nut Rocker *B. Bumble* (Top Rank)	–	–	–

	14	21	28
20 A Little Love A Little Kiss *Karl Denver* (Decca)	–	–	–
21 Our Favourite Melodies *Craig Douglas* (Columbia)	16	9	10
36 I Remember You *Frank Ifield* (Columbia)	11	2	1
25 Palisades Park *Freddy Cannon* (Stateside)	20	–	–
– Speedy Gonzales *Pat Boone* (London)	40	13	4
46 Right, Said Fred *Bernard Cribbins* (Parlophone)	21	17	15
32 Ya Ya Twist *Petula Clark* (Pye)	23	20	14
– Little Miss Lonely *Helen Shapiro* (Columbia)	48	23	13

AUGUST 1962

	11	18	25
4			
1 I Remember You *Frank Ifield* (Columbia)	1	1	1
2 I Can't Stop Loving You *Ray Charles* (HMV)	3	3	6
3 Speedy Gonzales *Pat Boone* (London)	2	2	2
4 A Picture Of You *Joe Brown* (Piccadilly)	4	6	13
5 Don't Ever Change *The Crickets* (Liberty)	5	9	10
6 Come Outside *Mike Sarne* (Parlophone)	9	17	18
7 Here Comes That Feeling *Brenda Lee* (Brunswick)	6	12	17
8 Little Miss Lonely *Helen Shapiro* (Columbia)	10	10	11
9 English Country Garden *Jimmy Rodgers* (Columbia)	14	19	19
10 Right, Said Fred *Bernard Cribbins* (Parlophone)	13	–	–
11 Let There Be Love *Nat 'King' Cole and George Shearing* (Capitol)	12	11	12
12 Our Favourite Melodies *Craig Douglas* (Columbia)	18	–	–
13 Good Luck Charm *Elvis Presley* (RCA)	–	–	–
14 Ya Ya Twist *Petula Clark* (Pye)	15	–	–
15 Sharing You *Bobby Vee* (Liberty)	20	–	–
16 Things *Bobby Darin* (London)	8	5	3
17 Ain't That Funny *Jimmy Justice* (Pye)	–	–	–
18 Ginny Come Lately *Brian Hyland* (HMV)	–	–	–
19 Cindy's Birthday *Shane Fenton* (Parlophone)	–	–	–
20 Stranger On The Shore *Acker Bilk* (Columbia)	19	18	–
23 Once Upon A Dream *Billy Fury* (Decca)	11	7	7
22 I'm Just A Baby *Louise Cordet* (Decca)	16	15	16
25 Breaking Up Is Hard To Do *Neil Sedaka* (RCA)	17	13	9
28 Guitar Tango *The Shadows* (Columbia)	7	4	4
43 Roses Are Red *Ronnie Carroll* (Philips)	23	8	5
40 Vacation *Connie Francis* (MGM)	24	14	14
50 Sealed With A Kiss *Brian Hyland* (HMV)	32	16	8
42 Roses Are Red *Bobby Vinton* (Columbia)	25	20	15
– Dancin' Party *Chubby Checker* (Columbia)	42	26	20

SEPTEMBER 1962

	8	15	22	29
1				
1 I Remember You *Frank Ifield* (Columbia)	1	2	2	4
2 Speedy Gonzales *Pat Boone* (London)	5	6	8	15
3 Things *Bobby Darin* (London)	2	4	5	6
4 Guitar Tango *The Shadows* (Columbia)	6	9	10	11
5 Sealed With A Kiss *Brian Hyland* (HMV)	3	5	6	7
6 Roses Are Red *Ronnie Carroll* (Philips)	4	3	4	5
7 Once Upon A Dream *Billy Fury* (Decca)	9	11	16	20
8 Breaking Up Is Hard To Do *Neil Sedaka* (RCA)	7	8	7	9
9 I Can't Stop Loving You *Ray Charles* (HMV)	10	16	–	–
10 Vacation *Connie Francis* (MGM)	15	–	–	–
11 Little Miss Lonely *Helen Shapiro* (Columbia)	18	–	–	–
12 Let There Be Love *Nat 'King' Cole and George Shearing* (Capitol)	13	19	–	–

79

	8	**15**	**22**	**29**
1				
13 I'm Just A Baby *Louise Cordet* (Decca)	20	–	–	–
14 So Do I *Kenny Ball* (Pye)	16	15	19	–
15 Pick A Bale Of Cotton *Lonnie Donegan* (Pye)	11	14	14	18
16 A Picture Of You *Joe Brown* (Piccadilly)	–	–	–	–
17 Ballad of Paladin *Duane Eddy* (RCA)	12	10	13	17
18 Don't Ever Change *The Crickets* (Liberty)	–	–	–	–
19 Dancing Party *Chubby Checker* (Columbia)	–	–	–	–
20 Main Theme From The Man With The Golden Arm *Jet Harris* (Decca)	14	12	15	16
34 She's Not You *Elvis Presley* (RCA)	8	1	1	1
41 Don't That Beat All *Adam Faith* (Parlophone)	19	13	9	8
– It'll Be Me *Cliff Richard* (Columbia)	17	7	3	2
50 Telstar *The Tornados* (Decca)	36	17	11	3
36 Will I What? *Mike Sarne* (Parlophone)	23	18	20	19
31 Spanish Harlem *Jimmy Justice* (Pye)	21	20	–	–
– Sheila *Tommy Roe* (HMV)	43	24	12	10
– Loco-Motion *Little Eva* (London)	42	25	17	13
38 What Now My Love *Shirley Bassey* (Columbia)	29	23	18	14
– You Don't Know Me *Ray Charles* (HMV)	–	47	23	12

OCTOBER 1962

	13	**20**	**27**
6			
1 Telstar *The Tornados* (Decca)	1	1	1
2 She's Not You *Elvis Presley* (RCA)	5	6	9
3 It'll Be Me *Cliff Richard* (Columbia)	6	9	11
4 Sheila *Tommy Roe* (HMV)	3	4	3
5 Loco-Motion *Little Eva* (London)	2	2	2
6 It Might As Well Rain Until September *Carole King* (London)	4	3	4
7 Sealed With A Kiss *Brian Hyland* (HMV)	14	20	–
8 I Remember You *Frank Ifield* (Columbia)	8	8	14
9 You Don't Know Me *Ray Charles* (HMV)	9	10	12
10 Don't That Beat All *Adam Faith* (Parlophone)	10	12	20
11 Roses Are Red *Ronnie Carroll* (Philips)	12	16	19
12 Things *Bobby Darin* (London)	13	18	–
13 What Now My Love *Shirley Bassey* (Columbia)	7	5	8
14 Breaking Up Is Hard To Do *Neil Sedaka* (RCA)	16	–	–
15 Guitar Tango *The Shadows* (Columbia)	–	–	–
16 It Started All Over Again *Brenda Lee* (Brunswick)	15	17	18
17 Speedy Gonzales *Pat Boone* (London)	19	–	–
18 Reminiscing *Buddy Holly* (Coral)	17	–	–
19 Ramblin' Rose *Nat 'King' Cole* (Capitol)	11	7	5
20 Main Theme From The Man With The Golden Arm *Jet Harris* (Decca)	18	–	–
27 Lonely *Acker Bilk* (Columbia)	20	14	17
41 Venus In Blue Jeans *Mark Wynter* (Pye)	22	11	6
46 Let's Dance *Chris Montez* (London)	21	13	7
42 Sherry *The Four Seasons* (Stateside)	25	15	15
– Swiss Maid *Del Shannon* (London)	42	19	10
40 Devil Woman *Marty Robbins* (CBS)	26	21	13
– Lovesick Blues *Frank Ifield* (Columbia)	–	–	16

	3	10	17	24
1 Telstar *The Tornados* (Decca)		10	17	24
2 Let's Dance *Chris Montez* (London)		3	4	4
3 Loco-Motion *Little Eva* (London)		2	2	2
4 Venus In Blue Jeans *Mark Wynter* (Pye)		5	7	7
5 Lovesick Blues *Frank Ifield* (Columbia)		6	5	6
6 It Might As Well Rain Until September *Carole King* (London)		1	1	1
7 Ramblin' Rose *Nat 'King' Cole* (Capitol)		7	11	12
8 Swiss Maid *Del Shannon* (London)		8	8	11
9 Sheila *Tommy Roe* (HMV)		4	3	3
10 She's Not You *Elvis Presley* (RCA)		10	10	14
11 Sherry *The Four Seasons* (Stateside)		17	–	–
12 Devil Woman *Marty Robbins* (CBS)		9	9	8
13 What Now My Love *Shirley Bassey* (Columbia)		11	12	9
14 You Don't Know Me *Ray Charles* (HMV)		12	16	20
15 It'll Be Me *Cliff Richard* (Columbia)		15	17	–
16 Lonely *Acker Bilk* (Columbia)		–	–	–
17 Bobby's Girl *Susan Maughan* (Philips)		–	–	–
18 I Remember You *Frank Ifield* (Columbia)		13	6	5
19 It Started All Over Again *Brenda Lee* (Brunswick)		16	15	17
20 No One Can Make My Sunshine Smile *The Everly Brothers* (Warner Bros.)		–	–	–
25 Because Of Love *Billy Fury* (Decca)		14	14	13
24 Oh Lonesome Me *Craig Douglas* (Decca)		18	–	–
33 Sun Arise *Rolf Harris* (Columbia)		19	19	16
– Dance With The Guitar Man *Duane Eddy* (RCA)		20	13	15
39 Must Be Madison *Joe Loss and his Orchestra* (HMV)		39	18	10
46 Love Me Tender *Richard Chamberlain* (MGM)		26	20	–
47 James Bond Theme *John Barry and his Orchestra* (Columbia)		27	23	18
		24	21	19

	1	8	15	22	29
1 Lovesick Blues *Frank Ifield* (Columbia)		1	2	3	5
2 Swiss Maid *Del Shannon* (London)		3	6	8	12
3 Bobby's Girl *Susan Maughan* (Philips)		4	4	5	9
4 Let's Dance *Chris Montez* (London)		5	7	12	10
5 Devil Woman *Marty Robbins* (CBS)		8	10	10	14
6 Dance With The Guitar Man *Duane Eddy* (RCA)		6	9	6	4
7 Venus In Blue Jeans *Mark Wynter* (Pye)		14	15	–	–
8 Sun Arise *Rolf Harris* (Columbia)		7	3	4	7
9 Telstar *The Tornados* (Decca)		9	8	9	8
10 Loco-Motion *Little Eva* (London)		17	–	–	–
11 No One Can Make My Sunshine Smile *The Everly Brothers* (Warner Bros.)		12	20	–	–
12 Ramblin' Rose *Nat 'King' Cole* (Capitol)		–	–	–	–
13 Sherry *The Four Seasons* (Stateside)		10	18	17	–
14 The Main Attraction *Pat Boone* (London)		15	12	14	16
15 Oh Lonesome Me *Craig Douglas* (Decca)		–	–	–	–
16 James Bond Theme *John Barry and his Orchestra* (Columbia)		13	–	16	–
17 Love Me Tender *Richard Chamberlain* (MGM)		19	16	15	–
18 It Might As Well Rain Until September *Carole King* (London)		–	–	–	–
19 I Remember You *Frank Ifield* (Columbia)		–	–	–	–
20 It Only Took A Minute *Joe Brown* (Piccadilly)		16	14	13	15
– Next Time *Cliff Richard* (Columbia)		18	5	2	2
24 Must Be Madison *Joe Loss and his Orchestra* (HMV)		20	–	–	–

	8	15	22	29
30 Rockin' Around The Christmas Tree *Brenda Lee* (Brunswick)	11	11	7	6
– Return To Sender *Elvis Presley* (RCA)	2	1	1	1
27 Desafinado *Stan Getz and Charlie Byrd* (HMV)	21	13	18	11
25 A Forever Kind Of Love *Bobby Vee* (Liberty)	22	17	19	19
21 Love Me Do *The Beatles* (Parlophone)	26	19	–	17
– Dance On! *The Shadows* (Columbia)	–	24	11	3
50 Like I Do *Maureen Evans* (Oriole)	31	27	20	–
– Your Cheating Heart *Ray Charles* (HMV)	–	50	25	13
34 We're Gonna Go Fishin' *Hank Locklin* (RCA)	35	34	27	18
– Me And My Shadow *Frank Sinatra* (Reprise)	–	43	32	20

The chart for 29 December is the official chart published in New Record Mirror *on 12 January 1963. The chart given in* Record Mirror *for 29 December 1962 was a temporary listing and corrected on 12 January 1963.*

1962–BEST-SELLING SINGLES

1 Stranger On The Shore *Acker Bilk* (Columbia)
2 I Remember You *Frank Ifield* (Columbia)
3 Rock-A-Hula Baby/Can't Help Falling In Love *Elvis Presley* (RCA)
4 Wonderful Land *The Shadows* (Columbia)
5 Let's Twist Again *Chubby Checker* (Columbia)
6 The Young Ones *Cliff Richard* (Columbia)
7 A Picture Of You *Joe Brown* (Piccadilly)
8 Come Outside *Mike Sarne* (Parlophone)
9 Good Luck Charm *Elvis Presley* (RCA)
10 I Can't Stop Loving You *Ray Charles* (HMV)
11 Telstar *The Tornados* (Decca)
12 Speedy Gonzales *Pat Boone* (London)
13 I'm Looking Out The Window/Do You Want To Dance *Cliff Richard* (Columbia)
14 Things *Bobby Darin* (London)
15 The Loco-Motion *Little Eva* (London)
16 Tell Me What He Said *Helen Shapiro* (Columbia)
17 Nut Rocker *B. Bumble* (Top Rank)
18 Roses Are Red *Ronnie Carroll* (Philips)
19 Ginny Come Lately *Brian Hyland* (HMV)
20 Wimoweh *Karl Denver* (Decca)

1963

1963 was definitely a year for British artists, for the charts produced names such as The Beatles, The Rolling Stones, Freddie and The Dreamers, Billy J. Kramer and The Dakotas, The Searchers, The Bachelors, Gerry and The Pacemakers, and Brian Poole and The Tremeloes.

The chart regulars also enjoyed various degrees of success. The Shadows had four hits which all entered the Top Ten, except for 'Geronimo'. Cliff also had four hits in 1963. One of these, 'Summer Holiday', was a Number One, 'It's All In The Game' and 'Don't Talk To Him' both reached the Number Two position, and 'Lucky Lips' settled at Number Four.

Billy Fury was another chart regular who achieved four chart successes in 1963, of which only one, 'Somebody Else's Girl', did not reach any of the Top Ten positions.

For the American contingent, Presley managed four hits, of which only 'Devil In Disguise' was a Number One. The other three hits did not make the Top Ten – a somewhat shattering change from 1962, when every Presley hit had been a Number One! However, what America did contribute to the British music scene of the time was a number of classic pop sounds, as opposed to successful artists. Some of these classics included 'He's So Fine' from The Chiffons; 'Rhythm Of The Rain' by The Cascades; 'Our Day Will Come' from Ruby and The Romantics; The Drifters' version of 'Up On The Roof'; 'Da Do Ron Ron', 'He's A Rebel' and 'Then He Kissed Me' all by The Crystals; The Surfaris with 'Wipeout'; and 'If I Had A Hammer' from Trini Lopez.

The Beatles had, of course, announced their arrival in December 1962 with 'Love Me Do', but this record had only achieved a brief Top Twenty innings. It was 'Please Please Me', their second release, which really set the ball rolling, though strangely this record failed to reach Number One. Their next 11 discs all reached the coveted Number One position, three of which were released in 1963 – 'From Me To You', 'She Loves You' and 'I Want To Hold Your Hand'.

Liverpool was the city with the sounds and Billy J. Kramer had a Number One with 'Bad To Me', though Kramer and his group, The Dakotas, are perhaps better remembered for their rendering of 'Do You Want To Know A Secret?', a disc which reached the Number Two position. Gerry and The Pacemakers hit the Number One spot with their first record, 'How Do You Do It?', which was followed by 'I Like It' and 'You'll Never Walk Alone', which both reached Number One, and so this Liverpudlian group ended 1963 with a hat-trick of hits.

Late in the year, Cilla Black, another Liverpudlian, entered the charts with 'Love Of The Loved' and Dusty Springfield made her first solo record, 'I Only Want To Be With You', which reached the Top Twenty in December. The Springfields, including Dusty, enjoyed several hits in 1963 including 'Island Of Dreams' and 'Say I Won't Be There'.

In America, The Beach Boys were becoming active and Bob Dylan arrived in Britain by means of one of his songs, 'Blowin' In The Wind', becoming a chart hit for Peter, Paul and Mary.

Amidst the Mersey Sound, The Beatles and other pop heroes such as 12-year-old Stevie Wonder came the march of the mods. The mod philosophy of life hinged onto French clothes, which were neat and casual, Italian scooters, and music drawn from the West Indies as well as from America and Britain. The mod life style was the complete antithesis of the rocker philosophy, and scooters and motorbikes clashed many times on pre-selected beaches or areas of waste ground. The two life styles, reflected in the music of the time, apparently could not exist side by side without essential ego-boosting and violent battles.

Television had done its best to fulfil the needs of the rockers, but with *Ready, Steady, Go* it set out to cater for the mods. Introduced by Cathy McGowan, the show poured forth the latest news for mods in terms of slang, clothes and music. Some of the mods later became involved in pop management, but in the end, as always, the movement burned itself out and pop continued in its usual habit of tottering between crazes, looking for something new to latch onto.

JANUARY 1963

	5	12	19	26
1 Next Time *Cliff Richard* (Columbia)		1	1	2
2 Return To Sender *Elvis Presley* (RCA)		2	3	6
3 Lovesick Blues *Frank Ifield* (Columbia)		5	4	11
4 Sun Arise *Rolf Harris* (Columbia)		7	8	15
5 Dance With The Guitar Man *Duane Eddy* (RCA)		4	7	9
6 Bobby's Girl *Susan Maughan* (Philips)		9	14	19
7 Dance On! *The Shadows* (Columbia)		3	2	1
8 It Only Took A Minute *Joe Brown* (Piccadilly)		6	11	–
9 Telstar *The Tornados* (Decca)		11	10	20
10 Let's Dance *Chris Montez* (London)		13	16	–
11 Swiss Maid *Del Shannon* (London)		14	20	–
12 Rockin' Around The Christmas Tree *Brenda Lee* (Brunswick)		–	–	–
13 A Forever Kind Of Love *Bobby Vee* (Liberty)		18	–	–
14 Up On The Roof *Kenny Lynch* (HMV)		12	13	10
15 Your Cheating Heart *Ray Charles* (HMV)		16	17	–
16 Devil Woman *Marty Robbins* (CBS)		–	–	–
17 Go Away Little Girl *Mark Wynter* (Pye)		8	6	7
18 Desafinado *Stan Getz and Charlie Byrd* (HMV)		15	–	–
19 Like I Do *Maureen Evans* (Oriole)		10	5	3
20 The Main Attraction *Pat Boone* (London)		20	–	–
30 He's A Rebel *The Crystals* (London)		19	–	–
24 Love Me Do *The Beatles* (Parlophone)		17	–	–
– Globe-Trotter *The Tornados* (Decca)		28	9	5
– Diamonds *Jet Harris and Tony Meehan* (Decca)		45	12	4
31 Don't You Think It's Time *Mike Berry and The Outlaws* (HMV)		21	15	8
44 Coming Home Baby *Mel Torme* (London)		24	18	13
26 Island Of Dreams *The Springfields* (Philips)		26	19	12
– Little Town Flirt *Del Shannon* (London)		–	41	14
– Some Kinda Fun *Chris Montez* (London)		–	42	16
– All Alone Am I *Brenda Lee* (Brunswick)		–	40	17
– Big Girls Don't Cry *The Four Seasons* (Stateside)		–	48	18

FEBRUARY 1963

	2	9	16	23
1 Diamonds *Jet Harris and Tony Meehan* (Decca)		1	1	3
2 Next Time/Bachelor Boy *Cliff Richard* (Columbia)		2	5	9
3 Like I Do *Maureen Evans* (Oriole)		5	7	14
4 Dance On! *The Shadows* (Columbia)		9	11	–
5 Globe-Trotter *The Tornados* (Decca)		6	13	16
6 Don't You Think It's Time *Mike Berry and The Outlaws* (HMV)		8	8	13
7 Little Town Flirt *Del Shannon* (London)		7	4	5
8 Return To Sender *Elvis Presley* (RCA)		17	–	–
9 Wayward Wind *Frank Ifield* (Columbia)		4	2	1
10 Some Kinda Fun *Chris Montez* (London)		12	20	20
11 Go Away Little Girl *Mark Wynter* (Pye)		20	–	–
12 Up On The Roof *Kenny Lynch* (HMV)		18	–	–
13 Big Girls Don't Cry *The Four Seasons* (Stateside)		13	15	18
14 Island Of Dreams *The Springfields* (Philips)		10	12	8
15 All Alone Am I *Brenda Lee* (Brunswick)		11	9	7
16 Please Please Me *The Beatles* (Parlophone)		3	3	2
17 Dance With The Guitar Man *Duane Eddy* (RCA)		–	–	–
18 Coming Home Baby *Mel Torme* (London)		–	–	–
19 Suki Yaki *Kenny Ball* (Pye)		14	10	10
20 Lovesick Blues *Frank Ifield* (Columbia)		–	–	–
29 Loop-De-Loop *Frankie Vaughan* (Philips)		15	6	6
21 A Taste Of Honey *Acker Bilk* (Columbia)		16	16	17

2	9	16	23
23 My Little Girl *The Crickets* (Liberty)	19	17	19
– The Night Has A Thousand Eyes *Bobby Vee* (Liberty)	30	14	4
39 Walk Right In *The Rooftop Singers* (Fontana)	21	18	11
45 Hava Nagila *The Spotnicks* (Oriole)	26	19	15
– That's What Love Will Do *Joe Brown* (Piccadilly)	50	26	12

MARCH 1963

2	9	16	23	30
1 Wayward Wind *Frank Ifield* (Columbia)	1	7	10	17
2 Please Please Me *The Beatles* (Parlophone)	3	2	5	7
3 The Night Has A Thousand Eyes *Bobby Vee* (Liberty)	4	5	6	13
4 Diamonds *Jet Harris and Tony Meehan* (Decca)	7	14	18	–
5 Loop-De-Loop *Frankie Vaughan* (Philips)	8	13	15	–
6 That's What Love Will Do *Joe Brown* (Piccadilly)	5	3	3	8
7 Summer Holiday *Cliff Richard and The Shadows* (Columbia)	2	1	1	2
8 Little Town Flirt *Del Shannon* (London)	13	18	–	–
9 Island Of Dreams *The Springfields* (Philips)	9	6	7	5
10 Suki Yaki *Kenny Ball and his Jazzmen* (Pye)	17	20	–	–
11 Walk Right In *The Rooftop Singers* (Fontana)	10	15	17	–
12 All Alone Am I *Brenda Lee* (Brunswick)	15	19	–	–
13 Hava Nagila *The Spotnicks* (Oriole)	16	–	–	–
14 Like I've Never Been Gone *Billy Fury* (Decca)	6	4	4	3
15 Like I Do *Maureen Evans* (Oriole)	–	–	–	–
16 Next Time/Bachelor Boy *Cliff Richard* (Columbia)	19	–	–	–
17 Hey Paula *Paul and Paula* (Philips)	11	8	9	12
18 Charmaine *The Bachelors* (Decca)	12	11	8	6
19 Don't You Think It's Time *Mike Berry and The Outlaws* (HMV)	–	–	–	–
20 Globe-Trotter *The Tornados* (Decca)	–	–	–	–
21 Tell Him *Billie Davis* (Decca)	14	10	11	15
42 One Broken Heart For Sale *Elvis Presley* (RCA)	18	12	12	14
25 Hi Lili-Hi Lo *Richard Chamberlain* (MGM)	20	–	–	–
– Foot Tapper *The Shadows* (Columbia)	25	9	2	1
30 From A Jack To A King *Ned Miller* (London)	21	16	13	4
46 Rhythm Of The Rain *The Cascades* (Warner Bros.)	30	17	14	9
– Say Wonderful Things *Ronnie Carroll* (Philips)	37	21	16	11
– Brown Eyed Handsome Man *Buddy Holly* (Coral)	–	32	19	16
– How Do You Do It? *Gerry and The Pacemakers* (Columbia)	–	39	20	10
– Let's Turkey Trot *Little Eva* (London)	44	26	21	18
– The Folk Singer *Tommy Roe* (HMV)	–	–	31	19
– In Dreams *Roy Orbison* (London)	38	28	25	20

APRIL 1963

6	13	20	27
1 How Do You Do It? *Gerry and The Pacemakers* (Columbia)	1	1	1
2 From A Jack To A King *Ned Miller* (London)	2	2	2
3 Summer Holiday *Cliff Richard and The Shadows* (Columbia)	6	9	13
4 Foot Tapper *The Shadows* (Columbia)	3	6	9
5 Like I've Never Been Gone *Billy Fury* (Decca)	9	11	17
6 Say Wonderful Things *Ronnie Carroll* (Philips)	7	8	14
7 Rhythm Of The Rain *The Cascades* (Warner Bros.)	5	5	7
8 Charmaine *The Bachelors* (Decca)	8	12	15
9 Brown Eyed Handsome Man *Buddy Holly* (Coral)	4	3	10
10 That's What Love Will Do *Joe Brown* (Piccadilly)	14	–	–
11 Please Please Me *The Beatles* (Parlophone)	17	–	–

6	13	20	27
12 Hey Paula *Paul and Paula* (Philips)	18	–	–
13 The Folk Singer *Tommy Roe* (HMV)	10	4	4
14 Let's Turkey Trot *Little Eva* (London)	13	18	19
15 Island Of Dreams *The Springfields* (Philips)	15	16	20
16 Tell Him *Billie Davis* (Decca)	–	–	–
17 In Dreams *Roy Orbison* (London)	12	10	8
18 The Night Has A Thousand Eyes *Bobby Vee* (Liberty)	–	–	–
19 One Broken Heart For Sale *Elvis Presley* (RCA)	–	–	–
20 Wayward Wind *Frank Ifield* (Columbia)	–	–	–
22 Say I Won't Be There *The Springfields* (Philips)	11	7	5
23 Walk Like A Man *The Four Seasons* (Stateside)	16	13	12
24 Robot *The Tornados* (Philips)	19	17	–
21 End Of The World *Skeeter Davis* (RCA)	20	19	18
– Nobody's Darlin' But Mine *Frank Ifield* (Columbia)	30	14	6
28 Can't Get Used To Losing You *Andy Williams* (CBS)	21	15	11
35 Losing You *Brenda Lee* (Brunswick)	27	20	16
– From Me To You *The Beatles* (Parlophone)	–	23	3

MAY 1963

4	11	18	25
1 From Me To You *The Beatles* (Parlophone)	1	1	1
2 How Do You Do It? *Gerry and The Pacemakers* (Columbia)	2	4	8
3 From A Jack To A King *Ned Miller* (London)	3	7	12
4 Nobody's Darlin' But Mine *Frank Ifield* (Columbia)	4	8	11
5 Say I Won't Be There *The Springfields* (Philips)	8	12	14
6 Can't Get Used To Losing You *Andy Williams* (CBS)	5	2	5
7 In Dreams *Roy Orbison* (London)	6	6	7
8 Rhythm Of The Rain *The Cascades* (Warner Bros.)	12	15	17
9 Brown Eyed Handsome Man *Buddy Holly* (Coral)	11	13	18
10 Foot Tapper *The Shadows* (Columbia)	15	20	–
11 The Folk Singer *Tommy Roe* (HMV)	13	17	19
12 Walk Like A Man *The Four Seasons* (Stateside)	14	18	–
13 Losing You *Brenda Lee* (Brunswick)	10	11	10
14 Summer Holiday *Cliff Richard* (Columbia)	19	–	–
15 Scarlett O'Hara *Jet Harris and Tony Meehan* (Decca)	7	3	2
16 Say Wonderful Things *Ronnie Carroll* (Philips)	20	–	–
17 Two Kinds Of Teardrops *Del Shannon* (London)	9	5	6
18 He's So Fine *The Chiffons* (Stateside)	16	16	16
19 Like I've Never Been Gone *Billy Fury* (Decca)	–	–	–
20 End Of The World *Skeeter Davis* (RCA)	–	–	–
43 Do You Want To Know A Secret? *Billy J. Kramer and The Dakotas* (Parlophone)	17	10	3
24 Young Lovers *Paul and Paula* (Philips)	18	14	9
– Lucky Lips *Cliff Richard* (Columbia)	21	9	4
29 Deck Of Cards *Wink Martindale* (London)	22	19	13
– When Will You Say I Love You? *Billy Fury* (Decca)	–	28	15
37 Pipeline *The Chantays* (London)	32	22	20

JUNE 1963

1	8	15	22	29
1 From Me To You *The Beatles* (Parlophone)	1	1	2	4
2 Do You Want To Know A Secret? *Billy J. Kramer and The Dakotas* (Parlophone)	2	3	4	7
3 Scarlett O'Hara *Jet Harris and Tony Meehan* (Decca)	4	5	7	11
4 Lucky Lips *Cliff Richard* (Columbia)	8	6	10	12
5 Can't Get Used To Losing You *Andy Williams* (CBS)	10	14	14	19
6 Two Kinds Of Teardrops *Del Shannon* (London)	6	13	15	16

1

	8	15	22	29
7 When Will You Say I Love You? *Billy Fury* (Decca)	3	4	5	10
8 In Dreams *Roy Orbison* (London)	11	10	11	13
9 Young Lovers *Paul and Paula* (Philips)	13	11	17	20
10 Deck Of Cards *Wink Martindale* (London)	9	9	8	8
11 Nobody's Darlin' But Mine *Frank Ifield* (Columbia)	14	15	18	—
12 Losing You *Brenda Lee* (Brunswick)	18	—	—	—
13 How Do You Do It? *Gerry and The Pacemakers* (Columbia)	15	20	19	—
14 Take These Chains From My Heart *Ray Charles* (HMV)	5	8	6	5
15 From A Jack To A King *Ned Miller* (London)	17	—	—	—
16 If You Gotta Make A Fool Of Somebody *Freddie and The Dreamers* (Columbia)	12	7	3	3
17 He's So Fine *The Chiffons* (Stateside)	20	—	—	—
18 Say I Won't Be There *The Springfields* (Philips)				
19 Pipeline *The Chantays* (London)	16	19	—	—
20 Harvest Of Love *Benny Hill* (Pye)	—	—	20	—
22 I Like It *Gerry and The Pacemakers* (Columbia)	7	2	1	1
33 Falling *Roy Orbison* (London)	19	17	12	9
– Atlantis *The Shadows* (Columbia)	27	12	9	2
– Bo Diddley *Buddy Holly* (Coral)	35	16	13	6
29 Forget Him *Bobby Rydell* (Cameo-Parkway)	21	18	16	14
– Welcome To My World *Jim Reeves* (RCA)	—	41	26	15
– Da Doo Ron Ron *The Crystals* (London)	—	—	37	17
– The Ice Cream Man *The Tornados* (Decca)	34	25	22	18

JULY 1963

6

	13	20	27
1 I Like It *Gerry and The Pacemakers* (Columbia)	1	2	7
2 Atlantis *The Shadows* (Columbia)	3	4	4
3 Confessin' *Frank Ifield* (Columbia)	2	1	1
4 If You Gotta Make A Fool Of Somebody *Freddie and The Dreamers* (Columbia)	8	14	16
5 Deck Of Cards *Wink Martindale* (London)	7	10	10
6 Take These Chains From My Heart *Ray Charles* (HMV)	5	6	8
7 Bo Diddley *Buddy Holly* (Coral)	4	8	13
8 From Me To You *The Beatles* (Parlophone)	13	16	15
9 Welcome To My World *Jim Reeves* (RCA)	6	12	11
10 Falling *Roy Orbison* (London)	11	13	14
11 Do You Want To Know A Secret? *Billy J. Kramer and The Dakotas* (Parlophone)	14	18	19
12 When Will You Say I Love You? *Billy Fury* (Decca)	16	19	—
13 Forget Him *Bobby Rydell* (Cameo-Parkway)	15	15	17
14 It's My Party *Lesley Gore* (Mercury)	9	9	9
15 In Dreams *Roy Orbison* (London)	20	—	—
16 Da Doo Ron Ron *The Crystals* (London)	12	5	6
17 Scarlett O'Hara *Jet Harris and Tony Meehan* (Decca)	—	—	—
18 The Ice Cream Man *The Tornados* (Decca)	—	—	—
19 Lucky Lips *Cliff Richard* (Columbia)	—	—	—
20 Two Kinds Of Teardrops *Del Shannon* (London)	—	—	—
27 Devil In Disguise *Elvis Presley* (RCA)	10	3	2
39 Sweets For My Sweet *The Searchers* (Pye)	17	7	3
22 You Can Never Stop Me Loving You *Kenny Lynch* (HMV)	18	20	18
48 Twist And Shout *Brian Poole and The Tremeloes* (Decca)	19	11	5
35 Suki Yaki *Kyu Sakamoto* (HMV)	25	17	12
– I Wonder *Brenda Lee* (Brunswick)	—	30	20

3		10	17	24	31
1 Devil In Disguise *Elvis Presley* (RCA)		3	5	11	15
2 Confessin' *Frank Ifield* (Columbia)		2	2	4	9
3 Sweets For My Sweet *The Searchers* (Pye)		1	1	2	3
4 Twist And Shout *Brian Poole and The Tremeloes* (Decca)		4	4	7	13
5 Da Doo Ron Ron *The Crystals* (London)		5	8	8	14
6 I Like It *Gerry and The Pacemakers* (Columbia)		9	16	20	–
7 Atlantis *The Shadows* (Columbia)		7	11	16	–
8 Suki Yaki *Kyu Sakamoto* (HMV)		6	9	14	16
9 Welcome To My World *Jim Reeves* (RCA)		15	13	13	18
10 It's My Party *Lesley Gore* (Mercury)		12	19	–	–
11 Take These Chains From My Heart *Ray Charles* (HMV)		17	18	19	–
12 You Can Never Stop Me Loving You *Kenny Lynch* (HMV)		10	15	17	–
13 Deck Of Cards *Wink Martindale* (London)		–	–	–	–
14 I Wonder *Brenda Lee* (Brunswick)		18	17	15	–
15 Theme From The Legion's Last Patrol *Ken Thorne and his Orchestra* (HMV)		14	7	6	4
16 Bo Diddley *Buddy Holly* (Coral)		–	–	–	–
17 From Me To You *The Beatles* (Parlophone)		20	–	–	–
18 Falling *Roy Orbison* (London)		–	–	–	–
19 In Summer *Billy Fury* (Decca)		8	6	5	8
20 Wipeout *The Surfaris* (London)		13	10	10	5
34 Bad To Me *Billy J. Kramer and The Dakotas* (Parlophone)		11	3	1	1
21 I'll Never Get Over You *Johnny Kidd and The Pirates* (HMV)		16	12	9	6
22 The Cruel Sea *The Dakotas* (Parlophone)		19	22	21	20
– I'm Telling You Now *Freddie and The Dreamers* (Columbia)		34	14	3	2
– You Don't Have To Be A Baby To Cry *The Caravelles* (Decca)		36	20	12	7
– Just Like Eddie *Heinz* (Decca)		38	26	18	11
– It's All In The Game *Cliff Richard* (Columbia)		–	–	25	10
– She Loves You *The Beatles* (Parlophone)		–	–	–	12
– Dance On *Kathy Kirby* (Decca)		–	42	27	17
– I Want To Stay Here *Steve Lawrence and Eydie Gorme* (CBS)		–	–	36	19

7		14	21	28
1 Bad To Me *Billy J. Kramer and The Dakotas* (Parlophone)		3	3	11
2 I'm Telling You Now *Freddie and The Dreamers* (Columbia)		5	6	14
3 She Loves You *The Beatles* (Parlophone)		1	1	1
4 It's All In The Game *Cliff Richard* (Columbia)		2	2	2
5 I'll Never Get Over You *Johnny Kidd and The Pirates* (HMV)		4	5	6
6 Sweets For My Sweet *The Searchers* (Pye)		12	17	–
7 You Don't Have To Be A Baby To Cry *The Caravelles* (Decca)		6	7	12
8 Wipeout *The Surfaris* (London)		8	10	13
9 Just Like Eddie *Heinz* (Decca)		9	8	5
10 I Want To Stay Here *Steve Lawrence and Eydie Gorme* (CBS)		7	4	3
11 Theme From The Legion's Last Patrol *Ken Thorne and his Orchestra* (HMV)		10	11	19
12 Confessin' *Frank Ifield* (Columbia)		15	20	–
13 In Summer *Billy Fury* (Decca)		14	19	–
14 Dance On *Kathy Kirby* (Decca)		11	14	16
15 Twist And Shout *Brian Poole and The Tremeloes* (Decca)		17	–	–
16 Da Doo Ron Ron *The Crystals* (London)		20	–	–
17 Still *Karl Denver* (Decca)		13	15	18

7	14	21	28
18 The Cruel Sea *The Dakotas* (Parlophone)	19	–	–
19 Suki Yaki *Kyu Sakamoto* (HMV)	–	–	–
20 Devil In Disguise *Elvis Presley* (RCA)	–	–	–
49 Applejack *Jet Harris and Tony Meehan* (Decca)	16	9	4
35 Wishing *Buddy Holly* (Coral)	18	13	10
– Do You Love Me? *Brian Poole and The Tremeloes* (Decca)	33	12	7
– If I Had A Hammer *Trini Lopez* (Reprise)	36	16	8
29 Whispering *The Bachelors* (Decca)	21	18	–
– Then He Kissed Me *The Crystals* (London)	–	22	9
– Shindig *The Shadows* (Columbia)	–	32	15
– Blue Bayou/Mean Woman Blues *Roy Orbison* (London)	–	41	17
38 Searchin' *The Hollies* (Parlophone)	32	26	20

OCTOBER 1963

5	12	19	26
1 She Loves You *The Beatles* (Parlophone)	3	3	3
2 Do You Love Me? *Brian Poole and The Tremeloes* (Decca)	1	1	1
3 Then He Kissed Me *The Crystals* (London)	2	2	4
4 It's All In The Game *Cliff Richard* (Columbia)	8	16	19
5 If I Had A Hammer *Trini Lopez* (Reprise)	4	6	7
6 I Want To Stay Here *Steve Lawrence and Eydie Gorme* (CBS)	11	14	–
7 Just Like Eddie *Heinz* (Decca)	15	17	20
8 Shindig *The Shadows* (Columbia)	6	8	12
9 Blue Bayou/Mean Woman Blues *Roy Orbison* (London)	5	4	5
10 I'll Never Get Over You *Johnny Kidd and The Pirates* (HMV)	20	–	–
11 Applejack *Jet Harris and Tony Meehan* (Decca)	9	12	15
12 Wishing *Buddy Holly* (Coral)	10	15	16
13 The First Time *Adam Faith* (Parlophone)	7	5	8
14 Still *Karl Denver* (Decca)	19	20	17
15 Bad To Me *Billy J. Kramer and The Dakotas* (Parlophone)	–	–	–
16 You Don't Have To Be A Baby To Cry *The Caravelles* (Decca)	–	–	–
17 Searchin' *The Hollies* (Parlophone)	12	13	13
18 Hello Little Girl *The Fourmost* (Parlophone)	14	11	9
19 I'm Telling You Now *Freddie and The Dreamers* (Columbia)	–	–	–
20 Hello Muddah! Hello Fadduh! *Alan Sherman* (Warner Bros.)	17	18	14
27 I Who Have Nothing *Shirley Bassey* (Columbia)	13	10	6
25 Everybody *Tommy Roe* (HMV)	16	9	11
28 Somebody Else's Girl *Billy Fury* (Decca)	18	19	–
– You'll Never Walk Alone *Gerry and The Pacemakers* (Columbia)	22	7	2
– Let It Rock/Memphis Tennessee *Chuck Berry* (Pye)	25	21	10
– Be My Baby *The Ronettes* (London)	–	32	18

NOVEMBER 1963

2	9	16	23	30
1 You'll Never Walk Alone *Gerry and The Pacemakers* (Columbia)	1	1	1	2
2 She Loves You *The Beatles* (Parlophone)	2	3	2	1
3 Do You Love Me? *Brian Poole and The Tremeloes* (Decca)	5	8	12	16
4 Blue Bayou/Mean Woman Blues *Roy Orbison* (London)	3	4	7	9
5 Then He Kissed Me *The Crystals* (London)	9	10	14	17
6 If I Had A Hammer *Trini Lopez* (Reprise)	10	13	15	15
7 I Who Have Nothing *Shirley Bassey* (Columbia)	8	9	8	11
8 Sugar And Spice *The Searchers* (Pye)	4	2	3	6
9 Let It Rock/Memphis Tennessee *Chuck Berry* (Pye)	7	6	10	12
10 The First Time *Adam Faith* (Parlophone)	11	14	19	–
11 Be My Baby *The Ronettes* (London)	6	5	4	8

2		9	16	23	30
12 Hello Little Girl *The Fourmost* (Parlophone)		13	20	–	–
13 Bossa Nova Baby *Elvis Presley* (RCA)		14	18	20	–
14 Hello Muddah! Hello Fadduh! *Alan Sherman* (Warner Bros.)		–	–	–	–
15 Everybody *Tommy Roe* (HMV)		17	–	–	–
16 Fools Rush In *Ricky Nelson* (Brunswick)		12	15	16	18
17 Miss You *Jimmy Young* (Columbia)		15	19	18	–
18 Shindig *The Shadows* (Columbia)		18	–	–	–
19 Searchin' *The Hollies* (Parlophone)		–	–	–	–
20 Still *Karl Denver* (Decca)		20	–	–	–
21 Blowin' In The Wind *Peter Paul and Mary* (Warner Bros.)		16	17	17	13
24 Memphis Tennessee *Dave Berry and The Cruisers* (Decca)		19	–	–	–
– Don't Talk To Him *Cliff Richard and The Shadows* (Columbia)		23	7	5	3
– I'll Keep You Satisfied *Billy J. Kramer and The Dakotas* (Parlophone)		–	11	9	4
– Secret Love *Kathy Kirby* (Decca)		–	12	6	5
44 Maria Elena *Los Indios Tabajaros* (RCA)		28	16	13	10
– You Were Made For Me *Freddie and The Dreamers* (Columbia)		39	23	11	7
– It's Almost Tomorrow *Mark Wynter* (Pye)		–	32	22	14
– Glad All Over *The Dave Clark Five* (Columbia)		–	–	38	19
– From Russia With Love *Matt Monro* (Parlophone)		–	43	27	20

DECEMBER 1963

7		14	22	28
1 She Loves You *The Beatles* (Parlophone)		2	2	2
2 Don't Talk To Him *Cliff Richard* (Columbia)		6	10	8
3 You Were Made For Me *Freddie and The Dreamers* (Columbia)		3	3	3
4 You'll Never Walk Alone *Gerry and The Pacemakers* (Columbia)		8	12	12
5 Secret Love *Kathy Kirby* (Decca)		4	5	4
6 I'll Keep You Satisfied *Billy J. Kramer and The Dakotas* (Parlophone)		11	16	13
7 Maria Elena *Los Indios Tabajaros* (RCA)		5	7	10
8 Glad All Over *The Dave Clark Five* (Columbia)		9	4	6
9 I Only Want To Be With You *Dusty Springfield* (Philips)		7	6	5
10 I Want To Hold Your Hand *The Beatles* (Parlophone)		1	1	1
11 Be My Baby *The Ronettes* (London)		–	–	–
12 It's Almost Tomorrow *Mark Wynter* (Pye)		14	20	–
13 Sugar And Spice *The Searchers* (Pye)		–	–	–
14 Blue Bayou/Mean Woman Blues *Roy Orbison* (London)		16	–	–
15 I Who Have Nothing *Shirley Bassey* (Columbia)		12	–	–
16 I Wanna Be Your Man *The Rolling Stones* (Decca)		15	13	14
17 Deep Purple *April Stevens and Nino Tempo* (London)		18	–	–
18 Let It Rock/Memphis Tennessee *Chuck Berry* (Pye)		–	–	–
19 Blowin' In The Wind *Peter Paul and Mary* (Warner Bros.)		–	–	–
20 Hungry For Love *Johnny Kidd* (HMV)		–	–	–
24 Dominique *The Singing Nun* (Philips)		10	8	7
28 Geronimo *The Shadows* (Columbia)		13	11	11
27 Stay *The Hollies* (Parlophone)		17	19	17
23 Money *Bern Elliott and The Fenmen* (Decca)		19	14	19
33 24 Hours From Tulsa *Gene Pitney* (UA)		20	9	9
35 Swinging On A Star *Big Dee Irwin* (Colpix)		27	15	15
– Not Too Little Not Too Much *Chris Sandford* (Decca)		30	17	18

31	If I Ruled The World *Harry Secombe* (Philips)	22 18 –
–	Kiss Me Quick *Elvis Presley* (RCA)	– 25 16
37	All I Want For Christmas is A Beatle *Dora Bryan* (Fontana)	24 21 20

1963–BEST-SELLING SINGLES

1 From Me To You *The Beatles* (Parlophone)
2 She Loves You *The Beatles* (Parlophone)
3 In Dreams *Roy Orbison* (London)
4 Island Of Dreams *The Springfields* (Philips)
5 From A Jack To A King *Ned Miller* (London)
6 Deck Of Cards *Wink Martindale* (London)
7 How Do You Do It? *Gerry and The Pacemakers* (Columbia)
8 Summer Holiday *Cliff Richard and The Shadows* (Columbia)
9 Confessin' *Frank Ifield* (Columbia)
10 Scarlett O'Hara *Jet Harris and Tony Meehan* (Decca)
11 Can't Get Used To Losing You *Andy Williams* (CBS)
12 Charmaine *The Bachelors* (Decca)
13 Please Please Me *The Beatles* (Parlophone)
14 I Like It *Gerry and The Pacemakers* (Columbia)
15 Atlantis *The Shadows* (Columbia)
16 Do You Want To Know A Secret? *Billy J. Kramer and The Dakotas*
    (Parlophone)
17 Take These Chains From My Heart *Ray Charles* (HMV)
18 Do You Love Me? *Brian Poole and The Tremeloes* (Decca)
19 Sweets For My Sweet *The Searchers* (Pye)
20 Foot Tapper *The Shadows* (Columbia)

1964

The excitement of new stars and new sounds from 1963 continued into 1964, and the British dominance in the charts continued with The Beatles and The Rolling Stones both going from strength to strength following their first year of real success in 1963. The previous year's tentative attempts for success from Dusty Springfield and Cilla Black became much more certain as both girls launched into their long hit runs:

The new names of 1964 included The Animals, who arrived in the charts with the old folk song 'The House Of The Rising Sun'. Manfred Mann, with their lead singer, Paul Jones, began with '5-4-3-2-1', the first of many hits for the group. A record entitled 'Rosalyn' created much interest in The Pretty Things but though they received magazine coverage and were well-known on the pop scene, their ratings in terms of chart successes were never very high.

Liverpool produced yet another chart group in the form of The Merseybeats, but their eventual track performance was disappointing after initial promise. Their chart careers began and ended in 1964 with three hits, though they managed one more hit in 1966 under the name of The Merseys. The Zombies were another new group who promised much, but who were perhaps ahead of their time. Several years later ex-members of the group such as Rod Argent, Russ Ballard and Colin Blunstone enjoyed hits in their own right.

Liverpool was not the only centre of music, as Eric Burdon and The Animals from Newcastle proved. From the Midlands came The Hollies, who had been overshadowed in 1963 by the Mersey Sound. However, 'Just One Look' reached Number Two early in 1964 and their chart residency began, with the group appearing in the charts with the regularity of clockwork.

The Beach Boys arrived in 1964 with 'I Get Around', a record which remained in the charts for two months. The Beach Boys then disappeared from the Top Twenty until 1966, when they returned with a much bigger impact.

The two main pop heroes of 1963, The Beatles and The Rolling Stones, dominated the charts for most of the year.

The Beatles had three Number Ones and lent inspiration to Peter and Gordon, another new chart act, with 'World Without Love' which also reached the Number One position. The Rolling Stones had two Number Ones with 'It's All Over Now' and 'Little Red Rooster', while 'Not Fade Away' reached Number Three.

For a time it seemed that The Dave Clark Five were destined to chase The Beatles up and down the charts, for they had entered the charts for the first time in late November 1963 to topple The Beatles from their Number One position, and, until the end of July 1964, they were continually in the Top Twenty with hits such as 'Glad All Over', 'Bits And Pieces' and 'Can't You See That She's Mine'. Although all these records sold thousands of copies, The Dave Clark Five then had to wait almost a year before they achieved their next Top Twenty hit. Lulu, with her group. The Luvvers, began her long chart career and while The Kinks arrived in the charts with 'You Really Got Me', The Bachelors achieved even more hits than The Beatles, for they managed five songs in the charts, all of which were in the Top Ten.

Ballads were in vogue, so Julie Rogers had a hit with 'The Wedding Song', as did Frankie Vaughan with 'Hello Dolly', and The Four Pennies with 'Juliet'. Songs by The Four Seasons, Dionne Warwick, Doris Day and P. J. Proby also kept ballads to the fore.

1964 also yielded The Supremes, and the birth of the Tamla Motown sound.

JANUARY 1964

4	11	18	25
1 I Want To Hold Your Hand *The Beatles* (Parlophone)	1	2	3
2 Glad All Over *The Dave Clark Five* (Columbia)	2	1	1
3 She Loves You *The Beatles* (Parlophone)	5	5	8
4 You Were Made For Me *Freddie and The Dreamers* (Columbia)	7	9	20
5 24 Hours From Tulsa *Gene Pitney* (UA)	6	6	5
6 I Only Want To Be With You *Dusty Springfield* (Philips)	4	4	4
7 Dominique *The Singing Nun* (Philips)	10	10	16
8 Maria Elena *Los Indios Tabajaros* (RCA)	13	11	19
9 Secret Love *Kathy Kirby* (Decca)	9	12	18
10 Don't Talk To Him *Cliff Richard* (Columbia)	14	–	–
11 Swinging On A Star *Big Dee Irwin* (Colpix)	8	7	7
12 Geronimo *The Shadows* (Columbia)	18	–	–
13 Hippy Hippy Shake *The Swinging Blue Jeans* (HMV)	3	3	2
14 Kiss Me Quick *Elvis Presley* (RCA)	15	15	14
15 I Wanna Be Your Man *The Rolling Stones* (Decca)	12	14	15
16 You'll Never Walk Alone *Gerry and The Pacemakers* (Parlophone)	17	20	–
17 Stay *The Hollies* (Parlophone)	11	8	12
18 Not Too Little Not Too Much *Chris Sandford* (Decca)	19	18	–
19 Money *Bern Elliott and The Fenmen* (Decca)	–	–	–
20 We Are In Love *Adam Faith* (Parlophone)	16	13	11
37 Do You Really Love Me Too? *Billy Fury* (Decca)	20	17	17
– Don't Blame Me *Frank Ifield* (Columbia)	38	19	13
– As Usual *Brenda Lee* (Brunswick)	29	16	9
– Needles And Pins *The Searchers* (Pye)	–	26	6
– I'm The One *Gerry and The Pacemakers* (Parlophone)	–	23	10

FEBRUARY 1964

1	8	15	22	29
1 Needles And Pins *The Searchers* (Pye)	1	1	3	3
2 Glad All Over *The Dave Clark Five* (Columbia)	4	6	10	14
3 Hippy Hippy Shake *The Swinging Blue Jeans* (HMV)	3	4	6	12
4 I'm The One *Gerry and The Pacemakers* (Columbia)	2	2	4	6
5 I Only Want To Be With You *Dusty Springfield* (Philips)	11	17	17	–
6 I Want To Hold Your Hand *The Beatles* (Parlophone)	7	15	15	17
7 24 Hours From Tulsa *Gene Pitney* (UA)	6	11	16	19
8 Stay *The Hollies* (Parlophone)	12	19	–	–
9 As Usual *Brenda Lee* (Brunswick)	5	7	7	9
10 Don't Blame Me *Frank Ifield* (Columbia)	10	8	12	15
11 We Are In Love *Adam Faith* (Parlophone)	18	–	–	–
12 Swinging On A Star *Big Dee Irwin* (Colpix)	16	20	–	–
13 Do You Really Love Me Too? *Billy Fury* (Decca)	14	–	–	–
14 5-4-3-2-1 *Manfred Mann* (HMV)	9	5	5	7
15 Kiss Me Quick *Elvis Presley* (RCA)	–	–	–	–
16 She Loves You *The Beatles* (Parlophone)	19	–	–	–
17 I Wanna Be Your Man *The Rolling Stones* (Decca)	–	–	–	–
18 Baby I Love You *The Ronettes* (London)	13	12	13	11
19 I Think Of You *The Merseybeats* (Fontana)	15	9	9	5
20 I'm In Love *The Fourmost* (Parlophone)	17	18	20	8
22 Diane *The Bachelors* (Decca)	8	3	1	1
26 Whispering *April Stevens and Nino Tempo* (London)	20	–	–	–
– Anyone Who Had A Heart *Cilla Black* (Parlophone)	28	10	2	2
42 Candy Man *Brian Poole and The Tremeloes* (Decca)	22	13	11	–
– I'm The Lonely One *Cliff Richard* (Columbia)	23	14	8	10
30 For You *Ricky Nelson* (Brunswick)	21	16	14	16

1		8	15	22	29
49	Boys Cry *Eden Kane* (Fontana)	33	24	18	13
–	Bits And Pieces *The Dave Clark Five* (Columbia)	–	–	19	4
–	Stay Awhile *Dusty Springfield* (Philips)	–	–	30	18
–	Over You *Freddie and The Dreamers* (Columbia)	–	–	44	20

MARCH 1964

7		14	21	28
1	Anyone Who Had A Heart *Cilla Black* (Parlophone)	1	3	4
2	Bits And Pieces *The Dave Clark Five* (Columbia)	2	2	5
3	Diane *The Bachelors* (Decca)	4	6	11
4	Needles And Pins *The Searchers* (Pye)	7	10	–
5	I Think Of You *The Merseybeats* (Fontana)	8	7	13
6	Candy Man *Brian Poole and The Tremeloes* (Decca)	11	15	20
7	I'm The One *Gerry and The Pacemakers* (Columbia)	12	19	–
8	5-4-3-2-1 *Manfred Mann* (HMV)	20	–	–
9	Little Children *Billy J. Kramer and The Dakotas* (Parlophone)	3	1	1
10	As Usual *Brenda Lee* (Brunswick)	17	20	–
11	Not Fade Away *The Rolling Stones* (Decca)	5	4	3
12	Boys Cry *Eden Kane* (Fontana)	9	8	9
13	Over You *Freddie and The Dreamers* (Columbia)	18	16	18
14	I'm The Lonely One *Cliff Richard* (Columbia)	–	–	–
15	Baby I Love You *The Ronettes* (London)	19	–	–
16	Stay Awhile *Dusty Springfield* (Philips)	13	13	19
17	Borne On The Wind *Roy Orbison* (London)	15	17	–
18	Let Me Go Lover *Kathy Kirby* (Decca)	10	11	15
19	For You *Ricky Nelson* (Brunswick)	–	–	–
20	Just One Look *The Hollies* (Parlophone)	6	5	2
21	I Love You Because *Jim Reeves* (RCA)	14	9	6
28	That Girl Belongs To Yesterday *Gene Pitney* (UA)	16	12	8
36	Theme For Young Lovers *The Shadows* (Columbia)	22	14	14
47	Tell Me When *The Applejacks* (Decca)	29	18	12
–	Can't Buy Me Love *The Beatles* (Parlophone)	–	–	7
–	I Believe *The Bachelors* (Decca)	–	28	10
–	World Without Love *Peter and Gordon* (Columbia)	39	36	16
–	Viva Las Vegas *Elvis Presley* (RCA)	46	29	17

APRIL 1964

4		11	18	25
1	Can't Buy Me Love *The Beatles* (Parlophone)	1	1	2
2	Little Children *Billy J. Kramer and The Dakotas* (Parlophone)	2	4	9
3	Just One Look *The Hollies* (Parlophone)	5	6	10
4	Not Fade Away *The Rolling Stones* (Decca)	6	8	8
5	I Love You Because *Jim Reeves* (RCA)	7	5	6
6	I Believe *The Bachelors* (Decca)	3	3	3
7	Bits And Pieces *The Dave Clark Five* (Columbia)	10	14	–
8	Diane *The Bachelors* (Decca)	13	16	–
9	That Girl Belongs To Yesterday *Gene Pitney* (UA)	8	9	15
10	Anyone Who Had A Heart *Cilla Black* (Parlophone)	11	15	19
11	Tell Me When *The Applejacks* (Decca)	9	7	7
12	Boys Cry *Eden Kane* (Decca)	–	–	–
13	World Without Love *Peter and Gordon* (Columbia)	4	2	1
14	Theme For Young Lovers *The Shadows* (Columbia)	12	19	20
15	I Think Of You *The Merseybeats* (Fontana)	20	–	–
16	Over You *Freddie and The Dreamers* (Columbia)	–	–	–
17	Let Me Go Lover *Kathy Kirby* (Decca)	19	–	–
18	Viva Las Vegas *Elvis Presley* (RCA)	17	18	–

	11	18	25
19 Stay Awhile *Dusty Springfield* (Philips)	–	–	–
20 Good Golly Miss Molly *The Swinging Blue Jeans* (HMV)	14	11	14
– Everything's All Right *The Mojos* (Decca)	18	13	12
– Move Over Darling *Doris Day* (CBS)	15	12	11
– My Boy Lollipop *Millie* (Fontana)	16	10	5
– Mockingbird Hill *The Migil Five* (Pye)	30	17	13
– Don't Throw Your Love Away *The Searchers* (Pye)	–	20	4
– Hubble Bubble Toil And Trouble *Manfred Mann* (HMV)	–	29	16
– Don't Let The Sun Catch You Crying *Gerry and The Pacemakers* (Columbia)	–	31	17
– Juliet *The Four Pennies* (Philips)	36	32	18

MAY 1964

2	9	16	23	30
1 World Without Love *Peter and Gordon* (Columbia)	4	5	12	–
2 Don't Throw Your Love Away *The Searchers* (Pye)	1	1	3	8
3 I Believe *The Bachelors* (Decca)	2	4	6	9
4 Can't Buy Me Love *The Beatles* (Parlophone)	7	13	15	–
5 My Boy Lollipop *Millie* (Fontana)	3	3	2	3
6 I Love You Because *Jim Reeves* (RCA)	10	8	10	12
7 Don't Let The Sun Catch You Crying *Gerry and The Pacemakers* (Columbia)	6	9	7	15
8 Move Over Darling *Doris Day* (CBS)	8	15	17	19
9 Everything's All Right *The Mojos* (Decca)	17	18	–	–
10 Mockingbird Hill *The Migil Five* (Pye)	12	14	18	–
11 Hubble Bubble Toil And Trouble *Manfred Mann* (HMV)	15	19	–	–
12 Juliet *The Four Pennies* (Philips)	5	2	1	2
13 Not Fade Away *The Rolling Stones* (Decca)	–	–	–	–
14 Tell Me When *The Applejacks* (Decca)	19	–	–	–
15 Walk On By *Dionne Warwick* (Pye)	9	11	11	11
16 Little Children *Billy J. Kramer and The Dakotas* (Parlophone)	–	–	–	–
17 Don't Turn Around *The Merseybeats* (Fontana)	13	16	16	16
18 Just One Look *The Hollies* (Parlophone)	–	–	–	–
19 A Little Lovin' *The Fourmost* (Parlophone)	11	10	8	6
20 Good Golly Miss Molly *The Swinging Blue Jeans* (HMV)	–	–	–	–
31 It's Over *Roy Orbison* (London)	14	6	5	4
30 Constantly *Cliff Richard* (Columbia)	16	7	9	5
28 If I Loved You *Richard Anthony* (Columbia)	18	20	19	–
38 I Will *Billy Fury* (Decca)	20	17	14	14
– You're My World *Cilla Black* (Parlophone)	30	12	4	1
– The Rise And Fall Of Flingel Bunt *The Shadows* (Columbia)	37	21	13	7
– No Particular Place To Go *Chuck Berry* (Pye)	42	26	20	10
– Someone, Someone *Brian Poole* (Decca)	49	34	26	13
– You're The One *Kathy Kirby* (Decca)	36	30	28	17
– Here I Go Again *The Hollies* (Parlophone)	–	–	46	18
36 Non Ho L'Eta Per Amarti *Gigliola Cinquetti* (Decca)	28	24	22	20

JUNE 1964

6	13	20	27
1 You're My World *Cilla Black* (Parlophone)	1	1	3
2 It's Over *Roy Orbison* (London)	2	2	1
3 Juliet *The Four Pennies* (Philips)	5	13	15
4 Constantly *Cliff Richard* (Columbia)	6	9	16
5 The Rise And Fall Of Flingel Bunt *The Shadows* (Columbia)	7	8	13
6 No Particular Place To Go *Chuck Berry* (Pye)	3	6	11

	13	20	27
6			
7 My Boy Lollipop *Millie* (Fontana)	15	–	–
8 Someone, Someone *Brian Poole* (Decca)	4	3	2
9 A Little Lovin' *The Fourmost* (Parlophone)	14	19	–
10 Walk On By *Dionne Warwick* (Pye)	13	17	19
11 Here I Go Again *The Hollies* (Parlophone)	8	4	7
12 My Guy *Mary Wells* (Stateside)	9	5	5
13 I Love You Because *Jim Reeves* (RCA)	12	15	14
14 I Believe *The Bachelors* (Decca)	–	–	–
15 Don't Throw Your Love Away *The Searchers* (Pye)	–	–	–
16 I Will *Billy Fury* (Decca)	20	–	–
17 Shout *Lulu and The Luvvers* (Decca)	10	7	9
18 Non Ho L'Eta Per Amartl *Gigliola Cinquetti* (Decca)	17	18	–
19 You're The One *Kathy Kirby* (Decca)	–	–	–
20 I Love You Baby *Freddie and The Dreamers* (Columbia)	16	20	–
21 Can't You See She's Mine *The Dave Clark Five* (Columbia)	11	11	10
37 Hello Dolly *Louis Armstrong* (London)	18	10	4
29 Ramona *The Bachelors* (Decca)	19	12	6
39 Nobody I Know *Peter and Gordon* (Columbia)	23	14	12
34 You're No Good *The Swinging Blue Jeans* (HMV)	25	16	8
32 Hold Me *P. J. Proby* (Decca)	31	22	17
41 Hello Dolly *Frankie Vaughan* (Philips)	28	26	18
45 Bamalama Bamaloo *Little Richard* (London)	29	25	20

JULY 1964

	11	18	25
4			
1 It's Over *Roy Orbison* (London)	5	7	10
2 Someone, Someone *Brian Poole* (Decca)	4	10	15
3 You're No Good *The Swinging Blue Jeans* (HMV)	7	8	14
4 Ramona *The Bachelors* (Decca)	6	12	18
5 Hold Me *P. J. Proby* (Decca)	3	5	7
6 House Of The Rising Sun *The Animals* (Columbia)	1	2	5
7 You're My World *Cilla Black* (Parlophone)	15	20	–
8 Hello Dolly *Louis Armstrong* (London)	9	13	17
9 My Guy *Mary Wells* (Stateside)	12	16	19
10 Nobody I Know *Peter and Gordon* (Columbia)	11	14	–
11 Can't You See She's Mine *The Dave Clark Five* (Columbia)	14	15	–
12 I Won't Forget You *Jim Reeves* (RCA)	8	4	4
13 Shout *Lulu and The Luvvers* (Decca)	17	19	–
14 Here I Go Again *The Hollies* (Parlophone)	16	–	–
15 The Rise And Fall Of Flingel Bunt *The Shadows* (Columbia)	19	–	–
16 I Love You Because *Jim Reeves* (RCA)	–	–	–
17 Kissin' Cousins *Elvis Presley* (RCA)	10	11	11
18 Hello Dolly *Frankie Vaughan* (Philips)	20	–	–
19 No Particular Place To Go *Chuck Berry* (Pye)	–	–	–
20 Like Dreamers Do *The Applejacks* (Decca)	–	–	–
25 It's All Over Now *The Rolling Stones* (Decca)	2	1	2
31 On The Beach *Cliff Richard* (Columbia)	13	9	8
42 I Just Don't Know What To Do With Myself *Dusty Springfield* (Philips)	18	6	3
– A Hard Day's Night *The Beatles* (Parlophone)	–	3	1
– Call Up The Groups *The Barron-Knights* (Columbia)	38	17	6
– Wishin' And Hopin' *The Merseybeats* (Fontana)	30	18	16
– Do Wah Diddy Diddy *Manfred Mann* (HMV)	–	30	9
– Tobacco Road *The Nashville Teens* (Decca)	48	26	12
– Someday We're Gonna Love Again *The Searchers* (Pye)	–	22	13
– I Get Around *The Beach Boys* (Capitol)	46	32	20

AUGUST 1964

1	8	15	22	29
1 A Hard Day's Night *The Beatles* (Parlophone)	1	2	2	5
2 It's All Over Now *The Rolling Stones* (Decca)	4	4	7	9
3 I Just Don't Know What To Do With Myself *Dusty Springfield* (Philips)	5	7	9	13
4 Call Up The Groups *The Barron-Knights* (Columbia)	3	3	5	10
5 Do Wah Diddy Diddy *Manfred Mann* (HMV)	2	1	1	2
6 Hold Me *P. J. Proby* (Decca)	13	18	–	–
7 House Of The Rising Sun *The Animals* (Columbia)	8	13	–	–
8 On The Beach *Cliff Richard* (Columbia)	7	9	11	15
9 I Won't Forget You *Jim Reeves* (RCA)	9	5	4	3
10 Tobacco Road *The Nashville Teens* (Decca)	6	6	6	6
11 I Get Around *The Beach Boys* (Capitol)	10	8	8	7
12 Someday We're Gonna Love Again *The Searchers* (Pye)	11	16	18	–
13 Wishin' And Hopin' *The Merseybeats* (Fontana)	14	15	17	–
14 It's Over *Roy Orbison* (London)	17	–	–	–
15 Kissin' Cousins *Elvis Presley* (RCA)	16	–	–	–
16 Someone, Someone *Brian Poole* (Decca)	20	–	–	–
17 You're No Good *The Swinging Blue Jeans* (HMV)	19	–	–	–
18 It's Only Make Believe *Billy Fury* (Decca)	12	10	12	17
19 Ramona *The Bachelors* (Decca)	–	–	–	–
20 Hello Dolly *Louis Armstrong* (London)	–	–	–	–
22 From A Window *Billy J. Kramer and The Dakotas* (Parlophone)	15	12	10	19
34 Have I The Right *The Honeycombs* (Pye)	18	11	3	1
25 I Found Out The Hard Way *The Four Pennies* (Philips)	23	14	14	18
– It's For You *Cilla Black* (Parlophone)	28	17	13	8
23 I Love You Because *Jim Reeves* (RCA)	26	19	16	14
46 You'll Never Get To Heaven *Dionne Warwick* (Pye)	25	20	–	–
– You Really Got Me *The Kinks* (Pye)	–	34	15	4
– As Tears Go By *Marianne Faithfull* (Decca)	–	27	19	16
41 The Crying Game *Dave Berry* (Decca)	41	21	20	12
– I Wouldn't Trade You For The World *The Bachelors* (Decca)	–	43	21	11
– Such A Night *Elvis Presley* (RCA)	–	–	31	20

SEPTEMBER 1964

4	11	18	25
1 Have I The Right *The Honeycombs* (Pye)	2	2	3
2 You Really Got Me *The Kinks* (Pye)	1	1	5
3 I Won't Forget You *Jim Reeves* (RCA)	3	4	7
4 Do Wah Diddy Diddy *Manfred Mann* (HMV)	6	8	15
5 The Crying Game *Dave Berry* (Decca)	5	6	10
6 A Hard Day's Night *The Beatles* (Parlophone)	10	15	19
7 It's For You *Cilla Black* (Parlophone)	11	18	–
8 I Wouldn't Trade You For The World *The Bachelors* (Decca)	4	7	6
9 I Get Around *The Beach Boys* (Capitol)	15	–	–
10 It's All Over Now *The Rolling Stones* (Decca)	17	20	–
11 Call Up The Groups *The Barron-Knights* (Columbia)	19	–	–
12 I Love You Because *Jim Reeves* (RCA)	14	11	14
13 Such A Night *Elvis Presley* (RCA)	13	14	18
14 Tobacco Road *The Nashville Teens* (Decca)	20	–	–
15 As Tears Go By *Marianne Faithfull* (Decca)	9	10	9
16 She's Not There *The Zombies* (Decca)	12	12	16
17 Rag Doll *The Four Seasons* (Philips)	8	5	2
18 I'm Into Something Good *Herman's Hermits* (Columbia)	7	3	1
19 The Wedding *Julie Rogers* (Mercury)	16	13	11

4		**11**	**18**	**25**
20	I Just Don't Know What To Do With Myself *Dusty Springfield* (Philips)	–	–	–
32	Where Did Our Love Go *The Supremes* (Stateside)	18	9	4
29	Everybody Loves Somebody *Dean Martin* (Reprise)	21	16	12
–	Oh Pretty Woman *Roy Orbison* (London)	36	17	8
39	Together *P. J. Proby* (Decca)	25	19	13
–	Is It True *Brenda Lee* (Brunswick)	30	23	17
–	I'm Crying *The Animals* (Columbia)	–	40	20

OCTOBER 1964

3		**10**	**17**	**24**	**31**
1	I'm Into Something Good *Herman's Hermits* (Columbia)	2	2	5	10
2	Rag Doll *The Four Seasons* (Philips)	4	5	12	16
3	Where Did Our Love Go *The Supremes* (Stateside)	3	3	4	5
4	Oh Pretty Woman *Roy Orbison* (London)	1	1	2	2
5	I Wouldn't Trade You For The World *The Bachelors* (Decca)	6	6	11	15
6	I Won't Forget You *Jim Reeves* (RCA)	7	10	14	17
7	The Wedding *Julie Rogers* (Mercury)	5	4	6	3
8	Have I The Right *The Honeycombs* (Pye)	13	18	–	–
9	As Tears Go By *Marianne Faithfull* (Decca)	12	15	19	–
10	You Really Got Me *The Kinks* (Pye)	16	20	–	–
11	Together *P. J. Proby* (Decca)	8	14	16	–
12	Everybody Loves Somebody *Dean Martin* (Reprise)	11	13	17	19
13	The Crying Game *Dave Berry* (Decca)	–	–	–	–
14	She's Not There *The Zombies* (Decca)	20	–	–	–
15	I'm Crying *The Animals* (Columbia)	10	8	9	14
16	When You Walk In The Room *The Searchers* (Pye)	9	7	3	4
17	I Love You Because *Jim Reeves* (RCA)	19	–	–	–
18	Is It True *Brenda Lee* (Brunswick)	18	–	–	–
19	Bread And Butter *The Newbeats* (Hickory)	15	19	–	–
20	We're Through *The Hollies* (Parlophone)	14	9	8	7
22	Walk Away *Matt Monro* (Parlophone)	17	12	7	6
–	(There's) Always Something There To Remind Me *Sandie Shaw* (Pye)	31	11	1	1
–	Twelfth Of Never *Cliff Richard* (Columbia)	30	16	13	8
31	How Soon *Henry Mancini* (RCA)	23	17	10	12
42	One Way Love *Cliff Bennett* (Parlophone)	29	23	15	9
–	Sha La La *Manfred Mann* (HMV)	–	43	18	11
–	Maybe I Know *Lesley Gore* (Mercury)	–	21	20	–
–	Baby Love *The Supremes* (Stateside)	–	–	24	13
–	He's In Town *The Rockin' Berries* (Piccadilly)	–	44	29	18
–	Um, Um, Um, Um, Um, Um *Wayne Fontana* (Fontana)	34	29	22	20

NOVEMBER 1964

7		**14**	**21**	**28**
1	(There's) Always Something There To Remind Me *Sandie Shaw* (Pye)	2	7	16
2	Oh Pretty Woman *Roy Orbison* (London)	1	4	8
3	The Wedding *Julie Rogers* (Mercury)	9	12	18
4	Walk Away *Matt Monro* (Parlophone)	4	8	14
5	Sha La La *Manfred Mann* (HMV)	3	5	11
6	When You Walk In The Room *The Searchers* (Pye)	11	15	–
7	Baby Love *The Supremes* (Stateside)	5	1	1
8	Twelfth Of Never *Cliff Richard* (Columbia)	13	18	–
9	Where Did Our Love Go *The Supremes* (Stateside)	16	–	–
10	We're Through *The Hollies* (Parlophone)	20	–	–

	14	21	28
11 How Soon *Henry Mancini* (RCA)	–	–	–
12 One Way Love *Cliff Bennett* (Parlophone)	14	–	–
13 Um, Um, Um, Um, Um, Um *Wayne Fontana* (Fontana)	8	6	5
14 He's In Town *The Rockin' Berries* (Piccadilly)	6	3	4
15 I'm Into Something Good *Herman's Hermits* (Columbia)	–	–	–
16 Google Eye *The Nashville Teens* (Decca)	10	13	–
17 Ain't That Lovin' You Baby *Elvis Presley* (RCA)	15	19	–
19 All Day And All Of The Night *The Kinks* (Pye)	7	2	2
19 I Won't Forget You *Jim Reeves* (RCA)	–	–	–
20 I Wouldn't Trade You For The World *The Bachelors* (Decca)	–	–	–
21 Tokyo Melody *Helmut Zacharias Orchestra* (Polydor)	12	9	12
29 Don't Bring Me Down *The Pretty Things* (Fontana)	17	10	13
26 Remember (Walkin' In The Sand) *The Shangri-Las* (Red Bird)	18	14	15
33 There's A Heartache Following Me *Jim Reeves* (RCA)	19	11	7
– I'm Gonna Be Strong *Gene Pitney* (Stateside)	34	16	6
28 Losing You *Dusty Springfield* (Philips)	22	17	10
– Downtown *Petula Clark* (Pye)	41	20	9
– Little Red Rooster *The Rolling Stones* (Decca)	–	24	3
30 Walk Tall *Val Doonican* (Decca)	25	23	17
– Pretty Paper *Roy Orbison* (London)	–	34	19
36 Black Girl *The Four Pennies* (Philips)	31	27	20

DECEMBER 1964

5	12	19	26
1 Little Red Rooster *The Rolling Stones* (Decca)	3	5	8
2 I'm Gonna Be Strong *Gene Pitney* (Stateside)	2	4	3
3 Baby Love *The Supremes* (Stateside)	8	10	15
4 Downtown *Petula Clark* (Pye)	4	2	2
5 All Day And All Of The Night *The Kinks* (Pye)	7	16	19
6 I Feel Fine *The Beatles* (Parlophone)	1	1	1
7 Um, Um, Um, Um, Um, Um *Wayne Fontana* (Fontana)	10	–	–
8 There's A Heartache Following Me *Jim Reeves* (RCA)	6	11	18
9 Losing You *Dusty Springfield* (Philips)	11	17	–
10 He's In Town *The Rocking Berries* (Pye)	13	–	–
11 Walk Tall *Val Doonican* (Decca)	5	3	4
12 Pretty Paper *Roy Orbison* (London)	9	6	6
13 Don't Bring Me Down *The Pretty Things* (Fontana)	17	–	–
14 Sha La La *Manfred Mann* (HMV)	–	–	–
15 Tokyo Melody *Helmut Zacharias Orchestra* (Polydor)	15	–	–
16 Oh Pretty Woman *Roy Orbison* (London)	–	–	–
17 I Understand *Freddie and The Dreamers* (Columbia)	12	7	5
18 Walk Away *Matt Monro* (Parlophone)	18	–	20
19 Show Me Girl *Herman's Hermits* (Columbia)	19	20	–
20 Black Girl *The Four Pennies* (Philips)	–	–	–
21 Message To Martha *Adam Faith* (Parlophone)	14	12	14
46 No Arms Could Ever Hold You *The Bachelors* (Decca)	16	8	7
– I Could Easily Fall *Cliff Richard* (Columbia)	20	9	9
44 Blue Christmas *Elvis Presley* (RCA)	26	13	11
– Somewhere *P. J. Proby* (Liberty)	30	14	10
30 Terry *Twinkle* (Decca)	24	15	12
– Girl Don't Come *Sandie Shaw* (Pye)	38	18	13
49 What Have They Done To The Rain *The Searchers* (Pye)	27	19	16
– Yeh, Yeh *Georgie Fame* (Columbia)	–	26	17

1964—BEST-SELLING SINGLES

1   I Love You Because *Jim Reeves* (RCA)
2   I Won't Forget You *Jim Reeves* (RCA)
3   It's Over *Roy Orbison* (London)
4   The Wedding *Julie Rogers* (Mercury)
5   Someone, Someone *Brian Poole* (Decca)
6   I Believe *The Bachelors* (Decca)
7   My Boy Lollipop *Millie* (Fontana)
8   It's All Over Now *The Rolling Stones* (Decca)
9   I Wouldn't Trade You For The World *The Bachelors* (Decca)
10 Oh Pretty Woman *Roy Orbison* (London)
11 Needles And Pins *The Searchers* (Pye)
12 Anyone Who Had A Heart *Cilla Black* (Parlophone)
13 A Hard Day's Night *The Beatles* (Parlophone)
14 Have I The Right *The Honeycombs* (Pye)
15 Do Wah Diddy Diddy *Manfred Mann* (HMV)
16 Diane *The Bachelors* (Decca)
17 You're My World *Cilla Black* (Parlophone)
18 I'm Into Something Good *Herman's Hermits* (Columbia)
19 I Think Of You *The Merseybeats* (Fontana)
20 Juliet *The Four Pennies* (Philips)

Album charts became valuable guides to the record industry and of interest to record buyers in the early part of the 1960s. From 1964 onwards album production grew rapidly and the leading albums from this period are recorded in the following listings.

1964—BEST-SELLING ALBUMS

1   West Side Story *Soundtrack of film*
2   With The Beatles *The Beatles*
3   The Rolling Stones *The Rolling Stones*
4   Please Please Me *The Beatles*
5   A Hard Day's Night *The Beatles*
6   In Dreams *Roy Orbison*
7   The Bachelors 16 Great Songs *The Bachelors*
8   Wonderful Life *Cliff Richard and The Shadows*
9   Stay With The Hollies *The Hollies*
10 Meet The Searchers *The Searchers*
11 How Do You Do It *Gerry and The Pacemakers*
12 Dance With The Shadows *The Shadows*
13 Moonlight And Roses *Jim Reeves*
14 Freddie And The Dreamers *Freddie and The Dreamers*
15 Gentleman Jim *Jim Reeves*
16 Shadows Greatest Hits *The Shadows*
17 Kissin' Cousins *Elvis Presley*
18 Born Free *Frank Ifield*
19 A Girl Called Dusty *Dusty Springfield*
20 It's The Searchers *The Searchers*

Every year since 1964 the industry trade paper has printed various interesting pieces of information, relating to that particular year, concerning artists and their success in chart terms. This information is printed here. Some years less information is given than others. The reason for this lies in lack of chart performance by artists in the category named.

A list of top artists for any one year is given from 1956, which is the first full year printed in this book. Data has been compiled from the Top Twenty; but, from the 1960s when a Top 50 chart came into being, information has been taken from that source.

1964–BEST-SELLING ARTISTS

Male Artists (Singles)

1 Jim Reeves
2 Roy Orbison
3 Cliff Richard
4 Elvis Presley
5 Gene Pitney
6 Billy Fury
7 P. J. Proby
8 Frank Ifield
9 Chuck Berry
10 Adam Faith

Female Arists (Singles)

1 Cilla Black
2 Brenda Lee
3 Dusty Springfield
4 Kathy Kirby
5 Dionne Warwick
6 Millie
7 Julie Rogers
8 Doris Day
9 Mary Wells

Only nine female artists accumulated enough points to qualify.

Groups (Male)

1 The Beatles
2 The Bachelors
3 The Searchers
4 The Rolling Stones
5 Manfred Mann
6 The Hollies
7 The Dave Clark Five
8 The Swinging Blue Jeans
9 Gerry and The Pacemakers
10 The Merseybeats
11 Brian Poole and The Tremeloes
12 The Shadows
13 The Four Pennies
14 The Animals
15 Billy J. Kramer and The Dakotas
16 Freddie and The Dreamers
17 Peter and Gordon
18 The Applejacks
19 The Fourmost
20 The Kinks

Groups (Female)

1 The Supremes
2 The Ronettes

Only two female groups accumulated enough points to qualify.

Best-Selling Singles Artists

1 Jim Reeves
2 The Beatles
3 The Bachelors
4 Roy Orbison
5 The Searchers
6 Cliff Richard
7 The Rolling Stones
8 Manfred Mann
9 The Hollies
10 The Dave Clark Five
11 Cilla Black
12 Brenda Lee
13 Dusty Springfield
14 Elvis Presley
15 The Swinging Blue Jeans
16 Gerry and The Pacemakers
17 The Merseybeats
18 Brian Poole and The Tremeloes
19 The Shadows
20 Gene Pitney

1965

1965 produced some exciting chart entries in its own right, even though 1963 and 1964 had provided two outstanding vintage pop years. The year had some classic records and saw the emergence of some new and exciting pop figures.

Many of the regulars such as Cliff Richard, The Beatles, The Rolling Stones, Elvis Presley and The Kinks accumulated hits, particularly the latter who had their finest year ever with no less than five Top Ten hits.

Not all previous chart regulars stayed the pace. There were notable absences from the Top Twenty of such stars as Freddie and The Dreamers, Billy Fury and Adam Faith. Fury had accumulated 19 hits during his career, while Faith had managed 16. Frank Ifield disappeared, so too Brenda Lee. Brian Poole and The Tremeloes just managed to remain in the charts with one hit only, before the group split up. It was the same story for Billy J. Kramer and The Dakotas, whose swan-song was 'Trains And Boats And Planes'.

The new names in the Top Twenty included The Who, heralded as a pop art group, The Yardbirds, The Moody Blues, Bob Dylan, Donovan, The Righteous Brothers, The Seekers, The Walker Brothers and Them, with Van Morrison as their lead singer.

There were the usual one-hit wonders, some of whom recorded songs which have become classics in pop history. Such was the case of Barry McGuire with 'Eve of Destruction'; 'Gettin' Mighty Crowded' from Betty Everett; 'She's About A Mover' by The Sir Douglas Quintet; The Shangri-Las with 'Leader Of The Pack'; and Dobie Gray's 'In Crowd'.

Beatle records remained in the charts for 29 weeks altogether, while The Kinks came a close second with a 28-week chart residency, and The Rolling Stones' records remained in the charts for a total of 27 weeks. These three top groups were ousted from their Number One positions at various times by artists such as The Righteous Brothers whose song, 'You've Lost That Loving Feeling', had a chart battle with a cover version by Cilla Black. A hit was achieved by the ballad singer Ken Dodd, whose record 'Tears' proved to be the single which reached the highest rating in 1965, and it stayed a staggering 21 weeks in the Top Twenty – a week longer than the chart residency achieved by 'Telstar' from The Tornados in 1962.

More sweet pop sounds came from The Seekers, who took the Number One spot with 'I'll Never Find Another You'. The Shadows did well with five hits during the year, but then finished their chart run with 'War Lord', although they were still voted the top instrumental group in a pop poll. However, they re-emerged in 1974 as a chart force, with vocals added to their distinctive sound.

Bob Dylan entered the British charts in April with 'The Times They Are A-Changin' ', which was quickly followed by 'Subterranean Homesick Blues', 'Like A Rolling Stone' and 'Positively Fourth Street'. Britain's answer to Dylan was in the form of Donovan, whose song 'Catch The Wind' made the charts. Donovan soon built his own fan following, but his music and lyrics seemed rather lightweight when compared to those of the mighty Mr Zimmerman.

Dylan's ex-girlfriend Joan Baez also made the 1965 charts with 'There But For Fortune' and she also entered the Top Fifty with the Dylan composition 'It's All Over Now Baby Blue'.

1965 saw the chart debut of a Cambridge University undergraduate, Jonathan King, with 'Everyone's Gone To The Moon'. He also wrote 'It's Good News Week' for Hedgehoppers Anonymous.

There was hope for the newcomers to the charts such as Bob Dylan, The Yardbirds, Donovan and The Walker Brothers, who all looked to 1966 with expectancy, but for several long-established chart artists, there was nothing but gloom awaiting them in 1966.

JANUARY 1965

2		9	16	23	30
1	I Feel Fine *The Beatles* (Parlophone)	1	2	7	13
2	Downtown *Petula Clark* (Pye)	3	8	10	16
3	Walk Tall *Val Doonican* (Decca)	5	7	9	15
4	I'm Gonna Be Strong *Gene Pitney* (Stateside)	6	12	15	–
5	I Understand *Freddie and The Dreamers* (Columbia)	12	14	18	–
6	I Could Easily Fall *Cliff Richard* (Columbia)	9	11	13	18
7	Yeh, Yeh *Georgie Fame* (Columbia)	2	1	1	4
8	No Arms Could Ever Hold You *The Bachelors* (Decca)	11	13	16	–
9	Somewhere *P. J. Proby* (Liberty)	8	6	6	14
10	Terry *Twinkle* (Decca)	4	4	4	7
11	Girl Don't Come *Sandie Shaw* (Pye)	7	5	3	8
12	Message To Martha *Adam Faith* (Parlophone)	15	16	–	–
13	Pretty Paper *Roy Orbison* (London)	–	–	–	–
14	Little Red Rooster *The Rolling Stones* (Decca)	16	18	–	–
15	Blue Christmas *Elvis Presley* (RCA)	–	–	–	–
16	What Have They Done To The Rain *The Searchers* (Pye)	13	15	17	–
17	Cast Your Fate To The Winds *Sounds Orchestral* (Piccadilly)	17	10	5	10
18	Baby Love *The Supremes* (Stateside)	–	–	–	–
19	Go Now! *The Moody Blues* (Decca)	10	3	2	1
20	There's A Heartache Following Me *Jim Reeves* (RCA)	18	20	–	–
22	Ferry 'Cross The Mersey *Gerry and The Pacemakers* (Columbia)	14	9	8	9
24	Genie With The Light Brown Lamp *The Shadows* (Columbia)	20	17	–	–
–	Baby Please Don't Go *Them* (Decca)	26	19	11	11
–	You've Lost That Loving Feeling *Cilla Black* (Parlophone)	–	28	12	2
–	Come Tomorrow *Manfred Mann* (HMV)	–	26	14	5
–	Keep Searchin' *Del Shannon* (Stateside)	–	30	19	12
–	You've Lost That Loving Feeling *The Righteous Brothers* (London)	–	35	20	3
–	Tired Of Waiting For You *The Kinks* (Pye)	–	–	31	6
–	Three Bells *Brian Poole and The Tremeloes* (Decca)	–	–	21	17
–	I'll Never Find Another You *The Seekers* (Columbia)	48	33	32	19
–	Leader Of The Pack *The Shangri-Las* (Red Bird)	–	42	27	20
–	All Day And All Of The Night *The Kinks* (Pye)	19	–	–	–

FEBRUARY 1965

6		13	20	27
1	You've Lost That Loving Feeling *The Righteous Brothers* (London)	1	3	4
2	Tired Of Waiting For You *The Kinks* (Pye)	2	1	5
3	Go Now! *The Moody Blues* (Decca)	4	10	18
4	Come Tomorrow *Manfred Mann* (HMV)	6	8	16
5	You've Lost That Loving Feeling *Cilla Black* (Parlophone)	9	13	–
6	Keep Searchin' *Del Shannon* (Stateside)	3	4	6
7	Cast Your Fate To The Winds *Sounds Orchestral* (Piccadilly)	8	12	19
8	Yeh, Yeh *Georgie Fame* (Columbia)	15	–	–
9	Girl Don't Come *Sandie Shaw* (Pye)	18	–	–
10	Terry *Twinkle* (Decca)	17	–	–
11	Baby Please Don't Go *Them* (Decca)	10	16	–
12	Ferry 'Cross The Mersey *Gerry and The Pacemakers* (Columbia)	12	18	–
13	The Special Years *Val Doonican* (Decca)	7	7	7
14	I'll Never Find Another You *The Seekers* (Columbia)	5	2	1

6		13	20	27
15 Somewhere *P. J. Proby* (Liberty)		–	–	–
16 I'm Lost Without You *Billy Fury* (Decca)		16	20	–
17 Three Bells *Brian Poole and The Tremeloes* (Decca)		–	–	–
18 Leader Of The Pack *The Shangri-Las* (Red Bird)		11	14	–
19 I Feel Fine *The Beatles* (Parlophone)		–	–	–
20 Downtown *Petula Clark* (Pye)		–	–	–
33 Don't Let Me Be Misunderstood *The Animals* (Columbia)		13	6	3
27 Game Of Love *Wayne Fontana* (Fontana)		14	5	2
39 Funny How Love Can Be *The Ivy League* (Piccadilly)		19	9	9
41 It Hurts So Much *Jim Reeves* (RCA)		20	11	8
25 Yes I Will *The Hollies* (Parlophone)		22	15	12
– Goodnight *Roy Orbison* (London)		36	17	14
– It's Not Unusual *Tom Jones* (Decca)		39	19	10
– I Must Be Seeing Things *Gene Pitney* (Stateside)		–	24	11
– Silhouettes *Herman's Hermits* (Columbia)		–	41	13
– Come And Stay With Me *Marianne Faithfull* (Decca)		–	26	15
– I'll Stop At Nothing *Sandie Shaw* (Pye)		–	44	17
– Mary Anne *The Shadows* (Columbia)		35	25	20

MARCH 1965

6		13	20	27
1 I'll Never Find Another You *The Seekers* (Columbia)		2	4	6
2 It's Not Unusual *Tom Jones* (Decca)		1	2	2
3 Game Of Love *Wayne Fontana* (Fontana)		5	10	14
4 Silhouettes *Herman's Hermits* (Columbia)		3	3	3
5 Don't Let Me Be Misunderstood *The Animals* (Columbia)		8	12	19
6 I Must Be Seeing Things *Gene Pitney* (Stateside)		9	7	9
7 The Special Years *Val Doonican* (Decca)		12	15	16
8 Funny How Love Can Be *The Ivy League* (Piccadilly)		11	17	–
9 Come And Stay With Me *Marianne Faithfull* (Decca)		7	5	4
10 Tired Of Waiting For You *The Kinks* (Pye)		15	–	–
11 I'll Stop At Nothing *Sandie Shaw* (Pye)		4	8	7
12 It Hurts So Much *Jim Reeves* (RCA)		17	16	–
13 You've Lost That Loving Feeling *The Righteous Brothers* (London)		–	–	–
14 Yes I Will *The Hollies* (Parlophone)		10	9	11
15 Goodnight *Roy Orbison* (London)		14	14	–
16 Keep Searchin' *Del Shannon* (Stateside)		20	–	–
17 Mary Anne *The Shadows* (Columbia)		18	20	–
18 I Apologise *P. J. Proby* (Liberty)		16	11	12
19 Come Tomorrow *Manfred Mann* (HMV)		–	–	–
20 Cast Your Fate To The Winds *Sounds Orchestral* (Piccadilly)		–	–	–
31 The Last Time *The Rolling Stones* (Decca)		6	1	1
44 Goodbye My Love *The Searchers* (Pye)		13	6	5
21 Honey I Need *The Pretty Things* (Fontana)		19	13	18
35 Concrete And Clay *Unit 4 Plus 2* (Decca)		27	18	8
– Do The Clam *Elvis Presley* (RCA)		32	19	20
– The Minute You're Gone *Cliff Richard* (Columbia)		38	26	10
– For Your Love *The Yardbirds* (Columbia)		–	32	13
33 I Can't Explain *The Who* (Brunswick)		26	23	15
– I Know A Place *Petula Clark* (Pye)		30	21	17

3		10	17	24
1	The Last Time *The Rolling Stones* (Decca)	2	9	14
2	Concrete And Clay *Unit 4 Plus 2* (Decca)	1	3	13
3	It's Not Unusual *Tom Jones* (Decca)	7	18	–
4	Goodbye My Love *The Searchers* (Pye)	11	–	–
5	For Your Love *The Yardbirds* (Columbia)	3	2	4
6	The Minute You're Gone *Cliff Richard* (Columbia)	4	1	3
7	Catch The Wind *Donovan* (Pye)	5	4	5
8	Come And Stay With Me *Marianne Faithfull* (Decca)	8	–	–
9	Silhouettes *Herman's Hermits* (Columbia)	9	14	20
10	I'll Never Find Another You *The Seekers* (Columbia)	15	–	–
11	I'll Stop At Nothing *Sandie Shaw* (Pye)	20	–	–
12	I Can't Explain *The Who* (Brunswick)	10	8	10
13	I Must Be Seeing Things *Gene Pitney* (Stateside)	–	–	–
14	Here Comes The Night *Them* (Decca)	6	5	2
15	Times They Are A-Changin' *Bob Dylan* (CBS)	13	7	7
16	You're Breaking My Heart *Keeley Smith* (Reprise)	14	16	16
17	Yes I Will *The Hollies* (Parlophone)	–	–	–
18	I Know A Place *Petula Clark* (Pye)	–	–	–
19	I'll Be There *Gerry and The Pacemakers* (Columbia)	16	12	17
20	I Apologise *P. J. Proby* (Liberty)	–	–	–
23	Stop In The Name Of Love *The Supremes* (Tamla Motown)	12	6	6
26	Little Things *Dave Berry* (Decca)	17	11	8
29	Everybody's Gonna Be Happy *The Kinks* (Pye)	18	15	11
32	Pop Go The Workers *The Barron-Knights* (Columbia)	19	13	15
–	Ticket To Ride *The Beatles* (Parlophone)	–	10	1
–	Bring It On Home To Me *The Animals* (Columbia)	34	17	12
33	All Over The World *Francoise Hardy* (Pye)	28	19	19
35	King Of The Road *Roger Miller* (Philips)	26	20	9
–	True Love Ways *Peter and Gordon* (Columbia)	39	24	18

1		8	15	22	29
1	Ticket To Ride *The Beatles* (Parlophone)	1	2	3	7
2	The Minute You're Gone *Cliff Richard* (Columbia)	7	9	17	–
3	Here Comes The Night *Them* (Decca)	3	6	19	–
4	King Of The Road *Roger Miller* (Philips)	2	1	4	5
5	Pop Go The Workers *The Barron-Knights* (Columbia)	6	8	10	15
6	Little Things *Dave Berry* (Decca)	10	15	–	–
7	Bring It On Home To Me *The Animals* (Columbia)	8	7	12	16
8	Concrete And Clay *Unit 4 Plus 2* (Decca)	13	19	–	–
9	Catch The Wind *Donovan* (Pye)	9	14	16	–
10	Stop In The Name Of Love *The Supremes* (Tamla Motown)	12	16	–	–
11	For Your Love *The Yardbirds* (Columbia)	18	–	–	–
12	The Last Time *The Rolling Stones* (Decca)	19	–	–	–
13	Times They Are A-Changin' *Bob Dylan* (CBS)	16	20	–	–
14	True Love Ways *Peter and Gordon* (Columbia)	5	4	2	3
15	World Of Our Own *The Seekers* (Columbia)	4	3	5	4
16	You're Breaking My Heart *Keeley Smith* (Reprise)	–	–	–	–
17	Oh No Not My Baby *Manfred Mann* (HMV)	11	12	11	13
18	I Can't Explain *The Who* (Brunswick)	–	–	–	–
19	Wonderful World *Herman's Hermits* (Columbia)	14	11	7	11
20	All Over The World *Francoise Hardy* (Pye)	20	–	18	17
25	Where Are You Now My Love *Jackie Trent* (Pye)	15	5	1	2
36	Subterranean Homesick Blues *Bob Dylan* (CBS)	17	10	9	9
–	This Little Bird *Marianne Faithfull* (Decca)	39	13	6	6
32	I've Been Wrong Before *Cilla Black* (Parlophone)	24	17	20	–

	1	8	15	22	29
31 Not Until The Next Time *Jim Reeves* (RCA)	31	27	18	15	14
– Long Live Love *Sandie Shaw* (Pye)	–	–	33	8	1
– Poor Man's Son *The Rocking Berries* (Columbia)	–	–	28	13	8
– The Clapping Song *Shirley Ellis* (London)	–	40	25	14	10
– Trains And Boats And Planes *Burt Bacharach* (London)	–	–	–	27	12
– Marie *The Bachelors* (Decca)	–	–	–	39	18
– The Price Of Love *The Everly Brothers* (Warner Bros.)	–	–	–	29	19
– Trains And Boats And Planes *Billy J. Kramer* (Parlophone)	–	–	–	35	20

JUNE 1965

	5	12	19	26
1 Long Live Love *Sandie Shaw* (Pye)	1	1	3	7
2 Where Are You Now My Love *Jackie Trent* (Pye)	2	9	18	–
3 World Of Our Own *The Seekers* (Columbia)	3	3	8	12
4 True Love Ways *Peter and Gordon* (Columbia)	4	13	15	18
5 Poor Man's Son *The Rocking Berries* (Columbia)	5	5	6	8
6 This Little Bird *Marianne Faithfull* (Decca)	6	8	12	15
7 The Clapping Song *Shirley Ellis* (London)	7	7	7	6
8 Trains And Boats And Planes *Burt Bacharach* (London)	8	6	5	4
9 King Of The Road *Roger Miller* (Philips)	9	16	–	–
10 Ticket To Ride *The Beatles* (Parlophone)	10	14	–	–
11 The Price Of Love *The Everly Brothers* (Warner Bros.)	11	4	2	3
12 Subterranean Homesick Blues *Bob Dylan* (CBS)	12	20	–	–
13 Not Until The Next Time *Jim Reeves* (RCA)	13	18	–	–
14 Crying In The Chapel *Elvis Presley* (RCA)	14	2	1	2
15 Wonderful World *Herman's Hermits* (Columbia)	15	19	–	–
16 All Over The World *Francoise Hardy* (Pye)	16	–	–	–
17 Marie *The Bachelors* (Decca)	17	11	9	11
18 You've Never Been In Love Like This Before *Unit 4 Plus 2* (Decca)	18	15	16	14
19 Trains And Boats And Planes *Billy J. Kramer* (Parlophone)	19	12	14	–
20 Bring It On Home To Me *The Animals* (Columbia)	20	–	–	–
23 I'm Alive *The Hollies* (Parlophone)	23	10	4	1
22 Set Me Free *The Kinks* (Pye)	22	17	13	9
32 Colours *Donovan* (Pye)	32	21	10	5
26 Anyway, Anyhow, Anywhere *The Who* (Brunswick)	26	24	11	13
– Looking Through The Eyes Of Love *Gene Pitney* (Stateside)	–	28	17	10
21 Come Home *The Dave Clark Five* (Columbia)	21	22	19	16
28 Love Her *The Walker Brothers* (Philips)	28	26	20	–
– On My Word *Cliff Richard* (Columbia)	–	32	21	17
– Stingray *The Shadows* (Columbia)	–	27	23	19
– Heart Full Of Soul *The Yardbirds* (Columbia)	–	–	32	20

JULY 1965

	3	10	17	24	31
1 Crying In The Chapel *Elvis Presley* (RCA)	1	2	5	6	14
2 I'm Alive *The Hollies* (Parlophone)	2	1	1	4	7
3 The Price Of Love *The Everly Brothers* (Warner Bros.)	3	6	9	15	20
4 Colours *Donovan* (Pye)	4	7	11	12	–
5 Looking Through The Eyes Of Love *Gene Pitney* (Stateside)	5	3	4	7	13
6 Trains And Boats And Planes *Burt Bacharach* (London)	6	12	–	–	–
7 Long Live Love *Sandie Shaw* (Pye)	7	15	17	–	–
8 The Clapping Song *Shirley Ellis* (London)	8	16	–	–	–
9 Set Me Free *The Kinks* (Pye)	9	14	20	–	–
10 Anyway, Anyhow, Anywhere *The Who* (Brunswick)	10	11	12	14	–
11 Heart Full Of Soul *The Yardbirds* (Columbia)	11	4	2	2	2

3	10	17	24	31
12 On My Word *Cliff Richard* (Columbia)	17	13	20	–
13 Leave A Little Love *Lulu* (Decca)	9	8	8	15
14 World Of Our Own *The Seekers* (Columbia)	18	–	–	–
15 To Know You Is To Love You *Peter and Gordon* (Columbia)	5	6	5	9
16 Marie *The Bachelors* (Decca)	–	–	–	–
17 Poor Man's Son *The Rocking Berries* (Piccadilly)	–	–	–	–
18 You've Never Been In Love Like This Before *Unit 4 Plus 2* (Decca)	–	–	–	–
19 Mr Tambourine Man *The Byrds* (CBS)	8	3	1	1
20 Come Home *The Dave Clark Five* (Columbia)	–	–	–	–
21 Tossing And Turning *The Ivy League* (Piccadilly)	10	7	3	4
23 In The Middle Of Nowhere *Dusty Springfield* (Philips)	13	10	9	8
25 She's About A Mover *Sir Douglas Quintet* (London)	19	15	16	–
28 Just A Little Bit Too Late *Wayne Fontana* (Fontana)	20	–	–	–
29 Wooly Bully *Sam The Sham and The Pharaohs* (MGM)	23	14	13	12
– There But For Fortune *Joan Baez* (Fontana)	32	16	11	10
– You've Got Your Troubles *The Fortunes* (Decca)	37	18	10	3
36 Goodbyee *Peter Cook and Dudley Moore* (Decca)	28	19	19	18
– We've Got To Get Out Of This Place *The Animals* (Columbia)	–	41	17	6
– He's Got No Love *The Searchers* (Pye)	48	31	18	16
– Catch Us If You Can *The Dave Clark Five* (Columbia)	–	38	23	11
– With These Hands *Tom Jones* (Decca)	49	33	21	17
– Let The Water Run Down *P. J. Proby* (Liberty)	33	24	22	19
– Help *The Beatles* (Parlophone)	–	–	–	5

AUGUST 1965

7	14	21	28
1 Help *The Beatles* (Parlophone)	1	1	2
2 Mr Tambourine Man *The Byrds* (CBS)	4	8	14
3 You've Got Your Troubles *The Fortunes* (Decca)	3	2	8
4 We've Got To Get Out Of This Place *The Animals* (Columbia)	2	3	6
5 Tossing And Turning *The Ivy League* (Piccadilly)	6	13	20
6 Heart Full Of Soul *The Yardbirds* (Columbia)	11	20	–
7 Catch Us If You Can *The Dave Clark Five* (Columbia)	5	7	9
8 There But For Fortune *Joan Baez* (Fontana)	8	12	17
9 In The Middle Of Nowhere *Dusty Springfield* (Philips)	16	–	–
10 I'm Alive *The Hollies* (Parlophone)	18	–	–
11 Wooly Bully *Sam The Sham and The Pharaohs* (MGM)	15	18	–
12 He's Got No Love *The Searchers* (Pye)	17	19	–
13 With These Hands *Tom Jones* (Decca)	13	15	–
14 Crying In The Chapel *Elvis Presley* (RCA)	19	–	–
15 Summer Nights *Marianne Faithfull* (Decca)	10	11	13
16 To Know You Is To Love You *Peter and Gordon* (Columbia)	–	–	–
17 Looking Through The Eyes Of Love *Gene Pitney* (Stateside)	–	–	–
18 Everyone's Gone To The Moon *Jonathan King* (Decca)	7	6	4
19 A Walk In The Black Forest *Horst Jankowski* (Mercury)	14	5	3
20 In Thoughts Of You *Billy Fury* (Decca)	9	10	11
22 Zorba's Dance *Marcello Minerbi* (Durium)	12	9	7
40 Don't Make My Baby Blue *The Shadows* (Columbia)	20	17	10
– I Got You Babe *Sonny and Cher* (Atlantic)	30	4	1
– All I Really Want To Do *The Byrds* (CBS)	26	14	5
39 See My Friend *The Kinks* (Pye)	24	16	12
– Satisfaction *The Rolling Stones* (Decca)	–	–	15
– What's New Pussycat *Tom Jones* (Decca)	47	21	16
– Make It Easy On Yourself *The Walker Brothers* (Philips)	–	31	18
– Like A Rolling Stone *Bob Dylan* (CBS)	–	42	19

SEPTEMBER 1965

4		11	18	25
1	I Got You Babe *Sonny and Cher* (Atlantic)	2	2	4
2	Help *The Beatles* (Parlophone)	5	8	13
3	Satisfaction *The Rolling Stones* (Decca)	1	1	2
4	All I Really Want To Do *The Byrds* (CBS)	7	12	–
5	A Walk In The Black Forest *Horst Jankowski* (Mercury)	4	6	7
6	Zorba's Dance *Marcello Minerbi* (Durium)	8	10	8
7	Everyone's Gone To The Moon *Jonathan King* (Decca)	15	19	–
8	Make It Easy On Yourself *The Walker Brothers* (Philips)	3	3	1
9	Like A Rolling Stone *Bob Dylan* (CBS)	6	4	6
10	See My Friend *The Kinks* (Pye)	18	–	–
11	What's New Pussycat *Tom Jones* (Decca)	12	14	20
12	We've Got To Get Out Of This Place *The Animals* (Columbia)	20	–	–
13	All I Really Want To Do *Cher* (Liberty)	9	11	17
14	You've Got Your Troubles *The Fortunes* (Decca)	19	–	–
15	Don't Make My Baby Blue *The Shadows* (Columbia)	17	–	–
16	In Thoughts Of You *Billy Fury* (Decca)	–	–	–
17	Catch Us If You Can *The Dave Clark Five* (Columbia)	–	–	–
18	That's The Way *The Honeycombs* (Pye)	13	13	12
19	Laugh At Me *Sonny* (Atlantic)	10	9	10
20	Summer Nights *Marianne Faithfull* (Decca)	–	–	–
32	Look Through Any Window *The Hollies* (Parlophone)	11	5	5
21	Unchained Melody *The Righteous Brothers* (London)	14	15	19
37	Tears *Ken Dodd* (Columbia)	16	7	3
30	Just A Little Bit Better *Herman's Hermits* (Columbia)	21	16	15
28	Il Silenzio *Nini Rosso* (Durium)	23	17	14
–	Eve Of Destruction *Barry McGuire* (RCA)	39	18	9
50	Hang On Sloopy *The McCoys* (Immediate)	29	20	16
–	If You Gotta Go, Go Now *Manfred Mann* (HMV)	–	37	11
–	Almost There *Andy Williams* (CBS)	–	27	18

OCTOBER 1965

2		9	16	23	30
1	Tears *Ken Dodd* (Columbia)	1	1	1	1
2	Make It Easy On Yourself *The Walker Brothers* (Philips)	3	6	7	15
3	Satisfaction *The Rolling Stones* (Decca)	8	10	15	20
4	Look Through Any Window *The Hollies* (Parlophone)	7	7	14	19
5	If You Gotta Go, Go Now *Manfred Mann* (HMV)	2	3	3	7
6	Eve Of Destruction *Barry McGuire* (RCA)	4	4	4	3
7	I Got You Babe *Sonny and Cher* (Atlantic)	14	15	20	–
8	Like A Rolling Stone *Bob Dylan* (CBS)	10	16	–	–
9	A Walk In The Black Forest *Horst Jankowski* (Mercury)	13	12	16	–
10	Il Silenzio *Nini Rosso* (Durium)	9	8	11	14
11	Hang On Sloopy *The McCoys* (Immediate)	6	5	5	8
12	Almost There *Andy Williams* (CBS)	5	2	2	2
13	That's The Way *The Honeycombs* (Pye)	16	18	–	–
14	Laugh At Me *Sonny* (Atlantic)	20	–	–	–
15	Just A Little Bit Better *Herman's Hermits* (Columbia)	17	19	–	–
16	Zorba's Dance *Marcello Minerbi* (Durium)	18	20	–	–
17	Baby Don't Go *Sonny and Cher* (Atlantic)	11	11	13	16
18	Help *The Beatles* (Parlophone)	–	–	–	–
19	Whatcha Gonna Do About It *The Small Faces* (Decca)	15	14	19	18
20	All I Really Want To Do *Cher* (Liberty)	–	–	–	–
23	Message Understood *Sandie Shaw* (Pye)	12	9	6	12
22	Some Of Your Lovin' *Dusty Springfield* (Philips)	19	13	8	11
31	In The Midnight Hour *Wilson Pickett* (Atlantic)	22	17	12	13
44	It's Good News Week *Hedgehoppers Anonymous* (Decca)	31	21	10	6

2

	9	16	23	30
– Evil Hearted You/Still I'm Sad *The Yardbirds* (Columbia)	–	22	9	4
– Here It Comes Again *The Fortunes* (Decca)	45	29	17	9
– Yesterday Man *Chris Andrews* (Decca)	44	31	18	5
– Get Off Of My Cloud *The Rolling Stones* (Decca)	–	–	–	17
– Yesterday *Matt Monro* (Parlophone)	–	–	26	10

NOVEMBER 1965

6

	13	20	27
1 Get Off Of My Cloud *The Rolling Stones* (Decca)	1	1	3
2 Tears *Ken Dodd* (Columbia)	2	4	5
3 Evil Hearted You/Still I'm Sad *The Yardbirds* (Columbia)	5	9	14
4 Yesterday Man *Chris Andrews* (Decca)	3	3	6
5 It's Good News Week *Hedgehoppers Anonymous* (Decca)	6	12	17
6 Here It Comes Again *The Fortunes* (Decca)	4	8	9
7 Almost There *Andy Williams* (CBS)	9	13	16
8 Yesterday *Matt Monro* (Parlophone)	8	11	13
9 Eve Of Destruction *Barry McGuire* (RCA)	13	17	–
10 It's My Life *The Animals* (Columbia)	7	7	7
11 Hang On Sloopy *The McCoys* (Immediate)	16	–	–
12 If You Gotta Go, Go Now *Manfred Mann* (HMV)	17	–	–
13 The Carnival Is Over *The Seekers* (Columbia)	10	2	1
14 Love Is Strange *The Everly Brothers* (Warner Bros.)	11	14	15
15 Positively 4th Street *Bob Dylan* (CBS)	12	10	10
16 Some Of Your Lovin' *Dusty Springfield* (Philips)	18	–	–
17 But You're Mine *Sonny and Cher* (Atlantic)	–	20	–
18 In The Midnight Hour *Wilson Pickett* (Atlantic)	–	–	–
19 Message Understood *Sandie Shaw* (Pye)	–	–	–
20 Until It's Time For You To Go *The Four Pennies* (Philips)	20	19	–
33 My Generation *The Who* (Brunswick)	14	5	2
31 1-2-3 *Len Barry* (Brunswick)	15	6	4
22 Baby I'm Yours *Peter and Gordon* (Columbia)	19	–	–
39 A Lover's Concerto *The Toys* (Stateside)	23	15	11
48 Wind Me Up *Cliff Richard* (Columbia)	29	16	8
46 Princess In Rags *Gene Pitney* (Stateside)	31	18	12
– Tell Me Why *Elvis Presley* (RCA)	40	22	18
– The River *Ken Dodd* (Columbia)	–	37	19
– Don't Bring Me Your Heartaches *Paul and Barry Ryan* (Decca)	38	26	20

DECEMBER 1965

4

	11	18	25
1 The Carnival Is Over *The Seekers* (Columbia)	1	2	4
2 My Generation *The Who* (Brunswick)	3	5	7
3 1-2-3 *Len Barry* (Brunswick)	6	4	8
4 Get Off Of My Cloud *The Rolling Stones* (Decca)	9	16	–
5 A Lover's Concerto *The Toys* (Stateside)	5	9	9
6 Tears *Ken Dodd* (Columbia)	8	7	5
7 Wind Me Up *Cliff Richard* (Columbia)	4	3	2
8 Positively 4th Street *Bob Dylan* (CBS)	11	15	17
9 Princess In Rags *Gene Pitney* (Stateside)	10	12	16
10 Yesterday Man *Chris Andrews* (Decca)	19	17	20
11 The River *Ken Dodd* (Columbia)	7	6	3
12 It's My Life *The Animals* (Columbia)	14	–	–
13 Don't Bring Me Your Heartaches *Paul and Barry Ryan* (Decca)	15	18	–
14 Maria *P. J. Proby* (Liberty)	12	8	12
15 Tell Me Why *Elvis Presley* (RCA)	17	20	–
16 Yesterday *Matt Monro* (Parlophone)	20	–	–
17 Is It Really Over *Jim Reeves* (RCA)	–	19	–

4

		11	**18**	**25**
18 Here It Comes Again *The Fortunes* (Decca)		–	–	–
19 Crawlin' Back *Roy Orbison* (London)		–	–	–
20 Let's Hang On *The Four Seasons* (Philips)		16	13	10
– Day Tripper/We Can Work It Out *The Beatles* (Parlophone)		2	1	1
38 My Ship Is Coming In *The Walker Brothers* (Philips)		13	10	6
33 Rescue Me *Fontella Bass* (Chess)		18	11	11
32 To Whom It Concerns *Chris Andrews* (Decca)		21	14	13
34 Till The End Of The Day *The Kinks* (Pye)		26	23	14
48 Keep On Runnin' *The Spencer Davis Group* (Fontana)		30	22	15
39 War Lord *The Shadows* (Columbia)		32	27	18
– Merrie Gentle Pops *The Barron-Knights* (Columbia)		–	36	19

1965–BEST-SELLING SINGLES

1 I'll Never Find Another You *The Seekers* (Columbia)
2 Tears *Ken Dodd* (Columbia)
3 A Walk In The Black Forest *Horst Jankowski* (Mercury)
4 World Of Our Own *The Seekers* (Columbia)
5 Crying In The Chapel *Elvis Presley* (RCA)
6 Help *The Beatles* (Parlophone)
7 I'm Alive *The Hollies* (Parlophone)
8 Zorba's Dance *Marcello Minerbi* (Durium)
9 King Of The Road *Roger Miller* (Philips)
10 The Minute You're Gone *Cliff Richard* (Columbia)
11 Tambourine Man *The Byrds* (CBS)
12 Eve Of Destruction *Barry McGuire* (RCA)
13 The Clapping Song *Shirley Ellis* (London)
14 Long Live Love *Sandie Shaw* (Pye)
15 True Love Ways *Peter and Gordon* (Columbia)
16 It's Not Unusual *Tom Jones* (Decca)
16 I Got You Babe *Sonny and Cher* (Atlantic)
18 Cast Your Fate To The Winds *Sounds Orchestral* (Piccadilly)
18 Almost There *Andy Williams* (CBS)
20 The Price Of Love *The Everly Brothers* (Warner Bros.)

1965—BEST-SELLING ALBUMS

1 Beatles For Sale *The Beatles*
2 Mary Poppins *Soundtrack of film*
3 Sound Of Music *Soundtrack of film*
4 Freewheelin' *Bob Dylan*
5 Rolling Stones Vol. II *The Rolling Stones*
6 Bringing It All Back Home *Bob Dylan*
7 13 Lucky Shades Of Val Doonican *Val Doonican*
8 Help *The Beatles*
9 Almost There *Andy Williams*
10 My Fair Lady *Soundtrack of film*
11 Joan Baez In Concert Vol. 5 *Joan Baez*
12 The Bachelors And 16 Great Songs *The Bachelors*
13 The Best Of Jim Reeves *Jim Reeves*
14 West Side Story *Soundtrack of film*
15 Animal Tracks *The Animals*
16 Kinks *The Kinks*
17 Hard Day's Night *The Beatles*
18 Hitmaker *Burt Bacharach*
19 Sound Of The Shadows *The Shadows*
20 Kinda Kinks *The Kinks*

1965—BEST-SELLING ARTISTS

1 The Seekers
2 Cliff Richard
3 Sandie Shaw
4 The Rolling Stones
5 The Beatles
6 Peter and Gordon
7 Bob Dylan
8 The Byrds
9 The Kinks
10 The Hollies
11 The Animals
12 Gene Pitney
13 Sonny and Cher
14 Herman's Hermits
15 The Yardbirds
16 Elvis Presley
17 Marianne Faithfull
18 Tom Jones
19 P. J. Proby
20 Jim Reeves

1966

Seven of the top 10 names of 1965 lost their chart ascendancy during 1966. The departure which perhaps left the largest gap was that of The Seekers. However, a new group who appeared on the scene continued to have hit after hit. This was the Fontana recording team with the endless name, Dave Dee, Dozy, Beaky, Mick and Tich. The last week of March saw their first assault on the charts with 'Hold Tight'. They did indeed 'hold tight' as far as 1966's charts were concerned, for they chalked up a further three successes before the year was finished.

The year's success story lay with The Beach Boys, who had enjoyed their first chart entry in 1964 with 'I Get Around', though they had no Top Twenty entry in 1965. Among their 1966 hits was 'Good Vibrations', a classic song which deservedly reached the Number One position.

For Dusty Springfield, 1966 saw further improvements on her career as a solo singer, for she had a major hit with 'You Don't Have To Say You Love Me'. Elvis Presley was to take the same song to the Number Nine position in 1971.

The year produced its classic songs such as Ike and Tina Turner's 'River Deep Mountain High', a song produced by Phil Spector and strangely unacclaimed in the United States, the land of its birth. There was also 'These Boots Are Made For Walkin'' from Nancy Sinatra, and two Beatle classics, 'Yellow Submarine' and the superb 'Eleanor Rigby'. The Walker Brothers had a huge hit with 'The Sun Ain't Gonna Shine Any More', and altogether the year was something of a revival for the Philips record company, whose stable of artists included the Dave Dee group, Dusty Springfield, Spencer Davis, The Walker Brothers, Manfred Mann, The Mindbenders and The Merseys.

As with most years, 1966 was host to one-hit wonders. The Overlanders promised much with the Beatle classic 'Michelle' taking them to Number One, but unfortunately this was their only Top Twenty entry in the annals of pop history. In much the same way, fortune awarded only two hits each to David and Jonathan, Crispian St. Peters, and the legendary Lovin' Spoonful.

For some artists, 1966 was the year which saw their total decline after some measure of success in previous years. This was true of Marianne Faithfull who, during 1964 and 1965, had achieved four Top Twenty hits. It was also true of P. J. Proby, who disappeared after six hit records. For some artists, 1966 was the beginning of a long spell with no hits; Sonny and Cher were just one duo who fall into this category. Since their first chart entry in 1965, they had achieved five hits, then 1966 saw a decline in their fortunes and chart appearances until 1972 when 'All I Ever Need Is You' brought them back into both the public eye and the charts.

Most artists disappear from the pop scene once their fortunes wane, and few make a comeback. However, at least one chart artist did make a reappearance on the pop scene as late as 1975. This was Chris Farlowe, who twice made The Rolling Stones' excellent song 'Out Of Time' a hit.

Apart from Dave Dee, Dozy, Beaky, Mick and Tich, 1966 also laid foundations for The Small Faces, another major chart force from whence other groups and singers eventually sprang. They entered the charts in September 1965 and 1966 saw four further hits, including 'All Or Nothing', their first Number One.

JANUARY 1966

1	8	15	22	29
1 Day Tripper/We Can Work It Out *The Beatles* (Parlophone)	1	1	2	4
2 Wind Me Up *Cliff Richard* (Columbia)	2	3	5	16
3 The River *Ken Dodd* (Columbia)	4	6	9	9
4 The Carnival Is Over *The Seekers* (Columbia)	3	4	7	14
5 Tears *Ken Dodd* (Columbia)	7	11	15	19
6 My Ship Is Coming In *The Walker Brothers* (Philips)	6	5	3	7
7 My Generation *The Who* (Brunswick)	12	16	–	–
8 1-2-3 *Len Barry* (Brunswick)	11	13	17	–
9 A Lover's Concerto *The Toys* (Stateside)	17	19	–	–
10 Let's Hang On *The Four Seasons* (Philips)	8	7	4	5
11 Rescue Me *Fontella Bass* (Chess)	13	14	18	–
12 Maria *P. J. Proby* (Liberty)	14	–	–	–
13 To Whom It Concerns *Chris Andrews* (Decca)	15	18	–	–
14 Till The End Of The Day *The Kinks* (Pye)	10	8	10	8
15 Keep On Runnin' *The Spencer Davis Group* (Fontana)	5	2	1	2
16 Princess In Rags *Gene Pitney* (Stateside)	18	–	–	–
17 Positively 4th Street *Bob Dylan* (CBS)	–	–	–	–
18 War Lord *The Shadows* (Columbia)	–	–	–	–
19 Merrie Gentle Pops *The Barron-Knights* (Columbia)	9	10	16	–
20 Yesterday Man *Chris Andrews* (Decca)	–	–	–	–
37 A Hard Day's Night *Peter Sellers* (Parlophone)	16	15	14	20
33 A Must To Avoid *Herman's Hermits* (Columbia)	19	9	8	6
22 My Girl *Otis Redding* (Atlantic)	20	17	12	11
30 Spanish Flea *Herb Alpert* (Pye)	21	12	6	3
– Michelle *The Overlanders* (Pye)	–	36	11	1
– Take Me To Your Heart Again *Vince Hill* (Columbia)	49	29	13	–
– England Swings *Roger Miller* (Pye)	31	24	19	13
31 Take Me For What I'm Worth *The Searchers* (Pye)	27	22	20	–
– You Were On My Mind *Crispian St. Peters* (Decca)	45	28	27	10
– Michelle *David and Jonathan* (Columbia)	–	39	24	12
– Love's Just A Broken Heart *Cilla Black* (Parlophone)	–	48	31	15
– Can You Please Crawl Out Your Window *Bob Dylan* (CBS)	–	–	–	17
– A Groovy Kind Of Love *The Mindbenders* (Fontana)	–	34	29	18
– If I Needed Someone *The Hollies* (Parlophone)	–	20	–	–

FEBRUARY 1966

5	12	19	26
1 Michelle *The Overlanders* (Pye)	1	5	11
2 Keep On Runnin' *The Spencer Davis Group* (Fontana)	6	8	20
3 Spanish Flea *Herb Alpert* (Pye)	3	4	6
4 You Were On My Mind *Crispian St. Peters* (Decca)	2	3	4
5 Love's Just A Broken Heart *Cilla Black* (Parlophone)	5	7	10
6 A Must To Avoid *Herman's Hermits* (Columbia)	8	11	–
7 Day Tripper/We Can Work It Out *The Beatles* (Parlophone)	13	–	–
8 Let's Hang On *The Four Seasons* (Philips)	15	–	–
9 My Ship Is Coming In *The Walker Brothers* (Philips)	17	–	–
10 Till The End Of The Day *The Kinks* (Pye)	20	–	–
11 Michelle *David and Jonathan* (Columbia)	16	20	–
12 The River *Ken Dodd* (Columbia)	–	–	–
13 My Girl *Otis Redding* (Atlantic)	12	16	–
14 A Groovy Kind Of Love *The Mindbenders* (Fontana)	7	6	3
15 The Carnival Is Over *The Seekers* (Columbia)	–	–	–
16 Like A Baby *Len Barry* (Brunswick)	10	13	19
17 England Swings *Roger Miller* (Philips)	–	–	–
18 These Boots Are Made For Walkin' *Nancy Sinatra* (Reprise)	4	1	1
19 Girl *St. Louis Union* (Decca)	11	12	16

5	12	19	26
20 Wind Me Up *Cliff Richard* (Columbia)	–	–	–
– Mirror, Mirror *Pinkerton's Assorted Colours* (Decca)	9	10	12
– 19th Nervous Breakdown *The Rolling Stones* (Decca)	14	2	2
37 Have Pity On The Boy *Paul and Barry Ryan* (Decca)	18	19	–
42 Tomorrow *Sandie Shaw* (Pye)	19	9	9
29 Second Hand Rose *Barbra Streisand* (CBS)	26	14	14
– My Love *Petula Clark* (Pye)	35	15	5
31 Little By Little *Dusty Springfield* (Philips)	21	17	17
– Sha La La La Lee *The Small Faces* (Decca)	30	18	7
– Barbara Ann *The Beach Boys* (Capitol)	–	35	8
– Inside Looking Out *The Animals* (Decca)	–	38	13
– Backstage *Gene Pitney* (Stateside)	–	45	15
40 Uptight *Stevie Wonder* (Tamla Motown)	31	26	18

MARCH 1966

5	12	19	26
1 These Boots Are Made For Walkin' *Nancy Sinatra* (Reprise)	1	9	12
2 19th Nervous Breakdown *The Rolling Stones* (Decca)	8	12	17
3 A Groovy Kind Of Love *The Mindbenders* (Fontana)	2	4	7
4 My Love *Petula Clark* (Pye)	9	14	16
5 Sha La La La Lee *The Small Faces* (Decca)	6	3	4
6 Barbara Ann *The Beach Boys* (Capitol)	3	5	5
7 Backstage *Gene Pitney* (Stateside)	4	7	9
8 Spanish Flea *Herb Alpert* (Pye)	5	13	19
9 You Were On My Mind *Crispian St. Peters* (Decca)	13	20	–
10 Make The World Go Away *Eddie Arnold* (RCA)	16	10	10
11 Tomorrow *Sandie Shaw* (Pye)	11	–	–
12 Inside Looking Out *The Animals* (Decca)	12	17	–
13 Love's Just A Broken Heart *Cilla Black* (Parlophone)	–	–	–
14 Uptight *Stevie Wonder* (Tamla Motown)	18	–	–
15 Girl *St. Louis Union* (Decca)	–	–	–
16 Lightning Strikes *Lou Christie* (MGM)	14	11	11
17 Mirror, Mirror *Pinkerton's Assorted Colours* (Decca)	–	–	–
18 I Can't Let Go *The Hollies* (Parlophone)	7	2	2
19 Michelle *The Overlanders* (Pye)	–	–	–
20 Little By Little *Dusty Springfield* (Philips)	–	–	–
26 The Sun Ain't Gonna Shine Any More *The Walker Brothers* (Philips)	10	1	1
31 This Golden Ring *The Fortunes* (Decca)	15	16	–
28 Shapes Of Things *The Yardbirds* (Columbia)	17	6	3
22 What Now My Love *Sonny and Cher* (Atlantic)	19	15	13
34 Dedicated Follower Of Fashion *The Kinks* (Pye)	20	8	6
– Substitute *The Who* (Reaction)	33	18	15
– May Each Day *Andy Williams* (CBS)	36	19	–
– Elusive Butterfly *Bob Lind* (Fontana)	48	21	8
44 Hold Tight *Dave Dee, Dozy, Beaky, Mick and Tich* (Fontana)	31	23	14
– Elusive Butterfly *Val Doonican* (Decca)	–	35	18
– Sound Of Silence *The Bachelors* (Decca)	–	39	20

APRIL 1966

2	9	16	23	30
1 The Sun Ain't Gonna Shine Any More *The Walker Brothers* (Philips)	1	2	7	14
2 I Can't Let Go *The Hollies* (Parlophone)	3	–	–	–
3 Shapes Of Things *The Yardbirds* (Columbia)	8	14	19	–
4 Dedicated Follower Of Fashion *The Kinks* (Pye)	4	9	13	20
5 Elusive Butterfly *Bob Lind* (Fontana)	5	7	11	–

118

2

	9	16	23	30
6 Elusive Butterfly *Val Doonican* (Decca)	7	6	5	16
7 Sha La La La Lee *The Small Faces* (Decca)	12	–	–	–
8 Make The World Go Away *Eddie Arnold* (RCA)	10	8	16	17
9 Barbara Ann *The Beach Boys* (Capitol)	14	19	–	–
10 Somebody Help Me *The Spencer Davis Group* (Fontana)	2	1	1	3
11 Hold Tight *Dave Dee, Dozy, Beaky, Mick and Tich* (Fontana)	6	4	4	5
12 Sound Of Silence *The Bachelors* (Decca)	9	3	3	7
13 What Now My Love *Sonny and Cher* (Atlantic)	17	–	–	–
14 Substitute *The Who* (Reaction)	11	5	8	11
15 A Groovy Kind Of Love *The Mindbenders* (Fontana)	–	–	–	–
16 Backstage *Gene Pitney* (Stateside)	–	–	–	–
17 These Boots Are Made For Walkin' *Nancy Sinatra* (Reprise)	20	–	–	–
18 Lightning Strikes *Lou Christie* (MGM)	–	–	–	–
19 Blue Turns To Grey *Cliff Richard* (Columbia)	15	16	18	18
20 Spanish Flea *Herb Alpert* (Pye)	–	–	–	–
34 Alfie *Cilla Black* (Parlophone)	13	18	12	10
41 You Don't Have To Say You Love Me *Dusty Springfield* (Philips)	16	10	2	1
39 Bang, Bang *Cher* (Liberty)	18	13	6	4
21 Someday One Day *The Seekers* (Columbia)	19	11	14	15
38 I Put A Spell On You *Alan Price* (Decca)	24	12	9	9
48 Pied Piper *Crispian St. Peters* (Decca)	26	15	10	8
29 Homeward Bound *Simon and Garfunkel* (CBS)	27	17	15	12
25 You Won't Be Leavin' *Herman's Hermits* (Columbia)	21	20	20	–
– Day Dream *The Lovin' Spoonful* (Pye)	–	23	17	6
– Pretty Flamingo *Manfred Mann* (HMV)	–	–	22	2
– Sloop John B. *The Beach Boys* (Capitol)	–	–	36	13
31 Super Girl *Graham Bonney* (Columbia)	32	27	24	19

MAY 1966

7

	14	21	28
1 Pretty Flamingo *Manfred Mann* (HMV)	1	1	4
2 Day Dream *The Lovin' Spoonful* (Pye)	2	3	11
3 Bang, Bang *Cher* (Liberty)	4	11	16
4 You Don't Have To Say You Love Me *Dusty Springfield* (Philips)	6	7	14
5 Sloop John B. *The Beach Boys* (Capitol)	3	2	6
6 Pied Piper *Crispian St. Peters* (Decca)	5	8	13
7 Hold Tight *Dave Dee, Dozy, Beaky, Mick and Tich* (Fontana)	7	13	18
8 Sound Of Silence *The Bachelors* (Decca)	8	18	–
9 Alfie *Cilla Black* (Parlophone)	11	20	–
10 Homeward Bound *Simon and Garfunkel* (CBS)	9	16	17
11 Somebody Help Me *The Spencer Davis Group* (Fontana)	16	–	–
12 Substitute *The Who* (Reaction)	18	–	–
13 I Put A Spell On You *Alan Price* (Decca)	17	–	–
14 Someday One Day *The Seekers* (Columbia)	20	–	–
15 Elusive Butterfly *Val Doonican* (Decca)	–	–	–
16 That's Nice *Neil Christian* (Strike)	14	–	–
17 Make The World Go Away *Eddie Arnold* (RCA)	–	–	–
18 Blue Turns To Grey *Cliff Richard* (Columbia)	–	–	–
19 Soul And Inspiration *The Righteous Brothers* (Verve)	15	19	19
20 Shotgun Wedding *Roy C.* (Island)	10	6	7
28 Sorrow *The Merseys* (Fontana)	12	9	5
42 Wild Thing *The Troggs* (Fontana)	13	4	2
27 How Does That Grab You Darlin' *Nancy Sinatra* (Reprise)	19	–	–
– Paint It, Black *The Rolling Stones* (Decca)	–	5	1
– Rainy Day Women *Bob Dylan* (CBS)	32	10	9
– Strangers In The Night *Frank Sinatra* (Reprise)	40	12	3

7

	14	21	28
– Promises *Ken Dodd* (Columbia)	26	14	12
– Hey Girl *The Small Faces* (Decca)	23	15	10
– Monday, Monday *The Mamas and Papas* (RCA)	31	17	8
– When A Man Loves A Woman *Percy Sledge* (Atlantic)	49	34	15
– I Love Her *Paul and Barry Ryan* (Decca)	44	30	20

JUNE 1966

4

	11	18	25
1 Strangers In The Night *Frank Sinatra* (Reprise)	1	1	2
2 Paint It, Black *The Rolling Stones* (Decca)	2	6	12
3 Wild Thing *The Troggs* (Fontana)	3	9	15
4 Sorrow *The Merseys* (Fontana)	4	4	9
5 Monday, Monday *The Mamas and Papas* (RCA)	5	3	3
6 Sloop John B. *The Beach Boys* (Capitol)	9	13	16
7 Rainy Day Women *Bob Dylan* (CBS)	10	15	–
8 Promises *Ken Dodd* (Columbia)	6	8	13
9 When A Man Loves A Woman *Percy Sledge* (Atlantic)	7	5	4
10 Hey Girl *The Small Faces* (Decca)	11	17	–
11 Shotgun Wedding *Roy C.* (Island)	12	–	–
12 Pretty Flamingo *Manfred Mann* (HMV)	13	–	–
13 Don't Bring Me Down *The Animals* (Decca)	8	7	6
14 Nothing Comes Easy *Sandie Shaw* (Pye)	14	16	17
15 Day Dream *The Lovin' Spoonful* (Pye)	20	–	–
16 Pied Piper *Crispian St. Peters* (Decca)	–	–	–
17 You Don't Have To Say You Love Me *Dusty Springfield* (Philips)	19	–	–
18 Come On Home *Wayne Fontana* (Fontana)	16	20	–
19 I Love Her *Paul and Barry Ryan* (Decca)	17	–	–
20 Once There Was A Time/Not Responsible *Tom Jones* (Decca)	18	19	18
21 Under Over Sideways Down *The Yardbirds* (Columbia)	15	10	10
– Paperback Writer *The Beatles* (Parlophone)	–	2	1
– Don't Answer Me *Cilla Black* (Parlophone)	25	11	7
– River Deep, Mountain High *Ike and Tina Turner* (London)	33	12	8
– Sunny Afternoon *The Kinks* (Pye)	31	14	5
– Nobody Needs Your Love *Gene Pitney* (Stateside)	37	18	11
– Hideaway *Dave Dee, Dozy, Beaky, Mick and Tich* (Fontana)	38	21	14
– Bus Stop *The Hollies* (Parlophone)	–	–	19
45 Opus 17 *The Four Seasons* (Philips)	34	25	20

JULY 1966

2

	9	16	23	30
1 Paperback Writer *The Beatles* (Parlophone)	2	7	14	19
2 Strangers In The Night *Frank Sinatra* (Reprise)	5	6	11	15
3 Sunny Afternoon *The Kinks* (Pye)	1	1	2	5
4 River Deep, Mountain High *Ike and Tina Turner* (London)	3	3	4	9
5 Nobody Needs Your Love *Gene Pitney* (Stateside)	4	2	5	11
6 Don't Answer Me *Cilla Black* (Parlophone)	8	12	17	–
7 When A Man Loves A Woman *Percy Sledge* (Atlantic)	9	13	19	–
8 Monday, Monday *The Mamas and Papas* (RCA)	11	15	20	–
9 Bus Stop *The Hollies* (Parlophone)	6	5	8	12
10 Hideaway *Dave Dee, Dozy, Beaky, Mick and Tich* (Fontana)	10	10	15	17
11 Don't Bring Me Down *The Animals* (Decca)	14	–	–	–
12 Get Away *Georgie Fame* (Columbia)	7	4	1	4
13 Over Under Sideways Down *The Yardbirds* (Columbia)	12	–	–	–
14 Promises *Ken Dodd* (Columbia)	16	–	–	–
15 Sorrow *The Merseys* (Fontana)	–	–	–	–

	9	16	23	30
2				
16 Paint It, Black *The Rolling Stones* (Decca)	–	–	–	–
17 I Am A Rock *Simon and Garfunkel* (CBS)	17	–	–	–
18 Wild Thing *The Troggs* (Fontana)	–	–	–	–
19 Sloop John B. *The Beach* Boys (Capitol)	19	–	–	–
20 Lana *Roy Orbison* (London)	15	16	16	20
21 It's A Man's Man's Man's World *James Brown* (Pye)	13	19	–	–
– Out Of Time *Chris Farlowe* (Immediate)	20	9	3	1
34 I Couldn't Live Without Your Love *Petula Clark* (Pye)	21	8	7	6
35 Black Is Black *Los Bravos* (Decca)	25	11	6	2
– Love Letters *Elvis Presley* (RCA)	37	14	9	8
– Goin' Back *Dusty Springfield* (Philips)	30	17	12	10
39 The More I See You *Chris Montez* (Pye)	26	18	13	7
23 This Door Swings Both Ways *Herman's Hermits* (Columbia)	18	20	–	–
– With A Girl Like You *The Troggs* (Fontana)	–	29	10	3
37 Mama *Dave Berry* (Decca)	34	25	18	14
– (Baby) You Don't Have To Tell Me *The Walker Brothers* (Philips)	–	27	21	13
– Summer In The City *The Lovin' Spoonful* (Kama Sutra)	–	43	28	16
– Visions *Cliff Richard* (Columbia)	–	–	29	18

AUGUST 1966

	13	20	27
6			
1 With A Girl Like You *The Troggs* (Fontana)	1	2	3
2 Out Of Time *Chris Farlowe* (Immediate)	2	9	15
3 Black Is Black *Los Bravos* (Decca)	4	4	6
4 The More I See You *Chris Montez* (Pye)	3	6	8
5 Get Away *Georgie Fame* (Columbia)	11	–	–
6 Love Letters *Elvis Presley* (RCA)	7	11	19
7 Mama *Dave Berry* (Decca)	6	5	5
8 I Couldn't Live Without Your Love *Petula Clark* (Pye)	10	13	20
9 Sunny Afternoon *The Kinks* (Pye)	13	–	–
10 Goin' Back *Dusty Springfield* (Philips)	14	19	–
11 River Deep, Mountain High *Ike and Tina Turner* (London)	18	–	–
12 Summer In The City *The Lovin' Spoonful* (Kama Sutra)	9	8	12
13 (Baby) You Don't Have To Tell Me *The Walker Brothers* (Philips)	–	–	–
14 Nobody Needs Your Love *Gene Pitney* (Stateside)	19	–	–
15 Visions *Cliff Richard* (Columbia)	12	7	7
16 God Only Knows *The Beach Boys* (Capitol)	5	3	2
17 Hi-Lili-Hi-Lo *The Alan Price Set* (Decca)	15	12	11
18 I Want You *Bob Dylan* (CBS)	16	17	18
19 Bus Stop *The Hollies* (Parlophone)	–	–	–
20 Strangers In The Night *Frank Sinatra* (Reprise)	20	–	–
– Yellow Submarine *The Beatles* (Parlophone)	8	1	1
24 I Saw Her Again *The Mamas and Papas* (RCA)	17	15	13
42 They're Coming To Take Me Away Ha-Haa! *Napoleon XIV* (Warner Bros.)	31	10	4
28 Lovers Of The World Unite *David and Jonathan* (Columbia)	24	14	10
34 More Than Love *Ken Dodd* (Columbia)	22	16	14
37 Just Like A Woman *Manfred Mann* (Fontana)	27	18	16
– All Or Nothing *The Small Faces* (Decca)	39	20	9
– Too Soon To Know *Roy Orbison* (London)	–	25	17

SEPTEMBER 1966

3	10	17	24
1 Yellow Submarine/Eleanor Rigby *The Beatles* (Parlophone)	1	3	5
2 God Only Knows *The Beach Boys* (Capitol)	3	5	8
3 All Or Nothing *The Small Faces* (Decca)	2	1	2
4 They're Coming To Take Me Away Ha-Haa! *Napoleon XIV* (Warner Bros.)	4	7	16
5 With A Girl Like You *The Troggs* (Fontana)	9	–	–
6 Mama *Dave Berry* (Decca)	8	11	15
7 Visions *Cliff Richard* (Columbia)	12	19	–
8 Too Soon To Know *Roy Orbison* (London)	5	4	3
9 Lovers Of The World Unite *David and Jonathan* (Columbia)	7	9	11
10 Summer In The City *The Lovin' Spoonful* (Kama Sutra)	17	–	–
11 I Saw Her Again *The Mamas and Papas* (RCA)	13	17	–
12 Hi-Lili-Hi-Lo *The Alan Price Set* (Decca)	14	20	–
13 Just Like A Woman *Manfred Mann* (Fontana)	11	10	20
14 The More I See You *Chris Montez* (Pye)	18	–	–
15 More Than Love *Ken Dodd* (Columbia)	16	18	–
16 Black Is Black *Los Bravos* (Decca)	19	–	–
17 Distant Drums *Jim Reeves* (RCA)	6	2	1
18 Got To Get You Into My Life *Cliff Bennett* (Parlophone)	15	6	9
19 Working In The Coal-Mine *Lee Dorsey* (Stateside)	10	8	10
20 I Want You *Bob Dylan* (CBS)	–	–	–
– Little Man *Sonny and Cher* (Atlantic)	35	12	6
– You Can't Hurry Love *The Supremes* (Tamla Motown)	38	13	7
– I'm A Boy *The Who* (Reaction)	20	14	4
38 When I Come Home *The Spencer Davis Group* (Fontana)	23	15	12
29 Ashes To Ashes *The Mindbenders* (Fontana)	22	16	14
– Bend It *Dave Dee, Dozy, Beaky, Mick and Tich* (Fontana)	–	38	13
– Walk With Me *The Seekers* (Columbia)	31	23	17
– Winchester Cathedral *New Vaudeville Band* (Fontana)	43	26	18
– All I See Is You *Dusty Springfield* (Philips)	–	41	19

OCTOBER 1966

1	8	15	22	29
1 Distant Drums *Jim Reeves* (RCA)	1	1	1	3
2 I'm A Boy *The Who* (Reaction)	3	3	5	8
3 You Can't Hurry Love *The Supremes* (Tamla Motown)	4	6	9	12
4 Little Man *Sonny and Cher* (Atlantic)	5	8	13	–
5 Too Soon To Know *Roy Orbison* (London)	8	14	15	20
6 Bend It *Dave Dee, Dozy, Beaky, Mick and Tich* (Fontana)	2	2	3	6
7 Winchester Cathedral *New Vaudeville Band* (Fontana)	6	4	6	5
8 All Or Nothing *The Small Faces* (Decca)	13	–	–	–
9 Yellow Submarine/Eleanor Rigby *The Beatles* (Parlophone)	18	–	–	–
10 Walk With Me *The Seekers* (Columbia)	11	11	12	16
11 All I See Is You *Dusty Springfield* (Philips)	9	10	11	11
12 Lovers Of The World Unite *David and Jonathan* (Columbia)	–	–	–	–
13 Working In The Coal-Mine *Lee Dorsey* (Stateside)	19	–	–	–
14 Sunny *Bobby Hebb* (Philips)	12	15	–	–
15 Got To Get You Into My Life *Cliff Bennett* (Parlophone)	–	–	–	–
16 God Only Knows *The Beach Boys* (Capitol)	–	–	–	–
17 Have You Seen Your Mother Baby, Standing In The Shadow *The Rolling Stones* (Decca)	7	5	8	10
18 Guantanamera *The Sandpipers* (Pye)	10	7	7	7
19 When I Come Home *The Spencer Davis Group* (Fontana)	20	–	–	–
20 Ashes To Ashes *The Mindbenders* (Fontana)	–	–	–	–

1	**8**	**15**	**22**	**29**
– Another Tear Falls *The Walker Brothers* (Philips)	14	12	18	–
– Sunny *Georgie Fame* (Columbia)	15	13	14	19
– I Don't Care *Los Bravos* (Decca)	16	17	19	–
– I Can't Control Myself *The Troggs* (Page One)	17	9	4	2
30 Lady Godiva *Peter and Gordon* (Columbia)	24	16	16	17
42 I've Got You Under My Skin *The Four Seasons* (Reprise)	29	18	20	14
– Reach Out I'll Be There *The Four Tops* (Tamla Motown)	–	19	2	1
– No Milk Today *Herman's Hermits* (Columbia)	35	20	17	9
– Stop Stop Stop *The Hollies* (Parlophone)	–	27	10	4
– Time Drags By *Cliff Richard* (Columbia)	–	34	21	13
– High Time *Paul Jones* (HMV)	49	39	28	15
– If I Were A Carpenter *Bobby Darin* (Atlantic)	–	44	29	18

NOVEMBER 1966

5	**12**	**19**	**26**
1 Reach Out I'll Be There *The Four Tops* (Tamla Motown)	1	3	4
2 Stop Stop Stop *The Hollies* (Parlophone)	2	7	8
3 I Can't Control Myself *The Troggs* (Page One)	6	8	11
4 Distant Drums *Jim Reeves* (RCA)	7	11	12
5 Winchester Cathedral *New Vaudeville Band* (Fontana)	10	14	–
6 High Time *Paul Jones* (HMV)	4	5	6
7 No Milk Today *Herman's Hermits* (Columbia)	9	12	18
8 Guantanamera *The Sandpipers* (Pye)	12	15	19
9 Bend It *Dave Dee, Dozy, Beaky, Mick and Tich* (Fontana)	15	19	–
10 Time Drags By *Cliff Richard* (Columbia)	11	18	–
11 Semi-Detached Suburban Mr James *Manfred Mann* (Fontana)	3	2	5
12 I've Got You Under My Skin *The Four Seasons* (Philips)	17	–	–
13 If I Were A Carpenter *Bobby Darin* (Atlantic)	13	9	10
14 A Fool Am I *Cilla Black* (Parlophone)	14	13	20
15 Good Vibrations *The Beach Boys* (Capitol)	5	1	1
16 I'm A Boy *The Who* (Reaction)	19	–	–
17 All I See Is You *Dusty Springfield* (Philips)	–	–	–
18 All That I Am *Elvis Presley* (RCA)	–	–	–
19 Have You Seen Your Mother Baby, Standing In The Shadow *The Rolling Stones* (Decca)	–	–	–
20 You Can't Hurry Love *The Supremes* (Tamla Motown)	–	–	–
26 Gimme Some Loving *The Spencer Davis Group* (Fontana)	8	4	2
25 Holy Cow *Lee Dorsey* (Stateside)	16	6	7
22 Beauty Is Only Skin Deep *The Temptations* (Tamla Motown)	18	–	–
27 Help Me Girl *Eric Burdon* (Decca)	20	17	14
– Green, Green Grass Of Home *Tom Jones* (Decca)	35	10	3
47 What Would I Be *Val Doonican* (Decca)	31	16	9
39 Friday On My Mind *The Easybeats* (UA)	33	20	17
– Just One Smile *Gene Pitney* (Stateside)	46	28	13
– My Mind's Eye *The Small Faces* (Decca)	–	29	15
32 A Love Like Yours *Ike and Tina Turner* (London)	26	21	16

DECEMBER 1966

3	**10**	**17**	**24**	**31**
1 Green, Green Grass Of Home *Tom Jones* (Decca)	1	1	1	1
2 Good Vibrations *The Beach Boys* (Capitol)	2	5	9	11
3 Gimme Some Loving *The Spencer Davis Group* (Fontana)	5	8	11	–
4 What Would I Be *Val Doonican* (Decca)	3	2	3	6
5 Semi-Detached Suburban Mr James *Manfred Mann* (Fontana)	7	12	15	–
6 Holy Cow *Lee Dorsey* (Stateside)	10	15	19	14
7 Reach Out I'll Be There *The Four Tops* (Tamla Motown)	13	18	–	–

3

	10	17	24	31
8 My Mind's Eye *The Small Faces* (Decca)	4	4	10	15
9 Just One Smile *Gene Pitney* (Stateside)	8	11	16	–
10 High Time *Paul Jones* (HMV)	16	20	–	–
11 Friday On My Mind *The Easybeats* (UA)	9	6	7	7
12 Distant Drums *Jim Reeves* (RCA)	14	14	14	16
13 Stop Stop Stop *The Hollies* (Parlophone)	19	–	–	–
14 What Becomes Of The Broken Hearted *Jimmy Ruffin* (Tamla Motown)	12	10	12	8
15 If I Were A Carpenter *Bobby Darin* (Atlantic)	17	–	–	–
16 Dead End Street *The Kinks* (Pye)	11	7	5	5
17 A Love Like Yours *Ike and Tina Turner* (London)	18	–	–	–
18 Morningtown Ride *The Seekers* (Columbia)	6	3	2	4
19 I Can't Control Myself *The Troggs* (Page One)	–	–	–	–
20 Help Me Girl *Eric Burdon* (Decca)	–	–	–	–
29 You Keep Me Hangin' On *The Supremes* (Tamla Motown)	15	9	8	10
– If Every Day Was Like Christmas *Elvis Presley* (RCA)	20	16	13	9
– Sunshine Superman *Donovan* (Pye)	–	13	4	2
– Save Me *Dave Dee, Dozy, Beaky, Mick and Tich* (Fontana)	–	17	6	3
– There Won't Be Many Coming Home *Roy Orbison* (London)	–	19	18	12
– Happy Jack *The Who* (Reaction)	–	–	17	13
– Under New Management *The Barron-Knights* (Columbia)	–	–	20	20
– In The Country *Cliff Richard* (Columbia)	–	36	21	17
– Sittin' In The Park *Georgie Fame* (Columbia)	–	–	43	18
– Any Way That You Want Me *The Troggs* (Page One)	–	39	25	19

1966—BEST-SELLING SINGLES

1 Distant Drums *Jim Reeves* (RCA)
2 Strangers In The Night *Frank Sinatra* (Reprise)
3 Spanish Flea *Herb Alpert* (Pye)
4 Hold Tight *Dave Dee, Dozy, Beaky, Mick and Tich* (Fontana)
5 Sloop John B. *The Beach Boys* (Capitol)
6 Mama *Dave Berry* (Decca)
7 These Boots Are Made For Walkin' *Nancy Sinatra* (Reprise)
8 God Only Knows *The Beach Boys* (Capitol)
9 A Groovy Kind Of Love *The Mindbenders* (Fontana)
10 Sunny Afternoon *The Kinks* (Pye)
11 When A Man Loves A Woman *Percy Sledge* (Atlantic)
12 Too Soon To Know *Roy Orbison* (London)
13 Yellow Submarine/Eleanor Rigby *The Beatles* (Parlophone)
13 Monday, Monday *The Mamas and Papas* (RCA)
15 Black Is Black *Los Bravos* (Decca)
16 You Don't Have To Say You Love Me *Dusty Springfield* (Philips)
17 River Deep, Mountain High *Ike and Tina Turner* (London)
17 The More I See You *Chris Montez* (Pye)
19 With A Girl Like You *The Troggs* (Fontana)
20 You Were On My Mind *Crispian St. Peters* (Decca)

1966–BEST-SELLING ALBUMS

1	The Beach Boys	11	The Small Faces
2	The Beatles	12	The Kinks
3	The Walker Brothers	13	Georgie Fame
4	The Rolling Stones	14	Otis Redding
5	Herb Alpert	15	Barbra Streisand
6	The Spencer Davis Group	16	The Seekers
7	Frank Sinatra	17	Elvis Presley
8	Bert Kaempfert	18	The Mamas and Papas
9	Jim Reeves	19	Bob Dylan
10	The Animals	20	Andy Williams

Album charts for this year did not list records by titles but rather in terms of artists and their album performance spread over a number of discs.

1966–BEST-SELLING ARTISTS

1	The Beach Boys	11	The Troggs
2	Dave Dee, Dozy, Beaky, Mick and Tich	12	The Hollies
		13	The Walker Brothers
3	The Kinks	14	The Who
4	Ken Dodd	15	Roy Orbison
5	Dusty Springfield	16	Manfred Mann
6	The Spencer Davis Group	17	Gene Pitney
7	The Small Faces	18	The Rolling Stones
8	Cliff Richard	19	The Seekers
9	The Beatles	20	Elvis Presley
10	Cilla Black		

1967

The charts of 1967 reflected Flower Power and its accompanying drug culture. The American West Coast world was given attention as a result of 'San Francisco' by Scott McKenzie, as well as the even more artificial 'Let's Go To San Francisco' from The Flowerpot Men.

The editor of a short-lived paper, *Flower Scene*, which was devoted to the movement wrote 'What the world needs now is love, just love, and let the people leading us to hatred and war go jump in a lake'. The magazine even ran a 'hippie of the month' campaign!

The underlying philosophy of Flower Power was a three-pronged edict stating that firstly people were to do their own thing, wherever and whenever they wanted; secondly, they were to drop out and leave conventional society; and thirdly hippies were to blow the mind of every 'straight' person with whom they came into contact and turn them on to beauty, love, honesty and fun.

Carnaby Street shop owners rubbed their hands in readiness for the wave of business in bells, beads, kaftans, frilly shirts and flower-patterned suits. Concert promoters staged shows featuring popular musicians and called them 'love ins'.

Flower Power and its consequent ethos also included The Move with two of their hits entitled 'I Can Hear The Grass Grow' and 'Flowers In The Rain'. The Rolling Stones sang 'We Love You', a double A-sided hit coupled with 'Dandelion', and produced the album 'Their Satanic Majesties Request'. The Beatles issued their famous 'Sergeant Pepper' album featuring tracks such as 'Lucy In The Sky With Diamonds' and 'A Day In The Life'.

One of 1967's greatest singles, 'A Whiter Shade Of Pale', came from Procol Harum in June. Even if the lyrics were beautifully incomprehensible, the record reached the Number One position and remained in the Top Twenty for three months all but a week. The disc was reissued in June 1972, but did not achieve anything like its previous success.

Jimi Hendrix arrived in 1967 and his songs, in the same way as the Procol Harum single, became vital material for alternative 'underground' groups. Hendrix had four hits – 'Hey Joe', 'Purple Haze', 'And The Wind Cries Mary' and 'Burning Of The Midnight Lamp'.

Another new group arrived, too, but they were a somewhat different kettle of fish. They were The Monkees, an American group who had been created originally for a television series about a group of comedy musicians. The Monkees became teen sensations as a result of this television show, and they achieved five hits in 1967, the first of which was 'I'm A Believer'.

Female hearts fluttered for Cat Stevens, another chart artist who emerged in 1967. His songs were among the first from British artists which reflected an individual's personal reflection on life as a young person. This song formula was particularly in evidence in 'Matthew And Son', his first hit.

Tongue-in-cheek nostaglia had been given a lift in 1961 with The Temperance Seven and in 1967, The New Vaudeville Band continued their success following their 1966 hit, 'Winchester Cathedral'. The year's most unlikely hits were The Dubliners with 'Seven Drunken Nights' and possibly from Prince Buster with 'Al Capone'. Pink Floyd, never in the future a singles chart force, arrived with a line-up including Syd Barrett and two singles, 'See Emily Play' and 'Arnold Layne'.

The Hollies, The Tremeloes, The Supremes, Stevie Wonder, Cliff Richard and Tom Jones all did very well in the charts of 1967, and there were three hits for the Small Faces, but the Spencer Davis group failed to maintain their 1966 momentum and could manage only one hit. The Beach Boys managed two chart entries and Elvis Presley had his only fruitless year since his arrival with a hit record in 1956!

JANUARY 1967

	7	14	21	28
1 Green, Green Grass Of Home *Tom Jones* (Decca)	1	1	2	4
2 Morningtown Ride *The Seekers* (Columbia)	2	2	4	8
3 Sunshine Superman *Donovan* (Pye)	3	3	5	14
4 Save Me *Dave Dee, Dozy, Beaky, Mick and Tich* (Fontana)	4	5	8	16
5 Happy Jack *The Who* (Reaction)	5	6	3	5
6 Dead End Street *The Kinks* (Pye)	6	9	15	20
7 What Would I Be *Val Doonican* (Decca)	7	10	18	18
8 You Keep Me Hangin' On *The Supremes* (Tamla Motown)	8	11	17	–
9 In The Country *Cliff Richard* (Columbia)	9	7	6	10
10 My Mind's Eye *The Small Faces* (Decca)	10	20	–	–
11 Good Vibrations *The Beach Boys* (Capitol)	11	15	–	–
12 Friday On My Mind *The Easybeats* (UA)	12	14	–	–
13 Any Way That You Want Me *The Troggs* (Page One)	13	8	9	13
14 What Becomes Of The Broken Hearted *Jimmy Ruffin* (Tamla Motown)	14	16	–	–
15 Under New Management *The Barron-Knights* (Columbia)	15	18	–	–
16 Pamela, Pamela *Wayne Fontana* (Fontana)	16	12	14	15
17 Distant Drums *Jim Reeves* (RCA)	17	–	–	–
18 Just One Smile *Gene Pitney* (Stateside)	18	–	–	–
19 Sittin' In The Park *Georgie Fame* (Columbia)	19	13	12	12
20 Reach Out I'll Be There *The Four Tops* (Tamla Motown)	20	–	–	–
42 I'm A Believer *The Monkees* (RCA)	42	4	1	1
32 Night Of Fear *The Move* (Deram)	32	17	7	2
23 (I Know) I'm Losing You *The Temptations* (Tamla Motown)	23	19	19	–
– Standing In The Shadows Of Love *The Four Tops* (Tamla Motown)	–	23	10	6
– Matthew And Son *Cat Stevens* (Deram)	–	33	11	3
25 I Feel Free *Cream* (Reaction)	25	21	13	11
41 Hey Joe *Jimi Hendrix* (Polydor)	41	32	16	9
48 A Place In The Sun *Stevie Wonder* (Tamla Motown)	48	46	20	–
– Let's Spend The Night Together/Ruby Tuesday *The Rolling Stones* (Decca)	–	–	26	7
– I've Been A Bad, Bad Boy *Paul Jones* (HMV)	–	–	38	17
43 Single Girl *Sandy Posey* (MGM)	43	36	27	19

FEBRUARY 1967

	4	11	18	25
1 I'm A Believer *The Monkees* (RCA)	1	1	2	3
2 Matthew And Son *Cat Stevens* (Deram)	2	2	5	9
3 Night Of Fear *The Move* (Deram)	3	4	7	17
4 Let's Spend The Night Together/Ruby Tuesday *The Rolling Stones* (Decca)	4	3	3	6
5 Green, Green Grass Of Home *Tom Jones* (Decca)	5	7	12	18
6 Hey Joe *Jimi Hendrix* (Polydor)	6	6	14	–
7 I've Been A Bad, Bad Boy *Paul Jones* (HMV)	7	5	6	11
8 Standing In The Shadows Of Love *The Four Tops* (Tamla Motown)	8	13	–	–
9 Happy Jack *The Who* (Reaction)	9	–	–	–
10 Morningtown Ride *The Seekers* (Columbia)	10	–	–	–
11 Pamela, Pamela *Wayne Fontana* (Fontana)	11	18	–	–
12 I Feel Free *Cream* (Reaction)	12	16	–	–
13 Sittin' In The Park *Georgie Fame* (Columbia)	13	20	–	–
14 Sugar Town *Nancy Sinatra* (Reprise)	14	10	8	14
15 Single Girl *Sandy Posey* (MGM)	15	19	19	20
16 In The Country *Cliff Richard* (Columbia)	16	–	–	–
17 Snoopy Vs The Red Baron *The Royal Guardsmen* (Stateside)	17	14	9	8

4	11	18	25
18 Let Me Cry On Your Shoulder *Ken Dodd* (Columbia)	11	15	–
19 I'm A Man *The Spencer Davis Group* (Fontana)	9	16	–
20 Any Way That You Want Me *The Troggs* (Page One)	–	–	–
43 This Is My Song *Petula Clark* (Pye)	8	1	1
23 Release Me *Engelbert Humperdinck* (Decca)	12	4	2
24 I Won't Come In While He's There *Jim Reeves* (RCA)	15	13	12
32 Peek-A-Boo *New Vaudeville Band* (Fontana)	17	11	7
34 Here Comes My Baby *The Tremeloes* (CBS)	24	10	4
– Mellow Yellow *Donovan* (Pye)	37	17	10
29 It Takes Two *Marvin Gaye and Kim Weston* (Tamla Motown)	22	18	16
– Edelweiss *Vince Hill* (Columbia)	40	20	13
– Penny Lane/Strawberry Fields Forever *The Beatles* (Parlophone)	–	–	5
– On A Carousel *The Hollies* (Parlophone)	–	34	15
– There's A Kind Of Hush *Herman's Hermits* (Columbia)	48	32	19

MARCH 1967

4	11	18	25
1 Release Me *Engelbert Humperdinck* (Decca)	1	1	1
2 Penny Lane/Strawberry Fields Forever *The Beatles* (Parlophone)	2	2	5
3 This Is My Song *Petula Clark* (Pye)	3	3	4
4 Here Comes My Baby *The Tremeloes* (CBS)	6	9	13
5 I'm A Believer *The Monkees* (RCA)	7	14	17
6 Edelweiss *Vince Hill* (Columbia)	4	5	2
7 On A Carousel *The Hollies* (Parlophone)	5	4	7
8 Mellow Yellow *Donovan* (Pye)	9	17	–
9 Peek-A-Boo *New Vaudeville Band* (Fontana)	13	15	20
10 Snoopy Vs The Red Baron *The Royal Guardsmen* (Stateside)	10	10	14
11 There's A Kind Of Hush *Herman's Hermits* (Columbia)	8	7	10
12 Let's Spend The Night Together/Ruby Tuesday *The Rolling Stones* (Decca)	18	–	–
13 Detroit City *Tom Jones* (Decca)	11	8	11
14 I Won't Come In While He's There *Jim Reeves* (RCA)	15	–	–
15 Matthew And Son *Cat Stevens* (Deram)	–	–	–
16 It Takes Two *Marvin Gaye and Kim Weston* (Tamla Motown)	16	19	–
17 Single Girl *Sandy Posey* MGM)	19	–	–
18 Georgy Girl *The Seekers* (Columbia)	12	6	3
19 Sugar Town *Nancy Sinatra* (Reprise)	–	–	–
20 I've Been A Bad, Bad Boy *Paul Jones* (HMV)	–	–	–
22 Give It To Me *The Troggs* (Page One)	14	12	15
31 This Is My Song *Harry Secombe* (Philips)	17	11	9
32 I'll Try Anything *Dusty Springfield* (Philips)	20	13	18
37 Memories Are Made Of This *Val Doonican* (Decca)	21	16	12
44 I Was Kaiser Bill's Batman *Whistling Jack Smith* (Deram)	29	18	8
– Simon Smith And His Amazing Dancing Bear *Alan Price* (Decca)	–	20	6
– Puppet On A String *Sandie Shaw* (Pye)	–	27	16
41 Love Is Here And Now You're Gone *The Supremes* (Tamla Motown)	24	22	19

APRIL 1967

	1	8	15	22	29
1 Release Me *Engelbert Humperdinck* (Decca)	1	2	5	8
2 This Is My Song *Harry Secombe* (Philips)	3	5	7	14
3 Edelweiss *Vince Hill* (Columbia)	7	10	17	20
4 Simon Smith And His Amazing Dancing Bear *Alan Price* (Decca)	5	7	11	18
5 I Was Kaiser Bill's Batman *Whistling Jack Smith* (Deram)	6	8	13	17
6 Puppet On A String *Sandie Shaw* (Pye)	4	3	2	1
7 Georgy Girl *The Seekers* (Columbia)	10	14	–	–
8 This Is My Song *Petula Clark* (Pye)	9	18	–	–
9 Somethin' Stupid *Frank and Nancy Sinatra* (Reprise)	2	1	1	2
10 Penny Lane/Strawberry Fields Forever *The Beatles* (Parlophone)	8	12	–	–
11 Memories Are Made Of This *Val Doonican* (Decca)	12	17	–	–
12 On A Carousel *The Hollies* (Parlophone)	16	–	–	–
13 There's A Kind Of Hush *Herman's Hermits* (Columbia)	15	–	–	–
14 It's All Over *Cliff Richard* (Columbia)	11	9	9	15
15 Touch Me, Touch Me *Dave Dee, Dozy, Beaky, Mick and Tich* (Fontana)	13	16	–	–
16 Detroit City *Tom Jones* (Decca)	19	–	–	–
17 Love Is Here And Now You're Gone *The Supremes* (Tamla Motown)	20	–	–	–
18 Give It To Me *The Troggs* (Page One)	–	–	–	–
19 I'll Try Anything *Dusty Springfield* (Philips)	–	–	–	–
20 Al Capone *Prince Buster* (Blue Beat)	18	–	–	–
– A Little Bit Me, A Little Bit You *The Monkees* (RCA)	14	4	3	3
46 Ha! Ha! Said The Clown *Manfred Mann* (Fontana)	17	6	4	4
39 Purple Haze *Jimi Hendrix* (Track)	22	11	6	5
33 Bernadette *The Four Tops* (Tamla Motown)	25	13	8	10
28 Because I Love You *Georgie Fame* (CBS)	23	15	15	–
36 Happy Together *The Turtles* (London)	27	19	12	12
23 Knock On Wood *Eddie Floyd* (Atlantic)	21	20	19	19
48 I'm Gonna Get Me A Gun *Cat Stevens* (Deram)	34	21	10	6
40 Seven Drunken Nights *The Dubliners* (Major Minor)	33	25	14	11
– I Can Hear The Grass Grow *The Move* (Deram)	39	30	16	7
– Dedicated To The One I Love *The Mamas and Papas* (RCA)	47	35	18	9
41 Arnold Layne *Pink Floyd* (Columbia)	31	26	20	–
– Funny Familiar Forgotten Feeling *Tom Jones* (Decca)	–	39	24	13
– The Boat That I Row *Lulu* (Columbia)	–	46	33	16

MAY 1967

	6	13	20	27
1 Puppet On A String *Sandie Shaw* (Pye)	1	3	5
2 Somethin' Stupid *Frank and Nancy Sinatra* (Reprise)	2	5	10
3 Purple Haze *Jimi Hendrix* (Track)	7	10	16
4 A Little Bit Me, A Little Bit You *The Monkees* (RCA)	10	11	18
5 I Can Hear The Grass Grow *The Move* (Deram)	9	13	20
6 Dedicated To The One I Love *The Mamas and Papas* (RCA)	3	2	3
7 Ha! Ha! Said The Clown *Manfred Mann* (Fontana)	12	18	–
8 I'm Gonna Get Me A Gun *Cat Stevens* (Deram)	13	20	–
9 Funny Familiar Forgotten Feeling *Tom Jones* (Decca)	8	7	11
10 The Boat That I Row *Lulu* (Columbia)	6	6	8
11 Release Me *Engelbert Humperdinck* (Decca)	15	–	19
12 Bernadette *The Four Tops* (Tamla Motown)	18	–	–
13 Seven Drunken Nights *The Dubliners* (Major Minor)	11	8	7
14 Happy Together *The Turtles* (London)	16	19	–

6	13	20	27
15 Silence Is Golden *The Tremeloes* (CBS)	4	1	1
16 Pictures Of Lily *The Who* (Track)	5	4	6
17 Hi Ho Silver Lining *Jeff Beck* (Columbia)	14	14	14
18 It's All Over *Cliff Richard* (Columbia)	–	–	–
19 Knock On Wood *Eddie Floyd* (Atlantic)	20	–	–
20 This Is My Song *Harry Secombe* (Philips)	–	–	–
37 New York Mining Disaster 1941 *The Bee Gees* (Polydor)	17	16	12
34 Then I Kissed Her *The Beach Boys* (Capitol)	19	12	4
– Waterloo Sunset *The Kinks* (Pye)	29	9	2
– The Wind Cries Mary *Jimi Hendrix* (Track)	27	15	9
– Sweet Soul Music *Arthur Conley* (Stax)	21	17	15
– The Happening *The Supremes* (Tamla Motown)	41	23	13
– Finchley Central *New Vaudeville Band* (Fontana)	46	25	17

JUNE 1967

3	10	17	24
1 Silence Is Golden *The Tremeloes* (CBS)	2	4	4
2 Waterloo Sunset *The Kinks* (Pye)	3	3	5
3 Dedicated To The One I Love *The Mamas and Papas* (RCA)	7	9	12
4 A Whiter Shade Of Pale *Procol Harum* (Deram)	1	1	1
5 Then I Kissed Her *The Beach Boys* (Capitol)	5	8	10
6 The Wind Cries Mary *Jimi Hendrix* (Track)	8	15	–
7 There Goes My Everything *Engelbert Humperdinck* (Decca)	4	2	2
8 The Happening *The Supremes* (Tamla Motown)	6	6	7
9 Pictures Of Lily *The Who* (Track)	10	–	–
10 Seven Drunken Nights *The Dubliners* (Major Minor)	12	16	–
11 Puppet On A String *Sandie Shaw* (Pye)	13	20	–
12 Somethin' Stupid *Frank and Nancy Sinatra* (Reprise)	18	–	–
13 Sweet Soul Music *Arthur Conley* (Stax)	9	7	9
14 The Boat That I Row *Lulu* (Columbia)	–	–	–
15 New York Mining Disaster 1941 *The Bee Gees* (Polydor)	15	–	–
16 Finchley Central *New Vaudeville Band* (Fontana)	11	11	13
17 Funny Familiar Forgotten Feeling *Tom Jones* (Decca)	20	–	–
18 Roses Of Picardy *Vince Hill* (Columbia)	16	13	18
19 Hi Ho Silver Lining *Jeff Beck* (Columbia)	–	–	–
20 Purple Haze *Jimi Hendrix* (Track)	–	–	–
24 Okay *Dave Dee, Dozy, Beaky, Mick and Tich* (Fontana)	14	10	6
41 Carrie Anne *The Hollies* (Parlophone)	17	5	3
22 The First Cut Is The Deepest *P. P. Arnold* (Immediate)	19	18	20
44 Paper Sun *Traffic* (Island)	26	12	8
36 Groovin' *The Young Rascals* (Atlantic)	23	14	11
25 If I Were A Rich Man *Topol* (CBS)	21	17	14
39 Night Of The Long Grass *The Troggs* (Page One)	25	19	17
48 Don't Sleep In The Subway *Petula Clark* (Pye)	34	22	15
– Here Comes The Nice *The Small Faces* (Immediate)	37	26	16
– She'd Rather Be With Me *The Turtles* (London)	–	40	19

JULY 1967

1	8	15	22	29
1 A Whiter Shade Of Pale *Procol Harum* (Deram)	1	1	4	7
2 There Goes My Everything *Engelbert Humperdinck* (Decca)	2	4	6	8
3 Carrie Anne *The Hollies* (Parlophone)	5	7	19	16
4 Okay *Dave Dee, Dozy, Beaky, Mick and Tich* (Fontana)	7	19	–	–
5 Paper Sun *Traffic* (Island)	8	15	–	–
6 She'd Rather Be With Me *The Turtles* (London)	4	5	7	5
7 Alternate Title *The Monkees* (RCA)	3	3	2	4

1	8	15	22	29
8 Groovin' *The Young Rascals* (Atlantic)	9	11	–	15
9 Silence Is Golden *The Tremeloes* (CBS)	20	–	–	–
10 The Happening *The Supremes* (Tamla Motown)	14	16	–	–
11 If I Were A Rich Man *Topol* (CBS)	10	9	9	–
12 Don't Sleep In The Subway *Petula Clark* (Pye)	16	20	–	–
13 Sweet Soul Music *Arthur Conley* (Stax)	13	12	–	–
14 Here Comes The Nice *The Small Faces* (Immediate)	12	14	17	18
15 Waterloo Sunset *The Kinks* (Pye)	–	–	–	–
16 Then I Kissed Her *The Beach Boys* (Capitol)	–	–	–	–
17 Seven Rooms Of Gloom *The Four Tops* (Tamla Motown)	15	18	12	19
18 Finchley Central *New Vaudeville Band* (Fontana)	–	–	–	–
19 Strange Brew *Cream* (Reaction)	18	17	18	–
20 It Must Be Him *Vikki Carr* (Liberty)	6	6	3	2
25 Respect *Aretha Franklin* (Atlantic)	11	10	16	12
28 See Emily Play *Pink Floyd* (Columbia)	17	8	8	6
29 Give Me Time *Dusty Springfield* (Philips)	19	–	–	–
– All You Need Is Love *The Beatles* (Parlophone)	–	2	1	1
– San Francisco (Flowers In Your Hair) *Scott McKenzie* (CBS)	–	13	5	3
45 With A Little Help From My Friends *The Young Idea* (Columbia)	35	29	10	–
– You Only Live Twice *Nancy Sinatra* (Reprise)	36	25	11	17
– When You're Young And In Love *The Marvelettes* (Tamla Motown)	28	21	13	–
– Somewhere My Love *The Michael Sammes Singers* (HMV)	–	31	14	–
30 Take Me In Your Arms And Love Me *Gladys Knight and The Pips* (Tamla Motown)	21	22	15	13
– Marta *The Bachelors* (Decca)	40	35	20	–
– Up, Up And Away *The Johnnie Mann Singers* (Liberty)	–	47	26	9
– Death Of A Clown *Dave Davies* (Pye)	–	–	23	10
42 Let's Pretend *Lulu* (Columbia)	32	32	35	11
– 007 *Desmond Dekker* (Pyramid)	–	49	27	14
43 Just Loving You *Anita Harris* (CBS)	30	33	39	20

AUGUST 1967

5	12	19	26
1 All You Need Is Love *The Beatles* (Parlophone)	2	2	3
2 San Francisco (Flowers In Your Hair) *Scott McKenzie* (CBS)	1	1	1
3 Death Of A Clown *Dave Davies* (Pye)	3	4	7
4 It Must Be Him *Vikki Carr* (Liberty)	5	10	13
5 Alternate Title *The Monkees* (RCA)	9	14	–
6 I'll Never Fall In Love Again *Tom Jones* (Decca)	4	3	2
7 She'd Rather Be With Me *The Turtles* (London)	6	11	15
8 I Was Made To Love Her *Stevie Wonder* (Tamla Motown)	7	5	8
9 See Emily Play *Pink Floyd* (Columbia)	10	13	–
10 A Whiter Shade Of Pale *Procol Harum* (Deram)	17	–	–
11 Up, Up And Away *The Johnnie Mann Singers* (Liberty)	8	6	10
12 There Goes My Everything *Engelbert Humperdinck* (Decca)	13	–	16
13 Let's Pretend *Lulu* (Columbia)	14	17	–
14 Just Loving You *Anita Harris* (CBS)	11	7	6
15 Respect *Aretha Franklin* (Atlantic)	–	–	–
16 Groovin' *The Young Rascals* (Atlantic)	–	–	–
17 Creeque Alley *The Mamas and Papas* (RCA)	12	12	9
18 Take Me In Your Arms And Love Me *Gladys Knight and The Pips* (Tamla Motown)	–	–	–
19 007 *Desmond Dekker* (Pyramid)	19	19	–
20 You Only Live Twice *Nancy Sinatra* (Reprise)	16	15	–
38 Even The Bad Times Are Good *The Tremeloes* (CBS)	15	8	4
27 Gin House *Amen Corner* (Deram)	18	16	12

	12	19	26
37 The House That Jack Built *The Alan Price Set* (Decca)	20	9	5
21 Tramp *Otis Redding and Carla Thomas* (Stax)	22	18	–
– Itchycoo Park *The Small Faces* (Immediate)	43	20	14
– Pleasant Valley Sunday *The Monkees* (RCA)	–	22	11
– We Love You/Dandelion *The Rolling Stones* (Decca)	–	–	17
– Excerpt From A Teenage Opera *Keith West* (Parlophone)	40	25	18
– Last Waltz *Engelbert Humperdinck* (Decca)	–	–	19
49 A Bad Night *Cat Stevens* (Deram)	26	24	20

SEPTEMBER 1967

2	9	16	23	30
1 San Francisco (Flowers In Your Hair) *Scott McKenzie* (CBS)	3	3	6	9
2 I'll Never Fall In Love Again *Tom Jones* (Decca)	2	2	5	8
3 Last Waltz *Engelbert Humperdinck* (Decca)	1	1	1	1
4 The House That Jack Built *The Alan Price Set* (Decca)	5	12	17	–
5 Even The Bad Times Are Good *The Tremeloes* (CBS)	6	7	11	12
6 All You Need Is Love *The Beatles* (Parlophone)	13	15	–	–
7 Just Loving You *Anita Harris* (CBS)	7	9	14	16
8 I Was Made To Love Her *Stevie Wonder* (Tamla Motown)	9	11	16	19
9 Death Of A Clown *Dave Davies* (Pye)	16	–	–	–
10 We Love You/Dandelion *The Rolling Stones* (Decca)	8	10	9	15
11 Pleasant Valley Sunday *The Monkees* (RCA)	11	17	–	–
12 Excerpt From A Teenage Opera *Keith West* (Parlophone)	4	4	2	2
13 Heroes And Villains *The Beach Boys* (Capitol)	12	8	12	13
14 Up, Up And Away *The Johnnie Mann Singers* (Liberty)	20	–	–	–
15 Creeque Alley *The Mamas and Papas* (RCA)	19	–	–	–
16 Gin House *Amen Corner* (Deram)	17	–	–	–
17 It Must Be Him *Vikki Carr* (Liberty)	–	–	–	–
18 Itchycoo Park *The Small Faces* (Immediate)	10	6	3	4
19 Everything *Engelbert Humperdinck* (Decca)	–	–	–	–
20 You Only Live Twice *Nancy Sinatra* (Reprise)	–	–	–	–
23 The Day I Met Marie *Cliff Richard* (Columbia)	14	14	15	10
25 Let's Go To San Francisco *The Flowerpot Men* (Deram)	15	5	4	6
32 Burning Of The Midnight Lamp *Jimi Hendrix* (Track)	18	19	19	20
43 Reflections *Diana Ross and The Supremes* (Tamla Motown)	23	13	7	5
33 There Must Be A Way *Frankie Vaughan* (Columbia)	27	16	13	11
22 You Keep Me Hanging On *Vanilla Fudge* (Atlantic)	22	18	20	–
– Flowers In The Rain *The Move* (Regal Zonophone)	40	20	8	3
– Hole In My Shoe *Traffic* (Island)	44	23	10	7
41 Black Velvet Band *The Dubliners* (Major Minor)	28	22	18	18
– The Letter *The Box Tops* (Stateside)	–	45	24	14
– Massachusetts *The Bee Gees* (Polydor)	–	–	31	17

OCTOBER 1967

7	14	21	28
1 Last Waltz *Engelbert Humperdinck* (Decca)	3	3	2
2 Flowers In The Rain *The Move* (Regal Zonophone)	2	4	5
3 Hole In My Shoe *Traffic* (Island)	4	2	3
4 Excerpt From A Teenage Opera *Keith West* (Parlophone)	5	9	13
5 Reflections *Diana Ross and The Supremes* (Tamla Motown)	8	10	11
6 Massachusetts *The Bee Gees* (Polydor)	1	1	1
7 Itchycoo Park *The Small Faces* (Immediate)	10	12	16
8 Let's Go To San Francisco *The Flowerpot Men* (Deram)	12	17	–
9 The Letter *The Box Tops* (Stateside)	6	5	6
10 The Day I Met Marie *Cliff Richard* (Columbia)	14	15	18

	14	21	28
11 There Must Be A Way *Frankie Vaughan* (Columbia)	7	7	10
12 Just Loving You *Anita Harris* (CBS)	17	–	17
13 I'll Never Fall In Love Again *Tom Jones* (Decca)	–	–	–
14 San Francisco *Scott McKenzie* (CBS)	20	–	–
15 Ode To Billy Joe *Bobby Gentry* (Capitol)	16	18	14
16 When Will The Good Apple Fall *The Seekers* (Columbia)	13	11	12
17 Even The Bad Times Are Good *The Tremeloes* (CBS)	–	–	–
18 From The Underworld *The Herd* (Fontana)	11	8	8
19 Black Velvet Band *The Dubliners* (Major Minor)	15	16	–
20 Good Times *Eric Burdon and The Animals* (MGM)	–	–	–
34 Homburg *Procol Harum* (Regal Zonophone)	9	6	9
22 King Midas In Reverse *The Hollies* (Parlophone)	18	20	19
23 Five Little Fingers *Frankie McBride* (Emerald)	19	–	–
48 Baby Now That I've Found You *The Foundations* (Pye)	21	13	4
– Zabadak *Dave Dee, Dozy, Beaky, Mick and Tich* (Fontana)	35	14	7
41 You've Not Changed *Sandie Shaw* (Pye)	23	19	20
– Autumn Almanac *The Kinks* (Pye)	–	42	15

NOVEMBER 1967

4	11	18	25
1 Massachusetts *The Bee Gees* (Polydor)	2	2	4
2 Baby Now That I've Found You *The Foundations* (Pye)	1	1	2
3 Zabadak *Dave Dee, Dozy, Beaky, Mick and Tich* (Fontana)	3	4	7
4 Last Waltz *Engelbert Humperdinck* (Decca)	4	5	8
5 Hole In My Shoe *Traffic* (Island)	11	16	20
6 From The Underworld *The Herd* (Fontana)	6	12	17
7 Homburg *Procol Harum* (Regal Zonophone)	9	14	19
8 Autumn Almanac *The Kinks* (Pye)	5	3	6
9 Flowers In The Rain *The Move* (Regal Zonophone)	12	18	–
10 The Letter *The Box Tops* (Stateside)	15	19	–
11 There Must Be A Way *Frankie Vaughan* (Columbia)	10	15	14
12 When Will The Good Apple Fall *The Seekers* (Columbia)	19	–	–
13 Ode To Billy Joe *Bobby Gentry* (Capitol)	20	–	–
14 Excerpt From A Teenage Opera *Keith West* (Parlophone)	–	–	–
15 San Franciscan Nights *Eric Burdon and The Animals* (MGM)	8	7	13
16 Love Is All Around *The Troggs* (Page One)	7	6	5
17 Reflections *Diana Ross and The Supremes* (Tamla Motown)	–	–	–
18 There Is A Mountain *Donovan* (Pye)	14	8	10
19 Just Loving You *Anita Harris* (CBS)	17	–	–
20 If The Whole World Stopped Loving *Val Doonican* (Pye)	16	11	9
21 I Can See For Miles *The Who* (Track)	13	10	12
22 You've Not Changed *Sandie Shaw* (Pye)	18	20	–
– Let The Heartaches Begin *Long John Baldry* (Pye)	31	9	1
49 Everybody Knows *The Dave Clark Five* (Columbia)	26	13	3
33 I Feel Love Coming On *Felice Taylor* (President)	25	17	11
42 Careless Hands *Des O'Connor* (Columbia)	28	27	15
– All My Love *Cliff Richard* (Columbia)	–	28	16
– Something's Gotten Hold Of My Heart *Gene Pitney* (Stateside)	–	36	18

DECEMBER 1967

2		9	16	23	30
1	Let The Heartaches Begin *Long John Baldry* (Pye)	2	3	6	8
2	Everybody Knows *The Dave Clark Five* (Columbia)	3	2	13	16
3	If The Whole World Stopped Loving *Val Doonican* (Pye)	4	4	4	4
4	Baby Now That I've Found You *The Foundations* (Pye)	8	17	–	–
5	Last Waltz *Engelbert Humperdinck* (Decca)	13	16	12	13
6	Love Is All Around *The Troggs* (Page One)	7	15	–	–
7	Something's Gotten Hold Of My Heart *Gene Pitney* (Stateside)	5	6	5	5
8	All My Love *Cliff Richard* (Columbia)	11	11	7	6
9	Hello, Goodbye *The Beatles* (Parlophone)	1	1	1	1
10	Careless Hands *Des O'Connor* (Columbia)	6	7	11	11
11	Zabadak *Dave Dee, Dozy, Beaky, Mick and Tich* (Fontana)	16	–	–	–
12	I Feel Love Coming On *Felice Taylor* (President)	12	14	19	–
13	I'm Coming Home *Tom Jones* (Decca)	10	5	2	3
14	There Is A Mountain *Donovan* (Pye)	–	–	–	–
15	World *The Bee Gees* (Polydor)	9	9	14	15
16	Massachusetts *The Bee Gees* (Polydor)	–	–	–	–
17	Autumn Almanac *The Kinks* (Pye)	20	–	–	–
18	I Can See For Miles *The Who* (Track)	–	–	–	–
19	Daydream Believer *The Monkees* (RCA)	15	13	8	7
20	San Franciscan Nights *Eric Burdon and The Animals* (MGM)	–	–	–	–
24	Thank U Very Much *The Scaffold* (Columbia)	14	10	9	9
21	Kites *Simon Dupree* (Columbia)	17	12	15	14
37	In And Out Of Love *The Supremes* (Tamla Motown)	18	18	17	17
42	Here We Go Round The Mulberry Bush *Traffic* (Island)	19	8	10	12
–	There Must Be A Way *Frankie Vaughan* (Columbia)	22	19	20	20
–	Magical Mystery Tour *The Beatles* (Parlophone)	–	20	3	2
–	Walk Away Renee *The Four Tops* (Tamla Motown)	–	25	16	10
–	Tin Soldier *The Small Faces* (Immediate)	49	29	18	19
–	Ballad Of Bonnie And Clyde *Georgie Fame* (CBS)	–	33	22	18

1967–BEST-SELLING SINGLES

1 Release Me *Engelbert Humperdinck* (Decca)
2 There Goes My Everything *Engelbert Humperdinck* (Decca)
3 Last Waltz *Engelbert Humperdinck* (Decca)
4 Just Loving You *Anita Harris* (CBS)
5 San Francisco (Flowers In Your Hair) *Scott McKenzie* (CBS)
6 Puppet On A String *Sandie Shaw* (Pye)
7 I'll Never Fall In Love Again *Tom Jones* (Decca)
8 There Must Be A Way *Frankie Vaughan* (Columbia)
9 A Whiter Shade Of Pale *Procol Harum* (Deram)
10 I'm A Believer *The Monkees* (RCA)
11 Somethin' Stupid *Frank and Nancy Sinatra* (Reprise)
12 Dedicated To The One I Love *The Mamas and Papas* (RCA)
13 It Must Be Him *Vikki Carr* (Liberty)
14 Excerpt From A Teenage Opera *Keith West* (Parlophone)
15 Massachusetts *The Bee Gees* (Polydor)
16 Silence Is Golden *The Tremeloes* (CBS)
17 Edelweiss *Vince Hill* (Columbia)
18 All You Need Is Love *The Beatles* (Parlophone)
19 This Is My Song *Petula Clark* (Pye)
20 If I Were A Rich Man *Topol* (CBS)

1967–BEST-SELLING ALBUMS

1 Sound Of Music *Soundtrack of film*
2 Best Of The Beach Boys Vol. 1 *The Beach Boys*
3 Dr Zhivago *Soundtrack of film*
4 Going Places *Herb Alpert*
5 Monkees *The Monkees*
6 Sgt. Pepper's Lonely Hearts Club Band *The Beatles*
7 Fiddler On The Roof *London cast of play*
8 Come The Day *The Seekers*
9 Four Tops Live *The Four Tops*
10 Drop Of The Hard Stuff *The Dubliners*
11 Green Green Grass Of Home *Tom Jones*
12 Release Me *Engelbert Humperdinck*
13 Are You Experienced *Jimi Hendrix*
14 This Is James Last *James Last*
15 Hand Clappin' Foot Stompin' *Geno Washington*

1967–BEST-SELLING ARTISTS

Male Artists (Singles)

1 Engelbert Humperdinck
2 Tom Jones
3 Cliff Richard
4 Val Doonican
5 Vince Hill
6 Frankie Vaughan
7 Cat Stevens
8 Donovan
9 Scott McKenzie
10 Stevie Wonder

Female Artists (Singles)

1 Sandie Shaw
2 Petula Clark
3 Anita Harris
4 Lulu
5 Nancy Sinatra

Groups (Singles)

1 The Monkees
2 The Supremes
3 The Tremeloes
4 The Beatles
5 Jimi Hendrix Experience
6 Dave Dee, Dozy, Beaky, Mick
   and Tich
7 The Four Tops
8 The Bee Gees
9 The Troggs
10 The Move

Male Artists (Albums)

1 Tom Jones
2 Engelbert Humperdinck
3 Geno Washington
4 Bob Dylan
5 Jim Reeves

Female Artists (Albums)

1 Dusty Springfield
2 Petula Clark
3 Vikki Carr

Groups (Albums)

1 The Beach Boys
2 The Monkees
3 Herb Alpert
4 The Beatles
5 The Four Tops

1968

Donovan continued his success of 1967 by providing songs which continued in the same vein as the previous year, seemingly preoccupied with flowers, beads, drugs, love, peace and happiness. He added two more hits in 1968 to his previous two of 1967, so obviously a market still existed for gentle, wafting lullabies which avoided the harshness of reality.

Music in 1968 lacked any real identity of its own, for there were few new stars, though the year did produce some fine songs. The outstanding records included two from The Beatles, 'Lady Madonna' and 'Hey Jude'. Early in January, The Beatles fought themselves for top chart placing as 'Hello, Goodbye' and 'Magical Mystery Tour' strove for the Number One position.

The Herd looked as though they would be labelled as the next 'teen' group and their key figure, Peter Frampton, received extensive teen magazine coverage. However, the group achieved only two hits in 1968, 'Paradise Lost' and 'I Don't Want Our Loving To Die', which followed their 1967 hit record, 'From The Underworld'. Peter Frampton, a good musician, was so horrified by the trimmings of teeny-bop fame that he made for the hills and The Herd were heard of no more. Later, Frampton was to emerge as an accepted and progressive musician.

There was also Julie Driscoll with Brian Auger and The Trinity, who excited the pop world and promised much, but 'This Wheel's On Fire' was their only Top Twenty hit. Blues-styled music continued from Chicken Shack and Christine Perfect but the group were to score only one hit in 1969 with 'I'd Rather Go Blind'.

The most unexpected hit was from a street busker called Don Partridge who sang 'Rosie', and many experienced pop commentators were thrown into confusion somewhat by the alarming speed with which 'Cinderella Rockafella' from Esther and Abi Ofarim travelled up the charts.

Amen Corner surfaced in style in 1968 under Andy Fairweather-Low after their first tentative chart entry with 'Gin House' during September 1967. Whereas 'Gin

House' had reached Number Twelve and no more, their two 1968 hits made the Top Six. Likewise Dave Dee, Dozy, Beaky, Mick and Tich had three hits, but the last of these three in October entitled 'Wreck Of The Antoinette' was the group's final chart appearance. Altogether, the group had achieved 10 Top Twenty discs.

Some noteworthy hits which emerged from the otherwise dull charts included The Love Affair's cover version of the American Robert Knight's smash hit 'Everlasting Love'; Joe Cocker with the superb 'With A Little Help From My Friends'; The Union Gap with 'Young Girl' and 'Lady Will Power'; Nina Simone's 'Ain't Got No – I Got Life'; 'Dock Of The Bay' by Otis Redding and, late in 1968, 'Son Of A Preacher Man' from Dusty Springfield.

Altogether, the music scene of 1968 leaned towards 'heavy' and progressive music, and audiences listened to lengthy tuning up sessions which were followed by long solos which hardly merited an admission fee. Many businessmen and concert promoters would have preferred a return to Flower Power, when they could sell the accessories which accompanied the music, but with the new progressive music, none of the trappings of fashion or cults were necessary.

JANUARY 1968

6		13	20	27
1	Hello, Goodbye *The Beatles* (Parlophone)	1	1	8
2	Magical Mystery Tour *The Beatles* (Parlophone)	2	4	5
3	I'm Coming Home *Tom Jones* (Decca)	7	7	16
4	Thank U Very Much *The Scaffold* (Columbia)	6	10	19
5	Walk Away Renee *The Four Tops* (Tamla Motown)	3	5	7
6	Daydream Believer *The Monkees* (RCA)	5	6	6
7	Something's Gotten Hold Of My Heart *Gene Pitney* (Stateside)	11	15	–
8	If The Whole World Stopped Loving *Val Doonican* (Pye)	8	9	18
9	Kites *Simon Dupree* (Columbia)	9	12	20
10	Ballad Of Bonnie And Clyde *Georgie Fame* (CBS)	4	2	1
11	Here We Go Round The Mulberry Bush *Traffic* (Island)	10	16	–
12	World *The Bee Gees* (Polydor)	12	11	12
13	In And Out Of Love *The Supremes* (Tamla Motown)	14	19	–
14	Careless Hands *Des O'Connor* (Columbia)	13	17	–
15	Let The Heartaches Begin *Long John Baldry* (Pye)	18	–	–
16	Last Waltz *Engelbert Humperdinck* (Decca)	19	–	–
17	Everybody Knows *The Dave Clark Five* (Columbia)	–	–	–
18	All My Love *Cliff Richard* (Columbia)	17	–	–
19	Tin Soldier *The Small Faces* (Immediate)	16	14	9
20	Jackie *Scott Walker* (Philips)	–	–	–
36	Everlasting Love *The Love Affair* (CBS)	15	3	2
22	The Other Man's Grass *Petula Clark* (Pye)	20	–	–
–	Am I That Easy To Forget *Engelbert Humperdinck* (Decca)	33	8	3
48	Judy In Disguise *John Fred and his Playboy Band* (Pye)	23	13	4
39	She Wears My Ring *Solomon King* (Columbia)	25	18	13
23	Paradise Lost *The Herd* (Fontana)	21	20	15
–	Everything I Am *Plastic Penny* (Page One)	27	22	10
–	Bend Me Shape Me *Amen Corner* (Deram)	–	33	11
–	Suddenly You Love Me *The Tremeloes* (CBS)	–	46	14
–	I Can Take Or Leave Your Loving *Herman's Hermits* (Columbia)	–	34	17

FEBRUARY 1968

3		10	17	24
1	Everlasting Love *The Love Affair* (CBS)	1	2	4
2	Ballad Of Bonnie And Clyde *Georgie Fame* (CBS)	7	14	–
3	Am I That Easy To Forget *Engelbert Humperdinck* (Decca)	4	4	6
4	Judy In Disguise *John Fred and his Playboy Band* (Pye)	3	6	9
5	Bend Me Shape Me *Amen Corner* (Deram)	5	3	5
6	Everything I Am *Plastic Penny* (Page One)	10	15	20
7	The Mighty Quinn *Manfred Mann* (Fontana)	2	1	1
8	She Wears My Ring *Solomon King* (Columbia)	9	5	3
9	Suddenly You Love Me *The Tremeloes* (CBS)	6	7	11
10	Tin Soldier *The Small Faces* (Immediate)	17	–	–
11	Daydream Believer *The Monkees* (RCA)	16	17	–
12	Magical Mystery Tour *The Beatles* (Parlophone)	18	–	–
13	Walk Away Renee *The Four Tops* (Tamla Motown)	20	–	–
14	I Can Take Or Leave Your Loving *Herman's Hermits* (Columbia)	11	11	16
15	Gimme Little Sign *Brenton Wood* (Liberty)	8	8	10
16	Hello, Goodbye *The Beatles* (Parlophone)	–	–	–
17	Darlin' *The Beach Boys* (Capitol)	15	12	14
18	World *The Bee Gees* (Polydor)	–	–	–
19	Paradise Lost *The Herd* (Fontana)	–	–	–
20	I'm Coming Home *Tom Jones* (Decca)	19	20	–
30	Pictures Of Matchstick Men *Status Quo* (Pye)	12	9	7

3	10	17	24
37 Don't Stop The Carnival *Alan Price* (Decca)	13	16	15
41 Words *The Bees Gees* (Polydor)	14	13	12
– Fire Brigade *The Move* (Regal Zonophone)	22	10	8
38 Back On My Feet Again *The Foundations* (Pye)	23	18	18
26 Nights In White Satin *The Moody Blues* (Deram)	21	19	–
– Cinderella Rockafella *Esther and Abi Ofarim* (Philips)	–	32	2
– Legend Of Xanadu *Dave Dee, Dozy, Beaky, Mick and Tich* (Fontana)	–	35	13
– Green Tambourine *The Lemon Pipers* (Kama Sutra)	40	23	17
– Rosie *Don Partridge* (Columbia)	35	22	19

MARCH 1968

2	9	16	23	30
1 Cinderella Rockafella *Esther and Abi Ofarim* (Philips)	1	1	2	4
2 The Mighty Quinn *Manfred Mann* (Fontana)	3	8	15	–
3 Legend Of Xanadu *Dave Dee, Dozy, Beaky, Mick and Tich* (Fontana)	2	2	1	5
4 Bend Me Shape Me *Amen Corner* (Deram)	8	14	18	–
5 She Wears My Ring *Solomon King* (Columbia)	9	12	12	15
6 Fire Brigade *The Move* (Regal Zonophone)	4	3	7	13
7 Pictures Of Matchstick Men *Status Quo* (Pye)	7	13	19	–
8 Words *The Bee Gees* (Polydor)	11	15	16	–
9 Everlasting Love *The Love Affair* (CBS)	17	20	–	–
10 Suddenly You Love Me *The Tremeloes* (CBS)	16	16	–	–
11 Green Tambourine *The Lemon Pipers* (Kama Sutra)	10	7	8	16
12 Gimme Little Sign *Brenton Wood* (Liberty)	15	18	–	–
13 Am I That Easy To Forget *Engelbert Humperdinck* (Decca)	18	19	–	–
14 Rosie *Don Partridge* (Columbia)	5	4	4	7
15 Jennifer Juniper *Donovan* (Pye)	6	5	6	9
16 Darlin' *The Beach Boys* (Capitol)	13	11	14	17
17 Judy In Disguise *John Fred and his Playboy Band* (Pye)	–	–	–	–
18 Don't Stop The Carnival *Alan Price* (Decca)	–	–	–	–
19 Back On My Feet Again *The Foundations* (Pye)	19	–	–	–
20 I Can Take Or Leave Your Loving *Herman's Hermits* (Columbia)	–	–	–	–
36 Delilah *Tom Jones* (Decca)	12	6	3	2
21 Dock Of The Bay *Otis Redding* (Stax)	14	9	5	3
34 Me, The Peaceful Heart *Lulu* (Columbia)	20	10	9	11
26 Wonderful World *Louis Armstrong* (HMV)	26	17	10	6
– Lady Madonna *The Beatles* (Parlophone)	–	–	11	1
– If I Were A Carpenter *The Four Tops* (Tamla Motown)	–	30	13	10
31 Love Is Blue *Paul Mauriat* (Philips)	24	21	17	14
24 Guitar Man *Elvis Presley* (RCA)	23	24	20	19
– Congratulations *Cliff Richard* (Columbia)	–	–	32	8
– Step Inside Love *Cilla Black* (Parlophone)	–	35	22	12
– If I Only Had Time *John Rowles* (MCA)	–	40	40	18
– Ain't Nothin' But A Houseparty *The Showstoppers* (Beacon)	–	38	29	20

APRIL 1968

6	13	20	27
1 Lady Madonna *The Beatles* (Parlophone)	4	6	18
2 Delilah *Tom Jones* (Decca)	2	4	5
3 Congratulations *Cliff Richard* (Columbia)	1	1	2
4 Dock Of The Bay *Otis Redding* (Stax)	6	8	9
5 Wonderful World *Louis Armstrong* (HMV)	3	2	1

	13	20	27
6 Cinderella Rockafella *Esther and Abi Ofarim* (Philips)	11	16	–
7 If I Were A Carpenter *The Four Tops* (Tamla Motown)	9	11	17
8 Legend of Xanadu *Dave Dee, Dozy, Beaky, Mick and Tich* (Fontana)	18	–	–
9 Step Inside Love *Cilla Black* (Parlophone)	8	9	14
10 Rosie *Don Partridge* (Columbia)	15	20	–
11 If I Only Had Time *John Rowles* (MCA)	5	3	4
12 Love Is Blue *Paul Mauriat* (Philips)	19	19	–
13 Jennifer Juniper *Donovan* (Pye)	–	–	–
14 Me, The Peaceful Heart *Lulu* (Columbia)	–	–	–
15 Captain Of Your Ship *Reparata and The Delrons* (Bell)	13	15	13
16 Ain't Nothin' But A Houseparty *The Showstoppers* (Beacon)	16	14	11
17 Fire Brigade *The Move* (Regal Zonophone)	–	–	–
18 Simon Says *The 1910 Fruitgum Co.* (Pye)	7	5	3
19 Valleri *The Monkees* (RCA)	12	12	16
20 Can't Take My Eyes Off You *Andy Williams* (CBS)	17	10	6
23 Jennifer Eccles *The Hollies* (Parlophone)	10	7	7
27 I Can't Let Maggie Go *The Honey Bus* (Deram)	14	13	8
24 Cry Like A Baby *The Box Tops* (Bell)	23	17	15
31 Something Here In My Heart *The Paper Dolls* (Pye)	22	18	12
– Lazy Sunday *The Small Faces* (Immediate)	–	31	10
– White Horses *Jacky* (Philips)	42	22	19
– Hello How Are You *The Easybeats* (UA)	35	26	20
42 Rock Around The Clock *Bill Haley* (MCA)	20	–	–

MAY 1968

	11	18	25
1 Wonderful World *Louis Armstrong* (HMV)	1	1	5
2 Simon Says *The 1910 Fruitgum Co.* (Pye)	3	6	7
3 Lazy Sunday *The Small Faces* (Immediate)	2	4	4
4 If I Only Had Time *John Rowles* (MCA)	8	8	11
5 Can't Take My Eyes Off You *Andy Williams* (CBS)	6	9	8
6 Congratulations *Cliff Richard* (Columbia)	11	12	17
7 Man Without Love *Engelbert Humperdinck* (Decca)	4	2	2
8 Jennifer Eccles *The Hollies* (Parlophone)	10	13	–
9 I Can't Let Maggie Go *The Honey Bus* (Deram)	14	18	–
10 Delilah *Tom Jones* (Decca)	15	20	–
11 Something Here In My Heart *The Paper Dolls* (Pye)	13	17	–
12 I Don't Want Our Loving To Die *The Herd* (Fontana)	5	7	6
13 Ain't Nothin' But A Houseparty *The Showstoppers* (Beacon)	16	16	16
14 White Horses *Jacky* (Philips)	12	10	10
15 Cry Like A Baby *The Box Tops* (Bell)	17	19	–
16 Young Girl *The Union Gap* (CBS)	7	3	1
17 Captain Of Your Ship *Reparata and The Delrons* (Bell)	–	–	–
18 Valleri *The Monkees* (RCA)	–	–	–
19 Somewhere In The Country *Gene Pitney* (Stateside)	20	–	–
20 Honey *Bobby Goldsboro* (UA)	9	5	3
24 Rainbow Valley *The Love Affair* (CBS)	18	11	9
22 Little Green Apples *Roger Miller* (Philips)	19	–	20
40 Sleepy Joe *Herman's Hermits* (Columbia)	22	14	12
38 Joanna *Scott Walker* (Philips)	23	15	13
– Helule Helule *The Tremeloes* (CBS)	41	25	14
– This Wheel's On Fire *Julie Driscoll, Brian Auger and The Trinity* (Marmalade)	26	23	15
– U.S. Male *Elvis Presley* (RCA)	–	40	18
– Do You Know The Way To San Jose *Dionne Warwick* (Pye)	–	32	19

JUNE 1968

1		8	15	22	29
1	Young Girl *The Union Gap* (CBS)	1	1	2	2
2	Honey *Bobby Goldsboro* (UA)	3	3	6	10
3	Man Without Love *Engelbert Humperdinck* (Decca)	2	4	10	14
4	Wonderful World *Louis Armstrong* (HMV)	11	12	20	20
5	Lazy Sunday *The Small Faces* (Immediate)	9	–	–	–
6	I Don't Want Our Loving To Die *The Herd* (Fontana)	6	10	14	–
7	Rainbow Valley *The Love Affair* (CBS)	5	5	11	17
8	Joanna *Scott Walker* (Philips)	7	11	15	19
9	Do You Know The Way To San Jose *Dionne Warwick* (Pye)	8	9	8	13
10	This Wheel's On Fire *Julie Driscoll, Brian Auger and The Trinity* (Marmalade)	10	6	5	8
11	Simon Says *The 1910 Fruitgum Co.* (Pye)	13	16	17	–
12	Sleepy Joe *Herman's Hermits* (Columbia)	12	17	16	–
13	Can't Take My Eyes Off You *Andy Williams* (CBS)	–	–	–	–
14	White Horses *Jacky* (Philips)	16	19	19	–
15	Helule Helule *The Tremeloes* (CBS)	14	15	18	–
16	U.S. Male *Elvis Presley* (RCA)	15	–	–	–
17	If I Only Had Time *John Rowles* (MCA)	18	–	–	–
18	Jumping Jack Flash *The Rolling Stones* (Decca)	4	2	1	1
19	Delilah *Tom Jones* (Decca)	–	–	–	–
20	Baby Come Back *The Equals* (President)	19	14	7	3
32	Blue Eyes *Don Partridge* (Columbia)	17	7	3	5
33	Hurdy Gurdy Man *Donovan* (Pye)	20	8	4	4
22	I Pretend *Des O'Connor* (Columbia)	22	13	9	6
43	Lovin' Things *The Marmalade* (CBS)	31	18	12	9
45	Son Of Hickory Hollers Tramp *O. C. Smith* (CBS)	30	20	13	7
–	My Name Is Jack *Manfred Mann* (Fontana)	–	50	21	11
–	Yummy Yummy *The Ohio Express* (Pye)	50	35	25	12
–	Boys *Lulu* (Columbia)	33	30	22	15
–	Yesterday Has Gone *Cupid's Inspiration* (NEMS)	–	–	37	16
–	Hush Not A Word To Mary *John Rowles* (MCA)	–	–	36	18

JULY 1968

6		13	20	27
1	Baby Come Back *The Equals* (President)	1	1	3
2	Son Of Hickory Hollers Tramp *O. C. Smith* (CBS)	2	2	6
3	Jumping Jack Flash *The Rolling Stones* (Decca)	5	9	19
4	Hurdy Gurdy Man *Donovan* (Pye)	6	20	–
5	I Pretend *Des O'Connor* (Columbia)	3	3	1
6	Lovin' Things *The Marmalade* (CBS)	7	14	–
7	Blue Eyes *Don Partridge* (Columbia)	10	11	16
8	Yesterday Has Gone *Cupid's Inspiration* (NEMS)	4	4	7
9	My Name Is Jack *Manfred Mann* (Fontana)	8	10	13
10	Young Girl *The Union Gap* (CBS)	13	15	–
11	Yummy Yummy *The Ohio Express* (CBS)	9	5	5
12	Hush Not A Word To Mary *John Rowles* (MCA)	14	12	14
13	This Wheel's On Fire *Julie Driscoll, Brian Auger and The Trinity* (Marmalade)	16	–	–
14	Mony Mony *Tommy James and The Shondells* (Ember)	11	6	2
15	One More Dance *Esther and Abi Ofarim* (Philips)	15	13	15
16	Honey *Bobby Goldsboro* (UA)	20	–	–
17	Do You Know The Way To San Jose *Dionne Warwick* (Pye)	19	–	–
18	Boys *Lulu* (Columbia)	–	–	–
19	Macarthur Park *Richard Harris* (RCA)	12	7	4
20	D. W. Washburn *The Monkees* (RCA)	17	–	–
30	Fire *The Crazy World of Arthur Brown* (Track)	18	8	8

6	13	20	27
46 This Guy's In Love *Herb Alpert* (A & M)	28	16	9
– Mrs Robinson *Simon and Garfunkel* (CBS)	42	17	10
31 Gotta See Jane *R. Dean Taylor* (Tamla Motown)	23	18	20
33 Where Will You Be *Sue Nicholls* (Pye)	24	19	17
– I Close My Eyes And Count To Ten *Dusty Springfield* (Philips)	31	22	11
48 Last Night In Soho *Dave Dee* (Fontana)	30	24	12
– Universal *The Small Faces* (Immediate)	37	23	18

AUGUST 1968

3	10	17	24	31
1 Mony Mony *Tommy James and The Shondells* (Major Minor)	1	2	1	4
2 I Pretend *Des O'Connor* (Columbia)	3	5	12	14
3 Fire *The Crazy World of Arthur Brown* (Track)	2	1	2	6
4 Macarthur Park *Richard Harris* (RCA)	8	15	–	–
5 Mrs Robinson *Simon and Garfunkel* (CBS)	4	6	11	17
6 Baby Come Back *The Equals* (President)	11	16	–	–
7 I Close My Eyes And Count To Ten *Dusty Springfield* (Philips)	6	4	6	13
8 Last Night In Soho *Dave Dee* (Fontana)	9	10	15	20
9 Son Of Hickory Hollers Tramp *O. C. Smith* (CBS)	16	–	–	–
10 Yummy Yummy *The Ohio Express* (Pye)	13	18	18	–
11 This Guy's In Love *Herb Alpert* (A & M)	5	3	3	3
12 Help Yourself *Tom Jones* (Decca)	7	9	5	5
13 Yesterday Has Gone *Cupid's Inspiration* (NEMS)	20	–	–	–
14 Dance To The Music *Sly and The Family Stone* (CBS)	12	7	10	10
15 Sunshine Girl *Herman's Hermits* (Columbia)	10	8	8	9
16 Universal *The Small Faces* (Immediate)	18	20	19	–
17 Gotta See Jane *R. Dean Taylor* (Tamla Motown)	–	–	–	–
18 Keep On *Bruce Channel* (Bell)	14	14	13	12
19 Days *The Kinks* (Pye)	15	12	14	15
20 Here Comes The Judge *Pigmeat Markham* (Chess)	19	19	–	–
26 Do It Again *The Beach Boys* (Capitol)	17	11	4	1
– I Gotta Get A Message To You *The Bee Gees* (Polydor)	27	13	7	2
44 High In The Sky *Amen Corner* (Deram)	23	17	9	7
37 On The Road Again *Canned Heat* (Liberty)	29	27	16	16
– Say A Little Prayer *Aretha Franklin* (Atlantic)	37	26	17	8
– Hold Me Tight *Johnny Nash* (Regal Zonophone)	42	38	20	11
– Dream A Little Dream Of Me *Mama Cass* (RCA)	–	46	28	18
46 Hard To Handle *Otis Redding* (Atlantic)	31	24	23	19

SEPTEMBER 1968

7	14	21	28
1 I Gotta Get A Message To You *The Bee Gees* (Polydor)	2	3	4
2 This Guy's In Love *Herb Alpert* (A & M)	6	10	15
3 Help Yourself *Tom Jones* (Decca)	8	14	13
4 Do It Again *The Beach Boys* (Capitol)	3	5	7
5 Say A Little Prayer *Aretha Franklin* (Atlantic)	4	4	6
6 High In The Sky *Amen Corner* (Deram)	9	11	11
7 Hold Me Tight *Johnny Nash* (Regal Zonophone)	5	7	5
8 Dance To The Music *Sly and The Family Stone* (CBS)	20	–	–
9 Mony Mony *Tommy James and The Shondells* (Major Minor)	14	–	–
10 Fire *The Crazy World of Arthur Brown* (Track)	15	–	–
11 Keep On *Bruce Channel* (Bell)	–	–	–
12 Dream A Little Dream Of Me *Mama Cass* (RCA)	11	12	14
13 Sunshine Girl *Herman's Hermits* (Columbia)	16	20	–
14 I Pretend *Des O'Connor* (Columbia)	18	18	–

	14	21	28
15 Lady Will Power *The Union Gap* (CBS)	13	9	10
16 Little Arrows *Leapy Lee* (MCA)	17	13	9
17 On The Road Again *Canned Heat* (Liberty)	10	8	8
18 Days *The Kinks* (Pye)	–	–	–
19 Hard To Handle *Otis Redding* (Atlantic)	19	15	16
20 Yesterday's Dream *The Four Tops* (Tamla Motown)	–	–	–
27 Hey Jude *The Beatles* (Apple)	1	1	2
– Those Were The Days *Mary Hopkin* (Apple)	7	2	1
26 Jezamine *The Casuals* (Decca)	12	6	3
29 Classical Gas *Mason Williams* (Warner Bros.)	25	16	12
33 Ice In The Sun *Status Quo* (Pye)	22	17	17
– Hello, I Love You *The Doors* (Elektra)	32	19	18
– Red Balloon *The Dave Clark Five* (Columbia)	–	39	19
31 I Live For The Sun *Vanity Fare* (Page One)	28	26	20

OCTOBER 1968

5

	12	19	26
1 Those Were The Days *Mary Hopkin* (Apple)	1	1	1
2 Hey Jude *The Beatles* (Apple)	4	3	2
3 Jezamine *The Casuals* (Decca)	3	2	3
4 Little Arrows *Leapy Lee* (MCA)	2	4	4
5 Hold Me Tight *Johnny Nash* (Regal Zonophone)	10	15	16
6 I Gotta Get A Message To You *The Bee Gees* (Polydor)	13	16	20
7 Lady Will Power *The Union Gap* (CBS)	5	5	9
8 Say A Little Prayer *Aretha Franklin* (Atlantic)	12	–	–
9 Red Balloon *The Dave Clark Five* (Columbia)	7	8	14
10 High In The Sky *Amen Corner* (Deram)	18	–	–
11 Ice In The Sun *Status Quo* (Pye)	8	14	18
12 Do It Again *The Beach Boys* (Capitol)	20	–	–
13 Classical Gas *Mason Williams* (Warner Bros.)	9	11	15
14 On The Road Again *Canned Heat* (Liberty)	–	–	–
15 Dream A Little Dream Of Me *Mama Cass* (RCA)	16	–	–
16 Hello, I Love You *The Doors* (Elektra)	15	19	19
17 A Day Without Love *The Love Affair* (CBS)	11	9	6
18 My Little Lady *The Tremeloes* (CBS)	6	6	8
19 Help Yourself *Tom Jones* (Decca)	–	–	–
20 Hard To Handle *Otis Redding* (Atlantic)	–	–	–
32 Les Bicyclettes De Belsize *Engelbert Humperdinck* (Decca)	14	7	5
23 Light My Fire *Jose Feliciano* (RCA)	17	10	10
43 Wreck Of The Antoinette *Dave Dee, Dozy, Beaky, Mick and Tich* (Fontana)	19	18	17
27 The Good, The Bad And The Ugly *Hugo Montenegro* (Warner Bros.)	21	12	7
33 Listen To Me *The Hollies* (Parlophone)	23	13	11
34 Only One Woman *The Marbles* (Polydor)	26	17	12
42 With A Little Help From My Friends *Joe Cocker* (Regal Zonophone)	38	20	13

NOVEMBER 1968

2

	9	16	23	30
1 Those Were The Days *Mary Hopkin* (Apple)	2	5	9	11
2 With A Little Help From My Friends *Joe Cocker* (Regal Zonophone)	1	2	5	10
3 The Good, The Bad And The Ugly *Hugo Montenegro* (RCA)	3	1	1	1
4 Little Arrows *Leapy Lee* (MCA)	8	14	13	20
5 Only One Woman *The Marbles* (Polydor)	6	8	8	12

2	9	16	23	30
6 Light My Fire *Jose Feliciano* (RCA)	7	7	11	13
7 Hey Jude *The Beatles* (Apple)	10	11	–	–
8 Jezamine *The Casuals* (Decca)	11	10	16	–
9 Les Bicyclettes De Belsize *Engelbert Humperdinck* (Decca)	12	12	19	–
10 My Little Lady *The Tremeloes* (CBS)	13	17	–	–
11 A Day Without Love *The Love Affair* (CBS)	15	20	–	–
12 Listen To Me *The Hollies* (Parlophone)	14	15	18	–
13 Red Balloon *The Dave Clark Five* (Columbia)	–	–	–	–
14 Wreck Of The Antoinette *Dave Dee, Dozy, Beaky, Mick and Tich* (Fontana)	18	–	–	–
15 Lady Will Power *The Union Gap* (CBS)	19	–	–	–
16 Eloise *Barry Ryan* (MGM)	4	3	2	2
17 Classical Gas *Mason Williams* (Warner Bros.)	20	–	–	–
18 All Along The Watchtower *Jimi Hendrix* (Track)	9	6	6	5
19 This Old Heart Of Mine *The Isley Brothers* (Tamla Motown)	5	4	3	3
20 Breaking Down The Walls Of Heartache *The Bandwagon* (Direction)	16	9	4	6
21 Mexico *Long John Baldry* (Pye)	17	16	15	19
41 Eleanore *The Turtles* (London)	23	13	7	8
35 Ain't Got No – I Got Life/Do What You Gotta Do *Nina Simone* (RCA)	28	18	10	7
23 You're All I Need To Get By *Marvin Gaye and Tammi Terrell* (Tamla Motown)	21	19	–	–
– Lily The Pink *The Scaffold* (Columbia)	41	23	12	4
34 If I Knew Then What I Know Now *Val Doonican* (Pye)	27	26	14	17
– I'm A Tiger *Lulu* (Columbia)	50	30	17	9
47 May I Have The Next Dream With You *Malcolm Roberts* (Major Minor)	31	24	20	14
27 Harper Valley P.T.A. *Jeannie C. Riley* (Polydor)	24	21	22	15
– One, Two, Three O'Leary *Des O'Connor* (Columbia)	–	–	31	16
– The Urban Spaceman *The Bonzo Dog Doo Dah Band* (Liberty)	44	34	25	18

DECEMBER 1968

7	14	21
1 The Good, The Bad And The Ugly *Hugo Montenegro* (RCA)	2	6
2 Lily The Pink *The Scaffold* (Columbia)	1	1
3 Eloise *Barry Ryan* (MGM)	8	18
4 This Old Heart Of Mine *The Isley Brothers* (Tamla Motown)	7	10
5 Breaking Down The Walls Of Heartache *The Bandwagon* (Direction)	10	11
6 One, Two, Three O'Leary *Des O'Connor* (Columbia)	4	4
7 Ain't Got No – I Got Life/Do What You Gotta Do *Nina Simone* (RCA)	3	2
8 May I Have The Next Dream With You *Malcolm Roberts* (Major Minor)	9	15
9 I'm A Tiger *Lulu* (Columbia)	12	12
10 Eleanore *The Turtles* (London)	14	–
11 All Along The Watchtower *Jimi Hendrix* (Track)	–	–
12 Harper Valley P.T.A. *Jeannie C. Riley* (Polydor)	15	17
13 The Urban Spaceman *The Bonzo Dog Doo Dah Band* (Liberty)	6	5
14 Build Me Up Buttercup *The Foundations* (Pye)	5	3
15 Race With The Devil *The Gun* (CBS)	13	8
16 Those Were The Days *Mary Hopkin* (Apple)	18	–
17 Only One Woman *The Marbles* (Polydor)	–	–
18 With A Little Help From My Friends *Joe Cocker* (Regal Zonophone)	–	–

7		14	21
19	Love Child *Diana Ross and The Supremes* (Tamla Motown)	17	19
20	If I Knew Then What I Know Now *Val Doonican* (Pye)	–	–
22	Sabre Dance *Love Sculpture* (Parlophone)	11	7
26	A Minute Of Your Time *Tom Jones* (Decca)	15	16
23	Private Number *Judy Clay and William Bell* (Stax)	19	14
30	Albatross *Fleetwood Mac* (Blue Horizon)	20	13
45	Ob-La-Di-Ob-La-Da *The Marmalade* (CBS)	22	9
44	Son Of A Preacher Man *Dusty Springfield* (Philips)	24	20

The chart for 28 December 1968 is a repeat of that for the previous week.

1968–BEST-SELLING SINGLES

1 What A Wonderful World *Louis Armstrong* (HMV)
2 I Pretend *Des O'Connor* (Columbia)
3 Those Were The Days *Mary Hopkin* (Apple)
4 Help Yourself *Tom Jones* (Decca)
5 Young Girl *The Union Gap* (CBS)
6 Deliiah *Tom Jones* (Decca)
7 Little Arrows *Leapy Lee* (MCA)
8 Baby Come Back *The Equals* (President)
9 The Good, The Bad And The Ugly *Hugo Montenegro* (RCA)
10 Jezamine *The Casuals* (Decca)
⌠11 She Wears My Ring *Solomon King* (Columbia)
⌡11 Hey Jude *The Beatles* (Apple)
13 If I Only Had Time *John Rowles* (MCA)
14 This Guy's In Love *Herb Alpert* (A & M)
15 Simon Says *The 1910 Fruitgum Co.* (Pye)
16 Honey *Bobby Goldsboro* (UA)
17 Man Without Love *Engelbert Humperdinck* (Decca)
18 Fire *The Crazy World Of Arthur Brown* (Track)
19 I Gotta Get A Message To You *The Bee Gees* (Polydor)
⌠20 Do It Again *The Beach Boys* (Capitol)
⎜20 Can't Keep My Eyes Off You *Andy Williams* (CBS)
⌡20 Son Of Hickory Hollers Tramp *O. C. Smith* (CBS)

1968–BEST-SELLING ALBUMS

1 Sound Of Music *Soundtrack of film*
2 Tom Jones Live At The Talk Of The Town *Tom Jones*
3 Diana Ross And The Supremes Greatest Hits *Diana Ross and The Supremes*
4 The Four Tops Greatest Hits *The Four Tops*
5 Best Of The Beach Boys *The Beach Boys*
6 15 Smash Hits *Tom Jones*
7 Jungle Book *Soundtrack of film*
8 History Of Otis Redding *Otis Redding*
9 Fleetwood Mac *Fleetwood Mac*
10 John Wesley Harding *Bob Dylan*
11 British Motown Chartbusters *Various artists*
12 Bookends *Simon and Garfunkel*
13 Delilah *Tom Jones*
14 The Hollies *The Hollies*
15 Otis Blue *Otis Redding*

Only 15 titles were listed by Record Retailer *for 1968.*

1968—BEST-SELLING ARTISTS

Male Artists (Singles)

1 Tom Jones
2 Engelbert Humperdinck
3 Des O'Connor

4 Cliff Richard
5 Louis Armstrong

Female Artists (Singles)

1 Aretha Franklin
2 Lulu
3 Mary Hopkin

4 Julie Driscoll
5 Dionne Warwick

Groups (Singles)

1 The Beatles
2 The Love Affair
3 The Bee Gees
4 The Beach Boys
5 Dave Dee, Dozy, Beaky, Mick
   and Tich

6 Herman's Hermits
7 The Four Tops
8 The Small Faces
9 Gary Puckett and The Union
   Gap
10 The Equals

Male Artists (Albums)

1 Tom Jones
2 Otis Redding
3 Engelbert Humperdinck

4 Bob Dylan
5 Val Doonican

Female Artists (Albums)

1 Aretha Franklin
2 Cilla Black

3 Dionne Warwick

1969

No big new stars came into 1969's chart reckoning, and the discs which became hits were, by and large, not exceptional.

For some people, the presence at the Number One spot of 'Je T'Aime, Moi Non Plus' from Jane Birkin and Serge Gainsbourg constituted the year's most sensational event. Certainly what appeared on disc as a simulated sound reproduction of the love act was novel and not altogether unpleasant. More interesting, however, was the extraordinary reaction of Philips, the recording company which originally released the record. Philips were presumably aware of the controversy which would surround the record when they recorded it, but when the disc reached the Number Two position they presumably decided that it was too controversial and sold the product to another record company. Record companies have often made hits of records which have failed with other companies, but 'Je T'Aime' would seem to be pop's only case of a hit record changing hands and reaching Number One with the new company, while it was already at a very high position in the charts with the original company.

Another newsworthy record in the charts was 'Give Peace A Chance' which reached Number Two. The song was recorded in a Canadian hotel room, with John Lennon and Yoko Ono being joined by a singing host who received the name of The Plastic Ono Band. Although John and Yoko formed a group of musicians for future recordings, the name of The Plastic Ono Band persisted, and was featured on 'Cold Turkey', one of the most realistic and horrific discs recorded as a single, for it was descriptive of someone coming off heroin.

Much more peaceful was a series of hit records such as 'Sugar Sugar', 'It Mek', 'Ragamuffin Man', and 'Where Do You Go To My Lovely'. The latter was sung by Peter Sarstedt, a brother of Eden Kane, the singer who had achieved several hits in the early 1960s.

Cliff Richard joined forces with Hank Marvin for 'Throw Down A Line', while a group known as Thunderclap Newman, whose line-up included Jimmy McCulloch, sang 'Something In The Air' – a song which has become one of pop's classics.

For a time 'Swamp' music became popular as an American singer, John Fogerty, assisted by his band known as Creedence Clearwater Revival, had three hits. The first two of these, 'Proud Mary' and 'Bad Moon Rising', were probably the most memorable, while the third, 'Green River' received, short shift, but Creedence Clearwater Revival had two hits in 1970.

The Rolling Stones had a Number One with 'Honky Tonk Women', while Marvin Gaye recorded 'I Heard It Through The Grapevine', one of Tamla Motown's finest singles. Gaye had another hit with 'Too Busy Thinking About My Baby' before joining forces with Tammi Terrell for the 'Onion Song'.

Hits came from Jethro Tull, Joe Cocker, Bob Dylan, and The Beatles bade farewell with 'Get Back' and 'The Ballad Of John And Yoko'. Surprisingly, 'Something', a double A-side with 'Come Together' only reached the Number Four position.

The most unusual hit was 'Babarabajagal' from Donovan and The Jeff Beck Group – a hybrid of artists if ever there was one.

The amount of festivals which were held, and the culture which accompanied them, enlivened what would otherwise have been a rather dull year for pop, and the Top Fifty in particular.

JANUARY 1969

4		11	18	25
1 Ob-La-Di-Ob-La-Da *The Marmalade* (CBS)		3	1	1
2 Lily The Pink *The Scaffold* (Columbia)		1	4	4
3 Build Me Up Buttercup *The Foundations* (Pye)		2	3	6
4 Albatross *Fleetwood Mac* (Blue Horizon)		4	2	2
5 The Urban Spaceman *The Bonzo Dog Doo Dah Band* (Liberty)		5	7	9
6 Sabre Dance *Love Sculpture* (Parlophone)		6	8	11
7 Ain't Go No – I Got Life/Do What You Gotta Do *Nina Simone* (RCA)		7	9	14
8 One, Two, Three O'Leary *Des O'Connor* (Columbia)		13	14	17
9 Son Of A Preacher Man *Dusty Springfield* (Philips)		9	11	13
10 Something's Happening *Herman's Hermits* (Columbia)		8	6	7
11 Race With The Devil *The Gun* (CBS)		14	19	–
12 For Once In My Life *Stevie Wonder* (Tamla Motown)		10	5	3
13 I'm A Tiger *Lulu* (Columbia)		11	18	20
14 Private Number *Judy Clay and William Bell* (Stax)		12	10	8
15 The Good, The Bad And The Ugly *Hugo Montenegro* (RCA)		16	15	19
16 May I Have The Next Dream With You *Malcolm Roberts* (Major Minor)		18	–	–
17 A Minute Of Your Time *Tom Jones* (Decca)		17	20	18
18 Love Child *Diana Ross and The Supremes* (Tamla Motown)		15	17	16
19 Breaking Down The Walls Of Heartache *The Bandwagon* (Direction)		19	–	–
20 Ob-La-Di-Ob-La-Da *The Bedrocks* (Columbia)		–	–	–
22 This Old Heart Of Mine *The Isley Brothers* (Tamla Motown)		20	–	–
32 Fox On The Run *Manfred Mann* (Fontana)		23	12	10
29 Blackberry Way *The Move* (Regal Zonophone)		29	13	5
31 S.O.S./Headline News *Edwin Starr* (Polydor)		22	16	12
– You Got Soul *Johnny Nash* (Major Minor)		37	23	15

FEBRUARY 1969

1		8	15	22
1 Albatross *Fleetwood Mac* (Blue Horizon)		2	2	6
2 Blackberry Way *The Move* (Regal Zonophone)		1	3	5
3 For Once In My Life *Stevie Wonder* (Tamla Motown)		3	4	10
4 Ob-La-Di-Ob-La-Da *The Marmalade* (CBS)		10	9	14
5 Fox On The Run *Manfred Mann* (Fontana)		11	13	16
6 Something's Happening *Herman's Hermits* (Columbia)		14	14	20
7 Lily The Pink *The Scaffold* (Columbia)		–	19	–
8 Private Number *Judy Clay and William Bell* (Stax)		13	–	–
9 You Got Soul *Johnny Nash* (Major Minor)		6	7	8
10 Build Me Up Buttercup *The Foundations* (Pye)		–	–	–
11 S.O.S./Headline News *Edwin Starr* (Polydor)		15	18	–
12 Dancing In The Street *Martha Reeves and The Vandellas* (Tamla Motown)		4	5	7
13 The Urban Spaceman *The Bonzo Dog Doo Dah Band* (Liberty)		–	–	–
14 To Love Somebody *Nina Simone* (RCA)		5	10	12
15 Sabre Dance *Love Sculpture* (Parlophone)		–	–	–
16 Please Don't Go *Donald Peers* (Columbia)		8	6	4
17 I Guess I'll Always Love You *The Isley Brothers* (Tamla Motown)		12	11	15
18 Love Child *Diana Ross and The Supremes* (Tamla Motown)		–	–	–
19 Quick Joey Small *Kasenatz Katz* (Buddah)		–	–	–
20 Ain't Got No – I Got Life/Do What You Gotta Do *Nina Simone* (RCA)		–	–	–
37 I'm Gonna Make You Love Me *The Supremes* (Tamla Motown)		7	8	3

		8	15	22
27	Mrs Robinson (E.P.) *Simon and Garfunkel* (CBS)	9	–	–
24	People *The Tymes* (Direction)	16	–	18
28	I'll Pick A Rose *Marv Johnson* (Tamla Motown)	17	16	13
33	Half As Nice *Amen Corner* (Immediate)	19	1	1
42	Soul Sister Brown Sugar *Sam and Dave* (Stax)	20	–	17
–	The Way It Used To Be *Engelbert Humperdinck* (Decca)	39	15	9
21	Hey Jude *Wilson Pickett* (Atlantic)	21	16	–
26	Going Up The Country *Canned Heat* (Liberty)	26	19	–
47	Wichita Lineman *Glen Campbell* (Ember)	24	26	11
–	Surround Yourself With Sorrow *Cilla Black* (Parlophone)	–	41	19
–	Where Do You Go To My Lovely *Peter Sarstedt* (UA)	18	12	2

MARCH 1969

		8	15	22	29
1	Where Do You Go To My Lovely *Peter Sarstedt* (UA)	1	1	1	2
2	Half As Nice *Amen Corner* (Immediate)	2	11	15	–
3	I'm Gonna Make You Love Me *Diana Ross and The Supremes and The Temptations* (Tamla Motown)	6	9	19	–
4	Please Don't Go *Donald Peers* (Columbia)	3	10	4	20
5	The Way It Used To Be *Engelbert Humperdinck* (Decca)	9	3	3	13
6	Dancing In The Street *Martha Reeves and The Vandellas* (Tamla Motown)	14	17	–	–
7	Blackberry Way *The Move* (Regal Zonophone)	18	–	–	–
8	Albatross *Fleetwood Mac* (Blue Horizon)	19	–	–	–
9	Wichita Lineman *Glen Campbell* (Ember)	7	8	8	14
10	I'll Pick A Rose *Marv Johnson* (Tamla Motown)	12	16	–	–
11	Surround Yourself With Sorrow *Cilla Black* (Parlophone)	4	4	6	3
12	You Got Soul *Johnny Nash* (Major Minor)	–	–	–	–
13	For Once In My Life *Stevie Wonder* (Tamla Motown)	20	–	–	–
14	I Guess I'll Always Love You *The Isley Brothers* (Tamla Motown)	–	–	–	–
15	You've Lost That Loving Feeling *The Righteous Brothers* (London)	13	12	10	17
16	To Love Somebody *Nina Simone* (RCA)	–	–	–	–
17	Gentle On My Mind *Dean Martin* (Capitol)	10	5	4	5
18	Soul Sister Brown Sugar *Sam and Dave* (Stax)	15	–	–	–
19	I Heard It Through The Grapevine *Marvin Gaye* (Tamla Motown)	5	2	2	1
20	Monsieur Dupont *Sandie Shaw* (Pye)	8	7	7	8
26	First Of May *The Bee Gees* (Polydor)	11	6	9	7
36	Good Times *Cliff Richard* (Columbia)	16	15	13	12
–	Sorry Suzanne *The Hollies* (Parlophone)	33	14	12	4
40	One Road *The Love Affair* (CBS)	21	18	16	19
36	Windmills Of Your Mind *Noel Harrison* (Reprise)	34	19	–	16
–	Games People Play *Joe South* (Capitol)	30	20	14	6
–	Get Ready *The Temptations* (Tamla Motown)	39	21	17	10
47	I Can Hear Music *The Beach Boys* (Capitol)	26	27	20	18
–	Boom Bang-A-Bang *Lulu* (Columbia)	–	22	22	9
–	If I Can Dream *Elvis Presley* (RCA)	17	13	11	11
–	In The Bad Bad Old Days *The Foundations* (Pye)	–	–	18	15

5		12	19	26
1	I Heard It Through The Grapevine *Marvin Gaye* (Tamla Motown)	1	3	6
2	Gentle On My Mind *Dean Martin* (Capitol)	4	5	5
3	Sorry Suzanne *The Hollies* (Parlophone)	5	7	18
4	Boom Bang-A-Bang *Lulu* (Columbia)	2	4	7
5	The Israelites *Desmond Dekker and The Aces* (Pyramid)	3	1	2
6	Monsieur Dupont *Sandie Shaw* (Pye)	11	13	–
7	Where Do You Go To My Lovely *Peter Sarstedt* (UA)	14	–	–
8	Games People Play *Joe South* (Capitol)	7	9	15
9	In The Bad Bad Old Days *The Foundations* (Pye)	8	8	10
10	First Of May *The Bee Gees* (Polydor)	17	–	–
11	Surround Yourself With Sorrow *Cilla Black* (Parlophone)	12	17	–
12	Good Times *Cliff Richard* (Columbia)	18	19	–
13	Get Ready *The Temptations* (Tamla Motown)	13	20	–
14	Windmills Of Your Mind *Noel Harrison* (Reprise)	15	10	9
15	If I Can Dream *Elvis Presley* (RCA)	19	–	–
16	The Way It Used To Be *Engelbert Humperdinck* (Decca)	–	–	–
17	Pinball Wizard *The Who* (Track)	9	6	4
18	I Can Hear Music *The Beach Boys* (Capitol)	10	11	12
19	Wichita Lineman *Glen Campbell* (Ember)	–	–	–
20	You've Lost That Loving Feeling *The Righteous Brothers* (London)	–	–	–
25	Goodbye *Mary Hopkin* (Apple)	6	2	3
28	Cupid *Johnny Nash* (Major Minor)	32	12	13
22	Hello World *The Tremeloes* (CBS)	16	14	19
35	Come Back And Shake Me *Clodagh Rodgers* (RCA)	27	15	8
21	Harlem Shuffle *Bob and Earl* (Island)	19	16	11
26	I Don't Know Why *Stevie Wonder* (Tamla Motown)	26	18	14
–	Man Of The World *Fleetwood Mac* (Blue Horizon)	–	20	–
–	Get Back *The Beatles* (Apple)	–	–	1
–	Road Runner *Jnr. Walker and The All Stars* (Tamla Motown)	–	26	16
–	Passing Strangers *Sarah Vaughan and Billy Eckstine* (Mercury)	–	23	17
–	Badge *Cream* (Polydor)	–	36	20

3		10	17	24	31
1	Get Back *The Beatles* (Apple)	1	1	1	1
2	Goodbye *Mary Hopkin* (Apple)	2	5	8	12
3	The Israelites *Desmond Dekker and The Aces* (Pyramid)	6	8	17	–
4	Pinball Wizard *The Who* (Track)	4	10	11	–
5	Come Back And Shake Me *Clodagh Rodgers* (RCA)	3	4	7	10
6	Cupid *Johnny Nash* (Major Minor)	10	14	19	–
7	Harlem Shuffle *Bob and Earl* (Island)	11	13	16	–
8	Windmills Of Your Mind *Noel Harrison* (Reprise)	19	17	–	–
9	I Heard It Through The Grapevine *Marvin Gaye* (Tamla Motown)	–	–	–	–
10	Boom Bang-A-Bang *Lulu* (Columbia)	–	17	–	–
11	Man Of The World *Fleetwood Mac* (Blue Horizon)	7	3	3	2
12	Gentle On My Mind *Dean Martin* (Reprise)	13	16	–	–
13	Road Runner *Jnr. Walker and The All Stars* (Tamla Motown)	12	12	12	17
14	In The Bad Bad Old Days *The Foundations* (Pye)	–	–	–	–
15	My Sentimental Friend *Herman's Hermits* (Columbia)	5	2	2	4
16	My Way *Frank Sinatra* (Capitol)	9	6	6	5
17	I Don't Know Why *Stevie Wonder* (Tamla Motown)	16	–	–	–

3	10	17	24	31
18 I Can Hear Music *The Beach Boys* (Capitol)	–	–	–	–
19 Games People Play *Joe South* (Capitol)	–	–	–	–
20 Behind The Painted Smile *The Isley Brothers* (Tamla Motown)	8	7	5	6
29 Living In Shame *Diana Ross and The Supremes* (Tamla Motown)	14	–	15	16
25 The Boxer *Simon and Garfunkel* (CBS)	15	9	9	7
24 Dizzy *Tommy Roe* (Stateside)	17	11	4	3
28 Badge *Cream* (Polydor)	18	–	20	–
21 Passing Strangers *Sarah Vaughan and Billy Eckstine* (Mercury)	20	20	–	–
36 Ragamuffin Man *Manfred Mann* (Fontana)	23	15	10	8
– Love Me Tonight *Tom Jones* (Decca)	–	19	14	9
35 Aquarius/Let The Sunshine In *Fifth Dimension* (Bell)	25	22	13	11
– Galveston *Glen Campbell* (Ember)	–	27	18	18
– Time Is Tight *Booker T. and The M.G.s* (Stax)	–	39	30	15
– Tracks Of My Tears *Smokey Robinson and The Miracles* (Tamla Motown)	–	37	30	19
– Higher And Higher *Jackie Wilson* (MCA)	–	–	39	20
– Dick-A-Dum-Dum *Des O'Connor* (Columbia)	–	46	28	14
– Oh Happy Day *The Edwin Hawkins Singers* (Buddah)	–	–	39	13

JUNE 1969

7	14	21	28
1 Dizzy *Tommy Roe* (Stateside)	2	3	6
2 Get Back *The Beatles* (Apple)	5	6	18
3 Man Of The World *Fleetwood Mac* (Immediate)	4	11	–
4 The Ballad Of John And Yoko *The Beatles* (Apple)	1	1	1
5 My Way *Frank Sinatra* (Capitol)	7	7	–
6 The Boxer *Simon and Garfunkel* (CBS)	8	10	–
7 My Sentimental Friend *Herman's Hermits* (Columbia)	18	–	–
8 Behind The Painted Smile *The Isley Brothers* (Tamla Motown)	20	–	–
9 Oh Happy Day *The Edwin Hawkins Singers* (Buddah)	3	2	2
10 Ragamuffin Man *Manfred Mann* (Fontana)	10	15	–
11 Love Me Tonight *Tom Jones* (Decca)	12	19	–
12 Time Is Tight *Booker T. and The M.G.s* (Stax)	6	4	4
13 Tracks Of My Tears *Smokey Robinson and The Miracles* (Tamla Motown)	9	12	10
14 Galveston *Glen Campbell* (Ember)	17	16	–
15 Higher And Higher *Jackie Wilson* (MCA)	11	13	13
16 Aquarius/Let The Sunshine In *Fifth Dimension* (Liberty)	16	–	–
17 I'd Rather Go Blind *Chicken Shack* (Blue Horizon)	19	14	17
18 Dick-A-Dum-Dum *Des O'Connor* (Columbia)	14	–	–
19 Come Back And Shake Me *Clodagh Rodgers* (RCA)	–	–	–
20 Goodbye *Mary Hopkin* (Apple)	–	–	–
25 Big Ship *Cliff Richard* (Columbia)	13	8	11
22 Living In The Past *Jethro Tull* (Island)	15	5	3
– In The Ghetto *Elvis Presley* (RCA)	36	9	5
– Something In The Air *Thunderclap Newman* (Track)	42	17	7
43 Way Of Life *The Family Dogg* (Bell)	34	18	15
35 Proud Mary *Creedence Clearwater Revival* (Liberty)	22	20	9
– Break-A-Way *The Beach Boys* (Capitol)	29	21	8
50 Frozen Orange Juice *Peter Sarstedt* (UA)	24	24	12
26 Gimme Gimme Good Lovin' *Crazy Elephant* (Major Minor)	21	22	14
38 What Is A Man? *The Four Tops* (Tamla Motown)	27	29	16
35 Happy Heart *Andy Williams* (CBS)	25	34	19
– Lights Of Cincinnati *Scott Walker* (Philips)	46	25	20

5		12	19	26
1 Something In The Air *Thunderclap Newman* (Track)		1	1	3
2 In The Ghetto *Elvis Presley* (RCA)		2	2	4
3 The Ballad Of John And Yoko *The Beatles* (Apple)		3	11	15
4 Living In The Past *Jethro Tull* (Island)		5	12	–
5 Oh Happy Day *The Edwin Hawkins Singers* (Buddah)		11	20	–
6 Time Is Tight *Booker T. and The M.G.s* (Stax)		10	17	19
7 Break-A-Way *The Beach Boys* (Capitol)		6	8	11
8 Way Of Life *The Family Dogg* (Bell)		7	6	10
9 Proud Mary *Creedence Clearwater Revival* (Liberty)		8	10	13
10 Frozen Orange Juice *Peter Sarstedt* (UA)		12	14	–
11 Big Ship *Cliff Richard* (Columbia)		15	–	–
12 Gimme Gimme Good Lovin' *Crazy Elephant* (Major Minor)		14	16	17
13 Dizzy *Tommy Roe* (Stateside)		19	22	–
14 Lights Of Cincinnati *Scott Walker* (Philips)		13	13	14
15 Hello Susie *Amen Corner* (Immediate)		4	5	6
16 Tracks Of My Tears *Smokey Robinson and The Miracles* (Tamla Motown)		–	–	–
17 Higher And Higher *Jackie Wilson* (MCA)		–	–	–
18 I'd Rather Go Blind *Chicken Shack* (Blue Horizon)		–	–	–
19 Baby Make It Soon *The Marmalade* (CBS)		18	9	9
20 My Way *Frank Sinatra* (Reprise)		–	–	–
– Honky Tonk Women *The Rolling Stones* (Decca)		9	3	1
27 It Mek *Desmond Dekker* (Pyramid)		16	7	7
24 What Is A Man? *The Four Tops* (Tamla Motown)		17	–	–
42 That's The Way God Planned It *Billy Preston* (Apple)		20	15	12
– Saved By The Bell *Robin Gibb* (Polydor)		25	18	5
32 Make Me An Island *Joe Dolan* (Pye)		29	19	16
– Goodnight Midnight *Clodagh Rodgers* (RCA)		31	23	8
– Babarabajagal *Donovan and The Jeff Beck Group* (Pye)		44	25	18
– Conversations *Cilla Black* (Parlophone)		32	24	20
– Give Peace A Chance *The Plastic Ono Band* (Apple)		21	4	2

2	9	16	23	30
1 Honky Tonk Women *The Rolling Stones* (Decca)	1	1	1	2
2 Give Peace A Chance *The Plastic Ono Band* (Apple)	2	4	6	15
3 Saved By The Bell *Robin Gibb* (Polydor)	3	2	2	3
4 In The Ghetto *Elvis Presley* (RCA)	5	11	16	20
5 Something In The Air *Thunderclap Newman* (Track)	12	–	–	–
6 Goodnight Midnight *Clodagh Rodgers* (RCA)	4	6	7	16
7 Make Me An Island *Joe Dolan* (Pye)	7	3	5	5
8 It Mek *Desmond Dekker* (Pyramid)	10	–	–	–
9 Baby Make It Soon *The Marmalade* (CBS)	9	18	–	–
10 Hello Susie *Amen Corner* (Immediate)	18	–	–	–
11 That's The Way God Planned It *Billy Preston* (Apple)	11	16	–	–
12 Babarabajagal *Donovan and The Jeff Beck Group* (Pye)	14	14	–	–
13 Conversations *Cilla Black* (Parlophone)	8	7	9	13
14 Way Of Life *The Family Dogg* (Bell)	20	–	–	–
15 Wet Dream *Max Romeo* (Unity)	–	10	13	18
16 My Cherie Amour *Stevie Wonder* (Tamla Motown)	6	5	4	4
17 Break-A-Way *The Beach Boys* (Capitol)	–	–	–	–
18 When Two Worlds Collide *Jim Reeves* (RCA)	–	17	–	–
19 Bringing On Back The Good Times *The Love Affair* (CBS)	13	9	11	12
20 Time Is Tight *Booker T. and The M.G.s* (Stax)	–	–	–	–
25 I Can Sing A Rainbow/Love Is Blue *The Dells* (Chelsea)	15	15	15	–
29 Peaceful *Georgie Fame* (CBS)	16	–	–	–
21 Early In The Morning *Vanity Fare* (Page One)	17	8	10	10

2	9	16	23	30
34 Curly *The Move* (Regal Zonophone)	19	19	12	14
28 Too Busy Thinking About My Baby *Marvin Gaye* (Tamla Motown)	32	12	8	7
– In The Year 2525 *Zager and Evans* (RCA)	21	13	3	1
37 Viva Bobbie Joe *The Equals* (President)	25	20	14	6
45 Je T'Aime, Moi Non Plus *Jane Birkin and Serge Gainsbourg* (Fontana)	-	32	17	17
– Don't Forget To Remember *The Bee Gees* (Polydor)	–	43	18	9
39 I'm A Better Man *Engelbert Humperdinck* (Decca)	–	28	19	–
– Bad Moon Rising *Creedence Clearwater Revival* (Liberty)	–	49	20	8
– Natural Born Boogie *Humble Pie* (Immediate)	–	–	23	11
– Good Morning Starshine *Oliver* (CBS)	48	31	26	19

SEPTEMBER 1969

6	13	20	27
1 In The Year 2525 *Zager and Evans* (RCA)	1	3	5
2 Bad Moon Rising *Creedence Clearwater Revival* (Liberty)	2	1	1
3 Honky Tonk Women *The Rolling Stones* (Decca)	9	10	18
4 My Cherie Amour *Stevie Wonder* (Tamla Motown)	8	11	16
5 Don't Forget To Remember *The Bee Gees* (Polydor)	3	2	3
6 Too Busy Thinking About My Baby *Marvin Gaye* (Tamla Motown)	5	6	8
7 Viva Bobbie Joe *The Equals* (President)	7	7	9
8 Je T'Aime, Moi Non Plus *Jane Birkin and Serge Gainsbourg* (Fontana)	6	4	2
9 Saved By The Bell *Robin Gibb* (Polydor)	10	12	–
10 Natural Born Boogie *Humble Pie* (Immediate)	4	5	6
11 Make Me An Island *Joe Dolan* (Pye)	12	13	–
12 Early In The Morning *Vanity Fare* (Page One)	14	–	–
13 Curly *The Move* (Regal Zonophone)	13	20	–
14 Good Morning Starshine *Oliver* (CBS)	11	8	7
15 Conversations *Cilla Black* (Parlophone)	–	–	–
16 Give Peace A Chance *The Plastic Ono Band* (Apple)	–	–	–
17 I'm A Better Man *Engelbert Humperdinck* (Decca)	15	18	–
18 Bringing On Back The Good Times *The Love Affair* (CBS)	–	–	–
19 Goodnight Midnight *Clodagh Rodgers* (RCA)	20	–	–
20 Wet Dream *Max Romeo* (Unity)	18	–	–
– Cloud Nine *The Temptations* (Tamla Motown)	16	–	15
– Marrakesh Express *Crosby, Stills and Nash* (Atlantic)	17	–	17
– I'll Never Fall In Love Again *Bobby Gentry* (Capitol)	19	9	4
– Throw Down A Line *Cliff Richard and Hank Marvin* (Columbia)	34	14	14
– A Boy Named Sue *Johnny Cash* (CBS)	41	15	10
– It's Getting Better *Mama Cass* (Stateside)	26	16	11
– Birth *The Peddlers* (CBS)	27	17	–
– Hare Krishna Mantra *Radha Krishna Temple* (Apple)	44	19	19
– Lay Lady Lay *Bob Dylan* (CBS)	30	31	12
– Put Yourself In My Place *The Isley Brothers* (Tamla Motown)	23	28	13
– Nobody's Child *Karen Young* (Major Minor)	35	30	20

Due to print schedules Record Mirror *did not publish a chart for 6 September 1969. However, it would have used the BMRB listing, and this we have done.*

4		11	18	25
1	Bad Moon Rising *Creedence Clearwater Revival* (Liberty)	3	12	18
2	I'll Never Fall In Love Again *Bobby Gentry* (Capitol)	2	1	2
3	Je T'Aime, Moi Non Plus *Jane Birkin and Serge Gainsbourg* (Major Minor)	1	2	4
4	A Boy Named Sue *Johnny Cash* (CBS)	4	4	10
5	Don't Forget To Remember *The Bee Gees* (Polydor)	7	16	16
6	Good Morning Starshine *Oliver* (CBS)	6	10	12
7	Throw Down A Line *Cliff Richard and Hank Marvin* (Columbia)	8	14	15
8	It's Getting Better *Mama Cass* (Stateside)	9	13	14
9	Lay Lady Lay *Bob Dylan* (CBS)	5	7	9
10	In The Year 2525 *Zager and Evans* (RCA)	18	–	–
11	Natural Born Boogie *Humble Pie* (Immediate)	17	–	–
12	Hare Krishna Mantra *Radha Krishna Temple* (Apple)	12	15	–
13	Viva Bobbie Joe *The Equals* (President)	–	–	–
14	Nobody's Child *Karen Young* (Major Minor)	10	6	7
15	Too Busy Thinking About My Baby *Marvin Gaye* (Tamla Motown)	–	–	–
16	Je T'Aime, Moi Non Plus *Jane Birkin and Serge Gainsbourg* (Fontana)	–	–	–
17	I'm Gonna Make You Mine *Lou Christie* (Buddah)	11	3	3
18	I Second That Emotion *Diana Ross and The Supremes and The Temptations* (Tamla Motown)	–	19	–
19	Love At First Sight *Sounds Nice* (Parlophone)	–	18	19
20	Space Oddity *David Bowie* (Philips)	13	8	6
34	Oh Well *Fleetwood Mac* (Reprise)	14	9	8
25	Put Yourself In My Place *The Isley Brothers* (Tamla Motown)	15	–	–
32	He Ain't Heavy, He's My Brother *The Hollies* (Parlophone)	16	5	5
27	Do What You Gotta Do *The Four Tops* (Tamla Motown)	19	17	11
31	Cloud Nine *The Temptations* (Tamla Motown)	20	–	–
–	Sugar Sugar *The Archies* (RCA)	43	11	1
50	Return Of Django/Dollar In The Teeth *The Upsetters* (Island)	37	20	17
44	Love's Been Good To Me *Frank Sinatra* (Capitol)	26	21	13
39	Delta Lady *Joe Cocker* (Regal Zonophone)	39	30	20

1		8	15	22	29
1	Sugar Sugar *The Archies* (RCA)	1	1	1	1
2	I'm Gonna Make You Mine *Lou Christie* (Buddah)	3	10	16	–
3	He Ain't Heavy, He's My Brother *The Hollies* (Parlophone)	4	4	11	18
4	Oh Well *Fleetwood Mac* (Reprise)	2	2	3	4
5	Space Oddity *David Bowie* (Philips)	7	16	18	–
6	I'll Never Fall In Love Again *Bobby Gentry* (Capitol)	9	15	–	–
7	Nobody's Child *Karen Young* (Major Minor)	6	9	8	11
8	Return Of Django/Dollar In The Teeth *The Upsetters* (Island)	5	5	5	8
9	Je T'Aime, Moi Non Plus *Jane Birkin and Serge Gainsbourg* (Major Minor)	14	20	–	–
10	A Boy Named Sue *Johnny Cash* (CBS)	12	18	–	–
11	Lay Lady Lay *Bob Dylan* (CBS)	20	–	–	–
12	Delta Lady *Joe Cocker* (Regal Zonophone)	10	11	14	–
13	Love's Been Good To Me *Frank Sinatra* (Reprise)	8	8	12	12
14	Do What You Gotta Do *The Four Tops* (Tamla Motown)	16	–	–	–
15	It's Getting Better *Mama Cass* (Stateside)	–	–	–	–
16	Bad Moon Rising *Creedence Clearwater Revival* (Liberty)	–	–	–	–

	1	8	15	22	29
17 Good Morning Starshine *Oliver* (CBS)		–	–	–	–
18 Wonderful World Beautiful People *Jimmy Cliff* (Trojan)	18	11	7	6	7
19 Don't Forget To Remember *The Bee Gees* (Polydor)	19	–	–	–	–
20 (Call Me) Number One *The Tremeloes* (CBS)	20	13	3	2	2
– Something/Come Together *The Beatles* (Apple)	–	15	6	4	6
22 What Does It Take *Jnr. Walker and The All Stars* (Tamla Motown)	22	17	13	13	13
38 Cold Turkey *The Plastic Ono Band* (Apple)	38	18	14	15	16
36 Sweet Dream *Jethro Tull* (Chrysalis)	36	19	12	7	10
31 The Liquidator *Harry J. and The All Stars* (Trojan)	31	24	17	17	9
45 Ruby Don't Take Your Love To Town *Kenny Rogers and The First Edition* (Reprise)	45	21	19	9	5
– Winter World Of Love *Engelbert Humperdinck* (Decca)	–	–	46	19	15
– Yester-Me, Yester-You, Yesterday *Stevie Wonder* (Tamla Motown)	–	–	31	10	3
49 Teresa *Joe Dolan* (Pye)	49	30	28	20	–
– Melting Pot *Blue Mink* (Philips)	–	–	50	27	14
– Two Little Boys *Rolf Harris* (Columbia)	–	–	–	32	17
– Onion Song *Mervin Gaye and Tammi Terrell* (Tamla Motown)	–	–	36	33	19
– Love Is All *Malcolm Roberts* (Major Minor)	–	–	–	30	20

DECEMBER 1969

	6	13	20
1 Sugar Sugar *The Archies* (RCA)	1	1	3
2 Yester-Me, Yester-You, Yesterday *Stevie Wonder* (Tamla Motown)	2	4	4
3 Ruby Don't Take Your Love To Town *Kenny Rogers and The First Edition* (Reprise)	3	2	2
4 (Call Me) Number One *The Tremeloes* (CBS)	4	6	9
5 Two Little Boys *Rolf Harris* (Columbia)	5	3	1
6 Oh Well *Fleetwood Mac* (Reprise)	6	18	–
7 Melting Pot *Blue Mink* (Philips)	7	5	5
8 Something/Come Together *The Beatles* (Apple)	8	11	18
9 Sweet Dream *Jethro Tull* (Chrysalis)	9	16	–
10 Suspicious Minds *Elvis Presley* (RCA)	10	8	6
11 Wonderful World Beautiful People *Jimmy Cliff* (Trojan)	11	10	17
12 Winter World Of Love *Engelbert Humperdinck* (Decca)	12	7	8
13 The Liquidator *Harry J. and The All Stars* (Trojan)	13	13	11
14 Return of Django/Dollar In The Teeth *The Upsetters* (Island)	14	–	–
15 Nobody's Child *Karen Young* (Major Minor)	15	14	–
16 Leavin' (Durham Town) *Roger Whittaker* (Columbia)	16	19	14
17 Onion Song *Marvin Gaye and Tammi Terrell* (Tamla Motown)	17	9	13
18 Love's Been Good To Me *Frank Sinatra* (Capitol)	18	–	–
19 Cold Turkey *The Plastic Ono Band* (Apple)	19	–	–
20 What Does It Take *Jnr. Walker and The All Stars* (Tamla Motown)	20	–	–
21 Love Is All *Malcolm Roberts* (Major Minor)	21	12	15
23 Tracy *The Cuff Links* (MCA)	23	15	10
27 All I Have To Do Is Dream *Bobby Gentry and Glen Campbell* (Capitol)	27	17	7
24 Green River *Creedence Clearwater Revival* (Liberty)	24	20	–
– Without Love *Tom Jones* (Decca)	–	21	12
30 Good Old Rock 'n' Roll *The Dave Clark Five* (Columbia)	30	25	16
26 Loneliness *Des O'Connor* (Columbia)	26	24	19
45 With The Eyes Of A Child *Cliff Richard* (Columbia)	45	39	20

1969—BEST-SELLING SINGLES

1 My Way *Frank Sinatra* (Capitol)
2 Je T'Aime, Moi Non Plus *Jane Birkin and Serge Gainsbourg* (Fontana/Major Minor)
3 Gentle On My Mind *Dean Martin* (Capitol)
4 Honky Tonk Women *The Rolling Stones* (Decca)
5 Nobody's Child *Karen Young* (Major Minor)
6 Saved By The Bell *Robin Gibb* (Polydor)
7 Please Don't Go *Donald Peers* (Columbia)
8 Get Back *The Beatles* (Apple)
9 I'll Never Fall In Love Again *Bobby Gentry* (Capitol)
10 Dizzy *Tommy Roe* (Stateside)
11 Albatross *Fleetwood Mac* (Blue Horizon)
12 In The Ghetto *Elvis Presley* (RCA)
13 I Heard It Through The Grapevine *Marvin Gaye* (Tamla Motown)
14 Sugar Sugar *The Archies* (RCA)
15 Bad Moon Rising *Creedence Clearwater Revival* (Liberty)
16 Make Me An Island *Joe Dolan* (Pye)
17 Where Do You Go To My Lovely *Peter Sarstedt* (UA)
18 My Cherie Amour *Stevie Wonder* (Tamla Motown)
19 Time Is Tight *Booker T. and The M.G.s* (Stax)
20 Don't Forget To Remember *The Bee Gees* (Polydor)

1969—BEST-SELLING ALBUMS

1 Best Of The Seekers *The Seekers*
2 Sound Of Music *Soundtrack of film*
3 His Orchestra His Singers *Ray Conniff*
4 Abbey Road *The Beatles*
5 Johnny Cash At San Quentin *Johnny Cash*
6 Oliver *Soundtrack of film*
7 According To My Heart *Jim Reeves*
8 Goodbye *Mary Hopkin*
9 Nashville Skyline *Bob Dylan*
10 Diana Ross And The Supremes Join The Temptations *Diana Ross and The Supremes with The Temptations*
11 Motown Chartbusters *Various artists*
12 Hair *London cast of play*
12 World Of Mantovani Vol. 1 *Mantovani*
14 World Of Val Doonican *Val Doonican*
15 On The Threshold Of A Dream *The Moody Blues*
15 World Of Mantovani Vol. 2 *Mantovani*
17 The Beatles (White Album) *The Beatles*
18 Flaming Star *Elvis Presley*
19 Stand Up *Jethro Tull*
20 This Is Tom Jones *Tom Jones*

1969—BEST-SELLING ARTISTS

Male Artists (Singles)

1 Stevie Wonder
2 Elvis Presley
3 Marvin Gaye
4 Frank Sinatra
5 Engelbert Humperdinck
6 Desmond Dekker
7 Peter Sarstedt
8 Cliff Richard
9 Dean Martin
10 Johnny Nash

Female Artists (Singles)

1 Clodagh Rodgers
2 Cilla Black
3 Lulu
4 Karen Young
5 Bobby Gentry
6 Mary Hopkin
7 Nina Simone
8 Sandie Shaw
9 Mama Cass
10 Dusty Springfield

Groups (Singles)

1 Fleetwood Mac
2 The Beatles
3 Creedence Clearwater Revival
4 The Isley Brothers
5 The Bee Gees
6 The Marmalade
7 Herman's Hermits
8 The Hollies
9 Jethro Tull
10 The Beach Boys

1970

If 1969 lacked a lively Top Fifty, let alone a Top Twenty, then 1970 hardly brought a vast improvement. Admittedly, there were several new names, of which The Jackson Five were the most interesting from a teen sensation point of view. They soon accumulated four Top Ten singles, though their chart positions did not reflect the furore which was created by teen journals and some record papers. 'I Want You Back' reached Number Two, but 'ABC' and 'The Love You Save' did not even enter the Top Five.

Marc Bolan, The Carpenters and Hot Chocolate all announced their arrival, though each had only one hit in 1970. For a while Mary Hopkin, a Welsh girl who had been discovered by Paul McCartney and who recorded on The Beatles' Apple label, had promised much, but very little happened for Mary after her third disc in 1970 failed to reach the Top Ten. Her previous records had all entered the Top Ten, and 'Those Were The Days', her first hit in 1968, had been a Number One, but her swan-song 'Think About Your Children' only managed a chart zenith of Number Nineteen.

The regulars from the 1960s found life a trifle sticky. Cliff Richard had one of his worst years since his arrival in 1958 and only managed one hit 'Goodbye Sam, Hello Samantha'. The Hollies had two hits, but Lulu did not appear in the charts at all. Tom Jones appeared in the listings for 1970 with 'Daughter Of Darkness' and 'I Who Have Nothing'. However, Elvis Presley showed resilience with three hits, including a Number One in the form of a powerful ballad with good lyrics called 'The Wonder Of You'. The Stones had no Top Twenty hits during 1970, but Simon and Garfunkel took their 'Bridge Over Troubled Water' into the Top Twenty, where it remained for a total of 13 weeks. Julie Felix, a veteran of Flower Power and folk music, signed with RAK Records, where she was guided by the successful Mickie Most. She recorded several successful songs and one, 'If I Could', gave her the Top Twenty placing for which she had so long strived. Alas, it was her only top disc, though one of her later records bubbled just under the Top Twenty.

Dana, an Irish girl with looks to melt, won the Eurovision Song Contest with 'All Kinds Of Everything', a record which sold two million copies around the world.

Black Sabbath appeared in the Top Five with 'Paranoid', while in completely different vein came Joni Mitchell with 'Big Yellow Taxi'. Hotlegs and their 'Neanderthal Man' entered the charts, an item which is interesting because of the fact that several members of Hotlegs were ex-members of The Mindbenders, Wayne Fontana's backing group in the 1960s. When Hotlegs disbanded, several of the members went on to form 10cc, a successful 1970s band.

Tamla Motown music reigned supreme, even without the aid of The Jackson Five, for many hits came for members of the Motown stable of artists, including Stevie Wonder, The Temptations, The Supremes, Diana Ross, Marvin Gaye, Jimmy Ruffin, The Four Tops, The Motown Spinners and Smokey Robinson.

JANUARY 1970

3		10	17	24	31
1	Two Little Boys *Rolf Harris* (Columbia)	1	1	1	2
2	Ruby Don't Take Your Love To Town *Kenny Rogers and The First Edition* (Reprise)	2	4	2	7
3	Sugar Sugar *The Archies* (RCA)	6	6	9	14
4	Suspicious Minds *Elvis Presley* (RCA)	7	2	6	6
5	Melting Pot *Blue Mink* (Philips)	3	7	10	16
6	Yester-Me, Yester-You, Yesterday *Stevie Wonder* (Tamla Motown)	9	14	–	–
7	All I Have To Do Is Dream *Bobby Gentry and Glen Campbell* (Capitol)	5	3	4	5
8	Winter World Of Love *Engelbert Humperdinck* (Decca)	14	16	–	–
9	Tracy *The Cuff Links* (MCA)	4	5	5	11
10	Without Love *Tom Jones* (Decca)	13	11	17	–
11	Onion Song *Marvin Gaye and Tammi Terrell* (Tamla Motown)	11	19	–	–
12	Good Old Rock 'n' Roll *The Dave Clark Five* (Columbia)	8	8	7	13
13	Leavin' (Durham Town) *Roger Whittaker* (Columbia)	12	12	19	18
14	(Call Me) Number One *The Tremeloes* (CBS)	15	–	–	–
15	Love Is All *Malcolm Roberts* (Major Minor)	–	–	–	–
16	The Liquidator *Harry J. and The All Stars* (Trojan)	10	17	15	17
17	But You Love Me Daddy *Jim Reeves* (RCA)	17	15	18	19
18	Loneliness *Des O'Connor* (Columbia)	–	–	–	–
19	Green River *Creedence Clearwater Revival* (Liberty)	–	–	–	–
20	Nobody's Child *Karen Young* (Major Minor)	–	–	–	–
30	Reflections Of My Life *The Marmalade* (Decca)	16	9	3	3
21	Something/Come Together *The Beatles* (Apple)	18	–	–	–
47	Comin' Home *Delaney and Bonnie* (Atlantic)	19	–	16	–
29	If I Thought You'd Ever Change Your Mind *Cilla Black* (Parlophone)	20	–	–	–
–	Friends *Arrival* (Decca)	–	18	11	8
–	Come And Get It *Badfinger* (Apple)	33	10	8	4
27	Some Day We'll Be Together *Diana Ross and The Supremes* (Tamla Motown)	24	13	14	15
22	With The Eyes Of A Child *Cliff Richard* (Columbia)	22	20	–	–
–	Leavin' On A Jet Plane *Peter, Paul and Mary* (Warner Bros.)	–	36	13	9
–	Love Grows *Edison Lighthouse* (Bell)	–	–	12	1
–	Witches Promise/Teacher *Jethro Tull* (Chrysalis)	–	–	30	10
–	I'm A Man *Chicago* (CBS)	–	23	20	12
–	I Can't Get Next To You *The Temptations* (Tamla Motown)	–	39	26	20

FEBRUARY 1970

7		14	21	28
1	Love Grows *Edison Lighthouse* (Bell)	1	1	1
2	Two Little Boys *Rolf Harris* (Columbia)	7	10	15
3	Reflections Of My Life *The Marmalade* (Decca)	6	15	–
4	Leavin' On A Jet Plane *Peter, Paul and Mary* (Warner Bros.)	2	3	6
5	Come And Get It *Badfinger* (Apple)	5	13	19
6	Witches Promise/Teacher *Jethro Tull* (Chrysalis)	4	8	12
7	Ruby Don't Take Your Love To Town *Kenny Rogers and The First Edition* (Reprise)	13	18	20
8	I'm A Man *Chicago* (CBS)	9	14	18
9	Friends *Arrival* (Decca)	11	–	–
10	Temma Harbour *Mary Hopkin* (Apple)	8	6	7
11	All I Have To Do Is Dream *Bobby Gentry and Glen Campbell* (Capitol)	15	–	–

7	14	21	28
12 Suspicious Minds *Elvis Presley* (RCA)	17	–	–
13 I Can't Get Next To You *The Temptations* (Tamla Motown)	14	17	17
14 Tracy *The Cuff Links* (MCA)	–	–	–
15 Let's Work Together *Canned Heat* (Liberty)	3	2	3
16 Hitchin' A Ride *Vanity Fare* (Page One)	20	16	–
17 Someday We'll Be Together *Diana Ross and The Supremes* (Tamla Motown)	19	–	–
18 Good Old Rock 'n' Roll *The Dave Clark Five* (Columbia)	–	–	–
19 Sugar Sugar *The Archies* (RCA)	–	–	–
20 The Liquidator *Harry J. and The All Stars* (Trojan)	–	–	–
21 Venus *Shocking Blue* (Penny Farthing)	10	9	8
30 I Want You Back *The Jackson Five* (Tamla Motown)	12	4	4
28 Wedding Bell Blues *Fifth Dimension* (Liberty)	16	–	–
36 Wanderin' Star *Lee Marvin* (Paramount)	18	5	2
– Instant Karma *John Lennon and Yoko Ono with The Plastic Ono Band* (Apple)	–	7	5
49 My Baby Loves Lovin' *White Plains* (Deram)	22	11	9
32 Years May Come, Years May Go *Herman's Hermits* (Columbia)	24	12	11
– United We Stand *Brotherhood Of Man* (Deram)	40	19	10
25 Both Sides Now *Judy Collins* (Elektra)	23	20	14
– Bridge Over Troubled Water *Simon and Garfunkel* (CBS)	–	42	13
41 Raindrops Keep Fallin' On My Head *Sacha Distel* (Warner Bros.)	32	26	16

MARCH 1970

7	14	21	28
1 Wanderin' Star *Lee Marvin* (Paramount)	1	1	2
2 I Want You Back *The Jackson Five* (Tamla Motown)	4	4	12
3 Let's Work Together *Canned Heat* (Liberty)	7	12	14
4 Love Grows *Edison Lighthouse* (Bell)	5	17	19
5 Instant Karma *John Lennon and Yoko Ono with The Plastic Ono Band* (Apple)	6	10	15
6 Leavin' On A Jet Plane *Peter, Paul and Mary* (Warner Bros.)	15	19	–
7 Bridge Over Troubled Water *Simon and Garfunkel* (CBS)	3	2	1
8 Years May Come, Years May Go *Herman's Hermits* (Columbia)	9	7	13
9 My Baby Loves Lovin' *White Plains* (Deram)	14	18	–
10 Temma Harbour *Mary Hopkin* (Apple)	19	–	–
11 United We Stand *Brotherhood Of Man* (Deram)	12	16	17
12 Venus *Shocking Blue* (Penny Farthing)	16	–	–
13 Na Na Hey Hey Kiss Him Goodbye *Steam* (Fontana)	13	9	10
14 Elizabethan Reggae *Boris Gardner* (Duke)	–	–	–
15 Raindrops Keep Fallin' On My Head *Sacha Distel* (Warner Bros.)	10	14	16
16 Something's Burning *Kenny Rogers and The First Edition* (Reprise)	18	13	11
17 Both Sides Now *Judy Collins* (Elektra)	–	–	–
18 Don't Cry Daddy *Elvis Presley* (RCA)	11	8	9
19 That Same Old Feeling *Pickettywitch* (Pye)	8	5	5
20 Two Little Boys *Rolf Harris* (Columbia)	–	20	–
– Let It Be *The Beatles* (Apple)	2	3	4
– Can't Help Falling In Love *Andy Williams* (CBS)	17	6	3
28 Everybody Get Together *The Dave Clark Five* (Columbia)	20	11	8
– Young, Gifted And Black *Bob and Marcia* (Harry J.)	22	15	6
– Knock Knock Who's There *Mary Hopkin* (Apple)	–	–	7
32 Farewell Is A Lonely Sound *Jimmy Ruffin* (Tamla Motown)	29	23	18
48 You're Such A Good Looking Woman *Joe Dolan* (Pye)	28	26	20

4		11	18	25
1	Bridge Over Troubled Water *Simon and Garfunkel* (CBS)	1	2	3
2	Knock Knock Who's There *Mary Hopkin* (Apple)	4	4	5
3	Can't Help Falling In Love *Andy Williams* (CBS)	3	3	4
4	Wanderin' Star *Lee Marvin* (Paramount)	5	8	13
5	Young, Gifted And Black *Bob and Marcia* (Harry J.)	8	7	7
6	That Same Old Feeling *Pickettywitch* (Pye)	7	11	19
7	Let It Be *The Beatles* (Apple)	11	16	–
8	Something's Burning *Kenny Rogers and The First Edition* (Reprise)	9	15	18
9	Everybody Get Together *The Dave Clark Five* (Columbia)	15	–	–
10	Don't Cry Daddy *Elvis Presley* (RCA)	14	20	–
11	Na Na Hey Hey Kiss Him Goodbye *Steam* (Fontana)	18	–	–
12	I Want You Back *The Jackson Five* (Tamla Motown)	20	–	–
13	All Kinds Of Everything *Dana* (Rex)	2	1	1
14	Farewell Is A Lonely Sound *Jimmy Ruffin* (Tamla Motown)	13	9	9
15	Spirit In The Sky *Norman Greenbaum* (Reprise)	6	5	2
16	Years May Come, Years May Go *Herman's Hermits* (Columbia)	–	–	–
17	I Can't Help Myself *The Four Tops* (Tamla Motown)	12	10	11
18	You're Such A Good Looking Woman *Joe Dolan* (Pye)	17	17	–
19	Who Do You Love *Juicy Lucy* (Vertigo)	–	14	20
20	Let's Work Together *Canned Heat* (Liberty)	–	–	–
21	Gimme Dat Ding *The Pipkins* (Columbia)	10	6	6
22	When Julie Comes Around *The Cuff Links* (MCA)	16	12	12
39	Never Had A Dream Come True *Stevie Wonder* (Tamla Motown)	19	13	8
37	Good Morning Freedom *Blue Mink* (Philips)	21	18	10
35	Travellin' Band *Creedence Clearwater Revival* (Liberty)	27	19	15
40	House Of The Rising Sun *Frijid Pink* (Deram)	39	21	14
47	Rag Mama Rag *The Band* (Capitol)	33	25	16
–	Daughter Of Darkness *Tom Jones* (Decca)	–	33	17

2		9	16	23	30
1	Spirit In The Sky *Norman Greenbaum* (Reprise)	1	2	2	4
2	All Kinds Of Everything *Dana* (Rex)	3	5	10	–
3	Back Home *The England World Cup Squad* (Pye)	2	1	1	1
4	Bridge Over Troubled Water *Simon and Garfunkel* (CBS)	4	12	14	–
5	Can't Help Falling In Love *Andy Williams* (CBS)	7	11	12	–
6	Never Had A Dream Come True *Stevie Wonder* (Tamla Motown)	9	16	15	–
7	Gimme Dat Ding *The Pipkins* (Columbia)	11	18	–	–
8	Farewell Is A Lonely Sound *Jimmy Ruffin* (Tamla Motown)	16	14	–	–
9	House Of The Rising Sun *Frijid Pink* (Deram)	6	4	6	7
10	When Julie Comes Around *The Cuff Links* (MCA)	12	13	–	–
11	Travellin' Band *Creedence Clearwater Revival* (Liberty)	8	9	11	16
12	Good Morning Freedom *Blue Mink* (Philips)	13	–	–	–
13	Young, Gifted And Black *Bob and Marcia* (Harry J.)	18	–	–	–
14	Knock Knock Who's There *Mary Hopkin* (Apple)	15	–	–	–
15	Daughter Of Darkness *Tom Jones* (Decca)	5	8	5	9
16	Rag Mama Rag *The Band* (Capitol)	19	17	–	–
17	I Can't Help Myself *The Four Tops* (Tamla Motown)	–	–	–	–
18	Who Do You Love *Juicy Lucy* (Vertigo)	–	–	–	–
19	I Can't Tell The Bottom From The Top *The Hollies* (Parlophone)	10	7	9	15
20	You're Such A Good Looking Woman *Joe Dolan* (Pye)	–	–	–	–
27	Brontosaurus *The Move* (Regal Zonophone)	14	10	7	10

2		9	16	23	30
23	I Don't Believe In If Anymore *Roger Whittaker* (Columbia)	17	15	8	8
35	Question *The Moody Blues* (Threshold)	20	3	4	2
44	Yellow River *Christie* (CBS)	28	6	3	3
26	The Seeker *The Who* (Track)	24	19	–	–
24	I've Got You On My Mind *White Plains* (Deram)	22	20	17	17
–	Honey Come Back *Glen Campbell* (Capitol)	38	28	13	5
–	Everything Is Beautiful *Ray Stevens* (CBS)	–	40	16	12
29	Do The Funky Chicken *Rufus Thomas* (Stax)	26	25	18	–
28	If I Could *Julie Felix* (RAK)	25	23	19	–
–	ABC *The Jackson Five* (Tamla Motown)	–	41	20	11
48	Up The Ladder To The Roof *The Supremes* (Tamla Motown)	39	30	30	6
–	Groovin' With Mr Bloe *Mr Bloe* (DJM)	37	36	21	13
–	Cottonfields *The Beach Boys* (Capitol)	–	46	32	14
–	The Green Manalishi *Fleetwood Mac* (Reprise)	–	–	49	18
50	Don't You Know *Butterscotch* (RCA)	41	31	22	19
–	Abraham, Martin And John *Marvin Gaye* (Tamla Motown)	35	33	24	20

JUNE 1970

6		13	20	27
1	Yellow River *Christie* (CBS)	2	2	4
2	Back Home *The England World Cup Squad* (Pye)	3	9	15
3	Question *The Moody Blues* (Threshold)	6	12	17
4	Honey Come Back *Glen Campbell* (Capitol)	5	6	8
5	Daughter Of Darkness *Tom Jones* (Decca)	16	20	–
6	Everything Is Beautiful *Ray Stevens* (CBS)	9	8	11
7	Groovin' With Mr Bloe *Mr Bloe* (DJM)	4	3	2
8	ABC *The Jackson Five* (Tamla Motown)	10	14	–
9	Spirit In The Sky *Norman Greenbaum* (Reprise)	15	–	–
10	Up The Ladder To The Roof *The Supremes* (Tamla Motown)	8	13	12
11	I Don't Believe In If Anymore *Roger Whittaker* (Columbia)	12	19	19
12	Cottonfields *The Beach Boys* (Capitol)	7	5	6
13	In The Summertime *Mungo Jerry* (Dawn)	1	1	1
14	Abraham, Martin And John *Marvin Gaye* (Tamla Motown)	14	11	9
15	Brontosaurus *The Move* (Regal Zonophone)	18	–	–
16	House Of The Rising Sun *Frijid Pink* (Deram)	19	–	–
17	The Green Manalishi *Fleetwood Mac* (Reprise)	13	10	10
18	Don't You Know *Butterscotch* (RCA)	17	–	20
19	I've Got You On My Mind *White Plains* (Deram)	–	–	–
20	Do The Funky Chicken *Rufus Thomas* (Stax)	–	–	–
25	Sally *Gerry Monroe* (Chapter One)	11	7	5
37	Goodbye Sam, Hello Samantha *Cliff Richard* (Columbia)	20	15	7
36	All Right Now *Free* (Island)	27	4	3
34	I Will Survive *Arrival* (Decca)	23	16	16
31	It's All In The Game *The Four Tops* (Tamla Motown)	24	17	13
29	Down The Dustpipe *Status Quo* (Pye)	21	18	14
–	Up Around The Bend *Creedence Clearwater Revival* (Liberty)	–	33	18

JULY 1970

4		11	18	25
1	In The Summertime *Mungo Jerry* (Dawn)	1	1	1
2	All Right Now *Free* (Island)	2	2	2
3	Groovin' With Mr Bloe *Mr Bloe* (DJM)	3	8	14
4	Sally *Gerry Monroe* (Chapter One)	7	6	13
5	Cottonfields *The Beach Boys* (Capitol)	6	7	10
6	Goodbye Sam, Hello Samantha *Cliff Richard* (Columbia)	8	9	12
7	Yellow River *Christie* (CBS)	15	17	18

167

4	11	18	25
8 It's All In The Game *The Four Tops* (Tamla Motown)	5	5	6
9 Up Around The Bend *Creedence Clearwater Revival* (Liberty)	4	3	5
10 The Green Manalishi *Fleetwood Mac* (Reprise)	10	16	17
11 Honey Come Back *Glen Campbell* (Capitol)	14	15	19
12 Down The Dustpipe *Status Quo* (Pye)	12	14	16
13 Abraham, Martin And John *Marvin Gaye* (Tamla Motown)	11	–	–
14 Everything Is Beautiful *Ray Stevens* (CBS)	18	–	–
15 Love Of The Common People *Nicky Thomas* (Trojan)	9	11	9
16 Something *Shirley Bassey* (UA)	13	10	7
17 I Will Survive *Arrival* (Decca)	17	–	–
18 Up The Ladder To The Roof *The Supremes* (Tamla Motown)	–	–	–
19 American Woman *Guess Who* (RCA)	–	–	–
20 Question *The Moody Blues* (Threshold)	–	–	–
22 Lola *The Kinks* (Pye)	16	4	4
28 Lady D'Arbanville *Cat Stevens* (Island)	19	12	11
– The Wonder Of You *Elvis Presley* (RCA)	20	13	3
39 (It's Like A) Sad Old Kinda Movie *Pickettywitch* (Pye)	27	18	–
45 I'll Say Forever My Love *Jimmy Ruffin* (Tamla Motown)	30	19	15
29 Love Like A Man *Ten Years After* (Deram)	24	20	–
48 Neanderthal Man *Hotlegs* (Fontana)	32	21	8
31 Big Yellow Taxi *Joni Mitchell* (Reprise)	25	28	20

AUGUST 1970

1	8	15	22	29
1 The Wonder Of You *Elvis Presley* (RCA)	1	1	1	1
2 All Right Now *Free* (Island)	4	5	12	14
3 Lola *The Kinks* (Pye)	2	3	4	5
4 In The Summertime *Mungo Jerry* (Dawn)	6	8	9	16
5 Something *Shirley Bassey* (UA)	5	4	6	8
6 Neanderthal Man *Hotlegs* (Fontana)	3	2	2	3
7 It's All In The Game *The Four Tops* (Tamla Motown)	9	14	–	–
8 Up Around The Bend *Creedence Clearwater Revival* (Liberty)	11	–	–	–
9 I'll Say Forever My Love *Jimmy Ruffin* (Tamla Motown)	7	9	10	13
10 Lady D'Arbanville *Cat Stevens* (Island)	8	12	17	20
11 Love Of The Common People *Nicky Thomas* (Trojan)	13	18	–	–
12 Love Like A Man *Ten Years After* (Deram)	10	10	13	12
13 Goodbye Sam, Hello Samantha *Cliff Richard* (Columbia)	18	20	–	–
14 Cottonfields *The Beach Boys* (Capitol)	19	19	–	–
15 Sally *Gerry Monroe* (Chapter One)	20	–	–	–
16 (It's Like A) Sad Old Kinda Movie *Pickettywitch* (Pye)	–	–	–	–
17 Big Yellow Taxi *Joni Mitchell* (Reprise)	12	13	11	–
18 Signed, Sealed, Delivered, I'm Yours *Stevie Wonder* (Tamla Motown)	15	15	16	18
19 Groovin' With Mr Bloe *Mr Bloe* (DJM)	–	–	–	–
20 Rainbow *The Marmalade* (Decca)	14	7	3	4
22 Song Of Joy *Miguel Rios* (A & M)	16	–	18	–
23 Natural Sinner *Fair Weather* (RCA)	17	6	8	6
29 Tears Of A Clown *Smokey Robinson and The Miracles* (Tamla Motown)	25	11	5	2
30 25 Or 6 To 4 *Chicago* (CBS)	28	16	14	7
37 The Love You Save *The Jackson Five* (Tamla Motown)	24	17	7	10
36 Sweet Inspiration *Johnny Johnson and The Bandwagon* (Bell)	29	23	15	11
– Mama Told Me Not To Come *Three Dog Night* (Stateside)	42	30	19	9
– Love Is Life *Hot Chocolate* (RAK)	–	43	20	17
46 Make It With You *Bread* (Elektra)	37	33	22	15
– Give Me Just A Little More Time *Chairmen Of The Board* (Invictus)	–	–	34	19

168

SEPTEMBER 1970

5		12	19	26
1	The Wonder Of You *Elvis Presley* (RCA)	2	4	5
2	Tears Of A Clown *Smokey Robinson and The Miracles* (Tamla Motown)	1	2	2
3	Mama Told Me Not To Come *Three Dog Night* (Stateside)	3	5	6
4	Rainbow *The Marmalade* (Decca)	9	11	–
5	Give Me Just A Little More Time *Chairmen Of The Board* (Invictus)	4	3	3
6	Neanderthal Man *Hotlegs* (Fontana)	13	19	–
7	Make It With You *Bread* (Elektra)	5	7	10
8	25 Or 6 To 4 *Chicago* (CBS)	7	12	17
9	Something *Shirley Bassey* (UA)	15	14	–
10	Sweet Inspiration *Johnny Johnson and The Bandwagon* (Bell)	12	16	–
11	Natural Sinner *Fair Weather* (RCA)	17	–	–
12	Lola *The Kinks* (Pye)	18	–	–
13	Wild World *Jimmy Cliff* (Island)	8	9	12
14	The Love You Save *The Jackson Five* (Tamla Motown)	–	–	–
15	Love Is Life *Hot Chocolate* (RAK)	10	6	11
16	I (Who Have Nothing) *Tom Jones* (Decca)	–	–	–
17	It's So Easy *Andy Williams* (CBS)	16	13	–
18	Love Like A Man *Ten Years After* (Deram)	–	–	–
19	I'll Say Forever My Love *Jimmy Ruffin* (Tamla Motown)	–	–	–
20	You Can Get It If You Really Want It *Desmond Dekker* (Trojan)	14	8	4
36	Band Of Gold *Freda Payne* (Invictus)	6	1	1
24	Which Way You Goin' Billy? *The Poppy Family* (Decca)	11	10	7
29	Don't Play That Song *Aretha Franklin* (Atlantic)	19	17	13
30	Montego Bay *Bobby Bloom* (Polydor)	20	15	8
26	Strange Band *Family* (Reprise)	22	18	14
32	Black Night *Deep Purple* (Harvest)	34	20	9
43	Close To You *The Carpenters* (A & M)	38	31	15
–	Ain't No Mountain High Enough *Diana Ross* (Tamla Motown)	32	21	16
–	Me And My Life *The Tremeloes* (CBS)	39	30	18
47	Paranoid *Black Sabbath* (Vertigo)	37	28	19
41	Long As I Can See The Light *Creedence Clearwater Revival* (Liberty)	29	26	20

OCTOBER 1970

3		10	17	24	31
1	Band Of Gold *Freda Payne* (Invictus)	1	1	1	3
2	You Can Get It If You Really Want It *Desmond Dekker* (Trojan)	2	3	8	12
3	Montego Bay *Bobby Bloom* (Polydor)	5	7	11	8
4	Tears Of A Clown *Smokey Robinson and The Miracles* (Tamla Motown)	12	16	–	–
5	Black Night *Deep Purple* (Harvest)	3	2	2	5
6	Give Me Just A Little More Time *Chairmen Of The Board* (Invictus)	9	18	–	–
7	Which Way You Goin' Billy? *The Poppy Family* (Decca)	10	9	12	–
8	Paranoid *Black Sabbath* (Vertigo)	4	5	5	6
9	The Wonder Of You *Elvis Presley* (RCA)	11	17	20	–
10	Love Is Life *Hot Chocolate* (RAK)	17	–	–	–
11	Strange Band *Family* (Reprise)	15	12	–	–
12	Mama Told Me Not To Come *Three Dog Night* (Stateside)	18	–	–	–
13	Ain't No Mountain High Enough *Diana Ross* (Tamla Motown)	7	6	7	9

3		10	17	24	31
14	Close To You *The Carpenters* (A & M)	6	8	6	11
15	Me And My Life *The Tremeloes* (CBS)	8	4	4	4
16	Make It With You *Bread* (Elektra)	20	–	–	–
17	Wild World *Jimmy Cliff* (Island)	–	–	–	–
18	Don't Play That Song *Aretha Franklin* (Atlantic)	13	–	–	–
19	It's So Easy *Andy Williams* (CBS)	–	–	–	–
20	Black Pearl *Horace Faith* (Trojan)	14	13	15	–
26	Ball Of Confusion *The Temptations* (Tamla Motown)	16	10	9	7
24	Our World *Blue Mink* (Philips)	19	–	17	–
39	Woodstock *Matthews Southern Comfort* (Uni)	24	11	10	1
–	Patches *Clarence Carter* (Atlantic)	39	14	3	2
35	The Tip Of My Fingers *Des O'Connor* (Columbia)	33	15	19	17
29	Gasoline Alley Bred *The Hollies* (Parlophone)	23	19	14	16
50	Still Waters *The Four Tops* (Tamla Motown)	27	20	13	10
–	War *Edwin Starr* (Tamla Motown)	–	–	16	15
37	Ruby Tuesday *Melanie* (Buddah)	29	21	18	13
49	The Witch *Rattles* (Decca)	41	25	22	14
–	It's Wonderful *Jimmy Ruffin* (Tamla Motown)	–	38	27	18
–	Indian Reservation *Don Fardon* (Young Blood)	11	18	–	–
–	New World In The Morning *Roger Whittaker* (Columbia)	44	28	24	20

NOVEMBER 1970

7		14	21	28
1	Woodstock *Matthews Southern Comfort* (Uni)	1	2	4
2	Patches *Clarence Carter* (Atlantic)	2	4	8
3	Black Night *Deep Purple* (Harvest)	11	11	–
4	Band Of Gold *Freda Payne* (Invictus)	10	17	–
5	War *Edwin Starr* (Tamla Motown)	3	5	6
6	Me And My Life *The Tremeloes* (CBS)	6	12	–
7	Ball Of Confusion *The Temptations* (Tamla Motown)	14	14	–
8	The Witch *Rattles* (Decca)	8	8	15
9	Ruby Tuesday *Melanie* (Buddah)	9	9	14
10	Paranoid *Black Sabbath* (Vertigo)	13	–	–
11	Still Waters *The Four Tops* (Tamla Motown)	15	18	–
12	Indian Reservation *Don Fardon* (Young Blood)	4	3	3
13	Ain't No Mountain High Enough *Diana Ross* (Tamla Motown)	–	–	–
14	Close To You *The Carpenters* (A & M)	20	–	–
15	Voodoo Chile *Jimi Hendrix Experience* (Track)	5	1	2
16	It's Wonderful *Jimmy Ruffin* (Tamla Motown)	12	6	12
17	Gasoline Alley Bred *The Hollies* (Parlophone)	–	–	–
18	San Bernadino *Christie* (CBS)	7	7	11
19	You Can Get It If You Really Want It *Desmond Dekker* (Trojan)	–	–	–
20	The Tip Of My Fingers *Des O'Connor* (Columbia)	–	–	–
24	Julie Do Ya Love Me *White Plains* (Deram)	16	13	10
21	New World In The Morning *Roger Whittaker* (Columbia)	17	–	20
32	Whole Lotta Love *C.C.S.* (RAK)	18	20	13
25	Think About Your Children *Mary Hopkin* (Apple)	19	–	19
31	Ride A White Swan *T. Rex* (Fly)	30	15	7
–	I Hear You Knocking *Dave Edmunds* (MAM)	–	16	1
–	You've Got Me Dangling On A String *Chairmen Of The Board* (Invictus)	40	19	16
–	I've Lost You *Elvis Presley* (RCA)	26	23	9
–	Home Lovin' Man *Andy Williams* (CBS)	–	45	17
–	It's Only Make Believe *Glen Campbell* (Capitol)	–	38	18
–	Cracklin' Rosie *Neil Diamond* (Uni)	29	10	5

5		12	19	26
1	I Hear You Knocking *Dave Edmunds* (MAM)	1	1	1
2	Voodoo Chile *Jimi Hendrix Experience* (Track)	5	11	19
3	Cracklin' Rosie *Neil Diamond* (Uni)	3	3	6
4	Indian Reservation *Don Fardon* (Young Blood)	9	13	14
5	You've Got Me Dangling On A String *Chairmen Of The Board* (Invictus)	8	10	12
6	When I'm Dead And Gone *McGuiness Flint* (Capitol)	2	2	3
7	Ride A White Swan *T. Rex* (Fly)	6	12	10
8	Julie Do Ya Love Me *White Plains* (Deram)	14	16	16
9	I've Lost You *Elvis Presley* (RCA)	10	14	15
10	It's Wonderful *Jimmy Ruffin* (Tamla Motown)	19	19	–
11	Woodstock *Matthews Southern Comfort* (Uni)	–	–	–
12	My Prayer *Gerry Monroe* (Chapter One)	12	9	9
13	War *Edwin Starr* (Tamla Motown)	20	–	–
14	San Bernadino *Christie* (CBS)	15	–	–
15	I'll Be There *The Jackson Five* (Tamla Motown)	13	5	5
16	Patches *Clarence Carter* (Atlantic)	–	–	–
17	Home Lovin' Man *Andy Williams* (CBS)	7	7	7
18	It's Only Make Believe *Glen Campbell* (Capitol)	4	4	4
19	Whole Lotta Love *C.C.S.* (RAK)	18	–	–
20	Ruby Tuesday *Melanie* (Buddah)	–	–	–
30	Nothing Rhymed *Gilbert O'Sullivan* (MAM)	11	8	8
24	Lady Barbara *Peter Noone and Herman's Hermits* (RAK)	16	17	13
32	Grandad *Clive Dunn* (Columbia)	17	6	2
27	Blame It On The Pony Express *Johnny Johnson and The Bandwagon* (Bell)	22	15	11
35	Brokenhearted *Ken Dodd* (Columbia)	30	18	17
26	It's A Shame *The Motown Spinners* (Tamla Motown)	26	20	–
25	My Way *Frank Sinatra* (Reprise)	24	26	18
–	Apeman *The Kinks* (Pye)	32	32	20

1970–BEST-SELLING SINGLES

1 The Wonder Of You *Elvis Presley* (RCA)
2 Yellow River *Christie* (CBS)
3 In The Summertime *Mungo Jerry* (Dawn)
4 Band Of Gold *Freda Payne* (Invictus)
5 Something *Shirley Bassey* (UA)
6 Wanderin' Star *Lee Marvin* (Paramount)
7 Spirit In The Sky *Norman Greenbaum* (Reprise)
8 Two Little Boys *Rolf Harris* (Columbia)
9 All Right Now *Free* (Island)
10 Cottonfields *The Beach Boys* (Capitol)

In 1970 only a top ten list of best-selling singles was printed.

1970–BEST-SELLING ALBUMS

1 Bridge Over Troubled Water *Simon and Garfunkel*
2 Led Zeppelin II *Led Zeppelin*
3 Easy Rider *Soundtrack of film*
4 Paint Your Waggon *Soundtrack of film*
5 Motown Chartbusters Vol. 3 *Various artists*
6 Abbey Road *The Beatles*
7 Let It Be *The Beatles*
8 Deep Purple In Rock *Deep Purple*
9 McCartney *Paul McCartney*
10 Andy Williams Greatest Hits *Andy Williams*
11 Johnny Cash At San Quentin *Johnny Cash*
12 Question Of Balance *Moody Blues*
13 Sound Of Music *Soundtrack of film*
14 Paranoid *Black Sabbath*
15 Motown Chartbusters Vol. 4 *Various artists*
16 Cosmo's Factory *Creedence Clearwater Revival*
17 Tom Jones Live In Las Vegas *Tom Jones*
18 Let It Bleed *The Rolling Stones*
19 Fire And Water *Free*
20 Black Sabbath *Black Sabbath*

1970–BEST-SELLING ARTISTS

Male Artists (Singles)

1 Elvis Presley
2 Jimmy Ruffin
3 Andy Williams
4 Roger Whittaker
5 Glen Campbell

6 Tom Jones
7 Stevie Wonder
8 Cliff Richard
9 Lee Marvin
10 Frank Sinatra

Female Artists (Singles)

1 Mary Hopkin
2 Freda Payne
3 Shirley Bassey

4 Julie Felix
5 Melanie

Groups (Singles)

1 The Jackson Five
2 Creedence Clearwater Revival
3 The Four Tops
4 Christie
5 White Plains
6 Kenny Rogers and The First Edition

7 Pickettywitch
8 Peter Noone and Herman's Hermits
9 Chicago
{10 The Cuff Links
{10 Blue Mink

Male Artists (Albums)

1 Andy Williams
2 Johnny Cash
3 Tom Jones
4 Elvis Presley
5 Bob Dylan

6 Leonard Cohen
7 Paul McCartney
8 Herb Alpert
9 Frank Sinatra
10 Frank Zappa

Female Artists (Albums)

1 Nana Mouskouri
2 Shirley Bassey
3 Melanie

4 Joni Mitchell
5 Dionne Warwick

Groups (Albums)

1 Simon and Garfunkel
2 Led Zeppelin
3 The Beatles
4 The Moody Blues
5 Motown Chartbusters

6 The Rolling Stones
7 Black Sabbath
8 Deep Purple
9 Creedence Clearwater Revival
10 Chicago

1971

Dave Edmunds had entered the 1970 charts in November with 'I Hear You Knocking', and the record continued to move upwards until it was the first Number One single of 1971. It was Edmunds' only hit for the MAM record label, for his future discs were recorded on Rockfield, his own label which was named after his Welsh recording studios. The wait for another hit for Edmunds was long, for his next Top Twenty entry was not until February 1973, when 'Baby I Love You' entered the charts at Number Thirty-Two.

Clive Dunn, from the *Dad's Army* television series, provided one of 1971's biggest surprises when the chart was only two weeks old with 'Grandad', a song which remained at the Number One position for three weeks.

For Andy Williams, 1971 was a quiet year with only one hit, 'Where Do I Begin (Love Story)'. This was a poor chart performance when compared to Williams' 1970 chart statistics, when he had achieved three hits.

Several major hits came into the charts at the end of January, one of which was 'My Sweet Lord' from the ex-Beatle, George Harrison. Another interesting entry so early in the year was 'Amazing Grace' from Judy Collins. However, The Royal Scots Dragoon Guards Band made another version of this song in 1972, and their version did better in terms of chart positions.

1971 was a good year for Marc Bolan and T. Rex. 'Ride A White Swan', which had entered the charts in 1970, remained in the 1971 charts until late February, and was quickly followed by more success. Bolan's hits were well spaced, for they were issued in March, July and November of 1971.

Elvis Presley achieved five Top Twenty hits, though none of these were very powerful when compared to his 1970 hit 'The Wonder Of You', which had remained in the Top Twenty for 16 weeks. Presley's biggest success of 1971 was achieved by the romantic ballad, 'I Just Can't Help Believing', which remained in the Top Twenty for a total of two months.

Humour of a kind reared its head during the year with

'Bridget The Midget' from Ray Stevens, and with the amazing 'Ernie (The Fastest Milkman In The West)' from Benny Hill. On the other hand there was a brief classical excursion in April called 'Mozart 40' from Waldo de Los Rios.

The Beatles as a group may have disbanded, but in 1971 each member had a chart triumph in his own right. For George Harrison it was 'My Sweet Lord' and 'Bangla Desh', and for John Lennon and his wife Yoko Ono, and The Plastic Ono Band it was a Top Ten triumph with 'Power To The People'. Meanwhile Paul McCartney as a solo artist achieved a hit with 'Another Day', a song which he had co-written with his wife, Linda. Ringo Starr, however, provided the biggest surprise of all with 'It Don't Come Easy', which was a hit on both sides of the Atlantic.

1971 saw the birth of Middle Of The Road with 'Chirpy Chirpy Cheep Cheep', and of The Sweet with 'Funny Funny' and 'Co-Co'. Whereas the latter group continued to achieve hit records, Middle Of The Road ceased to attract the public's attention – a strange phenomenon considering that all of their three 1971 hits reached the Top Five.

Reggae made some impact on the charts owing to the records of such artists as Dave and Ansil Collins, The Pioneers, Greyhound and Bob Andy and Marcia Griffiths.

Dawn, Rod Stewart, The Marmalade, Diana Ross and Tony Christie all had big hits in 1971, but the most significant arrivals in the charts were those of Elton John and Slade.

Slade's lead singer, Noddy Holder, stated 'The fans are fed up with paying to sit on their hands while watching musicians who clearly couldn't care less about the customers. What is wanted is more of a party atmosphere'. Slade certainly created a fun atmosphere, and the fans went back to stomping and leaping around and enjoying themselves. Slade had hit on the formula for success and provided exactly what the fans wanted at the time.

JANUARY 1971

2

	9	16	23	30
1 I Hear You Knocking *Dave Edmunds* (MAM)	2	2	6	7
2 Grandad *Clive Dunn* (Columbia)	1	1	1	2
3 When I'm Dead And Gone *McGuiness Flint* (Capitol)	3	3	3	17
4 It's Only Make Believe *Glen Campbell* (Capitol)	9	6	12	18
5 I'll Be There *The Jackson Five* (Tamla Motown)	5	5	4	6
6 Cracklin' Rosie *Neil Diamond* (UA)	6	7	14	10
7 Home Lovin' Man *Andy Williams* (CBS)	10	9	15	–
8 Nothing Rhymed *Gilbert O'Sullivan* (MAM)	8	10	17	–
9 My Prayer *Gerry Monroe* (Chapter One)	14	18	–	–
10 Ride A White Swan *T. Rex* (Fly)	4	4	2	4
11 Blame It On The Pony Express *Johnny Johnson and The Bandwagon* (Bell)	7	8	11	11
12 You've Got Me Dangling On A String *Chairmen Of the Board* (Invictus)	11	12	19	–
13 Lady Barbara *Peter Noone and Herman's Hermits* (RAK)	13	14	–	–
14 Indian Reservation *Don Fardon* (Young Blood)	16	–	–	–
15 I've Lost You *Elvis Presley* (RCA)	17	20	–	–
16 Julie Do Ya Love Me *White Plains* (Deram)	19	–	–	–
17 Broken Hearted *Ken Dodd* (Columbia)	15	16	20	–
18 My Way *Frank Sinatra* (Capitol)	–	–	–	–
19 Voodoo Chile *Jimi Hendrix Experience* (Track)	20	–	–	–
20 Apeman *The Kinks* (Pye)	12	11	5	5
31 Blackskin Blue Eyed Boy *The Equals* (President)	18	15	10	9
21 You're Ready Now *Frankie Valli* (Philips)	25	13	18	12
– You Don't Have To Say You Love Me *Elvis Presley* (RCA)	23	17	9	14
30 Amazing Grace *Judy Collins* (Elektra)	21	19	8	8
– My Sweet Lord *George Harrison* (Apple)	–	–	7	1
– The Pushbike Song *The Mixtures* (Polydor)	–	24	13	3
– No Matter What *Badfinger* (Apple)	35	34	16	13
– The Resurrection Shuffle *Ashton, Gardner and Dyke* (Capitol)	–	45	26	15
– She's A Lady *Tom Jones* (MAM)	–	42	21	16
– Stoned Love *The Supremes* (Tamla Motown)	–	48	24	19
– Candida *Dawn* (Bell)	–	40	22	20

FEBRUARY 1971

6

	13	20	27
1 My Sweet Lord *George Harrison* (Apple)	1	1	1
2 The Pushbike Song *The Mixtures* (Polydor)	2	2	2
3 Stoned Loved *The Supremes* (Tamla Motown)	3	4	5
4 Grandad *Clive Dunn* (Columbia)	9	9	12
5 No Matter What *Badfinger* (Apple)	6	6	10
6 Amazing Grace *Judy Collins* (Elektra)	5	5	6
7 Ride A White Swan *T. Rex* (Fly)	14	12	–
8 Ape Man *The Kinks* (Pye)	8	11	17
9 The Resurrection Shuffle *Ashton, Gardner and Dyke* (Capitol)	4	3	3
10 I'll Be There *The Jackson Five* (Tamla Motown)	11	–	–
11 You're Ready Now *Frankie Valli* (Philips)	12	15	–
12 Candida *Dawn* (Bell)	10	10	9
13 Your Song *Elton John* (DJM)	7	8	8
14 You Don't Have To Say You Love Me *Elvis Presley* (RCA)	18	18	–
15 Blackskin Blue Eyed Boy *The Equals* (President)	17	–	–
16 When I'm Dead And Gone *McGuiness Flint* (Capitol)	–	–	–
17 She's A Lady *Tom Jones* (MAM)	15	13	16
18 Cracklin' Rosie *Neil Diamond* (Uni)	20	–	–
19 I Hear You Knocking *Dave Edmunds* (MAM)	–	–	–

6		13	20	27
20	Blame It On The Pony Express *Johnny Johnson and The Bandwagon* (Bell)	–	–	–
31	It's Impossible *Perry Como* (RCA)	13	7	4
30	Rupert *Jackie Lee* (Pye)	16	16	14
21	It's The Same Old Song *The Weathermen* (B & C)	19	–	–
32	Baby Jump *Mungo Jerry* (Dawn)	–	14	7
39	(Come Round Here) I'm The One You Need *Smokey Robinson and The Miracles* (Tamla Motown)	24	17	13
23	Sunny Honey Girl *Cliff Richard* (Columbia)	22	19	–
22	It's Only Make Believe *Glen Campbell* (Capitol)	25	20	–
–	Sweet Caroline *Neil Diamond* (UA)	–	30	11
–	Forget Me Not *Martha Reeves and The Vandellas* (Tamla Motown)	32	22	15
–	I Think I Love You *The Partridge Family* (Bell)	34	35	18
–	Chestnut Mare *The Byrds* (CBS)	30	38	19
–	Everything's Tuesday *Chairmen Of The Board* (Invictus)	–	26	20

MARCH 1971

6		13	20	27
1	Baby Jump *Mungo Jerry* (Dawn)	1	2	4
2	My Sweet Lord *George Harrison* (Apple)	3	6	7
3	The Pushbike Song *The Mixtures* (Polydor)	6	7	11
4	Another Day *Paul McCartney* (Apple)	2	3	2
5	It's Impossible *Perry Como* (RCA)	5	5	5
6	The Resurrection Shuffle *Ashton, Gardner and Dyke* (Capitol)	11	10	16
7	Amazing Grace *Judy Collins* (Elektra)	9	13	6
8	Stoned Love *The Supremes* (Tamla Motown)	10	17	–
9	Sweet Caroline *Neil Diamond* (UA)	8	9	8
10	Rose Garden *Lynn Anderson* (CBS)	4	4	3
11	Forget Me Not *Martha Reeves and The Vandellas* (Tamla Motown)	15	–	–
12	Tomorrow Night *Atomic Rooster* (B & C)	13	11	14
13	Your Song *Elton John* (DJM)	20	–	–
14	Rupert *Jackie Lee* (Pye)	–	20	–
15	(Come Round Here) I'm The One You Need *Smokey Robinson and The Miracles* (Tamla Motown)	18	–	–
16	No Matter What *Badfinger* (Apple)	19	–	–
17	Hot Love *T. Rex* (Fly)	7	1	1
18	Grandad *Clive Dunn* (Columbia)	16	–	–
19	Everything's Tuesday *Chairmen Of The Board* (Invictus)	12	18	13
20	Candida *Dawn* (Bell)	–	–	–
21	Who Put The Lights Out *Dana* (Rex)	14	16	17
27	Rose Garden *New World* (RAK)	17	15	15
29	Strange Kind Of Woman *Deep Purple* (Purple)	22	8	18
–	Power To The People *John Lennon and The Plastic Ono Band* (Apple)	–	12	12
–	Bridget The Midget *Ray Stevens* (CBS)	34	14	9
26	I Will Drink The Wine *Frank Sinatra* (Capitol)	25	19	–
–	Jack In A Box *Clodagh Rodgers* (RCA)	–	23	10
–	There Goes My Everything *Elvis Presley* (RCA)	–	29	19
39	Walkin' *C.C.S.* (RAK)	32	21	20

APRIL 1971

3		10	17	24
1	Hot Love *T. Rex* (Fly)	1	1	1
2	Bridget The Midget *Ray Stevens* (CBS)	2	2	3
3	Rose Garden *Lynn Anderson* (CBS)	3	3	5
4	Another Day *Paul McCartney* (Apple)	5	11	17
5	Baby Jump *Mungo Jerry* (Dawn)	10	13	–
6	Jack In A Box *Clodagh Rodgers* (RCA)	4	5	10
7	Power To The People *John Lennon and The Plastic Ono Band* (Apple)	8	10	16
8	There Goes My Everything *Elvis Presley* (RCA)	6	7	11
9	It's Impossible *Perry Como* (RCA)	9	12	20
10	Walkin' *C.C.S.* (RAK)	7	9	8
11	Strange Kind Of Woman *Deep Purple* (Purple)	11	17	19
12	If Not For You *Olivia Newton-John* (Pye)	12	8	7
13	Sweet Caroline *Neil Diamond* (UA)	15	–	–
14	My Sweet Lord *George Harrison* (Apple)	14	–	–
15	The Pushbike Song *The Mixtures* (Polydor)	16	19	–
16	I Will Drink The Wine *Frank Sinatra* (Capitol)	–	16	–
17	Rose Garden *New World* (RAK)	19	–	–
18	Tomorrow Night *Atomic Rooster* (B & C)	–	–	–
19	Amazing Grace *Judy Collins* (Elektra)	18	–	–
20	Where Do I Begin (Love Story) *Andy Williams* (CBS)	13	6	4
21	Double Barrel *Dave and Ansil Collins* (Technique)	17	4	2
28	Funny Funny *The Sweet* (RCA)	20	15	14
–	Mozart 40 *Waldo de Los Rios* (A & M)	26	14	6
41	Remember Me *Diana Ross* (Tamla Motown)	28	18	13
–	Knock Three Times *Dawn* (Bell)	32	20	18
30	Something Old Something New *The Fantastics* (Bell)	21	21	9
–	It Don't Come Easy *Ringo Starr* (Apple)	–	29	12
–	Rosetta *Fame and Price* (CBS)	49	30	15

MAY 1971

1		8	15	22	29
1	Double Barrel *Dave and Ansil Collins* (Technique)	1	3	5	10
2	Hot Love *T. Rex* (Fly)	6	9	17	–
3	Knock Three Times *Dawn* (Bell)	2	1	1	1
4	Brown Sugar *The Rolling Stones* (RS)	3	2	2	2
5	Mozart 40 *Waldo de Los Rios* (A & M)	5	5	6	12
6	Bridget The Midget *Ray Stevens* (CBS)	10	18	–	–
7	It Don't Come Easy *Ringo Starr* (Apple)	4	4	4	8
8	Where Do I Begin (Love Story) *Andy Williams* (CBS)	8	10	15	–
9	Remember Me *Diana Ross* (Tamla Motown)	7	7	10	13
10	Walkin' *C.C.S.* (RAK)	16	–	–	–
11	If Not For You *Olivia Newton-John* (Pye)	14	–	–	–
12	Rose Garden *Lynn Anderson* (CBS)	17	–	–	–
13	There Goes My Everything *Elvis Presley* (RCA)	–	–	–	–
14	Funny Funny *The Sweet* (RCA)	13	13	–	–
15	Rosetta *Fame and Price* (CBS)	11	19	19	–
16	Something Old Something New *The Fantastics* (Bell)	9	–	–	–
17	Jack In The Box *Clodagh Rodgers* (RCA)	–	–	–	–
18	My Little One *The Marmalade* (Decca)	20	15	–	–
19	Another Day *Paul McCartney* (Apple)	–	–	–	–
20	Indiana Wants Me *R. Dean Taylor* (Tamla Motown)	12	6	3	3
22	Jig A Jig *East Of Eden* (Deram)	15	8	7	7
25	It's A Sin To Tell A Lie *Gerry Monroe* (Chapter One)	18	17	13	15
26	Sugar Sugar *Sakharin* (RCA)	19	12	14	14
32	Un Banc, Un Arbre, Une Rue *Severine* (Philips)	28	11	12	9

1

	8	15	22	29
48 Heaven Must Have Sent You *The Elgins* (Tamla Motown)	25	14	8	6
45 Malt And Barley Blues *McGuiness Flint* (Capitol)	23	16	9	5
50 My Brother Jake *Free* (Island)	24	20	11	4
– Good Old Arsenal *Arsenal 1st Team Squad* (Pye)	44	24	16	–
– I Am . . . I Said *Neil Diamond* (Uni)	33	28	18	11
42 Rain *Bruce Ruffin* (Trojan)	31	27	20	19
– Rags To Riches *Elvis Presley* (RCA)	–	43	23	16
– I Did What I Did For Maria *Tony Christie* (MCA)	47	34	24	17
– I Think Of You *Perry Como* (RCA)	–	38	27	18
– Oh You Pretty Thing *Peter Noone* (RAK)	–	–	34	20

JUNE 1971

5

	12	19	26
1 Knock Three Times *Dawn* (Bell)	1	2	7
2 Indiana Wants Me *R. Dean Taylor* (Tamla Motown)	3	10	15
3 Heaven Must Have Sent You *The Elgins* (Tamla Motown)	5	8	11
4 My Brother Jake *Free* (Island)	6	11	17
5 Brown Sugar *The Rolling Stones* (RS)	10	16	18
6 I Am . . . I Said *Neil Diamond* (Uni)	4	9	10
7 Malt And Barley Blues *McGuiness Flint* (Capitol)	11	14	19
8 I Did What I Did For Maria *Tony Christie* (MCA)	2	3	2
9 Rags To Riches *Elvis Presley* (RCA)	13	12	14
10 Jig A Jig *East Of Eden* (Deram)	14	–	–
11 I'm Gonna Run Away From You *Tammi Lynn* (Mojo)	8	5	4
12 Mozart 40 *Waldo de Los Rios* (A & M)	18	20	–
13 Lady Rose *Mungo Jerry* (Dawn)	7	6	5
14 I Think Of You *Perry Como* (RCA)	17	15	20
15 It Don't Come Easy *Ringo Starr* (Apple)	20	–	–
16 The Banner Man *Blue Mink* (Regal Zonophone)	9	4	3
17 Double Barrel *Dave and Ansil Collins* (Technique)	–	–	–
18 It's A Sin To Tell A Lie *Gerry Monroe* (Chapter One)	–	–	–
19 Oh You Pretty Thing *Peter Noone* (RAK)	12	13	12
20 Un Banc, Un Arbre, Une Rue *Severine* (Philips)	–	–	–
22 He's Gonna Step On You Again *John Kongos* (Fly)	15	7	6
36 Chirpy Chirpy Cheep Cheep *Middle Of The Road* (RCA)	16	1	1
23 Sugar Sugar *Sakharin* (RCA)	19	–	–
27 Just My Imagination *The Temptations* (Tamla Motown)	25	17	13
– Don't Let It Die *Hurricane Smith* (Columbia)	50	18	8
– Co-Co *The Sweet* (RCA)	33	19	9
40 I Don't Blame You At All *Smokey Robinson and The Miracles* (Tamla Motown)	32	22	16

JULY 1971

3

	10	17	24	31
1 Chirpy Chirpy Cheep Cheep *Middle Of The Road* (RCA)	1	1	2	2
2 Don't Let It Die *Hurricane Smith* (Columbia)	3	3	5	9
3 The Banner Man *Blue Mink* (Regal Zonophone)	4	8	9	14
4 He's Gonna Step On You Again *John Kongos* (Fly)	5	9	13	18
5 Co-Co *The Sweet* (RCA)	2	2	3	3
6 I Did What I Did For Maria *Tony Christie* (MCA)	7	18	18	–
7 I'm Gonna Run Away From You *Tammi Lynn* (Mojo)	6	10	14	–
8 Lady Rose *Mungo Jerry* (Dawn)	10	17	–	–
9 Knock Three Times *Dawn* (Bell)	15	–	–	–
10 Just My Imagination *The Temptations* (Tamla Motown)	8	11	10	15
11 I Don't Blame You At All *Smokey Robinson and The Miracles* (Tamla Motown)	12	15	19	–
12 Pied Piper *Bob and Marcia* (Trojan)	11	13	17	20

3

	10	17	24	31
13 Oh You Pretty Thing *Peter Noone* (RAK)	–	–	–	–
14 I Am . . . I Said *Neil Diamond* (UA)	19	–	–	–
15 Heaven Must Have Sent You *The Elgins* (Tamla Motown)	20	–	–	–
16 When You Are A King *White Plains* (Deram)	13	14	16	19
17 Monkey Spanner *Dave and Ansil Collins* (Technique)	17	7	7	7
18 Me And You And A Dog Named Boo *Lobo* (Philips)	14	5	4	4
19 Black And White *Greyhound* (Trojan)	9	6	6	8
20 Rags To Riches *Elvis Presley* (RCA)	–	–	–	–
22 River Deep Mountain High *The Supremes and The Four Tops* (Tamla Motown)	16	16	11	13
26 Tom-Tom Turnaround *New World* (RAK)	18	12	8	6
– Get It On *T. Rex* (Fly)	21	4	1	1
42 Tonight *The Move* (Harvest)	25	19	12	11
29 Leap Up and Down *St. Cecilia* (Polydor)	23	20	–	12
– Never Ending Song Of Love *The New Seekers* (Philips)	49	26	15	5
– Devil's Answer *Atomic Rooster* (B & C)	36	25	20	10
– I'm Still Waiting *Diana Ross* (Tamla Motown)	–	–	–	16
– Won't Get Fooled Again *The Who* (Track)	41	27	22	17

AUGUST 1971

7	14	21	28
1 Get It On *T. Rex* (Fly)	1	3	4
2 Never Ending Song Of Love *The New Seekers* (Philips)	2	2	2
3 Chirpy Chirpy Cheep Cheep *Middle Of The Road* (RCA)	8	8	13
4 Devil's Answer *Atomic Rooster* (B & C)	4	4	7
5 Co-Co *The Sweet* (RCA)	10	14	–
6 Me And You And A Dog Named Boo *Lobo* (Philips)	6	13	19
7 Tom-Tom Turnaround *New World* (RAK)	7	7	11
8 I'm Still Waiting *Diana Ross* (Tamla Motown)	3	1	1
9 Monkey Spanner *Dave and Ansil Collins* (Trojan)	11	18	–
10 Won't Get Fooled Again *The Who* (Track)	9	9	14
11 In My Own Time *Family* (Reprise)	5	5	5
12 Black And White *Greyhound* (Trojan)	15	20	–
13 Heartbreak Hotel *Elvis Presley* (RCA)	14	10	17
14 Tonight *The Move* (Harvest)	16	–	–
15 Leap Up And Down *St. Cecilia* (Polydor)	12	12	16
16 River Deep Mountain High *The Supremes and The Four Tops* (Tamla Motown)	20	–	–
17 Get Down Get With It *Slade* (Polydor)	17	16	18
18 Don't Let It Die *Hurricane Smith* (Columbia)	–	–	–
19 Just My Imagination *The Temptations* (Tamla Motown)	–	–	–
20 La-La Means I Love You *The Delfonics* (Bell)	19	–	–
27 What Are You Doing Sunday *Dawn* (Bell)	13	6	3
21 Soldier Blue *Buffy St. Marie* (RCA)	18	11	8
– Bangla Desh *George Harrison* (Apple)	27	15	10
44 Let Your Yeah Be Yeah *The Pioneers* (Trojan)	25	17	6
39 Hey Girl Don't Bother Me *The Tams* (Probe)	26	19	9
32 Move On Up *Curtis Mayfield* (Buddah)	22	22	12
49 It's Too Late *Carole King* (A & M)	32	24	15
34 We Will *Gilbert O'Sullivan* (MAM)	29	23	20

SEPTEMBER 1971

4		11	18	25
1	I'm Still Waiting *Diana Ross* (Tamla Motown)	1	2	10
2	Never Ending Song Of Love *The New Seekers* (Philips)	4	7	14
3	Hey Girl Don't Bother Me *The Tams* (Probe)	2	1	1
4	In My Own Time *Family* (Reprise)	11	14	20
5	What Are You Doing Sunday *Dawn* (*Bell*)	3	10	16
6	Let Your Yeah Be Yeah *The Pioneers* (Trojan)	5	13	18
7	Soldier Blue *Buffy St. Marie* (RCA)	7	9	12
8	It's Too Late *Carole King* (A & M)	10	6	15
9	Devil's Answer *Atomic Rooster* (B & C)	–	–	–
10	Get It On *T. Rex* (Fly)	13	–	–
11	Bangla Desh *George Harrison* (Apple)	12	–	–
12	Back-Street Luv *Curved Air* (Warner Bros.)	9	4	11
13	Tom-Tom Turnaround *New World* (RAK)	17	–	–
14	Move On Up *Curtis Mayfield* (Buddah)	16	–	–
15	Won't Get Fooled Again *The Who* (Track)	–	–	–
16	We Will *Gilbert O'Sullivan* (MAM)	18	20	–
17	Did You Ever . . .? *Nancy Sinatra and Lee Hazlewood* (Capitol)	6	3	2
18	Heartbreak Hotel *Elvis Presley* (RCA)	–	–	–
19	Nathan Jones *The Supremes* (Tamla Motown)	8	5	5
20	Leap Up And Down *St. Cecilia* (Polydor)	–	–	–
36	You've Got A Friend *James Taylor* (Warner Bros.)	14	12	9
25	I Believe (In Love) *Hot Chocolate* (RAK)	15	8	8
31	Maggie May *Rod Stewart* (Mercury)	19	11	3
37	Cousin Norman *The Marmalade* (Decca)	20	17	7
26	For All We Know *Shirley Bassey* (UA)	21	15	13
50	Tweedledee, Tweedledum *Middle Of The Road* (RCA)	23	16	4
39	Tap Turns On The Water *C.C.S.* (RAK)	26	18	6
24	When Love Comes Round Again *Ken Dodd* (Columbia)	28	19	–
28	Daddy Don't You Walk So Fast *Daniel Boone* (Penny Farthing)	24	21	17
–	Life Is A Long Song *Jethro Tull* (Chrysalis)	–	25	19

OCTOBER 1971

2		9	16	23	30
1	Hey Girl Don't Bother Me *The Tams* (Probe)	2	3	9	15
2	Maggie May *Rod Stewart* (Mercury)	1	1	1	1
3	Did You Ever . . .? *Nancy Sinatra and Lee Hazlewood* (Capitol)	3	5	8	13
4	Tweedledee, Tweedledum *Middle Of The Road* (RCA)	4	2	3	3
5	Tap Turns On The Water *C.C.S.* (RAK)	6	8	11	14
6	Cousin Norman *The Marmalade* (Decca)	8	7	17	–
7	Nathan Jones *The Supremes* (Tamla Motown)	12	16	–	–
8	You've Got A Friend *James Taylor* (Warner Bros.)	5	4	4	8
9	I Believe (In Love) *Hot Chocolate* (RAK)	10	17	–	–
10	For All We Know *Shirley Bassey* (UA)	7	6	7	6
11	Back-Street Luv *Curved Air* (Warner Bros.)	15	–	–	–
12	Life Is A Long Song *Jethro Tull* (Chrysalis)	11	11	16	–
13	I'm Still Waiting *Diana Ross* (Tamla Motown)	16	–	–	–
14	Never Ending Song Of Love *The New Seekers* (Philips)	20	–	–	–
15	It's Too Late *Carole King* (A & M)	–	–	–	–
16	Soldier Blue *Buffy St. Marie* (RCA)	–	–	–	–
17	Freedom Come, Freedom Go *The Fortunes* (Capitol)	9	10	6	7
18	Daddy Don't You Walk So Fast *Daniel Boone* (Penny Farthing)	19	20	–	–
19	Another Time, Another Place *Engelbert Humperdinck* (MAM)	–	15	13	16

2	9	16	23	30
20 Butterfly *Danyel Gerrard* (CBS)	–	13	12	11
21 You Don't Have To Be In The Army To Fight In The War				
Mungo Jerry (Dawn)	13	18	15	–
29 Witch-Queen Of New Orleans *Redbone* (Epic)	14	9	2	2
28 Sultana *Titanic* (CBS)	17	14	10	5
24 Simple Game *The Four Tops* (Tamla Motown)	18	12	5	4
26 Keep On Dancing *The Bay City Rollers* (Bell)	25	19	20	9
33 Spanish Harlem *Aretha Franklin* (Atlantic)	26	21	14	19
– The Night They Drove Old Dixie Down *Joan Baez*				
(Vanguard)	29	23	18	12
– Tired Of Being Alone *Al Green* (London)	37	28	19	10
46 Look Around *Vince Hill* (Columbia)	33	29	23	17
– Brandy *Scott English* (Horse)	44	33	25	18
– Till *Tom Jones* (Decca)	–	–	22	20

NOVEMBER 1971

6	13	20	27
1 Maggie May *Rod Stewart* (Mercury)	2	4	9
2 Witch-Queen Of New Orleans *Redbone* (Epic)	3	11	16
3 Simple Game *The Four Tops* (Probe)	5	12	20
4 Tired Of Being Alone *Al Green* (London)	6	9	11
5 Till *Tom Jones* (Decca)	4	2	6
6 The Night They Drove Old Dixie Down *Joan Baez* (Vanguard)	9	10	15
7 Sultana *Titanic* (CBS)	10	15	–
8 Coz I Luv You *Slade* (Polydor)	1	1	1
9 For All We Know *Shirley Bassey* (UA)	14	20	–
10 Tweedledee, Tweedledum *Middle Of The Road* (RCA)	15	–	–
11 Freedom Come, Freedom Go *The Fortunes* (Capitol)	19	–	–
12 Look Around *Vince Hill* (Columbia)	13	13	13
13 Brandy *Scott English* (Horse)	12	16	17
14 Spanish Harlem *Aretha Franklin* (Atlantic)	–	–	–
15 You've Got A Friend *James Taylor* (Warner Bros.)	–	–	–
16 Keep On Dancing *The Bay City Rollers* (Bell)	17	–	–
17 I Will Return *Springwater* (Polydor)	8	5	7
18 Butterfly *Danyel Gerrard* (CBS)	–	–	–
19 Johnny Reggae *The Piglets* (Bell)	7	3	5
20 Superstar *The Carpenters* (A & M)	18	19	–
21 The Banks Of The Ohio *Olivia Newton-John* (Pye)	11	6	8
32 Gypsies, Tramps And Thieves *Cher* (MCA)	16	7	4
24 Run Baby Run *The Newbeats* (London)	20	14	12
– Jeepster *T. Rex* (Fly)	37	8	2
– Ernie (The Fastest Milkman In The West) *Benny Hill*			
(Columbia)	29	17	3
27 Surrender *Diana Ross* (Tamla Motown)	22	18	10
– Tokoloshe Man *John Kongos* (Fly)	–	28	14
– Sing A Song Of Freedom *Cliff Richard* (Columbia)	45	29	18
30 Let's See Action *The Who* (Track)	27	24	19

DECEMBER 1971

4	11	18	25
1 Coz I Luv You *Slade* (Polydor)	3	3	14
2 Ernie (The Fastest Milkman In The West) *Benny Hill*			
(Columbia)	1	1	1
3 Jeepster *T. Rex* (Fly)	2	2	2
4 Gypsies, Tramps And Thieves *Cher* (MCA)	5	8	10
5 Johnny Reggae *The Piglets* (Bell)	10	14	–
6 Tokoloshe Man *John Kongos* (Fly)	4	6	7

4		11	18	25
7	Banks Of The Ohio *Olivia Newton-John* (Pye)	6	9	11
8	Till *Tom Jones* (Decca)	8	10	19
9	I Will Return *Springwater* (Polydor)	13	–	–
10	Run Baby Run *The Newbeats* (London)	11	11	–
11	Something Tells Me *Cilla Black* (Parlophone)	12	7	3
12	Surrender *Diana Ross* (Tamla Motown)	15	17	–
13	Sing A Song Of Freedom *Cliff Richard* (Columbia)	14	13	–
14	Maggie May *Rod Stewart* (Mercury)	19	–	–
15	No Matter How I Try *Gilbert O'Sullivan* (MAM)	9	5	8
16	Theme From Shaft *Isaac Hayes* (Stax)	7	4	5
17	For All We Know *Shirley Bassey* (UA)	–	–	–
18	The Night They Drove Old Dixie Down *Joan Baez* (Vanguard)	–	–	–
19	Look Around *Vince Hill* (Columbia)	–	–	–
20	Let's See Action *The Who* (Track)	16	–	–
27	It Must Be Love *Labi Siffre* (Pye)	17	16	15
21	Fireball *Deep Purple* (Purple)	18	15	17
28	Softly Whispering I Love You *The Congregation* (Columbia)	20	12	6
–	Soley Soley *Middle Of The Road* (RCA)	23	18	9
45	Morning *Val Doonican* (Philips)	26	19	12
25	Is This The Way To Amarillo *Tony Christie* (MCA)	21	20	20
–	I'd Like To Teach The World To Sing *The New Seekers* (Polydor)	–	32	4
–	Sleepy Shores *The Johnny Pearson Orchestra* (Penny Farthing)	–	26	13
41	I Just Can't Help Believing *Elvis Presley* (RCA)	22	22	16
–	Mother Of Mine *Neil Reid* (Decca)	–	–	18

1971–BEST-SELLING SINGLES

1. My Sweet Lord *George Harrison* (Apple)
2. Maggie May *Rod Stewart* (Mercury)
3. Chirpy Chirpy Cheep Cheep *Middle Of The Road* (RCA)
4. Knock Three Times *Dawn* (Bell)
5. Hot Love *T. Rex* (Fly)
6. The Pushbike Song *The Mixtures* (Polydor)
7. Never Ending Song Of Love *The New Seekers* (Philips)
8. I'm Still Waiting *Diana Ross* (Tamla Motown)
9. Hey Girl Don't Bother Me *The Tams* (Probe)
10. Get It On *T. Rex* (Fiy)

In their end of year analysis Music Week/BMRB *only published a top ten of best-selling singles.*

1971–BEST-SELLING ALBUMS

1. Bridge Over Troubled Water *Simon and Garfunkel*
2. Every Picture Tells A Story *Rod Stewart*
3. Sticky Fingers *The Rolling Stones*
4. Motown Chartbusters Vol. 5 *Various artists*
5. Electric Warrior *T. Rex*
6. Mud Slide Slim And The Blue Horizon *James Taylor*
7. Every Good Boy Deserves Favour *The Moody Blues*
8. Andy Williams Greatest Hits *Andy Williams*
9. Ram *Paul and Linda McCartney*
10. Tapestry *Carole King*

Only 10 albums were listed for 1971 in the Music Week *yearly market survey.*

1971–BEST-SELLING ARTISTS

Male Artists (Singles)

1 Elvis Presley
2 Dawn
3 Neil Diamond
4 Perry Como
5 George Harrison
6 Frank Sinatra
7 Tony Christie
8 Rod Stewart
9 Tom Jones
10 John Kongos

Female Artists (Singles)

1 Diana Ross
2 Judy Collins
3 Shirley Bassey
4 Olivia Newton-John
5 Lynn Anderson

Groups (Singles)

1 T. Rex
2 Middle Of The Road
3 Mungo Jerry
4 The Sweet
5 Dave and Ansil Collins
6 Curved Air
7 C.C.S.
8 New World
9 The Supremes
10 Atomic Rooster

Male Artists (Albums)

1 Andy Williams
2 James Taylor
3 Frank Sinatra
4 Rod Stewart
5 Jimi Hendrix
6 Neil Young
7 Johnny Cash
8 Waldo de Los Rios
9 Elvis Presley
10 Leonard Cohen

Groups (Albums)

1 Simon and Garfunkel
2 Motown Chartbusters
3 Led Zeppelin
4 The Rolling Stones
5 Deep Purple
6 Emerson Lake and Palmer
7 Yes
8 Paul and Linda McCartney
9 Santana
10 Crosby, Stills, Nash and Young

1972

'Morning Has Broken' from Cat Stevens rang through the early 1972 air; a hymn, though some people were probably not aware of the song's derivation. Another religious melody numbed the British public in April as 'Amazing Grace' from The Royal Scots Dragoon Guards Band tugged at the nation's heartstrings. The bagpipe hit also revived interest in the Judy Collins version of the song from 1971, for her version of the song enjoyed further Top Twenty success.

Two television themes also enjoyed chart success; the 'Theme From The Persuaders' from The John Barry Orchestra, and the 'Theme From The Onedin Line' by The Vienna Philharmonic Orchestra.

Some newcomers of 1971 did fairly well, for Slade had four hits, while The Sweet had three. However, Elton John appeared in the Top Twenty twice only with 'Rocket Man' and 'Crocodile Rock', the former being his most successful chart single. It is surprising that, despite all his album and American successes, John has never reached the Number One position in the British singles charts.

All other groups in 1972 appeared to live in the shadow of Marc Bolan and T. Rex, who had five hits in that year, including 'Debora', a disc which had been recorded in Bolan's Tyrannosaurus Rex days.

These hit makers, however, met fierce resistance from a new batch of stars of 1972. Whereas the year's most passionate, tear-jerking record was undoubtedly 'Mother Of Mine' from the schoolboy Neil Reid, a totally different kind of passion came into being, for 1972 saw the emergence of Donny Osmond with 'Puppy Love', his first British hit. It was also the beginning of a phenomenon which was given the label of Osmondmania. Donny and his brothers achieved a hit in November 1972 entitled 'Crazy Horses' and Donny on his own with 'Why' fought himself and his brothers with 'Crazy Horses' for the top chart placing.

The Osmonds and Donny were joined in their roles as heart-throbs by David Cassidy. Cassidy's chart run had begun in April 1972, two months before that of Donny and, strictly speaking, he had even preceded The Osmonds, for in February 1971 he had enjoyed success with The Partridge Family with 'I Think I Love You'.

Paul Gadd, alias Paul Raven, alias Gary Glitter came to the fore in 1972 as a major chart force. However, his 'Rock And Roll Part 2' took four months to make any chart impact.

The year saw the arrival of some classic songs, two of which came from Don MacLean with 'American Pie' and 'Vincent'. Together these records gave MacLean 20 weeks of chart occupancy. Another classic was Nilsson's 'Without You', surprisingly his only British hit. June 1972 saw 'The First Time Ever I Saw Your Face' become a world-wide hit sung by Roberta Flack. The song was written by the British folk writer Ewan McColl.

Apart from teen heroes, one other major chart artist, David Bowie, began his successive chart entries. He had achieved a hit, 'Space Oddity', in 1969 but with a change of image in the 1970s, Bowie had three hits in 1972. For Bowie, 1973 was to be even more successful.

1	8	15	22	29
1 Ernie (The Fastest Milkman In The West) *Benny Hill* (Columbia)	2	3	13	–
2 Jeepster *T. Rex* (Fly)	3	10	18	–
3 Something Tells Me *Cilla Black* (Parlophone)	7	6	12	–
4 I'd Like To Teach The World To Sing *The New Seekers* (Polydor)	1	1	1	1
5 Theme From Shaft *Isaac Hayes* (Stax)	6	14	14	–
6 Softly Whispering I Love You *The Congregation* (Columbia)	4	4	5	14
7 Tokoloshe Man *John Kongos* (Fly)	11	–	–	–
8 No Matter How I Try *Gilbert O'Sullivan* (MAM)	9	12	11	18
9 Soley Soley *Middle Of The Road* (RCA)	5	5	7	11
10 Gypsies, Tramps And Thieves *Cher* (MCA)	19	–	–	–
11 Banks Of The Ohio *Olivia Newton-John* (Pye)	–	–	–	–
12 Morning *Val Doonican* (Philips)	13	15	19	–
13 Sleepy Shores *The Johnny Pearson Orchestra* (Penny Farthing)	8	9	9	12
14 Coz I Luv You *Slade* (Polydor)	16	–	–	–
15 It Must Be Love *Labi Siffre* (Pye)	14	19	–	–
16 I Just Can't Help Believing *Elvis Presley* (RCA)	10	7	6	6
17 Fireball *Deep Purple* (Purple)	15	18	–	–
18 Mother Of Mine *Neil Reid* (Decca)	12	2	2	2
19 Till *Tom Jones* (Decca)	–	–	–	–
20 Is This The Way To Amarillo *Tony Christie* (MCA)	18	–	–	–
21 Kara Kara *New World* (RAK)	17	–	–	–
22 Sing A Song Of Freedom *Cliff Richard* (Columbia)	20	–	–	–
34 Brand New Key *Melanie* (Buddah)	24	8	4	5
– Horse With No Name *America* (Warner Bros.)	21	11	3	4
36 Morning Has Broken *Cat Stevens* (Island)	30	13	10	9
43 Stay With Me *The Faces* (Warner Bros.)	23	16	8	7
32 Theme From The Onedin Line *The Vienna Philharmonic Orchestra* (Decca)	25	17	15	16
– Where Did Our Love Go? *Donny Elbert* (London)	–	28	16	8
– Let's Stay Together *Al Green* (London)	–	29	17	10
– Moon River *Greyhound* (Trojan)	50	33	24	15
– Have You Seen Her? *The Chi-Lites* (MCA)	–	40	27	17
27 Theme From The Persuaders *The John Barry Orchestra* (CBS)	27	20	20	13
– Telegram Sam *T. Rex* (T. Rex)	–	–	–	3
– All I Ever Need Is You *Sonny and Cher* (MCA)	–	42	30	19
– Baby I'm A Want You *Bread* (Warner Bros.)	–	38	28	20

5	12	19	26
1 Telegram Sam *T. Rex* (T. Rex)	1	2	2
2 I'd Like To Teach The World To Sing *The New Seekers* (Polydor)	4	7	13
3 Mother Of Mine *Neil Reid* (Decca)	3	5	9
4 Horse With No Name *America* (Warner Bros.)	6	11	19
5 Brand New Key *Melanie* (Buddah)	8	14	18
6 Stay With Me *The Faces* (Warner Bros.)	11	–	–
7 Have You Seen Her? *The Chi-Lites* (MCA)	5	3	6
8 Where Did Our Love Go? *Donny Elbert* (London)	12	19	–
9 Let's Stay Together *Al Green* (London)	7	10	12
10 I Just Can't Help Believing *Elvis Presley* (RCA)	13	–	–
11 Son Of My Father *Chicory Tip* (CBS)	2	1	1

5	12	19	26
12 Moon River *Greyhound* (Trojan)	14	12	–
13 Morning Has Broken *Cat Stevens* (Island)	–	–	–
14 Baby I'm A Want You *Bread* (Elektra)	18	15	–
15 Family Affair *Sly and The Family Stone* (Epic)	19	18	–
16 All I Ever Need Is You *Sonny and Cher* (MCA)	10	8	11
17 American Pie *Don MacLean* (UA)	15	6	3
18 Soley Soley *Middle Of The Road* (RCA)	–	–	–
19 Sleepy Shores *The Johnny Pearson Orchestra* (Penny Farthing)	–	–	–
20 Theme From The Persuaders *The John Barry Orchestra* (CBS)	–	–	–
25 Look Wot You Dun *Slade* (Polydor)	9	4	4
23 Storm In A Tea Cup *The Fortunes* (Capitol)	16	9	7
28 Day After Day *Badfinger* (Apple)	17	13	10
26 My World *The Bee Gees* (Polydor)	20	17	16
50 Without You *Nilsson* (RCA)	27	16	5
22 If You Really Love Me *Stevie Wonder* (Tamla Motown)	22	20	20
– Got To Be There *Michael Jackson* (Tamla Motown)	39	22	8
46 Poppa Joe *The Sweet* (RCA)	30	26	14
– Blue Is The Colour *Chelsea F.C.* (Penny Farthing)	–	–	15
– Mother And Child Reunion *Paul Simon* (CBS)	–	28	17

MARCH 1972

4	11	18	25
1 Son Of My Father *Chicory Tip* (CBS)	3	4	12
2 American Pie *Don MacLean* (UA)	2	2	3
3 Without You *Nilsson* (RCA)	1	1	1
4 Look Wot You Dun *Slade* (Polydor)	8	13	18
5 Got To Be There *Michael Jackson* (Tamla Motown)	6	7	8
6 Have You Seen Her? *The Chi-Lites* (MCA)	14	–	–
7 Mother And Child Reunion *Paul Simon* (CBS)	7	5	6
8 Storm In A Tea Cup *The Fortunes* (Capitol)	11	14	–
9 Blue Is The Colour *Chelsea F.C.* (Penny Farthing)	5	8	11
10 Day After Day *Badfinger* (Apple)	13	16	–
11 Poppa Joe *The Sweet* (RCA)	12	12	17
12 Beg, Steal Or Borrow *The New Seekers* (Polydor)	4	3	2
13 Mother Of Mine *Neil Reid* (Decca)	15	10	15
14 Telegram Sam *T. Rex* (T. Rex)	18	–	–
15 I'd Like To Teach The World To Sing *The New Seekers* (Polydor)	–	–	20
16 My World *The Bee Gees* (Polydor)	20	–	–
17 Say You Don't Mind *Colin Blunstone* (CBS)	17	15	–
18 All I Ever Need Is You *Sonny and Cher* (MCA)	–	–	–
19 I Can't Help Myself *Donny Elbert* (Avco)	16	11	13
20 Let's Stay Together *Al Green* (London)	–	–	–
23 Alone Again (Naturally) *Gilbert O'Sullivan* (MAM)	9	6	4
22 Meet Me On The Corner *Lindisfarne* (Charisma)	10	9	5
21 Give Ireland Back To The Irish *Wings* (Apple)	19	17	16
50 Floy Joy *The Supremes* (Tamla Motown)	27	18	10
33 It's One Of Those Nights *The Partridge Family* (Bell)	25	19	14
– Desiderata *Les Crane* (Warner Bros.)	23	20	9
44 Hold Your Head Up *Argent* (Epic)	30	21	7
47 Too Beautiful To Last *Engelbert Humperdinck* (Decca)	37	26	19

APRIL 1972

1		8	15	22	29
1	Without You *Nilsson* (RCA)	1	2	2	3
2	Beg, Steal Or Borrow *The New Seekers* (Polydor)	2	3	6	12
3	Alone Again (Naturally) *Gilbert O'Sullivan* (MAM)	4	8	10	–
4	American Pie *Don MacLean* (UA)	7	16	–	–
5	Hold Your Head Up *Argent* (Epic)	5	6	8	16
6	Meet Me On The Corner *Lindisfarne* (Charisma)	6	13	–	–
7	Desiderata *Les Crane* (Warner Bros.)	9	9	12	19
8	Mother And Child Reunion *Paul Simon* (CBS)	14	–	–	–
9	Floy Joy *The Supremes* (Tamla Motown)	10	14	16	–
10	Got To Be There *Michael Jackson* (Tamla Motown)	–	–	–	–
11	It's One Of Those Nights *The Partridge Family* (Bell)	12	15	–	–
12	Blue Is The Colour *Chelsea F.C.* (Penny Farthing)	19	–	–	–
13	I Can't Help Myself *Donny Elbert* (Avco)	–	–	–	–
14	Too Beautiful To Last *Engelbert Humperdinck* (Decca)	17	20	–	–
15	Sweet Talking Guy *The Chiffons* (London)	8	5	4	4
16	Son Of My Father *Chicory Tip* (CBS)	–	–	–	–
17	Heart Of Gold *Neil Young* (Warner Bros.)	11	10	11	17
18	Back Off Boogaloo *Ringo Starr* (Apple)	15	4	3	2
19	The Young New Mexican Puppeteer *Tom Jones* (Decca)	13	7	7	6
20	What Is Life *Olivia Newton-John* (Pye)	16	18	17	–
31	Amazing Grace *Royal Scots Dragoon Guards Band* (RCA)	3	1	1	1
26	Until It's Time For You To Go *Elvis Presley* (RCA)	18	19	5	10
23	Crying, Laughing, Loving, Lying *Labi Siffre* (Pye)	20	11	13	15
41	Debora *Tyrannosaurus Rex* (Magni Fly)	27	12	15	7
29	Run Run Run *Jo Jo Gunne* (Asylum)	21	17	9	8
–	Come What May *Vicky Leandros* (Philips)	39	26	14	5
42	Radancer *The Marmalade* (Decca)	30	21	18	9
50	Stir It Up *Johnny Nash* (CBS)	43	24	19	13
–	Could It Be Forever *David Cassidy* (Bell)	35	34	20	11
–	A Thing Called Love *Johnny Cash and The Evangel Temple Choir* (CBS)	–	37	28	14
–	Tumbling Dice *The Rolling Stones* (RS)	–	–	–	18
33	I Am What I Am *Greyhound* (Trojan)	37	25	27	20

MAY 1972

6		13	20	27
1	Amazing Grace *Royal Scots Dragoon Guards Band* (RCA)	1	2	3
2	Back Off Boogaloo *Ringo Starr* (Apple)	11	12	–
3	Come What May *Vicky Leandros* (Philips)	2	4	4
4	Could It Be Forever *David Cassidy* (Bell)	3	3	2
5	Sweet Talking Guy *The Chiffons* (London)	10	11	–
6	Run Run Run *Jo Jo Gunne* (Asylum)	8	10	17
7	A Thing Called Love *Johnny Cash* (CBS)	4	6	7
8	Debora *Tyrannosaurus Rex* (Magni Fly)	12	16	–
9	Radancer *The Marmalade* (Decca)	6	9	13
10	Without You *Nilsson* (RCA)	15	–	–
11	The Young New Mexican Puppeteer *Tom Jones* (Decca)	13	–	–
12	Rocket Man *Elton John* (DJM)	7	5	5
13	Until It's Time For You To Go *Elvis Presley* (RCA)	16	–	–
14	Tumbling Dice *The Rolling Stones* (RS)	5	7	9
15	Stir It Up *Johnny Nash* (CBS)	14	18	–
16	Take A Look Around *The Temptations* (Tamla Motown)	17	13	18
17	Hold Your Head Up *Argent* (Epic)	–	–	–
18	Crying, Laughing, Loving, Lying *Labi Siffre* (Pye)	–	–	–
19	Runnin' Away *Sly and The Family Stone* (Epic)	–	17	–
20	Saturday Night At The Movies/At The Club *The Drifters* (Bell)	19	8	8

	13	20	27
– Metal Guru *T. Rex* (T. Rex)	9	1	1
27 Oh Babe What Would You Say *Hurricane Smith* (Columbia)	18	15	6
42 Leeds United *Leeds United F.C.* (Chapter One)	20	14	10
– Lady Eleanor *Lindisfarne* (Charisma)	29	19	12
24 Amazing Grace *Judy Collins* (Elektra)	23	20	–
– Vincent *Don MacLean* (UA)	36	29	11
32 A Whiter Shade Of Pale *Procol Harum* (Chrysalis)	26	22	14
28 Me And Julio Down By The School Yard *Paul Simon* (CBS)	24	23	15
– Sister Jane *New World* (RAK)	31	27	16
34 Isn't Life Strange *The Moody Blues* (Threshold)	39	24	19
– California Man *The Move* (Harvest)	46	34	20

JUNE 1972

3	10	17	24
1 Metal Guru *T. Rex* (T. Rex)	1	2	4
2 Rocket Man *Elton John* (DJM)	5	11	19
3 At The Club/Saturday Night At The Movies *The Drifters* (Bell)	6	4	5
4 Oh Babe What Would You Say *Hurricane Smith* (Columbia)	4	8	12
5 Vincent *Don MacLean* (UA)	2	1	1
6 Lady Eleanor *Lindisfarne* (Charisma)	3	6	10
7 Could It Be Forever *David Cassidy* (Bell)	7	14	–
8 Amazing Grace *Royal Scots Dragoon Guards Band* (RCA)	11	18	–
9 A Thing Called Love *Johnny Cash* (CBS)	19	–	–
10 Come What May *Vicky Leandros* (Philips)	17	–	–
11 California Man *The Move* (Harvest)	8	7	7
12 Leeds United *Leeds United F.C.* (Chapter One)	16	–	–
13 Isn't Life Strange *The Moody Blues* (Threshold)	15	15	–
14 Tumbling Dice *The Rolling Stones* (RS)	–	–	–
15 A Whiter Shade Of Pale *Procol Harum* (Chrysalis)	13	20	–
16 Sister Jane *New World* (RAK)	9	9	11
17 Take A Look Around *The Temptations* (Bell)	–	–	–
18 Doobedood'ndoobe *Diana Ross* (Tamla Motown)	18	12	–
19 Me And Julio Down By The School Yard *Paul Simon* (CBS)	20	–	–
20 Mary Had A Little Lamb *Wings* (Apple)	12	10	9
22 Rockin' Robin *Michael Jackson* (Tamla Motown)	10	5	3
25 Take Me Bak 'Ome *Slade* (Polydor)	14	3	2
31 Song Sung Blue *Neil Diamond* (Uni)	23	16	15
32 Supersonic Rocket Ship *The Kinks* (RCA)	24	17	16
35 Little Bit Of Love *Free* (Island)	28	19	20
– Rock And Roll Part 2 *Gary Glitter* (Bell)	37	21	6
– Little Willie *The Sweet* (RCA)	47	23	8
– Puppy Love *Donny Osmond* (MGM)	–	36	13
37 Oh Girl *The Chi-Lites* (MCA)	25	25	14
34 The First Time Ever I Saw Your Face *Roberta Flack* (Atlantic)	26	22	17
– Ooh-Wakka-Doo-Wakka-Day *Gilbert O'Sullivan* (MAM)	–	40	18
23 What's Your Name *Chicory Tip* (RCA)	21	13	–

JULY 1972

1	8	15	22	29
1 Take Me Bak 'Ome *Slade* (Polydor)	3	3	8	16
2 Vincent *Don MacLean* (UA)	5	8	19	–
3 Puppy Love *Donny Osmond* (MGM)	1	1	1	1
4 Little Willie *The Sweet* (RCA)	4	6	6	11
5 Rock And Roll Part 2 *Gary Glitter* (Bell)	2	2	2	3
6 Rockin' Robin *Michael Jackson* (Tamla Motown)	7	10	15	–
7 California Man *The Move* (Harvest)	10	14	–	–
8 An American Trilogy *Elvis Presley* (RCA)	9	9	10	18

1	8	15	22	29
9 Mary Had A Little Lamb *Wings* (Apple)	11	15	–	–
10 At The Club/Saturday Night At The Movies *The Drifters* (Bell)				
11 Circles *The New Seekers* (Polydor)	6	5	4	8
12 Ooh-Wakka-Doo-Wakka-Day *Gilbert O'Sullivan* (MAM)	8	11	11	–
13 Little Bit Of Love *Free* (Island)	15	18	–	–
14 Song Sung Blue *Neil Diamond* (Uni)	17	–	–	–
15 Metal Guru *T. Rex* (T. Rex)				
16 The First Time Ever I Saw Your Face *Roberta Flack* (Atlantic)	14	17	–	–
17 Sister Jane *New World* (RAK)	–	–	–	–
18 Oh Girl *The Chi-Lites* (MCA)	18	–	–	–
19 Supersonic Rocket Ship *The Kinks* (RCA)	–	–	–	–
20 Oh Babe What Would You Say *Hurricane Smith* (Columbia)	–	–	–	–
25 I Can See Clearly Now *Johnny Nash* (CBS)	12	7	5	7
28 Sylvia's Mother *Dr Hook and The Medicine Show* (CBS)	13	4	3	2
22 Join Together *The Who* (Track)	16	12	9	13
21 Walking In The Rain With The One You Love *Love Unlimited* (UA)	19	16	16	14
24 Nut Rocker *B. Bumble and The Stingers* (Stateside)	20	19	–	–
– Breaking Up Is Hard To Do *The Partridge Family* (Bell)	30	13	7	4
41 Starman *David Bowie* (RCA)	29	20	18	10
– Seaside Shuffle *Terry Dactyl and The Dinosaurs* (UK)	–	29	12	5
32 Betcha By Golly Wow *The Stylistics* (Avco)	25	25	13	15
43 Mad About You *Bruce Ruffin* (Rhino)	35	23	14	9
– School's Out *Alice Cooper* (Warner Bros.)	–	44	17	6
49 Silver Machine *Hawkwind* (UA)	40	37	20	12
– Automatically Sunshine *The Supremes* (Tamla Motown)	–	35	25	17
– Popcorn *Hot Butter* (Pye)	–	–	41	19
– My Guy *Mary Wells* (Tamla Motown)	48	38	26	20

AUGUST 1972

5	12	19	26
1 Puppy Love *Donny Osmond* (MGM)	4	4	10
2 School's Out *Alice Cooper* (Warner Bros.)	1	1	1
3 Sylvia's Mother *Dr Hook and The Medicine Show* (CBS)	5	8	16
4 Seaside Shuffle *Terry Dactyl and The Dinosaurs* (UK)	2	2	5
5 Breaking Up Is Hard To Do *The Partridge Family* (Bell)	3	6	8
6 Rock And Roll Part 2 *Gary Glitter* (Bell)	9	12	18
7 Silver Machine *Hawkwind* (UA)	7	3	3
8 I Can See Clearly Now *Johnny Nash* (CBS)	8	16	15
9 Circles *The New Seekers* (Polydor)	10	–	19
10 Automatically Sunshine *The Supremes* (Tamla Motown)	12	17	–
11 Popcorn *Hot Butter* (Pye)	6	5	6
12 Starman *David Bowie* (RCA)	11	18	–
13 Mad About You *Bruce Ruffin* (Rhino)	13	19	–
14 My Guy *Mary Wells* (Tamla Motown)	15	–	–
15 Join Together *The Who* (Track)	18	–	–
16 Betcha By Golly Wow *The Stylistics* (Avco)	14	–	–
17 Little Willy *The Sweet* (RCA)	20	–	–
18 Take Me Bak 'Ome *Slade* (Polydor)	–	–	–
19 Ooh-Wakka-Doo-Wakka-Day *Gilbert O'Sullivan* (MAM)	–	–	–
20 10538 Overture *The Electric Light Orchestra* (Harvest)	17	14	9
24 It's Four In The Morning *Faron Young* (Fontana)	16	10	12
26 Run To Me *The Bee Gees* (Polydor)	19	9	11
– You Wear It Well *Rod Stewart* (Mercury)	23	7	2
– All The Young Dudes *Mott The Hoople* (CBS)	22	11	4
– Layla *Derek and The Dominoes* (Polydor)	25	13	7

5

	12	19	26
27 The Locomotion *Little Eva* (London)	21	15	13
23 Working On A Building Of Love *Chairmen Of The Board* (Invictus)	24	20	–
– Standing In The Road *Blackfoot Sue* (JAM)	44	25	14
36 I Get The Sweetest Feeling *Jackie Wilson* (MCA)	31	24	17
– Sugar Me *Lynsey de Paul* (MAM)	–	47	20

SEPTEMBER 1972

2

	9	16	23	30
1 You Wear It Well *Rod Stewart* (Mercury)	2	2	4	11
2 Mama Weer All Crazee Now *Slade* (Polydor)	1	1	1	3
3 School's Out *Alice Cooper* (Warner Bros.)	11	16	–	–
4 Silver Machine *Hawkwind* (UA)	7	13	19	–
5 All The Young Dudes *Mott The Hoople* (CBS)	3	7	14	–
6 It's Four In The Morning *Faron Young* (Fontana)	5	3	6	7
7 Layla *Derek and The Dominoes* (Polydor)	9	11	–	–
8 Popcorn *Hot Butter* (Pye)	14	17	–	–
9 Standing In The Road *Blackfoot Sue* (JAM)	4	6	11	19
10 Seaside Shuffle *Terry Dactyl and The Dinosaurs* (UK)	15	–	–	–
11 The Locomotion *Little Eva* (London)	12	15	–	–
12 Sugar Me *Lynsey de Paul* (MAM)	6	5	5	15
13 Run To Me *The Bee Gees* (Polydor)	13	–	–	–
14 I Get The Sweetest Feeling *Jackie Wilson* (MCA)	10	9	13	13
15 10538 Overture *The Electric Light Orchestra* (Harvest)	17	–	–	–
16 Breaking Up Is Hard To Do *The Partridge Family* (Bell)	20	–	–	–
17 Puppy Love *Donny Osmond* (MGM)	19	–	–	–
18 Virginia Plain *Roxy Music* (Island)	8	4	7	10
19 I Can See Clearly Now *Johnny Nash* (CBS)	–	–	–	–
20 Ain't No Sunshine *Michael Jackson* (Tamla Motown)	16	8	8	8
25 Lean On Me *Bill Withers* (A & M)	18	18	–	–
– How Can I Be Sure *David Cassidy* (Bell)	–	10	3	1
– Living In Harmony *Cliff Richard* (Columbia)	21	12	12	12
– Children Of The Revolution *T. Rex* (T. Rex)	–	14	2	2
– Too Busy Thinking About My Baby *Mardi Gras* (Bell)	24	19	–	–
– Come On Over To My Place *The Drifters* (Bell)	27	20	10	9
– Too Young *Donny Osmond* (MGM)	–	22	9	5
– Wig-Wam Bam *The Sweet* (RCA)	48	25	15	6
38 Walk In The Night *Jnr. Walker and The All Stars* (Tamla Motown)	26	21	16	20
39 Big Six *Judge Dread* (Big Shot)	29	23	17	17
46 Suzanne Beware Of The Devil *Dandy Livingstone* (Horse)	33	28	18	16
– Mouldy Old Dough *Lieutenant Pigeon* (Decca)	–	38	20	4
– I Didn't Know I Loved You (Till I Saw You Rock 'n' Roll) *Gary Glitter* (Bell)	–	–	27	14
– You're A Lady *Peter Skellern* (Decca)	–	–	43	18

OCTOBER 1972

7

	14	21	28
1 How Can I Be Sure *David Cassidy* (Bell)	2	4	12
2 Children Of The Revolution *T. Rex* (T. Rex)	5	10	17
3 Mouldy Old Dough *Lieutenant Pigeon* (Decca)	1	1	1
4 Wig-Wam Bam *The Sweet* (RCA)	6	8	10
5 Too Young *Donny Osmond* (MGM)	7	14	–
6 You're A Lady *Peter Skellern* (Decca)	3	3	7
7 Mama Weer All Crazee Now *Slade* (Polydor)	16	–	–
8 I Didn't Know I Loved You (Till I Saw You Rock 'n' Roll) *Gary Glitter* (Bell)	4	5	6

7	**14**	**21**	**28**
9 It's Four In The Morning *Faron Young* (Fontana)	13	–	–
10 Come On Over To My Place *The Drifters* (Bell)	15	17	–
11 Burning Love *Elvis Presley* (RCA)	8	7	8
12 Big Six *Judge Dread* (Big Shot)	11	11	15
13 Ain't No Sunshine *Michael Jackson* (Tamla Motown)	–	–	–
14 Suzanne Beware Of The Devil *Dandy Livingstone* (Horse)	14	16	–
15 Virginia Plain *Roxy Music* (Island)	–	–	–
16 Living In Harmony *Cliff Richard* (Columbia)	–	–	–
17 Donna *10cc* (UK)	10	2	2
18 In A Broken Dream *Python Lee Jackson* (Young Blood)	9	6	3
19 Walk In The Night *Jnr. Walker and The All Stars* (Tamla Motown)	20	–	–
20 John I'm Only Dancing *David Bowie* (RCA)	12	13	13
34 Elected *Alice Cooper* (Warner Bros.)	17	9	4
22 Backstabbers *The O'Jays* (Philadelphia)	18	20	14
26 There Are More Questions Than Answers *Johnny Nash* (CBS)	19	12	9
– Clair *Gilbert O'Sullivan* (MAM)	–	15	5
– Goodbye To Love *The Carpenters* (A & M)	22	18	11
– Burlesque *Family* (Reprise)	23	19	19
– Guitar Man *Bread* (Elektra)	21	22	16
– Hallelujah Freedom *Jnr. Campbell* (Deram)	39	24	18
– Loop Di Love *Shag* (UK)	46	26	20

NOVEMBER 1972

4	**11**	**18**	**25**
1 Mouldy Old Dough *Lieutenant Pigeon* (Decca)	2	5	12
2 Clair *Gilbert O'Sullivan* (MAM)	1	1	3
3 Donna *10cc* (UK)	3	13	16
4 In A Broken Dream *Python Lee Jackson* (Young Blood)	7	12	–
5 Elected *Alice Cooper* (Warner Bros.)	4	11	17
6 Leader Of The Pack *The Shangri-Las* (Kama Sutra)	8	3	6
7 Loop Di Love *Shag* (UK)	5	4	7
8 You're A Lady *Peter Skellern* (Decca)	16	–	–
9 Burning Love *Elvis Presley* (RCA)	14	–	–
10 There Are More Questions Than Answers *Johnny Nash* (CBS)	12	18	–
11 Goodbye To Love *The Carpenters* (A & M)	9	15	15
12 I Didn't Know I Loved You (Till I Saw You Rock 'n' Roll) *Gary Glitter* (Bell)	17	–	–
13 Hallelujah Freedom *Jnr. Campbell* (Deram)	10	17	18
14 Burlesque *Family* (Reprise)	13	16	–
15 Big Six *Judge Dread* (Big Shot)	18	–	–
16 John I'm Only Dancing *David Bowie* (RCA)	–	–	–
17 Wig-Wam Bam *The Sweet* (RCA)	–	–	–
18 How Can I Be Sure *David Cassidy* (Bell)	–	–	–
19 Let's Dance *Chris Montez* (London)	15	9	11
20 Guitar Man *Bread* (Elektra)	–	–	–
23 My Ding-A-Ling *Chuck Berry* (Chess)	6	2	1
24 Here I Go Again *Archie Bell and The Drells* (Atlantic)	11	14	14
31 I'm Stone In Love With You *The Stylistics* (Avco)	19	10	9
42 Crocodile Rock *Elton John* (DJM)	20	8	5
– Why *Donny Osmond* (MGM)	21	6	4
– Crazy Horses *The Osmonds* (MGM)	27	7	2
21 New Orleans *Harley Quinne* (Bell)	23	19	–
32 Hi-Ho Silver Lining *Jeff Beck* (RAK)	22	20	19
– Gudbuy T'Jane *Slade* (Polydor)	–	–	8
– Angel/What Made Milwaukee Famous *Rod Stewart* (Mercury)	–	23	10
– Looking Through The Windows *The Jackson Five* (Tamla Motown)	40	21	13
34 Lay Down *The Strawbs* (A & M)	31	26	20

DECEMBER 1972

2	9	16	23/30
1 My Ding-A-Ling *Chuck Berry* (Chess)	1	1	2
2 Crazy Horses *The Osmonds* (MGM)	2	3	5
3 Why *Donny Osmond* (MGM)	6	6	9
4 Gudbuy T'Jane *Slade* (Polydor)	3	2	6
5 Crocodile Rock *Elton John* (DJM)	5	7	7
6 Angel/What Made Milwaukee Famous *Rod Stewart* (Mercury)	4	9	12
7 Clair *Gilbert O'Sullivan* (MAM)	14	–	–
8 Leader Of The Pack *The Shangri-Las* (Kama Sutra)	20	–	–
9 Looking Through The Windows *The Jackson Five* (Tamla Motown)	10	12	20
10 I'm Stone In Love With You *The Stylistics* (Avco)	15	–	–
11 Let's Dance *Chris Montez* (London)	–	–	–
12 Stay With Me *Blue Mink* (Regal Zonophone)	13	11	15
13 Lay Down *The Strawbs* (A & M)	12	14	–
14 Mouldy Old Dough *Lieutenant Pigeon* (Decca)	–	–	–
15 Loop Di Love *Shag* (UK)	19	–	–
16 Ben *Michael Jackson* (Tamla Motown)	7	8	8
17 Hi-Ho Silver Lining *Jeff Beck* (RAK)	17	17	–
18 Rock Me Baby *David Cassidy* (Bell)	11	13	17
19 Oh Carol *Neil Sedaka* (RCA)	–	–	–
20 Donna *10cc* (UK)	–	–	–
– Solid Gold Easy Action *T. Rex* (EMI)	8	4	3
27 Long Haired Lover From Liverpool *Little Jimmy Osmond* (MGM)	9	5	1
21 Shotgun Wedding *Roy C.* (UK)	16	10	11
28 Help Me Make It Through The Night *Gladys Knight and The Pips* (Tamla Motown)	18	19	14
33 Nights In White Satin *The Moody Blues* (Deram)	21	15	10
– Happy Christmas (War Is Over) *John Lennon and Yoko Ono, The Plastic Ono Band and The Harlem Community Choir* (Apple)	23	16	4
23 Keeper Of The Castle *The Four Tops* (Tamla Motown)	25	18	–
36 Little Drummer Boy *Royal Scots Dragoon Guards Band* (RCA)	28	20	13
– The Jean Genie *David Bowie* (RCA)	33	31	16
– Big Seven *Judge Dread* (Big Shot)	50	32	18
48 Getting A Drag *Lynsey de Paul* (MAM)	30	28	19

1972–BEST-SELLING SINGLES

1   Amazing Grace *Royal Scots Dragoon Guards Band* (RCA)
2   Mouldy Old Dough *Lieutenant Pigeon* (Decca)
3   Puppy Love *Donny Osmond* (MGM)
4   Without You *Nilsson* (RCA)
5   I'd Like To Teach The World To Sing *The New Seekers* (Polydor)
6   Son Of My Father *Chicory Tip* (CBS)
7   Rock And Roll Part 2 *Gary Glitter* (Bell)
8   Metal Guru *T. Rex* (T. Rex)
9   Mother Of Mine *Neil Reid* (Decca)
10 Telegram Sam *T. Rex* (T. Rex)
11 American Pie *Don MacLean* (UA)
12 Mama Weer All Crazee Now *Slade* (Polydor)
13 School's Out *Alice Cooper* (Warner Bros.)
14 You Wear It Well *Rod Stewart* (Mercury)
15 Beg, Steal Or Borrow *The New Seekers* (Polydor)
16 Vincent *Don MacLean* (UA)
17 Clair *Gilbert O'Sullivan* (MAM)
18 My Ding-A-Ling *Chuck Berry* (Chess)
19 How Can I Be Sure *David Cassidy* (Bell)
20 Sylvia's Mother *Dr Hook and The Medicine Show* (CBS)

1972–BEST-SELLING ALBUMS

1   20 Dynamic Hits *Various artists*
2   20 All-Time Hits Of The 50s *Various artists*
3   Simon And Garfunkel's Greatest Hits *Simon and Garfunkel*
4   Never A Dull Moment *Rod Stewart*
5   20 Fantastic Hits *Various artists*
6   Bridge Over Troubled Water *Simon and Garfunkel*
7   Fog On The Tyne *Lindisfarne*
8   Slade Alive *Slade*
9   25 Rockin' And Rollin' Greats *Various artists*
10 American Pie *Don MacLean*

1972–BEST-SELLING ARTISTS

Male Artists (Singles)

1 Gilbert O'Sullivan
2 Michael Jackson
3 Elvis Presley
4 Donny Osmond
5 Don MacLean

6 David Cassidy
7 Johnny Nash
8 Gary Glitter
9 Elton John
10 Harry Nilsson

Female Artists (Singles)

1 Vicky Leandros
2 Judy Collins
3 Lynsey de Paul

4 Melanie
5 Roberta Flack

Groups (Singles)

1 T. Rex
2 The New Seekers
3 Slade
4 The Sweet
5 Royal Scots Dragoon Guards Band

6 The Drifters
7 Alice Cooper
8 The Partridge Family
9 Lindisfarne
10 Chicory Tip

Male Artists (Albums)

1 Cat Stevens
2 Rod Stewart
3 Gilbert O'Sullivan
4 Don MacLean
5 Neil Young

6 David Cassidy
7 Neil Diamond
8 Andy Williams
9 Elvis Presley
10 David Bowie

Female Artists (Albums)

1 Carole King
2 Melanie
3 Shirley Bassey

4 Nana Mouskouri
5 Diana Ross

Groups (Albums)

1 Simon and Garfunkel
2 Lindisfarne
3 T. Rex
4 Slade
5 John Lenhon and The Plastic Ono Band

6 Deep Purple
7 The New Seekers
8 The Carpenters
9 Bread
10 Led Zeppelin

1973

Did 1973 begin with disaster? It could be said that it did, for Little Jimmy Osmond opened the New Year's charts at Number One with 'Long Haired Lover From Liverpool'. 1973 saw Little Jimmy have a follow-up hit with 'Tweedle Dee', while his big brother Donny achieved two Number Ones and a Number Four. His top chart positions were held by 'The Twelfth Of Never', which had been made popular by Johnny Mathis in the 1950s, and 'Young Love', which had given Hit Parade success to both Tab Hunter and Sonny James in 1957. Donny's other hit was 'When I Fall In Love', which had been a huge hit for Nat 'King' Cole in April 1957.

The Osmonds had two Top Five discs with 'Going Home' and 'Let Me In' and Marie Osmond, their younger sister, arrived on the scene with 'Paper Roses', a record which almost reached the Number One position.

David Cassidy had a good year with two hits in his own right and another two with The Partridge Family. At last David Essex found deserved fame and became a chart force with 'Rock On' which reached Number Three, and his follow-up, 'Lamplight', which entered the Top Ten.

Other teen heroes with chart success in 1973 included The Sweet, Slade, a slightly reticent Marc Bolan, Gary Glitter and Mud. Glitter's successes in the charts were very impressive statistically, for two of his discs reached Number Two in the charts, while another two, 'I'm The Leader Of The Gang' and 'I Love You Love Me Love' both reached Number One.

Mud achieved their first hit with 'Crazy' and were just one group signed to the RAK record label, a company owned by Mickie Most. The RAK label achieved 14 chart entries out of 18 releases and another successful label, Bell, achieved 16 hits out of 57 releases, i.e. a ratio of 1 : 3. This is very impressive when compared to the Decca record company's ratio of 1 : 31, or 20 hits out of 620 releases.

RAK's successes were achieved by Mud, Hot Chocolate, Cozy Powell, and Suzi Quatro, a girl singer discovered in Detroit by Mickie Most.

The record industry created a demand for teen stars, but most of these failed although minor hits were obtained by Andy and David Williams, The Dougal Brothers and The Handley Family.

Philadelphia groups came to the fore and successful discs were recorded by Billy Paul, The Stylistics, The Detroit Emeralds, The Detroit Spinners, Harold Melvin and The Bluenotes, The O'Jays, while artists on the Tamla Motown label also achieved a few hits.

A number of exciting new groups such as Mott The Hoople, Roxy Music, Wings and a re-born Status Quo all established themselves in the charts. Following on the heels of their late 1972 hit, 'Donna', 10cc continued to build upon their chart reputation. Perhaps the most memorable of all recording successes of 1973 were those of David Bowie, as his discs, act, personality and his 'cult' following made him a very important figure indeed.

JANUARY 1973

	6	13	20	27
1 Long Haired Lover From Liverpool *Little Jimmy Osmond* (MGM)		1	1	2
2 Solid Gold Easy Action *T. Rex* (EMI)		3	7	17
3 Crazy Horses *The Osmonds* (MGM)		4	8	18
4 The Jean Genie *David Bowie* (RCA)		2	3	3
5 Gudbuy T'Jane *Slade* (Polydor)		9	14	–
6 Happy Christmas (War Is Over) *John Lennon and Yoko Ono, The Plastic Ono Band and The Harlem Community Choir* (Apple)		15	–	–
7 My Ding-A-Ling *Chuck Berry* (Chess)		14	–	–
8 Shotgun Wedding *Roy C.* (UK)		11	12	–
9 Nights In White Satin *The Moody Blues* (Deram)		13	13	–
10 Hi Hi Hi/C. Moon *Wings* (Apple)		5	5	7
11 Big Seven *Judge Dread* (Big Shot)		8	10	12
12 Ben *Michael Jackson* (Tamla Motown)		12	19	–
13 Always On My Mind *Elvis Presley* (RCA)		10	9	11
14 Help Me Make It Through The Night *Gladys Knight and The Pips* (Tamla Motown)		18	11	–
15 Ball Park Incident *Wizzard* (Harvest)		6	6	6
16 Why *Donny Osmond* (MGM)		17	–	–
17 Crocodile Rock *Elton John* (DJM)		20	–	–
18 Getting A Drag *Lynsey de Paul* (MAM)		–	–	–
19 Little Drummer Boy *The Royal Scots Dragoon Guards Band* (RCA)		–	–	–
20 You're So Vain *Carly Simon* (Elektra)		7	4	4
– Blockbuster *The Sweet* (RCA)		16	2	1
22 Desperate Dan *Lieutenant Pigeon* (Decca)		19	17	20
– Wishing Well *Free* (Island)		26	15	8
28 Can't Keep It In *Cat Stevens* (Island)		21	16	13
– Papa Was A Rolling Stone *The Temptations* (Tamla Motown)		37	18	14
27 Come Softly To Me *The New Seekers* (Polydor)		24	20	30
– Do You Wanna Touch Me *Gary Glitter* (Bell)		–	34	5
– If You Don't Know Me By Now *Harold Melvin and The Blue notes* (CBS)		30	23	9
– Daniel *Elton John* (DJM)		–	38	10
– Paper Plane *Status Quo* (Vertigo)		40	24	15
– Me And Mrs Jones *Billy Paul* (Epic)		42	25	16
– Part Of The Union *The Strawbs* (A & M)		–	–	19

FEBRUARY 1973

	3	10	17	24
1 Blockbuster *The Sweet* (RCA)		1	1	1
2 Do You Wanna Touch Me *Gary Glitter* (Bell)		2	3	3
3 You're So Vain *Carly Simon* (Elektra)		4	8	12
4 Long Haired Lover From Liverpool *Little Jimmy Osmond* (MGM)		6	9	17
5 The Jean Genie *David Bowie* (RCA)		13	–	–
6 Daniel *Elton John* (DJM)		5	4	7
7 Part Of The Union *The Strawbs* (A & M)		3	2	2
8 Wishing Well *Free* (Island)		7	13	–
9 If You Don't Know Me By Now *Harold Melvin and The Bluenotes* (CBS)		11	15	–
10 Ball Park Incident *Wizzard* (Harvest)		19	–	–
11 Paper Plane *Status Quo* (Vertigo)		8	10	13
12 Me And Mrs Jones *Billy Paul* (Epic)		12	16	–
13 Hi Hi Hi/C. Moon *Wings* (Apple)		20	–	–

3		10	17	24
14 Always On My Mind *Elvis Presley* (RCA)		–	–	–
15 Can't Keep It In *Cat Stevens* (Island)		14	–	–
16 Big Seven *Judge Dread* (Big Shot)		–	–	–
17 Roll Over Beethoven *The Electric Light Orchestra* (Harvest)		10	6	8
18 Papa Was A Rolling Stone *The Temptations* (Tamla Motown)		15	–	–
19 Crazy Horses *The Osmonds* (MGM)		–	–	–
20 Help Me Make It Through The Night *Gladys Knight and The Pips* (Tamla Motown)		–	–	–
21 Sylvia *Focus* (Polydor)		9	5	4
23 Whisky In The Jar *Thin Lizzy* (Decca)		16	7	6
24 Superstition *Stevie Wonder* (Tamla Motown)		17	11	11
27 Take Me Home Country Roads *Olivia Newton-John* (Pye)		18	18	15
32 Baby I Love You *Dave Edmunds* (Rockfield)		28	12	10
49 Lookin' Through The Eyes Of Love *The Partridge Family* (Bell)		22	14	9
– Cindy Incidentally *The Faces* (Warner Bros.)		–	17	5
– Hello Hurray *Alice Cooper* (Warner Bros.)		44	19	14
34 Take Me Girl I'm Ready *Jnr. Walker and The All Stars* (Tamla Motown)		25	20	16
39 Reelin' And Rockin' *Chuck Berry* (Chess)		29	23	18
– Doctor My Eyes *The Jackson Five* (Tamla Motown)		–	27	19
33 Hocus Pocus *Focus* (Polydor)		30	22	20

MARCH 1973

3		10	17	24	31
1 Cum On Feel The Noize *Slade* (Polydor)		1	1	1	2
2 Part Of The Union *The Strawbs* (A & M)		4	12	20	–
3 Blockbuster *The Sweet* (RCA)		5	14	–	–
4 Sylvia *Focus* (Polydor)		12	9	–	–
5 Cindy Incidentally *The Faces* (Warner Bros.)		2	5	9	18
6 Do You Wanna Touch Me *Gary Glitter* (Bell)		13	–	–	–
7 Whisky In The Jar *Thin Lizzy* (Decca)		10	15	–	–
8 Baby I Love You *Dave Edmunds* (Rockfield)		11	10	–	20
9 Lookin' Through The Eyes Of Love *The Partridge Family* (Bell)		15	16	–	–
10 Feel The Need In Me *The Detroit Emeralds* (Janus)		6	4	5	6
11 Daniel *Elton John* (DJM)		–	–	–	–
12 Doctor My Eyes *The Jackson Five* (Tamla Motown)		9	11	15	–
13 Hello Hurray *Alice Cooper* (Warner Bros.)		7	6	8	15
14 Supersitition *Stevie Wonder* (Tamla Motown)		18	–	–	–
15 Roll Over Beethoven *The Electric Light Orchestra* (Harvest)		–	–	–	–
16 Gonna Make You An Offer You Can't Refuse *Jimmy Helms* (Cube)		17	8	10	14
17 Take Me Home Country Roads *Olivia Newton-John* (Pye)		–	–	–	–
18 Long Haired Lover From Liverpool *Little Jimmy Osmond* (MGM)		20	–	–	–
19 Killing Me Softly With His Song *Roberta Flack* (Atlantic)		8	7	6	9
20 Reelin' And Rockin' *Chuck Berry* (Chess)		–	–	–	–
– 20th Century Boy *T. Rex* (EMI)		3	3	3	5
– The Twelfth Of Never *Donny Osmond* (MGM)		14	2	2	1
22 Pinball Wizard/See Me Feel Me *The New Seekers* (Polydor)		16	17	17	19
29 Nice One Cyril *Cockerel Chorus* (Young Blood)		19	18	14	16
– Power To All Our Friends *Cliff Richard* (Columbia)		–	13	4	4
36 Heart Of Stone *Kenny* (RAK)		25	19	12	11
42 Never Never Never *Shirley Bassey* (UA)		31	20	11	10
– Get Down *Gilbert O'Sullivan* (MAM)		–	30	7	3
32 Why Can't We Live Together *Timmy Thomas* (Mojo)		28	23	13	12
– Tie A Yellow Ribbon *Dawn* (Bell)		38	32	16	7

3	10	17	24	31
28 That's When The Music Takes Me *Neil Sedaka* (RCA)	24	24	18	–
46 Love Train *The O'Jays* (CBS)	40	28	19	13
– I'm A Clown/Some Kind Of A Summer *David Cassidy* (Bell)	–	–	35	8
– Pyjamarama *Roxy Music* (Island)	45	31	23	17

APRIL 1973

7	14	21	28
1 Get Down *Gilbert O'Sullivan* (MAM)	1	3	3
2 The Twelfth Of Never *Donny Osmond* (MGM)	4	6	8
3 Tie A Yellow Ribbon *Dawn* (Bell)	2	1	1
4 Power To All Our Friends *Cliff Richard* (Columbia)	7	7	14
5 I'm A Clown/Some Kind Of A Summer *David Cassidy* (Bell)	3	5	4
6 Tweedle Dee *Little Jimmy Osmond* (MGM)	6	4	5
7 Cum On Feel The Noize *Slade* (Polydor)	13	19	–
8 Never Never Never *Shirley Bassey* (UA)	8	9	11
9 Love Train *The O'Jays* (CBS)	9	12	13
10 Killing Me Softly With His Song *Roberta Flack* (Atlantic)	19	20	–
11 Feel The Need In Me *The Detroit Emeralds* (Janus)	18	–	–
12 Heart Of Stone *Kenny* (RAK)	12	16	–
13 Pyjamarama *Roxy Music* (Island)	10	10	10
14 Why Can't We Live Together *Timmy Thomas* (Mojo)	15	–	–
15 20th Century Boy *T. Rex* (EMI)	17	–	–
16 Nice One Cyril *Cockerel Chorus* (Young Blood)	–	–	–
17 Hello Hello I'm Back Again *Gary Glitter* (Bell)	5	2	2
18 Crazy *Mud* (RAK)	14	14	12
19 Hello Hurray *Alice Cooper* (Warner Bros.)	–	–	–
20 Amanda *Stuart Gillies* (Philips)	20	13	15
21 All Because Of You *Geordie* (EMI)	11	11	6
– Drive-in Saturday *David Bowie* (RCA)	16	8	7
43 My Love *Wings* (Apple)	25	15	9
22 Duelling Banjos *Eric Weissberg and Steve Mandel* (Warner Bros.)	21	17	19
28 God Gave Rock 'n' Roll To You *Argent* (Epic)	29	18	–
– See My Baby Jive *Wizzard* (Harvest)	–	27	16
– Giving It All Away *Roger Daltrey* (Track)	31	24	17
– Brother Louie *Hot Chocolate* (RAK)	33	21	18
– Big Eight *Judge Dread* (Big Shot)	–	29	20

MAY 1973

5	12	19	26
1 Tie A Yellow Ribbon *Dawn* (Bell)	1	3	4
2 Hello Hello I'm Back Again *Gary Glitter* (Bell)	3	4	8
3 Drive-in Saturday *David Bowie* (RCA)	8	6	16
4 Hell Raiser *The Sweet* (RCA)	2	2	2
5 Tweedle Dee *Little Jimmy Osmond* (MGM)	16	20	–
6 See My Baby Jive *Wizzard* (Harvest)	4	1	1
7 All Because Of You *Geordie* (EMI)	11	12	–
8 Get Down *Gilbert O'Sullivan* (MAM)	12	–	–
9 Brother Louie *Hot Chocolate* (RAK)	7	8	9
10 I'm A Clown/Some Kind Of A Summer *David Cassidy* (Bell)	15	19	–
11 Giving It All Away *Roger Daltrey* (Track)	5	7	10
12 My Love *Wings* (Apple)	9	11	14
13 No More Mr Nice Guy *Alice Cooper* (Warner Bros.)	10	10	15
14 Pyjamarama *Roxy Music* (Island)	–	–	–
15 Crazy *Mud* (RAK)	–	–	–
16 Big Eight *Judge Dread* (Big Shot)	14	16	19

5		12	19	26
17 Amanda *Stuart Gillies* (Philips)		–	–	–
18 The Twelfth Of Never *Donny Osmond* (MGM)		–	–	–
19 Good Grief Christina *Chicory Tip* (CBS)		–	17	–
20 And I Love You So *Perry Como* (RCA)		6	5	3
25 Wonderful Dream *Ann-Marie David* (Epic)		13	13	13
29 The Right Thing To Do *Carly Simon* (Elektra)		17	–	–
21 Never Never Never *Shirley Bassey* (UA)		18	–	–
42 Also Sprach Zarathustra (2001) *Deodato* (Creed **Taylor**)		19	9	7
30 Could It Be I'm Falling In Love *The Detroit Spinners* (Atlantic)		20	18	12
34 One And One Is One *Medicine Head* (Polydor)		24	14	6
45 Brokendown Angel *Nazareth* (Mooncrest)		27	15	11
– Can The Can *Suzi Quatro* (RAK)		–	34	5
– Walk On The Wild Side *Lou Reed* (RCA)		32	24	17
– You Are The Sunshine Of My Life *Stevie Wonder* (Tamla Motown)		–	35	18
27 Mean Girl *Status Quo* (Pye)		22	21	20

JUNE 1973

2		9	16	23	30
1 See My Baby Jive *Wizzard* (Harvest)		1	3	6	15
2 Can The Can *Suzi Quatro* (RAK)		2	1	3	7
3 And I Love You So *Perry Como* (RCA)		4	7	11	14
4 One And One Is One *Medicine Head* (Polydor)		3	4	9	12
5 Hell Raiser *The Sweet* (RCA)		8	–	–	–
6 Tie A Yellow Ribbon *Dawn* (Bell)		9	14	13	16
7 You Are The Sunshine Of My Life *Stevie Wonder* (Tamla Motown)		7	9	17	–
8 Also Sprach Zarathustra (2001) *Deodato* (Creed Taylor)		14	–	–	–
9 Brokendown Angel *Nazareth* (Mooncrest)		12	17	–	–
10 Walk On The Wild Side *Lou Reed* (RCA)		13	13	–	–
11 Could It Be I'm Falling In Love *The Detroit Spinners* (Atlantic)		16	–	–	–
12 You Want It You Got It *The Detroit Emeralds* (Westbound)		15	19	–	–
13 Rubber Bullets *10cc* (UK)		5	2	1	2
14 Walking In The Rain *The Partridge Family* (Bell)		10	10	12	13
15 Hello Hello I'm Back Again *Gary Glitter* (Bell)		20	–	–	–
16 Giving It All Away *Roger Daltrey* (Track)		–	–	–	–
17 Albatross *Fleetwood Mac* (CBS)		6	5	2	3
18 Brother Louie *Hot Chocolate* (RAK)		–	–	–	–
19 Wonderful Dream *Ann-Marie David* (Epic)		–	–	–	–
20 Stuck In The Middle With You *Stealers Wheel* (A & M)		11	8	8	10
38 Give Me Love (Give Me Peace On Earth) *George Harrison* (Apple)		17	11	10	8
22 Armed And Extremely Dangerous *First Choice* (Bell)		18	16	16	–
26 Welcome Home *Peters and Lee* (Philips)		19	18	5	4
– The Groover *T. Rex* (EMI)		–	6	4	5
39 Snoopy Versus The Red Baron *The Hot Shots* (Mooncrest)		25	12	7	6
– Live And Let Die *Wings* (Apple)		37	15	14	9
35 Sweet Illusion *Jnr. Campbell* (Deram)		21	20	15	19
33 Frankenstein *The Edgar Winter Group* (Epic)		22	25	18	–
– Born To Be With You *Dave Edmunds* (Rockfield)		48	28	19	11
– Can You Do It *Geordie* (EMI)		–	31	20	18
– Skweeze Me Pleeze Me *Slade* (Polydor)		–	–	–	1
– Take Me To The Mardi Gras *Paul Simon* (CBS)		–	36	24	17
– Hallelujah Day *The Jackson Five* (Tamla Motown)		41	27	25	20

JULY 1973

7		**14**	**21**	**28**
1 Skweeze Me Pleeze Me *Slade* (Polydor)		1	4	6
2 Welcome Home *Peters and Lee* (Philips)		2	1	2
3 Rubber Bullets *10cc* (UK)		6	13	19
4 Life On Mars *David Bowie* (RCA)		3	3	3
5 Albatross *Fleetwood Mac* (CBS)		8	14	–
6 Snoopy Versus The Red Baron *The Hot Shots* (Mooncrest)		4	10	13
7 Born To Be With You *Dave Edmunds* (Rockfield)		5	8	10
8 The Groover *T. Rex* (EMI)		19	–	–
9 Take Me To The Mardi Gras *Paul Simon* (CBS)		7	9	11
10 Give Me Love (Give Me Peace On Earth) *George Harrison* (Apple)		10	–	–
11 Live And Let Die *Wings* (Apple)		11	16	20
12 Stuck In The Middle With You *Stealers Wheel* (A & M)		–	–	–
13 Can You Do It *Geordie* (EMI)		15	–	–
14 Honaloochie Boogie *Mott The Hoople* (CBS)		12	19	–
15 Rock-A-Doodle-Doo *Linda Lewis* (Raft)		17	17	–
16 Tie A Yellow Ribbon *Dawn* (Bell)		20	–	–
17 And I Love You So *Perry Como* (RCA)		16	20	–
18 Sweet Illusion *Jnr. Campbell* (Deram)		–	–	–
19 Can The Can *Suzi Quatro* (RAK)		–	–	–
20 Hallelujah Day *The Jackson Five* (Tamla Motown)		–	–	–
36 Saturday Night's Alright For Fighting *Elton John* (DJM)		9	7	7
23 Randy *Blue Mink* (EMI)		13	11	9
27 Step By Step *Joe Simon* (Mojo)		14	18	17
– Going Home *The Osmonds* (MGM)		18	6	5
– I'm The Leader Of The Gang (I Am) *Gary Glitter* (Bell)		–	2	1
43 Alright Alright Alright *Mungo Jerry* (Dawn)		23	5	4
32 Gaye *Clifford T. Ward* (Charisma)		24	12	8
30 Pillow Talk *Sylvia* (London)		22	15	14
47 Yesterday Once More *The Carpenters* (A & M)		34	26	12
– Touch Me In The Morning *Diana Ross* (Tamla Motown)		50	27	15
– Spanish Eyes *Al Martino* (Capitol)		42	31	16
– Bad Bad Boy *Nazareth* (Mooncrest)		–	34	18

AUGUST 1973

4		**11**	**18**	**25**
1 I'm The Leader Of The Gang (I Am) *Gary Glitter* (Bell)		1	1	3
2 Welcome Home *Peters and Lee* (Philips)		2	4	8
3 Alright Alright Alright *Mungo Jerry* (Dawn)		3	6	10
4 Going Home *The Osmonds* (MGM)		6	10	–
5 Life On Mars *David Bowie* (RCA)		7	13	19
6 48 Crash *Suzi Quatro* (RAK)		4	3	7
7 Yesterday Once More *The Carpenters* (A & M)		5	2	2
8 Spanish Eyes *Al Martino* (Capitol)		8	5	6
9 Touch Me In The Morning *Diana Ross* (Tamla Motown)		11	11	14
10 Randy *Blue Mink* (EMI)		14	–	–
11 Bad Bad Boy *Nazareth* (Mooncrest)		10	12	17
12 Gaye *Clifford T. Ward* (Charisma)		13	20	–
13 Ying Tong Song *The Goons* (Decca)		9	9	15
14 Saturday Night's Alright For Fighting *Elton John* (DJM)		20	–	–
15 Skweeze Me Pleeze Me *Slade* (Polydor)		–	–	–
16 Pillow Talk *Sylvia* (London)		17	–	–
17 Hypnosis *Mud* (RAK)		16	–	–
18 You Can Do Magic *Limmie and The Family Cookin'* (Avco)		12	7	5
19 Born To Be With You *Dave Edmunds* (Rockfield)		–	–	–
20 Snoopy Versus The Red Baron *The Hot Shots* (Mooncrest)		–	–	–

	11	18	25
21 All Right Now *Free* (Island)	15	15	18
34 Dancing On A Saturday Night *Barry Blue* (Bell)	18	8	4
23 Free Electric Band *Albert Hammond* (MUMS)	19	–	–
37 Smarty Pants *First Choice* (Bell)	24	14	9
– Young Love *Donny Osmond* (MGM)	–	16	1
32 Summer (The First Time) *Bobby Goldsboro* (UA)	26	17	12
36 Rising Sun *Medicine Head* (Polydor)	22	18	11
44 Like Sister And Brother *The Drifters* (Bell)	28	19	13
41 I'm Free *Roger Daltrey and The London Symphony Orchestra and Chamber Choir* (Ode)	34	24	16
31 I'm Doin' Fine Now *New York City* (RCA)	25	23	20

SEPTEMBER 1973

1	8	15	22	29
1 Young Love *Donny Osmond* (MGM)	1	1	7	15
2 Dancing On A Saturday Night *Barry Blue* (Bell)	2	4	8	19
3 You Can Do Magic *Limmie and The Family Cookin'* (Avco)	7	9	–	–
4 Yesterday Once More *The Carpenters* (A & M)	4	16	–	–
5 Spanish Eyes *Al Martino* (Capitol)	5	6	9	13
6 I'm The Leader Of The Gang (I Am) *Gary Glitter* (Bell)	17	–	–	–
7 Like Sister And Brother *The Drifters* (Bell)	8	11	16	–
8 Welcome Home *Peters and Lee* (Philips)	15	17	–	–
9 Summer (The First Time) *Bobby Goldsboro* (UA)	11	14	–	–
10 Smarty Pants *First Choice* (Bell)	16	19	–	–
11 Rising Sun *Medicine Head* (Polydor)	13	20	–	–
12 Angel Fingers *Wizzard* (Harvest)	3	2	1	3
13 Say, Has Anybody Seen My Sweet Gypsy Rose *Dawn* (Bell)	12	12	12	–
14 48 Crash *Suzi Quatro* (RAK)	–	–	–	–
15 I'm Free *Roger Daltrey and The London Symphony Orchestra and Chamber Choir* (Ode)	20	13	–	–
16 Rock On *David Essex* (CBS)	6	3	3	5
17 Pick Up The Pieces *Hudson Ford* (A & M)	10	8	13	–
18 Fool *Elvis Presley* (RCA)	19	15	19	20
19 Touch Me In The Morning *Diana Ross* (Tamla Motown)	–	–	–	–
20 I'm Doin' Fine Now *New York City* (RCA)	–	–	–	–
27 Angie *The Rolling Stones* (RS)	9	5	5	7
23 The Dean And I *10cc* (UK)	14	10	11	16
28 Dear Elaine *Roy Wood* (Harvest)	18	–	–	–
– Oh No Not My Baby *Rod Stewart* (Mercury)	22	7	6	6
33 I've Been Hurt *Guy Darrell* (Santa Ponsa)	24	18	15	12
– The Ballroom Blitz *The Sweet* (RCA)	–	–	2	2
43 Monster Mash *Bobby Pickett and The Crypt Kickers* (London)	30	21	4	4
36 For The Good Times *Perry Como* (RCA)	26	24	10	9
– Eye Level *The Simon Park Orchestra* (Columbia)	–	48	14	1
– All The Way From Memphis *Mott The Hoople* (CBS)	40	23	17	10
– Nutbush City Limits *Ike and Tina Turner* (UA)	47	32	18	8
– Joybringer *Manfred Mann Earthband* (Vertigo)	39	26	20	11
– The Laughing Gnome *David Bowie* (Deram)	–	42	25	14
– Caroline *Status Quo* (Vertigo)	44	28	23	17
– Ooh Baby *Gilbert O'Sullivan* (MAM)	–	31	26	18

OCTOBER 1973

6	13	20	27
1 Eye Level *The Simon Park Orchestra* (Columbia)	1	1	2
2 The Ballroom Blitz *The Sweet* (RCA)	3	7	12
3 Monster Mash *Bobby Pickett and The Crypt Kickers* (London)	5	5	13
4 My Friend Stan *Slade* (Polydor)	2	3	3
5 Nutbush City Limits *Ike and Tina Turner* (UA)	4	4	9
6 Angel Fingers *Wizzard* (Harvest)	11	15	–
7 For The Good Times *Perry Como* (RCA)	7	9	7
8 The Laughing Gnome *David Bowie* (Deram)	6	6	8
9 Joybringer *Manfred Mann Earthband* (Vertigo)	10	13	–
10 Rock On *David Essex* (CBS)	17	–	–
11 Caroline *Status Quo* (Vertigo)	9	8	5
12 Oh No Not My Baby *Rod Stewart* (Mercury)	13	–	–
13 All The Way From Memphis *Mott The Hoople* (CBS)	16	–	–
14 Angie *The Rolling Stones* (RS)	–	–	–
15 Spanish Eyes *Al Martino* (Capitol)	15	19	–
16 Goodbye Yellow Brick Road *Elton John* (DJM)	12	10	6
17 I've Been Hurt *Guy Darrell* (Santa Ponsa)	18	–	–
18 Ooh Baby *Gilbert O'Sullivan* (MAM)	19	–	–
19 Dancing On A Saturday Night *Barry Blue* (Bell)	–	–	–
20 Say, Has Anybody Seen My Sweet Gypsy Rose *Dawn* (Bell)	–	–	–
– Daydreamer/Puppy Song *David Cassidy* (Bell)	8	2	1
23 A Hard Rain's Gonna Fall *Bryan Ferry* (Island)	14	11	10
24 Ghetto Child *The Detroit Spinners* (Atlantic)	20	12	11
44 Showdown *The Electric Light Orchestra* (Harvest)	29	14	16
– Sorrow *David Bowie* (RCA)	–	16	4
25 That Lady *The Isley Brothers* (Epic)	22	17	14
34 Knockin' On Heaven's Door *Bob Dylan* (CBS)	26	18	17
– 5.15 *The Who* (Track)	40	20	–
37 Let There Be Peace On Earth (Let It Begin With Me) *Michael Ward* (Philips)	24	24	15
35 Deck Of Cards *Max Bygraves* (Pye)	38	26	18
– Top Of The World *The Carpenters* (A & M)	–	36	19
– This Flight Tonight *Nazareth* (Mooncrest)	45	23	20

NOVEMBER 1973

3	10	17	24
1 Daydreamer/Puppy Song *David Cassidy* (Bell)	1	3	11
2 Eye Level *The Simon Park Orchestra* (Columbia)	6	15	20
3 Sorrow *David Bowie* (RCA)	3	4	5
4 Let Me In *The Osmonds* (MGM)	2	2	2
5 Caroline *Status Quo* (Vertigo)	7	20	–
6 Goodbye Yellow Brick Road *Elton John* (DJM)	10	19	–
7 Ghetto Child *The Detroit Spinners* (Atlantic)	8	10	–
8 My Friend Stan *Slade* (Polydor)	16	–	–
9 Top Of The World *The Carpenters* (A & M)	5	7	9
10 For The Good Times *Perry Como* (RCA)	9	12	16
11 The Laughing Gnome *David Bowie* (Deram)	–	–	–
12 Showdown *The Electric Light Orchestra* (Harvest)	12	18	–
13 A Hard Rain's Gonna Fall *Bryan Ferry* (Island)	18	–	–
14 Knockin' On Heaven's Door *Bob Dylan* (CBS)	15	–	–
15 This Flight Tonight *Nazareth* (Mooncrest)	11	11	15
16 Nutbush City Limits *Ike and Tina Turner* (UA)	–	–	–
17 Deck Of Cards *Max Bygraves* (Pye)	14	13	19
18 Let There Be Peace On Earth (Let It Begin With Me) *Michael Ward* (Philips)	19	–	–
19 Won't Somebody Dance With Me *Lynsey de Paul* (MAM)	17	14	18

3

	10	17	24
20 Dyna-Mite *Mud* (RAK)	4	5	4
24 Photograph *Ringo Starr* (Apple)	13	8	10
31 Do You Wanna Dance *Barry Blue* (Bell)	20	9	7
– I Love You Love Me Love *Gary Glitter* (Bell)	–	1	1
– When I Fall In Love *Donny Osmond* (MGM)	23	6	6
28 Daytona Demon *Suzi Quatro* (RAK)	22	16	14
– Why Oh Why Oh Why *Gilbert O'Sullivan* (MAM)	48	17	12
– Paper Roses *Marie Osmond* (MGM)	–	24	3
50 My Coo-Ca-Choo *Alvin Stardust* (Magnet)	36	27	8
– Lamplight *David Essex* (CBS)	38	23	13
33 Helen Wheels *Wings* (Apple)	28	26	17

DECEMBER 1973

	1	8	15	22/29
1 I Love You Love Me Love *Gary Glitter* (Bell)		1	2	2
2 My Coo-Ca-Choo *Alvin Stardust* (Magnet)		4	3	5
3 Paper Roses *Marie Osmond* (MGM)		2	5	6
4 When I Fall In Love *Donny Osmond* (MGM)		12	12	15
5 Dyna-Mite *Mud* (RAK)		6	11	–
6 Why Oh Why Oh Why *Gilbert O'Sullivan* (MAM)		9	10	13
7 You Won't Find Another Fool Like Me *The New Seekers* (Polydor)		3	4	3
8 Lamplight *David Essex* (CBS)		7	7	8
9 Do You Wanna Dance *Barry Blue* (Bell)		10	19	–
10 Let Me In *The Osmonds* (MGM)		5	16	19
11 Photograph *Ringo Starr* (Apple)		14	–	–
12 Helen Wheels *Wings* (Apple)		15	15	–
13 Daydreamer/Puppy Song *David Cassidy* (Bell)		–	–	–
14 Top Of The World *The Carpenters* (A & M)		17	20	–
15 Sorrow *David Bowie* (RCA)		20	–	–
16 Street Life *Roxy Music* (Island)		11	9	10
17 Roll Away The Stone *Mott The Hoople* (CBS)		8	8	9
18 Daytona Demon *Suzi Quatro* (RAK)		18	–	–
19 Won't Somebody Dance With Me *Lynsey de Paul* (MAM)		–	–	–
20 Truck On (Tyke) *T. Rex* (EMI)		13	14	12
23 Amoureuse *Kiki Dee* (Rocket)		16	13	18
– I Wish It Could Be Christmas Every Day *Wizzard* (Harvest)		19	6	4
– Merry Xmas Everybody *Slade* (Polydor)		–	1	1
28 Love On A Mountain Top *Robert Knight* (Monument)		22	17	16
25 Keep On Truckin' *Eddie Kendricks* (Tamla Motown)		24	18	–
– The Show Must Go On *Leo Sayer* (Chrysalis)		–	24	7
42 Forever *Roy Wood* (Harvest)		32	31	11
– Gaudete *Steeleye Span* (Chrysalis)		48	27	14
– Dance With The Devil *Cozy Powell* (RAK)		46	38	17
– Pool Hall Richard/I Wish It Would Rain *The Faces* (Warner Bros.)		38	26	20

1973–BEST-SELLING SINGLES

1 Tie A Yellow Ribbon *Dawn* (Bell)
2 Eye Level *The Simon Park Orchestra* (Columbia)
3 Welcome Home *Peters and Lee* (Philips)
4 Blockbuster *The Sweet* (RCA)
5 Cum On Feel The Noize *Slade* (Polydor)
6 See My Baby Jive *Wizzard* (Harvest)
7 I'm The Leader Of The Gang (I Am) *Gary Glitter* (Bell)
8 I Love You Love Me Love *Gary Glitter* (Bell)
9 The Twelfth Of Never *Donny Osmond* (MGM)
10 Spanish Eyes *Al Martino* (Capitol)
11 Daydreamer/Puppy Song *David Cassidy* (Bell)
12 Long Haired Lover From Liverpool *Little Jimmy Osmond* (MGM)
13 Skweeze Me Pleeze Me *Slade* (Polydor)
14 And I Love You So *Perry Como* (RCA)
15 Hello Hello I'm Back Again *Gary Glitter* (Bell)
16 Get Down *Gilbert O'Sullivan* (MAM)
17 The Ballroom Blitz *The Sweet* (RCA)
18 Do You Wanna Touch Me *Gary Glitter* (Bell)
19 Young Love *Donny Osmond* (MGM)
20 Rubber Bullets *10cc* (UK)

1973–BEST-SELLING ALBUMS

1 Aladdin Sane *David Bowie*
2 Simon And Garfunkel's Greatest Hits *Simon and Garfunkel*
3 Don't Shoot Me I'm Only The Piano Player *Elton John*
4 We Can Make It *Peters and Lee*
5 The Beatles 1967–1970 *The Beatles*
6 The Dark Side Of The Moon *Pink Floyd*
7 Back To Front *Gilbert O'Sullivan*
8 Hunky Dory *David Bowie*
9 The Beatles 1962–1966 *The Beatles*
10 And I Love You So *Perry Como*
11 The Rise And Fall Of Ziggy Stardust *David Bowie*
12 Now And Then *The Carpenters*
13 Pin Ups *David Bowie*
14 Bridge Over Troubled Water *Simon and Garfunkel*
15 Sing It Again Rod *Rod Stewart*
16 Clockwork Orange *Soundtrack of film*
17 Billion Dollar Babies *Alice Cooper*
18 Goat's Head Soup *The Rolling Stones*
19 Slayed *Slade*
20 For Your Pleasure *Roxy Music*

1973–BEST-SELLING ARTISTS

Male Artists (Singles)

1 David Bowie
2 Gary Glitter
3 Perry Como
4 Donny Osmond
5 Paul McCartney

6 Jimmy Osmond
7 Gilbert O'Sullivan
8 Elton John
9 David Cassidy
10 Elvis Presley

Female Artists (Singles)

1 Suzi Quatro
2 Carly Simon
3 Shirley Bassey
4 Roberta Flack
5 Diana Ross

6 Olivia Newton-John
7 Lynsey de Paul
8 Marie Osmond
9 Sylvia
10 Linda Lewis

Groups (Singles)

1 Dawn
2 Slade
3 Wizzard
4 The Sweet
5 The Osmonds

6 T. Rex
7 Status Quo
8 Mud
9 The Carpenters
10 Peters and Lee

Male Artists (Albums)

1 David Bowie
2 Gilbert O'Sullivan
3 Donny Osmond
4 Max Bygraves
5 Elton John

6 Perry Como
7 Gary Glitter
8 Rod Stewart
9 Cat Stevens
10 David Cassidy

Female Artists (Albums)

1 Carly Simon
2 Diana Ross
3 Liza Minnelli
4 Shirley Bassey

5 Nana Mouskouri
6 Carole King
7 Suzi Quatro
8 Roberta Flack

Only eight female artists qualified for this chart.

Groups (Albums)

1 Simon and Garfunkel
2 The Beatles
3 The Carpenters
4 Slade
5 Pink Floyd

6 Status Quo
7 The Osmonds
8 Focus
9 Peters and Lee
10 Roxy Music

1974

Mud headed the top disc listing for 1974 with 'Tiger Feet', and by the year's end they were celebrating the fact that 'Lonely This Christmas' had sold more than half a million copies.

Also catching the public's imagination were David Essex, Showaddywaddy, The Three Degrees, Ringo Starr, Paper Lace and George McCrae. It was an outstanding year for Alvin Stardust, too, a singer who had been in the charts of 1962 with 'Cindy's Birthday' under the name of Shane Fenton. Stardust had made his first chart foray in the latter part of 1973 with 'My Coo-Ca-Choo' and this success continued into 1974 with 'Jealous Mind', 'You You You' and 'Red Dress'.

1974 also saw the emergence of The Wombles, whose music was carefully supervised by the ingenious Mike Batt. In mass popularity terms even the Wimbledon Common team's glory was stolen by the re-emergence of The Bay City Rollers, Scotland's major chart force.

The Bay City Rollers had entered the charts in 1971 with 'Keep On Dancing' and nothing had been seen of them since. However, their fortunes changed in 1974 and they spent endless weeks in the charts with hits such as 'All Of Me Loves All Of You', 'Remember' and 'Summerlove Sensation'. However, once their records slipped in the chart placings, they disappeared quickly which is why no Bay City Roller disc appears in the Top Thirty table of discs which have the longest individual disc residencies.

Several hits reflected certain occurences in the media. Abba achieved great success with their Eurovision-winning song 'Waterloo', and television helped Stephanie De Sykes with 'Born With A Smile On My Face'. The popularity of Kung Fu, as a result of the television programme of the same name, saw Carl Douglas in the Top Ten with 'Kung Fu Fighting'.

In the black music market, Britain's first soul group, Sweet Sensation, also entered the charts in 1974, while in 'soft' soul terms, the talking-singing Barry White had arrived. Reggae had a brief spell of chart fortune, and predictions of a mass outbreak of reggae in the charts were heard, but this was not to be, although two people in particular, Ken Boothe and John Holt, both had big hits.

Age proved to be no barrier for Charles Aznavour and Charlie Rich, as they both had hits with 'She' and 'The Most Beautiful Girl' respectively.

Humour was largely to be had from Ray Stevens with 'The Streak', and new names included Queen and Sparks. The reward for a record company's faith and patience came after six months of waiting for 'Y Viva Espana' to enter the charts, but when it did the disc threatened to stay forever.

When compared to the previous year, 1974 showed some startling changes for the worse for such artists as Jimmy, Marie and Donny Osmond, David Cassidy and The Sweet. However, of these names, only Marie and Jimmy Osmond failed to make a comeback in the charts during the following year.

JANUARY 1974

5	**12**	**19**	**26**
1 Merry Xmas Everybody *Slade* (Polydor)	1	3	12
2 You Won't Find Another Fool Like Me *The New Seekers* (Polydor)	2	1	5
3 I Love You Love Me Love *Gary Glitter* (Bell)	7	13	13
4 I Wish It Could Be Christmas Every Day *Wizzard* (Harvest)	4	16	–
5 My Coo-Ca-Choo *Alvin Stardust* (Magnet)	5	5	6
6 Paper Roses *Marie Osmond* (MGM)	14	8	14
7 The Show Must Go On *Leo Sayer* (Chrysalis)	3	2	3
8 Lamplight *David Essex* (CBS)	10	15	15
9 Roll Away The Stone *Mott The Hoople* (CBS)	13	17	18
10 Street Life *Roxy Music* (Island)	15	19	–
11 Forever *Roy Wood* (Harvest)	12	9	8
12 Why Oh Why Oh Why *Gilbert O'Sullivan* (MAM)	17	18	–
13 Love On A Mountain Top *Robert Knight* (Monument)	11	12	10
14 Dance With The Devil *Cozy Powell* (RAK)	6	4	4
15 Truck On (Tyke) *T. Rex* (EMI)	18	–	–
16 Pool Hall Richard/I Wish It Would Rain *The Faces* (Warner Bros.)	8	11	11
17 Gaudete *Steeleye Span* (Chrysalis)	16	–	–
18 When I Fall In Love *Donny Osmond* (MGM)	20	–	–
19 Amoureuse *Kiki Dee* (Rocket)	–	–	–
20 Vaya Con Dios *Millican and Nesbitt* (Pye)	–	–	–
26 Radar Love *Golden Earring* (Track)	9	7	7
22 Vado Via *Drupi* (A & M)	19	–	17
– Teenage Rampage *The Sweet* (RCA)	–	6	2
– Tiger Feet *Mud* (RAK)	–	10	1
36 Solitaire *Andy Williams* (CBS)	22	14	9
43 All Of My Life *Diana Ross* (Tamla Motown)	38	20	16
– Rockin' Roll Baby *The Stylistics* (Avco)	–	29	19
– How Come *Ronnie Lane* (GM)	49	25	20

FEBRUARY 1974

2	**9**	**16**	**23**
1 Tiger Feet *Mud* (RAK)	1	1	2
2 Teenage Rampage *The Sweet* (RCA)	2	4	11
3 You Won't Find Another Fool Like Me *The New Seekers* (Polydor)	8	20	–
4 The Show Must Go On *Leo Sayer* (Chrysalis)	7	10	–
5 Dance With The Devil *Cozy Powell* (RAK)	3	6	17
6 Solitaire *Andy Williams* (CBS)	4	5	7
7 Radar Love *Golden Earring* (Track)	11	17	–
8 My Coo-Ca-Choo *Alvin Stardust* (Magnet)	16	–	–
9 Forever *Roy Wood* (Harvest)	10	18	–
10 Love On A Mountain Top *Robert Knight* (Monument)	13	14	–
11 How Come *Ronnie Lane* (GM)	12	11	–
12 Rockin' Roll Baby *The Stylistics* (Avco)	6	8	12
13 The Man Who Sold The World *Lulu* (Polydor)	5	3	5
14 All Of My Life *Diana Ross* (Tamla Motown)	9	9	9
15 Pool Hall Richard/I Wish It Would Rain *The Faces* (Warner Bros.)	–	–	–
16 I Love You Love Me Love *Gary Glitter* (Bell)	–	–	–
17 Paper Roses *Marie Osmond* (MGM)	–	–	–
18 Teenage Lament '74 *Alice Cooper* (Warner Bros.)	15	12	–
19 Lamplight *David Essex* (CBS)	–	–	–
20 Living For The City *Stevie Wonder* (Tamla Motown)	17	15	19
– Devil Gate Drive *Suzi Quatro* (RAK)	14	2	1

2	9	16	23
– Teenage Dream *Marc Bolan* (EMI)	18	13	16
26 Wombling Song *The Wombles* (CBS)	19	7	4
34 Love's Theme *Love Unlimited Orchestra* (Pye)	20	19	10
– Ma He's Making Eyes At Me *Lena Zavaroni* (Philips)	30	16	13
– Jealous Mind *Alvin Stardust* (Magnet)	–	22	3
– Rebel Rebel *David Bowie* (RCA)	–	–	6
– The Air That I Breathe *The Hollies* (Polydor)	33	26	8
32 Never Never Gonna Give Ya Up *Barry White* (Pye)	23	21	14
– You're Sixteen *Ringo Starr* (Apple)	–	–	15
– Remember (Sha-La-La-La) *The Bay City Rollers* (Bell)	47	38	18
– The Most Beautiful Girl *Charlie Rich* (CBS)	–	46	20

MARCH 1974

2	9	16	23	30
1 Devil Gate Drive *Suzi Quatro* (RAK)	2	6	14	–
2 Jealous Mind *Alvin Stardust* (Magnet)	1	2	5	17
3 The Air That I Breathe *The Hollies* (Polydor)	3	3	2	4
4 Wombling Song *The Wombles* (CBS)	7	10	13	–
5 Rebel Rebel *David Bowie* (RCA)	5	13	16	–
6 Tiger Feet *Mud* (RAK)	16	–	–	–
7 You're Sixteen *Ringo Starr* (Apple)	4	5	4	7
8 Remember (Sha-La-La-La) *The Bay City Rollers* (Bell)	6	7	8	16
9 The Man Who Sold The World *Lulu* (Polydor)	17	–	–	–
10 Ma He's Making Eyes At Me *Lena Zavaroni* (Philips)	13	14	17	–
11 The Most Beautiful Girl *Charlie Rich* (Epic)	9	4	3	2
12 Love's Theme *Love Unlimited Orchestra* (Pye)	15	18	–	–
13 Solitaire *Andy Williams* (CBS)	20	–	–	–
14 Never Never Gonna Give Ya Up *Barry White* (Pye)	14	16	–	–
15 Billy, Don't Be A Hero *Paper Lace* (Bus Stop)	8	1	1	1
16 It's You *Freddie Starr* (Tiffany)	12	9	9	13
17 Jet *Wings* (Apple)	10	8	7	10
18 Rockin' Roll Baby *The Stylistics* (Avco)	–	–	–	–
19 Happiness Is Me And You *Gilbert O'Sullivan* (MAM)	19	20	–	–
20 Burn Baby Burn *Hudson Ford* (A & M)	18	15	19	–
28 Candle In The Wind *Elton John* (DJM)	11	12	11	14
– I Get A Little Sentimental Over You *The New Seekers* (Polydor)	24	11	6	5
50 School Love *Barry Blue* (Bell)	25	17	12	11
48 Jambalaya *The Carpenters* (A & M)	40	19	18	12
– Emma *Hot Chocolate* (RAK)	–	36	10	6
– Seven Seas Of Rhye *Queen* (EMI)	45	30	15	15
– Seasons In The Sun *Terry Jacks* (Bell)	–	–	20	3
– Remember Me This Way *Gary Glitter* (Bell)	–	–	–	8
– Angel Face *The Glitter Band* (Bell)	–	–	26	9
– Long Live Love *Olivia Newton-John* (Pye)	–	28	21	18
– You Are Everything *Diana Ross and Marvin Gaye* (Tamla Motown)	–	–	25	19
– Everlasting Love *Robert Knight* (Monument)	35	24	22	20

APRIL 1974

6	13	20	27
1 Seasons In The Sun *Terry Jacks* (Bell)	1	1	1
2 Billy, Don't Be A Hero *Paper Lace* (Bus Stop)	2	10	15
3 Emma *Hot Chocolate* (RAK)	6	6	14
4 Remember Me This Way *Gary Glitter* (Bell)	3	7	12
5 Angel Face *The Glitter Band* (Bell)	5	4	5
6 Everyday *Slade* (Polydor)	4	3	7

6

	13	20	27
7 I Get A Little Sentimental Over You *The New Seekers* (Polydor)	12	20	–
8 The Most Beautiful Girl *Charlie Rich* (Epic)	9	16	–
9 You Are Everything *Diana Ross and Marvin Gaye* (Tamla Motown)	7	5	6
10 The Air That I Breathe *The Hollies* (Polydor)	–	–	–
11 Seven Seas Of Rhye *Queen* (EMI)	10	14	17
12 You're Sixteen *Ringo Starr* (Apple)	–	–	–
13 School Love *Barry Blue* (Bell)	16	–	–
14 Jambalaya *The Carpenters* (A & M)	13	–	–
15 Jet *Wings* (Apple)	–	–	–
16 Long Live Love *Olivia Newton-John* (Pye)	11	19	–
17 Candle In The Wind *Elton John* (DJM)	19	–	–
18 It's You *Freddie Starr* (Tiffany)	–	–	–
19 Everlasting Love *Robert Knight* (Monument)	–	–	–
20 Rock Around The Clock *Bill Haley and The Comets* (MCA)	17	12	13
– The Cat Crept In *Mud* (RAK)	8	2	3
23 Doctor's Orders *Sunny* (CBS)	14	9	8
25 I'm Gonna Knock On Your Door *Jimmy Osmond* (MGM)	15	13	11
21 Golden Age Of Rock 'n' Roll *Mott The Hoople* (CBS)	18	18	16
36 Remember You're A Womble *The Wombles* (CBS)	20	8	4
28 Homely Girl *The Chi-Lites* (Brunswick)	22	11	9
38 A Walkin' Miracle *Limmie and The Family Cookin'* (Avco)	23	15	10
– Waterloo *Abba* (Epic)	–	17	2
43 Long Legged Woman Dressed In Black *Mungo Jerry* (Dawn)	36	25	18
– Don't Stay Away Too Long *Peters and Lee* (Philips)	–	38	19
– He's Misstra Know It All *Stevie Wonder* (Tamla Motown)	40	31	20

MAY 1974

4

	11	18	25
1 Waterloo *Abba* (Epic)	1	2	6
2 The Cat Crept In *Mud* (RAK)	12	17	–
3 Seasons In The Sun *Terry Jacks* (Bell)	9	20	–
4 Remember You're A Womble *The Wombles* (CBS)	3	5	13
5 Homely Girl *The Chi-Lites* (Brunswick)	7	8	15
6 A Walkin' Miracle *Limmie and The Family Cookin'* (Avco)	8	12	–
7 Doctor's Orders *Sunny* (CBS)	17	–	–
8 You Are Everything *Diana Ross and Marvin Gaye* (Tamla Motown)	15	–	–
9 Rock And Roll Winter *Wizzard* (Warner Bros.)	6	6	11
10 Angel Face *The Glitter Band* (Bell)	19	–	–
11 Don't Stay Away Too Long *Peters and Lee* (Philips)	4	3	4
12 Shang-A-Lang *The Bay City Rollers* (Bell)	5	4	2
13 Everyday *Slade* (Polydor)	–	–	–
14 Long Legged Woman Dressed In Black *Mungo Jerry* (Dawn)	13	19	20
15 I'm Gonna Knock On Your Door *Jimmy Osmond* (MGM)	–	–	–
16 Year Of Decision *The Three Degrees* (Philadelphia)	20	13	19
17 He's Misstra Know It All *Stevie Wonder* (Tamla Motown)	10	11	17
18 Emma *Hot Chocolate* (RAK)	–	–	–
19 Rock Around The Clock *Bill Haley and The Comets* (MCA)	–	–	–
20 Remember Me This Way *Gary Glitter* (Bell)	–	–	–
27 Sugar Baby Love *The Rubettes* (Polydor)	2	1	1
42 Red Dress *Alvin Stardust* (Magnet)	11	10	7
39 The Night Chicago Died *Paper Lace* (Bus Stop)	14	7	5
24 I Can't Stop *The Osmonds* (MGM)	16	15	12
28 Spiders And Snakes *Jim Stafford* (MGM)	18	14	14
48 This Town Ain't Big Enough For Both Of Us *Sparks* (Island)	27	9	3
21 Behind Closed Doors *Charlie Rich* (Epic)	23	16	–
38 Break The Rules *Status Quo* (Vertigo)	26	18	8

4		11	18	25
– There's A Ghost In My House *R. Dean Taylor* (Tamla Motown)		34	24	9
– If I Didn't Care *David Cassidy* (Bell)		29	21	10
46 Go *Gigliola Cinquetti* (CBS)		37	22	16
43 I See A Star *Mouth and McNeal* (Decca)		42	29	18

JUNE 1974

1	8	15	22	29
1 Sugar Baby Love *The Rubettes* (Polydor)	1	6	12	–
2 This Town Ain't Big Enough For Both Of Us *Sparks* (Island)	2	4	9	–
3 The Night Chicago Died *Paper Lace* (Bus Stop)	6	12	–	–
4 There's A Ghost In My House *R. Dean Taylor* (Tamla Motown)	5	3	4	5
5 Don't Stay Away Too Long *Peters and Lee* (Philips)	11	20	–	–
6 Hey Rock And Roll *Showaddywaddy* (Bell)	3	2	3	4
7 Shang-A-Lang *The Bay City Rollers* (Bell)	14	–	–	–
8 Go *Gigliola Cinquetti* (CBS)	12	11	–	–
9 If I Didn't Care *David Cassidy* (Bell)	9	15	–	–
10 Red Dress *Alvin Stardust* (Magnet)	19	–	–	–
11 Break The Rules *Status Quo* (Vertigo)	10	–	–	–
12 I See A Star *Mouth and McNeal* (Decca)	8	10	15	–
13 The Streak *Ray Stevens* (Janus)	4	1	2	3
14 I Can't Stop *The Osmonds* (MCA)	17	–	–	–
15 Waterloo *Abba* (Epic)	–	–	–	–
16 The In Crowd *Bryan Ferry* (Island)	13	14	19	–
17 Judy Teen *Cockney Rebel* (EMI)	7	7	5	12
18 Spiders And Snakes *Jim Stafford* (MGM)	–	–	–	–
19 Remember You're A Womble *The Wombles* (CBS)	20	–	–	–
20 (You Keep Me) Hanging On *Cliff Richard* (EMI)	15	13	–	–
22 A Touch Too Much *The Arrows* (RAK)	16	9	8	9
24 Jarrow Song *Alan Price* (Warner Bros.)	17	8	6	10
– Always Yours *Gary Glitter* (Bell)	–	5	1	2
30 Don't Let The Sun Go Down On Me *Elton John* (DJM)	24	16	17	16
28 Summer Breeze *The Isley Brothers* (Epic)	21	17	16	17
36 Liverpool Lou *The Scaffold* (Warner Bros.)	22	18	7	11
31 The Man In Black *Cozy Powell* (RAK)	26	19	20	18
– I'd Love You To Want Me *Lobo* (UK)	37	24	10	7
– She *Charles Aznavour* (Barclay)	–	–	11	1
– One Man Band *Leo Sayer* (Chrysalis)	–	25	13	6
– Kissin' In The Back Row *The Drifters* (Bell)	–	39	14	8
44 Guilty *The Pearls* (Bell)	29	22	18	13
– Going Down The Road *Roy Wood* (Harvest)	–	37	21	14
– Can't Get Enough *Bad Company* (Island)	27	21	23	15
– Wall Street Shuffle *10cc* (UK)	–	34	28	19
– Easy, Easy *The Scotland World Cup Squad* (Polydor)	–	–	30	20

JULY 1974

6	13	20	27
1 She *Charles Aznavour* (Barclay)	1	1	2
2 Kissin' In The Back Row *The Drifters* (Bell)	2	2	4
3 Always Yours *Gary Glitter* (Bell)	9	10	–
4 Bangin' Man *Slade* (Polydor)	3	5	8
5 Hey Rock And Roll *Showaddywaddy* (Bell)	11	16	–
6 I'd Love You To Want Me *Lobo* (UK)	5	7	10
7 The Streak *Ray Stevens* (Janus)	16	–	–
8 One Man Band *Leo Sayer* (Chrysalis)	6	18	–
9 Young Girl *Gary Puckett and The Union Gap* (CBS)	8	6	6

6	13	20	27
10 Guilty *The Pearls* (Bell)	15	–	–
11 Wall Street Shuffle *10cc* (UK)	10	12	13
12 Banana Rock *The Wombles* (CBS)	12	9	12
13 A Touch Too Much *The Arrows* (RAK)	–	–	–
14 Liverpool Lou *The Scaffold* (Warner Bros.)	–	–	–
15 Rock Your Baby *George McCrae* (Jayboy)	4	3	1
16 Going Down The Road *Roy Wood* (Harvest)	13	–	–
17 There's A Ghost In My House *R. Dean Taylor* (Tamla Motown)	–	–	–
18 Don't Let The Sun Go Down On Me *Elton John* (DJM)	19	–	–
19 Judy Teen *Cockney Rebel* (EMI)	–	–	–
20 Jarrow Song *Alan Price* (Warner Bros.)	–	–	–
27 Band On The Run *Wings* (Apple)	7	4	5
24 Too Big *Suzi Quatro* (RAK)	14	19	–
21 Beach Baby *The First Class* (UK)	17	13	18
– The Six Teens *The Sweet* (RCA)	18	11	9
26 If You Go Away *Terry Jacks* (Bell)	20	8	11
– Born With A Smile On My Face *Stephanie De Sykes and Rain* (Bradley's)	–	14	3
25 Laughter In The Rain *Neil Sedaka* (Polydor)	22	15	16
– When Will I See You Again *The Three Degrees* (Philadelphia)	33	17	7
47 She's A Winner *The Intruders* (Philadelphia)	29	20	19
– You Make Me Feel Brand New *The Stylistics* (Avco)	44	30	14
– Tonight *The Rubettes* (Polydor)	40	21	15
– Amateur Hour *Sparks* (Island)	–	42	17
50 My Girl Bill *Jim Stafford* (MGM)	31	23	20

AUGUST 1974

3	10	17	24	31
1 Rock Your Baby *George McCrae* (Jayboy)	1	2	6	16
2 Born With A Smile On My Face *Stephanie De Sykes and Rain* (Bradley's)	3	5	14	–
3 Band On The Run *Wings* (Apple)	8	12	–	–
4 When Will I See You Again *The Three Degrees* (Philadelphia)	2	1	1	2
5 She *Charles Aznavour* (Barclay)	17	–	–	–
6 Kissin' In The Back Row Of The Movies *The Drifters* (Bell)	9	–	–	–
7 Young Girl *Gary Puckett and The Union Gap* (CBS)	14	–	–	–
8 You Make Me Feel Brand New *The Stylistics* (Avco)	4	3	2	3
9 Amateur Hour *Sparks* (Island)	7	11	16	–
10 If You Go Away *Terry Jacks* (Bell)	–	–	–	–
11 The Six Teens *The Sweet* (RCA)	19	–	–	–
12 Tonight *The Rubettes* (Polydor)	12	13	18	–
13 Rocket *Mud* (RAK)	6	7	8	15
14 She's A Winner *The Intruders* (Philadelphia)	18	18	–	–
15 Rock The Boat *The Hues Corporation* (RCA)	10	6	7	11
16 Banana Rock *The Wombles* (CBS)	–	–	–	–
17 Summerlove Sensation *The Bay City Rollers* (Bell)	5	4	3	5
18 Laughter In The Rain *Neil Sedaka* (Polydor)	–	–	–	–
19 Beach Baby *The First Class* (UK)	–	–	–	–
20 Bangin' Man *Slade* (Polydor)	–	–	–	–
25 What Becomes Of The Broken Hearted *Jimmy Ruffin* (Tamla Motown)	11	8	4	6
22 It's Only Rock 'n' Roll *The Rolling Stones* (RS)	13	10	11	20
31 I Shot The Sheriff *Eric Clapton* (RSO)	15	9	9	13
21 Please Please Me *David Cassidy* (Bell)	16	16	–	–
26 My Girl Bill *Jim Stafford* (MGM)	20	–	–	–
33 I'm Leaving It All Up To You *Donny and Marie Osmond* (MGM)	21	14	5	4

3	10	17	24	31
42 Just For You *The Glitter Band* (Bell)	22	15	10	17
43 Hello Summertime *Bobby Goldsboro* (UA)	27	17	17	14
36 Honey Honey *Sweet Dreams* (Bradley's)	29	19	13	10
30 Your Baby Ain't Your Baby Anymore *Paul Da Vinci* (Penny Farthing)	23	20	–	–
– Mr Soft *Cockney Rebel* (EMI)	39	23	12	8
– Y Viva Espana *Sylvia* (Sonet)	46	28	15	7
– Love Me For A Reason *The Osmonds* (MGM)	–	–	19	1
– Na Na Na *Cozy Powell* (RAK)	48	29	20	12
– Kung Fu Fighting *Carl Douglas* (Pye)	–	42	29	9
– Annie's Song *John Denver* (RCA)	–	37	26	18
– Rock 'n' Roll Lady *Showaddywaddy* (Bell)	–	32	22	19

SEPTEMBER 1974

7	14	21	28
1 Love Me For A Reason *The Osmonds* (MGM)	1	2	4
2 I'm Leaving It All Up To You *Donny and Marie Osmond* (MGM)	3	5	11
3 When Will I See You Again *The Three Degrees* (Philadelphia)	7	15	–
4 Kung Fu Fighting *Carl Douglas* (Pye)	2	1	1
5 Y Viva Espana *Sylvia* (Sonet)	4	6	5
6 You Make Me Feel Brand New *The Stylistics* (Avco)	13	17	–
7 Annie's Song *John Denver* (RCA)	5	3	2
8 What Becomes Of The Broken Hearted *Jimmy Ruffin* (Tamla Motown)	8	12	18
9 Mr Soft *Cockney Rebel* (EMI)	11	20	–
10 Honey Honey *Sweet Dreams* (Bradley's)	12	13	–
11 Hang On In There Baby *Johnny Bristol* (MGM)	6	4	3
12 Summerlove Sensation *The Bay City Rollers* (Bell)	19	–	–
13 Na Na Na *Cozy Powell* (RAK)	10	10	14
14 Hello Summertime *Bobby Goldsboro* (UA)	20	18	–
15 Rock 'n' Roll Lady *Showaddywaddy* (Bell)	18	16	–
16 Queen Of Clubs *K. C. and The Sunshine Band* (Jayboy)	15	9	7
17 Rainbow *Peters and Lee* (Philips)	–	19	–
18 Just For You *The Glitter Band* (Bell)	–	–	–
19 You You You *Alvin Stardust* (Magnet)	9	7	6
20 Can't Get Enough Of Your Love Babe *Barry White* (Pye)	17	8	8
24 Baby Love *Diana Ross and The Supremes* (Tamla Motown)	14	14	12
22 The Black-Eyed Boys *Paper Lace* (Bus Stop)	16	11	13
29 Rock Me Gently *Andy Kim* (Capitol)	24	22	9
– Long Tall Glasses *Leo Sayer* (Chrysalis)	48	23	10
– Sad Sweet Dreamer *Sweet Sensation* (Pye)	44	34	15
– Gee Baby *Peter Shelley* (Magnet)	42	33	16
27 Smoke Gets In Your Eyes *Bryan Ferry* (Island)	22	21	17
28 Another Saturday Night *Cat Stevens* (Island)	23	24	19
– Knock On Wood *David Bowie* (RCA)	–	–	20

OCTOBER 1974

5	12	19	26
1 Kung Fu Fighting *Carl Douglas* (Pye)	4	14	–
2 Annie's Song *John Denver* (RCA)	1	5	12
3 Hang On In There Baby *Johnny Bristol* (MGM)	7	15	–
4 Long Tall Glasses *Leo Sayer* (Chrysalis)	6	6	14
5 Sad Sweet Dreamer *Sweet Sensation* (Pye)	3	1	3
6 Gee Baby *Peter Shelley* (Magnet)	5	4	5
7 You You You *Alvin Stardust* (Magnet)	8	–	–
8 Rock Me Gently *Andy Kim* (Capitol)	2	8	8
9 Can't Get Enough Of Your Love Babe *Barry White* (Pye)	9	–	–

5

	12	19	26
10 Queen Of Clubs *K. C. and The Sunshine Band* (Jayboy)	12	–	–
11 Y Viva Espana *Sylvia* (Sonet)	18	–	–
12 The Black-Eyed Boys *Paper Lace* (Bus Stop)	–	–	–
13 Everything I Own *Ken Boothe* (Trojan)	11	2	1
14 Love Me For A Reason *The Osmonds* (MGM)	–	–	–
15 The Bitch Is Back *Elton John* (DJM)	16	–	–
16 I'm Leaving It All Up To You *Donny and Marie Osmond* (MGM)	–	–	–
17 Knock On Wood *David Bowie* (RCA)	10	16	–
18 Reggae Tune *Andy Fairweather Low* (A & M)	13	10	13
19 Smoke Gets In Your Eyes *Bryan Ferry* (Island)	–	–	–
20 Machine Gun *The Commodores* (Tamla Motown)	20	20	–
31 I Get A Kick Out Of You *Gary Shearston* (Charisma)	14	9	7
27 Farewell/Bring It On Home To Me *Rod Stewart* (Mercury)	15	7	11
29 You're Having My Baby *Paul Anka* (UA)	17	12	6
21 I Got The Music In Me *The Kiki Dee Band* (Rocket)	19	–	–
– Far Far Away *Slade* (Polydor)	–	3	2
– All Of Me Loves All Of You *The Bay City Rollers* (Bell)	31	11	4
39 I Can't Leave You Alone *George McCrae* (Jayboy)	22	13	9
– All I Want Is You *Roxy Music* (Island)	49	17	16
28 You Little Trust Maker *The Tymes* (RCA)	23	18	20
– Gonna Make You A Star *David Essex* (CBS)	42	19	10
– Down On The Beach Tonight *The Drifters* (Bell)	46	25	15
44 Happy Anniversary *Slim Whitman* (UA)	33	28	17
– Hey There Lonely Girl *Eddie Holman* (ABC)	–	31	18
– Let's Get Together Again *The Glitter Band* (Bell)	–	48	19

NOVEMBER 1974

2

	9	16	23	30
1 Everything I Own *Ken Boothe* (Trojan)	1	3	5	16
2 Far Far Away *Slade* (Polydor)	5	6	–	–
3 Gonna Make You A Star *David Essex* (CBS)	2	1	1	1
4 All Of Me Loves All Of You *The Bay City Rollers* (Bell)	4	7	10	–
5 Killer Queen *Queen* (EMI)	3	2	2	5
6 Sad Sweet Dreamer *Sweet Sensation* (Pye)	18	–	–	–
7 You're Having My Baby *Paul Anka* (UA)	9	12	–	–
8 Down On The Beach Tonight *The Drifters* (Bell)	7	8	11	–
9 I Can't Leave You Alone *George McCrae* (Jayboy)	11	16	–	–
10 Let's Get Together Again *The Glitter Band* (Bell)	8	11	12	–
11 Hey There Lonely Girl *Eddie Holman* (ABC)	6	4	4	8
12 I Get A Kick Out Of You *Gary Shearston* (Charisma)	13	–	–	–
13 Gee Baby *Peter Shelley* (Magnet)	–	–	–	–
14 Let's Put It All Together *The Stylistics* (Avco)	10	9	9	14
15 All I Want Is You *Roxy Music* (Island)	12	14	19	–
16 Never Turn Your Back On Mother Earth *Sparks* (Island)	15	13	18	–
17 Minuetto Allegretto *The Wombles* (CBS)	16	19	–	–
18 Farewell/Bring It On Home To Me *Rod Stewart* (Mercury)	–	–	–	–
19 You Little Trust Maker *The Tymes* (RCA)	–	–	–	–
20 Reggae Tune *Andy Fairweather Low* (A & M)	–	–	–	–
21 Happy Anniversary *Slim Whitman* (UA)	14	–	–	–
26 Pepper Box *The Peppers* (Spark)	17	10	6	9
23 Da Doo Ron Ron *The Crystals* (Warner Spector)	19	15	17	19
38 You're The First, The Last, My Everything *Barry White* (20th Century)	20	5	3	2
40 Magic *Pilot* (EMI)	30	17	15	11
– The Wild One *Suzi Quatro* (RAK)	37	18	14	7
48 No Honestly *Lynsey de Paul* (Jet)	22	20	7	13
– Juke Box Jive *The Rubettes* (Polydor)	–	23	8	4
39 Too Good To Be Forgotten *The Chi-Lites* (Brunswick)	27	21	13	10
– Oh Yes You're Beautiful *Gary Glitter* (Bell)	–	–	16	3

2   **9 16 23 30**

	9	16	23	30
– You Ain't Seen Nothing Yet *Bachman Turner Overdrive* (Mercury)	–	34	20	6
– Tell Him *Hello* (Bell)	43	32	23	12
– My Boy *Elvis Presley* (RCA)	–	40	28	15
45 Costafine Town *Splinter* (Dark Horse)	28	22	22	17
– Lucy In The Sky With Diamonds *Elton John* (DJM)	–	–	34	18
– Ire Feelings (Skanga) *Rupie Edwards* (Cactus)	–	–	38	20

DECEMBER 1974

7	14	21/28
1 You're The First, The Last, My Everything *Barry White* (20th Century)	1	4
2 Gonna Make You A Star *David Essex* (CBS)	5	–
3 Juke Box Jive *The Rubettes* (Polydor)	8	3
4 Oh Yes You're Beautiful *Gary Glitter* (Bell)	2	9
5 You Ain't Seen Nothing Yet *Bachman Turner Overdrive* (Mercury)	3	2
6 Tell Him *Hello* (Bell)	7	10
7 Hey There Lonely Girl *Eddie Holman* (ABC)	–	–
8 My Boy *Elvis Presley* (RCA)	6	7
9 Killer Queen *Queen* (EMI)	–	–
10 Ire Feelings (Skanga) *Rupie Edwards* (Cactus)	9	14
11 Magic *Pilot* (EMI)	12	–
12 Pepper Box *The Peppers* (Spark)	–	–
13 Too Good To Be Forgotten *The Chi-Lites* (Brunswick)	13	–
14 Get Dancing *Discotex and The Sex-o-lettes* (Chelsea)	11	8
15 Lucy In The Sky With Diamonds *Elton John* (DJM)	10	11
16 The Wild One *Suzi Quatro* (RAK)	15	–
17 No Honestly *Lynsey de Paul* (Jet)	–	–
18 Costafine Town *Splinter* (Dark Horse)	17	–
19 Lonely This Christmas *Mud* (RAK)	4	1
20 How Long *Ace* (Anchor)	–	–
39 Streets Of London *Ralph McTell* (Reprise)	14	6
23 Junior's Farm *Wings* (Apple)	16	–
21 Where Did All The Good Times Go *Donny Osmond* (MGM)	18	–
24 Tell Me Why *Alvin Stardust* (Magnet)	19	16
34 Down Down *Status Quo* (Vertigo)	20	15
47 Wombling Merry Christmas *The Wombles* (CBS)	21	5
28 You Can Make Me Dance, Sing Or Anything *Rod Stewart and The Faces* (Warner Bros.)	23	12
41 Father Christmas Do Not Touch Me/The Inbetweenies *The Goodies* (Bradley's)	28	13
25 Sound Your Funky Horn *K. C. and The Sunshine Band* (Jayboy)	32	17
– Christmas Song *Gilbert O'Sullivan* (MAM)	44	18
– I Can Help *Billy Swann* (Monument)	27	19
22 Sha La La *Al Green* (London)	22	20

1974–BEST-SELLING SINGLES

1 Tiger Feet *Mud* (RAK)
2 Seasons In The Sun *Terry Jacks* (Bell)
3 Billy, Don't Be A Hero *Paper Lace* (Bus Stop)
4 When Will I See You Again *The Three Degrees* (Philadelphia)
5 Rock Your Baby *George McCrae* (Jayboy)
6 Gonna Make You A Star *David Essex* (CBS)
7 She *Charles Aznavour* (Barclay)
8 Kung Fu Fighting *Carl Douglas* (Pye)
9 Everything I Own *Ken Boothe* (Trojan)
10 Sugar Baby Love *The Rubettes* (Polydor)
11 Devil Gate Drive *Suzi Quatro* (RAK)
12 Love Me For A Reason *The Osmonds* (MGM)
13 Jealous Mind *Alvin Stardust* (Magnet)
14 The Air That I Breathe *The Hollies* (Polydor)
15 Annie's Song *John Denver* (RCA)
16 Waterloo *Abba* (Epic)
17 Wombling Song *The Wombles* (CBS)
18 You Make Me Feel Brand New *The Stylistics* (Avco)
19 The Most Beautiful Girl *Charlie Rich* (Epic)
20 Y Viva Espana *Sylvia* (Sonet)

1974–BEST-SELLING ALBUMS

1 The Singles 1969–1973 *The Carpenters*
2 Band On The Run *Paul McCartney and Wings*
3 Tubular Bells *Mike Oldfield*
4 Elvis Presley's 40 Greatest Hits *Elvis Presley*
5 The Dark Side Of The Moon *Pink Floyd*
6 Goodbye Yellow Brick Road *Elton John*
7 And I Love You So *Perry Como*
8 Rollin' *The Bay City Rollers*
9 Simon And Garfunkel's Greatest Hits *Simon and Garfunkel*
10 Old New Borrowed And Blue *Slade*
11 Another Time Another Place *Bryan Ferry*
12 Hergest Ridge *Mike Oldfield*
13 Super Bad *Various artists*
14 Diamond Dogs *David Bowie*
15 Caribou *Elton John*
16 Journey To The Centre Of The Earth *Rick Wakeman*
17 Elton John's Greatest Hits *Elton John*
18 Diana And Marvin *Diana Ross and Marvin Gaye*
19 Smiler *Rod Stewart*
20 Scott Joplin Piano Rags *Joshua Rifkin*

1974–BEST-SELLING ARTISTS

Male Artists (Singles)

1 Alvin Stardust
2 Barry White
3 Elton John
4 Gary Glitter
5 David Essex
6 George McCrae
7 David Bowie
8 Terry Jacks
9 Charlie Rich
10 Stevie Wonder

Female Artists (Singles)

1 Suzi Quatro
2 Sylvia
3 Diana Ross
4 Olivia Newton-John
5 Lena Zavaroni
6 Lulu
7 Sunny
8 Gigliola Cinquetti
9 Lynsey de Paul
10 Marie Osmond

Groups (Singles)

1 The Wombles
2 The Bay City Rollers
3 Mud
4 The Stylistics
5 Paper Lace
6 The Rubettes
7 Cozy Powell
8 Paul McCartney and Wings
9 The Three Degrees
10 The Glitter Band

Male Artists (Albums)

1 Elton John
2 Mike Oldfield
3 David Bowie
4 Perry Como
5 Stevie Wonder
6 Bryan Ferry
7 John Denver
8 Andy Williams
9 Rick Wakeman
10 Neil Diamond

Female Artists (Albums)

1 Diana Ross
2 Joni Mitchell
3 Carly Simon
4 Lena Zavaroni
5 Nana Mouskouri
6 Lena Martell
7 Olivia Newton-John
8 Carole King
9 Marie Osmond
10 Barbra Streisand

Groups (Albums)

1 The Carpenters
2 Simon and Garfunkel
3 Pink Floyd
4 Paul McCartney and Wings
5 The Beatles
6 Peters and Lee
7 Slade
8 Diana Ross and Marvin Gaye
9 Sparks
10 The Wombles

1975

Disco sounds continued to make their assault on the charts in 1975, a trend which had begun in 1974. It could be said that records were made popular by the discos and then entered the charts – a statement which could certainly be verified by a glance at the charts of 1975 with hits from K. C. and The Sunshine Band, Hamilton Bohannon, Jasper Carrott, Pete Wingfield, Chris Spedding, Wigan's Ovation, Jackie Wilson, The Sharonettes, Gloria Gaynor, B.T. Express and Silver Convention. The Chi-Lites' hit of January 1972 'Have You Seen Her?' became a hit all over again in July 1975, and there were many other disco records from the All Platinum record label. Other disco records which entered the charts came from The Tymes, Eddie Holman, Wayne Gibson, and Discotex and The Sex-o-lettes.

Girl artists came to the fore, and at one time about 18 girls made the Top Fifty – an unprecedented figure when taking into consideration the fact that in most other years it is hard to find even 10 girl artists entering the charts during a 12-month period.

1975 will be remembered as the year in which Johnny Mathis entered the charts again with 'I'm Stone In Love With You', his first hit single for 17 years, although an album of Mathis' had entered the Top Ten album charts in 1960.

For Dana, the Irish Eurovision song winner of 1970, 1975 showed compassion. In 1970 and 1971 she had achieved hits with 'All Kinds Of Everything' and 'Who Put The Lights Out', but fruitless years had followed until the welcome arrival of 'Please Tell Him That I Said Hello', a disc which made the 1975 charts in the last week of January at Number Thirty-Eight.

As far as the Top Twenty was concerned in 1975, The Glitter Band, The Rubettes, Status Quo, The Bay City Rollers, The Carpenters, Mac and Katie Kissoon, Pilot, Alvin Stardust and Kenny, a new teen group, all enjoyed success. Particularly pleasing was the appearance in the charts of The Average White Band with 'Pick Up The Pieces', a funky sound from a British group.

1975 promised much for some bands, but in fact yielded very little. Pilot seemed likely to become the next teen chart force, but this was not to be, while the Canadian exponents of the thudding bass, Bachman Turner Overdrive, did not live up to the potential they had shown in 1974. Another teen prospect, Arrows, floundered and even Suzi Quatro lost much of her chart appeal of the previous two years. Slade had Hit Parade successes with 'How Does It Feel' and 'Thanks For The Memory', but they were in America for most of the year, which could explain why their chart impact in Britain was not greater.

A new label, GTO, under the ex-Bell Records, hit-making prowess of Dick Leahy, not only made Dana a chart force with which to be reckoned again, but also signed Fox, an exciting new band who had two hits with 'Only You Can' and 'Imagine Me Imagine You'.

Rod Stewart, after months of legal disputes, returned to the charts with 'Sailing', and after years of non-action came two golden oldies, 'Sealed With A Kiss' from Brian Hyland and 'Honey' from Bobby Goldsboro.

Humour came from The Goodies, Mike Reid and Jasper Carrott, for those who examined words and vocal gesture rather than beat.

Frankie Valli of The Four Seasons patiently waited months for 'My Eyes Adored You' to enter the charts, and when it eventually did it gave the Private Stock record label its first major chart triumph. Telly Savalas of *Kojak* fame talked his way into the charts with 'If', while Barry White again talked and growled his way into the Top Ten.

Peter Shelley did well singing and producing records, but 1975 tended to lack any definite character and domination except by possibly The Bay City Rollers, who put the emphasis on teenage tartan clothes, half-mast trousers and Scottish scarves. It was estimated that The Rollers attracted merchandising of £2,000,000 in Britain in 1975 alone, while at least the same amount was projected for them in America, assuming that the much-planned Roller onslaught was successful. And if it wasn't, well, there was always next month's sensation.

The last three months saw one of the biggest selling singles for years with Queen's 'Bohemian Rhapsody', which some would regard as the peak of their careers.

There was even an old fashioned battle for chart supremacy with several versions of 'Paloma Blanca' vying for top honours; not surprisingly, Jonathan King was to the fore in this episode. Abba were gathering momentum for their major assault on the British charts in 1976 whilst a golden oldie, 'Space Oddity' from David Bowie, entered the charts once more and seemed as original as it did on its first outing in 1969.

Art Garfunkel topped the charts with a romantic ballad but it was a brief moment of solo glory after his familiar association with Paul Simon. Hot Chocolate ploughed on with another hit, but they were still searching for their first ever Number One. They finally succeeded on 2 July 1977, but in 1975 they were obstructed in their struggle for a Number One by Queen riding high.

The Stylistics continued their Top Twenty run of successes but the signs suggested their format needed a change. David Cassidy was back in the spotlight with an old Beach Boys hit 'Darlin'' but brief was his return. Comedian Billy Connolly brought humour into the Top Twenty with his own version of the Tammy Wynette hit 'D.I.V.O.R.C.E.', and for nostalgia-hunters there was Chubby Checker's return with 'Let's Twist Again'. There was a touch of the unusual with Laurel and Hardy reaching the charts thanks to 'The Trail Of The Lonesome Pine', but if Emerson Lake and Palmer member Greg Lake could reach Number Two with 'I Believe In Father Christmas', perhaps it wasn't so strange after all.

JANUARY 1975

4	11	18	25
1 Lonely This Christmas *Mud* (RAK)	1	8	17
2 Wombling Merry Christmas *The Wombles* (CBS)	5	20	–
3 Juke Box Jive *The Rubettes* (Polydor)	10	18	–
4 Streets Of London *Ralph McTell* (Reprise)	2	2	4
5 My Boy *Elvis Presley* (RCA)	13	14	16
6 You Ain't Seen Nothing Yet *Bachman Turner Overdrive* (Mercury)	12	16	–
7 The Inbetweenies/Father Christmas Do Not Touch Me *The Goodies* (Bradley's)	11	13	19
8 You're The First, The Last, My Everything *Barry White* (20th Century)	–	–	–
9 Oh Yes You're Beautiful *Gary Glitter* (Bell)	–	–	–
10 Down Down *Status Quo* (Vertigo)	3	1	5
11 Get Dancing *Discotex and The Sex-o-lettes* (Chelsea)	8	9	15
12 Christmas Song *Gilbert O'Sullivan* (MAM)	–	–	–
13 Hey Mister Christmas *Showaddywaddy* (Bell)	–	–	–
14 Lucy In The Sky With Diamonds *Elton John* (DJM)	17	19	–
15 Tell Him *Hello* (Bell)	–	–	–
16 You Can Make Me Dance, Sing Or Anything *Rod Stewart and The Faces* (Warner Bros.)	14	–	–
17 I Can Help *Billy Swann* (Monument)	9	6	12
18 Ire Feelings (Skanga) *Rupie Edwards* (Cactus)	–	–	–
19 Tell Me Why *Alvin Stardust* (Magnet)	–	–	–
20 Gonna Make You A Star *David Essex* (CBS)	–	–	–
21 The Bump *Kenny* (RAK)	4	3	3
23 Never Can Say Goodbye *Gloria Gaynor* (MGM)	6	4	2
27 Ms Grace *The Tymes* (RCA)	7	5	1
28 Are You Ready To Rock *Wizzard* (Warner Bros.)	15	10	8
26 Stardust *David Essex* (CBS)	16	7	10
29 Help Me Make It Through The Night *John Holt* (Trojan)	18	12	6
32 Crying Over You *Ken Boothe* (Trojan)	19	11	11
22 Under My Thumb *Wayne Gibson* (Pye)	20	17	–
40 The Morning Side Of The Mountain *Donny and Marie Osmond* (MGM)	26	15	7
– January *Pilot* (EMI)	–	27	9
– Promised Land *Elvis Presley* (RCA)	–	22	13
– Goodbye My Love *The Glitter Band* (Bell)	–	47	14
– Something For The Girl With Everything *Sparks* (Island)	–	44	18
– Purely By Coincidence *Sweet Sensation* (Pye)	–	49	20

FEBRUARY 1975

1	8	15	22
1 January *Pilot* (EMI)	1	1	2
2 Ms Grace *The Tymes* (RCA)	4	–	–
3 The Bump *Kenny* (RAK)	7	6	–
4 Never Can Say Goodbye *Gloria Gaynor* (MGM)	5	–	–
5 Morning Side Of The Mountain *Donny and Marie Osmond* (MGM)	6	8	–
6 Down Down *Status Quo* (Vertigo)	–	–	–
7 Help Me Make It Through The Night *John Holt* (Trojan)	9	16	–
8 Goodbye My Love *The Glitter Band* (Bell)	2	4	6
9 Promised Land *Elvis Presley* (RCA)	10	13	20
10 Sugar Candy Kisses *Mac and Katie Kissoon* (Polydor)	3	3	4
11 Are You Ready To Rock *Wizzard* (Warner Bros.)	20	–	–
12 Boogie On Reggae Woman *Stevie Wonder* (Tamla Motown)	15	19	–
13 Streets Of London *Ralph McTell* (Reprise)	19	–	–

	1	8	15	22
14 Purely By Coincidence *Sweet Sensation* (Pye)		11	18	–
15 Please Mr Postman *The Carpenters* (A & M)		8	2	3
16 Stardust *David Essex* (CBS)		–	–	–
17 Crying Over You *Ken Boothe* (Trojan)		–	–	–
18 Angie Baby *Helen Reddy* (Capitol)		13	5	8
19 I Can Help *Billy Swann* (Monument)		–	–	–
20 Now I'm Here *Queen* (EMI)		12	11	16
21 Black Superman (Muhammed Ali) *Johnny Wakelin and The Kinshasa Band* (Pye)		14	7	10
25 Footsee *Wigan's Chosen Few* (Pye)		16	10	9
22 Something For The Girl With Everything *Sparks* (Island)		17	–	–
24 Star On A TV Show *The Stylistics* (Avco)		18	12	14
– Make Me Smile (Come Up And See Me) *Steve Harley and Cockney Rebel* (EMI)		33	9	1
30 Your Kiss Is Sweet *Syreeta* (Tamla Motown)		25	14	13
– Shame Shame Shame *Shirley and Company* (All Platinum)		38	15	7
40 Good Love Can Never Die *Alvin Stardust* (Magnet)		22	17	11
28 It May Be Winter Outside *Love Unlimited* (20th Century)		24	20	15
– The Secrets That You Keep *Mud* (RAK)		–	26	5
39 My Eyes Adored You *Frankie Valli* (Private Stock)		31	21	12
32 I'm Stone In Love With You *Johnny Mathis* (CBS)		28	24	17
37 Please Tell Him That I Said Hello *Dana* (GTO)		29	25	18
– Only You Can *Fox* (GTO)		–	50	19

MARCH 1975

	1	8	15	22	29
1 Make Me Smile (Come Up And See Me) *Steve Harley and Cockney Rebel* (EMI)		2	3	13	–
2 If *Telly Savalas* (MCA)		1	1	2	4
3 Please Mr Postman *The Carpenters* (A & M)		6	14	–	–
4 The Secrets That You Keep *Mud* (RAK)		3	5	7	–
5 Only You Can *Fox* (GTO)		4	4	3	7
6 Shame Shame Shame *Shirley and Company* (All Platinum)		7	12	–	–
7 My Eyes Adored You *Frankie Valli* (Private Stock)		5	6	12	–
8 Sugar Candy Kisses *Mac and Katie Kissoon* (Polydor)		–	–	–	–
9 January *Pilot* (EMI)		–	–	–	–
10 Footsee *Wigan's Chosen Few* (Pye)		10	–	–	–
11 It May Be Winter Outside *Love Unlimited* (20th Century)		14	–	–	–
12 Your Kiss Is Sweet *Syreeta* (Tamla Motown)		17	–	–	–
13 Good Love Can Never Die *Alvin Stardust* (Magnet)		16	–	–	–
14 Angie Baby *Helen Reddy* (Capitol)		20	–	–	–
15 Black Superman (Muhammed Ali) *Johnny Wakelin and The Kinshasa Band* (Pye)		–	–	–	–
16 Goodbye My Love *The Glitter Band* (Bell)		–	–	–	–
17 Please Tell Him That I Said Hello *Dana* (GTO)		12	8	16	18
18 Star On A TV Show *The Stylistics* (Avco)		–	–	–	–
19 I'm Stone In Love With You *Johnny Mathis* (CBS)		11	10	18	20
20 Now I'm Here *Queen* (EMI)		–	–	–	–
– Bye Bye Baby *The Bay City Rollers* (Bell)		8	2	1	1
22 Pick Up The Pieces *The Average White Band* (Atlantic)		9	7	6	12
24 Dreamer *Supertramp* (A & M)		13	15	15	17
21 How Does It Feel *Slade* (Polydor)		15	16	–	–
29 Young Americans *David Bowie* (RCA)		18	–	19	–
30 Sweet Music *Showaddywaddy* (Bell)		19	18	14	16
44 There's A Whole Lot Of Loving *Guys and Dolls* (Magnet)		26	9	4	2
26 Mandy *Barry Manilow* (Arista)		21	11	11	13
– What Am I Gonna Do With You *Barry White* (20th Century)		30	13	5	5
– Girls *Moments and Whatnauts* (All Platinum)		35	17	9	3
– Fancy Pants *Kenny* (RAK)		36	19	8	6

226

1	8	15	22	29
– I Can Do It *The Rubettes* (State)	31	20	10	9
– Play Me Like You Play Your Guitar *Duane Eddy and The Rebelettes* (GTO)	47	29	17	11
– Philadelphia Freedom *The Elton John Band* (DJM)	29	24	20	15
– The Funky Gibbon/Sick Man Blues *The Goodies* (Bradley's)	–	37	23	8
– Fox On The Run *The Sweet* (RCA)	–	42	21	10
– Swing Your Daddy *Jim Gilstrap* (Chelsea)	–	44	26	14
– Reach Out I'll Be There *Gloria Gaynor* (MGM)	45	31	22	19

APRIL 1975

5	12	19	26
1 Bye Bye Baby *The Bay City Rollers* (Bell)	1	1	1
2 There's A Whole Lot Of Loving *Guys and Dolls* (Magnet)	3	6	19
3 Girls *Moments and Whatnauts* (All Platinum)	6	7	–
4 Fancy Pants *Kenny* (RAK)	5	8	–
5 Fox On The Run *The Sweet* (RCA)	2	2	3
6 What Am I Gonna Do With You *Barry White* (20th Century)	15	19	–
7 I Can Do It *The Rubettes* (State)	9	12	–
8 Swing Your Daddy *Jim Gilstrap* (Chelsea)	7	4	5
9 Play Me Like You Play Your Guitar *Duane Eddy and The Rebelettes* (GTO)	10	11	–
10 The Funky Gibbon/Sick Man Blues *The Goodies* (Bradley's)	4	5	8
11 Love Me Love My Dog *Peter Shelley* (Magnet)	8	3	4
12 Let Me Be The One *The Shadows* (EMI)	13	15	–
13 Philadelphia Freedom *The Elton John Band* (DJM)	12	17	20
14 Reach Out I'll Be There *Gloria Gaynor* (MGM)	14	20	–
15 Only You Can *Fox* (GTO)	–	–	–
16 The Ugly Duckling *Mike Reid* (Pye)	11	10	15
17 If *Telly Savalas* (MCA)	18	–	–
18 Pick Up The Pieces *The Average White Band* (Atlantic)	–	–	–
19 Sweet Music *Showaddywaddy* (Bell)	–	–	–
20 Mandy *Barry Manilow* (Arista)	–	–	–
21 Skiing In The Snow *Wigan's Ovation* (Spark)	16	13	12
23 Lady Marmalade *Labelle* (Epic)	17	–	17
31 Honey *Bobby Goldsboro* (UA)	19	9	2
39 A Little Love And Understanding *Gilbert Becaud* (Decca)	20	–	13
49 Life Is A Minestrone *10cc* (Mercury)	23	14	9
– The Tears I Cried *The Glitter Band* (Bell)	29	16	14
– Ding-A-Dong *Teach-In* (Polydor)	26	18	18
– Oh Boy *Mud* (RAK)	–	–	6
– Loving You *Minnie Riperton* (Epic)	49	23	7
45 Hurt So Good *Susan Cadogan* (Magnet)	34	25	10
– Take Good Care Of Yourself *The Three Degrees* (Philadelphia)	40	22	11
36 Hold On To Love *Peter Skellern* (Decca)	21	24	16

MAY 1975

3	10	17	24	31
1 Oh Boy *Mud* (RAK)	1	2	3	15
2 Loving You *Minnie Riperton* (Epic)	2	3	4	13
3 Honey *Bobby Goldsboro* (UA)	5	8	–	–
4 Hurt So Good *Susan Cadogan* (Magnet)	4	4	8	17
5 Bye Bye Baby *The Bay City Rollers* (Bell)	8	19	–	–
6 Love Me Love My Dog *Peter Shelley* (Magnet)	16	–	–	–
7 Life Is A Minestrone *10cc* (Mercury)	15	20	–	–
8 The Tears I Cried *The Glitter Band* (Bell)	11	18	–	–
9 Take Good Care Of Yourself *The Three Degrees* (Philadelphia)	9	15	–	–

3	**10**	**17**	**24**	**31**
10 Fox On The Run *The Sweet* (RCA)	–	–	–	–
11 Swing Your Daddy *Jim Gilstrap* (Chelsea)	18	–	–	–
12 A Little Love And Understanding *Gilbert Becaud* (Decca)	10	13	–	–
13 Ding-A-Dong *Teach-In* (Polydor)	19	–	–	–
14 Hold On To Love *Peter Skellern* (Decca)	20	–	–	–
15 The Funky Gibbon/Sick Man Blues *The Goodies* (Bradley's)	–	–	–	–
16 The Night *Frankie Valli and The Four Seasons* (Mowest)	7	9	15	19
17 Let Me Try Again *Tammy Jones* (Epic)	6	5	7	9
18 Only Yesterday *The Carpenters* (A & M)	14	7	10	14
19 Skiing In The Snow *Wigan's Ovation* (Spark)	–	–	–	–
20 We'll Find Our Day *Stephanie De Sykes* (Bradley's)	17	17	–	–
23 Stand By Your Man *Tammy Wynette* (Epic)	3	1	1	1
21 I Wanna Dance Wit Choo *Discotex and The Sex-o-lettes* (Chelsea)	12	6	11	8
25 Love Like You And Me *Gary Glitter* (Bell)	13	10	20	–
32 The Way We Were *Gladys Knight and The Pips* (Buddah)	22	11	5	4
– Sing Baby Sing *The Stylistics* (Avco)	36	12	6	3
– Thanks For The Memory *Slade* (Polydor)	–	14	12	7
46 Don't Do It Baby *Mac and Katie Kissoon* (State)	27	16	9	12
– Whispering Grass *Windsor Davies and Don Estelle* (EMI)	–	28	2	2
– Three Steps To Heaven *Showaddywaddy* (Bell)	–	50	13	5
– Send In The Clowns *Judy Collins* (Elektra)	–	39	14	6
– Roll Over Lay Down *Status Quo* (Vertigo)	–	37	16	10
– Autobahn *Kraftwerk* (Vertigo)	38	22	17	16
43 Once Bitten Twice Shy *Ian Hunter* (CBS)	28	25	18	20
– The Israelites *Desmond Dekker* (Cactus)	40	21	19	11
– The Proud One *The Osmonds* (MGM)	–	–	34	18

JUNE 1975

7	**14**	**21**	**28**
1 Whispering Grass *Windsor Davies and Don Estelle* (EMI)	1	1	2
2 Stand By Your Man *Tammy Wynette* (Epic)	5	7	16
3 Three Steps To Heaven *Showaddywaddy* (Bell)	2	3	3
4 Sing Baby Sing *The Stylistics* (Avco)	4	8	14
5 Try To Remember/The Way We Were *Gladys Knight and The Pips* (Buddah)	7	9	19
6 Send In The Clowns *Judy Collins* (Elektra)	8	11	–
7 The Proud One *The Osmonds* (MGM)	6	5	7
8 I'm Not In Love *10cc* (Mercury)	3	2	1
9 Roll Over Lay Down *Status Quo* (Vertigo)	13	18	–
10 The Israelites *Desmond Dekker* (Cactus)	14	19	–
11 Autobahn *Kraftwerk* (Vertigo)	12	16	–
12 Thanks For The Memory *Slade* (Polydor)	17	–	–
13 I Wanna Dance Wit Choo *Discotex and The Sex-o-lettes* (Chelsea)	–	–	–
14 Once Bitten Twice Shy *Ian Hunter* (CBS)	18	20	–
15 Imagine Me, Imagine You *Fox* (GTO)	19	–	–
16 Let Me Try Again *Tammy Jones* (Epic)	–	–	–
17 Don't Do It Baby *Mac and Katie Kissoon* (State)	–	–	–
18 Listen To What The Man Said *Wings* (Apple)	10	6	9
19 Swing Low Sweet Chariot *Eric Clapton* (RSO)	–	–	–
20 Disco Queen *Hot Chocolate* (RAK)	11	12	17
22 The Hustle *Van McCoy* (Avco)	9	4	4
30 Oh What A Shame *Roy Wood* (Jet)	15	13	15
23 Disco Stomp *Hamilton Bohannon* (Brunswick)	16	10	8
21 I'll Do For You Anything You Want Me To *Barry White* (20th Century)	20	–	–
– Tears On My Pillow *Johnny Nash* (CBS)	29	14	5

7	**14**	**21**	**28**
42 Baby I Love You, OK *Kenny* (RAK)	24	15	12
40 Mr Raffles (Man It Was Mean) *Steve Harley and Cockney Rebel* (EMI)	23	17	13
– Doing Alright With The Boys *Gary Glitter* (Bell)	–	22	6
– Misty *Ray Stevens* (Janus)	–	35	10
– Moonshine Sally *Mud* (RAK)	–	26	11
– My White Bicycle *Nazareth* (Mooncrest)	36	24	18
– I Don't Love You But I Think I Like You *Gilbert O'Sullivan* (MAM)	41	25	20

JULY 1975

5	**12**	**19**	**26**
1 I'm Not In Love *10cc* (Mercury)	4	8	14
2 Tears On My Pillow *Johnny Nash* (CBS)	1	2	3
3 The Hustle *Van McCoy* (Avco)	3	4	7
4 Whispering Grass *Windsor Davies and Don Estelle* (EMI)	9	15	–
5 Misty *Ray Stevens* (Janus)	2	3	4
6 Disco Stomp *Hamilton Bohannon* (Brunswick)	8	9	15
7 Three Steps To Heaven *Showaddywaddy* (Bell)	12	–	–
8 Doing Alright With The Boys *Gary Glitter* (Bell)	6	18	–
9 Have You Seen Her/Oh Girl *The Chi-Lites* (Brunswick)	5	6	6
10 Moonshine Sally *Mud* (RAK)	11	13	–
11 The Proud One *The Osmonds* (MGM)	–	–	–
12 Listen To What The Man Said *Wings* (Apple)	–	–	–
13 Baby I Love You, OK *Kenny* (RAK)	16	–	–
14 I Don't Love You But I Think I Like You *Gilbert O'Sullivan* (MAM)	17	–	–
15 Eighteen With A Bullet *Pete Wingfield* (Island)	10	7	8
16 Mr Raffles (Man It Was Mean) *Steve Harley and Cockney Rebel* (EMI)	–	–	
17 My White Bicycle *Nazareth* (Mooncrest)	14	17	
18 Make The World Go Away *Donny and Marie Osmond* (MGM)	18	–	–
19 Foe-Dee-O-Dee *The Rubettes* (State)	15	–	19
20 Oh What A Shame *Roy Wood* (Jet)	–	–	–
– Give A Little Love *The Bay City Rollers* (Bell)	7	1	1
37 Barbados *Typically Tropical* (Gull)	13	5	2
32 Je T'Aime *Judge Dread* (Cactus)	19	10	9
30 D.I.V.O.R.C.E. *Tammy Wynette* (Epic)	20	16	12
47 Rolling Stone *David Essex* (CBS)	26	11	5
28 Jive Talkin' *The Bee Gees* (RSO)	23	12	11
33 Sealed With A Kiss *Brian Hyland* (ABC)	24	14	10
23 Black Pudding Bertha *The Goodies* (Bradley's)	22	19	–
21 Mama Never Told Me *Sister Sledge* (Atlantic)	27	20	–
– It's In His Kiss *Linda Lewis* (Arista)	41	28	13
– If You Think You Know How To Love Me *Smokey* (RAK)	–	40	16
– Action *The Sweet* (RCA)	47	27	17
36 I Write The Songs *David Cassidy* (RCA)	30	23	18
– New York City *T. Rex* (EMI)	39	30	20

AUGUST 1975

2	**9**	**16**	**23**	**30**
1 Give A Little Love *The Bay City Rollers* (Bell)	2	4	11	–
2 Barbados *Typically Tropical* (Gull)	1	2	4	8
3 Tears On My Pillow *Johnny Nash* (CBS)	10	14	–	–
4 Misty *Ray Stevens* (Janus)	20	–	–	–
5 Jive Talkin' *The Bee Gees* (RSO)	5	6	9	17
6 If You Think You Know How To Love Me *Smokey* (RAK)	4	3	5	10

	9	16	23	30
7 Sealed With A Kiss *Brian Hyland* (ABC)	7	12	16	–
8 It's In His Kiss *Linda Lewis* (Arista)	6	9	13	–
9 The Hustle *Van McCoy* (Avco)	–	–	–	–
10 Je T'Aime *Judge Dread* (Cactus)	9	16	–	–
11 Rolling Stone *David Essex* (CBS)	17	–	–	–
12 Can't Give You Anything (But My Love) *The Stylistics* (Avco)	3	1	1	1
13 Have You Seen Her/Oh Girl *The Chi-Lites* (Brunswick)	–	–	–	–
14 Eighteen With A Bullet *Pete Wingfield* (Island)	–	–	–	–
15 Action *The Sweet* (RCA)	19	–	–	–
16 Delilah *The Sensational Alex Harvey Band* (Vertigo)	8	7	17	15
17 I Write The Songs/For Love *David Cassidy* (RCA)	11	18	–	–
18 D.I.V.O.R.C.E. *Tammy Wynette* (Epic)	–	–	–	–
19 New York City *T. Rex* (EMI)	15	17	–	–
20 Highwire *Linda Carr and The Love Squad* (Chelsea)	–	15	–	–
22 Sherry *Adrian Baker* (Magnet)	12	10	12	16
28 It's Been So Long *George McCrae* (Jayboy)	13	8	6	4
29 The Last Farewell *Roger Whittaker* (EMI)	14	5	3	3
21 Blanket On The Ground *Billie Jo Spears* (UA)	16	11	7	6
23 Dolly My Love *The Moments* (All Platinum)	18	13	10	11
33 El Bimbo *Bimbo Jet* (EMI)	26	19	14	12
50 Best Thing That Ever Happened *Gladys Knight and The Pips* (Buddah)	30	20	15	7
– Sailing *Rod Stewart* (Warner Bros.)	–	24	2	2
48 That's The Way I Like It *K. C. and The Sunshine Band* (Jayboy)	38	23	8	5
45 Summer Of '42 *The Biddu Orchestra* (Epic)	35	26	18	14
41 Fame *David Bowie* (RCA)	33	30	19	–
– Super Womble *The Wombles* (CBS)	36	28	20	–
– Summertime City *Mike Batt* (Epic)	–	49	36	9
– Funky Moped/Magic Roundabout *Jasper Carrott* (DJM)	–	50	45	13
– Love In The Sun *The Glitter Band* (Bell)	44	40	29	18
– Julie-Ann *Kenny* (RAK)	–	47	35	19
– A Child's Prayer *Hot Chocolate* (RAK)	50	43	28	20

SEPTEMBER 1975

6	13	20	27
1 Sailing *Rod Stewart* (Warner Bros.)	1	1	1
2 Can't Give You Anything (But My Love) *The Stylistics* (Avco)	3	12	–
3 The Last Farewell *Roger Whittaker* (EMI)	2	3	6
4 That's The Way (I Like It) *K. C. and The Sunshine Band* (Jayboy)	5	10	19
5 It's Been So Long *George McCrae* (Jayboy)	11	15	–
6 Summertime City *Mike Batt* (Epic)	6	4	13
7 Blanket On The Ground *Billie Jo Spears* (UA)	14	–	–
8 A Child's Prayer *Hot Chocolate* (RAK)	7	8	9
9 Best Thing That Ever Happened *Gladys Knight and The Pips* (Buddah)	9	17	–
10 Funky Moped/Magic Roundabout *Jasper Carrott* (DJM)	8	5	5
11 Moonlighting *Leo Sayer* (Chrysalis)	4	2	3
12 Julie-Ann *Kenny* (RAK)	10	11	15
13 El Bimbo *Bimbo Jet* (EMI)	–	–	–
14 Dolly My Love *Moments* (All Platinum)	–	–	–
15 Summer Of '42 *The Biddu Orchestra* (Epic)	17	–	–
16 Love In The Sun *The Glitter Band* (Bell)	15	20	–
17 Fame *David Bowie* (RCA)	–	–	–
18 Barbados *Typically Tropical* (Gull)	–	–	–
19 If You Think You Know How To Love Me *Smokey* (RAK)	–	–	–
20 Super Womble *The Wombles* (CBS)	–	–	–

6	**13**	**20**	**27**
30 I'm On Fire *5000 Volts* (Philips)	12	6	4
29 Heartbeat *Showaddywaddy* (Bell)	13	7	7
28 Fool *Al Matthews* (CBS)	16	–	17
21 Pandora's Box *Procol Harum* (Chrysalis)	18	16	18
22 Motor Biking *Chris Spedding* (RAK)	19	14	14
25 Don't Throw It All Away *Gary Benson* (State)	20	–	–
– Hold Me Close *David Essex* (CBS)	48	9	2
46 There Goes My First Love *The Drifters* (Bell)	26	13	8
– Fattie Bum-Bum *Carl Malcolm* (UK)	36	18	11
44 Una Paloma Blanca *Jonathan King* (UK)	24	19	12
40 Like A Butterfly *Mac and Katie Kissoon* (State)	31	30	20
24 Sing A Little Song *Desmond Dekker* (Cactus)	22	21	16
— I Only Have Eyes For You *Art Garfunkel* (CBS)	44	24	10

OCTOBER 1975

4	**11**	**18**	**25**
1 Hold Me Close *David Essex* (CBS)	1	1	2
2 Sailing *Rod Stewart* (Warner Bros.)	11	20	–
3 There Goes My First Love *The Drifters* (Bell)	3	3	3
4 I Only Have Eyes For You *Art Garfunkel* (CBS)	2	2	1
5 Moonlighting *Leo Sayer* (Chrysalis)	18	–	–
6 Funky Moped/Magic Roundabout *Jasper Carrott* (DJM)	7	16	19
7 Heartbeat *Showaddywaddy* (Bell)	16	–	–
8 I'm On Fire *5000 Volts* (Philips)	4	19	–
9 Fattie Bum-Bum *Carl Malcolm* (UK)	8	13	–
10 Una Paloma Blanca *Jonathan King* (UK)	5	9	11
11 Paloma Blanca *George Baker* (Warner Bros.)	10	15	13
12 The Last Farewell *Roger Whittaker* (EMI)	–	–	–
13 Scotch On The Rocks *The Band of the Black Watch* (Spark)	12	8	10
14 Who Loves You *The Four Seasons* (Warner Bros.)	9	6	9
15 It's Time For Love *The Chi-Lites* (Brunswick)	6	5	7
16 S.O.S. *Abba* (Epic)	13	7	6
17 Motor Biking *Chris Spedding* (RAK)	–	–	–
18 Like A Butterfly *Mac and Katie Kissoon* (State)	19	18	–
19 Big Ten *Judge Dread* (Cactus)	17	14	15
20 Sing A Little Song *Desmond Dekker* (Cactus)	–	–	–
23 Feelings *Morris Albert* (Decca)	14	4	5
27 L-L-Lucy *Mud* (Private Stock)	15	10	14
26 Feel Like Makin' Love *Bad Company* (Island)	20	–	–
– Space Oddity *David Bowie* (RCA)	23	11	4
44 Don't Play Your Rock And Roll To Me *Smokey* (RAK)	24	12	8
42 What A Difference A Day Makes *Esther Phillips* (Kudu)	25	17	12
49 Rhinestone Cowboy *Glen Campbell* (Capitol)	32	25	17
– Hold Back The Night *Trammps* (Buddah)	43	28	18
43 Island Girl *Elton John* (DJM)	26	22	20
– Love Is The Drug *Roxy Music* (Island)	37	27	16

NOVEMBER 1975

1	**8**	**15**	**22**	**29**
1 I Only Have Eyes For You *Art Garfunkel* (CBS)	3	13	–	–
2 Space Oddity *David Bowie* (RCA)	1	1	2	10
3 There Goes My First Love *The Drifters* (Bell)	11	–	–	–
4 Feelings *Morris Albert* (Decca)	8	15	–	–
5 Love Is The Drug *Roxy Music* (Island)	2	3	4	11
6 S.O.S. *Abba* (Epic)	7	–	–	–
7 Hold Me Close *David Essex* (CBS)	18	–	–	–
8 What A Difference A Day Makes *Esther Phillips* (Kudu)	6	11	–	–

1	8	15	22	29
9 Don't Play Your Rock And Roll To Me *Smokey* (RAK)	12	–	–	–
10 Rhinestone Cowboy *Glen Campbell* (Capitol)	4	4	7	13
11 Scotch On The Rocks *The Band of the Black Watch* (Spark)	19	20	–	–
12 It's Time For Love *The Chi-Lites* (Brunswick)	–	–	–	–
13 Who Loves You *The Four Seasons* (Warner Bros.)	–	–	–	–
14 Island Girl *Elton John* (DJM)	20	–	–	–
15 Hold Back The Night *Trammps* (Buddah)	5	7	15	–
16 L-L-Lucy *Mud* (Private Stock)	–	–	–	–
17 I Ain't Lyin' *George McCrae* (Jayboy)	14	12	18	–
18 Highfly *John Miles* (Decca)	17	18	–	–
19 Blue Guitar *Justin Hayward and John Lodge* (Threshold)	10	8	11	17
20 Funky Moped/Magic Roundabout *Jasper Carrott* (DJM)	–	–	–	–
26 D.I.V.O.R.C.E. *Billy Connolly* (Polydor)	9	2	1	3
28 Love Hurts *Jim Capaldi* (Island)	13	5	5	4
23 New York Groove *Hello* (Bell)	15	9	12	14
25 Ride A Wild Horse *Dee Clark* (Chelsea)	16	19	20	–
43 Imagine *John Lennon* (Apple)	25	6	6	6
– You Sexy Thing *Hot Chocolate* (RAK)	38	10	3	2
48 Sky High *Jigsaw* (Splash)	26	14	10	9
45 Right Back Where We Started From *Maxine Nightingale* (UA)	30	16	14	8
– Bohemian Rhapsody *Queen* (EMI)	47	17	9	1
– This Old Heart Of Mine *Rod Stewart* (Riva)	–	27	8	7
– Money Honey *The Bay City Rollers* (Bell)	–	–	13	5
31 Darlin' *David Cassidy* (RCA)	33	22	16	18
– All Around My Hat *Steeleye Span* (Chrysalis)	–	42	17	12
– Why Did You Do It *Stretch* (Anchor)	48	30	19	20
– Na Na Is The Saddest Word *The Stylistics* (Avco)	–	43	25	15
– Let's Twist Again *John Asher* (Creole)	–	42	26	16
– In For A Penny *Slade* (Polydor)	–	–	27	19

DECEMBER 1975

6	13	20	27
1 Bohemian Rhapsody *Queen* (EMI)	1	1	1
2 You Sexy Thing *Hot Chocolate* (RAK)	2	4	7
3 Money Honey *The Bay City Rollers* (Bell)	4	12	15
4 This Old Heart Of Mine *Rod Stewart* (Riva)	7	14	–
5 All Around My Hat *Steeleye Span* (Chrysalis)	6	9	19
6 Na Na Is The Saddest Word *The Stylistics* (Avco)	5	7	8
7 D.I.V.O.R.C.E. *Billy Connolly* (Polydor)	18	–	–
8 Love Hurts *Jim Capaldi* (Island)	12	–	–
9 The Trail Of The Lonesome Pine *Laurel and Hardy* (UA)	3	2	3
10 Imagine *John Lennon* (Apple)	10	–	–
11 In For A Penny *Slade* (Polydor)	16	–	–
12 Sky High *Jigsaw* (Splash)	11	–	–
13 Right Back Where We Started From *Maxine Nightingale* (UA)	20	–	–
14 Let's Twist Again *Chubby Checker* (London)	9	6	5
15 Show Me You're A Woman *Mud* (Private Stock)	8	10	11
16 Why Did You Do It *Stretch* (Anchor)	19	–	–
17 Darlin' *David Cassidy* (RCA)	–	–	–
18 Let's Twist Again *John Asher* (Creole)	14	–	–
19 Happy To Be On An Island In The Sun *Demis Roussos* (Philips)	13	5	6
20 Space Oddity *David Bowie* (RCA)	–	–	–
24 Golden Years *David Bowie* (RCA)	15	8	9
40 I Believe In Father Christmas *Greg Lake* (Manticore)	16	3	2
36 Renta Santa *Chris Hill* (Philips)	22	11	10
43 Wide Eyed And Legless *Andy Fairweather Low* (A & M)	26	15	13
22 First Impressions *The Impressions* (Curtom)	23	16	–

6

			13	**20**	**27**
47	Christmas In Dreadland *Judge Dread* (Cactus)		24	17	14
–	It's Gonna Be A Cold Cold Christmas *Dana* (GTO)		48	18	4
32	Art For Art's Sake *10cc* (Mercury)		27	19	17
44	Glass Of Champagne *Sailor* (Epic)		32	20	18
50	If I Could *David Essex* (CBS)		25	21	16
–	Make A Daft Noise For Christmas *The Goodies* (Bradley's)		47	27	20
27	Can I Take You Home Little Girl *The Drifters* (Bell)		21	13	12

1975–BEST-SELLING SINGLES

1 Bye Bye Baby *The Bay City Rollers* (Bell)
2 Sailing *Rod Stewart* (Warner Bros.)
3 Can't Give You Anything (But My Love) *The Stylistics* (Avco)
4 Whispering Grass *Windsor Davies and Don Estelle* (EMI)
5 Stand By Your Man *Tammy Wynette* (Epic)
6 Give A Little Love *The Bay City Rollers* (Bell)
7 Hold Me Close *David Essex* (CBS)
8 The Last Farewell *Roger Whittaker* (EMI)
9 I Only Have Eyes For You *Art Garfunkel* (CBS)
10 Tears On My Pillow *Johnny Nash* (CBS)
11 I'm Not In Love *10cc* (Mercury)
12 Barbados *Typically Tropical* (Gull)
13 If *Telly Savalas* (MCA)
14 There Goes My First Love *The Drifters* (Bell)
15 Three Steps To Heaven *Showaddywaddy* (Bell)
16 The Hustle *Van McCoy* (Avco)
17 Space Oddity *David Bowie* (RCA)
18 January *Pilot* (EMI)
19 Funky Moped/Magic Roundabout *Jasper Carrott* (DJM)
20 Make Me Smile (Come Up And See Me) *Steve Harley and Cockney Rebel* (EMI)

1975–BEST-SELLING ALBUMS

1 Best Of The Stylistics *The Stylistics*
2 Once Upon A Star *The Bay City Rollers*
3 Atlantic Crossing *Rod Stewart*
4 Horizon *The Carpenters*
5 40 Golden Greats *Jim Reeves*
6 Elvis Presley's 40 Greatest Hits *Elvis Presley*
7 Tubular Bells *Mike Oldfield*
8 Elton John's Greatest Hits *Elton John*
9 Venus And Mars *Wings*
10 The Singles 1969–1973 *The Carpenters*
11 40 Greatest Hits *Perry Como*
12 Captain Fantastic And The Brown Dirt Cowboy *Elton John*
13 Simon And Garfunkel's Greatest Hits *Simon and Garfunkel*
14 20 Greatest Hits *Tom Jones*
15 His Greatest Hits *Engelbert Humperdinck*
16 Rollin' *The Bay City Rollers*
17 The Original Soundtrack *10cc*
18 Favourites *Peters and Lee*
19 The Dark Side Of The Moon *Pink Floyd*
20 Get Dancing *Various artists*

1975–BEST-SELLING ARTISTS

Male Artists (Singles)

1 David Essex
2 David Bowie
3 George McCrae
4 Rod Stewart
5 Hamilton Bohannon
6 Judge Dread
7 Elvis Presley
8 Gary Glitter
9 John Lennon
10 Barry White

Female Artists (Singles)

1 Tammy Wynette
2 Gloria Gaynor
3 Susan Cadogan
4 Billie Jo Spears
5 Dana
6 Minnie Riperton
7 Tammy Jones
8 Syreeta
9 Judy Collins
10 Linda Lewis

Groups (Singles)

1 Mud
2 The Stylistics
3 The Bay City Rollers
4 Kenny
5 Showaddywaddy
6 Hot Chocolate
7 The Goodies
8 Gladys Knight and The Pips
9 Mac and Katie Kissoon
10 10cc

Male Artists (Albums)

1 Elton John
2 Mike Oldfield
3 Perry Como
4 Barry White
5 David Essex
6 Rod Stewart
7 John Lennon
8 Engelbert Humperdinck
9 Neil Diamond
10 Cat Stevens

Female Artists (Albums)

1 Shirley Bassey
2 Tammy Wynette
3 Judy Collins
4 Helen Reddy
5 Gloria Gaynor
6 Diane Solomon
7 Minnie Riperton
8 Joni Mitchell
9 Linda Lewis
10 Olivia Newton-John

Groups (Albums)

1 The Bay City Rollers
2 The Carpenters
3 Simon and Garfunkel
4 The Stylistics
5 Pink Floyd
6 Paul McCartney and Wings
7 10cc
8 The Eagles
9 Peters and Lee
10 Mud

1976

Was it really that long ago when The Sex Pistols hit the headlines? In Top Twenty terms their time, amid extensive, hysterical media coverage, was the Jubilee year of 1977. However, in the lower regions of the industry's charts of 1976 they made a brief outing with 'Anarchy In The UK'. In the meantime, while punks gathered strength for their assault on the charts and record company executives subsequently reached for their cheque books, 1976 for the most part gave the impression of tranquility with a few pleasant differences from any other year.

Two Radio One disc jockeys, Dave Lee Travis and Paul Burnett, renamed themselves Laurie Lingo and The Dipsticks for the purpose of one record, and almost made Number One with their comedy version of C. W. McCall's 'Convoy'. The industry played its favourite game of trying to find a so-called 'teen' group and produced for a short period Our Kid and Slik. For fans of the 1960s and the Mersey Sound there was a Beatles revival and 'Yesterday' was released in Britain for the first time as a single. Another 1960s figure, Peter Frampton, made a comeback after his years with The Herd with 'Show Me The Way', but his success in Britain was relatively small compared with the enormity of fortune he met in America.

Cliff Richard struggled until suddenly in May he sparkled and ceased the sing-along medleys with which he had become associated. He sounded earthy and 'Devil Woman' gained him more appreciation, save perhaps from elderly ladies who had come to love his former somewhat bland performances. Manfred Mann came back with a Bruce Springsteen number, 'Blinded By The Light' and there was romance in the air when Dr Hook sang 'If Not You', Yvonne Elliman implored 'Love Me' and with real class Joan Armatrading sang of 'Love And Affection'.

Eurovision produced a British winner, Number One for Brotherhood of Man and a million seller in 'Save Your Kisses For Me'. There were smiles abounding from Guys and Dolls as 'You Don't Have To Say You Love Me' had a third very happy chart outing. The Four Seasons seem-

235

ingly consolidated their Top Twenty return, which had begun with 'Who Loves You' in 1975, by reaching the Number One position with 'December '63'.

There were suspicions about the lyrics of The Who's 'Squeeze Box' but the better informed said it was a tribute to a musical instrument, which was comforting.

Hank Mizell's 'Jungle Rock' did well but for the great mass of record buyers the most popular figures seemed to be Abba, The Drifters and Rod Stewart, although some were not too happy with the lyrics of Rod's 'The Killing Of Georgie'. The subject of homosexuality was to come in much more overt form in 1978, due to The Tom Robinson Band with 'Glad To Be Gay'.

The Liverpool Football Team performed as well on disc as they did on the field, as did such notables as Status Quo, Gladys Knight and The Pips, 10cc, Leo Sayer and Wings. There were even a number of singles from such album specialists as Steve Miller, The Eagles, War, Chicago, and The Sutherland Brothers and Quiver.

JANUARY 1976

10		17	24	31
1 Bohemian Rhapsody *Queen* (EMI)		1	1	3
2 The Trail Of The Lonesome Pine *Laurel and Hardy* (UA)		11	–	–
3 I Believe In Father Christmas *Greg Lake* (Manticore)		18	–	–
4 Glass Of Champagne *Sailor* (Epic)		2	2	5
5 Let's Twist Again/The Twist *Chubby Checker* (London)		6	17	–
6 Wide Eyed And Legless *Andy Fairweather Low* (A & M)		7	8	19
7 Art For Art's Sake *10cc* (Mercury)		5	11	15
8 Golden Years *David Bowie* (RCA)		12	19	–
9 It's Gonna Be A Cold Cold Christmas *Dana* (GTO)		14	–	–
10 Can I Take You Home Little Girl *The Drifters* (Bell)		19	15	–
11 Happy To Be On An Island In the Sun *Demis Roussos* (Philips)		10	–	–
12 Mama Mia *Abba* (Epic)		3	3	1
13 If I Could *David Essex* (CBS)		13	–	–
14 You Sexy Thing *Hot Chocolate* (RAK)		–	–	–
15 Money Honey *The Bay City Rollers* (Bell)		–	–	–
16 Christmas In Dreadland/Come Outside *Judge Dread* (Cactus)		–	–	–
17 Na Na Is The Saddest Word *The Stylistics* (Avco)		–	–	–
18 King Of The Cops *Billy Howard* (Penny Farthing)		8	6	9
19 First Impressions *The Impressions* (Curtom)		–	–	–
20 Show Me You're A Woman *Mud* (Private Stock)		–	–	–
21 In Dulce Jubilo/On Horseback *Mike Oldfield* (Virgin)		4	4	8
23 Itchycoo Park *The Small Faces* (Immediate)		9	13	13
28 Let The Music Play *Barry White* (20th Century)		15	9	11
45 Love Machine *The Miracles* (Tamla Motown)		16	5	4
43 We Do It *R. & J. Stone* (RCA)		17	7	7
24 Do The Bus Stop *The Fatback Band* (Polydor)		20	18	–
30 Midnight Rider *Paul Davidson* (Tropical)		25	10	12
– Forever And Ever *Slik* (Bell)		39	12	2

236

10		**17**	**24**	**31**
46 Evil Woman *The Electric Light Orchestra* (Jet)		27	14	10
– Love To Love You Baby *Donna Summer* (GTO)		37	16	6
– Answer Me *Barbara Dickson* (RSO)		41	22	14
– Walk Away Love *David Ruffin* (Tamla Motown)		42	29	16
– Sunshine Day *Osibisa* (Bronze)		46	23	17
– No Regrets *The Walker Brothers* (GTO)		33	26	20
31 Milkyway *Sheer Elegance* (Pye)		22	20	18

FEBRUARY 1976

7	**14**	**21**	**28**
1 Mama Mia *Abba* (Epic)	2	5	13
2 Forever And Ever *Slik* (Bell)	1	2	5
3 Love Machine *The Miracles* (Tamla Motown)	4	8	14
4 Love To Love You Baby *Donna Summer* (GTO)	5	6	12
5 We Do It *R. & J. Stone* (RCA)	6	9	17
6 Bohemian Rhapsody *Queen* (EMI)	16	–	–
7 Glass Of Champagne *Sailor* (Epic)	–	–	–
8 December '63 *The Four Seasons* (Warner Bros.)	3	1	1
9 King Of The Cops *Billy Howard* (Penny Farthing)	20	–	–
10 In Dulce Jubilo/On Horseback *Mike Oldfield* (Virgin)	–	–	–
11 Evil Woman *The Electric Light Orchestra* (Jet)	11	–	–
12 Midnight Rider *Paul Davidson* (Tropical)	13	–	–
13 No Regrets *The Walker Brothers* (GTO)	7	11	8
14 Itchycoo Park *The Small Faces* (Immediate)	14	–	–
15 Moonlight Seranade/Little Brown Jug/In The Mood *Glen Miller* (RCA)	17	13	15
16 Let The Music Play *Barry White* (20th Century)	–	–	–
17 Answer Me *Barbara Dickson* (RSO)	9	–	–
18 Walk Away From Love *David Ruffin* (Tamla Motown)	10	16	–
19 Milkyway *Sheer Elegance* (Pye)	–	–	–
20 Low Rider *War* (Island)	15	12	16
21 Rodrigo's Guitar Concerto *Manuel and The Music of the Mountains* (EMI)	8	4	3
23 Baby Face *Wing and A Prayer Fife and Drum Corps* (Atlantic)	12	19	–
22 Sunshine Day *Osibisa* (Bronze)	18	–	–
26 Squeeze Box *The Who* (Polydor)	19	15	10
48 I Love To Love *Tina Charles* (CBS)	23	3	2
– Convoy *C. W. McCall* (MGM)	41	7	4
46 Dat *Pluto Shervington* (Opal)	29	10	7
29 It Should Have Been Me *Yvonne Fair* (Tamla Motown)	21	14	6
– Rain *Status Quo* (Vertigo)	36	17	9
45 Let's Call It Quits *Slade* (Polydor)	25	18	11
31 I Love Music *The O'Jays* (Philadelphia)	30	20	–
– Funky Weekend *The Stylistics* (Avco)	44	22	18
30 Something's Been Making Me Blue *Smokie* (RAK)	27	21	19
– Love Really Hurts Without You *Billy Ocean* (GTO)	–	34	20

MARCH 1976

6	**13**	**20**	**27**
1 I Love To Love *Tina Charles* (CBS)	1	1	3
2 December '63 *The Four Seasons* (Warner Bros.)	2	9	17
3 Convoy *C. W. McCall* (MGM)	3	2	8
4 Rodrigo's Guitar Concerto *Manuel and The Music of the Mountains* (EMI)	5	14	–
5 It Should Have Been Me *Yvonne Fair* (Tamla Motown)	6	10	–
6 Dat *Pluto Shervington* (Opal)	11	16	–
7 Rain *Status Quo* (Vertigo)	8	15	–
8 Love Really Hurts Without You *Billy Ocean* (GTO)	4	3	2

6   13   20   27

	13	20	27
9 Forever And Ever *Slik* (Bell)	–	–	–
10 Funky Weekend *The Stylistics* (Avco)	13	13	–
11 Squeeze Box *The Who* (Polydor)	17	20	–
12 You Don't Have To Say You Love Me *Guys and Dolls* (Magnet)	9	5	6
13 I Love Music *The O'Jays* (Philadelphia)	18	19	–
14 Let's Call It Quits *Slade* (Polydor)	–	–	–
15 (Do) The Spanish Hustle *The Fatback Band* (Polydor)	10	11	14
16 People Like You And People Like Me *The Glitter Band* (Bell)	7	7	5
17 Something's Been Making Me Blue *Smokie* (RAK)	–	–	–
18 Moonlight Serenade/Little Brown Jug/In The Mood *Glenn Miller* (RCA)			
19 Miss You Nights *Cliff Richard* (EMI)	16	18	15
20 Low Rider *War* (Island)	–	–	–
22 I Wanna Stay With You *Gallagher and Lyle* (A & M)	12	8	7
27 Falling Apart At The Seams *The Marmalade* (Target)	19	12	9
25 Let's Do The Latin Hustle *Eddie Drennon and BBS Unlimited* (Pye)	20	26	20
– Save Your Kisses For Me *Brotherhood of Man* (Pye)	14	4	1
43 You See The Trouble With Me *Barry White* (20th Century)	15	6	4
– Yesterday *The Beatles* (Apple)	41	17	10
40 Concrete And Clay *Randy Edelman* (20th Century)	25	22	11
44 Take It To The Limit *The Eagles* (Asylum)	27	25	12
– Music *John Miles* (Decca)	–	44	13
26 Let's Do The Latin Hustle *M. and O. Band* (Creole)	21	24	16
– I'm Mandy Fly Me *10cc* (Mercury)	–	31	18
– Hello Happiness *The Drifters* (Bell)	46	28	19

APRIL 1976

3   10   17   24

	10	17	24
1 Save Your Kisses For Me *Brotherhood of Man* (Pye)	1	1	1
2 You See The Trouble With Me *Barry White* (20th Century)	2	4	9
3 Love Really Hurts Without You *Billy Ocean* (GTO)	5	19	–
4 Music *John Miles* (Decca)	3	3	3
5 I Love To Love *Tina Charles* (CBS)	–	–	–
6 I Wanna Stay With You *Gallagher and Lyle* (A & M)	13	15	–
7 Pinball Wizard *Elton John* (DJM)	8	10	15
8 Yesterday *The Beatles* (Apple)	9	13	18
9 Falling Apart At The Seams *The Marmalade* (Target)	11	14	–
10 People Like You And People Like Me *The Glitter Band* (Bell)	15	–	–
11 I'm Mandy Fly Me *10cc* (Mercury)	6	6	6
12 Hello Happiness *The Drifters* (Bell)	12	16	16
13 Take It To The Limit *The Eagles* (Asylum)	17	–	–
14 Fernando *Abba* (Epic)	4	2	2
15 You Don't Have To Say You Love Me *Guys and Dolls* (Magnet)	–	–	–
16 Hey Mr Music Man *Peters and Lee* (Philips)	–	–	–
17 Concrete And Clay *Randy Edelman* (20th Century)	16	–	–
18 Jungle Rock *Hank Mizell* (Charley)	7	5	4
19 Convoy *C. W. McCall* (MGM)	–	–	–
20 Don't Stop It Now *Hot Chocolate* (RAK)	19	11	13
25 Do You Know Where You're Going To *Diana Ross* (Tamla Motown)	10	7	5
21 Girls Girls Girls *Sailor* (Epic)	14	9	7
22 Hey Jude *The Beatles* (Apple)	18	12	12
– Love Me Like I Love You *The Bay City Rollers* (Bell)	20	8	8
33 Disco Connection *Isaac Hayes Movement* (ABC)	25	17	14
– S-S-S-Single Bed *Fox* (GTO)	41	18	11
42 Life Is Too Short *Sheer Elegance* (Pye)	29	20	17
45 Get Up And Boogie *Silver Convention* (Magnet)	26	21	10

3

	10	17	24
– Convoy GB *Laurie Lingo and The Dipsticks* (State)	–	50	19
– All By Myself *Eric Carmen* (Arista)	46	26	20

MAY 1976

1

	8	15	22	29
1 Save Your Kisses For Me *Brotherhood of Man* (Pye)	2	2	8	16
2 Fernando *Abba* (Epic)	1	1	1	1
3 Jungle Rock *Hank Mizell* (Charley)	3	3	9	13
4 Love Me Like I Love You *The Bay City Rollers* (Bell)	17	–	–	–
5 S-S-S-Single Bed *Fox* (GTO)	5	4	10	15
6 Do You Know Where You're Going To *Diana Ross* (Tamla Motown)	8	–	–	–
7 Girls Girls Girls *Sailor* (Epic)	13	–	–	–
8 I'm Mandy Fly Me *10cc* (Mercury)	–	–	–	–
9 Get Up And Boogie *Silver Convention* (Magnet)	7	8	12	19
10 Disco Connection *Isaac Hayes Movement* (ABC)	10	18	–	–
11 Music *John Miles* (Decca)	15	–	–	–
12 Life Is Too Short Girl *Sheer Elegance* (Pye)	9	12	20	–
13 All By Myself *Eric Carmen* (Arista)	12	19	–	–
14 Convoy GB *Laurie Lingo and The Dipsticks* (State)	4	7	13	–
15 Don't Stop It Now *Hot Chocolate* (RAK)	–	–	–	–
16 Silver Star *The Four Seasons* (Warner Bros.)	6	9	3	–
17 More More More *Andrea True Connection* (Buddah)	18	5	6	5
18 Hey Jude *The Beatles* (Apple)	–	–	–	–
19 Arms Of Mary *The Sutherland Brothers and Quiver* (CBS)	16	6	5	6
20 Can't Help Falling In Love *The Stylistics* (Avco)	14	10	4	14
22 Fallen Angel *Frankie Valli* (Private Stock)	11	13	18	–
24 Love Hangover *Diana Ross* (Tamla Motown)	19	15	15	10
28 Let Your Love Flow *The Bellamy Brothers* (Warner Bros.)	20	17	17	9
35 No Charge *J. J. Barrie* (Power Exchange)	26	11	2	2
43 Fool To Cry *The Rolling Stones* (Rolling Stones)	22	14	7	8
32 I'm Your Puppet *James and Bobby Purify* (Mercury)	27	16	19	12
29 Reggae Like It Used To Be *Paul Nicholas* (RSO)	23	20	26	17
– My Resistance Is Low *Robin Sarstedt* (Decca)	46	22	11	4
– Combine Harvester (Brand New Key) *The Wurzels* (EMI)	–	33	14	3
– Silly Love Songs *Wings* (Parlophone)	–	29	16	7
– Midnight Train To Georgia *Gladys Knight and The Pips* (Buddah)	48	30	24	18
– This Is It *Melba Moore* (Buddah)	–	41	29	20
– Devil Woman *Cliff Richard* (EMI)	41	24	21	11

JUNE 1976

5

	12	19	26
1 No Charge *J. J. Barrie* (Power Exchange)	3	5	14
2 Combine Harvester (Brand New Key) *The Wurzels* (EMI)	1	1	2
3 My Resistance Is Low *Robin Sarstedt* (Decca)	6	9	–
4 Fernando *Abba* (Epic)	4	18	–
5 Silly Love Songs *Wings* (Parlophone)	2	3	3
6 Fool To Cry *The Rolling Stones* (Rolling Stones)	7	12	–
7 Let Your Love Flow *The Bellamy Brothers* (Warner Bros.)	8	11	19
8 Arms Of Mary *The Sutherland Brothers and Quiver* (CBS)	10	–	–
9 Devil Woman *Cliff Richard* (EMI)	12	15	–
10 Midnight Train To Georgia *Gladys Knight and The Pips* (Buddah)	11	16	–
11 Love Hangover *Diana Ross* (Tamla Motown)	14	–	–
12 Shake It Down *Mud* (Private Stock)	22	13	–
13 I'm Your Puppet *James and Bobby Purify* (Mercury)	18	–	–
14 More More More *Andrea True Connection* (Buddah)	20	–	–

5	**12**	**19**	**26**
15 Show Me The Way *Peter Frampton* (A & M)	16	10	12
16 Silver Star *The Four Seasons* (Warner Bros.)	–	–	–
17 Can't Help Falling In Love *The Stylistics* (Avco)	17	7	9
18 Jolene *Dolly Parton* (RCA)	19	6	8
19 Heart On My Sleeve *Gallagher and Lyle* (A & M)	–	–	–
20 Save Your Kisses For Me *Brotherhood of Man* (Pye)	5	2	1
22 You To Me Are Everything *The Real Thing* (Pye)	13	8	5
42 Tonight's The Night *Rod Stewart* (Riva)	15	4	4
29 You Just Might See Me Cry *Our Kid* (Polydor)	9	14	17
21 This Is It *Melba Moore* (Buddah)	24	17	10
37 The Boys Are Back In Town *Thin Lizzy* (Vertigo)	26	19	6
34 Young Hearts Run Free *Candi Staton* (Warner Bros.)	34	20	7
– Let's Stick Together *Bryan Ferry* (Island)	43	21	11
48 Leader Of The Pack *The Shangri-Las* (Charley/Contempo)	21	22	13
24 Soul City Walk *Archie Bell and The Drells* (Philadelphia)	28	23	15
38 You're My Everything *Lee Garrett* (Chrysalis)	27	25	16
31 The Wanderer *Dion* (Philips)	–	43	18
– Kiss And Say Goodbye *The Manhattans* (CBS)	32	24	20
45 The Continental *Maureen McGovern* (20th Century)			

JULY 1976

3	**10**	**17**	**24**	**31**
1 You To Me Are Everything *The Real Thing* (Pye)	1	6	7	17
2 You Just Might See Me Cry *Our Kid* (Polydor)	4	9	14	–
3 Young Hearts Run Free *Candi Staton* (Warner Bros.)	2	4	4	6
4 Let's Stick Together *Bryan Ferry* (Island)	5	8	10	16
5 Tonight's The Night *Rod Stewart* (Riva)	8	12	16	–
6 Heart On My Sleeve *Gallagher and Lyle* (A & M)	14	18	–	–
7 Leader Of The Pack *The Shangri-Las* (Charley/Contempo)	10	11	17	–
8 The Boys Are Back In Town *Thin Lizzy* (Vertigo)	12	15	–	–
9 Combine Harvester (Brand New Key) *The Wurzels* (EMI)	–	–	–	–
10 Silly Love Songs *Wings* (Parlophone)	11	–	–	–
11 Kiss And Say Goodbye *The Manhattans* (CBS)	6	5	5	4
12 The Roussos Phenomenon *Demis Roussos* (Philips)	3	1	3	3
13 Jolene *Dolly Parton* (RCA)	17	–	–	–
14 A Little Bit More *Dr Hook* (Capitol)	7	3	2	2
15 Show Me The Way *Peter Frampton* (A & M)	–	–	–	–
16 The Continental *Maureen McGovern* (20th Century)	–	–	–	–
17 I Love To Boogie *T. Rex* (EMI)	18	13	20	20
18 You're My Everything *Lee Garrett* (Chrysalis)	–	–	–	–
19 Misty Blue *Dorothy Moore* (Contempo)	13	10	6	7
20 Soul City Walk *Archie Bell and The Drells* (Philadelphia)	–	–	–	–
49 Don't Go Breaking My Heart *Elton John and Kiki Dee* (Rocket)	9	2	1	1
24 You're My Best Friend *Queen* (EMI)	15	7	8	10
21 You Are My Love *Liverpool Express* (Warner Bros.)	19	16	11	11
26 It Only Takes A Minute *One Hundred Ton and A Feather* (UK)	20	14	9	9
29 Man To Man *Hot Chocolate* (RAK)	22	17	15	14
27 I Recall A Gypsy Woman *Don Williams* (ABC)	28	20	–	13
– Heaven Must Be Missing An Angel *Tavares* (Capitol)	39	23	12	5
46 Good Vibrations *The Beach Boys* (Capitol)	31	35	18	–
– Back In The USSR *The Beatles* (Parlophone)	35	29	19	19
– Jeans On *David Dundas* (Air)	–	–	25	8
– Harvest For The World *The Isley Brothers* (Epic)	37	27	23	12
– Mystery Song *Status Quo* (Vertigo)	48	34	27	18
– Now Is The Time *Jimmy James and The Vagabonds* (Pye)	–	48	21	15
23 The Boston Tea Party *Sensational Alex Harvey Band* (Mountain)	16	19	13	–

AUGUST 1976

7	14	21	28
1 Don't Go Breaking My Heart *Elton John and Kiki Dee* (Rocket)	1	1	1
2 A Little Bit More *Dr Hook* (Capitol)	2	2	3
3 Jeans On *David Dundas* (Air)	3	3	4
4 The Roussos Phenomenon *Demis Roussos* (Philips)	6	16	20
5 Misty Blue *Dorothy Moore* (Contempo)	9	12	19
6 Heaven Must Be Missing An Angel *Tavares* (Capitol)	4	6	7
7 Kiss And Say Goodbye *The Manhattans* (CBS)	12	–	–
8 Now Is The Time *Jimmy James and The Vagabonds* (Pye)	5	7	10
9 Young Hearts Run Free *Candi Staton* (Warner Bros.)	19	–	–
10 Harvest For The World *The Isley Brothers* (Epic)	14	15	–
11 In Zaire *Johnny Wakelin* (Pye)	7	4	5
12 Dr Kiss Kiss *5000 Volts* (Philips)	8	8	8
13 It Only Takes A Minute *One Hundred Ton and A Feather* (UK)	–	–	–
14 You Are My Love *Liverpool Express* (Warner Bros.)	18	–	–
15 Mystery Song *Status Quo* (Vertigo)	11	13	17
16 You're My Best Friend *Queen* (EMI)	–	–	–
17 The Boston Tea Party *Sensational Alex Harvey Band* (Mountain)	–	–	–
18 Man To Man *Hot Chocolate* (RAK)	–	–	–
19 Love On Delivery *Billy Ocean* (GTO)	20	20	–
20 You Should Be Dancing *The Bee Gees* (RSO)	10	9	6
28 Let 'Em In *Wings* (Parlophone)	13	5	2
40 Extended Play *Bryan Ferry* (Island)	15	14	14
24 Here Comes The Sun *Steve Harley and Cockney Rebel* (EMI)	16	10	15
32 You Don't Have To Go *The Chi-Lites* (Brunswick)	17	17	9
23 What I've Got In Mind *Billie Jo Spears* (UA)	22	11	13
34 You'll Never Find Another Love Like Mine *Lou Rawls* (Philadelphia)	21	18	11
43 16 Bars *The Stylistics* (H & L)	27	19	12
– Dancing Queen *Abba* (Epic)	–	23	16
– The Killing Of Georgie *Rod Stewart* (Riva)	–	22	18

SEPTEMBER 1976

4	11	18	25
1 Dancing Queen *Abba* (Epic)	1	1	1
2 Let 'Em In *Wings* (Parlophone)	2	6	13
3 Don't Go Breaking My Heart *Elton John and Kiki Dee* (Rocket)	4	14	–
4 What I've Got In Mind *Billie Jo Spears* (UA)	9	16	–
5 A Little Bit More *Dr Hook* (Capitol)	12	–	–
6 In Zaire *Johnny Wakelin* (Pye)	18	–	–
7 Extended Play *Bryan Ferry* (Island)	11	17	–
8 The Killing Of Georgie *Rod Stewart* (Riva)	6	2	8
9 You Don't Have To Go *The Chi-Lites* (Brunswick)	3	8	12
10 Jeans On *David Dundas* (Air)	–	–	–
11 16 Bars *The Stylistics* (H & L)	7	7	14
12 You'll Never Find Another Love Like Mine *Lou Rawls* (Philadelphia)	10	–	–
13 You Should Be Dancing *The Bee Gees* (RSO)	5	–	20
14 Dr Kiss Kiss *5000 Volts* (Philips)	16	–	–
15 Here Comes The Sun *Steve Harley and Cockney Rebel* (EMI)	–	–	–
16 (Light Of Experience) Doina De Jale *Gheorghe Zamfir* (Epic)	8	4	10
17 Nice And Slow *Jesse Green* (EMI)	33	20	–

	11	18	25
18 Afternoon Delight *The Starland Vocal Band* (RCA)	–	–	–
19 Heaven Must Be Missing An Angel *Tavares* (Capitol)	–	–	–
20 Now Is The Time *Jimmy James and The Vagabonds* (Pye)	–	–	–
37 Can't Get By Without You *The Real Thing* (Pye)	13	3	2
26 Blinded By The Light *Manfred Mann's Earthband* (Bronze)	14	11	6
21 Baby We Better Try To Get It Together *Barry White* (20th Century)	15	15	16
22 Aria *Acker Bilk* (Pye)	17	5	7
24 Here I Go Again *Twiggy* (Mercury)	19	19	18
– I Am A Cider Drinker *The Wurzels* (EMI)	23	9	3
– I Only Wanna Be With You *The Bay City Rollers* (Bell)	25	10	4
29 Mississippi *Pussycat* (Sonet)	21	12	5
50 Sailing *Rod Stewart* (Warner Bros.)	36	23	11
27 Dance Little Lady Dance *Tina Charles* (CBS)	22	13	9
– Loving And Free *Kiki Dee* (Rocket)	45	26	15
– Disco Duck *Rick Dees and his Cast of Idiots* (RSO)	–	34	19
20 I Can't Ask For Any More Than You *Cliff Richard* (EMI)	–	–	21

OCTOBER 1976

	9	16	23	30
1 Dancing Queen *Abba* (Epic)	1	2	6	8
2 Can't Get By Without You *The Real Thing* (Pye)	3	7	11	19
3 Mississippi *Pussycat* (Sonet)	2	1	1	1
4 I Am A Cider Drinker *The Wurzels* (EMI)	5	16	–	–
5 I Only Wanna Be With You *The Bay City Rollers* (Bell)	7	12	16	–
6 Dance Little Lady Dance *Tina Charles* (CBS)	8	8	17	–
7 Sailing *Rod Stewart* (Warner Bros.)	4	3	3	10
8 Aria *Acker Bilk* (Pye)	10	17	–	–
9 Blinded By The Light *Manfred Mann's Earthband* (Bronze)	9	20	–	–
10 Disco Duck *Rick Dees and his Cast of Idiots* (RSO)	6	6	10	13
11 The Killing Of Georgie *Rod Stewart* (Riva)	16	–	–	–
12 (Light Of Experience) Doina De Jale *Gheorghe Zamfir* (Epic)	17	–	–	–
13 Girl Of My Best Friend *Elvis Presley* (RCA)	11	9	13	12
14 Loving And Free *Kiki Dee* (Rocket)	13	15	18	–
15 16 Bars *The Stylistics* (H & L)	–	–	–	–
16 The Best Disco In Town *The Ritchie Family* (Polydor)	12	10	14	14
17 Here I Go Again *Twiggy* (Mercury)	19	–	–	–
18 Let 'Em In *Wings* (Parlophone)	–	–	–	–
19 Baby We Better Try To Get It Together *Barry White* (20th Century)	–	–	–	–
23 I Can't Ask For Any More Than You *Cliff Richard* (EMI)		20	18	17
22 Howzat *Sherbet* (Epic)	14	4	8	4
35 When Forever Has Gone *Demis Roussos* (Philips)	15	5	2	2
36 I'll Meet You At Midnight *Smokie* (RAK)	18	19	11	11
40 Hurt *The Manhattans* (CBS)	20	11	5	5
– Summer Of My Life *Simon May* (Pye)	39	13	7	7
– If You Leave Me Now *Chicago* (CBS)	38	14	4	3
– Don't Take Away The Music *Tavares* (Capitol)	23	18	9	6
– Dancing With The Captain *Paul Nicholas* (RSO)	49	24	15	9
32 Rubber Band Man *The Detroit Spinners* (Atlantic)	24	22	19	16
– Play That Funky Music *Wild Cherry* (Epic)	34	22	20	15
– Couldn't Get It Right *Climax Blues Band* (BTM)	47	28	22	17
– Jaws *Lalo Schifrin* (CTI)	46	36	23	18
– Love And Affection *Joan Armatrading* (A & M)	–	39	26	20

Two records occupied Number 11 on 23 October, an unusual occurrence that two records should tie in the BMRB listings.

6		13	20	27
1 Mississippi *Pussycat* (Sonet)		2	4	6
2 If You Leave Me Now *Chicago* (CBS)		1	1	1
3 When Forever Has Gone *Demis Roussos* (Philips)		5	11	–
4 Hurt *The Manhattans* (CBS)		6	6	19
5 Don't Take Away The Music *Tavares* (Capitol)		4	8	12
6 Howzat *Sherbert* (Epic)		8	18	–
7 Summer Of My Life *Simon May* (Pye)		9	16	–
8 Dancing With The Captain *Paul Nicholas* (RSO)		12	14	–
9 Sailing *Rod Stewart* (Warner Bros.)		18	–	–
10 Play That Funky Music *Wild Cherry* (Epic)		7	9	7
11 Couldn't Get It Right *Climax Blues Band* (BTM)		11	10	17
12 I'll Meet You At Midnight *Smokie* (RAK)		–	–	–
13 Dancing Queen *Abba* (Epic)		20	–	–
14 Jaws *Lalo Schifrin* (CTI)		15	17	–
15 Substitute *The Who* (Polydor)		16	7	18
16 You Make Me Feel Like Dancing *Leo Sayer* (Chrysalis)		3	2	3
17 Girl Of My Best Friend *Elvis Presley* (RCA)		–	–	–
18 Rubber Band Man *The Detroit Spinners* (Atlantic)		17	–	–
19 Love And Affection *Joan Armatrading* (A & M)		10	12	16
20 If Not You *Dr Hook* (Capitol)		14	5	5
23 Beautiful Noise *Neil Diamond* (CBS)		13	13	14
36 Under The Moon Of Love *Showaddywaddy* (Bell)		19	3	2
29 Lost In France *Bonnie Tyler* (RCA)		22	15	9
28 Rock'n Me *The Steve Miller Band* (Mercury)		24	19	11
43 Love Me *Yvonne Elliman* (RSO)		27	20	8
– Somebody To Love *Queen* (EMI)		–	–	4
– Money Money Money *Abba* (Epic)		–	34	10
– Livin' Thing *The Electric Light Orchestra* (Jet)		49	23	13
– Get Back *Rod Stewart* (Riva)		–	47	15
45 So Sad The Song *Gladys Knight and The Pips* (Buddah)		32	35	20

4		11	18	25
1 Under The Moon Of Love *Showaddywaddy* (Bell)		1	1	2
2 If You Leave Me Now *Chicago* (CBS)		4	8	16
3 You Make Me Feel Like Dancing *Leo Sayer* (Chrysalis)		6	10	–
4 Somebody To Love *Queen* (EMI)		2	3	4
5 Livin' Thing *The Electric Light Orchestra* (Jet)		5	4	6
6 Money Money Money *Abba* (Epic)		3	5	3
7 Love Me *Yvonne Elliman* (RSO)		7	6	7
8 If Not You *Dr Hook* (Capitol)		9	–	–
9 Lost In France *Bonnie Tyler* (RCA)		10	15	–
10 Mississippi *Pussycat* (Sonet)		20	–	–
11 Sorry Seems To Be The Hardest Word *Elton John* (Rocket)		13	17	–
12 Get Back *Rod Stewart* (Riva)		11	13	18
13 Rock'n Me *The Steve Miller Band* (Mercury)		15	–	–
14 When A Child Is Born *Johnny Mathis* (CBS)		8	2	1
15 Beautiful Noise *Neil Diamond* (CBS)		–	–	–
16 Lean On Me *Mud* (Private Stock)		14	7	12
17 Don't Make Me Wait Too Long *Barry White* (20th Century)		17	–	–
18 Couldn't Get It Right *Climax Blues Band* (BTM)		–	–	–
19 Substitute *The Who* (Polydor)		–	–	–
20 Play That Funky Music *Wild Cherry* (Epic)		–	–	–
25 Stop Me (If You've Heard It All Before) *Billy Ocean* (GTO)		12	16	20
26 Portsmouth *Mike Oldfield* (Virgin)		16	9	5
22 Little Does She Know *The Kursaal Flyers* (CBS)		18	14	14
23 Fairy Tale *Dana* (GTO)		19	–	13

	11	18	25
43 Bionic Santa *Chris Hill* (Philips)	28	11	10
46 Dr Love *Tina Charles* (CBS)	24	18	8
– Wild Side Of Life *Status Quo* (Vertigo)	32	19	17
48 Grandma's Party *Paul Nicholas* (RSO)	27	20	15
38 Living Next Door To Alice *Smokie* (RAK)	21	12	9
– Don't Give Up On Us *David Soul* (Private Stock)	–	37	11
– Things We Do For Love *10cc* (Mercury)	37	27	19

1976–BEST-SELLING SINGLES

1 Save Your Kisses For Me *Brotherhood of Man* (Pye)
2 Don't Go Breaking My Heart *Elton John and Kiki Dee* (Rocket)
3 Mississippi *Pussycat* (Sonet)
4 Dancing Queen *Abba* (Epic)
5 A Little Bit More *Dr Hook* (Capitol)
6 If You Leave Me Now *Chicago* (CBS)
7 Fernando *Abba* (Epic)
8 I Love To Love *Tina Charles* (CBS)
9 The Roussos Phenomenon *Demis Roussos* (Philips)
10 December '63 *The Four Seasons* (Warner Bros.)
11 Under The Moon Of Love *Showaddywaddy* (Bell)
12 You To Me Are Everything *The Real Thing* (Pye)
13 Forever And Ever *Slik* (Bell)
14 Sailing *Rod Stewart* (Warner Bros.)
15 Young Hearts Run Free *Candi Staton* (Warner Bros.)
16 Combine Harvester (Brand New Key) *The Wurzels* (EMI)
17 When Forever Has Gone *Demis Roussos* (Philips)
18 Jungle Rock *Hank Mizell* (Charley)
19 Can't Get By Without You *The Real Thing* (Pye)
20 You Make Me Feel Like Dancing *Leo Sayer* (Chrysalis)

1976–BEST-SELLING ALBUMS

1 Greatest Hits *Abba*
2 20 Golden Greats *The Beach Boys*
3 Forever And Ever *Demis Roussos*
4 Wings At The Speed Of Sound *Wings*
5 A Night On The Town *Rod Stewart*
6 Live In London *John Denver*
7 Laughter And Tears *Neil Sedaka*
8 Their Greatest Hits 1971–1975 *The Eagles*
9 20 Golden Greats *Glen Campbell*
10 Very Best Of Slim Whitman *Slim Whitman*
11 Best Of Roy Orbison *Roy Orbison*
12 A Night At The Opera *Queen*
13 Desire *Bob Dylan*
14 Greatest Hits Vol. 2 *Diana Ross*
15 Instrumental Gold *Various artists*
16 Frampton Comes Alive *Peter Frampton*
17 Changesonebowie *David Bowie*
18 Rock Follies *Rock Follies*
19 How Dare You *10cc*
20 The Best Of Gladys Knight And The Pips *Gladys Knight and The Pips*

1976–BEST-SELLING ARTISTS

Male Artists (Singles)

1 Rod Stewart
2 Demis Roussos
3 Barry White
4 Billy Ocean
5 Bryan Ferry
6 Paul Nicholas
7 Hank Mizell
8 Elton John
9 Elvis Presley
10 Mike Oldfield

Female Artists (Singles)

1 Tina Charles
2 Diana Ross
3 Candi Staton
4 Dana
5 Dorothy Moore
6 Donna Summer
7 Billie Jo Spears
8 Yvonne Fair
9 Dolly Parton
10 Yvonne Elliman

Groups (Singles)

1 Abba
2 The Stylistics
3 Dr Hook
4 Tavares
5 The Beatles
6 Queen
7 The Real Thing
8 Wings
9 The Manhattans
10 Brotherhood of Man

Male Artists (Albums)

1 Demis Roussos
2 John Denver
3 Mike Oldfield
4 David Bowie
5 Peter Frampton
6 Neil Sedaka
7 Elton John
8 Neil Diamond
9 Roy Orbison
10 Bob Dylan

Female Artists (Albums)

1 Diana Ross
2 Nana Mouskouri
3 Helen Reddy
4 Joan Armatrading
5 Pam Ayres
6 Shirley Bassey
7 Donna Summer
8 Emmylou Harris
9 Joni Mitchell
10 Linda Ronstadt

Groups (Albums)

1 Abba
2 Queen
3 The Eagles
4 Wings
5 Gladys Knight and The Pips
6 The Stylistics
7 The Beach Boys
8 Thin Lizzy
9 10cc
10 Pink Floyd

1977

Did punk and new wave really stem from figures such as Lou Reed, Iggy Pop and The New York Dolls? Whatever the case, 1977 saw the emergence of endless hitherto unknown groups, record companies and record labels. Discs appeared in coloured vinyl and special picture covers and there was the buying phenomenon of the 12-inch single. The year would certainly have seemed to belong to The Sex Pistols. They were signed up by both EMI and A & M and subsequently parted company, until finally coming home to roost with Virgin. After the enormous amount of controversy and media coverage afforded to the band, it was hardly surprising that the public tired of hearing of them and little more was heard of The Sex Pistols the following year until a reformed group, without Johnny Rotten, crashed into the Top Ten during July. For all the influence punk and new wave had on the general record scene, in strict Top Twenty terms it made little impression. When the year's points were allotted to compile a top 50 singles list, no new wave bands were prominent, which proves how distorting even a Top Twenty can be.

Although The Sex Pistols made 1977 the year for their 'God Save The Queen', 'Pretty Vacant' and 'Holiday In The Sun', a quite different artist constantly featuring in the charts was Donna Summer. With records on both the Casablanca and GTO labels, she consistently reached the top of the charts with the frequency of a Presley or Richard of old. Sadly Elvis died and so triggered a flurry of re-releases and successes with new titles. Alas the Top Twenty does not indicate how he monopolised the Top Fifty for many weeks. Many groups, particularly new ones, must have bewailed a situation where valuable chart positions were taken by The King, but the secret of his success lay in his nickname.

However, new artists with definite promise of a long future did appear, among which were The Boomtown Rats, Heatwave, The Stranglers, and Deniece Williams, but some such as Mr Big, Racing Cars and Patsy Gallant, who showed great potential, did not fulfil their promise.

Elkie Brooks, although hardly a newcomer to the music scene, arrived in the charts with a flourish with 'Pearl's A Singer', whilst Rod Stewart, Showaddywaddy, Hot Chocolate (who finally reached the milestone of a Number One with 'So You Win Again'), Status Quo, Leo Sayer, Thin Lizzy and David Soul were still firm favourites. Abba of course did well, and from Paul McCartney and Wings came 'Mull Of Kintyre', the biggest selling British single ever, with some two million sales. It was a remarkable achievement.

The 1977 Top Twenty listings did not hold many surprises apart from perhaps the appearance in the charts of The Muppets. There were few classic singles in the charts but Darts, a group with enormous potential, and Boney M., a band which took many people by surprise with their sales consistency, both appeared in the limelight. At long last Nazareth put their world hit version of the old classic 'Love Hurts' into the British listings.

Re-releases from Roxy Music and Deep Purple attracted interest, while The Detroit Emeralds bounced back with a re-recording of 'Feel The Need'. Legendary names such as Yes, Bob Marley and Boz Scaggs, who had previously only attracted minimal attention in terms of the Top Twenty, appeared in the charts. Carly Simon fulfilled her promise of the early part of the 1970s by coming back strongly with 'Nobody Does It Better'.

Some of the hitherto consistently successful artists found life getting harder. Elton John was one, David Essex another, and where were The Wombles, Linda Lewis, The Bellamy Brothers, Tammy Wynette, Emmylou Harris, Gilbert O'Sullivan and R. and J. Stone? However, some of the veterans of the music business continued to enter the Top Twenty, and these included Bryan Ferry, The Jacksons, Barbra Streisand, Stevie Wonder, Marvin Gaye, Cliff Richard, 10cc and The Bee Gees, who were to enjoy such a huge measure of success in 1978.

JANUARY 1977

8	**15**	**22**	**29**
1 When A Child Is Born *Johnny Mathis* (CBS)	2	13	–
2 Under The Moon Of Love *Showaddywaddy* (Bell)	4	12	11
3 Portsmouth *Mike Oldfield* (Virgin)	9	7	19
4 Money Money Money *Abba* (Epic)	3	8	17
5 Living Next Door To Alice *Smokie* (RAK)	10	10	14
6 Somebody To Love *Queen* (EMI)	13	–	–
7 Dr Love *Tina Charles* (CBS)	8	4	12
8 Don't Give Up On Us *David Soul* (Private Stock)	1	1	1
9 Grandma's Party *Paul Nicholas* (RSO)	12	14	16
10 Lean On Me *Mud* (Private Stock)	17	–	–
11 Bionic Santa *Chris Hill* (Philips)	20	–	–
12 Things We Do For Love *10cc* (Mercury)	6	6	7
13 Wild Side Of Life *Status Quo* (Vertigo)	11	9	9
14 Fairy Tale *Dana* (GTO)	15	19	–
15 Livin' Thing *The Electric Orchestra* (Jet)	19	–	–
16 Little Does She Know *The Kursaal Flyers* (CBS)	16	–	–
17 I Wish *Stevie Wonder* (Tamla Motown)	14	5	6
18 Love Me *Yvonne Elliman* (RSO)	–	–	–
19 You Make Me Feel Like Dancing *Leo Sayer* (Chrysalis)	–	–	–
20 Side Show *Barry Biggs* (Dynamic)	5	3	3
25 Don't Cry For Me Argentina *Julie Covington* (MCA)	7	2	2
22 You're More Than A Number In My Little Red Book *The Drifters* (Arista)	18	11	5
– Isn't She Lovely *David Parton* (Pye)	35	15	4
27 Car Wash *Rose Royce* (MCA)	21	16	10
26 Haitian Divorce *Steely Dan* (ABC)	27	17	–
– Daddy Cool *Boney M.* (Atlantic)	23	18	8
– Suspicion *Elvis Presley* (RCA)	24	20	13
– When I Need You *Leo Sayer* (Chrysalis)	–	–	15
– Don't Believe A Word *Thin Lizzy* (Vertigo)	38	21	18
29 Every Man Must Have A Dream *Liverpool Express* (Warner Bros.)	25	24	20

FEBRUARY 1977

5	**12**	**19**	**26**
1 Don't Give Up On Us *David Soul* (Private Stock)	2	3	3
2 Don't Cry For Me Argentina *Julie Covington* (MCA)	1	2	2
3 Side Show *Barry Biggs* (Dynamic)	4	4	9
4 Isn't She Lovely *David Parton* (Pye)	5	5	14
5 When I Need You *Leo Sayer* (Chrysalis)	3	1	1
6 Daddy Cool *Boney M.* (Atlantic)	7	9	13
7 You're More Than A Number In My Little Red Book *The Drifters* (Arista)	11	14	–
8 Things We Do For Love *10cc* (Mercury)	15	–	–
9 Suspicion *Elvis Presley* (RCA)	10	10	19
10 Car Wash *Rose Royce* (MCA)	9	13	15
11 Wild Side Of Life *Status Quo* (Vertigo)	12	–	–
12 Don't Believe A Word *Thin Lizzy* (Vertigo)	13	15	–
13 I Wish *Stevie Wonder* (Tamla Motown)	14	–	–
14 Don't Leave Me This Way *Harold Melvin and The Bluenotes* (Philadelphia)	6	7	5
15 Dr Love *Tina Charles* (CBS)	–	–	–
16 Jack In The Box *The Moments* (All Platinum)	8	8	7
17 Grandma's Party *Paul Nicholas* (RSO)	–	–	–
18 Portsmouth *Mike Oldfield* (Virgin)	–	–	–
19 Boogie Nights *Heatwave* (GTO)	16	6	4
20 New Kid In Town *The Eagles* (Asylum)	20	–	–

5		12	19	26
23 Every Man Must Have A Dream *Liverpool Express* (Asylum)		17	20	–
40 Chanson D'Amour *Manhattan Transfer* (Atlantic)		18	12	6
21 Sing Me *The Brothers* (Bus Stop)		19	11	8
– Romeo *Mr Big* (EMI)		30	16	11
50 This Is Tomorrow *Bryan Ferry* (Polydor)		21	17	10
38 Don't Leave Me This Way *Thelma Houston* (Tamla Motown)		24	18	–
27 What Can I Say *Boz Scaggs* (CBS)		22	19	12
– They Shoot Horses Don't They *Racing Cars* (Chrysalis)		33	21	16
– Baby I Know *The Rubettes* (State)		43	22	17
– Torn Between Two Lovers *Mary MacGregor* (Ariola)		–	38	18
– Sound And Vision *David Bowie* (RCA)		–	46	20

MARCH 1977

5		12	19	26
1 When I Need You *Leo Sayer* (Chrysalis)		2	7	11
2 Boogie Nights *Heatwave* (GTO)		3	3	7
3 Chanson D'Amour *Manhattan Transfer* (Atlantic)		1	1	1
4 Romeo *Mr Big* (EMI)		5	4	9
5 Don't Cry For Me Argentina *Julie Covington* (MCA)		8	12	–
6 Don't Give Up On Us *David Soul* (Private Stock)		14	–	–
7 Don't Leave Me This Way *Harold Melvin and The Bluenotes* (Philadelphia)		10	19	–
8 Sing Me *The Brothers* (Bus Stop)		13	16	–
9 Jack In The Box *The Moments* (All Platinum)		16	–	–
10 What Can I Say *Boz Scaggs* (CBS)		12	11	–
11 This Is Tomorrow *Bryan Ferry* (Polydor)		9	13	17
12 Torn Between Two Lovers *Mary MacGregor* (Ariola)		4	8	6
13 Don't Leave Me This Way *Thelma Houston* (Tamla Motown)		17	15	–
14 They Shoot Horses Don't They *Racing Cars* (Chrysalis)		18	18	–
15 Sound And Vision *David Bowie* (RCA)		6	5	3
16 Side Show *Barry Biggs* (Dynamic)		–	–	–
17 Baby I Know *The Rubettes* (State)		11	10	12
18 Knowing Me Knowing You *Abba* (Epic)		7	2	2
19 Isn't She Lovely *David Parton* (Pye)		–	–	–
20 Rockaria *The Electric Light Orchestra* (Jet)		15	9	10
50 When *Showaddywaddy* (Arista)		19	6	4
25 You'll Never Know What You're Missing *The Real Thing* (Pye)		20	–	16
40 Moody Blue *Elvis Presley* (RCA)		22	14	8
22 Saturday Nite *Earth Wind and Fire* (CBS)		21	17	19
45 My Kinda Life *Cliff Richard* (EMI)		38	20	–
– Going In With My Eyes Open *David Soul* (Private Stock)		–	–	5
– I Don't Want To Put A Hold On You *Bernie Flint* (EMI)		–	29	14
– Sunny *Boney M.* (Atlantic)		48	22	15
30 Another Suitcase In Another Hall *Barbara Dickson* (MCA)		23	28	18
– Red Light Spells Danger *Billy Ocean* (GTO)		–	48	20
37 Oh Boy *Brotherhood of Man* (Pye)		30	26	13

APRIL 1977

2		9	16	23	30
1 Knowing Me Knowing You *Abba* (Epic)		1	1	1	1
2 Going In With My Eyes Open *David Soul* (Private Stock)		2	2	5	8
3 Chanson D'Amour *Manhattan Transfer* (Atlantic)		5	11	17	–
4 When *Showaddywaddy* (Arista)		3	4	6	18
5 Sound And Vision *David Bowie* (RCA)		4	9	11	–
6 Moody Blue *Elvis Presley* (RCA)		7	7	–	–
7 Sunny *Boney M.* (Atlantic)		9	3	8	10
8 I Don't Want To Put A Hold On You *Bernie Flint* (EMI)		6	5	3	5

249

2		9	16	23	30
9	Torn Between Two Lovers *Mary MacGregor* (Ariola)	13	19	–	–
10	Boogie Nights *Heatwave* (GTO)	16	–	–	–
11	Oh Boy *Brotherhood of Man* (Pye)	10	8	12	11
12	Love Hit Me *Maxine Nightingale* (UA)	11	13	–	–
13	Red Light Spells Danger *Billy Ocean* (GTO)	8	6	2	2
14	Rockaria *The Electric Light Orchestra* (Jet)	–	–	–	–
15	Romeo *Mr Big* (EMI)	–	–	–	–
16	My Kinda Life *Cliff Richard* (EMI)	15	18	–	–
17	Baby I Know *The Rubettes* (Polydor)	17	–	–	–
18	Lay Back In The Arms Of Someone *Smokie* (RAK)	14	12	13	16
19	Another Suitcase In Another Hall *Barbara Dickson* (MCA)	–	–	–	–
20	Saturday Nite *Earth Wind and Fire* (CBS)	–	–	–	–
23	You Don't Have To Be A Star *Marilyn McCoo and Billy Davis* (ABC)	12	10	10	7
24	Gimme Some *Brendon* (Magnet)	18	14	14	15
34	Have I The Right *Dead End Kids* (CBS)	19	16	7	6
35	Free *Deniece Williams* (CBS)	20	15	4	3
–	Sir Duke *Stevie Wonder* (Tamla Motown)	39	17	9	4
43	Pearl's A Singer *Elkie Brooks* (A & M)	24	20	16	9
–	Whodunit *Tavares* (Capitol)	35	25	15	12
–	How Much Love *Leo Sayer* (Chrysalis)	44	26	18	20
29	Rock Bottom *Lynsey de Paul and Mike Moran* (Polydor)	21	23	19	–
42	Lonely Boy *Andrew Gold* (Asylum)	27	22	20	19
–	I Don't Want To Talk About It/First Cut Is The Deepest *Rod Stewart* (Riva)	–	–	48	13
47	I Wanna Get Next To You *Rose Royce* (MCA)	33	21	26	14
–	Solsbury Hill *Peter Gabriel* (Charisma)	41	29	23	17

MAY 1977

7		14	21	28
1	Free *Deniece Williams* (CBS)	1	2	7
2	Sir Duke *Stevie Wonder* (Tamla Motown)	3	8	11
3	Red Light Spells Danger *Billy Ocean* (GTO)	13	17	–
4	I Don't Want To Talk About It/First Cut Is The Deepest *Rod Stewart* (Riva)	2	1	1
5	Whodunit *Tavares* (Capitol)	5	7	12
6	Have I The Right *Dead End Kids* (CBS)	7	14	–
7	Knowing Me Knowing You *Abba* (Epic)	12	–	–
8	Pearl's A Singer *Elkie Brooks* (A & M)	10	18	–
9	I Don't Want To Put A Hold On You *Bernie Flint* (EMI)	20	–	–
10	How Much Love *Leo Sayer* (Chrysalis)	17	16	–
11	Lonely Boy *Andrew Gold* (Asylum)	18	15	–
12	Ain't Gonna Bump No More *Joe Tex* (Epic)	4	3	2
13	The Shuffle *Van McCoy* (H & L)	6	4	6
14	You Don't Have To Be A Star *Marilyn McCoo and Billy Davis* (ABC)	–	–	–
15	Hotel California *The Eagles* (Asylum)	8	9	10
16	Solsbury Hill *Peter Gabriel* (Charisma)	14	13	14
17	Gimme Some *Brendon* (Magnet)	–	–	–
18	Oh Boy *Brotherhood of Man* (Pye)	–	–	–
19	A Star Is Born (Evergreen) *Barbra Streisand* (CBS)	11	6	3
20	Lay Back In The Arms Of Someone *Smokie* (RAK)	–	–	–
24	Good Morning Judge *10cc* (Mercury)	9	10	5
23	Mah Na Mah Na *Piero Umiliani* (EMI International)	15	11	8
22	Lucille *Kenny Rogers* (UA)	16	5	4
28	I Wanna Get Next To You *Rose Royce* (MCA)	19	–	–
32	Got To Give It Up *Marvin Gaye* (Tamla Motown)	25	12	9
39	Too Hot To Handle/Slip Your Disc To This *Heatwave* (GTO)	29	19	–
–	Lido Shuffle *Boz Scaggs* (CBS)	41	20	17

7	14	21	28
– O.K. *Rock Follies* (Polydor)	–	48	13
– We Can Do It *Liverpool Football Team* (State)	–	–	15
42 It's A Game *The Bay City Rollers* (Arista)	24	21	16
– Disco Inferno *Trammps* (Atlantic)	37	23	18
35 Gonna Capture Your Heart *Blue* (Rocket)	27	24	19
– Tokyo Joe *Bryan Ferry* (Polydor)	49	29	20

JUNE 1977

4	11	18	25
1 I Don't Want To Talk About It/First Cut Is The Deepest *Rod Stewart* (Riva)	1	2	5
2 Lucille *Kenny Rogers* (UA)	3	1	2
3 Ain't Gonna Bump No More *Joe Tex* (Epic)	5	9	13
4 A Star Is Born (Evergreen) *Barbra Streisand* (CBS)	4	5	4
5 The Shuffle *Van McCoy* (H & L)	8	10	15
6 Good Morning Judge *10cc* (Mercury)	9	11	19
7 Got To Give It Up *Marvin Gaye* (Tamla Motown)	11	12	14
8 Halfway Down The Stairs *The Muppets* (Pye)	10	7	11
9 Mah Na Mah Na *Piero Umiliani* (EMI International)	20	–	–
10 O.K. *Rock Follies* (Polydor)	12	18	–
11 God Save The Queen *The Sex Pistols* (Virgin)	2	4	9
12 Hotel California *The Eagles* (Asylum)	–	–	–
13 Lido Shuffle *Boz Scaggs* (CBS)	14	13	17
14 Spot The Pigeon *Genesis* (Chrysalis)	22	16	–
15 Too Hot To Handle/Slip Your Disc To This *Heatwave* (GTO)	17	15	18
16 We Can Do It *Liverpool Football Team* (State)	19	–	–
17 You're Moving Out Today *Carole Bayer Sager* (Elektra)	7	6	6
18 Telephone Line *The Electric Light Orchestra* (Jet)	13	8	10
19 Free *Deniece Williams* (CBS)	–	–	–
20 Whodunit *Tavares* (Capitol)	–	–	–
23 Show You The Way To Go *The Jacksons* (Epic)	6	3	1
26 Tokyo Joe *Bryan Ferry* (Polydor)	15	–	–
25 Disco Inferno *Trammps* (Atlantic)	16	–	–
28 Gonna Capture Your Heart *Blue* (Rocket)	18	–	–
22 Baby Don't Change Your Mind *Gladys Knight and The Pips* (Buddah)	21	14	7
48 Fanfare For The Common Man *Emerson Lake and Palmer* (Atlantic)	25	17	8
27 Peaches/Go Buddy Go *The Stranglers* (UA)	23	19	16
– Sam *Olivia Newton-John* (EMI)	33	23	12
– So You Win Again *Hot Chocolate* (RAK)	–	20	3
46 You're Gonna To Get Next To Me *Bo Kirkland and Ruth Davis* (EMI International)	26	22	20

JULY 1977

2	9	16	23	30
1 So You Win Again *Hot Chocolate* (RAK)	1	1	2	5
2 Show You The Way To Go *The Jacksons* (Epic)	2	6	12	–
3 Fanfare For The Common Man *Emerson Lake and Palmer* (Atlantic)	3	2	4	3
4 Lucille *Kenny Rogers* (UA)	7	18	–	–
5 Baby Don't Change Your Mind *Gladys Knight and The Pips* (Buddah)	4	5	6	7
6 You're Moving Out Today *Carole Bayer Sager* (Elektra)	9	13	–	–
7 A Star Is Born (Evergreen) *Barbra Streisand* (CBS)	10	16	18	–
8 Telephone Line *The Electric Light Orchestra* (Jet)	13	20	–	–
9 Sam *Olivia Newton-John* (EMI)	6	8	8	13

2		9	16	23	30
10	Peaches/Go Buddy Go *The Stranglers* (UA)	8	9	11	19
11	Halfway Down The Stairs *The Muppets/Jerry Nelson* (Pye)	16	–	–	–
12	God Save The Queen *The Sex Pistols* (Virgin)	19	–	–	–
13	I Don't Want To Talk About It/First Cut Is The Deepest *Rod Stewart* (Riva)	–	–	–	–
14	Ma Baker *Boney M.* (Atlantic)	5	4	3	2
15	Lido Shuffle *Boz Scaggs* (CBS)	–	–	–	–
16	You're Gonna Get Next To Me *Bo Kirkland and Ruth Davis* (EMI International)	12	14	15	–
17	Good Old Fashioned Loverboy *Queen* (EMI)	–	19	17	–
18	Too Hot To Handle/Slip Your Disc To This *Heatwave* (GTO)	17	–	–	–
19	Spot The Pigeon *Genesis* (Charisma)				
20	Oh Lori *Alessi* (A & M)	14	11	9	8
21	Do What You Wanna Do *T. Connection* (TK)	11	15	13	–
–	I Feel Love *Donna Summer* (GTO)	15	3	1	1
24	Slow Down *John Miles* (Decca)	18	17	10	11
22	Feel The Need *The Detroit Emeralds* (Atlantic)	20	12	14	12
–	Pretty Vacant *The Sex Pistols* (Virgin)	45	7	7	6
–	Angelo *Brotherhood of Man* (Pye)	25	10	5	4
40	One Step Away *Tavares* (Capitol)	22	25	16	17
38	We're All Alone *Rita Coolidge* (A & M)	30	24	19	9
43	Easy *The Commodores* (Tamla Motown)	28	21	20	10
26	Exodus *Bob Marley and The Wailers* (Island)	23	22	27	14
–	You Got What It Takes *Showaddywaddy* (Arista)	–	–	50	15
–	Float On *The Floaters* (ABC)	–	–	38	16
–	It's Your Life *Smokie* (RAK)	–	44	24	18
–	The Crunch *The Rah Band* (Good Earth)	49	32	21	20

AUGUST 1977

6		13	20	27
1	I Feel Love *Donna Summer* (GTO)	1	3	5
2	Angelo *Brotherhood of Man* (Pye)	2	1	2
3	Ma Baker *Boney M.* (Atlantic)	5	7	11
4	So You Win Again *Hot Chocolate* (RAK)	15	16	–
5	Fanfare For The Common Man *Emerson Lake and Palmer* (Atlantic)	8	19	–
6	We're All Alone *Rita Coolidge* (A & M)	6	8	7
7	It's Your Life *Smokie* (RAK)	10	5	13
8	Pretty Vacant *The Sex Pistols* (Virgin)	12	–	–
9	You Got What It Takes *Showaddywaddy* (Arista)	3	2	3
10	Oh Lori *Alessi* (A & M)	14	17	–
11	Easy *The Commodores* (Tamla Motown)	9	11	15
12	Slow Down *John Miles* (Decca)	20	–	–
13	The Crunch *The Rah Band* (Good Earth)	7	6	6
14	Float On *The Floaters* (ABC)	4	4	1
15	Something Better Change/Straighten Out *The Stranglers* (UA)	13	9	12
16	Feel The Need *The Detroit Emeralds* (Atlantic)	16	18	20
17	One Step Away *Tavares* (Capitol)	–	–	–
18	Sam *Olivia Newton-John* (EMI)	–	–	–
19	Exodus *Bob Marley and The Wailers* (Island)	18	20	–
20	All Around The World *The Jam* (Polydor)	23	13	18
24	Roadrunner Once Roadrunner Twice *Jonathan Richman* (Beserkley)	11	12	14
26	Nights On Broadway *Candi Staton* (Warner Bros.)	17	15	9
30	That's What Friends Are For *Deniece Williams* (CBS)	19	10	8
43	Nobody Does It Better *Carly Simon* (Elecktra)	21	14	10
–	Way Down *Elvis Presley* (RCA)	46	42	4

6

		13	20	27
–	Magic Fly *Space* (Pye)	48	27	16
44	Tulane *The Steve Gibbons Band* (Polydor)	28	22	17
–	Do Anything You Wanna Do *The Rods* (Island)	39	29	19

SEPTEMBER 1977

3

		10	17	24
1	Way Down *Elvis Presley* (RCA)	1	1	1
2	Float On *The Floaters* (ABC)	3	6	15
3	Angelo *Brotherhood of Man* (Pye)	6	9	19
4	You Got What It Takes *Showaddywaddy* (Arista)	12	16	–
5	Magic Fly *Space* (Pye)	2	2	2
6	Nights On Broadway *Candi Staton* (Warner Bros.)	7	8	12
7	The Crunch *The Rah Band* (Good Earth)	13	17	–
8	That's What Friends Are For *Deniece Williams* (CBS)	9	11	10
9	Nobody Does It Better *Carly Simon* (Elektra)	10	7	7
10	Silver Lady *David Soul* (Private Stock)	8	3	3
11	I Feel Love *Donna Summer* (GTO)	–	–	–
12	Oxygene *Jean Michel Jarre* (Polydor)	4	4	4
13	Tulane *The Steve Gibbons Band* (Polydor)	15	12	–
14	Down Deep Inside *Donna Summer* (Casablanca)	5	5	5
15	Dancin' In The Moonlight *Thin Lizzy* (Vertigo)	14	15	17
16	We're All Alone *Rita Coolidge* (A & M)	18	–	–
17	Something Better Change/Straighten Out *The Stranglers* (UA)	–	–	–
18	All Around The World *The Jam* (Polydor)	–	–	–
19	Ma Baker *Boney M.* (Atlantic)	–	–	–
20	It's Your Life *Smokie* (RAK)	–	–	–
24	Do Anything You Wanna Do *The Rods* (Island)	11	20	9
26	Telephone Man *Meri Wilson* (Pye)	16	10	6
27	Gary Gilmour's Eyes *The Adverts* (Anchor)	19	25	18
21	Spanish Stroll *Mink DeVille* (Capitol)	20	–	–
–	Best Of My Love *The Emotions* (CBS)	27	14	8
25	Sunshine After The Rain *Elkie Brooks* (A & M)	21	18	–
23	Think I'm Gonna Fall In Love With You *The Dooleys* (GTO)	22	19	–
–	Wonderous Stories *Yes* (Atlantic)	–	31	13
–	Black Is Black *La Belle Epoque* (Harvest)	30	27	14
–	From New York To LA *Patsy Gallant* (EMI)	42	26	16
29	I Can't Get You Outa My Mind *Yvonne Elliman* (RSO)	23	21	20
28	Looking After Number One *The Boomtown Rats* (Ensign)	17	13	11

OCTOBER 1977

1

		8	15	22	29
1	Way Down *Elvis Presley* (RCA)	2	6	10	19
2	Silver Lady *David Soul* (Private Stock)	1	1	1	4
3	Magic Fly *Space* (Pye)	5	11	–	–
4	Oxygene *Jean Michel Jarre* (Polydor)	11	18	–	–
5	Down Deep Inside *Donna Summer* (Casablanca)	10	15	–	–
6	Telephone Man *Meri Wilson* (Pye)	9	10	17	–
7	Best Of My Love *The Emotions* (CBS)	4	5	6	14
8	Black Is Black *La Belle Epoque* (Harvest)	3	2	2	2
9	From New York To LA *Patsy Gallant* (EMI)	6	8	12	–
10	Sunshine After The Rain *Elkie Brooks* (A & M)	12	20	–	–
11	I Remember Elvis Presley *Danny Mirror* (Sonet)	8	4	5	9
12	Nobody Does It Better *Carly Simon* (Elektra)	20	–	–	–
13	Think I'm Gonna Fall In Love With You *The Dooleys* (GTO)	19	–	–	–
14	Looking After Number One *The Boomtown Rats* (Ensign)	15	–	–	–
15	Do Anything You Wanna Do *The Rods* (Island)	18	–	–	–

253

1		8	15	22	29
16 Wondrous Stories *Yes* (Atlantic)		7	14	13	18
17 I Can't Get You Outa My Mind *Yvonne Elliman* (RSO)		–	19	19	–
18 Black Betty *Ram Jam* (Epic)		16	12	9	7
19 Nights On Broadway *Candi Staton* (Warner Bros.)		–	–	–	–
20 No More Heroes *The Stranglers* (UA)		13	9	8	12
24 Yes Sir I Can Boogie *Baccara* (RCA)		14	3	3	1
21 I Remember Yesterday *Donna Summer* (GTO)		17	16	14	16
– You're In My Heart *Rod Stewart* (Riva)		–	7	4	3
44 Star Wars Theme *Meco* (RCA)		24	13	7	10
– Rockin' All Over The World *Status Quo* (Vertigo)		32	17	11	6
– Holiday In The Sun *The Sex Pistols* (Virgin)		–	–	15	8
30 From Here To Eternity *Giorgio* (Oasis)		25	21	16	–
– Calling Occupants Of Interplanetary Craft *The Carpenters* (A & M)		49	25	18	11
– Name Of The Game *Abba* (Epic)		–	–	20	5
– We Are The Champions *Queen* (EMI)		–	–	30	13
– 2.4.6.8. Motorway *The Tom Robinson Band* (EMI)		–	–	37	15
– Virginia Plain *Roxy Music* (Polydor)		–	–	29	20
– Needles And Pins *Smokie* (RAK)		–	48	22	17

NOVEMBER 1977

5		12	19	26
1 Name Of The Game *Abba* (Epic)		1	1	1
2 Yes Sir I Can Boogie *Baccara* (RCA)		2	4	9
3 You're In My Heart *Rod Stewart* (Riva)		3	6	12
4 Black Is Black *La Belle Epoque* (Harvest)		7	12	–
5 Rockin' All Over The World *Status Quo* (Vertigo)		4	3	3
6 We Are The Champions *Queen* (EMI)		6	2	2
7 Silver Lady *David Soul* (Private Stock)		15	–	–
8 2.4.6.8. Motorway *The Tom Robinson Band* (EMI)		5	5	8
9 Holiday In The Sun *The Sex Pistols* (Virgin)		13	17	–
10 Calling Occupants Of Interplanetary Craft *The Carpenters* (A & M)		9	10	16
11 Black Betty *Ram Jam* (Epic)		8	19	–
12 Star Wars Theme *Meco* (RCA)		20	–	–
13 Needles And Pins *Smokie* (RAK)		10	11	15
14 No More Heroes *The Stranglers* (UA)		–	–	–
15 Virginia Plain *Roxy Music* (Polydor)		11	13	19
16 I Remember Elvis Presley *Danny Mirror* (Sonet)		–	–	–
17 From Here To Eternity *Giorgio* (Oasis)		19	18	–
18 Wondrous Stories *Yes* (Atlantic)		–	–	–
19 I Remember Yesterday *Donna Summer* (GTO)		–	–	–
20 Love Hurts Etc *Nazareth* (Mountain)		16	15	20
22 How Deep Is Your Love *The Bee Gees* (RSO)		12	9	6
23 Live In Trouble *The Barron Knights* (Epic)		14	7	10
41 Dancin' Party *Showaddywaddy* (Arista)		17	8	4
25 She's Not There *Santana* (CBS)		18	16	11
37 Daddy Cool *Darts* (Magnet)		21	14	7
21 I Believe You *Dorothy Moore* (Epic)		23	20	–
– Mull Of Kintyre/Girls School *Wings* (EMI)		–	48	5
– Floral Dance *The Brighouse and Rastrick Band* (Transatlantic)		50	30	13
45 I Will *Ruby Winters* (Creole)		29	22	14
42 Egyptian Reggae *Jonathan Richman and The Modern Lovers* (Beserkley)		31	23	18
34 Belfast *Boney M.* (Atlantic)		22	21	17

3		10	17	24
1	Mull Of Kintyre *Wings* (EMI)	1	1	1
2	We Are The Champions *Queen* (EMI)	7	10	–
3	Rockin' All Over The World *Status Quo* (Vertigo)	8	11	–
4	Name Of The Game *Abba* (Epic)	11	18	–
5	How Deep Is Your Love *The Bee Gees* (RSO)	3	3	3
6	Dancin' Party *Showaddywaddy* (Arista)	4	7	12
7	Daddy Cool *Darts* (Magnet)	6	6	8
8	I Will *Ruby Winters* (Creole)	5	4	4
9	Floral Dance *The Brighouse and Rastrick Brass Band* (Transatlantic)	2	2	2
10	Live In Trouble *The Barron Knights* (Epic)	17	–	–
11	Egyptian Reggae *Jonathan Richman and The Modern Lovers* (Beserkley)	9	5	9
12	2.4.6.8. Motorway *The Tom Robinson Band* (EMI)	–	–	–
13	Yes Sir I Can Boogie *Baccara* (RCA)	–	–	–
14	She's Not There *Santana* (CBS)	14	–	–
15	You're In My Heart *Rod Stewart* (Riva)	–	–	–
16	Needles And Pins *Smokie* (RAK)	–	–	–
17	Calling Occupants Of Interplanetary Craft *The Carpenters* (A & M)	–	–	15
18	Watchin' The Detectives *Elvis Costello* (Stiff)	20	16	15
19	Belfast *Boney M.* (Atlantic)	10	8	11
20	Mary Of The Fourth Form *The Boomtown Rats* (Ensign)	15	15	16
23	Put Your Love In Me *Hot Chocolate* (RAK)	12	17	10
37	Love's Unkind *Donna Summer* (GTO)	16	13	6
22	Turn To Stone *The Electric Light Orchestra* (Jet)	18	21	20
34	It's A Heartache *Bonnie Tyler* (RCA)	19	14	7
48	White Christmas *Bing Crosby* (MCA)	25	12	5
–	My Way *Elvis Presley* (RCA)	26	19	14
29	Don't It Make My Brown Eyes Blue *Crystal Gayle* (UA)	21	20	18
25	Dance Dance Dance *Chic* (Atlantic)	22	22	19
–	Let's Have A Quiet Night In *David Soul* (Private Stock)	–	31	17
21	Love Of My Life *The Dooleys* (GTO)	13	9	13

1977–BEST-SELLING SINGLES

1. Don't Give Up On Us *David Soul* (Private Stock)
2. Don't Cry For Me Argentina *Julie Covington* (MCA)
3. When I Need You *Leo Sayer* (Chrysalis)
4. Silver Lady *David Soul* (Private Stock)
5. Knowing Me Knowing You *Abba* (Epic)
6. I Feel Love *Donna Summer* (GTO)
7. Way Down *Elvis Presley* (RCA)
8. So You Win Again *Hot Chocolate* (RAK)
9. Angelo *Brotherhood of Man* (Pye)
10. Chanson D'Amour *Manhattan Transfer* (Atlantic)
11. Yes Sir I Can Boogie *Baccara* (RCA)
12. Black Is Black *La Belle Epoque* (Harvest)
13. Mull Of Kintyre *Wings* (EMI)
14. Fanfare For The Common Man *Emerson Lake and Palmer* (Atlantic)
15. Ma Baker *Boney M.* (Atlantic)
16. A Star Is Born (Evergreen) *Barbra Streisand* (CBS)
17. Name Of The Game *Abba* (Epic)
18. Lucille *Kenny Rogers* (UA)
19. Rockin' All Over The World *Status Quo* (Vertigo)
20. Magic Fly *Space* (Pye)

The above compilation by Music Week *(*BMRB*) covered the period 1 January–10 December.*

1977–BEST-SELLING ALBUMS

1. Arrival *Abba*
2. 20 Golden Greats *The Shadows*
3. 20 Golden Greats *Diana Ross and The Supremes*
4. Rumours *Fleetwood Mac*
5. A Star Is Born *Soundtrack of film*
6. The Sound Of Bread *Bread*
7. Disco Fever *Various artists*
8. Hotel California *The Eagles*
9. Greatest Hits *Abba*
10. Endless Flight *Leo Sayer*
11. The Johnny Mathis Collection *Johnny Mathis*
12. Animals *Pink Floyd*
13. Never Mind The Bollocks *The Sex Pistols*
14. Portrait Of Sinatra *Frank Sinatra*
15. Going For The One *Yes*
16. A New World Record *The Electric Light Orchestra*
17. 20 All-Time Greats *Connie Francis*
18. Songs In The Key Of Life *Stevie Wonder*
19. Oxygene *Jean Michel Jarre*
20. Stranglers IV *The Stranglers*

1977–BEST-SELLING ARTISTS

Male Artists (Singles)

1 David Soul
2 Elvis Presley
3 Rod Stewart
4 Leo Sayer
5 Stevie Wonder
6 Barry Biggs
7 Boz Scaggs
8 David Bowie
9 Kenny Rogers
10 Van McCoy

Female Artists (Singles)

1 Donna Summer
2 Deniece Williams
3 Barbra Streisand
4 Julie Covington
5 Elkie Brooks
6 Yvonne Elliman
7 Rita Coolidge
8 Carly Simon
9 Tina Charles
10 Olivia Newton-John

Groups (Singles)

1 Boney M.
2 Showaddywaddy
3 Abba
4 Smokie
5 The Electric Light Orchestra
6 The Stranglers
7 Brotherhood of Man
8 Queen
9 The Sex Pistols
10 Status Quo

Male Artists (Albums)

1 Elvis Presley
2 Leo Sayer
3 Rod Stewart
4 David Soul
5 Stevie Wonder
6 Johnny Mathis
7 David Bowie
8 Neil Diamond
9 Slim Whitman
10 Cliff Richard

Female Artists (Albums)

1 Donna Summer
2 Connie Francis
3 Joan Armatrading
4 Elkie Brooks
5 Lena Martell
6 Linda Ronstadt
7 Deniece Williams
8 Barbra Streisand
9 Emmylou Harris
10 Petula Clark

Groups (Albums)

1 Abba
2 The Eagles
3 Pink Floyd
4 Fleetwood Mac
5 The Stranglers
6 The Electric Light Orchestra
7 The Shadows
8 Queen
9 Bob Marley and The Wailers
10 Yes

1978

Kate Bush, with her shaggy red hair, pink trousers, red socks and high-heeled shoes, was 1978's first singles sensation with 'Wuthering Heights', before the familiar faces made their presence felt. Abba starred in their own film, reached the top of the album listings with 'Abba – The Album', and did very well in the singles charts with 'Take A Chance On Me'. Darts strengthened their 1977 position with 'Come Back My Love', and showed another side of their musical character as they quickly moved towards the top during May with an excellent single 'Boy From New York City'. Most mysterious was the late-selling and entry into the charts of the Christmas-flavoured 'If I Had Words' from Scott Fitzgerald and Yvonne Keeley. Reggae hit the top with two fun Jamaican girls, Althia and Donna, and for once no one scored strings and watered down the song for the benefit of supposed white audiences. Blondie's presence with 'Denis' (the old Randy and The Rainbows American hit of 1964) cheered many, not in the least because it realised endless magazine, pop paper and television coverage of the group's leading lady, Debbie Harry.

Disco music continued unabated in chart influence during the first half of the year, while the Eurovision Song Contest provided Britain's entrants CoCo with a British Top Twenty chart entry which gave them some comfort after being placed low down in the Eurovision voting after many thought they were firm favourites.

Most deserving of praise was Patti Smith finding herself a hit single with 'Because The Night', a song co-written with Bruce Springsteen. Some feel that one of the greatest injustices ever perpetrated by the record-buying public was the non-appearance in the charts several years previously of Springsteen's masterpiece 'Born To Run'. 'Because The Night' at least gave the east coast of America a slice of British chart action.

The Stranglers found themselves in the charts once more, after an amazing run of hits in 1977, and by contrast Brian and Michael enjoyed success with 'Matchstalk Men And Matchstalk Cats And Dogs', which illustrates the point that singles buying covers a wide range of the public these days. The Bee Gees reigned supreme, both with their own records and with writing hits for others such as Yvonne Elliman, Samantha Sang, Andy Gibb and Tavares.

By May there were some amazing things taking place on the record manufacturing front. Outstripping all previous levels of demand for the 45 records in WEA history came the disc 'Rivers Of Babylon' by Boney M. British presses could not keep up with customer demand, as eight British plants tried to cope and the company finally had to go to Holland for further pressing. A 12-inch version was pressed late in the day so that more of the firm's West Drayton presses could continue operating. The shipping figure by the second week of May was 700,000, with 150,000 orders on extend. In Germany the figure was one million, and in France 500,000. Also causing manufacturing problems was The Bee Gees single, 'Night Fever', and this record was pressed outside Britain to keep up with demand. By June Boney M. were past the million mark.

More million sellers followed. 1978 was indeed the year when singles came back with a bang with total sales by the year's end hovering around an amazing figure of 100 million. That was a third more than the previous year and certainly far ahead of albums. All kinds of reason can be advanced for the sudden spectacular increase. New wave bands came more to the fore and they're basically into 45s. Endless record shapes, coloured vinyl, packaging of the wierd and wonderful helped. The Gibb brothers could do no wrong and from films Saturday Night Fever and Grease came hits. And 1978 had big groups and whatever they did the public bought. In this list must come Abba, Boney M, Darts, Travolta – Olivia Newton-John, Bee Gees, Commodores, Boomtown Rats, Rose Royce and Blondie.

JANUARY 1978

7		14	21	28
1	Mull Of Kintyre *Wings* (EMI)	1	1	1
2	Floral Dance *The Brighouse and Rastrick Band* (Transatlantic)	2	5	12
3	How Deep Is Your Love *The Bee Gees* (RSO)	7	7	–
4	Love's Unkind *Donna Summer* (GTO)	3	3	3
5	I Will *Ruby Winters* (Creole)	9	13	–
6	It's A Heartache *Bonnie Tyler* (RCA)	4	4	6
7	Daddy Cool/The Girl Can't Help It *Darts* (Magnet)	12	18	–
8	Don't It Make My Brown Eyes Blue *Crystal Gayle* (UA)	5	6	7
9	My Way *Elvis Presley* (RCA)	16	20	–
10	Dance Dance Dance *Chic* (Atlantic)	6	9	9
11	Who Pays The Ferry Man *Yannis Markopoulus* (BBC)	11	15	19
12	Belfast *Boney M.* (Atlantic)			
13	Let's Have A Quiet Night In *David Soul* (Private Stock)	8	10	13
14	Put Your Love In Me *Hot Chocolate* (RAK)	18	–	–
15	Dancin' Party *Showaddywaddy* (Arista)	–	–	–
16	White Christmas *Bing Crosby* (MCA)	–	–	–
17	Love Of My Life *The Dooleys* (GTO)	–	–	–
18	Uptown Top Ranking *Althia and Donna* (Lightning)	13	2	2
19	Only Women Bleed *Julie Covington* (Virgin)	14	12	15
20	Rockin' All Over The World *Status Quo* (Vertigo)	–	–	–
30	I Love You *Donna Summer* (Casablanca)	10	16	18
–	As Time Goes By *Dooley Wilson* (UA)	15	19	20
23	Jamming/Punky Reggae Party *Bob Marley and The Wailers* (Island)	17	11	11
–	Don't Dilly Dally On The Way/Waiting At The Church *The Muppets*	19	–	–
22	Native New Yorker *Odyssey* (RCA)	20	8	5
–	Figaro *Brotherhood of Man* (Pye)	45	14	4
–	Lovely Day *Bill Withers* (CBS)	30	17	8
–	If I Had Words *Scott Fitzgerald and Yvonne Keeley* (Pepper)	31	27	10
–	Galaxy *War* (MCA)	33	26	14
–	On Fire *T. Connection* (TK)	21	24	16
–	The Groove Line *Heatwave* (GTO)	34	21	17

FEBRUARY 1978

4		11	18	25
1	Uptown Top Ranking *Althia and Donna* (Lightning)	3	7	17
2	Mull Of Kintyre/Girls School *Wings* (Parlophone)	5	12	–
3	Figaro *Brotherhood of Man* (Pye)	1	2	2
4	If I Had Words *Scott Fitzgerald and Yvonne Keeley* (Pepper)	4	3	5
5	Native New Yorker *Odyssey* (RCA)	6	13	16
6	Love's Unkind *Donna Summer* (GTO)	9	–	–
7	Lovely Day *Bill Withers* (CBS)	7	11	15
8	It's A Heartache *Bonnie Tyler* (RCA)	–	–	–
9	Jamming/Punky Reggae Party *Bob Marley and The Wailers* (Island)	10	–	–
10	Take A Chance On Me *Abba* (Epic)	2	1	1
11	Dance Dance Dance *Chic* (Atlantic)	19	–	–
12	The Groove Line *Heatwave* (GTO)	13	14	20
13	Sorry I'm A Lady *Baccara* (RCA)	8	10	8
14	Don't It Make My Brown Eyes Blue *Crystal Gayle* (UA)	–	–	–
15	Galaxy *War* (MCA)	17	–	–
16	Mr Blue Sky *The Electric Light Orchestra* (Jet)	16	8	6
17	Who's Gonna Love Me *The Imperials* (Power Exchange)	20	–	–
18	Hot Legs/I Was Only Joking *Rod Stewart* (Riva)	14	5	7
19	Let's Have A Quiet Night In *David Soul* (Private Stock)	–	–	–
20	Come Back My Love *Darts* (Magnet)	12	4	3

4		11	18	25
26	Wishing On A Star *Rose Royce* (Warner Bros.)	11	6	4
32	Drummer Man *Tonight* (TDS)	15	15	14
21	Love Is Like Oxygen *The Sweet* (Polydor)	18	9	10
49	Just One More Night *Yellow Dog* (Virgin)	26	16	9
28	For A Few Dollars More *Smokie* (RAK)	25	17	19
34	Stayin' Alive *The Bee Gees* (RSO)	31	18	12
27	Theme From Which Way Is Up *Stagard* (MCA)	29	19	–
43	Emotions *Samantha Sang* (Private Stock)	33	20	–
50	5 Minutes *The Stranglers* (UA)	22	21	11
–	Wuthering Heights *Kate Bush* (EMI)	42	27	13
–	Free EP *Free* (Island)	–	25	18

MARCH 1978

4		11	18	25
1	Take A Chance On Me *Abba* (Epic)	2	3	8
2	Come Back My Love *Darts* (Magnet)	3	4	7
3	Wishing On A Star *Rose Royce* (Warner Bros.)	4	5	6
4	Stayin' Alive *The Bee Gees* (RSO)	6	8	9
5	Wuthering Heights *Kate Bush* (EMI)	1	1	1
6	Figaro *Brotherhood of Man* (Pye)	13	18	–
7	Mr Blue Sky *The Electric Light Orchestra* (Jet)	9	9	11
8	Just One More Night *Yellow Dog* (Virgin)	10	15	–
9	Love Is Like Oxygen *The Sweet* (Polydor)	16	–	–
10	If I Had Words *Scott Fitzgerald and Yvonne Keeley* (Pepper)	17	–	–
11	Denis *Blondie* (Chrysalis)	5	2	2
12	Free EP *Free* (Island)	11	17	–
13	Hot Legs/I Was Only Joking *Rod Stewart* (Riva)	20	–	–
14	Baker Street *Gerry Rafferty* (UA)	8	6	4
15	I Can't Stand The Rain *Eruption* (Atlantic)	7	7	5
16	Emotions *Samantha Sang* (Private Stock)	14	12	12
17	Is This Love *Bob Marley and The Wailers* (Island)	12	11	13
18	Glad To Be Gay *The Tom Robinson Band* (EMI)	–	–	–
19	Just The Way You Are *Billy Joel* (CBS)	–	–	–
20	Sorry I'm A Lady *Baccara* (RCA)	–	–	–
21	Fantasy *Earth Wind and Fire* (CBS)	15	14	15
37	Matchstalk Men And Matchstalk Cats And Dogs *Brian and Michael* (Pye)	18	10	3
23	5 Minutes *The Stranglers* (UA)	19	–	–
32	Ally's Tartan Army *Andy Cameron* (Klub)	21	13	16
30	Rumour Has It *Donna Summer* (Casablanca)	28	19	19
36	Every 1's A Winner *Hot Chocolate* (RAK)	27	20	14
–	I Love The Sound Of Breaking Glass *Nick Lowe* (Radar)	33	21	10
44	Whenever You Want My Love *The Real Thing* (Pye)	31	29	18
–	If You Can't Give Me Love *Suzi Quatro* (RAK)	–	42	20
27	Lilac Wine *Elkie Brooks* (A & M)	22	16	17

On 18 March incorrect positions for Abba and Blondie were printed in one of the two chart listings supplied in Music Week *and also in* Record Mirror. *The correct placings are given above.*

APRIL 1978

1		8	15	22	29
1	Wuthering Heights *Kate Bush* (EMI)	3	8	15	–
2	Denis *Blondie* (Chrysalis)	2	5	10	20
3	Baker Street *Gerry Rafferty* (UA)	4	3	8	9
4	Matchstalk Men And Matchstalk Cats And Dogs *Brian and Michael* (Pye)	1	1	1	2
5	I Can't Stand The Rain *Eruption* (Atlantic)	7	11	17	–

1	8	15	22	29
6 Ally's Tartan Army *Andy Cameron* (Klub)	9	18	–	–
7 I Love The Sound Of Breaking Glass *Nick Lowe* (Radar)	10	12	–	–
8 Come Back My Love *Darts* (Magnet)	17	–	–	–
9 Is This Love *Bob Marley and the Wailers* (Island)	14	–	–	–
10 If You Can't Give Me Love *Suzi Quatro* (RAK)	6	4	4	4
11 Emotions *Samantha Sang* (Private Stock)	15	20	–	–
12 Wishing On A Star *Rose Royce* (Warner Bros.)	–	–	–	–
13 Every 1's A Winner *Hot Chocolate* (RAK)	12	19	16	–
14 I Wonder Why *Showaddywaddy* (Arista)	5	2	3	3
15 Take A Chance On Me *Abba* (Epic)	19	–	–	–
16 Fantasy *Earth Wind and Fire* (CBS)	–	–	–	–
17 Chelsea *Elvis Costello and the Attractions* (Radar)	–	16	–	–
18 Follow You Follow Me *Genesis* (Charisma)	8	7	9	7
19 Stayin' Alive *The Bee Gees* (Polydor)	–	–	–	–
20 Walk In Love *Manhattan Transfer* (Atlantic)	16	13	12	19
25 Never Let Her Slip Away *Andrew Gold* (Asylum)	11	6	6	6
12 With A Little Luck *Wings* (Parlophone)	13	9	5	8
26 Sometimes When We Touch *Dan Hill* (20th Century)	18	15	13	18
27 Too Much Too Little Too Late *Johnny Mathis and Deniece Williams* (CBS)	20	10	7	5
– Night Fever *The Bee Gees* (RSO)	–	14	2	1
30 More Like The Movies *Dr Hook* (Capitol)	23	17	14	14
32 Singing In The Rain *Sheila B. Devotion* (Carrere)	30	22	11	11
38 Everybody Dance *Chic* (Atlantic)	33	24	18	12
– She's So Modern *The Boomtown Rats* (Ensign)	–	23	19	15
43 Let's All Chant *The Michael Zager Band* (Private Stock)	49	29	20	10
– Automatic Lover *Dee D. Jackson* (Mercury)	–	–	27	13
– Bad Old Days *CoCo* (Ariola)	–	–	39	16
49 It Takes Two To Tango *Richard Myhill* (Mercury)	35	26	21	17

MAY 1978

6	13	20	27
1 Night Fever *The Bee Gees* (RSO)	2	2	2
2 Rivers Of Babylon *Boney M.* (Atlantic/Hansa)	1	1	1
3 Matchstalk Men And Matchstalk Cats And Dogs *Brian and Michael* (Pye)	6	17	–
4 Too Much Too Little Too Late *Johnny Mathis/Deniece Williams* (CBS)	3	4	6
5 Never Let Her Slip Away *Andrew Gold* (Asylum)	5	7	12
6 Automatic Lover *Dee D. Jackson* (Mercury)	4	5	11
7 I Wonder Why *Showaddywaddy* (Arista)	15	–	–
8 If You Can't Give Me Love *Suzi Quatro* (RAK)	11	–	–
9 With A Little Luck *Wings* (EMI)	–	–	–
10 Let's All Chant *The Michael Zager Band* (Magnet)	8	9	16
11 Follow You Follow Me *Genesis* (Charisma)	18	–	–
12 Singing In The Rain *Sheila B. Devotion* (Carrere)	16	–	–
13 Bad Old Days *CoCo* (Ariola)	14	–	–
14 Everybody Dance *Chic* (Atlantic)	9	19	–
15 She's So Modern *Boomtown Rats* (Ensign)	12	14	17
16 Jack And Jill *Raydio* (Arista)	13	11	13
17 Baker Street *Gerry Rafferty* (United Artists)	–	–	–
18 Sometimes When We Touch *Dan Hill* (20th Century)	–	–	–
19 Take Me I'm Yours *Squeeze* (A&M)	–	–	–
20 More Like The Movies *Dr Hook* (Capitol)	20	–	–
23 Because The Night *Patti Smith* (Arista)	7	6	5
30 Boy From New York City *Darts* (Magnet)	10	3	3
22 Do It Again *Raffaella Carra* (Epic)	17	12	9
35 (I'm Always Touched By Your) Presence Dear *Blondie* (Chrysalis)	19	20	10

6

		13	20	27
24	Love Is In The Air *John Paul Young* (Ariola)	23	8	8
45	If I Can't Have You *Yvonne Elliman* (RSO)	21	10	4
38	More Than A Woman *Tavares* (Capitol)	28	13	7
28	Come To Me *Ruby Winters* (Creole)	32	15	15
31	It Makes You Feel Like Dancin' *Rose Royce* (Warners)	37	16	20
27	Nice 'n' Sleazy *The Stranglers* (United Artists)	29	18	18
37	What A Waste *Ian Dury* (Stiff)	35	28	14
–	Ca Plane Pour Moi *Plastic Bertrand* (Sire)	58	33	19

JUNE 1978

3

		10	17	24
1	Rivers Of Babylon *Boney M* (Atlantic Hansa)	1	2	3
2	Boy From New York City *Darts* (Magnet)	3	4	9
3	Night Fever *Bee Gees* (RSO)	6	11	14
4	If I Can't Have You *Yvonne Elliman* (RSO)	5	8	13
5	Love Is In The Air *John Paul Young* (Ariola)	8	12	16
6	You're The One That I Want *John Travolta/Olivia Newton John* (RSO)	2	1	1
7	Because The Night *Patti Smith* (Arista)	9	16	27
8	More Than A Woman *Tavares* (Capitol)	7	15	18
9	What a Waste *Ian Dury* (Stiff)	11	14	–
10	Ca Plane Pour Moi *Plastic Bertrand* (Sire)	10	9	8
11	Come To Me *Ruby Winters* (Creole)	20	22	36
12	Oh Carol *Smokie* (RAK)	12	5	10
13	Hi Tension *Hi Tension* (Island)	14	18	–
14	Jack & Jill *Raydio* (Arista)	–	–	–
15	(I'm Always Touched By Your) Presence Dear *Blondie* (Chrysalis)	17	–	–
16	Too Much Too Little Too Late *Johnny Mathis/Deniece Williams* (CBS)	–	–	–
17	Ole Ola *Rod Stewart* (RIVA)	4	13	–
18	Do It Do It Again *Raffaella Carra Sugar* (Epic)	16	–	–
19	It Makes You Feel Like Dancin' *Rose Royce* (Warner)	–	–	–
20	A Bi Ni Bi *Izhar Cohen & Alphabeta* (Polydor)	–	–	–
22	Davy's On The Road Again *Manfred Mann's Earth Band* (Bronze)	13	6	6
27	Annie's Song *James Galway* (Red Seal)	15	7	5
28	It Sure Brings Out The Love In Your Eyes *David Soul* (Private Stock)	18	19	12
35	Angels With Dirty Faces *Sham 69* (Polydor)	19	–	–
32	Miss You *Rolling Stones* (EMI)	23	3	4
44	Smurf Song *Father Abraham* (Decca)	25	10	2
36	Making Up Again *Goldie* (Bronze)	24	17	7
24	On A Little Street In Singapore *Manhattan Transfer* (Atlantic)	37	20	–
–	Airport *Motors* (Virgin)	47	28	11
37	Beautiful Lover *Brotherhood Of Man* (Pye)	27	21	15
–	Man With The Child In His Eyes *Kate Bush* (EMI)	60	30	17
58	Dancing In The City *Marshall Hain* (Harvest)	40	23	19
38	Rosalie *Thin Lizzy* (Vertigo)	21	32	20

JULY 1978

1

		8	15	22	29
1	You're The One That I Want *John Travolta/Olivia Newton John* (RSO)	1	1	1	1
2	Smurf Song *Father Abraham* (Decca)	2	2	2	2
3	**Annie's Song *James Galway* (Red Seal)**	3	4	13	16
4	Miss You *Rolling Stones* (EMI)	7	10	19	–

1	8	15	22	29
5 Airport *Motors* (Virgin)	4	5	8	9
6 Rivers Of Babylon *Boney M* (Atlantic Hansa)	10	18	20	18
7 Man With The Child In His Eyes *Kate Bush* (EMI)	6	9	9	15
8 Dancing In The City *Marshall Hain* (Harvest)	5	3	3	4
9 Davy's On The Road Again *Manfred Mann's Earth Band* (Bronze)	12	–	–	–
10 Making Up Again *Goldie* (Bronze)	9	20	–	–
11 Oh Carol *Smokie* (RAK)	16	–	–	–
12 Mind Blowing Decisions *Heatwave* (GTO)	13	14	15	–
13 Like Clockwork *Boomtown Rats* (Ensign)	8	6	6	6
14 Ca Plane Pour Moi *Plastic Bertrand* (Sire)	20	–	–	–
15 Night Fever *Bee Gees* (RSO)	–	–	–	–
16 Beautiful Lover *Brotherhood Of Man* (Pye)	17	–	–	–
17 Boy From New York City *Darts* (Magnet)	–	–	–	–
18 (Don't Fear) The Reaper *Blue Oyster Cult* (CBS)	19	16	18	20
19 It Sure Brings Out The Love In Your Eyes *David Soul* (Private Stock)	–	–	–	–
20 If I Can't Have You *Yvonne Elliman* (RSO)	–	–	–	–
25 A Little Bit Of Soap *Showaddywaddy* (Arista)	11	8	5	7
26 Argentine Melody *San Jose* (MCA)	14	15	17	–
22 Use Ta Be My Girl *O'Jays* (Philadelphia)	15	13	12	14
– No-One Is Innocent/My Way *Sex Pistols* (Virgin)	18	7	11	11
24 Boogie Oogie Oogie *A Taste Of Honey* (Capitol)	22	11	10	5
29 Run For Home *Lindisfarne* (Mercury)	23	12	14	10
34 Substitute *Clout* (Carrere)	25	17	4	3
36 Wild West Hero *Electric Light Orchestra* (Jet)	24	19	7	8
52 Come On Dance *Saturday Night Band* (CBS)	32	26	16	17
58 Stay *Jackson Browne* (Asylum)	44	32	31	12
38 From East To West/Scots Machine (GTO)	34	30	27	13
53 How Can This Be Love *Andrew Gold* (Asylum)	46	29	37	19

AUGUST 1978

5	12	19	26
1 You're The One That I Want *John Travolta/Olivia Newton-John* (RSO)	1	2	2
2 Substitute *Clout* (Carrere)	2	3	7
3 Smurf Song *Father Abraham* (Decca)	4	12	19
4 Dancing In The City *Marshall Hain* (Harvest)	8	16	–
5 Boogie Oogie Oogie *A Taste Of Honey* (Capitol)	3	7	9
6 Wild West Hero *Electric Light Orchestra* (Jet)	10	19	–
7 A Little Bit Of Soap *Showaddywaddy* (Arista)	14	–	–
8 Like Clockwork *Boomtown Rats* (Ensign)	15	–	–
9 5–7–0–5 *City Boy* (Vertigo)	12	8	13
10 Rivers Of Babylon/Brown Girl In The Ring* *Boney M* (Atlantic/Hansa)	6	5	4
11 Forever Autumn *Justin Hayward* (CBS)	7	6	5
12 Run For Home *Lindisfarne* (Mercury)	17	–	–
13 If The Kids Are United *Sham 69* (Polydor)	9	9	14
14 Life's Been Good *Joe Walsh* (Asylum)	20	17	–
15 Stay *Jackson Browne* (Asylum)	13	22	20
16 Use Ta Be My Girl *O'Jays* (Philadelphia)	–	–	–
17 Come Back And Finish What You Started *Gladys Knight & The Pips* (Buddah)	19	15	17
18 Airport *Motors* (Virgin)	–	–	–
19 From East to West/Scots Machine (GTO)	16	–	–
20 No-One Is Innocent/My Way *Sex Pistols* (Virgin)	–	–	–
46 Three Times A Lady *Commodores* (Motown)	5	1	1
23 Northern Lights *Renaissance* (Warners)	11	10	11
52 It's Raining *Darts* (Magnet)	18	4	3
30 Supernature *Cerrone* (Atlantic)	23	11	8

5	12	19	26
26 Baby Stop Crying *Bob Dylan* (CBS)	21	13	15
27 It's Only Make Believe *Child* (Ariola)	28	14	16
– Dreadlock Holiday *10cc* (Mercury)	54	18	6
28 Who Are You *The Who* (Polydor)	26	20	18
– Jilted John *Jilted John* (EMI)	37	25	10
– Oh What A Circus *David Essex* (Mercury)	–	36	12

* With airplay, consumer shop demand asking for Brown Girl In The Ring the Bony M record became a double-sided hit. Often records may start as double A sides but rarely is their case of a former number one song finding itself at later date ranked only equal with its previous ignored B track.

SEPTEMBER 1978

2	9	16	23	30
1 Three Times A Lady *Commodores* (Motown)	1	1	2	5
2 It's Raining *Darts* (Magnet)	3	4	8	17
3 Rivers of Babylon/Brown Girl in the Ring *Boney M* (Atlantic/Hansa)	2	3	5	10
4 Dreadlock Holiday *10cc* (Mercury)	4	2	1	2
5 You're The One That I Want *John Travolta/Olivia Newton-John* (RSO)	7	12	18	–
6 Oh What A Circus *David Essex* (Mercury)	5	5	3	6
7 Jilted John *Jilted John* (EMI)	6	6	4	9
8 Supernature *Cerrone* (Atlantic)	8	9	–	–
9 Forever Autumn *Justin Hayward* (CBS)	12	–	–	–
10 It's Only Make Believe *Child* (Ariola)	11	18	–	–
11 Boogie Oogie Oogie *A Taste of Honey* (Capitol)	–	–	–	–
12 Substitute *Clout* (Carrere)	18	–	–	–
13 Baby Stop Crying *Bob Dylan* (CBS)	14	20	–	–
14 5–7–0–5 *City Boy* (Vertigo)	–	–	–	–
15 Northern Lights *Renaissance* (Warners)	20	–	–	–
16 If the Kids are United *Sham 69* (Polydor)	–	–	–	–
17 British Hustle/Peace on Earth *Hi Tension* (Island)	9	8	14	15
18 Who Are You *Who* (Polydor)	–	–	–	–
19 An Everlasting Love *Andy Gibb* (RSO)	10	11	16	20
20 Come Back And Finish What You Started *Gladys Knight & The Pips* (Buddah)	–	–	–	–
26 Forget About You *Motors* (Virgin)	13	16	15	18
25 Hong Kong Garden *Siouxsie & The Banshees* (Polydor)	15	7	10	11
23 Picture This *Blondie* (Chrysalis)	16	13	12	12
24 Top Of The Pops *Rezillos* (Sire)	17	17	–	–
33 Kiss You All Over *Exile* (RAK)	19	10	6	7
39 Again And Again *Status Quo*	23	14	13	14
27 I Thought It Was You *Herbie Hancock* (CBS)	25	15	19	–
31 Grease *Franki Valli* (RSO)	24	19	9	3
– Summer Night City *Abba* (Epic	–	21	7	8
– Summer Nights *John Travolta/Olivia Newton-John* (RSO)	–	56	11	1
– Love Don't Live Here Anymore *Rose Royce* (Whitfield)	–	46	17	4
32 You Make Me Feel (Mighty Real) *Sylvester* (Fantasy)	30	26	20	16
62 A Rose Has To Die *Dooleys* (GTO)	38	25	27	13
– I Can't Stop Lovin' You *Leo Sayer* (Chrysalis)	–	66	29	19

OCTOBER 1978

7	14	21	28
1 Summer Nights *John Travolta/Olivia Newton-John* (RSO)	1	1	1
2 Love Don't Live Here Anymore *Rose Royce* (Whitfield)	2	5	8
3 Grease *Franki Valli* (RSO)	5	8	–
4 Dreadlock Holiday *10cc* (Mercury)	15	–	–

265

7	14	21	28
5 Summer Night City *Abba* (Epic)	12	20	–
6 Lucky Stars *Dean Friedman* (Lifesong)	4	3	4
7 I Can't Stop Lovin' You *Leo Sayer* (Chrysalis)	6	7	10
8 You Make Me Feel (Mighty Real) *Sylvester* (Fantasy)	9	10	–
9 Rasputin *Boney M* (Atlantic/Hansa)	3	2	2
10 Kiss You All Over *Exile* (RAK)	16	–	–
11 On What A Circus *David Essex* (Mercury)	19	–	–
12 Three Times A Lady *Commodores* (Motown)	17	–	–
13 Jilted John *Jilted John* (EMI)	–	–	–
14 Picture This *Blondie* (Chrysalis)	18	–	–
15 Talking In Your Sleep *Crystal Gayle* (United Artists)	14	13	11
16 A Rose Has To Die *Dooleys* (GTO)	11	18	–
17 Sweet Talkin' Woman *Electric Light Orchestra* (Jet)	7	6	6
18 Now That We've Found Love *Third World* (Island)	10	11	12
19 Hong Kong Garden *Siouxsie & The Banshees* (Polydor)	–	–	–
20 Again And Again *Status Quo* (Vertigo)	–	–	–
36 Sandy *John Travolta* (Midsong/Polydor)	8	4	3
23 Blame It On The Boogie *Jacksons* (Epic)	13	14	9
27 Mexican Girl *Smokie* (RAK)	20	19	20
– Rat Trap *Boomtown Rats* (Ensign)	22	9	7
– Macarthur Park *Donna Summer* (Casablanca)	29	12	5
32 Blame It On The Boogie *Mick Jackson* (Atlantic)	38	15	17
30 Ever Fallen In Love (With Someone You Shouldn't Have) *Buzzcocks* (United Artists)	24	16	14
– Hurry Up Harry *Sham 69* (Polydor)	37	17	16
– Public Image *Public Image* (Virgin)	–	21	13
45 Givin' Up Givin' In *Three Degrees* (Ariola)	33	29	15
41 Dippety Day *Father Abraham & The Smurfs* (Decca)	27	26	18
– Darlin' *Frankie Miller* (Chrysalis)	34	28	19

NOVEMBER 1978

4	11	18	25
1 Summer Nights *John Travolta/Olivia Newton-John* (RSO)	1	3	7
2 Sandy *John Travolta* (Midsong)	3	4	10
3 Rat Trap *Boomtown Rats* (Ensign)	2	1	1
4 Rasputin *Boney M* (Atlantic/Hansa)	7	11	–
5 Macarthur Park *Donna Summer* (Casablanca)	5	9	15
6 Sweet Talkin' Woman *Electric Light Orchestra* (Jet)	9	15	34
7 Lucky Stars *Dean Friedman* (Lifesong)	14	–	–
8 Blame It On The Boogie *Jacksons* (Epic)	8	10	13
9 Public Image *Public Image* (Virgin)	11	17	–
10 Hurry Up Harry *Sham 69* (Polydor)	18	19	–
11 Darlin' *Frankie Miller* (Chrysalis)	6	6	6
12 Ever Fallen In Love (With Someone You Shouldn't Have) *Buzzcocks* (United Artists)	19	20	–
13 Dippety Day *Father Abraham & The Smurfs* (Decca)	15	16	20
14 Givin' Up Givin' In *Three Degrees* (Ariola)	12	12	17
15 Down In The Tube Station At Midnight *The Jam* (Polydor)	20	–	–
16 Love Don't Live Here Anymore *Rose Royce* (Whitfield)	–	–	–
17 I Can't Stop Lovin' You *Leo Sayer* (Chrysalis)	–	–	–
18 Talking In Your Sleep *Crystal Gayle* (United Artists)	–	–	–
19 Blame It On The Boogie *Mick Jackson* (Atlantic)	–	–	–
20 Instant Replay *Dan Hartman* (Blue Sky)	17	8	8
24 Hopelessly Devoted To You *Olivia Newton-John* (RSO)	4	2	2
– My Best Friend's Girl *Cars* (Elektra)	10	5	3
21 Bicycle Race/Fat Bottomed Girls *Queen* (EMI)	13	13	11
28 Pretty Little Angel Eyes *Showaddywaddy* (Arista)	16	7	5
– Do You Think I'm Sexy *Rod Stewart* (Riva)	–	14	4
– Hanging On The Telephone *Blondie* (Chrysalis)	27	18	9

	11	18	25
57 I Love America *Patrick Juvet* (Casablanca)	28	22	12
36 Always And Forever/Mind Blowing Decisions *Heatwave* (GTO)	26	23	14
30 Part Time Love *Elton John* (Rocket)	24	24	16
68 Toast/Hold On *Streetband* (Logo)	29	25	18
63 Germ Free Adolescence *X-ray Spex* (EMI)	34	30	19

DECEMBER 1978

2	**9**	**16**	**23**
1 Do You Think I'm Sexy *Rod Stewart* (Riva)	2	3	8
2 Rat Trap *Boomtown Rats* (Ensign)	5	13	–
3 Hopelessly Devoted To You *Olivia Newton-John* (RSO)	10	–	–
4 My Best Friend's Girl *Cars* (Elektra)	11	–	–
5 Hanging On The Telephone *Blondie* (Chrysalis)	7	10	17
6 Pretty Little Angel Eyes *Showaddywaddy* (Arista)	14	14	–
7 Mary's Boy Child *Boney M* (Atlantic/Hansa)	1	1	1
8 Instant Replay *Dan Hartman* (Blue Sky)	15	–	–
9 I Lost My Heart To A Starship Trooper *Sarah Brightman/Hot Gossip* (Ariola)	6	6	7
10 Darlin' *Frankie Miller* (Chrysalis)	16	–	–
11 Always And Forever/Mind Blowing Decisions *Heatwave* (GTO)	9	9	12
12 Don't Cry Out Loud *Elkie Brooks* (A&M)	13	12	15
13 Bicycle Race/Fat Bottomed Girls *Queen* (EMI)	–	–	–
14 Too Much Heaven *Bee Gees* (RSO)	3	5	4
15 Summer Nights *John Travolta/Olivia Newton-John* (RSO)	–	–	–
16 Part Time Love *Elton John* (Rocket)	20	15	–
17 I Love America *Patrick Juvet* (Casablanca)	18	–	–
18 Le Freak *Chic* (Atlantic)	8	7	9
19 A Taste Of Aggro *Barron Knights* (Epic)	4	4	3
20 Don't Let It Fade Away *Darts* (Magnet)	19	18	–
25 YMCA *Village People* (Mercury)	12	2	2
26 In The Bush *Musique* (CBS)	17	16	16
30 You Don't Bring Me Flowers *Barbra Streisand* (CBS)	25	8	5
40 Lay Your Love On Me *Racey* (RAK)	24	11	6
37 Greased Lightning *John Travolta*	23	17	11
27 Shooting Star *Dollar* (Carrere)	26	19	18
29 Tommy Gun *Clash* (CBS)	27	20	20
– Song For Guy *Elton John* (Rocket)	–	22	10
– Hit Me With Your Rhythm Stick *Ian Dury & The Blockheads* (Stiff)	44	30	13
44 I'm Every Woman *Chaka Khan* (Warner)	32	31	14
68 Christmas In Smurfland *Father Abraham* (Decca)	40	32	19

1978-BEST-SELLING SINGLES

1. Rivers Of Babylon/Brown Girl In The Ring *Boney M* (Atlantic/Hansa)
2. You're The One That I Want *John Travolta/Olivia Newton-John* (RSO)
3. Summer Nights *John Travolta/Olivia Newton-John* (RSO)
4. Three Times A Lady *Commodores* (Motown)
5. Smurf Song *Father Abraham* (Decca)
6. Night Fever *Bee Gees* (RSO)
7. Take A Chance On Me *Abba* (Epic)
8. Matchstalk Men And Matchstalk Cats & Dogs *Brian & Michael* (Pye)
9. Rat Trap *Boomtown Rats* (Ensign)
10. Dreadlock Holiday *10cc* (Mercury)
11. Wuthering Heights *Kate Bush* (EMI)
12. Sandy *John Travolta* (Midsong)
13. Rasputin' *Boney M* (Atlantic/Hansa)
14. Substitute *Clout* (Carrere)
15. Denis *Blondie* (Chrysalis)
16. Baker Street *Gerry Rafferty* (United Artists)
17. Figaro *Brotherhood Of Man* (Pye)
18. Come Back My Love *Darts* (Magnet)
19. Love Don't Live Here Anymore *Rose Royce* (Whitfield)
20. It's Raining *Darts* (Magnet)

1978-BEST-SELLING ALBUMS

1. Saturday Night Fever *Various*
2. Grease *Various*
3. The Album *Abba*
4. Nightflight To Venus *Boney M*
5. 20 Golden Greats *Nat King Cole*
6. Rumours *Fleetwood Mac*
7. Out Of The Blue *Electric Light Orchestra*
8. 20 Golden Greats *Buddy Holly & The Crickets*
9. The Kick Inside *Kate Bush*
10. Images *Don Williams*
11. War Of The Worlds *Jeff Wayne's Musical Version*
12. And Then There Were Three *Genesis*
13. Classic Rock *London Symphony Orchestra*
14. New Boots And Panties *Ian Dury*
15. Live And Dangerous *Thin Lizzy*
16. Reflections *Andy Williams*
17. The Sound Of Bread *Bread*
18. Street Legal *Bob Dylan*
19. The Stud *Various*
20. 20 Golden Greats *Hollies*

Male Artists (Singles)

1 Andrew Gold
2 Rod Stewart
3 Sylvester
4 John Travolta
5 Dean Friedman

6 James Galway
7 Leo Sayer
8 Plastic Bertrand
9 Elton John
(Only 9 listed)

Female Artists (Singles)

1 Donna Summer
2 Kate Bush
3 Crystal Gayle
4 Ruby Winters
5 Elkie Brooks

6 Yvonne Elliman
7 Suzi Quatro
8 Olivia Newton-John
9 Evelyn Champagne-King
10 Dee D Jackson

Groups (Singles)

1 Boney M
2 John Travolta/Olivia Newton-John
3 Darts
4 Bee Gees
5 Boomtown Rats

6 Blondie
7 Father Abraham & The Smurfs
8 Showaddywaddy
9 Electric Light Orchestra
10 Rose Royce

Male Artists (albums)

1 Don Williams
2 Johnny Mathis
3 Nat King Cole
4 Rod Stewart
5 Gerry Rafferty

6 Bob Dylan
7 Andy Williams
8 Leo Sayer
9 Billy Joel
10 Andrew Lloyd Webber

Female Artists (Album)

1 Kate Bush
2 Donna Summer
3 Rita Coolidge
4 Lena Martell
5 Shirley Bassey

6 Tammy Wynette
7 Crystal Gayle
8 Elkie Brooks
9 Joan Armatrading
10 Olivia Newton-John

Groups (Albums)

1 Abba
2 Electric Light Orchestra
3 Fleetwood Mac
4 Ian Dury & The Blockheads
5 Bob Marley & The Wailers

6 Manhattan Transfer
7 Genesis
8 Blondie
9 Darts
10 Boney M

1979

There may have been some exciting records thrown up by small companies and a wide assortment of interesting discs were played as usual on John Peel's BBC Radio One show, but in pop chart-land the real sales accumulated for the familiar names. Blondie, Dr Hook, Boomtown Rats, Bee Gees and Abba were hardly new. Nor were Michael Jackson, Art Garfunkel and (an admittedly revived) Cliff Richard. Also Queen, Three Degrees, Sex Pistols, Boney M, Roxy Music, Status Quo and the Jacksons were other oldies with high-selling singles. But there were a few new names.

Tubeway Army was in reality Gary Numan, and if some said Numan had borrowed from the likes of John Foxx and Kraftwerk, he was to build his own pop empire and make small-time Beggars Banquet of south-west London the most valuable licensed label-company for the mighty worldwide WEA group. Numan could do no wrong with two chart-toppers. His Tubeway Army began a career, which still continues, with the hit Are Friends Electric. Cars came next and Complex was the slight let-down, but still providing his year's hat-trick. Two top ten hits for B. A. Robertson suggested he had a future. There was vocalist and multi-instrumentalist Robin Scott – as M – with the classic 45 called Pop Muzik, but who missed the 20 with his other hit of the year Moonlight And Muzak. And there came a cool chick by the name of Lene Lovich who packed supreme self-confidence and talent into a formula which gave her hits Lucky Number and Say When. Another 75 hit was Bird Song. It reached 39, some way off the magical Top 20.

Some artists consolidated their debut performance of 1978. Squeeze from Deptford had made the 20 in 1978 with Take Me I'm Yours but then came poor showings from Bang Bang and Goodbye which made the 75 but far below the 20. Their singing and songwriting talent blossomed in 1979 as Cool for Cats and Up The Junction both made Number Two. Squeeze had of course been around since 1974 and members of Sad Cafe had been in several Manchester groups. They emerged on the scene with a haunting number Every Day Hurts and they were joined in the one-hit for the year stakes by artistes like Janet Kay, Bellamy Brothers, Buggles, Lena Martell and promising new outfit Selecter.

Disco fared well with major hits, ranging from Ring My Bell by schoolteacher Anita Ward to gay pastures of Village People who's pounding YMCA haunted the British clubs. Mixed groups continued successfully. The Dooleys ended the year with two ten tenners, Abba had no less than five in the top four, Boney M had three in the 20 and Blondie had four in the Top Twenty with two chart-toppers Heart Of Glass and Sunday Girl and at two, Dreaming. It was Union City Blues, reaching only 13, which rather tarnished an otherwise almost unblemished year. A duo called Dollar had charted with Shooting Star in 1978 and here in 1979 they made the 20 three times and continue having major success. For Thereze and David a mix of glamour and love song spelt fortune.

The song of the year – in sales terms – was Bright Eyes from Art Garfunkel. Four years back he had his last solo hit and oddly enough it too was a chart-topper – I Only Have Eyes For You.

JANUARY 1979

6	13	20	27
1 YMCA *Village People* (Mercury)	1	1	2
2 Mary's Boy Child *Boney M* (Atlantic/Hansa)	7	–	–
3 Lay Your Love On Me *Racey* (RAK)	3	3	7
4 A Taste Of Aggro *Barron Knights* (Epic)	6	17	–
5 Song For Guy *Elton John* (Rocket)	4	8	14
6 Hit Me With Your Rhythm Stick *Ian Dury & The Blockheads* (Stiff)	2	2	1
7 You Don't Bring Me Flowers *Barbra Streisand/Neil Diamond*	8	12	–
8 Too Much Heaven *Bee Gees* (RSO)	10	14	19
9 I Lost My Heart To A Starship Trooper *Sarah Brightman/Hot Gossip* (Ariola)	11	16	–
10 Le Freak *Chic* (Atlantic)	9	7	10
11 Do You Think I'm Sexy *Rod Stewart* (Riva)	20	–	–
12 Always And Forever/Mind Blowing Decisions (GTO)	17	19	–
13 Greased Lightning *John Travolta* (Midsong)	15	–	–
14 Shooting Star *Dollar* (Carrere)	19	–	–
15 I'm Every Woman *Chaka Khan* (Warners)	14	11	16
16 I'll Put You Together Again *Hot Chocolate* (RAK)	16	13	18
17 In The Bush *Musique* (CBS)	–	–	–
18 September *Earth Wind & Fire* (CBS)	5	4	3
19 Tommy Gun *Clash* (CBS)	–	–	–
20 Promises *Buzzcocks* (United Artists)	–	–	–
21 A Little More Love *Olivia Newton-John* (EMI)	12	5	4
24 Hello This Is Joannie *Paul Evans* (Spring)	13	6	8
28 One Nation Under a Groove *Funkadelic* (Warners)	18	9	13
40 Car 67 *Driver 67* (Logo)	27	10	11
29 Just The Way You Are *Barry White* (20th Century)	22	15	12
– Women In Love *Three Degrees* (Ariola)	64	18	5
41 Rama Lama Ding Dong *Rockey Sharpe & The Replays* (Chiswick)	24	20	17
– Heart Of Glass *Blondie* (Chrysalis)	–	–	6
43 Don't Cry For Me Argentina *Shadows* (EMI)	35	23	9
38 My Life *Billy Joel* (CBS)	29	26	15
42 Take That To The Bank *Shalamar* (RCA)	31	30	20

FEBRUARY 1979

3	10	17	24
1 Heart Of Glass *Blondie* (Chrysalis)	1	1	1
2 Hit Me With Your Rhythm Stick *Ian Dury & The Blockheads* (Stiff)	4	8	16
3 Women In Love *Three Degrees* (Ariola)	3	3	4
4 YMCA *Village People* (Mercury)	6	–	–
5 September *Earth Wind & Fire* (CBS)	8	14	–
6 A Little More Love *Olivia Newton John* (EMI)	10	16	–
7 Car 67 *Driver 67* (Logo)	9	10	–
8 Chiquitita *Abba* (Epic)	2	2	3
9 Lay Your Love On Me *Racey* (RAK)	19	–	–
10 Don't Cry For Me Argentina *Shadows* (EMI)	5	5	9
11 Hello This Is Joannie *Paul Evans* (Spring)	15	–	–
12 Le Freak *Chic* (Atlantic)	–	–	–
13 Just The Way You Are *Barry White* (20th Century)	14	18	–
14 My Life *Billy Joel* (CBS)	12	12	–
15 One Nation Under A Groove *Funkadelic* (Warner)	–	–	–
16 Milk And Alcohol *Dr Feelgood* (United Artists)	13	9	10
17 Cool Meditation *Third World* (Island)	18	17	19
18 I'm Every Woman *Chaka Khan* (Warner)	–	–	–

3	10	17	24
19 Mirrors *Sally Oldfield* (Bronze)	–	–	–
20 Rama Lama Ding Dong *Rockey Sharpe & The Replays* (Chiswick)	–	–	–
23 I Was Made For Dancin' *Leif Garrett* (Atlantic)	7	4	6
27 Contact *Edwin Starr* (20th Century)	11	6	8
28 King Rocker *Generation X* (Chrysalis)	16	11	17
25 This Is It *Dan Hartmann* (Blue Sky)	17	20	20
31 Take On The World *Judas Priest* (CBS)	20	15	14
– Tragedy *Bee Gees* (RSO)	–	7	2
– Oliver's Army *Elvis Costello & The Attractions* (Radar)	45	13	5
44 Ain't Love A Bitch *Rod Stewart* (Riva)	29	19	11
47 I Will Survive *Gloria Gaynor* (Polydor)	32	21	7
73 Get Down *Gene Chandler* (20th Century)	21	22	12
37 Sound Of The Suburbs *Member* (Virgin)	23	25	13
– Bat Out Of Hell *Meat Loaf* (Epic)	34	37	15
– Can You Feel The Force? *Real Thing* (Pye)	–	60	18

MARCH 1979

3	10	17	24	31
1 Tragedy *Bee Gees* (RSO 27)	1	3	6	11
2 Heart Of Glass *Blondie* (Chrysalis CHS2275)	6	8	24	38
3 Oliver's Army *Elvis Costello* (Radar ADA 31)	2	2	2	4
4 I Will Survive *Gloria Gaynor* (Polydor 2095 097)	3	1	1	1
5 Chiquitita *Abba* (Epic 7030)	9	17	30	52
6 Contact *Edwin Starr* (20th Century BT2396)	8	10	31	45
7 I Was Made For Dancing *Leif Garrett* (Scotti Bros K11202)	17	38	61	–
8 Lucky Number *Lene Lovich* (Stiff BUY 42)	4	4	3	5
9 Woman In Love *Three Degrees* (Ariola ARO 141)	18	40	58	–
10 Get It *Darts* (Magnet MAG 140)	12	14	19	49
11 Get Down *Gene Chandler* (20th Century BT 2352)	11	12	12	32
12 Sound Of The Suburbs *Members* (Virgin VS 242)	16	16	34	56
13 Ain't Love A Bitch *Rod Stewart* (Riva 18)	20	23	70	–
14 Can You Feel The Force? *Real Thing* (Pye 7N46147)	5	5	5	7
15 Milk And Alcohol *Dr Feelgood* (United Artists UP34648)	24	48	–	–
16 Take On The World *Judas Priest* (CBS 6915)	23	46	69	–
17 Bat Out Of Hell *Meat Loaf* (Epic EPC 7018)	21	47	65	–
18 King Rocker *Generation X* (Chrysalis CHS 2261)	43	60	–	–
19 Don't Cry For Me Argentina *Shadows* (EMI 2890)	38	59	–	–
20 Into The Valley *Skids* (Virgin VS 241)	13	13	10	13
24 Something Else/Friggin' In The Riggin' *Sex Pistols* (Virgin VS240)	7	6	4	3
26 Painter Man *Boney M* (Atlantic/Hansa K11255)	10	11	11	22
23 Keep On Dancing *Gary's Gang* (CBS 7109)	14	9	8	10
25 I Want Your Love *Chic* (Atlantic LV 16)	15	7	7	6
33 You Bet Your Love *Herbie Hancock* (CBS 7010)	19	19	18	21
46 Waiting For An Alibi *Thin Lizzy* (Vertigo LIZZY 3)	25	15	9	12
31 Hold The Line *Toto* (CBS 6784)	35	18	14	15
29 Just What I Needed *Cars* (Elektra K12312)	36	20	21	17
28 Don't Stop Me Now *Queen* (EMI 2910)	22	22	13	9
36 Money In My Pocket *Dennis Brown* (Atlantic LV5)	26	21	15	14
– In The Navy *Village People* (Mercury 6007 209)	–	27	16	2
40 Clog Dance *Violinski* (Jet 136)	29	26	17	20
– Turn The Music Up *Players Association* (Vanguard VS 5011)	41	25	20	8
– Cool For Cats *Squeeze* (A&M AMS 7426)	–	–	33	16
– Sultans of Swing *Dire Straits* (Vertigo 6059 208)	45	28	23	18
66 Bright Eyes *Art Garfunkel* (CBS 6947)	50	45	27	19

7	14	21	28
1 I Will Survive *Gloria Gaynor* (Polydor 2095 017)	5	9	30
2 In The Navy *Village People* (Mercury 6007 209)	4	8	15
3 Bright Eyes *Art Garfunkel* (CBS 6947)	1	1	1
4 I Want Your Love *Chic* (Atlantic LV 16)	12	15	31
5 Something Else/Friggin' In The Riggin' *Sex Pistols* (Virgin VS 240)	11	18	26
6 Cool For Cats *Squeeze* (A&M AMS 7426)	2	3	3
7 Lucky Number *Lene Lovich* (Stiff BUY 42)	19	33	60
8 Sultans Of Swing *Dire Straits* (Vertigo 6059 206)	8	12	13
9 Turn The Music Up *Players Association* (Vanguard VS5011)	13	21	32
10 Oliver's Army *Elvis Costello & The Attractions* (Radar ADA 31)	17	30	55
11 Some Girls *Racey* (RAK 291)	3	2	2
12 Can You Feel The Force? *Real Thing* (Pye 7N 46147)	33	34	66
13 Don't Stop Me Now *Queen* (EMI 2910)	16	32	49
14 Money In My Pocket *Dennis Brown* (Atlantic LV5)	18	26	75
15 Keep On Dancing *Gary's Gang* (CBS 7109)	38	40	70
16 Strange Town *Jam* (Polydor POSP 34)	15	20	22
17 Waiting For An Alibi *Thin Lizzy* (Vertigo LIZZY 3)	21	38	–
18 He's The Greatest Dancer *Sister Sledge* (Atlantic K11257)	6	7	11
19 Into The Valley *Skids* (Virgin VS 241)	36	36	64
20 Just What I Needed *Cars* (Elektra K 12312)	23	48	–
24 Silly Thing/Who Killed Bambi *Sex Pistols* (Virgin VS256)	7	6	8
23 Shake Your Body (Down To The Ground) *Jacksons* (Epic EPC7181)	9	4	4
21 The Runner *Three Degrees* (Ariola ARO 154)	10	10	10
27 Wow *Kate Bush* (EMI 2911)	14	14	14
33 Questions and Answers *Sham 69* (Polydor POSP 27)	20	22	18
– Hallelujah *Milk & Honey* (Polydor 2001 870)	35	5	6
32 I Don't Wanna Lose You *Kandidate* (RAK 289)	22	11	12
53 Pop Muzik *M* (MCA 413)	28	13	5
26 Forever In Blue Jeans *Neil Diamond* (CBS 7047)	26	16	16
35 Remember Then *Showaddywaddy* (Arista ARIST 247)	27	17	17
43 Goodnight Tonight *Wings* (Parlophone R6023)	25	19	9
37 The Logical Song *Supertramp* (A&M AMS 7427)	24	23	7
– Hooray Hooray It's A Holi Holiday *Boney M* (Atlantic/Hansa 11279)	–	–	19
64 Knock On Wood *Amii Stewart* (Atlantic/Hansa K11214)	31	24	20

5	12	19	26
1 Bright Eyes *Art Garfunkel* (CBS 6947)	1	1	6
2 Some Girls *Racey* (RAK 291)	5	15	26
3 Pop Muzik *M* (MCA 413)	2	2	3
4 Hooray Hooray It's A Holi Holiday *Boney M* (Atlantic/Hansa K11279)	3	3	7
5 Goodnight Tonight *Wings* (Parlophone R6023)	8	14	31
6 Shake Your Body (Down To The Ground) *Jacksons* (Epic EPC 7181)	12	18	38
7 Hallelujah *Milk & Honey* (Polydor 2001 870)	14	22	49
8 Cool For Cats *Squeeze* (A&M AMS 7426)	16	32	56
9 The Logical Song *Supertramp* (A&M AMS 7427)	10	13	17
10 Knock On Wood *Amii Stewart* (Atlantic/Hansa K11214)	9	6	11
11 I Don't Wanna Lose You *Kandidate* (RAK 289)	17	20	39
12 The Runner *Three Degrees* (Ariola ARO 154)	27	40	68
13 Love You Inside Out *Bee Gees* (RSO 31)	13	16	22

	12	19	26
14 He's The Greatest Dancer *Sister Sledge* (Atlantic K11257)	37	49	75
15 Haven't Stopped Dancing Yet *Gonzalez* (Sidewalk SID 102)	19	21	40
16 Silly Thing/Who Killed Bambi *Sex Pistols* (Virgin VS256)	33	47	66
17 Wow *Kate Bush* (EMI 2911)	45	69	–
18 Forever In Blue Jeans *Neil Diamond* (CBS 7047)	23	61	–
19 Does Your Mother Know *Abba* (Epic EPC 7316)	4	4	4
20 One Way Ticket *Eruption* (Atlantic/Hansa K1266)	11	9	10
21 Reunited *Peaches & Herb* (Polydor POSP 43)	6	5	5
22 Banana Splits *Dickies* (A&M AMS 7431)	7	11	15
31 Boys Keep Swingin' *David Bowie* (RCA BOW 2)	15	19	9
27 Roxanne *Police* (A&M AMS 7348)	18	12	13
34 Dance Away *Roxy Music* (Polydor POSP 44)	20	7	2
25 Parisienne Walkways *Gary Moore* (MCA 419)	21	8	12
– Sunday Girl *Blondie* (Chrysalis CHS 2320)	–	10	1
28 Jimmy Jimmy *Undertones* (Sire SIR 4015)	24	17	16
– Boogie Wonderland *Earth Wind & Fire* (CBS 7292)	30	24	8
– Shine A Little Love *Electric Light Orchestra* (JET 144)	–	33	14
40 The Number One Song In Heaven *Sparks* (Virgin VS244)	34	25	18
32 Nice Legs Shame About Her Face *Monks* (Carrere CAR104)	25	23	19
44 Love Song *The Damned* (Chiswick CHIS 112)	26	27	20

JUNE 1979

	9	16	23	30
2				
1 Sunday Girl *Blondie* (Chrysalis CHS 2320)	1	2	4	7
2 Dance Away *Roxy Music* (Polydor POSP 44)	2	3	3	6
3 Pop Muzik *M* (MCA 413)	7	19	23	50
4 Reunited *Peaches & Herb* (Polydor POSP 43)	5	11	20	32
5 Boogie Wonderland *Earth Wind & Fire* (CBS 7292)	4	4	5	4
6 Does Your Mother Know *Abba* (Epic EPC 7316)	12	25	41	73
7 Boys Keep Swingin' *David Bowie* (RCA BOW 2)	9	15	26	48
8 Bright Eyes *Art Garfunkel* (CBS 6947)	18	22	30	47
9 Theme From Deer Hunter *Shadows* (EMI 2939)	10	9	10	12
10 Parisienne Walkways *Gary Moore* (MCA 419)	13	20	38	61
11 Hot Stuff *Donna Summer* (Casablanca CAN 151)	11	12	17	28
12 Roxanne *Police* (A&M AMS 7348)	16	32	51	–
13 One Way Ticket *Eruption* (Atlantic/Hansa K1266)	15	31	49	–
14 Knock On Wood *Amii Stewart* (Atlantic/Hansa K11214)	23	35	59	–
15 Ain't No Stoppin' Us Now *McFadden & Whitehead* (Philadelphia PIR 7365)	8	5	7	8
16 Shine A Little Love *Electric Light Orchestra* (Jet 144)	6	6	11	17
17 Hooray Hooray It's A Holi Holiday *Boney M* (Atlantic/Hansa K11279)	29	48	74	–
18 The Number One Song In Heaven *Sparks* (Virgin VS244)	14	17	18	38
19 Ring My Bell *Anita Ward* (TK TKR 7543)	3	1	1	2
20 Jimmy Jimmy *Undertones* (Sire SIR 4015)	19	21	46	74
21 Masquerade *The Skids* (Virgin VS 262)	17	14	15	16
25 Are Friends Electric *Tubeway Army* (Beggars Banquet BEG 18)	20	7	2	1
24 H.A.P.P.Y. Radio *Edwin Starr* (RCA TC 2408)	22	10	12	9
50 Up The Junction *Squeeze* (A&M AMS 7444)	25	13	6	3
41 The Lone Ranger *Quantum Jump* (Electric WOT 33)	33	16	8	5
30 Who Were You With In The Moonlight *Dollar* (Carrere CAR 110)	28	18	16	14
33 We Are Family *Sister Sledge* (Atlantic K11293)	21	8	9	11
37 Night Owl *Gerry Rafferty* (United Artists UP 3651)	34	26	13	10
38 Cavatina *John Williams* (Cube BUG 80)	32	30	14	13
31 Say When *Lene Lovich* (Stiff BUY 46)	37	24	19	19
48 Living On The Front Line *Eddy Grant* (Ice/Ensign ENY 26)	45	29	21	15

	9	**16**	**23**	**30**
– Light My Fire/137 Disco Heaven *Amii Stewart* (Atlantic/Hansa K11278)	–	44	24	18
42 Gertcha *Chas & Dave* (EMI 2947)	38	27	27	20

JULY 1979

	14	**21**	**28**
7			
1 Are Friends Electric *Tubeway Army* (Beggars Banquet BEG 18)	1	1	2
2 Up The Junction *Squeeze* (A&M AMS 7444)	4	9	29
3 Silly Games *Janet Kay* (Scope SC2)	2	2	3
4 Ring My Bell *Anita Ward* (TK TKR 7543)	10	32	44
5 Night Owl *Gerry Rafferty* (United Artists UP 3651)	6	7	28
6 Light My Fire/137 Disco Heaven *Amii Stewart* (Atlantic/Hansa 11278)	5	8	11
7 The Lone Ranger *Quantum Jump* (Electric WOT 33)	9	27	40
8 Boogie Wonderland *Earth Wind & Fire* (CBS 7282)	23	30	52
9 C'Mon Everybody *Sex Pistols* (Virgin VS 272)	3	3	8
10 Dance Away *Roxy Music* (Polydor POSP 44)	29	41	59
11 Sunday Girl *Blondie* (Chrysalis CHS 2320)	31	35	68
12 Living On The Front Line *Eddy Grant* (Ice/Ensign ENY 26)	11	18	24
13 Ain't No Stoppin' Us Now *McFadden & Whitehead* (Philadelphia PIR 7365)	39	52	–
14 Who Were You With In The Moonlight *Dollar* (Carrere CAR 110)	20	34	53
15 H.A.P.P.Y. Radio *Edwin Starr* (RCA TC 2408)	18	40	65
16 Cavatina *John Williams* (Cube BUG 80)	19	48	72
17 We Are Family *Sister Sledge* (Atlantic K11293)	35	37	64
18 Go West *Village People* (Mercury 6007 221)	15	17	22
19 Theme From Deer Hunter (Cavatina) *Shadows* (EMI 2939)	37	59	57
20 Maybe *Thom Pace* (RSO 34)	17	14	16
21 Babylon's Burning *Ruts* (Virgin VS 271)	7	11	17
28 Lady Lynda *Beach Boys* (Caribou CRB 7427)	8	6	9
22 Good Times *Chic* (Atlantic K 11310)	12	5	7
27 Wanted *Dooleys* (GTO GT 249)	13	10	5
26 Do Anything You Want To *Thin Lizzy* (Vertigo LIZZY 4)	14	16	19
31 Space Bass *Slick* (Fantasy FTC 176)	16	21	25
29 Girls Talk *Dave Edmunds* (Swan Song SSK 19418)	21	4	4
32 Breakfast In America *Supertramp* (A&M AMS 7451)	26	12	10
30 Born To Be Alive *Patrick Hernandez* (Gem/Aquarius GEM 4)	25	13	13
– Don't Like Mondays *Boomtown Rats* (Ensign ENY 30)	–	15	1
60 Can't Stand Losing You *Police* (A&M AMS 7381)	38	19	15
34 Death Disco *Public Image Ltd* (Virgin VS 274)	32	20	26
41 My Sharona *Knack* (Capitol CL 16087)	24	24	6
39 Bad Girls *Donna Summer* (Casablanca CAN 155)	22	22	14
– Angel Eyes/Voulez Vous *Abba* (Epic EPC 7499)	48	23	12
36 Chuck E's In Love *Rickie Lee Jones* (Warner Bros K17390)	30	31	18
54 If I Had You *Korgis* (Rialto TREB 103)	34	25	20

AUGUST 1979

	11	**18**	**25**
4			
1 I Don't Like Mondays *Boomtown Rats* (Ensign ENY 30)	1	1	2
2 Can't Stand Losing You *Police* (A&M AMS 7381)	4	7	19
3 Wanted *Dooleys* (GTO GT 249)	5	8	16
4 Girls Talk *Dave Edmunds* (Swan Song SSK 19418)	9	15	28
5 Angel Eyes/Voulez Vous *Abba* (Epic EPC 7499)	3	5	9
6 Silly Games *Janet Kay* (Scope SC2)	20	31	47

4		11	18	25
7 Are Friends Electric *Tubeway Army* (Beggars Banquet BEG 18)		19	38	52
8 My Sharona *Knack* (Capitol CL 16087)		12	25	41
9 Breakfast In America *Supertramp* (A&M AMS 7451)		13	24	38
10 Beat The Clock *Sparks* (Virgin VS 270)		11	12	14
11 Born To Be Alive *Patrick Hernandez* (Gem/Aquarius GEM 4)		10	18	21
12 Good Times *Chic* (Atlantic K11310)		15	26	40
13 If I Had You *Korgis* (Rialto TREB 103)		16	21	24
14 We Don't Talk Anymore *Cliff Richard* (EMI 2975)		2	2	1
15 Bad Girls *Donna Summer* (Casablanca CAN 155)		21	28	45
16 C'Mon Everybody *Sex Pistols* (Virgin VS 272)		26	47	61
17 The Diary of Horace Wimp *Electric Light Orchestra* (Jet 150)		8	10	10
18 Lady Lynda *Beach Boys* (Caribou CRB 7427)		22	46	66
19 Babylon Burning *Ruts* (Virgin VS 271)		50	61	67
20 Chuck E's In Love *Rickie Lee Jones* (Warner Bros K17390)		28	62	–
45 Reasons To Be Cheerful *Ian Dury & The Blockheads* (Stiff BUY 50)		6	3	4
23 Hersham Boys *Sham 69* (Polydor POSP 64)		7	6	7
26 After The Love Has Gone *Earth Wind & Fire* (CBS 7721)		14	4	5
22 Duke of Earl *Darts* (Magnet MAG 147)		17	9	6
27 Stay With Me Till Dawn *Judy Tzuke* (Rocket XPRES 17)		18	16	20
44 Bang Bang *B. A. Robertson* (Asylum K13152)		27	11	3
– Angel Eyes *Roxy Music* (Polydor POSP 67)		32	13	12
41 Gangsters *Specials* (2 Tone TT1)		24	14	8
31 Sweet Little Rock 'n' Roller *Showaddywaddy* (Arista 278)		29	17	15
30 Ooh What A Life *Gibson Brothers* (Island WIP 6503)		25	19	11
29 Morning Dance *Spyro Gyra* (Infinity INF 111)		23	20	17
66 Is She Really Going Out With Him *Joe Jackson* (A&M AMS 7459)		30	23	13
68 Money *Flying Lizards* (Virgin VS276)		47	30	18

SEPTEMBER 1979

1		8	15	22	29
1 We Don't Talk Anymore *Cliff Richard* (EMI 2976)		1	1	2	6
2 Don't Like Mondays *Boomtown Rats* (Ensign ENY 30)		8	16	24	55
3 Bang Bang *B. A. Robertson* (Asylum K 13152)		2	3	7	19
4 Angel Eyes *Roxy Music* (Polydor POSP 67)		4	6	10	20
5 After The Love Has Gone *Earth Wind & Fire* (CBS 7721)		10	15	37	56
6 Gangsters *Specials* (2 Tone TT1)		6	11	19	36
7 Duke Of Earl *Darts* (Magnet MAG 147)		18	19	41	62
8 Money *Flying Lizards* (Virgin VS 276)		5	10	17	33
9 Reasons To Be Cheerful *Ian Dury & The Blockheads* (Stiff BUY 50)		20	39	47	–
10 Ooh What A Life *Gibson Brothers* (Island WIP 6502)		12	13	31	42
11 Just When I Needed You Most *Randy Vanwarmer* (Island WIP 6516)		9	8	9	17
12 Hersham Boys *Sham 69* (Polydor POSP 64)		22	34	49	71
13 Is She Really Going Out With Him *Joe Jackson* (A&M AMS 7459)		15	20	39	60
14 Angel Eyes/Voulez Vous *Abba* (Epic EPC 7499)		29	40	66	–
15 Gotta Go Home *Boney M* (Atlantic/Hansa 11351)		13	12	13	22
16 Street Life *Crusaders* (MCA 513)		7	5	6	9
17 Sweet Little Rock 'n' Roller *Showaddywaddy* (Arista 278)		21	36	60	–
18 When You Are Young *Jam* (Polydor POSP 69)		17	22	32	35
19 The Diary of Horace Wimp *Electric Light Orchestra* (Jet 150)		31	52	–	–
20 Cars *Gary Numan* (Beggars Banquet BEG 23)		3	2	1	2

277

1		8	15	22	29
38	Don't Bring Me Down *Electric Light Orchestra* (Jet 153)	11	4	3	5
25	Duchess *Stranglers* United Artists BP 308)	14	14	18	25
23	Love's Gotta Hold On Me *Dollar* (Carrere CAR 122)	16	9	5	4
22	If I Said You Had A Beautiful . . . *Bellamy Brothers* (Warner Bros K 17405)	19	7	4	3
24	Lost In Music *Sister Sledge* (Atlantic K 11337)	24	17	20	27
30	Reggae For It Now *Bill Loveladay* (Charisma CB 337)	27	18	12	15
–	Message In A Bottle *Police* (A&M AMS 7474)	–	–	8	1
35	Strut Your Funky Stuff *Frantique* (Philadelphia PIR 7728)	26	23	11	10
48	Sail On *Commodores* (Motown TMG 1155)	34	24	14	8
28	Gone Gone Gone *Johnny Mathis* (CBS 7730)	25	21	15	18
44	Cruel To Be Kind *Nick Lowe* (Radar ADA 43)	32	26	16	14
–	Dreaming *Blondie* (Chrysalis CHS 2350)	–	–	–	7
–	Since You've Been Gone *Rainbow* (Polydor POSP 70)	–	33	26	11
–	What Ever You Want *Status Quo* (Vertigo 6059)	–	–	35	12
67	Time For Action *Secret Affair* (I SPY SEE 1)	40	27	21	13
–	Don't Stop 'Til You Get Enough *Michael Jackson* (Epic EPC 7763)	–	51	29	16

OCTOBER 1979

6		13	20	27
1	Message In A Bottle *Police* (A&M AMS 7474)	1	2	8
2	Dreaming *Blondie* (Chrysalis CHS 2350)	3	4	10
3	Cars *Gary Numan* (Beggars Banquet BEG 23)	7	14	37
4	What Ever You Want *Status Quo* (Vertigo 6059 242)	5	8	13
5	If I Said You Had A Beautiful . . . *Bellamy Brothers* (Warner Bros K17405)	8	16	30
6	Video Killed The Radio Star *Buggles* (Island WIP 6524)	2	1	2
7	Don't Stop 'Till You Get Enough *Michael Jackson* (Epic EPC 7763)	4	3	4
8	Since You've Been Gone *Rainbow* (Polydor POSP 70)	6	7	12
9	Love's Gotta Hold On Me *Dollar* (Carrere CAR 122)	12	26	38
10	Don't Bring Me Down *Electric Light Orchestra* (JET 153)	20	36	61
11	Kate Bush Live On Stage (EMI MIEP 2991)	10	13	25
12	Cruel To Be Kind *Nick Lowe* (Radar ADA 43)	14	19	31
13	Sail On *Commodores* (Motown TMG 1155)	13	38	51
14	Strut Your Funky Stuff *Frantique* (Philadelphia PIR 7728)	17	34	47
15	Time For Action *Secret Affair* (I SPY SEE 1)	21	24	56
16	The Prince *Madness* (2 Tone CHSTT 3)	19	22	28
17	We Don't Talk Anymore *Cliff Richard* (EMI 2975)	22	59	–
18	Street Life *Crusaders* (MCA 513)	24	49	71
19	Reggae For It Now *Bill Lovelady* (Charisma CB 337)	31	54	–
20	Queen Of Hearts *Dave Edmunds* (Swan Song SSK 19419)	18	11	14
28	One Day At A Time *Lena Martell* (Pye 7N 46021)	9	5	1
21	Every Day Hurts *Sad Cafe* (RCA PB 5180)	11	6	5
22	You Can Do It *Al Hudson & The Soul Partners* (MCA 511)	15	15	19
30	Chosen Few *Dooleys* (GTO GT 258)	16	10	7
40	When You're In Love *Dr Hook* (Capitol CL 16039)	26	9	3
34	O.K. Fred *Erroll Dunkley* (Scope SC 6)	23	12	11
27	Back Of My Hand *Jags* (Island WIP 6501)	28	17	20
53	Tusk *Fleetwood Mac* (Warner Bros K 17468)	30	18	9
38	The Devil Went Down To Georgia *Charlie Daniels* (Epic EPC 7737)	27	20	15
–	Gimme Gimme Gimme *Abba* (Epic EPC 7914)	–	30	6
64	Gonna Get Along Without You Now *Viola Wills* (Ariola/Hansa AHA 546)	47	27	16
42	Making Plans for Nigel *XTC* (Virgin VS 282)	37	28	17
–	My Forbidden Lover *Chic* (Atlantic K 11385)	51	23	18

NOVEMBER 1979

3		10	17	24
1	One Day At A Time *Lena Martell* (Pye 7N46021)	1*	2	5
2	When You're In Love *Dr Hook* (Capitol CL16039)	2	1	1
3	Every Day Hurts *Sad Cafe* (RCA PB5180)	4	7	24
4	Gimme Gimme Gimme *Abba* (Epic EPC 7914)	3	6	7
5	Video Killed The Radio Star *Buggles* (Island WIP 6524)	12	25	42
6	Don't Stop 'Till You Get Enough *Michael Jackson* (Epic EPC 7763)	16	31	41
7	Chosen Few *Dooleys* (GTO GT258)	14	28	40
8	Tusk *Fleetwood Mac* (Warner Bros K 17468)	6	9	25
9	Gonna Get Along Without You Now *Viola Wills* (Ariola/Hansa AHA546)	8	12	19
10	Crazy Little Thing Called Love *Queen* (EMI 5001)	5	3	2
11	O.K. Fred *Erroll Dunkley* (Scope SC6)	13	19	37
12	Message In A Bottle *Police* (A&M AMS 7474)	23	47	56
13	Dreaming *Blondie* (Chrysalis CHS 2350)	35	51	–
14	The Devil Went Down To Georgia *Charlie Daniels* (Epic EPC 7737)	24	30	57
15	My Forbidden Lover *Chic* (Atlantic K11385)	20	23	59
16	Star *Earth Wind & Fire* (CBS 7902)	18	21	43
17	Queen Of Hearts *Dave Edmunds* (Swan Song SSK 19419)	36	53	–
18	Since You've Been Gone *Rainbow* (Polydor POSP 70)	31	45	–
19	What Ever You Want *Status Quo* (Vertigo 6059 242)	38	54	–
20	She's In Love With You *Suzi Quatro* (RAK 299)	11	11	14
29	Eton Rifles *Jam* (Polydor POSP 83)	7	4	3
21	On My Radio *Selecter* (Two Tone CHSTT4)	9	8	16
32	Still *Commodores* (Motown TMG 1166)	10	5	4
26	The Sparrow *Ramblers* (Decca F1380)	15	13	11
23	Making Plans For Nigel *XTC* (Virgin VS 282)	17	20	33
28	Message To You Rudy/Nite Klub *Specials* (2 Tone TT5)	19	10	12
72	No More Tears (Enough Is Enough) *Donna Summer and Barbra Streisand* (Casablanca/CBS CAN 114 CBS 8000)	27	14	6
42	Knocked It Off *B. A. Robertson* (Asylum K 1296)	25	15	8
33	Ladies Night *Kool & The Gang* (Mercury KOOL 7/12)	21	16	9
31	Rise *Herb Alpert* (A&M AMS 7465)	26	17	13
30	He Was Beautiful (Cavatina) *Iris Williams* (Columbia DB 9070)	29	18	22
–	One Step Beyond *Madness* (Stiff BUY 56)	51	22	10
–	Complex *Gary Numan* (Beggars Banquet BEG 29)	–	–	15
–	Confusion/Last Train to London *Electric Light Orchestra* (JET 166)	–	33	17
–	Que Sera Mi Vida *Gibson Brothers* Island WIP 6525	–	34	18
35	I Don't Want To Be A Freak *Dynasty* (Solar FB 1694)	30	26	20

*In some printed charts the Lena Martell record was listed at Number 2; this was incorrect.

DECEMBER 1979

1		8	15	22
1	When You're In Love *Dr Hook* (Capitol CL 16039)	4	8	21
2	Crazy Little Thing Called Love *Queen* (EMI 5001)	7	12	26
3	No More Tears (Enough Is Enough) *Donna Summer and Barbra Streisand* (Casablanca/CBS CAN 114 CBS 8000)	3	5	11
4	Still *Commodores* (Motown TMG 1166)	11	17	42
5	Walking On The Moon *Police* (A&M AMS 7494)	1	2	3
6	Complex *Gary Numan* (Beggars Banquet BEG 29)	8	15	23
7	One Step Beyond *Madness* (Stiff BUY 56)	10	9	19

1		8	15	22
8	Confusion/Last Train To London *Electric Light Orchestra* (HET166)	9	11	15
9	Eton Rifles *Jam* (Polydor POSP 83)	13	43	54
10	Knocked It Off *B. A. Robertson* (Asylum K12396)	20	41	58
11	Ladies Night *Kool & The Gang* (Mercury KOOL 7/12)	18	33	49
12	Que Sera Mi Vida *Gibson Brothers* (Island WIP 6525)	5	6	8
13	Diamond Smiles *Boomtown Rats* (Ensign ENY 33)	15	16	27
14	It's A Disco Night (Rock Don't Stop) *Isley Brothers* (Epic EPC7911)	17	22	44
15	The Sparrow *Ramblers* (Decca F13860)	19	28	31
16	One Day At A Time *Lena Martell* (Pye 7N46021)	27	32	40
17	Message To You Rudy/Nite Klub *Specials* (2 Tone TT5)	32	54	74
18	Rockabilly Rebel *Matchbox* (Magnet MAG 155)	21	19	22
19	Gimme Gimme Gimme *Abba* (Epic EPC 7914)	34	52	68
20	Rise *Herb Alpert* (A&M AMS 7465)	23	46	66
26	Another Brick In The Wall *Pink Floyd* (Harvest HAR 5194)	2	1	1
22	I Only Want To Be With You *Tourists* (Logo GO370)	6	4	5
38	Rapper's Delight *Sugarhill Gang* (Sugarhill SHL 101)	12	3	6
23	Nights In White Satin *Moody Blues* (Deram DM 161)	14	14	18
21	Union City Blue *Blondie* (Chrysalis CHS2400)	16	13	14
25	Off The Wall *Michael Jackson* (Epic EPC 8045)	22	7	12
26	My Simple Heart *Three Degrees* (Ariola ARO 202)	31	10	9
36	Living On An Island *Status Quo* (Vertigo 6059 248)	30	18	16
61	Wonderful Christmas Time *Paul McCartney* (Parlophone R6029)	31	20	7
–	I Have A Dream *Abba* (Epic EPC 8088)	–	21	2
–	Day Trip To Bangor *Fiddler's Dram* (Dingles SID211)	–	26	4
47	Brass In Pocket *The Pretenders* (Real ARE 11)	33	30	10
–	John I'm Only Dancing (Again) *David Bowie* (RCA BOW4)	–	23	13
34	Is It Love You're After *Rose Royce* (Whitfield K17456)	29	24	17
–	Tears Of A Clown/Ranking Full Stop *Beat* (2 Tone CHSTT6)	67	31	20

There was no chart for December 29.

1979 – BEST-SELLING SINGLES

1 Bright Eyes *Art Garfunkel* (CBS)
2 Heart Of Glass *Blondie* (Chrysalis)
3 We Don't Talk Anymore *Cliff Richard* (EMI)
4 Don't Like Mondays *Boomtown Rats* (Ensign)
5 When You're In Love *Dr Hook* (Capitol)
6 I Will Survive *Gloria Gaynor* (Polydor)
7 Are Friends Electric *Tubeway Army* (Beggars Banquet)
8 Dance Away *Roxy Music* (Polydor)
9 Sunday Girl *Blondie* (Chrysalis)
10 One Day At A Time *Lena Martell* (Pye)
11 Message In A Bottle *Police* (A&M)
12 Pop Muzik *M* (MCA)
13 Hit Me With Your Rhythm Stick *Ian Dury & The Blockheads* (Stiff)
14 Oliver's Army *Elvis Costello & The Attractions*, (Radar)
15 Tragedy *Bee Gees* (RSO)
16 Chiquitita *Abba* (Epic)
17 Video Killed The Radio Star *Buggles* (Island)
18 Cars *Gary Numan* (Beggars Banquet)
19 Every Day Hurts *Sad Cafe* (RCA)
20 Ring My Bell *Anita Ward* (TK)

1979 – BEST-SELLING ALBUMS

1 Parallel Lines *Blondie* (Chrysalis)
2 Discovery *Electric Light Orchestra* (Jet)
3 The Very Best Of Leo Sayer *Leo Sayer* (Chrysalis)
4 Breakfast In America *Supertramp* (A&M)
5 Voulez Vous *Abba* (Epic)
6 Barbra Streisand's Greatest Hits Volume 2 *Barbra Streisand* (CBS)
7 Spirits Having Flown *Bee Gees* (RSO)
8 Greatest Hits Volume 2 *Abba* (Epic)
9 Regatta De Blanc *Police* (A&M)
10 Manilow Magic *Barry Manilow* (Arista)
11 Greatest Hits *Rod Stewart* (Riva)
12 Last The Whole Night Long *James Last* (Polydor)
13 Armed Forces *Elvis Costello & The Attractions* (Radar)
14 Outlandos D'Amour *Police* (A&M)
15 The Best Disco Album In The World *Various* (WEA)
16 Replicas *Tubeway Army* (Beggars Banquet)
17 I Am *Earth Wind & Fire* (CBS)
18 C'Est Chic *Chic* (Atlantic)
19 Dire Straits *Dire Straits* (Vertigo)
20 Manifesto *Roxy Music* (Polydor/EG)

1979 – BEST-SELLING ARTISTS

Male Artists (Singles)

1 Art Garfunkel
2 Edwin Starr
3 Dave Edmunds
4 B. A. Robertson
5 Cliff Richard
6 Gary Numan
7 Gerry Rafferty
8 Michael Jackson
9 David Bowie
10 Gene Chandler

Female Artists (Singles)

1 Lene Lovich
2 Donna Summer
3 Amii Stewart
4 Gloria Gaynor
5 Kate Bush
6 Lena Martell
7 Janet Kay
8 Anita Ward
9 Olivia Newton-John
10 Anne Murray

Groups (Singles)

1 Blondie
2 Abba
3 Earth Wind & Fire
4 Chic
5 Police
6 Electric Light Orchestra
7 Sex Pistols
8 Boney M
9 Roxy Music
10 Three Degrees

Male Artists (Albums)

1 Barry Manilow
2 Jeff Wayne
3 Neil Diamond
4 James Last
5 Rod Stewart
6 Rod Stewart
7 Bob Dylan
8 Mike Oldfield
9 Gerry Rafferty
10 Billy Joel

Female Artists (Albums)

1 Kate Bush
2 Barbra Streisand
3 Donna Summer
4 Judy Tzuke
5 Rickie Lee Jones
6 Billy Jo Spears
7 Lena Martell
8 Diana Ross
9 Doris Day
10 Ruby Winters

Groups (Albums)

1 Electric Light Orchestra
2 Blondie
3 Earth Wind & Fire
4 Police
5 Abba
6 Dire Straits
7 Sex Pistols
8 Supertramp
9 Ian Dury & The Blockheads
10 Meat Loaf

Top Producer (Singles)

1 Bernard Edwards/Nile Rodgers
1 Mike Chapman
3 Mickie Most
4 Georgio Moroder
5 Andersson/Ulvaeus

Top Producer (Albums)

1 Mike Chapman
2 Jeff Lynne
3 Ron Dante/Barry Manilow
4 Gary Numan
5 Todd Rundgren

1980

It took a 1979 chart release to set the year in real motion. Once Pink Floyd's first hit in 11 years, Another Brick In The Wall, had disappeared it was replaced by class pop with disco flavour as former pop paper photographer and writer Chrissie Hynde and her Pretenders sang of Brass In Pocket.

And quite a few did coin the money. There were four hits for The Police, three in the 20 for newcomer Sheena Easton, four Top Tenners for fun band Madness busily consolidating their '79 entry, two Number One's for the Jam who also saw a re-issue of their old hits, Abba followed the Jam score-card, exciting new outfit Dexy's Midnight Runners hit the top with Geno and 7 with There There My Dear but even their success, or that or The Police, or anyone, slightly paled against the relentless success of Blondie. Debbie and her musicians performed the hat-trick with Atomic, Call Me and The Tide Is High.

That disco remained a potent force was illustrated by the high placing, in the year's listing of the Top 100 singles, by records such as Feels Like I'm In Love from Kelly Marie, the infectious D.I.S.C.O. from Ottowan, the pacey Working My Way Back To You from a returning Detroit Spinners, Upside Down from long-lasting Diana Ross, If You're Looking For A Way Out by Odyssey and the curious infatuation that people had with Theme From Mash.

Romance had its place. Fern Kinney made lovers happy with Together We Are Beautiful which is always an easier expression than Everyone Thinks We Are Beautiful. Randy Crawford had hearts fluttering with One Day I'll Fly Away, both deliciously sung and arranged. The male romance was headed by Johnny Logan, though more plaintive and reflective than passionate in What's Another Year.

For some, 1980 was anything but 'another' for they will remember it as the time when they had their first hit. Into this category came Sheena Easton, the Nolans (first time in the 20), Jona Lewie (as himself), Linx, Lipps Inc. the amazingly titled Splodgenessabounds, Ottowan, Bad

283

Manners, Liquid Gold (first in 20) and the Vapors. Of course, there were others.

The familiars had their place of course – Barbra Streisand scored well with Woman In Love and it came with one of the best-ever promotional videos, there was Kenny Rogers and Don McLean, David Bowie and Stevie Wonder.

But the year was overshadowed with the tragic death of John Lennon and it came as the former Beatle was re-launching his career, he had come out of hibernation, there was a new record company and the song at the time of his death now seems a rather sick co-incidence (Just Like) Starting Over. It began a flurry of Lennon singles buying. Imagine and the splendid Happy Christmas (War Is Over) charted and early in '81 he monopolised the top of the chart.

Don't Stand So Close To Me from Police was the year's most successful single, but for me at any rate some of the best 45's came from The Specials – Too Much Too Young (EP), Rat Race, Stereotype and at the year's end Do Nothing. It was the time when the 'Coventry sound' was at its selling height as The Specials were joined by The Selecter and The Beat; great sounds and in live performance they were all spot on.

JANUARY 1980

5		12	19	26
1 Another Brick In The Wall *Pink Floyd* (Harvest HAR5194)		1	5	10
2 I Have A Dream *Abba* (Epic EPC 8088)		2	7	13
3 Day Trip To Bangor *Fiddler's Dram* (Dingles SID211)		4	9	24
4 I Only Want To Be With You *Tourists* (Logo GO370)		5	10	25
5 Brass In Pocket *Pretenders* (Real ARE 11)		3	1	1
6 Wonderful Christmas Time *Paul McCartney* (Parlophone R6029)		18	51	–
7 Rapper's Delight *Sugarhill Gang* (Sugarhill SHL 101)		8	15	23
8 Walking On The Moon *Police* (A&M AMS 7494)		9	33	58
9 Que Sera Mi Vida *Gibson Brothers* (Island WIP6525)		16	23	52
10 My Simple Heart *Three Degrees* (Ariola ARO 202)		10	16	38
11 Off The Wall *Michael Jackson* (Epic EPC8045)		25	29	57
12 John I'm Only Dancing (Again) *David Bowie* (RCA BOW 4)		12	18	43
13 It Won't Seem Like Christmas Without You *Elvis Presley* (RCA PB9464)		24	42	–
14 No More Tears *Donna Summer* (Casablanca/CBS CAN 174 CBS 8000)		29	48	66
15 Is It Love You're After *Rose Royce* (Whitfield K17456)		13	13	19
16 Union City Blue *Blondie* (Chrysalis CHS2400)		23	35	59
17 Tears Of A Clown/Ranking Full Stop *Beat* (2 Tone CHSTT6)		6	8	11
18 Living On An Island *Status Quo* (Vertigo 6059 248)		17	28	42
19 Nights In White Satin *Moody Blues* (Deram DM 161)		39	46	65
20 Please Don't Go *K. C. & The Sunshine Band* (T.K. TKR 7558)		7	3	5
24 With You I'm Born Again *Billy Preston/Syreeta* (Motown TMG1159)		11	2	2
54 My Girl *Madness* (Stiff BUY 62)		14	4	3
29 London Calling *Clash* (CBS 8087)		15	11	14
27 Blue Peter *Mike Oldfield* (Virgin VS 317)		19	24	32
40 I'm In The Mood For Dancing *Nolan Sisters* (Epic EPC8068)		20	6	4
39 Green Onions *Booker T & The M.G.'s* (Atlantic K10109)		26	12	7
58 Better Love Next Time *Dr Hook* (Capitol CL 16112)		31	14	8
69 Babe *Styx* (A&M AMS 7489)		37	17	6
42 I Wanna Hold Your Hand *Dollar* (Carrere CAR 131)		30	19	9
23 Working For The Yankee Dollar *Skids* (Virgin VS 306)		21	20	28
– It's Different For Girls *Joe Jackson* (A&M AMS 7493)		50	27	12
– Too Much Too Young *Specials* (2 Tone CHSTT7)		–	–	15
61 Spirits (Having Flown) *Bee Gees* (RSO 52)		38	26	16
72 I Hear You Now *Jon & Vangelis* (Polydor POSP 96)		45	25	17
65 We Got The Funk *Positive Force* (Sugarhill SHL102)		34	32	18
33 Spacer *Sheila and B. Devotion* (Carrere CAR 128)		28	22	20

FEBRUARY 1980

2		9	16	23
1 Too Much Too Young/Guns Of Navarone *Specials* (2 Tone CHSTT 7)		1	2	4
2 Brass In Pocket *Pretenders* (Real ARE 11)		7	19	42
3 My Girl *Madness* (Stiff BUY 62)		4	10	29
4 I'm In The Mood For Dancing *Nolans* (Epic EPC 8068)		3	3	11
5 It's Different For Girls *Joe Jackson* (A&M AMS 7493)		5	7	19
6 With You I'm Born Again *Billy Preston/Syreeta* (Motown TMG1159)		9	32	51
7 Babe *Styx* (A&M AMS7489)		6	9	17
8 Please Don't Go *K.C. & The Sunshine Band* (T.K. TKR 7558)		14	33	47
9 Green Onions *Booker T. & The M.G.'s* (Atlantic K10109)		10	25	36
10 Coward Of The County *Kenny Rogers* (United Artists UP614)		2	1	1

2

	9	16	23
11 I Wanna Hold Your Hand *Dollar* (Carrere CAR 131)	16	35	58
12 7Teen *Regents* (Rialto TREB 111)	11	15	15
13 Better Love Next Time *Dr Hook* (Capitol CL16112)	17	24	56
14 Someone's Looking At You *Boomtown Rats* (Ensign ENY34)	8	4	7
15 I Hear You Now *Jon & Vangelis* (Polydor POSP 96)	12	8	13
16 London Calling *Clash* (CBS 8087)	34	62	–
17 Tears Of A Clown/Ranking Full Stop *Beat* (2 Tone CHSTT6)	37	52	–
18 Spacer *Sheila and B. Devotion* (Carrere CAR 128)	19	30	53
19 Jazz Carnival *Azymuth* (Milestone MRC 101)	22	29	49
20 Living By Numbers *New Muzik* (GTO GT261)	13	14	22
40 Captain Beaky *Keith Michell* (Polydor POSP 106)	15	5	5
37 And The Beat Goes On *Whispers* (Solar SO 1)	18	6	2
30 Save Me *Queen* (EMI 5022)	20	11	20
– Rock With You *Michael Jackson* (Epic EPC 8206)	35	12	12
62 Carrie *Cliff Richard* (EMI 5006)	27	13	6
29 Three Minute Hero *Selecter* (2 Tone CHSTT8)	21	16	21
– I Can't Stand Up For Falling Down *Elvis Costello* (F.Beat XX1)	–	17	9
– So Good To Be Back Home Again *Tourists* (Logo TOUR1)	46	18	10
36 Baby I Love You *Ramones* (Sire SIR 4031)	25	20	8
– Atomic *Blondie* (Chrysalis CHS 2410)	–	–	3
– Take That Look Off Your Face *Marti Webb* (Polydor POSP100)	57	49	14
52 Riders In The Sky *Shadows* (EMI 5027)	26	21	16
35 Living In The Plastic Age *Buggles* (Island WIP 6540)	28	27	18

MARCH 1980

1

	8	15	22	29
1 Atomic *Blondie* (Chrysalis CHS2410)	1	2	7	18
2 Coward Of The County *Kenny Rogers* (United Artists UP614)	6	15	18	39
3 And The Beat Goes On *Whispers* (Solar SO1)	5	10	17	33
4 Carrie *Cliff Richard* (EMI5006)	7	11	19	46
5 I Can't Stand Up For Falling Down *Elvis Costello* (F Beat XX1)	4	12	22	55
6 Take That Look Off Your Face *Marti Webb* (Polydor POSP 100)	3	3	3	6
7 Rock With You *Michael Jackson* (Epic EPC 8206)	9	13	21	48
8 So Good To Be Back Home Again *Tourists* (Logo TOUR 1)	11	19	37	62
9 Together We Are Beautiful *Fern Kinney* (WEA K 7911)	2	1	2	2
10 Captain Beaky *Keith Michell* (Polydor POSP 106)	17	27	44	64
11 Baby I Love You *Ramones* (Sire SIR 4031)	14	22	47	–
12 Riders In The Sky *Shadows* (EMI 5027)	13	17	32	53
13 Too Much Too Young/Guns Of Navarone *Specials* (2 Tone CHSTT7)	21	48	64	71
14 Someone's Looking At You *Boomtown Rats* (Ensign ENY 34)	22	50	62	–
15 I'm In The Mood For Dancing *Nolans* (Epic EPC 8068)	27	42	70	72
16 Living In The Plastic Age *Buggles* (Island WIP 6540)	20	32	–	–
17 Games Without Frontiers *Peter Gabriel* (Charisma CB354)	8	4	6	9
18 I Hear You Now *Jon & Vangelis* (Polydor POSP 96)	36	61	–	–
19 So Lonely *Police* (A&M AMS 7402)	12	6	11	16
20 Hands Off – She's Mine *The Beat* (Go-Feet FEET 1)	16	9	13	15
22 All Night Long *Rainbow* (Polydor POSP104)	10	5	9	7
25 At The Edge *Stiff Little Fingers* (Chrysalis CHS 2406)	15	18	20	22
34 Turning Japanese *Vapors* (United Artists BP334)	18	8	4	3

1	8	15	22	29
40 Cuba/Better Do It Salsa *Gibson Brothers* (Island WIP6540)	19	16	12	14
30 Do That To Me One More Time *Captain & Tennille* (Casablanca CAN175)	25	7	10	8
47 Dance Yourself Dizzy *Liquid Gold* (Polo 1)	23	14	5	4
48 Working My Way Back To You/Forgive Me Girl *Detroit Spinners* (Atlantic K11432)	31	20	8	5
– Going Underground *Jam* (Polydor POSP 113)	–	–	1	1
44 Stomp *Brothers Johnson* (A&M AMS7509)	32	25	14	11
67 Echo Beach *Martha & The Muffins* (Dindisc DIN9)	39	21	15	10
– Spirit of Radio *Rush* (Mercury RADIO 7)	–	23	16	13
69 Poison Ivy *Lambrettas* (Rocket XPRES 25)	44	28	27	12
65 Another Nail In The Heart *Squeeze* (A&M AMS 7507)	40	27	26	17
– January February *Barbara Dickson* (Epic EPC 8115)	–	59	29	19
– King – Food For Thought *UB40* (Graduate GRAD 6)	65	55	40	20

APRIL 1980

5	12	19	26
1 Going Underground/Dreams Of Children *Jam* (Polydor POSP 113)	3	6	20
2 Dance Yourself Dizzy *Liquid Gold* (Polo 1)	2	3	8
3 Working My Way Back To You/Forgive Me Girl *Detroit Spinners* (Atlantic K11432)	1	1	3
4 Turning Japanese *Vapors* (United Artists BP334)	7	17	34
5 Together We Are Beautiful *Fern Kinney* (WEA K79111)	14	28	46
6 Stomp *Brothers Johnson* (A&M AMS7509)	9	15	29
7 Poison Ivy *Lambrettas* (Rocket XPRES 25)	8	10	15
8 Turn It On Again *Genesis* (Charisma CB 356)	10	13	16
9 Sexy Eyes *Dr Hook* (Capitol CL 16127)	4	5	5
10 King – Food For Thought *UB40* (Graduate GRAD6)	5	4	4
11 Echo Beach *Martha & The Muffins* (Dindisc DIN9)	15	21	42
12 January February *Barbara Dickson* (Epic EPC8115)	11	11	13
13 All Night Long *Rainbow* (Polydor POSP 104)	20	35	55
14 Night Boat To Cairo EP *Madness* (Stiff BUY 71)	6	7	10
15 Living After Midnight *Judas Priest* (CBS 8379)	12	16	18
16 Do That To Me One More Time *Captain & Tennille* (Casablanca CAN175)	27	45	–
17 My World *Secret Affair* (I-SPY SEE5)	16	18	19
18 Another Nail In The Heart *Squeeze* (A&M AMS 7507)	23	27	25
19 Don't Push It, Don't Force It *Leon Haywood* (20th Century TC2443)	18	14	12
20 Happy House *Siouxsie & The Banshees* (Polydor POSP 117)	17	20	22
26 Talk Of The Town *Pretenders* (Real ARE12)	13	8	9
40 Silver Dream Machine *David Essex* (Mercury BIKE 1)	19	9	6
– Call Me *Blondie* (Chrysalis CHS 2414)	21	2	1
37 Geno *Dexy's Midnight Runners* (Parlophone R6033)	29	12	2
25 Kool In The Kaftan *B. A. Robertson* (Asylum K 12427)	25	19	17
– Coming Up *Paul McCartney* (Parlophone R6035)	–	62	7
61 Toccata *Sky* (Ariola ARO 300)	46	24	11
31 My Oh My *Sad Cafe* (RCA SDA 3)	24	23	14

MAY 1980

3	10	17	24	31
1 Geno *Dexy's Midnight Runners* (Parlophone R6033)	1	2	5	10
2 Coming Up *Paul McCartney* (Parlophone R6035)	3	3	11	24
3 Call Me *Blondie* (Chrysalis CHS 2414)	4	14	37	57

3	10	17	24	31
4 Silver Dream Machine *David Essex* (Mercury BIKE 1)	5	10	15	34
5 Toccata *Sky* (Ariola ARO 300)	6	15	21	47
6 King – Food For Thought *UB40* (Graduate GRAD 6)	13	35	51	68
7 Working My Way Back To You/Forgive Me Girl *Detroit Spinners* (Atlantic K11432)	18	42	69	–
8 Sexy Eyes *Dr Hook* (Capitol CL 16127)	16	34	54	–
9 Talk Of The Town *Pretenders* (Real ARE 12)	22	36	73	–
10 Check Out The Groove *Bobby Thurston* (Epic EPC8348)	12	16	22	56
11 My Perfect Cousin *Undertones* (Sire SIR 4038)	10	9	29	41
12 Don't Push It, Don't Force It *Leon Haywood* (20th Century TC2443)	19	28	60	–
13 The Groove *Rodney Franklin* (CBS 8429)	7	11	14	46
14 Night Boat To Cairo EP *Madness* (Stiff BUY 71)	29	49	70	–
15 What's Another Year *Johnny Logan* (Epic EPC8572)	2	1	1	3
16 My Oh My *Sad Cafe* (RCA SAD 3)	24	53	74	–
17 Dance Yourself Dizzy *Liquid Gold* (Polo 1)	40	54	71	–
18 January February *Barbara Dickson* (Epic EPC 8115)	46	66	–	–
19 I Shoulda Loved Ya *Narada Michael Walden* (Atlantic K11413)	11	8	9	16
20 Wheels of Steel *Saxon* (Carrere CAR 143)	20	27	38	65
23 Golden Years (Live EP) *Motorhead* (Bronze BRO 92)	8	12	20	28
31 No Doubt About It *Hot Chocolate* (RAK 310)	9	6	2	2
36 Hold On To My Love *Jimmy Ruffin* (RSO 57)	14	7	8	11
25 Don't Make Waves *Nolans* (Epic EPC 8349)	15	13	12	15
58 Mirror In The Bathroom *Beat* (Go Feet 2)	17	4	4	7
55 She's Out Of My Life *Michael Jackson* (Epic EPC8384)	25	5	3	4
39 Let's Go Round Again *Average White Band* (RCA AWB1)	28	17	17	12
– Over You *Roxy Music* (Polydor POSP 93)	–	18	7	6
29 Breathing *Kate Bush* (EMI 5058)	26	19	16	30
30 Fool For Your Loving *Whitesnake* (United Artists BP352)	21	20	13	14
– Theme From Mash *Mash* (CBS 8536)	42	23	6	1
– We Are Glass *Gary Numan* (Beggars Banquet BEG36)	–	–	10	5
– Rat Race/Rude Buoys Outa Jail *Specials* (2 Tone CHSTT11)	–	–	18	8
61 You Gave Me Love *Crown Heights Affair* (Mercury MER 9)	35	25	19	17
– Funky Town *Lipps Inc.* (Casablanca CAN 194)	–	70	25	9
– Crying *Don McLean* (EMI 5051)	41	40	28	13
– Midnite Dynamos *Matchbox* (Magnet MAG 169)	67	33	26	18
– You'll Always Find Me In The Kitchen At Parties *Jona Lewie* (Stiff BUY 73)	73	30	27	19
– D-A-A-Ance *Lambrettas* (Rocket XPRES 33)	–	–	48	20

JUNE 1980

7	14	21	28
1 Theme From Mash *Mash* (CBS 8536)	1	2	4
2 No Doubt About It *Hot Chocolate* (RAK 310)	4	5	15
3 Funky Town *Lipps Inc.* (Casablanca CAN 194)	3	3	2
4 Crying *Don McLean* (EMI5061)	2	1	1
5 Rat Race/Rude Buoys Outa Jail *Specials* (2 Tone CHSTT)	7	11	10
6 Over You *Roxy Music* (Polydor POSP 93)	5	9	17
7 We Are Glass *Gary Numan* (Beggars Banquet BEG 36)	9	19	48
8 She's Out Of My Life *Michael Jackson* (Epic EPC 8384)	11	32	53
9 Let's Get Serious *Jermaine Jackson* (Motown TMG 1183)	8	8	9
10 What's Another Year *Johnny Logan* (Epic EPC 8572)	32	50	–
11 Mirror In The Bathroom *The Beat* (Go-Feet FEET2)	26	41	59
12 You Gave Me Love *Crown Heights Affair* (Mercury MER 9)	10	10	12

7	14	21	28
13 Let's Go Round Again *Average White Band* (RCA AWB1)	13	34	48
14 Back Together Again *Roberta Flack/Donny Hathaway* (Atlantic K11481)	6	4	3
15 Hold On To My Love *Jimmy Ruffin* (RSO 57)	33	42	–
16 Midnite Dynamos *Matchbox* (Magnet MAG 169)	15	14	21
17 Geno *Dexy's Midnight Runners* (Parlophone R6033)	35	54	–
18 Fool For Your Loving *Whitesnake* (United Artists BP 352)	38	52	
19 You'll Always Find Me In The Kitchen At Parties *Jona Lewie* (Stiff BUY 73)	16	21	28
20 Just Can't Give You Up *Mystic Merlin* (Capitol CL16133)	24	33	–
21 D-A-A-A-N-C-E *Lambrettas* (Rocket XPRES 33)	12	15	22
26 Messages *Orchestral Manoeuvres In The Dark* (Dindisc DIN 15)	14	13	13
29 Behind The Groove *Teena Marie* (Motown TMG 1185)	17	7	6
23 Breaking The Law *Judas Priest* (CBS8644)	18	12	18
27 Everybody's Got To Learn Sometime *Korgis* (Rialto TREB 115)	19	6	5
22 I'm Alive *Electric Light Orchestra* (Jet 179)	20	20	26
32 Substitute *Liquid Gold* (Polo POLO4)	21	16	8
– Six Pack *Police* (A&M AMPP 6001)	31	17	34
– Play The Game *Queen* (EMI 5076)	34	18	16
– Simon Templer/Two Pints of Lager *Splodgenessabounds* (Deram BUM 1)	42	22	7
– Jump To The Beat *Stacy Lattisaw* (Atlantic K11496)	57	31	11
– Xanadu *Olivia Newton-John* (JET185)	–	39	14
– My Way of Thinking/I Think It's Going to Rain *UB40* (Graduate GRA8)	72	29	19
– Waterfalls *Paul McCartney* (Parlophone R6037)	–	53	20

JULY 1980

5	12	19	26
1 Crying *Don McLean* (EMI 5051)	4	8	18
2 Funky Town *Lipps Inc.* (Casablanca CAN 194)	6	12	24
3 Xanadu *Olivia Newton-John/Electric Light Orchestra* (Jet 185)	1	1	2
4 Back Together Again *Roberta Flack/Donny Hathaway* (Atlantic K11481)	13	18	49
5 Everybody's Got To Learn Sometime *Korgis* (Rialto TREB115)	8	14	35
6 Jump To The Beat *Stacy Lattisaw* (Atlantic K11496)	3	3	4
7 Simon Templer/Two Pints Of Lager *Splodgenessabounds* (Deram BUM 1)	10	14	40
8 My Way Of Thinking/I Think It's Going to Rain *UB40* (Graduate GRAD8)	7	6	10
9 To Be Or Not To Be *B. A. Robertson* (Asylum K12449)	12	11	27
10 Behind The Groove *Teena Marie* (Motown TMG1185)	15	30	44
11 Waterfalls *Paul McCartney* (Parlophone R6037)	11	9	16
12 Use It Up And Wear It Out *Odyssey* (RCA PC1962)	2	2	1
13 Substitute *Liquid Gold* (Polo POLO4)	19	37	62
14 Play The Game *Queen* (EMI 5076)	17	22	30
15 Theme From Mash *The Mash* (CBS 8536)	32	55	71
16 Cupid/I've Loved You For A Long Time *Detroit Spinners* (Atlantic K11498)	5	4	6
17 Midnite Dynamos *Matchbox* (Magnet MAG 169)	27	41	61
18 Let's Get Serious *Jermaine Jackson* (Motown TMG 1183)	38	65	–
19 747 (Strangers In The Night) *Saxon* (Carrere CAR 151)	14	13	15
20 Messages *Orchestral Manoeuvres In The Dark* (Dindisc DIN15)	39	51	–

	12	19	26
21 Could You Be Loved *Bob Marley & The Wailers* (Island WIP 6610)	9	5	5
63 Babooshka *Kate Bush* (EMI 5085)	16	7	7
30 Love Will Tear Us Apart *Joy Division* (Factory FACT23)	18	17	13
56 Emotional Rescue *Rolling Stones* (Rolling Stones PSR 105)	20	19	9
51 More Than I Can Say *Leo Sayer* (Chrysalis CHS 2442)	22	10	3
29 Let's Hang On *Darts* (Magnet MAG 174)	24	16	11
– There There My Dear *Dexy's Midnight Runners* (Parlophone R6038)	45	20	12
– Upside Down *Diana Ross* (Motown TMG1195)	–	31	8
35 A Lovers Holiday/Glow Of Love *Change* (WEA K7914)	29	23	14
36 Theme From The Invaders *Yellow Magic Orchestra* (A&M AMS7502)	25	26	17
– Oops Upside Your Head *Gap Band* (Mercury MER 22)	59	38	19
61 Wednesday Week *Undertones* (Sire SIR4042)	30	32	20

AUGUST 1980

2	9	16	23	30
1 Use It Up And Wear It Out *Odyssey* (RCA PC1962)	3	9	18	31
2 More Than I Can Say *Leo Sayer* (Chrysalis CHS2442)	4	8	14	23
3 Upside Down *Diana Ross* (Motown TMG1195)	2	2	5	7
4 Xanadu *Olivia Newton-John/Electric Light Orchestra* (JET 185)	13	20	35	47
5 Babooshka *Kate Bush* (EMI 5085)	6	12	22	41
6 Could You Be Loved *Bob Marley & The Wailers* (Island WIP 6610)	8	14	23	35
7 There There My Dear *Dexy's Midnight Runners* (Parlophone R6038)	11	19	16	46
8 Jump To The Beat *Stacy Lattisaw* (Atlantic K11496)	17	32	53	–
9 Winner Takes It All *Abba* (Epic EPC 8835)	1	1	2	4
10 Cupid/I've Loved You For A Long Time *Detroit Spinners* (Atlantic K11498)	20	37	58	71
11 Wednesday Week *Undertones* (Sire SIR 4042)	12	23	34	75
12 Emotional Rescue *Rolling Stones* (Rolling Stones PSR106)	19	41	71	–
13 Let's Hang On *Darts* (Magnet MAG174)	18	21	46	68
14 My Way Of Thinking/I Think It's Going To Rain *UB40* (Graduate GRAD8)	34	52	–	–
15 Lip Up Fatty *Bad Manners* (Magnet MAG 176)	15	15	19	26
16 Love Will Tear Us Apart *Joy Division* (Factory AC23)	22	49	67	–
17 A Lovers Holiday/Glow Of Love *Change* (WEA K79141)	23	45	–	–
18 Oops Upside Your Head *Gap Band* (Mercury MER 22)	7	6	7	9
19 Theme From The Invaders *Yellow Magic Orchestra* (A&M AMS 7502)	27	28	48	–
20 9 To 5 *Sheena Easton* (EMI 5066)	5	3	4	3
30 Oh Yeah *Roxy Music* (Polydor 2001 972)	9	5	6	11
22 Give Me The Night *George Benson* (Warner LV40)	10	7	10	12
23 Mariana *Gibson Brothers* (Island WIP 6617)	14	11	15	21
24 Funkin' For Jamaica *Tom Browne* (Arista ARIST 357)	16	10	12	16
– Ashes To Ashes *David Bowie* (RCA BOW 6)	–	4	1	1
56 Tom Hark *Piranhas* (Sire/Hansa SIR 4044)	26	13	9	6
61 Feels Like I'm In Love *Kelly Marie* (Calibre 1)	29	16	8	5
27 Are You Getting Enough *Hot Chocolate* (RAK 318)	21	17	29	36
57 All Over The World *Electric Light Orchestra* (JET195)	24	18	11	15
– Start *Jam* (Polydor 2069 266)	–	–	3	2
48 Sunshine Of Your Smile *Mike Berry* (Polydor 2059 261)	37	22	13	10
31 Private Life *Grace Jones* (Island WIP6629)	25	24	17	24
– Dreamin' *Cliff Richard* (EMI 5095)	–	50	20	14

290

2

	9	16	23	30
– I Die You Die *Gary Numan* (Beggars Banquet BEG46)	–	–	–	8
– Eighth Day *Hazel O'Connor* (A&M AMS 7553)	–	70	27	13
– Can't Stop The Music *Village People* (Mercury MER 16)	64	27	21	17
– Bank Robber *Clash* (CBS8323)	60	31	24	19
– It's Still Rock & Roll To Me *Billy Joel* (CBS8753)	68	33	30	20
– Modern Girl *Sheena Easton* (EMI 5042)	74	35	25	18

SEPTEMBER 1980

6

	13	20	27
1 Start *Jam* (Polydor 2059 266)	2	5	11
2 Ashes To Ashes *David Bowie* (RCA BOW6)	3	7	15
3 Feels Like I'm In Love *Kelly Marie* (Calibre 1)	1	1	4
4 9 to 5 *Sheena Easton* (EMI 5066)	6	11	17
5 Eighth Day *Hazel O'Connor* (A&M AMS7553)	5	6	10
6 I Die You Die *Gary Numan* (Beggars Banquet BEG46)	12	18	34
7 Tom Hark *Piranhas* (Sire/Hansa SIR 4044)	9	17	32
8 Winner Takes It All *Abba* (Epic EPC8835)	16	30	41
9 Sunshine Of Your Smile *Mike Berry* (Polydor POSP 2059 261)	11	12	18
10 Dreamin' *Cliff Richard* (EMI 5095)	8	9	12
11 Can't Stop The Music *Village People* (Mercury MER 16)	14	13	23
12 Bank Robber *Clash* (CBS8323)	13	16	26
13 Modern Girl *Sheena Easton* (EMI 5042)	10	8	9
14 Upside Down *Diana Ross* (Motown TMG 1195)	23	33	47
15 Oops Upside Your Head *Gap Band* (Mercury MER 22)	19	31	36
16 Give Me The Night *George Benson* (Warner Brothers LV40)	28	38	56
17 It's Only Love/Beyond The Reef *Elvis Presley* (RCA4)	7	3	6
18 All Over The World *Electric Light Orchestra* (JET 195)	29	48	–
19 Oh Yeah *Roxy Music* (Polydor 2001 972)	33	56	–
20 It's Still Rock And Roll To Me *Billy Joel* (CBS8753)	15	15	14
26 One Day I'll Fly Away *Randy Crawford* (Warner Brothers K17680)	4	2	2
24 Paranoid *Black Sabbath* (NEMS BSS101)	17	14	19
54 Another One Bites The Dust *Queen* (EMI5102)	18	10	7
22 A Walk In The Park *Nick Straker Band* (CBS 8525)	20	20	20
– Masterblaster (Jammin') *Stevie Wonder* (Motown TMG 1204)	30	4	3
21 Marie Marie *Shakin' Stevens* (Epic EPC 8725)	21	19	21
– Don't Stand So Close To Me *Police* (A&M ANS7564)	–	–	1
– Baggy Trousers *Madness* (Stiff BUY 84)	36	21	5
– D.I.S.C.O. *Ottowan* (Carrere CAR 161)	66	28	8
– My Old Piano *Diana Ross* (Motown TMG 1202)	–	36	13
32 I Owe You One *Shalamar* (Solar SO 11)	24	23	16

OCTOBER 1980

4

	11	18	25
1 Don't Stand So Close To Me *Police* (A&M AMS7564)	1	1	3
2 Masterblaster (Jammin') *Stevie Wonder* (Motown TMG1204)	4	6	14
3 D.I.S.C.O. *Ottowan* (Carrere CAR 161)	2	2	2
4 Baggy Trousers *Madness* (Stiff BUY 84)	3	3	5
5 One Day I'll Fly Away *Randy Crawford* (Warner Brothers K17680)	8	19	30
6 My Old Piano *Diana Ross* (Motown TMG1202)	5	8	11
7 Feels Like I'm In Love *Kelly Marie* (Calibre 1)	12	27	34
8 Another One Bites The Dust *Queen* (EMI5102)	16	23	36
9 It's Only Love *Elvis Presley* (RCA 4)	20	31	49
10 Amigo *Black Slate* (Ensign ENY 42)	9	11	16
11 Searching *Change* (WEA K79156)	13	16	21
12 I Got You *Split Enz* (A&M AMS 7546)	18	28	45

4

	11	18	25
13 I Owe You One *Shalamar* (Solar SO11)	21	30	39
14 Eighth Day *Hazel O'Connor* (A&M AMS 7553)	24	40	67
15 Modern Girl *Sheena Easton* (EMI 5042)	29	38	56
16 It's Still Rock & Roll To Me *Billy Joel* (CBS 8753)	28	46	–
17 Three Little Birds *Bob Marley & The Wailers* (Island WIP 6641)	17	17	22
18 Killer On The Loose *Thin Lizzy* (Vertigo LIZZY 7)	10	12	18
19 Paranoid *Black Sabbath* (NEMS BSS 101)	30	39	58
20 If You're Lookin' For A Way Out *Odyssey* (RCA 5)	7	7	7
25 Stereotype/International Jet Set *Specials* (2 Tone CHSTT 13)	6	22	23
51 And The Birds Were Singing *Sweet People* (Polydor POSP 179)	11	4	8
22 Trouble *Gillan* (Virgin VS 377)	14	20	25
38 When You Ask About Love *Matchbox* (Magnet MAG 191)	15	10	6
29 Casanova *Coffee* (De-Lite MER38)	19	13	13
– What You're Proposing *Status Quo* (Vertigo QUO3)	27	5	4
48 Woman In Love *Barbra Srteisand* (CBS 8966)	22	9	1
28 Gotta Pull Myself Together *Nolans* (Epic EPC 8878)	25	14	9
23 You're Lying *Linx* (Chrysalis CHS 2461)	23	15	17
59 Enola Gay *Orchestral Manoeuvres In The Dark* (Dindisc DIN22)	35	18	12
45 Love X Love *George Benson* (Warner Brothers K17699)	26	21	10
41 Special Brew *Bad Manners* (Magnet MAG 180)	38	25	15
– Dog Eat Dog *Adam & The Ants* (CBS9039)	50	37	19
43 All Out Of Love *Air Supply* (Arista ARIST 362)	31	24	20

NOVEMBER 1980

1

	8	15	22	29
1 Woman In Love *Barbra Streisand* (CBS 8966)	1	2	3	6
2 What You're Proposing *Status Quo* (Vertigo QUO 3)	2	5	10	21
3 D.I.S.C.O. *Ottowan* (Carrere CAR 161)	10	21	27	34
4 When You Ask About Love *Matchbox* (Magnet MAG 191)	6	11	17	28
5 Special Brew *Bad Manners* (Magnet MAG 180)	3	3	7	14
6 If You're Lookin' For A Way Out *Odyssey* (RCA 5)	7	10	16	24
7 Baggy Trousers *Madness* (Stiff BUY 84)	13	23	38	45
8 Enola Gay *Orchestral Manoeuvres In The Dark* (Dindisc DIN22)	9	8	9	13
9 Gotta Pull Myself Together *Nolans* (Epic EPC 8878)	11	16	24	41
10 Don't Stand So Close To Me *Police* (A&M AMS 7564)	16	31	49	73
11 All Out Of Love *Air Supply* (Arista ARIST 362)	12	19	21	37
12 Love X Love *George Benson* (Warner Brothers K17699)	20	27	58	–
13 Dog Eat Dog *Adam & The Ants* (CBS 9039)	4	7	8	19
14 And The Birds Were Singing *Sweet People* (Polydor POSP 179)	27	41	71	–
15 Casanova *Coffee* (De-Lite MER 38)	24	38	54	70
16 Army Dreamers *Kate Bush* (EMI 5106)	17	25	29	68
17 One Man Woman *Sheena Easton* (EMI 5114)	14	18	25	30
18 You're Lying *Linx* (Chrysalis CHS 2463)	28	42	55	–
19 What's In A Kiss *Gilbert O'Sullivan* (CBS 8929)	26	29	63	–
20 Fashion *David Bowie* (RCA BOW 7)	8	6	5	5
– The Tide Is High *Blondie* (Chrysalis CHS 2465)	5	1	1	2
25 Suddenly *Olivia Newton-John/Cliff Richard* (Jet 7002)	15	17	20	27
26 Never Knew Love Like This Before *Stephanie Mills* (20th Century TC2460)	18	9	6	4
31 I Could Be So Good For You *Dennis Waterman* (EMI 5009)	19	4	4	3
– Same Old Scene *Roxy Music* (Polydor ROXY 1)	29	12	14	16

292

1	8	15	22	29
– Super Trouper *Abba* (Epic EPC 9089)	–	13	2	1
34 Earth Dies Screaming/Dream A Lie *UB40* (Graduate GRAD 10)	25	14	11	10
38 Ace Of Spades *Motorhead* (Bronze BRO 106)	21	15	15	22
– (Just Like) Starting Over *John Lennon/Yoko Ono* (Geffen K 79186)	30	20	13	8
72 Celebration *Kool and the Gang* (De-Lite KOOL 10)	33	22	12	7
– I'm Coming Out *Diana Ross* (Motown TMG 1210)	–	34	18	18
– To Cut A Long Story Short *Spandau Ballet* (Reformation/Chrysalis CHS2473)	–	43	19	11
– Banana Republic *Boomtown Rats* (Ensign BONGO 1)	–	–	23	9
– Embarrassment *Madness* (Stiff BUY 102)	–	–	31	12
– Do You Feel My Love *Eddy Grant* (Ensign ENY 46)	–	67	30	15
22 Passion *Rod Stewart* (Riva 26)	37	26	22	17
55 I Like What You're Doing To Me *Young and Co.* (Excalibur EXC501)	39	30	26	20

DECEMBER 1980

6	13	20	27
1 Super Trouper *Abba* (Epic EPC 9089)	1	4	5
2 The Tide Is High *Blondie* (Chrysalis CHS2465)	7	14	20
3 Banana Republic *Boomtown Rats* (Ensign BONGO 1)	5	7	11
4 Embarrassment *Madness* (Stiff BUY 102)	4	6	8
5 To Cut A Long Story Short *Spandau Ballet* (Reformation/Chrysalis CHS2473)	6	8	16
6 I Could Be So Good For You *Dennis Waterman* (EMI5009)	14	26	30
7 Never Knew Love Like This Before *Stephanie Mills* (20th Century TC2460)	13	20	39
8 Celebration *Kool and the Gang* (De-Lite KOOL 10)	11	16	25
9 Do You Feel My Love *Eddy Grant* (Ensign/ICE ENY 45)	8	11	21
10 (Just Like) Starting Over *John Lennon/Yoko Ono* (WEA/Geffen K79186)	21	1	2
11 Earth Dies Screaming/Dream A Lie *UB40* (Graduate GRAD 10)	18	22	38
12 Fashion *David Bowie* (RCA BOW7)	24	42	56
13 I'm Coming Out *Diana Ross* (Motown TMG 1210)	19	21	35
14 Woman In Love *Barbra Streisand* (CBS 8966)	27	43	48
15 Stop The Cavalry *Jona Lewie* (Stiff BUY 104)	3	3	3
16 There's No One Quite Like Grandma *St Winifred's School Choir* (MFP FP900)	2	2	1
17 Rock 'n' Roll Ain't Noise Pollution *AC/DC* (Atlantic K11630)	15	17	27
18 Ace Of Spades *Motorhead* (Bronze BRO 106)	30	37	42
19 Passion *Rod Stewart* (Riva 26)	28	29	45
20 I Like What You're Doing To Me *Young and Co.* (Excalibur EXC501)	26	28	44
– De Do Do Do De Da Da Da *Police* (A&M AMS 7578)	9	5	6
23 Runaway Boys *Stray Cats* (Arista SCAT 1)	10	9	10
22 Lady *Kenny Rogers* (United Artists UP 635)	12	13	14
31 Antmusic *Adam & The Ants* (CBS 9352)	16	10	7
34 Lies *Status Quo* (Vertigo QUO 4)	17	15	12
30 Flash *Queen* (EMI 5126)	20	12	15
43 Rabbit *Chas & Dave* (Rockney 9)	34	18	13
27 Love On The Rocks *Neil Diamond* (Capitol CL 16173)	22	19	18
– Happy Christmas (War Is Over) *John Lennon* (Apple R5970)	–	45	4
– Imagine *John Lennon* (Parlophone R6009)	–	–	9
69 Never Mind The Presents *Barron Knights* (Epic EPC 9070)	36	27	17
38 Over The Rainbow/You Belong To Me *Matchbox* (Magnet MAG 192)	31	24	19

1980 – BEST SELLING RECORDS

Music Week discontinued its practice of collating information resulting in best selling artists in singles and album field, which along with other data, was printed early in the following year. Instead we give here the Top 50 selling singles and 50 albums for 1980.

Singles

1 Don't Stand So Close To Me *Police* (A&M)
2 Woman In Love *Barbra Streisand* (CBS)
3 Feels Like I'm In Love *Kelly Marie* (Calibre)
4 D.I.S.C.O. *Ottowan* (Carrere)
5 Geno *Dexy's Midnight Runners* (Parlophone)
6 Together We Are Beautiful *Fern Kinney* (WEA)
7 Coward Of The County *Kenny Rogers* (United Artists)
8 Working My Way Back To You *Detroit Spinners* (Atlantic)
9 9 to 5 *Sheena Easton* (EMI)
10 Ashes To Ashes *David Bowie* (RCA)
11 Baggy Trousers *Madness* (Stiff)
12 Theme From Mash *Mash* (CBS)
13 The Tide Is High *Blondie* (Chrysalis)
14 Going Underground/Dreams Of Children (Polydor)
15 Crying *Don McLean* (EMI)
16 Winner Takes It All *Abba* (Epic)
17 Dance Yourself Dizzy *Liquid Gold* (Polo)
18 Atomic *Blondie* (Chrysalis)
19 Upside Down *Diana Ross* (Motown)
20 Use It Up And Wear It Out *Odyssey* (RCA)
21 Start *Jam* (Polydor)
22 Masterblaster (Jammin') *Stevie Wonder* (Motown)
23 Funky Town *Lipps Inc.* (Casablanca)
24 I'm In The Mood For Dancing *Nolans* (Epic)
25 One Day I'll Fly Away *Randy Crawford* (Warner)
26 If You're Looking For A Way Out *Odyssey (RCA)*
27 *Too Much Too Young Specials* (2 Tone)
28 Super Trouper *Abba* (Epic)
29 Take That Look Off Your Face *Marti Webb* (Polydor)
30 No Doubt About It *Hot Chocolate* (RAK)
31 What You're Proposing *Status Quo* (Vertigo)
32 Brass In Pocket *Pretenders* (Real)
33 What's Another Year *Johnny Logan* (Epic)
34 Xanadu *Olivia Newton-John/ELO* (Jet)
35 Oops Upside Your Head *Gap Band* (Casablanca)
36 King – Food For Thought *UB40* (Graduate)
37 And The Beat Goes On *Whispers* (Solar)
38 Special Brew *Bad Manners* (Magnet)
39 Turning Japanese *Vapors* (United Artists)
40 When You Ask About Love *Matchbox* (Magnet)
41 My Girl *Madness* (Stiff)
42 Call Me *Blondie* (Chrysalis)
43 Enola Gay *Orchestral Manoeuvres In The Dark* (Dindisc)
44 More Than I Can Say *Leo Sayer* (Chrysalis)
45 Could You Be Loved *Bob Marley & The Wailers* (Island)
46 Tom Hark *Piranhas* (Sire/Hansa)
47 Modern Girl *Sheena Easton* (EMI)
48 All Night Long *Rainbow* (Polydor)
49 Coming Up *Paul McCartney* (Parlophone)
50 Eighth Day *Hazel O'Connor* (A&M)

Albums

1 Zenyatta Mondatta *Police* (A&M)
2 Greatest Hits *Rose Royce* (Whitfield)
3 Pretenders *Pretenders* (Real)
4 Super Trouper *Abba* (Epic)
5 Regatta De Blanc *Police* (A&M)
6 Flesh and Blood *Roxy Music* (EG/Polydor)
7 Off The Wall *Michael Jackson* (Epic)
8 Duke *Genesis* (Charisma)
9 Guilty *Barbra Streisand* (CBS)
10 Sky 2 *Sky* (Ariola)
11 One Step Beyond *Madness* (Stiff)
12 Manilow Magic *Barry Manilow* (Arista)
13 String Of Hits *Shadows* (EMI)
12 12 Gold Bars *Status Quo* (Vertigo)
15 The Last Dance *Shadows* (EMI)
16 Greatest Hits Vol. 2 *Various* (Motown)
17 The Magic Of Boney M *Boney M* (Atlantic/Hansa)
18 Outlandos D'Amour *Police* (A&M)
19 Tell Me On A Sunday *Marti Webb* (Polydor)
20 Tears And Laughter *Johnny Mathis* (CBS)
21 Scary Monsters & Super Creeps *David Bowie* (RCA)
22 The Wall *Pink Floyd* (Harvest)
23 Specials *Specials* (2 Tone)
24 Never For Ever *Kate Bush* (EMI)
25 Get Happy *Elvis Costello* (Radar)
26 Greatest Hits *Rod Stewart* (Riva)
27 I Just Can't Stop It *The Beat* (Go-Feet)
28 Signing Off *UB40* (Graduate)
29 Me, Myself, I *Joan Armatrading* (A&M)
30 Give Me The Night *George Benson* (Warner Brothers)
31 McCartney 11 *Paul McCartney* (Parlophone)
32 Emotional Rescue *Rolling Stones* (Rolling Stones)
33 Peter Gabriel *Peter Gabriel* (Charisma)
34 Eat To The Beat *Blondie* (Chrysalis)
35 Bat Out Of Hell *Meatloaf* (Epic/Cleveland Int.)
36 Absolutely *Madness* (Stiff)
37 Back In Black *AC/DC* (Atlantic)
38 Sometimes You Win *Dr Hook* (Capitol)
39 Parallel Lines *Blondie* (Chrysalis)
40 Wheels Of Steel *Saxon* (Carrere)
41 The Game *Queen* (EMI)
42 Bee Gees Greatest *Bee Gees* (RSO)
43 20 Hottest Hits *Hot Chocolate* (RAK)
44 Xanadu *Original Soundtrack* (Jet)
45 Breaking Glass *Hazel O'Connor* (A&M)
46 War Of The Worlds *Jeff Wayne's Musical Version* (CBS)
47 Deepest Purple *Deep Purple* (Harvest)
48 Permanent Waves *Rush* (Mercury)
49 Telekon *Gary Numan* (Beggars Banquet)
50 Glass Houses *Billy Joel* (CBS)

1981

It was not exactly all change – even if some of the pop music bandwagon did their best to believe Roxy Music, Electric Light Orchestra, Stevie Wonder, Rainbow, Queen, Bowie and Cliff Richard were long ago dead and well buried. Nevertheless, it was a year which saw a drastically new look in the top names in the end of year singles listing.

Soft Cell, Adam and the Ants, Shakin' Stevens, Kim Wilde, Toyah, Altered Images, Duran Duran were some of the better new faces (for it is hard to welcome the Tweets).

'New' is of course a slightly risky word, for Adam and Shaky' has been trying for some time. Others, like Orchestral Manoeuvres In The Dark, Spandau Ballet, Human League, Tenpole Tudor and Teardrop Explodes, heralded the synthesized, (so-called) futurist sounds. Here fashion and image went along with the 'sound'. Twelve-inch records were mandatory for these acts and so too the expensive video for Top Of The Pops and other TV shows. They sold records and they helped the circulation of some pop papers to surprising heights at a time when general record buying habits flucutated. Shakin' Stevens was of course good old rock 'n' roll, a shade and touch of Elvis somewhere, and given a fine producer in Stuart Colman with some rolling, danceable material.

Adam and the Ants has in previous guise played the late punk clubs and joints and achieved nothing of significance. Suddenly, a change of image, a fetching style of dress and a general souping up of the theatrical glamour, excellent videos and some talent to help things along, and wham! there were six hits on CBS! Their earlier recordings re-surfaced and one of them Young Parisians made Number Nine.

It was a year which had the unexpected. Few would have predicted Kraftwerk at the top even if synthesizers were 'in' and the guitar unheard. Also there was the 'compilation' record with bits and pieces fo earlier hit sounds slung together in masterful fashion. It all began with Dutch producer Jaap Eggermont and his Star Sound and soon Tight Fit, Gidea Park, Lobo, and even the Royal

Philharmonic Orchestra were among those who followed suit.

There was jazz-funk from Freeez, Linx, Shakatak and among some others there was none better than Imagination with their exquisite Body Talk; it was superb stuff.

One-time 'independent chart' material also made inroads, with Toyah Willcox leading the fray. Eurovision produced a group called Bucks Fizz and for once in this anaemic contest, here was an outfit which suggested they had future. Scotland gave us Altered Images and onwards marched Bad Manners, Madness, Diana Ross, Kool & The Gang, and the evergreen Cliff.

It was a year of fine records with too many interesting groups for this small and generalised commentary to cover, but there was Echo And The Bunnymen, Classix Nouveaux, Japan, Ultravox, ever-present Abba and a rush of heavy sounds from the likes of Gillan, Motorhead, Saxon and Rainbow. Many others charted, many of them failed the 20 mark. Disco gave us fine stuff from Tom Tom Club and others. For the mellow there was still life in two languages from Julio Iglesias and slap-stick comedy from Italian-Australian Joe Dolce.

Soft Cell had the year's most successful record, but for me the top of the pops was at 11, Ghost Town from the Specials and closely followed by Imagination's Body Talk. In conclusion, 1981 was one of pop's best-ever years.

JANUARY 1981

10		17	24	31
1	Imagine John Lennon (Parlophone R6009)	1	1	1
2	Happy Christmas (War Is Over) John Lennon (Apple R5970)	3	9	23
3	Stop The Cavalry Jona Lewie (Stiff BUY 104)	6	19	32
4	Antmusic Adam & The Ants (CBS 9352)	2	2	4
5	(Just Like) Starting Over John Lennon/Yoko Ono (Geffen K79186)	5	15	22
6	There's No One Quite Like Grandma St Winifred's School Choir (MFP 900)	22	58	70
7	De Do Do Do De Da Da Da Police (A&M AMS7578)	9	24	54
8	Super Trouper Abba (Epic EPC9089)	28	48	71
9	Embarrassment Madness (Stiff BUY102)	13	28	38
10	Flash Queen (EMI 5126)	10	10	14
11	Rabbit Chas & Dave (Rockney 9)	8	18	30
12	Runaway Boys Stray Cats (Arista SCAT 1)	16	35	59
13	Banana Republic Boomtown Rats (Ensign BONGO 1)	30	52	74
14	Lies/Don't Drive My Car Status Quo (Vertigo QUO 4)	11	26	36
15	Do Nothing/Maggies Farm Specials (2-Tone CHSTT 16)	4	5	11
16	To Cut A Long Story Short Spandau Ballet (Reformation/Chrysalis CHS2473)	35	55	–
17	Love On The Rocks Neil Diamond (Capitol CL 16173)	21	37	64
18	Over The Rainbow/You Belong To Me Matchbox (Magnet MAG 192)	15	21	31
19	Lady Kenny Rogers (United Artists UP 636)	26	47	63
20	Too Nice To Talk To The Beat (Go Feet FEET4)	7	7	13
24	Who's Gonna Rock You Nolans (Epic EPC 9325)	12	17	27
30	I Am The Beat The Look (MCA 647)	14	6	8
31	I Ain't Gonna Stand For It Stevie Wonder (Motown TMG 1215)	17	12	10
29	Runaround Sue Racey (RAK 326)	18	13	15
35	Don't Stop The Music Yarborough & Peoples (Mercury MER 53)	19	8	7
27	This Wreckage Gary Numan (Beggars Banquet BEG 50)	20	31	43
–	Woman John Lennon (Geffen K79195)	–	3	2
–	In The Air Tonight Phil Collins (Virgin VSK 102)	36	4	3
39	Young Parisians Adam & The Ants (Decca F 13903)	23	11	9
–	Rapture Blondie (Chrysalis CHS 2485)	–	14	5
–	Vienna Ultravox (Chrysalis CHS 2481)	52	16	6
49	Scary Monsters David Bowie (RCA BOW 8)	25	20	20
44	Fade To Grey Visage (Polydor POSP 194)	33	23	12
–	Romeo & Juliet Dire Straits (Vertigo MOVIE 1)	49	25	16
–	A Little In Love Cliff Richard (EMI 5123)	–	33	17
–	Return Of The Los Palmas 7 Madness (Stiff BUY 108)	–	38	18
–	Gangsters Of The Groove Heatwave (GTO GT285)	59	29	19

FEBRUARY 1981

7		14	21	28
1	Woman John Lennon (Geffen K79195)	1	3	4
2	In The Air Tonight Phil Collins (Virgin VSK 102)	4	5	12
3	Vienna Ultravox (Chrysalis CHS 2481)	2	2	2
4	Imagine John Lennon (Parlophone R6009)	6	17	23
5	Rapture Blondie (Chrysalis CHS2485)	8	13	27
6	Ant Music Adam & The Ants (CBS 9352)	9	18	20
7	Don't Stop The Music Yarborough & Peoples (Mercury MER 53)	11	19	33
8	Fade To Grey Visage (Polydor POSP 194)	13	12	16

7		14	21	28
9	Young Parisians *Adam & The Ants* (Decca F13803)	15	22	32
10	I Am The Beat *The Look* (MCA 647)	20	31	47
11	Romeo & Juliet *Dire Straits* (Vertigo MOVIE 1)	12	8	14
12	I Surrender *Rainbow* (Polydor POSP 221)	5	4	3
13	I Ain't Gonna Stand For It *Stevie Wonder* (Motown TMG 1215)	25	47	67
14	Return Of The Los Palmas 7 *Madness* (Stiff BUY 108)	10	7	7
15	A Little In Love *Cliff Richard* (EMI 5123)	16	20	28
16	It's My Turn *Diana Ross* (Motown TMG 1217)	22	30	49
17	The Freeze *Spandau Ballet* (Chrysalis CHS 2486)	18	24	30
18	Do Nothing/Maggies Farm *Specials* (2-Tone CHSTT 16)	30	57	–
19	Oldest Swinger In Town *Fred Wedlock* (Rocket XPRES 46)	7	6	10
20	Gangsters Of The Groove *Heatwave* (GTO GT 285)	23	27	35
30	Shaddup You Face *Joe Dolce* (Epic EPC 9518)	3	1	1
35	Rock This Town *Stray Cats* (Arista SCAT 2)	14	9	11
31	We'll Bring The House Down *Slade* (Cheapskate CHEAP 16)	17	10	13
28	Sgt Rock (Is Going To Help Me) *XTC* (Virgin VS 384)	19	16	18
–	Message Of Love *Pretenders* (Real ARE 15)	28	11	15
44	Do The Hucklebuck *Coast To Coast* (Polydor POSP 214)	39	14	8
–	St Valentine's Day Massacre EP *Motorhead/Girlschool* (Bronze BRO 116)	–	15	5
–	Jealous Guy *Roxy Music* (Polydor/E.G. ROXY 2)	–	21	6
54	Southern Freeez *Freeez* (Beggars Banquet BEG 51)	34	23	9
–	Kings Of The Wild Frontier *Adam & The Ants* (CBS 8877)	–	39	17
–	Something 'Bout You Baby I Like *Status Quo* (Vertigo QUO 5)	–	–	19

MARCH 1981

7		14	21	28
1	Shaddup You Face *Joe Dolce* (Epic EPC 9518)	3	10	25
2	Vienna *Ultravox* (Chrysalis CHS 2481)	4	7	16
3	Jealous Guy *Roxy Music* (Polydor/E.G. ROXY 2)	1	1	3
4	I Surrender *Rainbow* (Polydor POSP 221)	12	22	38
5	St Valentine's Day Massacre EP *Motorhead/Girlschool* (Bronze BRON 116)	10	15	33
6	Kings Of The Wild Frontier *Adam & The Ants* (CBS 8877)	2	4	5
7	Do The Hucklebuck *Coast To Coast* (Polydor POSP 214)	5	5	7
8	Southern Freeez *Freeez* (Beggars Banquet BEG 51)	8	11	21
9	Something 'Bout You Baby I Like *Status Quo* (Vertigo QUO 5)	9	12	22
10	Return Of The Los Palmas 7 *Madness* (Stiff BUY 108)	18	27	41
11	Woman *John Lennon* (Geffen K79195)	23	32	48
12	Rock This Town *Stray Cats* (Arista SCAT 2)	19	29	44
13	Oldest Swinger In Town *Fred Wedlock* (Rocket XPRES 46)	24	38	46
14	Once In A Lifetime *Talking Heads* (Sire SIR 4048)	14	16	27
15	(Somebody) Help Me Out *Beggar & Co.* (Ensign ENY 201)	15	19	30
16	Four From Toyah *Toyah* (Safari TOY 1)	11	8	4
17	Romeo & Juliet *Dire Straits* (Vertigo MOVIE 1)	33	48	69
18	Kids In America *Kim Wilde* (RAK 327)	6	3	2
19	Message Of Love *Pretenders* (Real ARE 15)	29	50	74
20	We'll Bring The House Down *Slade* (Cheapskate CHEAP 16)	30	60	71
29	This Ole House *Shakin' Stevens* (Epic EPC 9555)	7	2	1
25	Reward *Teardrop Explodes* (Mercury TEAR 2)	13	6	8
35	You Better You Bet *The Who* (Polydor WHO 4)	16	9	9
27	Star *Kiki Dee* (Ariola ARO 251)	17	13	15
45	I Missed Again *Phil Collins* (Virgin VS 402)	20	14	17
57	Lately *Stevie Wonder* (Motown TMG 1226)	27	18	6

	14	21	28
31 Jones Vs Jones/Summer Madness/Funky Stuff *Kool & The Gang* (De-Lite KOOL 11/1112/Gang11)	21	17	18
47 Planet Earth *Duran Duran* (EMI 5137)	26	20	12
– Capstick Comes Home/Sheffield Grinder *Tony Capstick* (Dingles SID27)	–	54	10
56 Einstein A Go-Go *Landscape* (RCA 22)	38	21	11
65 Intuition *Linx* (Chrysalis CHS 2500)	41	25	13
– Mind Of A Toy *Visage* (Polydor POSP 236)	32	24	14
– What Becomes Of The Broken Hearted *Dave Stewart/Colin Blunstone* (Stiff BROKEN 1)	57	30	19
– It's A Love Thing *Whispers* (Solar SO 16)	43	26	20

APRIL 1981

4	11	18	25
1 This Ole House *Shakin' Stevens* (Epic EPC 9555)	1	2	3
2 Kids In America *Kim Wilde* (RAK 327)	4	11	14
3 Capstick Comes Home/Sheffield Grinder *Tony Capstick* (Dingles SID 27)	6	17	24
4 Lately *Stevie Wonder* (Motown TMG 1226)	3	3	5
5 Making Your Mind Up *Bucks Fizz* (RCA 56)	2	1	1
6 Four From Toyah *Toyah* (Safari TOY 1)	8	16	27
7 Jealous Guy *Roxy Music* (E.G./Polydor ROXY 2)	18	34	47
8 Einstein A Go-Go *Landscape* (RCA 22)	5	5	6
9 Do The Hucklebuck *Coast To Coast* (Polydor POSP 214)	17	22	31
10 Intuition *Linx* (Chrysalis CHS 2500)	7	10	11
11 It's A Love Thing *Whispers* (Solar SO 16)	9	9	9
12 D-Days *Hazel O'Connor* (Albion ION 1009)	10	12	16
13 Mind Of A Toy *Visage* (Polydor POSP 236)	16	21	32
14 You Better You Bet *The Who* (Polydor POSP WHO 4)	23	44	64
15 Reward *Teardrop Explodes* (Mercury TEAR 2)	21	42	51
16 Planet Earth *Duran Duran* (EMI 5137)	22	23	40
17 What Becomes Of The Broken Hearted *Dave Stewart and Colin Blunstone* (Stiff BROKE 1)	13	13	19
18 Kings Of The Wild Frontier *Adam & The Ants* (CBS 8877)	26	31	38
19 Star *Kiki Dee* (Ariola ARO 251)	28	51	67
20 Jones Vs Jones/Summer Madness/Funky Stuff *Kool & The Gang* (De-Lite KOOL 11/112 Gang11)	25	27	52
23 Can You Feel It *Jacksons* (Epic EPC 9554)	11	8	7
26 Night Games *Graham Bonnet* (Vertigo VER 1)	12	6	8
31 Good Thing Going *Sugar Minott* (RCA 58)	14	7	4
21 Attention To Me *Nolans* (Epic EPC 9571)	15	14	10
– Chi Mai Theme Tune Life & Times of Lloyd George *Ennio Morricone* (BBC RESL92)	19	4	2
29 Just A Feeling *Bad Manners* (Magnet MAG 187)	20	15	13
53 Muscle Bound/Glow *Spandau Ballet* (Reformation/Chrysalis CHS 2508)	29	18	15
– And The Bands Played On *Saxon* (Carrere CAR 180)	27	19	12
25 New Orleans *Gillan* (Virgin VS 406)	24	20	18
– Stars On 45 *Star Sound* (CBS 1102)	–	45	17
– Grey Day *Madness* (Stiff BUY 112)	–	–	20

MAY 1981

2	9	16	23	30
1 Making Your Mind Up *Bucks Fizz* (RCA 56)	4	6	16	26
2 Chi Mai Theme Tune (Life & Times Of Lloyd George) *Ennio Morricone* (BBC RESL 92)	3	5	9	20
3 Stars On 45 *Star Sound* (CBS 1102)	2	3	3	3

2		9	16	23	30
4	Good Thing Going *Sugar Minott* (RCA 58)	7	13	29	40
5	Grey Day *Madness* (Stiff BUY 112)	6	4	8	15
6	Can You Feel It *Jacksons* (Epic EPC 9554)	8	11	27	39
7	This Ole House *Shakin' Stevens* (Epic EPC 9554)	19	28	41	50
8	Night Games *Graham Bonnet* (Vertigo VER 1)	11	31	33	57
9	Einstein A Go-Go *Landscape* (RCA 22)	20	34	48	–
10	Lately *Stevie Wonder* (Motown TMG 1226)	25	35	59	73
11	It's A Love Thing *Whispers* (Solar SO 16)	14	36	47	–
12	Attention To Me *Nolans* (Epic EPC 9571)	9	12	20	41
13	Muscle Bound/Glow *Spandau Ballet* (Reformation/Chrysalis CHS 2509)	10	15	22	46
14	Only Crying *Keith Marshall* (Arrival PIK 2)	12	17	17	29
15	And The Bands Played On *Saxon* (Carrere CAR 180)	16	30	52	61
16	Just A Feeling *Bad Manners* (Magnet MAG 187)	18	32	44	–
17	New Orleans *Gillan* (Virgin VS 408)	23	33	45	–
18	Can't Get Enough Of You *Eddy Grant* (Ice/Ensign ENY 207)	13	18	24	35
19	Intuition *Linx* (Chrysalis CHS 2500)	40	52	–	–
20	D-Days *Hazel O'Connor* (Albion ION 1009)	33	61	–	–
–	Stand & Deliver *Adam & The Ants* (CBS A 1065)	1	1	1	1
39	You Drive Me Crazy *Shakin' Stevens* (Epic EPC 1165)	5	2	2	2
26	Bermuda Triangle *Barry Manilow* (Arista ARIST 406)	15	19	30	42
25	Don't Break My Heart Again *Whitesnake* (Liberty BP 395)	17	21	31	52
29	Keep On Loving You *Reo Speedwagon* (Epic EPC 9544)	21	7	7	8
–	Ossie's Dream (Way To Wembley) *Spurs FA Cup Final Squad* (Shelf 1)	45	8	5	5
–	Chequered Love *Kim Wilde* (RAK 330)	32	9	4	4
37	Swords Of A Thousand Men *Tenpole Tudor* (Stiff BUY 109)	22	10	6	6
31	Stray Cat Strut *Stray Cats* (Arista SCAT 3)	26	14	11	14
27	Ai No Corrida *Quincy Jones* (A&M AMS 8109)	24	16	14	22
–	Bette Davis Eyes *Kim Carnes* (EMI America EA 121)	51	20	10	10
42	When He Shines *Sheena Easton* (EMI 5166)	27	23	12	19
–	I Want To Be Free *Toyah* (Safari SAFE 34)	–	37	13	9
53	The Sound Of The Crowd *Human League* (Virgin VS 416)	34	27	15	12
56	Treason (It's Just A Story) *Teardrop Explodes* (Mercury TEAR 3)	30	25	18	21
46	Killers Live EP *Thin Lizzy* (Vertigo LIZZY 8)	28	24	19	27
–	Being With You *Smokey Robinson* (Motown TMG 1223)	63	39	23	7
–	How 'Bout Us *Champaign* (CBS A 1046)	74	42	28	11
–	All Those Years Ago *George Harrison* (Dark Horse K 17807)	–	–	58	13
–	Don't Let It Pass You By/Don't Slow Down *UB40* (DEP International DEP 1)	–	–	35	16
–	Ain't No Stopping *Enigma* (Creole CR 9)	–	–	32	17
61	It's Going To Happen *The Undertones* (Ardeck ARDS 8)	36	29	21	18

JUNE 1981

6		13	20	27
1	Stand & Deliver *Adam & The Ants* (CBS A 1065)	5	7	13
2	You Drive Me Crazy *Shakin' Stevens* (Epic EPC 1165)	7	10	16
3	Being With You *Smokey Robinson* (Motown TMG 1223)	1	1	2
4	Funeral Pyre *Jam* (Polydor POSP 257)	4	12	24
5	Chequered Love *Kim Wilde* (RAK 330)	18	26	44
6	How 'Bout Us *Champaign* (CBS A 1046)	6	5	7
7	Stars On 45 *Star Sound* (CBS A102)	13	24	36
8	I Want To Be Free *Toyah* (Safari SAFE 34)	10	11	14

6 | **13 20 27**

9 Swords Of A Thousand Men *Tenpole Tudor* (Stiff BUY 109) — 16 16 38
10 Will You *Hazel O'Connor* (A&M AMS 8131) — 9 8 10
11 Bette Davis Eyes *Kim Carnes* (EMI America EA 121) — 14 25 45
12 One Day In Your Life *Michael Jackson* (Motown TMG 976) — 3 2 1
13 More Than In Love *Kate Robbins* (RCA 69) — 2 3 3
14 Keep On Loving You *Reo Speedwagon* (Epic EPC 9544) — 20 29 51
15 All Those Years Ago *George Harrison* (Dark Horse K17807) — 15 20 37
16 Ain't No Stopping *Enigma* (Creole CR 9) — 11 13 19
17 Ossie's Dream (Way To Wembley) *Spurs FA Cup Final Squad* (Shelf 1) — 26 50 69
18 The Sound Of The Crowd *Human League* (Virgin VS 416) — 21 30 52
19 Chariots Of Fire (Main Theme) *Vangelis* (Polydor POSP 246) — 12 14 21
20 Stray Cat Strut *Stray Cats* (Arista SCAT 3) — 27 55 66
– Teddy Bear *Red Sovine* (Starday SD 142) — 22 4 4
66 Memory *Elaine Paige* (Polydor POSP 279) — 34 15 9
57 Piece Of The Action *Bucks Fizz* (RCA 88) — 25 17 12
43 Body Talk *Imagination* (Red Bus RBS 201) — 31 19 11
– Ghost Town *Specials* (2-Tone CHSTT) — – 21 6
33 Take It To The Top *Kool & The Gang* (De-Lite DE2) — 24 22 15
44 If Leaving Me Is Easy *Phil Collins* (Virgin VS 423) — 29 27 17
– Can Can *Bad Manners* (Magnet MAG 190) — – – 18
– No Woman No Cry *Bob Marley & The Wailers* (Island WIP 6244) — 63 38 20
46 All Stood Still *Ultravox* (Chrysalis CHS 2522) — 17 9 8
23 Going Back To Our Roots *Odyssey* (RCA 85) — 8 6 5
21 Don't Let It Pass You By/Don't Slow Down *UB40* (DEP International) — 19 18 25

JULY 1981

4 | **11 18 25**

1 One Day In Your Life *Michael Jackson* (Motown TMG 976) — 2 5 13
2 Ghost Town *Specials* (2-Tone CHSTT) — 1 1 1
3 Can Can *Bad Manners* (Magnet MAG 190) — 3 3 3
4 Going Back To Our Roots *Odyssey* (RCA 85) — 5 9 17
5 Being With You *Smokey Robinson* (Motown TMG 1223) — 8 27 39
6 Memory *Elaine Paige* (Polydor POSP 279) — 7 10 19
7 Body Talk *Imagination* (Red Bus RBS 201) — 6 4 5
8 More Than In Love *Kate Robbins & Beyond* (RCA 69) — 17 29 40
9 Teddy Bear *Red Sovine* (Starday SO 142) — 19 35 54
10 How 'Bout Us *Champaign* (CBS A 1046) — 18 28 42
11 All Stood Still *Ultravox* (Chrysalis CHS 2522) — 20 24 37
12 No Woman No Cry *Bob Marley & The Wailers* (Island WIP 6244) — 9 8 12
13 Piece Of The Action *Bucks Fizz* (RCA 88) — 15 16 34
14 (You Don't Stop) Wordy Rappinghood *Tom Tom Club* (Island WIP 6694) — 10 7 8
15 Stars On 45 (Vol. 2) *Star Sound* (CBS A 1407) — 4 2 2
16 Razzamatazz *Quincy Jones* (A&M AMS 8140) — 11 13 21
17 You Might Need Somebody *Randy Crawford* (Warner Brothers K17803) — 12 11 14
18 Take It To The Top *Kool & The Gang* (De-Lite DE 2) — 25 31 62
19 Will You *Hazel O'Connor* (A&M AMS 8131) — 29 45 74
20 Wikka Wrap *Evasions* (Groove GP 107) — 23 23 32
25 Dancing On The Floor *Third World* (CBS A 1214) — 13 12 10
– Motorhead (Live) *Motorhead* (Bronze BRO 124) — 14 6 6
22 There's A Guy Works Down The Chip Shop *Kirsty McColl* (Polydor POSP 250) — 16 14 24
– Sat In Your Lap *Kate Bush* (EMI 5201) — 26 15 11

	11	18	25
– Lay All Your Love On Me *Abba* (Epic EPC A1456)	–	17	7
– Chant No. 1 *Spandau Ballet* (Reformation/Chrysalis CHS 2528)	–	18	4
27 New Life *Depeche Mode* (Mute MUTE 014)	21	19	15
29 Can't Happen Here *Rainbow* (Polydor POSP 251)	24	20	26
– Happy Birthday *Stevie Wonder* (Motown TMG 1235)	–	–	9
34 For Your Eyes Only *Sheena Easton* (EMI 5195)	27	21	16
– Never Surrender *Saxon* (Carrere CAR 204)	–	26	18
70 Walk Right Now *Jacksons* (Epic EPC A1294)	46	30	20

AUGUST 1981

1	8	15	22	29
1 Green Door *Shakin' Stevens* (Epic EPCA 1354)	1	1	1	4
2 Ghost Town *Specials* (2-Tone CHSTT 17)	5	12	22	30
3 Chant No. 1 *Spandau Ballet* (Reformation/Chrysalis CHSTT 17)	4	5	12	20
4 Happy Birthday *Stevie Wonder* (Motown TMG 1235)	2	3	7	11
5 Stars On 45 (Vol. 2) *Star Sound* (CBS A 1407)	9	26	31	54
6 Can Can *Bad Manners* (Magnet MAG 190)	6	16	26	36
7 Hooked On Classics *Louis Clarke/RPO* (RCA 109)	3	2	2	3
8 Body Talk *Imagination* (Red Bus RBS 201)	13	20	34	43
9 Lay All Your Love On Me *Abba* (Epic EPCA 131456)	14	24	28	66
10 Dancing On The Floor *Third World* (CBS A1214)	12	17	24	38
11 For Your Eyes Only *Sheena Easton* (EMI 5196)	8	10	15	23
12 New Life *Depeche Mode* (Mute MUTE 014)	11	15	18	31
13 Sat In Your Lap *Kate Bush* (EMI 5201)	18	29	35	–
14 Back To The Sixties *Tight Fit* (Jive JIVE 002)	10	4	8	9
15 Walk Right Now *Jacksons* (Epic EPC A 1294)	7	8	17	24
16 (You Don't Stop) Wordy Rappinghood *Tom Tom Club* (Island WIP 6694)	22	38	–	–
17 You Might Need Somebody *Randy Crawford* (Warner 17803)	24	32	63	–
18 No Woman No Cry *Bob Marley & The Wailers* (Island WIP 6244)	23	43	60	–
19 Motorhead (Live) *Motorhead* (Bronze BRO 124)	33	46	69	–
20 Never Surrender *Saxon* (Carrere CAR 204)	26	37	65	–
23 Girls On Film *Duran Duran* (EMI 5206)	15	6	5	7
24 Show Me *Dexy's Midnight Runners* (Mercury DEXYS 6)	16	18	23	39
35 Water On Glass/Boys *Kim Wilde* (RAK 334)	17	13	11	13
40 Hold On Tight *Electric Light Orchestra* (Jet 7011)	19	9	6	5
25 Beach Boy Gold *Gidea Park* (Sonet STONE 2162)	20	11	13	14
– Love Action (I Believe In Love) *Human League* (Virgin VS 435)	29	7	3	6
33 Caribbean Disco *Lobo* (Polydor POSP 302)	27	14	10	8
– Japanese Boy *Aneka* (Hansa/Ariola HANSA 5)	60	19	4	1
62 Tainted Love *Soft Cell* (Bizzare TMG 1235)	45	26	9	2
36 Si, Si, Je Suis Un Rock Star *Bill Wyman* (A&M AMS 8144)	28	22	14	17
– One In Ten *UB40* (Dep Int. DEP 2)	54	23	16	10
26 Take It On The Run *Reo Speedwagon* (Epic EPC A 1207)	25	25	19	21
51 Wunderbar *Tenpole Tudor* (Stiff BUY 120)	36	21	20	16
– Abacab *Genesis* (Charisma CB 388)	–	–	27	12
– She's Got Claws *Gary Numan* (Beggars Banquet BEG 62)	–	–	–	15
47 Startrax Club Disco *Various* (Pickay KSY 1001)	34	27	21	18
– The Thin Wall *Ultravox* (Chrysalis CHS 2540)	–	–	37	19

SEPTEMBER 1981

5		12	19	26
1 Tainted Love *Soft Cell* (Bizarre BZS 2)		1	2	2
2 Japanese Boy *Aneka* (Hansa/Ariola HANSA 5)		3	6	13
3 Love Action (I Believe In Love) *Human League* (Virgin VS 435)		6	10	15
4 Hold On Tight *Electric Light Orchestra* (Jet 7011)		5	7	14
5 Hooked On Classics *Louis Clark/RPO* (RCA 109)		15	31	44
6 She's Got Claws *Gary Numan* (Beggars Banquet BEG 62)		10	16	33
7 One In Ten *UB40* (Dep. Int. DEP 2)		9	12	26
8 Green Door *Shakin' Stevens* (Epic EPCA 1354)		21	32	47
9 Abacab *Genesis* (Charisma CB 388)		13	18	28
10 Caribbean Disco *Lobo* (Polydor POSP 302)		17	23	35
11 Wired For Sound *Cliff Richard* (EMI 5221)		4	5	6
12 Girls On Film *Duran Duran* (EMI 5206)		19	27	41
13 Start Me Up *Rolling Stones* (EMI RSR 108)		7	9	16
14 The Thin Wall *Ultravox* (Chrysalis CHS 2540)		14	15	25
15 Chemistry *Nolans* (Epic EPC A1485)		20	26	34
16 Everybody Salsa *Modern Romance* (WEA K18815)		12	14	23
17 Wunderbar *Tenpole Tudor* (Stiff BUY 120)		27	36	69
18 Back To The Sixties *Tight Fit* (Jive JIVE 002)		25	39	62
19 Happy Birthday *Stevie Wonder* (Motown TMG 1235)		30	34	56
20 Rainy Night In Georgia *Randy Crawford* (Warner Brothers K 17840)		18	21	31
– Prince Charming *Adam & The Ants* (CBS CBSA 1408)		2	1	1
23 Souvenir *Orchestral Manoeuvres In The Dark* (Dindisc DIN 24)		8	3	4
28 Hands Up (Give Me Your Heart) *Ottowan* (Carrere CAR 183)		11	4	3
29 Slow Hand *Pointer Sisters* (Planet K12530)		16	11	10
43 Pretend *Alvin Stardust* (Stiff BUY 124)		26	8	5
– Endless Love *Diana Ross* (Motown TMG 1240)		39	13	7
30 You'll Never Know *Hi Gloss* (Epic EPCA 1387)		23	17	12
72 So This Is Romance *Linx* (Chrysalis CHS 2546)		33	19	18
32 One Of Those Nights *Bucks Fizz* (RCA 114)		22	20	20
– Birdie Song *Tweets* (PRT 7P 219)		44	25	8
– Invisible Sun *Police* (A&M AMS 8164)		–	–	9
– Under Your Thumb *Godley & Creme* (Polydor POSP 322)		64	30	33
– Stars On 45 (Vol. 3) *Star Sound* (CBS A1521)		–	53	17
31 Hand Held In Black & White *Dollar* (WEA BUCK 1)		24	24	19

OCTOBER 1981

3		10	17	24	31
1 Prince Charming *Adam & The Ants* (CBS CBSA 1408)		1	4	14	23
2 Invisible Sun *Police* (A&N ANS 8164)		3	9	22	26
3 Hands Up (Give Me Your Heart) *Ottowan* (Carrere CAR 183)		5	7	13	20
4 Pretend *Alvin Stardust* (Stiff BUY 124)		6	15	20	30
5 Souvenir *Orchestral Manoeuvres In The Dark* (Virgin Dindisc DIN 24)		10	17	25	32
6 Under Your Thumb *Godley & Creme* (Polydor POSP 322)		4	3	8	15
7 Birdie Song *Tweets* (PRT 7P 219)		2	2	3	5
8 Tainted Love *Soft Cell* (Bizarre BZS 2)		12	20	22	28
9 Endless Love *Diana Ross* (Motown TMG 1240)		9	13	17	25
10 Shut Up *Madness* (Stiff BUY 126)		7	12	15	19
11 Slow Hand *Pointer Sisters* (Planet K12530)		14	22	33	51
12 Just Can't Get Enough *Depeche Mode* (Mute MUTE 016)		11	8	12	17
13 You'll Never Know *Hi Gloss* (Epic EPCA 1387)		15	23	34	48

3	10	17	24	31
14 Wired For Sound *Cliff Richard* (EMI 5221)	20	37	45	–
15 So This Is Romance *Linx* (Chrysalis CHS2546)	17	27	35	59
16 In & Out Of Love *Imagination* (Red Bus RBS 202)	18	26	30	54
17 It's My Party *Dave Stewart/Barbara Gaskin* (Stiff/Broken BROKEN 2)	8	1	1	1
18 Stars On 45 (Vol. 3) *Star Sound* (CBS A 1521)	26	32	43	–
19 Hand Held In Black & White *Dollar* (WEA BUCK 1)	24	28	44	68
20 Hold On Tight *Electric Light Orchestra* (Jet 7011)	38	56	–	–
32 Thunder In Mountains *Toyah* (Safari SAFE 38)	13	5	4	7
30 Walkin' In The Sunshine *Bad Manners* (Magnet MAG 197)	16	10	11	16
26 Quiet Life *Japan* (Hansa/Ariola 6)	19	19	21	24
– Open Your Heart *Human League* (Virgin VS 453)	21	6	6	11
– It's Raining *Shakin' Stevens* (Epic EPCA 1643)	40	11	10	10
47 Good Year For The Roses *Elvis Costello* (F-Beat XX17)	23	14	9	8
48 Happy Birthday *Altered Images* (Epic EPCA 1522)	28	16	5	2
– O Superman *Laurie Anderson* Warner K 17870	–	18	2	3
– Absolute Beginners *Jam* (Polydor POSP 322)	–	–	7	4
35 Let's Hang On *Barry Manilow* (Arista ARIST 429)	30	21	16	12
– Hold Me *B. A. Robertson & Maggie Bell* (Swansong BAM 1)	–	36	18	13
– Labelled With Love *Squeeze* (A&M AMS 8166)	72	31	19	9
– Every Little Thing She Does Is Magic *Police* (A&M AMS 8174)	–	–	27	6
– When She Was My Girl *Four Tops* (Casablanca CAN 1005)	–	42	29	14
– Tonight I'm Yours *Rod Stewart* (Riva RIVA 33)	–	47	28	18

NOVEMBER 1981

7	14	21	28
1 It's My Party *Dave Stewart/Barbara Gaskin* (Stiff/Broken BROKEN 2)	6	15	29
2 Happy Birthday *Altered Images* (Epic EPCA 1522)	2	11	16
3 Every Little Thing She Does Is Magic *Police* (A&M AMS 8174)	1	2	9
4 Labelled With Love *Squeeze* (A&M AMS 8166)	4	10	17
5 When She Was My Girl *Four Tops* (Casablanca CAN 1005)	3	6	13
6 Good Year For The Roses *Elvis Costello* (F.Beat XX 17)	12	16	34
7 Joan Of Arc *Orchestral Manoeuvres In The Dark* (Dindisc DIN 36)	5	5	6
8 Absolute Beginners *Jam* (Polydor POSP 350)	19	27	61
9 Birdie Song *Tweets* (PRT 7P 219)	16	22	22
10 Open Your Heart *Human League* (Virgin VS 453)	15	21	40
11 Hold Me *B. A. Robertson/Maggie Bell* (Swansong BAM 1)	13	20	35
12 Let's Hang On *Barry Manilow* (Arista ARIST 429)	17	24	58
13 Tonight I'm Yours *Rod Stewart* (Riva RIVA 33)	10	8	11
14 It's Raining *Shakin' Stevens* (Epic EPCA 1643)	18	28	46
15 O Superman *Laurie Anderson* (Warners K 17870)	24	54	–
16 Thunder In Mountains *Toyah* (Safari SAFE 38)	21	39	51
17 When You Were Sweet Sixteen *Fureys & Davie Arthur* (Ritz RITZ 003)	14	14	20
18 Physical *Olivia Newton-John* (EMI 5234)	11	7	8
19 Favourite Shirts *Haircut One Hundred* (Arista CLIP 1)	9	4	4
20 Walkin' In The Sunshine *Bad Manners* (MAG 197)	34	56	–
– Under Pressure *Queen/David Bowie* (EMI 5250)	8	1	1
21 Begin The Beguine (Volver A Empezar) *Julio Iglesias* (CBA CBSA 1612)	7	3	2
38 Let's Groove *Earth Wind & Fire* (CBS CBSA 1679)	20	9	3

7	14	21	28
− I Go To Sleep *Pretenders* (Real ARE 18)	29	12	10
− Bed Sitter *Soft Cell* (Some Bizarre BZS 6)	28	13	5
45 Ay Ay Ay Ay Moosey *Modern Romance* (WEA K18883)	23	17	12
32 Steppin' Out *Kool & The Gang* (De Lite DE4)	25	18	14
40 Why Do Fools Fall In Love? *Diana Ross* (Capitol CL 226)	22	19	7
− Daddy's Home *Cliff Richard* (EMI 5251)	−	37	15
49 Voice *Ultravox* (Chrysalis CHS 2559)	27	23	18
50 Tears Are Not Enough *ABC* (Neutron NT 101)	39	26	19

DECEMBER 1981

5	12	19	26
1 Begin The Beguine (Volver A Empezar) *Julio Iglesias* (CBS CBSA 1612)	3	6	14
2 Under Pressure *Queen/David Bowie* (EMI 5250)	8	16	35
3 Let's Groove *Earth Wind & Fire* (CBS CBSA1679)	5	11	25
4 Bed Sitter *Soft Cell* (Some Bizarre BZS 6)	6	9	16
5 Why Do Fools Fall In Love *Diana Ross* (Capitol CL 226)	4	7	13
6 Daddy's Home *Cliff Richard* (EMI 5251)	2	2	2
7 I Go To Sleep *Pretenders* (Real ARE 18)	13	17	34
8 Favourite Shirts *Haircut One Hundred* (Arista CLIP 1)	21	39	48
9 Don't You Want Me *Human League* (Virgin VS 466)	1	1	1
10 Ay Ay Ay Ay Moosey *Modern Romance* (WEA K 18883)	15	21	38
11 Physical *Olivia Newton-John* (EMI 5234)	19	35	36
12 Steppin' Out *Kool & The Gang* (De Lite DE4)	18	24	43
13 Joan Of Arc *Orchestral Manoeuvres In The Dark* (Dindisc DIN36)	32	41	56
14 Four More From Toyah (Safari TOY2)	14	22	29
15 Tonight I'm Yours *Rod Stewart* (Riva RIVA 33)	37	51	66
16 Voice *Ultravox* (Chrysalis CHS 2559)	23	25	53
17 Every Little Thing She Does Is Magic *Police* (A&M AMS 8174)	38	54	71
18 Cambodia *Kim Wilde* (RAK 336)	12	15	17
19 Tears Are Not Enough *ABC* (Neutron NT 101)	30	32	−
20 The Lunatics Have Taken Over The Asylum *Fun Boy Three* (Chrysalis CGS2563	20	20	27
− Ant Rap *Adam & The Ants* (CBS CBS A1738)	9	4	4
24 It Must Be Love *Madness* (Stiff BUY 134)	7	5	6
21 Wedding Bells *Godley & Creme* (Polydor POSP 369)	10	8	7
− One Of Us *Abba* (Epic EPCA 1740)	11	3	3
23 Flashback *Imagination* (Red Bus RBS 206)	16	18	23
27 Rock 'n' Roll *Status Quo* (Vertigo QUO 6)	17	12	8
35 The Land Of Make Believe *Bucks Fizz* (RCA 163)	24	10	5
− Spirits In The Material World *Police* (A&M AM8194)	28	13	12
26 My Own Way *Duran Duran* (EMI 5254)	22	14	15
37 Mirror Mirror *Dollar* (WEA BUCK 2)	26	19	9
− I'll Find My Way Home *Jon/Vangelis* (Polydor JV1)	46	26	10
− Young Turks *Rod Stewart* (Riva RIVA 34)	41	23	11
− Hokey Cokey *The Snowmen* (Stiff ODB 1)	68	40	18
− Waiting For A Girl Like You *Foreigner* (Atlantic K11696)	58	30	19
− I Could Be Happy *Altered Images* (Epic EPCA 1834)	51	29	20

1981 – BEST SELLING RECORDS

Singles:

1 Tainted Love *Soft Cell* (Some Bizzare)
2 Stand & Deliver *Adam & The Ants* (CBS)
3 Prince Charming *Adam & The Ants* (CBS)
4 This Ole House *Shakin' Stevens* (Epic)
5 Vienna *Ultravox* (Chrysalis)
6 One Day In Your Life *Michael Jackson* (Motown)
7 Making Your Mind Up *Bucks Fizz* (RCA)
8 Shaddup You Face *Joe Dolce* (Epic)
9 Birdie Song *Tweets* (PRT)
10 You Drive Me Crazy *Shakin' Stevens* (CBS)
11 Ghost Town *Specials* (2-Tone)
12 Being With You *Smokey Robinson* (Motown)
13 It's My Party *Dave Stewart and Barbara Gaskin* (Broken)
14 Woman *John Lennon* (Geffen)
15 Happy Birthday *Altered Images* (Epic)
16 Hands Up (Give Me Your Heart) *Ottowan* (Carrere)
17 Stars On 45 *Star Sound* (CBS)
18 Green Door *Shakin' Stevens* (Epic)
19 Imagine *John Lennon* (Parlophone)
20 Jealous Guy *Roxy Music* (Polydor/EG)
21 Kids In America *Kim Wilde* (RAK)
22 Japanese Boy *Aneka* (Hansa)
23 Chi Mai Theme (Tune Life And Times Of Lloyd George) *Ennio Morricone* (BBC)
24 Begin the Beguine (Volver A Empezar) *Julio Iglesias* (CBS)
25 Hooked On Classics *Louis Clark/Royal Philharmonic Orchestra* (RCA)
26 Souvenir *Orchestral Manoeuvres In The Dark* (Dindisc)
27 Can Can *Bad Manners* (Magnet)
28 Ant Music *Adam & The Ants* (CBS)
29 Do The Hucklebuck *Coast To Coast* (Polydor)
30 Hold On Tight *Electric Light Orchestra* (Jet)
31 More Than In Love *Kate Robbins And Beyond* (RCA)
32 Body Talk *Imagination* (Red Bus)
33 Love Action (I Believe In Love) *Human League* (Virgin)
34 Stars On 45 (Vol. 2) *Star Sound* (CBS)
35 Lately *Stevie Wonder* (Motown)
36 In The Air Tonight *Phil Collins* (Virgin)
37 Going Back To Our Roots *Odyssey* (RCA Victor)
38 Under Your Thumb *Godley & Creme* (Polydor)
39 Happy Birthday *Stevie Wonder* (Motown)
40 Kings Of The Wild Frontier *Adam & The Ants* (CBS)
41 Every Little Thing She Does Is Magic *Police* (A&M)
42 I Surrender *Rainbow* (Polydor)
43 Under Pressure *Queen/David Bowie* (EMI)
44 Pretend *Alvin Stardust* (Stiff)
45 How 'Bout Us *Champaign* (CBS)
46 Four From Toyah *Toyah* (Safari)
47 Endless Love *Diana Ross & Lionel Ritchie* (Motown)
48 Einstein A Go-Go *Landscape* (RCA)
49 Hand Held In Black & White *Dollar* (WEA)
50 Can You Feel It *Jacksons* (Epic)

Albums:

1 Kings Of The Wild Frontier *Adam & The Ants* (CBS)
2 Queen's Greatest Hits *Queen* (EMI)
3 Face Value *Phil Collins* (Virgin)
4 Shaky *Shakin' Stevens* (Epic)
5 Ghost In The Machine *Police* (A&M)
6 Love Songs *Cliff Richard* (EMI)
7 Dare *Human League* (Virgin)
8 Double Fantasy *John Lennon* (Geffen)
9 Jazz Singer *Neil Diamond* (Capitol)
10 Stars On 45 *Star Sound* (CBS)
11 Hotter Than July *Stevie Wonder* (Motown)
12 Making Movies *Dire Straits* (Vertigo)
13 Vienna *Ultravox* (Chrysalis)
14 Prince Charming *Adam & The Ants* (CBS)
15 Secret Combination *Randy Crawford* (Warner Brothers)
16 Chart Hits '81 *Various* (K-Tel)
17 Manilow Magic *Barry Manilow* (Arista)
18 Time *Electric Light Orchestra* (Jet)
19 Bat Out Of Hell *Meatloaf* (Epic/Cleveland International)
20 The Best Of Blondie *Blondie* (Chrysalis)
21 Dead Ringer *Meat Loaf* (Epic)
22 Guilty *Barbra Streisand* (CBS)
23 Anthem *Toyah* (Safari)
24 Hooked On Classics *Louis Clark/RPO* (RCA)
25 Present Arms *UB40* (Dep. International)
26 This Ole House *Shakin' Stevens* (Epic)
27 Superhits 1 & 2 *Various* (Ronco)
28 Duran Duran *Duran Duran* (EMI)
29 Disco Daze And Disco Nites *Various* (Ronco)
30 Abacab *Genesis* (Charisma)
31 Tattoo You *Rolling Stones* (Rolling Stones)
32 Hi Infidelity *Reo Speedwagon* (Epic)
33 The Very Best Of David Bowie *David Bowie* (RCA)
34 Pearls *Elkie Brooks* (A&M)
35 Architecture & Morality *Orchestral Manoeuvres In The Dark* (Dindisc)
36 If I Should Love Again *Barry Manilow* (Arista)
37 Super Trouper *Abba* (Epic)
39 Official BBC Album Of The Royal Wedding *Various* (BBC)
40 Christopher Cross *Christopher Cross* (Warner Brothers)
41 Wired For Sound *Cliff Richard* (EMI)
42 The River *Bruce Springsteen* (CBS)
43 Difficult To Cure *Rainbow* (Polydor)
44 Barry *Barry Manilow* (Arista)
45 Dr Hook's Greatest Hits *Dr Hook* (Capitol)
46 The Simon and Garfunkel Collection *Simon and Garfunkel* (CBS)
47 Journey To Glory *Spandau Ballet* (Reformation/Chrysalis)
48 Signing Off *UB40* (Graduate)
49 Chariots Of Fire *Vangelis* (Polydor)
50 Sky 3 *Sky* (Ariola)

1982

You could say the 1982 charts had something for everyone. A look at the Top Fifty selling singles or albums reveals an interesting mix. The former throws up people like Dexy's, Irene Cara, Survivor, Toni Basil, Haircut One Hundred, Dionne Warwick, PhD, Nicole, Meatloaf, Pigbag, Shakin' Stevens and Imagination, while the latter's bedmates can bring together Barbra Streisand, Iron Maiden, ABC, Vangelis, Barry Manilow, Shalamar, Commodores, Japan, Status Quo, Julio Iglesias, Roxy Music, Paul McCartney and Soft Cell. And there you have diversity of musical style and general image.

The music business itself said 1982 was a hard year and the record companies forecast no change for 1983. Album sales fell, though singles held up well—even if they had to be boosted by endless 12 inch discs (both black and other colours), three-track and special-mix editions, a picture disc and (at very least) a bright sleeve. The pessimists said the companies were fighting for a slightly smaller piece of the profit cake. Others thought there was a glimmer of hope, especially if new bands could translate success from singles to albums and achieve some career longevity.

Phonogram was one company which found 1982 a very friendly year. They had ABC, Soft Cell, Dexy's, Kool & The Gang, Crown Heights Affair, David Essex, Status Quo, Teardrop Explodes and Tears for Fears among their success roster. They pressed themselves or pressed and distributed through PolyGram major acts of other companies such as Charisma and Arista. The Managing Director of Phonogram Brian Shepherd said the company's success relied on the oldest blueprint in the business. He told *Record Business* it was the case of signing the right acts, marketing them aggressively with hit singles, and then turning that success into hit albums.

Yet not even the best of companies can prevent a group splitting and Polydor must have shed a corporate tear or two as The Jam said their days were finished and as they played out the year with a series of sell-out concerts. During the year, their instant Number One—Beat

309

Surrender—gave them a hatrick of records achieving this chart feat.

Not even the best sales force in the world amongst any major company can prevent the unexpected monster smash from a small independent. The example in 1982 was Save Your Love by Renée and Renato on Hollywood. The company had been started by husband-and-wife team John and Sue Edwards and the hit 45 was only the company's second single. It was also the first Number One for Pinnacle, who distributed the record, and making it the first indie-distributed chart-topper (and as it happens, the first Number One for Bromley-based independent record pressing company Continental Production Services). By the record's third week in the top spot, it had sailed past the half-million sales mark.

Music Week, December 25th issue, expressed surprise at Barbra Streisand having the year's best selling album. For other unexpected happenings in 1982, there was a spate of 12-inch three track oldies being issued. This arose because two releases, The House Of The Rising Sun and Layla, charted high. Thus, EMI decided they would issue once more, the first Beatles chart hit, Love Me Do, twenty years on from its first release; they found themselves with a hit.

Dionne Warwick bounced back into the limelight with a Bee Gees based number Heartbreaker and before the year was out had a follow-up hit from the same writing source with All The Love In The World. Few would have predicted 1982 as the backcloth for the lady's return.

RCA issued David Bowie and Bing Crosby with Peace On Earth and Little Drummer Boy after digging into their vinyl vaults. Another surprising release was I'm Alright from Young Steve And The Afternoon Boys, Young Steve being the rapidly improving afternoon Radio One disc jockey Steve Wright. And did anyone expect Captain Sensible to sing Happy Talk? or Pigbag with Papa's Got A Brand New Pigbag? But the major excitement, outside of the Phonogram acts, settled around people like Wham, Culture Club, Talk Talk, Yazoo and Depeche Mode. Equally fast-becoming veterans like Duran Duran, Human League, Stranglers, Bow Wow Wow, Japan kept on having hits and joined real chart oldies like Hot Chocolate, David Essex, Queen, Eddy Grant, Kraftwerk and The Steve Miller Band in the charts.

Of course, Paul McCartney, Adam Ant, Abba, Madness were all there as well, and nobody was surprised.

JANUARY 1982

9		16	23	30
1	Don't You Want Me *Human League* (Virgin VS 466)	2	5	12
2	The Land Of Make Believe *Bucks Fizz* (RCA 163)	1	1	2
3	Ant Rap *Adam & The Ants* (CBS A 1738)	5	15	23
4	It Must Be Love *Madness* (Stiff BUY 134)	9	12	18
5	One Of Us *Abba* (Epic EPCA 1740)	6	17	22
6	Daddy's Home *Cliff Richard* (EMI 5251)	12	24	28
7	Get Down On It *Kool & The Gang* (De Lite DE 5)	3	4	5
8	Mirror Mirror *Dollar* (WEA BUCK 2)	4	11	8
9	I'll Find My Way Home *Jon/Vangelis* (Polydor JV1)	8	6	7
10	I Could Be Happy *Altered Images* (Epic EPCA 1834)	7	10	13
11	Wedding Bells *Godley & Creme* (Polydor POSP 369)	17	30	45
12	Waiting For A Girl Like You *Foreigner* (Atlantic K 11696)	11	8	11
13	Rock 'n' Roll *Status Quo* (Vertigo QUO 6)	15	25	27
14	Young Turks *Rod Stewart* (Riva 34)	14	21	25
15	Spirits In The Material World *Police* (A&M AMS 8194)	18	38	54
16	My Own Way *Duran Duran* (EMI 5254)	16	27	44
17	Birdie Song *Tweets* (PRT 7P219)	21	29	35
18	Flashback *Imagination* (Red Bus RBS 206)	31	28	41
19	Cambodia *Kim Wilde* (RAK 336)	39	43	68
20	Why Do Fools Fall In Love? *Diana Ross* (Capitol CL 226)	34	53	–
21	The Model/Computer Love *Kraftwerk* (EMI 5207)	10	2	3
–	Oh Julie *Shakin' Stevens* (Epic EPCA 1742)	13	3	1
53	Bein' Boiled *Human League* (EMI FAST 4)	19	9	6
31	I Wanna Be A Winner *Brown Sauce* (BBC RESL 101)	20	23	15
30	Dead Ringer For Love *Meat Loaf* (Epic EPCA 1697)	26	7	9
48	Drowning In Berlin *Mobiles* (Rialto RIA 3)	30	13	14
25	Yellow Pearl *Philip Lynott* (Vertigo SOLO 3)	22	14	21
67	Golden Brown *The Stranglers* (Liberty BP 407)	25	16	4
54	Arthur's Theme (Best That You Can Do) *Christopher Cross* (Warner Brothers K17847)	27	18	10
26	Don't Walk Away *Four Tops* (Casablanca CAN 1006)	23	19	16
62	I Just Wanna (Spend Some Time With You) *Alton Edwards* (Streetwave STRA 1897)	33	20	20
–	Maid Of Orleans *Orchestral Manoeuvres In The Dark* (Dindisc 40)	–	31	17
42	Easier Said Than Done *Shakatak* (Polydor POSP 375)	36	22	19

FEBRUARY 1982

6		13	20	27
1	The Model/Computer Love *Kraftwerk* (EMI 5207)	4	5	13
2	Oh Julie *Shakin' Stevens* (Epic EPCA 1742)	3	7	14
3	Golden Brown *The Stranglers* (Liberty BP 407)	2	2	6
4	The Land Of Make Believe *Bucks Fizz* (RCA 163)	9	19	31
5	Dead Ringer For Love *Meat Loaf* (Epic EPCA 1697)	5	9	15
6	Maid Of Orleans (The Waltz Joan Of Arc) *Orchestral Manoeuvres In The Dark* (Dindisc/Virgin 40)	6	4	7
7	Arthur's Theme (Best That You Can Do) *Christopher Cross* (Warner K17847)	7	8	12
8	Get Down On It *Kool & The Gang* (De Lite Phonogram DE 5)	14	20	32
9	Drowning In Berlin *Mobiles* (Rialto RIA 3)	10	16	24
10	Being Boiled *Human League* (Fast Product FAST 4)	16	23	38
11	I'll Find My Way Home *Jon & Vangelis* (Polydor JV1)	19	25	47
12	Easier Said Than Done *Shakatak* (Polydor POSP 375)	13	15	26
13	Waiting For A Girl Like You *Foreigner* (Atlantic K11706)	15	39	43
14	Let's Get It Up *AC/DC* (Atlantic K11706)	22	13	21
15	Senses Working Overtime *XTC* (Virgin VS 462)	17	10	16

311

6		13	20	27
16 Mirror Mirror (Mon Amour) *Dollar* (WEA BUCK 2)		24	38	63
17 I Could Be Happy *Altered Images* (Epic EPCA 1834)		27	37	57
18 Don't Walk Away *Four Tops* (Casablanca CAN 1006)		21	27	58
19 I Wanna Be A Winner *Brown Sauce* (BBC RES 101)		25	34	51
20 Say Hello, Wave Goodbye *Soft Cell* (Some Bizzare/Phonogram BZS 7)		18	3	5
– Town Called Malice/Precious *The Jam* (Polydor POSP 400)		1	1	1
29 The Lion Sleeps Tonight *Tight Fit* (Jive JIVE 9)		8	6	2
27 I Can't Go For That (No Can Do) *Daryl Hall & Joan Oates* (RCA 172)		11	12	8
36 Love Plus One *Haircut One Hundred* (Arista CLIP 2)		12	11	4
23 I Just Wanna (Spend Some Time With You) *Alton Edwards* (Streetwave STRA1897)		20	22	44
21 Never Give Up On A Good Thing *George Benson* (Warner Brothers K17902)		23	14	18
– Centerfold *J. Geils Band* (EMI America EA135)		26	17	3
44 Landslide *Olivia Newton-John* (EMI 5257)		32	18	27
– T'aint What You Do (It's The Way You Do It) *Funboy Three with Bananarama* (Chrysalis CHS 2570)		43	36	9
– See You *Depeche Mode* (Mute MUTE 018)		40	31	10
64 Mickey *Toni Basil* (Radialchoice TIC 4)		39	24	11
41 Fool If You Think It's Over *Elkie Brooks* (A&M AMS 8187)		29	21	17
– Run To The Hills *Iron Maiden* (EMI 5263)		–	33	19
– Deutscher Girls *The Original Adam & The Ants* (EG EGO 05)		–	–	20

MARCH 1982

6		13	20	27
1 The Lion Sleeps Tonight *Tight Fit* (Jive JIVE 9)		1	1	2
2 Mickey *Toni Basil* (Radialchoice TIC 4)		2	3	5
3 Town Called Malice/Precious *The Jam* (Polydor POSP 400)		11	20	39
4 Love Plus One *Haircut One Hundred* (Arista CLIP 2)		3	4	10
5 Centerfold *J. Geils Band* (EMI America EA 135)		5	9	17
6 T'Aint What You Do (It's The Way That You Do It) *Fun Boy Three with Bananarama* (Chrysalis CHS 2570)		4	5	12
7 Say Hello, Wave Goodbye *Soft Cell* (Some Bizzare/Phonogram BZS 7)		17	24	40
8 See You *Depeche Mode* (Mute MUTE 018)		6	11	13
9 Golden Brown *The Stranglers* (Liberty BP 407)		23	39	68
10 Maid Of Orleans (The Waltz Joan Of Arc) *Orchestral Manoeuvres In The Dark* (Virgin/Dindisc 40)		19	27	49
11 Run To The Hills *Iron Maiden* (EMI 5263)		7	13	15
12 I Can't Go For That (No Can Do) *Daryl Hall & John Oates* (RCA 172)		20	28	55
13 Deutscher Girls *The Original Adam & The Ants* (EG EGO 5)		13	19	30
14 Cardiac Arrest *Madness* (Stiff BUY 140)		15	14	20
15 Poison Arrow *A.B.C.* (Neutron/Phonogram NT 102)		10	6	6
16 Go Wild In The Country *Bow Wow Wow* (RCA 175)		9	7	11
17 Never Give Up On A Good Thing *George Benson* (Warner Brothers K17992)		31	47	73
18 Classic *Adrian Gurvitz* (RAK 339)		12	10	8
19 Senses Working Overtime *XTC* (Virgin VS 462)		46	67	–
20 Stars On Stevie *Star Sound* (CBS A2041)		14	17	24
39 Seven Tears *Goombay Dance Band* (Epic EPC A1242)		8	2	1
23 Some Guys Have All The Luck *Robert Palmer* (Island WIP 6754)		16	18	25
40 Just An Illusion *Imagination* (Red Bus RBS 208)		18	8	4
47 Quiereme Mucho (Yours) *Julio Iglesias* (CBS A1939)		24	12	3
38 Party Fears Two *The Associates* (Associates ASC 1)		25	15	9

	6	13	20	27
68 Layla *Derek & The Dominoes* (RSO 87)		30	16	7
– Ain't No Pleasing You *Chas & Dave* (Rockney KOR 14)		61	31	14
– Ghosts *Japan* (Virgin VS 472)		–	42	16
– Damned Don't Cry *Visage* (Polydor POSP 390)		33	23	18
35 Music For Chameleons *Gary Numan* (Beggars Banquet BEG 70)		22	21	19

APRIL 1982

	3	10	17	24
1 Seven Tears *Goombay Dance Band* (Epic EPCA 1242)		1	4	13
2 Just An Illusion *Imagination* (Red Bus R&BS 208)		3	8	15
3 Quiereme Mucho (Yours) *Julio Iglesias* (CBS A1939)		9	23	33
4 Layla *Derek & The Dominoes* (RSO 87)		8	18	24
5 My Camera Never Lies *Bucks Fizz* (RCA 202)		2	1	2
6 The Lion Sleeps Tonight *Tight Fit* (Jive JIVE 9)		20	31	50
7 Ain't No Pleasing You *Chas & Dave* (Rockney KOR 14)		4	2	5
8 Poison Arrow *A.B.C.* (Neutron/Phonogram NT 102)		15	27	40
9 Ghosts *Japan* (Virgin VS 472)		5	7	14
10 Party Fears Two *The Associates* (Associates ASC1)		22	33	52
11 Damned Don't Cry *Visage* (Polydor POSP 390)		12	22	25
12 Classic *Adrian Gurvitz* (RAK 339)		21	41	66
13 Mickey *Toni Basil* (Radialchoice/Virgin TIC4)		26	35	46
14 Have You Ever Been In Love *Leo Sayer* (Chrysalis CHS 2596)		10	13	23
15 Give Me Back My Heart *Dollar* (WEA BUCK 3)		7	5	4
16 Is It A Dream *Classix Nouveaux* (Liberty BP 409)		11	12	21
17 See Those Eyes *Altered Images* (Epic EPC A2918)		17	11	19
18 More Than This *Roxy Music* (EG/Polydor ROXY 3)		6	6	7
19 Your Honour *Pluto* (KR KR4)		28	36	59
20 Go Wild In The Country *Bow Wow Wow* (RCA 175)		33	38	56
25 Dear John *Status Quo* (Vertigo/Phonogram QUO 7)		13	10	16
21 Don't Love Me Too Hard *Nolans* (Epic EPC A1927)		14	14	20
37 Night Birds *Shakatak* (Polydor POSP 407)		16	15	9
24 A Bunch Of Thyme *Foster & Allen* (RITZ 005)		18	21	32
– Ebony And Ivory *Paul McCartney with Stevie Wonder* (Parlophone R6054)		19	3	1
50 Papa's Got A Brand New Pigbag *Pigbag* (Y Records Y10)		30	9	3
– One Step Further *Bardo* (Epic EPCA 2265)		43	16	6
31 Blue Eyes *Elton John* (Rocket/Phonogram XPRES 71)		23	17	8
– Fantastic Day *Haircut One Hundred* (Arista CLIP 3)		32	19	12
35 I Can Make You Feel Good *Shalamar* (Solar K12599)		27	20	10
– This Time (We'll Get It Right) We'll Fly The Flag *England W.C. Squad* (England ER1)		35	25	11
– Really Saying Something *Bananarama with Fun Boy Three* (Deram NANA 1)		37	24	17
57 Ever So Lonely *Monsoon* (Mobile Corp/Phonogram CORP 2)		39	28	18

MAY 1982

	1	8	15	22	29
1 Ebony And Ivory *Paul McCartney with Stevie Wonder* (Parlophone R6054)		1	2	9	25
2 One Step Further *Bardo* (Epic EPC A2265)		6	21	33	61
3 Papa's Got A Brand New Pigbag *Pigbag* (Y Records Y10)		7	17	27	40
4 This Time (We'll Get It Right) We'll Fly The Flag *England W.C. Squad* (England ER1)		2	8	15	26
5 Really Saying Something *Bananarama with Fun Boy Three* (Deram NANA 1)		5	6	12	23

1	8	15	22	29
6 Shirley *Shakin' Stevens* (Epic EPC A 2087)	11	23	36	64
7 I Can Make You Feel Good *Shalamar* (Solar K12599)	9	16	25	44
8 Give Me Back My Heart *Dollar* (WEA BUCK3)	20	29	54	–
9 Fantastic Day *Haircut One Hundred* (Arista CLIP 3)	10	14	23	51
10 Blue Eyes *Elton John* (Rocket/Phonogram XPRES 71)	19	28	38	70
11 My Camera Never Lies *Bucks Fizz* (RCA 202)	26	46	–	–
12 Ain't No Pleasing You *Chas & Dave* (Rockney KOR 14)	22	36	61	–
13 I Won't Let You Down *PhD.* (WEA K79209)	3	3	3	7
14 More Than This *Roxy Music* (EG/Polydor ROXY 3)	28	58	72	–
15 Night Birds *Shakatak* (Polydor POSP 407)	24	32	67	–
16 Ever So Lonely *Monsoon* (Mobile Suit Corp/Phonogram CORP 2)	12	20	29	38
17 I Love Rock 'n' Roll *Joan Jett & The Blackhearts* (Epic EPC A2152)	4	4	4	10
18 View From A Bridge *Kim Wilde* (RAK 342)	16	25	32	66
19 Promised You A Miracle *Simple Minds* (Virgin VS 488)	15	13	18	22
20 Dear John *Status Quo* (Vertigo/Phonogram QUO 7)	38	70	–	–
– A Little Peace *Nicole* (CBS A2365)	8	1	1	4
24 We Have A Dream *The Scottish World Cup Squad* (WEA K19145)	13	5	6	13
31 Only You *Yazoo* (Mute MUTE 020)	14	7	2	3
22 Instinction *Spandau Ballet* (Reformation/Chrysalis CHS2602)	17	10	16	18
26 Girl Crazy *Hot Chocolate* (RAK 341)	18	9	7	11
37 Forget Me Nots *Patrice Rushen* (Elektra K13173)	27	11	10	8
– The Meaning Of Love *Depeche Mode* (Mute MUTE 022)	34	12	17	15
56 Fantasy Island *Tightfit* (Jive JIVE 3)	32	15	11	5
41 Mama Used To Say *Junior* (Mercury/Phonogram MER 98)	31	18	14	9
43 Tottenham Tottenham *Tottenham Hotspur FA Cup Team* (Rockney SHELF2)	30	19	24	27
– Goody Two Shoes *Adam Ant* (CBS A2387)	–	–	5	2
– House Of Fun *Madness* (Stiff BUY 146)	–	–	8	1
– The Look Of Love *A.B.C.* (Neutron/Phonogram NT 103)	–	23	13	6
34 Shout! Shout! (Knock Yourself Out) *Rocky Sharpe & The Replays* (Chiswick DICE 3)	21	22	19	20
– Hungry Like The Wolf *Duran Duran* (EMI 5295)	–	35	20	12
– Island Of Lost Souls *Blondie* (Chrysalis CHS 2608)	39	24	21	14
– Torch *Soft Cell* (Some Bizarre/Phonogram BZ9)	–	–	–	16
– Club Country *The Associates* (Associates ASC 2)	35	30	22	17
– The Number Of The Beast *Iron Maiden* (EMI 5287)	–	33	26	19

JUNE 1982

5	12	19	26
1 House Of Fun *Madness* (Stiff BUY 146)	2	5	14
2 Goody Two Shoes *Adam Ant* (CBS A2367)	1	1	2
3 Torch *Soft Cell* (Some Bizarre/Phonogram BZS 9)	3	2	3
4 Only You *Yazoo* (Mute MUTE 020)	8	13	21
5 The Look Of Love *A.B.C.* (Neutron/Phonogram NT 103)	4	4	6
6 Fantasy Island *Tightfit* (Jive JIVE 13)	5	8	15
7 Mama Used To Say *Junior* (Mercury/Phonogram MER 98)	7	12	17
8 Hungry Like The Wolf *Duran Duran* (EMI 5295)	6	6	5
9 I Won't Let You Down *Ph.D.* (WEA K 79209)	15	34	47
10 A Little Peace *Nicole* (CBS A2365)	16	41	50
11 Forget Me Nots *Patrice Rushen* (Elektra K13173)	12	22	48
12 Island Of Lost Souls *Blondie* (Chrysalis CHS 2068)	11	20	30
13 Girl Crazy *Hot Chocolate* (RAK 341)	19	40	55
14 Club Country *The Associates* (Associates ASC 2)	13	16	29

5	12	19	26
15 I've Never Been To Me *Charlene* (Motown TMG 1260)	9	3	1
16 I Love Rock 'n' Roll *Joan Jett & The Blackhearts* (Epic EPCA2152)	33	58	69
17 The Meaning Of Love *Depeche Mode* (Mute MUTE 022)	21	46	72
18 We Have A Dream *The Scottish World Cup Squad* (WEA K19145)	36	45	53
19 Paperplate (EP) *Genesis* (Charisma/Phonogram GEN 1)	10	11	20
20 The Number Of The Beast *Iron Maiden* (EMI 5287)	18	26	49
38 I Want Candy *Bow Wow Wow* (RCA 238)	14	14	9
24 I'm A Wonderful Thing (Baby) *Kid Creole & The Coconuts* (Ze/Island WIP 6756)	17	7	4
21 The Telephone Always Rings *The Fun Boy Three* (Chrysalis CHS 2609)	20	17	27
– We Take Mystery *Gary Numan* (Beggars Banquet BEG 77)	–	9	11
29 Work That Body *Diana Ross* (Capitol CL 241)	22	10	8
42 Do I Do *Stevie Wonder* (Motown TMG 1269)	27	15	10
– Inside Out *Odyssey* (RCA 226)	56	18	7
27 The Back Of Love *Echo and The Bunnymen* (Korova KOW 24)	24	19	23
– Abracadabra *The Steve Miller Band* (Mercury/Phonogram STEVE 3)	–	38	12
– Avalon *Roxy Music* (EG/Polydor ROXY 4)	–	33	13
54 Iko Iko *Natasha* (Towerbell TOW 22)	38	24	16
56 Beatles Movie Medley *The Beatles* (Parlophone R6055)	34	25	18
– No Regrets *Midge Ure* (Chrysalis CHS 2618)	73	27	19

JULY 1982

3	10	17	24	31
1 Happy Talk *Captain Sensible* (A&M GAP 1)	1	3	16	30
2 I've Never Been To Me *Charlene* (Motown TMG 260)	7	22	34	65
3 Inside Out *Odyssey* (RCA 260)	3	4	10	13
4 Abracadabra *The Steve Miller Band* (Mercury/Phonogram STEVE 3)	2	2	3	8
5 Music & Lights *Imagination* (Red Bus RBS 210)	5	6	12	18
6 I'm A Wonderful Thing (Baby) *Kid Creole & The Coconuts* (Ze/Island WIP 6756)	14	25	50	–
7 Work That Body *Diana Ross* (Capitol CL 241)	10	17	37	41
8 Hungry Like The Wolf *Duran Duran* (EMI 5295)	16	27	43	68
9 Goody Two Shoes *Adam Ant* (CBS A2367)	28	45	61	75
10 Beatles Movie Medley *The Beatles* (Parlophone R6055)	11	18	27	53
11 No Regrets *Midge Ure* (Chrysalis CHS 2618)	9	11	19	26
12 Torch *Soft Cell* (Some Bizarre/Phonogram BZS 9)	25	41	65	–
13 Just Who Is The 5 O'Clock Hero *The Jam* (Polydor 2059 504)	8	16	33	40
14 Iko Iko *Natasha* (Towerbell TOW 22)	12	10	15	21
15 I Want Candy *Bow Wow Wow* (RCA 238)	24	34	70	–
16 Avalon *Roxy Music* (EG/Polydor ROXY 4)	19	29	57	–
17 A Night To Remember *Shalamar* (Solar K 13162)	6	5	7	10
18 The Look Of Love *A.B.C.* (Neutron/Phonogram NT 103)	23	44	64	–
19 Do I Do *Stevie Wonder* (Motown TMG 1269)	26	32	–	–
20 Now Those Days Are Gone *Bucks Fizz* (RCA 241)	13	8	11	16
51 Fame *Irena Cara* (RSO 90)	4	1	1	1
25 For Those About To Rock (We Salute You) *AC/DC* (Atlantic K11721)	15	15	24	31
22 Las Palabras De Amor *Queen* (EMI 5316)	17	19	29	36
21 Murphy's Law *Cheri* (21/Polydor POSP 459)	18	13	18	22
41 Shy Boy *Bananarama* (London NANA 2)	20	9	4	6

	10	17	24	31
54 Da Da Da *Trio* (Mobile Suit Corporation/Phonogram CORP5)	30	7	2	5
– It Started With A Kiss *Hot Chocolate* (RAK 344)	36	12	8	7
34 Night Train *Visage* (Polydor POSP 441)	21	14	13	12
56 I Second That Emotion *Japan* (Hansa HANSA 12)	31	20	14	9
– Don't Go *Yazoo* (Mute YAZ 001)	–	24	5	3
– Driving My Car *Madness* (Stiff BUY 153)	–	–	6	4
63 Come On Eileen *Dexy's Midnight Runners & The Emerald Express* (Mercury/Phonogram DEXYS 9)	41	31	9	2
– The Only Way Out *Cliff Richard* (EMI 5138)	–	35	17	14
42 Me And My Girl (Night-Clubbing) *David Essex* (Mercury/Phonogram MER107)	32	28	20	15
– Stool Pigeon *Kid Creole & The Coconuts* (Ze/Island WIP6793)	–	–	26	11
30 Videotheque *Dollar* (WEA BUCK 4)	29	26	21	17
– Strange Little Girl *The Stranglers* (Liberty BP 412)	–	–	35	19
47 Take It Away *Paul McCartney* (Parlophone R6056)	33	30	25	20

AUGUST 1982

7	14	21	28
1 Come On Eileen *Dexy's Midnight Runners* (Mercury/Phonogram DEXYS 9)	1	1	1
2 Fame *Irena Cara* (Polydor/RSO 90)	2	3	6
3 Don't Go *Yazoo* (Mute YAZ 001)	3	4	8
4 Driving In My Car *Madness* (Stiff BUY 153)	4	8	18
5 It Started With A Kiss *Hot Chocolate* (RAK 344)	5	5	12
6 Da Da Da *Trio* (Mobile Suit Corporation/Phonogram CORP 5)	13	22	44
7 Shy Boy *Bananarama* (London NANA 2)	10	19	39
8 Stool Pigeon *Kid Creole & The Coconuts* (Ze/Island WIP 6793)	7	9	17
9 I Second That Emotion *Japan* (Hansa HANSA 12)	11	20	38
10 The Only Way Out *Cliff Richard* (EMI 5318)	14	25	34
11 Strange Little Girl *The Stranglers* (Liberty BP 412)	8	7	13
12 Abrcadabra *The Steve Miller Band* (Mercury/Phonogram STEVE 3)	28	41	63
13 Me And My Girl (Night-Clubbing) *David Essex* (Phonogram MER 107)	17	32	36
14 A Night To Remember *Shalamar* (Solar K13162)	31	46	66
15 Take It Away *Paul McCartney* (Parlophone R6056)	15	23	33
16 Night Train *Visage* (Polydor POSP 441)	24	53	72
17 Arthur Daley ('e's Alright) *The Firm* (Bark/Stiff HID 1)	16	14	25
18 Videotheque *Dollar* (WEA BUCK 4)	29	44	–
19 The Clapping Song *The Belle Stars* (Stiff BUY 155)	12	11	16
20 Chalk Dust – The Umpire Strikes Back *The Brat* (Hansa SMASH 1)	19	30	37
29 Eye Of The Tiger *Survivor* (Scotti Brothers SCT A2411)	6	2	2
21 My Girl Lollopop (My Boy Lollipop) *Bad Manners* (Magnet MAG 232)	9	10	15
22 Love Is In Control (Finger On The Trigger) *Donna Summer* (Warner Brothers K79302)	18	24	23
25 Too Late *Junior* (Mercury/Phonogram MER 112)	20	29	35
39 Can't Take My Eyes Off You *Boystown Gang* (ERC ERC101)	21	6	4
70 I Eat Cannibals Part 1 *Toto Coelo* (Radialchoice/Virgi TIC 10)	34	12	9
47 What! *Soft Cell* (Some Bizarre/Phonogram BZS 11)	–	13	3
47 Big Fun *Kool & The Gang* (De Lite/Phonogram DE7)	23	15	14
26 John Wayne Is Big Leggy *Haysi Fantayzee* (Regard RG 100)	22	16	11
27 Hurry Home *Wavelength* (Ariola ARO 281)	27	17	21
31 Summertime *The Fun Boy Three* (Chrysalis CHS 2629)	26	18	24

7

	14	21	28
– Save A Prayer *Duran Duran* (EMI 5327)	–	27	5
– Hi-Fidelity *The Kids from 'Fame' featuring Valerie Landsburg* (RCA 254)	46	26	7
– Nobody's Fool *Haircut One Hundred* (Arista CLIP 4)	–	33	10
– Walking On Sunshine *Rockers Revenge featuring Donnie Calvin* (London LON 11)	67	37	19
– White Boys And Heroes *Gary Numan* (Beggars Banquet BEG 81)	–	–	20

SEPTEMBER 1982

4

	11	18	25
1 Eye Of The Tiger *Survivor* (Scott Brothers SCT A2411)	1	1	1
2 Come On Eileen *Dexy's Midnight Runners & The Emerald Express* (Mercury/Phonogram DEXYS 9)	3	9	14
3 Save A Prayer *Duran Duran* (EMI 5327)	2	3	7
4 What! *Soft Cell* (Some Bizarre/Phonogram BZS 11)	7	15	23
5 Hi-Fidelity *The Kids from 'Fame' featuring Valerie Landsburg* (RCA 254)	6	7	13
6 Can't Take My Eyes Off You *Boystown Gang* (ERC ERC 101)	10	19	20
7 Walking On Sunshine *Rockers Revenge featuring Donnie Calvin* (London LON 11)	5	4	4
8 I Eat Cannibals Part 1 *Toto Coelo* (Radialchoice/Virgin TIC 10)	9	13	21
9 Nobody's Fool *Haircut One Hundred* (Arista CLIP 4)	12	16	24
10 Fame *Irene Cara* (Polydor/RSO 90)	20	29	37
11 John Wayne Is Big Leggy *Haysi Fantayzee* (Regard RG 100)	18	26	49
12 Give Me Your Heart Tonight *Shakin' Stevens* (Epic EPC A2656)	11	11	11
13 – Private Investigations *Dire Straits* (Vertigo/Phonogram DSTR1)	4	2	3
14 Big Fun *Kool & The Gang* (De Lite/Phonogram DE 7)	23	30	69
15 Today *Talk Talk* (EMI 5314)	14	14	16
16 Cherry Pink And Apple Blossom White *Modern Romance featuring John Du Prez* (WEA K19245)	15	20	28
17 It Started With A Kiss *Hot Chocolate* (RAK 344)	35	48	65
18 Spread A Little Happiness *Sting* (A&M AMS 8242)	16	21	29
19 The Message *Grand Master Flash & The Furious Five* (Sugar Hill SHL117)	13	8	8
20 White Boys And Heroes *Gary Numan* (Beggars Banquet BEG 81)	25	37	–
28 All Of My Heart *A.B.C.* (Neutron/Phonogram NT 104)	8	6	5
34 There It Is *Shalamar* (Solar K 13194)	17	10	6
32 Saddle Up *David Christie* (KR KR 9)	19	12	9
– The Bitterest Pill (I Ever Had To Swallow) *The Jam* (Polydor POSP 5)	–	5	2
40 Why *Carly Simon* (WEA K79300)	24	17	12
39 Love Come Down *Evelyn King* (RCA 249)	29	18	15
– Friend Or Foe *Adam Ant* (CBS A2736)	–	22	10
– Zoom *Fat Larry's Band* (WMOT/Virgin VS 546)	–	40	17
33 Leave In Silence *Depeche Mode* (BONG 1)	21	23	18
– Just What I Always Wanted *Mari Wilson* (Compact PINK 4)	61	36	19

OCTOBER 1982

2

	9	16	23	30
1 Pass The Dutchie *Musical Youth* (MCA YOU 1)	1	1	2	5
2 The Bitterest Pill (I Ever Had To Swallow) *The Jam* (Polydor POSP 505)	10	16	40	65

317

	9	16	23	30
2				
3 Zoom *Fat Larry's band* (WMOT/Virgin VS546)	2	3	4	8
4 Eye Of The Tiger *Survivor* (Scotti Brothers SCT A2411)	11	19	32	45
5 There It Is *Shalamar* (Solar K13194)	6	9	19	41
6 Walking On Sunshine *Rockers Revenge* (London LON 11)	12	17	34	44
7 Love Come Down *Evelyn King* (RCA 249)	7	7	15	20
8 Private Investigations *Dire Straits* (Vertigo/Phonogram DSTR1)	18	26	55	–
9 Friend Or Foe *Adam Ant* (CBS A2736)	9	11	21	28
10 Why *Carly Simon* (WEA K79300)	13	12	23	26
11 Hard To Say I'm Sorry *Chicago* (Full Moon K79301)	4	5	6	9
12 All Of My Heart *A.B.C.* (Neutron/Phonogram NY104)	17	23	47	–
13 Saddle Up *David Christie* (KR KR9)	15	21	44	63
14 Just What I Always Wanted *Marie Wilson* (Compact/London PINK 4)	8	8	14	23
15 Do You Really Want To Hurt Me *Culture Club* (Virgin VS518)	3	2	1	1
16 The Message *Grand Master* (Sugar Hill SH 117)	20	43	56	–
17 Glittering Prize *Simple Minds* (Virgin VS 511)	16	18	25	31
18 Save A Prayer *Duran Duran* (EMI 5327)	34	62	–	–
19 Leave In Silence *Depeche Mode* (Mute BONG 1)	22	25	50	70
20 Come On Eileen *Dexy's Midnight Runners & The Emerald Express* (Mercury/Phonogram DEXYS 9)	36	52	66	–
26 Jackie Wilson Said *Dexy's Midnight Runners & The Emerald Express* (Mercury/Phonogram DEXYS 10)	5	6	10	17
38 Starmaker *The Kids from 'Fame'* (RCA 280)	14	4	3	3
28 The House Of The Rising Sun *The Animals* (RAK RR1)	19	13	11	14
57 Lifeline *Spandau Ballet* (Reformation/Chrysalis CHS 2642)	28	10	7	7
– Love Me Do *The Beatles* (Parlophone R4949)	–	14	5	4
– Annie, I'm Not Your Daddy *Kid Creole & The Coconuts* (Ze/Island WIP 6801)	39	15	9	2
29 Reap The Wild Wind *Ultravox* (Chrysalis CHS 2639)	21	20	12	13
30 Danger Games *The Pinkees* (Creole CR 39)	30	27	8	12
– I Wanna Do It With You *Barry Manilow* (Arista ARIST 495)	–	36	13	10
65 Mad World *Tears For Fears* (Mercury/Phonogram IDEA 3)	47	38	16	6
33 Should I Stay Or Should I Go/Straight To Hell *Clash* (CBS A2646)	24	24	17	18
– Ziggy Stardust *Bauhaus* (Beggars Banquet BEG 83)	42	22	18	15
– I'll Be Satisfied *Shakin' Stevens* (Epic EPC A2846)	–	44	20	19
– I Don't Wanna Dance *Eddy Grant* (Ice ICE 56)	–	63	30	11
– Ooh La, La, La (Let's Go Dancin') *Kool & The Gang* (De Lite/Phonogram DE 9)	–	64	31	16

NOVEMBER 1982

	13	20	27
6			
1 Do You Really Want To Hurt Me *Culture Club* (Virgin VS 518)	4	7	18
2 I Don't Wanna Dance *Eddy Grant* (Ice ICE 56)	1	1	1
3 Mad World *Tears for Fears* (Mercury/Phonograph IDEA 3)	3	3	6
4 Starmaker *The Kids From 'Fame'* (RCA 280)	7	19	36
5 Heartbreaker *Dionne Warwick* (Arista ARIST 496)	2	2	3
6 Annie, I'm Not Your Daddy *Kid Creole & The Coconuts* (Ze/Island WIP 6801)	12	23	45
7 Love Me Do *The Beatles* (Parlophone R4949)	15	29	64
8 I Wanna Do It With You *Barry Manilow* (Arista ARIST 495)	8	16	23
9 Lifeline *Spandau Ballet* (Reformation/Chrysalis CHS2642)	18	48	61

6 | | 13 | 20 | 27

		13	20	27
10	I'll Be Satisfied *Shakin' Stevens* (Epic EPC A2846)	13	22	30
11	Ooh La, La, La (Let's Go Dancing) *Kool & The Gang* (De-Lite/Phonogram DE9)	6	11	22
12	Hard To Say I'm Sorry *Chicago* (Full Moon K 79301)	30	38	55
13	Caroline (Live At The N.E.C.) *Status Quo* (Vertigo/Phonogram Quo 10)	14	17	25
14	Pass The Dutchie *Musical Youth* (MCA YOU 1)	34	43	65
15	Love's Comin' At Ya *Melba Moore* (EMI America EA 146)	16	26	33
16	Zoom *Fat Larry's Band* (WMOT/Virgin VS 546)	39	46	74
17	Back On The Chain Gang *Pretenders* (Real ARE 19)	22	30	39
18	(Sexual) Healing *Marvin Gaye* (CBS A2855)	5	4	5
19	Ziggy Stardust *Bauhaus* (Beggars Banquet BEG 83)	26	42	–
20	Maneater *Daryl Hall & John Oates* (RCA 290)	10	6	10
28	Muscles *Diana Ross*	23	15	19
33	The Girl Is Mine *Michael Jackson/Paul McCartney* (Epic EPCA2729)	9	8	12
46	Theme From Harry's Game *Clannad* (RCA 292)	11	5	8
22	Zambezi *The Piranhas featuring Bob Grover* (Dakota DAK 6)	17	20	27
37	Living On The Ceiling *Blancmange* (London BLANC 3)	19	12	7
24	Never Give You Up *Sharon Redd* (Prelude PRL A2755)	20	25	31
–	Mirror Man *Human League* (Virgin VS 522)	–	9	2
42	Young Guns (Go For It) *Wham!* (Innervision IVL A2766)	24	10	4
–	Rio *Duran Duran* (EMI 5346)	32	13	11
52	State Of Independence *Donna Summer* (Warner Bros K 79344)	29	14	15
27	Do It To The Music *Raw Silk* (KR KR14)	27	18	24
41	Save Your Love *Renée And Renato* (Hollywood HWD 003)	38	24	9
34	Cry Boy Cry *Blue Zoo* (Magnet MAG 234)	21	21	13
62	Wishing (If I Had A Photograph Of You) *A Flock Of Seagulls* (Jive JIVE 25)	41	28	14
–	Youth Of Today *Musical Youth* (MCA YOU 2)	–	31	16
–	Truly *Lionel Richie* (Motown TMG 1284)	–	35	17
–	The Other Side Of Love *Yazoo* (Mute YAZ 002)	–	34	20

DECEMBER 1982

4 | | 11 | 18 | 25

		11	18	25
1	Beat Surrender *The Jam* (Polydor POSP 540)	1	2	10
2	Mirror Man *The Human League* (Virgin VS522)	2	7	12
3	Young Guns (Go For It) *Wham!* (Innervision IVL A2766)	4	8	13
4	I Don't Wanna Dance *Eddy Grant* (Ice ICE 56)	8	25	30
5	Save Your Love *Renée and Renato* (Hollywood HWD 003)	3	1	1
6	Truly *Lionel Richie* (Motown TMG 1284)	6	6	9
7	Living On The Ceiling *Blancmange* (London BLANC 3)	7	11	22
8	Heartbreaker *Dionne Warwick* (Arista ARIST 496)	15	37	41
9	Time (Clock Of The Heart) *Culture Club* (Virgin VS 558)	5	3	4
10	Rio *Duran Duran* (EMI 5346)	9	14	21
11	Wishing (If I Had A Photograph Of You) *A Flock Of Seagulls* (Jive JIVE26)	10	15	24
12	(Sexual) Healing *Marvin Gaye* (CBS A2855)	17	33	37
13	Youth of Today *Musical Youth* (MCA YOU 2)	16	23	38
14	The Other Side of Love *Yazoo* (Mute YAZ 002)	13	16	25
15	Mad World *Tears For Fears* (Mercury/Phonogram IDEA 3)	23	38	47
16	Hymn *Ultravox* (Chrysalis CHS 2657)	14	13	16
17	Our House *Madness* (Stiff BUY 163)	12	5	5
18	Best Years Of Our Lives *Modern Romance* (WEA ROM 1)	11	9	8
19	State Of Independence *Donna Summer* (Warner Brothers K79344)	20	36	54
20	Theme From Harry's Game *Clannad* (RCA 292)	25	44	53

4   **11 18 25**

	11	18	25
35 Let's Get This Straight (From The Start) *Dexy's Midnight Runners* (Old Mercury DEXYS 11)	18	18	17
25 Friends *Shalamar* (Solar CHUM 1)	19	12	15
— The Shakin' Stevens EP *Shakin' Stevens* (Epic SHAKY 1)	35	4	2
39 Peace On Earth/Little Drummer Boy *David Bowie and Bing Crosby* (RCA BOW12)	22	10	3
52 You Can't Hurry Love *Phil Collins* (Virgin VS 531)	27	17	6
38 Buffalo Gals *Malcolm McLaren & The World's Famous Supreme Team* (Charisma MALC 1)	24	19	18
37 If You Can't Stand The Heat *Bucks Fizz* (RCA 300)	29	20	20
— A Winter's Tale *David Essex* (Mercury/Phonogram MER 127)	65	30	7
63 Little Town *Cliff Richard* (EMI 5348)	38	21	11
— All The Love In The World *Dionne Warwick* (Arista ARIST 507)	73	27	14
— Singalong-A-Santa (Medley) *Santa Claus & The Christmas Trees* (Polydor IVY1)	58	28	19

1982 BEST SELLING RECORDS

Singles:

1 Come On Eileen *Dexy's Midnight Runners* (Mercury/Phonogram)
2 Fame *Irene Cara* (RSO/Polydor)
3 Eye Of The Tiger *Survivor* (Scotti Brothers)
4 The Lion Sleeps Tonight *Tightfit* (Jive)
5 Do You Really Want To Hurt Me *Culture Club* (Virgin)
6 Pass The Dutchie *Musical Youth* (MCA)
7 I Don't Wanna Dance *Eddy Grant* (Ice)
8 Seven Tears *Goombay Dance Band* (Epic)
9 Ebony And Ivory *Paul McCartney with Stevie Wonder* (Parlophone)
10 Town Called Malice/Precious *The Jam* (Polydor)
11 Golden Brown *The Stranglers* (Liberty)
12 Mad World *Tears For Fears* (Mercury/Phonogram)
13 Mickey *Toni Basil* (Radialchoice/Virgin)
14 Love Plus One *Haircut One Hundred* (Arista)
15 The Model/Computer Love *Kraftwerk* (EMI)
16 Oh Julie *Shakin' Stevens* (Epic)
17 Goody Two Shoes *Adam Ant* (CBS)
18 Only You *Yazoo* (Mute)
19 Heartbreaker *Dionne Warwick* (Arista)
20 Don't Go *Yazoo* (Mute)
21 Walkin' On Sunshine *Rockers Revenge featuring Donnie Calvin* (London)
22 Zoom *Fat Larry's Band* (WMOT/Virgin)
23 I Won't Let You Down *PhD* (WEA)
24 Just An Illusion *Imagination* (R&B)
25 Hard To Say I'm Sorry *Chicago* (Full Moon)
26 Abracadabra *The Steve Miller Band* (Mercury/Phonogram)
27 Starmaker *The Kids From 'Fame'* (RCA)
28 Centrefold *J. Geils Band* (EMI America)
29 House Of Fun *Madness* (Stiff)
30 The Land Of Make Believe *Bucks Fizz* (RCA)
31 Maid Of Orleans *Orchestral Manoeuvres In The Dark* (Virgin)
32 The Look Of Love *ABC* (Neutron/Phonogram)
33 Ain't No Pleasing You *Chas & Dave* (Rockney)
34 Save A Prayer *Duran Duran* (EMI)
35 T'Aint What You Do *The Fun Boy Three with Bananarama* (Chrysalis)
36 A Little Peace *Nicole* (CBS)
37 Hungry Like A Wolf *Duran Duran* (EMI)
38 My Camera Never Lies *Bucks Fizz* (RCA)
39 It Started With A Kiss *Hot Chocolate* (RAK)
40 Fantasy Island *Tightfit* (Jive)
41 Dead Ringer For Love *Meatloaf* (Epic)
42 Inside Out *Odyssey* (RCA)
43 Young Guns (Go For It) *Wham!* (Innervision)
44 Torch *Soft Cell* (Some Bizzare/Phonogram)
45 This Time/England We'll Fly *The England World Cup Squad* (England)
46 Say Hello, Wave Goodbye *Soft Cell* (Some Bizzare/Phonogram)
47 I've Never Been To Me *Charlene* (Motown)
48 Papa's Got A Brand New Pigbag *Pigbag* (Y Records)
49 Private Investigations *Dire Straits* (Mercury/Phonogram)
50 Poison Arrow *ABC* (Nuetron/Phonogram)

Albums:

1 Love Songs *Barbra Streisand* (CBS)
2 The Kids From Fame *Various* (BBC)
3 Complete Madness *Madness* (Stiff)
4 The Lexicon Of Love *ABC* (Neutron/Phonogram)
5 Rio *Duran Duran* (EMI)
6 Love Over Gold *Dire Straits* (Vertigo/Phonogram)
7 Pelican West *Haircut One Hundred* (Arista)
8 Dare *Human League* (Virgin)
9 Avalon *Roxy Music* (EG(Polydor))
10 Too Rye Ay *Kevin Rowland and Dexy's Midnight Runners* (Mercury)
11 Pearls *Elkie Brooks* (A&M)
12 All For A Song *Barbara Dickson* (Epic)
13 Upstairs At Erics *Yazoo* (Mute)
14 Tropical Gangsters *Kid Creole & The Coconuts* (Ze/Island)
15 The Gift *The Jam* (Polydor)
16 Tug Of War *Paul McCartney* (Parlophone)
17 Bat Out Of Hell *Meatloaf* (Epic)
18 The Number Of The Beast *Iron Maiden* (EMI)
19 Non-Stop Erotic Cabaret *Soft Cell* (Some Bizzare/Phonogram)
20 Architecture & Morality *Orchestral Manoeuvres In The Dark* (Virgin)
21 Chariots Of Fire *Vangelis* (Polydor)
22 The John Lennon Collection *John Lennon* (Parlophone)
23 Love And Dancing *The League Unlimited Orchestra* (Virgin)
24 Barry Live In Britain *Barry Manilow* (Arista)
25 Queen's Greatest Hits *Queen* (EMI)
26 Friends *Shalamar* (Solar)
27 Fame *Original Soundtrack* (RSO/Polydor)
28 4 *Foreigner* (Atlantic)
29 Night Birds *Shakatak* (Polydor)
30 Action Trax *Various* (K-Tel)
31 Asia *Asia* (Geffen)
32 Tin Drum *Japan* (Virgin)
33 Love Songs *Commodores* (K-Tel)
34 The Kids From 'Fame' Again *Various* (K-Tel)
35 Still Life *Rolling Stones* (Rolling Stones Records)
36 The Singles — The First Ten Years *Abba* (Epic)
37 Dead Ringer *Meatloaf* (Epic)
38 Three Sides Live *Genesis* (Charisma/Phonogram)
39 Reflections *Various* (CBS)
40 The Concert In Central Park *Simon & Garfunkel* (Geffen)
41 Mirage *Fleetwood Mac* (Warner)
42 Give Me You Heart Tonight *Shakin' Stevens* (Epic)
43 1982 *Status Quo* (Vertigo/Phonogram)
44 Begin The Beguine *Julio Iglesias* (CBS)
45 Heartbreaker *Dionne Warwick* (Arista)
46 Kissing To Be Clever *Culture Club* (Virgin)
47 Chart Beat/Chart Heat *Various* (K-Tel)
48 Hot Space *Queen* (EMI)
49 Pictures At Eleven *Robert Plant* (Swansong)
50 The Visitors *Abba* (Epic)

1983

No one could really claim that 1983 was a vintage year for pop, but it had some interesting moments. The year provided the highest selling single yet of the 1980s in Culture Club's 'Karma Chameleon'. By December it had sold 1.3 million and that made it the U.K.'s eleventh highest selling single of all time. The year also saw Michael Jackson milk his world 20 million plus selling album 'Thriller' for five UK hits and six Stateside. In fact, Jackson established a dubious though honourable new record of having the most hits from one album.

There were some other lengthy stays at the top, including Billy Joel's 'Uptown Girl', which with 'Karma Chameleon', gave the chart the only two chart-toppers between September 24 and December 3.

1983 was a year that saw some oldies return in a big way. Rod Stewart ended a period of struggle by topping the chart with 'Baby Jane'; Elton John was more like his old self with hits 'Cold As Christmas', 'I Guess That's Why They Call It The Blues', 'I'm Still Standing' and 'Kiss The Bride'; and just before the year ended the heroes of the 1970's Slade found the Top Ten after only four weeks with 'My, Oh My'. Earlier The Kinks did well with 'Come Dancing'. Other veterans continued their story with expected hits and Paul McCartney, Cliff Richard, Genesis, David Bowie, David Essex, KC & The Sunshine Band, Robert Plant (solo), The Rolling Stones and Police were amongst them.

The 'newish' outfits consolidated their hold and in their number came Duran Duran (whose 'Is There Something I Should Know' was an instant chart-topper in week-ending March 26th), Depeche Mode, Bananerama, Blancmange, The Fun Boy Three, Wham!, Heaven 17 and the Eurythmics. Nick Heyward, The Creatures and The Style Council also provided 'something new' though in reality each had already successful pedigree. Disco remained as strong as ever and refused to fade away.

UB40, Kim Wilde, Spandau Ballet, George Benson, Freeze, Madness, Paul Young and New Order kept capturing the turntables and music paper columns, whilst from unexpected quarters came a revival of Joy Division's 'Love Will Tear Us Apart' (though it had always sold in 'indie' territory), a jazzy flavoured 'Bad Day' from Carmel, a return for Joe Cocker in company of Jennifer Warnes with 'Up Where We Belong', and sudden stardom again for the well liked Eddy Grant. Incantation's success with 'Cacharpaya' caught many by surprise and few surely expected 'Only You' from The Flying Pickets to top the chart after a mere three weeks in the overall Top 75.

The strangest happening for chart collators was the sudden about-turn of 'Say Say Say' from Paul McCartney and Michael Jackson. It had fallen to 14 and bounced upwards to 3 in the November 12th listing. Records rise in the charts very rarely once they have moved downwards, and while a handful of discs have gone against an almost irreversible trend, none has achieved anything like the extent of this about-turn. Reports suggested a massive promotional effort to stem the decline and otherwise lack-lustre charting for the famed two — and it worked.

Much more can be said of 1983 but one last comment remains; it was a year that saw few records chart unless they appeared at come stage or the other in 12-inch form. Numerous records appeared in three or more forms — 7-inch, 12-inch and picture discs for starters — and some fans bought all three and obeyed the whims and fancies of marketing techniques. Other marketing gestures included 10-inch records, four to six-track editions, coloured vinyl and unusually shaped discs for the buyer, whilst some dealers had records for nothing, tapes and videos, shop aids and special deals. With much of this running out of hand and with stories of chart hyping, the industry's own organization the BPI and the new chart compilers Gallup eventually took their own steps to curb such wildness.

JANUARY 1983

8		15	22	29
1	Save Your Love *Renee and Renato* (Hollywood HWD 003)	3	13	20
2	You Can't Hurry Love *Phil Collins* (Virgin VS 531)	1	1	2
3	A Winter's Tale *David Essex* (Mercury/Phonogram MER 127)	2	6	15
4	Best Years Of Our Lives *Modern Romance* (WEA ROM 1)	5	14	28
5	Our House *Madness* (Stiff BUY 163)	13	10	21
6	Time (Clock Of The Heart) *Culture Club* (Virgin VS 558)	8	17	26
7	The Shakin' Stevens EP *Shakin' Stevens* (Epic SHAKY 1)	25	58	–
8	Orville's Song *Keith Harris and Orville* (BBC RESL 124)	4	5	9
9	Peace On Earth/Little Drummer Boy *David Bowie and Bing Crosby* (RCA BOW 12)	46	–	–
10	All The Love In The World *Dionne Warwick* (Arista ARIST 507)	12	15	23
11	Buffalo Gals *Malcolm McLaren and The World's Famous Supreme Team* (Charisma/Phonogram MALC 1)	9	11	16
12	Hymn *Ultravox* (Chrysalis CHS 2657)	11	18	27
13	If You Can't Stand The Heat *Bucks Fizz* (RCA 300)	10	16	32
14	Young Guns (Go For It) *Wham!* (Innervision IVL A2766)	18	29	41
15	Beat Surrender *The Jam* (Polydor POSP 540)	24	44	62
16	Cacharpaya (Andres Pumpsa Desi) *Incantation* (Beggars Banquet BEG84)	14	12	14
17	Truly *Lionel Richie* (Motown TMG 1284)	27	39	71
18	Little Town *Cliff Richard* (EMI 5348)	44	–	–
19	Friends *Shalamar* (Solar CHUM 1)	20	30	47
20	Mirror Man *The Human League* (Virgin VS 522)	29	57	–
34	The Story Of The Blues *Wah!* (Eternal JF 1)	6	3	4
38	Down Under *Men At Work* (Epic EPC A1980)	7	2	1
29	Heartache Avenue *The Maisonettes* (Ready Steady Go! RSG 1)	15	7	7
40	European Female *The Stranglers* (Epic EPC A2893)	16	9	13
24	Theme From E.T. (The Extra Terrestrial) *John Williams* (MCA 800)	17	21	30
50	Steppin' Out *Joe Jackson* (A&M AMS 8262)	19	8	6
–	Electric Avenue *Eddy Grant* (Ice ICE 57)	22	4	3
–	Sign Of The Times *The Belle Stars* (Stiff BUY 167)	51	19	5
41	Gloria *Laura Branigan* (Atlantic K11759)	32	20	8
–	Too Shy *Kajagoogoo* (EMI5359)	–	33	10
–	The Cutter *Echo & The Bunnymen* (Korova KOW 26)	–	27	11
–	New Year's Day *U2* (Island UWIP 6848)	–	23	12
–	Twisting By The Pool *Dire Straits* (Vertigo/Phonogram DSTR 2)	–	24	17
48	Oh Diane *Fleetwood Mac* (Warner Brothers FLEET 1)	37	26	18
68	Hold Me Tighter In The Rain *Billy Griffin* (CBS A2935)	38	28	19

FEBRUARY 1983

5		12	19	26
1	Down Under *Men At Work* (Epic EPC A1980)	1	2	6
2	Electric Avenue *Eddy Grant* (Ice ICE 57)	4	10	23
3	You Can't Hurry Love *Phil Collins* (Virgin VS 531)	8	17	26
4	Sign Of The Times *The Belle Stars* (Stiff BUY 167)	3	3	5
5	Too Shy *Kajagoogoo* (EMI 5359)	2	1	1
6	Gloria *Laura Brannigan* (Atlantic K11759)	6	11	20
7	The Story Of The Blues *Wah!* (Eternal JF 1)	12	20	28
8	The Cutter *Echo & The Bunnymen* (Korova KOW 26)	11	18	32

		12	19	26
5				
9	Steppin' Out *Joe Jackson* (A&M AMS 8262)	16	30	43
10	New Year's Day *U2* (Island UW1P 6848)	13	21	36
11	Wham Rap! (Enjoy What You Do) *Wham!* (Innervision IVL A2442)	9	8	10
12	Up Where We Belong *Joe Cocker and Jennifer Warnes* (Island WIP 6830)	7	7	7
13	Heartache Avenue *The Maisonettes* (Ready Steady Go! RSG 1)	23	43	68
14	Twisting By The Pool *Dire Straits* (Vertigo/Phonogram DSTR 2)	15	19	38
15	Last Night A D.J. Saved My Life *Indeep* (Sound Of New York SNY 1)	14	13	18
16	Oh Diane *Fleetwood Mac* (Warner Brothers FLEET 1)	10	9	13
17	Hold Me Tighter In The Rain *Billy Griffin* (CBS A2935)	20	31	45
18	Orville's Song *Keith Harris and Orville* (BBC RESL 124)	31	46	60
19	Change *Tears For Fears* (Mercury/Phonogram IDEA 4)	5	4	4
20	Billie Jean *Michael Jackson* (Epic EPC A3084)	17	5	2
22	Christian *China Crisis* (Virgin VS562)	18	12	15
39	Africa *Toto* (CBS A2510)	19	6	3
68	Tunnel Of Love *The Fun Boy Three* (Chrysalis CHS 2678)	26	14	11
38	Love On Your Side *Thompson Twins* (Arista ARIST 504)	27	15	12
—	Never Gonna Give You Up *Musical Youth* (MCA YOU 3)	40	16	8
—	Tomorrow's (Just Another Day)/Madness (Is All In The Mind) *Madness* (Stiff BUY 169)	—	24	9
—	Total Eclipse Of The Heart *Bonnie Tyler* (CBS TYLER 1)	—	49	14
36	Shiny Shiny *Haysi Fantayzee* (Regard RG 106)	28	23	16
48	Hey Little Girl *Icehouse* (Chrysalis CHS 2670)	39	34	17
88	Baby, Come To Me *Patti Austin and James Ingram* (Qwest K 15005)	38	35	19

MARCH 1983

		12	19	26
5				
1	Billie Jean *Michael Jackson* (Epic EPC A3084)	2	3	8
2	Total Eclipse Of The Heart *Bonnie Tyler* (CBS TYLER 1)	1	1	2
3	Too Shy *Kajagoogoo* (EMI 5359)	6	14	29
4	Africa *Toto* (CBS A2510)	5	7	23
5	Sweet Dreams (Are Made Of This) *Eurythmics* (RCA DA 2)	3	2	3
6	Never Gonna Give You Up *Musical Youth* (MCA YOU 3)	10	17	35
7	Change *Tears For Fears* (Mercury/Phonogram IDEA 4)	16	25	44
8	Tomorrow's (Just Another Day)/Madness (Is All In The Mind) *Madness* (Stiff BUY 169)	8	15	30
9	Love On Your Side *Thompson Twins* (Arista ARIST 504)	9	12	22
10	The Tunnel Of Love *The Fun Boy Three* (Chrysalis CHS 2678)	13	18	34
11	Up Where We Belong *Joe Cocker and Jennifer Warnes* (Island WIP 6830)	19	23	37
12	Rock The Boat *Forrest* (CBS A3163)	4	4	6
13	Get The Balance Right! *Depeche Mode* (Mute 7BONG 2)	15	26	40
14	Wham Rap! (Enjoy What You Do) *Wham!* (Inner Vision IVL A2442)	23	39	54
15	Communication *Spandau Ballet* (Reformation/Chrysalis CHS 2668)	12	13	20
16	Sign Of The Times *The Belle Stars* (Stiff BUY 167)	27	46	68
17	Hey Little Girl *Icehouse* (Chrysalis CHS 2670)	17	20	33
18	Baby, Come To Me *Patti Austin and James Ingram* (Qwest K 15005)	11	11	18
19	She Means Nothing To Me *Phil Everly and Cliff Richard* (Capitol CL276)	14	9	16

5

	12	19	26
20 Shiny Shiny *Haysi Fantayzee* (Regard RG 106)	26	41	66
21 Na Na Hey Hey Kiss Him Goodbye *Bananarama* (London NANA 4)	7	5	7
28 High Life *Modern Romance* (WEA ROM 2)	18	8	10
25 Genetic Engineering *Orchestral Manoeuvres In The Dark* (Telegraph/Virgin VS 527)	20	22	32
– Speak Like A Child *The Style Council* (Polydor TSC 1)	–	6	4
31 Rip It Up *Orange Juice* (Polydor POSP 547)	22	10	9
30 You Can't Hide (Your Love From Me) *David Joseph* (Island IS 101)	24	16	13
26 Waves *Blancmange* (London BLANC 4)	21	19	19
– Is There Something I Should Know? *Duran Duran* (EMI 5371)	–	–	1
– Let's Dance *David Bowie* (EMI America EA 152)	–	–	5
39 Drop The Pilot *Joan Armatrading* (A&M AMS8306)	29	28	11
– Don't Talk To Me About Love *Altered Images* (Epic EPC A3083)	–	36	12
– Run For Your Life *Bucks Fizz* (RCA FIZ 1)	31	21	14
– Visions In Blue *Ultravox* (Chrysalis CHS 2676)	–	30	15
61 Garden Party *Mezzoforte* (Steinar STE 705)	40	29	17

APRIL 1983

2	9	16	23	30
1 Is There Something I Should Know? *Duran Duran* (EMI 5371)	2	3	11	27
2 Let's Dance *David Bowie* (EMI America EA 152)	1	1	1	6
3 Total Eclipse Of The Heart *Bonnie Tyler* (CBS TYLER 1)	8	16	27	34
4 Speak Like A Child *The Style Council* (Polydor TSC 1)	4	11	23	36
5 Sweet Dreams (Are Made Of This) *Eurythmics* (RCA DA 2)	5	15	25	33
6 Boxerbeat *JoBoxers* (RCA BOX 1)	3	6	7	19
7 Don't Talk To Me About Love *Altered Images* (Epic EPC A3083)	11	17	33	55
8 Rip It Up *Orange Juice* (Polydor POSP 547)	12	18	32	49
9 Na Na Hey Hey Kis Him Goodbye *Bananarama* (London NANA 4)	16	21	40	71
10 Rock The Boat *Forrest* (CBS A3163)	17	24	43	66
11 Billie Jean *Michael Jackson* (Epic EPC3084)	20	25	36	41
12 Drop the Pilot *Joan Armatrading* (A&M AMS 8306)	22	29	57	–
13 Fields of Fire (400 Miles) *Big Country* (Mercury COUNT 2)	13	10	15	29
14 You Can't Hide (Your Love From Me) *David Joseph* (Island IS101)	25	31	56	–
15 Whistle Down The Wind *Nick Heyward* (Arista HEY1)	15	13	17	30
16 Orchard Road *Leo Sayer* (Chrysalis CHS2677)	19	26	35	61
17 Blue Monday *New Order* (Factory FAC73)	14	14	12	13
18 Breakaway *Tracy Ullman* (Stiff BUY 168)	6	4	5	10
19 Garden Party *Mezzoforte* (Steinar STE 705)	26	30	50	72
20 Ooh To Be Ah *Kajagoogoo* (EMI 5383)	7	7	8	16
– Church Of The Poisoned Mind *Culture Club* (Virgin VS 571)	9	2	2	5
27 Snot Rap *Kenny Everett* (RCA KEN1)	10	9	13	26
24 Two Hearts Beat As One *U2* (Island IS109)	18	22	42	68
– Beat It *Michael Jackson* (Epic EPC A3258)	30	5	3	3
39 Words *F.R. David* (Carrere CAR 248)	21	8	4	2
38 The House That Jack Built *Tracie* (Respond KOB 701)	23	12	9	15
32 I Am (I'm Me) *Twisted Sister* (Atlantic A 9854)	29	19	18	18

		9	16	23	30
36	The Celtic Soul Brothers *Kevin Rowland & Dexys Midnight Runners* (Mercury/Phonogram DEXYS 12)	24	20	22	32
–	Love Is A Stranger *Eurythmics* (RCA DA 1)	49	23	6	7
–	True *Spandau Ballet* (Reformation/Chrysalis SPAN 1)	–	–	10	1
–	True Love Ways *Cliff Richard* (EMI 5385)	–	37	14	8
–	(Keep Feeling) Fascination *Human League* (Virgin VS569)	–	–	16	4
–	Rosanna *Toto* (CBS A2079)	50	36	19	12
40	Young Free And Single *Sunfire* (Warner Brothers W 9897)	34	28	20	21
–	We Are Detective *Thompson Twins* (Arista ARIST 526)	–	40	21	9
–	Flight Of Icarus *Iron Maiden* (EMI 5378)	–	–	28	11
–	Temptation *Heaven 17* (B.E.F./Virgin VS 570)	–	43	31	14
–	Friday Night (Live Version) *The Kids From Fame* (RCA 320)	64	38	24	17
–	Dancing Tight *Galaxy featuring Phil Fearon* (Ensign/Island ENY 501)	–	–	39	20

MAY 1983

7		14	21	28
1	True *Spandau Ballet* (Reformation/Chrysalis SPAN 1)	1	1	2
2	Words *F.R. David* (Carrere CAR 248)	4	9	17
3	(Keep Feeling) Fascination *Human League* (Virgin VS569)	2	6	15
4	Beat It *Michael Jackson* (Epic EPC A3258)	11	16	26
5	Pale Shelter *Tears For Fears* (Mercury/Phonogram IDEA 5)	6	8	18
6	Dancing Tight *Galaxy featuring Phil Fearson* (Ensign/Island ENY 501)	5	4	6
7	We Are Detective *Thompson Twins* (Arista ARIST 526)	8	11	24
8	Temptation *Heaven 17* (B.E.F./Virgin VS 570)	3	2	4
9	Let's Dance *David Bowie* (EMI America EA 152)	13	24	37
10	Church Of The Poison Mind *Culture Club* (Virgin VS 571)	16	29	43
11	True Love Ways *Cliff Richard* (EMI 5385)	14	25	39
12	Love Is A Stranger *Eurythmics* (RCA DA 1)	17	31	52
13	Friday Night (Live Version) *The Kids From Fame* (RCA 320)	15	18	31
14	Flight Of Icarus *Iron Maiden* (EMI 5378)	23	40	67
15	Rosanna *Toto* (CBS A2079)	20	30	57
16	Our Lips Are Sealed *The Fun Boy Three* (Chrysalis FUNB1)	9	7	9
17	Blue Monday *New Order* (Factory FAC 73)	18	26	32
18	Breakaway *Tracey Ullman* (Stiff BUY 168)	25	39	66
19	Last Film *Kissing The Pink* (Magnet KTP3)	19	19	36
20	I Am (I'm Me) *Twisted Sister* (Atlantic A9854)	31	56	–
30	Candy Girl *New Edition* (London LON21)	7	3	1
29	Can't Get Used To Losing You *The Beat* (Go Feet FEET 17)	10	5	3
28	Blind Vision *Blancmange* (London BLANC 5)	12	10	14
–	Bad Boys *Wham!* (Inner Vision A3143)	37	12	5
64	What Kinda Boy You're Lookin' For (Girl) *Hot Chocolate* (RAK 357)	35	13	10
43	Don't Stop That Crazy Rhythm *Modern Romance* (WEA ROM3)	26	14	21
35	Family Man *Daryl Hall and John Oates* (RCA 323)	24	15	22
56	Buffalo Soldier *Bob Marley and The Wailers* (Island/Tuff Gong IS108)	33	17	11
–	Nobody's Diary *Yazoo* (Mute YAZ 003)	–	20	8
–	Every Breath You Take *The Police* (A&M AM 117)	–	–	7
–	Money Go Round (Part 1) *The Style Council* (Polydor TSC2)	–	–	12
–	Glory, Glory, Man. United *Manchester United Football Team* (EMI 5390)	–	35	13

	14	21	28
– Just Got Lucky *JoBoxers* (RCA BOXX2)	–	38	16
– Love Town *Booker Newbury III* (Polydor POSP 613)	–	–	19
– Feel The Need In Me *Forrest* (CBS A3411)	69	28	20

JUNE 1983

4	11	18	25
1 Every Breath You Take *The Police* (A&M AM 117)	1	1	1
2 Bad Boys *Wham!* (Inner Vision A3143)	2	3	5
3 Candy Girl *New Edition* (London LON 21)	5	17	31
4 Nobody's Diary *Yazoo* (Mute YAZ 003)	3	5	9
5 Can't Get Used To Losing You *The Beat* (Go Feet FEET 17)	10	22	28
6 Buffalo Soldier *Bob Marley and The Wailers* (Island/Tuff Gong IS 108)	4	7	14
7 Just Got Lucky *JoBoxers* (RCA BOXX 2)	7	12	22
8 Love Town *Booker Newbury III* (Polydor/Montage POSP 613)	6	8	13
9 Temptation *Heaven 17* (B.E.F./Virgin VS 570)	14	25	32
10 True *Spandau Ballet* (Reformation/Chrysalis SPAN 1)	16	29	35
11 Money Go Round *The Style Council* (Polydor TSC 2)	13	26	47
12 What Kinda Boy You're Looking For (Girl) *Hot Chocolate* (RAK 357)	20	28	38
13 Glory, Glory, Man. United *Manchester United Football Team* (EMI 5390)	25	49	–
14 Our Lips Are Sealed *The Fun Boy Three* (Chrysalis FUNB 1)	23	34	48
15 Lady Love Me (One More Time) *George Benson* (Warner Brothers W 9614)	11	11	11
16 Dancing Tight *Galaxy featuring Phil Fearon* (Ensign/Island ENY 501)	22	31	44
17 Feel The Need In Me *Forrest* (CBS A 3411)	21	30	45
18 In A Big Country *Big Country* (Mercury/Phonogram COUNT 3)	17	21	26
19 Stop And Go *David Grant* (Chrysalis GRAN 1)	26	35	64
20 Blind Vision *Blancmange* (London BLANC 5)	35	51	68
– China Girl *David Bowie* (EMI America EA 157)	8	2	3
30 Flashdance . . . What A Feeling *Irene Cara* (Casablanca Phonogram CAN 1016)	9	4	4
21 Waiting For A Train *Flash & The Pan* (Easy Beat/Ensign EASY 1)	12	10	7
39 Hang On Now *Kajagoogoo* (EMI 5394)	15	13	18
27 I Guess That's Why They Call It The Blues *Elton John* (Rocket/Phonogram XPRES 91)	18	9	6
37 Baby Jane *Rod Stewart* (Warner Brothers W 9608)	19	6	2
– Wanna Be Startin' Somethin' *Michael Jackson* (Epic A3427)	38	14	8
51 Dark Is The Night *Shakatak* (Polydor POSP 595)	30	15	15
– Pills And Soap *The Imposter* (IMP/Demon IMP 001)	29	16	27
– We Came To Dance *Ultravox* (Chrysalis VOX 1)	24	18	20
40 Dream To Sleep *H20* (RCA 330)	27	19	17
– Dead Giveaway *Shalamar* (Solar E 9819)	33	20	12
– When We Were Young *Bucks Fizz* (RCA 342)	–	23	10
– Garden Party *Marillion* (EMI 5393)	–	24	16
– Moonlight Shadow *Mike Oldfield* (Virgin VS 586)	42	27	19

JULY 1983

2	9	16	23	30
1 Baby Jane *Rod Stewart* (Warner Brothers W9608)	1	1	3	9
2 Every Breath You Take *The Police* (A&M AM 117)	9	20	28	40

2		9	16	23	30
3	Flashdance . . . What A Feeling *Irene Cara* (Casablanca/Phonogram CAN 1016)	2	5	8	13
4	Moonlight Shadow *Mike Oldfield* (Virgin VS586)	4	4	5	7
5	I Guess That's Why They Call It The Blues *Elton John* (Rocket/Phonogram XPRES 91)	10	15	26	39
6	China Girl *David Bowie* (EMI America EA 157)	17	27	49	64
7	I.O.U. *Freeez* (Beggars Banquet BEG 96)	5	3	2	2
8	Dead Giveaway *Shalamar* (Solar E 9819)	8	11	22	32
9	Bad Boys *Wham!* (Inner Vision A 3143)	16	24	36	45
10	When We Were Young *Bucks Fizz* (RCA 342)	13	22	43	55
11	Waiting For A Train *Flash & The Pan* (Easy Beat/Ensign EASY 1)	18	25	37	54
12	Wherever I Lay My Hat (That's My Home) *Paul Young* (CBS A3371)	3	2	1	1
13	Wanna Be Startin' Somethin' *Michael Jackson* (Epic A3427)	21	28	50	53
14	Take That Situation *Nick Heyward* (Arista HEY 2)	11	14	24	43
15	Rock 'N' Roll Is King *ELO* (Jet A3500)	14	13	17	23
16	Come Live With Me *Heaven 17* (B.E.F./Virgin VS 607)	7	6	6	5
17	War Baby *Tom Robinson* (Panic NIC 2)	6	7	9	18
18	Dream To Sleep *H20* (RCA 330)	22	31	59	—
19	Lady Love Me (One More Time) *George Benson* (Warner Brothers W 9614)	25	37	61	—
20	Nobody's Diary *Yazoo* (Mute YAZ 003)	28	35	57	71
26	The Trooper *Iron Maiden* (EMI 5397)	12	12	19	24
29	It's Over *The Funk Masters* (Master Funk Records 7MF 004)	15	8	10	14
42	Double Dutch *Malcolm McLaren* (Charisma/Phonogram MALC 3)	19	10	7	4
28	Forbidden Colours *David Sylvan and Riuichi Sakamoto* (Virgin VS601)	20	18	16	20
—	Who's That Girl? *Eurythmics* (RCA DA3)	29	9	4	3
31	All Night Long *Mary Jane Girls* (Gordy TMG 1309)	24	16	13	21
—	The Walk *The Cure* (Fiction FICS18)	34	17	12	16
35	Tantalise (Wo Wo Ee Yeh Yeh) *Jimmy The Hoover* (Inner Vision A3406)	26	19	18	22
—	Cruel Summer *Bananarama* (London NANA 5)	36	21	11	10
—	Wrapped Around Your Finger *The Police* (A&M AM 127)	—	—	14	8
—	Never Stop *Echo & The Bunnymen* (Korova KOW 28)	—	30	15	17
40	Don't Try To Stop It *Roman Holiday* (Jive JIVE 39)	32	23	20	15
—	The Crown *Gary Byrd & The G.B. Experience* (Motown TMGT 1312)	—	—	21	6
—	Do It Again/Billie Jean *Club House* Island IS 132)	—	—	29	11
—	It's Late *Shakin' Stevens* (Epic A3565)	—	—	23	12
—	Give It Up *KC & The Sunshine Band* (Epic A3017)	—	64	30	19

AUGUST 1983

6		13	20	27
1	Wherever I Lay My Hat (That's My Home) *Paul Young* (CBS A3371)	2	9	20
2	I.O.U. *Freeez* (Beggars Banquet BRG96)	3	10	16
3	Double Dutch *Malcolm McLaren* (Charisma/Phonogram MALC 3)	4	7	11
4	Who's That Girl? *Eurythmics* (RCA DA 3)	7	13	24
5	Give It Up *KC & The Sunshine Band* (Epic A3017)	1	1	1
6	The Crown *Gary Byrd & The G.B. Experience* (Motown TMGT 1312)	6	11	18

		13	20	27
6				
7	Wrapped Around Your Finger *The Police* (A&M AM127)	18	26	39
8	Cruel Summer *Bananarama* (London NANA 5)	13	16	30
9	Come Live With Me *Heaven 17* (B.E.F./Virgin VS607)	19	27	34
10	Club Tropicana *Wham!* (Inner Vision A3613)	5	4	5
11	It's Late *Shakin' Stevens* (Epic A3565)	14	22	32
12	Moonlight Shadow *Mike Oldfield* (Virgin VS 586)	16	18	29
13	Do It Again/Billie Jean *Club House* (Island IS132)	22	38	55
14	Don't Try To Stop It *Roman Holiday* (Jive JIVE 39)	20	32	51
15	Big Log *Robert Plant* (WEA B 9848)	11	12	17
16	Everything Counts *Depeche Mode* (Mute 7BONG 3)	10	6	7
17	Flashdance . . . What A Feeling *Irene Cara* (Casablanca/Phonogram CAN 1016)	25	34	48
18	The Walk *The Cure* (Fiction FICS 18)	30	42	75
19	Baby Jane *Rod Stewart* (Warner Brothers W 9608)	27	40	57
20	Right Now *The Creatures* (Wonderland/Polydor SHE 2)	17	14	19
–	Long Hot Summer *The Style Council* (Polydor TSC(X)3)	8	3	3
24	I'm Still Standing *Elton John* (Rocket/Phonogram EJS1)	9	5	4
–	Gold *Spandau Ballet* (Reformation/Chrysalis SPAN(X)2)	12	2	2
25	Rockit *Herbie Hancock* (CBS (T) A3577)	15	8	8
23	The First Picture Of You *The Lotus Eaters* (Sylvan/Arista SYL(12)1)	21	15	15
40	Watching You, Watching Me *David Grant* (Chrysalis GRAN(X)2)	34	17	10
–	Wings Of A Dove *Madness* (Stiff BUY(IT) 181)	–	19	6
37	Wait Until Tonight (My Love) *Galaxy featuring Phil Fearon* (Ensign/Island (12) ENY 503)	26	20	21
–	Red Red Wine *UB40* (DEP International 7(12)DEP 7)	–	36	9
65	Come Dancing *The Kinks* (Arista ARIST(12) 502)	43	29	12
45	Walking In The Rain *Modern Romance* (WEA X 9733(T))	39	30	13
38	The Sun Goes Down (Living It Up) *Level 42* (Polydor POSP(X)622)	33	21	14

SEPTEMBER 1983

		10	17	24
3				
1	Red Red Wine *UB40* (DEP International 7(12)DEP 7)	1	1	2
2	Give It Up *KC & The Sunshine Band* (Epic(T)A3017)	4	13	18
3	Gold *Spandau Ballet* (Reformation/Chrysalis SPAN(X) 2)	6	16	24
4	Wings Of A Dove *Madness* (Stiff BUY(IT) 181)	2	8	13
5	I'm Still Standing *Elton John* (Rocket/Phonogram EJS 1(12))	8	15	23
6	Club Tropicana *Wham!* (Inner Vision(T)A3613)	11	18	25
7	Long Hot Summer/Paris Match *The Style Council* (Polydor TSC(X)3)	13	24	38
8	What Am I Gonna Do *Rod Stewart* (Warner Brothers W 9564(T))	3	7	10
9	Walking In The Rain *Modern Romance* (WEA X 9733(T))	9	9	7
10	Watching You, Watching Me *David Grant* (Chrysalis GRAN(X)2)	14	19	27
11	The Sun Goes Down (Living It Up) *Level 42* (Polydor POSP(X)622)	10	10	14
12	Rockit *Herbie Hancock* (CBS(T)A3577)	17	23	34
13	Come Dancing *The Kinks* (Arista ARIST(12) 502)	18	25	32
14	Everything Counts *Depeche Mode* (Mute 7(12)BONG 3)	22	28	46
15	Bad Day *Carmel* (London LON(X)29)	16	26	40
16	Tonight I Celebrate My Love *Peabo Bryson and Roberta Flack* (Capitol (12) CL 302)	7	2	3
17	Confusion *New Order* (Factory FAC 93)	12	14	22
18	Disappearing Act *Shalamar* (Solar E 9807(T))	19	22	35

OCTOBER 1983

1	8	15	22	29
23 68 Guns *The Alarm* (I.R.S. PFP(PFSX) 1023)	19	17	20	33
62 (Hey You) The Rocksteady Crew *The Rocksteady Crew* (Charisma/Virgin RSC 1(12))	29	11	6	6
28 Blue Hat For A Blue Day *Nick Heyward* (Arista HEY(12)3)	24	15	14	19
56 All Night Long (All Night) *Lionel Richie* (Motown TMG(T)1319)	31	16	4	2
– Say Say Say *Paul McCartney and Michael Jackson* (Parlophone(12)R 6062)	–	25	10	13
– The Safety Dance *Men Without Hats* (Statik TAK 1(12))	68	36	13	8
– Please Don't Make Me Cry *UB40* (DEP International/Virgin 7(12) DEP 8)	–	38	15	12
32 Midnight At The Lost and Found (Remix) *Meat Loaf* (Cleveland International/Epic(T)A3748)	28	21	17	17
50 Superstar *Lydia Murdock* (Korova KOW 30(T))	40	30	18	14
– Union Of The Snake *Duran Duran* (EMI(12)EMI 5429)	–	–	–	4
– Uptown Girl *Billy Joel* (CBS(T) A3775)	–	54	25	7

NOVEMBER 1983

5	12	19	26
1 Uptown Girl *Billy Joel* (CBS(T)A 3775)	1	1	1
2 All Night Long (All Night) *Lionel Richie* (Motown TMG(T)1319)	2	4	6
3 Union Of The Snake *Duran Duran* (EMI(12)EMI 5429)	6	13	28
4 Karma Chameleon *Culture Club* (Virgin VS 612(12))	8	9	18
5 They Don't Know *Tracey Ullman* (Stiff (S)BUY 180)	13	27	39
6 The Safety Dance *Men Without Hats* (Statik TAK 1(12))	7	8	19
7 New Song *Howard Jones* (WEA HOW 1 (T))	14	26	38
8 (Hey You) The Rocksteady Crew *The Rocksteady Crew* (Charisma/Virgin RSC 1(12))	12	18	27
9 Puss'N Boots *Adam Ant* (CBS (T)A3614)	5	6	12
10 Please Don't Make Me Cry *UB40* (DEP International/Virgin 7(12) DEP 8)	11	15	31
11 Superman (Gioca Jouer) *Black Lace* (Flair FLA 105)	23	34	41
12 The Love Cats *The Cure* (Fiction FICS(X) 19)	10	7	8
13 In Your Eyes *George Benson* (Warner Brothers W 9487 (T))	19	33	47
14 Say Say Say *Paul McCartney/Michael Jackson* (Parlophone(12)R 6062)	3	2	2
15 Dear Prudence *Siouxsie And The Banshees* (Wonderland/Polydor SHE(X) 4)	34	53	–
16 Superstar *Lydia Murdock* (Korova KOW 30(T))	28	46	–
17 Kissing With Confidence *Will Powers* (Island (12) IS 134)	22	40	57
18 Blue Monday *New Order* (Factory FAC 73)	25	38	50
19 Cry Just A Little Bit *Shakin' Stevens* (Epic(T)A3774)	4	3	3
20 Kiss The Bride *Elton John* (Rocket/Phonogram EJS 2(12))	24	39	69
21 The Sun And The Rain *Madness* (Stiff BUY (IT) 192)	9	5	7
24 A Mess Of Blues *Status Quo* (Verrtigo/Phonogram QUO 12)	15	20	24
22 Unconditional Love *Donna Summer* (Mercury/Phonogram DONNA 2(12))	16	14	22
26 Synchronicity II *The Police* (A&M AM(X) 153)	17	25	45
25 That Was Then But This Is Now *ABC* (Neutron/Phonogram NT(X) 105)	18	22	44
34 Only For Love *Limahl* (EMI(12)LML 1)	20	16	17
– Never Never *The Assembly* (Mute (12) TINY 1)	30	10	4
– Undercover Of The Night *The Rolling Stones* (Rolling Stones(12)RSR 113)	21	11	13
– A Solid Bond In Your Heart *The Style Council* (Polydor TSC 4)	–	12	11

5	12	19	26
— Love Of The Common People *Paul Young* (CBS(T) A3585)	—	17	5
42 Love Will Tear Us Apart *Joy Division* (Factory FAC 23(12))	30	19	21
47 Calling Your Name *Marilyn* (Mercury/Phonogram MAZ 1(12))	32	21	9
— Thriller *Michael Jackson* (Epic (T)A3643)	—	24	10
— Hold Me Now *Thompson Twins* (Arista TWINS(12)2)	—	31	14
45 Right By Your Side *Eurythmics* (RCA DA(T) 4)	27	23	15
— Let's Stay Together *Tina Turner* (Capitol (12)CL 316)	—	26	16
61 Oblivious *Aztec Camera* (WEA AZTEC 1(T))	35	29	20

DECEMBER 1983

3	10	17	24
1 Uptown Girl *Billy Joel* (CBS (T)A3775)	3	10	14
2 Love Of The Common People *Paul Young* (CBS (T)A3585)	2	2	4
3 Say Say Say *Paul McCartney/Michael Jackson* (Parlophone (12)R6062)	12	18	25
4 Calling Your Name *Marilyn* (Mercury/Phonogram MAZ 1(12))	7	13	23
5 Hold Me Now *Thompson Twins* (Arista TWINS (12)2)	4	5	6
6 Never Never *The Assembly* (Mute (12) TINY 1)	10	22	30
7 Let's Stay Together *Tina Turner* (Capitol (12)CL 316)	6	6	9
8 Cry Just A Little Bit *Shakin' Stevens* (Epic (T)A3774)	13	17	24
9 Only You *Flying Pickets* (10 Records/Virgin TEN 14(12))	1	1	1
10 Right By Your Side *Eurythmics* (RCA DA (T)4)	14	19	28
11 Thriller *Michael Jackson* (Epic (T)A3643)	16	12	13
12 A Solid Bond In Your Heart *The Style Council* (Polydor TSC 4)	25	39	56
13 Waterfront *Simple Minds* (Virgin VS 636)	17	21	31
14 The Love Cats *The Cure* (Fiction FICS(X) 19)	26	31	54
15 My Oh My *Slade* (RCA(T)373)	5	3	2
16 All Night Long (All Night) *Lionel Richie* (Motown TMG(T) 1319)	24	34	42
17 The Sun And The Rain *Madness* (Stiff BUY(T)192)	27	36	50
18 Oblivious *Aztec Camera* (WEA AZTEC1(T))	20	27	40
19 Undercover Of The Night *The Rolling Stones* (Rolling Stones (12)RSR143)	32	47	60
20 Please Don't Fall In Love *Cliff Richard* (EMI 5437)	9	7	10
21 Move Over Darling *Tracey Ullman* (Stiff BUY(T)195)	8	9	12
— Victims *Culture Club* (Virgin VS641(12))	11	4	3
26 Islands In The Stream *Kenny Rogers & Dolly Parton* (RCA378)	15	11	8
30 Club Fantastic (Megamix) *Wham!* (Inner Vision (T)A3586)	18	15	21
23 That's All *Genesis* (Charisma/Virgin TATA 1(12))	19	16	18
— Tell Her About It *Billy Joel* (CBS (T)A3655)	22	8	7
31 What Is Love *Howard Jones* (WEA HOW2(T))	23	14	11
— Read 'Em And Weep *Barry Manilow* (Arista (12)551)	40	20	17
— Marguerita Time *Status Quo* (Vertigo/Phonogram QUO 14)	36	25	5
44 2000 Miles *The Pretenders* (Real ARE 20(T))	35	23	15
— Many Rivers To Cross *UB40* (DEP International/Virgin DEP9(12))	38	24	16
— Staight Ahead *Kool & The Gang* (De Lite/Phonogram DE(X)15)	49	30	19
— Merry Xmas Everybody *Slade* (Polydor 2058 422)	72	35	20

1983 BEST SELLING RECORDS

Singles:

1. Karma Chameleon *Culture Club* (Virgin VS 612)
2. Uptown Girl *Billy Joel* (CBS A3775)
3. Red Red Wine *UB40* (DEP International/Virgin DEP 7)
4. Let's Dance *David Bowie* (EMI America EA 152)
5. Total Eclipse Of The Heart *Bonnie Tyler* (CBS TYLER 1)
6. True *Spandau Ballet* (Reformation/Chrysalis SPAN 1)
7. Down Under *Men At Work* (Epic A1980)
8. Billie Jean *Michael Jackson* (Epic A3084)
9. All Night Long (All Night) *Lionel Richie* (Motown TMG 1319)
10. Sweet Dreams (Are Made Of This) *Eurythmics* (RCA DA 2)
11. You Can't Hurry Love *Phil Collins* (Virgin VS 531)
12. Too Shy *Kajagoogoo* (EMI 5359)
13. Wherever I Lay My Hat (That's My Home) *Paul Young* (CBS A3371)
14. Every Breath You Take *The Police* (A&M AM 117)
15. Is There Something I Should Know? *Duran Duran* (EMI 5371)
16. Give It Up *KC & The Sunshine Band* (Epic A3017)
17. Blue Monday *New Order* (Factory FAC 73)
18. I.O.U. *Freeez* (Beggars Banquet BEG 96)
19. Baby Jane *Rod Stewart* (Warner Brothers W 9608)
20. They Don't Know *Tracey Ullman* (Stiff BUY 180)
21. Say Say Say *Paul McCartney/Michael Jackson* (Parlophone R6062)
22. Words *F.R. David* (Carrere CAR 248)
23. Tonight I Celebrate My Love *Bryson/Flack* (Capitol CL 302)
24. Bad Boys *Wham!* (Inner Vision A3143)
25. Flashdance . . .What A Feeling *Irene Cara* (Casablanca/Phonogram CAN 1016)
26. Only You *The Flying Pickets* (10 Records/Virgin TEN 14)
27. New Song *Howard Jones* (WEA HOW 1)
28. Love Of The Common People *Paul Young* (CBS A3585)
29. Moonlight Shadow *Mike Oldfield* (Virgin VS 586)
30. Sign Of The Times *The Belle Stars* (Stiff BUY 167)
31. Candy Girl *New Edition* (London LON 21)
32. Temptation *Heaven 17* (B.E.F./Virgin VS 570)
33. Church Of The Poison Mind *Culture Club* (Virgin VS 571)
34. Electric Avenue *Eddy Grant* (Ice ICE 57)
35. Mama *Genesis* (Charisma/Virgin MAMA1)
36. Beat It *Michael Jackson* (Epic A3258
37. Double Dutch *Malcolm McLaren* (Charisma/Phonogram/Virgin MALC 3)
38. Africa *Toto* (CBS A2510)
39. Club Tropicana *Wham!* (Inner Vision A3613)
40. (Keep Feeling) Fascination *The Human League* (Virgin VS 569)
41. Cry Just A Bit *Shakin' Stevens* (Epic A3774)
42. Gold *Spandau Ballet* (Reformation/Chrysalis SPAN 2)
43. Modern Love *David Bowie* (EMI America EA 158)
44. Come Back And Stay *Paul Young* (CBS A3636)
45. I'm Still Standing *Elton John* (Rocket/Phonogram EJS 1)
46. (Hey You) The Rocksteady Crew *Rocksteady Crew* (Charisma/Virgin RSC 1)
47. The Story Of The Blues *Wah!* (Eternal JF 1)
48. Up Where We Belong *Joe Cocker & Jennifer Warnes* (Island WIP 6830)
49. Nobody's Diary *Yazoo* (Mute 7YAZ003)
50. Dancing Tight *Galaxy featuring Phil Fearon* (Ensign/Island ENY 501)

Albums:

1 Thriller *Michael Jackson* (Epic EPC 85930)
2 Let's Dance *David Bowie* (EMI America AML 3029)
3 Colour By Numbers *Culture Club* (Virgin V 2285)
4 No Parlez *Paul Young* (CBS 25521)
5 True *Spandau Ballet* (Reformation/Chrysalis CDL 1403)
6 Fantastic *Wham!* (Inner Vision IVL 25328)
7 Business As Usual *Men At Work* (Epic EPC 85669)
8 Synchronicity *The Police* (A&M AMLX 63735)
9 Genesis *Genesis* (Charisma/Virgin GENLP 1)
10 18 Greatest Hits *Michael Jackson plus The Jackson 5* (Telstar STAR 2232)
11 Sweet Dreams (Are Made Of This) *Eurythmics* (RCA RCALP 6063)
12 Can't Slow Down *Lionel Richie* (Motown STMA 8041)
13 Labour Of Love *UB40* (DEP International/Virgin LP DEP 5)
14 The Luxury Gap *Heaven 17* (B.E.F./Virgin V 2253)
15 The Hurting *Tears For Fears* (Mercury/Phonogram MERS 17)
16 Stages *Elaine Paige* (K-Tel WEA NE 1262)
17 The Very Best Of The Beach Boys *The Beach Boys* (Capitol BBTV 1867193)
18 Too Low For Zero *Elton John* (Rocket/Phonogram HISPD 24)
19 Snap! *The Jam* (Polydor SNAP 1)
20 Rio *Duran Duran* (EMI EMC 3411)
21 Now That's What I Call Music *Various* (EMI/Virgin NOW 1)
22 The Crossing *Big Country* (Mercury/Phonogram MERS 27)
23 In Your Eyes *George Benson* (Warner Brothers 9237441)
24 War *U2* (Island ILPS 9733)
25 Richard Clayderman *Richard Clayderman* (Delphine/Decca SKL 5329)
26 Hello, I Must Be Going *Phil Collins* (Virgin V2252)
27 The John Lennon Collection *John Lennon* (Parlophone EMTV 37)
28 Faster Than The Speed Of Night *Bonnie Tyler* (CBS 25304)
29 The Final Cut *Pink Floyd* (Harvest SHPF 1983)
30 Quick Step And Side Kick *Thompson Twins* (Arista 204 924)
31 Seven And The Ragged Tiger *Duran Duran* (EMI EMC 1654541)
32 You And Me Both *Yazoo* (Mute STUMM 12)
33 Toto IV *Toto* (CBS 85529)
34 Raiders Of The Pop Charts *Various* (Ronco RTL 2088)
35 Crises *Mike Oldfield* (Virgin V 2262)
36 Body Wishes *Rod Stewart* (Warner Brothers 9238771)
37 An Innocent Man *Billy Joel* (CBS 25554)
38 Voice Of The Heart *Carpenters* (A&M MALX 64954)
39 Twice As Kool *Kool & The Gang* (De-Lite/Phonogram PROLP 2)
40 Heartbreaker *Dionne Warwick* (Arista 204 974)
41 U2 Live Under A Blood Red Sky *U2* (Island IMA 3)
42 Chas 'n' Dave's Knees-Up *Chas 'n' Dave* (Rockney/Towerball ROC 911)
43 Lionel Richie *Lionel Richie* (Motown STMA 8037)
44 Kissing To Be Clever *Culture Club* (Virgin V 2232)
45 The Two Of Us *Various* (K-tel NE 1222)
46 Visions *Various* (K-tel ONE 1199)
47 Chart Hits '83 *Various* (K-tel NE 1256)
48 Love Over Gold *Dire Straits* (Vertigo/Phonogram 6359109)
49 The Look *Shalamar* (Solar 9602391)
50 Complete Madness *Madness* (Stiff HITTV 1)

1984

George Michael had a very good year. He wrote chart-toppers 'Wake Me Up Before You Go' and 'Freedom' for his group Wham! and co-penned his solo number one 'Careless Whisper'. When 'Freedom' made the top spot in the week ending 20 October he had written three of the last five singles to reach Number One, a sequence only bettered in 1963 by Lennon and McCartney. And it was only the undeniable sales thrust of the charity Live Aid single 'Do They Know It's Christmas?' that prevented his co-penned Wham! Yuletide single 'Last Christmas' coupled with the equally popular 'Everything She Wants' from giving him and Wham! another Number One. Both records roared into the 15 December chart at Number One and Number Two, consecutively, and shouldered out of the way 'The Power of Love' from Frankie Goes To Hollywood.

Frankie might well have felt the year's top credits were stolen from them, almost at the last gasp. They were the first outfit to have a trio of chart-toppers since Blondie in 1980. 'Relax' sold amidst controversy over its lyrics and 'Two Tribes' came packaged with a superlative video. Pop sales statistics are notoriously unreliable, but it seems Frankie sold more singles in any year save for the Beatles and Boney M during their respective heydays.

There were other artists selling singles and albums by the million: Michael Jackson, dishy Duran Duran, Lionel Richie (particularly for 'Hello', another hit accompanied by a powerful video), Paul Young, McCartney (naturally), Stevie Wonder; and Queen had five chart hits after a barren 1983, the most they've achieved since they broke into the chart world with 'Seven Seas Of Rhye' in 1974.

For some girls it was a very good year. Alison Moyet and Sade caught most people's eye and ears. Both had three hits and enjoyed huge album sales. Cyndi Lauper couldn't repeat her astounding US chart year in Britain, though four of her records charted: 'Girls Just Want To Have Fun' and 'Time After Time' made the Top Three, but 'She Bop' and 'All Through The Night' did not make the Top 20. Back home she was the first woman in American chart history to place her first three hits in the top three of the US listings.

337

Continued record company 'push' on Prince ensured three hits for an artist who has first featured in the total UK listings in 1980 and the same British group of record companies WEA went to town on Madonna whose four hits included three in the Top 20.

But, as in any other year, there was too much activity to summarise accurately. Familiar and new names arrived weekly and industry hype regularly announced a new 'sensation' — but as in the case of delicious Nena from Germany it was all to often seemingly short-lived. However, sales were often colossal for the big acts and records. When Stevie Wonder's 'I Just Called To Say I love You' hit the top it was the third consecutive single to sell more than a million, and so set a record. Thus 1984 joined 1978 and 1979 as being the best years for record sales, and this was evident even *before* Live Aid became operative; that was just the icing on the sales cake. Nevertheless, record companies were not flush with money; they spent heavily on promotional aids such as the video. Indeed a video became necessary in order to generate initial interest and then to push a record even higher. Thus in some quarters style became almost as essential as talent; and in disco music, the remix engineer more important than the artist!

JANUARY 1984

7	14	21	28
1 Only You *The Flying Pickets* (Ten 14 (12))	10	25	47
2 My Oh My *Slade* (RCA(T) 373)	11	30	55
3 Love Of The Common People *Paul Young* (CBS(T)A3585)	5	14	28
4 Victims *Culture Club* (Virgin VS641(12))	7	22	38
5 Marguerita Time *Status Quo* (Vertigo/Phonogram QUO14)	3	7	15
6 Tell Her About It *Billy Joel* (CBS(T)3655)	4	8	18
7 Islands In The Stream *Kenny Rogers & Dolly Parton* (RCA 378)	8	10	24
8 Hold Me Now *Thompson Twins* (Arista TWINS (12)2)	9	12	25
9 Pipes of Peace *Paul McCartney* (Parlophone R6064)	1	1	2
10 What Is Love? *Howard Jones* (WEA NOW2(T))	2	3	4
11 Thriller *Michael Jackson* (Epic (T)A3643)	12	18	27
12 Let's Stay Together *Tina Turner* (Capitol (12)CL316)	17	27	37
13 Please Don't Fall In Love *Cliff Richard* (EMI5437)	26	46	–
14 Uptown Girl *Billy Joel* (CBS (T)A3775)	16	33	45
15 Move Over Darling *Tracey Ullman* (Stiff BUY(IT)195)	21	36	60
16 2000 Miles *The Pretenders* (Real ARE 20(T))	25	56	–
17 Many Rivers To Cross *UB40* (Dep International/Virgin DEP9(12))	20	32	52
18 Rat Rapping *Roland Rat* (Rodent/Magnet(12)RAT 1)	14	21	32
19 Straight Ahead *Kool & The Gang* (De-Lite/Phonogram DE(X)15)	15	19	23
20 Merry Xmas Everybody *Slade* (Polydor 2058)	83	–	–
35 Relax *Frankie Goes To Hollywood* (ZTT/Island(12)TAS)	6	2	1
57 A Rockin' Good Way *Shaky & Bonnie* (Epic(T)A4071)	13	5	5
43 That's Living (Alright) (from *Auf Wiedersehen Pet*) *Joe Fagin* (Towerbell TOW46)	18	4	3
40 Bird of Paradise *Snowy White* (Towerbell(12)TOW42)	19	6	7
36 Running With The Night *Lionel Richie* (Motown TMG(T)1324)	22	9	16
– Nobody Told Me *John Lennon* (Ono Music/Polydor POSP700)	–	11	6
– Wonderland *Big Country* (Mercury/Phonogram COUNT5(12))	–	13	8
52 Love Is A Wonderful Colour *The Icicle Works* (Beggars Banquet BEG99(T))	28	15	19
– Wishful Thinking *China Crisis* (Virgin VS647(12))	36	16	9
– King Of Pain *The Police* (A&M AM(X)176)	32	17	21
– Here Comes The Rain *The Eurythmics* (RCA DA(T)5)	–	20	11
– Girls Just Want To Have Fun *Cyndi Lauper* (Portrait/Epic (T)A3943)	50	32	10
– (Feels Like) Heaven *Fiction Factory* (CBS(T)A3996)	56	28	12
56 I Am What I Am (from *La Cage Aux Folles*) (Chrysalis CHS (12))	38	24	13
– Break My Stride *Matthew Wilder* (Epic(T)A3908)	–	31	14
– The Killing Moon *Echo & The Bunnymen* (Korova KOW32(T))	–	–	17
– Speed Your Love To Me *Simple Minds* (Virgin VS649)	–	–	20

FEBRUARY 1984

4	11	18	25
1 Relax *Frankie Goes To Hollywood* (ZTT/Island(12)ZTAS)	1	1	1
2 Girls Just Want To Have Fun *Cyndi Lauper* (Portrait/Epic (T)A3943)	3	4	8

3 That's Living Alright (from *Auf Wiedersehen Pet*) *Joe Fagin* (Towerbell TOW46)	6	7	17
4 Radio Ga Ga *Queen* (EMI(12)QUEEN 1)	2	2	4
5 Break My Stride *Matthew Wilder* (Epic (T)A3908)	4	5	6
6 (Feels Like) Heaven *Fiction Factory* (CBS(T)A3996)	8	16	26
7 Pipes Of Peace *Paul McCartney* (Parlophone R6064)	18	42	51
8 Here Comes The Rain Again *Eurythmics* (RCA DA(T)5)	10	18	29
9 The Killing Moon *Echo & The Bunnymen* (Korova KOW32(T))	11	25	40
10 Wonderland *Big Country* (Mercury/Phonogram COUNT 5(12))	14	21	37
11 A Rockin' Good Way *Shaky & Bonnie* (Epic(T)A407)	16	33	45
12 New Moon On Monday *Duran Duran* (EMI(12)DURAN 1)	9	9	20
13 Holiday *Madonna* (Sire W9405)	7	6	13
14 Nobody Told Me *John Lennon* (Ono Music/Polydor POSP700)	21	41	62
15 Wishful Thinking *China Crisis* (Virgin VS647(12))	17	37	44
16 What Is Love? *Howard Jones* (WEA HOW2)	25	44	49
17 I Am What I Am (from *La Cage Aux Folles*) Gloria Gaynor (Chrysalis CHS(12)2765)	15	23	32
18 Doctor! Doctor! *Thompson Twins* (AristaTWINS(12)3)	5	3	3
19 Bird Of Paradise *Snowy White* (Towerbell (12)TOW 42)	22	39	53
20 What Difference Does It Make? *The Smiths* Rough Trade (RT(T)145)	13	12	18
25 Love Theme From The Thorn Birds (WEA X9518)	12	10	24
26 Spice Of Life *The Manhattan Transfer* (Atlantic A9728(T))	19	22	30
29 Hyperactive *Thomas Dolby* (Parlophone Odeon (12) R6055)	20	17	22
– My Ever Changing Moods *The Style Council* (Polydor TSC(X)5)	–	8	5
58 99 Red Balloons *Nena* (Epic (T)A4074)	31	11	2
– Michael Caine *Madness* (Stiff BUY(T)196)	26	13	11
38 Wouldn't It Be Good *Nik Kershaw* (MCA NIK(T))	32	14	9
52 Somebody's Watching Me *Rockwell* (Motown TMG(T)1331)	30	15	7
35 Let The Music Play *Shannon* (Club/Phonogram LET 1(12))	27	19	14
41 Soul Train *Swans Way* (Exit International/Phonogram EXT3(12))	34	20	23
– Joanna/Tonight *Kool & The Gang* (De-Lite/Phonogram DE(X)16)	50	26	10
– An Innocent Man *Billy Joel* (CBS(T)A4142)	–	28	12
– Hide And Seek *Howard Jones* (WEA HOW3(T))	–	24	15
50 Street Dance *Break Machine* (Record Shack SOHO(T)13)	36	27	16
54 Run Runaway *Slade* (RCA(T)385)	40	34	19

MARCH 1984

3	10	17	24	31
1 99 Red Balloons *Nena* (Epic(T)A4074)	1	1	2	11
2 Relax *Frankie Goes To Hollywood* (ZTT/Island (12)ZTAS)	3	6	16	21
3 Joanna (Tonight) *Kool & The Gang* (De-Lite/Phonogram DE(X)16)	2	2	4	10
4 Wouldn't It Be Good *Nik Kershaw* (MCA NIK(T)2)	4	4	6	12
5 Doctor! Doctor! *Thompson Twins* (Arista TWINS(12)3)	9	19	26	39
6 Somebody's Watching Me *Rockwell* (Motown TMG(T)1331)	6	9	17	26
7 Radio Ga Ga *Queen* (EMI(12)QUEEN 1)	16	28	37	60
8 An Innocent Man *Billy Joel* (CBS(T)A4142)	8	8	11	17
9 My Ever Changing Moods *The Style Council* (Polydor TSC(X)5)	17	27	35	51

340

10 Run Runaway *Slade* (RCA(T)385)	7	14	20	32
11 Street Dance *Break Machine* (Record Shack (SOHO(T)13)	5	3	3	8
12 Break My Stride *Matthew Wilder* (Epic (T)A3908)	18	25	34	58
13 Girls Just Want To Have Fun *Cyndi Lauper* (Portrait/Epic (T)3943)	20	32	41	67
14 Hide And Seek *Howard Jones* (WEA HOW3(T))	12	12	18	23
15 Let The Music Play *Shannon* (Club/Phonogram LET1(12))	14	21	27	31
16 Michael Caine *Madness* (Stiff BUY (T)196)	22	33	46	66
17 Get Out Of Your Lazy Bed *Matt Bianco* (WEA BIANCO1(T))	15	23	31	50
18 Holiday *Madonna* (Sire W9405(T))	26	35	66	–
19 I Gave You My Heart (Didn't I?) *Hot Chocolate* (RAK369)	13	16	24	35
20 Jump *Van Halen* (Warner Brothers W9384(T))	10	7	10	16
26 Torvill & Dean (EP) (Bolero/Barnum) (Safari SKATE(R)1)	11	10	13	14
38 Breaking Down (Sugar Samba) *Julia & Company* (London LON(46)46)	19	15	19	24
– Hello *Lionel Richie* (Motown (TMG)(T) 1330)	25	5	1	1
47 It's Raining Men *The Weather Girls* (CBS(T)A2924)	36	11	5	2
– What Do I Do *Phil Fearon & Galaxy* (Ensign/Island (12ENY) 510)	27	13	7	5
39 To Be Or Not To Be (The Hitler Rap) *Mel Brooks* (Island (12)IS 158)	31	17	12	18
35 'Ullo John! Gotta New Motor *Alexei Sayle* (Island (12)IS162)	21	18	15	19
59 Your Love Is King *Sade* (Epic (T)A4137)	37	20	9	6
48 Robert De Niro's Waiting *Bananarama* (London NANA6(12inch) NANX6)	38	22	8	3
– It's A Miracle *Culture Club* (Virgin VS662(12))	–	–	14	4
– A Love Worth Waiting For *Shakin' Stevens* (Epic(T)A4291)	–	–	22	7
– People Are People *Depeche Mode* (Mute 7BONG 5 (12"-12BONG5))	–	–	29	9
– You Take Me Up *Thompson Twins* (Arista TWINS(12)4)	–	–	–	13
– Cherry Oh Baby *UB40* (Dep International/Virgin DEP10(12))	–	42	28	15
– P.Y.T. (Pretty Young Thing) *Michael Jackson* (Epic(T)A4136)	–	–	–	20

APRIL 1984

7	14	21	28
1 Hello *Lionel Richie* (Motown (TMG)T 1330)	1	1	1
2 A Love Worth Waiting For *Shakin' Stevens* (Epic(T)A4291)	2	3	6
3 Robert De Niro's Waiting *Bananarama* (London NANA6(12"-NANX(6))	5	12	23
4 You Take Me Up *Thompson Twins* (Arista TWINS (12)4)	3	2	4
5 People Are People *Depeche Mode* (Mute BONG5)(12"-12BONG)	4	6	9
6 It's Raining Men *The Weather Girls* (CBS(T)A2924)	8	18	27
7 It's A Miracle *Culture Club* (Virgin VS662(12))	7	16	28
8 What Do I Do? *Phil Fearon & Galaxy* (Ensign/Island (12ENY510)	11	23	37
9 Torvill & Dean (EP) (Bolero/Barnum) (Safari SKAT(R)1)	23	39	51
10 Your Love Is King *Sade* (Epic (T)A4137)	15	30	42
11 P.Y.T. (Pretty Young Thing) *Michael Jackson* (Epic(T)A4138)	12	21	32
12 Cherry Oh Baby *UB40* (Dep International/Virgin DEP101)	16	28	44
13 Street Dance *Break Machine* (Record Shack SOHO(T)13)	19	34	48

14 Nelson Mandela *The Special AKA* (2 Tone CHS TT(12)26)   9   9 16

15 Glad It's All Over/Damned On 45 *Captain Sensible* (A&M
CAP(X)6)   6   7   8

16 Lucky Star *Madonna* (Sire W522)   14 20 34

17 Joanna/Tonight *Kool & The Gang* (De-Lite/Phonogram
DE(X)16)   33   –   –

18 Ain't Nobody *Rufus and Chaka Khan* (Warner Brothers
RCK1(T))   13   8 12

19 An Innocent Man *Billy Joel* (CBS (T)A4074)   40   –   –

20 99 Red Balloons *Nena* (Epic (T)A4142)   39   –   –

26 Against All Odds (Take A Look At Me Now) *Phil Collins*
(Virgin VS674)   10   4   2

25 Wood Beez (Pray Like Aretha Franklin) *Scritti Politti* (Virgin
VS 657(12))   17 10 14

– I Want To Break Free *Queen* (EMI(12)QUEEN 2)   18   5   3

31 The Caterpillar *The Cure* (Fiction/Polydor FICS(X)20)   20 14 19

– The Reflex *Duran Duran* (EMI(12)DURAN 2)   –   –   5

– When You're Young And In Love *The Flying Pickets* (10
Records TEN20(12))   – 37 13

41 I'm Falling *The Bluebells* (London LON(X)45)   36 26 15

– Dancing Girls *Nik Kershaw* (MCA (NIK)(T)3)   35 25 18

– Automatic *Pointer Sisters* (Planet RPS(T)105)   59 38 20

– (When You Say You Love Somebody) In The Heart *Kool &
The Gang* (De-Lite/Phonogram DE(X)17)   30 11   7

50 Just Be Good To Me *The S.O.S. Band* (Tabu/Epic(T)A3626)   26 13 17

– Don't Tell me *Blancmange* (London
BLANC7/12" – BLANX7)   32 15 11

40 Someday *The Gap Band* (Total Experience/Phonogram
TE(X)5)   22 17 25

– Locomotion *OMD* (Virgin VS660(– 12))   28 19 10

MAY 1984

5	12	19	26
1 The Reflex *Duran Duran* (EMI(12)DURAN 2)	1	1	1
2 Against All Odds (Take A Look At Me Now) *Phil Collins* (Virgin VS674)	2	3	8
3 I Want To Break Free *Queen* (EMI (12) QUEEN 2)	3	4	5
4 Hello *Lional Richie* (Motown TMG (T)1330)	10	15	29
5 Automatic *Pointer Sisters* (Planet RPS(T)105)	4	2	2
6 Locomotion *OMD* (Virgin VS660(12))	5	7	12
7 When You're Young And In Love *The Flying Pickets* (10 Records 20(12))	7	10	16
8 Don't Tell Me *Blancmange* (London BLANC 7"(12" – BLANX7)	8	9	15
9 One People/People Get Ready *Bob Marley & The Wailers* (Island(12)IS 169)	6	5	6
10 You Take Me Up *Thompson Twins* (Arista TWINS(12)4)	21	34	55
11 I'm Falling *The Bluebells* (London LON(X)45)	14	19	33
12 (When You Say You Love Somebody) In The Heart *Kool & The Gang* (De-Lite/Phonogram DE(X)17)	15	23	37
13 Ain't Nobody *Rufus and Chakha Khan* (Warner Brothers RCK1(T))	19	26	38
14 Dancing Girls *Nik Kershaw* (MCA NIK(T)3)	13	14	27
15 A Love Worth Waiting For *Shakin' Stevens* (Epic(T)A4291)	27	39	57
16 Glad It's All Over/Damned on 45 *Captain Sensible* (A&M CAP(X)6)	29	37	68
17 Just Be Good To Me *The S.O.S. Band* (Tabu/Epic(T)A3626)	20	20	30
18 Thieves Like Us *New Order* (Factory FAC103)	22	38	59

19 The Lebanon *Human League* (Virgin VS672(12))   11   12   22
20 People Are People *Depeche Mode* (Mute
   7BONG5(12″-12BONG)   36   50   74
28 Footloose *Kenny Loggins* (CBS(T)4332)   9   6   7
21 Love Games *Belle And The Devotions* (CBS(T)A4332)   12   11   24
25 Somebody Else's Guy *Jocelyn Brown* (Fourth &
   Broadway/Island(12)BRW5)   16   13   20
24 To All The Girls I've Loved Before *Julio Iglesias & Willie
   Nelson* (CBS A4252)   17   21   31
41 Let's Hear It For The Boy (from *Footloose*) *Deniece
   Williams* (CBS(T)A4319)   18   8   3
– Break Dance Party *Break Machine* (Record Shack
   SOHO(T)20)   32   16   9
46 I'll Be Around *Terri Wells* (Philly World/London LON(X)48)   28   17   18
38 Stay With Me Tonight *Jeffrey Osbourne* (A&M AM(X)188)   24   18   19
– Wake Me Up Before You Go *Wham!* (Epic (T)A4440)   –   –   4
– Dancing With Tears In My Eyes *Ultravox* (Chrysalis UV(X)1)   –   29   10
– Groovin' (You're The Best Thing/The Big Boss Groove) *The
   Style Council* (Polydor TSC(X)6)   –   –   11
49 Searchin' *Hazel Dean* (Proto ENA(T)109)   40   28   13
50 Love Wars *Womack and Womack* (Elektra E9799(T))   35   25   14
60 I Feel Like Buddy Holly *Alvin Stardust* (Chrysalis
   CHS(12)2784)   42   31   17

Thieves Like Us also charted on Factory Benelux as the flip side of
Murder (FBN 22) and was at 92 on May 26.

JUNE 1984

2	9	16	23	30
1 Wake Me Up Before You Go *Wham!* (Epic(T)A4440)	1	2	2	5
2 Let's Hear It For The Boy (from *Footloose*) *Deniece Williams* (CBS(T)A4319)	2	9	16	26
3 The Reflex *Duran Duran* (EMI(12)DURAN2)	4	19	27	35
4 Automatic *Pointer Sisters* (Planet RPS(T)105)	14	24	32	48
5 Groovin' (You're The Best Thing/The Big Boss Groove) *The Style Council* (Polydor TSC(X)6)	7	13	17	32
6 Dancing With Tears In My Eyes *Ultravox* (Chrysalis CHS(12)2784)	3	6	14	23
7 I Feel Like Buddy Holly *Alvin Stardust* (Chrysalis CHS(12)2784)	11	16	18	34
8 Searchin' *Hazel Dean* (Pronto ENA(T)109)	6	12	15	24
9 I Want To Break Free *Queen* (EMI(12) QUEEN2)	15	22	28	41
10 Against All Odds (Take A Look At Me Now) *Phil Collins* (Virgin VS674)	22	28	39	51
11 High Energy *Evelyn Thomas* (Record Shack SOHO(T)18)	9	5	9	14
12 One Love/People Get Ready *Bob Marley* (Island (12)IS 169)	24	34	47	65
13 Break Dance Party *Break Machine* (Record Shack SOHO(T)20)	20	30	37	54
14 Footloose *Kenny Loggins* (CBS(T)A4101)	21	32	43	73
15 Pearl In The Shell *Howard Jones* (WEA HOW4(T))	8	7	10	22
16 Love Wars *Womack & Womack* (Elektra E9799)	23	29	42	61
17 Relax *Frankie Goes To Hollywood* (ZTT/Island(12)ZTAS1)	16	11	5	3
18 Locomotion *OMD* (Virgin VS 660(12))	28	41	63	–
19 Heaven Knows (I'm Miserable Now) *The Smiths* (Rough Trade RT(T)156)	10	10	13	20
20 Going Down Town Tonight *Status Quo* (Vertigo/Phonogram QUO5)	27	35	51	–

343

	– Only When You Leave *Spandau Ballet* (Reformation/Chrysalis SPAN(X) 3)	5	3	6	16
22	Sad Songs (Say So Much) *Elton John* (Rocket/Phonogram PH7(12))	12	8	7	9
35	Smalltown Boy *Bronski Beat* (Forbidden Fruit/London BITE(X)1)	13	4	3	4
21	Red Guitar *David Sylvian* (Virgin VS633)	17	25	33	59
30	One Better Day *Madness* (Stiff BUY(IT)201)	18	17	25	38
23	Thinking Of You *Sister Sledge* (Cotillon/AtlanticB9744)	19	14	11	11
	– Two Tribes *Frankie Goes To Hollywood* (ZTT/Island(12)ZTAS 3)	–	1	1	1
45	Farewell My Summer Love *Michael Jackson* (Motown TMG(T)1342)	26	15	8	7
	– I Won't Let The Sun Go Down On Me *Nik Kershaw* (MCA NIK(T)4)	–	18	4	2
43	Susanna *The Art Company* (Epic(T)A4174)	31	20	12	13
58	Change Of Heart *Change* (WEA YZ7(T))	39	26	19	17
29	So Tired *Ozzy Osbourne* (Epic(T)A4452)	25	21	20	21
	– Jump (For My Love) *Pointer Sisters* (Planet RPS(T)106)	–	–	24	6
	– Breakin' . . . There's No Stopping Us *Ollie & Jerry* (Polydor POSP (X)690)	–	–	35	8
	– Time After Time *Cyndi Lauper* (Portrait/Epic(T)A4290)	–	62	36	10
52	White Lines (Don't Don't Do It) *Grandmaster & Melle Mel* (Sugar Hill (L)130)	46	36	21	12
	– Talking Loud And Clear *Orchestral Manoeuvres In The Dark* (Virgin VS 685(12))	–	39	23	15
	– Stuck On You *Lionel Richie* (Motown TMG(T)134)	–	–	34	18
	– Absolute *Scritti Politti* (Virgin 6801(12))	43	33	22	19

JULY 1984

7		14	21	28
1	Two Tribes *Frankie Goes To Hollywood* (ZTT/Island (12)ZTAS 3)	1	1	1
2	Relax *Frankie Goes To Hollywood* (ZTT/Island (12)ZTAS 1)	2	3	3
3	I Won't (Let The Sun Go Down On Me) *Nik Kershaw* (MCA NIK(T)4)	4	7	9
4	Time After Time *Cyndi Lauper* (Portrait/Epic (T)A4290)	3	4	6
5	Breakin' . . . There's No Stopping Us *Ollie & Jerry* (Polydor POSP (X) 690)	6	13	14
6	Jump (For My Love) *Pointer Sisters* (Planet RPS(T)106)	7	9	11
7	Smalltown Boy *Bronski Beat* (Forbidden Fruit/London BITE(X)1)	12	19	26
8	Farewell My Summer Love *Michael Jackson* (Motown TMG(T)1342)	16	20	29
9	Wake Me Up Before You Go *Wham!* (Epic (T)A4440)	18	22	28
10	White Lines (Don't Do It) *Grandmaster & Melle Mel* (Sugar Hill (SHL)130)	9	8	7
11	Talking Loud And Clear *Orchestral Manoeuvres In The Dark* (Virgin VS685(12))	15	16	24
12	Stuck On You *Lionel Richie* (Motown TMG(T)1341)	17	18	27
13	Thinking Of You *Sister Sledge* (Cotillon/Atlantic B9744)	19	24	38
14	Love Resurrection *Alison Moyet* (CBS(T)A4497)	13	12	10
15	Sad Songs (Say So Much) *Elton John* (Rocket/Phonogram PH7(12))	23	27	36
16	Life On Your Own *Human League* (Virgin VS688(12))	21	29	37
17	Absolute *Scritti Politti* (Virgin VS6801(12))	24	32	39
18	What's Love Got To Do With It *Tina Turner* (Capitol (12)CL334)	10	6	5

344

19 Change of Heart *Change* (WEA Y27(T))	27	31	45
20 Young At Heart *The Bluebells* (London LON(X)49)	14	10	8
– Hole In My Shoe *Neil* (WEA YZ10)	5	2	2
21 When Doves Cry *Prince* (Warner Brothers W9286)	8	5	4
28 Sisters of Mercy *Thompson Twins* (Arista TWINS(12)5)	11	11	13
37 State Of Shock *Jacksons* (Epic(T)4431)	20	14	19
– Everybody's Laughing *Phil Fearnon & Galaxy* (Ensign/Island(12)ENY 514)	28	15	12
– Seven Seas *Echo and the Bunneymen* (Korova KOW35(T))	26	17	16
45 Down On The Street *Shakatak* (Polydor POSP (X)688)	33	21	15
– You Think You're A Man *Divine* (Proto ENA(T)18)	38	26	17
56 Closest Thing To Heaven *The Kane Gang* (Kitchenware/London SK(X)15)	42	30	18
42 Come Back *The Mighty Wah!* (Eternal/Beggars Banquet BEG11(T))	40	28	20

AUGUST 1984

4	11	18	25
1 Two Tribes *Frankie Goes To Hollywood* (ZTT/Island (12)ZTAS 3)	1	3	5
2 Hole In My Shoe *Neil* (WEA YZ10)	7	13	25
3 Relax *Frankie Goes To Hollywood* (ZTT/Island (12) ZTAS3)	6	7	12
4 When Doves Cry *Prince* (Warner Brothers W9286)	5	8	14
5 What's Love Got To Do With It *Tina Turner* (Capitol (12)CL 334)	3	5	8
6 It's A Hard Life *Queen* (EMI(12) QUEEN3)	9	12	17
7 White Lines (Don't Do It) *Grandmaster & Melle Mel* (Sugar Hill SHL 130)	10	9	10
8 Time After Time *Cyndi Lauper* (Portrait/Epic (T)4290)	16	21	30
9 Down On The Street *Shakatak* (Polydor POSP (X)688)	14	17	24
10 Everybody's Laughing *Phil Fearnon & Galaxy* (Ensign/Island(12)ENY 514)	11	16	26
11 Young At Heart *The Bluebells* (London LON(X)49)	17	23	32
12 Careless Whisper *George Michael* (Epic(T)A4603)	2	1	1
13 Whatever I Do (Wherever I Go) *Hazell Dean* (Proto ENA(T)119)	8	4	7
14 Love Resurrection *Alison Moyet* (CBS(T)A4497)	21	31	42
15 Closest Thing To Heaven *The Kane Gang* (Kitchenware/London SK(X)15)	12	14	20
16 You Think You're A Man *Divine* (Proto ENA(T)18)	18	22	31
17 I Won't Let The Sun Go Down On Me *Nik Kershaw* (MCA NIK(T)4)	27	33	38
18 Eyes Without A Face *Billy Idol* (Chrysalis IDOL(X)3)	19	25	33
19 Agadoo *Black Lace* (Flair FLA 107(T))	4	2	2
20 On The Wings Of Love *Jeffrey Osbourne* (A&M AM(X)198)	15	11	13
25 Self Control *Laura Branigan* (Atlantic A9676(T))	13	6	6
21 Tossing and Turning *Windjammer* (MCA MCA(T) 897)	20	18	21
– Like To Get To Know You Well *Howard Jones* (WEA HOW5(T))	33	10	4
44 Stuck On You *Trevor Walters* (I&S Productions IS(T)002)	23	15	9
32 Some Guys Have All The Luck *Rod Stewart* (Warner Brothers W9204(T))	25	20	19
– I Just Called To Say I Love You (from *The Woman In Red*) *Stevie Wonder* (Motown TMG1349)	–	–	3
– 2 Minutes To Midnight *Iron Maiden* (EMI(12)EMI5489)	–	27	11
– Passengers (re-mix) *Elton John* (Rocket/Phonogram EJS 5(12)	52	30	15
– Dr. Beat *Miami Sound* (Epic(T)A4614)	41	28	16
36 Sunglasses *Tracey Ullman* (Stiff BUY(IT)205)	26	19	18

	8	15	22	29
1				
1 Careless Whisper *George Michael* (Epic(T)A4603)	2	2	3	5
2 I Just Called To Say I Love You (from *The Woman In Red*) *Stevie Wonder* (Motown TMG1349)	1	1	1	1
3 Agadoo *Black Lace* (Flair FLA 107(T))	3	4	5	8
4 Like To Get To Know You Well *Howard Jones* (WEA HOW5 (T))	4	5	12	20
5 Self Control *Laura Branigan* (Atlantic A9676)	8	10	14	24
6 Passengers (re-mix) *Elton John* (Rocket/Phonogram EJS5(12))	5	6	10	22
7 Dr Beat *Miami Sound* (Epic(T)A4614)	7	7	6	11
8 Whatever I Do (Wherever I Go) *Hazell Dean* (Proto ENA(T)119)	10	16	32	35
9 Two Tribes *Frankie Goes To Hollywood* (ZTT/Island(12)ZTAS3)	13	17	29	34
10 Stuck On You *Trevor Walters* (I&S Productions IS(T)002)	16	22	35	50
11 I'll Fly For You *Spandau Ballet* (Reformation/Chrysalis SPAN(X)4)	9	12	15	26
12 What's Love Got To Do With It *Tina Turner* (Capitol(12)CL334)	19	27	40	48
13 White Lines (Don't Do It) *Grandmaster & Melle Mel* (Sugar Hill SHL130)	18	20	23	31
14 2 Minutes To Midnight *Iron Maiden* (EMI(12)EMI5489)	25	39	65	–
15 Some Guys Have All The Luck *Rod Stewart* (Warner Brothers W9204(T))	20	25	44	55
16 On The Wings Of Love *Jeffrey Osbourne* (A&M AM(X)198)	23	35	49	–
17 Mothers Talk *Tears For Fears* (Mercury/Phonogram IDEA7(12))	14	18	30	40
18 Ghostbusters *Ray Parker Jr.* (Arista ARIST(12)580)	6	3	2	2
19 When Doves Cry *Prince* (Warner Brothers W9286(T))	24	32	47	56
20 Relax *Frankie Goes To Hollywood* (ZTT/Island(12)ZTAS3)	22	29	41	47
22 Big In Japan *Alphaville* (WEA X9505)	11	9	8	9
24 Master And Servant *Depeche Mode* (Mute 7BONG6(12" – 12BONG 6))	12	11	9	14
32 Madame Butterfly (Un Bel Vi Vedromo) *Malcolm McLaren* (Charisma/Virgin MALC5(12)	15	13	13	18
23 William. It Was Really Nothing *The Smiths* (Rough Trade RT(T)166)	17	21	38	43
– Pride (In The Name Of Love) *U2* (Island (12)IS202)	–	8	4	3
– Lost In Music *Sister Sledge* (Cotilion/Atlantic B9718)	32	14	7	4
34 Talking In Your Sleep *Bucks Fizz* (RCAFIZ(T)2)	21	15	16	25
37 Hot Water *Level 42* (Polydor POSP(X)697)	26	19	18	21
– A Letter To You *Shakin' Stevens* (Epic A4677)	–	23	11	10
– Blue Jeans *David Bowie* (EMI America EA181)	–	–	17	6
– Hammer To Fall *Queen* (EMI(12)QUEEN4)	–	–	19	13
– Human Racing *Nik Kershaw* (MCA NIK(T)5)	–	38	20	19
– Why? *Bronski Beat* (Forbidden Fruit/London BITE(X)2)	–	–	22	7
– Love Kills (from *Metropolis*) *Freddie Mercury* (CBS(T)A4735)	–	–	27	12
– Apollo 9 *Adam Ant* (CBS(T)A4719)	–	–	28	15
– Purple Rain *Prince and the Revolution* (Warner Brothers W9174(T))	–	–	25	16
– If It Happens Again *UB40* (Dep International/Virgin DEP11(12))	–	–	33	17

346

OCTOBER 1984

	13	**20**	**27**
6			
1 I Just Called To Say I Love You (from *A Woman In Red*) Stevie Wonder (Motown TMG(T)1349)	1	2	4
2 Ghostbusters *Ray Parker Jr.* (Arista ARIST(12)580)	4	8	14
3 The War Song *Culture Club* (Virgin VS694(12))	2	3	6
4 Pride (In The Name Of Love) *U2* (Island(12)Is 202)	8	13	19
5 Lost In Music *Sister Sledge* (Cotilion/Atlantic B9718(T))	11	17	24
6 Why? *Bronski Beat* (Forbidden Fruit/London BITE(X)2)	7	11	16
7 Blue Jean *David Bowie* (EMI America EMI EA1181)	17	27	39
8 Purple Rain *Prince and the Revolution* (Warner Brothers W9174(T))	10	14	21
9 If It Happens Again *UB40* (Dep International/Virgin DEP11(12)	12	16	27
10 Love Kills (from *Metropolis*) *Freddie Mercury* (CBS(T)A4735)	14	18	28
11 Careless Whisper *George Michael* (Epic (T)A4603)	18	20	26
12 A Letter To You *Shakin' Stevens* (Epic A4677)	19	28	37
13 Apollo 9 *Adam Ant* (CBS(T)4719)	15	21	33
14 Big In Japan *Alphaville* (WEA X9505)	23	31	38
15 Drive *The Cars* (Elektra E9706)	5	6	7
16 Agadoo *Black Lace* (Flair FLA107(T))	25	24	31
17 East Of Eden *Big Country* (Mercury/Phonogram MER(X)175)	24	34	49
18 Dr. Beat *Miami Sound Machine* (Epic(T)A4614)	26	35	43
19 Hammer To All *Queen* (EMI(12)QUEEN4)	28	37	53
20 Human Racing *Nik Kershaw* (MCA NIK(T)5)	30	44	59
– Freedom *Wham!* (Epic(T)A4743)	3	1	1
28 No More Lonely Nights (Ballad) *Paul McCartney* (Parlophone(12)R6080)	6	4	2
21 Together In Electric Dreams (from *Electric Dreams*) *Giorgio Moroder* (Virgin VS713(12))	9	5	3
– Shout To The Top *The Style Council* (Polydor (TSC(X)7)	13	7	10
38 Missing You *John Waite* (EMI America(12)EA 182)	16	10	9
– I'm Gonna Tear Your Playhouse Down *Paul Young* (CBS(T)A4677)	20	9	11
– All Cried Out *Alison Moyet* (CBS(T)A4757)	35	12	8
32 Skin Deep *The Stranglers* (Epic(T)A4738)	21	15	18
22 Smooth Operator *Sade* (Epic A4655(12 inch – TX4655))	22	19	20
– I Feel For You *Chaka Khan* (Warner Brothers W9209(T))	–	22	5
71 Too Late For Goodbyes *Julian Lennon* (Charisma/Virgin JL1(12)	43	30	12
– Love's Great Adventure *Ultravox* (Chrysalis UV(X)3)	–	23	13
– Highly Strung *Spandau Ballet* (Reformation/Chrysalis SPAN(X)5)	–	25	15
46 Modern Girl *Meat Loaf* (Arista ARIST(12) 585)	34	26	17

NOVEMBER 1984

	10	**17**	**24**
3			
1 Freedom *Wham!* (Epic(T)A4743)	2	4	9
2 I Feel For You *Chaka Kahn* (Warner Brothers W9209(T))	1	1	1
3 No More Lonely Nights (Ballad) *Paul McCartney* (Parlophone(12)R6080)	4	13	22
4 Together In Electric Dreams (from *Electric Dreams*) *Giorgio Moroder* (Virgin VS713 (12))	5	15	21
5 The Wild Boys *Duran Duran* (Parlophone (12)DURAN 3)	3	2	3
6 Too Late For Goodbyes *Julian Lennon* (Charisma/VirginJL1(12))	6	9	19
7 The Wanderer *Status Quo* (Vertigo/Phonogram QUO16)	7	7	10

8 All Cried Out *Alison Moyet* (CBS(T)A4757)	8	8	13
9 I Just Called To Say I Love You (from *Woman In Red*) *Stevie Wonder* (Motown TMG(T)1349)	14	19	25
10 Missing You *John Waite* (EMI America EA(12)182)	15	20	31
11 Drive *The Cars* (Elektra E9706)	17	27	40
12 Carribean Queen (No More Love On The Run) *Billy Ocean* (Jive K77)	9	6	6
13 Love's Great Adventure *Ultravox* (Chrysalis UV(X)3)	12	12	16
14 The War Song *Culture Club* (Virgin VS694(12))	23	30	54
15 Gimme All Your Lovin' *ZZ Top* (Warner Brothers W9693)	11	10	15
16 Shout To The Top *The Style Council* (Polydor TSC(X)7)	26	33	55
17 Modern Girl *Meat Loaf* (Arista ARIST (12) 585)	19	21	37
18 Penny Lover *Lionel Richie* (Motown TMG(T)1356)	18	22	30
19 Ghostbusters *Ray Parker Jr.* (Arista ARIST (12)580)	27	32	46
20 Never Ending Story *Limahl* (EMI (12)ML3)	10	5	4
40 I Should Have Known Better *Jim Diamond* (A&M AM(X)220)	13	3	2
28 I'm So Excited *Pointer Sisters* (Planet/RCA RPS(T)108)	16	14	11
32 Aces High *Iron Maiden* (EMI(12)EMI 5502)	20	25	43
39 Hard Habit To Break *Chicago* (Full Moon WEA W9214)	21	11	8
– Blasphemous Rumours/Someday *Depeche Mode* (Mute7BONG12" – 12BONG7)	26	16	17
– The Riddle *Nik Kershaw* (MCA NIK(T)6)	–	17	5
24 Gotta Get You Home Tonight *Eugene Wilde* (Fourth & Broadway/Island (12)BRW15)	22	18	23
62 Sexcrime (nineteen eighty-four) *Eurythmics* (Virgin VS728(12))	44	24	7
– Treat Her Like A Lady *The Temptations* (Motown TMG(T)1365)	–	26	12
50 Let It All Blow *Daz Band* (Motown TMG(T)1361)	35	28	14
75 I Won't Run Away *Alvin Stardust* (Chrysalis CHS(12)2829)	51	31	18
– All Join Hands *Slade* (RCA RCA(T)455)	–	38	20

DECEMBER 1984

1	8	15	22	29
1 I Should Have Known Better *Jim Diamond* (A&M AM(X)220)	2	6	18	20
2 I Feel For You *Chaka Khan* (Warner Brothers W9209(T))	6	14	21	25
3 The Power Of Love *Frankie Goes To Hollywood* (ZTT/Island (12)ZTAS5)	1	3	5	6
4 The Riddle *Nik Kershaw* (MCA NIK(T)6)	3	8	8	12
5 Never Ending Story *Limahl* (EMI(12)ML3)	10	18	27	33
6 Sexcrime (nineteen eighty-four) *Eurythmics* (Virgin VS728(12))	4	9	17	17
7 Teardrops *Shakin' Stevens* (Epic(T)A4882)	5	7	11	16
8 Hard Habit To Break *Chicago* (Full Moon WEA W9214)	11	24	29	34
9 The Wild Boys *Duran Duran* (Parlophone(12)DURAN3)	19	29	32	31
10 Caribbean Queen (No More Love On The Run) *Billy Ocean* (Jive(T)K77)	17	31	38	43
11 I Won't Run Away *Alvin Stardust* (Chrysalis CHS(12)289)	7	10	16	18
12 Let It All Blow *Daz Band* (Motown TMG(T)1361)	14	27	30	36
13 Treat Her Like A Lady *The Temptations* (Motown TMG(T)1365)	18	28	31	41
14 Louise *Human League* (Virgin VS723(12))	13	15	24	28
15 All Join Hands *Slade* (RCA RCA(T)455)	20	23	25	27
16 I'm So Excited *Pointer Sisters* (Planet RCA(T)455)	22	39	51	60
17 One Night In Bangkok *Murray Head* (RCA CHESS(T)1)	16	12	14	15

18 The Wanderer *Status Quo* (Vertigo/Phonogram QUO(P)16)	31	43	53	5!
19 Fresh *Kool & The Gang* (De-Lite/Phonogram DE(X)18)	12	11	12	1:
20 Freedom *Wham!* (Epic (T)A4743)	25	36	41	3!
27 Like A Virgin *Madonna* (Sire W9210(T))	8	5	4	!
39 We All Stand Together (from *Rupert and The Frog Song*) Paul McCartney (Parlophone R6086)	9	4	3	
26 Do The Conga *Black Lace* (Flair FLA108(T))	15	13	10	1
— Do They Know It's Christmas? *Band Aid* (Mercury/Phonogram FEED1(12))	−	1	1	
— Last Christmas/Everything She Wants *Wham!* (Epic(T)GA4949(12 − TA4949))	−	2	2	2
63 Nellie The Elephant *The Toy Dolls* (Volume VOL(T)11)	42	16	6	4
— Everything Must Change *Paul Young* (CBS(T)A4972)	39	17	9	9
— Round & Round *Spandau Ballet* (Reformation/Chrysalis SPAN(X)6)	23	19	19	22
— Lay Your Hands On Me *Thompson Twins* (Arista TWINS(12)6)	30	20	20	19
72 Another Rock And Roll Christmas *Gary Glitter* (MLM/Arista ARIST(12)592)	56	22	7	8
45 Shout *Tears For Fears* (Mercury/Phonogram IDEA8(12))	35	32	13	10
46 Ghostbusters *Ray Parker Jr.* (Arista ARIST(12)580)	43	33	15	7
— I Want To Know What Love Is *Foreigner* (Atlantic A9596(T))	67	41	26	11

1984 TOP SELLING RECORDS

Singles:

1 Do They Know It's Christmas *Band Aid* (Mercury/Phonogram)
2 I Just Called To Say I Love You *Stevie Wonder* (Motown)
3 Relax *Frankie Goes To Hollywood* (ZTT/Island)
4 Two Tribes *Frankie Goes To Hollywood* (ZTT/Island)
5 Careless Whisper *George Michael* (Epic)
6 Everything She Wants (Remix)/Last Christmas *Wham!* (Epic)
7 Hello *Lionel Richie* (Motown)
8 Agadoo *Black Lace* (Flair)
9 Ghostbusters *Ray Parker Jr.* (Arista)
10 Freedom *Wham!* (Epic)
11 Wake Me Up Before You Go *Wham!* (Epic)
12 I Feel For You *Chaka Khan* (Warner Brothers)
13 White Lines (Don't Do It) *Grandmaster & Melle Mel* (Sugar Hill)
14 We All Stand Together *Paul McCartney & The Frog Chorus* (Parlophone)
15 99 Red Balloons *Nena* (Epic)
16 The Power Of Love *Frankie Goes To Hollywood* (ZTT/Island)
17 The Reflex *Duran Duran* (EMI)
18 Like A Virgin *Madonna* (Sire)
19 Against All Odds (Take A Look At Me Now) *Phil Collins* (Virgin)
20 What's Love Got To Do With It *Tina Turner* (Capitol)
21 I Should Have Known Better *Jim Diamond* (A&M)
22 No More Lonely Nights (Ballad) *Paul McCartney* (Parlophone)
23 I Want To Break Free *Queen* (EMI)
24 Hole In My Shoe *Neil* (WEA)
25 Time After Time *Cyndi Lauper* (Portrait/Epic)
26 Radio Ga Ga *Queen* (EMI)
27 Together In Electric Dreams *Giorgio Moroder with Philip Oakey* (Virgin)
28 When Doves Cry *Prince* (Warner Brothers)
29 Doctor! Doctor! *Thompson Twins* (Arista)
30 Self Control *Laura Branigan* (Atlantic)
31 The War Song *Culture Club* (Virgin)
32 Girls Just Want To Have Fun *Cyndi Lauper* (Portrait/Epic)
33 The Wild Boys *Duran Duran* (EMI)
34 I Won't Let The Sun Go Down On Me *Nik Kershaw* (MCA)
35 Like To Get To Know You Well *Howard Jones* (WEA)
36 Nellie The Elephant *The Toy Dolls* (Volume)
37 Pride (In The Name Of Love) *U2* (Island)
38 Automatic *Pointer Sisters* (Planet/RCA)
39 Joanna *Kool & The Gang* (De-Lite/Phonogram)
40 That's Living Alright *Joe Fagin* (Towerbell)
41 Wouldn't It Be Good *Nik Kershaw* (MCA)
42 Street Dance *Break Machine* (Record Shack)
43 Smalltown Boy *Bronski Beat* (Forbidden Fruit/London)
44 Break My Stride *Matthew Wilder* (Epic)
45 The Riddle *Nik Kershaw* (MCA)
46 Dr Beat *Miami Sound Machine* (Epic)
47 Let's Hear It For The Boy *Deniece Williams* (CBS)
48 Never Ending Story *Limahl* (EMI)
49 Caribbean Queen (No More Love On The Run) *Billy Ocean* (Jive)
50 Whatever I Do (Wherever I Go) *Hazel Dean* (Probe)

Albums:

1 Can't Slow Down *Lionel Richie* (Motown)
2 The Hits Album/The Hits Tape *Various* (CBS/WEA)
3 Legend *Bob Marley & The Wailers* (Island)
4 Make It Big *Wham!* (Epic)
5 Now That's What I Call Music, 3 *Various* (Virgin/EMI)
6 Thriller *Michael Jackson* (Epic)
7 Diamond Life *Sade* (Epic)
8 Now That's What I Call Music, 4 *Various* (Virgin/EMI)
9 An Innocent Man *Billy Joel* (CBS)
10 The Pleasuredome *Frankie Goes To Hollywood* (ZTT/Island)
11 The Collection *Ultravox* (Chrysalis)
12 Into The Gap *Thompson Twins* (Arista)
13 Now That's What I Call Music, 2 *Various* (Virgin/EMI)
14 The Works *Queen* (EMI)
15 'Alf' *Alison Moyet* (CBS)
16 Human's Lib *Howard Jones* (WEA)
17 Eliminator *ZZ Top* (Warner Brothers)
18 Private Dancer *Tina Turner* (Capitol)
19 Party Time *Black Lace* (Telstar)
20 Parade *Spandau Ballet* (Reformation/Chrysalis)
21 The Unforgettable Fire *U2* (Island)
22 Human Racing *Nik Kershaw* (MCA)
23 Shakin' Stevens Greatest Hits *Shakin' Stevens* (Epic)
24 No Parlez *Paul Young* (CBS)
25 Alchemy — Dire Straits Live *Dire Straits* (Vertigo/Phonogram)
26 Touch *Eurythmics* (RCA)
27 Give My Love To Broad Street *Paul McCartney* (Parlophone)
28 U2 Live 'Under A Blood Red Sky' *U2* (Island)
29 Now That's What I Call Music *Various* (Virgin/EMI)
30 'Woman In Red' *Stevie Wonder/Dionne Warwick* (Motown)
31 Arena *Duran Duran* (Parlophone)
32 Yesterday Once More *Carpenters* (EMI)
33 Breaking Hearts *Elton John* (Rocket/Phonogram)
34 Break Out *Pointer Sisters* (Planet/RCA)
35 Colour By Numbers *Culture Club* (Virgin)
36 Cafe Bleu *The Style Council* (Polydor)
37 Born In The U.S.A. *Bruce Springsteen* (CBS)
38 The Smiths *The Smiths* (Rough Trade)
39 Cinema *Elaine Page* (K-Tel/WEA)
40 The Crossing *Big Country* (Mercury/Phonogram)
41 The Art Garfunkel Album *Art Garfunkel* (CBS)
42 The Riddle *Nik Kershaw* (MCA)
43 Music from 'Purple Rain' *Prince & The Revolution* (Warner Brothers)
44 Tonight *David Bowie* (EMI America)
45 Labour Of Love *UB40* (Dep International/Virgin)
46 Sparkle In The Rain *Simple Minds* (Virgin)
47 Queen's Greatest Hits *Queen* (EMI)
48 Original Soundtrack 'Footloose' *Various* (CBS)
49 Twelve Gold Bars Volume Two (And One) *Status Quo* (Vertigo)
50 The Age Of Consent *Bronski Beat* (Forbidden Fruit/London).

1985

Record Mirror readers voted Madonna the top female singer of 1985 − but she was more than that. The lady was *the* chart artist of the year. No-one had previously achieved eight singles in the Top Ten over a twelve-month period. Five of her hits came from the million-plus selling album Like A Virgin. Michael Jackson had been the only other artist to have had five Top Ten singles from an album, and in his case it was Thriller. One of those hits, 'The Girl Is Mine', was a duet with Paul McCartney. But interestingly, the same readers placed only Madonna's 'Into The Groove' amongst the top ten favourite singles of 1985. The lady with the top reader single was Kate Bush with her marvellous 'Running Up That Hill' from the stunning Hounds Of Love album.

Other artists had a good year, when it came to totting up the hits. Elton John, Phil Collins, Shakin' Stevens, Eurythmics (including the killer cut of Annie vocalising with guest Aretha Franklin on 'Sisters Are Doin' It For Themselves'), Go West (thanks to a late burst with 'Don't Look Down'), Level 42, Tears For Fears, Simple Minds, Bronski Beat and Wham! all had strong selling times.

Outside of the aforementioned excellent partnership between Annie Lennox and soul star Aretha Franklin, there was an equally much applauded merger of Chrissie Hynde with UB40 on the old Sonny and Cher smash 'I Got You Babe'.

The year had its familiars, from time to time, as with the chart veterans Siouxsie and the Banshees (first hit 1978), Queen (first hit 1974), Paul McCartney (1962 with the Beatles; 1972 Wings; McCartney 1971), Bruce Springsteen enjoying some of his finest British chart successes (UK album chart first in 1975), Dire Straits (1979), Alvin Stardust (1973 under this name; 1961 with Shane Fenton) and David Bowie (first hit 1969).

For others, 1985 will not be remembered with affection. Two mighty names from 1984, Frankie Goes To Hollywood and Culture Club (Boy George) achieved little. Gary Numan, Tracie, Howard Jones, The Human League, even Michael

Jackson, Kim Wilde and Nena, though hardly forgotten, saw little singles chart action during 1985; and Kim should have had more success than a mere single hit 'Rage To Love'. And there were others in similar plight. Duran Duran split into Arcadia and Power Station, but promised they would be together again to ensure Duran hits in 1986. Nick Beggs saw Kajagoogoo fold and Kaja take its place, and then that too died a death. Most had expected Beggs to ride the image and reach heights along with Weller of Style Council, Paul King of King, Pete Burns of Dead Or Alive, Robert Smith of The Cure and Morrissey of The Smiths — all artists whose varying styles helped to sell and chart records.

U2 and Bono, Paul Young, a returning Bryan Ferry, a triumphantly re-functioning Tina Turner, Midge Ure without Ultravox, Nik Kershaw and chart newcomer Jennifer Rush were much in evidence. Ms Rush's 'The Power Of Love' passed one million sales and became the year's best selling single. It also made her the first female singer to have a million seller, for until her record, only Elaine Paige and Barbara Dickson had come close, selling around 900,000 of their 'I Know Him So Well', a song that found its way on to at least six albums. But while those three ladies could rejoice, Madness could have shed a tear when their Uncle Sam (it reached 21!) failed to give them the 21st consecutive Top Twenty hit!

JANUARY 1985

5	12	19	26
1 Do They Know It's Christmas *Band Aid* (Mercury/Phonogram) FEED(1(12))	1	2	9
2 Everything She Wants (Remix)/Last Christmas *Wham!* (EpicQA4949(12" – QTA4949))	2	3	8
3 We All Stand Together (from *Rupert and The Frog Song*) *Paul McCartney* (Parlophone R6086)	5	11	27
4 Like A Virgin *Madonna* (Sire 9210(T))	3	4	7
5 Nellie The Elephant *Toy Dolls* (Volume VOL(T)11)	6	14	32
6 Ghostbusters *Ray Parker Jr.* (Arista ARIST(12) 580)	8	7	16
7 The Power Of Love *Frankie Goes To Hollywood* (ZTT/Island(12)ZTAS5)	10	20	35
8 Shout *Tears For Fears* (Mercury/Phonogram (IDEA8(12))	7	5	4
9 Everything Must Change *Paul Young* (CBS(T)A4972)	9	9	14
10 I Want To Know What Love Is *Foreigner* (Atlantic A9596)	4	1	1
11 The Riddle *Nik Kershaw* (MCA NIK(T)6)	14	32	55
12 Another Rock And Roll Christmas *Gary Glitter* (MLM/Arista ARIST(12)592)	31	–	–
13 Do The Conga *Black Lace* (Flair FLA108(T))	18	53	–
14 Fresh *Kool & The Gang* (De-Lite/Phonogram DE(X)18)	12	24	39
15 One Night In Bangkok *Murray Head* (RCA CHESS (T)1)	16	30	43
16 Lay Your Hands On Me *Thompson Twins* (Arista TWINS(12)6)	13	23	42
17 Sexcrime (nineteen eighty-four) *Eurythmics* (Virgin VS728(12))	22	47	72
18 Round & Round *Spandau Ballet* (Reformation/Chrysalis SPAN(X)6)	20	33	48
19 I Should Have Known Better *Jim Diamond* (A&M AM(X)220)	28	46	57
20 Teardrops *Shakin' Stevens* (Epic (T)A 4882)	27	71	–
30 Step Off *Grandmaster Melle Mel/Furious Five* (Sugar Hill/PRT SH(L)139)	11	8	11
34 Police Officer *Smiley Culture* (Fashion FAD7012(12" – FAD026))	15	12	15
37 San Damiano (Heart & Soul) *Sal Solo* (MCA MCA(T)930)	17	15	19
24 It Ain't Necessarily So *Bronski Beat* (Forbidden Fruit/London BITE(X)3)	19	16	23
63 I Know Him So Well *Elaine Page and Barbara Dickson* (RCA CHESS(T)1)	34	6	3
45 Since Yesterday *Strawberry Switchblade* (Korova KOW38(T))	32	10	5
– 1999/Little Red Corvette *Prince* (Warner Brothers W1999(T))	–	13	2
69 Friends *Amii Stewart* (RCA RCA(T)471)	39	17	12
52 Atmosphere *Russ Abbot* (Spirit FIRE(T)4)	40	18	10
50 Say Yeah *The Limit* (Portrait/Epic(T)A4808)	37	19	17
– Love & Pride *King* (CBS A4988(12" – TX4988))	45	21	6
75 Solid *Ashford & Simpson* (Capitol(12)CL345)	54	27	13
– This Is My Night *Chaka Khan* (Warner Brothers W9097)	–	28	18
– Dancing In The Dark *Bruce Springsteen* (CBS(T)A4436)	62	36	20

FEBRUARY 1985

2	9	16	23
1 I Want To Know What Love Is *Foreigner* (Atlantic A9596(T))	3	5	12
2 I Know Him So Well *Elaine Page and Barbara Dickson* (RCA CHESS(T)1)	1	1	1
3 Little Red Corvette/1999 *Prince* (Warner Brothers W1999(T))*	5	6	10

354

4	Love & Pride *King* (CBS A4988(12" – TX4988))	2	2	2
5	Solid *Ashford & Simpson* (Capitol(12) CL345)	4	3	3
6	Shout *Tears For Fears* (Mercury/Phonogram IDEA8(12))	8	16	23
7	Since Yesterday *Strawberry Switchblade* (Korova KOW38(T))	9	18	25
8	Atmosphere *Russ Abbot* (Spirit FIRE(T)4)	7	8	15
9	Like A Virgin *Madonna* (Sire 9210(T))	15	23	31
10	Dancing In The Dark *Bruce Springsteen* (CBS(T)A4436)	6	4	4
11	Everything She Wants (Remix) /Last Christmas *Wham!* (EpicQA4949(12" – QTA 4949))	21	33	38
12	Yah Mo B There (Remix) *James Ingram/Michael McDonald* (QWEST Q9394(T))	14	25	33
13	Friends *Amii Stewart* (RCA RCA(T)471)	20	27	36
14	This Is My Night *Chaka Khan* (Warner Brothers W9097(T))	24	35	52
15	Step Off *Grandmaster Melle Mel/Furious Five* (Sugar Hill/PRT SH(L)139)	28	38	37
16	Loverboy *Billy Ocean* (Jive JIVE(T)80)	16	15	16
17	Do They Know It's Christmas *Band Aid* (Mercury/Phonogram)FEED1(12)	30	38	37
18	Run To You (Specially Remixed Version) *Bryan Adams* (A&M AM(Y)224)	11	11	11
19	Sussudio *Phil Collins* (Virgin VS 736(12))	12	12	18
20	Ghostbusters *Ray Parker Jr.* (Arista ARIST (12) 580)	26	32	35
21	Close (To The Edit) *Art of Noise* (ZTT/Island(12)ZTPS01)	10	9	8
22	A New England *Kirsty MacColl* (Stiff BUY(IT)216)	13	10	7
31	Thinking Of You *The Colourfield* (Chrysalis COLF(X)3)	17	13	13
–	Things Can Only Get Better *Howard Jones* (WEA HOW6(T))	18	7	6
32	Nightshift *Commodores* (Motown TMG(T)1371)	19	17	9
–	This Is Not America *David Bowie* (EMI America (12)EA190)	22	14	17
42	You Spin Me Round (Like A Record) *Dead or Alive* (EpicA4861(12" – TX 4861))	40	19	5
41	You're The Inspiration *Chicago* (Full Moon/WEA W9126)	34	20	14
46	Love Like Blood *Killing Joke* (EG/Polydor EGO(X)20)	32	24	19
–	Change Your Mind *Sharpe and Numan* (Polydor POSP(X)722)	43	28	20

*Warner Brothers reversed the title credits for this record from those operative in January.

MARCH 1985

2		9	16	23	30
1	I Know Him So Well *Elaine Page and Barbara Dickson* (RCA CHESS(T)1)	2	8	10	28
2	You Spin Me Round (Like A Record) *Dead Or Alive* (Epic A4861(12" – TC4861))	1	1	6	12
3	Love & Pride *King* (CBS A4988(12" – TX4988))	8	17	24	41
4	Solid *Ashford & Simpson* (Capitol(12)CL 345)	6	12	21	32
5	Dancing In The Dark *Bruce Springsteen* (CBS(T)A4436)	9	13	13	27
6	Nightshift *Commodores* (Motown TMG(T)1371)	3	5	11	17
7	Things Can Only Get Better *Howard Jones* (WEA HOW6(T))	10	19	30	45
8	A New England *Kirsty MacColl* (Stiff BUY(IT)216)	14	25	47	–
9	Let's Go Crazy/Take Me With You *Prince and the Revolution* (Warner Brothers W2000(T))	7	10	16	30
10	Close (To The Edit) *Art Of Noise* (ZTT/Island(12)ZTPS01)	21	34	54	70
11	Run To You (Specially Remixed Version) *Bryan Adams* (A&M AM(Y)224)	17	27	36	66
12	Thinking Of You *The Colourfield* (Chrysalis COLF(X)3)	22	30	52	75
13	The Boys Of Summer *Don Henley* (Geffen(T)A4945)	12	20	23	37

14 You're The Inspiration *Chicago* (Full Moon/WEA W9126(T))	23	31	44	72
15 Little Red Corvette/1999 *Prince* (Warner Brothers W1999)	28	39	60	–
16 Love Like Blood *Killing Joke* (EG/Polydor EGO(X)20)	19	28	46	65
17 Change Your Mind *Sharpe & Numan* (Polydor POSP(X)722)	24	32	56	74
18 Loverboy *Billy Ocean* (Jive JIVE(T)80)	27	35	57	–
19 Theme From Shaft *Eddy & The Southband* (Club/Phonogram JAB(X)11)	13	23	27	46
20 Atmosphere *Russ Abbot* (Spirit FIRE(T)4)	35	49	69	–
22 Kiss Me *Stephen 'Tintin' Duffy* (10/Virgin TIN2(12))	4	4	5	9
24 Material Girl *Madonna* (Sire W9083(T))	5	3	3	7
34 The Last Kiss *David Cassidy* (MLM/Arista ARIST(12)589)	11	6	8	11
30 Breakin' Up My Heart *Shakin' Stevens* (Epic (T) A6072)	15	14	22	35
26 Legs (US Remix) *ZZ Top* (Warner Brothers W9272(T))	16	18	29	42
39 Do What You Do *Jermaine Jackson* (Arista ARIST(12)609)	18	7	7	6
– Easy Lover *Philip Bailey and Phil Collins* (CBS/Virgin(T)A4915)	20	2	1	1
– Every Time You Go Away *Paul Young* (CBS(T)A6300)	26	9	4	4
– That Ole Devil Called Love *Alison Moyet* (CBS(T)A6044)	–	11	2	2
– Wide Boy *Nik Kershaw* (MCA NIK(T)7)	–	15	12	10
44 We Close Our Eyes *Go West* (Chrysalis CHS(12)2850)	31	16	9	8
– Pie Jesu *Sarah Brightman and Paul Miles-Kingston* (His Master's Voice/EMI (12) WEBBER 1)	–	–	14	3
– Between The Wars (EP) *Billy Bragg* (Go!Discs AGEOP 1)	–	33	15	15
– Some Like It Hot *The Power Station* (Parlophone(12)R6091)	–	37	17	14
56 The Belle Of St. Mark *Sheila E* (Warner Brothers W9180)	39	24	18	22
47 Mr Telephone Man *New Edition* (MCA MCA(T)938)	40	26	19	20
42 Hangin' On A String (Contemplating) *Loose Ends* (Virgin VS748(12))	37	22	20	13
– Welcome To The Pleasure Dome *Frankie Goes To Hollywood* (ZTT/Island (12)ZTAS7)	–	–	–	5
– Everybody Wants To Rule The World *Tears For Fears* (Mercury/Phonogram (IDEA 9(12))	–	–	–	16
– Cover Me *Bruce Springsteen* (CBS(T)A4662)	–	–	32	18
58 Move Closer *Phyllis Nelson* (Carrere CAR(T)337)	48	44	28	19

APRIL 1985

6	13	20	27
1 Easy Lover *Philip Bailey and Phil Collins* (CBS/Virgin(T)A4915)	1	3	13
2 Welcome To The Pleasure Dome (Remix) *Frankie Goes To Hollywood* (ZTT/Island(12)ZTAS 7)	2	5	12
3 Pie Jesu *Sarah Brightman and Paul Miles Kingston* (His Master's Voice/EMI(12)WEBBER 1)	4	10	26
4 That Ole Devil Called Love *Alison Moyet* (CBS(T)A6044)	6	14	24
5 Everybody Wants To Rule The World *Tears For Fears* (Mercury/Phonogram IDEA 9(12))	3	2	2
6 We Close Our Eyes *Go West* (Chrysalis CHS(12)2850)	5	6	9
7 Every Time You Go Away *Paul Young* (CBS(T)A6300)	9	13	25
8 Do What You Do *Jermaine Jackson* (Arista ARIST(12)609)	12	21	38
9 Wide Boy *Nik Kershaw* (MCA NIK(T) 7)	11	18	29
10 Kiss Me *Stephen 'Tintin' Duffy* (10/Virgin TIN2(12))	15	27	40
11 Material Girl *Madonna* (Sire W 9083(T))	16	31	44

12 Could It Be I'm Falling In Love *David Grant & Jaki Graham* (Chrysalis GRAN(X)6)	10	7	5
13 Hangin' On A String (Contemplating) *Loose Ends* (Virgin VS748(12))	17	29	32
14 Move Closer *Phyllis Nelson* (Carrere CAR(T)337)	8	4	3
15 Some Like It Hot *The Power Station* (Parlophone (12)R6091)	21	28	43
16 Cover Me *Bruce Springsteen* (CBS(T)A4662)	20	34	42
17 The Heat Is On (from 'Beverly Hills Cop') *Glen Frey* (MCA MCA(T)941)	14	12	18
18 Spend The Night *The Cool Notes* (Abstract Dance/Priority AD(T)3)	13	11	16
19 The Last Kiss *David Cassidy* (MLM/Arista ARIST(12)589)	33	49	–
20 You Spin Me Round (Like A Record) *Dead Or Alive* (Epic A4861(12"TX 4861))	30	36	49
– We Are The World *USA for Africa* (CBS USAID(T)1)	7	1	1
27 Clouds Across The Moon *Rah Band* (RCA PB 40025(12" – PT40026))	18	9	6
28 Can't Fight This Feeling *Reo Speedwagon* (Epic(T)A4880)	19	16	21
– One More Night *Phil Collins* (Virgin VS755(12))	27	8	4
38 Life In A Northern Town *Dream Academy* (Blanco y negro WEA NEG10(T))	25	15	15
29 Love Is A Battlefield *Pat Benatar* (Chrysalis PAT(X)1)	23	17	17
40 Black Man Ray *China Crisis* (Virgin VS 752)	32	19	14
– Look Mama *Howard Jones* (WEA HOW 7(T))	–	20	10
– I Feel Love (Medley) *Bronski Beat* (Forbidden Fruit/LondonBITE(X)4)	–	24	7
– Don't You (Forget About Me) *Simple Minds* (Virgin VS749(12))	–	22	8
– Lover Come Back To Me *Dead Or Alive* (Epic(T)A6086)	–	23	11
– Eye To Eye (Remix) *Chaka Khan* (Warner Brothers W9009)	–	40	19
– Feel So Real *Steve Arrington* (Atlantic A9576(T))	–	–	20

The month's third week chart was dated incorrectly in *Music Week* for 27 April.

MAY 1985

4	11	18	25
1 Move Closer *Phyllis Nelson* (Carrere CAT(T)337)	2	2	4
2 We Are The World *USA For Africa* (CBS USAID(T)1)	5	17	33
3 Everybody Wants To Rule The World *Tears For Fears* (Mercury/Phonogram IDEA9(12))	4	9	15
4 19 *Paul Hardcastle* (Chrysalis CHS(12)2860)	1	1	1
5 I Feel Love (Medley) *Bronski Beat* (Forbidden Fruit/London BITE(X)4)	3	3	5
6 One More Night *Phil Collins* (Virgin VS755(12))	10	16	34
7 Don't You (Forget About Me) *Simple Minds* (Virgin VS749(12))	8	10	13
8 The Unforgettable Fire *U2* (Island (12)IS220)	6	12	26
9 Clouds Across The Mood *Rah Band* (RCA PB40025(12" – PT40026))	12	21	41
10 Could It Be That I'm Falling In Love *David Grant & Jaki Graham* (Chrysalis GRAN(X)6)	15	30	45
11 Feel So Real *Steve Arrington* (Atlantic A9576)	7	5	8
12 Lover Come Back To Me *Dead Or Alive* (Epic(T)A6086)	14	27	32
13 Look Mama *Howard Jones* (WEA-HOW7(T))	18	29	48
14 I Was Born To Love You *Freddie Mercury* (CBS(T)A6019)	11	11	12
15 Black Man Ray *China Crisis* (Virgin VS752(12))	24	42	58
16 Eye To Eye (Remix) *Chaka Khan* (Warner Brothers W9009)	21	37	55
17 Rhythm Of The Night *Debarge* (Gordy TMG(T)1376)	9	4	6

18 We Close Our Eyes *Go West* (Chrysalis CHS(12)2850)	27	43	70
19 Easy Lover *Philip Bailey and Phil Collins* (CBS/Virgin(T)A4915)	34	46	60
20 So Far Away *Dire Straits* (Vertigo/Phonogram DSTR9(12))	23	41	64
− Walls Come Tumbling Down *The Style Council* (Polydor TSC(X)8)	13	6	9
22 I Want Your Lovin' (Just A Little Bit) *Curtis Hairston* (London LON(X)66)	16	13	22
25 Would I Lie To You *Eurythmics* (RCA PB40101 (12" − PT40102))	17	18	25
29 Cry *Godley & Creme* (Polydor POSP(X)732)	19	19	23
39 Love Don't Live Here Anymore *Jimmy Nail* (Virgin VS 764)	20	8	3
− A View To Kill *Duran Duran* (Parlophone DURAN 007)	−	7	2
− Slave To Love *Bryan Ferry* (EG Records/Polydor FERRY1(12" − FERRx1))	30	14	11
− Kayleigh *Marillion* (EMI(12)MARIL3)	−	15	7
− Magic Touch *Loose Ends* (Virgin VS761(12))	33	20	16
− We All Follow Man. United *Manchester United Football Team* (Columbia DB9107)	−	35	10
− Here We Go *Everton 1985* (The Official Team Record) (Columbia DB9106)	44	32	14
− Call Me *Go West* (Chrysalis GOW(X))	36	24	17
− Out In The Fields *Gary Moore & Phil Lynott* (10/Virgin TEN49(12))	−	31	18
38 Rage To Love *Kim Wilde* (MCA KIM(T)3)	29	22	19
56 Walking On Sunshine *Katrina and the Waves* (Capitol(12) CL354)	41	39	20

JUNE 1985

	8	15	22	29
1 1 19 *Paul Hardcastle* (Chrysalis CHS(12)2860)	1	3	14	16
2 A View To Kill *Duran Duran* (Parlophone DURAN 007)	2	6	11	15
3 Love Don't Live Here Anymore *Jimmy Nail* (Virgin VS764(12))	7	18	25	42
4 Kayleigh *Marillion* (EMI(12)MARIL3)	3	2	4	7
5 Rhythm Of The Night *DeBarge* (Gordy TMG(T)1376)	11	22	27	40
6 Move Closer *Phyllis Nelson* (Carrere CAR(T)337)	17	25	29	39
7 I Feel Love (Medley) *Bronski Beat* (Forbidden Fruit/London BITE(X)4)	15	27	35	55
8 Out In The Fields *Gary Moore* (10/Virgin TEN49(12))	5	7	16	20
9 Walking On Sunshine *Katrina and the Waves* (Capitol (12)CL354)	8	12	17	24
10 Slave To Love *Bryan Ferry* (EG/Polydor FERRx 1)	13	26	34	47
11 I Feel So Real *Steve Arrington* (Atlantic A9576(T))	20	33	47	72
12 Obsession *Animotion* (Mercury/Phonogram PH34(12))	6	5	8	13
13 Call Me *Go West* (Chrysalis GOW(X)1)	12	17	23	31
14 We All Follow Man. United *Manchester United Football Team* (Columbia DB9107)	33	58	−	−
15 The Word Girl *Scritti Politti* (Virgin VS 747(12))	10	8	6	10
16 Walls Come Tumbling Down *The Style Council* (Polydor TSC(X)8)	28	46	74	−
17 Magic Touch *Loose Ends* (Virgin VS761(12))	26	35	52	−
18 I Was Born To Love You *Freddie Mercury* (CBS (T)A6019)	31	36	51	−
19 Suddenly *Billy Ocean* (Jive JIVE(T)90)	9	4	5	6
20 Icing On The Cake *Stephen 'Tintin' Duffy* (10/Virgin TIN3(12))	14	14	20	27
52 You'll Never Walk Alone *The Crowd* (Spartan BRAD1)	4	1	1	3

JULY 1985

359

		39	18	10
–	Living On Video ('85 Re-Mix) *Trans-X* (Boiling Point/Polydor POSP (X)650)	39	18	10
30	She Sells Sanctuary *The Cult* (Beggars Banquet BEG 135(T))	26	19	19
–	Into The Groove *Madonna* (Sire W8934(T))	–	–	4
–	We Don't Need Another Hero (Thunderdome) *Tina Turner* (Capitol(12)CL364)	–	37	11
65	Money For Nothing *Dire Straits* (Vertigo/Phonogram DSTR10(12))	47	39	15
–	White Wedding *Billy Idol* (Chrysalis IDOL(X)5)	52	34	18
–	All Night Holiday *Russ Abbot* (Spirit FREE(T)6)	35	25	20

AUGUST 1985

3		10	17	24	31
1	Into The Groove *Madonna* (Sire W8394(T)	1	1	1	2
2	There Must Be An Angel (Playing With My Fire) *Eurythmics* (RCA PB 40247(12″ – PT40248)	2	6	9	14
3	We Don't Need Another Hero (Thunderdome) *Tina Turner* (Capitol(12)CL364)	3	4	7	10
4	Frankie *Sister Sledge* (Atlantic A9547(T))	10	17	21	32
5	Axel F *Harold Faltermeyer* (MCA MCA(T)949)	12	16	23	25
6	Live Is Life *Opus* (Polydor POSP(X)743)	9	12	16	24
7	Cherish *Kool & The Gang* (De-Lite/Phonogram DE(X)743)	8	14	18	20
8	Money For Nothing *Dire Straits* (Vertigo/Phonogram DSTR(10)12)	4	5	6	8
9	Living On Video ('85 Re-Mix) *Trans-X* (Boiling Point/Polydor POSP(X)650)	13	18	28	41
10	Round And Around *Jaki Graham* (EMI(12)JAKI4)	14	21	30	35
11	White Wedding *Billy Idol* (Chrysalis IDOL(X)5)	6	7	8	11
12	Crazy For You *Madonna* (Geffen A6323)	15	19	24	31
13	My Toot Toot *Denise LaSalle* (Epic A6334(12″ – TX6334))	18	30	37	55
14	In Your Car *The Cool Notes* (Abstract Dance/Priority AD(T)4)	20	32	35	51
15	She Sells Sanctuary *The Cult* (Beggars Banquet BEG135(T))	19	24	31	53
16	Money's Too Tight (To Mention) *Simply Red* (Elektra EKR9(T))	24	37	50	66
17	Dare Me *Pointer Sisters* (Planet PB49957(12″ – PT49958))	22	31	38	50
18	Let Me Be The One *Five Star* (Tent/RCA PB40193(12″ – PT40194))	21	22	27	29
19	I'm On Fire/Born In The USA *Bruce Springsteen* (CBS(T)A6342)	29	36	41	69
20	In Between Days *The Cure* (Fiction/Polydor FICS(X)22)	16	15	20	28
32	Holiday *Madonna* (Sire W9405)	5	2	3	6
22	I Got You Babe *UB40, guest vocals by Chrissie Hynde* (DEP International/Virgin DEP20(12))	7	3	2	1
23	Don Quixote *Nik Kershaw* (MCA NIK(T)8)	11	10	14	21
21	Glory Days *Bruce Springsteen* (CBS(T)A6375)	17	20	33	52
56	Drive *The Cars* (Elektra E9706(T))	32	8	5	4
54	Say I'm Your Number One *Princess* (Supreme SUPE(T)101)	31	11	10	7
–	Running Up That Hill *Kate Bush* (EMI(12)KB1)	–	9	4	3
35	Excitable *Amazulu* (Island(12)IS201)	25	13	12	13
–	Tarzan Boy *Baltimore* (Columbia(12)DB9102)	51	33	11	5
–	Alone Without You *King* (CBS(T)A6308)	–	29	13	9

53 I Wonder If I Take You Home *Lisa Lisa and Cult Jam with Full Force* (CBS(T)A6057)   39 26 15 12
43 You're The One For Me (Paul Hardcastle Mix) *D Train* (Prelude/RCAZB40301 (12" – ZT40302))   40 27 17 15
38 Take Me Home *Phil Collins* (Virgin VS777(12))   28 28 19 19
– I Can Dream About You *Dan Hartman* (MCA MCA(T)988)   – – 40 16
65 Takes A Little Time *Total Contrast* (London LON(X)71)   49 40 22 17
64 Body And Soul *Mai Tai* (Hot Melt/Virgin VS801(12))   43 41 36 18

SEPTEMBER 1985

7		14	21	28
1 Dancing In The Street *David Bowie And Mick Jagger* (EMI America(12)FA204)		1	1	1
2 I Got You Babe *UB40, guest vocals by Chrissie Hynde* (DEP International Virgin DEP20(12))		3	6	14
3 Tarzan Boy *Baltimore* (Columbia(12)DB 9102)		4	4	9
4 Into The Groove *Madonna* (Sire W8934(T))		7	12	20
5 Running Up The Hill *Kate Bush* (EMI(12)KB1)		8	15	23
6 Drive *The Cars* (Electra E9706(T))		6	13	19
7 Say I'm Your Number One *Princess* (Supreme SUPE(T)101)		9	14	26
8 Alone Without You *King* (CBS(T)A6308)		11	19	29
9 Money For Nothing *Dire Straits* (Vertigo/Phonogram DSTR10(12))		14	21	27
10 Holding Out For A Hero *Bonnie Tyler* (CBS(T)A4251)		2	2	2
11 Body And Soul *Mai Tai* (Hot Melt/Virgin VS801(12))		10	9	10
12 I Can Dream About You *Dan Hartman* (MCA MCA(T)988)		15	22	33
13 I Wonder If I Take You Home *Lisa Lisa and Cult Jam with Full Force* (CBS(T)A6057)		17	24	30
14 Holiday *Madonna* (Sire W9405(T))		23	33	42
15 Don't Mess With Dr. Dream *Thompson Twins* (Arista TWINS(12)9)		16	26	37
16 Knock On Wood/Light My Fire (Remix) *Amii Stewart* (Sedition EDIT(L)3303)		12	7	8
17 White Wedding *Billy Idol* (Chrysalis IDOL(X)5)		20	30	39
18 We Don't Need Another Hero (Thunderdome) *Tina Turner* (Capitol(12)CL364)		25	32	41
19 You're The One For Me (Paul Hardcastle Mix) *D Train* (Prelude/RCA ZB 40301(12" – ZT40302)		24	34	45
20 Part-Time Lover *Stevie Wonder* (Motown ZB40351(12" – ZT40352))		5	3	3
23 Lavender *Marillion* (EMI(12)MARIL4)		13	5	7
21 Yesterday's Men *Madness* (Zarjazz/Virgin JAZZ5(12))		18	20	28
31 Power Of Love *Huey Lewis And The News* (Chrysalis HUEY(X)1)		19	11	12
– If I Was *Midge Ure* (Chrysalis URE(X)1)		29	8	4
– Angel *Madonna* (Sire W8881(T))		–	10	5
38 Body Rock (Original Soundtrack) *Maria Vidal* (EMI America(12)EA189)		26	16	11
– She's So Beautiful (from the Musical 'Time') *Cliff Richard* (EMI(12)EMI5531)		33	17	18
43 Lean On Me (ah-li-ayo) *Red Box* (Sire W8926(T))		30	18	6
– Rebel Yell *Billy Idol* (Chrysalis IDOL(X)6)		38	25	13
49 The Power Of Love *Jennifer Rush* (CBS A5003(12" – TX5003)		42	36	15
41 Trapped *Colonel Abrams* (MCA MCA(T)997)		34	28	16
– The Lodgers *Style Council* (Polydor TSC(X)10)		–	–	17

OCTOBER 1985

	12	19	26
5			
1 If I Was *Midge Ure* (Chrysalis URE(X)1)	2	2	8
2 The Power Of Love *Jennifer Rush* (CBS A 5003(12″ – TX5003))	1	1	1
3 Dancing In The Street *David Bowie and Mick Jagger* (EMI America(12)EA204)	7	13	21
4 Lean On Me (ah-li-ayo) *Red Box* (Sire W8926(T))	3	4	10
5 Part-Time Lover *Stevie Wonder* (Motown ZB-40351(12″-ZT40352)	5	11	16
6 Angel *Madonna* (Sire W8881(T))	8	16	30
7 Holding Out For A Hero *Bonnie Tyler* (CBS(T)A4251)	9	12	18
8 Rebel Yell *Billy Idol* (Chrysalis IDOL(X)6)	6	9	11
9 Lavender *Marillion* (EMI (12)MARIL4)	13	32	42
10 Trapped *Colonel Abrams* (MCA MCA(T)997)	4	3	3
11 The Power Of Love *Huey Lewis and the News* (Chrysalis HUEY(X)1)	15	26	40
12 Body Rock (Original Soundtrack) *Maria Vidal* (EMI America(12)EA189)	11	20	22
13 The Lodgers *The Style Council* (Polydor TSC(X)10)	18	34	44
14 Knock On Wood/Light My Fire (Remix) *Amii Stewart* (Sedition/PRT EDIT(L)3303)	21	35	55
15 Body and Soul *Mai Tai* (Hot Melt/Virgin VS801(12)	27	44	64
16 Tarzan Boy *Baltimora* (Columbia (12)DB9102)	28	43	73
17 She's So Beautiful (from the musical Time) *Cliff Richard* (EMI(12)EMI5531)	17	22	25
18 It's Called A Heart *Depeche Mode* (Mute 7BONG9(12″-12BONG9)	36	53	–
19 Brand New Friend *Lloyd Cole and the Commotions* (Polydor COLE(X)4)	29	38	57
20 Running Free *Iron Maiden* (EMI (12)EMI 5532)	19	27	43
27 St. Elmo's Fire (Man In Motion) *John Parr* (London LON(X)73)	10	6	6
– Alive & Kicking *Simple Minds* (Virgin VS817(12))	12	8	7
36 Take On Me *Aha* (Warner Brothers W9006)	14	5	2
21 Single Life *Cameo* (Club/Phonogram JAB(X)21)	16	15	19
– Gambler *Madonna* (Geffen A6585)	20	7	4
– Miami Vice Theme *Jan Hammer* (MCA MCA(T)1000)	30	10	5
– Slave To The Rhythm *Grace Jones* (ZTT/Island(12)IS206)	33	14	12
31 Rain *The Cult* (Beggars Banquet BEG14(T))	26	17	17
– Lipstick, Powder And Paint *Shakin' Stevens* (Epic A6610)	39	18	15
– Nikita *Elton John* (Rocket/Phonogram EJS9(12)	41	19	9
39 Something About You *Level 42* (Polydor POSP(X) 759)	31	21	13
– Election Day *Arcadia* (Parlophone Odeon Series(12)NSR1)	–	–	14
– The Taste Of Your Tears *King* (CBS(T)A6618)	–	37	20

NOVEMBER 1985

	9	16	23	30
2				
1 The Power Of Love *Jennifer Rush* (CBS A5003(12″ – TX5003))	1	2	4	5
2 Take On Me *A-Ha!* (Warner Brothers W9006(T))	2	3	5	12
3 Trapped *Colonel Abrams* (MCA MCA(T)997)	5	7	13	20
4 Nikita *Elton John* (Rocket/Phonogram EJS9(12)	3	4	6	15
5 Gambler *Madonna* (Geffen(T)A6585)	8	14	22	38
6 St. Elmo's Fire (Man In Motion) *John Parr* (London LON(X)73)	9	17	27	44

		9	6	23	30
7	Election Day *Arcadia* (Parlophone Odeon Series(12)NSR1)	10	16	32	52
8	Miami Vice Theme *Jon Hammer* (MCA MCA(T)1000)	14	23	31	48
9	Something About You *Level 42* (Polydor POSP(X)759)	6	6	8	13
10	Alive & Kicking *Simple Minds* (Virgin VS817(12))	11	18	34	43
11	Lipstick, Powder And Paint *Shakin' Stevens* Epic ((T)A6610)	15	20	35	46
12	A Good Heart *Feargal Sharkey* (Virgin VS808(12))	4	1	1	2
13	Slave To The Rhythm *Grace Jones* (ZTT/Island(12)IS206)	19	26	38	50
14	Lean On Me, etc. *Red Box* (Sire WB8926(T))	25	36	55	–
15	The Taste Of Your Tears *King* (CBS(T)A6618)	12	11	15	23
16	If I Was *Midge Ure* (Chrysalis URE(X)1)	24	37	58	–
17	Yeh Yeh *Matt Bianco* (WEA YZ46(T))	13	15	30	47
18	Rebel Yell *Billy Idol* (Chrysalis IDOL(X)6)	26	35	60	73
19	Don't Break My Heart *UB40* (Dep International/Virgin DEP22(12))	7	5	3	3
20	Cloudbusting *Kate Bush* (EMI (12)KB2)	20	27	43	60
23	Stairway To Heaven *Far Corporation* (Arista ARIST(12)639)	16	8	11	17
26	Road To Nowhere *Talking Heads* (EMI(12)EMI5530)	17	12	10	6
38	Sisters Are Doin' It For Themselves *Eurythmics and Aretha Franklin* (RCA PB 40339 (12″ PT 0440)	18	10	9	14
–	One Vision *Queen* (EMI(12)QUEEN 6)	–	9	7	8
–	The Show *Doug E Fresh & The Get Fresh Crew* (Cooltempo/Chrysalis COOL(X)116)	22	13	12	7
–	Just For Money *Paul Hardcastle* (Chrysalis CASH(X)1)	31	19	20	36
–	I'm Your Man *Wham!* (Epic(T)A6716)	–	–	2	1
–	Say You, Say Me *Lionel Richie* (Motown ZB 40422(12″-ZT40422))	–	34	14	11
39	Brothers In Arms *Dire Straits* (Vertigo/Phonogram DSTR11(12))	23	22	16	18
–	Lost Weekend *Lloyd Cole And The Commotions* (Polydor COLE(X)5)	37	24	17	19
–	See The Day *Dee C. Lee* (CBS A6570(12″-TX6570))	51	38	18	4
–	That's What Friends Are For *Dionne Warwick & Friends* (Arista (12)ARIST638)	49	33	19	16
–	Saving All My Love For You *Whitney Houston* (Arista ARIST(12)640)	–	60	23	9
–	Separate Lives *Phil Collins & Marilyn Martin* (Virgin VS 818)	–	–	25	10

7		14	21	28
1	I'm Your Man *Wham!* (Epic (T)A6716)	2	4	8
2	Saving All My Love For You *Whitney Houston* (Arista ARIST(12)640)	1	1	2
3	See The Day *Dee C. Lee* (CBS A6570(12"-TX6570))	3	6	10
4	A Good Heart *Feargal Sharkey* (Virgin VS 808(12))	7	13	18
5	Separate Lives *Phil Collins & Marilyn Martin* (Virgin VS818(12))	4	7	7
6	Don't Break My Heart *UB40* (Dep International/Virgin DEP22(12))	12	20	27
7	The Show *Dough E Fresh & The Get Fresh Crew* (Cooltempo/Chrysalis COOL(X)116)	11	18	24
8	Road To Nowhere *Talking Heads* (EMI(12)EMI5530)	15	24	29
9	Say You Say Me *Lionel Richie* (Motown ZB 40421(12"-ZT40422)	8	11	14
10	The Power Of Love *Jennifer Rush* (CBS A5003(12"-ZTX5003))	27	21	22
11	Nikita *Elton John* (Rocket/Phonogram EJS9(12))	18	33	45
12	Dress You Up *Madonna* (Sire W8848)	5	8	9
13	Don't Look Down — The Sequel *Go West* (Chrysalis GOW(X)3)	13	15	19
14	Take On Me *Aha* (Warner Brothers W9006(T))	23	34	37
15	One Vision *Queen* (EMI(12) QUEEN6)	25	38	46
16	That's What Friends Are For *Dionne Warwick & Friends* (Arista ARIST 638)	21	31	35
17	Spies Like Us *Paul McCartney* (Parlophone (12)&6118)	16	16	16
18	Sisters Are Doin' It For Themselves *Eurythmics and Aretha Franklin* (RCA PB 40339(12"-PT40340))	29	37	49
19	We Built This City *Starship* (RCA PB49929(12"-FT 49930))	14	12	12
20	Mated *David Grant/Jaki Graham* (EMI(12)JAK16)	20	30	41
24	Do They Know Its Christmas? *Band Aid* (Mercury/Phonogram FEED1(12))	6	3	3
23	West End Girls *Pet Shop Boys* (Parlophone(12)R6115)	9	5	4
38	Merry Christmas Everyone *Shakin' Stevens* (Epic(T)A6769)	10	2	1
–	Santa Claus Is Comin' To Town/My Hometown *Bruce Springsteen* (CBS A6773)	17	9	11
33	Don't You Just Know It *Amazulu* (Island (12)S 233)	19	19	17
–	Last Christmas *Wham!* (Epic WHAM(T)1)	32	10	6
45	Walking In The Air *Aled Jones* (EMI(12) ALED1)	37	14	5
39	Hit That Perfect Beat *Bronski Beat* Forbidden Fruit/London BITE(X)6	26	17	13
61	Girlie Girlie *Sophie George* (Winner WIN(T)01)	39	25	15
43	Wrap Her Up *Elton John* (Rocket/Phonogram EJS10(12))	34	23	20

1985 BEST SELLING RECORDS

Singles:

1 The Power of Love *Jennifer Rush* (CBS)
2 I Know Him So Well *Elaine Paige and Barbara Dickson* (RCA)
3 Into the Groove *Madonna* (Sire)
4 19 *Paul Hardcastle* (Chrysalis)
5 Frankie *Sister Sledge* (Atlantic)
6 Dancing In The Street *David Bowie and Mick Jagger* (EMI America)
7 Move Closer *Phyllis Nelson* (Carrere)
8 A Good Heart *Feargal Sharkey* (Virgin)
9 Take On Me *a-ha* (Warner Brothers)
10 Love & Pride *King* (CBS)
11 I Want To Know What Love Is *Foreigner* (Atlantic)
12 Easy Lover *Philip Bailey/Phil Collins* (CBS/Virgin)
13 Axel F *Harold Faltermeyer* (MCA)
14 Do They Know It's Christmas? *Band Aid* (Mercury/Phonogram)
15 I Got You Babe *UB40 Guest Vocals by Chrissie Hynde* (DEP International/Virgin)
16 Crazy For You *Madonna* (Geffen)
17 Saving All My Love For You *Whitney Houston* (Arista)
18 Solid *Ashford & Simpson* (Capitol)
19 You Spin Me Round (Like A Record) *Dead Or Alive* (Epic)
20 There Must Be An Angel (Playing With My Heart) *Eurythmics* (RCA)
21 I'm Your Man *Wham!* (Epic)
22 Trapped *Colonel Abrams* (MCA)
23 Cherish *Kool & The Gang* (De-Lite/Phonogram)
24 Everybody Want's To Rule The World *Tears For Fears* (Mercury/Phonogram)
25 Merry Christmas Everyone *Shakin' Stevens* (Epic)
26 You'll Never Walk Alone *The Crowd* (Spartan)
27 If I Was *Midge Ure* (Chrysalis)
28 Nikita *Elton John* (Rocket/Phonogram)
29 Dancing In The Dark *Bruce Springsteen* (CBS)
30 Little Red Corvette/1999 *Prince* (Warner Brothers)
31 Holding Out For A Hero *Bonnie Tyler* (CBS)
32 Kayleigh *Marillion* (EMI)
33 Last Christmas *Wham!* (Epic)
34 A View To A Kill *Duran Duran* (Parlophone)
35 We Are The World *USA For Africa* (CBS)
36 Lean On Me (ah-li-ayo) *Red Box* (Sire)
37 Part-Time Lover *Stevie Wonder* (Motown)
38 Money For Nothing *Dire Straits* (Vertigo/Phonogram)
39 Don't Break My Heart *UB40* (DEP International/Virgin)
40 We Close Our Eyes *Go West* (Chrysalis)
41 Nightshift *Commodores* (Motown)
42 That Old Devil Called Love *Alison Moyet* (CBS)
43 We Don't Need Another Hero (Thunderdome) *Tina Turner* (Capitol)
44 Tarzan Boy *Baltimora* (Columbia)
45 See The Day *Dee C. Lee* (CBS)
46 Kiss Me *Stephen 'Tintin' Duffy* (10/Virgin)
47 I Feel Love (Medley) *Bronski Beat/Marc Almond* (Forbidden Fruit/London)
48 Welcome to the Pleasuredome *Frankie Goes to Hollywood* (ZTT)
49 Suddenly *Billy Ocean* (Jive)
50 Shout *Tears For Fears* (Mercury/Phonogram)

Albums:

1 Brothers In Arms *Dire Straits* (Vertigo/Phonogram)
2 No Jacket Required *Phil Collins* (Virgin)
3 Like A Virgin *Madonna* (Sire)
4 Born In The U.S.A. *Bruce Springsteen* (CBS)
5 Songs From The Big Chair *Tears For Fears* (Mercury)
6 Now, That's What I Call Music 6 *Various* (EMI/Virgin)
7 Now – The Christmas Album *Various* (EMI/Virgin)
8 Now, That's What I Call Music 5 *Various* (EMI/Virgin)
9 Hits 2 *Various* (CBS/WEA)
10 The Secret Of Assiciation *Paul Young* (CBS)
11 Alf *Alison Moyet* (CBS)
12 Hits 3 *Various* (CBS/WEA)
13 The Love Songs *George Benson* (K-tel/WEA)
14 Hounds of Love *Kate Bush* (EMI)
15 Be Yourself Tonight *Eurythmics* (RCA)
16 Private Dancer *Tina Turner* (Capitol)
17 Promise *Sade* (Epic)
18 Make It Big *Wham!* (Epic)
19 Diamond Life *Sade* (Epic)
20 Misplaced Childhood *Marillion* (EMI)
21 Eliminator *ZZ Top* (Warner Brothers)
22 The Singles Collection *Spandau Ballet* (Chrysalis)
23 Boys and Girls *Bryan Ferry* (EG/Polydor)
24 Go West *Go West* (Chrysalis)
25 Agent Provocateur *Foreigner* (Atlantic)
26 Reckless *Bryan Adams* (A&M)
27 The Kenny Rogers Story *Kenny Rogers* (Liberty)
28 Greatest Hits Volume 1 & 2 *Billy Joel* (CBS)
29 Greatest Hits of 1985 *Various* (Telstar)
30 The Unforgettable Fire *U2* (Island)
31 Out Now *Various* (Chrysalis/MCA)
32 Hits Out Of Hell *Meat Loaf* (Cleveland International/Epic)
33 Welcome To The Pleasure Dome *Frankie Goes To Hollywood* (ZTT/Island)
34 The Age Of Consent *Bronski Beat* (Forbidden Fruit/London)
35 Live "Under A Blood Red Sky" *U2* (Island)
36 Once Upon A Time *Simple Minds* (Virgin)
37 The Dream of Blue Turtles *Sting* (A&M)
38 The First Album *Madonna* (Sire)
39 Dream Into Action *Howard Jones* (WEA)
40 The Love Album *Various* (Telstar)
41 The Collection *Ultravox* (UTV)
42 The Hita Album/The Hits Tape *Various* (CBS/WEA)
43 Queen Greatest Hits *Queen* (EMI)
44 Voices From The Holy Land *Aled Jones* (BBC)
45 Ice On Fire *Elton John* (Rocket)
46 All Through The Night *Aled Jones with BBC Welsh Symph. Orch.* (BBC)
47 Now, That's What I Call Music 4 *Various* (EMI/Virgin)
48 Requiem – Andrew Lloyd Webber *Placido Domingo/Sarah Brightman* (HMV/EMI)
49 Love Hurts *Elaine Paige* (WEA)
50 Face Value *Phil Collins* (Virgin)

1986

The chart artist of 1985, Madonna was soon achieving more statistical success with her January hit 'Borderline' and so giving her ten successive Top 20 hits. In its previous 1984 incarnation, 'Borderline' achieved no more than position 56. To come were other hit singles, 'Live to Tell' 'Papa Don't Preach', 'True Blue' and 'Open Your Heart'. Along with Madonna, women were well to the fore. Cherrelle helped Alexander O'Neal, Aretha Franklin asked 'Who's Zoomin' Who?' Nana Mouskouri almost made number one and with Denise LaSalle (51) and Gracie Fields (59) became one of the oldest women ever to make the charts. Grace Jones, the girls of Five Star, Sarah Brightman (with Steve Harley), Su Pollard, Rochelle, Diana Ross and Whitney Houston were other females who charted. Houston sold a cool thirteen million worldwide of her debut self-titled album. Sinatra's surprise major hit 'Theme From New York, New York' could thank disco land for better times than its Number 59 peak in 1980. Diana Ross had her first chart-topper in fifteen years with the Gibb Brothers composition 'Chain Reaction;' it was her 36th single hit. The Young Ones release became the fifth charity record of its kind to top the chart, and gave Cliff Richard his eleventh Number One. Another Revival was The Real Thing's, 'You To Me Are Everything'. Michael Jackson's sister Janet had her first Top 20 hit with 'What Have You Done For Me Lately'. It was the year that saw the successful marriage of old hits with television advertising, producing offspring such as Sam Cooke's 'Wonderful World', Marvin Gaye's 'I Heard It Through The Grapevine' and Jackie Wilson's 'Reet Petite.' Wham! made history by taking the first 7-inch double-pack to Number One with 'The Edge of Heaven', previously there had been limited editions. 'I Can't Stop' was Gary Numan's twenty-first successive hit, excluding a release from his old company. Lulu remade her old hit 'Shout' after 22 years and the song proved very good for her once more, while the oldie version also sold a few copies. The BBC television series *Eastenders* spawned major hits for Anita Dobson and Nick Berry but other artists from the show were not so well received. Status Quo reached their twentieth Top Ten single with 'In The Army Now', only the third group ever to do so. Film themes have always proved useful for record companies and artists seeking hits and career exposure. Berlin's theme from *Top Gun*, 'Take My Breath Away' was the year's most successful, and was yet another hit for the 'fifty hits and more man', Georgio Moroder. Another remake, 'You Keep Me Hangin' On' gave Kim Wilde her second Number Two since Kids In America back in 1981; she also found the top spot in the USA. Arguably, Madonna again took the year. But even she didn't achieve the record of Whitney Houston's three successive Number One's when 'Greatest Love Of My Life' during 1986 provided her third top hit.

Because record label matrix numbers became so complex – a result of multi-format releases, independent and major joint distributions and an increasing use of origination credit within the matrix – charts hereon omit such details in the interests of primary information preceding ancillary data within a limited amount of space.

4	11	18	25
1 Merry Christmas Everyone *Shakin' Stevens* (Epic)	3	20	42
2 Saving All My Love For You *Whitney Houston* (Arista)	2	9	19
3 West End Girls *Pet Shop Boys* (Parlophone)	1	1	3
4 Do They Know It's Christmas *Band Aid* (Mercury)	13	47	–
5 Walking In The Air *Aled Jones* (HMV)	8	18	30
6 Last Christmas *Wham!* (Epic)	14	36	68
7 Dress You Up *Madonna* (Sire)	6	21	32
8 I'm Your Man *Wham!* (Epic)	9	27	33
9 Separate Lives *Phil Collins & Marilyn Martin* (Virgin)	11	19	26
10 See The Day *Dee C Lee* (CBS)	16	33	45
11 Hit That Perfect Beat *Bronski Beat* (Forbidden Fruit)	4	3	7
12 We Built This City *Starship* (Grunt/RCA)	15	24	35
13 Spies Like Us *Paul McCartney* (Parlophone)	18	26	43
14 Girlie Girlie *Sophia George* (Winner)	7	7	16
15 Don't You Just Know It *Amazulu* (Island)	17	28	39
16 Say You Say Me *Lionel Richie* (Motown)	22	37	64
17 A Good Heart *Feargal Sharkey* (Virgin)	24	39	52
18 Don't Look Down *Go West* (Chrysalis)	19	31	50
19 Wrap Her Up *Elton John* (Rocket/Phonogram)	12	16	35
20 Santa Claus Is Comin' To Town *Bruce Springsteen* (CBS)	47	–	–
27 The Sun Always Shines On TV *A Ha* (Warner Brothers)	5	2	1
21 Saturday Love *Cherrelle & Alexander O'Neal* (Tabu)	10	6	6
25 Russians *Sting* (A&M)	20	12	14
– Walk of Life *Dire Straits* (Vertigo)	30	4	2
50 You Little Thief *Feargal Sharkey* (Virgin)	26	5	5
49 Broken Wings *Mr Mister* (RCA)	31	8	4
36 Alice, I Want You Just For Me *Full Force* (CBS)	27	10	9
38 Who's Zoomin' Who? *Aretha Franklin* (Arista)	25	11	11
– It's Alright (Baby's Coming Back) *Eurythmics* (RCA)	39	13	12
29 Ring of Ice *Jennifer Rush* (CBS)	23	14	18
23 Leaving Me Now *Level 42* (Polydor)	21	15	17
– Suspicious Minds *Fine Young Cannibals* (London)	35	17	10
– Only Love *Nana Mouskouri* (Carrere/Philips)	59	25	8
– System Addict *Five Star* (Tent)	42	22	13
– Borderline *Madonna* (Sire)	–	–	15
– Pull Up To The Bumper *Grace Jones* (Island)	–	40	20

1	8	15	22
1 The Sun Always Shines On TV *A Ha* (Warner Bros)	2	6	16
2 Only Love *Nana Mouskouri* (Carrere/Philips)	4	7	12
3 Walk of Life *Dire Straits* (Vertigo/Phonogram)	5	13	14
4 Borderline *Madonna* (Sire)	3	2	6
5 Broken Wings *Mr Mister* (RCA)	11	21	29
7 When The Going Gets Tough, The Tough Get Going *Billy Ocean* (Jive)	1	1	1
7 West End Girls *Pet Shop Boys* (Parlophone)	23	38	42
8 Suspicious Minds *Fine Young Cannibals* (London)	9	17	26
9 Saturday Love *Cherrelle with Alexander O'Neal* (Tabu)	13	27	37
10 System Addict *Five Star* (Tent/RCA)	6	3	7
11 You Little Thief *Feargal Sharkey* (Virgin)	15	29	38
12 The Phantom of the Opera *Sarah Brightman & Steve Harley* (Polydor)	7	11	18
13 Alice, I Want You (Just For Me) *Full Force* (CBS)	22	35	46

	8	15	22
1			
14 It's Alright (Baby's Coming Back) *Eurythmics* (RCA)	17	33	40
15 Pull Up To The Bumper/La Vie En Rose *Grace Jones* (Island)	12	16	21
16 Hit That Perfect Beat *Bronski Beat* (Forbidden Fruit/London)	28	37	58
17 Sanctify Yourself *Simple Minds* (Virgin)	10	18	25
18 Who's Zoomin' Who *Aretha Franklin* (Arista)	29	36	49
19 Living In America *James Brown* (Scotti Brothers)	8	5	9
20 In A Lifetime *Clannad (Additional vocals, Bono)* (RCA)	26	31	52
34 The Captain of Your Heart *Double* (Polydor)	14	8	10
22 Life's What You Make It *Talk Talk* (EMI)	16	19	22
– Eloise *Damned* (MCA)	18	4	3
23 How Will I Know *Whitney Houston* (Arista)	19	10	5
37 Rise *Public Image Limited* (Virgin)	20	12	11
56 Starting Together *Su Pollard* (Rainbow)	34	9	2
44 Chain Reaction *Diana Ross* (Capitol)	31	14	4
70 Burning Heart *Survivor* (Scotti Brothers)	30	15	8
29 Shot In The Dark *Ozzy Osbourne* (Epic)	21	20	28
53 Don't Waste My Time *Paul Hardcastle* (Chrysalis)	35	25	13
– Turning Away *Shakin' Stevens* (Epic)	39	23	15
25 Imagination *Belouis Some* (Parlophone)	25	22	17
42 Radio Africa *Latin Quarter* (Rockin' Horse/Arista)	36	24	19
– And She Was *Talking Heads* (EMI)	45	32	20

MARCH 1986

	8	15	22	29
1				
1 When The Going Gets Tough, The Tough Get Going *Billy Ocean* (Jive)	2	5	14	23
2 Chain Reaction *Diana Ross* (Capitol)	1	1	1	2
3 Starting Together *Su Pollard* (Rainbow)	5	11	29	41
4 Eloise *Damned* (MCA)	8	19	33	50
5 Burning Heart *Survivor* (Scotti Brothers)	6	10	23	38
6 How Will I Know *Whitney Houston* (Arista)	7	12	24	31
7 Love Missile F1–11 *Sigue Sigue Sputnik* (Parlophone)	3	3	10	17
8 Don't Waste My Time *Paul Hardcastle* (Chrysalis)	9	15	27	36
9 System Addict *Five Star* (Tent/RCA)	21	37	51	–
10 Manic Monday *Bangles* (CBS)	4	2	3	8
11 Borderline *Madonna* (Sire)	23	41	63	–
12 Rise *Public Image Limited* (Virgin)	15	36	53	–
13 Living In America *James Brown* (Polydor)	19	35	45	61
14 Only Love *Nana Mouskouri* (Carrere/Philips)	34	32	66	–
15 Stripped *Depeche Mode* (Bong)	22	41	56	–
16 Turning Away *Shakin' Stevens* (Epic)	28	44	69	–
17 The Captain of Your Heart *Double* (Polydor)	26	43	62	–
18 The Power of Love/Do You Believe In Love *Huey Lewis and the News* (Chrysalis)	11	9	11	18
19 And She Was *Talking Heads* (EMI)	17	30	39	63
20 Imagination *Belouis Some* (Parlophone)	30	56	63	74
28 Theme From New York, New York *Frank Sinatra* (Reprise)	10	4	9	22
25 Heaven Must Be Missing An Angel *Tavares* (Capitol)	12	16	25	29
24 If You Were Here Tonight (Remix) *Alexander O'Neal* (Tabu)	13	14	20	28
34 (Nothing Serious) Just Buggin' *Whistle* (Champion)	14	7	8	15
37 Hi Ho Silver *Jim Diamond* (A&M)	16	6	5	7
26 Hounds of Love *Kate Bush* (EMI)	18	24	38	58
27 One Dance Won't Do *Audrey Hall* (Germain)	20	25	35	48
– Absolute Beginners *David Bowie* (Virgin)	–	8	2	3
– Kiss *Prince and the Revolution* (Paisley Park/Warner Bros)	27	13	6	9
– Move Away *Culture Club* (Virgin)	–	17	7	10
50 Kyrie *Mr Mister* (RCA)	29	18	15	11

1	8	15	22	29
48 Digging Your Scene *The Blow Monkeys* (RCA)	32	20	12	13
– Living Doll *Cliff Richard and the Young Ones* (WEA)	–	–	4	1
– Harlem Shuffle *Rolling Stones* (Rolling Stones)	–	27	13	14
– No One Is To Blame *Howard Jones* (WEA)	–	23	16	20
45 The Honey Thief *Hipsway* (Mercury)	31	22	17	21
41 Rock Me Tonight (For Old Times Sake) *Freddie Jackson* (Capitol)	36	26	18	26
– You To Me Are Everything *Real Thing* (PRT)	53	38	19	6
– Touch Me (I Want Your Body) *Samantha Fox* (Jive)	–	–	22	4
– Wonderful World *Sam Cooke* (RCA)	–	–	30	5
– Peter Gunn *Art of Noise & Duana Eddy* (China)	–	–	26	12
– A Kind Of Magic *Queen* (EMI)	–	–	–	16
– Love Comes Quickly *Pet Shop Boys* (Parlophone)	52	31	21	19

APRIL 1986

5	12	19	26
1 Living Doll *Cliff Richard & The Young Ones* (WEA)	1	2	4
2 Wonderful World *Sam Cooke* (RCA)	3	6	12
3 Touch Me (I Want Your Body) *Samantha Fox* (Jive)	4	5	9
4 A Different Corner *George Michael* (Epic)	2	1	1
5 You To Me Are Everything *The Decade* (Remix '76–'86) (PRT)	6	7	14
6 Chain Reaction *Diana Ross* (Capitol)	12	18	35
7 A Kind Of Magic *Queen* (EMI)	7	4	3
8 Absolute Beginners *David Bowie* (Virgin)	13	21	34
9 Peter Gunn *Art of Noise & Duane Eddy* (China)	8	12	22
10 Rock Me Amadeus (The American Edit) *Falco* (A&M)	5	3	2
11 Hi Ho Silver *Jim Diamond* (A&M)	17	19	33
12 Manic Monday *Bangles* (CBS)	20	31	55
13 Kyrie *Mr Mister* (RCA)	16	25	49
14 Secret Lovers *Atlantic Starr* (A&M)	10	11	15
15 Kiss *Prince and the Revolution* (Paisley Park/Warner Bros)	26	32	47
16 Move Away *Culture Club* (Virgin)	27	40	64
17 Overjoyed *Stevie Wonder* (Motown)	19	24	50
18 Digging Your Scene *The Blow Monkeys* (RCA)	24	29	48
19 Love Comes Quickly *Pet Shop Boys* (Parlophone)	21	30	44
20 E=MC² *Big Audio Dynamite* (CBS)	11	13	19
23 Train of Thought (Remix) *A Ha* (Warner Brothers)	9	8	13
27 Have You Ever Had It Blue *The Style Council* (Polydor)	14	15	25
– All The Things She Said *Simple Minds* (Virgin)	15	9	11
– Look Away *Big Country* (Mercury/Phonogram)	18	10	7
– Can't Wait Another Minute *Five Star* (Tent/RCA)	36	14	8
45 What Have You Done For Me Lately *Janet Jackson* (A&M)	37	16	6
35 The Finest *S.O.S. Band* (Tabu)	23	17	17
29 C'Mon! C'Mon! *Bronski Beat* (Forbidden Fruit/London)	25	20	24
– Just Say No *Grange Hill Cast* (BBC)	–	26	5
– Live To Tell *Madonna* (Sire)	–	–	10
– Greatest Love Of All *Whitney Houston* (Arista)	46	33	16
– Driving Away From Home (Jim's Tune) *It's Immaterial* (Siren)	58	28	18
– You And Me Tonight *Aurra* (10 Records)	–	39	20

MAY 1986

3	10	17	24	31
1 A Different Corner *George Michael* (Epic)	6	12	21	36
2 Rock Me Amadeus (The American Edit) *Falco* (A&M)	1	4	7	15
3 What Have You Done For Me Lately *Janet Jackson* (A&M)	5	6	15	31

3

	10	17	24	31
4 Live To Tell *Madonna* (Sire)	2	5	10	17
5 Just Say No *Grange Hill Cast* (BBC)	12	27	49	–
6 A Kind of Magic *Queen* (EMI)	9	15	26	44
7 Can't Wait Another Minute *Five Star* (Tent/RCA)	7	10	14	19
8 Look Away *Big Country* (Mercury/Phonogram)	14	21	33	54
9 Lessons In Love *Level 42* (Polydor)	3	3	3	5
10 Greatest Love Of All *Whitney Houston* (Arista)	10	8	11	24
11 I Heard It Through The Grapevine *Marvin Gaye* (Tamla Motown)	8	9	18	37
12 You And Me Tonight *Aurra* (10/Virgin)	13	18	22	40
13 Living Doll *Cliff Richard & The Young Ones* (WEA)	21	31	46	61
14 Touch Me (I Want Your Body) *Samantha Fox* (Jive)	24	33	48	–
15 All The Things She Said *Simple Minds* (Virgin)	20	35	45	73
16 Secret Lovers *Atlantic Starr* (A&M)	17	24	36	57
17 The Finest *S.O.S. Band* (Tabu)	19	28	42	57
18 Wonderful World *Sam Cooke* (RCA)	25	32	44	68
19 On My Own *Patti La Belle & Michael McDonald* (MCA)	4	2	2	2
20 You To Me Are Everything *The Decade* (Remix '76–'86) (PRT)	28	43	51	–
– The Chicken Song *Spitting Image* (Virgin)	11	1	1	1
30 Sledgehammer *Peter Gabriel* (Charisma/Virgin)	15	7	4	4
24 I'll Keep On Loving You *Princess* (Supreme)	16	19	24	39
25 All And All *Joyce Sims* (London)	18	16	17	23
58 Snooker Loopy *The Matchroom Mob with Chas and Dave* (Rockney/Towerbell)	37	11	6	7
31 Why Can't This Be Love? *Van Halen* (Warner Brothers)	22	13	8	8
29 There'll Be Sad Songs (To Make You Cry) *Billy Ocean* (Jive)	27	14	13	12
– Spirit In The Sky *Dr and the Medics* (ILR/MCA)	40	17	5	3
– Rock Lobster/Planet Claire *B 52's* (Island)	35	20	12	14
– Rolling Home *Status Quo* (Vertigo/Phonogram)	–	25	9	11
– Addicted To Love *Robert Palmer* (Island)	63	34	16	10
– Holding Back The Years *Simply Red* (WEA)	–	55	19	6
62 Set Me Free *Jaki Graham* (EMI)	45	35	20	9
– Everybody Wants To Run The World *Tears For Fears* (Mercury/Phonogram)	–	–	–	13
– Who Made Who *AC/DC* (Atlantic)	–	–	27	16
– Mine All Mine/Party Freak *Cashflow* (Club/Phonogram)	–	–	30	18
66 Sinful *Pete Wylie* (MDM/Virgin)	49	39	28	20

JUNE 1986

7

	14	21	28
1 Spirit In The Sky *Dr and the Medics* (IRS/MCA)	1	1	4
2 Holding Back The Years *Simply Red* (WEA)	2	4	9
3 The Chicken Song *Spitting Image* (Virgin)	12	25	36
4 Sledgehammer *Peter Gabriel* (Virgin)	4	8	18
5 Everybody Wants To Run The World *Tears for Fears* (Mercury/Phonogram)	8	27	41
7 On My Own *Patti La Belle & Michael McDonald* (MCA)	9	20	25
7 Lessons In Love *Level 42* (Polydor)	13	23	33
8 Addicted To Love *Robert Palmer* (Island)	5	6	10
9 Set Me Free *Jaki Graham* (EMI)	7	16	22
10 Can't Wait *Nu Shooz* (Atlantic)	3	3	2
11 I Can't Get By Without You (The Second Decade Remix) *The Real Thing* (PRT)	6	7	11
12 Snooker Loopy *The Matchroom Mob with Chas and Dave* (Rockney/Towerbell)	28	33	59
13 Sinful *Pete Wylie* (MDM/Virgin)	14	24	40
14 Why Can't This Be Love? *Van Halen* (Warner Bros)	23	37	54
15 Mine All Mine/Party Freak *Cashflow* (Club/Phonogram)	17	28	39
16 Invisible Touch *Genesis* (Virgin)	15	17	23

7	**14**	**21**	**28**
17 Opportunities (Let's Make Lots of Money) *Pet Shop Boys*			
(Parlophone)	11	15	20
18 There'll Be Sad Songs (To Make You Cry) *Billy Ocean* (Jive)	27	40	62
19 Vienna Calling – The New 86 Edit/Mix *Falco* (A&M)	10	10	17
20 Rollin' Home *Status Quo* (Vertigo/Phonogram)	33	50	–
– Hunting High and Low (Remix) *A Ha* (Warner Bros)	16	5	6
21 Bad Boy *Miami Sound Machine* (Epic)	18	18	16
37 Amityville (The House On The Hill) *Lovebug Starski* (Epic)	19	13	12
22 21st Century Boy *Sigue Sigue Sputnik* (EMI)	20	31	46
– The Edge of Heaven *Wham!* (Epic)	–	2	1
33 Too Good To Be Forgotten *Amazulu* (Island)	21	9	5
55 New Beginning (Mamba Seyra) *Bucks Fizz* (Polydor)	24	11	8
58 Happy Hour *Housemartins* (Go! Discs)	30	12	3
43 My Favourite Waste of Time *Owen Paul* (Epic)	25	14	7
30 Nasty *Janet Jackson* (A&M)	22	19	19
– Papa Don't Preach *Madonna* (Sire)	–	–	13
– Friends Will Be Friends *Queen* (EMI)	–	21	14
36 Venus *Bananarama* (London)	26	22	15

JULY 1986

5	**12**	**19**	**26**
1 The Edge of Heaven *Wham!* (Epic)	2	5	12
2 Papa Don't Preach *Madonna* (Sire)	1	1	1
3 Happy Hour *The Housemartins* (Go! Discs)	4	7	10
4 My Favourite Waste of Time *Owen Paul* (Epic)	3	4	6
5 I Can't Wait *Nu Shooz* (Atlantic)	7	13	22
6 Too Good To Be Forgotten *Amazulu* (Island)	5	9	18
7 Hunting High and Low (Remix) *A Ha* (Warner Brothers)	11	22	31
8 New Beginning (Mamba Seyra) *Bucks Fizz* (RCA)	9	18	29
9 Venus *Bananarama* (London)	8	8	9
10 Spirit In The Sky *Dr and The Medics* (IRS/MCA)	15	26	34
11 Can't Get By Without You (The Second Decade Remix)			
The Real Thing (PRT)	18	25	36
12 Do Ya Do Ya (Wanna Please Me) *Samantha Fox* (Jive)	10	16	26
13 Amityville (The House On The Hill) *Lovebug Starski* (Epic)	23	36	55
14 Friends Will Be Friends *Queen* (EMI)	20	27	39
15 Holding Back The Years *Simply Red* (WEA)	19	28	35
16 Addicted To Love *Robert Palmer* (Island)	21	29	40
17 Headlines *Midnight Star* (Solar/MCA)	16	20	27
18 (Bang Zoom) Let's go *The Real Roxanne With Hitman Howie Tee*			
(Cooltempo/Chrysalis)	12	11	15
19 It's 'Orrible Being In Love (When You're 8½) *Claire and Friends*			
(BBC)	13	15	24
20 Bad Boy *Miami Sound Machine* (Epic)	30	42	63
23 Let's Go All The Way *Sly Fox* (Capitol)	6	3	4
26 Paranoimia *The Art of Noise* (China)	14	12	17
– Every Beat Of My Heart *Rod Stewart* (Warner Brothers)	17	2	3
– Sing Our Own Song *UB40* (Dep International/Virgin)	22	6	5
– The Lady In Red *Chris De Burgh* (A&M)	40	10	2
38 Higher Love *Steve Winwood* (Island)	24	14	13
57 Camaflage *Stan Ridgway* (IRS/MCA)	38	17	7
40 Roses *Haywoode* (CBS)	25	19	14
84 What's The Colour of Money? *Hollywood Beyond* (WEA)	59	24	8
– I Didn't Mean To Turn You On *Robert Palmer* (Island)	–	30	11
52 So Macho/Cruising *Sinitta* (Fanfare)	46	33	16
51 Smile *Audrey Hall* (London)	37	23	19
– Some Candy Talking *The Jesus and Mary Chain* (blanco y negro/			
WEA)	–	–	20

AUGUST 1986

2	9	16	23	30
1 The Lady In Red *Chris De Burgh* (A&M)	1	1	2	3
2 Papa Don't Preach *Madonna* (Sire)	7	7	13	22
3 Let's Go All The Way *Sly Fox* (Capitol)	6	12	22	27
4 Every Beat Of My Heart *Rod Stewart* (Warner)	9	14	26	38
5 So Macho/Cruising *Sinitta* (Fanfare)	2	3	3	2
6 Camaflage *Stan Ridgway* (IRS)	4	6	9	21
7 What's The Colour Of Money? *Hollywood Beyond* (WEA)	8	13	20	22
8 Sing Our Own Song *UB40* (DEP International/Virgin)	13	27	37	52
9 I Didn't Mean To Turn You On *Robert Palmer* (Island)	10	15	24	40
10 Find The Time *Five Star* (Tent/RCA)	7	9	16	24
11 Roses *Haywoode* (CBS)	14	20	33	53
12 My Favourite Waste of Time *Owen Paul* (Epic)	21	32	50	72
13 Some Candy Talking *Jesus and Mary Chain* (blanco y negro/ WEA)	20	35	55	–
14 Smile *Audrey Hall* (London)	18	23	39	57
15 Fight For Ourselves *Spandau Ballet* (Reformation/CBS)	15	16	30	45
17 Ain't Nothin' Goin' But The Rent *Gwen Guthrie* (Boiling Point/ Polydor)	12	5	5	8
18 Panic *The Smiths* (Rough Trade)	11	11	14	23
19 Higher Love *Steve Winwood* (Island)	24	34	53	–
20 Happy Hour *The Housemartins* (Go! Discs)	27	36	52	62
27 I Want To Wake Up With You *Boris Gardener* (Revue/Creole)	5	2	1	1
26 Shout *Lulu* (Decca/London)	16	8	10	19
36 Calling All The Heroes *It Bites* (Virgin)	17	10	6	13
21 Red Sky *Status Quo* (Vertigo/Phonogram)	19	19	27	37
– Anyone Can Fall In Love *Anita Dobson* (BBC)	28	4	4	7
44 I Can Prove It *Phil Fearon* (Ensign/Chrysalis)	31	17	8	14
24 Dancing On The Ceiling *Lionel Richie* (Motown)	23	18	7	11
– Girls And Boys (Edit) *Prince & The Revolution* (Paisley Park/Warner Brothers)	–	27	11	12
– Brother Louie *Modern Talking* (RCA)	–	37	12	4
– We Don't Have To *Jermaine Stewart* (10/Virgin)	68	33	15	6
– Breaking Away *Jaki Graham* (EMI)	38	22	17	16
75 Glory Of Love (From Karate Kid Pt 11) *Peter Cetera* (Full Moon/Warner Brothers)	54	38	18	9
– Human *Human League* (Virgin)	–	–	19	10
– Don't Leave Me This Way *Communards* (London)	–	–	28	5
– When I Think Of You *Janet Jackson* (A&M)	43	30	21	15
– A Question Of Time (Remix) *Depeche Mode* (Mute/Bong)	–	–	25	17
47 The Way It Is *Bruce Hornsby & The Range* (RCA)	35	28	23	18
– Love Can't Turn Around *Farley 'Jackmaster' Funk* (Chicago/ London)	–	–	36	20

SEPTEMBER 1986

6	13	20	27
1 I Want To Wake Up With You *Boris Gardiner* (Revue/Creole)	2	5	9
2 Don't Leave Me This Way *The Communards* (London)	1	1	1
3 We Don't Have To *Jermaine Stewart* (10/Virgin)	3	2	2
4 Brother Louie *Modern Talking* (RCA)	7	12	17
5 Glory Of Love (From Karate Kid) *Peter Cetera* (Full Moon/Warner Brothers)	5	3	6
6 Rage Hard *Frankie Goes To Hollywood* (ZTT/Island)	4	7	16
7 So Macho/Cruising *Sinitta* (Fanfare)	9	14	21
8 Human *Human League* (Virgin)	10	16	25

6	13	20	27
9 The Lady In Red *Chris De Burgh* (A&M)	19	25	38
10 When I Think Of You *Janet Jackson* (A&M)	12	19	27
11 Ain't Nothing Goin' On But The Rent *Gwen Guthrie* (Polydor)	20	30	40
12 Dancing On The Ceiling *Lionel Richie* (Motown)	21	32	42
13 Girls and Boys (Edit) *Prince & The Revolution* (Paisley Park/ Warner Brothers)	22	34	49
14 (I Just) Died In Your Arms *Cutting Crew* (Siren/Virgin)	8	4	5
15 The Way It Is *Bruce Hornsby and The Range* (RCA)	17	23	39
16 Love Can't Turn Around *Farley 'Jackmaster' Funk* (Chicago/ London)	11	11	10
17 Anyone Can Fall In Love *Anita Dobson*/Simon May Orchestra (BBC)	30	40	50
18 Calling All The Heroes *It Bites* (Virgin)	28	45	61
19 I Can Prove It *Phil Fearon* (Ensign/Chrysalis)	32	43	66
20 A Question Of Time (Remix) *Depeche Mode* (Mute/Bong)	33	42	68
23 Holiday Rap *M.C. Miker 'G' & Deejay Sven* (Debut)	6	8	11
28 Word Up *Cameo* (Club/Phonogram)	13	6	3
22 You Give Love A Bad Name *Bon Jovi* (Vertigo/Phonogram)	14	15	20
37 Walk This Way *Run D.M.C.* (London)	15	9	8
29 Thorn In My Side *Eurythmics* (RCA)	16	10	7
24 Wasted Years *Iron Maiden* (EMI)	18	28	46
– Rain Or Shine *Five Star* (Tent/RCA)	31	13	4
41 Sweet Freedom *Michael McDonald* (MCA)	27	17	12
38 Pretty In Pink *Psychedelic Furs* (CBS)	25	18	18
– Rumors *Timex Social Club* (Cooltempo/Chrysalis)	34	20	13
52 (Forever) Live And Die *Orchestral Manoeuvres In The Dark* (Virgin)	38	24	14
26 Stuck With You *Huey Lewis And The News* (Chrysalis)	24	21	15
– One Great Thing *Big Country* (Mercury/Phonogram)	–	27	19

OCTOBER 1986

4	11	18	25
1 Don't Leave Me This Way *Communards* (London)	3	6	9
2 Rain Or Shine *Five Star* (Tent/RCA)	2	3	7
3 True Blue *Madonna* (Sire)	1	2	2
4 Word Up *Cameo* (Club/Phonogram)	6	12	18
5 Thorn In My Side *Eurythmics* (RCA)	7	11	17
7 We Don't Have To *Jermaine Stewart* (10/Virgin)	11	18	28
7 (I Just) Died In Your Arms *Cutting Crew* (Siren/Virgin)	14	21	33
8 Walk This Way *Run D.M.C.* (London)	13	19	32
9 You Can Call Me Al *Paul Simon* (Warner Brothers)	5	4	5
10 Glory of Love (From Karate Kid Pt 11) *Peter Cetera* (Full Moon/Warner Brothers)	23	31	43
11 (Forever) Live And Die *Orchestral Manoeuvres In The Dark* (Virgin)	12	15	20
12 Stuck With You *Huey Lewis and The News* (Chrysalis)	15	17	24
13 Love Can't Turn Around *Farley 'Jackmaster' Funk* (Chicago/ London)	21	30	35
14 I've Been Losing You *A Ha* (Warner Brothers)	8	10	16
15 Always There *Marti Webb/Simon May Orchestra* (BBC)	17	14	13
16 Rumours *Timex Social Club* (Cooltempo/Chrysalis)	22	27	31
17 Sweet Freedom *(Michael McDonald* (MCA)	26	33	48
18 Montego Bay *Amazulu* (Island)	16	16	23
19 In Too Deep (From the Film 'Mona Lisa') *Genesis* (Virgin)	25	36	58
20 I Want To Wake Up With You *Boris Gardiner* (Revue/Creole)	30	34	41
66 Every Loser Wins *Nick Berry* (BBC)	4	1	1
29 In The Army Now *Status Quo* (Vertigo)	9	5	4
23 Suburbia *Pet Shop Boys* (Parlophone)	10	8	8
21 True Colors *Cyndi Lauper* (Portrait)	18	13	12
45 All I Ask Of You *Cliff Richard & Sarah Brightman* (Polydor)	19	7	3

4 | | **11** | **18** | **25**

	11	18	25
26 Walk Like An Egyptian *Bangles* (CBS)	20	9	6
34 Shut Your Mouth *Julian Cope* (Island)	28	20	19
37 Midas Touch *Midnight Star* (Solar/MCA)	27	22	10
45 You're Everything To Me *Boris Gardiner* (Revue/Creole)	38	25	11
– Don't Get Me Wrong *The Pretenders* (Real/WEA)	45	32	14
– The Wizard *Paul Hardcastle* (Chrysalis)	34	23	15

NOVEMBER 1986

1	8	15	22	29
1 Every Loser Wins *Nick Berry* (BBC)	2	7	21	28
2 In The Army Now *Status Quo* (Vertigo/Phonogram)	3	6	17	24
3 All I Ask Of You *Cliff Richard & Sarah Brightman* (Polydor)	5	10	15	20
4 Walk Like An Egyptian *Bangles* (CBS)	4	3	8	14
5 True Blue *Madonna* (Sire)	11	19	30	40
6 You Can Call Me Al *Paul Simon* (Warner Brothers)	13	24	38	53
7 Take My Breath Away (Love Theme from 'Top Gun'). *Berlin* (CBS)	1	1	1	1
8 Midas Touch *Midnight Star* (Solar/MCA)	9	17	27	42
9 Suburbia *Pet Shop Boys* (Parlophone)	18	29	42	75
10 Don't Get Me Wrong *The Pretenders* (Real/WEA)	10	15	25	37
11 You're Everything To Me *Boris Gardiner* (Revue/Creole)	21	35	50	–
12 True Colors *Cyndi Lauper* (Portrait)	19	30	39	50
13 Rain Or Shine *Five Star* (Tent/RCA)	27	37	58	–
14 Notorious *Duran Duran* (EMI)	7	12	20	36
15 You Keep Me Hanging On *Kim Wilde* (MCA)	7	2	2	3
16 Ask *The Smiths* (Rough Trade)	14	21	33	58
17 To Have And To Hold *Catherine Stock* (Sierra)	29	40	69	–
18 Think For A Minute *The Housemartins* (Go! Discs)	28	34	68	–
19 The Wizard *Paul Hardcastle* (Chrysalis)	32	52	–	–
20 Always There *Martin Webb/ Simon May Orchestra* (BBC)	34	39	52	67
24 Showing Out *Mel & Kim* (Supreme)	8	4	3	4
26 Something Outa Nothing *Letitia Dean & Paul Medford* (BBC)	12	16	32	45
27 Livin' On A Prayer *Bon Jovi* (Vertigo/Phonogram)	15	11	7	6
31 Don't Give Up *Peter Gabriel & Kate Bush* (Virgin)	16	9	9	12
36 Breakout *Swing Out Sister* (Mercury/Phonogram)	17	5	4	5
– Through The Barricades *Spandau Ballet* (Reformation/ Chrysalis)	20	8	6	11
33 For America *Red Box* (Sire/WEA)	22	13	10	10
71 The Final Countdown *Europe* (Epic)	35	14	5	2
39 Because I Love You *Shakin' Stevens* (Epic)	24	18	14	18
– (Waiting For) The Ghost Train *Madness* (Zarrjazz/Virgin)	33	20	18	23
– French Kissin' in the USA *Debbie Harry* (Chrysalis)	–	27	11	9
– Each Time You Break My Heart *Nick Kamen* (WEA)	54	26	12	8
– Ghostdancing *Simple Minds* (Virgin)	–	22	13	16
57 Sometimes *Erasure* (Mute)	43	33	16	7
– Sweet Love *Anita Baker* (Elektra)	–	36	19	13
– If I Say Yes *Five Star* (Tent/RCA)	–	–	23	15
– The Skye Boat Song *Roger Whittaker & Des O'Connor* (Tembo)	53	46	22	17
– Warriors (Of The Wasteland) *Frankie Goes To Hollywood* (ZTT/ Island)	–	–	24	19

6		13	20	27
1	The Final Countdown *Europe* (Epic)	1	3	3
2	Take My Breath Away (Theme From 'Top Gun') *Berlin* (CBS)	5	11	14
3	Sometimes *Erasure* (Mute)	2	5	5
4	Livin' On A Prayer *Bon Jovi* (Vertigo/Phonogram)	7	9	10
5	Each Time You Break My Heart *Nick Kamen* (WEA)	9	13	21
6	Breakout *Swing Out Sister* (Mercury/Phonogram)	12	19	23
7	You Keep Me Hanging On *Kim Wilde* (MCA)	15	22	28
8	French Kissin' In The USA *Debbie Harry* (Chrysalis)	11	14	19
9	Showing Out *Mel & Kim* (Supreme)	18	24	30
10	The Skye Boat Song *Roger Whittaker & Des O'Connor* (Tembo)	13	18	20
11	For America *Red Box* (Sire)	20	36	56
12	The Rain (Short Version) *Oran 'Juice' Jones* (Def Jam)	4	6	6
13	Sweet Love *Anita Baker* (Elektra)	22	23	38
14	So Cold The Night *Communards* (London)	10	8	11
15	Shake You Down *Gregor Abbott* (CBS)	6	7	9
16	If I Say Yes *Five Star* (Tent/RCA)	26	31	39
17	Through The Barricades *Spandau Ballet* (Reformation/CBS)	28	35	40
18	War *Bruce Springsteen* (CBS)	23	32	42
19	Warriors (Of The Wasteland) *Frankie Goes To Hollywood* (ZTT/ Island)	32	42	53
20	Land Of Confusion *Genesis* (Virgin)	17	16	16
23	Caravan Of Love *The Housemartins* (Go! Discs)	3	1	2
–	Open Your Heart (Remix) *Madonna* (Sire)	8	4	4
30	Reet Petite (The Sweetest Girl In Town) *Jackie Wilson* (SMP/SKM)	14	2	1
28	Cry Wolf *A Ha* (Warner Brothers)	16	10	7
21	Shiver *George Benson* (Warner Brothers)	19	21	26
32	Is This Love *Alison Moyet* (CBS)	24	12	8
–	Big Fun *The Gap Band* (Total Experience/RCA)	39	15	12
26	Step Right Up *Jaki Graham* (EMI)	21	17	15
39	Because Of You *Dexy's Midnight Runners* (Mercury/Phonogram)	25	20	13
44	Dreamin' *Status Quo* (Vertigo/Phonogram)	34	25	17
50	No More The Fool *Elkie Brooks* (Legend)	38	30	18

1986 – BEST-SELLING RECORDS

Singles:
1. Don't Leave Me This Way *Communards* (London)
2. Every Loser Wins *Nick Berry* (BBC)
3. I Want To Wake Up With You *Boris Gardiner* (Revue)
4. Living Doll *Cliff Richard & The Young Ones* (WEA)
5. Chain Reaction *Diana Ross* (Capitol)
6. The Lady In Red *Chris De Burgh* (A&M)
7. When The Going Gets Tough, The Tough Get Going *Billy Ocean* (Jive)
8. Papa Don't Preach *Madonna* (Sire)
9. Take My Breath Away *Berlin* (CBS)
10. So Macho/Cruising *Sinitta* (Fanfare)
11. True Blue *Madonna* (Sire)
12. A Different Corner *George Michael* (Sire)
13. Rock Me Amadeus *Falco* (A&M)
14. We Don't Have To *Jermaine Stewart* (10)
15. Spirit In The Sky *Dr And The Medics* (IRS)
16. The Final Countdown *Europe* (Epic)
17. Reet Petite (The Sweetest Girl In Town) *Jackie Wilson* (SMP)
18. Rain Or Shine *Five Star* (Tent)
19. Caravan Of Love *The Housemartins* (Go! Discs)
20. The Chicken Song/A Nice South African *Spitting Image* (Virgin)
21. The Sun Always Shines on TV *A Ha* (Warner Brothers)
22. On My Own *Patti LaBelle with Michael McDonald* (MCA)
23. Walk Like An Egyptian *Bangles* (CBS)
24. In The Army Now *Status Quo* (Vertigo/Phonogram)
25. Lessons In Love *Level 42* (Polydor)
26. Glory Of Love *Peter Cetera* (Full Moon)
27. The Edge of Heaven *Wham!* (Epic)
28. Sledgehammer *Peter Gabriel* (Virgin)
29. All I Ask Of You *Cliff Richard & Sarah Brightman* (Polydor)
30. Touch Me (I Want Your Body) *Samantha Fox* (Jive)
31. Wonderful World *Sam Cooke* (RCA)
32. A Kind of Magic *Queen* (EMI)
33. Holding Back The Years *Simply Red* (Elektra)
34. You Keep Me Hangin' On *Kim Wilde* (MCA)
35. Let's Go All The Way *Sly Fox* (Capitol)
36. Word Up *Cameo* (Club)
37. Manic Monday *Bangles* (CBS)
38. I Can't Wait *Nu Shooz* (Atlantic)
39. My Favourite Waste Of Time *Owen Paul* (Epic)
40. You Can Call Me Al *Paul Simon* (Warner Brothers)
41. Livin' On A Prayer *Bon Jovi* (Vertigo/Phonogram)
42. Sometimes *Erasure* (Mute)
43. Showing Out *Mel & Kim* (Supreme)
44. (I Just) Died In Your Arms *Cutting Crew* (Siren)
45. You To Me Are Everything *The Real Thing* (PRT)
46. Happy Hour *The Housemartins* (Go! Discs)
47. Starting Together *Su Pollard* (Rainbow)
48. Thorn In My Side *Eurythmics* (RCA)
49. Walk Of Life *Dire Straits* (Vertigo)
50. Borderline *Madonna* (Sire)

Albums:

1 True Blue *Madonna* (Sire)
2 Brothers In Arms *Dire Straits* (Vertigo/Phonogram)
3 Now, That's What I Call Music *Various* (EMI/Virgin/Polygram)
4 Graceland *Paul Simon* (Warner Brothers)
5 Whitney Houston *Whitney Houston* (Arista)
6 Now, That's What I Call Music 7 *Various* (EMI/Virgin/Polygram)
7 Hunting High And Low *A Ha* (Warner Brothers)
8 A Kind Of Magic *Queen* (EMI)
9 Silk And Steel *Five Star* (Tent)
10 Revenge *Eurythmics* (RCA)
11 Hits 5 *Various* (CBS/WEA/RCA)
12 Hits 4 *Various* (CBS/WEA/RCA)
13 The Final *Wham!* (Epic)
14 Invisible Touch *Genesis* (Virgin)
15 Every Breath You Take – The Singles *The Police* (A&M)
16 The Whole Story *Kate Bush* (EMI)
17 Into The Light *Chris De Burgh* (A&M)
18 Street Life – 20 Great Hits *Bryan Ferry/Roxy Music* (EG/Polydor)
19 So *Peter Gabriel* (Virgin)
20 Picture Book *Simply Red* (Elektra)
21 Once Upon A Lifetime *Simple Minds* (Virgin)
22 No Jacket Required *Phil Collins* (Virgin)
23 World Machine *Level 42* (Polydor)
24 Dancing On The Ceiling *Lionel Richie* (Motown)
25 London 0 Hull 4 *The Housemartins* (Go! Discs)
26 Slippery When Wet *Bon Jovi* (Vertigo/Phonogram)
27 Top Gun *Original Soundtrack* (CBS)
28 Like A Virgin *Madonna* (Sire)
29 Fore! *Huey Lewis and The News* (Chrysalis)
30 Be Yourself Tonight *Eurythmics* (RCA)
31 Scoundrel Days *A Ha* (Warner Brothers)
32 Communards *Communards* (London)
33 Go West/Bangs and Crashes *Go West* (Chrysalis)
34 Please *Pet Shop Boys* (Parlophone)
35 Queen Greatest Hits *Queen* (EMI)
36 Different Light *Bangles* (CBS)
37 Love Zone *Billy Ocean* (Jive)
38 Live Magic *Queen* (EMI)
39 Riptide *Robert Palmer* (Island)
40 Island Life *Grace Jones* (Island)
41 The Dream Of The Blue Turtles *Sting* (A&M)
42 South Pacific *Te Kanawa/Carreras/Vaughan* (CBS)
43 The Broadway Album *Barbra Streisand* (CBS)
44 Rocky VI *Original Soundtrack* (Scotti Brothers)
45 Luxury Of Life *Five Star* (Tent)
46 Suzanne Vega *Suzanne Vega* (A&M)
47 Hounds Of Love *Kate Bush* (EMI)
48 Break Every Rule *Tina Turner* (Capitol)
49 In The Army Now *Status Quo* (Vertigo)
50 Every Beat Of My Heart *Rod Stewart* (Warner Brothers)

1987

Oldies but goodies, whether in songs or artists, continued their good times. The first Top 20 entry for the long lasting Siouxsie and The Banshees was a revival of the 1968, Dylan-penned hit for Julie Driscoll, Brian Auger and The Trinity. Before February had passed there was a chart topper for 'Stand By Me' from Ben E King and readying to replace there was Percy Sledge and his 'When A Man Loves A Woman'; 'I Get The Sweetest Feeling' from Jackie Wilson charted in March.

George Michael and Aretha Franklin became the fourth Anglo–American duettists to hit the top. At the end of March both British and US charts were headed by remakes of songs that had success during the 1970s. Club Nouveau triumphed with the old Bill Wither's number 'Lean On Me' and Boy George revived the 13-year-old hit of Ken Boothe, 'Everything I Own'. 'Respectable' by Mel and Kim became the 587th Number One and only the fourth by a female duo. Of course, Madonna had to make her appearance. Her Top Five 'La Isla Bonita' was her fourteenth to reach the higher end of the chart, and gave her (for the second time) five Top Five singles from an album, the relevant long-players being *Like A Virgin* and *True Blue*. Album plundering, loved by such artists as Michael Jackson and Elton John, had a seeming peak when Five Star lifted a sixth hit off *Silk And Steel*, and so equalled the six taken from Jackson's mega-selling *Thriller*. Seven singles had come from Five Star's *Luxury Of Life* album but only five became hits. Tom Jones at 46 years old had his first hit for ten years with 'A Boy From Nowhere'. And yes, by the month of May, Madonna had set another record. When 'La Isla Bonita' gave her a fourth Number One in the UK, she overtook Sandie Shaw with the most hits at the top by any female solo artist. 'Star Trekkin' ' gave The Firm a 61-place chart jump from 74 to 13 (but failed by one place to equal the previous biggest positional movement held by Nick Berry in 1986 with his 66 to 4 with 'Every Loser Wins'. At July's end Madonna had set yet another record: 'Who's That Girl' brought her tally of Top Ten hits to fifteen beating the previous 1980s success of Madness with their fourteen. 'Who's That Girl' and 'La Bamba' provided the first consecutive film Number One's since 'Summer Holiday' and 'Foot Tapper' in 1963. Paul Carrack revived the 1964 Searcher's hit 'When You Walk In The Room', Dusty Springfield had her first Top Ten hit in nineteen years, in the company of The Pet Shop Boys. 'Some People' from Cliff Richard was his twenty-ninth Top Five hit though Elvis had thirty-four. The Bee Gees returned to chartland as artists when 'You Win Again' became the 57th Gibb Brothers hit and their 30th to reach the Top Ten. They were the second-oldest chart group entrants; the Detroit Spinners had an average of 40 when they charted in 1980. But in a year seemingly punctuated by revivals and old connections, none was more surprising, though pleasurable, than the arrival of 'My Baby Just Cares For Me' by Nina Simone: 57-years-old as a song, first recorded by her in 1957, and a hit for the 54-year-old singing genius, it was her first hit since her cover of the Bee Gees 'To Love Somebody' in 1969.

Shakin' Stevens had a third consecutive hit with a re-make when 'What Do You Want To Make Those Eyes At Me For' gave him his twenty-fourth hit in the 1980s (though the second of these, 'Come See About Me,' failed to make the Top 20 listing). And as the year ended, The Tams after a sixteen-year absence, Joe Cocker after seventeen, and Wilson Pickett likewise, were poised for the Top 20 . . . oldies but goodies.

JANUARY 1987

3	10	17	24	31
1 Reet Petite (The Sweetest Girl In Town) *Jackie Wilson* (SMP/SKM)	1	1	2	6
2 Caravan Of Love *The Housemartins* (Go! Discs)	2	7	25	38
3 The Final Countdown *Europe* (Epic)	4	14	32	41
4 Open Your Heart (Remix) *Madonna* (Sire)	6	12	31	40
5 Cry Wolf *A Ha* (Warner Brothers)	5	13	30	46
6 The Rain (Short Version) *Oran 'Juice' Jones* (Def Jam)	8	11	18	32
7 Sometimes *Erasure* (Mute)	7	9	17	31
8 Is This Love? *Alison Moyet* (CBS)	3	3	3	4
9 Shake You Down *Gregory Abbott* (CBS)	10	19	28	37
10 Livin' On A Prayer *Bon Jovi* (Vertigo/Phonogram)	13	22	37	52
11 So Cold The Night *Communards* (London)	12	21	38	56
12 Big Fun *The Gap Band* (Total Experience/RCA)	9	4	6	11
13 Take My Breath Away (Love Theme from 'Top Gun') *Berlin* (CBS)	16	25	45	60
14 Land of Confusion *Genesis* (Virgin)	14	16	27	45
15 Dreamin' *Status Quo* (Vertigo/Phonogram)	17	27	48	–
16 Because Of You *Dexy's Midnight Runners* (Mercury/Phonogram)	27	41	54	–
17 Step Right Up *Jaki Graham* (EMI)	15	23	43	62
18 No More The Fool *Elkie Brooks* (Legend)	11	5	5	5
19 French Kissin' In The USA *Debbie Harry* (Chrysalis)	22	53	–	–
20 Each Time You Break My Heart *Nick Kamen* (WEA)	21	52	62	70
– Jack Your Body *Steve 'Silk' Hurley* (London)	18	2	1	1
25 Hymn To Her *The Pretenders* (Real)	19	8	8	16
31 Over The Hills And Far Away *Gary Moore* (10/Virgin)	20	20	29	43
42 C'Est La Vie *Robbie Nevil* (Manhattan/EMI)	32	6	4	3
– Surrender *Swing Out Sister* (Mercury/Phonogram)	38	10	7	9
– It Didn't Matter *The Style Council* (Polydor)	–	15	9	19
33 Ballerina Girl/Deep River Woman *Lionel Richie* (Motown)	24	17	19	26
43 Real Wild Child (Wild One) *Iggy Pop* (A&M)	36	18	10	17
– Wasteland *The Mission* (Mercury)	–	24	11	13
– Something In My House *Dead Or Alive* (Epic)	57	29	12	14
– Rat In Mi Kitchen *UB40* (Dep International)	–	31	13	12
– This Wheel's On Fire *Siouxsie and The Banshees*	–	30	14	18
50 Down To Earth *Curiosity Killed The Cat* (Mercury/Phonogram)	49	32	15	8
– Walking Down Your Street *Bangles* (CBS)	53	28	16	22
60 Almaz *Randy Crawford* (Warner Brothers)	56	35	20	10
– I Knew You Were Waiting (For Me) *Aretha Franklin & George Michael* (Epic)	–	–	–	2
– Heartache *Pepsi & Shirlie* (Polydor)	–	50	22	7
– I Love My Radio *Taffy* (Transglobal/Rhythm King/Mute)	63	36	24	15
69 Jack The Groove *Raze* (Champion)	59	40	21	20

FEBRUARY 1987

7	14	21	28
1 I Knew You Were Waiting For Me *Aretha Franklin & George Michael* (Epic)	1	2	5
2 Heartache *Pepsi and Shirlie* ((Polydor)	2	4	6
3 Jack Your Body *Steve 'Silk' Hurley* (DJ International)	8	20	35
4 Almaz *Randy Crawford* (Warner Brothers)	4	7	22
5 Down To Earth *Curiosity Killed The Cat* (Mercury)	3	3	3
6 C'Est La Vie *Robbie Nevil* (Manhattan)	16	30	51
7 I Love My Radio *Taffy* (Transglobal)	6	12	25

7		14	21	28
8 No More The Fool *Elkie Brooks* (Legend)		13	27	41
9 Surrender *Swing Out Sister* (Mercury)		21	31	50
10 Is This Love *Alison Moyet* (CBS)		15	28	48
11 It Doesn't Have To Be This Way *Blow Monkeys* (RCA)		5	8	14
12 Shoplifters Of The World *Smiths* (Rough Trade)		12	24	45
13 Reet Petite *Jackie Wilson* (SMP)		23	33	38
14 You Sexy Thing *Hot Chocolate* (EMI)		10	13	20
15 Rat In Mi Kitchen *UB40* (Dep International)		24	34	54
16 Once Bitten Twice Shy *Vesta Williams* (A&M)		14	16	26
17 Big Fun *The Gap Band* (Total Experience)		26	39	62
18 Hymn To Her *Pretenders* (Real)		32	47	75
19 The Music of the Night *Michael Crawford & Sarah Brightman* (Polydor)		7	11	19
20 Jack The Groove *Raze* (Champion)		36	56	–
25 Male Stripper *Man 2 Meets Man Parrish* (Bolts)		9	6	4
24 Stay Out Of My Life *Five Star* (Tent/RCA)		11	9	13
23 Behind The Mask (Edit) *Eric Clapton* (Duck/Warner Brothers)		17	15	16
– Running In The Family *Level 42* (Polydor)		18	10	7
– Stand By Me *Ben E King* (Atlantic)		19	1	1
28 Rock The Night *Europe* (Epic)		20	17	12
– When A Man Loves A Woman *Percy Sledge* (Atlantic)		28	5	2
38 Coming Round Again *Carly Simon* (Arista)		22	14	10
47 Crush On You *The Jets* (MCA)		30	18	9
60 Live It Up *Mental As Anything* (Epic)		39	19	8
– Sonic Boom Boy *Westworld* (RCA)		–	22	11
– The Right Thing *Simply Red* (WEA)		45	23	15
– Manhattan Skyline *A Ha* (Warner Brothers)		–	–	17
– Love Removal Machine *The Cult* (Beggars Banquet)		–	–	18

MARCH 1987

7		14	21	28
1 Stand By Me *Ben E King* (Atlantic)		2	6	14
2 When A Man Loves A Woman *Percy Sledge* (Atlantic)		6	9	19
3 Live It Up *Mental As Anything* (Epic)		5	5	8
4 Male Stripper *Man 2 Meets Man Parrish* (Bolts)		9	13	20
5 Crush On You *The Jets* (MCA)		8	10	17
6 Running In The Family *Level 42* (Polydor)		10	12	21
7 Everything I Own *Boy George* (Virgin)		1	1	2
8 Down To Earth *Curiosity Killed The Cat* (Mercury/Phonogram)		15	23	37
9 The Great Pretender *Freddie Mercury* (Parlophone)		4	4	5
10 I Get The Sweetest Feeling *Jackie Wilson* (SMP)		3	3	3
11 The Right Thing *Simply Red* (WEA)		12	18	28
12 Coming Round Again *Carly Simon* (Arista)		13	20	31
13 Manhattan Skyline *A Ha* (Warner Brothers)		24	21	36
14 Sonic Boom Boy *Westworld* (RCA)		18	24	35
15 Heartache *Pepsi & Shirlie* (Polydor)		27	27	44
16 Rock The Night *Europe* (Epic)		23	30	51
17 I Knew You Were Waiting For Me *Aretha Franklin & George Michael* (Epic)		28	35	58
18 Love Removal Machine *The Cult* (Beggars Banquet)		19	29	43
19 Stay Out Of My Life *Five Star* (Tent/RCA)		30	39	55
20 It Doesn't Have To Be *Erasure* (Mute)		17	15	12
25 Respectable *Mel & Kim* (Supreme)		7	2	1
29 Moonlighting 'Theme' *Al Jarreau* (WEA International)		11	8	13
30 Weak In The Presence Of Beauty *Alison Moyet* (CBS)		16	7	6
– Sign of The Times *Prince* (Paisley Park/Warner Brothers)		20	16	10
47 Respect Yourself *Bruce Willis* (Motown)		31	11	7

	14	21	28
7			
26 (You Gotta) Fight For Your Right (To Party) *Beastie Boys* (Def Jam)	21	14	11
39 Loving You Is Sweeter Than Ever *Nick Kamen* (WEA)	25	17	16
– Tonight, Tonight, Tonight (Remix) *Genesis* (Virgin)	24	19	18
– With Or Without You *U2* (Island)	–	–	4
– Let's Wait Awhile – Remix *Janet Jackson* (Breakout/A&M)	–	31	9
– Big Time *Peter Gabriel* (Virgin)	–	–	15

APRIL 1987

	11	18	25
4			
1 Let It Be *Ferry Aid* (The Sun/Zeebrugge Disaster Fund)	1	1	4
2 Respectable *Mel & Kim* (Supreme)	2	6	5
3 Let's Wait Awhile – Remix *Janet Jackson* (Breakout/A&M)	4	5	9
4 With Or Without You *U2* (Island)	5	8	11
5 La Isla Bonita (Remix) *Madonna* (Sire)	3	2	1
6 Everything I Own *Boy George* (Virgin)	13	28	38
7 Lean On Me *Club Nouveau* (King Joy/Warner Brothers)	6	3	3
8 Weak In The Presence Of Beauty *Alison Moyet* (CBS)	9	15	30
9 I Get The Sweetest Feeling *Jackie Wilson* (SMP)	12	24	37
10 The Great Pretender *Freddie Mercury* (Parlophone)	20	27	40
11 Respect Yourself *Bruce Willis* (Motown)	18	22	32
12 Sign of The Times *Prince* (Paisley Park/Warner Brothers)	15	21	34
13 Big Time *Peter Gabriel* (Virgin)	16	25	44
14 Live It Up *Mental As Anything* (Epic)	21	33	43
15 If You Let Me Stay *Terence Trent D'Arby* (CBS)	7	7	7
16 (You Gotta) Fight For Your Right (To Party) *Beastie Boys* (Def Jam)	25	34	39
17 Ever Fallen In Love *Fine Young Cannibals* (London)	10	9	10
18 Loving You Is Sweeter Than Ever *Nick Kamen* (WEA)	27	38	46
19 It Doesn't Have To Be *Erasure* (Mute)	29	50	60
20 Moonlighting 'Theme' *Al Jarreau* (WEA International)	34	48	64
21 The Irish Rover *The Pogues and The Dubliners* (Stiff)	8	11	20
22 Ordinary Day *Curiosity Killed The Cat* (Mercury/Phonogram)	11	12	19
37 Can't Be Without You Tonight *Judy Boucher* (Orbitone)	14	4	2
– Wanted Dead Or Alive *Bon Jovi* (Vertigo/Phonogram)	17	13	16
30 Day-In-Day-Out *David Bowie* (EMI America)	19	17	28
42 Living In A Box *Living In A Box* (Chrysalis)	23	10	6
– The Slightest Touch *Five Star* (Tent/RCA)	–	14	8
27 Still Of The Night *Whitesnake* (EMI)	22	16	23
34 Let My People Go-Go *The Rainmakers* (Mercury/Phonogram)	28	18	22
33 Keep Your Eye On Me – Special Mix *Herb Alpert* (Breakout/A&M)	26	19	26
52 Another Step (Closer To You) *Kim Wilde & Junior* (MCA)	32	20	14
– A Boy From Nowhere *Tom Jones* (Epic)	–	32	12
– Sheila Take A Bow *The Smiths* (Rough Trade)	–	–	13
– Nothing's Gonna Stop Us Now *Starship* (Grunt/RCA)	50	29	15
– Diamond Lights *Glenn & Chris* (Record Shack)	–	30	17
65 (Something Inside) So Strong *Labi Siffre* (China)	46	31	18

MAY 1987

	9	16	23	30
2				
1 La Isla Bonita (Remix) *Madonna* (Sire)	3	7	17	24
2 Can't Be With You Tonight *Judy Boucher* (Orbitone)	2	2	3	8
3 Nothing's Gonna Stop Us Now *Starship* (Grunt/RCA)	1	1	1	1
4 The Slighest Touch *Five Star* (Tent/RCA)	5	8	15	22
5 Lean On Me *Club Nouveau* (King Joy/Warner Brothers)	11	17	34	42
7 Living In A Box *Living In A Box* (Chrysalis)	6	5	7	14
7 A Boy From Nowhere *Tom Jones* (Epic)	4	3	2	4

	9	16	23	30
8 If You Let Me Stay *Terence Trent D'Arby* (CBS)	12	20	33	51
9 Another Step (Closer To You) *Kim Wilde & Junior* (MCA)	9	6	8	17
10 Sheila Take A Bow *The Smiths* (Rough Trade)	15	29	53	–
11 Respectable *Mel & Kim* (Supreme)	18	25	40	40
12 Diamond Lights *Chris & Glenn* (Record Shack)	14	23	38	45
13 Ever Fallen In Love *Fine Young Cannibals* (London)	20	31	49	–
14 To Be With You Again *Level 42* (Polydor)	10	15	29	38
15 Let's Wait Awhile (Remix) *Janet Jackson* (Breakout/A&M)	21	36	60	–
16 (Something Inside) So Strong *Labi Siffre* (China)	7	4	4	9
17 Let It Be *Ferry Aid* (The Sun/Zeebrugge Disaster Fund)	34	58	–	–
18 With Or Without You *U2* (Island)	24	28	43	59
19 April Skies *The Jesus and Mary Chain* (Blanco y negro/WEA)	8	10	24	36
20 Wanted Dead Or Alive *Bon Jovi* (Vertigo/Phonogram)	33	44	69	–
21 Big Love *Fleetwood Mac* (Warner Brothers)	13	9	9	12
30 Back & Forth (Remix) *Cameo* (Club/Phonogram)	16	13	11	11
32 Lil' Devil *The Cult* (Beggars Banquet)	17	11	13	20
23 Never Take Me Alive *Spear Of Destiny* (10/Virgin)	19	14	16	21
29 Boops (Here To Go) *Sly & Robbie* (Fourth & Broadway/Island)	22	12	12	19
– Strangelove *Depeche Mode* (Mute)	23	16	20	30
40 Shattered Dreams *Johnny Hates Jazz* (Virgin)	30	18	5	5
37 Real Fashion (Reggae Style) *Cary Johnson* (Oval/10/Virgin)	25	19	22	25
– Incommunicado *Marillion* (EMI)	–	–	6	6
– I Wanna Dance With Somebody (Who Loves Me) *Whitney Houston* (Arista)	–	–	10	2
39 Wishing I Was Lucky *Wet Wet Wet* (The Precious Organization/Phonogram)	29	21	14	10
– Hot Shot Tottenham *Tottenham Hotspur Squad/Chas and Dave* (Rainbow)	44	35	18	32
– Prime Mover *Zodiac Mindwarp* (Mercury/Phonogram)	40	24	19	18
– Hold Me Now *Johnny Logan* (Epic)	–	–	25	3
– Jack Mix II *Mirage* (Debut/Passion)	57	38	21	7
– Five Get Excited *The Housemartins* (Go! Discs)	–	–	28	13
56 Serious *Donna Allen* (Portrait)	42	33	26	15
– Born To Run *Bruce Springsteen* (CBS)	–	–	23	16

JUNE 1987

6	13	20	17
1 I Wanna Dance With Somebody (Who Loves Me) *Whitney Houston* (Arista)	1	2	2
2 Nothing's Gonna Stop Us Now *Starship* (Grunt/RCA)	3	5	10
3 Hold Me Now *Johnny Logan* (Epic)	2	4	6
4 Jack Mix II/III *Mirage* (Debut/Passion)	5	11	20
5 Shattered Dreams *Johnny Hates Jazz* (Virgin)	7	18	31
6 Wishing I Was Lucky *Wet Wet Wet* (The Precious Organization/Phonogram)	10	15	33
7 Victim Of Love *Erasure* (Mute)	8	10	15
8 Serious *Donna Allen* (Portrait)	12	22	39
9 A Boy From Nowhere *Tom Jones* (Epic)	20	36	42
10 Goodbye Stranger *Pepsi & Shirlie* (Polydor)	9	12	19
11 Five Get Over Excited *The Housemartins* (Go! Discs)	19	40	66
12 Incommunicado *Marillion* (EMI)	30	54	–
13 I Still Haven't Found What I'm Looking For *U2* (Island)	6	7	13
14 Can't Be With You Tonight *Judy Boucher* (Orbitone)	24	33	43
15 (Something Inside) So Strong *Labi Siffre* (China)	26	45	67
16 No Sleep Till Brooklyn *Beastie Boys* (Def Jam)	14	19	29
17 Back & Forth (Remix) *Cameo* (Club/Phonogram)	32	64	–

6		13	20	17
18 Nothing's Gonna Stop Me Now *Samantha Fox* (Jive)		11	8	8
19 Big Love *Fleetwood Mac* (Warner Brothers)		31	50	–
20 Living In A Box *Living In A Box* (Chrysalis)		33	51	72
– I Want Your Sex *George Michael* (Epic)		4	3	4
74 Star Trekkin' *The Firm* (Bark)		13	1	1
22 You're The Voice *John Farnham* (Wheatley)		15	9	7
27 It's Tricky *Run DMC* (London)		16	17	24
36 Under The Boardwalk *Bruce Willis* (Motown)		17	6	3
24 Looking For A New Love *Jody Watley* (MCA)		18	13	16
37 When Smokey Sings *ABC* (Neutro/Phonogram)		21	14	12
30 Is This Love? *Whitesnake* (EMI)		22	16	11
34 It's Not Unusual *Tom Jones* (Decca/London)		33	20	17
– It's A Sin *Pet Shop Boys* (Parlophone)		–	–	5
– Misfit *Curiosity Killed The Cat* (Mercury/Phonogram)		–	21	9
– Wishing Well *Terence Trent D'Arby* (CBS)		–	31	14
39 Let's Dance *Chris Rea* (Magnet)		27	25	18

JULY 1987

4		11	18	25
1 It's A Sin *Pet Shop Boys* (Parlophone)		1	1	2
2 Star Trekkin' *The Firm* (Bark)		3	10	14
3 Under The Boardwalk *Bruce Willis* (Motown)		2	2	4
4 I Wanna Dance With Somebody (Who Loves Me) *Whitney Houston* (Arista)		8	12	18
5 Wishing Well *Terence Trent D'Arby* (CBS)		4	4	8
6 You're The Voice *John Farnham* (Wheatley/RCA)		9	17	29
7 Misfit *Curiosity Killed The Cat* (Mercury/Phonogram)		10	16	28
8 I Want Your Sex Rhythm 1 Lust *George Michael* (Epic)		19	29	40
9 Is This Love *Whitesnake* (EMI)		11	19	24
10 My Pretty One *Cliff Richard* (EMI)		6	11	16
11 When Smokey Sings *ABC* (Neutron/Phonogram)		14	22	31
12 Let's Dance *Chris Rea* (Magnet)		13	20	30
13 Hold Me Now *Johnny Logan* (Epic)		20	33	45
14 Nothing's Gonna Stop Me Now *Samantha Fox* (Jive)		23	40	49
15 Nothing's Gonna Stop Us Now *Starship* (Grunt/RCA)		28	30	38
16 Always *Atlantic Star* (Warner Brothers)		7	5	3
17 The Living Daylights *A Ha* (Warner Brothers)		5	6	11
18 Comin' On Strong *Broken English* (EMI)		18	26	39
19 Promised You A Miracle *Simple Minds* (Virgin)		25	36	52
20 If I Was Your Girlfriend *Prince* (Paisley Park/Warner Brothers)		24	31	51
26 Sweetest Smile *Black* (A&M)		12	8	9
28 Alone *Heart* (Capitol)		15	9	6
– F.L.M. Mel & Kim (Supreme)		16	7	7
23 Sweet Sixteen *Billy Idol* (Chrysalis)		17	18	23
– Who's That Girl *Madonna* (Sire)		–	3	1
44 A Little Bit Of Boogie Woogie (In The Back Of . . .) *Shakin' Stevens* (Epic)		26	13	13
75 Jive Talkin' *Boogie Box High* (Hardback)		31	14	10
39 (Your Love Keeps Lifting Me) Higher And Higher) *Jackie Wilson* (SMP)		21	15	9
– La Bamba *Los Lobos* (Slash/FRR/London)		–	32	5
52 Just Don't Want To Be Lonely *Freddie McGregor* (Germain)		37	23	12
– I Heard A Rumour *Bananarama* (London)		55	28	15
47 Labour Of Love *Hue & Cry* (Circa/Virgin)		50	34	17
– She's On It *Beastie Boys* (Def Jam)		–	42	20

386

1		8	15	22	29
1	La Bamba *Los Lobos* (Slash/FRR/London)	1	2	7	15
2	Who's That Girl *Madonna* (Sire)	2	8	15	20
3	Always *Atlantic Starr* (Warner Brothers)	4	7	17	27
4	It's A Sin *Pet Shop Boys* (Parlophone/EMI)	11	19	38	43
5	Alone *Heart* (Capitol)	3	5	14	24
6	Under The Boardwalk *Bruce Willis* (Motown)	13	20	36	40
7	Jive Talkin' *Boogie Box High* (Hardback)	9	17	26	36
8	F.L.M. *Mel & Kim* (Supreme)	14	23	37	63
9	Just Don't Want To Be Lonely *Freddie McGregor* (Germain)	12	15	32	41
10	She's On It *Beastie Boys* (Def Jam)	10	18	39	42
11	Wishing Well *Terence Trent D'Arby* (CBS)	21	27	45	57
12	A Little Boogie Woogie (In The Back Of . . .) *Shakin' Stevens* (Epic)	19	28	48	67
13	Labour Of Love *Hue & Cry* (Circa/Virgin)	6	6	12	17
14	I Heard A Rumour *Bananarama* (London)	15	16	28	37
15	Sweetest Smile *Black* (A&M)	27	39	59	69
16	I Really Didn't Mean It *Luther Vandross* (Epic)	18	21	31	58
17	The Living Daylights *A Ha* (Warner Brothers)	30	40	52	51
18	You Caught My Eye *Judy Boucher* (Orbitone)	20	22	42	58
19	True Faith *New Order* (Factory)	7	4	5	7
20	Oops Upside Your Head ('87 Mix) *The Gap Band* (Club/Phonogram)	25	32	46	68
–	I Just Can't Stop Loving You *Michael Jackson* (Epic)	5	1	1	3
28	Call Me *Spagna* (CBS)	8	3	2	5
34	Animal *Def Leppard* (Bludgeon Riffola/Phonogram)	16	9	6	9
30	Roadblock *Stock Aitken Waterman* (Breakout/A&M)	17	13	16	21
33	Toy Boy *Sinitta* (Fanfare)	22	10	4	4
38	Somewhere Out There (From An American Tail) *Linda Ronstadt & James Ingram* (MCA)	23	11	8	10
43	Sweet Little Mystery *Wet Wet Wet* (The Precious Organization/Phonogram)	31	12	9	6
–	Never Gonna Give You Up *Rick Astley* (RCA)	32	14	3	1
–	What Have I Done To Deserve This? *Pet Shop Boys & Dusty Springfield* (Parlophone)	–	–	10	2
44	Funky Town *Pseudo Echo* (RCA)	36	24	11	8
–	Girlfriend In A Coma *The Smiths* (Rough Trade)	–	–	13	16
–	Whenever You're Ready *Five Star* (Tent/RCA)	–	–	18	11
–	U Got The Look *Prince & Sheena Easton* (Paisley Park/Warner Brothers)	–	38	19	13
72	Bridge To Your Heart *Wax* (RCA)	42	34	20	12
–	Didn't We Almost Have It All *Whitney Houston* (Arista)	–	–	22	14
–	Wonderful Life *Black* (A&M)	–	–	33	18
–	Wipeout *Fat Boys & The Beach Boys* (Urban/Polydor)	–	–	41	19

SEPTEMBER 1987

5	12	19	26
1 Never Gonna Give You Up *Rick Astley* (RCA)	1	1	1
2 What Have I Done To Deserve This? *Pet Shop Boys & Dusty Springfield* (Parlophone)	3	8	15
3 Wipeout *Fat Boys & The Beach Boys* (Urban/Polydor)	2	3	7
4 Toy Boy *Sinitta* (Fanfare)	6	10	14
5 Sweet Little Mystery *Wet Wet Wet* (The Precious Organization/ Phonogram)	8	14	21
6 Call Me *Spagna* (CBS)	14	21	29
7 I Just Can't Stop Loving You *Michael Jackson/Siedah Garrett* (Epic)	17	30	37
8 Wonderful Life *Black* (A&M)	9	13	17
9 Heart And Soul *T'Pau* (Siren/Virgin)	5	4	6
10 Funky Town *Pseudo Echo* (RCA)	20	27	38
11 U Got The Look *Prince & Sheena Easton* (Paisley Park/Warner Brothers)	13	23	30
12 Bridge To Your Heart *Wax* (RCA)	12	16	24
13 Whenever You're Ready *Five Star* (Tent/RCA)	23	37	57
14 Didn't We Almost Have It All *Whitney Houston* (Arista)	21	28	36
15 Some People *Cliff Richard* (EMI)	7	6	3
16 Somewhere Out There (From 'An American Tail') *Linda Ronstadt & James Ingram* (MCA)	22	32	40
17 Animal *Def Leppard* (Bludgeon/Riffola/Phonogram)	25	40	54
18 The Motive (Living Without You) *Then Jericho* (London)	18	22	32
19 True Faith *New Order* (Factory)	27	38	50
20 Sasanova *Levert* (Atlantic)	10	9	12
– Where The Streets Have No Name *U2* (Island)	4	5	13
35 Pump Up The Volume/Anita *M/A/R/R/S* (4AD)	11	2	2
27 Me And The Farmer *The Housemartins* (Go! Discs)	15	17	28
21 The Hourglass *Squeeze* (A&M)	16	19	27
34 I Don't Want To Be A Hero *Johnny Hates Jazz* (Virgin)	19	15	11
– Causing A Commotion *Madonna* (Sire)	–	7	4
– It's Over (Remix) *Level 42* (Polydor)	24	11	10
– House Nation *The House Master Boys & The Rude boy Of House* (Magnet/Dance)	28	12	8
38 Lies *Jonathan Butler* (Jive)	29	18	18
58 Hey Matthew *Karel Fialka* (IRS/MCA)	36	20	9
– Bad *Michael Jackson* (Epic)	–	–	5
76 I Need Love *L.L. Cool J.* (Def Jam)	48	26	16
– Crockett's Theme (Instrumental New Mix) *Jan Hammer* (MCA)	–	36	19
– Pour Some Sugar On Me *Def Leppard* (Bludgeon Riffola/ Phonogram)	–	31	20

OCTOBER 1987

3	10	17	24	31
1 Pump Up The Volume *M/A/R/R/S* (4AD)	1	3	6	16
2 Never Gonna Give You Up *Rick Astley* (RCA)	4	10	22	28
3 Bad *Michael Jackson* (Epic)	3	6	20	27
4 Some People *Cliff Richard* (EMI)	8	14	27	41
5 Causing A Commotion *Madonna* (Sire)	10	15	28	35
6 Crockett's Theme (Instrumental New Mix) *Jan Hammer* (MCA)	5	4	2	4
7 Full Metal Jacket (I Wanna Be Your . . .) *Abigail Mead & Nigel Goulding* (Warner Brothers)	2	2	3	12
8 House Nation *The House Master Boys & The Rude Boy Of House* (Magnetic)	11	24	36	63
9 I Need Love *L.L. Cool J.* (Def Jam)	9	8	16	29

388

3	10	17	24	31
10 Hey Matthew *Karel Fialka* (IRS/MCA)	14	28	49	–
11 Heart And Soul *T'Pau* (Siren/Virgin)	17	31	39	58
12 Wipeout *Fat Boys & The Beach Boys* (Urban/Polydor)	18	32	45	71
13 The Corrosion *The Sisters Of Mercy* (Merciful Release/WEA)	7	11	26	46
14 I Don't Want To Be A Hero *Johnny Hates Jazz* (Virgin)	13	25	32	64
15 It's Over (Remix) *Level 42* (Polydor)	19	27	33	57
16 Cars ('E' Reg Model) *Gary Numan* (Beggars Banquet)	16	23	40	72
17 Casanova *Levert* (Atlantic)	26	39	56	–
18 Pour Some Sugar On Me *Def Leppard* (Bludgeon Riffola/ Phonogram)	28	51	72	–
19 Jack Le Freak *Chic* (Atlantic)	25	40	64	–
20 Toy Boy *Sinitta* (Fanfare)	32	43	57	–
22 You Win Again *Bee Gees* (Warner Brothers)	6	1	1	1
32 Crazy Crazy Nights *Kiss* (Vertigo/Phonogram)	12	5	4	9
34 I Found Lovin' *Fatback Band* (Master Mix)	15	7	9	17
21 Brilliant Disguise *Bruce Springsteen* (CBS)	20	38	54	70
39 I Found Lovin' *Steve Walsh* (A.I.)	22	9	14	21
38 The Circus (Remix) *Erasure* (Mute)	21	12	7	6
40 The Real Thing *Jellybean Feat/Steve Dante* (Chrysalis)	29	13	13	13
– Strong As Steel *Five Star* (Tent/RCA)	34	16	19	23
59 Mony Mony *Billy Idol* (Chrysalis)	35	17	8	7
65 Walk The Dinosaur *Was Not Was* (Fontana/Phonogram)	38	18	12	10
36 Valerie *Steve Winwood* (Island)	23	19	25	33
– Rain In The Summertime *The Alarm* (IRS/MCA)	–	20	18	24
– Love In The First Degree/Mr Sleaze *Bananarama* (London)	46	22	5	3
– Faith *George Michael* (Epic)	–	–	10	2
42 Little Lies *Fleetwood Mac* (Warner Brothers)	39	21	11	5
– Maybe Tomorrow *UB40* (DEP International/Virgin)	41	29	15	14
– Rent *Pet Shop Boys* (Parlophone)	–	–	17	8
– Whenever You Need Somebody *Rick Astley* (RCA)	–	–	–	11
68 I Don't Think That Man Should . . . *Ray Parker Jnr.* (Geffen)	48	36	34	15
41 Come On, Let's Go *Los Lobos* (Slash/London)	37	26	21	18
– China In Your Hand *T'Pau* (Siren)	–	–	43	19
– Dance Little Sister *Terence Trent D'Arby* (CBS)	44	30	23	20

NOVEMBER 1987

7	14	21	28
1 You Win Again *Bee Gees* (Warner Brothers)	3	7	15
2 Faith *George Michael* (Epic)	5	12	21
3 Whenever You Need Somebody *Rick Astley* (RCA)	4	3	3
4 Love In The First Degree/Mr Sleaze *Bananarama* (London)*	7	13	16
5 China In Your Hand *T'Pau* (Siren)	1	1	1
6 Little Lies *Fleetwood Mac* (Warner Brothers)	9	15	22
7 Got My Mind Set On You *George Harrison* (Dark Horse/WEA)	2	2	2
8 Mony Mony (Live) *Billy Idol* (Chrysalis)	14	19	32
9 Crockett's Theme (Instrumental New Mix) *Jan Hammer* (MCA)	17	22	37
10 Walk The Dinosaur *Was Not Was* (Fontana/Phonogram)	18	21	38
11 The Circus (Remix) *Erasure* (Mute)	19	29	42
12 Barcelona *Freddie Mercury & Montserrat Caballe* (Polydor)	8	10	17
13 I Don't Think That Man Should Sleep *Ray Parker Jnr.* (Geffen)	16	24	41
14 Rent *Pet Shop Boys* (Parlophone)	21	32	56
15 Never Can Say Goodbye *The Communards* (London)	6	4	4
16 Crazy Crazy Nights *Kiss* (Vertigo/Phonogram)	26	36	51
17 Here I Go Again *Whitesnake* (EMI)	12	11	9
18 Full Metal Jacket (I Wanna Be . . .) *Abigail Mead & Nigel Goulding* (Warner Brothers)	30	38	55
19 The Real Thing *Jellybean & Steve Dante* (Chrysalis)	27	35	50

7		**14**	**21**	**28**
20 Wanted *The Style Council* (Polydor)		25	43	–
24 I've Had The Time Of My Life *Bill Medley & Jennifer Warnes* (RCA)		10	6	6
26 My Baby Just Cares For Me *Nina Simone* (Charly)		11	5	7
29 Jack Mix IV *Mirage* (Debut/Passion)		13	8	11
28 Paid In Full *Eric B & Rakim* (4th & B'way Island)		15	16	20
– So Emotional *Whitney Houston* (Arista)		20	9	5
46 Criticize *Alexander O'Neal* (Tabu)		28	14	8
39 Dinner With Gershwin *Donna Summer* (Warner Brothers)		23	17	13
51 Some Guys Have All The Luck *Maxi Priest* (10/Virgin)		32	18	12
56 Sho' You Right *Barry White* (Breakout/A&M)		38	20	14
– Letter From America *The Proclaimers* (Chrysalis)		51	25	10
– To Be Reborn *Boy George* (Virgin)		–	26	18
– Build *The Housemartins* (Go! Discs)		–	30	19

* the titles were flipped with 'Mr Sleaze' becoming the 'A' side in the chart of November 28

DECEMBER 1987

5		**12**	**19**	**26**
1 China In Your Hand *T'Pau* (Siren/Virgin)		1	5	9
2 Got My Mind Set On You *George Harrison* (Dark Horse/WEA)		7	13	18
3 Letter From America *The Proclaimers* (Chrysalis)		6	12	16
4 Criticize *Alexander O'Neal* (Tabu)		8	11	17
5 Never Can Say Goodbye *The Communards* (London)		14	18	26
6 So Emotional (Remix) *Whitney Houston* (Arista)		12	16	22
7 What Do You Want To Make Those Eyes At Me For *Shakin' Stevens* (Epic)		5	7	10
8 Whenever You Need Somebody *Rick Astley* (RCA)		24	35	43
9 (I've Had) The Time Of My Life *Bill Medley & Jennifer Warnes* (RCA)		21	29	36
10 Here I Go Again *Whitesnake* (EMI)		26	32	42
11 My Baby Just Cares For Me *Nina Simone* (Charly)		28	33	29
12 Some Guys Have All The Luck *Maxi Priest* (10/Virgin)		16	27	34
13 To Be Reborn *Boy George* (Virgin)		18	38	50
14 Once Upon A Long Ago *Paul McCartney* (Parlophone)		10	14	21
15 Build *The Housemartins* (Go! Discs)		17	31	45
16 The Way You Make Me Feel *Michael Jackson* (Epic)		3	3	6
17 Sho' You Right *Barry White* (Breakout/A&M)		37	62	–
18 Who Found Who *Jellybean & Elisa Fiorillo* (Chrysalis)		11	10	12
19 Jack Mix IV *Mirage* (Debut/Passion)		35	54	61
20 Dinner With Gershwin *Donna Summer* (Warner Brothers)		34	53	75
– When I Fall In Love *Rick Astley* (RCA)		2	2	4
– Always On My Mind *Pet Shop Boys* (Parlophone)		4	1	1
30 Love Letters *Alison Moyet* (CBS)		9	4	5
39 Rockin' Around The Christmas Tree *Kim Wilde & Mel Smith* (10/Virgin)		13	6	3
– The Look Of Love *Madonna* (Sire)		15	9	14
40 Fairytale Of New York *The Pogues & Kirsty MacColl* (Pogue Mahone/ Stiff)		19	8	2
35 I'm The Man (DEF) Uncensored Version *Anthrax* (Island)		20	23	58
27 Turn Back The Clock *Johnny Hates Jazz* (Virgin)		27	15	15
41 Ev'ry Time We Say Goodbye *Simply Red* (WEA)		33	17	11
– Heaven Is A Place On Earth *Belinda Carlisle* (Virgin)		43	19	8
– When I Fall In Love *Nat 'King' Cole* (Capitol)		51	20	7
44 Angel Eyes (Home And Away) *Wet Wet Wet* (Precious/Phonogram)		32	21	13
– Jingo *Jellybean* (Chrysalis)		50	30	19
– Touched By The Hand Of God *New Order* (Factory)		–	25	20

Record Mirror in its issue of 9 January 1988 changed its chart dating from 'week ending' to 'week beginning' and so this gave another list for December that would otherwise be week ending January 2, 1988. Since the source of these charts *Music Week* has kept to a week ending, we have not changed accordingly.

However, to help *Record Mirror* addicts and general chart compilers the chart printed reads 1 Always On My Mind; 2 Fairytale Of New York; 3 Rockin' Around The Christmas Tree; 4 When I Fall In Love (NKC); 5 Heaven Is A Place On Earth; 6 Love Letters; 7 When I Fall In Love (RA); 8 The Way You Make Me Feel; 9 China In Your Hand; 10 Angel Eyes; 11 Ev'ry Time We Say Goodbye; 12 What Do You Want; 13 Turn Back The Clock; 14 Who Found Who; 15 Letter From America; 16 The Look Of Love; 17 Criticize; 18 Got My Mind Set On You; 19 Jingo; 20 House Arrest – Krush. The Krush record was the only newcomer. This chart will form the first week's layout in the next edition of this book.

Singles

1 Never Gonna Give You Up *Rick Astley* (RCA)
2 Nothing's Gonna Stop Us Now *Starship* (RCA)
3 I Wanna Dance With Somebody *Whitney Houston* (Arista)
4 You Win Again *Bee Gees* (Warner Bros)
5 China In Your Hand *T'Pau* (Siren)
6 Respectable *Mel & Kim* (Supreme)
7 Stand By Me *Ben E King* (Atlantic)
8 It's A Sin *Pet Shop Boys* (Parlophone)
9 Star Trekkin' *Firm* (Bark)
10 Pump Up The Volume *M/A/R/R/S* (4AD)
11 I Knew You Were Waiting (For Me) *George Michael & Aretha Franklin* (Epic)
12 Under The Boardwalk *Bruce Willis* (Motown)
13 Let It Be *Ferry Aid* (The Sun)
14 Always On My Mind *Pet Shop Boys* (Parlophone)
15 Got My Mind Set On You *George Harrison* (Dark Horse)
16 Can't Be Without You Tonight *Judy Boucher* (Orbitone)
17 La Isla Bonita *Madonna* (Sire)
18 La Bamba *Los Lobos* (Slash)
19 Hold Me Now *Johnny Logan* (Epic)
20 Who's That Girl *Madonna* (Sire)
21 Everything I Own *Boy George* (Virgin)
22 Down To Earth *Curiosity Killed The Cat* (Mercury)
23 When A Man Loves A Woman *Percy Sledge* (Atlantic)
24 Heartache *Pepsi and Shirley* (Polydor)
25 Always *Atlantic Starr* (Warner Bros)
26 Whenever You Need Somebody *Rick Astley* (RCA)
27 Toy Boy *Sinitta* (Fanfare)
28 I Get The Sweetest Feeling *Jackie Wilson* (SMP)
29 Faith *George Michael* (Epic)
30 I Just Can't Stop Loving You *Michael Jackson/Siedah Garrett* (Epic)
31 Live It Up (From Crocodile Dundee) *Mental As Anything* (CBS)
32 Mr Sleaze/Love In The First Degree *Bananarama* (London)
33 Crockett's Theme *Jan Hammer* (MCA)
34 Alone *Heart* (Capitol)
35 Wipe Out *Fat Boys & Beach Boys* (Urban)
36 Call Me *Spagna* (CBS)
37 Let's Wait Awhile *Janet Jackson* (A&M)
38 Jack Your Body *Steve 'Silk' Hurley* (DJ International)
39 The Great Pretender *Freddie Mercury* (Parlophone)
40 Male Stripper *Man 2 Meets Man Parrish* (Bolts)
41 Lean On Me *Club Nouveau* (King Jay/Warner)
42 What Have I Done To Deserve This *Petshop Boys and Dusty Springfield* (Parlophone)
43 Some People *Cliff Richard* (EMI)
44 A Boy From Nowhere *Tom Jones* (Epic)
45 With Or Without You *U2* (Island)
46 Wishing Well *Terence Trent D'Arby* (CBS)
47 Heart And Soul *T'Pau* (Siren)
48 Fairytale Of New York *Pogues/Kirsty MacColl* (Pogue Mahone)
49 I Wanna Be Your Drill Instructor *Abigail Mead/Nigel Goulding* (Warner Bros)
50 My Arms Keep Missing You *Rick Astley* (RCA)

Albums

1 Bad *Michael Jackson* (Epic)
2 The Joshua Tree *U2* (Island)
3 Whitney *Whitney Houston* (Arista)
4 Now That's What I Call Music 10 *Various* (EMI/Virgin/PolyGram)
5 Hits 6 *Various* (CBS/WEA/BMG)
6 Tango In The Night *Fleetwood Mac* (Warner Bros)
7 Whenever You Need Somebody *Rick Astley* (RCA)
8 Bridge of Spies *T'Pau* (Siren)
9 The Phantom Of The Opera *Original Cast* (Polydor)
10 Hits 10 *Various* (CBS/WEA/BMG)
11 Running In The Family *Level 42* (Polydor)
12 Now That's What I Call Music 9 *Various* (EMI/Polydor/PolyGram)
13 Raindancing *Alison Moyet* (CBS)
14 Graceland *Paul Simon* (Warner Bros)
15 Pet Shop Boys, Actually *Pet Shop Boys* (Parlophone)
16 Introducing The Hardline According *Terence Trent D'Arby* (CBS)
17 All The Best *Paul McCartney* (Parlophone)
18 Invisible Touch *Genesis* (Virgin)
19 Men And Women *Simply Red* (Elektra)
20 The Best Of UB40 Vol 1 (Virgin)
21 True Blue *Madonna* (Sire)
22 Live In The City Of Light *Simple Minds* (Virgin)
23 The Singles *The Pretenders* (Real)
24 Keep Your Distance *Curiosity Killed The Cat* (Mercury)
25 Faith *George Michael* (Epic)
26 The Cream Of Eric Clapton *Eric Clapton* (Polydor)
27 Solitude Standing *Suzanna Vega* (A&M)
28 Always Guaranteed *Cliff Richard* (EMI)
29 The Very Best Of Hot Chocolate *Hot Chocolate* (EMI)
30 Sixties Mix *Various* (Stylus)
31 Circus *Erasure* (Mute)
32 Give Me The Reason *Luther Vandross* (Epic)
33 Silk And Steel *Five Star* (Tent)
34 Hysteria *Def Leppard* (Bludgeon Riff)
35 F.L.M. *Mel & Kim* (Supreme)
36 Brothers In Arms *Dire Straits* (Vertigo)
37 Popped In Souled Out *Wet Wet Wet* (Precious Organization)
38 So *Peter Gabriel* (Virgin)
39 Whitesnake 1987 *Whitesnake* (EMI)
40 It's Better To Travel *Swing Out Sister* (Mercury)
41 Who's That Girl *Original Soundtrack* (Sire)
42 Simply Shadows *Shadows* (Polydor)
43 You Can Dance *Madonna* (Sire)
44 Dancing With Strangers *Chris Rea* (Magnet)
45 The Return of Bruno *Bruce Willis* (Motown)
46 Bad Animals *Heart* (Capitol)
47 Hearsay *Alexander O'Neal* (Tabu)
48 Move Closer *Various* (CBS)
49 Tunnel Of Love *Bruce Springsteen* (CBS)
50 Licensed To Kill *Beastie Boys* (Def Jam/CBS)

1988

The year of Stock, Aitken and Waterman: producers, hit-song writers, publishers, and more. Not everyone loved them or their success, since they produced uncomplicated pop. This music enabled a magazine such as *Smash Hits* to sail into a sales region hitherto thought of as only in the past. At its peak the 'teen' journal hit 875,000 copies per issue, with heroes including Rick Astley (formerly an office boy with SA&W), Jason Donovan, and Kylie Minogue and many more beside giving image to that journal. Kylie was the star of the year, spending most weeks on the chart, solo, or with Jason, her star friend from television soap opera *Neighbours*. Her debut record 'I Should Be So Lucky' was in the Top Three best sellers of the year.

Yet some dispute awarding Kylie her 'star of the year', others suggesting the amazing Cliff Richard. By Christmas he was topping the singles and album chart simultaneously, the third time he had achieved this feat. Outside of the usual listings, he also topped the Compact Disc chart, the Video chart and the book charts! Yet there were still those who said he had peaked long time before, that he was old-fashioned, etc., etc. His double album 'Private Collection' went on to sell around 1,400,000 copies! It was his sixth Number One album.

While Cliff charted high at the year's end, chart statisticians were fascinated to see 'Brothers In Arms' from Dire Straits – with a sale of over three million – leave the album chart after 186 consecutive weeks. Even that feat made it only the fifteenth longest chart running act in pop history; but more pertinent, in 'consecutive' week terms, only five albums can better its performance.

1988 was a good year for women as Yazz (and the Plastic Population), Joyce Sims, Belinda Carlisle, Whitney Houston, Salt 'N' Pepa, Carol Decker (with T'Pau), Tiffany, Enya and Debbie Gibson were among those riding high. Indeed, only one male, Rick Astley, could find a way into the top solo acts of the year. When

Kylie Minogue was followed by Tiffany, who was followed by Belinda Carlisle, this was the first time in chart history that three consecutive Number One's had come from women; but it was repeated with a succession of Robin Beck, Enya and Whitney Houston.

Bros provided the teen market with something other than Kylie and Jason. *Neighbours* not only gave us Jason and Kylie, but also Angry Anderson, formerly a throaty rockster, who sang 'Suddenly', the song used in the *Neighbours* wedding scene, when Kylie and Jason came together.

In albumsville, Terence Trent D'Arby hovered around the million mark for his 'The Hardline According To' . . . while U2 and Fleetwood Mac accumulated more sales for their 'Tango In The Night' (carried over from 1987), and 'Rattle And Hum', respectively.

Wet Wet Wet, who also were flung at the younger end of the market, did well with 'Popped In, Souled Out', some said they might be the next Beatles, but time has not borne out such a suggestion.

As in any year of the late eighties, there were revived oldies, and a second time success for remixed records – none more so than for 'Blue Monday' from New Order, the best-selling 12-inch of all time and first to chart in 1983, and only issued in 7-inch form in 1988!

In the trade, CD singles picked up momentum, but as with cassette shorties, still needed total marketing dedication from the companies to ensure real success.

Please note that the dates given at the top of a listing are those of the week-ending. However, from 1988 the actual chart received its first airplay the previous Sunday, and was then broadcast during the week, with *Top of the Pops* on television still giving its rundown each Thursday.

2		9	16	23	30
1	Always On My Mind Pet Shop Boys (Parlophone)	1	2	11	20
2	Fairytale Of New York The Pogues feat. Kirsty MacColl (Pogue Mahone/Staff)	4	19	39	68
3	Rockin' Around The Christmas Tree Mel & Kim (10/Virgin)	10	31	–	–
4	When I Fall In Love Nat King Cole (Capitol)	14	27	57	–
5	Heaven Is A Place On Earth Belinda Carlisle (Virgin)	2	1	1	2
6	Love Letters Alison Moyet (CBS)	6	18	31	59
7	When I Fall In Love/My Arms Keep Missing You* Rick Astley (RCA)	11	14	21	29
8	The Way You Make Me Feel Michael Jackson (Epic)	3	16	26	43
9	China In Your Hand T'Pau (Siren/Virgin)	13	28	40	63
10	Angel Eyes (Home And Away) Wet Wet Wet (Precious/Phonogram)	5	6	9	15
11	Ev'ry Time We Say Goodbye Simply Red (WEA)	24	40	50	–
12	What Do You Want to Make Those Eyes Shakin' Stevens (Epic)	22	50	–	–
13	Turn Back The Clock Johnny Hates Jazz (Virgin)	12	20	28	52
14	Who Found Who Jellybean feat. Elisa Fiorillo (Chrysalis)	16	25	46	70
15	Letter From America The Proclaimers (Chrysalis)	30	57	–	–
16	The Look Of Love Madonna (Sire)	15	36	65	–
17	Criticize Alexander O'Neal (Tabu)	18	30	50	–
18	Got My Mind Set On You George Harrison (Dark Horse/WEA)	28	41	69	–
19	Jingo Jellybean (Chrysalis)	17	12	17	28
20	House Arrest Krush (Club/Phonogram)	7	3	4	4
23	Stutter Rap (No Sleep Til Bedtime) Morris Minor & The Majors	8	4	5	5
21	I Found Someone Cher (Geffen)	9	5	6	11
–	All Day And All Of The Night The Stranglers (Epic)	19	7	7	13
30	G.T.O. Sinitta (Fanfare)	20	15	19	37
–	Sign Your Name Terence Trent D'Arby (CBS)	29	8	2	3
–	Come Into My Life Joyce Sims (ffrr)	21	9	8	7
31	Rise To The Occasion Climie Fisher (EMI)	23	10	10	10
–	Father Figure George Michael (Epic)	35	11	13	23
–	I Think We're Alone Now Tiffany (MCA)	–	13	3	1
–	Heatseeker AC/DC (Atlantic)	–	17	12	12
–	Rok Da House Beatmasters/Cookie Crew (Rhythm King/Mute)	50	26	14	8
26	Ideal World (Remix) The Christians (Island)	27	22	15	14
–	When Will I Be Famous Bros (CBS)	51	39	16	6
73	O L'Amour Dollar (London)	59	33	18	9
–	I Can't Help it Bananarama (London)	45	23	20	22
–	Candle In The Wind (Live) Elton John (Rocket)	77	47	30	16
–	Shake Your Love Debbie Gibson (Atlantic)	–	–	35	17
–	Hot In The City Billy Idol (Chrysalis)	76	45	27	18
76	The House That Jack Built Jack n' Chill (Oval/10/Virgin)	56	46	33	19

* The Rick Astley single was flipped with 'My Arms Keep Missing You' listed on January 9.

FEBRUARY 1988

6		13	20	27
1	I Think We're Alone Now *Tiffany* (MCA)	1	2	5
2	When Will I Be Famous *Bros* (CBS)	3	6	11
3	Heaven Is A Place On Earth *Belinda Carlisle* (Virgin)	13	20	36
4	Sign Your Name *Terence Trent D'Arby* (CBS)	12	15	30
5	Rok Da House *Beatmasters/Cookie Crew* (Rhythm King/Mute)	9	14	27
6	House Arrest *Krush* (Club/Phonogram)	16	22	40
7	O L'Amour *Dollar* (London)	11	19	43
8	Tell It To My Heart *Taylor Dayne* (Arista)	4	3	4
9	Shake Your Love *Debbie Gibson* (Atlantic)	7	10	13
10	Candle In The Wind (Live) *Elton John* (Rocket/Phonogram)	5	7	16
11	Come Into My Life *Joyce Sims* (ffrr/London)	17	23	45
12	The Jack That House Built *Jack 'n' Chill* (Oval/10/Virgin)	6	11	18
13	Hot In The City *Billy Idol* (Chrysalis)	14	16	28
14	Stutter Rap (No Sleep Til Bedtime) *Morris Minor & The Majors* (Ten/Virgin)	23	40	68
15	Ideal World (Remix) *The Christians* (Island)	21	38	71
16	I Should Be So Lucky *Kylie Minogue* (PWL)	2	1	1
17	Say It Again *Jermaine Stewart* (10/Virgin)	10	8	7
18	Tired Of Getting Pushed Around *2 Men, a Drum Machine & a Trumpet* (ffrr/London)	19	28	64
19	Rise To The Occasion *Climie Fisher* (EMI)	27	48	–
20	Valentine *T'Pau* (Siren/Virgin)	15	9	15
27	Get Outta My Dreams, Get Into My Car *Billy Ocean* (Jive)	8	4	3
25	Give Me All Your Love *Whitesnake* (EMI)	18	18	38
–	Tower of Strength (Bombay Mix) *The Mission* (Mercury/Phonogram)	20	13	12
–	Beat Dis *Bomb The Bass* (Mister-Ron Mute/Rhythm King)	–	5	2
36	Gimme Hope Jo'Anna *Eddy Grant* (Ice)	25	12	8
29	Mandinka *Sinead O'Connor* (Ensign/Chrysalis)	22	17	23
–	Suedehead *Morrissey* (HMV)	–	–	6
–	Together Forever *Rick Astley* (RCA)	–	–	9
–	Doctorin' The House *Coldcut feat. Yazz and the Plastic Population* (Ahead of Our Time)	–	25	10
–	Joe Le Taxi *Vanessa Paradis* (FA Productions/Polydor)	56	29	14
–	Dominion *The Sisters of Mercy* (Merciful Release/WEA)	–	–	17
–	C'Mon Everybody *Eddie Cochran* (Liberty)	43	32	19
55	Hazy Shade Of Winter (Remix) *Bangles* (Def Jam)	41	30	20

MARCH 1988

5		12	19	26
1	I Should Be So Lucky *Kylie Minogue* (PWL)	1	1	3
2	Beat Dis *Bomb The Bass* (Mister-Ron/Rhythm King/Mute)	3	8	23
3	Get Outta My Dreams, Get Into My Car *Billy Ocean* (Jive)	5	10	21
4	Together Forever *Rick Astley* (RCA)	2	2	11
5	Suedehead *Morrissey* (HMV)	8	28	46
6	Tell It To My Heart *Taylor Dane* (Arista)	14	23	36
7	Joe Le Taxi *Vanessa Paradis* (FA Production/Virgin)	4	3	6
8	Gimme Hope Jo'Anna *Eddy Grant* (Ice)	7	14	30
9	Doctorin' The House *Coldcut feat. Yazz & The Plastic Population* (Ahead Of Our Time)	6	9	20
10	I Think We're Alone Now *Tiffany* (MCA)	19	33	43
11	Say It Again *Jermaine Stewart* (10/Virgin)	24	39	54

5		12	19	26
12	Hazy Shade Of Winter (Remix) *Bangles* (Def Jam)	11	21	38
13	Dominion *Sisters of Mercy* (Merciful Release/WEA)	15	25	45
14	C'Mon Everybody *Eddie Cochran* (Liberty)	18	34	52
15	Crash *The Primitives* (RCA)	9	5	7
16	That's The Way It Is *Mel & Kim* (Supreme)	10	15	28
17	I Get Weak *Belinda Carlisle* (Virgin)	13	11	10
18	Tower of Strength (Bombay Mix) *The Mission* (Mercury/Phonogram)	29	50	73
19	Goodgroove *Derek B* (Music Of Life)	16	24	39
20	Ship Of Fools *Erasure* (Mute)	12	6	9
28	Love Is Contagious *Taja Sevelle* (Paisley Park/Reprise/WEA)	17	7	12
35	Never/These Dreams *Heart* (Capitol)	20	12	8
37	Don't Turn Around *Aswad* (Mango/Island)	22	4	1
–	I Know You Got Soul *Eric B. & Rakim* (Cooltempo/Chrysalis)	21	13	19
–	Where Do Broken Hearts Go *Whitney Houston* (Arista)	30	16	15
–	Drop The Boy *Bros* (CBS)	–	17	2
40	Reckless *Afrika Bambaattaa/UB40* (EMI)	27	18	17
32	Heart Of Gold *Johnny Hates Jazz* (Virgin)	23	19	24
38	I'm Not Scared *Eighth Wonder* (CBS)	26	20	13
–	Can I Play With Madness *Iron Maiden* (EMI)	–	–	4
–	Could've Been *Tiffany* (MCA)	–	22	5
–	Cross My Broken Heart (Remix) *Sinitta* (Fanfare)	–	30	14
–	Bass (How Low Can You Go) *Simon Harris* (ffrr/London)	–	29	16
–	Stay On These Roads *a-ha* (Warner Brothers)	–	–	18

APRIL 1988

2		9	16	23	30
1	Don't Turn Around *Aswad* (Mango/Island)	3	10	22	31
2	Drop The Boy *Bros* (CBS)	2	2	9	20
3	Can I Play With Madness *Iron Maiden* (EMI)	5	18	34	59
4	Could've Been *Tiffany* (MCA)	4	4	12	21
5	Stay On These Roads *a-ha* (Warner Brothers)	8	17	32	53
6	Cross My Broken Heart (Remix) *Sinitta* (Fanfare)	6	6	20	27
7	Heart *Pet Shop Boys* (Parlophone)	1	1	1	2
8	I Should Be So Lucky *Kylie Minogue* (PWL)	10	21	37	41
9	Never/These Dreams *Heart* (Capitol)	14	32	48	74
10	I'm Not Scared *Eighth Wonder* (CBS)	9	7	18	25
11	Love Changes (Everything) *Climie Fisher* (EMI)	7	3	2	7
12	Bass (How Low Can You Go) *Simon Harris* (ffrr/London)	18	36	55	–
13	Only In My Dreams *Debbie Gibson* (Atlantic)	11	16	27	46
14	Where Do Broken Hearts Go *Whitney Houston* (Arista)	17	23	52	68
15	Crash *The Primitives* (Lazy/RCA)	27	38	58	72
16	I Get Weak *Belinda Carlisle* (Virgin)	26	41	65	–
17	Temptation *Wet Wet Wet* (Precious/Phonogram)	12	19	31	54
18	Ship Of Fools *Erasure* (Mute)	23	48	74	–
19	Reckless *Afrika Bambaataa/UB40* (EMI)	30	45	–	–
20	Joe Le Taxi *Vanessa Paradis* (FA Productions/Polydor)	35	44	–	–
29	Everywhere *Fleetwood Mac* (Warner Brothers)	13	5	4	10
25	Prove Your Love *Taylor Dane* (Arista)	15	8	11	19
24	Dreaming *Glen Goldsmith* (Reproduction/RCA)	16	12	16	22
22	Ain't Complaining *Status Quo* (Vertigo/Phonogram)	19	24	42	73
37	Who's Leaving Who *Hazell Dean* (EMI)	20	9	6	4
34	Pink Cadillac *Natalie Cole* (Manhattan)	24	11	5	6

2		9	16	23	30
31	Girlfriend *Pebbles* (MCA)	23	13	8	11
–	I Want You Back *Bananarama* (London)	36	14	7	5
28	Just A Mirage *Jellybean feat. Adele Bertei* (Chrysalis)	21	15	13	18
–	Armageddon It (Atomix Mix) *Def Leppard* (Bludgeon Riffola/Phonogram)	28	20	23	37
–	Theme From S'Express *S'Express* (Rhythm King/Mute)	–	25	3	1
–	I Want You Back '88 *Michael Jackson with The Jackson 5* (Motown)	–	31	10	9
–	One More Try *George Michael* (Epic)	–	–	14	8
69	Mary's Prayer *Danny Wilson* (Virgin)	62	35	15	3
51	Get Lucky *Jermaine Stewart* (Sire/Virgin)	40	22	17	13
–	Let's All Chant *Mick and Pat* (PWL)	42	29	19	15
–	Perfect *Fairground Attraction* (RCA)	–	59	35	12
–	The Payback Mix Part One *James Brown* (Urban/Polydor)	–	–	25	14
56	A Love Supreme *Will Downing* (4th+Broadway/Island)	41	34	21	16
50	She's Like The Wind *Patrick Swayze feat. Wendy Fraser* (RCA)	47	39	24	17

MAY 1988

7		14	21	28
1	Theme From S'Express *S'Express* (Rhythm King/Mute)	2	7	10
2	Perfect *Fairground Attraction* (RCA)	1	2	3
3	Mary's Prayer *Danny Wilson* (Virgin)	7	10	20
4	Who's Leaving Who *Hazell Dean* (EMI)	8	13	26
5	I Want You Back *Bananarama* (London)	6	9	21
6	Pink Cadillac *Natalie Cole* (Manhattan)	11	15	24
7	Heart *Pet Shop Boys* (Parlophone)	18	28	48
8	I Want You Back '88 *Michael Jackson with The Jackson 5* (Motown)	10	18	32
9	One More Try *George Michael* (Epic)	19	26	43
10	Blue Monday 1988 *New Order* (Factory)	3	5	5
11	Let's All Chant *Mick and Pat* (PWL)	14	23	39
12	The Payback Mix *James Brown* (Urban/Polydor)	20	40	66
13	Love Changes (Everything) *Climie Fisher* (EMI)	29	47	70
14	A Love Supreme *Will Downing* (4th + Broadway/Island)	17	24	42
15	Pump Up The Bitter (Brutal Mix) *Star Turn On 45* (Pacific/Immaculate)	12	21	46
16	Everywhere *Fleetwood Mac* (Warner Brothers)	21	32	50
17	Loadsamoney (Doin' Up The House) *Harry Enfield* (Mercury/Phonogram)	4	6	12
18	Alphabet Street *Prince* (Paisley Park/Warner Brothers)	9	11	29
19	Get Lucky *Jermaine Stewart* (Siren/Virgin)	30	49	68
20	She's Like The Wind *Patrick Swayze feat. Wendy Fraser* (RCA)	24	29	51
–	With A Little Help/She's Leaving Home *Wet Wet Wet/ Billy Bragg* (Childline)	5	1	1
–	Anfield Rap (Red Machine In Full Effect) *Liverpool F.C.* (Virgin)	13	3	4
–	Got To Be Certain *Kylie Minogue* (PWL)	15	4	2
–	Divine Emotions *Narada* (Reprise/Warner Brothers)	16	8	9
–	Circle In The Sand *Belinda Carlisle* (Virgin)	31	12	6
39	The King of Rock 'n' Roll *Prefab Sprout* (Kitchenware/CBS)	28	14	7
36	Bad Young Brother *Derek B* (Tuff Audio/Phonogram)	26	16	16
44	Somewhere In My heart *Aztec Camera* (WEA)	33	17	8
–	What About Love *Heart* (Capitol)	40	19	14
30	Broken Land *The Adventures* (Elektra)	23	20	23

7	14	21	28
– Don't Go *Hothouse Flowers* (ffrr/London)	47	22	11
– Check This Out *L.A. Mix* (Breakout/A&M)	–	34	13
46 Im Nin'Alu *Ofra Haza* (WEA)	38	25	15
51 My One Temptation *Mica Paris* (4th + Broadway Island)	42	30	17
54 Oh Patti (Don't Feel Sorry For Loverboy) *Scritti Politti* (Virgin)	41	31	18
47 Out Of The Blue *Debbie Gibson* (Atlantic)	37	27	19

JUNE 1988

4	11	18	25
1 With A Little/She's Leaving Home *Wet Wet Wet/ Billy Bragg* (Childline)	1	3	10
2 Got To Be Certain *Kylie Minogue* (PWL)	2	6	12
3 Perfect *Fairground Attraction* (RCA)	10	17	30
4 Circle In The Sand *Belinda Carlisle* (Virgin)	6	13	23
5 Somewhere In My Heart *(Aztec Camera* (WEA)	3	8	14
6 Check This Out *L.A. Mix* (Breakout/A&M)	9	18	38
7 The King Of Rock 'n' Roll *Prefab Sprout* (Kitchenware/CBS)	13	23	41
8 My One Temptation *Mica Paris* (4th+Broadway/Island)	7	12	19
9 Blue Monday 1988 *New Order* (Factory)	20	34	46
10 Love Will Save The Day *Whitney Houston* (Arista)	16	31	42
11 Don't Go *Hothouse Flowers* (ffrr/London)	17	27	51
12 Anfield Rap (Red Machine In Full Effect) *Liverpool F.C.* (Virgin)	21	58	–
13 Oh Patti (Don't Feel Sorry For Loverboy) *Scritti Politti* (Virgin)	14	24	37
14 Voyage Voyage (Remix) *Desireless* (CBS)	5	5	7
15 What About Love *Heart* (Capitol)	26	45	–
16 Im Nin'Alu *Ofra Haza* (WEA)	29	54	–
17 Theme From S'Express *S'Express* (Rhythm King/Mute)	27	36	45
18 Give A Little Love *Aswad* (Mango/Island)	11	14	28
19 Out Of The Blue *Debbie Gibson* (Atlantic)	28	47	–
20 Divine Emotions *Narada* (Reprise/Warner Brothers)	34	51	74
22 Doctorin' The Tardis *Time Lords* (Communications)	4	1	2
23 I Saw Him Standing There *Tiffany* (MCA)	8	10	15
– Everday Is Like Sunday *Morrisey* (HMV)	12	9	13
32 Wild World *Maxi Priest* (10)	15	7	5
25 Another Weekend *Five Star* (Tent)	18	22	48
– Chains Of Love (Remix) *Erasure* (Mute)	19	11	11
– I Owe You Nothing *Bros* (CBS)	–	2	1
– Boys (Summertime Love) *Sabrina* (Ibiza)	24	4	3
27 Don't Call Me Baby *Voice Of The Beehive* (London)	23	15	16
43 Tribute (Right On) *The Pasadenas* (CBS)	33	16	6
– The Twist (Yo Ywist) *Fat Boys & Chubby Checker* (Urban)	–	19	4
– Lucretia My Reflection *Sisters Of Mercy* (Merciful Release)	–	20	22
– In The Air Tonight (88 Remix) *Phil Collins* (Virgin)	–	35	8
– Breakfast in Bed *UB40 with Chrissie Hynde* (Dep International/Virgin)	–	30	9
53 Don't Blame It On That Girl/Wam-Bam/Boogie *Matt Bianco* (WEA)	36	21	17
– You Have Placed A Chill In My Heart *Eurythmics* (RCA)	37	25	18
– Car Wash/Is It Love You're After *Rose Royce* (MCA)	46	28	20

2		9	16	23	30
1	I Owe You Nothing *Bros* (CBS)	4	4	11	16
2	The Twist (Yo, Twist) *Fat Boys/Chubby Checker* (Tin Pan Apple/Urban/Polydor)	2	3	6	13
3	Boys (Summertime Love) *Sabrina* (Ibiza/London)	6	8	15	25
4	In The Air Tonight (88 Remix) *Phil Collins* (Virgin)	5	10	19	37
5	Tribute (Right On) *The Pasadenas* (CBS)	9	11	18	20
6	Breakfast In Bed *UB40 with Chrissie Hynde* (Dep International/Virgin)	8	7	10	17
7	Push It/Tramp *Salt 'N Pepa* (Champion)	33	2	2	2
8	Doctorin' The Tardis *The Timelords* (KLF Communications) The Timelords	12	27	35	57
9	Wild World *Maxi Priest* (10/Virgin)	10	17	27	48
10	Fast Car *Tracey Chapman* (Elektra)	7	5	7	12
11	Nothing's Gonna Change My Love For You *Glen Medeiros* (London)	1	1	1	1
12	Voyage Voyage (Remix) *Desireless* (CBS)	17	26	31	45
13	Chains Of Love (Remix) *Erasure* (Mute)	26	39	64	–
14	Wap-Bam-Boogie (Don't Blame It On That Girl) *Matt Bianco* (WEA)	11	12	17	18
15	Tougher Than The Rest *Bruce Springsteen* (CBS)	13	16	23	33
16	You Have Placed A Chill In My Heart *Eurythmics* (RCA)	19	33	51	73
17	I Will Be With You *T'Pau* (Siren/Virgin)	14	21	30	54
18	Maybe (We Should Call it A Day) *Hazell Dean* (EMI)	15	22	32	75
19	Got To Be Certain *Kylie Minogue* (PWL)	27	37	46	65
20	Car Wash/Is It Love You're After *Rose Royce* (MCA)	25	40	62	–
32	Roses Are Red *Mac Band* (MCA)	16	9	8	8
23	Don't Believe The Hype *Public Enemy* (Def Jam/CBS)	18	31	42	74
21	There's More To Love *Communards* (London)	20	23	33	62
–	I Don't Want To Talk About It *Everything But The Girl* (Bianco Y Negro/WEA)	23	6	3	3
36	Cross My Heart *Eighth Wonder* (CBS)	22	13	14	19
–	Dirty Diana *Michael Jackson* (Epic)	–	14	4	4
48	I Want Your Love *Transvision Vamp* (MCA)	32	15	5	5
–	Foolish Beat *Debbie Gibson* (Atlantic)	34	18	9	9
–	Monkey *George Michael* (Epic)	–	19	13	14
–	Love Bites *Def Leppard* (Bludgeon Riffola)	–	20	12	11
–	You Came *Kim Wilde* (MCA)	–	38	16	6
–	Superfly Guy *S'Express* (Rhythm King/Mute)	–	–	20	7
–	The Only Way Is Up *Yazz & The Plastic Population* (Big Life)	–	–	28	10
–	Reach Out, I'll Be There *The Four Tops* (Motown)	–	–	36	15

6		13	20	27
1	The Only Way Is Up *Yazz & The Plastic Population* (Big Life)	1	1	1
2	The Loco-Motion *Kylie Minogue* (PWL)	2	2	2
3	Nothing's Gonna Change My Love *Glenn Medeiros* (London)	7	12	27
4	You Came *Kim Wilde* (MCA)	3	4	8
5	Push It/Tramp *Salt 'N Pepa* (Champion)	9	16	22
6	Superfly Guy *S'Express* (Rhythm King/Mute)	5	9	11
7	I Need You *B.V.S.M.P.* (Debut/Passion)	4	3	5
8	I Don't Walk To Talk About It *Everything But The Girl* (Bianco Y Negro/WEA)	12	20	32

6	13	20	27
9 I Want Your Love *Transvision Vamp* (MCA)	10	14	23
10 Dirty Diana *Michael Jackson* (Epic)	16	27	44
11 Roses Are Red *Mac Band/The McCampbell Brothers* (MCA)	14	18	30
12 Reach Out I'll Be There *The Four Tops* (Motown)	11	11	13
13 Foolish Beat *Debbie Gibson* (Atlantic)	19	21	38
14 Find My Love *Fairground Attraction* (RCA)	8	7	7
15 Love Bites *Def Leppard* (Bludgeon/Riffola/Phonogram)	21	33	49
16 Peek A Boo *Siouxsie/Banshees* (Wonderland/Polydor)	18	25	47
17 Hustle! (To The Music) *The Funky Worm* (FON/WEA)	13	13	19
18 Fast Car *Tracey Chapman* (Elektra)	30	50	61
19 All Fired Up *Pat Benatar* (Chrysalis)	20	26	45
20 Monkey *George Michael* (Epic)	32	54	–
– The Evil That Men Do *Iron Maiden* (EMI)	6	5	9
22 Martha's Harbour *All About Eve* (Mercury/Phonogram)	15	10	14
37 Hands To Heaven *Breathe* (Siren/Virgin)	17	6	4
34 The Harder I Try *Brother Beyond* (Parlophone)	24	8	3
36 Good Tradition *Tanita Tikaram* (WEA)	23	15	10
56 My Love *Julio Iglesias feat. Stevie Wonder* (CBS)	33	17	6
– On The Beach Summer '88 *Chris Rea* (WEA)	36	19	12
41 Somewhere Down The Crazy River *Robbie Robertson* (Geffen)	35	22	15
– King of Emotion *Big Country* (Mercury/Phonogram)	–	24	16
– Running All Over The World *Status Quo* (Vertigo/Phonogram)	–	30	17
66 Teardrops *Womack & Womack* (4th+Broadway/Island)	55	37	18
– Megablast/Don't Make Me Wait *Bomb the Bass* (Mister-ron/Mute)	–	–	20

SEPTEMBER 1988

3	10	17	24
1 The Only Way is Up *Yazz & The Plastic Population* (Big Life)	3	7	10
2 The Harder I Try *Brother Beyond* (Parlophone)	2	5	13
3 The Loco-Motion *Kylie Minogue* (PWL)	9	8	26
4 Hands To Heaven *Breathe* (Siren/Virgin)	10	16	25
5 My Love *Julio Iglesias feat. Stevie Wonder* (CBS)	7	11	23
6 Megablast/Don't Make Me Wait *Bomb The Bass* (Rhythm King)	6	9	14
7 Teardrops *Womack & Womack* (4th+Broadway/Island)	4	3	3
8 I Need You *B.V.M.P.* (Debut/Passion)	14	24	35
9 A Groovy Kind Of Love *Phil Collins* (Virgin)	1	1	2
10 Find My Love *Fairground Attraction* (RCA)	18	31	44
11 Good Tradition *Tanita Tikaram* (WEA)	17	39	46
12 Touchy! *a-ha* (Warner Brothers)	11	19	27
13 You Came *Kim Wilde* (MCA)	22	34	50
14 The Race *Yello* (Mercury/Phonogram)	8	8	7
15 Rush Hour *Jane Wiedlin* (Manhattan/EMI)	13	12	17
16 Somewhere Down The Crazy River *Robbie Robertson* (Geffen)	29	38	61
17 Running All Over The World *Status Quo* (Vertigo/Phonogram)	30	35	49
18 Heaven In My Hands *Level 42* (Polydor)	12	21	36
19 Anything For You *Gloria Estefan & Miami Sound Machine* (Epic)	15	10	11
20 Harvester Of Sorrow *Metallica* (Vertigo/Phonogram)	32	–	–
28 He Ain't Heavy, He's My Brother *The Hollies*	5	2	1
– Another Part Of Me *Michael Jackson* (Epic)	16	15	19
34 I'm Gonna Be *The Proclaimers* (Chrysalis)	19	14	12
40 Easy *Commodores* (Motown)	20	17	15
– Lovely Day (Sunshine Mix) *Bill Withers* (CBS)	21	6	4
– Nothing Can Divide Us *Jason Donovan* (PWL)	37	13	5

	10	17	24
– I Quit *Bros* (CBS)	–	4	6
48 Big Fun *Inner City feat. Kevin Saunderson* (10/Virgin)	31	20	8
– Domino Dancing *Pet Shop Boys* (Parlophone)	–	–	9
– She Wants To Dance With Me *Rick Astley* (RCA)	–	–	16
– Bad Medicine *Bon Jovi* (Vertigo/Phonogram)	–	–	18
– Riding On A Train *Pasadenas* (CBS)	–	29	20

OCTOBER 1988

1	8	15	22	29
1 He Ain't Heavy, He's My Brother *The Hollies* (Parlophone)	2	5	14	20
2 A Groovy Kind Of Love *Phil Collins* (Virgin)	5	10	13	16
3 Desire *U2* (Island)	1	2	17	30
4 Teardrops *Womack & Womack* (4th+Broadway/Island)	4	4	10	12
5 Lovely Day (Sunshine Mix) *Bill Withers* (CBS)	8	14	24	37
6 Nothing Can Divide Us *Jason Donovan* (PWL)	6	9	12	20
7 Domino Dancing *Pet Shop Boys* (Parlophone)	9	12	21	33
8 One Moment In Time *Whitney Houston* (Arista)	3	1	1	3
9 Big Fun *Inner City feat. Kevin Saunderson* (10/Virgin)	10	11	16	15
10 She Wants To Dance With Me *Rick Astley* (RCA)	7	6	8	13
11 I'm Gonna Be *The Proclaimers* (Chrysalis)	15	24	33	54
12 The Race *Yello* (Mercury/Phonogram)	18	26	34	55
13 Riding On A Train *The Pasadenas* (CBS)	13	13	19	24
14 I Quit *Bros* (CBS)	24	33	55	66
15 Anything For You *Gloria Estefan & Miami Sound Machine* (Epic)	20	28	39	58
16 The Only Way Is Up *Yazz & The Plastic Population* (Big Life)	23	30	43	71
17 Bad Medicine *Bon Jovi* (Vertigo/Phonogram)	19	27	40	62
18 Easy *Commodores* (Motown)	26	38	56	–
19 A Little Respect *Erasure* (Mute)	12	7	4	5
20 I Don't Want Your Love *Duran Duran* (EMI)	14	18	28	67
25 Don't Worry Be Happy *Bobby McFerrin* (Manhattan)	11	3	2	6
24 Fake 88 *Alexander O'Neal* (Tabu)	16	17	26	42
34 Wee Rule *Wee Papa Girl Rappers* (Jive)	17	8	6	7
50 Never Trust A Stranger *Kim Wilde* (MCA)	32	15	7	9
44 Burn It Up *The Beatmasters with P. P. Arnold* (Rhythm King)	35	16	15	14
37 Secret Garden *T'Pau* (Siren/Virgin)	22	19	18	23
– We Call it Acieed *D. Mob* (featuring Gary Haisman)	–	20	3	4
– Orinoco Flow *Enya* (WEA)	–	29	5	1
– Harvest For The World *The Christians* (Island)	–	21	9	8
– Je Ne Sais Pas Pourquoi *Kylie Minogue* (PWL)	–	–	11	2
69 Girl You Know It's True *Milli Vanilli* (Cooltempo/Chrysalis)	56	40	20	10
– Stand Up For Your Love Rights *Yazz* (The Beatmasters)	–	–	–	11
45 Can You Party *Royal House* (Champion)	49	52	30	17
– She Makes My Day *Robert Palmer* (EMI)	–	71	38	18
– Kiss *Art Of Noise feat. Tom Jones* (China)	–	–	–	19

NOVEMBER 1988

5	12	19	26
1 Orinoco Flow *Enya* (WEA)	1	5	13
2 Je Ne Sais Pas Pourquoi *Kylie Minogue* (PWL)	2	3	10
3 Girl You Know It's True *Milli Vanilli* (Cooltempo/Chrysalis)	4	7	11
4 Stand Up For Your Love Rights *Yazz* (Big Life)	3	2	5
5 Kiss *Art Of Noise feat. Tom Jones* (China)	7	15	26
6 One Moment In Time *Whitney Houston* (Arista)	13	19	38

	12	19	26
7 We Call it Acieed *D. Mob* (ffrr/London)	11	17	28
8 She Makes My Day *Robert Palmer* (EMI)	6	9	15
9 Wee Rule *Wee Papa Girl Rapperes* (Jive)	19	27	50
10 A Little Respect *Erasure* (Mute)	14	20	36
11 Harvest For The World *The Christians* (Island)	16	26	44
12 Don't Worry Be Happy *Bobby McFerrin* (Manhattan)	21	25	53
13 Never Trust A Stranger *Kim Wilde* (MCA)	20	23	43
14 Can You Party *Royal House* (Champion)	17	18	34
15 Real Gone Kid *Deacon Blue* (CBS)	10	10	8
16 Burn It Up *Beatmasters with P. P. Arnold* (Rhythm King/Mute)	27	47	74
17 The First Time *Robin Beck* (Mercury/Phonogram)	5	1	1
18 A Groovy Kind Of Love *Phil Collins* (Virgin)	28	37	59
19 Teardrops *Womack & Womack* (4th + Broadway/Island)	31	40	62
20 She Wants To Dance With Me *Rick Astley* (RCA)	30	49	68
30 He Ain't No Competition *Brother Beyond* (Parlophone)	8	6	9
24 1-2-3 *Gloria Estefan & Miami Sound Machine* (Epic)	9	11	14
28 Let's Stick Together 88 Remix *Bryan Ferry* (EG/Virgin)	12	14	22
39 Missing You *Chris De Burgh* (A&M)	15	8	3
– Need You Tonight *INXS* (Mercury/Phonogram)	18	4	2
– Twist And Shout *Salt 'N' Pepa* (ff/London)	22	12	4
– The Clairvoyant *Iron Maiden* (EMI)	–	13	6
66 Till I Loved You (Love Theme from Goya) *Barbara Streisand* (CBS)	32	16	17
– Left To My Own Devices *Pet Shop Boys* (Parlophone)	–	–	7
– Smooth Criminal *Michael Jackson* (Epic)	–	–	12
– Two Hearts *Phil Collins* (Virgin)	–	–	16
– Take Me To Your Heart *Rick Astley* (RCA)	–	–	18
– Say A Little Prayer *Bomb The Bass feat. Maureen* (Rhythym King/Mute)	–	–	19
– Nathan Jones *Bananarama* (London)	–	30	20

DECEMBER 1988

3	10	17	24	31
1 First Time *Robin Beck* (Mercury/Phonogram)	5	12	18	22
2 Cat Among The Pigeons/Silent Night *Bros* (Epic)	4	5	6	8
3 Missing You *Chris De Burgh* (A&M)	10	17	22	30
4 Left To My Own Devices *Pet Shop Boys* (Parlophone)	11	19	26	33
5 I Need You Tonight *INXS* (Mercury/Phonogram)	13	21	25	25
6 Two Hearts *Phil Collins* (Virgin)	6	7	8	10
7 Mistletoe & Wine *Cliff Richard* (EMI)	1	1	1	1
8 Smooth Criminal *Michael Jackson* (Epic)	9	11	14	13
9 Twist And Shout *Salt 'N Pepa* (ffrr/London)	19	33	42	47
10 Say A Little Prayer *Bomb The Bass feat. Maureen* (Rhythm King/Mute)	12	14	17	26
11 Real Gone Kid *Deacon Blue* (CBS)	21	32	41	45
12 Take Me To Your Heart *Rick Astley* (RCA)	8	8	12	16
13 Radio Romance *Tiffany* (MCA)	14	18	24	27
14 Jack To The Sound Of The Underground *Hithouse* (Supreme)	16	24	29	36
15 He Ain't No Competition *Brother Beyond* (Parlophone)	26	44	60	68
16 Suddenly *Angry Anderson* (Food For Thought)	3	3	4	4
17 Stand Up For Your Love Rights *Yazz* (Big Life)	29	37	44	44
18 Stakker Humanoid *Humanoid* (Westside)	17	20	31	38
19 Nathan Jones *Bananarama* (London)	15	16	16	24
20 The Clairvoyant *Iron Maiden* (EMI)	39	61	72	64
– Especially For You *Kylie Minogue* (PWL)	2	2	2	2
– Crackers International EP *Erasure* (Mute)	7	4	3	3

3	10	17	24	31
24 Kissing A Fool *George Michael* (Epic)	18	26	37	42
34 Burning Bridges (On And Off) *Status Quo* (Vertigo/ Phonogram)	20	9	7	5
– Good Life *Inner City* (10/Virgin)	22	6	5	6
– Angel of Harlem *U2* (Island)	–	10	9	12
37 Downtown '88 *Petula Clark* (PRT)	24	13	10	11
– Fine Time *New Order* (Factory)	23	15	11	17
– Buffalo Stance *Neneh Cherry* (Circa/Virgin)	44	31	13	7
46 Loco In Acapulco *Four Tops* (Arista)	30	23	15	9
51 Four Letter Word *Kim Wilde* (MCA)	34	28	19	14
42 You Are The One *a-ha* (Warner Brothers)	28	25	20	18
– Keeping The Dream Alive *Freiheit* (CBS)	–	47	27	15
43 9 A.M. (The Comfort Zone) *Londonbeat* (Anxious/RCA)	38	29	21	19
– Evening Falls *Enya* (WEA)	–	–	36	20

1988 – BEST-SELLING RECORDS

Singles:

1. Mistletoe & Wine *Cliff Richard* (EMI)
2. The Only Way Is Up *Yazz & The Plastic Population* (Big Life)
3. I Should Be So Lucky *Kylie Minogue* (PWL)
4. Especially For You *Kylie Minogue & Jason Donovan* (PWL)
5. I Think We're Alone Now *Tiffany* (MCA)
6. Nothing's Gonna Change My Love For You *Glenn Medeiros* (London)
7. A Groovy Kind Of Love *Phil Collins* (Virgin)
8. He Ain't Heavy, He's My Brother *The Hollies* (EMI)
9. With A Little Help From My Friends/She's Leaving Home *Wet Wet Wet/Billy Bragg* (Childline)
10. Teardrops *Womack & Womack* (4th + Broadway/Island)
11. The Loco-Motion *Kylie Minogue* (PWL)
12. First Time *Robin Beck* (Mercury/Phonogram)
13. Perfect *Fairground Attraction* (RCA)
14. One Moment In Time *Whitney Houston* (Arista)
15. Push It/Tramp *Salt 'N Pepa* (Champion)
16. Suddenly *Angry Anderson* (Food for Thought)
17. Heaven Is A Place On Earth *Belinda Carlisle* (Virgin)
18. Orinoco Flow *Enya* (WEA)
19. Theme from *S'Express* (Rhythm King/Mute)
20. Je Ne Sais Pas Pourquoi *Kylie Minogue* (PWL)
21. Got To Be Certain *Kylie Minogue* (PWL)
22. The Harder I Try *Brother Beyond* (Parlophone)
23. Tell It To My Heart *Taylor Dayne* (Arista)
24. Crackers International EP *Erasure* (Mute)
25. I Owe You Nothing *Bros* (CBS)
26. Heart *Pet Shop Boys* (Parlophone)
27. Get Outta My Dreams, Get Into My Car *Billy Ocean* (Jive)
28. Don't Turn Around *Aswad* (Mango/Island)
29. Nothing Can Divide Us *Jason Donovan* (PWL)
30. Beat Dis *Bomb The Bass* (Mister-Ron/Rhythm King/Mute)
31. Drop The Boy *Bros* (CBS)
32. Sign Your Name *Terence Trent D'Arby* (CBS)
33. The Twist (Yo Twist) *Fat Boys & Chubby Checker* (Urban/Polydor)
34. When Will I Be Famous? *Bros* (CBS)
35. Boys (Summertime Love) *Sabrina* (Ibiza/London)
36. House Arrest *Krush* (Fontana/Club/Phonogram)
37. You Came *Kim Wilde* (MCA)
38. Lovely Day (Sunshine Mix) *Bill Withers* (CBS)
39. I Need You *B.V.S.M.P.* (Debut/Passion)
40. Girl You Know It's True *Milli Vanilli* (Cooltempo/Chrysalis)
41. Stand Up For Your Love Rights *Yazz* (Big Life)
42. Cat Among The Pigeons/Silent Night *Bros* (CBS)
43. Don't Worry, be Happy *Bobby McFerrin* (EMI Manhattan)
44. Hands To Heaven *Breathe* (Siren/Virgin)
45. Desire *U2* (Island)
46. A Little Respect *Erasure* (Mute)
47. Big Fun *Inner City/Kevin Saunderson* (10/Virgin)
48. Love Changes (Everything) *Climie Fisher* (EMI)
49. Together Forever *Rick Astley* (RCA)
50. Missing You *Chris De Burgh* (A&M)

Albums:

1　Kylie *Kylie Minogue* (PWL)
2　Private Collection *Cliff Richard* (EMI)
3　Bad *Michael Jackson* (Epic)
4　Push *Bros* (CBS)
5　Now That's What I Call Music 13 *Various* (EMI/Virgin/PolyGram)
6　Popped In Souled Out *Wet Wet Wet* (Precious Organisation/Phonogram)
7　Tracy Chapman *Tracy Chapman* (Elektra)
8　Introducing The Hardline According to . . . *Terence Trent D'Arby* (CBS)
9　Tango In The Night *Fleetwood Mac* (Warner Brothers)
10　Rattle And Hum *U2* (Island)
11　Money For Nothing *Dire Straits* (Vertigo/Phonogram)
12　Now That's What I Call Music 12 *Various* (EMI/Virgin/PolyGram)
13　Now That's What I Call Music Music 11 *Various* (EMI/Virgin/PhonoGram)
14　Dirty Dancing (OST) *Various* (RCA)
15　Kick *INXS* (Mercury/Phonogram)
16　Premiere Collection *Andrew Lloyd Webber Various* (Really Useful/Polydor)
17　Whitney *Whitney Houston* (Arista)
18　Christians *Christians* (Island)
19　The Greatest Hits Collection *Bananarama* (London)
20　Heaven On Earth *Belinda Carlisle* (A&M)
21　The Innocents *Erasure* (Mute)
22　Hearsay/All Mixed Up *Alexander O'Neal* (Tabu)
23　Turn Back The Clock *Johnny Hates Jazz* (Virgin)
24　Introspective *Pet Shop Boys* (Parlophone)
25　Bridge of Spies *T'Pau* (Siren/Virgin)
26　The Best of OMD *OMD* (Virgin)
27　Greatest Hits *Fleetwood Mac* (Warner Brothers)
28　Idol Songs: 11 Of The Berst *Billy Idol* (Chrysalis)
29　New Light Through Old Windows *Chris Rea* (WEA)
30　The First Of A Million Kisses *Fairground Attraction* (RCA)
31　The Greatest Love *Various* (Telstar)
32　The Ultimate Collection *Bryan Ferry/Roxy Music* (E.G. Virgin)
33　Buster (OST) *Various* (Virgin)
34　Nite Flite *Various* (CBS)
35　Pet Shop Boys, Actually *Pet Shop Boys* (Parlophone)
36　Flying Colours *Chris De Burgh* (A&M)
37　Faith *George Michael* (Epic)
38　Greatest Hits *Human League* (Virgin)
39　Whenever You Need Somebody *Rick Astley* (RCA)
40　Soft Metal *Various* (Stylus)
41　The Hits Album *Various* (CBS/WEA/BMG)
42　To Whom It May Concern *Pasadenas* (CBS)
43　Watermark *Enya* (WEA)
44　The Hits Album 8 *Various* (CBS/WEA/BMG)
45　More Dirty Dancing (OST) *Various* (RCA)
46　Give Me The Reason *Luther Vandross* (Epic)
47　Smash Hits Party 88 *Various* (Dover/Chrysalis)
48　Wanted *Yazz* (Big Life)
49　The Legendary *Roy Orbison* (Telstar)
50　Hot City Nights *Various* (Vertigo/Phonogram)

1989

'Do They Know It's Christmas' became the only song in the eighties to hit the top twice, and was the twelfth Number One for the production team of Stock, Aitken and Waterman, with ten acts helping the dozen.

S,A&W were not the only ones to have a good year, Neneh Cherry had three hit singles, a gold album and a second child. Teens screamed and bought Bros, Kylie Minogue, Jason Donovan, new American sensations New Kids On The Block; and among the dance people there came Paula Abdul, Black Box, Technotronic, and quality outfit Soul II Soul.

The most unexpected comeback came from a duo of Marc Almond and Gene Pitney. For Almond it was his most successful single since 'Stories of Johnny' in 1985, and that only reached 23; for the American, he hadn't tasted chart life since days with Bronze Records in 1974.

The best kept secret lay with hit duo Milli Vanilli, for it was not until 1990 that we would learn the two merely fronted their credited records.

Familiars were present, not least Alice Cooper, and three American women; Linda Ronstadt, Natalie Cole, and Cher. Cooper had last seen a Top Twenty 20 hit in 1974.

By the year's end, Madonna could claim to have had more Top Ten hits, more weeks in the Top Ten, and having sold more records than any other act of the eighties decade. Sometimes the razzamatazz surrounding the admittedly often odd American girl hid her stupendous chart achievements, not-withstanding an endless supply of top class singles and albums. Among the SAW class of '89 was Cliff Richard, busily enjoying a run of hits to equal his splendid chart times of the early Sixties, and benefitting from the pacey 'I Just Don't Have The Heart.' The same trio gave Donna Summer a fresh lease of life. And yes, the three were behind another major 'charity' hit, the reworking of 'Ferry Cross The Mersey' by Holly Johnson, Paul McCartney, The Christians – and the original man from 1964, Gerry Marsden, without his Pacemakers.

Any year sees a diminution of a long running hit

artist, and 1989 was the one to see Shakin' Stevens suffering; when 'Love Attack' failed, it was his fifth to miss the Top Twenty, and once that was an area that he knew so well, 21 singles in a row made the Top Twenty between 1980 and 1987. The Eurythmics belied their fame in chart performance, with 'Revival' being the sixth of the then last seven releases not to make the Top Twenty. 'Thorn In My Side' in the Autumn of 1986 had been the last Top Ten hit.

It was the year when Roy Orbison had his first Top Ten hit since 1966; this time it was 'You Got It' and in 1966 it had been 'Too Soon to Know'. But alas, Orbison was no longer with us. Jive Bunny and the Mastermixers sold 600,000 plus of their 'Swing The Mood'. They collected a platinum award, the first act to do so since 1985. Previously for such an award you had to sell a cool million, as did 'The Power of Love' for Jennifer Rush.

The marketing of singles in endless formats sometimes helps artists (see foreword to Iron Maiden in 1991). Thus 1989, had nine different editions of 'Lay Your Hands On Me' from Bon Jovi. But it never made the Top Ten for all the effort and expense!

JANUARY 1989

	14	21	28
7			
1 Especially For You *Kylie Minogue & Jason Donovan* (PWL)	1	1	3
2 Crackers International EP *Erasure* (Mute)	2	2	6
3 Suddenly *Angry Anderson* (Food For Thought)	5	15	25
4 Good Life *Inner City* (10/Virgin)	4	8	12
5 Mistletoe & Wine *Cliff Richard* (EMI)	18	58	–
6 Buffalo Stance *Neneh Cherry* (Circa/Virgin)	3	3	8
7 Loco In Acapulco *Four Tops* (Arista)	7	14	24
8 Burning Bridges (On & Off) *Status Quo* (Vertigo/Phonogram)	11	26	42
9 Four Letter Word *Kim Wilde* (MCA)	6	12	18
10 Cat Among The Pigeons/Silent Night *Bros* (CBS)	21	51	–
11 Two Hearts *Phil Collins* (Virgin)	15	32	44
12 Smooth Criminal *Michael Jackson* (Epic)	20	36	57
13 Downtown '88 *Petula Clark* (PRT)	25	39	61
14 Take Me To Your Heart *Rick Astley* (RCA)	23	43	68
15 You Are The One *a-ha* (Warner Brothers)	13	20	32
16 Keeping The Dream Alive *Freheit* (CBS)	14	16	24
17 Angel Of Harlem *U2* Island)	35	53	–
18 First Time *Robin Beck* (Mercury/Phonogram)	43	–	–
19 Fine Time *New Order* (Factory)	28	41	62
20 Radio Romance *Tiffany* (MCA)	27	46	–
29 She Drives Me Crazy *Fine Young Cannibals* (London)	8	5	5
25 All She Wants Is *Duran Duran* (EMI)	9	13	26
39 Baby I Love Your Way/Freebird *Will To Power* (Epic)	10	6	9
31 Waiting For A Star To Fall *Boy Meets Girl* (RCA)	12	9	11
28 Rhythm Is Gonna Get You *Gloria Estefan/Miami Sound Machine* (Epic)	16	10	29
– The Living Years *Mike & The Mechanics* (WEA)	17	4	2
– Something's Gotten Hold Of My Heart *Marc Almond feat. Gene Pitney* (Parlophone)	19	10	1
– You Got It *Roy Orbison* (Virgin)	24	7	4
– Cuddly Toy *Roachford* (CBS)	31	11	7
– Get On The Dance Floor *Rose Base & DJ E-Z Rock* (Supreme)	30	17	14
42 Baby Don't Forget My Number *Milli Vanilli* (Cooltempo/Chrysalis)	32	19	16
– Love Train *Holly Johnson* (MCA)	44	21	10
– Wait *Robert Howard & Kim Mazelle* (RCA)	38	22	13
– Be My Twin *Brother Beyond* (Parlophone)	–	29	15
– That's The Way Love Is *Ten City* (Atlantic)	–	33	17
– Where Is The Love *Will Downing & Mica Paris* (4th + Broadway/Island)	–	28	19
– Respect *Adeva* (Cooltempo/Chrysalis)	40	24	20

FEBRUARY 1989

	11	18	25
4			
1 Something's Gotten Hold Of My Heart *Marc Almond feat. Gene Pitney* (Parlophone)	1	1	3
2 The Living Years *Mike & The Mechanics* (WEA)	2	4	7
3 You Got it *Roy Orbison* (Virgin)	3	7	11
4 Cuddly Toy *Roachford* (CBS)	5	12	26
5 Love Train *Holly Johnson*	4	5	8
6 She Drives Me Crazy *Fine Young Cannibals* (London)	10	19	22
7 Especially For You *Kylie Minogue & Jason Donovan* (PWL)	16	23	19
8 That's The Way Love Is *Ten City* (Atlantic)	8	13	19
9 Crackers International EP *Erasure* (Mute)	17	26	36

410

4	11	18	25
10 Wait *Robert Howard & Kym Mazelle* (RCA)	7	10	17
11 Baby I Love Your Way/Freebird (Medley) *Will To Power* (Epic)	19	27	40
12 Buffalo Stance *Neneh Cherry* (Circa/Virgin)	24	28	42
13 Big Area *Then Jericho* (London)	14	22	37
14 Be My Twin *Brother Beyond* (Parlophone)	21	30	49
15 Waiting For A Star To Fall *Boy Meets Girl* (RCA)	27	36	54
16 Baby Don't Forget My Number *Milli Vanilli* (Cooltempo/ Chrysalis)	22	35	51
17 Respect *Adeva* (Cooltempo/Chrysalis)	18	25	38
18 My Prerogative *Bobby Brown* (MCA)	9	6	6
19 Good Life *Inner City* (10/Virgin)	30	39	59
20 Get On The Dance Floor *Rot Base & DJ E-2* (Supreme)	29	44	64
– Last Of The Famous Int. Playboys *Morrisey* (HMV)	6	8	21
27 Fine Time *Yazz* (Big Life)	11	9	9
24 Love Changes Everything *Michael Ball* (Really Useful/Polydor)	12	3	2
22 It's Only Love *Simply Red* (Elektra)	13	14	24
23 The Lover In Me *Sheena Easton* (MCA)	15	15	25
29 I Only Wanna Be With You *Samantha Fox* (Jive)	20	16	18
– Belfast Child *Simple Minds* (Virgin)	–	2	1
– Hold Me In Your Arms *Rick Astley* (RCA)	26	11	10
69 Stop *Sam Brown* (A&M)	37	17	5
31 Looking For Linda *Hue & Cry* (Circa/Virgin)	23	18	16
– Rocket *Def Leppard* (Bludgeon/Riffola/Phonogram)	31	20	15
– Leave Me Alone *Michael Jackson* (Epic)	–	–	4
– Help *Bananarama-La na nee nee noo noo* (London)	–	–	12
15 I Don't Want A Lover *Texas* (Mercury/Phonogram)	32	21	13
– Hey Music Lover *S'Express* (Rhythm King/Mute)	–	29	14
– Every Rose Has Its Thorn *Poison* (Enigma/Capitol)	33	24	20

MARCH 1989

4	11	18	25
1 Belfast Child *Simple Minds* (Virgin)	6	13	22
2 Leave Me Alone *Michael Jackson* (Epic)	5	11	15
3 Love Changes Everything *Michael Ball* (Really Useful/Polydor)	2	8	11
4 Stop *Sam Brown* (A&M)	4	5	9
5 Help *Bananarama-LaNaNeeNeeNooNoo* (London)	3	3	6
6 Hey Music Lover *S'Express feat. Eric & Billy* (Rhythm King/ Mute)	7	9	12
7 My Prerogative *Bobby Brown* (MCA)	14	26	36
8 I Don't Want A Lover *Texas* (Mercury/Phonogram)	9	14	19
9 Too Many Broken Hearts *Jason Donovan* (PWL)	1	1	2
10 Can't Stay Away From You *Gloria Estefan & Miami Sound Machine* (Epic)	8	7	7
11 Hold me In Your Arms *Rick Astley* (RCA)	19	33	27
12 Something's Gotten Hold Of My Heart *Marc Almond feat. Gene Pitney* (Parlophone)	20	39	50
13 Love Train *Holly Johnson* (MCA)	26	40	59
14 Every Rose Has Its Thorn *Poison* (Enigma/Capitol)	13	18	25
15 Looking For Linda *Hue & Cry* (Circa/Virgin)	23	34	51
16 Turn Up The Bass *Tyree feat. Kool Rock Steady* (ffrr/London)	12	16	23
17 Blow The House Down *Living In A Box* (Chrysalis)	10	10	14
18 Fine Time *Yazz* (Big Life)	31	46	62
19 Rocket *Def Leppard* (Bludgeon/Riffola/Phonogram)	33	49	70
20 Nothing Has Been Proved *Dusty Springfield* (Parlophone)	16	17	26
30 This Time I Know It's For Real *Donna Summer* (Warner Brothers)	11	4	3
34 Straight Up *Paula Abdul* (Siren/Virgin)	15	6	4
32 I'd Rather Jack *The Reynolds Girls* (PWL)	17	12	10

		11	18	25
26	Wages Day *Deacon Blue* (CBS)	18	20	28
–	Like A Prayer *Madonna* (Sire)	–	2	1
–	Keep On Movin' *Soul II Soul feat. Caron Wheeler* (Virgin)	–	15	5
33	Celebrate The World *Womack & Womack* (4th+Broadway/ Island)	24	19	20
–	Paradise City *Guns N' Roses* (Geffen)	–	21	8
43	International Rescue *We've Got A Fuzzbox* (WEA)	30	23	13
–	One Man *Chanelle* (Cooltempo/Chrysalis)	36	25	16
69	I Beg Your Pardon *Kon Kan* (Atlantic)	47	32	17
48	Sleep Talk *Alyson Williams* (Def Jam)	39	28	18

APRIL 1989

1		8	15	22	29
1	Like A Prayer *Madonna* (Sire)	1	3	8	18
2	Too Many Broken Hearts *Jason Donovan* (PWL)	2	6	11	20
3	This Time I Know It's For Real *Donna Summer* (Warner Brothers)	4	8	10	19
4	Straight Up *Paula Abdul* (Siren/Virgin)	3	4	7	16
5	Keep On Movin' *Soul II Soul feat. Caron Wheeler* (10/Virgin)	6	10	16	22
6	Paradise City *Guns 'N' Roses* (Geffen)	7	13	19	32
7	Can't Stay Away From You *Gloria Estefan & Miami Sound Machine* (Epic)	17	26	46	61
8	I'd Rather Jack *The Reynolds Girls* (PWL)	10	17	37	48
9	Help *Bananarama-LaNaNeeNeeNooNoo* (London)	24	37	68	–
10	I Beg Your Pardon *Kon Kan* (Atlantic)	8	5	5	6
11	International Rescue *We've Got A Fuzzbox* (WEA)	11	18	40	55
12	Stop *Sam Brown* (A&M)	26	44	69	–
13	Eternal Flame *Bangles* (CBS)	5	1	1	1
14	Don't Be Cruel *Bobby Brown* (MCA)	13	15	27	38
15	People Hold On *Coldcut feat. Lisa Stansfield* (Ahead Of Our Time)	12	11	15	25
16	I Haven't Stopped Dancing Yet *Pat & Mick* (PWL)	9	14	22	28
17	Sleep Talk *Alyson Williams* (Def Jam)	20	30	50	66
18	Love Changes Everything *Michael Ball* (Really Useful/ Polydor)	30	46	56	64
19	One Man *Chanelle* (Cooltempo/Chrysalis)	23	32	53	73
20	Leave Me Alone *Michael Jackson* (Epic)	31	41	67	–
28	Americanos *Holly Johnson* (MCA)	14	9	4	4
22	Fire Woman *The Cult* (Beggars Banquet)	15	20	52	–
33	Baby I Don't Care *Transvision Vamp* (MCA)	16	7	3	3
26	The Beat (En) Generation *The The* (Epic)	18	25	43	70
–	If You Don't Know Me By Now *Simply Red* (Elektra)	19	2	2	2
–	When Love Comes To Town *US with B.B. King* (Island)	–	12	6	14
–	Mistify *INXS* (Mercury/Phonogram)	21	16	14	21
–	Good Thing *Fine Young Cannibals* (London)	–	19	9	7
–	Lullaby *The Cure* (Fiction/Polydor)	–	–	12	5
–	This Is Your Land *Simple Minds* (Virgin)	–	–	13	15
52	Got to Keep On *Cookie Crew* (ffrr/London)	37	21	17	17
–	One *Metallica* (Vertigo/Phonogram)	–	–	18	13
–	Ain't Nobody Better *Inner City* (10/Virgin)	–	–	20	10
–	Who's In The House *The Beatmasters with Merlin* (Rhythm King/Mute)	–	–	23	8
–	Interesting Drug *Morrissey* (HMV/EMI)	–	–	–	9
55	Requiem *London Boys* (Teldec/WEA)	42	38	24	11
48	Beds Are Burning *Midnight Oil* (Sprint/CBS)	44	33	21	12

6		13	20	27
1	Eternal Flame *Bangles* (CBS)	2	7	11
2	Hand On Your Heart *Kylie Minogue* (PWL)	1	2	2
3	If You Don't Know Me By Now *Simply Red* (Elektra)	12	15	28
4	Baby I Don't Care *Transvision Vamp* (MCA)	9	11	20
5	Requiem *London Boys* (Teldec/WEA)	4	4	4
6	Americanos *Holly Johnson* (MCA)	10	13	24
7	Miss You Like Crazy *Natalie Cole* (EMI USA)	5	3	3
8	Who's In The House *The Beatmasters with Merlin* (Rhythm King/Mute)	11	12	25
9	Beds Are Burning *Midnight Oil* (Sprint/CBS)	6	9	17
10	Good Thing *Fine Young Cannibals* (London)	17	27	43
11	Lullaby *The Cure* (Fiction/Polydor)	24	52	70
12	Interesting Drug *Morrissey* (HMV/EMI)	32	64	–
13	Ain't Nobody Better *Inner City* (10/Virgin)	19	37	54
14	One *Metallica* (Vertigo/Phonogram)	20	36	62
15	I Beg Your Pardon *Kon Kan* (Atlantic)	23	33	52
16	Your Mama Don't Dance *Poison* (Capitol)	13	18	30
17	Where Has All The Love Gone *Yazz* (Big Life)	16	19	32
18	I'll Be There For You *Bon Jovi* (Vertigo/Phonogram)	18	24	34
19	Got To Keep On *Cookie Crew* (ffrr/London)	26	46	60
20	Straight Up *Paula Abdul* (Siren/Virgin)	31	44	67
–	I Want It All *Queen* (EMI)	3	5	9
28	Bring Me Edelweiss *Edelweiss* (WEA)	7	6	5
23	I'm Every Woman (Remix) *Chaka Khan* (Warner Brothers)	8	8	10
26	The Look *Roxette* (EMI)	14	10	7
21	Electric Youth *Debbie Gibson* (Atlantic)	15	14	15
–	Ferry 'Cross the Mersey *Marsden/McCartney/Johnson/Christians* (PWL)	–	1	1
37	Rooms On Fire *Stevie Nicks* (Modern/EMI)	21	16	21
39	Don't It Make You Feel Good *Stefan Dennis* (Sublime)	22	17	16
–	Every Little Step *Bobby Brown* (MCA)	–	20	6
–	Manchild *Neneh Cherry* (Circa/Virgin)	–	26	8
45	Helyom Halib *Cappella* (Music Man)	38	23	12
58	On The Inside (Theme 'Prisoner Cell Block H') *Lynne Hamilton* (A.I.)	51	30	13
14	Fergus Sings The Blues *Deacon Blue* (CBS)	–	25	14
–	My Brave Face *Paul McCartney* (Parlophone)	–	22	18
–	I Don't Wanna Get Hurt *Donna Summer* (Warner Brothers)	–	–	19

3		10	17	24
1	Ferry 'Cross The Mersey *Christians/Johnson/McCartney/Marsden* (PWL)	3	14	34
2	Miss You Like Crazy *Natalie Cole* (EMI USA)	4	7	12
3	On The Inside (Theme 'Prisoner Cell Block H') *Lynne Hamilton* (A.I.)	7	13	22
4	Hand On Your Heart *Kylie Minogue* (PWL)	11	18	29
5	Manchild *Neneh Cherry* (Circa/Virgin)	9	10	18
6	Requiem *London Boys* (Teldec/WEA)	13	21	32
7	I Don't Wanna Get Hurt *Donna Summer* (Warner Brothers)	10	9	16
8	Bring Me Edelweiss *Edelweiss* (WEA)	15	25	43
9	Every Little Step *Bobby Brown* (MCA)	14	23	36
10	Express Yourself *Madonna* (Sire)	5	5	10

8	10	17	24
11 Helyom Halib *Capella* (Music Man)	20	26	46
12 The Look *Roxette* (EMI)	24	32	58
13 Funky Cold Medina/On Fire *Tone Loc* (4th+ Broadway/Stark)	16	9	23
14 Sweet Child O'Mine (Remix) *Guns N' Roses* (Geffen)	8	6	9
15 Can I Get Witness *Sam Brown* (A&M)	21	27	52
16 Fergus Sings The Blues *Deacon Blue* (CBS)	28	47	69
17 I'm Every Woman (Remix) *Chaka Khan* (Warner Brothers)	32	44	65
18 I Want It All *Queen* (Parlophone)	31	53	73
19 Right Back Where We Started From *Sinitta* (Fanfare)	6	4	4
20 Just Keep Rockin' *Double Trouble & The Rebel MC* (Desire)	18	16	13
– Sealed With A Kiss *Jason Donovan* (PWL)	1	1	2
– The Best Of Me *Cliff Richard* (EMI)	2	2	6
– Back To Life (However Do You Want Me) *Soul II Soul/Caron Wheeler* (Ten/Virgin)	12	3	1
22 I Drove All Night *Cyndi Lauper* (Epic)	17	8	7
25 It Is Time To Get Funky *D Mob feat. LRS* (London)	19	12	11
35 Song For Whoever *The Beautiful South* (Go! Discs)	23	11	8
– The Only One *Transvision Vamp* (MCA)	25	15	17
24 Pink Sunshine *Fuzzbox* (WEA)	22	17	14
– Cruel Summer (Swing Beat Version) *Bananarama* (London)	33	20	19
– Batdance *Prince* (Warner Brothers)	–	–	3
– All I Want Is You *U2* (Island)	–	–	5
42 Joy and Pain *Donna Allen* (BCM)	38	22	15
– Licence To Kill *Gladys Knight* (MCA)	58	40	20

JULY 1989

1	8	15	22	29
1 Back To Life (However Do You Want Me) *Soul II Soul/Caron Wheeler* (10/Virgin)	1	1	3	9
2 Batdance *Prince* (Warner Brothers)	4	10	14	24
3 Song For Whoever *The Beautiful South* (Go!Discs)	2	4	8	19
4 All I Want Is You *U2* (Island)	8	23	34	60
5 Sealed With A Kiss *Jason Donovan* (PWL)	14	21	30	38
6 Right Back Where We Started From *Sinitta* (Fanfare)	13	20	28	41
7 I Drove All Night *Cyndi Lauper* (Epic)	9	15	24	45
8 Licence To Kill *Gladys Knight* (MCA)	6	7	10	13
9 It Is Time To Get Funky *D Mob feat. LRS* (London)	16	26	35	53
10 Joy and Pain *Donna Allen* (BCM)	17	24	33	57
11 Just Keep Rockin' *Double Trouble & The Rebel MC* (Desire)	11	16	22	29
12 Sweet Child O'Mine (Remix) *Guns N' Roses* (Geffen)	20	32	40	69
13 Breakthru' *Queen* (Parlophone)	7	13	21	42
14 The Best Of Me *Cliff Richard* (EMI)	35	53	68	–
15 Express Yourself *Madonna* (Sire)	24	34	37	58
16 Pink Sunshine *Fuzzbox* (WEA)	28	39	51	–
17 In A Lifetime *Clannad/additional vocals Bono* (RCA)	19	36	52	–
18 Atomic City *Holly Johnson* (MCA)	25	43	–	–
19 London Nights *London Boys* (Teldec/WEA)	3	3	2	4
20 Pop Muzik (The 1989 Remix) *M* (Freestyle)	15	17	26	44
– It's Alright *Pet Shop Boys* (Parlophone)	5	5	7	12
22 Patience *Guns N' Roses* (Geffen)	10	14	19	31
38 You'll Never Stop Me Loving You *Sonia* (Chrysalis)	12	2	1	1
– Ain't Nobody *Rufus & Chaka Khan* (Warner Brothers)	18	6	6	7
– On Our Own (from Ghostbusters II) *Bobby Brown* (MCA)	–	8	4	5
42 Wind Beneath My Wings *Bette Midler* (Atlantic)	30	9	5	8
25 Superwoman *Karyn White* (Warner Brothers)	21	11	11	11
26 Voodoo Ray EP *A Guy Called Gerald* (Rham)	26	12	12	15
– Liberian Girl *Michael Jackson* (Epic)	–	18	13	16

1	8	15	22	29
37 Grandpa's Party *Monie Love* (Cooltempo/Chrysalis)	22	19	16	21
– Don't Wanna Lose You *Gloria Estefan* (Epic)	–	30	9	6
59 Days *Kirsty MacColl* (Virgin)	36	28	15	14
33 Cry *Waterfront* (Polydor)	27	25	17	18
– Say No Go *De La Soul* (Tommy Boy/Big Life)	33	22	18	20
– A New Flame *Simply Red* (WEA)	51	33	20	17
– Too Much *Bros* (CBS)	–	–	–	2
– Swing The Mood *Jive Bunny & The Mastermixers* (Music Factory)	–	54	13	3
– French Kiss *Lil Louis* (ffrr/London)	–	–	–	10

AUGUST 1989

5	12	19	26
1 Swing The Mood *Jive Bunny & The Mastermixers* (Music Factory)	1	1	1
2 Wouldn't Change A Thing *Kylie Minogue* (PWL)	2	3	6
3 You'll Never Stop Me Loving You *Sonia* (Chrysalis)	4	10	16
4 Too Much *Bros* (CBS)	7	15	27
5 French Kiss *Lil Louis* (ff/London)	3	2	4
6 Don't Wanna Lose You *Gloria Estefan* (Epic)	6	9	15
7 On Our Own (From Ghostbusters II) *Bobby Brown* (MCA)	8	12	22
8 London Nights *London Boys* (Teldec/WEA)	12	27	43
9 Ain't Nobody *Rufus & Chaka Khan* (Warner Brothers)	10	20	29
10 Wind Beneath My Wings *Bette Midler* (Atlantic)	11	19	33
11 Back To Life (However Do You Want Me) *Soul II Soul/Caron Wheeler* (10/Virgin)	19	29	42
12 Days *Kirsty MacColl* (Virgin)	15	28	44
13 Poison *Alice Cooper* (Epic)	5	4	2
14 Superwoman *Karyn White* (Warner Brothers)	22	33	47
15 Kick It In *Simple Minds* (Virgin)	20	37	57
16 Do You Love What You Feel *Inner City* (10/Virgin)	17	21	38
17 A New Flame *Simply Red* (WEA)	21	34	53
18 Licence To Kill *Gladys Knight* (MCA)	33	50	–
19 Landslide of Love *Transvision Vamp* (MCA)	14	18	31
20 Voodoo Ray *A Guy Called Gerald* (Rham)	29	45	64
27 Toy Soldiers *Martika* (CBS)	9	5	5
26 You're History *Shakespeare's Sister* (ff/London)	13	7	9
32 Pure *The Lightning Seeds* (Ghetto)	16	16	25
30 This One *Paul McCartney* (Parlophone)	18	22	41
– Losing My Mind *Liza Minnelli* (Epic)	24	6	7
– Blame It On The Boogie *Big Fun* (Jive)	25	8	8
– Ride On Time *Black Box* (deConstruction/RCA)	28	11	3
36 Do The Right Thing *Redhead Kingpin & The FBI* (10/Virgin)	23	13	14
– Hey DJ I Can't Dance *Beatmasters/Betty Boo* (Rhythm King)	35	14	11
– This Is The Right Time *Lisa Stansfield* (Arista)	37	17	13
– Kisses On The Wind *Neneh Cherry* (Circa/Virgin)	39	23	20
– I Just Don't Have The Heart *Cliff Richard* (EMI)	–	–	10
– The Invisible Man *Queen* (EMI)	–	26	12
– Numero Uno *Starlight* (City Beat/Beggars Banquet)	–	39	17
– Warning *Adeva* (Cooltempo/Chrysalis)	47	36	18
– I Need Your Lovin' *Alyson Williams* (Def Jam)	–	40	19

SEPTEMBER 1989

		9	16	23	30
2					
1	Swing The Mood *Jive Bunny & The Mastermixers* (Music Factory)	2	4	11	15
2	Ride On Time *Black Box* (deConstruction/RCA)	1	1	1	1
3	I Just Don't Have The Heart *Cliff Richard* (EMI)	5	12	18	31
4	Poison *Alice Cooper* (Epic)	8	15	23	36
5	Toy Soldiers *Martika* (CBS)	10	20	27	43
6	Blame It On The Boogie *Big Fun* (Jive)	4	6	12	21
7	Hey DJ/I Can't Dance . . ./Ska Train *Beatmasters/Betty Boo* (Rhythm King)	7	11	15	24
8	French Kiss *Lil Louis* (ffrr/London)	13	27	37	45
9	Sowing The Seeds Of Love *Tears For Fears* (Fontana/ Phonogram)	6	5	9	10
10	Wouldn't Change A Thing *Kylie Minogue* (PWL)	14	26	36	48
11	Numero Uno *Starlight* (Citybeat/Beggars Banquet)	9	9	13	18
12	I Need Your Lovin' *Alyson Williams* (Def Jam)	11	8	10	11
13	You're History *Shakespeare's Sister* (ffrr/London)	21	34	52	–
14	Losing My Mind *Liza Minnelli* (Epic)	27	42	60	–
15	This Is The Right Time *Lisa Stansfield* (Arista)	23	32	49	64
16	The Invisible Man *Queen* (Parlophone)	31	44	71	–
17	Warning *Adeva* (Cooltempo/Chrysalis)	19	28	34	44
18	Lay Your Hands On Me *Bon Jovi* (Vertigo/Phonogram)	18	21	35	49
19	Do The Right Thing *Redhead Kingpin & The FBI* (10/Virgin)	28	39	59	–
20	Love's About To Change My Heart *Donna Summer* (Warner Brothers)	24	29	33	53
–	Every Day (I Love You More) *Jason Donovan* (PWL)	3	2	8	16
21	The Time Warp (PWL Remix) *Damian* (Jive)	12	7	7	8
32	Right Here Waiting *Richard Marx* (EMI/USA)	15	3	2	2
31	The Best *Tina Turner* (Capitol)	16	10	5	5
26	Nightrain *Guns N' Roses* (Geffen)	17	22	45	50
–	Partyman *Prince* (Warner Brothers)	20	14	16	26
–	Personal Jesus *Depeche Mode* (Mute)	25	13	14	19
–	Cherish *Madonna* (Sire)	–	16	3	7
41	If Only I Could *Sydney Youngblood* (Circa/Virgin)	36	17	6	4
44	Lovesong *The Cure* (Fiction/Polydor)	33	18	20	32
53	Pump Up The Jam *Technotronic feat. Felly* (Swanyard)	37	19	4	3
–	Love In An Elevator *Aerosmith* (Geffen)	34	23	17	13
–	Don't Let Me Down Gently *The Wonder Stuff* (Polydor)	–	–	19	20
–	Drama *Erasure* (Mute)	–	–	–	6
–	You Keep It All In *The Beautiful South* (Go!Discs)	–	–	31	9
–	The Sensual World *Kate Bush* (EMI)	–	–	–	12
–	Sweet Surrender *Wet Wet Wet* (Precious/Phonogram)	–	–	–	14
–	Harlem Desire *London Boys* (WEA)	–	37	21	17

OCTOBER 1989

		14	21	28
7				
1	Ride on Time *Black Box* (deConstruction/RCA)	1	2	5
2	Pump Up The Jam *Technotronic feat. Felly* (Swanyard/SYR)	2	4	8
3	If Only I Could *Sydney Youngblood* (Circa/Virgin)	3	5	10
4	Drama! *Erasure* (Mute)	6	14	27
5	Right Here Waiting *Richard Marx* (EMI USA)	11	18	30
6	Sweet Surrender *Wet Wet Wet* (Precious/Phonogram)	7	12	18
7	The Best *Tina Turner* (Capitol)	12	19	24
8	You Keep It All In *The Beautiful South* (Go! Discs)	9	13	20

7		14	21	28
9 Chocolate Box *Bros* (CBS)		15	23	36
10 Cherish *Madonna* (Sire)		20	30	41
11 We Didn't Start The Fire *Billy Joel* (CBS)		8	7	9
12 Street Tuff *Rebel MC/Double Trouble* (Desire)		5	6	3
13 The Time Warp (PWL Remix) *Damian* (Jive)		25	32	38
14 Name And Number *Curiosity* (Mercury/Phonogram)		16	16	22
15 The Sensual World *Kate Bush* (EMI)		29	44	65
16 Oye Mi Canto (Hear My Voice) *Gloria Estefan* (Epic)		19	25	35
17 Love In An Elevator *Aerosmith* (Geffen)		27	39	56
18 If I Could Turn Back Time *Cher* (Geffen)		13	9	6
19 Harlem Desire *London Boys* (WEA)		31	40	55
20 I Need Your Lovin' *Alyson Williams* (Def Jam)		30	41	61
– That's What I Like *Jive Bunny & The Mastermixers* (Music Factory Dance)		4	1	1
24 Girl I'm Gonna Miss You *Milli Vanilli* (Cooltempo/Chrysalis)		10	3	2
28 Leave A Light On *Belinda Carlisle* (Virgin)		14	8	4
27 Can't Forget You *Sonia* (Chrysalis)		17	22	34
31 Room In Your Heart *Living In A Box* (Chrysalis)		18	11	7
40 Wishing On A Star *Fresh 4* (10/Virgin)		22	10	11
– The Road To Hell *Chris Rea* (EMI)		26	15	12
– Lean On You *Cliff Richard* (EMI)		28	17	21
32 Love On A Mountain Top *Sinitta* (Fanfare)		23	20	26
– All Around The World *Lisa Stansfield* (Arista)		–	–	13
52 I Want That Man *Deborah Harry* (Chrysalis)		36	21	14
– I Feel The Earth Move *Martika* (CBS)		45	33	15
– Eye Know *De La Soul* (Tommy Boy/Big Life)		–	24	16
– I Thank You *Adeva* (Cooltempo/Chrysalis)		–	28	17
– Don't Make Me Over *Sybil* (Champion)		41	34	19

NOVEMBER 1989

4		11	18	25
1 That's What I Like *Jive Bunny & The Mastermixers* (Music Factory Dance)		3	8	14
2 Girl I'm Gonna Miss You *Milli Vanilli* (Cooltempo/Chrysalis)		2	5	8
3 All Around The World *Lisa Stansfield* (Arista)		1	1	2
4 Street Tuff *Rebel MC/Double Trouble* (Desire)		5	10	16
5 Room In Your Heart *Living In A Box* (Chrysalis)		6	11	19
6 Leave A Light On *Belinda Carlisle* (Virgin)		9	14	23
7 If I Could Turn Back Time *Cher* (Geffen)		10	19	35
8 We Didn't Start The Fire *Billy Joel* (CBS)		18	21	40
9 Ride On Time *Black Box* (deConstruction/RCA)		14	18	26
10 The Road to Hell *Chris Rea* (WEA)		11	17	32
11 Pump Up The Jam *Technotronic feat. Felly* (Swanyard)		19	26	36
12 I Feel The Earth Move *Martika* (CBS)		7	7	9
13 I Want That Man *Deborah Harry* (Chrysalis)		15	16	25
14 Eye Know *De La Soul* (Tommy Boy/Big Life)		17	22	38
15 If Only I Could *Sydney Youngblood* (Circa/Virgin)		20	29	43
16 Wishing On A Star *Fresh 4* (10/Virgin)		24	42	66
17 Never Too Late *Kylie Minogue* (PWL)		4	4	5
18 I Thank You *Adeva* (Cooltempo/Chrysalis)		21	40	55
19 Never Too Much (Remix '89) *Luther Vandross* (Epic)		13	13	22
20 Don't Make Me Over *Sybil* (Champion)		27	43	–
22 Another Day In Paradise *Phil Collins* (Virgin)		8	2	4
23 Grand Piano *The Mixmaster* (BCM)		12	9	10
21 C'mon And Get My Love *D Mob intr. Cathy Dennis* (ffrr/London)		16	15	15
– You Got It (The Right Stuff) *New Kids On The Block* (CBS)		23	3	1

4		11	18	25
– Don't Know Much *Linda Ronstadt* (Elektra)		25	6	3
– Infinite Dreams *Iron Maiden* (EMI)		–	12	6
– Pacific *808 State* (ZTT/WEA Zang)		–	20	12
– Homely Girl *UB40* (Dep International/Virgin)		–	24	7
49 Lambada *Kaoma* (CBS)		40	27	11
– What The World Is Waiting For *The Stone Roses* (Silvertone)		–	–	13
– Whatcha Gonna Do With My Lovin' *Inner City* (10/Virgin)		–	28	17
– Ouija Board, Ouija Board *Morrissey* (HMV/EMI)		–	–	18
– Comment Te Dire Adieu *Jimmy Somerville/June Miles Kingston* (London)		46	33	20

DECEMBER 1989

2	9	16	23	30
1 You've Got It (The Right Stuff) *New Kids On The Block* (CBS)	1	4	10	14
2 Don't Know Much *Linda Ronstadt feat. Aaron Neville* (Elektra)	2	7	9	9
3 All Around The World *Lisa Stansfield* (Arista)	10	21	29	32
4 The Eve Of The War (Ben Liebrand Remix) *Jeff Wayne* (CBS)	3	6	11	16
5 Another Day In Paradise *Phil Collins* (Virgin)	12	22	27	33
6 Homely Girl *UB40* (DEP International)	6	12	21	26
7 Lambada *Kaoma* (CBS)	4	5	5	7
8 Fools Gold/What The World Is Waiting For *The Stone Roses* (Ore)	9	17	24	29
9 Can't Shake The Feeling *Big Fun* (Jive)	8	11	17	22
10 Pacific *808 State* (ZTT)	13	29	43	51
11 Never Too Late *Kylie Minogue* (PWL)	24	30	35	41
12 Whatcha Gonna Do With My Lovin' *Inner City* (10/Virgin)	15	26	37	42
13 I Feel The Earth Move *Martika* (CBS)	26	39	49	55
14 Comment Te Dire Adieu *Jimmy Somerville/June Miles Kingston* (London)	17	28	38	44
15 Girl I'm Gonna Miss You *Milli Vanilli* (Cooltempo/Chrysalis)	31	44	55	58
16 Grand Piano *The Mixmaster* (BCM)	36	53	70	70
17 C'Mon And Get My Love *D Mob intr. Cathy Dennis* (ffrr/London)	34	58	74	–
18 That's What I Like *Jive Bunny & The Mastermixers* (Music Factory Dance)	33	38	51	47
19 Manchester Rave On EP *Happy Mondays* (Factory)	28	50	55	56
20 I'm Not The Man I Used To Be *Fine Young Cannibals* (London)	20	33	50	54
– Get A Life *Soul II Soul* (10/Virgin)	5	3	4	6
– When You Come Back To Me *Jason Donovan* (PWL)	7	2	3	3
33 I Don't Wanna Lose You *Tina Turner* (Capitol)	11	8	8	8
32 Got To Get *Rab 'n' Raz feat. Leila K.* (Arista)	14	13	14	11
– You Surround Me *Erasure* (Mute)	16	15	22	23
– The Amsterdam EP *Simple Minds* (Virgin)	18	19	28	37
34 In Private *Dusty Springfield* (Parlophone)	19	14	15	15
– Let's Party *Jive Bunny & The Mastermixers* (Music Factory Dance)	–	1	2	2
– Dear Jesse *Madonna* (Sire)	–	9	7	5
– Donald Where's Your Troosers *Donald Stewart* (Stone)	30	10	6	4
– Sit And Wait *Sydney Youngblood* (Circa/Virgin)	27	16	18	21
36 Deep Heat '89 *Latino Rave* (Deep Heat)	22	18	16	17
– Hitmix (Official Bootleg Mega-Mix) *Alexander O'Neal* (Tabu)	38	20	19	24
– Do They Know It's Christmas *Band Aid II* (PWL/Polydor)	–	–	1	1

2		9	16	23	30
–	Sister *Bros* (CBS)	–	32	12	10
–	Getting Away With It *Electronic* (Factory)	–	23	13	12
–	Whenever God Shines His Light *Van Morrison with Cliff Richard* (Polydor)	35	25	20	20
–	The Magic Number/Buddy *De La Soul* (Big Life/Tommy Boy)	–	–	25	13
–	Words *The Christians* (Island)	–	–	33	18
39	Broke Away *Wet Wet Wet* (Precious/Phonogram)	39	24	23	19

Singles:

1 Ride On Time *Black Box* (de Construction/RCA)
2 Swing The Mood *Jive Bunny & The Mastermixers* (Music Factory Dance).
3 Eternal Flame *Bangles* (CBS)
4 Too Many Broken Hearts *Jason Donovan* (PWL)
5 Back To Life *Soul II Soul feat. Caron Wheeler* (10/Virgin)
6 Something's Gotton Hold Of My Heart *Marc Almond featuring Gene Pitney* (Parlophone)
7 That's What I Like *Jive Bunny & The Mastermixers* (Music Factory Dance)
8 Pump Up The Jam *Technotronic feat. Felly* (Swanyard)
9 Do They Know It's Christmas *Band Aid II* (PWL/Polydor)
10 Hand On Your Heart *Kylie Minogue* (PWL)
11 Like A Prayer *Madonna* (Sire/Warner Brothers)
12 All Around The World *Lisa Stansfield* (Arista)
13 If Only I Could *Sydney Youngblood* (Circa/Virgin)
14 Love Changes Everything *Michael Ball* (Really Useful/Polydor)
15 Girl I'm Gonna Miss You *Milli Vanilli* (Cooltempo/Chrysalis)
16 You'll Never Stop Me Loving You *Sonia* (Chrysalis)
17 You Got It (The Right Stuff) *New Kids On The Block* (CBS)
18 The Living Years *Mike & The Mechanics* (WEA)
19 Ferry 'Cross The Mersey *Christians/Johnson/McCartney/Marsden/SAW* (PWL)
20 Miss You Like Crazy *Natalie Cole* (EMI)
21 Wouldn't Change A Thing *Kylie Minogue* (PWL)
22 This Time I Know It's For Real *Donna Summer* (Warner Brothers)
23 Don't Know Much *Linda Ronstadt feat. Aaron Neville* (Elektra)
24 Let's Party *Jive Bunny & The Mastermixers* (Music Factory Dance)
25 Street Tuff *Rebel MC and Double Trouble* (Desire)
26 Belfast Child *Simple Minds* (Virgin)
27 Requiem *London Boys* (Teldec/WEA)
28 French Kiss *Lil Louis* (ffrr/London)
29 Sealed With A Kiss *Jason Donovan* (PWL)
30 Right Here Waiting *Richard Marx* (EMI USA)
31 Straight Up *Paula Abdul* (Siren/Virgin)
32 Especially For You *Kylie Minogue & Jason Donovan* (PWL)
33 You Got It *Roy Orbison* (Virgin)
34 Lambada *Kaoma* (CBS)
35 Help *Bananarama/Lananeeneenoonoo* (London)
36 Stop *Sam Brown* (A&M)
37 When You Come Back To Me *Jason Donovan* (PWL)
38 If You Don't Know Me By Now *Simple Red* (Elektra)
39 London Nights *London Boys* (Teldec/WEA)
40 Poison *Alice Cooper* (Epic)
41 The Best *Tina Turner* (Capitol)
42 Love Train *Holly Johnson* (MCA)
43 If I Could Turn Back Time *Cher* (Geffen)
44 Leave Me Alone *Michael Jackson* (Epic)
45 Room In Your Heart *Living In A Box* (Chrysalis)
46 Another Day In Paradise *Phil Collins* (Virgin)
47 Song For Whoever *The Beautiful South* (Go! Discs)
48 Get A Life *Soul II Soul* (10/Virgin)
49 Baby I Don't Care *Transvision Vamp* (MCA)
50 Leave A Light On *Belinda Carlisle* (Virgin)

Albums:

1 Ten Good Reasons *Jason Donovan* (PWL)
2 A New Flame *Simply Red* (Elektra)
3 . . . But Seriously *Phil Collins* (Virgin)
4 Anything For You *Gloria Estefan & Miami Sound Machine* (Epic)
5 Cuts Both Ways *Gloria Estefan* (Epic)
6 Enjoy Yourself *Kylie Minogue* (PWL)
7 The Raw And The Cooked *Fine Young Cannibals* (London)
8 Foreign Affair *Tina Turner* (Capitol)
9 Like A Prayer *Madonna* (Sire/Warner Brothers)
10 Club Classics Volume One *Soul II Soul* (Virgin)
11 Don't Be Cruel *Bobby Brown* (MCA)
12 The Road To Hell *Chris Rea* (WEA)
13 When The World Knows Your Name *Deacon Blue* (CBS)
14 Jive Bunny – The Album *Jive Bunny & The Mastermixers* (Telstar)
15 Appetite For Destruction *Guns N' Roses* (Geffen)
16 Street Fighting Years *Simple Minds* (Virgin)
17 The Miracle *Queen* (Parlophone)
18 Wild! *Erasure* (Mute)
19 The Twelve Commandments of Dance *London Boys* (Teldec/WEA)
20 We Too Are One *Eurythmics* (RCA)
21 The Seeds of Love *Tears For Fears* (Fontana/Phonogram)
22 Raw Like Sushi *Neneh Cherry* (Circa/Virgin)
23 Affection *Lisa Stansfield* (Arista)
24 Watermark *Enya* (WEA)
25 Velveteen *Transvision Vamp* (MCA)
26 The Legend Of Roy Orbison *Roy Orbison* (Telstar/CBS)
27 Spark To A Flame – The Very Best Of *Chris De Burgh* (A&M)
28 Ancient Heart *Tanita Tikaram* (WEA)
29 Holding Back The River *Wet Wet Wet* (Precious Organisation/Phonogram)
30 Batman – The Original Soundtrack *Prince* (Warner Brothers)
31 PastPresent *Clannad* (RCA)
32 Kylie – The Album *Kylie Minogue* (PWL)
33 The Best Of Rod Stewart *Rod Stewart* (Warner Brothers)
34 Bad *Michael Jackson* (Epic)
35 Kick *INXS* (Mercury/Phonogram)
36 The Innocents *Erasure* (Mute)
37 Paradise *Inner City* (10/Virgin)
38 Stronger *Cliff Richard* (EMI)
39 The Sensual World *Kate Bush* (EMI)
40 All Or Nothing *Milli Vanilli* (Cooltempo/Chrysalis)
41 Everything *Bangles* (CBS)
42 Level Best *Level 42* (Polydor)
43 Mystery Girl *Roy Orbison* (Virgin)
44 Crossroads *Tracy Chapman* (Elektra)
45 Remote/The Bitter Suite *Hue & Cry* (Circa/Virgin)
46 Runaway Horses *Belinda Carlisle* (A&M)
47 Greatest Hits *Billy Ocean* (Jive)
48 Welcome The The Beautiful South *The Beautiful South* (Go! Discs)
49 Blast *Holly Johnson* (MCA)
50 Aspects Of Love *Original Cast* (Really Useful/Polydor)

In 1989, compilation albums were deleted from the main chart and during the year appeared weekly in their own Top Twenty listing. Obviously, this process disguised the true nature of weekly sales title comparison, but it was done in order to prevent the main chart being little more than a compilation rundown, and to aid the sales of single artist/group material.

1990

Manchester was the music city of 1990, providing Britain with one group or artist after another. Yet for all the media buzz surrounding these outfits, the top selling single and album acts came from elsewhere.

Elton John had his first chart single in 1971, and (amazingly) had his very first number one in 1990 with 'Sacrifice'/'Healing Hands'. Cliff Richard took the prestigious Christmas week Number One for the third year running, adding 'Saviour's Day' to 'Mistletoe And Wine' in 1988, and his principal role on Band Aid II in 1989.

New Kids On The Block registered eight Top Ten hits but couldn't better Madonna's Top Five, eight-hit listing of 1985; 1990 was good for her especially in the album field – plus her constant ability to create furore, as she did with the video for her hit 'Justify My Love'.

Oldies – and presumably goodies – were ever present, particularly for The Righteous Brothers', 'You've Lost That Lovin Feeling' and 'Unchained Melody' reminding some of 1965. Oddly, Bill Medley, the other half with Bobby Hatfield of the American duo, charted once more with Jennifer Warnes on '(I've Had The Time Of My Life', from the *Dirty Dancing* soundtrack. Film and television provided other hits, with the latter most evident in 'Falling' from the cult show *Twin Peaks* and vocalised by Julee Cruise.

Dance hits were in abundance, and of the new acts, none was more recognised than Betty Boo. Irish girl Sinead O'Connor took the UK charts, and the world by storm for her heart-rending vocal of Prince's 'Nothing Compares 2U'. Other acts blatantly and fragrantly borrowed odd bits from elsewhere. Sampling with Vanilla Ice's 'Ice Ice Baby' debuting at Number Three, the highest ever by a new chart act. Similarly, DNA utilised Suzanne Vega before she knew about it when they struck big with 'Tom's Diner': and Snap borrowed some mighty vocalising from Jocelyn Brown for their chart topper 'Power!'

The S,A&W people were still present, but star names Kylie Minogue and Jason Donovan appeared to be losing impetus, with Jason Donovan's 'I'm Doing Fine' suffering a November eclipse and being his first not to make the Top Twenty.

The unfashionable continued to make hits, none more so than Phil Collins. Then there was Paul Simon, Status Quo, Paul McCartney – and even Steve Miller, thanks to a television advertisement to assert veteran power.

Of the new outfits in major chart success, EMF, KLF, The Beautiful South and Jesus Jones suggested they would be the 'stars' of the decade's first half, while the less predictable Depeche Mode, The Cure, Jimmy Somerville and Erasure ensured there would be life beyond the sound machine people.

Manchester? Well, there was Happy Mondays, Stone Roses, New Order, a partially firing Morrissey, 808 State, Northside, Lisa Stansfield (so good) and absent for much of the time Simply Red, MC Tunes, and the people at Factory Records, unrecognised and shunned by majors down South . . . And yes, classical music of a kind penetrated the usually pop occupancy of best selling lists.

6		13	20	27
1	Do They Know It's Christmas? *Band Aid II* (PWL/Polydor)	4	32	66
2	When You Come Back To Me *Jason Donovan* (PWL)	2	9	17
3	Get A Life *Soul II Soul* (10/Virgin)	3	6	11
4	Let's Party *Jive Bunny & The Mastermixers* (Music Factory Dance)	19	50	–
5	Dear Jesse *Madonna* (Sire)	5	16	28
6	Donald Where's Your Troosers *Andy Stewart* (Stone)	18	43	67
7	Lambada *Kaoma* (CBS)	9	15	21
8	The Magic Number/Buddy *De La Soul* (Big Life/Tommy)	7	11	20
9	Hangin' Tough *New Kids On The Block* (CBS)	1	1	2
10	You Got It (The Right Stuff) *New Kids On The Block* (CBS)	26	39	49
11	Got To Get *Rob 'n' Raz feat. Leila K.* (Arista)	8	8	10
12	Deep Heat '89 *Latina Rave* (Deep Heat)	13	22	37
13	Getting Away With It *Electronic* (Factory)	15	21	35
14	Sister *Bros* (CBS)	28	54	–
15	Can't Shake The Feeling *Big Fun* (Jive)	41	65	–
16	I Don't Wanna Lose You *Tina Turner* (Capitol)	29	45	60
17	The Eve Of The War (Ben Liebrand Remix) *Jeff Wayne* (CBS)	32	53	73
18	20 Seconds To Comply *Silver Bullet* (Tom Tom)	11	17	25
19	Sit and Wait *Sydney Youngblood* (Circa/Virgin)	23	36	50
20	Listen To Your Heart *Sonia* (Chrysalis)	10	14	22
23	Touch Me *49ers* (4th + Broadway/Island)	6	3	4
32	Got To Have Your Love *Mantronix (feat. Wondress)* (Capitol)	12	4	5
25	Going Back To My Roots/Rich In Paradise *FPI Project* (Rumour)	14	10	9
36	Put Your Hands Together *D. Mob feat. Nuff Juice* (ffrr/London)	16	7	8
–	Butterfly On A Wheel *The Mission* (Mercury/Phonogram)	17	12	29
24	Hey You *Quireboys* (Parlophone)	20	19	14
–	Tears On My Pillow *Kylie Minogue* (PWL)	–	2	1
–	You Make Me Feel (Mighty Real) *Jimmy Somerville* (London)	24	5	7
41	Could Have Told You So *Halo James* (Epic)	30	13	6
–	No More Mr. Nice Guy *Megadeth* (SBK)	36	18	13
–	I Called U *Lil Louis* (ffrr/London)	35	20	16
–	Nothing Compares 2U *Sinead O'Connor* (Ensign/Chrysalis)	–	30	3
–	N-R-G *Adamski* (MCA)	–	27	12
–	More Than You Know *Martika* (CBS)	39	23	15
–	Welcome To The Terrordome *Public Enemy* (Def Jam)	–	26	18
–	Welcome *Gino Latino* (ffrr/London)	–	28	19

3		10	17	24
1	Nothing Compares 2U *Sinead O'Connor* (Ensign/Chrysalis)	1	1	1
2	Tears On My Pillow *Kylie Minogue* (PWL)	3	9	15
3	Get Up (Before The Night Is Over) *Technotronic feat. Ya Kid K* (Swanyard)	2	2	3
4	Got To Have Your Love *Mantronix* (Capitol)	5	8	12
5	Touch Me *49ers* (4th + Broadway/Island)	6	12	18
6	Could Have Told You So *Halo James* (Epic)	8	18	30
7	Hangin' Tough *New Kids On The Block* (CBS)	14	26	39
8	You Make Me Feel (Mighty Real) *Jimmy Somerville* (London)	16	30	40
9	Happenin' All Over Again *Lonnie Gordon* (Supreme)	4	4	7
10	I Wish It Would Rain Down *Phil Collins* (Virgin)	7	7	9
11	Instant Replay *Yell!* (Fanfare)	10	11	14

3	Title	10	17	24
12	N-R-G *Adamski* (MCA)	22	42	62
13	Going Back To My Roots/Rich In *FPI Project* (Rumour)	21	36	55
14	Put Your Hands Together *D Mob/Nuff Juice* (ffrr/London)	23	46	59
15	Nothing Ever Happens *Del Amitri* (A&M)	11	14	20
16	More Than You Know *Martika* (CBS)	25	29	49
17	Welcome *Gino Latino* (ffrr/London)	17	23	35
18	Got To Get *Rob 'n' Raz feat. Leila K.* (Arista)	28	47	68
19	Walk On By *Sybil* (PWL)	9	6	8
20	The Face *And Why Not?* (Island)	13	16	26
23	18 and Life *Skid Row* (Atlantic)	12	13	23
–	Dub Be Good To Me *Beats International feat. Lindy Layton* (Go Beat)	15	3	2
25	Just Like Jesse James *Cher* (Geffen)	18	15	11
–	Live Together *Lisa Stansfield* (Arista)	19	10	10
22	Shine On *The House of Love* (Fontana/Phonogram)	20	28	50
–	I Don't Know Anybody Else *Black Box* (deConstruction)	–	5	4
–	Enjoy The Silence *Depeche Mode* (Mute)	–	17	6
36	Hello *The Beloved* (East West)	24	19	25
38	Come Back To Me *Janet Jackson* (Breakout/A&M)	27	20	21
–	How Am I Supposed To Live Without You *Michael Bolton* (CBS)	–	22	5
–	Steamy Windows *Tina Turner* (Capitol)	–	27	13
45	Downtown Train *Rod Stewart* (Warner Brothers)	32	21	16
–	96 Tears *The Stranglers* (Epic)	–	31	17
–	Stronger Than That *Cliff Richard* (EMI)	–	–	19

MARCH 1990

3	Title	10	17	24	31
1	Dub Be Good To Me *Beats International feat. Lindy Layton* (Go Beat)	1	1	1	5
2	Nothing Compares 2U *Sinead O'Connor* (Ensign/Chrysalis)	4	9	13	20
3	How Am I Supposed To Live Without You *Michael Bolton* (CBS)	3	3	8	10
4	Get Up (Before The Night Is Over) *Technotronic/Ya Kid K.* (Swanyard)	9	15	26	45
5	I Don't Know Anybody Else *Black Box* (deConstruction)	7	13	27	37
6	Enjoy The Silence *Depeche Mode* (Mute)	6	12	20	32
7	The Brits 1990 *Various Artists* (RCA)	2	2	9	19
8	Elephant Stone *The Stone Roses* (Silvertone)	10	25	39	51
9	Infinity *Guru Josh* (deConstruction)	5	5	10	11
10	Downtown Train *Rod Stewart* (Warner Brothers)	11	19	35	46
11	Happenin' All Over Again *Lonnie Gordon* (Supreme)	19	35	47	74
12	Walk On By *Sybil* (PWL)	25	47	72	–
13	Room At The Top *Adam Ant* (MCA)	16	26	44	71
14	Stronger Than That *Cliff Richard* (EMI)	14	22	51	73
15	Black Betty (Ben Liebrand Remix) *Ram Jam* (Epic)	13	17	24	41
16	Steamy Windows *Tina Turner* (Capitol)	26	42	62	–
17	Just Like Jesse James *Cher* (Geffen)	28	50	70	–
18	I Wish It Would Rain Down *Phil Collins* (Virgin)	37	60	68	–
19	96 Tears *The Stranglers* (Epic)	31	53	65	–
20	Dude (Looks Like A Lady) *Aerosmith* (Geffen)	21	32	45	–
22	Moments In Soul *JT And The Big Family* (Champion)	8	7	11	13
–	Blue Savannah *Erasure* (Mute)	12	8	3	4
33	Love Shack *B52s* (Reprise/Warner Brothers)	14	6	2	2
–	Madly In Love *Bros* (CBS)	15	14	30	52
34	Lily Was Here *David A. Stewart feat. Candy Dulfer* (Anxious/RCA)	17	10	7	6
29	I Might *Shakin' Stevens* (Epic)	18	21	23	42

3		10	17	24	31
31	Natural Thing *Innocence* (Cooltempo/Chrysalis)	20	16	18	29
–	That Sounds Good To Me *Jive Bunny & The Mastermixers* (Music Factory Dance)	–	4	4	9
–	I'll Be Loving You (Forever) *New Kids On The Block* (CBS)	–	11	5	7
–	Strawberry Fields Forever *Candy Flip* (Debut/Passion)	–	18	6	3
–	Made Of Stone *The Stone Roses* (Silvertone)	–	20	25	49
–	The Power *Snap* (Arista)	–	–	12	1
–	This Is How It Feels *Inspiral Carpets* (Cow/Mute)	–	22	15	14
–	Don't You Love Me *49ers* (4th+Broadway/Island)	–	28	14	12
47	Loaded *Primal Scream* (Creation)	32	24	16	16
74	Birdhouse In Your Soul *They Might Be Giants* (Elektra)	47	34	17	8
–	Everything Starts With An 'E' *E-Zee Possee* (More Protein/Virgin)	–	36	19	15
–	Chime *Orbital* (ffrr/London)	–	–	28	17
–	Mamma Gave Birth To The . . . *Queen Latifah + De La Soul* (Tommy Boy/Gee St)	–	–	34	18

APRIL 1990

7		14	21	28
1	The Power *Snap* (Arista)	2	3	4
2	Love Shack *B52s* (Reprise/Warner Brothers)	6	10	14
3	Strawberry Fields Forever *Candy Flip* (Debut/Passion)	9	13	19
4	Vogue *Madonna* (Sire)	1	1	1
5	Blue Savannah *Erasure* (Mute)	14	16	22
6	Birdhouse In Your Soul *They Might Be Giants* (Elektra)	10	11	17
7	Lily Was Here *David A. Stewart feat. Candy Duffer* (Anxious/RCA)	12	15	21
8	Don't Miss The Partyline *Bizz Nizz* (Cooltempo/Chrysalis)	7	7	9
9	Hang On To Your Love *Jason Donovan* (PWL)	8	9	13
10	Dub Be Good To Me *Beats International feat. Lindy Layton*	20	24	32
11	Kingston Town *UB40* (Dep International/Virgin)	4	4	5
12	I'll Be Loving You (Forever) *New Kids On The Block* (CBS)	22	23	31
13	Ghetto Heaven *The Family Stand* (Atlantic/East West)	13	12	10
14	Mamma Gave Birth To The . . . *Queen Latifa + De La Soul* (Tommy Boy/Gee St)	16	19	27
15	All I Wanna Do Is Make Love To You *Heart* (Capitol)	11	8	8
16	Step On *Happy Mondays* (Factory)	5	6	6
17	Black Velvet *Alannah Myles* (Atlantic/East West)	3	2	2
18	This Is How It Feels *Inspiral Carpets* (Cow/Mute)	25	31	43
19	Another Day In Paradise *Jam Tronik* (Debut Passion)	19	27	37
20	Better World *Rebel MC* (Desire)	21	26	36
23	This Beat Is Technotronic *Technotronic feat. MC Eric* (Swanyard)	15	14	15
36	Opposites Attract *Paula Abdul (duet with The Wild Pair)* (Siren/Virgin)	17	5	3
21	Escapade *Janet Jackson (feat. Jimmy Jam/Terry Lewis* (Breakout/A&M)	18	17	18
46	Everybody Needs Somebody To Love *The Blues Brothers* (Atlantic/East West)	31	18	12
–	Dirty Cash *Adventures of Stevie V* (Mercury/Phonogram)	–	28	11
45	Killer *Adamski*	39	20	7
41	Counting Every Minute *Sonia* (Chrysalis)	30	21	16
26	Real Real Real *Jesus Jones* (Food/EMI)	23	22	20

426

5		12	19	26
1 Vogue *Madonna* (Sire)		4	6	8
2 Opposites Attract *Paula Abdul (duet with The Wild Pair)* (Siren/Virgin)		3	5	7
3 Black Velvet *Alannah Myles* (Atlantic/East West)		7	8	13
4 Killer *Adamski* (MCA)		1	1	1
5 Dirty Cash *Adventures of Stevie V* (Mercury/Phonogram)		2	3	3
6 Kingston Town *UB40* (Dep International/Virgin)		9	12	15
7 The Power *Snap* (Arista)		10	13	17
8 A Dreams A Dream *Soul II Soul* (10/Virgin)		6	9	14
9 All I Wanna Do I Make Love To You *Heart* (Capitol)		11	15	18
10 Ghetto Heaven *The Family Stand* (Atlantic/East West)		12	17	19
11 Step On *Happy Mondays* (Factory)		13	18	29
12 November Spawned A Monster *Morrissey* (HMV)		16	43	73
13 Don't Miss The Partyline *Bizz Nizz* (Cooltempo/Chrysalis)		21	24	38
14 Everybody Needs Somebody To Love *The Blues Brothers* (Atlantic/EMI)		23	37	58
15 Something Happened On The Way To . . . *Phil Collins* (Virgin)		15	19	26
16 Wild Women Do *Natalie Cole* (EMI)		17	23	31
17 Counting Every Minute *Sonia* (Chrysalis)		37	51	–
18 Tattooed Millionaire *Bruce Dickinson* (EMI)		26	55	74
19 Real Real Real *Jesus Jones* (Food/EMI)		30	40	64
20 Tomorrow *Tongue 'n' Cheek* (Syncopate/EMI)		27	42	65
– Better The Devil You Know *Kylie Minogue* (Sire)		5	2	2
– Cover Girl *New Kids On The Block* (CBS)		8	4	4
33 Hold On *En Vogue* (Atlantic/East West)		14	7	5
– Won't Talk About It (Remix) *Beats International* (Go Beat)		18	10	9
– Take Your Time *Mantronix feat. Wondress* (Capitol)		19	11	10
– Circlesquare *The Wonder Stuff* (Polydor)		20	20	28
38 How Can We Be Lovers *Michael Bolton* (CBS)		22	14	11
– I Still Haven't Found What I'm Looking For *The Chimes* (CBS)		–	16	6
– Venus *Don Pablo's Animals* (Rumour)		–	30	12
– Policy Of Truth *Depeche Mode* (Mute)		–	28	16
– Roam *B52s* (Reprise/Warner Brothers)		–	38	20

2		9	16	23	30
1 Killer *Adamski* (MCA)		2	4	11	16
2 World In Motion *England New Order* (Factory/MCA)		1	1	2	4
3 Better The Devil You Know *Kylie Minogue* (PWL)		6	15	24	31
4 Dirty Cash *Adventures of Stevie V* (Mercury/Phonogram)		5	11	16	22
5 Hold On *En Vogue* (Atlantic/East West)		7	14	22	34
6 I Still Haven't Found What I'm Looking For *Chimes* (CBS)		9	19	27	38
7 Venus *Don Pablo's Animals* (Rumour)		4	8	13	19
8 Cover Girl *New Kids On The Block* (CBS)		14	29	42	65
9 Vogue *Madonna* (Sire)		15	27	36	48
10 How Can We Be Lovers *Michael Bolton* (CBS)		20	26	40	58
11 Won't Talk About It (Remix) *Beats International* (Go Beat)		19	35	54	–
12 Hear The Drummer (Get Wicked) *Chad Jackson* (Big Wave)		3	3	7	10
13 Papa Was A Rollin' Stone *Was Not Was* (Fontana/Phonogram)		12	17	22	30
14 Opposites Attract *Paula Abdul (duet with The Wild Pair)* (Siren/Virgin)		17	33	53	72
15 Doin' The Do *Betty Boo* (Rhythm King/Mute)		8	7	9	9

2

	9	16	23	30
16 Take Your Time *Mantronix (feat/ Wondress)*	25	42	64	–
17 Roam *B52s* (Reprise/Warner Brothers)	18	25	34	55
18 Policy Of Truth *Depeche Mode* (Mute)	30	51	70	–
19 Star *Erasure* (Mute)	11	12	17	26
20 It's My Life *Talk Talk* (Parlophone)	13	16	21	28
24 The Only One I Know *The Charlatans* (Dead Dead Good/Situation Two)	10	9	10	15
22 Everybody Everybody *Black Box* (deConstruction/RCA)	16	41	64	–
– Step By Step *New Kids On The Block* (CBS)	–	2	5	12
– Sacrifice/Healing Hands *Elton John* (Rocket/Phonogram)	26	5	1	1
38 It Must Have Been Love *Roxette* (EMI)	21	6	4	3
36 Hold On *Wilson Phillips* (SBK)	23	10	8	6
– Ooops Up *Snap* (Arista)	–	13	6	5
47 The Only Rhyme That Bites *MC Tunes Versus 808 State* (ZTT/WEA)	31	18	12	11
40 Yaaah/Techno Trance *D-Shake* (Cooltempo/Chrysalis)	29	20	28	42
– Nessun Dorma *Luciano Pavarotti* (Decca)	–	21	3	2
– The Free Style Mega-Mix *Bobby Brown* (MCA)	39	22	14	18
– Close To You *Maxi Priest* (10/Virgin)	55	36	15	8
– Thinking Of You *Maureen* (Urban/Polydor)	–	38	18	17
– You've Got A Friend *Big Fun and Sonia* (Jive)	–	–	19	14
– Mona *Craig McLachlan & Check 1-2* (Epic)	–	44	20	7
– U Can't Touch This *M.C. Hammer* (Capitol)	66	41	25	13
– Treat Me Good *Yazz* (Big Life)	–	–	30	20

JULY 1990

7

	14	21	28
1 Sacrifice/Healing Hands *Elton John* (Rocket/Phonogram)	1	1	2
2 Nessun Dorma *Luciano Pavarotti* (Decca)	2	3	17
3 It Must Have Been Love *Roxette* (EMI)	5	6	7
4 Mona *Craig McLachlan & Check 1-2* (Epic)	3	2	3
5 Oops Up *Snap* (Arista)	10	9	11
6 World In Motion *England New Order* (Factory)	8	10	18
7 Close To You *Maxi Priest* (10/Virgin)	9	11	15
8 Hold On *Wilson Phillips* (SBK)	11	16	20
9 U Can't Touch This *M.C. Hammer* (Capitol)	6	7	5
10 The Only Rhyme That Bites *MC Tunes Versus 808 State* (ZTT/WEA)	12	20	30
11 Thinking Of You *Maureen* (Urban/Polydor)	14	22	26
12 Thunderbirds Are Go *FAB feat. MC Parker* (Brothers Org.)	7	5	6
13 Doin' The Do *Betty Boo* (Rhythm King/Mute)	16	24	38
14 Hear The Drummer (Get Wicked) *Chad Jackson* (Big Wave)	24	35	52
15 The Great Song Of Indifference *Bob Geldof* (Mercury/Phonogram)	17	30	53
16 You've Got A Friend *Big Fun and Sonia* (Jive)	19	40	58
17 Unskinny Bop *Poison* (Enigma/Capitol)	15	19	24
18 Another Night *Jason Donovan* (PWL)	23	38	62
19 The Only One I Know *The Charlatans* (Dead Dead Good/Situation)	31	44	71
20 Killer *Adamski* (MCA)	18	26	37
– One Love *The Stone Roses* (Silvertone)	4	8	14
21 She Ain't Worth It *Glenn Medeiros/Bobby Brown* (London)	13	12	12
29 Alright *Janet Jackson* (A&M)	20	25	42
– Turtle Power *Partners In Kryme* (SBK)	–	4	1
– I'm Free *Soup Dragons feat. Junior Reid* (Raw TV/Big Life)	28	13	10
– Hanky Panky *Madonna* (Sire)	–	14	4
– Rockin' Over The Beat *Technotronic feat. Ya Kid K.* (Swanyard)	26	15	9

		14	21	28
7				
49	Naked In The Rain *Blue Pearl* (W.A.U!Mr Modo/Big Life)	34	17	8
35	Carry The Blame/California Dreamin' *River City People* (EMI)	27	18	16
–	Tom's Diner *DNA feat. Suzanne Vega* (A&M)	–	–	13
–	Wash Your Face In My Sink *Dream Warriors* (4th+ Broadway/Island)	48	31	19

AUGUST 1990

		11	18	25
4				
1	Turtle Power *Partners In Kryme* (SBK)	1	1	3
2	Hanky Panky *Madonna* (Sire)	6	8	19
3	Tom's Diner *DNA feat. Suzanne Vega* (A&M)	2	2	2
4	Sacrifice/Healing Hands *Elton John* (Rocket/Phonogram)	9	11	24
5	U Can't Touch This *M.C.Hammer* (Capitol)	3	5	7
6	Naked In The Rain *Blue Pearl* (W.A.U! Mr. Modo/Big Life)	4	4	5
7	Mona *Craig McLachlan* (Epic)	13	33	71
8	I'm Free *Soup Dragons feat. Junior Reid* (Raw TV/Big Life)	5	7	10
9	Rockin' Over The Beat *Technotronic feat. Ya Kid K.* (Swanyard)	10	15	25
10	It Must Have Been Love *Roxette* (EMI)	18	28	43
11	Thieves In The Temple *Prince* (Paisley Park/Warner Brothers)	7	10	27
12	Thunderbirds Are Go *FAB feat. MC Parker* (Brothers Org.)	25	42	63
13	California Dreamin'/Carry The Blame *River City People* (EMI)	14	20	35
14	LFO *LFO* (Warp/Outer Rhythm)	12	16	26
15	Oops Up *Snap* (Arista)	22	31	49
16	Wash Your Face In My Sink *Dream Warriors* (4th Street+ Broadway/Island)	16	22	41
17	Tonight *New Kids On The Block* (CBS)	8	6	4
18	She Ain't Worth It *Glenn Medeiros/Bobby Brown* (London)	27	41	72
19	One Love *The Stone Roses* (Silvertone)	42	51	64
20	Poison *Bell Biv Devoe* (MCA)	19	21	33
25	Itsy Bitsy Teeny Weeny *Bombalurina* (Carpet/Polydor)	11	3	1
22	Tricky Disco *Tricky Disco* (Warp/ Outer Rhythm)	15	14	20
24	Hardcore Uproar *Together* (ffrr/London)	17	12	12
23	Violence Of Summer (Love's . . .) *Duran Duran* (Parlophone)	20	32	54
–	Listen To Your Heart *Roxette* (EMI)	21	9	6
42	Blaze Of Glory *Jon Bon Jovi* (Vertigo/Phonogram)	24	13	13
–	Where Are You Baby? *Betty Boo* (Rhythm King)	35	17	9
–	Englishman In N.Y. (Liebrand Remix) *Sting* (A&M)	26	18	15
36	Amanda *Craig McLachlan & Check 1-2* (Epic)	23	19	21
–	Praying For Time *George Michael* (Epic)	–	–	8
–	Four Bacharach & David Songs *Deacon Blue* (CBS)	–	–	11
–	Can Can You Party *Jive Bunny and The Mastermixers* (Music Factory/Mastermix)	–	–	14
–	What Time Is Love *The KLF/The Children of the Revolution* (KLF Communications)	34	25	16
–	Silhouettes *Cliff Richard* (EMI)	–	–	17
46	The King Of Wishful Thinking *Go West* (Chrysalis)	40	24	18

SEPTEMBER 1990

		8	15	22	29
1					
1	Itsy Bitsy Teeny Weeny *Bombalurina* (Carpet/Polydor)	1	3	7	20
2	Four Bacarach & David Songs (EP) *Deacon Blue* (CBS)	2	4	5	14
3	Tonight *New Kids On The Block* (CBS)	5	8	20	30
4	Where Are You Baby? *Betty Boo* (Rhythm King)	3	6	13	23
5	Tom's Diner *DNA feat. Suzanne Vega* (A&M)	15	25	39	57

	8	15	22	29
1	8	15	22	29
6 Praying For Time *George Michael* (Epic)	10	12	29	47
7 Listen To Your Heart/Dangerous *Roxette* (EMI)	13	20	30	51
8 Can Can You Party *Jive Bunny & The Mastermixers* (Music Factory Dance)	11	21	37	64
9 Naked In The Rain *Blue Pearl* (W.A.U! Mr Modo/Big Life)	8	17	26	48
10 Silhouettes *Cliff Richard* (EMI)	12	19	33	52
11 What Time Is Love? *The KLF/The Children Of The Revolution* (KLF Communications)	7	5	6	7
12 Turtle Power *Partners In Kryme* (SBK)	16	30	44	–
13 Groove Is In The Heart/What. . . *Dee-Lite* (Elektra)	4	2	2	3
14 The Joker *Steve Miller Band* (Capitol)	6	1	1	2
15 U Can't Touch This *M.C.Hammer* (Capitol)	18	33	35	–
16 Vision Of Love *Mariah Carey* (CBS)	14	9	10	17
17 I'm Free *Soup Dragons feat. Junior Reid* (Raw TV/Big Life)	17	24	36	63
18 Blaze Of Glory *Jon Bon Jovi* (Vertigo/Phonogram)	22	31	46	–
19 Hardcore Uproar *Together* (ffrr/London)	26	43	68	–
20 The King Of Wishful Thinking *Go West* (Chrysalis)	20	28	43	–
23 Rhythm Of The Rain *Jason Donovan* (PWL)	9	10	24	35
24 End Of The World *Sonia* (Chrysalis)	19	18	22	41
– The Space Jungle *Adamski* (MCA)	23	7	8	10
40 Groovy Train *The Farm* (Produce)	28	11	9	6
34 Don't Be A Fool *Loose Ends* (Ten/Virgin)	21	13	17	27
– Livin' In The Light *Caron Wheeler* (RCA)	29	14	18	26
– Black Cat *Janet Jackson* (A&M)	32	15	15	25
– Suicide Blonde *INXS* (Mercury/Phonogram)	–	16	11	18
– Holy Smoke *Iron Maiden* (EMI)	–	–	3	5
– Show Me Heaven *Maria McKee* (Epic)	–	26	4	1
56 I've Been Thinking About You *London Beat* (Anxious)	45	22	12	4
34 Fascinating Rhythm *Bass-O-Matic* (Guerilla/Virgin)	38	22	14	9
– Thunderstruck *AC/DC* (Atco/East West)	–	–	16	13
– Then *The Charlatans* (Situation Two)	–	–	19	12
– Cult Of Snap *Snap* (Arista)	–	–	21	8
– I Can't Stand It *Twenty 4 Seven* (BCM)	–	–	28	11
– Never Enough *The Cure* (Fiction/Polydor)	–	–	–	15
– Blue Velvet *Bobby Vinton* (Epic)	–	–	–	16
– Tunes Split The Atom *MC Tunes Versus 808 State* (ZTT/WEA)	–	44	31	19

OCTOBER 1990

	13	20	27
6	13	20	27
1 Show Me Heaven *Maria McKee* (Epic)	1	1	2
2 I've Been Thinking About You *London Beat* (Anxious)	3	5	10
3 Blue Velvet *Bobby Vinton* (Epic)	2	3	6
4 So Hard *Pet Shop Boys* (Parlophone)	5	9	21
5 The Anniversary Waltz – Part 1 *Status Quo* (Vertigo/Phonogram)	4	2	4
6 The Joker *Steve Miller* (Capitol)	12	29	40
7 I Can't Stand It *Twenty 4 Seven* (BCM)	7	7	11
8 Groove Is In The Heart/What Is *Dee-Lite* (Elektra)	11	17	28
9 Fascinating Rhythm *Bass-O-Matic* (Guerilla/Virgin)	10	13	24
10 Groovy Train *The Farm* (Produce)	13	21	30
11 Cult Of Snap *Snap* (Arista)	15	31	43
12 Megamix *Technotronic* (Swanyard)	6	6	9
13 Never Enough *The Cure* (Fiction/Polydor)	22	47	61
14 What Time Is Love? *The KLF feat. The Children Of The Revolution* (KLF Communications)	28	49	73
15 Then *The Charlatans* (Dead Dead Good/Situation Two)	23	55	–

6		13	20	27
16	It's A Shame (My Sister) *Monie Love feat. True Image* (Cooltempo/Chrysalis)	14	12	18
17	The Space Jungle *Adamski* (MCA)	26	45	71
18	Tunes Split The Atom *MC Tunes Versus 808 State* (ZTT/WEA)	20	37	66
19	Have You Seen Her *M.C.Hammer* (Capitol)	8	10	15
20	Thunderstruck *AC/DC* (Atco/East West)	37	58	–
30	A Little Time *The Beautiful South* (Go!Disc)	9	4	1
–	Let's Try Again/Didn't I Blow *New Kids On The Block* (CBS)	16	8	16
21	World In My Eyes *Depeche Mode* (Mute)	17	22	46
24	Spin That Wheel (Turtles . . .) *Hi Tek 3 feat. Ya Kid K.* (Brothers Organisation)	18	15	20
–	From A Distance *Cliff Richard* (EMI)	19	11	17
–	More *Sisters Of Mercy* (Merciful Release/East West)	21	14	27
–	I'm Your Baby Tonight *Whitney Houston* (Arista)	–	16	7
–	Piccadilly Palace *Morrissey* (HMV)	–	18	39
–	Crying In The Rain *a-ha* (Warner Brothers)	27	19	13
–	Kinky Afro *Happy Mondays* (London/Factory)	–	20	5
–	Unchained Melody *The Righteous Brothers* (Verve/Polydor)	–	–	3
–	Take My Breath Away *Berlin* (CBS)	41	27	8
60	Working Man *Rita MacNeil* (Polydor)	40	24	12
–	(We Want) The Same Thing *Belinda Carlisle*	43	28	14
52	Good Morning Britain *Aztec Camera and Mick Jones* (WEA)	36	23	19

NOVEMBER 1990

3		10	17	24
1	Unchained Melody *The Righteous Brothers* (Verve/Polydor)	1	1	1
2	A Little Time *The Beautiful South* (Go!Discs)	2	4	9
3	Take My Breath Away *Berlin* (CBS)	3	7	14
4	Show Me Heaven *Maria McKee* (Epic)	8	14	24
5	I'm Your Baby Tonight *Whitney Houston* (Arista)	7	10	20
6	(We Want) The Same Thing *Belinda Carlisle* (Virgin)	6	9	16
7	Kinky Afro *Happy Mondays* (Factory)	14	24	38
8	The Anniversary Waltz – Part 1 *Status Quo* (Vertigo/ Phonogram)	16	27	46
9	Step Back In Time *Kylie Minogue* (PWL)	4	8	13
10	Blue Velvet *Bobby Vinton* (Epic)	17	20	28
11	Working Man *Rita McNeil* (Polydor)	12	18	30
12	Megamix *Technotronic* (Swanyard)	21	37	63
13	Crying In The Rain *a-ha* (Warner Brothers)	19	31	59
14	I've Been Thinking About You *Londonbeat* (Anxious)	24	33	51
15	Close To Me *The Cure* (Fiction/Polydor)	13	17	32
16	Don't Worry *Kim Appleby* (Parlophone)	5	3	2
17	I Can't Stand It *Twenty 4 Seven* (BCM)	27	39	69
18	The Obvious Child *Paul Simon* (Warner Brothers)	15	16	26
19	I'll Be Your Baby Tonight *Robert Palmer and UB40* (EMI)	10	6	7
20	Good Morning Britain *Aztec Camera and Mick Jones* (WEA)	26	36	72
21	Fantasy *Black Box* (deConstruction/RCA)	9	5	6
–	Fog On The Tyne (Revisited) *Gazza and Lindisfarne* (Best/RCA)	11	2	4
22	Dressed For Success *Roxette* (EMI)	18	19	22
39	There She Goes *The La's* (Go! Discs)	20	13	15
–	Cubik/Olympic *808 State* (ZTT)	29	11	10
44	To Love Somebody *Jimmy Somerville* (London)	28	12	8
55	Unbelievable *E.M.F.* (Parlophone)	25	15	5
–	Ice Ice Baby *Vanilla Ice* (SBK)	–	–	3
–	Falling *Julee Cruise* (Warner Brothers)	64	35	11
–	It Takes Two *Rod Stewart & Tina Turner* (Warner Brothers)	–	–	12

	10	17	24
– King Of The Road (EP) *The Proclaimers* (Chrysalis)	–	–	17
– Time To Make The Floor Burn *Megabass* (Brothers Organisation)	36	22	18
– Let's Swing Again *Jive Bunny & The Mastermixers* (Music Factory Dance)	–	25	19

DECEMBER 1990

1	8	15	22	29
1 Ice Ice Baby *Vanilla Ice* (SBK)	1	1	1	2
2 Unchained Melody *The Righteous Brothers* (Verve/Polydor)	2	5	9	12
3 Unbelievable *E.M.F.* (Parlophone)	3	6	7	10
4 Don't Worry *Kim Appleby* (Parlophone)	4	7	17	27
5 It Takes Two *Rod Stewart/Tina Turner* (Warner Brothers)	7	19	32	33
6 Fantasy *Black Box* (deConstruction)	10	20	33	35
7 Falling *Julee Cruise* (Warner Brothers)	8	16	30	31
8 I'll Be Your Baby Tonight *Robert Palmer and UB40* (EMI)	17	29	40	46
9 King Of The Road (EP) *The Proclaimers* (Chrysalis)	14	26	35	36
10 To Love Somebody *Jimmy Somerville* (London)	15	23	37	42
11 Fog On The Tyne (Revisited) *Gazza and Lindisfarne* (Best)	23	33	49	48
12 Cubik/Olympic *808 State* (ZTT)	28	53	59	53
13 My Definition Of A Bombastic Jazz Style *Dream Warriors* (4th+Broadway/Island)	16	21	34	40
14 Kinky Boots *Patrick Macnee & Honor Blackman* (Deram)	5	8	16	24
15 A Little Time *The Beautiful South* (Go!Discs)	34	41	53	55
16 Time To Make The Floor Burn *Megabass* (Brothers Organisation)	21	36	50	59
17 There She Goes *The Las* (Go!Discs)	36	58	72	75
18 Seven Little Girls Sitting In The Backseat *Bombalurina featuring Timmy Mallett* (Carpet)	19	28	42	44
19 Take My Breath Away *Berlin* (CBS)	33	51	57	65
20 Being Boring *Pet Shop Boys* (Parlophone)	26	45	54	–
– Saviour's Day *Cliff Richard* (EMI)	6	3	2	1
– Justify My Love *Madonna* (Sire)	9	2	3	7
24 Wicked Game *Chris Isaak* (London)	11	10	12	11
– All Together Now *The Farm* (Produce)	12	4	5	6
– This One's For The Children *New Kids On The Block* (CBS)	13	9	13	20
21 Sucker DJ *Dimples D* (FBI)	18	17	22	28
– Pray *M.C.Hammer* (Capitol)	20	11	10	9
– Mary Had A Little Boy *Snap* (Arista)	24	12	8	8
– You've Lost That Lovin' Feeling *The Righteous Brothers* (Verve/Polydor)	–	13	4	3
44 Just This Side of Love *Malandra Burrows* (YTV Enterprises)	29	15	11	14
– Situation *Yazz* (Mute)	22	14	18	21
27 Are You Dreaming? *Twenty 4 Seven feat. Captain Hollywood* (BCM)	25	18	19	17
– Sadness *Enigma* (Virgin International)	–	27	6	4
– The Grease Megamix *John Travolta/Olivia Newton John* (Polydor)	–	–	14	5
– The Total Mix *Black Box* (deConstruction)	–	22	15	18
– The Anniversary Waltz Part Two *Status Quo* (Vertigo)	–	35	20	16
– The Crazy Party Mixes *Jive Bunny & The Mastermixers* (Music Factory Dance)	–	–	25	13
– Crazy *Seal* (ZTT)	45	32	23	15
– The Best Christmas Of Them All *Shakin' Stevens* (Epic)	–	34	24	19

1990 – BEST-SELLING RECORDS

Singles:

1 Unchained Melody *The Righteous Brothers* (Verve)
2 Nothing Compares 2U *Sinead O'Connor* (Ensign)
3 Sacrifice/Healing Hands *Elton John* (Rocket)
4 Ice Ice Baby *Vanilla Ice* (SBK)
5 Killer *Adamski* (MCA)
6 Show Me Heaven *Maria McKee* (Epic)
7 Dub Be Good To Me *Beats International* (Go!)
8 Vogue *Madonna* (Sire)
9 World In Motion *England/New Order* (Factory/MCA)
10 The Power *Snap!* (Arista)
11 Nessun Dorma *Luciano Pavarotti* (Decca)
12 A Little Time *The Beautiful South* (Go!)
13 Turtle Power *Partners In Kryme* (SBK)
14 It Must Have Been Love *Roxette* (EMI)
15 U Can't Touch This *MC Hammer* (Capitol)
16 Its Bitsy Teeny Weeny Yellow Polka Dot Bikini *Bombalurina* (Carpet)
17 Get Up (Before The Night Is Over) *Technotronic featuring Ya Kid K.* (Swanyard)
18 Black Velvet *Alannah Myles* (Atlantic)
19 Dirty Cash *Adventures of Stevie V* (Mercury)
20 Don't Worry *Kim Appleby* (Parlophone)
21 Saviour's Day *Cliff Richard* (EMI)
22 Mona *Craig McLachlan & Check 1-2* (Epic)
23 Love Shack *B-52s* (WEA)
24 The Joker *Steve Miller* (Capitol)
25 Opposites Attract *Paula Abdul With The Wild Pair* (Siren)
26 Groove Is In The Heart *Dee-Lite* (Elektra)
27 Blue Velvet *Bobby Vinton* (Epic)
28 How Am I Supposed To Live Without You *Michael Bolton* (CBS)
29 I've Been Thinking About You *Londonbeat* (Anxious)
30 Unbelievable *E.M.F.* (EMI)
31 Naked In The Rain *Blue Pearl* (Big Life)
32 Tom's Diner *DNA featuring Suzanne Vega* (A&M)
33 Oops Up *Snap!* (Arista)
34 Tears On My Pillow *Kylie Minogue* (PWL)
35 Kingston Town *UB40* (Dep International)
36 The Anniversary Waltz *Status Quo* (Vertigo)
37 Take My Breath Away *Berlin* (CBS)
38 Better The Devil You Know *Kylie Minogue* (PWL)
39 Tonight *New Kids On The Block* (CBS)
40 I'm Free *Soup Dragons featuring Junior Reid* (Big Life)
41 Lily Was Here *David A. Stewart/Candy Dulfer* (Anxious)
42 Blue Savannah *Erasure* (Mute)
43 Justify My Love *Madonna* (Sire)
44 Four Bacharach & David Songs (EP) *Deacon Blue* (CBS)
45 Hold On *Wilson Phillips* (SBK)
46 Hear The Drummer (Get Wicked) *Chad Jackson* (Big Wave)
47 Fantasy *Black Box* (deConstruction)
48 What Time Is Love *KLF* (KLF Communication)
49 Got To Have Your Love *Mantronix feat. Wondress* (Capitol)
50 Step On *Happy Mondays* (Factory)

Albums:

1 . . . But Seriously *Phil Collins* (Virgin)
2 The Immaculate Conception *Madonna* (Sire)
3 In Concert *Carreras/Domingo/Pavorotti* (Decca)
4 The Very Best Of Elton John *Elton John* (Rocket)
5 Soul Provider *Michael Bolton* (CBS)
6 The Essential Pavarotti *Luciano Pavarotti* (Reprise)
7 Only Yesterday *Carpenters* (A&M)
8 Now That's What I Call Music 18 *Various* (EMI/Virgin/Polygram)
9 Sleeping With The Past *Elton John* (Rocket)
10 Serious Hits . . . Live *Phil Collins* (Virgin)
11 Listen Without Prejudice Vol. 1 *George Michael* (Epic)
12 Just The Two Of Us *Various* (Epic)
13 The Rhythm Of The Saints *Paul Simon* (Warner Brothers)
14 Vivaldi Four Seasons *Nigel Kennedy/ECO* (EMI)
15 Foreign Affair *Tina Turner* (Capitol)
16 Rocking All Over The Years *Status Quo* (Vertigo)
17 Labour Of Love II *UB40* (Dep International)
18 I Do Not Want What I Haven't Got *Sinead O'Connor* (Chrysalis)
19 From A Distance (The Event) *Cliff Richard* (EMI)
20 The Singles Collection 1984/1990 *Jimmy Somerville* (Various)
21 The Road To Hell *Chris Rea* (East West)
22 Step By Step *New Kids On The Block* (CBS)
23 Hangin' Tough *New Kids On The Block* (CBS)
24 Pump Up The Jam *Technotronic* (Swanyard)
25 Choke *The Beautiful South* (Go!)
26 Pretty Woman *Original Soundtrack* (EMI USA)
27 Vol II – 1990 A New Decade *Soul II Soul* (Ten)
28 I'm Your Baby Tonight *Whitney Houston* (Arista)
29 Changes Bowie *David Bowie* (EMI)
30 I'm Breathless *Madonna* (Sire)
31 Heart Of Stone *Cher* (Geffen)
32 Missing You – An Album Of Love *Various* (EMI)
33 Now Dance 902 *Various* (EMI/Virgin/PolyGram)
34 The Very Best Of The Bee Gees *Bee Gees* (Polydor)
35 Now That's What I Call Music 17 *Various* (EMI/Virgin/PolyGram)
36 Affection *Lisa Stansfield* (Arista)
37 Classic Experience II *Various* (EMI)
38 Smash Hits 1990 *Various* (Dover)
39 Pure Soft Metal *Various* (Stylus)
40 The Best Of Rod Stewart *Rod Stewart* (WEA)
41 Journey Man *Eric Clapton* (Reprise/Duck)
42 That Loving Feeling Volume III *Various* (EMI/Virgin/PolyGram)
43 Now Dance 90! *Various* (EMI/Virgin/PolyGram)
44 Summer Dreams *Beach Boys* (Capitol)
45 Look Sharp! *Roxette* (EMI)
46 X *INXS* (Mercury)
47 Please Hammer Don't Hurt 'Em *MC Hammer* (Capitol)
48 Cuts Both Ways *Gloria Estefan* (Epic)
49 Between The Lines *Jason Donovan* (PWL)
50 Violator *Depeche Mode* (Mute)

1955

January	22	Mambo Italiano *Rosemary Clooney* (Philips)
	29	Mambo Italiano *Rosemary Clooney* (Philips)
February	5	Mambo Italiano *Rosemary Clooney* (Philips)
	12	Naughty Lady Of Shady Lane *Dean Martin* (Capitol)
	19	Give Me Your Word *Tennessee Ernie Ford* (Capitol)
	26	Give Me Your Word *Tennessee Ernie Ford* (Capitol)
March	5	Give Me Your Word *Tennessee Ernie Ford* (Capitol)
	12	Softly Softly *Ruby Murray* (Columbia)
	19	Give Me Your Word *Tennessee Ernie Ford* (Capitol)
	26	Give Me Your Word *Tennessee Ernie Ford* (Capitol)
April	2	Give Me Your Word *Tennessee Ernie Ford* (Capitol)
	9	Give Me Your Word *Tennessee Ernie Ford* (Capitol)
	16	Give Me Your Word *Tennessee Ernie Ford* (Capitol)
	23	Give Me Your Word *Tennessee Ernie Ford* (Capitol)
	30	Give Me Your Word *Tennessee Ernie Ford* (Capitol)
May	7	Stranger In Paradise *Tony Bennett* (Philips)
	14	Stranger In Paradise *Tony Bennett* (Philips)
	21	Stranger In Paradise *Tony Bennett* (Philips)
	28	Stranger In Paradise *Tony Bennett* (Philips)
June	4	Stranger In Paradise *Tony Bennett* (Philips)
	11	Unchained Melody *Al Hibbler* (Brunswick)
	18	Unchained Melody *Al Hibbler* (Brunswick)
	25	Unchained Melody *Al Hibbler* (Brunswick)
July	2	Unchained Melody *Al Hibbler* (Brunswick)
	9	Dreamboat *Alma Cogan* (HMV)
	16	Dreamboat *Alma Cogan* (HMV)
	23	Rose Marie *Slim Whitman* (London)
	30	Rose Marie *Slim Whitman* (London)
August	13	Rose Marie *Slim Whitman* (London)
	20	Rose Marie *Slim Whitman* (London)
	27	Rose Marie *Slim Whitman* (London)
September	3	Rose Marie *Slim Whitman* (London)
	10	Rose Marie *Slim Whitman* (London)
	17	Rose Marie *Slim Whitman* (London)
	24	Rose Marie *Slim Whitman* (London)
October	1	Cool Water *Frankie Laine* (Philips)
	8	The Man From Laramie *Jimmy Young* (Decca)
	15	The Man From Laramie *Jimmy Young* (Decca)
	22	The Man From Laramie *Jimmy Young* (Decca)
	29	The Man From Laramie *Jimmy Young* (Decca)
November	5	The Man From Laramie *Jimmy Young* (Decca)
	12	Rock Around The Clock *Bill Haley* (Brunswick)
	19	Rock Around The Clock *Bill Haley* (Brunswick)
	26	Rock Around The Clock *Bill Haley* (Brunswick)
December	3	Rock Around The Clock *Bill Haley* (Brunswick)
	10	Rock Around The Clock *Bill Haley* (Brunswick)
	17	Rock Around The Clock *Bill Haley* (Brunswick)
	24	Rock Around The Clock *Bill Haley* (Brunswick)

Total Number One records: 11.
Record with most weeks at top: Give Me Your Word *Tennessee Ernie Ford*
(Capitol) 10 weeks. The record achieved this on a combination of two spells
at the top. Rose Marie *Slim Whitman* (London) achieved 9 consecutive
weeks at the top.

January	7	Rock Around The Clock *Bill Haley* (Brunswick)
	14	Sixteen Tons *Tennessee Ernie Ford* (Capitol)
	21	Sixteen Tons *Tennessee Ernie Ford* (Capitol)
	28	Sixteen Tons *Tennessee Ernie Ford* (Capitol)
February	4	Sixteen Tons *Tennessee Ernie Ford* (Capitol)
	11	Sixteen Tons *Tennessee Ernie Ford* (Capitol)
	18	Zambesi *Lou Busch* (Capitol)
	25	Zambesi *Lou Busch* (Capitol)
March	3	Memories Are Made Of This *Dean Martin* (Capitol)
	10	Memories Are Made Of This *Dean Martin* (Capitol)
	17	It's Almost Tomorrow *The Dream Weavers* (Brunswick)
	24	It's Almost Tomorrow *The Dream Weavers* (Brunswick)
	31	It's Almost Tomorrow *The Dream Weavers* (Brunswick)
April	7	Poor People Of Paris *Winifred Atwell* (Decca)
	14	Poor People Of Paris *Winifred Atwell* (Decca)
	21	Poor People Of Paris *Winifred Atwell* (Decca)
	28	Poor People Of Paris *Winifred Atwell* (Decca)
May	5	Poor People Of Paris *Winifred Atwell* (Decca)
	12	No Other Love *Ronnie Hilton* (HMV)
	19	No Other Love *Ronnie Hilton* (HMV)
	26	No Other Love *Ronnie Hilton* (HMV)
June	2	No Other Love *Ronnie Hilton* (HMV)
	9	I'll Be Home *Pat Boone* (London)
	16	I'll Be Home *Pat Boone* (London)
	23	I'll Be Home *Pat Boone* (London)
	30	I'll Be Home *Pat Boone* (London)
July	7	I'll Be Home *Pat Boone* (London)
	14	I'll Be Home *Pat Boone* (London)
	21	Why Do Fools Fall In Love *Frankie Lymon and The Teenagers* (Columbia)
	28	Why Do Fools Fall In Love *Frankie Lymon and The Teenagers* (Columbia)
August	4	Why Do Fools Fall In Love *Frankie Lymon and The Teenagers* (Columbia)
	11	Whatever Will Be Will Be *Doris Day* (Philips)
	18	Whatever Will Be Will Be *Doris Day* (Philips)
	25	Whatever Will Be Will Be *Doris Day* (Philips)
September	1	Whatever Will Be Will Be *Doris Day* (Philips)
	8	Whatever Will Be Will Be *Doris Day* (Philips)
	15	Whatever Will Be Will Be *Doris Day* (Philips)
	22	Lay Down Your Arms *Anne Shelton* (Philips)
	29	Lay Down Your Arms *Anne Shelton* (Philips)
October	6	Lay Down Your Arms *Anne Shelton* (Philips)
	13	Lay Down Your Arms *Anne Shelton* (Philips)
	20	Woman In Love *Frankie Laine* (Philips)
	27	Woman In Love *Frankie Laine* (Philips)
November	3	Woman In Love *Frankie Laine* (Philips)
	10	Just Walking In The Rain *Johnny Ray* (Philips)
	17	Just Walking In The Rain *Johnny Ray* (Philips)
	24	Just Walking In The Rain *Johnny Ray* (Philips)
December	1	Just Walking In The Rain *Johnny Ray* (Philips)
	8	Just Walking In The Rain *Johnny Ray* (Philips)
	15	Just Walking In The Rain *Johnny Ray* (Philips)
	22	Just Walking In The Rain *Johnny Ray* (Philips)

Total Number One records: 13.
Record with most weeks at top: Just Walking In The Rain *Johnny Ray* (Philips) 7 weeks.

January	5	Singing The Blues *Guy Mitchell* (Philips)
	12	Singing The Blues *Guy Mitchell* (Philips)
	19	Singing The Blues *Tommy Steele* (Decca)
	26	Singing The Blues *Guy Mitchell* (Philips)
February	2	Garden Of Eden *Frankie Vaughan* (Philips)
	9	Garden Of Eden *Frankie Vaughan* (Philips)
	16	Garden Of Eden *Frankie Vaughan* (Philips)
	23	Young Love *Tab Hunter* (London)
March	2	Young Love *Tab Hunter* (London)
	9	Young Love *Tab Hunter* (London)
	16	Young Love *Tab Hunter* (London)
	23	Young Love *Tab Hunter* (London)
	30	Young Love *Tab Hunter* (London)
April	6	Young Love *Tab Hunter* (London)
	13	Cumberland Gap *Lonnie Donegan* (Pye/Nixa)
	20	Cumberland Gap *Lonnie Donegan* (Pye/Nixa)
	27	Cumberland Gap *Lonnie Donegan* (Pye/Nixa)
May	4	Cumberland Gap *Lonnie Donegan* (Pye/Nixa)
	11	Butterfly *Andy Williams* (London)
	18	Butterfly *Andy Williams* (London)
	25	Butterfly *Andy Williams* (London)
June	1	Butterfly *Andy Williams* (London)
	8	Yes Tonight Josephine *Johnny Ray* (Philips)
	15	Yes Tonight Josephine *Johnny Ray* (Philips)
	22	Yes Tonight Josephine *Johnny Ray* (Philips)
	29	Yes Tonight Josephine *Johnny Ray* (Philips)
July	6	Gambling Man *Lonnie Donegan* (Pye/Nixa)
	13	All Shook Up *Elvis Presley* (RCA)
	20	All Shook Up *Elvis Presley* (RCA)
	27	All Shook Up *Elvis Presley* (RCA)
August	3	All Shook Up *Elvis Presley* (RCA)
	10	All Shook Up *Elvis Presley* (RCA)
	17	All Shook Up *Elvis Presley* (RCA)
	24	All Shook Up *Elvis Presley* (RCA)
	31	Diana *Paul Anka* (Columbia)
September	7	Diana *Paul Anka* (Columbia)
	14	Diana *Paul Anka* (Columbia)
	21	Diana *Paul Anka* (Columbia)
	28	Diana *Paul Anka* (Columbia)
October	5	Diana *Paul Anka* (Columbia)
	12	Diana *Paul Anka* (Columbia)
	19	Diana *Paul Anka* (Columbia)
	26	That'll Be The Day *The Crickets* (Vogue/Coral)
November	2	That'll Be The Day *The Crickets* (Vogue/Coral)
	9	That'll Be The Day *The Crickets* (Vogue/Coral)
	16	That'll Be The Day *The Crickets* (Vogue/Coral)
	23	Mary's Boy Child *Harry Belafonte* (RCA)
	30	Mary's Boy Child *Harry Belafonte* (RCA)
December	7	Mary's Boy Child *Harry Belafonte* (RCA)
	14	Mary's Boy Child *Harry Belafonte* (RCA)
	21	Mary's Boy Child *Harry Belafonte* (RCA)

Total Number One records: 11
Record with most weeks at top: Diana *Paul Anka* (Columbia) 8 weeks.
Guy Mitchell regained the top spot after losing it to Tommy Steele.

1958

January	4	Ma He's Making Eyes At Me *Johnny Otis Show* (Capitol)
	11	Ma He's Making Eyes At Me *Johnny Otis Show* (Capitol)
	18	Great Balls Of Fire *Jerry Lee Lewis* (London)
	25	Jailhouse Rock *Elvis Presley* (RCA)
February	1	Jailhouse Rock *Elvis Presley* (RCA)
	8	Jailhouse Rock *Elvis Presley* (RCA)
	15	The Story Of My Life *Michael Holliday* (Columbia)
	22	The Story Of My Life *Michael Holliday* (Columbia)
March	1	Magic Moments/Catch A Falling Star *Perry Como* (RCA)
	8	Magic Moments/Catch A Falling Star *Perry Como* (RCA)
	15	Magic Moments/Catch A Falling Star *Perry Como* (RCA)
	22	Magic Moments/Catch A Falling Star *Perry Como* (RCA)
	29	Magic Moments/Catch A Falling Star *Perry Como* (RCA)
April	5	Magic Moments/Catch A Falling Star *Perry Como* (RCA)
	12	Magic Moments/Catch A Falling Star *Perry Como* (RCA)
	19	Whole Lotta Woman *Marvin Rainwater* (MGM)
	26	Whole Lotta Woman *Marvin Rainwater* (MGM)
May	3	Whole Lotta Woman *Marvin Rainwater* (MGM)
	10	Whole Lotta Woman *Marvin Rainwater* (MGM)
	17	Who's Sorry Now *Connie Francis* (MGM)
	24	Who's Sorry Now *Connie Francis* (MGM)
	31	Who's Sorry Now *Connie Francis* (MGM)
June	7	Who's Sorry Now *Connie Francis* (MGM)
	14	Who's Sorry Now *Connie Francis* (MGM)
	21	Who's Sorry Now *Connie Francis* (MGM)
	28	All I Have To Do Is Dream/Claudette *The Everly Brothers* (London)
July	5	All I Have To Do Is Dream/Claudette *The Everly Brothers* (London)
	12	All I Have To Do Is Dream/Claudette *The Everly Brothers* (London)
	19	All I Have To Do Is Dream/Claudette *The Everly Brothers* (London)
	26	All I Have To Do Is Dream/Claudette *The Everly Brothers* (London)
August	2	All I Have To Do Is Dream/Claudette *The Everly Brothers* (London)
	9	All I Have To Do Is Dream/Claudette *The Everly Brothers* (London)
	16	All I Have To Do Is Dream/Claudette *The Everly Brothers* (London)
	23	All I Have To Do Is Dream/Claudette *The Everly Brothers* (London)
	30	When *The Kalin Twins* (Brunswick)
September	6	When *The Kalin Twins* (Brunswick)
	13	When *The Kalin Twins* (Brunswick)
	20	When *The Kalin Twins* (Brunswick)
	27	When *The Kalin Twins* (Brunswick)
October	4	Stupid Cupid *Connie Francis* (MGM)
	11	Stupid Cupid *Connie Francis* (MGM)
	18	Stupid Cupid *Connie Francis* (MGM)
	25	Stupid Cupid *Connie Francis* (MGM)
November	1	Stupid Cupid *Connie Francis* (MGM)
	8	Bird Dog *The Everly Brothers* (London)
	15	Bird Dog *The Everly Brothers* (London)
	22	Bird Dog *The Everly Brothers* (London)
	29	Hoots Mon *Lord Rockingham's XI* (Decca)

December	5	Hoots Mon *Lord Rockingham's XI* (Decca)
	12	Hoots Mon *Lord Rockingham's XI* (Decca)
	19	Hoots Mon *Lord Rockingham's XI* (Decca)
	26	It's Only Make Believe *Conway Twitty* (MGM)

Total Number One records: 13.
Record with most weeks at top: All I Have To Do Is Dream/Claudette *The Everly Brothers* (London) 9 weeks.

1959

January	3	It's Only Make Believe *Conway Twitty* (MGM)
	10	It's Only Make Believe *Conway Twitty* (MGM)
	17	It's Only Make Believe *Conway Twitty* (MGM)
	24	I Got Stung/One Night *Elvis Presley* (RCA)
	31	I Got Stung/One Night *Elvis Presley* (RCA)
February	7	I Got Stung/One Night *Elvis Presley* (RCA)
	14	I Got Stung/One Night *Elvis Presley* (RCA)
	21	I Got Stung/One Night *Elvis Presley* (RCA)
	28	Smoke Gets In Your Eyes *The Platters* (Mercury)
March	7	Smoke Gets In Your Eyes *The Platters* (Mercury)
	14	Smoke Gets In Your Eyes *The Platters* (Mercury)
	21	Smoke Gets In Your Eyes *The Platters* (Mercury)
	28	Smoke Gets In Your Eyes *The Platters* (Mercury)
April	4	Side Saddle *Russ Conway* (Columbia)
	11	Side Saddle *Russ Conway* (Columbia)
	18	Side Saddle *Russ Conway* (Columbia)
	25	It Doesn't Matter Any More *Buddy Holly* (Coral)
May	2	A Fool Such As I/I Need Your Love Tonight *Elvis Presley* (RCA)
	9	A Fool Such As I/I Need Your Love Tonight *Elvis Presley* (RCA)
	16	A Fool Such As I/I Need Your Love Tonight *Elvis Presley* (RCA)
	23	A Fool Such As I/I Need Your Love Tonight *Elvis Presley* (RCA)
	30	A Fool Such As I/I Need Your Love Tonight *Elvis Presley* (RCA)
June	6	A Fool Such As I/I Need Your Love Tonight *Elvis Presley* (RCA)
	13	A Fool Such As I/I Need Your Love Tonight *Elvis Presley* (RCA)
	20	Roulette *Russ Conway* (Columbia)
August	8	Livin' Doll *Cliff Richard* (Columbia)
	15	Livin' Doll *Cliff Richard* (Columbia)
	22	Livin' Doll *Cliff Richard* (Columbia)
	29	Only Sixteen *Craig Douglas* (Top Rank)
September	5	Only Sixteen *Craig Douglas* (Top Rank)
	12	Only Sixteen *Craig Douglas* (Top Rank)
	19	Only Sixteen *Craig Douglas* (Top Rank)
	26	Only Sixteen *Craig Douglas* (Top Rank)
October	3	Only Sixteen *Craig Douglas* (Top Rank)
	10	Only Sixteen *Craig Douglas* (Top Rank)
	17	Travellin' Light *Cliff Richard* (Columbia)
	24	Travellin' Light *Cliff Richard* (Columbia)
	31	Travellin' Light *Cliff Richard* (Columbia)
November	7	Travellin' Light *Cliff Richard* (Columbia)
	14	Travellin' Light *Cliff Richard* (Columbia)
	21	Travellin' Light *Cliff Richard* (Columbia)
	28	Travellin' Light *Cliff Richard* (Columbia)

December	5	What Do You Want *Adam Faith* (Parlophone)
	12	What Do You Want *Adam Faith* (Parlophone)
	19	What Do You Want *Adam Faith* (Parlophone)
	26	What Do You Want *Adam Faith* (Parlophone)

Total Number One records: 11.
Record with most weeks at top: Only Sixteen *Craig Douglas* (Top Rank), Travellin' Light *Cliff Richard* (Columbia), A Fool Such As I *Elvis Presley* (RCA) 7 weeks.

1960

January	9	What Do Want To Make Those Eyes At Me For? *Emile Ford* (Pye)
	16	What Do Want To Make Those Eyes At Me For? *Emile Ford* (Pye)
	23	Why? *Anthony Newley* (Decca)
	30	Why? *Anthony Newley* (Decca)
February	6	Why? *Anthony Newley* (Decca)
	13	Why? *Anthony Newley* (Decca)
	20	Why? *Anthony Newley* (Decca)
	27	Why? *Anthony Newley* (Decca)
March	5	Poor Me *Adam Faith* (Parlophone)
	12	Running Bear *Johnny Preston* (Mercury)
	19	Running Bear *Johnny Preston* (Mercury)
	26	My Old Man's A Dustman *Lonnie Donegan* (Pye)
April	2	My Old Man's A Dustman *Lonnie Donegan* (Pye)
	9	My Old Man's A Dustman *Lonnie Donegan* (Pye)
	16	My Old Man's A Dustman *Lonnie Donegan* (Pye)
	23	My Old Man's A Dustman *Lonnie Donegan* (Pye)
	30	Cathy's Clown *The Everly Brothers* (Warner Bros.)
May	7	Cathy's Clown *The Everly Brothers* (Warner Bros.)
	14	Cathy's Clown *The Everly Brothers* (Warner Bros.)
	21	Cathy's Clown *The Everly Brothers* (Warner Bros.)
	28	Cathy's Clown *The Everly Brothers* (Warner Bros.)
June	4	Cathy's Clown *The Everly Brothers* (Warner Bros.)
	11	Cathy's Clown *The Everly Brothers* (Warner Bros.)
	18	Cathy's Clown *The Everly Brothers* (Warner Bros.)
	25	Cathy's Clown *The Everly Brothers* (Warner Bros.)
July	2	Good Timin' *Jimmy Jones* (MGM)
	9	Good Timin' *Jimmy Jones* (MGM)
	16	Good Timin' *Jimmy Jones* (MGM)
	23	Good Timin' *Jimmy Jones* (MGM)
	30	Please Don't Tease *Cliff Richard* (Columbia)
August	6	Please Don't Tease *Cliff Richard* (Columbia)
	13	Please Don't Tease *Cliff Richard* (Columbia)
	20	Apache *The Shadows* (Columbia)
	27	Apache *The Shadows* (Columbia)
September	3	Apache *The Shadows* (Columbia)
	10	Apache *The Shadows* (Columbia)
	17	Apache *The Shadows* (Columbia)
	24	Apache *The Shadows* (Columbia)
October	1	Tell Laura I Love Her *Ricky Valance* (Columbia)
	8	Tell Laura I Love Her *Ricky Valance* (Columbia)
	15	Only The Lonely *Roy Orbison* (London)
	22	Only The Lonely *Roy Orbison* (London)
	29	Only The Lonely *Roy Orbison* (London)
November	5	It's Now Or Never *Elvis Presley* (RCA)
	12	It's Now Or Never *Elvis Presley* (RCA)
	19	It's Now Or Never *Elvis Presley* (RCA)
	26	It's Now Or Never *Elvis Presley* (RCA)

December	3	It's Now Or Never *Elvis Presley* (RCA)
	10	It's Now Or Never *Elvis Presley* (RCA)
	17	It's Now Or Never *Elvis Presley* (RCA)
	31	It's Now Or Never *Elvis Presley* (RCA)

Total Number One records: 12.
Record with most weeks at top: It's Now or Never *Elvis Presley* (RCA) nine (including same chart of 31 for 24 December), Cathy's Clown *The Everly Brothers* (Warner Bros.) nine.

1961

January	7	Poetry in Motion *Johnny Tillotson* (London)
	14	Poetry In Motion *Johnny Tillotson* (London)
	21	Poetry in Motion *Johnny Tillotson* (London)
	28	Are You Lonesome Tonight EP *Elvis Presley* (RCA)
February	4	Are You Lonesome Tonight EP *Elvis Presley* (RCA)
	11	Are You Lonesome Tonight EP *Elvis Presley* (RCA)
	18	Are You Lonesome Tonight EP *Elvis Presley* (RCA)
	25	Walk Right Back *The Everly Brothers* (Warner Bros.)
March	4	Walk Right Back *The Everly Brothers* (Warner Bros.)
	11	Walk Right Back *The Everly Brothers* (Warner Bros.)
	18	Walk Right Back *The Everly Brothers* (Warner Bros.)
	25	Wooden Heart *Elvis Presley* (RCA)
April	1	Wooden Heart *Elvis Presley* (RCA)
	8	Wooden Heart *Elvis Presley* (RCA)
	15	Are You Sure *The Allisons* (Fontana)
	22	Are You Sure *The Allisons* (Fontana)
	29	You're Driving Me Crazy *Temperance Seven* (Parlophone)
May	6	You're Driving Me Crazy *Temperance Seven* (Parlophone)
	13	Blue Moon *The Marcels* (Pye)
	20	Blue Moon *The Marcels* (Pye)
	27	Runaway *Del Shannon* (London)
June	3	Surrender *Elvis Presley* (RCA)
	10	Surrender *Elvis Presley* (RCA)
	17	Surrender *Elvis Presley* (RCA)
	24	Surrender *Elvis Presley* (RCA)
July	1	Runaway *Del Shannon* (London) Surrender *Elvis Presley* (RCA)
	8	Temptation *The Everly Brothers* (Warner Bros.)
	15	Temptation *The Everly Brothers* (Warner Bros.)
	22	Temptation *The Everly Brothers* (Warner Bros.)
	29	Temptation *The Everly Brothers* (Warner Bros.)
August	5	Well I Ask You *Eden Kane* (Decca)
	12	You Don't Know *Helen Shapiro* (Columbia)
	19	You Don't Know *Helen Shapiro* (Columbia)
	26	Johnny Remember Me *John Leyton* (Top Rank)
September	2	Johnny Remember Me *John Leyton* (Top Rank)
	9	Johnny Remember Me *John Leyton* (Top Rank)
	16	Johnny Remember Me *John Leyton* (Top Rank)
	23	Johnny Remember Me *John Leyton* (Top Rank)
	30	Kon Tiki *The Shadows* (Columbia)
October	7	Michael Row The Boat *The Highwaymen* (HMV)
	14	Walkin' Back To Happiness *Helen Shapiro* (Columbia)
	21	Walkin' Back To Happiness *Helen Shapiro* (Columbia)
	28	Walkin' Back To Happiness *Helen Shapiro* (Columbia)
November	4	Walkin' Back To Happiness *Helen Shapiro* (Columbia)
	11	His Latest Flame EP *Elvis Presley* (RCA)
	18	His Latest Flame EP *Elvis Presley* (RCA)
	25	His Latest Flame EP *Elvis Presley* (RCA)

December 2 Take Good Care Of My Baby *Bobby Vee* (London)
9 Tower Of Strength *Frankie Vaughan* (Philips)
16 Tower Of Strength *Frankie Vaughan* (Philips)
23 Tower Of Strength *Frankie Vaughan* (Philips)
30 Tower Of Strength *Frankie Vaughan* (Philips)

Total Number One records: 19.
Record with most weeks at top: Johnny Remember Me *John Leyton* (Top
Rank) 5 weeks.

1962

January 6 Stranger On The Shore *Acker Bilk* (Columbia)
13 Stranger On The Shore *Acker Bilk* (Columbia)
20 The Young Ones *Cliff Richard* (Columbia)
27 The Young Ones *Cliff Richard* (Columbia)
February 3 The Young Ones *Cliff Richard* (Columbia)
10 The Young Ones *Cliff Richard* (Columbia)
17 The Young Ones *Cliff Richard* (Columbia)
24 Rock-A-Hula Baby/Can't Help Falling In Love *Elvis Presley* (RCA)
March 3 Rock-A-Hula-Baby/Can't Help Falling In Love *Elvis Presley* (RCA)
10 Rock-A-Hula Baby/Can't Help Falling In Love *Elvis Presley* (RCA)
17 Rock-A-Hula Baby/Can't Help Falling In Love *Elvis Presley* (RCA)
24 Wonderful Land *The Shadows* (Columbia)
31 Wonderful Land *The Shadows* (Columbia)
April 7 Wonderful Land *The Shadows* (Columbia)
14 Wonderful Land *The Shadows* (Columbia)
21 Wonderful Land *The Shadows* (Columbia)
28 Wonderful Land *The Shadows* (Columbia)
May 5 Wonderful Land *The Shadows* (Columbia)
12 Wonderful Land *The Shadows* (Columbia)
19 Nut Rocker *B. Bumble and The Stingers* (Top Rank)
26 Good Luck Charm *Elvis Presley* (RCA)
June 2 Good Luck Charm *Elvis Presley* (RCA)
9 Good Luck Charm *Elvis Presley* (RCA)
16 Good Luck Charm *Elvis Presley* (RCA)
23 Good Luck Charm *Elvis Presley* (RCA)
30 Come Outside *Mike Sarne* (Parlophone)
July 7 Come Outside *Mike Sarne* (Parlophone)
14 I Can't Stop Loving You *Ray Charles* (HMV)
21 I Can't Stop Loving You *Ray Charles* (HMV)
28 I Remember You *Frank Ifield* (Columbia)
August 4 I Remember You *Frank Ifield* (Columbia)
11 I Remember You *Frank Ifield* (Columbia)
18 I Remember You *Frank Ifield* (Columbia)
25 I Remember You *Frank Ifield* (Columbia)
September 1 I Remember You *Frank Ifield* (Columbia)
8 I Remember You *Frank Ifield* (Columbia)
15 She's Not For You *Elvis Presley* (RCA)
22 She's Not For You *Elvis Presley* (RCA)
29 She's Not For You *Elvis Presley* (RCA)
October 6 Telstar *The Tornados* (Decca)
13 Telstar *The Tornados* (Decca)
20 Telstar *The Tornados* (Decca)
27 Telstar *The Tornados* (Decca)
November 3 Telstar *The Tornados* (Decca)
10 Lovesick Blues *Frank Ifield* (Columbia)
17 Lovesick Blues *Frank Ifield* (Columbia)
24 Lovesick Blues *Frank Ifield* (Columbia)

December **1** Lovesick Blues *Frank Ifield* (Columbia)
8 Lovesick Blues *Frank Ifield* (Columbia)
15 Return To Sender *Elvis Presley* (RCA)
22 Return To Sender *Elvis Presley* (RCA)
29 Return To Sender *Elvis Presley* (RCA)

Total Number One records: 13.
Record with most weeks at top: Wonderful Land *The Shadows* (Columbia)
8 weeks.

1963

January **5** The Next Time/Bachelor Boy *Cliff Richard* (Columbia)
12 The Next Time/Bachelor Boy *Cliff Richard* (Columbia)
19 The Next Time/Bachelor Boy *Cliff Richard* (Columbia)
26 Dance On *The Shadows* (Columbia)
February **2** Diamonds *Jet Harris and Tony Meehan* (Decca)
9 Diamonds *Jet Harris and Tony Meehan* (Decca)
16 Diamonds *Jet Harris and Tony Meehan* (Decca)
23 Wayward Wind *Frank Ifield* (Columbia)
March **2** Wayward Wind *Frank Ifield* (Columbia)
9 Wayward Wind *Frank Ifield* (Columbia)
16 Summer Holiday *Cliff Richard* (Columbia)
23 Summer Holiday *Cliff Richard* (Columbia)
30 Foot Tapper *The Shadows* (Columbia)
April **6** How Do You Do It *Gerry and The Pacemakers* (Columbia)
13 How Do You Do It *Gerry and The Pacemakers* (Columbia)
20 How Do You Do It *Gerry and The Pacemakers* (Columbia)
27 How Do You Do It *Gerry and The Pacemakers* (Columbia)
May **4** From Me To You *The Beatles* (Parlophone)
11 From Me To You *The Beatles* (Parlophone)
18 From Me To You *The Beatles* (Parlophone)
25 From Me To You *The Beatles* (Parlophone)
June **1** From Me To You *The Beatles* (Parlophone)
8 From Me To You *The Beatles* (Parlophone)
15 From Me To You *The Beatles* (Parlophone)
22 I Like It *Gerry and The Pacemakers* (Columbia)
29 I Like It *Gerry and The Pacemakers* (Columbia)
July **6** I Like It *Gerry and The Pacemakers* (Columbia)
13 I Like It *Gerry and The Pacemakers* (Columbia)
20 Confessin' *Frank Ifield* (Columbia)
27 Confessin' *Frank Ifield* (Columbia)
August **3** Devil In Disguise *Elvis Presley* (RCA)
10 Sweets For My Sweet *The Searchers* (Pye)
17 Sweets For My Sweet *The Searchers* (Pye)
24 Bad To Me *Billy J. Kramer and The Dakotas* (Parlophone)
31 Bad To Me *Billy J. Kramer and The Dakotas* (Parlophone)
September **7** Bad To Me *Billy J. Kramer and The Dakotas* (Parlophone)
14 She Loves You *The Beatles* (Parlophone)
21 She Loves You *The Beatles* (Parlophone)
28 She Loves You *The Beatles* (Parlophone)
October **5** She Loves You *The Beatles* (Parlophone)
12 Do You Love Me *Brian Poole and The Tremeloes* (Decca)
19 Do You Love Me *Brian Poole and The Tremeloes* (Decca)
26 Do You Love Me *Brian Poole and The Tremeloes* (Decca)
November **2** You'll Never Walk Alone *Gerry and The Pacemakers*
(Columbia)
9 You'll Never Walk Alone *Gerry and The Pacemakers*
(Columbia)
16 You'll Never Walk Alone *Gerry and The Pacemakers*
(Columbia)

443

23 You'll Never Walk Alone *Gerry and The Pacemakers*
(Columbia)
30 She Loves You *The Beatles* (Parlophone)
December 7 She Loves You *The Beatles* (Parlophone)
14 I Want To Hold Your Hand *The Beatles* (Parlophone)
21 I Want To Hold Your Hand *The Beatles* (Parlophone)

Total Number One records: 17.
Record with most weeks at top: From Me To You *The Beatles* (Parlophone)
7 weeks.

1964

January	4	I Want To Hold Your Hand *The Beatles* (Parlophone)
	11	I Want To Hold Your Hand *The Beatles* (Parlophone)
	18	Glad All Over *The Dave Clark Five* (Columbia)
	25	Glad All Over *The Dave Clark Five* (Columbia)
February	1	Needles And Pins *The Searchers* (Pye)
	8	Needles And Pins *The Searchers* (Pye)
	15	Needles And Pins *The Searchers* (Pye)
	22	Diane *The Bachelors* (Decca)
	29	Diane *The Bachelors* (Decca)
March	7	Anyone Who Had A Heart *Cilla Black* (Parlophone)
	14	Anyone Who Had A Heart *Cilla Black* (Parlophone)
	21	Little Children *Billy J. Kramer and The Dakotas* (Parlophone)
	28	Little Children *Billy J. Kramer and The Dakotas* (Parlophone)
April	4	Can't Buy Me Love *The Beatles* (Parlophone)
	11	Can't Buy Me Love *The Beatles* (Parlophone)
	18	Can't Buy Me Love *The Beatles* (Parlophone)
	25	World Without Love *Peter and Gordon* (Columbia)
May	2	World Without Love *Peter and Gordon* (Columbia)
	9	Don't Throw Your Love Away *The Searchers* (Pye)
	16	Don't Throw Your Love Away *The Searchers* (Pye)
	23	Juliet *The Four Pennies* (Philips)
	30	You're My World *Cilla Black* (Parlophone)
June	6	You're My World *Cilla Black* (Parlophone)
	13	You're My World *Cilla Black* (Parlophone)
	20	You're My World *Cilla Black* (Parlophone)
	27	It's Over *Roy Orbison* (London)
July	4	It's Over *Roy Orbison* (London)
	11	House Of The Rising Sun *The Animals* (Columbia)
	18	It's All Over Now *The Rolling Stones* (Decca)
	25	A Hard Day's Night *The Beatles* (Parlophone)
August	1	A Hard Day's Night *The Beatles* (Parlophone)
	8	A Hard Day's Night *The Beatles* (Parlophone)
	15	Doo Wah Diddy Diddy *Manfred Mann* (HMV)
	22	Doo Wah Diddy Diddy *Manfred Mann* (HMV)
	29	Have I The Right *The Honeycombs* (Pye)
September	4	Have I The Right *The Honeycombs* (Pye)
	11	You Really Got Me *The Kinks* (Pye)
	18	You Really Got Me *The Kinks* (Pye)
	25	I'm Into Something Good *Herman's Hermits* (Columbia)
October	3	I'm Into Something Good *Herman's Hermits* (Columbia)
	10	Oh Pretty Woman *Roy Orbison* (London)
	17	Oh Pretty Woman *Roy Orbison* (London)
	24	There's Always Something There To Remind Me *Sandie Shaw* (Pye)
	31	There's Always Something There To Remind Me *Sandie Shaw* (Pye)

November	7	There's Always Something There To Remind Me *Sandie Shaw* (Pye)
	14	Oh Pretty Woman *Roy Orbison* (London)
	21	Baby Love *The Supremes* (Stateside)
	28	Baby Love *The Supremes* (Stateside)
December	5	Little Red Rooster *The Rolling Stones* (Decca)
	12	I Feel Fine *The Beatles* (Parlophone)
	19	I Feel Fine *The Beatles* (Parlophone)
	26	I Feel Fine *The Beatles* (Parlophone)

Total Number One records: 24.
Record with most weeks at top: You're My World *Cilla Black* (Parlophone)
4 weeks.

1965

January	2	I Feel Fine *The Beatles* (Parlophone)
	9	I Feel Fine *The Beatles* (Parlophone)
	16	Yeh Yeh *Georgie Fame* (Columbia)
	23	Yeh Yeh *Georgie Fame* (Columbia)
	30	Go Now *The Moody Blues* (Decca)
February	6	You've Lost That Loving Feeling *The Righteous Brothers* (London)
	13	You've Lost That Loving Feeling *The Righteous Brothers* (London)
	20	Tired Of Waiting For You *The Kinks* (Pye)
	27	I'll Never Find Another You *The Seekers* (Columbia)
March	6	I'll Never Find Another You *The Seekers* (Columbia)
	13	It's Not Unusual *Tom Jones* (Decca)
	20	The Last Time *The Rolling Stones* (Decca)
	27	The Last Time *The Rolling Stones* (Decca)
April	3	The Last Time *The Rolling Stones* (Decca)
	10	Concrete And Clay *Unit 4 Plus 2* (Decca)
	17	The Minute You're Gone *Cliff Richard* (Columbia)
	24	Ticket To Ride *The Beatles* (Parlophone)
May	1	Ticket To Ride *The Beatles* (Parlophone)
	8	Ticket To Ride *The Beatles* (Parlophone)
	15	King Of The Road *Roger Miller* (Philips)
	22	Where Are You Now My Love *Jackie Trent* (Pye)
	29	Long Live Love *Sandie Shaw* (Pye)
June	5	Long Live Love *Sandie Shaw* (Pye)
	12	Long Live Love *Sandie Shaw* (Pye)
	19	Crying In The Chapel *Elvis Presley* (RCA)
	26	I'm Alive *The Hollies* (Parlophone)
July	3	Crying In The Chapel *Elvis Presley* (RCA)
	10	I'm Alive *The Hollies* (Parlophone)
	17	I'm Alive *The Hollies* (Parlophone)
	24	Mr Tambourine Man *The Byrds* (CBS)
	31	Mr Tambourine Man *The Byrds* (CBS)
August	7	Help *The Beatles* (Parlophone)
	14	Help *The Beatles* (Parlophone)
	21	Help *The Beatles* (Parlophone)
	28	I Got You Babe *Sonny and Cher* (Atlantic)
September	4	I Got You Babe *Sonny and Cher* (Atlantic)
	11	Satisfaction *The Rolling Stones* (Decca)
	18	Satisfaction *The Rolling Stones* (Decca)
	25	Make It Easy On Yourself *The Walker Brothers* (Philips)
October	2	Tears *Ken Dodd* (Columbia)
	9	Tears *Ken Dodd* (Columbia)
	16	Tears *Ken Dodd* (Columbia)
	23	Tears *Ken Dodd* (Columbia)
	30	Tears *Ken Dodd* (Columbia)

November	6	Get Off Of My Cloud *The Rolling Stones* (Decca)
	13	Get Off Of My Cloud *The Rolling Stones* (Decca)
	20	Get Off Of My Cloud *The Rolling Stones* (Decca)
	27	The Carnival Is Over *The Seekers* (Coiumbia)
December	4	The Carnival Is Over *The Seekers* (Columbia)
	11	The Carnival Is Over *The Seekers* (Columbia)
	18	Day Tripper/We Can Work It Out *The Beatles* (Parlophone)
	25	Day Tripper/We Can Work It Out *The Beatles* (Parlophone)

Total Number One records: 25.
Record with most weeks at top: Tears *Ken Dodd* (Columbia) 5 weeks.

1966

January	1	Day Tripper/We Can Work It Out *The Beatles* (Parlophone)
	8	Day Tripper/We Can Work It Out *The Beatles* (Parlophone)
	15	Day Tripper/We Can Work It Out *The Beatles* (Parlophone)
	22	Keep On Running *The Spencer Davis Group* (Fontana)
	29	Michelle *The Overlanders* (Pye)
February	5	Michelle *The Overlanders* (Pye)
	12	Michelle *The Overlanders* (Pye)
	19	These Boots Are Made For Walkin' *Nancy Sinatra* (Reprise)
	26	These Boots Are Made For Walkin' *Nancy Sinatra* (Reprise)
March	5	These Boots Are Made For Walkin' *Nancy Sinatra* (Reprise)
	12	These Boots Are Made For Walkin' *Nancy Sinatra* (Reprise)
	19	The Sun Ain't Gonna Shine Any More *The Walker Brothers* (Philips)
	26	The Sun Ain't Gonna Shine Any More *The Walker Brothers* (Philips)
April	2	The Sun Ain't Gonna Shine Any More *The Walker Brothers* (Philips)
	9	The Sun Ain't Gonna Shine Any More *The Walker Brothers* (Philips)
	16	Somebody Help Me *The Spencer Davis Group* (Fontana)
	23	Somebody Help Me *The Spencer Davis Group* (Fontana)
	30	You Don't Have To Say You Love Me *Dusty Springfield* (Philips)
May	7	Pretty Flamingo *Manfred Mann* (HMV)
	14	Pretty Flamingo *Manfred Mann* (HMV)
	21	Pretty Flamingo *Manfred Mann* (HMV)
	28	Paint It Black *The Rolling Stones* (Decca)
June	4	Strangers In The Night *Frank Sinatra* (Reprise)
	11	Strangers In The Night *Frank Sinatra* (Reprise)
	18	Strangers In The Night *Frank Sinatra* (Reprise)
	25	Paperback Writer *The Beatles* (Parlophone)
July	2	Paperback Writer *The Beatles* (Parlophone)
	9	Sunny Afternoon *The Kinks* (Pye)
	16	Sunny Afternoon *The Kinks* (Pye)
	23	Get Away *Georgie Fame* (Columbia)
	30	Out Of Time *Chris Farlowe* (Immediate)
August	6	With A Girl Like You *The Troggs* (Fontana)
	13	With A Girl Like You *The Troggs* (Fontana)
	20	Yellow Submarine/Eleanor Rigby *The Beatles* (Parlophone)
	27	Yellow Submarine/Eleanor Rigby *The Beatles* (Parlophone)

September	3	Yellow Submarine/Eleanor Rigby *The Beatles* (Parlophone)
	10	Yellow Submarine/Eleanor Rigby *The Beatles* (Parlophone)
	17	All Or Nothing *The Small Faces* (Decca)
	24	Distant Drums *Jim Reeves* (RCA)
October	1	Distant Drums *Jim Reeves* (RCA)
	8	Distant Drums *Jim Reeves* (RCA)
	15	Distant Drums *Jim Reeves* (RCA)
	22	Distant Drums *Jim Reeves* (RCA)
	29	Reach Out I'll Be There *The Four Tops* (Tamla Motown)
November	5	Reach Out I'll Be There *The Four Tops* (Tamla Motown)
	12	Reach Out I'll Be There *The Four Tops* (Tamla Motown)
	19	Good Vibrations *The Beach Boys* (Capitol)
	26	Good Vibrations *The Beach Boys* (Capitol)
December	3	Green Green Grass Of Home *Tom Jones* (Decca)
	10	Green Green Grass Of Home *Tom Jones* (Decca)
	17	Green Green Grass Of Home *Tom Jones* (Decca)
	24	Green Green Grass Of Home *Tom Jones* (Decca)
	31	Green Green Grass Of Home *Tom Jones* (Decca)

Total Number One records: 21.
Records with most weeks at top: Distant Drums *Jim Reeves* (RCA) and Green Green Grass Of Home *Tom Jones* (Decca) 5 weeks.

1967

January	7	Green Green Grass Of Home *Tom Jones* (Decca)
	14	Green Green Grass Of Home *Tom Jones* (Decca)
	21	I'm A Believer *The Monkees* (RCA)
	28	I'm A Believer *The Monkees* (RCA)
February	4	I'm A Believer *The Monkees* (RCA)
	11	I'm A Believer *The Monkees* (RCA)
	18	This Is My Song *Petula Clark* (Pye)
	25	This Is My Song *Petula Clark* (Pye)
March	4	Release Me *Engelbert Humperdinck* (Decca)
	11	Release Me *Engelbert Humperdinck* (Decca)
	18	Release Me *Engelbert Humperdinck* (Decca)
	25	Release Me *Engelbert Humperdinck* (Decca)
April	1	Release Me *Engelbert Humperdinck* (Decca)
	8	Release Me *Engelbert Humperdinck* (Decca)
	15	Somethin' Stupid *Frank and Nancy Sinatra* (Reprise)
	22	Somethin' Stupid *Frank and Nancy Sinatra* (Reprise)
	29	Puppet On A String *Sandie Shaw* (Pye)
May	6	Puppet On A String *Sandie Shaw* (Pye)
	13	Puppet On A String *Sandie Shaw* (Pye)
	20	Silence Is Golden *The Tremeloes* (CBS)
	27	Silence Is Golden *The Tremeloes* (CBS)
June	3	Silence Is Golden *The Tremeloes* (CBS)
	10	A Whiter Shade Of Pale *Procol Harum* (Deram)
	17	A Whiter Shade Of Pale *Procol Harum* (Deram)
	24	A Whiter Shade Of Pale *Procol Harum* (Deram)
July	1	A Whiter Shade Of Pale *Procol Harum* (Deram)
	8	A Whiter Shade Of Pale *Procol Harum* (Deram)
	15	A Whiter Shade Of Pale *Procol Harum* (Deram)
	22	All You Need Is Love *The Beatles* (Parlophone)
	29	All You Need Is Love *The Beatles* (Parlophone)
August	5	All You Need Is Love *The Beatles* (Parlophone)
	12	San Francisco (Flowers In Your Hair) *Scott McKenzie* (CBS)

	19	San Francisco (Flowers In Your Hair) *Scott McKenzie* (CBS)
	26	San Francisco (Flowers In Your Hair) *Scott McKenzie* (CBS)
September	2	San Francisco (Flowers In Your Hair) *Scott McKenzie* (CBS)
	9	Last Waltz *Engelbert Humperdinck* (Decca)
	16	Last Waltz *Engelbert Humperdinck* (Decca)
	23	Last Waltz *Engelbert Humperdinck* (Decca)
	30	Last Waltz *Engelbert Humperdinck* (Decca)
October	7	Last Waltz *Engelbert Humperdinck* (Decca)
	14	Massachusetts *The Bee Gees* (Polydor)
	21	Massachusetts *The Bee Gees* (Polydor)
	28	Massachusetts *The Bee Gees* (Polydor)
November	4	Massachusetts *The Bee Gees* (Polydor)
	11	Baby Now That I've Found You *The Foundations* (Pye)
	18	Baby Now That I've Found You *The Foundations* (Pye)
	25	Let The Heartaches Begin *Long John Baldry* (Pye)
December	2	Let The Heartaches Begin *Long John Baldry* (Pye)
	9	Hello, Goodbye *The Beatles* (Parlophone)
	16	Hello, Goodbye *The Beatles* (Parlophone)
	23	Hello, Goodbye *The Beatles* (Parlophone)
	30	Hello, Goodbye *The Beatles* (Parlophone)

Total Number One records: 15.
Records with most weeks at top: Release Me *Engelbert Humperdinck* (Decca) and A Whiter Shade Of Pale *Procol Harum* (Deram) 6 weeks.

1968

January	6	Hello, Goodbye *The Beatles* (Parlophone)
	13	Hello, Goodbye *The Beatles* (Parlophone)
	20	Hello, Goodbye *The Beatles* (Parlophone)
	27	Ballad Of Bonnie And Clyde *Georgie Fame* (CBS)
February	3	Everlasting Love *The Love Affair* (CBS)
	10	Everlasting Love *The Love Affair* (CBS)
	17	The Mighty Quinn *Manfred Mann* (Fontana)
	24	The Mighty Quinn *Manfred Mann* (Fontana)
March	2	Cinderella Rockafella *Esther and Abi Ofarim* (Philips)
	9	Cinderella Rockafella *Esther and Abi Ofarim* (Philips)
	16	Cinderella Rockafella *Esther and Abi Ofarim* (Philips)
	23	Legend Of Xanadu *Dave Dee, Dozy, Beaky, Mick and Tich* (Fontana)
	30	Lady Madonna *The Beatles* (Parlophone)
April	6	Lady Madonna *The Beatles* (Parlophone)
	13	Congratulations *Cliff Richard* (Columbia)
	20	Congratulations *Cliff Richard* (Columbia)
	27	Wonderful World *Louis Armstrong* (HMV)
May	4	Wonderful World *Louis Armstrong* (HMV)
	11	Wonderful World *Louis Armstrong* (HMV)
	18	Wonderful World *Louis Armstrong* (HMV)
	25	Young Girl *The Union Gap* (CBS)
June	1	Young Girl *The Union Gap* (CBS)
	8	Young Girl *The Union Gap* (CBS)
	15	Young Girl *The Union Gap* (CBS)
	22	Jumping Jack Flash *The Rolling Stones* (Decca)
	29	Jumping Jack Flash *The Rolling Stones* (Decca)
	6	Baby Come Back *The Equals* (President)
	13	Baby Come Back *The Equals* (President)
	20	Baby Come Back *The Equals* (President)
	27	I Pretend *Des O'Connor* (Columbia)

August	3	Mony Mony *Tommy James and The Shondells* (Major Minor)
	10	Mony Mony *Tommy James and The Shondells* (Major Minor)
	17	Fire *The Crazy World Of Arthur Brown* (Track)
	24	Mony Mony *Tommy James and The Shondells* (Major Minor)
	31	Do It Again *The Beach Boys* (Capitol)
September	7	I Gotta Get A Message To You *The Bee Gees* (Polydor)
	14	Hey Jude *The Beatles* (Apple)
	21	Hey Jude *The Beatles* (Apple)
	28	Those Were The Days *Mary Hopkin* (Apple)
October	5	Those Were The Days *Mary Hopkin* (Apple)
	12	Those Were The Days *Mary Hopkin* (Apple)
	19	Those Were The Days *Mary Hopkin* (Apple)
	26	Those Were The Days *Mary Hopkin* (Apple)
November	2	Those Were The Days *Mary Hopkin* (Apple)
	9	With A Little Help From My Friends *Joe Cocker* (Regal Zonophone)
	16	The Good, The Bad And The Ugly *Hugo Montenegro* (RCA)
	23	The Good, The Bad And The Ugly *Hugo Montenegro* (RCA)
	30	The Good, The Bad And The Ugly *Hugo Montenegro* (RCA)
December	7	The Good, The Bad And The Ugly *Hugo Montenegro* (RCA)
	14	Lily The Pink *The Scaffold* (Columbia)
	21	Lily The Pink *The Scaffold* (Columbia)

Total Number One records: 22.
Record with most weeks at top: Those Were The Days *Mary Hopkin* (Apple) 6 weeks.

1969

January	4	Ob-La-Di-Ob-La-Da *The Marmalade* (CBS)
	11	Lily The Pink *The Scaffold* (Columbia)
	18	Ob-La-Di-Ob-La-Da *The Marmalade* (CBS)
	25	Ob-La-Di-Ob-La-Da *The Marmalade* (CBS)
February	1	Albatross *Fleetwood Mac* (Blue Horizon)
	8	Blackberry Way *The Move* (Regal Zonophone)
	15	Half As Nice *Amen Corner* (Immediate)
	22	Half As Nice *Amen Corner* (Immediate)
March	1	Where Do You Go To My Lovely *Peter Sarstedt* (UA)
	8	Where Do You Go To My Lovely *Peter Sarstedt* (UA)
	15	Where Do You Go To My Lovely *Peter Sarstedt* (UA)
	22	Where Do You Go To My Lovely *Peter Sarstedt* (UA)
	29	I Heard It Through The Grapevine *Marvin Gaye* (Motown)
April	5	I Heard It Through The Grapevine *Marvin Gaye* (Motown)
	12	I Heard It Through The Grapevine *Marvin Gaye* (Motown)
	19	The Israelites *Desmond Dekker* (Pyramid)
	26	Get Back *The Beatles* (Apple)
May	3	Get Back *The Beatles* (Apple)
	10	Get Back *The Beatles* (Apple)
	17	Get Back *The Beatles* (Apple)
	24	Get Back *The Beatles* (Apple)
	31	Get Back *The Beatles* (Apple)
June	7	Dizzy *Tommy Roe* (Stateside)
	14	The Ballad Of John And Yoko *The Beatles* (Apple)
	21	The Ballad Of John And Yoko *The Beatles* (Apple)
	28	The Ballad Of John And Yoko *The Beatles* (Apple)

July	5	Something In The Air *Thunderclap Newman* (Track)
	12	Something In The Air *Thunderclap Newman* (Track)
	19	Something In The Air *Thunderclap Newman* (Track)
	26	Honky Tonk Women *The Rolling Stones* (Decca)
August	2	Honky Tonk Women *The Rolling Stones* (Decca)
	9	Honky Tonk Women *The Rolling Stones* (Decca)
	16	Honky Tonk Women *The Rolling Stones* (Decca)
	23	Honky Tonk Women *The Rolling Stones* (Decca)
	30	In The Year 2525 *Zager and Evans* (RCA)
September	6	In The Year 2525 *Zager and Evans* (RCA)
	13	In The Year 2525 *Zager and Evans* (RCA)
	20	Bad Moon Rising *Creedence Clearwater Revival* (Liberty)
	27	Bad Moon Rising *Creedence Clearwater Revival* (Liberty)
October	4	Bad Moon Rising *Creedence Clearwater Revival* (Liberty)
	11	Je T'Aime, Moi Non Plus *Jane Birkin and Serge Gainsbourg* (Major Minor)
	18	I'll Never Fall In Love Again *Bobby Gentry* (Capitol)
	25	Sugar Sugar *The Archies* (RCA)
November	1	Sugar Sugar *The Archies* (RCA)
	8	Sugar Sugar *The Archies* (RCA)
	15	Sugar Sugar *The Archies* (RCA)
	22	Sugar Sugar *The Archies* (RCA)
	29	Sugar Sugar *The Archies* (RCA)
December	6	Sugar Sugar *The Archies* (RCA)
	13	Sugar Sugar *The Archies* (RCA)
	20	Two Little Boys *Rolf Harris* (Columbia)

Total Number One records: 19.
Record with most weeks at top: Sugar Sugar *The Archies* (RCA) 8 weeks.

1970

January	3	Two Little Boys *Rolf Harris* (Columbia)
	10	Two Little Boys *Rolf Harris* (Columbia)
	17	Two Little Boys *Rolf Harris* (Columbia)
	24	Two Little Boys *Rolf Harris* (Columbia)
	31	Love Grows *Edison Lighthouse* (Bell)
February	7	Love Grows *Edison Lighthouse* (Bell)
	14	Love Grows *Edison Lighthouse* (Bell)
	21	Love Grows *Edison Lighthouse* (Bell)
	28	Love Grows *Edison Lighthouse* (Bell)
March	7	Wanderin' Star *Lee Marvin* (Paramount)
	14	Wanderin' Star *Lee Marvin* (Paramount)
	21	Wanderin' Star *Lee Marvin* (Paramount)
	28	Bridge Over Troubled Water *Simon and Garfunkel* (CBS)
April	4	Bridge Over Troubled Water *Simon and Garfunkel* (CBS)
	11	Bridge Over Troubled Water *Simon and Garfunkel* (CBS)
	18	All Kinds Of Everything *Dana* (Rex)
	25	All Kinds Of Everything *Dana* (Rex)
May	2	Spirit In The Sky *Norman Greenbaum* (Reprise)
	9	Spirit In The Sky *Norman Greenbaum* (Reprise)
	16	Back Home *England World Cup Squad* (Pye)
	23	Back Home *England World Cup Squad* (Pye)
	30	Back Home *England World Cup Squad* (Pye)
June	6	Yellow River *Christie* (CBS)
	13	In The Summertime *Mungo Jerry* (Dawn)
	20	In The Summertime *Mungo Jerry* (Dawn)
	27	In The Summertime *Mungo Jerry* (Dawn)
July	4	In The Summertime *Mungo Jerry* (Dawn)
	11	In The Summertime *Mungo Jerry* (Dawn)
	18	In The Summertime *Mungo Jerry* (Dawn)
	25	In The Summertime *Mungo Jerry* (Dawn)

August	1	The Wonder Of You *Elvis Presley* (RCA)
	8	The Wonder Of You *Elvis Presley* (RCA)
	15	The Wonder Of You *Elvis Presley* (RCA)
	22	The Wonder Of You *Elvis Presley* (RCA)
	29	The Wonder Of You *Elvis Presley* (RCA)
September	5	The Wonder Of You *Elvis Presley* (RCA)
	12	Tears Of A Clown *Smokey Robinson and The Miracles* (Tamla Motown)
	19	Band Of Gold *Freda Payne* (Invictus)
	26	Band Of Gold *Freda Payne* (Invictus)
October	3	Band Of Gold *Freda Payne* (Invictus)
	10	Band Of Gold *Freda Payne* (Invictus)
	17	Band Of Gold *Freda Payne* (Invictus)
	24	Band Of Gold *Freda Payne* (Invictus)
	31	Woodstock *Matthews Southern Comfort* (UA)
November	7	Woodstock *Matthews Southern Comfort* (UA)
	14	Woodstock *Matthews Southern Comfort* (UA)
	21	Voodoo Chile *Jimi Hendrix Experience* (Track)
	28	I Hear You Knocking *Dave Edmunds* (MAM)
December	5	I Hear You Knocking *Dave Edmunds* (MAM)
	12	I Hear You Knocking *Dave Edmunds* (MAM)
	19	I Hear You Knocking *Dave Edmunds* (MAM)
	26	I Hear You Knocking *Dave Edmunds* (MAM)

Total Number One records: 15.
Record with most weeks at top: In The Summertime *Mungo Jerry* (Dawn)
7 weeks.

1971

January	2	I Hear You Knocking *Dave Edmunds* (MAM)
	9	Grandad *Clive Dunn* (Columbia)
	16	Grandad *Clive Dunn* (Columbia)
	23	Grandad *Clive Dunn* (Columbia)
	30	My Sweet Lord *George Harrison* (Apple)
February	6	My Sweet Lord *George Harrison* (Apple)
	13	My Sweet Lord *George Harrison* (Apple)
	20	My Sweet Lord *George Harrison* (Apple)
	27	My Sweet Lord *George Harrison* (Apple)
March	6	Baby Jump *Mungo Jerry* (Dawn)
	13	Baby Jump *Mungo Jerry* (Dawn)
	20	Hot Love *T. Rex* (Fly)
	27	Hot Love *T. Rex* (Fly)
April	3	Hot Love *T. Rex* (Fly)
	10	Hot Love *T. Rex* (Fly)
	17	Hot Love *T. Rex* (Fly)
	24	Hot Love *T. Rex* (Fly)
May	1	Double Barrel *Dave and Ansil Collins* (Trojan)
	8	Double Barrel *Dave and Ansil Collins* (Trojan)
	15	Knock Three Times *Dawn* (Bell)
	22	Knock Three Times *Dawn* (Bell)
	29	Knock Three Times *Dawn* (Bell)
June	5	Knock Three Times *Dawn* (Bell)
	12	Knock Three Times *Dawn* (Bell)
	19	Chirpy Chirpy Cheep Cheep *Middle of the Road* (MCA)
	26	Chirpy Chirpy Cheep Cheep *Middle of the Road* (MCA)
July	3	Chirpy Chirpy Cheep Cheep *Middle of the Road* (MCA)
	10	Chirpy Chirpy Cheep Cheep *Middle of the Road* (MCA)
	17	Chirpy Chirpy Cheep Cheep *Middle of the Road* (MCA)
	24	Get It On *T. Rex* (Fly)
	31	Get It On *T. Rex* (Fly)

August	7	Get It On *T. Rex* (Fly)
	14	Get It On *T. Rex* (Fly)
	21	I'm Still Waiting *Diana Ross* (Tamla Motown)
	28	I'm Still Waiting *Diana Ross* (Tamla Motown)
September	4	I'm Still Waiting *Diana Ross* (Tamla Motown)
	11	I'm Still Waiting *Diana Ross* (Tamla Motown)
	18	Hey Girl Don't Bother Me *The Tams* (Probe)
	25	Hey Girl Don't Bother Me *The Tams* (Probe)
October	2	Hey Girl Don't Bother Me *The Tams* (Probe)
	9	Maggie May *Rod Stewart* (Mercury)
	16	Maggie May *Rod Stewart* (Mercury)
	23	Maggie May *Rod Stewart* (Mercury)
	30	Maggie May *Rod Stewart* (Mercury)
November	6	Maggie May *Rod Stewart* (Mercury)
	13	Coz I Luv You *Slade* (Polydor)
	20	Coz I Luv You *Slade* (Polydor)
	27	Coz I Luv You *Slade* (Polydor)
December	4	Coz I Luv You *Slade* (Polydor)
	11	Ernie (The Fastest Milkman In The West) *Benny Hill* (Columbia)
	18	Ernie (The Fastest Milkman In The West) *Benny Hill* (Columbia)
	25	Ernie (The Fastest Milkman In The West) *Benny Hill* (Columbia)

Total Number One records: 14.
Record with most weeks at top: Hot Love *T. Rex* (Fly) 6 weeks.

1972

January	1	Ernie (The Fastest Milkman In The West) *Benny Hill* (Columbia)
	8	I'd Like To Teach The World To Sing *The New Seekers* (Polydor)
	15	I'd Like To Teach The World To Sing *The New Seekers* (Polydor)
	22	I'd Like To Teach The World To Sing *The New Seekers* (Polydor)
	29	I'd Like To Teach The World To Sing *The New Seekers* (Polydor)
February	5	Telegram Sam *T. Rex* (T. Rex)
	12	Telegram Sam *T. Rex* (T. Rex)
	19	Son Of My Father *Chicory Tip* (CBS)
	26	Son Of My Father *Chicory Tip* (CBS)
March	4	Son Of My Father *Chicory Tip* (CBS)
	11	Without You *Nilsson* (RCA)
	18	Without You *Nilsson* (RCA)
	25	Without You *Nilsson* (RCA)
April	1	Without You *Nilsson* (RCA)
	8	Without You *Nilsson* (RCA)
	15	Amazing Grace *Royal Scots Dragoon Guards Band* (RCA)
	22	Amazing Grace *Royal Scots Dragoon Guards Band* (RCA)
	29	Amazing Grace *Royal Scots Dragoon Guards Band* (RCA)
May	6	Amazing Grace *Royal Scots Dragoon Guards Band* (RCA)
	13	Amazing Grace *Royal Scots Dragoon Guards Band* (RCA)
	20	Metal Guru *T. Rex* (EMI)
	27	Metal Guru *T. Rex* (EMI)
June	3	Metal Guru *T. Rex* (EMI)
	10	Metal Guru *T. Rex* (EMI)
	17	Vincent *Don MacLean* (UA)
	24	Vincent *Don MacLean* (UA)

July	1	Take Me Bak 'Ome *Slade* (Polydor)
	8	Puppy Love *Donny Osmond* (MGM)
	15	Puppy Love *Donny Osmond* (MGM)
	22	Puppy Love *Donny Osmond* (MGM)
	29	Puppy Love *Donny Osmond* (MGM)
August	5	Puppy Love *Donny Osmond* (MGM)
	12	School's Out *Alice Cooper* (Warner Bros.)
	19	School's Out *Alice Cooper* (Warner Bros.)
	26	School's Out *Alice Cooper* (Warner Bros.)
September	2	You Wear It Well *Rod Stewart* (Mercury)
	9	Mama Weer All Crazee Now *Slade* (Polydor)
	16	Mama Weer All Crazee Now *Slade* (Polydor)
	23	Mama Weer All Crazee Now *Slade* (Polydor)
	30	How Can I Be Sure *David Cassidy* (Bell)
October	7	How Can I Be Sure *David Cassidy* (Bell)
	14	Mouldy Old Dough *Lieutenant Pigeon* (Decca)
	21	Mouldy Old Dough *Lieutenant Pigeon* (Decca)
	28	Mouldy Old Dough *Lieutenant Pigeon* (Decca)
November	4	Mouldy Old Dough *Lieutenant Pigeon* (Decca)
	11	Clair *Gilbert O'Sullivan* (MAM)
	18	Clair *Gilbert O'Sullivan* (MAM)
	25	My Ding-A-Ling *Chuck Berry* (Chess)
December	2	My Ding-A-Ling *Chuck Berry* (Chess)
	9	My Ding-A-Ling *Chuck Berry* (Chess)
	16	My Ding-A-Ling *Chuck Berry* (Chess)
	23/30	Long Haired Lover From Liverpool *Little Jimmy Osmond* (MGM)

Total Number One records: 18.
Records with most weeks at top: Without You *Nilsson* (RCA), Amazing Grace *Royal Scots Dragoon Guards Band* (RCA) and Puppy Love *Donny Osmond* (MGM) 5 weeks.

1973

January	6	Long Haired Lover From Liverpool *Little Jimmy Osmond* (MGM)
	13	Long Haired Lover From Liverpool *Little Jimmy Osmond* (MGM)
	20	Long Haired Lover From Liverpool *Little Jimmy Osmond* (MGM)
	27	Blockbuster *The Sweet* (RCA)
February	3	Blockbuster *The Sweet* (RCA)
	10	Blockbuster *The Sweet* (RCA)
	17	Blockbuster *The Sweet* (RCA)
	24	Blockbuster *The Sweet* (RCA)
March	3	Cum On Feel The Noize *Slade* (Polydor)
	10	Cum On Feel The Noize *Slade* (Polydor)
	17	Cum On Feel The Noize *Slade* (Polydor)
	24	Cum On Feel The Noize *Slade* (Polydor)
	31	The Twelfth Of Never *Donny Osmond* (MGM)
April	7	Get Down *Gilbert O'Sullivan* (MAM)
	14	Get Down *Gilbert O'Sullivan* (MAM)
	21	Tie A Yellow Ribbon *Dawn* (Bell)
	28	Tie A Yellow Ribbon *Dawn* (Bell)
May	5	Tie A Yellow Ribbon *Dawn* (Bell)
	12	Tie A Yellow Ribbon *Dawn* (Bell)
	19	See My Baby Jive *Wizzard* (Harvest)
	26	See My Baby Jive *Wizzard* (Harvest)
June	2	See My Baby Jive *Wizzard* (Harvest)
	9	See My Baby Jive *Wizzard* (Harvest)
	16	Can The Can *Suzi Quatro* (RAK)
	23	Rubber Bullets *10cc* (UK)
	30	Skweeze Me Pleeze Me *Slade* (Polydor)

July	7	Skweeze Me Pleeze Me *Slade* (Polydor)
	14	Skweeze Me Pleeze Me *Slade* (Polydor)
	21	Welcome Home *Peters and Lee* (Philips)
	28	I'm The Leader Of The Gang (I Am) *Gary Glitter* (Bell)
August	4	I'm The Leader Of The Gang (I Am) *Gary Glitter* (Bell)
	11	I'm The Leader Of The Gang (I Am) *Gary Glitter* (Bell)
	18	I'm The Leader Of The Gang (I Am) *Gary Glitter* (Bell)
	25	Young Love *Donny Osmond* (MGM)
September	1	Young Love *Donny Osmond* (MGM)
	8	Young Love *Donny Osmond* (MGM)
	15	Young Love *Donny Osmond* (MGM)
	22	Angel Fingers *Wizzard* (Harvest)
	29	Eye Level *Simon Park Orchestra* (Columbia)
October	6	Eye Level *Simon Park Orchestra* (Columbia)
	13	Eye Level *Simon Park Orchestra* (Columbia)
	20	Eye Level *Simon Park Orchestra* (Columbia)
	27	Daydreamer/Puppy Song *David Cassidy* (Bell)
November	3	Daydreamer/Puppy Song *David Cassidy* (Bell)
	10	Daydreamer/Puppy Song *David Cassidy* (Bell)
	17	I Love You Love Me Love *Gary Glitter* (Bell)
December	1	I Love You Love Me Love *Gary Glitter* (Bell)
	8	I Love You Love Me Love *Gary Glitter* (Bell)
	15	Merry Xmas Everybody *Slade* (Polydor)
	22/29	Merry Xmas Everybody *Slade* (Polydor)

Total Number One records: 18.
Record with most weeks at top: Blockbuster *The Sweet* (RCA) 5 weeks.

1974

January	5	Merry Xmas Everybody *Slade* (Polydor)
	12	Merry Xmas Everybody *Slade* (Polydor)
	19	You Won't Find Another Fool Like Me *The New Seekers* (Polydor)
	26	Tiger Feet *Mud* (RAK)
February	2	Tiger Feet *Mud* (RAK)
	9	Tiger Feet *Mud* (RAK)
	16	Tiger Feet *Mud* (RAK)
	23	Devil Gate Drive *Suzi Quatro* (RAK)
March	2	Devil Gate Drive *Suzi Quatro* (RAK)
	9	Jealous Mind *Alvin Stardust* (Magnet)
	16	Billy, Don't Be A Hero *Paper Lace* (Bus Stop)
	23	Billy, Don't Be A Hero *Paper Lace* (Bus Stop)
	30	Billy, Don't Be A Hero *Paper Lace* (Bus Stop)
April	6	Seasons In The Sun *Terry Jacks* (Bell)
	13	Seasons In The Sun *Terry Jacks* (Bell)
	20	Seasons In The Sun *Terry Jacks* (Bell)
	27	Seasons In The Sun *Terry Jacks* (Bell)
May	4	Waterloo *Abba* (Epic)
	11	Waterloo *Abba* (Epic)
	18	Sugar Baby Love *The Rubettes* (Polydor)
	25	Sugar Baby Love *The Rubettes* (Polydor)
June	1	Sugar Baby Love *The Rubettes* (Polydor)
	8	Sugar Baby Love *The Rubettes* (Polydor)
	15	The Streak *Ray Stevens* (Janus)
	22	Always Yours *Gary Glitter* (Bell)
	29	She *Charles Aznavour* (Barclay)
July	6	She *Charles Aznavour* (Barclay)
	13	She *Charles Aznavour* (Barclay)
	20	She *Charles Aznavour* (Barclay)
	27	Rock Your Baby *George McCrae* (Jayboy)

August	3	Rock Your Baby *George McCrae* (Jayboy)
	10	Rock Your Baby *George McCrae* (Jayboy)
	17	When Will I See You Again *The Three Degrees* (Philadelphia)
	24	When Will I See You Again *The Three Degrees* (Philadalphia)
	31	Love Me For A Reason *The Osmonds* (MGM)
September	7	Love Me For A Reason *The Osmonds* (MGM)
	14	Love Me For A Reason *The Osmonds* (MGM)
	21	Kung Fu Fighting *Carl Douglas* (Pye)
	28	Kung Fu Fighting *Carl Douglas* (Pye)
October	5	Kung Fu Fighting *Carl Douglas* (Pye)
	12	Annie's Song *John Denver* (RCA)
	19	Sad Sweet Dreamer *Sweet Sensation* (Pye)
	26	Everything I Own *Ken Boothe* (Trojan)
November	2	Everything I Own *Ken Boothe* (Trojan)
	9	Everything I Own *Ken Boothe* (Trojan)
	16	Gonna Make You A Star *David Essex* (CBS)
	23	Gonna Make You A Star *David Essex* (CBS)
	30	Gonna Make You A Star *David Essex* (CBS)
December	7	You're The First, The Last, My Everything *Barry White* (20th Century)
	14	You're The First, The Last, My Everything *Barry White* (20th Century)
	21	Lonely This Christmas *Mud* (RAK)

Total Number One records: 22.
Records with most weeks at top: Tiger Feet *Mud* (RAK) Seasons In The Sun *Terry Jacks* (Bell), Sugar Baby Love *The Rubettes* (Polydor) and She *Charles Aznavour* (Barclay) 4 weeks.

1975

January	4	Lonely This Christmas *Mud* (RAK)
	11	Lonely This Christmas *Mud* (RAK)
	18	Down Down *Status Quo* (Vertigo)
	25	Ms Grace *The Tymes* (RCA)
February	1	January *Pilot* (EMI)
	8	January *Pilot* (EMI)
	15	January *Pilot* (EMI)
	22	Make Me Smile (Come Up And See Me) *Steve Harley and Cockney Rebel* (EMI)
March	1	Make Me Smile (Come Up And See Me) *Steve Harley and Cockney Rebel* (EMI)
	8	If *Telly Savalas* (MCA)
	15	If *Telly Savalas* (MCA)
	22	Bye Bye Baby *The Bay City Rollers* (Bell)
	29	Bye Bye Baby *The Bay City Rollers* (Bell)
April	5	Bye Bye Baby *The Bay City Rollers* (Bell)
	12	Bye Bye Baby *The Bay City Rollers* (Bell)
	19	Bye Bye Baby *The Bay City Rollers* (Bell)
	26	Bye Bye Baby *The Bay City Rollers* (Bell)
May	3	Oh Boy *Mud* (RAK)
	10	Oh Boy *Mud* (RAK)
	17	Stand By Your Man *Tammy Wynette* (Epic)
	24	Stand By Your Man *Tammy Wynette* (Epic)
	31	Stand By Your Man *Tammy Wynette* (Epic)
June	7	Whispering Grass *Windsor Davies and Don Estelle* (EMI)
	14	Whispering Grass *Windsor Davies and Don Estelle* (EMI)
	21	Whispering Grass *Windsor Davies and Don Estelle* (EMI)
	28	I'm Not In Love *10cc* (Mercury)

July	5	I'm Not In Love *10cc* (Mercury)
	12	Tears On My Pillow *Johnny Nash* (CBS)
	19	Give A Little Love *The Bay City Rollers* (Bell)
	26	Give A Little Love *The Bay City Rollers* (Bell)
August	2	Give A Little Love *The Bay City Rollers* (Bell)
	9	Barbados *Typically Tropical* (Gull)
	16	I Can't Give You Anything (But My Love) *The Stylistics* (Avco)
	23	I Can't Give You Anything (But My Love) *The Stylistics* (Avco)
	30	I Can't Give You Anything (But My Love) *The Stylistics* (Avco)
September	6	Sailing *Rod Stewart* (Warner Bros.)
	13	Sailing *Rod Stewart* (Warner Bros.)
	20	Sailing *Rod Stewart* (Warner Bros.)
	27	Sailing *Rod Stewart* (Warner Bros.)
October	4	Hold Me Close *David Essex* (CBS)
	11	Hold Me Close *David Essex* (CBS)
	18	Hold Me Close *David Essex* (CBS)
	25	I Only Have Eyes For You *Art Garfunkel* (CBS)
November	1	I Only Have Eyes For You *Art Garfunkel* (CBS)
	8	Space Oddity *David Bowie* (RCA)
	15	Space Oddity *David Bowie* (RCA)
	22	D.I.V.O.R.C.E. *Billy Connolly* (Polydor)
	29	Bohemian Rhapsody *Queen* (EMI)
December	6	Bohemian Rhapsody *Queen* (EMI)
	13	Bohemian Rhapsody *Queen* (EMI)
	20	Bohemian Rhapsody *Queen* (EMI)
	27	Bohemian Rhapsody *Queen* (EMI)

Total Number One records: 21.
Record with most weeks at top: Bye Bye Baby *The Bay City Rollers* (Bell)
6 weeks.

1976

January	3	Bohemian Rhapsody *Queen* (EMI)
	10	Bohemian Rhapsody *Queen* (EMI)
	17	Bohemian Rhapsody *Queen* (EMI)
	24	Bohemian Rhapsody *Queen* (EMI)
	31	Mama Mia *Abba* (Epic)
February	7	Mama Mia *Abba* (Epic)
	14	Forever and Forever *Slik* (Bell)
	21	December '63 *The Four Seasons* (Warner Bros.)
	28	December '63 *The Four Seasons* (Warner Bros.)
March	6	I Love To Love *Tina Charles* (CBS)
	13	I Love To Love *Tina Charles* (CBS)
	20	I Love To Love *Tina Charles* (CBS)
	27	Save Your Kisses For Me *Brotherhood of Man* (Pye)
April	3	Save Your Kisses For Me *Brotherhood of Man* (Pye)
	10	Save Your Kisses For Me *Brotherhood of Man* (Pye)
	17	Save Your Kisses For Me *Brotherhood of Man* (Pye)
	24	Save Your Kisses For Me *Brotherhood of Man* (Pye)
May	1	Save Your Kisses For Me *Brotherhood of Man* (Pye)
	8	Fernando *Abba* (Epic)
	15	Fernando *Abba* (Epic)
	22	Fernando *Abba* (Epic)
	29	Fernando *Abba* (Epic)
June	5	No Charge *J. J. Barrie* (Power Exchange)
	12	Combine Harvester (Brand New Key) *Wurzels* (EMI)
	19	Combine Harvester (Brand New Key) *Wurzels* (EMI)
	26	You To Me Are Everything *The Real Thing* (Pye)

July	3	You To Me Are Everything *The Real Thing* (Pye)
	10	You To Me Are Everything *The Real Thing* (Pye)
	17	The Roussos Phenomenon *Demis Roussos* (Philips)
	24	Don't Go Breaking My Heart *Elton John and Kiki Dee* (Rocket)
	31	Don't Go Breaking My Heart *Elton John and Kiki Dee* (Rocket)
August	7	Don't Go Breaking My Heart *Elton John and Kiki Dee* (Rocket)
	14	Don't Go Breaking My Heart *Elton John and Kiki Dee* (Rocket)
	21	Don't Go Breaking My Heart *Elton John and Kiki Dee* (Rocket)
	28	Don't Go Breaking My Heart *Elton John and Kiki Dee* (Rocket)
September	4	Dancing Queen *Abba* (Epic)
	11	Dancing Queen *Abba* (Epic)
	18	Dancing Queen *Abba* (Epic)
	25	Dancing Queen *Abba* (Epic)
October	2	Dancing Queen *Abba* (Epic)
	9	Dancing Queen *Abba* (Epic)
	16	Mississippi *Pussycat* (Sonet)
	23	Mississippi *Pussycat* (Sonet)
	30	Mississippi *Pussycat* (Sonet)
November	6	Mississippi *Pussycat* (Sonet)
	13	If You Leave Me Now *Chicago* (CBS)
	20	If You Leave Me Now *Chicago* (CBS)
	27	If You Leave Me Now *Chicago* (CBS)
December	4	Under The Moon Of Love *Showaddywaddy* (Bell)
	11	Under The Moon Of Love *Showaddywaddy* (Bell)
	18	Under The Moon Of Love *Showaddywaddy* (Bell)

Total Number One records: 15.
Records with most weeks at top: Save Your Kisses For Me *Brotherhood of Man* (Pye), Don't Go Breaking My Heart *Elton John and Kiki Dee* (Rocket) and Dancing Queen *Abba* (Epic) 6 weeks.

1977

January	8	When A Child Is Born *Johnny Mathis* (CBS)
	15	Don't Give Up On Us *David Soul* (Private Stock)
	22	Don't Give Up On Us *David Soul* (Private Stock)
	29	Don't Give Up On Us *David Soul* (Private Stock)
February	5	Don't Give Up On Us *David Soul* (Private Stock)
	12	Don't Cry For Me Argentina *Julie Covington* (MCA)
	19	When I Need You *Leo Sayer* (Chrysalis)
	26	When I Need You *Leo Sayer* (Chrysalis)
March	5	When I Need You *Leo Sayer* (Chrysalis)
	12	Chanson D'Amour *Manhattan Transfer* (Atlantic)
	19	Chanson D'Amour *Manhattan Transfer* (Atlantic)
	26	Chanson D'Amour *Manhattan Transfer* (Atlantic)
April	2	Knowing Me, Knowing You *Abba* (Epic)
	9	Knowing Me, Knowing You *Abba* (Epic)
	16	Knowing Me, Knowing You *Abba* (Epic)
	23	Knowing Me, Knowing You *Abba* (Epic)
	30	Knowing Me, Knowing You *Abba* (Epic)
May	7	Free *Deniece Williams* (CBS)
	14	Free *Deniece Williams* (CBS)
	21	I Don't Want To Talk About It/The First Cut Is The Deepest *Rod Stewart* (Riva)
	28	I Don't Want To Talk About It/The First Cut Is The Deepest *Rod Stewart* (Riva)

June	4	I Don't Want To Talk About It/The First Cut Is The Deepest *Rod Stewart* (Riva)
	11	I Don't Want To Talk About It/The First Cut Is The Deepest *Rod Stewart* (Riva)
	18	Lucille *Kenny Rogers* (UA)
	25	Show You The Way To Go *The Jacksons* (Epic)
July	2	So You Win Again *Hot Chocolate* (RAK)
	9	So You Win Again *Hot Chocolate* (RAK)
	16	So You Win Again *Hot Chocolate* (RAK)
	23	I Feel Love *Donna Summer* (GTO)
	30	I Feel Love *Donna Summer* (GTO)
August	6	I Feel Love *Donna Summer* (GTO)
	13	I Feel Love *Donna Summer* (GTO)
	20	Angelo *Brotherhood of Man* (Pye)
	27	Float On *The Floaters* (ABC)
September	3	Way Down *Elvis Presley* (RCA)
	10	Way Down *Elvis Presley* (RCA)
	17	Way Down *Elvis Presley* (RCA)
	24	Way Down *Elvis Presley* (RCA)
October	1	Way Down *Elvis Presley* (RCA)
	8	Silver Lady *David Soul* (Private Stock)
	15	Silver Lady *David Soul* (Private Stock)
	22	Silver Lady *David Soul* (Private Stock)
	29	Yes Sir I Can Boogie *Baccara* (RCA)
November	5	The Name Of The Game *Abba* (Epic)
	12	The Name Of The Game *Abba* (Epic)
	19	The Name Of The Game *Abba* (Epic)
	26	The Name Of The Game *Abba* (Epic)
December	3	Mull Of Kintyre/Girls School *Wings* (Parlophone)
	10	Mull Of Kintyre/Girls School *Wings* (Parlophone)
	17	Mull Of Kintyre/Girls School *Wings* (Parlophone)
	24	Mull Of Kintyre/Girls School *Wings* (Parlophone)

Total Number One records: 19.
Records with most weeks at top: Knowing Me, Knowing You *Abba* (Epic)
and Way Down *Elvis Presley* (RCA) 5 weeks.

1978

January	7	Mull Of Kintyre/Girls School *Wings* (Parlophone)
	14	Mull Of Kintyre/Girls School *Wings* (Parlophone)
	21	Mull Of Kintyre/Girls School *Wings* (Parlophone)
	28	Mull Of Kintyre/Girls School *Wings* (Parlophone)
February	4	Uptown Top Ranking *Althia and Donna* (Lightning)
	11	Figaro *Brotherhood of Man* (Pye)
	18	Take A Chance On Me *Abba* (Epic)
	25	Take A Chance On Me *Abba* (Epic)
March	4	Take A Chance On Me *Abba* (Epic)
	11	Wuthering Heights *Kate Bush* (EMI)
	18	Wuthering Heights *Kate Bush* (EMI)
	25	Wuthering Heights *Kate Bush* (EMI)
April	1	Wuthering Heights *Kate Bush* (EMI)
	8	Matchstalk Men And Matchstalk Cats And Dogs *Brian and Michael* (Pye)
	15	Matchstalk Men And Matchstalk Cats And Dogs *Brian and Michael* (Pye)
	22	Matchstalk Men And Matchstalk Cats And Dogs *Brian and Michael* (Pye)
	29	Night Fever *The Bee Gees* (RSO)
May	6	Night Fever *The Bee Gees* (RSO)
	13	Rivers Of Babylon *Boney M.* (Atlantic)
	20	Rivers Of Babylon *Boney M.* (Atlantic)
	27	Rivers Of Babylon *Boney M.* (Atlantic)

June	3	Rivers Of Babylon *Boney M* (Atlantic/Hansa)
	10	Rivers Of Babylon *Boney M* (Atlantic/Hansa)
	17	You're The One That I Want *John Travolta/Olivia Newton-John* (RSO)
	24	You're The One That I Want *John Travolta/Olivia Newton-John* (RSO)
July	1	You're The One That I Want *John Travolta/Olivia Newton-John* (RSO)
	8	You're The One That I Want *John Travolta/Olivia Newton-John* (RSO)
	15	You're The One That I Want *John Travolta/Olivia Newton-John* (RSO)
	22	You're The One That I Want *John Travolta/Olivia Newton-John* (RSO)
	29	You're The One That I Want *John Travolta/Olivia Newton-John* (RSO)
August	5	You're The One That I Want *John Travolta/Olivia Newton-John* (RSO)
	12	You're The One That I Want *John Travolta/Olivia Newton-John* (RSO)
	19	Three Times A Lady *Commodores* (Motown)
	26	Three Times A Lady *Commodores* (Motown)
September	2	Three Times A Lady *Commodores* (Motown)
	9	Three Times A Lady *Commodores* (Motown)
	16	Three Times A Lady *Commodores* (Motown)
	23	Dreadlock Holiday *10cc* (Mercury)
	30	Summer Nights *John Travolta/Olivia Newton-John* (RSO)
October	7	Summer Nights *John Travolta/Olivia Newton-John* (RSO)
	14	Summer Nights *John Travolta/Olivia Newton-John* (RSO)
	21	Summer Nights *John Travolta/Olivia Newton-John* (RSO)
	28	Summer Nights *John Travolta/Olivia Newton-John* (RSO)
November	4	Summer Nights *John Travolta/Olivia Newton-John* (RSO)
	11	Summer Nights *John Travolta/Olivia Newton-John* (RSO)
	18	Rat Trap *Boomtown Rats* (Ensign)
	25	Rat Trap *Boomtown Rats* (Ensign)
December	2	Do You Think I'm Sexy *Rod Stewart* (Riva)
	9	Mary's Boy Child *Boney M* (Atlantic/Hansa)
	16	Mary's Boy Child *Boney M* (Atlantic/Hansa)
	23	Mary's Boy Child *Boney M* (Atlantic/Hansa)

Total Number One records: 15
Record with most weeks at the top: You're The One That I Want *John Travolta & Olivia Newton-John* (RSO) 9 weeks.

1979

January	6	YMCA *Village People* (Mercury)
	13	YMCA *Village People* (Mercury)
	20	YMCA *Village People* (Mercury)
	27	Hit Me With Your Rhythm Stick *Ian Dury & The Blockheads* (Stiff)
February	3	Heart Of Glass *Blondie* (Chrysalis)
	10	Heart Of Glass *Blondie* (Chrysalis)
	17	Heart Of Glass *Blondie* (Chrysalis)
	24	Heart Of Glass *Blondie* (Chrysalis)
March	3	Tragedy *Bee Gees* (RSO)
	10	Tragedy *Bee Gees* (ROS)
	17	I Will Survive *Gloria Gaynor* (Polydor)
	24	I Will Survive *Gloria Gaynor* (Polydor)

	31	I Will Survive *Gloria Gaynor* (Polydor)
April	7	I Will Survive *Gloria Gaynor* (Polydor)
	14	Bright Eyes *Art Garfunkel* (CBS)
	21	Bright Eyes *Art Garfunkel* (CBS)
	28	Bright Eyes *Art Garfunkel* (CBS)
May	5	Bright Eyes *Art Garfunkel* (CBS)
	12	Bright Eyes *Art Garfunkel* (CBS)
	19	Bright Eyes *Art Garfunkel* (CBS)
	26	Sunday Girl *Blondie* (Chrysalis)
June	2	Sunday Girl *Blondie* (Chrysalis)
	9	Sunday Girl *Blondie* (Chrysalis)
	16	Ring My Bell *Anita Ward* (TK)
	23	Ring My Bell *Anita Ward* (TK)
	30	Are Friends Electric *Gary Numan* (Beggars Banquet)
July	7	Are Friends Electric *Gary Numan* (Beggars Banquet)
	14	Are Friends Electric *Gary Numan* (Beggars Banquet)
	21	Are Friends Electric *Gary Numan* (Beggars Banquet)
	28	Don't Like Mondays *Boomtown Rats* (Ensign)
August	4	Don't Like Mondays *Boomtown Rats* (Ensign)
	11	Don't Like Mondays *Boomtown Rats* (Ensign)
	18	Don't Like Mondays *Boomtown Rats* (Ensign)
	25	We Don't Talk Anymore *Cliff Richard* (EMI)
September	1	We Don't Talk Anymore *Cliff Richard* (EMI)
	8	We Don't Talk Anymore *Cliff Richard* (EMI)
	15	We Don't Talk Anymore *Cliff Richard* (EMI)
	22	Cars *Gary Numan* (Beggars Banquet)
	29	Message In A Bottle *Police* (A&M)
October	6	Message In A Bottle *Police* (A&M)
	13	Message In A Bottle *Police* (A&M)
	20	Video Killed The Radio Star *Buggles* (Island)
	27	One Day At A Time *Lena Martell* (Pye)
November	3	One Day At A Time *Lena Martell* (Pye)
	10	One Day At A Time *Lena Martell* (Pye)
	17	When You're In Love *Dr Hook* (Capitol)
	24	When You're In Love *Dr Hook* (Capitol)
December	1	When You're In Love *Dr Hook* (Capitol)
	8	Walking On The Moon *Police* (A&M)
	15	Another Brick In The Wall *Pink Floyd* (Harvest)
	22	Another Brick In The Wall *Pink Floyd* (Harvest)

Total Number One records: 18
Record with most weeks at top: Bright Eyes *Art Garfunkel* (CBS) 6 weeks.

1980

January	5	Another Brick In The Wall *Pink Floyd* (Harvest)
	12	Another Brick In The Wall *Pink Floyd* (Harvest)
	19	Brass In Pocket *Pretenders* (Real)
	26	Brass In Pocket *Pretenders* (Real)
February	2	Too Much Too Young/Guns Of Navarone *Specials* (2 Tone)
	9	Too Much Too Young/Guns Of Navarone *Specials* (2 Tone)
	16	Coward Of The County *Kenny Rogers* (United Artists)
	23	Coward Of The County *Kenny Rogers* (United Artists)
March	1	Atomic *Blondie* (Chrysalis)
	8	Atomic *Blondie* (Chrysalis)
	15	Together We Are Beautiful *Fern Kinney* (Atlantic)
	22	Going Underground/Dreams Of Children *Jam* (Polydor)
	20	Going Underground/Dreams Of Children *Jam* (Polydor)

April	5	Going Underground/Dreams Of Children *Jam* (Polydor)
	12	Working My Way Back To You/Forgive Me Girl *Detroit Spinners* (Atlantic)
	19	Working My Way Back To You/Forgive Me Girl *Detroit Spinners* (Atlantic)
	26	Call Me *Blondie* (Chrysalis)
May	3	Geno *Dexy's Midnight Runners* (Parlophone)
	10	Geno *Dexy's Midnight Runners* (Parlophone)
	17	What's Another Year *Johnny Logan* (Epic)
	24	What's Another Year *Johnny Logan* (Epic)
	31	Theme From Mash *Mash* (CBS)
June	7	Theme From Mash *Mash* (CBS)
	14	Theme From Mash *Mash* (CBS)
	21	Crying *Don McLean* (EMI)
	28	Crying *Don McLean* (EMI)
July	5	Crying *Don McLean* (EMI)
	12	Xanadu *Olivia Newton-John/ELO* (Jet)
	19	Xanadu *Olivia Newton-John/ELO* (Jet)
	26	Use It Up And Wear It Out *Odyssey* (RCA)
August	2	Use It Up And Wear It Out *Odyssey* (RCA)
	9	Winner Takes It All *Abba* (Epic)
	16	Winner Takes It All *Abba* (Epic)
	23	Ashes To Ashes *David Bowie* (RCA)
	30	Ashes To Ashes *David Bowie* (RCA)
September	6	Start *Jam* (Polydor)
	13	Feels Like I'm In Love *Kelly Marie* (Calibre)
	20	Feels Like I'm In Love *Kelly Marie* (Calibre)
	27	Don't Stand So Close To Me *Police* (A&M)
October	4	Don't Stand So Close To Me *Police* (A&M)
	11	Don't Stand So Close To Me *Police* (A&M)
	18	Don't Stand So Close To Me *Police* (A&M)
	25	Woman In Love *Barbra Streisand* (CBS)
November	1	Woman In Love *Barbra Streisand* (CBS)
	8	Woman In Love *Barbra Streisand* (CBS)
	15	The Tide Is High *Blondie* (Chrysalis)
	22	The Tide Is High *Blondie* (Chrysalis)
	29	Super Trouper *Abba* (Epic)
December	6	Super Trouper *Abba* (Epic)
	13	Super Trouper *Abba* (Epic)
	20	(Just Like) Starting Over *John Lennon & Yoko One* (Geffen)
	27	There's No One Quite Like Grandma *St Winifred's School Choir* (MFP)

Total Number One records: 25
Record with most weeks at top: Don't Stand So Close To Me *Police* 4 weeks.

1981

January	10	Imagine *John Lennon* (Parlophone)
	17	Imagine *John Lennon* (Parlophone)
	24	Imagine *John Lennon* (Parlophone)
	31	Imagine *John Lennon* (Parlophone)
February	7	Woman *John Lennon* (Geffen)
	14	Woman *John Lennon* (Geffen)
	21	Shaddup You Face *Joe Dolce* (Epic)
	28	Shaddup You Face *Joe Dolce* (Epic)
March	7	Shaddup You Face *Joe Dolce* (Epic)
	14	Jealous Guy *Roxy Music* (EG/Polydor)
	21	Jealous Guy *Roxy Music* (EG/Polydor)
	28	This Ole House *Shakin' Stevens* (Epic)

April	4	This Ole House *Shakin' Stevens* (Epic)
	11	This Ole House *Shakin' Stevens* (Epic)
	18	Making Your Mind Up *Bucks Fizz* (RCA)
	25	Making Your Mind Up *Bucks Fizz* (RCA)
May	2	Making Your Mind Up *Bucks Fizz* (RCA)
	9	Stand & Deliver *Adam & The Ants* (CBS)
	16	Stand & Deliver *Adam & The Ants* (CBS)
	23	Stand & Deliver *Adam & The Ants* (CBS)
	30	Stand & Deliver *Adam & The Ants* (CBS)
June	6	Stand & Deliver *Adam & The Ants* (CBS)
	13	Being With You *Smokey Robinson* (Motown)
	20	Being With You *Smokey Robinson* (Motown)
	27	One Day In Your Life *Michael Jackson* (Motown)
July	4	One Day In Your Life *Michael Jackson* (Motown)
	11	Ghost Town *Specials* (2 Tone)
	18	Ghost Town *Specials* (2 Tone)
	25	Ghost Town *Specials* (2 Tone)
August	1	Green Door *Shakin' Stevens* (Epic)
	8	Green Door *Shakin' Stevens* (Epic)
	15	Green Door *Shakin' Stevens* (Epic)
	22	Green Door *Shakin' Stevens* (Epic)
	29	Japanese Boy *Aneka* (Hansa/Ariola)
September	5	Tainted Love *Soft Cell* (Bizarre)
	12	Tainted Love *Soft Cell* (Bizarre)
	19	Prince Charming *Adam & The Ants* (CBS)
	26	Prince Charming *Adam & The Ants* (CBS)
October	3	Prince Charming *Adam & The Ants* (CBS)
	10	Prince Charming *Adam & The Ants* (CBS)
	17	It's My Party *Dave Stewart & Barbara Gaskin* (Stiff/Broken)
	24	It's My Party *Dave Stewart & Barbara Gaskin* (Stiff/Broken)
	31	It's My Party *Dave Stewart & Barbara Gaskin* (Stiff/Broken)
November	7	It's My Party *Dave Stewart & Barbara Gaskin* (Stiff/Broken)
	14	Every Little Thing She Does Is Magic *Police* (A&M)
	21	Under Pressure *Queen/David Bowie* (EMI)
	28	Under Pressure *Queen/David Bowie* (EMI)
December	5	Begin The Beguine (Volver A Empezar) *Julio Iglesias* (CBS)
	12	Don't You Want Me *Human League* (Virgin)
	19	Don't You Want Me *Human League* (Virgin)
	26	Don't You Want Me *Human League* (Virgin)

Total Number One records: 19
Record with most weeks at top: Stand And Deliver *Adam & The Ants* 5 weeks

1982

January	9	Don't You Want Me *Human League* (Virgin)
	16	The Land Of Make Believe *Bucks Fizz* (RCA)
	23	The Land Of Make Believe *Bucks Fizz* (RCA)
	30	Oh Julie *Shakin' Stevens* (Epic)
February	6	The Model/Computer Love *Kraftwerk* (EMI)
	13	Town Called Malice/Precious *The Jam* (Polydor)
	20	Town Called Malice/Precious *The Jam* (Polydor)
	27	Town Called Malice/Precious *The Jam* (Polydor)
March	6	The Lion Sleeps Tonight *Tight Fit* (Jive)
	13	The Lion Sleeps Tonight *Tight Fit* (Jive)
	20	The Lion Sleeps Tonight *Tight Fit* (Jive)
	27	Seven Tears *Goombay Dance Band* (Epic)

April	3	Seven Tears *Goombay Dance Band* (Epic)
	10	Seven Tears *Goombay Dance Band* (Epic)
	17	My Camera Never Lies *Bucks Fizz* (RCA)
	24	Ebony And Ivory *Paul McCartney with Stevie Wonder* (Parlophone)
May	1	Ebony And Ivory *Paul McCartney with Stevie Wonder* (Parlophone)
	8	Ebony And Ivory *Paul McCartney with Stevie Wonder* (Parlophone)
	15	A Little Peace *Nicole* (CBS)
	22	A Little Peace *Nicole* (CBS)
	29	House Of Fun *Madness* (Stiff)
June	5	House Of Fun *Madness* (Stiff)
	12	Goody Two Shoes *Adam Ant* (CBS)
	19	Goody Two Shoes *Adam Ant* (CBS)
	26	I've Never Been To Me *Charlene* (Motown)
July	3	Happy Talk *Captain Sensible* (A&M)
	10	Happy Talk *Captain Sensible* (A&M)
	17	Fame *Irene Cara* (RSO)
	24	Fame *Irene Cara* (RSO)
	31	Fame *Irene Cara* (Polydor/RSO)
August	7	Come On Eileen *Dexy's Midnight Runners & The Emerald Express* (Mercury/Phonogram)
	14	Come On Eileen *Dexy's Midnight Runners & The Emerald Express* (Mercury/Phonogram)
	21	Come On Eileen *Dexy's Midnight Runners & The Emerald Express* (Mercury/Phonogram)
	28	Come On Eileen *Dexy's Midnight Runners & The Emerald Express* (Mercury/Phonogram)
September	4	Eye Of The Tiger *Survivor* (Scotti Brothers)
	11	Eye Of The Tiger *Survivor* (Scotti Brothers)
	18	Eye Of The Tiger *Survivor* (Scotti Brothers)
	25	Eye Of The Tiger *Survivor* (Scotti Brothers)
October	2	Pass The Dutchie *Musical Youth* (MCA)
	9	Pass The Dutchie *Musical Youth* (MCA)
	16	Pass The Dutchie *Musical Youth* (MCA)
	23	Do You Really Want To Hurt Me *Culture Club* (Virgin)
	30	Do You Really Want To Hurt Me *Culture Club* (Virgin)
November	6	Do You Really Want To Hurt Me *Culture Club* (Virgin)
	13	I Don't Wanna Dance *Eddy Grant* (Ice)
	20	I Don't Wanna Dance *Eddy Grant* (Ice)
	27	I Don't Wanna Dance *Eddy Grant* (Ice)
December	4	Beat Surrender *The Jam* (Polydor)
	11	Beat Surrender *The Jam* (Polydor)
	18	Save Your Love *Renée and Renato* (Hollywood)
	25	Save Your Love *Renée and Renato* (Hollywood)

Total Number One records: 22.
Records with most weeks at top: Come On Eileen *Dexy's Midnight Runners & The Emerald Express* (Mercury/Phonogram) 4 weeks and Eye Of The Tiger *Survivor* (Scotti Brothers) 4 weeks.

January	8	Save Your Love *Renee and Renato* (Hollywood)
	15	You Can't Hurry Love *Phil Collins* (Virgin)
	22	You Can't Hurry Love *Phil Collins* (Virgin)
	29	Down Under *Men At Work* (Epic)
February	5	Down Under *Men At Work* (Epic)
	12	Down Under *Men At Work* (Epic)
	19	Too Shy *Kajagoogoo* (EMI)
	26	Too Shy *Kajagoogoo* (EMI)
March	5	Billie Jean *Michael Jackson* (Epic)
	12	Total Eclipse Of The Heart *Bonnie Tyler* (CBS)
	19	Total Eclipse Of The Heart *Bonnie Tyler* (CBS)
	26	Is There Something I Should Know? *Duran Duran* (EMI)
April	2	Is There Something I Should Know? *Duran Duran* (EMI)
	9	Let's Dance *David Bowie* (EMI America)
	16	Let's Dance *David Bowie* (EMI America)
	23	Let's Dance *David Bowie* (EMI America)
	30	True *Spandau Ballet* (Chrysalis/Reformation)
May	7	True *Spandau Ballet* (Chrysalis/Reformation)
	14	True *Spandau Ballet* (Chrysalis/Reformation)
	21	True *Spandau Ballet* (Chrysalis/Reformation)
	28	Candy Girl *New Edition* (London)
June	4	Every Breath You Take *The Police* (A&M)
	11	Every Breath You Take *The Police* (A&M)
	18	Every Breath You Take *The Police* (A&M)
	25	Every Breath You Take *The Police* (A&M)
July	2	Baby Jane *Rod Stewart* (Warners)
	9	Baby Jane *Rod Stewart* (Warners)
	16	Baby Jane *Rod Stewart* (Warners)
	23	Wherever I Lay My Hat (That's My Home) *Paul Young* (CBS)
	30	Wherever I Lay My Hat (That's My Home) *Paul Young* (CBS)
August	6	Wherever I Lay My Hat (That's My Home) *Paul Young* (CBS)
	13	Give It Up *KC & The Sunshine Band* (Epic)
	20	Give It Up *KC & The Sunshine Band* (Epic)
	27	Give It Up *KC & The Sunshine Band* (Epic)
September	3	Red Red Wine *UB40* (DEP International)
	10	Red Red Wine *UB40* (DEP International)
	17	Red Red Wine *UB40* (DEP International)
	24	Karma Chameleon *Culture Club* (Virgin)
October	1	Karma Chameleon *Culture Club* (Virgin)
	8	Karma Chameleon *Culture Club* (Virgin)
	15	Karma Chameleon *Culture Club* (Virgin)
	22	Karma Chameleon *Culture Club* (Virgin)
	29	Karma Chameleon *Culture Club* (Virgin)
November	5	Uptown Girl *Billy Joel* (CBS)
	12	Uptown Girl *Billy Joel* (CBS)
	19	Uptown Girl *Billy Joel* (CBS)
	26	Uptown Girl *Billy Joel* (CBS)
December	3	Uptown Girl *Billy Joel* (CBS)
	10	Only You *Flying Pickets* (10Records/Virgin)

17 Only You *Flying Pickets* (10Records/Virgin)
24 Only You *Flying Pickets* (10Records/Virgin)

Total Number One records: 18
Record with most weeks at top: Karma Chameleon *Culture Club* (Virgin) 6 weeks.

1984

January	7	Only You *The Flying Pickets* (Ten)
	14	Pipes of Peace *Paul McCartney* (Parlophone)
	21	Pipes of Peace *Paul McCartney* (Parlophone)
	28	Relax *Frankie Goes To Hollywood* (ZTT/Island)
February	4	Relax *Frankie Goes To Hollywood* (ZTT/Island)
	11	Relax *Frankie Goes To Hollywood* (ZTT/Island)
	18	Relax *Frankie Goes To Hollywood* (ZTT/Island)
	25	Relax *Frankie Goes To Hollywood* (ZTT/Island)
March	3	99 Balloons *Nena* (Epic)
	10	99 Balloons *Nena* (Epic)
	17	99 Balloons *Nena* (Epic)
	24	Hello *Lionel Richie* (Motown)
	31	Hello *Lionel Richie* (Motown)
April	7	Hello *Lionel Richie* (Motown)
	14	Hello *Lionel Richie* (Motown)
	21	Hello *Lionel Richie* (Motown)
	28	Hello *Lionel Richie* (Motown)
May	5	The Reflex *Duran Duran* (EMI)
	12	The Reflex *Duran Duran* (EMI)
	19	The Reflex *Duran Duran* (EMI)
	26	The Reflex *Duran Duran* (EMI)
June	2	Wake Me Up Before I Go *Wham!* (Epic
	9	Wake Me Up Before I Go *Wham!* (Epic)
	16	Two Tribes *Frankie Goes To Hollywood* (ZTT/Island)
	23	Two Tribes *Frankie Goes To Hollywood* (ZTT/Island)
	30	Two Tribes *Frankie Goes To Hollywood* (ZTT/Island)
July	7	Two Tribes *Frankie Goes To Hollywood* (ZTT/Island)
	14	Two Tribes *Frankie Goes To Hollywood* (ZTT/Island)
	21	Two Tribes *Frankie Goes To Hollywood* (ZTT/Island)
	28	Two Tribes *Frankie Goes To Hollywood* (ZTT/Island)
August	4	Two Tribes *Frankie Goes To Hollywood* (ZTT/Island)
	11	Two Tribes *Frankie Goes To Hollywood* (ZTT/Island)
	18	Careless Whisper *George Michael* (Epic)
	25	Careless Whisper *George Michael* (Epic)
September	1	Careless Whisper *George Michael* (Epic)
	8	I Just Called To Say I Love You *Stevie Wonder* (Motown)
	15	I Just Called To Say I Love You *Stevie Wonder* (Motown)
	22	I Just Called To Say I Love You *Stevie Wonder* (Motown)
	29	I Just Called To Say I Love You *Stevie Wonder* (Motown)
October	6	I Just Called To Say I Love You *Stevie Wonder* (Motown)
	13	I Just Called To Say I Love You *Stevie Wonder* (Motown)
	20	Freedom *Wham!* (Epic)
	27	Freedom *Wham!* (Epic)
November	3	Freedom *Wham!* (Epic)
	10	I Feel For You *Chaka Khan* (Warner Brothers)
	17	I Feel For You *Chaka Khan* (Warner Brothers)
	24	I Feel For You *Chaka Khan* (Warner Brothers)
December	1	I Should Have Known Better *Jim Diamond* (A&M)
	8	The Power Of Love *Frankie Goes To Hollywood* (ZTT/Island)
	15	Do They Know It's Christmas? *Band Aid* (Mercury/Phonogram)
	22	Do They Know It's Christmas? *Band Aid* (Mercury/Phonogram)
	29	Do They Know It's Christmas? *Band Aid* (Mercury/Phonogram)

Total Number One records: 15.
Record with most weeks at top: Two Tribes *Frankie Goes To Hollywood* (ZTT/Island) 9 weeks.

January	5	Do They Know It's Christmas? *Band Aid* (Mercury/Phonogram)
	12	Do They Know It's Christmas? *Band Aid* (Mercury/Phonogram)
	19	I Want To Know What Love Is *Foreigner* (Atlantic)
	26	I Want To Know What Love Is *Foreigner* (Atlantic)
February	2	I Know Him So Well *Elaine Paige and Barbara Dickson* (RCA)
	9	I Know Him So Well *Elaine Paige and Barbara Dickson* (RCA)
	16	I Know Him So Well *Elaine Paige and Barbara Dickson* (RCA)
	23	I Know Him So Well *Elaine Paige and Barbara Dickson* (RCA)
March	2	I Know Him So Well *Elaine Paige and Barbara Dickson* (RCA)
	9	You Spin Me Round (Like A Record) *Dead Or Alive* (Epic)
	16	You Spin Me Round (Like A Record) *Dead Or Alive* (Epic)
	23	Easy Lover *Philip Bailey and Phil Collins* (CBS/Virgin)
	30	Easy Lover *Philip Bailey and Phil Collins* (CBS/Virgin)
April	6	Easy Lover *Philip Bailey and Phil Collins* (CBS/Virgin)
	13	Easy Lover *Philip Bailey and Phil Collins* (CBS/Virgin)
	20	We Are The World *USA for Africa* (CBS)
	27	We Are The World *USA for Africa* (CBS)
May	4	Move Closer *Phyllis Nelson* (Carrere)
	11	19 *Paul Hardcastle* (Chrysalis)
	18	19 *Paul Hardcastle* (Chrysalis)
	25	19 *Paul Hardcastle* (Chrysalis)
June	1	19 *Paul Hardcastle* (Chrysalis)
	8	19 *Paul Hardcastle* (Chrysalis)
	15	You'll Never Walk Alone *The Crowd* (Spartan)
	22	You'll Never Walk Alone *The Crowd* (Spartan)
	29	Frankie *Sister Sledge* (Atlantic)
July	6	Frankie *Sister Sledge* (Atlantic)
	13	Frankie *Sister Sledge* (Atlantic)
	20	Frankie *Sister Sledge* (Atlantic)
	27	There Must Be An Angel (Playing With My Heart) *Eurythmics* (RCA)
August	3	Into The Groove *Madonna* (Sire)
	10	Into The Groove *Madonna* (Sire)
	17	Into The Groove *Madonna* (Sire)
	24	Into The Groove *Madonna* (Sire)
	31	I Got You Babe *UB40, Guest Vocals Chrissie Hynde* (Dep International/Virgin)
September	7	Dancing In The Street *David Bowie And Mick Jagger* (EMI America)
	14	Dancing In The Street *David Bowie And Mick Jagger* (EMI America)
	21	Dancing In The Street *David Bowie And Mick Jagger* (EMI America)
	28	Dancing In The Street *David Bowie And Mick Jagger* (EMI America)
October	5	If I Was *Midge Ure* (Chrysalis URE(X)1)
	12	The Power Of Love *Jennifer Rush* (CBS A 5003(12"-TX5003)
	19	The Power Of Love *Jennifer Rush* (CBS A 5003(12"-TX5003)
	26	The Power Of Love *Jennifer Rush* (CBS A 5003(12"-TX5003)

November	2	The Power Of Love *Jennifer Rush* (CBS A 5003(12"-TX5003)
	9	The Power Of Love *Jennifer Rush* (CBS A 5003(12"-TX5003)
	16	A Good Heart *Feargal Sharkey* (Virgin)
	23	A Good Heart *Feargal Sharkey* (Virgin)
	30	I'm Your Man *Wham!* (Epic)
December	7	I'm Your Man *Wham!* (Epic)
	14	Saving All My Love For You *Whitney Houston* (Arista)
	21	Saving All My Love For You *Whitney Houston* (Arista)
	28	Merry Christmas Everyone *Shakin' Stevens* (Epic)

Total Number One records: 20
Record with most weeks at top: I Know Him So Well *Elaine Paige and Barbara Dickson* (RCA); 19 *Paul Hardcastle* (Chrysalis); The Power of Love *Jennifer Rush* (CBS); all three 5 weeks.

1986

January	4	Merry Christmas Everyone *Shakin' Stevens* (Epic)
	11	West End Girls *Pet Shop Boys* (Parlophone)
	18	West End Girls *Pet Shop Boys* (Parlophone)
	25	The Sun Always Shines On TV *A Ha* (Warner Brothers)
February	1	The Sun Always Shines On TV *A Ha* (Warner Brothers)
	8	When The Going Gets Tough, The Tough Get Going *Billy Ocean* (Jive)
	15	When The Going Gets Tough, The Tough Get Going *Billy Ocean* (Jive)
	22	When The going Gets Tough, The Tough Get Going *Billy Ocean* (Jive)
March	1	When The Going Gets Tough, The Tough Get Going *Billy Ocean* (Jive)
	8	Chain Reaction *Diana Ross* (Capitol)
	15	Chain Reaction *Diana Ross* (Capitol)
	22	Chain Reaction *Diana Ross* (Capitol)
	29	Living Doll *Cliff Richard & The Young Ones* (WEA)
April	5	Living Doll *Cliff Richard & The Young Ones* (WEA)
	12	Living Doll *Cliff Richard & The Young Ones* (WEA)
	19	A Different Corner *George Michael* (Epic)
	26	A Different Corner *George Michael* (Epic)
May	3	A Different Corner *George Michael* (Epic)
	10	Rock Me Amadeus (The American Edit) *Falco* (A&M)
	17	The Chicken Song *Spitting Image* (Virgin)
	24	The Chicken Song *Spitting Image* (Virgin)
	31	The Chicken Song *Spitting Image* (Virgin)
June	7	**Spirit In The Sky** *Dr and The Medics* (IRS/MCA)
	14	Spirit In The Sky *Dr and The Medics* (IRS/MCA)
	21	Spirit In The Sky *Dr and The Medics* (IRS/MCA)
	28	The Edge Of Heaven *Wham!* (Epic)
July	5	The Edge Of Heaven *Wham!* (Epic)
	12	Papa Don't Preach *Madonna* (Epic)
	19	Papa Don't Preach *Madonna* (Sire)
	26	Papa Don't Preach *Madonna* (Sire)
August	2	The Lady In Red *Chris De Burgh* (A&M)
	9	The Lady In Red *Chris De Burgh* (A&M)
	16	The Lady In Red *Chris De Burgh* (A&M)
	23	I Want To Wake Up With You *Boris Gardiner* (Revue/Creole)
	30	I Want To Wake Up With You *Boris Gardiner* (Revue/Creole)

468

September	6	I Want To Wake Up With You *Boris Gardiner* (Revue/Creole)
	13	Don't Leave Me This Way *The Communards* (London)
	20	Don't Leave Me This Way *The Communards* (London)
	27	Don't Leave Me This Way *The Communards* (London)
October	4	Don't Leave Me This Way *The Communards* (London)
	11	True Blue *Madonna* (Sire)
	18	Every Loser Wins Nick Berry (Sire)
	25	Every Loser Wins *Nick Berry* (Sire)
November	1	Every Loser Wins *Nick Berry* (Sire)
	8	Take My Breath Away (Love Theme from Top Gun) *Berlin* (CBS)
	15	Take My Breath Away (Love Theme from Top Gun) *Berlin* (CBS)
	22	Take My Breath Away (Love Theme from Top Gun) *Berlin* (CBS)
	29	Take My Breath Away (Love Theme from Top Gun) *Berlin* (CBS)
December	6	The Final Countdown *Europe* (Epic)
	13	The Final Countdown *Europe* (Epic)
	20	Caravan Of Love *The Housemartins* (Go! Discs)
	27	Reet Petite (The Sweetest Girl In Town) *Jackie Wilson* (SMP/SKM)

Total Number One Records: 21
Records with most weeks at the top: When The Going Gets Tough, The Tough Get Going *Billy Ocean* (Jive) 4 weeks; Don't Leave Me This Way *The Communards* (London) 4 weeks; Take My Breath Away (Love Theme from Top Gun) *Berlin* (CBS) 4 weeks.

1987

January	3	Reet Petite (The Sweetest Girl In Town) *Jackie Wilson* (SMP/SKM)
	10	Reet Petite (The Sweetest Girl In Town) *Jackie Wilson* (SMP/SKM)
	17	Reet Petite (The Sweetest Girl In Town) *Jackie Wilson* (SMP/SKM)
	24	Jack Your Body *Steve 'Silk' Hurley* (London)
	31	Jack Your Body *Steve 'Silk' Hurley* (London)
February	7	I Knew You Were Waiting For Me *Aretha Franklin & George Michael* (Epic)
	14	I Knew You Were Waiting For Me *Aretha Franklin & George Michael* (Epic)
	21	Stand By Me *Ben E King* (Atlantic)
	28	Stand By Me *Ben E King* (Atlantic)
March	7	Stand By Me *Ben E King* (Atlantic)
	14	Everything I Own *Boy George* (Virgin)
	21	Everything I Own *Boy George* (Virgin)
	28	Respectable *Mel & Kim* (Supreme)
April	4	Let It Be *Ferry Aid* (The Sun/Zeebrugge Disaster Fund)
	11	Let It Be *Ferry Aid* (The Sun/Zeebrugge Disaster Fund)
	18	Let It Be *Ferry Aid* (The Sun/Zeebrugge Disaster Fund)
	25	La Isla Bonita (Remix) *Madonna* (Sire)
May	2	La Isla Bonita (Remix) *Madonna* (Sire)
	9	Nothing's Gonna Stop Us Now *Starship* (Grunt/RCA)
	16	Nothing's Gonna Stop Us Now *Starship* (Grunt/RCA)
	23	Nothing's Gonna Stop Us Now *Starship* (Grunt/RCA)
	30	Nothing's Gonna Stop Us Now *Starship* (Grunt/RCA)
June	6	I Wanna Dance With Somebody (Who Loves Me) *Whitney Houston* (Arista)
	13	I Wanna Dance With Somebody (Who Loves Me) *Whitney Houston* (Arista)

	20	Star Trekkin' *The Firm* (Bark)
	27	Star Trekkin' *The Firm* (Bark)
July	4	It's A Sin *Pet Shop Boys* (Parlophone)
	11	It's A Sin *Pet Shop boys* (Parlophone)
	18	It's A Sin *Pet Shop Boys* (Parlophone)
	25	Who's That Girl *Madonna* (Sire)
August	1	La Bamba *Los Lobos* (Slash/FRR/London)
	8	La Bamba *Los Lobos* (Slash/FRR/London)
	15	I Just Can't Stop Loving You *Michael Jackson* (Epic)
	22	I Just Can't Stop Loving You *Michael Jackson* (Epic)
	29	Never Gonna Give You Up *Rick Astley* (RCA)
September	5	Never Gonna Give You Up *Rick Astley* (RCA)
	12	Never Gonna Give You Up *Rick Astley* (RCA)
	19	Never Gonna Give You Up Rick *Astley* (RCA)
	26	Never Gonna Give You Up *Rick Astley* (RCA)
October	3	Pump Up The Volume *M/A/R/R/S* (4AD)
	10	Pump Up The Volume *M/A/R/R/S* (4AD)
	17	You Win Again *Bee Gees* (Warner Brothers)
	24	You Win Again *Bee Gees* (Warner Brothers)
	31	You Win Again *Bee Gees* (Warner Brothers)
November	7	You Win Again *Bee Gees* (Warner Brothers)
	14	China In Your Hand *T'Pau* (Siren)
	21	China In Your Hand *T'Pau* (Siren)
	28	China In Your Hand *T'Pau* (Siren)
December	6	China In Your Hand *T'Pau* (Siren)
	13	China In Your Hand *T'Pau* (Siren)
	19	Always On My Mind *Pet Shop Boys* (Parlophone)
	26	Always On My Mind *Pet Shop Boys* (Parlophone)

Total Number One Records: 20.
Most week's at the top: Never Gonna Give You Up *Rick Astley* and China In Your Hand *T'Pau* 5 weeks.

1988

January	2	Always On My Mind *Pet Shop Boys* (Parlophone)
	9	Always On My Mind *Pet Shop Boys* (Parlophone)
	16	Heaven Is A Place On Earth *Belinda Carlisle* (Virgin)
	23	Heaven Is A Place On Earth *Belinda Carlisle* (Virgin)
	30	I Think We're Alone Now *Tiffany* (MCA)
February	6	I Think We're Alone Now *Tiffany* (MCA)
	13	I Think We're Alone Now *Tiffany* (MCA)
	20	I Should Be So Lucky *Kylie Minogue* (PWL)
	27	I Should Be So Lucky *Kylie Minogue* (PWL)
March	5	I Should Be So Lucky *Kylie Minogue* (PWL)
	12	I Should Be So Lucky *Kylie Minogue* (PWL)
	19	I Should Be So Lucky *Kylie Minogue* (PWL)
	26	Don't Turn Around *Aswad* (Mango/Island)
April	2	Don't Turn Around *Aswad* (Mango/Island)
	9	Heart *Pet Shop Boys* (Parlophone)
	16	Heart *Pet Shop Boys* (Parlophone)
	23	Heart *Pet Shop Boys* (Parlophone)
	30	Theme From S-Express *S'Express* (Rhythm King/Mute)
May	7	Theme From S-Express *S'Express* (Rhythm King/Mute)
	14	Perfect *Fairground Attraction* (RCA)
	21	With A Little/She's Leaving Home *Wet Wet Wet/Billy Bragg* (Childline)
	28	With A Little/She's Leaving Home *Wet Wet Wet/Billy Bragg* (Childline)

June	4	With A Little/She's Leaving Home *Wet Wet Wet/Billy Bragg* (Childline)
	11	With A Little/She's Leaving Home *Wet Wet Wet/Billy Bragg* (Childline)
	18	Doctorin' The Tardis *Time Lords* (KLF Communications)
	25	I Owe You Nothing *Bros* (CBS)
July	2	I Owe You Nothing *Bros* (CBS)
	9	Nothing's Gonna Change My Love *Glenn Medeiros* (London)
	16	Nothing's Gonna Change My Love *Glenn Medeiros* (London)
	23	Nothing's Gonna Change My Love *Glenn Medeiros* (London)
	30	Nothing's Gonna Change My Love *Glenn Medeiros* (London)
August	6	The Only Way Is Up *Yazz And The Plastic Population* (Big Life)
	13	The Only Way Is Up *Yazz And The Plastic Population* (Big Life)
	20	The Only Way Is Up *Yazz And The Plastic Population* (Big Life)
	27	The Only Way Is Up *Yazz And The Plastic Population* (Big Life)
September	3	The Only Way Is Up *Yazz And The Plastic Population* (Big Life)
	10	A Groovy Kind Of Love *Phil Collins* (Virgin)
	17	A Groovy Kind Of Love *Phil Collins* (Virgin)
	24	He Ain't Heavy, He's My Brother *The Hollies* (EMI)
October	1	He Ain't Heavy, He's My Brother *The Hollies* (EMI)
	8	Desire *U2* (Island)
	15	One Moment In Time *Whitney Houston* (Arista)
	22	One Moment In Time *Whitney Houston* (Arista)
	29	Orinoco Flow *Enya* (WEA)
November	5	Orinoco Flow *Enya* (WEA)
	12	Orinoco Flow *Enya* (WEA)
	19	First Time *Robin Beck* (Mercury/Phonogram)
	26	First Time *Robin Beck* (Mercury/Phonogram)
December	3	First Time *Robin Beck* (Mercury/Phonogram)
	10	Mistletoe & Wine *Cliff Richard* (EMI)
	17	Mistletoe & Wine *Cliff Richard* (EMI)
	24	Mistletoe & Wine *Cliff Richard* (EMI)
	31	Mistletoe & Wine *Cliff Richard* (EMI)

Total number one records: 20
Records with most weeks at the top: I Should Be So Lucky *Kylie Minogue* (PWL); The Only Way Is Up *Yazz And The Plastic Population* (Big Life); both five weeks.

January	7	Especially For You *Kylie Minogue* (PWL)
	14	Especially For You *Kylie Minogue* (PWL)
	21	Especially For You *Kylie Minogue* (PWL)
	28	Something's Gotten Hold Of My Heart *Marc Almond featuring Gene Pitney* (Parlophone)
February	4	Something's Gotten Hold Of My Heart *Marc Almond featuring Gene Pitney* (Parlophone)
	11	Something's Gotten Hold Of My Heart *Marc Almond featuring Gene Pitney* (Parlophone)
	18	Something's Gotten Hold Of My Heart *Marc Almond featuring Gene Pitney* (Parlophone)
	25	Belfast Child *Simple Minds* (Virgin)
March	4	Belfast Child *Simple Minds* (Virgin)
	11	Too Many Broken Hearts *Jason Donovan* (PWL)
	18	Too Many Broken Hearts *Jason Donovan* (PWL)
	25	Like A Prayer *Madonna* (Sire)
April	1	Like A Prayer *Madonna* (Sire)
	8	Like A Prayer *Madonna* (Sire)
	15	Eternal Flame *Bangles* (CBS)
	22	Eternal Flame *Bangles* (CBS)
	29	Eternal Flame *Bangles* (CBS)
May	6	Eternal Flame *Bangles* (CBS)
	13	Hand On Your Heart *Kylie Minogue* (PWL)
	20	Ferry Cross The Mersey *Marsden/McCartney/Johnson/ Christian* (PWL)
	27	Ferry Cross The Mersey *Marsden/McCartney/ Johnson/Christian* (PWL)
June	3	Ferry Cross The Mersey *Marsden/McCartney/ Johnson/Christian* (PWL)
	10	Sealed With A Kiss *Jason Donovan* (PWL)
	17	Sealed With A Kiss *Jason Donovan* (PWL)
	24	Back To Life/However Do You Want Me *Soul II Soul* (10/Virgin)
July	1	Back To Life/However Do You Want Me *Soul II Soul* (10/Virgin)
	8	Back To Life/However Do You Want Me *Soul II Soul* (10/Virgin)
	15	Back To Life/However Do You Want Me *Soul II Soul* (10/Virgin)
	22	You'll Never Stop Me Loving You *Sonia* (Chrysalis)
	29	You'll Never Stop Me Loving You *Sonia* (Chrysalis)
August	5	Swing The Mood *Jive Bunny & The Mastermixers* (Music Factory)
	12	Swing The Mood *Jive Bunny & The Mastermixers* (Music Factory)
	19	Swing The Mood *Jive Bunny & The Mastermixers* (Music Factory)
	26	Swing The Mood *Jive Bunny & The Mastermixers* (Music Factory)
September	2	Swing The Mood *Jive Bunny & The Mastermixers* (Music Factory)
	9	Ride On Time *Black Box* (deConstruction/RCA)
	16	Ride On Time *Black Box* (deConstruction/RCA)
	23	Ride On Time *Black Box* (deConstruction/RCA)
	30	Ride On Time *Black Box* (deConstruction/RCA)
October	7	Ride On Time *Black Box* (deConstruction/RCA)
	14	Ride On Time *Black Box* (deConstruction/RCA)

	21	That's What I Like *Jive Bunny & The Mastermixers* (Music Factory Dance)
	28	That's What I Like *Jive Bunny & The Mastermixers* (Music Factory Dance)
November	4	That's What I Like *Jive Bunny & The Mastermixers* (Music Factory Dance)
	11	All Around The World *Lisa Stansfield* (Arista)
	18	All Around The World *Lisa Stansfield* (Arista)
	25	You Got It (The Right Stuff) *New Kids On The Block* (CBS)
December	2	You Got It (The Right Stuff) *New Kids On The Block* (CBS)
	9	You Got It (The Right Stuff) *New Kids On The Block* (CBS)
	16	Let's Party *Jive Bunny & The Mastermixers* (Music Factory Dance)
	23	Do They Know It's Christmas? *Band Aid II* (PWL/Polydor)
	30	Do They Know It's Christmas? *Band Aid II* (PWL/Polydor)

Total number one records: 18
Record with most weeks at the top: Ride On Time *Black Box* (deConstruction/RCA); six weeks

---

1990

January	6	Do They Know It's Christmas *Band Aid II* (PWL)
	13	Hangin' Tough *New Kids On The Block* (CBS)
	20	hangin' Tough *New Kids On The Block* (CBS)
	27	Tears On My Pillow *Kylie Minogue* (PWL)
February	3	Nothing Compares 2U *Sinead O'Connor* (Enigma/Chrysalis)
	10	Nothing Compares 2U *Sinead O'Connor* (Enigma/Chrysalis)
	17	Nothing Compares 2U *Sinead O'Connor* (Enigma/Chrysalis)
	24	Nothing Compares 2U *Sinead O'Connor* (Enigma/Chrysalis)
March	3	Dub Be Good To Me *Beats International featuring Linda Layton* (Go Beat)
	10	Dub Be Good To Me *Beats International featuring Linda Layton* (Go Beat)
	17	Dub Be Good To Me *Beats International featuring Linda Layton* (Go Beat)
	24	Dub Be Good To Me *Beats International featuring Linda Layton* (Go Beat)
	31	The Power *Snap* (Arista)
April	7	The Power *Snap* (Arista)
	14	Vogue *Madonna* (Sire)
	21	Vogue *Madonna* (Sire)
	28	Vogue *Madonna* (Sire)
May	5	Vogue *Madonna* (Sire)
	12	Killer *Adamski* (MCA)
	19	Killer *Adamski* (MCA)
	26	Killer *Adamski* (MCA)
June	2	Killer *Adamski* (MCA)
	9	World In Motion *England New Order* (Factory/MCA)
	16	World In Motion *England New Order* (Factory/MCA)
	23	Sacrifice/Healing Hands *Elton John* (Rocket/Phonogram)
	30	Sacrifice/Healing Hands *Elton John* (Rocket/Phonogram)
July	7	Sacrifice/Healing Hands *Elton John* (Rocket/Phonogram)
	14	Sacrifice/Healing Hands *Elton John* (Rocket/Phonogram)
	21	Sacrifice/Healing Hands *Elton John* (Rocket/Phonogram)
	28	Turtle Power *Partners In Kryme* (SBK)
August	4	Turtle Power *Partners In Kryme* (SBK)
	11	Turtle Power *Partners In Kryme* (SBK)

473

	18	Turtle Power *Partners In Kryme* (SBK)
	25	Itsy Bitsy Teeny Weeny *Bombalurina* (Carpet/Polydor)
September	1	Itsy Bitsy Teeny Weeny *Bombalurina* (Carpet/Polydor)
	8	Itsy Bitsy Teeny Weeny *Bombalurina* (Carpet/Polydor)
	15	The Joker *Steve Miller Band* (Capitol)
	22	The Joker *Steve Miller Band* (Capitol)
	29	Show Me Heaven *Maria McKee* (Epic)
October	6	Show Me Heaven *Maria McKee* (Epic)
	13	Show Me Heaven *Maria McKee* (Epic)
	20	Show Me Heaven *Maria McKee* (Epic)
	27	A Little Time *The Beautiful South* (Go! Disc)
November	3	Unchained Melody *The Righteous Brothers* (Verve/Polydor)
	10	Unchained Melody *The Righteous Brothers* (Verve/Polydor)
	17	Unchained Melody *The Righteous Brothers* (Verve/Polydor)
	24	Unchained Melody *The Righteous Brothers* (Verve/Polydor)
December	1	Ice Ice Baby *Vanilla Ice* (SBK)
	8	Ice Ice Baby *Vanilla Ice* (SBK)
	15	Ice Ice Baby *Vanilla Ice* (SBK)
	22	Ice Ice Baby *Vanilla Ice* (SBK)
	29	Saviour's Day *Cliff Richard* (EMI)

Total Number One Records: 18
Record with most weeks at the top: Sacrifice/Healing Hands *Elton John* (Rocket/
Phonogram); 5 weeks

This index lists song titles. The date of the record's first entry, as related to its appearance in the Top 20, is given. It should be remembered that a record may well have been in the Top 75 (but not Top 20) in preceding weeks prior to the month when it first made its Top 20 appearance.

Some titles appear here that are not listed in other music publications. This book takes its chart continuously from *Record Mirror* and later from the industry charts that became the province of the BBC for radio and television programmes. Other sources derive early listings from the *New Musical Express* and then later from the industry chart. In early times there were differences between the two music papers; especially in the 15–20 positions of the chart. Several missing titles, either from the main section or index of other books that have listed artists and their hits (but not charts), will also be found; and in a few instances the title has been corrected.

The following information per entry reads sequentially:
song/record title; *artist's name*; date of first entry into the chart.

Borderline *Madonna* 26.1.86
Born In The USA *Bruce Springsteen* 15.6.85
Born To Be Alive *Patrick Hernandez* 7.7.79
Born To Be With You *Chordettes* 1.9.56
Born To Be With You *Dave Edmunds* 9.6.73
Born To Run *Bruce Springsteen* 30.5.87
Born Too Late *Poni-Tails* 27.9.58
Born With A Smile On My Face *Stephanie De Sykes* 20.7.74
Borne On The Wind *Roy Orbison* 7.3.64
Boston Tea Party *Sensational Alex Harvey Band* 3.7.76
Both Sides Now *Judy Collins* 7.2.70
Boxer *Simon and Garfunkel* 3.5.69
Boxer Beat *Jo Boxers* 2.4.83
Boy *Lulu* 8.6.68
Boy From New York City *Darts* 6.5.78
Boy From Nowhere, A *Tom Jones* 25.4.87
Boy Named Sue *Johnny Cash* 13.9.69
Boys *Kim Wilde* 1.8.81
Boys (Summertime Love) *Sabrina* 11.6.88
Boys Are Back In Town *Thin Lizzy* 5.6.76
Boys Cry *Eden Kane* 1.2.64
Boys Keep Swinging *David Bowie* 5.5.79
Boys Of Summer *Don Henley* 2.3.85
Brand New Friend *Lloyd Cole and the Commotions* 5.10.85
Brand New Key *Melanie* 1.1.72
Brandy *Scott English* 9.10.71
Brass In Pocket *Pretenders* 1.12.79
Bread And Butter *Newsbeats* 3.10.64
Break Away *Beach Boys* 14.6.69
Break My Stride *Matthew Wilder* 21.1.84
Break The Rules *Status Quo* 4.5.74
Breakaway *Tracey Ullman* 2.4.83
Breakdance Party *Break Machine* 12.5.84
Breakfast In America *Supertramp* 7.7.79
Breakfast In Bed *UB40* 18.6.88
Breaking Down (Samba) *Julia and Company* 3.3.84
Breaking Away *Jaki Graham* 23.8.86
Breaking Down The Walls Of Heartache *Johnny Johnson and the Bandwagon* 2.11.68
Breakin' In A Brand New Broken Heart *Connie Francis* 8.7.61
Breakin'... There's No Stopping Us *Ollie and Jerry* 23.6.84
Breaking The Law *Judas Priest* 7.6.80
Breaking Up Is Hard To Do *Partridge Family starring Shirley Jones and David Cassidy* 8.7.72
Breaking Up Is Hard To Do *Neil Sedaka* 4.8.62
Breaking Up My Heart *Shakin' Stevens* 2.3.85
Breakout *Swing Out Sister* 8.11.86
Breakthru' *Queen* 1.7.89
Breathing *Kate Bush* 3.5.80
Breathless *Jerry Lee Lewis* 12.4.58
Breeze And I *Caterina Valente* 27.8.55
Bridge over Troubled Wate *Simon and Garfunkel* 21.2.70
Bridge To Your Heart *Wax* 22.8.87
Bridget The Midget *Ray Stevens* 13.3.71
Bright Eyes *Art Garfunkel* 3.3.79
Brilliant Disguise *Bruce Springsteen* 10.10.87
Bring A Little Water Sylvie *Lonnie Donegan* 15.9.56
Bring It On Home *Animals* 10.4.56
Bring It On Home To Me *Rod Stewart* 5.10.74
Bring Me Edelweis *Edelweiss* 6.5.89
Bringing On Back The Good Times *Love Affair* 2.8.69
Bring Your Smile Along *Frankie Laine* 29.10.55
British Hustle *Hi Tension* 2.9.78

Brits, The *Various* 3.3.90
Broke Away *Wet Wet Wet* 9.12.89
Broken Down Angel *Nazareth* 5.5.73
Broken Hearted Melody *Sarah Vaughan* 26.9.59
Broken Land *Adventures, The* 7.5.88
Broken Wings *Mr Mister* 18.1.86
Brontosaurus *Move* 2.5.70
Brothers In Arms *Dire Straits* 2.11.85
Brother Louie *Hot Chocolate* 14.4.73
Brother Louie *Modern Talking* 23.8.86
Brown Sugar *Rolling Stones* 1.5.71
Brown-Eyed Handsome Man *Buddy Holly* 16.3.63
Buddy *De La Soul* 23.12.89
Buffalo Girls *Malcolm Mclaren and the World's Famous Supreme Team* 4.12.82
Buffalo Soldier *Bob Marley* 7.5.83
Buffalo Stance *Neneh Cherry* 10.12.88
Build *The Housemartins* 28.11.87
Build Me Up Buttercup *Foundations* 7.12.68
Build Your Love *Johnnie Ray* 14.9.57
Bump, The *Kenny* 4.1.75
Bunch Of Thyme *Foster and Allen* 3.4.82
Buona Sera *Acker Bilk* 7.1.61
Burlesque *Family* 14.10.72
Burn, Baby Burn *Hudson-Ford* 2.3.74
Burn It Up *Beatmasters with P. P. Arnold* 1.10.88
Burning Bridges (On And Off) *Status Quo* 3.12.88
Burning Heart *Survivor* 15.2.86
Burning Love *Elvis Presley* 7.10.72
Burning Of The Midnight Lamp *Jimi Hendrix* 2.9.67
Bus Stop *Hollies* 26.6.66
But I Do *Clarence 'Frogman' Henry* 20.5.61: 12.8.61
But You Love Me Daddy *Jim Reeves* 3.1.70
But You're Mine *Sonny and Cher* 6.11.65
Butterfingers *Tommy Steele* 27.4.57
Butterfly *Andy Williams* 20.4.57
Butterfly *Danyel Gerard* 2.10.71
Butterfly *Charlie Gracie* 27.4.57
Butterfly On A Wheel *The Mission* 13.1.90
By The Light Of The Silvery Moon *Little Richard* 4.4.59
Bye Bye Baby *Bay City Rollers* 8.3.75
Bye Bye Baby *Johnny Otis Show* 25.1.58
Bye Bye Love *Everly Brothers* 20.7.57
C'Moon *Wings* 6.1.73
Ca Plane pour Moi *Plastic Bertrand* 13.5.78
Cacharpaya *Incantation* 8.1.83
Calcutta *Lawrence Welk* 18.2.61
Calendar Girl *Neil Sedaka* 4.2.61
California *River city People* 7.7.90
California Man *Move* 13.5.72
Call Me *Blondie* 12.4.80
Call Me *Go West* 11.5.85
Call Me *Spanga* 8.8.87
(Call Me) Number One *Tremeloes* 1.11.69
Call Rosie On The Phone *Guy Mitchell* 19.10.57
Call Up The Groups *Barron Knights* 11.7.64
Calling All The Heroes *It Bites* 9.8.86
Calling Recognised Occupants Of Interplanetary Craft *Carpenters* 8.10.77
Calling Your Name *Marilyn* 5.12.81
Cambodia *Kim Wilde* 5.12.83
Camouflage *Stan Ridgeway* 19.7.86
Can Can *Bad Manners* 27.6.81
Can Can You Party *Jive Bunny & The Mastermixers* 25.8.90
Can I Get A Witness *Sam Brown* 3.6.89
Can I Play With Madness *Iron Maiden* 26.3.88
Can I Take You Home Little Girl *Drifters* 6.12.75

482

Cruising *Sinitta*		26.7.86
Crushed By The Wheels Of Industry *Heaven 17*		10.9.83
Crush On You *The Jets*		21.2.87
Cry *Godley Creme*		4.5.85
Cry *Waterfront*		1.7.89
Cry Boy Cry *Blue Zoo*		6.11.82
Cry Just A Little Bit *Shakin' Stevens*		5.11.83
Cry Like A Baby *Box Tops*		6.4.68
Cry Wolf *a-ha*		13.12.86
Cryin' In The Rain *Everly Brothers*		27.1.62
Crying *Don McLean*		10.5.80
Crying Game *Dave Berry*		1.8.64
Crying In The Chapel *Elvis Presley*		5.6.65
Crying In The Rain *a-ha*		13.10.90
Crying Laughing Loving Lying *Labi Siffre*		1.4.72
Crying Over You *Ken Boothe*		4.1.75
Cuba (Re-Issue) *Gibson Brothers*		1.3.80
Cubik *808 State*		10.11.90
Cuddley Toy *Roachford*		14.1.89
Cult Of Snap *Snap*		22.9.90
Cum On Feel The Noize *Slade*		3.1.73
Cumberland Gap *Lonnie Donegan*		6.4.57
Cumberland Gap *Vipers Skiffle Group*		30.3.57
Cupid *Sam Cooke*		12.8.61
Cupid/I've Loved You For a Long Time *Detroit Spinners*		5.7.80
Curly *Move*		2.8.69
Cutter *Echo and the Bunnymen*		22.1.83
D.W.Washburn *Monkees*		6.7.68
Da Da Da *Trio*		3.7.82
Da Doo Ron Ron *Crystals*		22.6.63; 2.11.74
D-a-a-ance *Lambrettas*		24.5.80
Daddy Cool *Boney M*		15.1.77
Daddy Cool/The Girl Can't Help It *Darts*		5.11.77
Daddy Don't You Walk So Fast *Daniel Boone*		4.9.71
Daddy's Home *Cliff Richard*		2.11.81
Dambusters March *The Central Band of the Royal Air Force*		8.10.55
Dambusters March *Billy Cotton*		5.11.55
Damned Don't Cry *Visage*		13.3.82
Damned On 45 *Captain Sensible*		7.4.84
Dance Away *Roxy Music*		5.5.79
Dance Dance Dance *Chic*		3.12.77
Dance Little Lady Dance *Tina Charles*		24.4.76
Dance Little Sister *Terence Trent D'Arby*		31.10.87
Dance On *Kathy Kirby*		17.8.63
Dance On *Shadows*		15.12.62
Dance To The Music *Sly and the Family Stone*		3.8.68
Dance With Me *Drifters*		23.1.60
Dance With The Devil *Cozy Powell*		8.12.73
Dance With The Guitar Man *Duane Eddy*		10.11.62
Dance Yourself Dizzy *Liquid Gold*		1.3.80
Dancin' Girls *Nik Kershaw*		14.4.84
Dancin' In the Moonlight *Thin Lizzy*		3.9.77
Dancin' Party *Chubby Checker*		11.8.62
Dancin' Party *Showaddywaddy*		5.11.77
Dancing In The City *Marshall Hain*		3.6.78
Dancing In The Dark *Bruce Springsteen*		12.1.85
Dancing In The Street *David Bowie and Mick Jagger*		7.9.85
Dancing In The Street *Martha Reeves and the Vandellas*		1.2.69
Dancing On A Saturday Night *Barry Blue*		4.8.73
Dancing On The Ceiling *Lionel Richie*		16.8.86
Dancing On The Floor (Hooked On Love) *Third World*		4.7.81
Dancing Queen *Abba*		21.8.76
Dancing Tight *Phil Fearon and Galaxy*		23.4.83
Dancing With Tears In My Eyes *Ultravox*		19.5.84
Dancing With The Captain *Paul Nicholas*		9.10.76
Dandelion *Rolling Stones*		26.8.67
Danger Games *Pinkees*		2.10.82
Dangerous *Roxette*		11.8.89
Daniel *Elton John*		20.1.73
Dare Me *Pointer Sisters*		3.8.85
Dark Is The Night *Shakatak*		4.6.83
Darlin' *Beach Boys*		3.2.68
Darlin' *David Cassidy*		1.11.75
Darlin' *Frankie Miller*		4.11.78
Dat *Pluto Shervington*		7.2.76
Daughter Of Darkness *Tom Jones*		18.4.70
Davy's On The Road Again *Manfred Mann's Earth Band*		3.6.78
Day After Day *Badfinger*		5.2.72
Day I Met Marie *Cliff Richard*		2.9.67
Day-In-Day-Out *David Bowie*		11.4.78
Day The Rains Came *Jane Morgan*		12.12.58
Day Trip To Bangor *Fiddlers Dram*		5.12.79
Day Tripper *Beatles*		11.12.65
Day Without Love *Love Affair*		5.10.68
Daydream *Lovin' Spoonful*		16.4.66
Daydream Believer *Monkees*		2.12.67
Daydreamer *David Cassidy*		13.10.73
Days *Kinks*		3.8.68
Days *Kirsty MacColl*		1.7.89
Daytona Demon *Suzi Quatro*		3.11.73
D-Days *Hazel O'Connor*		11.4.81
De Do Do Do, De Da Da Da *Police*		13.12.80
Dead End Street *Kinks*		3.12.66
Dead Giveaway *Shalamar*		11.6.83
Dead Or Alive *Lonnie Donegan*		5.5.56
Dead Ringer For Love *Meat Loaf*		9.1.82
Dean And I *10CC*		1.9.73
Dear Elaine *Roy Wood*		1.9.73
Dear Jesse *Madonna*		16.12.89
Dear John *Status Quo*		3.4.82
Dear Prudence *Souxsie and the Banshees*		1.10.83
Death Disco (Parts 1 & 2) *Public Image Limited*		7.7.79
Death Of A Clown *Dave Davies*		22.7.67
Debora *T-Rex*		1.4.72
December '63 (Oh What A Night) *Four Seasons*		7.2.76
Deck Of Cards *Max Bygraves*		6.10.73
Deck Of Cards *Wink Martindale*		19.12.59; 4.5.63
Dedicated Follower Of Fashion *Kinks*		5.3.66
Dedicated To The One I Love *Mamas and Papas*		8.4.67
Deep Heat '89 *Latino Rave*		2.12.89
Deep In The Heart Of Texas *Duane Eddy*		2.6.62
Deep Purple *Nino Tempo and April Stevens*		7.12.63
Deep River Woman/Ballerina Girl *Lionel Richie*		17.1.87
Theme From The Deer Hunter (Cavatina) *Shadows*		2.6.79
Delaware *Perry Como*		27.2.60
Delilah *Tom Jones*		2.3.68
Delilah *Sensational Alex Harvey Band*		2.8.75
Delta Lady *Joe Cocker*		4.10.69
Denis *Blondie*		4.3.78
Desafinado *Stan Getz and Charlie Byrd*		1.12.62
Desiderata *Les Crane*		11.3.72
Desire *U2*		1.10.88
Desperate Dan *Lieutenant Pigeon*		6.1.73
Detroit City *Tom Jones*		4.3.67
Deutscher Girls *Adam and the Ants*		27.2.82
Devil Gate Drive *Suzi Quatro*		9.2.74

484

485

486

Exodus (Theme From)	Ferrante and Teicher	11.3.61
Experiments With Mice	Johnny Dankworth	23.6.56
Expresso Bongo (EP)	Cliff Richard	23.1.60
Express Yourself	Madonna	3.6.89
Extended Play (EP)	Bryan Ferry	7.8.76
Eye Know	De La Soul	21.10.89
Eye Level	Simon Park Orchestra	15.9.73
Eye Of The Tiger	Survivor	3.8.82
Eye Of The World	Sonia	1.9.90
Eye To Eye	Chaka Chan	20.4.85
Eyes Without A Face	Billy Idol	4.8.84
F.B.I.	Shadows	11.2.61
Fabulous	Charlie Gracie	29.6.57
Face, The	And Why Not	3.2.90
Fade To Grey	Visage	10.1.81
Fairytale	Dana	4.12.76
Fairytale Of New York	The Pogues	12.12.87
Faith	George Michael	24.10.87
Faithful Hussar, The	Ted Heath	4.8.56
Fake 88	Alexander O'Neal	1.10.88
Fall In Love With You	Cliff Richard	26.3.60
Fallen Angel	Frankie Valli	1.5.76
Fallin'	Connie Francis	29.11.58
Falling	Julee Cruise	10.11.90
Falling	Roy Orbison	1.6.63
Falling Apart At The Seams	Marmalade	6.3.76
Fame	David Bowie	2.8.75
Fame	Irene Cara	3.7.82
Family Affair	Sly and the Family Stone	5.2.72
Family Man	Daryl Hall and John Oates	7.5.83
Fancy Pants	Kenny	8.3.75
Fanfare For The Common Man	Emerson, Lake and Palmer	4.6.77
Fantastic Day	Haircut 100	10.4.82
Fantasy	Black Box	3.11.90
Fantasy	Earth, Wind & Fire	4.3.78
Fantasy Island	Tight Fit	1.5.82
Far Away Eyes	Rolling Stones	3.6.78
Far Far Away	Slade	19.10.74
Farewell	Rod Stewart	5.10.74
Farewell Is A Lonely Sound	Jimmy Ruffin	7.3.70
Farewell My Summer Love	Michael Jackson	2.6.84
Fascinating Rhythm	Bass-O-Matic	1.9.90
Fashion	David Bowie	1.11.80
Fast Car	Tracy Chapman	2.7.88
Fat Bottomed Girls	Queen	4.11.78
Father Christmas Do Not Touch Me	Goodies	7.12.74
Father Figure	George Michael	9.1.88
Fattie Bum Bum	Carl Malcolm	13.9.75
Favourite Shirts (Boy Meets Girl)	Haircut 100	7.11.81
Feel Like Makin' Love	Bad Company	4.10.75
Feel So Real	Steve Arrington	27.4.85
Feel The Need In Me	Detroit Emeralds	3.3.73; 2.7.77
Feel The Need In Me	Forrest	14.5.83
Feelings	Morris Albert	4.10.75
(Feels Like) Heaven	Fiction Factory	7.1.84
Feels Like I'm In Love	Kelly Marie	2.8.80
Fergus Sings The Blues	Deacon Blue	20.5.89
Fernando	Abba	1.5.76
Ferry Cross The Mersey	Marsden, McCartney, Johnson, Christians	20.5.89
Ferry Across The Mersey	Gerry and the Pacemakers	2.1.65
Fever	Peggy Lee	30.8.58
Fields Of Fire (400 Miles)	Big Country	2.4.83
Figaro	Brotherhood Of Man	14.1.78
Fight For Ourselves	Spandau Ballet	2.8.86
Final Countdown, The	Europe	15.11.86
Finchley Central	New Vaudeville Band	13.5.67

Find My Love	Fairground Attraction	6.8.88
Find The Time	Five Star	2.8.86
Finest, The	S.O.S. Band	19.4.86
Fine Time	New Order	10.12.88
Fine Time	Yazz	4.2.89
Finger Of Suspicion	Dickie Valentine	22.1.55
Fings Ain't Wot they Used T'Be	Max Bygraves	19.3.60
Fire	Arthur Brown	6.7.68
Fire Brigade	Move	10.2.68
Fire Woman	The Cult	1.4.89
Fireball	Deep Purple	4.12.71
First Cut Is The Deepest	P.P. Arnold	3.6.67
First Cut Is The Deepest	Rod Stewart	23.4.77
First Impressions	Impressions	6.12.75
First Of May	Bee Gees	1.3.69
First Picture Of You	Lotus Eaters	6.8.83
First Taste Of Love	Ben E King	28.1.61
First Time	Robin Beck	5.11.88; 7.1.89
First Time	Adam Faith	5.10.63
First Time Ever I Saw Your Face	Roberta Flack	3.6.72
Fish Man	Ian Menzies	24.9.60
5:15	Who	13.10.73
5-4-3-2-1	Manfred Mann	1.2.64
Five Get Over Excited	The Housemartins	30.5.87
Five Little Fingers	Frankie McBride	7.10.67
Five Miles Out	Mike Oldfield	4.3.82
Five Minutes	Stranglers	4.2.78
5.7.0.5	City Boy	5.8.78
Flash	Queen	6.12.80
Flashback	Imagination	5.12.81
Flashdance	Irene Cara	4.6.83
Flight Of Icarus	Iron Maiden	23.4.83
F.L.M.	Mel & Kim	11.7.87
Float On	Floaters	23.7.77
Floral Dance	Brighouse and Rastrick Brass Band	12.11.77
Flowers In The Rain	Move	9.9.67
Floy Joy	Supremes	4.3.72
Foe-Dee-O-Dee	Rubettes	5.7.75
Fog On The Tyne	Gazza & Lindisfarne	10.11.90
Folk Singer	Tommy Roe	23.3.63
Follow You Follow Me	Genesis	1.4.78
Fool	Al Matthews	6.9.75
Fool	Elvis Presley	1.9.73
Fool Am I	Cilla Black	5.11.66
Fool For Your Loving	Whitesnake	3.5.80
Fool If You Think It's Over	Elkie Brooks	6.2.82
Fool Number One	Brenda Lee	25.11.61
Fool Such As I	Elvis Presley	25.4.59
Fool To Cry	Rolling Stones	1.5.76
Foot Tapper	Shadows	9.3.63
Fools Rush In	Rick Nelson	2.11.63
Foolish Beat	Debbie Gibson	9.7.88
Footsee	Wigan's Chosen Few	1.2.75
Footloose	Kenny Loggins	5.5.74
Footsteps	Steve Lawrence	16.4.60
For A Few Dollars More	Smokie	4.2.78
For All We Know	Shirley Bassey	4.9.71
For America	Red Box	15.11.86
For Once In My Life	Stevie Wonder	4.1.69
For The Good Times	Perry Como	1.9.73
For Those About To Rock	AC/DC	3.7.82
For You	Rick Nelson	1.2.64
For Your Eyes Only	Sheena Easton	4.7.81
For Your Love	Yardbirds	20.3.65
Forbidden Colours	Sylvan Sakamoto	2.7.83
Forever	Roy Wood	1.12.73

488

Harvest Of Love *Benny Hill*	1.6.63
Harvester Of Sorrow *Metallica*	3.9.88
Hats Off To Larry *Del Shannon*	9.9.61
Hava Nagila *Spotnicks*	2.2.63
Have A Drink On Me *Lonnie Donegan*	13.5.61
Have I The Right *Dead End Kids*	2.4.77
Have I The Right *Honeycombs*	1.8.64
Have Pity On The Boy *Paul and Barry Ryan*	5.2.66
Have You Ever Been In Love *Leo Sayer*	3.4.82
Have You Ever Had It Blue *The Style Council*	12.4.86
Have You Seen Her *MC Hammer*	6.10.90
Have You Seen Her *Chi-Lites*	15.1.72; 5.7.75
Have You Seen Your Mother Baby Standing In The	
Shadows *Rolling Stones*	1.10.66
Hawkeye *Frankie Laine*	26.11.55
Haven't Stopped Dancing Yet *Gonzalez*	5.5.79
Hazy Shade Of Winter (Remix) *Bangles*	6.2.88
He Ain't Heavy He's My Brother *Hollies*	4.10.69;
	3.9.88
He Ain't No Competition *Brother Beyond*	12.11.88
He Was Beautiful (Cavatina) *Iris Williams*	3.11.79
Head Over Heels *Tears for Fears*	22.6.85
Headline News *Edwin Starr*	4.1.69
Headlines *Midnight Starr*	5.7.86
Healing Hands *Elton John*	9.6.90
Hear The Drummer(Get Wicked) *Chad*	
Jackson	2.6.90
Heart *Max Bygraves*	6.4.57
Heart *Pet Shop Boys*	2.4.88
Heart And Soul *T'Pau*	5.9.87
Heart Full Of Soul *Yardbirds*	19.6.65
Heart Of A Teenage Girl *Craig Douglas*	23.4.60
Heart Of Glass *Blondie*	27.1.79
Heart Of Gold *Johnny Hates Jazz*	5.7.88
Heart Of Gold *Neil Young*	1.4.72
Heart Of Man *Frankie Vaughan*	8.8.59
Heart Of Stone *Kenny*	3.3.73
Heart On My Sleeve *Gallagher and Lyle*	5.6.76
Heartache *Pepsi & Shirlie*	31.8.87
Heartache Avenue *Maisonettes*	8.1.83
Heartaches By The Number *Guy Mitchell*	28.11.59;
	23.1.60
Heartbeat *Ruby Murray*	26.2.55
Heartbeat *Showaddywaddy*	6.10.75
Heartbreak Hotel *Elvis Presley*	19.5.56; 4.9.71
Heartbreaker *Dionne Warwick*	6.11.82
Heat Is On *Glenn Frey*	6.4.85
Heatseeker *AC/DC*	16.1.88
Heaven In My Hands *Level 42*	3.10.90
Heaven Is A Place On Earth *Belinda*	
Carlisle	19.12.87; 23.1.88
Heaven Knows I'm Miserable Now *The Smiths*	2.6.84
Heaven Must Be Missing An Angel *Tavares*	10.7.76;
	8.3.86
Heaven Must Have Sent You *Elgins*	1.5.71
Heavenly Hands *Level 42*	3.9.88
Helen Wheels *Wings*	3.11.73
He'll Have To Go *Jim Reeves*	16.4.60
Hell Raiser *Sweet*	5.5.73
Hello *The Beloved*	3.2.90
Hello *Lionel Richie*	10.3.84
Hello Dolly *Louis Armstrong*	6.6.64
Hello Dolly *Frankie Vaughan*	6.6.64
Hello Goodbye *Beatles*	2.12.67
Hello Happiness *Drifters*	13.3.76
Hello Hello I'm Back Again *Gary Glitter*	7.4.73
Hello How Are You *Easybeats*	13.4.68
Hello Hurray *Alice Cooper*	10.2.73
Hello I Love You *Doors*	7.9.68
Hello Little Girl *Fourmost*	5.10.63
Hello Mary-Lou *Rick Nelson*	3.6.61
Hello Muddah Hello Faddah *Alan Sherman*	5.10.63
Hello Summertime *Bobby Goldsboro*	3.8.74
Hello Suzie *Amen Corner*	5.7.69
Hello This Is Joanie *Paul Evans*	6.1.79
Hello World *Tremeloes*	5.4.69
Help! *Beatles*	31.7.65
Help *Bananarama Lananeeneenoono*	25.2.89
Help Me Girl *Eric Burdon*	5.11.66
Help Me Make It Through The Night *John Holt*	4.1.75
Help Me Make It Through The Night *Gladys Knight*	
and the Pips	2.12.72
Help Yourself *Tom Jones*	3.8.68
Helule Helule *Tremeloes*	11.5.68
Helyom Halib *Cappella*	6.5.89
Here Comes My Baby *Tremeloes*	4.2.67
Here Comes Summer *Jerry Keller*	29.8.59
Here Comes That Feeling *Brenda Lee*	7.7.62
Here Comes The Judge *Pigmeat Markham*	3.6.68
Here Comes The Nice *Small Faces*	10.6.67
Here Comes The Night *Them*	3.4.65
Here Comes The Rain Again *Eurythmics*	21.1.84
Here Comes The Sun *Cockney Rebels*	7.8.76
Here I Go Again *Archie Bell and the Drells*	4.11.72
Here I Go Again *Hollies*	23.5.64
Here I Go Again *Twiggy*	4.9.76
Here I Go Again *Whitesnake*	7.11.87
Here It Comes Again *Fortunes*	9.10.65
Here We Go *Everton F.C. 1985*	11.5.85
Here We Go Round The Mulberry	
Bush *Traffic*	2.12.67
Hernandos Hideaway *Johnston Brothers*	8.10.55
Hernandos Hideaway *Johnnie Ray*	8.10.55
Heroes and Villains *Beach Boys*	2.9.67
Herseham Boys *Sham 69*	4.8.79
He's A Rebel *Crystals*	5.1.63
He's Gonna Step On You Again *John Kongos*	5.6.71
He's Got No Love *Searchers*	10.7.65
He's Got The Whole Wide World In His Hands	
Laurie London	19.11.57
He's In Town *Rockin' Berries*	17.10.64
He's Misstra Know It All *Stevie Wonder*	13.4.74
He's So Fine *Chiffons*	4.5.63
He's The Greatest Dancer *Sister Sledge*	7.4.79
Hey! Baby *Bruce Channel*	24.3.62
Hey DJ, I Can't Dance *Beatmasters and Betty*	
Boo	12.8.89
Hey Girl *Small Faces*	14.5.66
Hey Girl Don't Bother Me *Tams*	7.8.71
Hey Joe *Jimi Hendrix Experience*	7.1.67
Hey Jude *Beatles*	7.9.68; 3.4.76
Hey Jude *Wilson Pickett*	1.2.69
Hey Little Girl *Ice House*	5.2.83
Hey Little Girl *Del Shannon*	24.3.62
Hey Little Lucy *Conway Twitty*	20.5.59
Hey Matthew *Farel Falka*	19.9.87
Hey Mr. Christmas *Showaddywaddy*	4.1.75
Hey Mr. Music Man *Peters and Lee*	3.4.76
Hey Music Lover *S'Express*	18.2.89
Hey Paula *Paul and Paula*	2.3.63
Hey Rock And Roll *Showaddywaddy*	1.6.74
Hey There *Rosemary Clooney*	8.10.55
Hey There *Sammy Davis Jnr.*	15.10.55
Hey There *The Johnston Brothers*	22.10.55
Hey There *Johnnie Ray*	8.10.55
(Hey There) Lonely Girl *Eddie Holman*	19.10.74
Hey You *Quireboys*	6.1.90

(Hey You) the Rocksteady Crew *Rocksteady Crew*		1.10.83
Hi Fidelity *Kids From Fame*		14.8.82
Hi Hi Hi *Wings*		6.1.73
Hi Ho Silver *Jim Diamond*		8.3.86
Hi Ho Silver Lining *Jeff Beck*	4.11.67; 11.11.72
Hi Lilli Hi Lo *Richard Chamberlain*		2.3.63
Hi Lilli Hi Lo *Alan Price*		6.8.66
Hi Tension *Hi Tension*		3.6.78
Hide And Seek *Howard Jones*		18.2.84
Hideaway *Dave Dee, Dozy, Beaky, Mick and Tich*		11.6.66
High Class Baby *Cliff Richard*		29.11.58
High Energy *Evelyn Thomas*		2.6.84
High Fly *John Miles*		1.11.75
High Hopes *Frank Sinatra*		19.9.59
High Life *Modern Romance*		5.3.83
High School Confidential *Jerry Lee Lewis*		24.1.59
High Time *Paul Jones*		8.10.66
Higher Love *Steve Winwood*		19.7.86
Highly Strung *Spandau Ballet*		20.10.84
Highwire *Linda Carr and the Love Squad*		2.8.75
Hippy Hippy Shake *Swinging Blue Jeans*		4.1.64
His Latest Flame *Elvis Presley*		4.11.61
History *Mai Tai*		1.6.85
Hit And Miss *John Barry*		5.3.60
Hit Me With Your Rhythm Stick *Ian Dury*		9.12.78
Hit The Road Jack *Ray Charles*		28.10.61
Hit That Perfect Beat *Bronski Beat*		7.12.85
Hitmix (Official Bootleg Mega-Mix) *Alexander O'Neal*		9.12.89
Hitchin' A Ride *Vanity Fair*		7.2.70
Hocus Pocus *Focus*		3.2.73
Hokey Cokey *Snowmen*		12.12.81
Hold Back The Night *Trammps*		11.10.75
Hold Back Tomorrow *Micki and Griff*		3.10.59
Hold Me *P. J. Proby*		6.6.64
Hold Me *B.A. Robertson and Maggie Bell*		3.10.81
Hold Me Close *David Essex*		13.10.75
Hold Me In Your Arms *Rick Astley*		11.2.89
Hold Me Now *Johnny Logan*		30.5.87
Hold Me Now *Thompson Twins*		19.11.83
Hold Me Tight *Johnny Nash*		10.8.68
Hold Me Tighter In The Rain *Billy Griffin*		8.1.83
Hold On *En Vogue*		5.5.90
Hold On *Streetband*		4.11.78
Hold On *Wilson Phillips*		2.6.90
Hold On Tight *Electric Light Orchestra*		1.8.81
Hold On To Love *Peter Skellern*		5.4.75
Hold On To My Love *Jimmy Ruffin*		3.5.80
Hold The Line *Toto*		3.3.79
Hold Tight *Dave Dee, Dozy, Beaky, Mick and Tich*		5.3.66
Hold Your Head Up *Argent*		4.3.72
Holding Back The Years *Simply Red*		24.5.86
Holding Out For A Hero *Bonnie Tyler*		7.9.85
Hole In My Shoe *Neil*		14.7.84
Hole In My Shoe *Traffic*		9.9.67
Hole In The Ground *Bernard Cribbins*		24.2.62
Holiday *Madonna*	4.2.84; 3.8.85
Holiday Rap *M.C.Miker*		13.9.86
Holidays In The Sun *Sex Pistols*		22.10.77
Holy Cow *Lee Dorsey*		5.11.66
Holy Smoke *Iron Maiden*		22.9.90
Homburg *Procul Harum*		7.10.67
Home Lovin' Man *Andy Williams*		21.11.70
Homely Girl *Chi-Lites*		6.4.74
Homely Girl *UB40*		18.11.89
Homeward Bound *Simon and Garfunkel*		2.4.66
Honey *Bobby Goldsboro*	5.4.68; 5.4.75
Honey Come Back *Glen Campbell*		9.2.70
Honey Honey *Sweet Dreams*		3.8.74
Honey I Need *Pretty Things*		6.3.65
Honey Thief (The) *Hipsway*		22.3.86
Honeycomb *Jimmie Rodgers*		19.4.57
Hong Kong Garden *Siouxsi and the Banshees*		2.9.78
Honky Tonk Women *Rolling Stones*		12.7.69
Hooked On Classics *Royal Philharmonic Orchestra, Louis Clark*		1.8.81
Hooray! Hooray! It's A Holi Day *Boney M*		28.4.79
Hoots Mon *Lord Rockinham's XI*		1.11.58
Hopelessly Devoted To You *Olivia Newton-John*		4.11.78
Horse With No Name *America*		8.1.72
Hot Diggity *Perry Como*		26.5.56
Hot Diggity *Michael Holliday*		16.6.56
Hot Diggity *Stargazers*		9.6.58
Hot Legs *Rod Stewart*		4.2.78
Hot Love *T.Rex*		6.3.71
Hot In The City *Billy Idol*		9.1.88
Hot Shot Tottenham *Tottenham Hotspur Squad/ Chas and Dave*		23.5.87
Hot Stuff *Donna Summer*		2.6.79
Hot Tracks (EP) *Nazareth*		5.11.77
Hot Water *Level 42*		1.9.84
Hotel California *Eagles*		7.5.77
Hound Dog *Elvis Presley*	22.9.56; 7.8.71
Hounds Of Love *Kate Bush*		8.3.86
Hourglass *Squeeze*		12.9.87
House Arrest *Krush*		2.1.88
House Nation *The House Master Boys and The Rude Boy of House*		19.9.87
House Of Fun *Madness*		22.5.82
House of The Rising Sun *Animals*	4.7.64; 2.10.72
House Of The Rising Sun *Frijid Pink*		4.4.70
House That Jack Built *Alan Price*		5.8.67
House That Jack Built, The *Jack 'n' Chill*		2.1.88
House That Jack Built, The *Tracie*		2.4.83
House With Love In It *Vera Lynn*		5.1.57
How About That *Adam Faith*		17.9.60
How Am I Supposed To Live Without You *Michael Bolton*		17.2.90
How 'Bout Us *Champagne*		9.5.81
How Can I Be Sure *David Cassidy*		16.9.82
How Can I Meet Her *Everly Brothers*		2.6.62
How Can This Be Love *Andrew Gold*		1.7.78
How Can We Be Lovers *Michael Bolton*		5.5.90
How Come *Ronnie Lane*		12.1.74
How Deep Is Your Love *Bee Gees*		5.11.77
How Do You Do It *Gerry and the Pacemakers*		16.3.63
How Does It Feel *Slade*		1.3.75
How Does That Grab You Darlin' *Nancy Sinatra*		7.5.66
How Long *Ace*		7.12.74
How Many Tears *Bobby Vee*		19.8.61
How Much Love *Leo Sayer*		9.4.77
How Soon *Henry Mancini*		3.10.64
How Will I Know *Whitney Houston*		8.2.86
Howzat *Sherbert*		2.10.76
Hubble Bubble Toil and Trouble *Manfred Mann*		18.4.64
Human *Human League*		23.8.86
Humming Bird *Frankie Laine*		8.10.55
Human Racing *Nik Kershaw*		15.9.84
Hundred Pounds Of Clay *Craig Douglas*		15.4.61
Hungry For Love *Johnny Kid and the Pirates*		7.12.83
Hungry Like A Wolf *Duran Duran*		15.5.82

493

Song	Artist	Date
I Get Weak	Belinda Carlisle	5.3.88
I Go Ape	Neil Sedaka	2.5.59
I Go To Sleep	Pretenders	14.11.81
I Got Stung	Elvis Presley	31.1.59
I Got You	Split Enz	4.10.80
I Got You Babe	Sonny and Cher	14.8.65
I Got You Babe	UB40, guest vocals Chrissie Hynde	3.8.85
I Guess I'll Always Love You	Isley Brothers	1.2.69
I Guess That's Why They Call It The Blues	Elton John	4.6.83
(I've Had) The Time Of My Life	Bill Medley and Jennifer Warnes	14.11.87
I Have A Dream	Abba	15.12.79
I Haven't Stopped Dancing Yet	Pat and Mick	1.4.89
I Hear You Knocking	Dave Edmunds	21.11.70
I Hear You Knocking	Gale Storm	17.3.56
I Hear You Now	Jon and Vangelis	5.1.80
I Heard A Rumour	Bananarama	25.7.87
I Heard It Through The Grapevine	Marvin Gaye	1.3.69; 3.5.86
I Just Called To Say I Love You	Stevie Wonder	25.8.84
I Just Can't Help Believing	Elvis Presley	11.12.71
I Just Can't Stop Loving You	Michael Jackson	8.8.87
(I Just) Died In Your Arms	Cutting Crew	6.9.86
I Just Don't Have The Heart	Cliff Richard	26.8.89
I Just Don't Know About Anybody Else	Black Box	17.2.90
I Just Don't Know What To Do With Myself	Dusty Springfield	4.7.64
I Just Wanna (Spend Some Time With You)	Alton Edwards	9.1.82
I Knew You Were Waiting (For Me)	Aretha Franklin and George Michael	31.1.87
I Know	Perry Como	8.8.59
I Know A Place	Petula Clark	13.3.65
I Know Him So Well	Elaine Page and Barbara Dickson	5.1.85
(I Know) I'm Losing You	Temptations	7.1.67
I Know You Got Soul	Eric B. Rakim	12.3.88
I Like It	Gerry and the Pacemakers	1.6.63
I Like (What You're Doing To Me)	Young and Company	1.11.80
I Like Your Kind Of Love	Andy Williams	6.7.57
I Live For The Sun	Vanity Fair	7.9.68
I Lost My Heart To A Starship Trooper	Sarah Brightman	2.12.78
I Love America	Patrick Juvet	4.11.78
I Love Her	Paul and Barry Ryan	14.5.66
I Love How You Love Me	Jimmy Crawford	23.12.61
I Love Music	O'Jays	7.2.76
I Love My Radio	Taffy	31.1.87
I Love Rock 'N' Roll	Joan Jett and the Blackhearts	1.5.82
I Love The Sound Of Breaking Glass	Nick Lowe	11.3.78
I Love To Boogie	T. Rex	3.7.76
I Love To Love (But My Baby Loves To Dance)	Tina Charles	7.2.76
I Love You	Cliff Richard	3.12.60
I Love You	Donna Summer	7.1.78
I Love You Baby	Paul Anka	9.11.57
I Love You Baby	Freddie and the Dreamers	6.6.64
I Love You Because	Jim Reeves	7.3.64
I Love You Love Me Love	Gary Glitter	17.11.73
I Love You So Much It Hurts	Charlie Gracie	31.8.57
I May Never Pass This Way Again	Perry Como	12.7.58
I May Never Pass This Way Again	Robert Earl	10.5.58
I Might	Shakin' Stevens	3.3.90
I Missed Again	Phil Collins	7.3.81
I Must Be Seeing Things	Gene Pitney	20.2.65
I Need Love	L.L. Cool J.	26.9.87
I Need You	BVSMP	6.8.88
I Need Your Love Tonight	Elvis Presley	25.4.59
I Need Your Lovin'	Alyson Williams	12.8.89
I Only Have Eyes For You	Art Garfunkel	13.10.75
I Only Wanna Be With You	Bay City Rollers	11.9.76
I Only Wanna Be With You	Samantha Fox	4.2.89
I Only Want To Be With You	Dusty Springfield	7.12.63
I Only Want To Be With You	Tourists	1.12.79
I Owe You Nothing	Bros	18.6.88
I Owe You One	Shalamar	6.9.80
I Pretend	Des O'Connor	1.6.68
I Quit	Bros	17.9.88
I Really Didn't Mean It	Luther Vandross	1.8.87
I Recall A Gypsy Woman	Don Williams	3.7.76
I Remember Elvis Presley (The King Is Dead)	Danny Mirror	1.10.77
I Remember Yesterday	Donna Summer	1.10.77
I Remember You	Frank Ifield	7.7.62
I Saw Her Again	Mamas and Papas	6.8.66
I Saw Him Standing There	Tiffany	11.6.88
I Say A Little Prayer	Aretha Franklin	10.8.68
I Second That Emotion	Japan	3.7.82
I Second That Emotion	Diana Ross and the Supremes/Temptations	4.10.69
I See A Star	Mouth and Macneal	4.5.74
I Shot The Sheriff	Eric Clapton	3.8.74
I Should Be So Lucky	Kylie Minogue	6.2.88
I Should Have Lovedya	Michael Walden	3.5.80
I Should Have Known Better	Jim Diamond	3.11.84
I Still Haven't Found What I'm Looking For	Chimes	19.5.90
I Still Haven't Found What I'm Looking For	U2	6.6.87
I Still Love You All	Kenny Ball and his Jazzmen	3.6.61
I Surrender	Rainbow	₹7.2.81
I Thank You	Adeva	21.10.89
I Think I Love You	Partridge Family starring Shirley Jones and David Cassidy	13.2.71
I Think It's Going to Rain	UB40	5.7.80
I Think Of You	Perry Como	15.5.71
I Think Of You	Merseybeats	1.2.64
I Think We're Alone Now	Tiffany	16.1.88
I Thought It Was You	Herbie Hancock	2.9.78
I Understand	Freddie and the Dreamers	5.12.64
I Understand	G-Clefs	23.12.61
I Wanna Be A Winner	Brown Sauce	9.1.82
I Wanna Be Your Man	Rolling Stones	7.12.63
I Wanna Dance With Choo	Disco Tex and the Sex-O-Lettes	3.5.75
I Wanna Dance With Somebody (Who Loves Me)	Whitney Houston	22.5.87
I Wanna Do It With You	Barry Manilow	16.10.82
I Wanna Get Next To You	Rose Royce	2.4.77
I Wanna Go Home	Lonnie Donegan	28.5.60
I Wanna Hold Your Hand	Dollar	5.7.80
I Wanna Stay With You	Gallagher and Lyle	6.3.76
I Want Candy	Bow Wow Wow	5.6.82
I Want It All	Queen	13.5.89
I Want That Man	Deborah Harry	7.10.89

I Want To Be Free *Toyah*	16.5.81	
I Want To Break Free *Queen*	14.4.84	
I Want To Hold Your Hand *Beatles*	7.12.63	
I Want To Know What Love Is *Foreigner*	8.12.84	
I Want To Stay Here *Steve and Eydie*	24.8.63	
I Want To Wake Up With You *Boris Gardiner*	9.8.86	
I Want To Walk You Home *Fats Domino*	7.11.59	
I Want You *Bob Dylan*	6.8.66	
I Want You Back *Bananarama*	9.4.88	
I Want You Back *Jackson Five*	7.2.70	
I Want You Back '88 *Michael Jackson*	16.4.88	
I Want You I Need You I Love You *Elvis Presley*	18.8.56	
I Want Your Love *Chic*	3.3.79	
I Want Your Love *Transvision Vamp*	2.7.88	
I Want Your Lovin' (Just A Little Bit) *Curtis Hairston*	4.5.85	
I Want Your Sex, Rhythm I Lust *George Michael*	13.6.87	
I Was Kaiser Bill's Batman *Whistling Jack Smith*	4.3.67	
I Was Born To Love You *Freddie Mercury*	4.5.85	
I Was Made For Dancin' *Leif Garrett*	3.2.79	
I Was Made To Love Her *Stevie Wonder*	5.8.67	
I Was Only Joking *Rod Stewart*	4.2.78	
I (Who Have Nothing) *Shirley Bassey*	5.10.63	
I (Who Have Nothing) *Tom Jones*	5.9.70	
I Will *Billy Fury*	2.5.64	
I Will *Ruby Winters*	5.11.77	
I Will Be With You *T'Pau*	2.7.88	
I Will Drink The Wine *Frank Sinatra*	6.3.71	
I Will Return *Springwater*	6.11.71	
I Will Survive *Arrival*	6.6.70	
I Will Survive *Gloria Gaynor*	3.2.79	
I Wish *Stevie Wonder*	8.1.77	
I Wish It Could Be Christmas Everyday *Wizzard*	15.12.73	
I Wish It Would Rain *Faces*	8.12.73	
I Wish It Would Rain Down *Phil Collins*	3.2.90	
I Wonder *Dickie Valentine*	2.7.55	
I Wonder *Brenda Lee*	20.7.63	
I Wonder If It Take You Home *Lisa Lisa and the Cult Jam Force*	3.8.85	
I Wonder Why *Showaddywaddy*	1.4.78	
I Won't Come In While He's There *Jim Reeves*	4.2.67	
I Won't Forget You *Jim Reeves*	4.7.64	
I Won't Last A Day Without You *Carpenters*	14.10.72	
I Won't Let The Sun Go Down On Me *Nik Kershaw*	16.6.84	
I Won't Let You Down *PhD*	1.5.82	
I Won't Run Away *Alvin Stardust*	3.11.84	
I Wouldn't Trade You for The World *Bachelors*	15.8.64	
I Write The Songs *David Cassidy*	2.8.75	
I've Been Losing You *a-ha*	4.10.86	
I.O.U. *Freeze*	2.7.83	
Ice Cream Man *Tornados*	8.6.63	
Ice Ice Baby *Vanilla Ice*	24.11.90	
Ice In The Sun *Status Quo*	7.9.68	
Icing On The Cake *Stephen 'Tin Tin' Duffy*	1.6.85	
I'd Like To Teach The World To Sing *New Seekers*	18.12.71	
I'd Love You To Want Me *Lobo*	8.6.74	
I'd Never Find Another You *Billy Fury*	16.12.61	
I'd Rather Go Blind *Chicken Shack*	7.6.69	
I'd Rather Jack *Reynolds Girls*	4.3.89	
Ideal World *The Christians*	2.1.88	
Idle On Parade *Anthony Newley*	2.5.59	
If *Telly Savalas*	1.3.75	

If Anyone Finds This I Love You *Ruby Murray*	26.3.55	
If Dreams Came True *Pat Boone*	20.9.58	
If Everyday Was Like Christmas *Elvis Presley*	10.12.66	
If I Can Dream *Elvis Presley*	8.3.69	
If I Can't Have You *Yvonne Elliman*	6.5.78	
If I Could *David Essex*	6.12.75	
If I Could (El Condor Pasa) *Julie Felix*	2.5.70	
If I Could Turn Back Time *Cher*	7.10.89	
If I Didn't Care	11.5.74	
If I Found Someone *Cher*	2.1.89	
If I Had A Hammer *Trini Lopez*	14.9.63	
If I Had Words *Scott Fitzgerald and Yvonne Keeley*	14.1.78	
If I Had You *Korgis*	7.7.79	
If I Knew Then What I Know Now *Val Doonican*	2.11.68	
If I Loved You *Richard Anthony*	2.5.64	
If I Needed Someone *Hollies*	15.11.66	
If I Only Had Time *John Rowles*	16.3.68	
If I Ruled The World *Harry Secombe*	7.12.63	
If I Said You Have A Beautiful Body Would You Hold It Against Me *Bellamy Brothers*	1.9.79	
If I Say Yes *Five Star*	29.11.86	
If I Thought You'd Ever Change Your Mind *Cilla Black*	3.1.70	
If I Was *Midge Ure*	14.9.85	
If I Was Your Girlfriend *Prince*	4.7.87	
If I Were A Carpenter *Bobby Darin*	15.10.66	
If I Were A Carpenter *Four Tops*	16.3.68	
If I Were A Rich Man *Topol*	3.6.67	
If It Happens Again *UB40*	22.9.84	
If Leaving Me Is Easy *Phil Collins*	6.6.81	
If Not For You *Dr. Hook*	6.11.76	
If Not For You *Olivia Newton-John*	3.4.71	
If Only I Could *Sydney Youngblood*	2.9.89	
(If Paradise Is) Half As Nice *Amen Corner*	1.2.69	
If She Should Come To You *Anthony Newley*	23.7.60	
If The Kids Are United *Sham 69*	5.8.78	
If The Whole World Stopped Loving You *Val Doonican*	4.11.67	
If You Believe *Johnnie Ray*	12.3.55	
If You Can't Give Me Love *Suzi Quatro*	18.3.78	
If You Can't Stand The Heat *Buck's Fizz*	4.12.82	
If You Don't Know Me By Now *Harold Melvin and the Bluenotes*	13.1.73	
If You Don't Know Me By Now *Simply Red*	8.4.89	
If You Go Away *Terry Jacks*	6.7.74	
If You Gotta Go Go Now *Manfred Mann*	18.9.65	
If You Gotta Make A Fool Of Somebody *Freddie and the Dreamers*	1.6.63	
If You Leave Me Now *Chicago*	9.10.76	
If You Let Me Stay *Terence Trent D'Arby*	4.4.87	
If You Really Love Me *Stevie Wonder*	5.2.72	
If You Think You Know How To Love Me *Smokie*	19.7.75	
If You Were Here Tonight (Remix) *Alexander O'Neal*	8.3.86	
If You're Looking For A Way Out *Odyssey*	4.10.80	
Iko Iko *Natasha*	5.6.82	
Il Silenzioo *Nini Rosso*	4.9.65	
I'll Be Around *Terri Wells*	5.5.84	
I'll Be Home *Pat Boone*	21.4.56	
I'll Be Loving You (Forever) *New Kids On The Block*	17.3.90	
I'll Be Satisfied *Shakin' Stevens*	16.10.82	
I'll Be There *Gerry and the Pacemakers*	3.4.65	
I'll Be There *Jackson Five*	5.12.70	

It's My Turn *Diana Ross*	7.2.81	
It's Not Unusual *Tom Jones*	13.2.65; 20.6.87	
It's Now Or Never *Elvis Presley*	5.11.60	
It's One Of Those Nights (Yes Love) *Partridge Family starring Shirley Jones and David Cassidy*	4.3.72	
It's Only Love *Elvis Presley*	6.9.80	
It's Only Love *Simply Red*	4.2.89	
It's Only Make Believe *Glen Campbell*	21.11.70	
It's Only Make Believe *Child*	5.8.78	
It's Only Make Believe *Billy Fury*	1.8.64	
It's Only Make Believe *Conway Twitty*	22.11.58	
It's Only Rock And Roll *Rolling Stones*	3.8.74	
It's 'Orrible Being In Love (When You're 8½) *Claire and Friends*	5.7.86	
It's Over *Fun Masters*	2.7.83	
It's Over (Remix) *Level 42*	19.9.87	
It's Over *Roy Orbison*	2.5.64	
It's Raining *Darts*	5.8.78	
It's Raining *Shakin' Stevens*	10.10.81	
It's Raining Men *Weather Girls*	3.3.84	
It's So Easy *Andy Williams*	5.8.70	
It's Still Rock And Roll To Me *Billy Joel*	9.8.80	
It's The Same Old Song *Weathermen*	6.2.71	
It's Time For Love *Chi-Lites*	4.10.75	
It's Time To Get Funky *D.Mob featuring LRS*	3.6.89	
It's Too Late *Carole King*	7.8.71	
It's Too Soon To Know *Pat Boone*	5.4.58	
It's Tricky *Run DMC*	13.6.87	
It's Wonderful *Jimmy Ruffin*	17.10.70	
It's You *Freddie Starr*	2.3.74	
It's You That I Have *Marion Ryan*	31.12.60	
It's Your Life *Smokie*	16.7.77	
Itsy Bitsy Teeny Weeny *Bombalurina*	4.8.90	
Itsy Bitsy Teeny Weeny Yellow Polka Dot Bikini *Brian Hyland*	16.7.60	
I've Been A Bad Bad Boy *Paul Jones*	2.1.67	
I've Been Hurt *Guy Darrel*	1.9.73	
I've Been Losing You *a-ha*	4.10.86	
I've Been Wrong Before *Cilla Black*	1.5.65	
I've Been Thinking About You *Londonbeat*	1.9.90	
I've Got You On My Mind *White Plains*	2.5.70	
I've Got You Under My Skin *Four Seasons*	1.10.66	
I've Gotta Get A Message To You *Bee Gees*	10.8.68	
I've Lost You *Elvis Presley*	14.11.70	
I've Never Been to Me *Charlene*	4.5.82	
I've Told Every Little Star *Linda Scott*	10.6.61	
I've Waited So Long *Anthony Newley*	2.5.59	
Ivy Will Cling *Arnold Stang*	5.12.59	
Jack And Jill *Raydio*	6.5.78	
Jack In The Box *Moments*	5.2.77	
Jack In The Box *Clodagh Rodgers*	20.3.71	
Jack Le Freak *Chic*	3.10.87	
Jack Mix II *Mirage*	30.5.87	
Jack Mix III *(same record as II, titles flipped)*	6.6.87	
Jack Mix IV *Mirage*	14.11.87	
Jack O'Diamonds *Lonnie Donegan*	4.1.58	
Jack The Groove *Raze*	31.1.87	
Jack To The Sound Of The Underground *Hithouse*	3.12.88	
Jack Your Body *Steve 'Silk' Hurley*	10.1.87	
Jackie *Scott Walker*	6.1.68	
Jackie Wilson Said *Dexy's Midnight Runners*	2.10.82	
Jackson *Nancy Sinatra*	8.7.67	
Ja-Da *Johnny and the Hurricanes*	25.3.61	
Jailhouse Rock *Elvis Presley*	25.1.58	
Jailhouse Rock EP *Elvis Presley*	8.2.58	
Jambalaya (On The Bayou) *Carpenters*	2.3.74	
James Bond Theme *John Barry*	3.11.62	
Jamming *Bob Marley and the Wailers*	7.1.78	
January *Pilot*	18.1.75	
January February *Barbara Dickson*	15.3.80	
Japanese Boy *Aneka*	8.8.81	
Jarrow Song *Alan Price*	1.6.74	
Jaws *Lalo Schifrin*	9.10.76	
Jazz Carnival *Azymuth*	2.2.80	
Je Ne Sais Par Pourquoi *Kylie Minogue*	22.10.89	
Je T'Aime ... Moi Non Plus *Jane Birkin and Serge Gainsbourg*	2.8.69	
Je T'Aime ... Moi Non Plus *Judge Dread*	5.7.75	
Jealous Guy *Roxy Music*	21.2.81	
Jealous Mind *Alvin Stardust*	16.2.74	
Jealousy *Billy Fury*	16.9.61	
Jean Genie *David Bowie*	9.12.72	
Jeannie *Danny Williams*	10.2.62	
Jeans On *David Dundas*	24.7.76	
Jeepster *T. Rex*	13.11.71	
Jennifer Eccles *Hollies*	6.4.68	
Jennifer Juniper *Donovan*	2.3.68	
Jenny Jenny *Little Richard*	14.9.57	
Jesamine *Casuals*	7.9.68	
Jet *Wings*	2.3.74	
Jezebel *Marty Wilde*	2.6.62	
Jig A Jig *East of Eden*	1.5.71	
Jilted John *Jilted John*	12.8.78	
Jimmy Jimmy *Undertones*	5.5.79	
Jimmy Unknown *Lita Roza*	3.3.56	
Jingle Bell Rock *Max Bygraves*	26.12.59	
Jingo *Jellybean*	26.12.87	
Jive Talkin' *Bee Gees*	5.7.75	
Jive Talking *Boogie Box High*	18.7.87	
Joan Of Arc *Orchestral Manoeuvres in the Dark*	7.11.81	
Joanna *Kool and the Gang*	11.2.84	
Joanna *Scott Walker*	4.5.68	
Joe Le Taxi *Vanessa Paradis*	13.2.88	
John And Julie *Eddie Calvert*	3.9.55	
John I'm Only Dancing *David Bowie*	7.10.72; 15.12.79	
John Wayne Is Big Leggy *Haysi Fantazyee*	7.8.82	
Johnny B. Goode *Chuck Berry*	7.6.58	
Johnny Come Home *Fine Young Cannibals*	8.6.85	
Johnny Reggae *Piglets*	6.11.71	
Johnny Remember Me *John Leyton*	5.8.61	
Johnny Staccato Theme *Elmer Bernstein*	19.12.59	
Johnny Will *Pat Boone*	9.12.61; 10.2.62	
Join In And Sing Again *Johnston Brothers*	19.11.55	
Join In And Sing Again	1.7.72	
Join Together *Who*	1.9.90	
Joker, The *Steve Miller*	5.6.76	
Jolene *Dolly Parton*	7.3.81	
Jones Vs Jones *Koole and the Gang*	3.6.89	
Joy And Pain *Donna Allen*	8.9.73	
Joybringer *Manfred Mann's Earth Band*	6.1.68	
Judy In Disguise (With Glasses) *John Fred and the Playboy Band*	6.1.68	
Judy Teen *Steve Harley and Cockney Rebel*	1.6.74	
Juke Box Jive *Rubettes*	16.11.74	
Julie Ann *Kenny*	16.8.75	
Julie Do Ya Love Me *White Plains*	7.11.70	
Juliet *Four Pennies*	11.4.64	
Jump *Van Halen*	3.3.84	
Jump (For My Love) *Pointer Sisters*	23.6.84	
Jump To The Beat *Stacy Lattisaw*	14.6.80	
Jumpin' Jack Flash *Rolling Stones*	1.6.68	
Jungle Rock *Hank Mizell*	3.4.76	
Junior's Farm *Wings*	7.12.74	
Just A Feeling *Bad Manners*	4.4.81	

498

Just A Little Bit Better *Herman's Hermits*	4.9.65	
Just A Little Bit Too Late *Wayne Fontana and the Mindbenders*	3.7.65	
Just A Little Too Much *Rick Nelson*	5.9.59	
Just A Mirage *Jellybean feat. Adele Bertei*	2.4.88	
Just An Illusion *Imagination*	6.3.82	
Just Be Good To Me *S.O.S. Band*	7.4.84	
Just Can't Get Enough *Depeche Mode*	3.10.81	
Just Can't Give You Up *Mystic Merlin*	7.6.80	
Just Don't Want To Be Lonely *Freddie McGregor*	25.7.87	
Just For Money *Paul Hardcastle*	9.11.85	
Just For You *Glitter Band*	3.8.74	
Just Got Lucky *Jo Boxers*	21.5.83	
Just Keep It Up *Dee Clark*	12.9.59	
Just Keep Rockin' *Double Trouble and The Rebel MC*	3.6.89	
Just Like A Woman *Manfred Mann*	6.8.66	
Just Like Eddie *Heinz*	10.8.63	
Just Like Jesse James *Cher*	3.2.90	
(Just Like) Starting Over *John Lennon*	8.11.80	
Just Loving You *Anita Harris*	1.7.67	
Just My Imagination *Temptations*	5.6.71	
Just One Look *Hollies*	7.3.64	
Just One More Night *Yellow Dog*	4.2.78	
Just One Smile *Gene Pitney*	12.11.66	
Just Say No *Grange Hill*	26.4.86	
Just The Way You Are *Billy Joel*	4.3.78	
Just The Way You Are *Billy White*	6.1.79	
Just This Side Of Love *Malandra Burrows*	8.12.90	
Just Walkin' In The Rain *Johnny Ray*	20.10.56	
Just What I Always Wanted *Mari Wilson*	11.9.82	
Just What I Needed *Cars*	3.3.79	
Just When I Needed You Most *Randy Vanwarmer*	1.9.79	
Just Who Is The Five O'Clock Hero *Jam*	13.7.82	
Justify My Love *Madonna*	8.12.90	
Kar Kara *New World*	1.1.72	
Karma Chameleon *Culture Club*	17.9.83	
Kate Bush On Stage (EP) *Kate Bush*	6.10.79	
Kayleigh *Marillion*	18.5.85	
(Keep Feeling) Fascination *Human League*	23.4.83	
Keep On *Bruce Channel*	3.8.63	
Keep On Dancin' *Gary's Gang*	3.3.79	
Keep On Dancin' *Bay City Rollers*	2.10.71	
Keep On Loving You *Reo Speedwagon*	2.5.81	
Keep On Movin' *Soul II Soul feat. Caron Wheeler*	11.3.89	
Keep On Running *Spencer Davis Group*	4.12.65	
Keep On Truckin' *Eddie Kendricks*	1.12.73	
Keep On Searchin' (We'll follow The Sun) *Del Shannon*	16.1.65	
Keep Your Eye On Me – Special Mix *Herb Alpert*	18.4.87	
Keep Of The Castle *Four Tops*	2.12.72	
Keeping The Dream Alive *Freiheit*	7.12.88	
Kewpie Doll *Perry Como*	17.5.58	
Kewpie Doll *Frankie Vaughan*	24.5.58	
Kick It In *Simple Minds*	5.8.89	
Kicking Up The Leaves *Mark Wynter*	3.12.60	
Kids In America *Kim Wilde*	7.3.81	
Killer *Adamski*	7.4.90	
Killer On The Loose *Thin Lizzy*	4.10.80	
Killer Queen *Queen*	2.11.74	
Killers Live (EP) *Thin Lizzy*	2.5.81	
Killing Me Softly With His Song *Roberta Flack*	3.3.73	
Killing Moon *Echo and the Bunnymen*	28.1.84	
Killing Of Georgie *Rod Stewart*	21.8.76	
Kind Of Magic, A *Queen*	29.3.86	

King *UB40*	8.3.80	
King Creole *Elvis Presley*	11.10.58	
King In A Catholic Style (Wake Up) *China Crisis*	5.6.85	
King Midas In Reverse *Hollies*	7.10.67	
King Of Emotion *Big Country*	20.8.88	
King Of Pain *Police*	14.1.84	
King Of Rock 'N' Roll *Prefab Sprout*	7.5.88	
King Of The Cops *Billy Howard*	7.2.76	
King Of The Road *Roger Miller*	3.4.65	
King Of The Road (EP) *The Proclaimers*	24.11.90	
King Of Wishful Thinking *Go West*	4.9.90	
King Rocker *Generation X*	3.2.79	
Kings Of The Wild Frontier *Adam and the Ants*	21.2.81	
Kingston Town *UB40*	7.4.90	
Kinky Afro *Happy Mondays*	20.10.90	
Kinky Boots *Patrick Macnee and Honor Blackman*	1.12.90	
Kiss *Art Of Noise*	29.10.88	
Kiss *Prince and the Revolution*	15.3.86	
Kiss And Say Goodbye *Manhattans*	19.6.76	
Kiss Me *Stephen 'Tintin' Duffy*	2.3.85	
Kiss Me Honey *Shirley Bassey*	3.1.59	
Kiss Me Quick *Elvis Presley*	18.12.63	
Kiss The Bride *Elton John*	5.11.83	
Kiss You All Over *Exile*	2.9.78	
Kisses On The Wind *Neneh Cherry*	12.8.89	
Kisses Sweeter Than Wine *Jimmy Rodgers*	11.1.58	
Kisses Sweeter Than Wine *Frankie Vaughan*	11.1.58	
Kissin' Cousins *Elvis Presley*	4.7.64	
Kissing A Fool *George Michael*	3.12.88	
Kissing In The Back Row Of The Movies *Drifters*	15.6.74	
Kissing With Confidence *Will Powers*	5.11.83	
Kites *Simon Dupree and the Big Sound*	2.12.67	
Knee Deep In The Blues *Guy Mitchell*	23.2.57	
Knee Deep In The Blues *Tommy Steele*	23.2.57	
Knock Knock Who's There *Mary Hopkin*	28.3.70	
Knock On Wood *David Bowie*	28.9.74	
Knock On Wood *Eddie Floyd*	1.4.67	
Knock On Wood *Amii Stewart*	10.4.79; 7.9.85	
Knock Three Times *Dawn*	10.4.71	
Knocked It Off *B.A. Robertson*	3.11.79	
Knockin' On Heaven's Door *Bob Dylan*	6.10.73	
Knowing Me Knowing You *Abba*	5.3.77	
Komotion *Duane Eddy*	12.11.60	
Kon-Tiki *Shadows*	9.9.61	
Kookie Kookie (Lend Me Your Comb) *Edward Byrnes and Connie Stevens*	7.5.60	
Kool In The Kaftan *B.A. Robertson*	5.4.80	
Kung Fu Fighting *Carl Douglas*	17.8.74	
Kyrie *Mr Mister*	15.3.86	
La Dee Dah *Jackie Dennis*	29.3.58	
La Bamba *Los Lobos*	25.7.87	
La Isla Bonita (Remix) *Madonna*	4.4.87	
La La Means I Love You *Delfonics*	7.8.71	
La Vien En Rose *Grace Jones*	15.2.86	
Labelled With Love *Squeeze*	10.10.81	
Labour Of Love *Hue & Cry*	25.7.87	
Ladies Night *Kool and the Gang*	3.11.79	
Lady *Kenny Rogers*	6.12.80	
Lady Barbara *Herman's Hermits*	5.12.70	
Lady D'Arbanville *Cat Stevens*	4.7.70	
Lady Eleanor *Lindisfarne*	13.5.72	
Lady Godiva *Peter and Gordon*	1.10.66	
Lady In Red, The *Chris De Burgh*	19.7.86	
Lady Is A Tramp (EP) *Frank Sinatra*	5.7.58	

L-L-Lucy   *Mud*   4.10.75
Loaded   *Primal Scream*   3.3.90
Loadsamoney (Doin' Up The House)   *Harry Enfield*   7.5.89
Loco In Acapulco   *Four Tops*   3.12.88
Loco-Motion   *Little Eva*   8.9.62; 5.8.72
Loco-Motion   *Kylie Minogue*   6.8.88
Locomotion   *Orchestral Manoeuvres in the Dark*   14.4.84
L.O.D. (Love On Delivery)   *Billy Ocean*   7.8.76
Lodgers   *The Style Council*   28.9.85
Logical Song   *Supertramp*   7.5.79
Lola   *Kinks*   4.7.70
Lollilop   *Chordettes*   26.4.58
Lollipop   *Mudlarks*   3.5.58
London Calling   *Clash*   5.1.80
London Nights   *London Boys*   1.7.89
Lone Ranger   *Quantum Jump*   2.6.79
Loneliness   *Des O'Connor*   6.12.69
Lonely   *Acker Bilk*   6.10.62
Lonely   *Eddie Cochran*   8.10.60
Lonely Boy   *Paul Anka*   8.8.59
Lonely Boy   *Andrew Gold*   9.4.77
Lonely City   *John Leyton*   5.5.62
Lonely One   *Duane Eddy*   4.4.59
Lonely Pup (In A Christmas Shop)   *Adam Faith*   10.12.60
Lonely This Christmas   *Mud*   7.12.74
Lonesome   *Adam Faith*   3.2.62
Long As I Can See The Light   *Creedence Clearwater Revival*   5.9.70
Long Haired Lover From Liverpool   *Little Jimmy Osmond*   2.12.72
Long Hot Summer   *Style Council*   13.8.83
Long Live Love   *Olivia Newton-John*   16.3.74
Long Live Love   *Sandie Shaw*   15.5.65
Long Tall Glasses   *Leo Sayer*   14.9.74
Long Tall Sally   *Little Richard*   25.8.56; 16.2.57
Longlegged Woman Dressed In Black   *Mungo Jerry*   6.4.74
Look Around   *Vince Hill*   2.10.71
Look Away   *Big Country*   12.4.86
Look For A Star   *Garry Mills*   9.7.60
Look Homeward Angel   *Johnny Ray*   16.3.57
Look Mama   *Howard Jones*   20.4.85
Look Of Love   *ABC*   15.5.82
Look Of Love, The   *Madonna*   12.12.87
Look, The   *Roxette*   6.5.89
Look Through Any Window   *Hoolies*   4.9.65
Look Wot You Dun   *Slade*   5.2.72
Lookin' Through The Windows   *Jackson Five*   11.11.72
Looking After Number 1   *Boomtown Rats*   3.9.77
Looking For Linda   *Hue & Cry*   4.2.89
Looking For New Love   *Jody Whatley*   13.6.87
Looking High High High   *Bryan Johnson*   9.4.60
Looking Through The Eyes Of Love   *Partridge Family starring Shirley Jones and David Cassidy*   3.2.73
Looking Through The Eyes Of Love   *Gene Pitney*   12.6.65
Loop Di Love   *Shag*   14.10.72
Loop De-Loop   *Frankie Vaughan*   2.2.63
Lorelei   *Lonnie Donegan*   27.8.60
Losing My Mind   *Lisa Minelli*   12.8.89
Losing You   *Brenda Lee*   6.4.63
Losing You   *Dusty Springfield*   7.11.64
Lost In France   *Bonnie Tyler*   6.11.76
Lost In Music   *Sister Sledge*   1.9.79; 8.9.84
Lost John   *Lonnie Donegan*   28.4.56

Lost Weekend   *Lloyd Cole and the Commotions*   9.11.85
Louise   *Human League*   1.12.84
Love Action (I Believe In Love)   *Human League*   8.8.81
Love And Affection   *Joan Armatrading*   16.10.76
Love And Marriage   *Frank Sinatra*   14.1.56
Love At First Sight (Je T'Aime ... Mon Non Plus)   *Sounds Nice*   4.10.69
Love And Pride   *King*   12.1.85
Love Bites   *Def Leppard*   16.7.88
Love Can't Turn Around   *Farley 'Jackmaster' Funk*   30.8.86
Love Cats   *Cure*   5.11.83
Love Changes Everything   *Michael Ball*   4.2.89
Love Changes (Everything)   *Climie Fisher*   2.4.88
Love Child   *Supremes*   7.12.68
Love Come Down   *Evelyn King*   4.9.82
Love Comes Quickly   *Pet Shop Boys*   29.3.86
Love Don't Live Here Anymore   *Rose Royce*   16.9.78
Love Don't Live Here Anymore   *Jimmy Nail*   11.5.85
Love Grows (Where My Rosemary Goes)   *Edison Lighthouse*   24.1.70
Love Games   *Belle and the Devotions*   5.5.84
Love Hangover   *Diana Ross*   1.5.76
Love Her   *Walker Brothers*   5.6.65
Love Hit Me   *Maxine Nightingale*   2.4.77
Love Hurts   *Jim Capaldi*   1.11.75
Love Hurts   *Nazareth*   5.11.77
Love In An Elevator   *Aerosmith*   9.9.89
Love In The First Degree   *Bananarama*   24.10.87
Love In The Sun   *Glitter Band*   9.8.75
Love Is A Battlefield   *Pat Benatar*   6.4.85
Love Is A Golden Ring   *Frankie Laine*   20.4.57
Love Is A Many Splendoured Thing   *Four Aces*   5.11.55
Love Is A Stranger   *Eurythmics*   9.4.83
Love Is A Wonderful Colour   *Icicle Works*   7.1.84
Love Is All   *Malcolm Roberts*   22.11.69
Love Is All Around   *Troggs*   4.11.67
Love Is Blue   *Jeff Beck*   2.3.68
Love Is Blue (L'Amour Est Bleu)   *Paul Mauriat*   6.4.68
Love Is Contagious   *Taja Seville*   5.3.88
Love Is Here And Now You're Gone   *Supremes*   4.3.67
Love Is In Control (Finger On The Trigger)   *Donna Summer*   7.8.82
Love Is In The Air   *John Paul Young*   6.5.78
Love Is Life   *Hot Chocolate*   15.8.70
Love Is Like A Violin   *Ken Dodd*   23.7.60; 6.8.60
Love Is Like Oxygen   *Sweet*   4.2.78
Love Is Strange   *Everly Brothers*   6.11.65
Love Is The Drug   *Roxy Music*   11.10.75
Love Kills   *Freddie Mercury*   15.9.84
Love Letters   *Ketty Lester*   5.5.62
Love Letters   *Elvis Presley*   9.7.66
Love Letters   *Alison Moyet*   12.12.87
Love Letters In The Sand   *Pat Boone*   13.7.57
Love Like A Man   *Ten Years After*   4.7.70
Love Like Blood   *Killing Joke*   2.2.85
Love Like You And Me   *Gary Glitter*   3.5.75
Love Like Yours   *Ike and Tina Turner*   5.11.66
Love Machine   *Miracles*   10.1.76
Love Makes The World Go Round   *Perry Como*   15.11.58
Love Me   *Yvonne Elliman*   6.11.76
Love Me As If There Were No Tomorrow   *Nat 'King' Cole*   3.11.56
Love Me Do   *Beatles*   1.12.62; 16.10.82

Love Me For A Reason *Osmonds*	24.8.74
Love Me Forever *Eydie Gorme*	8.2.58
Love Me Forever *Marion Ryan*	1.2.58
Love Me Like I Love You *Bay City Rollers*	10.4.76
Love Me Love My Dog *Peter Shelley*	5.4.75
Love Me Or Leave Me *Sammy Davis Jnr*	17.9.55
Love Me Or Leave Me *Doris Day*	15.10.55
Love Me Tender *Richard Chamberlain*	3.11.62
Love Me Tender *Elvis Presley*	8.12.56
Love Me Tonight *Tom Jones*	17.5.69
Love Me Warm And Tender *Paul Anka*	7.4.62
Love Missile F1-11 *Sigue Sigue Sputnik*	1.3.86
Love Of My Life *Dooleys*	3.12.77
Love Of The Common People *Nicky Thomas*	4.7.70
Love Of The Common People *Paul Young*	19.11.83
Love On A Mountain Top *Robert Knight*	1.12.73
Love On A Mountain Top *Sinitta*	7.10.89
Love On The Rocks *Neil Diamond*	6.12.80
Love On Your Side *Thompson Twins*	5.2.83
Love Plus One *Haircut 100*	6.2.82
Love Really Hurts Without You *Billy Ocean*	21.2.76
Love Removal Machine *The Cult*	28.2.87
Love Resurrection *Alison Moyet*	7.7.84
Love Shack *B52's*	3.3.90
Love Song *Damned*	5.5.79
Love Supreme, A *Will Downing*	2.4.88
Love Theme From The Thorn Birds *Juan Martin*	4.2.84
Love To Love You Baby *Donna Summer*	17.1.76
Love Town *Booker Newbury III*	28.5.83
Love Train *O Jays*	3.3.73
Love Train *Holly Johnson*	14.1.89
Love Wars *Womack and Womack*	5.5.84
Love Will Save The Day *Whitney Houston*	4.6.89
Love Will Tear Us Apart *Joy Division*	5.7.80
Love Worth Waiting For *Shakin' Stevens*	24.3.84
Love X Love *George Benson*	4.10.80
Love You Inside Out *Bee Gees*	5.5.79
Love You Save *Jackson Five*	1.8.70
Lovely Day *Bill Withers*	14.1.78
Loverboy *Billy Ocean*	2.2.85
Lover Come Back To Me *Dead or Alive*	20.4.85
Lover In The (The) *Sheena Easton*	4.2.89
Lover Please *Vernon Girls*	2.6.82
Lover's Concerto *Toys*	6.11.65
Lover's Holiday *Change*	5.7.80
Lovers Of The World Unite *David and Jonathan*	6.8.66
Love's About To Change My Heart *Donna Summer*	2.9.89
Love's Been Good To Me *Frank Sinatra*	4.10.69
Love's Comin' At Ya *Melba Moore*	6.11.82
Love's Gotta Hold On Me *Dollar*	1.9.79
Love's Great Adventure *Ultravox*	20.10.84
Love's Just A Broken Heart *Cilla Black*	15.1.66
Love's Theme *Love Unlimited Orchestra*	2.2.74
Love's Unkind *Donna Summer*	3.12.77
Lovesick Blues *Frank Ifield*	27.10.62
Lovesong *The Cure*	16.9.89
Lovin' Things *Marmalade*	1.6.68
Loving And Free *Kiki Dee*	11.9.76
Loving The Alien *David Bowie*	8.6.85
Loving You *Minnie Ripperton*	12.4.75
Loving You Is Sweeter Than Ever *Nick Kamen*	21.3.87
Low Rider *War*	7.2.76
Lucille *Everly Brothers*	24.9.60
Lucille *Little Richard*	6.7.57
Lucille *Kenny Rogers*	7.5.77

Lucky Five *Russ Conway*	28.5.60
Lucky Lips *Cliff Richard*	11.5.63
Lucky Number *Lene Lovich*	3.3.79
Lucky Star *Madonna*	7.4.84
Lucky Stars *Dean Friedman*	4.11.78
Lucretia (My Reflection) *Sisters Of Mercy*	18.6.88
Lucy In The Sky With Diamonds *Elton John*	23.11.74
Lullaby *The Cure*	22.4.89
Lumbered *Lonnie Donegan*	16.9.61
Lunatics (Have Taken Over The Asylum) *Funboy Three*	5.12.81
Lute *Boney M*	2.7.77
Ma Baker *Boney M*	2.7.77
Ma He's Making Eyes At Me *Johnny Otis Show*	23.11.57
Ma He's Making Eyes At Me *Lena Zavaroni*	9.2.74
Macarthur Park *Richard Harris*	6.7.68
Macarthur Park *Donna Summer*	4.11.78
MacDonalds Cave *Piltdown Men*	15.10.60
Machine Gun *Commodores*	5.10.74
Mack the Knife *Bobby Darin*	3.10.59
Mack The Knife *Ella Fitzgerald*	7.5.60
Mad About You *Bruce Ruffin*	1.7.72
Mad Passionate Love *Bernard Bresslaw*	20.9.58
Mad World *Tears For Fears*	2.10.82
Madam Butterfly *Malcolm McLaren*	1.9.84
Madchester Rave On (EP) *Happy Mondays*	2.12.89
Made Of Stone *Stone Roses*	17.3.90
Made You *Adam Faith*	25.6.60
Madly In Love *Bros*	10.3.90
Maggie May *Rod Stewart*	4.9.71
Maggie May *Vipers*	20.4.57
Maggie's Farm *Specials*	10.1.81
Magic *Pilot*	2.11.74
Magic Fly *Space*	13.8.77
Magic Moments *Perry Como*	15.2.58
Magic Number, The/Buddy *De La Soul*	23.12.89
Magic Roundabout *Jasper Carrott*	16.8.75
Magic Touch *Loose Ends*	11.5.85
Magical Mystery Tour EP *Beatles*	16.12.67
Mah Na Mah Na *Piero Umiliani*	7.5.77
Mahogany (Do You Know Where You're Going To) *Diana Ross*	3.4.76
Maid Of Orleans (The Waltz Joan Of Arc) *Orchestral Manoeuvres in the Dark*	23.1.82
Maigret Theme *Joe Loss*	7.4.62
Main Attraction *Pat Boone*	1.12.62
Main Title *Billy May*	28.4.56
Make A Daft Noise For Christmas *Goodies*	13.12.75
Make It A Party *Winifred Atwell*	3.11.56
Make It Easy On Yourself *Walker Brothers*	21.8.65
Make It With You *Bread*	1.8.70
Make Me An Island *Joe Dolan*	5.7.69
Make Me Smile (Come Up And See Me) *Steve Harley and Cockney Rebel*	8.2.75
Make The World Go Away *Eddy Arnold*	5.3.66
Make The World Go Away *Donny and Marie Osmond*	5.7.75
Makin' Love *Floyd Robinson*	17.10.59
Making Plans For Nigel *XTC*	6.10.79
Making Up Again *Goldie*	3.6.78
Making Your Mind Up *Buck's Fizz*	4.4.81
Male Stripper *Man 2 Man Meets Man*	14.2.87
Malt And Barley Blues *McGuiness Flint*	1.5.71
Mama *Dave Berry*	2.7.66
Mama *Connie Francis*	2.5.60
Mama *Genesis*	3.9.83
Mama *David Whitfield*	23.7.55
Mama Never Told Me *Sister Sledge*	5.7.75

Mama Gave Birth To The . . . *Queen Latifah*
+ *De La Soul*   24.3.90
Mama Told Me Not To Come   *Three Dog*   8.8.70
Mama Used To Say   *Junior*   1.5.82
Mama Weer All Crazee Now   *Slade*   2.9.72
Mambo Italiano   *Rosemary Clooney*   22.1.55
Mambo Rock   *Bill Haley and his Comets*   2.4.55
Mamma Mia   *Abba*   10.1.76
Man From Laramie   *Jimmy Young*   10.9.55
Man In Black   *Cozy Powell*   1.6.74
Man Of Mystery   *Shadows*   12.11.60
Man Of The World   *Fleetwood Mac*   19.4.69
Man On Fire   *Frankie Vaughan*   14.9.57
Man To Man   *Hot Chocolate*   3.7.76
Man Who Sold The World   *Lulu*   2.2.74
Man With The Child In His Eyes   *Kate Bush*   10.6.78
Man With The Golden Arm (Main Title Theme)
Jet Harris   1.9.62
Man With The Golden Arm (Main Title Theme)
Billy May   28.4.56
Man Without Love   *Engelbert Humperdinck*   4.5.68
Manchild   *Neneh Cherry*   20.5.89
Mandinka   *Sinead O'Connor*   6.2.88
Mandolins In The Moonlight   *Perry Como*   15.1.58
Mandy   *Eddie Calvert*   22.2.58
Mandy   *Barry Manilow*   1.3.75
Maneater   *Daryl Hall and John Oates*   6.11.82
Manhattan Skyline   *a-ha*   28.2.87
Manhattan Spiritual   *Reg Owen*   7.2.59
Manic Monday   *Bangles*   1.3.86
Many Rivers To Cross   *UB40*   10.12.83
Many Tears Ago   *Connie Francis*   28.1.61
March Of The Siamese Children   *Kenny Ball
and his Jazzmen*   24.2.62
Marcheta   *Karl Denver*   1.7.61
Margie   *Fats Domino*   30.5.59
Marguerita Time   *Status Quo*   10.12.83
Maria   *P.J. Proby*   4.12.65
Maria Elena   *Indios Tabajaras*   2.11.63
Marianna   *Gibson Brothers*   2.8.80
Marie   *Bachelors*   22.5.65
Marie Marie   *Shakin' Stevens*   6.9.80
Marrakesh Express   *Crosby, Stills and Nash*   13.9.69
Married   *Brook Brothers*   18.11.61
Marry Me   *Mike Preston*   25.3.61
Marta   *Bachelors*   8.7.67
Martha's Harbour   *All About Eve*   6.8.88
Mary Anne   *Shadows*   13.2.65
Mary Had A Little Boy   *Snap*   8.12.90
Mary Of The Fourth Form   *Boomtown Rats*   3.12.77
Mary's Boy Child   *Harry Belafonte* 16.11.67; 26.12.58
Mary's Boy Child – Oh My Lord   *Boney M*   2.12.78
Mary's Prayer   *Danny Wilson*   2.4.88
Masquerade   *Skids*   2.6.79
Massachusetts   *Bee Gees*   23.9.67
Master And Servant   *Depeche Mode*   1.9.84
Masterblaster (Jammin')   *Stevie Wonder*   13.9.80
Matchstalk Men And Matchstalk Cats And
Dogs   *Brian and Michael*   4.3.78
Mated   *David Grant/Jaki Graham*   7.12.85
Material Girl   *Madonna*   2.3.85
Matthew And Son   *Cat Stevens*   14.1.67
May Each Day   *Andy Williams*   12.3.66
May I Have The Next Dream With You   *Malcolm
Roberts*   2.11.68
May You Always   *Joan Regan*   6.6.59
Maybe   *Hazel Dean*   2.7.88
Maybe   *Thomas Pace*   7.7.79
Maybe Baby   *Crickets*   15.3.58

Maybe I Know   *Lesley Gore*   17.10.64
Maybe Tomorrow   *Billy Fury*   11.4.59
Maybe Tomorow   *UB40*   24.10.87
Me & Julio Down By The Schoolyard   *Paul
Simon*   6.5.72
Me & Mrs. Jones   *Billy Paul*   13.1.73
Me And My Girl (Night Clubbing)   *David
Essex*   10.7.82
Me And My Life   *Tremeloes*   12.9.70
Me And My Shadow   *Frank Sinatra and
Sammy Davis Jnr.*   15.12.62
Me And The Farmer   *The Housemartins*   12.9.87
Me And You And A Dog Named Boo   *Lobo*   3.7.71
Me The Peaceful Heart   *Lulu*   2.3.68
Mean Girl   *Status Quo*   5.5.73
Mean Streak   *Cliff Richard*   24.5.59
Mean Woman Blues   *Roy Orbison*   21.9.63
Meaning Of Love   *Depeche Mode*   8.5.82
Meet Me On The Corner   *Max Bygraves*   12.11.55
Meet Me On The Corner   *Lindisfarne*   4.3.72
Megablast (Don't Make Me Wait)   *Bomb The
Bass*   27.8.88
Megamix   *Technotronic*   6.10.90
Mellow Yellow   *Donovan*   11.2.67
Melting Pot   *Blue Mink*   15.11.69
Memories Are Made Of This   *Val Doonican*   4.3.67
Memories Are Made Of This   *Dave King*   18.2.56
Memories Are Made Of This   *Dean Martin*   11.2.56
Memory   *Elaine Page*   6.6.81
Memphis Tennessee   *Chuck Berry*   12.10.63
Memphis Tennessee   *Dave Berry*   2.11.63
La Mer (Beyond The Sea)   *Bobby Darin*   6.2.60
Merry Christmas Everyone   *Shakin' Stevens* 14.12.85
Merry Gentle Pops   *Barron Knights*   18.12.65
Merry Xmas Everybody   *Slade*   15.12.73; 10.12.83
Mess Of Blues   *Elvis Presley*   30.7.60
Mess Of The Blues   *Status Quo*   5.11.83
Message In A Bottle   *Police*   22.9.79
Message Of Love   *Pretenders*   14.2.81
Message, The   *Grandmaster Flash and the
Furious Five*   4.9.82
Message To Martha   *Adam Faith*   5.12.64
Message To You Rudy   *Specials*   3.11.79
Message Understood   *Sandie Shaw*   2.10.65
Messages   *Orchestral Manoeuvres in the
Dark*   17.6.80
Messing About On The River   *Josh McCrae*   4.2.61
Metal Guru   *T. Rex*   13.5.72
Mexicali Rose   *Karl Denver*   21.10.61
Mexican Girl   *Smokie*   7.10.78
Mexico   *Long John Baldry*   2.1.68
Miami Vice Theme   *Jan Hammer*   12.10.85
Michael   *Highwaymen*   16.9.61
Michael Caine   *Madness*   11.2.84
Michael Row The Boat   *Lonnie Donegan*   9.9.61
Michelle   *David and Jonathan*   15.1.66
Michelle   *Overlanders*   15.1.66
Mickey   *Toni Basil*   6.2.82
Midas Touch   *Midnight Star*   25.10.86
Midnight At The Lost And Found   *Meat Loaf*   1.10.83
Midnight In Moscow   *Kenny Ball and his
Jazzmen*   18.11.61
Midnight Rider   *Paul Davidson*   10.1.76
Midnight Train To Georgia   *Gladys Knight & The
Pips*   8.5.76
Midnite Dynamo   *Matchbox*   10.5.80
Mighty Quinn   *Manfred Mann*   3.2.68
Milk And Alcohol   *Dr. Feelgood*   3.2.79
Milky Way   *Elegance*   17.1.76

505

My Best Friend's Girl *Cars*	11.11.78
My Boomerang Won't Come Back *Charlie Drake*	14.10.61
My Boy *Elvis Presley*	16.11.74
My Boy Lollipop *Millie*	11.4.64
My Brave Face *Paul McCartney*	20.5.89
My Brother Jake *Free*	1.5.71
My Camera Never Lies *Buck's Fizz*	3.4.82
My Cheri Amour *Stevie Wonder*	2.8.69
My Coo-Ca-Choo *Alvin Stardust*	3.11.73
My Definition Of A Bombastic Jazz Style *Dream Warriors*	1.12.90
My Ding-A-Ling *Chuck Berry*	4.11.72
My Dixie Darling *Lonnie Donegan*	12.1.57
My Ever Changing Moods *Style Council*	18.2.84
My Eyes Adored You *Frankie Valli*	1.2.75
My Favourite Waste Of Time *Owen Paul*	21.6.86
My Forbidden Lover *Chic*	13.10.79
My Friend Stan *Slade*	6.10.73
My Friend The Sea *Petula Clark*	25.11.61; 16.12.61
My Generation *Who*	6.11.65
My Girl *Madness*	5.1.80
My Girl *Otis Redding*	1.1.66
My Girl Bill *Jim Stafford*	6.7.74
My Girl Lollipop (My Boy Lollipop) *Bad Manners*	7.8.82
My Guy *Mary Wells*	6.6.64; 8.7.72
My Happiness *Connie Francis*	21.2.59
My Heart Has A Minds Of Its Own *Connie Francis*	5.11.60
My Hometown *Bruce Springsteen*	14.12.85
My Kind Of Girl *Matt Monroe*	11.3.61
My Kinda Life *Cliff Richard*	5.3.77
My Life *Billy Joel*	6.1.79
My Little Girl *Crickets*	2.2.63
My Little Lady *Tremeloes*	5.10.68
My Little One *Marmalade*	1.5.71
My Love *Petula Clark*	12.2.66
My Love *Julio Iglesias feat. Stevie Wonder*	6.8.88
My Love *Wings*	7.4.73
My Love For You *Johnny Mathis*	8.10.60
My Mind's Eye *Small Faces*	19.11.66
My Name is Jack *Manfred Mann*	15.6.68
My Oh My *Sad Cafe*	5.4.80
My Oh My *Slade*	3.12.83
My Old Man's A Dustman *Lonnie Donegan*	26.3.60
My Old Piano *Diana Ross*	20.9.80
My One Temptation *Mica Paris*	7.5.88
My Own Way *Duran Duran*	5.12.81
My Perfect Cousin *Undertones*	3.5.80
My Prayer *Gerry Monroe*	5.12.70
My Prayer *Platters*	3.11.56
My Prerogative *Bobby Brown*	4.2.89
My Pretty One *Cliff Richard*	4.7.87
My Resistance Is Low *Peter Sarstedt*	8.5.76
My Sentimental Friend *Herman's Hermits*	3.5.69
My September Love *David Whitfield*	10.3.56
My Sharona *Knack*	7.7.79
My Ship Is Coming In *Walker Brothers*	4.12.65
My Simple Heart *Three Degrees*	1.12.79
My Son John *David Whitfield*	25.8.56
My Special Angel *Bobby Helms*	7.12.57
My Special Angel *Malcolm Vaughan*	7.12.57
My Sweet Lord *George Harrison*	23.1.71
My Toot Toot *Denise LaSalle*	6.7.85
My True Love *Jack Scott*	8.11.58
My Ukelele *Max Bygraves*	10.1.59
My Way *Sex Pistols*	5.8.78
My Way *Elvis Presley*	10.12.77
My Way *Frank Sinatra*	3.5.69; 5.12.70
My Way Of Thinking *UB40*	14.4.60
My White Bicycle *Nazareth*	14.6.75
My World *Bee Gees*	5.2.72
My World *Secret Affair*	5.4.80
Mystery Song *Status Quo*	10.7.76
Mystify *INXS*	8.4.89
Na Na Hey Hey Kiss Him Goodbye *Bananarama*	5.3.83
Na Na Hey Hey Kiss Him Goodbye *Steam*	7.3.70
Na Na Na *Cozy Powell*	10.8.74
Na Na Is The Saddest Word *Stylistics*	15.1.75
Nairobi *Tommy Steele*	8.3.58
Naked In The Rain *Blue Pearl*	7.7.90
Name And Number *Curiosity*	7.10.89
Name Of The Game *Abba*	22.10.77
Nasty *Janet Jackson*	21.6.86
Nathan Jones *Bananarama*	19.11.88
Nathan Jones *Supremes*	4.9.71
Native New Yorker *Odyssey*	7.1.78
Natural Born Boogie *Humble Pie*	2.8.69
Natural Sinner *Fair Weather*	1.8.70
Natural Thing *Innocence*	3.3.90
Naughty Lady Of Shady Lane *Dean Martin*	22.1.55
Neanderthal Man *Hotlegs*	4.7.70
Need You Tonight *INXS*	12.9.88
Needles And Pins *Searchers*	18.1.64
Needles And Pins *Smokie*	15.10.77
Nellie The Elephant *Toy Dolls*	1.12.84
Nelson Mandela *Special A.K.A.*	7.4.84
Nessun Dorma *Luciano Pavarotti*	16.6.90
Never Can Say Goodbye *Gloria Gaynor*	4.1.75
Never Can Say Goodbye *The Communards*	7.11.87
Never Do A Tango With An Eskimo *Alma Cogan*	7.1.56
Never Ending Song Of Love *New Seekers*	10.7.71
Never Ending Story *Limahl*	3.11.84
Never Enough *The Cure*	29.9.90
Never Give Up On A Good Thing *George Benson*	6.2.82
Never Give You Up *Sharon Redd*	6.11.82
Never Gonna Give You Up *Musical Youth*	12.3.83
Never Gonna Give You Up *Rick Astley*	15.8.87
Never Goodbye *Karl Denver*	7.4.62
Never Had A Dream Come True *Stevie Wonder*	4.4.70
Never Knew Love Like This Before *Stephanie Mills*	1.11.80
Never Let Her Slip Away *Andrew Gold*	1.4.78
Never Mind *Cliff Richard*	25.4.59
Never Mind The Presents *Barron Knights*	6.12.80
Never Never *Assembly*	12.10.83
Never Never Gonna Give Ya Up *Barry White*	2.2.74
Never Never Never *Shirley Bassey*	3.3.73
Never On Sunday *Lynn Cornell*	22.9.60
Never Say Die (Give A Little Bit More) *Cliff Richard*	3.9.83
Never Stop *Echo and the Bunnymen*	16.7.83
Never Surrender *Saxon*	18.7.81
Never Take Me Alive *Spear of Destiny*	9.5.87
Never/These Dreams *Heart*	5.3.88
Never Too Late *Kylie Minogue*	4.11.89
Never Too Much/Remix '89 *Luther Vandross*	4.11.89
Never Trust A Stranger *Kim Wilde*	1.10.88
Never Turn Your Back On Mother Earth *Sparks*	2.11.74
New Beginning (Mamba Seyra) *Buck's Fizz*	21.6.86
New England *Kirsty MacColl*	2.2.85
New Flame, A *Simply Red*	8.7.89

Oh I'm Falling In Love *Jimmy Rodgers*	5.4.58
Oh Julie *Shakin' Stevens*	16.1.82
Oh Lonesome Me *Craig Douglas*	3.11.62
Oh Lori *Alessi*	2.7.77
Oh No Not My Baby *Manfred Mann*	1.5.65
Oh No Not My Baby *Rod Stewart*	8.9.73
Oh Patti (Don't Feel Sorry For Loverboy) *Scritti Politti*	7.5.88
Oh Pretty Woman *Roy Orbison*	11.9.64
Oh Well *Fleetwood Mac*	4.10.69
Oh What A Circus *David Essex*	19.8.78
Oh What A Shame *Roy Wood*	7.6.75
Oh Yeah (On The Radio) *Roxy Music*	2.8.80
Oh Yes You're Beautiful *Gary Glitter*	23.11.74
Oh You Pretty Thing *Peter Noone*	22.5.71
O.K.? *Rock Follies*	21.5.77
O.K. Fred *Errol Dunkley*	6.10.79
Okay? *Dave Dee, Dozy, Beaky, Mick and Tich*	3.6.67
Ol' MacDonald *Frank Sinatra*	26.11.60
Ol' Rag Blues *Status Quo*	10.9.83
Old *Dexy's Midnight Runners*	4.12.82
Old Smokey *Johnny and the Hurricanes*	15.7.61
Oldest Swinger In Town *Fred Wedlock*	7.2.81
Ole La (Muhler Brasileira) *Rod Stewart*	3.6.78
Oliver's Army *Elvis Costello and the Attractions*	10.2.79
Olympic *808 State*	10.11.90
On A Carousel *Hollies*	18.2.67
On A Little Street In Singapore *Manhattan Transfer*	3.6.78
On A Slow Boat To China *Emile Ford and the Checkmates*	6.2.60
On Fire *T-Connection*	14.1.78
On Horseback *Mike Oldfield*	10.1.76
On My Own *Patti Le Balle*	31.5.86
On My Radio *Selecter*	3.11.79
On My Word *Cliff Richard*	12.6.75
On Our Own from 'Ghostbusters II' *Bobby Brown*	15.7.89
On The Beach *Cliff Richard*	4.7.64
On The Beach Summer '88 *Chris Rea*	13.8.88
On The Inside (Theme 'Prisoner Cell Block H') *Lynne Hamilton*	6.5.89
On The Rebound *Floyd Cramer*	29.4.61
On The Road Again *Canned Heat*	3.6.68
On The Street Where You Live *Vic Damone*	24.5.58
On The Street Where You Live *David Whitfield*	17.5.58; 21.6.58; 5.7.58
On The Wings Of Love *Jeffrey Osbourne*	4.8.84
Once Bitten Twice Shy *Ian Hunter*	3.5.75
Once Bitten Twice Shy *Vesta Williams*	7.2.87
Once In A Lifetime *Talking Heads*	7.3.81
Once There Was A Time *Tom Jones*	4.6.66
Once Upon A Dream *Billy Fury*	4.8.62
Once Upon A Long Time Ago *Paul McCartney*	5.12.87
One *Metallica*	22.4.89
One And One Is One *Medicine Head*	5.5.73
One Better Day *Madness*	2.6.84
One Broken Heart For Sale *Elvis Presley*	2.3.63
One Dance Won't Do *Audrey Hall*	8.3.86
One Day At A Time *Lena Martell*	6.10.79
One Day I'll Fly Away *Randy Crawford*	6.9.80
One Day In Your Life *Michael Jackson*	6.6.81
One Great Thing *Big Country*	27.9.86
One In Ten *UB40*	8.8.81
One Inch Rock *T. Rex*	1.4.72
One Love *Bob Marley and the Wailers*	5.5.84
One Love *Stone Roses*	14.7.90
One Man *Chanelle*	11.3.89
One Man Band *Leo Sayer*	15.6.74
One Man Woman *Sheena Easton*	1.11.80
One Moment In Time *Whitney Houston*	1.10.88
One More Dance *Esther and Abi Ofarim*	6.7.68
One More Night *Phil Collins*	13.4.85
One More Sunrise *Dickie Valentine*	31.10.59
One More Try *George Michael*	23.4.88
One Nation Under A Groove, Part 1 *Funkadelic*	6.1.79
One Night *Elvis Presley*	24.1.59
One Night In Bangkok *Murray Head*	1.12.84
One Of Those Nights *Buck's Fizz*	5.9.81
One Of Us *Abba*	12.12.81
One Road *Love Affair*	8.3.69
One Step Away *Tavares*	2.7.77
One Step Beyond *Madness*	10.11.79
One Step Further *Bardo*	10.4.82
137 Disco Heaven (Medley) *Amii Stewart*	16.6.79
1-2-3 *Len Barry*	6.11.65
1-2-3 *Gloria Estefan*	5.11.88
1-2-3 O'Leary *Des O'Connor*	23.11.68
One Vision *Queen*	16.11.85
One Way Love *Cliff Bennett and the Rebel Rousers*	3.10.64
One Way Ticket *Eruption*	7.4.79
Onedin Line Theme *Vienna Philarmonic Orchestra*	1.1.72
Onion Song *Marvin Gaye and Tammi Terrell*	15.11.69
Only Crying *Keith Marshall*	2.5.81
Only For Love *Limahl*	5.11.83
Only In My Dreams *Debbie Gibson*	2.4.88
Only Love *Nana Mouskouri*	25.1.86
Only Man On The Island *Tommy Steele*	1.2.7.58
Only One I Know *The Charlatans*	2.6.90
Only One, The *Transvision Vamp*	10.6.89
Only One Woman *Marbles*	5.10.68
Only Rhyme That Bites *MC Tunes Versus 808 State*	2.6.90
Only Sixteen *Sam Cook*	22.8.59
Only Sixteen *Craig Douglas*	13.8.59
Only Sixteen *Al Saxon*	29.8.59
Only The Lonely *Roy Orbison*	20.8.60
Only Way Out *Cliff Richard*	17.7.82
Only Way I Know *Charlatans*	2.6.90
Only Way Is Up, The *Yazz & The Plastic Population*	23.7.88
Only When You Leave *Spandau Ballet*	9.6.84
Only Women Bleed *Julie Covington*	7.1.78
Only Yesterday *Carpenters*	3.5.75
Only You *Flying Pickets*	3.12.83
Only You *Hilltoppers*	28.1.56
Only You *Platters*	6.9.56; 23.3.57
Only You *Yazoo*	1.5.82
Only You Can *Fox*	12.2.75
Ooh Baby *Gilbert O'Sullivan*	15.9.73
Ooh La La *Keith Kelly*	23.4.60
Ooh La La La (Let's Go Dancin') *Kool and the Gang*	16.10.82
Ooh To Be Ah *Kajagoogoo*	2.4.83
Ooh! What A Life *Gibson Brothers*	4.8.79
Ooh-Wakka-Doo-Wakka-Day *Gilbert O'Sullivan*	17.6.72
Ooops Up *Snap*	16.6.90
Oops Up Side Your Head *Gap Band*	12.7.80
Oops Up Side Your Head ('87 Mix) *The Gap Band*	1.8.87

Open Your Heart *Human League*		10.10.81
Open Your Heart (Remix) *Madonna*		13.12.86
Opportunities (Let's Make Lots Of Money)		
Pet Shop Boys		7.6.86
Opposites Attract *Paula Abdul (duet with*		
The Wild Pair)		7.4.90
Opus 17 (Don't You Worry 'Bout Me) *Four*		
Seasons		4.6.66
Orchard Road *Leo Sayer*		2.4.83
Ordinary Day *Curiosity Killed The Cat*		11.4.87
Orinico Flow *Enya*		15.10.88
Orville's Song *Keith Harris and Orville*		8.1.83
Ossie's Dream *Tottenham Hotspur F.C. Cup*		
Final Squad		9.5.81
Other Man's Grass *Petula Clark*		6.1.68
Other Side Of Love *Yazoo*		20.11.82
Ouija Board, Ouija Board *Morrissey*		25.11.90
Our Favourite Melodies *Craig Douglas*		4.8.62
Our House *Madness*		4.12.82
Our Lips Are Sealed *Funboy Three*		7.5.83
Our World *Blue Mink*		3.10.70
Out In The Fields *Gary Moore and Phil*		
Lynott		18.5.85
Out Of The Blue *Debbie Gibson*		7.5.88
Out Of Time *Chris Farlowe*		9.7.66
Out Of Town *Max Bygraves*		9.6.56
Overjoyed *Stevie Wonder*		5.4.86
Over The Hills And Far Away *Gary Moore*		10.1.87
Over The Rainbow/You Belong To Me (Medley)		
Matchbox		6.12.80
Over Under Sideways Down *Yardbirds*		4.6.66
Over You *Freddie and the Dreamers*		22.2.64
Over You *Roxy Music*		17.5.80
Oxygene Part IV *Jean-Michel Jarre*		3.9.77
Oye Mi Canto (Hear My Voice) *Gloria*		
Estefan		7.10.89
Pacific *808 State*		18.11.89
Paid In Full *Eric B and Rakim*		14.11.87
Paint It Black *Rolling Stones*		21.5.66
Painter Man *Boney M*		3.3.79
Paisley Park *Prince and the Revolution*		1.6.85
Pale Shelter *Tears for Fears*		7.5.83
Palisades Park *Freddy Cannon*		7.7.62
Paloma Blanca *George Baker Selection*		4.10.75
Paloma Blanca *Jonathan King*		6.9.75
Pamela Pamela *Wayne Fontana*		7.1.67
Pandora's Box *Procol Harum*		6.10.75
Panic *The Smiths*		2.8.86
Papa Was A Rollin' Stone *Temptations*		13.1.73
Papa Was A Rollin' Stone *Was Not Was*		2.6.90
Papa Don't Preach *Madonna*		28.6.86
Papa's Got A Brand New Bag *James Brown*		3.4.65
Paper Plane *Status Quo*		13.1.73
Paper Roses *Kaye Sisters*		6.8.60
Paper Roses *Marie Osmond*		17.11.73
Paper Sun *Traffic*		3.6.67
Paperback Writer *Beatles*		18.6.66
Paperplate *Genesis*		5.6.82
Paradise City *Guns 'N' Roses*		18.3.89
Paradise Lost *Herd*		6.1.68
Paralysed *Elvis Presley*		31.8.57
Paranoid *Black Sabbath*		5.9.70;6.9.80
Paranoimia *The Art of Noise*		12.7.86
Parisienne Walkways *Gary Moore*		5.5.79
Part Of The Union *Strawbs*		27.1.73
Part Time Love *Elton John*		4.11.78
Part-Time Lover *Stevie Wonder*		7.9.85
Party *Elvis Presley*		4.1.58
Party Doll *Buddy Knox*		25.5.57
Party Fears Two *Associates*		6.3.82
Partyman *Prince*		9.9.89
Party's Over *Lonnie Donegan*		7.4.62
Pasadena *Temperance Seven*		17.6.61
Pass The Dutchie *Musical Youth*		2.10.82
Passengers *Elton John*		18.8.84
Passing Strangers *Billy Eckstine and Sarah*		
Vaughan		19.4.69
Passion *Rod Stewart*		1.11.80
Patches *Clarence Carter*		10.10.70
Patience *Guns N' Roses*		1.7.89
Patricia *Perez Prado*		26.7.58
Payback Mix Pt. One *James Brown*		23.4.88
Peace On Earth *Hi-Tension*		2.9.78
Peace On Earth/Little Drummer Boy *Bing Crosby*		
and David Bowie		4.12.84
Peaceful *Georgie Fame*		2.8.69
Peaches *Stranglers*		4.6.77
Pearls In Shell *Howard Jones*		2.6.84
Pearl's A Singer *Elkie Brooks*		2.4.77
Peek-A-Boo *New Vaudeville Band*		4.2.67
Peek A Boo *Siouxsie and the Banshees*		6.8.88
Peggy Sue *Buddy Holly*		4.1.58
Peggy Sue Got Married *Buddy Holly*		12.9.59
Penny Lane *Beatles*		25.2.67
Penny Lover *Lionel Richie*		3.11.84
People *Tymes*		1.2.69
People Are Ready *Depeche Mode*		24.3.84
People Hold On *Coldcut feat. Lisa Stansfield*		1.4.89
People Like You And People Like Me *Glitter*		
Band		6.3.76
Pepe *Russ Conway*		31.12.60; 21.1.61
Pepe *Duane Eddy*		14.1.61
Pepper Box *Peppers*		2.11.74
Peppermint Twist *Joey Dee and the*		
Starliners		13.1.62
Pepys' Diary *Benny Hill*		18.2.61
Perfect *Fairground Attraction*		16.4.88
Perfidia *Ventures*		10.12.60
Personal Jesus *Depeche Mode*		9.9.89
Personality *Anthony Newley*		20.6.59
Personality *Lloyd Price*		13.6.59
Persuaders *John Barry*		1.1.72
Peter Gunn Theme *Duane Eddy*		13.6.59
Peter Gunn *Art Of Noise and Duane Eddy*		29.3.86
Petite Fleur *Chris Barber's Jazz Band*		14.2.59
Phantom Of The Opera *Sarah Brightman and*		
Steve Harley		1.2.86
Philadelphia Freedom *Elton John*		8.3.75
Photograph *Ringo Starr*		3.11.73
Physical *Olivia Newton-John*		7.11.81
Piano Party *Winifred Atwell*		5.12.59
Piccadilly Palare *Morrissey*		20.10.90
Pick A Bale Of Cotton *Lonnie Donegan*		1.9.62
Pick Up The Pieces *Average White Band*		1.3.75
Pick Up The Pieces *Hudson Ford*		1.9.73
Pickin' A Chicken *Eve Boswell*		24.12.55
Picture Of You *Joe Brown*		2.6.62
Picture This *Blondie*		2.9.78
Pictures Of Lily *Who*		6.5.67
Pictures Of Matchstick Men *Status Quo*		3.2.68
Pie Jesu *Sarah Brightman and Paul Miles*		
Kingston		23.3.85
Piece Of The Action *Buck's Fizz*		6.6.81
Pied Piper *Bob and Marcia*		3.7.71
Pillow Talk *Sylvia*		7.7.73
Pills And Soap *Imposter*		11.6.83
Piltdown Rides Again *Piltdown Men*		14.1.61
Pinball Wizard *Elton John*		3.4.76

Pinball Wizard *Who*		5.4.69
Pinball Wizard/See Me Tell Me (Medley) *New*		
Seekers		3.3.73
Pink Cadillac *Natalie Cole*		2.4.88
Pink Sunshine *Fuzz Box*		3.6.89
Piped Piper *Chrispian St. Peters*		2.4.66
Pipeline *Chantays*		4.5.63
Pipes Of Peace *Paul McCartney*		7.1.84
Pistol Packin' Mama *Gene Vincent*		18.6.60
Place In The Sun *Stevie Wonder*		7.1.67
Planet Earth *Duran Duran*		7.3.81
Plastic Age *Buggles*		2.2.80
Play Me Like You Play Your Guitar *Duane*		
Eddy		8.3.75
Play That Funky Music *Wild Cherry*		9.10.76
Play The Game *Queen*		14.6.80
Pleasant Valley Sunday *Monkees*		19.8.67
Please Don't Fall In Love *Cliff Richard*		3.12.83
Please Don't Go *K.C. and the Sunshine Band*		5.1.80
Please Don't Go *Donald Peers*		1.2.69
Please Don't Make Me Cry *UB40*		15.10.83
Please Don't Tease *Cliff Richard*		2.7.60
Please Help Me I'm Falling *Hank Locklin*		10.9.60
Please Help Me *Brooks Brothers*		20.8.60
Please Mr. Postman *Carpenters*		1.2.75
Please Please Me *Beatles*		2.2.63
Please Tell Him That I Said Hello *Dana*		1.2.75
Poetry In Motion *Johnny Tilotson*		26.11.60
Poison *Alice Cooper*		5.8.89
Poison *Bell Biv Devoe*		4.8.90
Poison Arrow *ABC*		6.3.82
Poison Ivy *Coasters*		21.11.59
Poison Ivy *Lambrettas*		1.3.80
Police Officer *Smiley Culture*		5.1.85
Policy Of Truth *Depeche Mode*		19.5.90
Pony Time *Chubby Checker*		8.4.61
Pool Hall Richard *Faces*		8.12.73
Poor Jenny *Everly Brothers*		30.5.59
Poor Little Fool *Rick Nelson*		23.8.58
Poor Man's Son *Rockin' Berries*		15.5.65
Poor Me *Adam Faith*		6.2.60
Poor People Of Paris *Winifred Atwell*		10.3.56
Pop Go The Workers *Barron Knights*		3.4.65
Pop Goes The Weasel *Anthony Newley*		17.6.61
Pop Muzik *M*		7.4.79
Pop Muzik (1989 Remix) *Robin Scott*		1.7.89
Popcorn *Hot Butter*		22.7.72
Poppa Joe *Sweet*		5.2.72
Port Au Prince *Winifred Atwell*		19.5.56
Portrait Of My Love *Matt Monroe*		31.12.60
Portsmouth *Mike Oldfield*		4.12.76
Portuguese Washerwoman *Joe 'Fingers'*		
Carr		30.6.56
Positively Fourth Street *Bob Dylan*		6.11.65
Pour Some Sugar On Me *Def Leppard*		26.9.87
Power Of Love *Frankie Goes To Hollywood*		1.12.84
Power Of Love *Huey Lewis and the News*		7.9.85
Power Of Love *Jennifer Rush*		7.9.85
Power Of Love/Do You Believe In Love *Huey Lewis*		
And The News		1.3.86
Power, The *Snap*		17.3.90
Power To All Our Friends *Cliff Richard*		17.3.73
Power To The People *John Lennon*		20.3.71
Pray *MC Hammer*		8.12.90
Praying For Time *George Michael*		25.8.90
Precious *Jam*		13.2.82
Pretend *Alvin Stardust*		5.9.81
Pretty Blue Eyes *Craig Douglas*		30.1.60
Pretty Flamingo *Manfred Mann*		23.4.66

Pretty In Pink *Psychedelic Furs*		20.9.86
Pretty Little Angel Eyes *Showaddywaddy*		4.11.78
Pretty Paper *Roy Orbison*		2.11.64
Pretty Vacant *Sex Pistols*		9.7.77
Price Of Love *Everly Brothers*		22.5.65
Pride (In The Name Of Love) *U2*		15.9.84
Prime Mover *Zodiac Mindwarp*		23.5.87
Prince Charming *Adam and the Ants*		12.9.81
Prince, The *Madness*		6.10.79
Princess *Tommy Steele*		19.4.58
Princes In Rags *Gene Pitney*		6.11.65
Private Investigations *Dire Straits*		4.9.82
Private Life *Grace Jones*		2.8.80
Private Number *Judy Clay and William Bell*		7.12.68
Prize Of Gold *Joan Regan*		2.4.55
Problems *Everly Brothers*		24.1.59
Promised Land *Elvis Presley*		18.1.75
Promised You A Miracle *Simple Minds*		1.5.82; 4.7.87
Promises *Buzzcocks*		6.1.79
Promises *Ken Dodd*		14.5.66
Proud Mary *Creedance Clearwater Revival*		7.6.69
Proud One *The Osmonds*		24.5.75
Prove Your Love *Taylor Dayne*		2.4.88
Pub With No Beer *Slim Dusty*		14.2.59
Public Image *Public Image Limited*		21.10.78
Pull Up To The Bumper *Grace Jones*		25.1.86
Pump Up The Bitter *Star Turn On*		7.5.88
Pump Up The Jam *Technotronic*		2.9.89
Pump Up The Volume/Anitna *M/A/R/R/S*		12.9.87
Punky Reggae Party *Bob Marley and the*		
Wailers		7.1.78
Puppet On A String *Sandie Shaw*		18.3.67
Puppy Love *Donny Osmond*		17.6.72
Puppy Song *David Cassidy*		13.10.73
Pure *The Lightning Seeds*		5.8.89
Purely By Coincidence *Sweet Sensation*		18.1.75
Purple Haze *Jimi Hendrix*		1.4.67
Purple People Eater *Sheb Wooley*		21.6.58
Purple Rain *Prince*		22.9.84
Push It/Tramp *Salt 'N Pepa*		2.7.88
Pushbike Song *Mixtures*		16.1.71
Puss 'N' Boots *Adam and the Ants*		5.11.83
Put A Light In The Window *Southlanders*		15.2.58
Put Your Hands Together *D-Mob*		6.1.90
Put Your Head On My Shoulder *Paul Anka*		31.10.59
Put Your Love In Me *Hot Chocolate*		3.12.77
Put Yourself In My Place *Isley Brothers*		13.9.69
Putting On The Style *Lonnie Donegan*		15.6.57
Pyjamarama *Roxy Music*		10.3.73
PYT (Pretty Young Thing) *Michael Jackson*		31.3.84
Quarter To Three *Gary U.S. Bonds*		29.7.61
Que Sera Mi Vida (If You Should Go) *Gibson*		
Brothers		17.11.79
Queen Of Clubs *KC and the Sunshine Band*		7.9.74
Queen Of Hearts *Dave Edmunds*		6.10.79
Queen's First (EP) *Queen*		2.7.77
Question *Moody Blues*		2.5.70
Question Of Time, A (Remix) *Depeche*		
Mode		30.8.86
Questions And Answers *Sham 69*		7.4.79
Quick Joey Small (Run Joey Run) *Kasenetz-Katz*		
Singing Orchestral Circus		1.2.69
Quiereme Mucho (Yours) *Julio Inglesias*		6.3.82
Quiet Life *Japan*		3.10.81
Quite A Party *Fireballs*		12.8.61
Rabbit *Chas and Dave*		6.12.80
Race, The *Yello*		3.9.90
Race With The Devil *Gun*		7.12.68
Radancer *Marmalade*		1.4.72

Radar Love   *Golden Earring*   5.1.74
Radio Africa   *Latin Quarter*   22.2.86
Radio Gaga   *Queen*   4.2.84
Radio Romance   *Tiffany*   3.12.88; 7.1.89RE
Rag Doll   *Four Seasons*   4.9.64
Rag Mama Rag   *The Band*   4.4.78
Rage Hard   *Frankie Goes To Hollywood*   6.9.86
Rage To Love   *Kim Wilde*   4.5.85
Ragtime Cowboy Joe   *Chipmunks*   8.8.59
Rain   *The Cult*   5.10.85
Rain   *Bruce Ruffin*   1.5.71
Rain   *Status Quo*   14.2.76
Rain, The   *Oran 'Juice' Ones*   6.2.86
Rain In The Summertime   *The Alarm*   17.10.87
Rain Or Shine   *Five Star*   20.9.86
Rainbow   *Marmalade*   1.8.70
Rainbow   *Peters and Lee*   7.9.74
Rainbow Valley   *Love Affair*   4.5.68
Raindrops Keep Falling On My Head   *Sacha Distel*   7.2.70
Rainy Day Woman Nos 12 & 35   *Bob Dylan*   14.5.66
Rainy Night In Georgia   *Randy Crawford*   5.9.81
Rama Lama Ding Dong   *Rocky Sharpe and the Replays*   6.1.79
Ramblin' Rose   *Nat 'King' Cole*   6.10.62
Ramona   *Bachelors*   6.6.64
Randy   *Blue Mink*   7.7.73
Ranking Full Stop   *Beat*   8.12.79
Rapper's Delight   *Sugarhill Gang*   1.12.79
Rapture   *Blondie*   24.1.81
Rasputin   *Boney M*   7.10.78
Rat In My Kitchen   *UB40*   24.1.87
Rat Race   *Specials*   24.5.80
Rat Rapping   *Roland Rat Superstar*   7.1.84
Rat Trap   *Boomtown Rats*   14.10.78
Raunchy   *Bill Justis*   22.2.58
Rave On   *Buddy Holly*   28.6.58
Rawhide   *Frankie Laine*   14.11.59; 13.2.60
Razzamatazz   *Quincy Jones*   4.7.81
Razzle Dazzle   *Bill Haley and his Comets*   6.10.56
Reach For The Stars   *Shirley Bassey*   5.8.51
Reach Out I'll Be There   *Four Tops*   15.10.66; 23.7.88
Reach Out I'll Be There   *Gloria Gaynor*   8.3.75
Reach 'Em And Weep   *Barry Manilow*   3.12.83
Ready Willing And Able   *Doris Day*   30.4.55
Real Fashion (Reggae Style)   *Carey Johnson*   16.5.87
Real Gone Kid   *Deacon Blue*   5.11.88
Real Real Real   *Jesus Jones*   7.4.90
Real Thing, The   *Jellybean featuring Steve Dante*   17.10.87
Real Wild Child (The Wild One)   *Iggy Pop*   17.1.87
Really Saying Something   *Bananarama*   10.4.82
Reap The Wild Wind   *Ultravox*   2.10.82
Reason To Believe   *Rod Stweart*   4.9.71
Reasons To Be Cheerful   *Ian Dury and the Blockheads*   4.8.79
Rebel Rebel   *David Bowie*   23.2.74
Rebel Rouser   *Duane Eddy*   20.9.58
Rebel Yell   *Billy Idol*   14.9.85
Reckless   *Afrika Babaataa*   5.3.88
Red Balloon   *Dave Clark Five*   21.9.68
Red Dress   *Alvin Stardust*   4.5.74
Red Guitar   *David Sylvian*   2.6.84
Red Light Spells Danger   *Billy Ocean*   19.3.77
Red Red Wine   *UB40*   20.8.83
Red River Rock   *Johnny and the Hurricanes*   10.10.59
Red Sky   *Status Quo*   9.8.86
Reelin' and Rockin'   *Chuck Berry*   3.2.73

Reet Petite (The Sweetest Girl In Town)   *Jackie Wilson*   16.11.57; 13.12.86
Relax   *Frankie Goes To Hollywood*   14.1.84; 2.6.84
Reflections   *Supremes*   2.9.67
Reflections Of My Life   *Marmalade*   3.1.70
Reflex   *Duran Duran*   28.4.84
Reggae For it Now   *Bill Loveday*   1.9.79
Reggae Like It Used To Be   *Paul Nicholas*   1.5.76
Reggae Tune   *Andy Fairweather-Low*   5.10.74
Release Me   *Engelbert Humperdinck*   4.2.67
Remember Me   *Diana Ross*   3.4.71
Remember Me This Way   *Gary Glitter*   30.3.74
Remember (Sha-La-La)   *Bay City Rollers*   9.2.74
Remember Then   *Showaddywaddy*   7.4.79
Remember (Walkin' In The Sand)   *Shangri-Las*   7.10.64
Remember You're A Womble   *Wombles*   6.4.74
Remember You're Mine   *Pat Boone*   5.10.57
Reminiscing   *Buddy Holly*   6.10.62
Rent   *Pet Shop Boys*   24.10.87
Renta Santa   *Chris Hill*   6.12.75
Requiem   *London Boys*   1.4.89
Rescue Me   *Fontella Bass*   4.12.65
Respect   *Adeva*   14.1.89
Respect   *Aretha Franklin*   1.7.67
Respect Yourself   *Bruce Willis*   21.3.87
Respectable   *Mel & Kim*   14.3.87
Restless   *Johnny Kidd and the Pirates*   15.10.60
Resurrection Shuffle   *Ashton, Gardner and Dyke*   16.1.71
Return of Django   *Upsetters*   4.10.69
Return Of the Los Palmas Seven   *Madness*   24.1.81
Return To Me   *Dean Martin*   28.7.58
Return To Sender   *Elvis Presley*   1.12.62
Reunited   *Peaches and Herbs*   5.5.79
Reveille Rock   *Johnny and the Hurricanes*   26.12.59
Reward   *Teardrop Explodes*   7.3.71
Rhinestone Cowboy   *Glen Campbell*   4.10.75
Rhythm Is Gonna Get You   *Gloria Estefan/Miami Sound Machine*   7.1.89
Rhythm Of The Night   *Debarge*   4.5.85
Rhythm Of The Rain   *Cascades*   2.3.63
Rhythm Of The Rain   *Jason Donovan*   1.8.90
Rich In Paradise   *FPI Project*   13.1.90
Riddle, The   *Nik Kershaw*   24.11.84
Ride A White Swan   *T. Rex*   7.11.70
Ride A Wild Horse   *Dee Clark*   1.11.75
Ride On Time   *Blackbox*   12.8.89
Riders In The Sky   *Ramrods*   18.2.61
Riders In The Sky   *Shadows*   2.2.80
Riding On A Train   *Pasadenas*   17.9.88
Right Back Where We Started From   *Sinitta*   3.6.89
Right Back Where You Started Back   *Maxine Nightingale*   1.11.75
Right By Your Side   *Eurythmics*   5.11.83
Right Here Waiting   *Richard Marx*   2.8.89
Right Now   *Creatures*   6.8.83
Right Said Fred   *Bernard Cribbins*   7.7.62
Right Thing, The   *Simply Red*   28.2.87
Right Thing To Do   *Carly Simon*   5.5.73
Ring My Bell   *Anita Ward*   2.6.79
Ring Of Fire   *Duane Eddy*   24.6.61
Ring Of Ice   *Jennifer Rush*   18.1.86
Rio   *Duran Duran*   13.11.82
Rip It Up   *Bill Haley and the Comets*   10.11.56
Rip It Up   *Little Richard*   5.1.57
Rip It Up   *Orange Juice*   5.3.83
Rise   *Herb Alpert*   3.11.79
Rise   *Public Image Limited*   8.2.86

Rise & Fall Of Flingel Bunt   *Shadows*   9.5.64
Rise To The Occasion   *Climie Fisher*   16.1.88
Rising Sun   *Medicine Head*   4.8.73
River, The   *Ken Dodd*   20.8.65
River Deep Mountain High   *Supremes and Four*
   Tops   3.7.71
River Deep Mountain High   *Ike and Tina*
   Turner   11.6.66
River Stay 'Way From My Door   *Frank Sinatra* 18.6.60
Rivers Of Babylon   *Boney M*   6.5.78
Roadblock   *Stock, Aitken and Waterman*   8.8.87
Road Runner   *Jnr Walker*   19.4.69
Road To Hell   *Chris Rea*   14.10.89
Road To Nowhere   *Talking Heads*   2.11.85
Roadrunner   *Jonathan Richman and the Modern*
   Lovers   6.8.77
Roam   *B52s*   19.5.90
Robert De Niro's Waiting   *Bananarama*   3.3.84
Robin Hood   *Dick James*   21.1.56
Robin Hood   *Gary Miller*   14.1.56
Robot   *Tornados*   6.4.63
Robot Man   *Connie Francis*   21.5.60
Rock A Hula Baby   *Elvis Presley*   3.2.62
Rock and Roll Waltz   *Kay Starr*   18.2.58
Rock Around The Clock   *Bill Haley* 15.10.55; 22.9.56;
   6.4.68; 6.4.74
Rock Bottom   *Lynsey De Paul and Mike Moran* 9.4.77
Rock Island Line   *Lonnie Donegan*   7.1.56
Rock Lobster/Planet Claire   *B52s*   17.5.86
Rock Me Amadeus (The American Edit)   *Falco* 5.4.86
Rock Me Baby   *David Cassidy*   2.12.72
Rock Me Gently   *Andy Kim*   7.9.74
Rock Me Tonight (For Old Times Sake)   *Freddie*
   Jackson   22.3.86
Rock On   *David Essex*   1.9.73
Rock the Boat   *Forrest*   5.3.83
Rock the Boat   *Hues Corporation*   3.8.74
Rock The Joint   *Bill Haley and his Comets*   2.2.57
Rock The Night   *Europe*   14.2.87
Rock This Town   *Stray Cats*   7.2.81
Rock With The Caveman   *Tommy Steele*   27.10.56
Rock With You   *Michael Jackson*   9.2.80
Rock Your Baby   *George McCrae*   6.7.74
Rock-A-Beatin' Boogie   *Bill Haley and his*
   Comets   7.1.56
Rock-A-Billy   *Guy Mitchell*   4.5.57
Rock-A-Bye Your Baby (With A Dixie Melody)   *Jerry*
   Lewis   16.2.57
Rock-A-Doodle Doo   *Linda Lewis*   7.7.73
Rock & Roll (Parts 1 & 2)   *Gary Glitter*   10.6.72
Rock 'N' Me   *Steve Miller*   6.11.76
Rock 'N' Roll   *Status Quo*   5.12.81
Rock 'N' Roll Ain't Noise Pollution   *AC/DC*   6.12.80
Rock 'N' Roll Is King   *Electric Light Orchestra* 2.7.83
Rock 'N' Roll Lady   *Showaddywaddy*   17.8.74
Rock 'N' Roll Winter   *Wizzard*   4.5.74
Rockabilly Rebel   *Matchbox*   1.12.79
Rockaria   *Electric Light Orchestra*   5.3.77
Rocket   *Def Leppard*   11.2.89
Rocket   *Mud*   3.8.74
Rocket Man   *Elton John*   6.5.72
Rockin' All Over The World   *Status Quo*   8.10.77
Rockin' Around The Christmas Tree   *Brenda*
   Lee   1.12.62
Rockin' Around The Christmas Tree   *Mel Smith*
   & Kim Wilde   12.12.87
Rockin' Good Way   *Shaky and Bonnie*   14.1.84
Rockin' Goose   *Johnny and the*
   Hurricanes   22.10.60

Rockin' Over The Beat   *Technotronic feat.*
   Ya Kid   14.7.90
Rockin' Robin   *Michael Jackson*   3.6.72
Rockin' Roll Baby   *Stylistics*   19.1.74
Rockin' Through The Rye   *Bill Haley and his*
   Comets   18.8.56
Rockit   *Herbie Hancock*   6.8.83
Rodrigo's Guitar Concerto   *Manuel*   7.2.76
Rok Da House   *Beatmasters feat. Cookie*
   Crew   23.1.88
Roll Away The Stone   *Mott the Hoople*   1.12.73
Roll Over Beethoven   *Electric Light Orchestra* 3.2.73
Roll Over Lay Down   *Status Quo*   17.5.75
Rollin' Home   *Status Quo*   24.5.86
Rollin' Stone   *David Essex*   5.7.75
Romeo   *Mr. Big*   12.2.77
Romeo   *Petula Clark*   15.7.61
Romeo & Juliet   *Dire Straits*   17.1.81
Room At The Top   *Adam Ant*   3.3.90
Room In Your Heart   *Living In A Box*   7.10.89
Rooms On Fire   *Stevie Nicks*   6.5.89
Rosalie   *Thin Lizzy*   3.6.78
Rosanna   *Toto*   9.4.83
Rose Garden   *Lyn Anderson*   6.3.71
Rose Garden   *New World*   6.3.71
Rose Has To Die   *Dooleys*   2.9.78
Rose Marie   *Slim Whitman*   16.7.55
Roses   *Haywoode*   19.7.86
Roses Are Red   *Mac Band*   2.7.88
Roses Are Red   *Ronnie Caroll*   4.8..62
Roses Are Red   *Bobbie Vinton*   4.8.62
Roses Of Picardy   *Vince Hill*   3.6.67
Rosetta   *Fame and Price Together*   10.4.71
Rosie   *Don Partridge*   10.2.68
Roulette   *Russ Conway*   23.5.59
Round and Round   *Jaki Graham*   6.7.85
Round and Round   *Spandau Ballet*   8.12.84; 5.1.85
Roussos Phenomenon   *Demis Roussos*   7.8.76
Roxanne   *Police*   5.5.79
Royal Event   *Russ Conway*   27.2.60
Rubber Ball   *Bobby Vee*   21.1.61
Rubber Ball   *Marty Wilde*   28.1.61
Rubber Bullets   *10cc*   2.6.73
Rubberband Man   *Detroit Spinners*   2.10.76
Ruby Don't Take Your Love To Town   *Kenny*
   Rogers   1.11.69
Ruby Tuesday   *Melanie*   3.10.70
Ruby Tuesday   *Rolling Stones*   21.1.67
Rudder and Rock   *David Whitfield*   17.3.56
Rude Boys Outa Jail   *Specials*   24.5.80
Rudy's Rock   *Bill Haley and his Comets*   24.11.56
Rumors   *Timex Social Club*   20.9.86
Rumour Has It   *Donna Summer*   4.3.78
Run Boy Run   *Newbeats*   6.11.71
Run For Home   *Lindisfarne*   1.7.78
Run For Your Life   *Buck's Fizz*   12.3.83
Run Run Away   *Slade*   4.2.84
Run Run Run   *Jo Jo Gunne*   1.4.72
Run To Him   *Bobby Vee*   6.1.62
Run To Me   *Bee Gees*   5.8.72
Run To The Hills   *Iron Maiden*   20.2.82
Run To You   *Bryan Adams*   2.2.85
Runaround Sue   *Dion*   11.11.61
Runaround Sue   *Racey*   10.1.81
Runaway   *Del Shannon*   6.5.61
Runaway Boys   *Stray Cats*   6.12.80
Runner, The   *Three Degrees*   7.4.79
Runnin' Away   *Sly and the Family Stone*   6.5.72
Running All Over The World   *Status Quo*   20.8.88

Running Bear *Johnny Preston*		13.2.60
Running Free *Iron Maiden*		5.10.85
Running In The Family *Level 42*		14.2.87
Running Scared *Roy Orbison*		3.6.61
Running Up That Hill *Kate Bush*		17.8.85
Running With the Night *Lionel Richie*		9.1.84
Rupert *Jackie Lee*		6.2.71
Rush Hour *Jane Wiedlin*		3.9.88
Russians *Sting*		11.1.86
S.O.S. *Abba*		4.10.75
S.O.S. *Edwin Starr*		4.1.69
Sabre Dance *Love Sculpture*		7.12.68
Sacrifice/Healing Hands *Elton John*		9.6.90
Sad Songs (Say So Much) *Elton John*		2.6.84
Sad Sweet Dreamer *Sweet Sensation*		14.9.74
Saddle Up *David Christie*		4.9.82
Sadness Pt. 1 *Enigma*		15.12.90
Safety Dance *Men Without Hats*		8.10.83
Sail On *Commodores*		1.9.79
Sailing *Rod Stewart*		4.9.76; 16.8.75
Sailor *Petula Clark*		28.1.68
Sailor *Ann Shelton*		28.1.61
St. Elmo's Fire (Man In Motion) *John Parr*		5.10.85
St. Theresa Of The Roses *Malcolm Vaughan*		17.11.56
St. Valentine's Day Massacre *Motorhead*		21.2.81
Saints Rock 'N' Roll *Bill Haley and his Comets*		2.6.56
Sally *Gerry Munroe*		6.6.70
Sally Don't You Grieve *Lonnie Donegan*		5.7.58
Sal's Got A Sugar Lip *Lonnie Donegan*		19.9.59
Sam *Olivia Newton-John*		1.6.77
Samantha *Kenny Ball and his Jazzmen*		4.3.61
Same Old Scene *Roxy Music*		1.11.80
San Bernadino *Christie*		7.11.70
San Damiano (Heart And Soul) *Sal Solo*		5.1.85
San Franciscan Nights *Eric Burdon*		4.11.67
San Francisco *Scott McKenzie*		15.7.67
Sanctify Yourself *Simple Minds*		1.2.86
Sandy *John Travolta*		7.10.78
Santa Bring My Baby Back To Me *Elvis Presley*		16.11.57
Santa Claus Is Comin' To Town *Bruce Springsteen*		14.12.85
Sat In Your Lap *Kate Bush*		11.7.81
Saturday Love *Cherrelle and Alexander O'Neal*		18.1.86
Saturday Night At The Movies *Drifters*		6.5.72
Saturday Night's Alright For Fighting *Elton John*		7.7.73
Saturday Nite *Earth Wind and Fire*		5.3.77
Savage Shadows		18.11.61
Save A Prayer *Duran Duran*		21.8.82
Save Me *Dave Dee, Dozy, Beaky, Mick and Tich*		17.12.66
Save Me *Queen*		2.2.80
Save The Last Dance For Me *Drifters*		29.10.60
Save Your Kisses For Me *Brotherhood Of Man*		13.3.76
Save Your Love *Renée and Renato*		6.11.82
Saved By The Bell *Robin Gibb*		12.7.69
Saving All My Love For You *Whitney Houston*		16.11.85
Saviour's Day *Cliff Richard*		8.12.90
Say A Little Prayer *Bomb The Bass feat. Maureen*		26.11.88
Say Hello Wave Goodbye *Soft Cell*		6.2.82
Say I Won't Be There *Springfields*		6.4.63
Say It Again *Jermaine Stewart*		6.2.88
Say I'm Your Number One *Princess*		3.8.85

Say No Go *De La Soul*		1.7.89
Say Say Say *Michael Jackson and Paul McCartney*		15.10.83
Say When *Lene Lovich*		2.6.79
Say Wonderful Things *Ronnie Carroll*		9.3.63
Say Yeah *The Limit*		5.1.85
Say You Don't Mind *Colin Blunstone*		4.3.72
Say You, Say Me *Lionel Richie*		16.11.85
Scarlet O'Hara *Jet Harris and Tony Meehan*		4.5.63
Scary Monsters (And Super Creeps) *David Bowie*		10.1.81
School Love *Barry Blue*		2.3.74
School's Out *Alice Cooper*		15.7.72
Scotch On The Rocks *Band of the Black Watch*		4.10.75
Scots Machine *Voyage*		8.7.78
Sea Of Heartbreak *Don Gibson*		7.9.61
Sea Of Love *Marty Wilde*		26.9.59
Sealed With A Kiss *Jason Donovan*		10.6.89
Sealed With A Kiss *Brian Hyland*		4.8.62; 5.7.75
Searchin' *Hazel Dean*		5.5.84
Searchin' *Hollies*		7.9.63
Searching *Change*		4.10.80
Seaside Shuffle *Terry Dactyl and the Dinosurs*		15.7.72
Seasons In The Sun *Terry Jacks*		23.3.74
Second Hand Rose *Barbra Streisand*		5.2.66
Secret Garden *T'Pau*		11.10.88
Secret Love *Kathy Kirby*		16.11.63
Secret Lovers *Atlantic Starr*		5.4.86
Secrets That You Keep *Mud*		15.2.75
See Emily Play *Pink Floyd*		1.7.67
See My Baby Jive *Wizzard*		21.4.73
See My Friend *Kinks*		7.8.65
See The Day *Dee C. Lee*		9.11.85
See Those Eyes *Altered Images*		3.4.82
See You *Depeche Mode*		6.2.82
See You Later Alligator *Bill Haley and the Comets*		10.3.56
Seeker, The *Who*		2.5.70
Self Control *Laura Branigan*		4.8.84
Semi-Detached Suburban Mr. James *Manfred Mann*		5.11.66
Send In The Clowns *Judy Collins*		17.5.75
Senses Working Overtime *XTC*		6.2.82
Sensual World, The *Kate Bush*		30.9.89
Separate Lives *Phil Collins and Marilyn Martin*		2.11.85
September *Earth Wind and Fire*		6.1.79
September In The Rain *Dinah Washington*		2.12.61
Serenade *Mario Lanza*		19.2.55
Serenade *Slim Whitman*		28.7.56
Serious *Donna Allen*		30.5.87
Set Me Free *Kinks*		5.6.65
Set Me Free *Jaki Graham*		24.5.86
Seven Days *Ann Shelton*		24.3.56
Seven Drunken Nights *Dubliners*		1.4.67
747 Strangers In The Night *Saxon*		5.7.80
Seven Little Girls Sitting In The Back Seat *Avons*		21.11.59
Seven Little Girls Sitting In The Back Seat *Bombalurina*		7.12.90
Seven Little Girls Sitting In The Back Seat *Paul Evans*		28.11.59
Seven Rooms Of Gloom *Four Tops*		1.7.67
Seven Seas *Echo and the Bunnymen*		14.7.84
Seven Seas Of Rhye *Queen*		9.3.74
Seven Tears *Goombay Dance Band*		6.3.82
7Teen *Regents*		2.2.80

Seventeen *Fontaine Sisters* 19.11.55
Sexcrime (Nineteen Eighty Four) *Eurythmics* 3.11.84
(Sexual) Healing *Marvin Gaye* 6.11.82
Sexy Eyes *Dr. Hook* 5.4.80
Sgt. Rock (Is Going To Help Me) *XTC* 7.2.81
Sha-La-La *Manfred Mann* 17.10.64
Sha-La-La *Small Faces* 12.2.66
Shaddap You Face *Joe Dolce Music Theatre* 7.2.81
Shaft Theme *Isaac Hayes* 4.12.71
Shake It Down *Mud* 5.6.76
Shake Rattle and Roll *Bill Haley and his Comets* 22.1.55
Shake You Down *Gregory Abbott* 6.12.87
Shake Your Body (Down To The Ground) *Jacksons* 7.4.79
Shake Your Love *Debbie Gibson* 23.1.88
Shakin' All Over *Johnny Kidd and the Pirates* 2.7.60
Shakin' Stevens EP *Shakin' Stevens* 11.12.82
Shake The Disease *Depeche Mode* 1.6.85
Sha La La (Make Me Happy) *Al Green* 7.12.74
Shame Shame Shame *Shirley and Company* 8.2.75
Shang-A-Lang *Bay City Rollers* 4.5.74
Shapes Of Things *Yardbirds* 5.3.66
Sharing You *Bobby Vee* 9.6.62
Shattered Dreams *Johnny Hates Jazz* 16.5.87
Shazam *Duane Eddy* 30.4.60
She *Charles Aznavour* 22.6.74
She Ain't Worth It *Glenn Medeiros and Bobby Brown* 7.7.90
She Drives Me Crazy *Fine Young Cannibals* 7.1.89
She Loves You *Beatles* 31.8.63
She Makes My Day *Robert Palmer* 15.10.88
She Means Nothing To Me *Phil Everly and Cliff Richard* 5.3.83
She Sells Sanctuary *The Cult* 6.7.85
She Wants To Dance With Me *Rick Astley* 24.9.88
She Wears My Ring *Solomon King* 6.1.68
She'd Rather Be With Me *Turtles* 17.6.67
Sheffield Grinder *Tony Capstick and the Carlton Main Frickley Collier Band* 21.3.81
Sheila *Tommy Roe* 8.9.62
Sheila Take A Bow *The Smiths* 25.4.87
Sherry *Adrian Baker* 2.8.75
Sherry *Four Seasons* 6.10.62
She's A Lady *Tom Jones* 16.1.71
She's A Winner *The Intruders* 6.7.74
She's About A Mover *Sir Douglas Quintet* 3.7.65
She's Got Claws *Gary Numan* 29.8.81
She's Got It *Little Richard* 23.3.57
She's In Love With You *Suzi Quatro* 3.11.79
She's Leaving Home *Wet Wet Wet* 14.5.88
She's Like The Wind *Patrick Swayze feat. Wendy Fraser* 2.4.88
She's Not There *Santana* 5.11.77
She's Not There *Zombies* 4.9.64
She's Not You *Elvis Presley* 8.9.62
She's On It *The Beastie Boys* 25.7.87
She's Out Of My Life *Michael Jackson* 23.5.80
She's So Beautiful *Cliff Richard* 14.9.85
She's So Modern *Boomtown Rats* 15.4.78
Shifting Whispering Sands *Eammon Andrews* 28.1.56
Shifting Whispering Sands *Billy Vaughan* 17.12.55
Shindig *Shadows* 21.9.63
Shine A Little Love *Electric Light Orchestra* 19.5.79
Shine On *The House Of Love* 3.2.90
Shiny Shiny *Haysi Fantayzee* 5.2.83
Ships Of Fools *Erasure* 5.3.88
Shiralee *Tommy Steele* 31.8.57

Shirley *Shakin' Stevens* 1.5.82
Shiver *George Benson* 13.12.86
Sho' You Right *Barry White* 21.11.87
Shooting Star *Dollar* 2.12.78
Shoplifters Of The World Unite *The Smiths* 7.2.87
Short Fat Fanny *Larry Williams* 21.9.57
Short'nin' Bread *Viscounts* 22.10.60
Shot In The Dark *Ozzy Osbourne* 15.2.86
Shotgun Wedding *Roy C* 7.5.66; 2.12.72
Should I Stay Or Should I Go *Clash* 2.10.82
Shout *Lulu* 6.6.64; 9.8.86
Shout *Tears for Fears* 1.12.84
Shout Shout (Knock Yourself Out) *Rockey Sharpe and the Replays* 8.5.82
Shout To The Top *Style Council* 13.10.84
Show Me *Dexy's Midnight Runners* 1.8.81
Show Me Girl *Herman's Hermits* 5.12.64
Show Me Heaven *Maria McKee* 15.9.90
Show Me The Way *Peter Frampton* 5.6.76
Show Me You're A Woman *Mud* 6.12.75
Show Must Go On, The *Leo Sayer* 15.12.73
Show, The *Doug E. Fresh & The Get Fresh Crew* 9.11.85
Show You The Way To Go *Jacksons* 4.6.77
Showdown *Electric Light Orchestra* 6.10.73
Showing Out *Mel & Kim* 8.11.86
Shuffle, The *Van McCoy* 7.5.77
Shut Up *Madness* 3.10.81
Shy Boy *Bananarama* 3.7.82
(Si Si) Je Suis Un Rock Star *Bill Wyman* 8.8.81
Sick Man Blues *Goodies* 15.3.75
Side Saddle *Russ Conway* 28.2.59
Sideshow *Barry Briggs* 8.1.77
Sign Of The Times *Belle Stars* 15.1.83
Sign O The Times *Prince* 14.3.87
Sign Your Name *Terence Trent D'Arby* 9.1.88
Signature Tune Of The Army Game *Michael Medwin, Bernard Bresslaw, Alfie Bass and Leslie Fyson* 7.6.58
Signed Sealed Delivered (I'm Yours) *Stevie Wonder* 1.8.70
Silence Is Golden *Tremeloes* 6.5.67
Silent Night *Bros* 3.12.88
Silhouettes *Herman's Hermits* 20.2.65
Silhouettes *Cliff Richard* 25.8.90
Silly Games *Janet Kay* 7.7.79
Silly Love Songs *Wings* 15.5.76
Silly Thing *Sex Pistols* 7.4.79
Silver Dream Machine (Part 1) *David Essex* 5.4.80
Silver Lady *David Soul* 3.9.77
Silver Machine *Hawkwind* 1.7.72
Silver Stars *Four Seasons* 1.5.76
Simon Says *1910 Fruitgum Company* 6.4.68
Simon Smith & His Amazing Dancing Bear *Alan Price* 18.3.67
Simon Templar *Splodgenessabounds* 14.6.80
Simple Game *Four Tops* 2.10.71
Since Yesterday *Strawberry Switchblade* 5.1.85
Since You've Been Gone *Rainbow* 15.9.79
Sinful *Pete Wylie* 31.5.86
Sing A Little Song *Desmond Decker and The Aces* 6.9.75
Sing A Song Of Freedom *Cliff Richard* 13.11.71
Sing Baby Sing *Stylistics* 10.5.75
Sing Little Birdie *Pearl Carr and Teddy Johnson* 21.3.59
Sing Me *Brothers* 5.2.77
Sing Our Own Song *UB40* 12.7.87
Sing With Shand *Jimmy Shand* 1.12.56

Single Life *Cameo*	5.10.85	
Singalong-A-Santa *Santa Clause and the Christmas Trees*	11.12.82	
Singin' In The Rain Part 1 *Sheila and B. Devotion*	1.4.78	
Singing Dogs (Medley) *Singing Dogs*	19.11.55	
Singing The Blues *Guy Mitchell*	8.12.56	
Singing The Blues *Tommy Steele*	15.12.56	
S-S-S-Single Bed *Fox*	3.4.76	
Single Girl *Sandy Posey*	7.1.67	
Single Life *Cameo*	5.10.85	
Sir Duke *Stevie Wonder*	9.4.77	
Sister *Bros*	16.12.89	
Sister Jane *New World*	13.5.72	
Sister Of Mercy *Thompson Twins*	7.7.84	
Sisters Are Doing It For Themselves *Eurythmics and Aretha Franklin*	2.11.85	
Sit And Wait *Sydney Youngblood*	9.12.89	
(Sittin' On) The Dock Of The Bay *Otis Redding*	2.3.68	
Sitting In The Park *Georgie Fame*	24.12.66	
Situation *Yazoo*	8.12.90	
Six Packs *Police*	14.6.80	
Six Teens *Sweet*	13.7.74	
16 Bars *Stylistics*	7.8.76	
Sixteen Reasons *Connie Stevens*	21.5.50	
Sixteen Tons *Tennessee Ernie Ford*	7.1.56	
Sixteen Tons *Frankie Laine*	7.1.56	
68 Guns *Alarm*	1.10.83	
Skiffle Session (EP) *Lonnie Donegan*	7.7.56	
Skiing In The Snow *Wigab's Ovation*	5.4.75	
Skin Deep *Stranglers*	6.10.84	
Skweeze Me Pleeze Me *Slade*	30.6.73	
Sky High *Jigsaw*	8.11.75	
Slave To Love *Bryan Ferry*	11.5.85	
Slave To The Rhythm *Grace Jones*	12.10.85	
Sleep Talk *Alyson Williams*	4.3.89	
Sleep Walk *Santo and Johnny*	10.10.59	
Sleepy Joe *Herman's Hermits*	4.5.68	
Sleepy Shores *Johnny Pearson*	18.12.71	
Slightest Touch *Five Star*	18.4.87	
Slip your Disc To This *Heatwave*	7.5.77	
Sloop John B. *Beach Boys*	23.4.66	
Slow Boat To China *Emile Ford*	6.2.60	
Slow Down *John Miles*	2.7.77	
Slowhand *Pointer Sisters*	5.9.81	
Smalltown Boy *Bronski Beat*	2.6.84	
Smarty Pants *First Choice*	4.8.73	
Smoke Gets In Your Eyes *Bryan Ferry*	14.9.74	
Smoke Gets In Your Eyes *Platters*	17.1.59	
Smooth Criminal *Michael Jackson*	26.11.88	
Smooth Operator *Sade*	6.10.84	
Smurf Song *Father Abraham and the Smurfs*	3.6.78	
Snoopy Vs. The Red Baron *Hotshots*	2.6.73	
Snoopy Vs. The Red Baron *Royal Guardsmen*	4.2.67	
Snot Rap *Kenny Everett*	2.4.83	
Snow Coat *Russ Conway*	14.11.59	
Sledgehammer *Peter Gabriel*	3.5.86	
Slightest Touch (The) *Five Star*	18.4.87	
Smile *Audrey Hall*	26.7.86	
Snooker Loopy *The Matchroom Mob with Chas and Dave*	17.5.86	
So Cold The Night *The Communards*	6.12.87	
So Do I *Kenny Ball and his Jazzmen*	1.9.62	
So Emotional (Remix) *Whitney Houston*	14.11.87	
So Far Away *Dire Straits*	4.5.85	
So Good to Be Back Home Again *Tourists*	9.12.80	
So Hard *Pet Shop Boys*	6.10.90	
So Lonely *Police*	1.3.80	
So Long Baby *Del Shannon*	16.12.61	
So Macho/Cruising *Sinitta*	26.7.88	
So Sad The Song *Gladys Knight and the Pips*	6.11.76	
So Sad (To Watch Good Love Go By) *Everly Brothers*	24.9.60	
So This Is Romance *Linx*	5.9.81	
So Tired *Ozzy Osbourne – Blizzard of Oz*	2.6.84	
So You Win Again *Hot Chocolate*	18.6.77	
Softly As I Leave You *Matt Monroe*	3.3.62	
Softly Softly *Ruby Murray*	22.1.55	
Softly Whispering I Love You *Congregation*	4.12.71	
Soldier Blue *Buffy Sainte-Marie*	7.8.71	
Soley Soley *Middle Of The Road*	11.12.71	
Solid *Ashford and Simpson*	5.1.85	
Solid Bond In Your Heart *Style Council*	19.11.83	
Solid Gold Easy Action *T. Rex*	9.12.72	
Solitaire *Andy Williams*	5.1.74	
Solsbury Hill *Peter Gabriel*	9.4.77	
Some Girls *Racey*	7.4.79	
Some Guys Have All The Luck *Robert Palmer*	6.3.82	
Some Guys Have All The Luck *Rod Stewart*	4.8.84	
Some Guys Have All The Luck *Maxi Priest*	21.11.87	
Some Kind Of A Summer *David Cassidy*	7.4.73	
Some Kinda Earthquake *Duane Eddy*	12.12.59	
Some Kinda Fun *Chris Montez*	19.1.63	
Some Like It Hot *Power Station*	16.3.85	
Some Of Your Lovin' *Dusty Springfield*	2.10.65	
Some People *Cliff Richard*	5.9.87	
Somebody *Depeche Mode*	10.12.84	
Somebody Else's Girl *Billy Fury*	5.10.63	
Somebody Else's Guy *Jocelyn Brown*	5.5.84	
Somebody Help Me *Spencer Davis Group*	2.4.66	
(Somebody) Help Me Out *Beggar and Co*	7.3.81	
Somebody To Love *Queen*	27.11.76	
Somebody's Watching Me *Rockwell*	4.2.84	
Someday *The Gap Band*	7.4.84	
Someday *Rick Nelson*	22.11.58	
Someday *Jodie Sands*	18.10.58	
Someday One Day *Seekers*	2.4.66	
Someday We'll Be Together *Supremes*	3.1.70	
Someday We're Gonna Love Again *Searchers*	18.7.64	
Someone *Johnny Mathis*	8.8.59	
Someone Else's Baby *Adam Faith*	16.4.60	
Someone Someone *Brian Poole and the Tremeloes*	9.5.64	
Someone's Looking At You *Boomtown Rats*	2.2.80	
Somethin' Stupid *Nancy Sinatra and Frank Sinatra*	1.4.67	
Something *Shirley Bassey*	4.7.70	
Something *Beatles*	8.11.69	
Something About You *Level 42*	5.10.85	
Something Better Change *Stranglers*	6.8.77	
Something 'Bout You Baby I Like *Status Quo*	28.2.81	
Something Else *Sex Pistols*	3.3.79	
Something For The Girl With Everything *Sparks*	18.1.75	
Something Happened On The Way To *Phil Collins*	5.5.90	
Something Here In My Heart (Keeps A-Tellin' Me No) *Paper Dolls*	6.4.68	
Something In My House *Dead Or Alive*	24.1.87	
Something In The Air *Thunderclap Newman*	14.6.69	
(Something Inside) So Strong *Labi Siffre*	25.4.87	
Something Old, Something New *Fantastics*	3.4.71	
Something Outa Nothing *Letitia Dean and Paul Medford*	8.11.86	

Step Right Up *Jaki Graham*	20.12.86
Steppin' Out *Joe Jackson*	8.1.83
Steppin' Out *Kool and the Gang*	7.11.81
Stereotype *Specials*	4.10.80
Still *Commodore*	3.11.79
Still *Karl Denver*	7.9.63
Still I'm Sad *Yardbirds*	16.10.65
Still Of The Night *Whitesnake*	18.4.87
Still Water (Love) *Four Tops*	3.10.70
Stingray *Shadows*	12.6.65
Stir It Up *Johnny Nash*	1.4.72
Stomp *Brothers Johnson*	1.3.80
Stoned Love *Supremes*	16.1.71
Stood Up *Rick Nelson*	22.2.58
Stop *Sam Brown*	4.2.89
Stop And Go *David Grant*	4.6.83
Stop Her On Sight (SOS) *Edwin Starr*	4.1.69
Stop In The Name Of Love *Supremes*	3.4.65
Stop Me (If You've Heard It All Before) *Billy Ocean*	4.12.76
Stop Stop Stop *Hollies*	15.10.66
Stop The Cavalry *Jona Lewie*	6.12.80
Storm In A Teacup *fortunes*	5.2.72
Story Of My Life *Gary Miller*	25.1.58
Story Of My Life *Michael Holliday*	18.1.58
Story Of The Blues *Wah!*	8.1.83
Straight Ahead *Kool and the Gang*	10.12.83
Straight To Hell *Clash*	2.10.82
Straight Up *Paula Abdul*	4.3.89
Straighten Out *Stranglers*	3.9.77
Strange Band *Family*	5.9.70
Strange Brew *Cream*	1.7.67
Strange Kind Of Woman *Deep Purple*	6.3.71
Strange Lady In Town *Frankie Laine*	30.7.55
Strange Little Girl *Stranglers*	24.7.82
Strange Town *Jam*	7.4.79
Stranger In Paradise *Tony Bennett*	16.4.55
Stranger In Paradise *Four Aces*	21.5.55
Stranger In Paradise *Tony Martin*	30.4.55
Stranger On The Shore *Acker Bilk*	2.12.61
Stranger, The *Shadows*	3.12.60
Strangers In The Night *Frank Sinatra*	14.5.66
Strangelove *Depeche Mode*	16.5.87
Strawberry Blonde *Frank D'rone*	31.12.60
Strawberry Fair *Anthony Newley*	26.11.60
Strawberry Fields Forever *Beatles*	25.2.67
Strawberry Fields Forever *Candy Flip*	17.3.90
Stray Cat Strut *Stray Cats*	2.5.81
Streak, The *Ray Stevens*	1.6.74
Street Dance *Break Machine*	4.2.84
Street Life *Crusaders*	4.9.79
Street Life *Roxy Music*	1.12.73
Street Tuff *Rebel MC/Double Trouble*	7.10.89
Streets Of London *Ralph McTell*	7.12.74
Stripped *Depeche Mode*	1.3.86
Strong As Steel *Five Star*	17.10.87
Stronger Than That *Cliff Richard*	24.2.90
Strut Your Funky Stuff *Frantique*	1.9.79
Stuck In The Middle With You *Stealer's Wheel*	2.6.73
Stuck On You *Elvis Presley*	9.4.60
Stuck On You *Lionel Richie*	23.6.84
Stuck On You *Trevor Walters*	4.8.84
Stuck With You *Huey Lewis and the News*	27.9.86
Stupid Cupid *Connie Francis*	6.9.58
Stutter Rap *Morris Minor and the Majors*	2.1.88
Substitute *Clout*	17.7.78
Substitute *Liquid Gold*	7.6.80
Substitute *Who*	12.3.66; 6.11.76
Subterranean Homesick blues *Bob Dylan*	1.5.65

Suburbia *Pet Shop Boys*	11.10.86
Such A Night *Elvis Presley*	22.8.64
Succi Succi *Laurie Johnson*	7.10.61
Succi Suci *Nina and Frederick*	14.10.61
Sucker DJ *Dimples D*	8.12.90
Suddenly *Angry Anderson*	3.2.88
Suddenly *Olivia Newton-John and Cliff Richard*	1.11.80
Suddenly *Billy Ocean*	1.6.85
Suddenly There's A Valley *Petula Clark*	3.12.55
Suddenly There's A Valley *Lee Lawrence*	26.11.56
Suddenly There's A Valley *Julius La Rosa*	17.12.55
Suddenly You Love Me *Tremeloes*	20.1.68
Suedehead *Morrissey*	27.2.88
Sugar And Spice *Searchers*	2.11.63
Sugar Baby Love *Rubettes*	4.5.74
Sugar Candy Kisses *Mac and Katie Kissoon*	1.2.75
Sugar Me *Lynsey de Paul*	19.8.72
Sugar Moon *Pat Boone*	5.7.58
Sugar Sugar *Archies*	11.10.69
Sugar Sugar *Sakkarin*	1.5.71
Sugar Town *Nancy Sinatra*	4.2.67
Sugartime *Jim Dale*	8.3.58
Sugartime *McGuire Sisters*	1.3.58
Suicide Blonde *INXS*	15.9.90
Sukiyaki *Kenny Ball*	2.2.63
Sutana *Titanic*	2.10.71
Sultans Of Swing *Dire Straits*	10.3.79
Summer Breeze *Isley Brothers*	1.6.74
Summer Holiday *Cliff Richard*	2.3.63
Summer In The City *Lovin' Spoonful*	16.7.66
Summer Madness *Kool and the Gang*	7.3.81
Summer Night City *Abba*	16.9.78
Summer Nights *Marianne Faithful*	7.8.65
Summer Nights *John Travolta and Olivia Newton-John*	16.9.78
Summer Of My Life *Simon May*	9.10.76
Summer of '42 *Biddu*	2.8.75
'Summer Place', Theme From 'A *Percy Faith*	5.3.60
Summer Set *Acker Bilk*	23.1.60
Summer (The First Time) *Bobby Goldsboro*	4.8.73
Summerlove Sensation *Bay City Rollers*	3.8.74
Summertime *Funboy Three*	7.8.82
Summertime City *Mike Batt*	16.8.75
Sun Ain't Gonna Shine Anymore *Walker Brothers*	5.3.66
Sun Always Shines, The *a-ha*	11.1.86
Sun And The Rain *Madness*	5.11.83
Sun Arise *Rolf Harris*	3.11.62
Sun Goes Down *Thin Lizzy*	6.8.83
Sunday Girl *Blondie*	5.5.79
Sunglasses *Tracey Ullman*	4.8.84
Sunny *Boney M*	12.3.77
Sunny *Georgie Fame*	8.10.66
Sunny *Bobby Hebb*	1.10.66
Sunny Afternoon *Kinks*	11.6.66
Sunny Honey Girl *Cliff Richard*	6.2.71
Sunshine After The Rain *Elkie Brooks*	3.9.77
Sunshine Day *Osibisa*	17.1.86
Sunshine Girl *Herman's Hermits*	3.8.68
Sunshine Of Your Smile *Mike Berry*	2.8.80
Sunshine Superman *Donovan*	17.12.66
Super Nature *Cerrone*	17.12.66
Super Trouper *Abba*	15.11.80
Super Womble *Wombles*	9.8.75
Superfly Guy *S'Express*	23.7.88
Supergirl *Graham Bonney*	2.4.66
Superman (Gioca Jouer) *Black Lace*	1.10.83
Supersonic Rocket Ship *Kinks*	3.6.72

Superstar *Carpenters*		6.11.71
Superstar *Lydia Murdock*		22.10.83
Superstition *Stevie Wonder*		3.2.73
Superwoman *Karyn White*		1.7.89
Surrender *Elvis Presley*		27.5.61
Surrender *Diana Ross*		6.11.71
Surrender *Swing Out Sister*		17.1.87
Surround Yourself With Sorrow *Cilla Black*		15.2.69
Susanna *Art Company*		2.6.84
Suspicion *Elvis Presley*		15.1.77
Suspicious Minds *Elvis Presley*		6.12.69
Suspicious Minds *Fine Young Cannibals*		18.1.86
Sussudio *Phil Collins*		2.2.85
Suzanne Beware Of the Devil *Dandy Livingstone*		2.9.72
Sway *Bobby Rydell*		14.1.61
Surrender *Swing Out Sister*		17.1.87
Sweet Caroline *Neil Diamond*		20.2.71
Sweet Child Of Mine *Guns N' Roses*		3.6.89
Sweet Dream *Jethro Tull*		1.11.69
Sweet Dreams (Are Made Of This) *Eurythmics*		5.3.83
Sweet Freedom *Michael McDonald*		20.9.86
Sweet Illusion *Junior Campbell*		2.6.73
Sweet Inspiration *Johnny Johnson and the Bandwagon*		1.8.70
Sweet Little Mystery *Wet Wet Wet*		15.8.87
Sweet Little Rock 'N' Roller *Showaddywaddy*		4.8.79
Sweet Little Sixteen *Chuck Berry*		19.4.58
Sweet Love *Anita Baker*		22.11.86
Sweet Music *Showaddywaddy*		1.3.75
Sweet Nuthins *Brenda Lee*		9.4.60
Sweet Old Fashioned Girl *Teresa Brewer*		21.7.56
Sweet Sixteen *Billy Idol*		11.7.87
Sweet Soul Music *Arthur Conley*		13.5.67
Sweet Surrender *Wet Wet Wet*		30.9.89
Sweet Talkin' Guy *Chiffons*		1.4.72
Sweet Talkin' Woman *Electric Light Orchestra*		7.10.78
Sweeter Than You *Rick Nelson*		5.9.59
Sweetest Smile *Black*		11.7.87
Sweetie Pie *Eddie Cochran*		6.7.60
Sweets For My Sweet *Searches*		6.7.63
Swing Low Sweet Chariot *Eric Clapton*		7.6.75
Swing The Mood *Jive Bunny & The Mastermixers*		29.7.89
Swing Your Daddy *Jim Gilstrap*		15.3.75
Swingin' Shepherd Blues *Ella Fitzgerald*		24.5.58
Swingin' Shepherd Blues *Ted Heath*		5.4.58
Swingin' Shepherd Blues *Mo Koffman*		22.3.58
Swinging On A Star *Big Dee Irwin*		7.12.63
Swiss Maid *Del Shannon*		13.10.62
Swords Of A Thousand Men *Ten Pole Tudor*		2.5.81
Sylvia *Focus*		3.2.73
Sylvia's Mother *Dr Hook*		1.7.72
Synchronicity II *Police*		5.11.83
System Addict *Five Star*		18.1.86
Tahiti *David Essex*		3.9.83
Tainted Love *Soft Cell*		8.8.81
Take A Chance On Me *Abba*		4.2.78
Take A Message To Mary *Everly Brothers*		30.5.59
Take Five *Dave Brubeck Quartet*		28.10.61
Take Good Care Of My Baby *Bobby Vee*		4.11.61
Take Good Care Of Yourself *Three Degrees*		12.4.75
Take It Away *Paul McCartney*		3.7.82
Take It On The Run *Reo Speedwagon*		1.8.81
Take It Satch (EP) *Louis Armstrong*		9.6.56
Take It To The Limit *Eagles*		6.3.76
Take It To The Top *Kool and the Gang*		6.6.81
Take Me Bak 'Ome *Slade*		3.6.72
Take Me Girl I'm Ready *Jnr Walker and the All-Stars*		3.2.73
Take Me Home *Phil Collins*		3.8.85
Take Me Home Country Roads *Olivia Newton-John*		3.2.73
Take Me I'm Yours *Squeeze*		6.5.78
Take Me In Your Arms And Love Me *Gladys Knight and the Pips*		1.7.67
Take Me To The Mardi Gras *Paul Simon*		16.6.73
Take Me To Your Heart *Rick Astley*		26.11.88
Take Me To Your Heart Again *Vince Hill*		8.1.66
Take My Breath Away *Berlin*		13.10.90
Take My Breath Away (Love Theme from Top Gun) *Berlin*		1.11.86
Take On Me *a-ha*		5.10.85
Take On The World *Judas Priest*		3.2.79
Take That Look Off Your Face *Marti Webb*		9.2.80
Take That Situation *Nick Heyward*		2.7.83
Take That To The Bank *Shalamar*		6.1.79
Take These Chains From My Heart *Ray Charles*		1.6.63
Take Your Time *Mantronix feat. Wondress*		12.5.90
Takes A Little Time *Total Contrast*		3.8.85
Talk Of The Town *Pretenders*		5.4.80
Talking Army Blues *Josh McCrae*		25.6.60
Talking In Your Sleep *Buck's Fizz*		1.9.84
Talking In Your Sleep *Crystal Gayle*		7.10.78
Talking Loud And Clear *Orchestral Manoeuvres in the Dark*		16.6.84
Tallahassee Lassie *Freddy Cannon*		22.8.59
Tammy *Debbie Reynolds*		7.9.57
Tantalise (Wo Woo Ee Yeh Yeh) *Jimmy the Hoover*		2.7.83
Tap Turns On The Water *C.C.S.*		4.9.71
Tarzan Boy *Baltimora*		10.8.85
Taste Of Aggro *Barron Knights*		2.12.78
Taste Of Honey *Acker Bilk*		2.2.63
Taste Of Your Tears *King*		19.10.85
Tattooed Millionaire *Bruce Dickinson*		5.5.90
Tea For Two Cha-Cha *Tommy Dorsey Orchestra starring Warren Covington*		1.11.58
Teacher *Jethro Tull*		24.1.70
Tear Fell, A *Teresa Brewer*		31.3.56
Teardrops *Shakin' Stevens*		1.12.84
Teardrops *Womack & Womack*		6.8.88
Tears *Ken Dodd*		4.9.65
Tears Are Not Enough *ABC*		7.11.81
Tears I Cried *Glitter Band*		12.4.75
Tears Of A Clown *The Beat*		8.12.79
Tears Of A Clown *Smokey Robinson and the Miracles*		1.8.70
Tears On My Pillow *Johnny Nash*		14.6.75
Tears On My Pillow *Kylie Minogue*		20.1.90
Tease Me *Keith Kelly*		7.5.60
Techno Dance *D-Shake*		2.6.90
Teddy Bear *Elvis Presley*		13.7.57
Teddy Bear *Red Sovine*		13.6.81
Teen Beat *Sandy Nelson*		31.10.59
Teenage Dream *T. Rex*		9.2.74
Teenage Lament '74 *Alice Cooper*		2.2.74
Teenage Opera, Excerpt From A *Keith West*		12.8.67
Teenage Rampage *Sweet*		19.1.74
Teenager In Love *Craig Douglas*		13.6.59
Teenager In Love *Marty Wilde*		6.6.59
Telegram Sam *T. Rex*		29.1.72
Telephone Always Rings *Funboy Three*		5.6.82
Telephone Line *Electric Light Orchestra*		4.6.77
Telephone Man *Meri Wilson*		3.9.77
Tell Her About It *Billy Joel*		10.12.83

Tell It To My Heart   Taylor Dayne   6.2.88
Tell Him   Billy Davis   2.3.63
Tell Him   Hellow   9.11.74
Tell Laura I Love Her   Ricky Valance   27.8.60
Tell Me What He Said   Helen Shapiro   24.2.62
Tell Me When   Applejacks   7.3.64
Tell Me Why   Elvis Presley   4.12.65
Tell Me Why   Alvin Stardust   7.12.74
Telstar   Tornados   1.9.62
Temma Harbour   Mary Hopkin   7.2.70
Temptation   Everly Brothers   17.6.61
Temptation   Heaven 17   16.4.83
Temptation   Wet Wet Wet   2.4.88
Ten Swinging Bottles   Pete Chester and the
   Chestnuts   31.12.60
10538 Overture   Electric Light Orchestra   5.8.72
Tender Trap   Frank Sinatra   21.1.56
Tequila   Champs   5.4.58
Teresa   Joe Dolan   1.11.69
Terry   Twinkle   5.12.64
Thank U Very Much   Scaffold   2.12.67
Thanks For The Memory (Wam Bam Thank You
   Mam)   Slade   17.5.75
That Girl Belongs To Yesterday   Gene Pitney   7.3.64
That Lady   Isley Brothers   6.10.73
That Old Black Magic   Sammy Davis Jr   29.10.55
That Ole Devil Called Love   Alison Moyet   16.3.85
That Same Old Feeling   Pickettywitch   7.3.70
That Sounds Good To Me   Jive Bunny & The
   Mastermixers   17.3.90
That Was Then But This Is Now   ABC   5.11.83
That'll Be The Day   Crickets   28.9.57
That's All   Genesis   3.12.83
That's How It Feels   Inspiral Carpets   17.3.90
That's Livin' Alright   Joe Fagin   14.1.84
That's Love   Billy Fury   11.6.60
That's My Home   Acker Bilk   29.7.61; 19.8.61
That's Nice   Neil Christian   7.5.66
That's The Way   Honeycombs   4.9.65
That's The Way God Planned It   Billy Preston   5.7.69
That's The Way (I Like It)   KC and the Sunshine
   Band   2.8.75
That's The Way It Is   Mel & Kim   5.3.88
That's The Way Love Is   Ten City   21.1.89
That's What Friends Are For   Dionne
   Warwick   9.11.85
That's What Friends Are For   Deniece Williams   6.8.77
That's What I Like   Jive Bunny & The
   Mastermixers   14.10.89
That's What Love Will Do   Joe Brown   9.2.63
That's When Music Takes Me   Neil Sedaka   2.3.73
That's You   Nat 'King' Cole   28.5.60
The Skye Boat Song   Roger Whittaker & Des
   O'Connor   29.11.86
Theme For A Dream   Cliff Richard   4.3.61
Theme For Young Lovers   Shadows   7.3.64
Theme For A Summer Place   Percy Faith   5.3.60
Theme From Dixie   Duane Eddy   22.4.61
Theme From E.T.   John Williams   8.1.83
Theme From Mash (Suicide Is Painless)
   Mash   10.5.80
Theme From New York New York   Frank
   Sinatra   8.3.85
Theme From Picnic   Morris Stoloff   9..56
Theme From S'Express   S'Express   16.4.88
Theme From Shaft   Eddy and the Southband   2.3.85
Theme From Shaft   Isaac Hayes   4.12.71
Theme From The Invaders (Computer Game)
   Yellow Magic Orchestra   5.7.80

Theme From The Film The Legion's Last Patrol   Ken
   Thorne   3.8.63
Theme From The Onedin Line   Vienna
   Philharmonic   1.1.72
Theme From The Persuaders   John Barry   1.1.72
Theme From The Threepenny Opera   Dick
   Hyman Trio   24.3.56
Theme From The Threepenny Opera   Billy
   Vaughan   24.3.56
Theme From Which Way Is Up   Stargard   4.2.78
Theme From Z Cars   Johnny Keating   10.3.62
Then   The Charlatans   22.9.90
Then He Kissed Me   Crystals   21.9.63
Then I Kissed her   Beach Boys   6.5.67
There Are More Questions Than Answers   Johnny
   Nash   7.10.72
There But For Fortune   Joen Baez   10.7.65
There Goes My Everything   Engelbert
   Humperdinck   3.6.67
There Goes My Everything   Elvis Presley   20.3.71
There Goes My First Love   Drifters   6.10.75
There Is A Mountain   Donovan   4.11.67
There It Is   Shalamar   4.9.83
There Must Be A Way   Frankie Vaughan   2.9.67;
                                                                        9.12.67
There Must Be An Angel   Eurythmics   6.7.85
There She Goes   LA's   3.11.90
There There My Dear   Dexy's Midnight
   Runners   12.7.80
There Won't Be Many Coming Home   Roy
   Orbison   17.12.66
There'll Be Sad Songs (To Make You Cry)
   Billy Ocean   17.5.86
There'll Never Be Anyone Else But You
   Ricky Nelson   18.4.59
There's A Ghost In My House   R. Dean Taylor 11.5.74
There's A Guy Works Down The Chipshop Swears
   He's Elvis   Kirsty McColl   4.7.81
There's A Heartache Following Me   Jim
   Reeves   7.11.64
There's A Kind Of Hush   Herman's Hermits   11.2.67
There's More To Love   The Communards   27.7.88
There's No One Quite Like Grandma   St Winifred's
   School Choir   6.12.80
There's A Whole Lot Of Loving   Guys and
   Dolls   1.3.75
(There's) Always Something There To Remind
   Me   Sandie Shaw   10.10.64
These Boots are Made For Walkin'   Nancy
   Sinatra   5.2.66
They Don't Know   Tracey Ullman   1.10.83
(They Long To Be) Close To You   Carpenters   5.8.70
They Shoot Horses Don't They   Racing Cars 12.2.77
They're Coming To Take Me Away Ha-
   Haaa!   Napoleon XIV   6.8.66
Thieves In The Temple   Prince   4.8.90
Thieves Like Us   New Order   5.5.84
Thin Wall   Ultravox   29.8.81
Thing Called Love   Johnny Cash   15.4.72
Things   Bobby Darin   4.8.62
Things Can Only Get Better   Howard Jones   9.2.85
Things We Do For Love   10CC   4.12.76
Think About Your Children   Mary Hopkin   7.11.70
Think For A Minute   The Housemartins   1.11.86
Think I'm Gonna Fall In Love With You
   Dooleys   3.9.77
Think It Over   Crickets   2.8.58
Thinking Of You   Colourfield   2.2.85
Thinking Of You   Maureen   16.6.90

Tonight I'm Yours (Don't Hurt Me)   Rod
   Stewart   17.10.81
Tonight's The Night   Rod Stewart   5.6.76
Too Beautiful To Last   Engelbert Humperdinck 1.4.72
Too Big   Suzi Quatro   6.7.74
Too Busy Thinking 'Bout My Baby   Marvin
   Gaye   2.8.69
Too Busy Thinking 'Bout My Baby   Mardi Gras 9.9.72
Too Good   Little Tony   9.1.60
Too Good to Be Forgotten   Chi-Lites   2.11.74
Too Good To Be Forgotten   Amazulu   21.6.86
Too Hot To Handle   Heatwave   7.5.77
Too Late   Junior   7.8.82
Too Late For Goodbyes   Julian Lennon   6.10.84
Too Many Beautiful Girls   Clinton Ford 26.8.61
Too Many Broken Hearts   Jason Donovan 4.3.89
Too Much   Bros   29.7.89
Too Much   Elvis Presley   11.5.57
Too Much Heaven   Bee Gees   12.2.78
Too Much Too Little Too Late   Johnny Mathis and
   Deniece Williams   1.4.78
Too Much Too Young (EP)   Specials   26.1.80
Too Sky   Kajagoogoo   22.1.83
Too Soon To Know   Roy Orbison   20.8.66
Too Young   Donny Osmond   16.9.72
Too Young To Go Steady   Nat 'King' Cole 19.5.56
Top Of The Pops   Rezillos   2.9.78
Top Of The World   Carpenters   20.10.73
Top Teen Baby   Garry Mills   29.10.60
Torch   Soft Cell   29.5.82
Torn Between Two Lovers   Mary MacGregor 19.2.77
Torvill & Dean (EP)   Richard Hartly   3.3.84
Tossing And Turning   Ivy League   3.7.65
Tossing And Turning   Windjammer   4.8.84
Total Eclipse Of The Heart   Bonnie Tyler 19.2.83
Total Mix   Black Box   15.12.90
Tottenham Tottenham   Tottenham Hotspur
   F.A. Cup Final Squad   1.5.82
Touch Me   49ers   6.1.90
Touch Me (I Want Your Body)   Samantha Fox 29.3.86
Touch Me In The Morning   Diana Ross   14.7.73
Touch Me Touch Me   Dave Dee, Dozy, Beaky,
   Mick and Tich   1.4.67
Touch Too Much   Arrows   1.6.74
Touched By The Hand Of God   New Order 26.12.87
Touchy   a-ha   3.9.90
Tougher Than The Rest   Bruce Springsteen 2.7.88
Tower Of Strength (Bombay Mix)   The
   Mission   13.2.88
Tower Of Strength   Frankie Vaughan   18.11.61
Town Called Malice   Jam   6.2.82
Toy Ballons   Russ Conway   9.12.61
Toy Boy   Sinitta   15.8.87
Toy Soldiers   Martika   5.8.89
Tracks Of My Tears   Smokey Robinson and
   the Miracles   17.5.69
Tracy   Cuff Links   6.12.69
Tragedy   Bee Gees   17.2.79
Trail Of The Lonesome Pine, The   Laurel and Hardy
   Avalon Boys   6.12.75
Train Of Thought (Remix)   a-ha   12.4.86
Trains And Boats And Planes   Burt
   Bacharach   22.5.65
Trains And Boats And Planes   Billy J. Kramer 22.5.65
Tramp   Otis Redding and Carla Thomas   5.8.67
Trapped   Colonel Abrams   7.9.85
Travellin' Band   Creedence Clearwater
   Revival   4.4.70
Travellin' Light   Cliff Richard   10.10.59

Travellin' Man   Rick Nelson   27.5.61
Treason (It's Just A Story)   Teardrop Explodes 2.5.81
Treat Her Like A Lady   Temptations   17.11.84
Treat Me Good   Yazz   23.6.90
Tribute (Right On)   Pasadenas   4.6.88
Tribute To Buddy Holly   Mike Berry   4.11.61
Tricky Disco   Tricky Disco   4.8.90
Trooper   Iron Maiden   2.7.83
Trouble   Gillan   4.10.80
Truck On (Tyke)   T. Rex   1.2.73
True Blue   Madonna   4.10.86
True Faith   New Order   1.8.87
True Love   Bing Crosby and Grace Kelly 24.11.56
True   Spandau Ballet   23.4.83
True Colors   Cyndi Lauper   11.10.86
True Love Ways   Peter and Gordon   10.4.65
True Love Ways   Cliff Richard   16.4.83
Truly   Lionel Richie   20.11.82
Try To Remember (Medley)   Gladys Knight and
   the Pips   7.6.75
Trying To Get To You   Elvis Presley   2.11.57
Tulane   Steve Gibbons Band   6.8.77
Tulips From Amsterdam   Max Bygraves   17.5.58
Tumbling Dice   Rolling Stones   29.4.72
Tumbling Tumbleweeds   Slim Whitman   3.3.56
Tunes Split The Atom   MC Tunes Versus 808 15.9.90
Tunnel Of Love   Dire Straits   5.2.83
Turn Back The Clock   Johnny Hates Jazz 19.12.87
Turn It On Again   Genesis   5.4.80
Turn It Up   Conway Brothers   6.7.85
Turn The Music Up   Players Assoication 10.3.79
Turn To Stone   Electric Light Orchestra 3.12.77
Turn Up The Bass   Tyree feat. Kool   4.3.89
Turning Away   Shakin' Stevens   15.2.86
Turning Japanese   Vapors   1.3.80
Turtle Power   Partners In Kryme   21.7.90
Tusk   Fleetwood Mac   6.10.79
Tutti Frutti   Little Richard   6.4.57
TV Game   The Army Game   7.6.58
Tweedle Dee   Little Jimmy Osmond   7.4.73
Twelfth Of Never   Donny Osmond   10.3.73
Twelfth Of Never   Cliff Richard   10.10.64
20 Seconds To Comply   Silver Bullet   6.1.90
20th Century Boy   T.Rex   10.3.73
21st Century Boy   Sigue Sigue Sputnik 14.6.86
25 To 6 To 4   Chicago   8.8.70
Twenty Four Hours From Tulsa   Gene Pitney 7.12.63
Twenty Tiny Fingers   Stargazers   19.11.55
Twilight Time   Platters   3.5.58
Twist, The   Chubby Checker   13.1.62
Twist And Shout   Brian Poole and the
   Tremeloes   6.7.63
Twist And Shout   Salt 'N Pepa   11.11.88
Twist (Yo Twist)   Fat Boys & Chubby
   Checker   18.6.88
Twistin' By The Pool   Dire Straits   22.1.83
Twistin' The Night Away   Sam Cooke   17.3.63
'Twixt Twelve And Twenty   Pat Boone   8.8.59
Two Different Worlds   Ronnie Hilton   1.12.56
Two Hearts   Phil Collins   26.11.88
Two Hearts Beat As One   U2   2.4.83
Two Kinds Of Teardrop   Del Shannon   4.5.63
Two Little Boys   Rolf Harris   22.11.69
Two Pints Of Lager And A Packet Of Crisps
   Please   Splodgenessabounds   14.6.80
2 Minutes To Midnight   Iron Maiden   18.8.64
2000 Miles   Pretenders   10.12.83
Two Tribes   Frankie Goes To Hollywood 16.6.84
2-4-6-8 Motorway   Tom Robinson Band   22.10.77

U Can't Touch This *MC Hammer*	9.6.90
U Got The Look *Prince and Sheena Easton*	22.8.87
U.S. Male *Elvis Presley*	18.5.68
Ugly Duckling *Mike Reid*	5.4.75
'Ullo John Got A New Motor? *Alexei Sayle*	3.3.84
Um Um Um Um Um Um *Wayne Fontana and the*	
Mindbenders	10.10.64
Un Banc, Un Arbre, Une Rue *Severine*	1.5.71
Una Paloma Blanca *Jonathan King*	6.9.75
Unbelievable *E.M.F.*	3.11.90
Unchained Melody *Les Baxter*	21.5.55
Unchained Melody *Al Hibbler*	14.5.55
Unchained Melody *Righteous Brothers*	4.9.65;
	27.10.90
Unchained Melody *Jimmy Young*	28.5.55
Unconditional Love *Donna Summer*	5.11.83
Under My Thumb *Wayne Gibson*	4.1.75
Under New Management *Barron Knights*	24.12.66
Under Pressure *Queen and David Bowie*	14.11.81
Under The Boardwalk *Bruce Willis*	13.6.87
Under The Bridges Of Paris *Eartha Kitt*	16.4.55
Under The Moon Of Love *Showaddywaddy*	6.11.76
Under Your Thumb *Godley and Creme*	12.9.81
Undercover Of The Night *Rolling Stones*	12.11.83
Unforgettable Fire *U2*	4.5.85
Union City Blues *Blondie*	1.12.79
Union Of The Snake *Duran Duran*	29.10.83
United We Stand *Brotherhood Of Man*	14.2.70
Universal *Small Faces*	13.7.68
Unsquare Dance *Dave Brubeck Quartet*	2.6.62
Unskinny Bop *Poison*	7.7.90
Until It's Time For You To Go *Four Pennies*	6.11.69
Until It's Time For You To Go *Elvis Presley*	1.4.72
Up And Around The Bend *Creedence Clearwater*	
Revival	20.6.70
Up The Junction *Squeeze*	2.6.79
Up The Ladder To The Roof *Supremes*	2.5.70
Up The Pool *Jethro Tull*	18.9.71
Up Town Top Ranking *Althia and Donna*	7.1.78
Up, Up And Away *Johnny Mann Singers*	15.7.67
Up Where We Belong *Joe Cocker and Jennifer*	
Warnes	5.2.83
Upside Down *Diana Ross*	19.7.80
Uptight *Stevie Wonder*	5.2.66
Uptown Girl *Billy Joel*	15.10.83
Urge, The *Freddy Cannon*	28.5.60
Use It Up And Wear It Out *Odyssey*	5.7.80
Used Ta Be My Girl *O'Jays*	1.7.78
Vacation *Connie Francis*	4.8.62
Vada Via *Drupi*	5.1.74
Valentine *T'Pau*	6.2.88
Valerie *Steve Winwood*	17.10.87
Valleri *Monkees*	6.4.68
Valley Of Tears *Buddy Holly*	15.7.61
Vaya Con Dios *Millican and Nesbitt*	5.1.74
Venus *Don Pablo's Animals*	19.5.90
Venus *Shocking Blue*	5.2.70
Venus *Bananarama*	28.6.86
Venus In Blue Jeans *Mark Wynter*	6.10.62
Very First Christmas Of All *Ruby Murray*	10.12.55
Very Precious Love *Doris Day*	19.7.58
Victim *Erasure*	6.6.87
Victims *Culture Club*	10.12.83
Video Killed The Radio Star *Buggles*	6.10.79
Videotheque *Dollar*	3.7.82
Vienna *Ultravox*	17.1.81
Vienna Calling *Falco*	7.6.86
View From A Bridge *Kim Wilde*	1.5.82
View To A Kill *Duran Duran*	18.5.85

Vincent *Don McLean*	13.5.72
Violence Of Summer (Love's) *Duran Duran*	4.8.90
Virginia Plain *Roxy Music*	2.9.72; 22.10.77
Vision Of Love *Mariah Carey*	1.9.90
Visions *Cliff Richard*	23.7.66
Visions In Blue *Ultravox*	19.3.83
Viva Bobby Joe *Equals*	2.8.69
Viva Las Vagas *Elvis Presley*	14.3.64
Vogue *Madonna*	7.4.90
Voice In The Wilderness *Cliff Richard*	23.1.60
Voice, The *Ultravox*	7.11.81
Volare *Marino Marino*	18.10.58
Volare *Dean Martin*	6.9.58
Volare *Domenico Modugno*	13.9.58
Voodoo Chile *Jimi Hendrix Experience*	7.11.70
Voodoo Ray (EP) *A Guy Called Gerald*	8.7.89
Voulez-Vous *Abba*	14.7.79
Voyage Voyage *Desireless*	4.6.88
Wages Day *Deacon Blue*	4.3.89
Wait *Robert Howard & Kym Mazelle*	14.1.89
Wait For Me *Malcolm Vaughan*	28.2.59; 4.4.59
Wait Until Tonight (My Love) *Phil Fearon and*	
Galaxy	6.8.83
Waiting For A Girl Like You *Foreigner*	12.12.81
Waiting For A Star To Fall *Boy Meets Girl*	7.1.88
Waiting For A Train *Flash and the Pan*	4.6.83
Waiting For An Alibi *Thin Lizzy*	3.3.79
(Waiting For) The Ghost Run *Madness*	15.11.86
Wake Me Up Before You Go *Wham!*	26.5.84
Wake Up Little Susie *Everly Brothers*	9.11.57
Wake Up Little Susie *King Brothers*	21.12.57
Walk Away *Matt Moroe*	3.10.64
Walk, The *The Cure*	2.7.83
Walk Away From Love *David Ruffin*	17.1.76
Walk Away Renee *Four Tops*	16.12.67
Walk Don't Run *John Barry*	24.9.60
Walk Don't Run *Ventures*	17.9.60
Walk Hand In Hand *Ronnie Carroll*	4.8.56
Walk Hand In Hand *Tony Martin*	21.7.56
Walk Hand In Hand *Jimmy Parkinson*	4.8.56
Walk In Love *Manhattan Transfer*	1.4.78
Walk In The Black Forest *Horst Jankowski*	7.8.65
Walk In The Night *Junior Walker and*	
the All-Stars	2.9.72
Walk In The Park *Nick Straker Band*	6.9.80
Walk Like A Man *Four Seasons*	6.4.63
Walk Like An Egyptian *Bangles*	11.10.86
Walk Of Life *Dire Straits*	18.1.86
Walk On By *Leroy Van Dyke*	13.1.62
Walk On By *Sybil*	3.2.90
Walk On By *Dionne Warwick*	2.5.64
Walk On The Wild Side *Lou Reed*	12.5.73
Walk Right Back *Everly Brothers*	11.2.61
Walk Right In *Rooftop Singers*	2.2.63
Walk Right Now *Jacksons*	4.7.81
Walk Tall *Val Doonican*	7.11.64
Walk The Dinosaur *Was Not Was*	17.10.87
Walk This Way *Run DMC*	13.9.86
Walk With Me *Seekers*	10.9.66
Walking *C.C.S.*	6.3.71
Walkin' Back To Happiness *Helen Shapiro*	30.9.61
Walkin' In The Rain With The One I Love *Love*	
Unlimited	1.7.72
Walkin' Miracle *Limmie and the Family*	
Cookin'	6.4.74
Walking In The Air *Aled Jones*	7.12.85
Walking In The Rain *Modern Romance*	6.8.83
Walking Down Your Street *Bangles*	24.1.87

523

White Wedding *Billy Idol* 13.7.85
Whiter Shade Of Pale, A *Procol Harum* 3.6.67
Who Am I *Adam Faith* 11.2.61
Who Are We *Ronnie Hilton* 14.7.56
Who Are You *Who* 5.8.78
Who Could Be Bluer *Jerry Lordan* 27.2.60
Who Do You Love *Juicy Lucy* 2.5.70
Who Found Who *Jellybean featuring Elisa Florillo* 5.2.87
Who Killed Bambi *Sex Pistols* 7.4.79
Who Loves You *Four Seasons* 4.10.75
Who Made Who *AC/DC* 31.5.86
Who Pays The Ferryman *Yannis Markopoulos* 7.1.78
Who Put The Bomp *Viscounts* 14.10.61
Who Put The Lights Out *Dana* 6.3.71
Who Were You With In The Moonlight *Dollar* 2.6.79
Whodunit *Tavares* 9.4.77
Whole Lotta Love *C.C.S.* 7.11.70
Whole Lotta Shakin' Goin' On *Jerry Lee Lewis* 28.9.57
Whole Lotta Woman *Marvin Rainwater* 1.3.58
Who's Gonna Love Me *Imperials* 4.2.78
Who's Gonna Rock You *Nolan Sisters* 10.1.81
Who's In The House *Beatmasters with Merlin* 22.4.89
Who's Leaving Who *Hazel Dean* 2.4.88
Who's Sorry Now *Connie Francis* 12.4.58
Who's Sorry Now *Johnnie Ray* 18.2.56
Who's That Girl *Eurythmics* 9.7.83
Who's That Girl *Madonna* 18.7.87
Who's Zoomin' Who *Aretha Franklin* 18.1.86
Why *Frankie Avalon* 23.1.60
Why *Bronski Beat* 22.9.84
Why *Anthony Newley* 16.1.60
Why *Donny Osmond* 11.11.72
Why *Carly Simon* 4.9.82
Why Baby Why *Pat Boone* 18.5.57
Why Can't This Be Love *Van Halen* 10.5.86
Why Can't We Live Together *Timmy Thomas* 3.3.73
Why Did You Do It *Stretch* 8.11.75
Why Do Fools Fall In Love *Alma Cogan* 18.8.56
Why Do Fools Fall In Love *Frankie Lymon and the Teenagers* 30.6.56
Why Do Fools Fall In Love *Diana Ross* 7.11.81
Why Don't They Understand *George Hamilton* 15.3.58
Why Oh Why Oh Why *Gilbert O'Sullivan* 10.11.73
Wichita Lineman *Glen Campbell* 1.2.69
Wicked Game *Chris Isaak* 8.12.90
Wide Boy *Nick Kershaw* 16.3.85
Wide Eyed and Legless *Andy Fairweather-Low* 6.12.75
Wig-Wam-Bam *Sweet* 9.9.72
Wikka Wrap *Evasions* 4.7.81
Wild Boys *Duran Duran* 3.11.84
Wild In The Country *Elvis Presley* 9.9.61
Wild One *Bobby Rydell* 19.3.60
Wild One *Suzi Quatro* 9.11.74
Wild Side Of Life *Status Quo* 11.12.76
Wild Thing *Troggs* 7.5.66
Wild West Hero *Electric Light Orchestra* 1.7.78
Wild Wind *John Leyton* 7.10.61
Wild Women Do *Natilie Cole* 5.5.90
Wild World *Jimmy Cliff* 5.9.70
Wild World *Maxi Priest* 4.6.88
Wilfred The Weasel *Keith Mitchell* 2.2.80
Will I What *Mike Sarne* 1.9.62
Will You *Hazel O'Connor* 6.6.81
Will You Love Me Tomorrow *Shirelles* 11.2.61

William, It Was Really Nothing *Smiths* 1.9.84
Willie And The Hand Jive *Cliff Richard* 2.4.69
Willie Can *Alma Cogan* 31.3.56
Wimoweh *Karl Denver* 3.2.62
(Win A Place Or Show) She's A Winner *Intruders* 6.7.74
Winchester Cathedral *New Vaudeville Band* 10.9.66
Wind Beneath My Wings *Bette Midler* 1.7.89
Wind Cries Mary *Jimi Hendrix Experience* 13.5.67
Wind Me Up (Let Me Go) *Cliff Richard* 6.11.65
Windmills Of Your Mind *Noel Harrison* 1.3.69
Wings Of A Dove *Madness* 20.8.83
Winner Takes It All *Abba* 2.8.80
Winter World Of Love *Engelbert Humperdinck* 15.11.69
Winter's Tale *David Essex* 11.12.62
Wipe Out *Surfaris* 3.8.63
Wipeout *Fat Boys And The Beach Boys* 29.8.87
Wired For Sound *Cliff Richard* 5.9.81
Wisdom Of A Fool *Norman Wisdom* 16.3.57
Wishful Thinking *China Crisis* 14.1.84
Wishin' And Hopin' *Merseybeats* 11.7.64
Wishing *Buddy Holly* 7.9.63
Wishing (If I Had A Photograph Of You) *A Flock Of Seagulls* 6.11.82
Wishing I Was Lucky *Wet Wet Wet* 23.5.87
Wishing On A Star *Fresh 4* 7.10.89
Wishing On A Star *Rose Royce* 4.2.78
Wishing Well *Free* 13.1.73
Wishing Well *Terence Trent D'Arby* 27.6.87
Witch Doctor *Don Lang* 31.5.58
Witch Doctor *David Seville* 31.5.58
Witch Queen Of New Orleans *Redbone* 2.10.71
Witch, The *Rattles* 3.10.70
Witchcraft *Frank Sinatra* 1.3.58
Witch's Promise *Jethro Tull* 24.1.70
With A Girl Like You *Troggs* 16.7.66
With A Little Help *Wet Wet Wet* 14.5.88
With A Little Help From My Friends *Joe Cocker* 5.10.68
With A Little Help From My Friends *Young Idea* 1.7.67
With A Little Luck *Wings* 1.4.78
With All My Heart *Petula Clark* 3.8.57
With Or Without You *U2* 28.3.87
With The Eyes Of A Child *Cliff Richard* 6.12.69
With These Hands *Tom Jones* 10.7.65
With You I'm Born Again *Billy Preston and Syreeta* 5.1.80
With Your Love *Robert Earl* 25.2.56
With Your Love *Malcolm Vaughan* 4.2.56
Without Love *Tom Jones* 13.12.69
Without You *Nilsson* 5.2.72
Wizard, The *Paul Hardcastle* 25.10.86
Woman *John Lennon* 24.1.81
Woman In Love *Four Aces* 22.8.56
Woman In Love *Frankie Laine* 15.9.56
Woman In Love *Barbra Streisand* 4.10.80
Woman In Love *Three Degrees* 13.1.79
Wombling Merry Christmas *Wombles* 7.12.74
Wombling Song *Wombles* 2.2.74
Wonder Of You *Elvis Presley* 11.7.70
Wonderful Christmastime *Paul McCartney* 1.12.79
Wonderful Dream *Ann-Marie David* 5.5.73
Wonderful Land *Shadows* 3.3.62
Wonderful Life *Black* 29.8.87
Wonderful Time Up There *Pat Boone* 5.4.58
Wonderful World *Herman's Hermits* 1.5.65
Wonderful World *Sam Cooke* 29.3.86

(You Don't Stop) Wordy Rapping Hood   Tom Tom
   Club   4.7.81
You Drive Me Crazy   Shakin' Stevens   9.4.81
You Gave Me Love   Crown Heights Affair   3.5.80
You Give Love A Bad Name   Bon Jovi   13.9.86
You Got It   Roy Orbison   14.1.89
You Got It (The Right Stuff)   New Kids On The
   Block   11.11.89
You Got Soul   Johnny Nash   4.1.69
You Got What It Takes   Showaddywaddy   23.7.77
(You Gotta) Fight For Your Right (To Party)   Beastie
   Boys   21.3.87
You Have Placed A Chill In My
   Heart   Eurythmics   11.6.88
You Just Might See Me Cry   Our Kid   5.6.76
You Keep It All In   The Beautiful South   23.9.89
(You Keep Me) Hangin' On   Cliff Richard   1.6.74
You Keep Me Hangin' On   Supremes   3.12.66
You Keep Me Hangin' On   Vanilla Fudge   2.9.67
You Keep Me Hangin' On   Kim Wilde   1.11.86
You Little Thief   Feargal Sharkey   18.1.86
You Little Trust Maker   Tymes   5.10.74
You Make Me Feel Brand New   Stylistics   13.7.74
You Make Me Feel Like Dancing   Leo Sayer   6.11.76
You Make Me Feel (Mighty Real)   Jimmy
   Somerville   13.1.90
You Make Me Feel (Mighty Real)   Sylvester   2.9.78
You Me And Us   Alma Cogan   23.2.57
You Might Need Somebody   Randy Crawford   4.7.81
You Must Have Been A Beautiful Baby   Bobby
   Darin   21.10.61
You My Love   Frank Sinatra   7.5.55
You Need Hands   Max Bygraves   17.5.58
You Only Live Twice   Nancy Sinatra   8.7.67
You Really Got Me   Kinks   15.8.64
You See The Trouble With Me   Barry White   6.3.76
You Send Me   Rod Stewart   5.10.74
You Sexy Thing   Hot Chocolate   8.11.75; 7.2.87
You Should Be Dancing   Bee Gees   7.8.76
You Spin Me Round (Like A Record)   Dead Or
   Alive   2.2.85
You Surround Me   Erasure   9.12.89
You Take Me Up   Thompson Twins   31.3.84
You Think You're A Man   Divine   7.7.84
You To Me Are Everything   Real Thing   5.6.76;
                                             22.3.86
You Want It You Got It   Detroit Emeralds   2.6.73
You Wear It Well   Rod Stewart   12.8.72
You Were Made For Me   Freddie and the
   Dreamers   9.11.63
You Were On My Mind   Crispian St. Peters   8.1.66
You Win Again (Fade)   Bee Gees   10.10.87
You Won't Be Leaving   Herman's Hermits   2.4.66
You Won't Find Another Fool Like Me   New
   Seekers   1.12.73
You You You   Alvin Stardust   7.9.74
You'll Always Find Me In The Kitchen At Parties   Jona
   Lewie   10.5.80
You'll Answer To Me   Cleo Laine   23.9.61
You'll Never Find Another Love Like Mine   Lou
   Rawls   7.8.76
You'll Never Get to Heaven   Dionne Warwick 1.8.64
You'll Never Know   Shirley Bassey   20.5.61
You'll Never Know   Hi Gloss   5.9.81
You'll Never Know What You're Missing   Real
   Thing   5.3.77
You'll Never Stop Me Loving You   Sonia   1.7.89
You'll Never Walk Alone   Gerry and the
   Pacemakers   12.10.63

You'll Never Walk Alone   The Crowd   1.6.85
Young Americans   David Bowie   1.3.75
Young And Foolish   Ronnie Hilton   11.2.56
Young And Foolish   Edmund Hockridge   11.2.56
Young And Foolish   Dean Martin   25.2.56
Young At Heart   Bluebells   7.7.84
Young, Free And Single   Sunfire   2.4.83
Young Gifted And Black   Bob and Marcia   14.3.70
Young Girl   Gary Puckett and the Union Gap 4.5.68;
                                             6.7.74
Young Guns (Go For It)   Wham!   6.11.82
Young Hearts Run Free   Candi Staton   5.6.76
Young Love   Tab Hunter   9.2.57
Young Love   Sonny James   16.2.57
Young Love   Donny Osmond   18.8.72
Young Lovers   Paul and Paula   4.5.63
Young New Mexican Puppeteer   Tom Jones   1.4.72
Young Ones   Cliff Richard   13.1.62
Young Parisians   Adam and the Ants   10.1.81
Young Turks   Rod Stewart   12.12.81
Young World   Rick Nelson   5.5.62
Your Baby Ain't Your Baby Anymore   Paul Da
   Vinci   3.8.74
Your Cheating Heart   Ray Charles   15.12.62
Your Honour   Pluto Shervington   3.4.82
Your Kiss Is Sweet   Syreeta   1.2.75
Your Love Is King   Sade   3.3.84
(Your Love Keeps Lifting Me) Higher and
   Higher   Jackie Wilson   24.5.69; 18.7.87
Your Mama Don't Dance   Poison   6.5.89
Your Song   Elton John   6.2.71
You're A Lady   Peter Skellern   23.9.72
You're All That I Need To Get By   Marvin Gaye and
   Tammi Terrell   2.11.68
You're Breaking My Heart   Keely Smith   3.4.65
You're Driving Me Crazy   Temperance Seven   8.4.61
You're Everything To Me   Boris Gardener   25.10.86
You're Gonna Get Next To Me   Bo Kirkland and
   Ruth Davis   00.00.00
You're Having My Baby   Paul Anka   5.10.74
You're History   Shakespeare Sister   5.8.89
You're In My Heart   Rod Stewart   15.10.77
You're Lying   Linx   4.10.80
You're More Than A Number In My Little Red
   Book   Drifters   8.1.77
You're Moving Out Today   Carol Bayer Sager 4.6.77
You're My Best Friend   Queen   3.7.76
You're My Everything   Lee Garrett   5.6.76
(You're My) Soul and Inspiration   Righteous
   Brothers   7.5.66
You're My World   Cilla Black   9.5.64
You're No Good   Swinging Blue Jeans   6.6.64
You're Ready Now   Frankie Valli   2.1.71
You're Sixteen   Johnny Burnette   21.1.61
You're Sixteen   Ringo Star   23.2.74
You're So Vain   Carly Simon   6.1.73
You're Such A Good Looking Woman   Joe
   Dolan   7.3.70
You're The First The Last My Everything   Barry
   White   2.11.74
You're The Inspiration   Chicago   2.2.85
You're The One   Kathy Kirby   9.5.64
You're The One For Me   D Train   3.8.85
You're The One That I Want   John Travolta and
   Olivia Newton-John   3.6.78
You're The Only Good Thing   Jim Reeves   9.12.61
You're The Voice   John Farnham   13.6.87
Youth Of Today   Musical Youth   20.11.82
You've Got A Friend   Big Fun and Sonia   23.6.90

You've Got A Friend *James Taylor* 4.9.71
You've Got Me Dangling On A String *Chairmen of the Board* 14.11.70
You've Got Your Troubles *Fortunes* 10.7.65
You've Lost That Lovin' Feeling *Cilla Black* 16.1.65
You've Lost That Lovin' Feeling *Righteous Brothers* 16.1.65; 1.3.69; 15.12.90
You've Never Been In Love Like This Before *Unit Four Plus Two* 5.6.65
You've Not Changed *Sandie Shaw* 7.10.67

Yummy Yummy Yummy *Ohio Express* 8.6.68
Zabadak! *Dave Dee, Dozy, Beaky, Mick and Tich* 14.10.67
Zambesi *Lou Busch* 28.1.56
Zambesi *Eddie Calvert* 24.3.56
Zambesi *Piranhas* 6.11.82
Ziggy Stardust *Bauhaus* 9.10.82
Zoom *Fat Larry's Band* 18.9.82
Zorba's Dance *Marcello Minerbi* 7.8.65